APPLYING EDUCATIONAL RESEARCH

How to Read, Do, and Use Research to Solve Problems of Practice

SEVENTH EDITION

M. D. Gall
Professor Emeritus, University of Oregon

Joyce P. Gall
Independent Researcher

Walter R. Borg
Late of Utah State University

PEARSON

Boston   Columbus   Indianapolis   New York   San Francisco   Hoboken
Amsterdam   Cape Town   Dubai   London   Madrid   Milan   Munich   Paris   Montreal   Toronto
Delhi   Mexico City   São Paulo   Sydney   Hong Kong   Seoul   Singapore   Taipei   Tokyo

Vice President and Editorial Director:
  Jeffery W. Johnston
Vice President and Publisher: Kevin M. Davis
Editorial Assistant: Caitlin Griscom
Executive Field Marketing Manager:
  Krista Clark
Senior Product Marketing Manager: Christopher
  Barry
Program Manager: Carrie Mollette
Project Manager: Lauren Carlson
Procurement Specialist: Michelle Klein
Senior Art Director: Jayne Conte

Text Designer: Aptara®, Inc.
Cover Designer: Suzanne Behnke
Cover Art: Susan Law Cain/Shutterstock
Development Project Management:
  Aptara®, Inc.
Full-Service Project Management:
  Aptara®, Inc.
Composition: Aptara®, Inc.
Printer/Binder: Courier-Kendallville
Cover Printer: Moore Langen
Text Font: ITC Garamond Std 10/12

Credits and acknowledgments for material borrowed from other sources and reproduced, with permission, in this textbook appear on the appropriate page within the text.

Every effort has been made to provide accurate and current Internet information in this book. However, the Internet and information posted on it are constantly changing, so it is inevitable that some of the Internet addresses listed in this textbook will change.

Library of Congress Cataloging-in-Publication Data
Gall, Meredith D.
  Applying educational research: How to read, do, and use research to solve problems of practice/M. D. Gall, Joyce P. Gall, Walter R. Borg,—Seventh edition.
    pages cm
  ISBN-13: 978-0-13-286863-1
  ISBN-10: 0-13-286863-6
  1. Education—Research—Handbooks, manuals, etc.   I. Title.
  LB1028.B59 2014
  370.72—dc23   2013042148

10 9 8 7 6 5 4 3 2 1

PEARSON

ISBN 10:   0-13-286863-6
ISBN 13: 978-0-13-286863-1

About the Authors

Meredith "Mark" Gall, professor emeritus, has a bachelor's degree and master's degree in education from Harvard University and a PhD in psychology from the University of California at Berkeley. He was an R & D project director at the Far West Laboratory for Educational Research and Development and then a professor of education at the University of Oregon, where he served in various capacities, including head of teacher education and director of graduate studies in curriculum and instruction. His specializations include research methodology, teacher development, teaching strategies, and the psychology of studying. He has served on the editorial boards of several journals, including the *Journal of Experimental Education*, *Journal of Educational Research*, and *Elementary School Journal*. Among his other book publications are *Educational Research: An Introduction* and *Clinical Supervision and Teacher Development*.

Joyce P. "Joy" Gall has a bachelor's degree in psychology from the University of Illinois at Urbana-Champaign and a PhD in psychology from the University of California at Berkeley. She has worked as a trainer-developer at the Far West Laboratory for Educational Research and Development, the American Institutes for Research, ROLM Corporation, and the University of Oregon. Her specializations include educational leadership, the psychology of studying, and training and development in education and industry. Her other books include *Educational Research: An Introduction, Making the Grade, Help Your Son or Daughter Study for Success*, and *Tools for Learning: A Guide to Teaching Study Skills*.

Preface

GOALS OF THIS BOOK
Relating Research to Practice

This book on research methods differs most significantly from other books of its type in its emphasis on helping educators see the relevance of research to their daily work. This goal of making research relevant is accomplished by focusing on "problems of practice," a phrase that we use to refer to the ongoing calls for curriculum improvement, the urgent demands of new federal and state policies for schools, and the compelling unmet needs of students and their teachers. Throughout the book, we demonstrate how empirical research helps educators think methodically about problems of practice and work toward their solution.

Each chapter begins with a list of the problems of practice featured in the chapter's research examples and full-text article reprint. Here are examples of the problems, stated in the form of questions:

Chapter 1. What can be done to improve high school graduation rates?

Chapter 5. What can be done to increase the currently small percentage of females who take courses and pursue careers in STEM disciplines (science, technology, engineering, math)?

Chapter 9. Is an online course sufficient, or does it need to be blended with some form of classroom instruction?

Chapter 12. What can be done to improve middle school students' life skills, especially avoidance of harmful drugs?

Chapter 14. How can YouTube and other social websites help us understand students' interests and perspectives on the world around them?

Chapter 19. Should the evaluation of schools and teachers be focused primarily on how well their students perform on achievement tests?

This book includes these and more than 100 other problems of practice that educators are likely to encounter in their careers and research-based efforts to help solve them. In other words, educators learn research skills in a context that contributes to their work lives and professional development.

iv

Comprehending Research Terms and Procedures

In order to read or conduct research studies, educators need to learn research terminology and procedures. Therefore, we have sought to explain all of the research terms and procedures that educators are likely to come across as they review or conduct research studies. For this reason, *Applying Educational Research* can serve both as a textbook for a research methods course and as a reference book for professional use.

Locating Relevant Research Studies

As educators encounter problems of practice, they need efficient procedures for locating relevant research studies. Chapter 4 and Appendix 2 teach these procedures. If educators need to prepare a formal literature review to synthesize what they have learned from their search, Chapter 3 teaches the requisite skills.

Evaluating Research Studies

Any research study is likely to have both strengths and weaknesses. Therefore, one of our goals is to help educators develop skills for evaluating research studies. Most chapters in this book provide criteria for evaluating studies that used the research design presented in that chapter. Also, three of the appendices include questions that educators can ask themselves when evaluating quantitative and qualitative research studies in general, supplemented by questions for evaluating the specific design of a study.

Conducting Research Studies

Many educators will need to conduct a research study as a requirement for earning an advanced degree. Therefore, one of our goals is to explain all of the skills that novice researchers will need to conduct their study. These skills also provide a foundation for educators whose careers require advanced training in research methodology. Chapter 2 provides an overview of all aspects of a research study, from the initial design and pilot study to the preparation of a final report of the study's findings. Once educators have this overview, they can study the specialized steps for conducting a study using any of the research designs in Parts Three, Four, and Five of the book.

NEW TO THIS EDITION

This book is a substantial revision of the sixth edition of *Applying Educational Research*. It updates the problems of practice that concern educators and also the research studies within the chapters and the resources for further study, and it provides more recent reprinted articles at the end of chapters as well. It also presents new developments in research methodology.

- We present 136 examples of current problems of practice distributed across 19 chapters. A new feature of the book is that the problems are stated as questions and put in list form at the beginning of each chapter. We selected problems that confront educators at all levels of schooling, from kindergarten through graduate school, and educators who serve in a variety of roles, including teachers, administrators, counselors, school psychologists, higher education personnel, staff development specialists, and teacher educators.
- The book includes 18 full-text research articles, 13 of which are new to this edition. Nine of the new articles were published in 2010 or later, and all address significant problems of practice that confront educators today.
- The chapters illustrate various research procedures by referring to more than 90 research studies and literature reviews conducted in the United States and other countries. Approximately one-third of the studies have publication years of 2010 or later.
- All but two of the chapters describe a problem of practice that has been brought to the public's attention by a newspaper or other news service. Most of these news reports are new to this edition.
- The previous edition had two chapters (Chapters 4 and 5) to present skills in using search engines and making use of available literature reviews. We combined them into one chapter (Chapter 4), because user input indicated that many educators learn how to

use search engines prior to taking a research methods course. Educators who wish to build on these skills can study Appendix 2, which focuses specifically on the ERIC search engine because it is the one that educators are most likely to use.
- We switched the order of the chapters on tests of statistical significance and the practical significance of statistical results. This change was based on user input that the issue of practical significance is more meaningful to educators if they first study tests of statistical significance.
- We switched the order of the chapter on ethnography and critical research and the chapter on narrative research. Users of the sixth edition noted that qualitative case study research developed to a large extent from ethnography, and, therefore the chapter on ethnography should immediately follow the chapter on case studies.
- The *Resources for Further Study* section of each chapter has been updated to include articles, books, and other publications that have appeared since the previous edition.

ORGANIZATION OF THE BOOK

The first chapter of Part One is an overview of the nature of educational research and its relevance to solving problems of practice in education. Chapter 2 summarizes all of the steps involved in designing and completing a research study. It is supplemented by Appendix 1, which contains a form for outlining a research proposal.

The first chapter of Part Two (Chapter 3) describes a systematic process for conducting and writing a literature review. Chapter 4 describes the use of search engines and published literature reviews.

Part Three begins with Chapter 5, which is an overview about how to read and evaluate reports of quantitative research studies. The next three chapters explain various types of statistical analysis: descriptive statistics in Chapter 6, tests of statistical significance in Chapter 7, and ways to determine the practical significance of statistical results in Chapter 8. The remaining chapters in Part Three explain various quantitative research designs: descriptive (Chapter 9), group comparison (Chapter 10), correlational (Chapter 11), and experimental (Chapter 12).

Part Four starts with Chapter 13, which describes the methods used in the most basic type of qualitative research—case studies. The remaining chapters explain specialized qualitative designs: ethnography and critical research in Chapter 14, narrative research in Chapter 15, and historical research in Chapter 16.

Part Five includes a single chapter (Chapter 17), which is about mixed-methods research. This approach to research design is discussed separately because it incorporates elements of both quantitative designs, the subject of Part Three, and qualitative designs, the subject of Part Four.

Part Six includes chapters on action research (Chapter 18) and evaluation research (Chapter 19). These research methods can employ either quantitative or qualitative designs, or elements of both.

ORGANIZATION OF THE CHAPTERS

Beginning of Chapter

Each chapter begins with a list of the problems of practice that are featured in the full-text article reprint and in the research studies discussed in the body of the chapter. Next comes a list of the chapter's important ideas. This list provides an initial overview when one is starting to read a chapter, and it then serves as a convenient summary when reviewing the chapter later.

The third list includes the chapter's key terms. Each key term is boldfaced at the point where it is defined in the chapter. Definitions also appear in the book's glossary.

Body of Chapter

The main text of each chapter describes the techniques for using a particular research design or statistical method, or for conducting a literature search. Published research studies, each focused on a particular problem of practice, are used to illustrate these procedures. Another significant feature of most chapters is a section on how to analyze and evaluate reports of studies that used a particular research design. Most chapters also include a section that illustrates how particular research designs can be used to investigate a problem of practice that was brought to the public's attention by an actual news article.

End of Chapter

This section includes a self-check test (with answers provided at the end of the book), chapter references, and resources for further study. Most chapters also include a full-text article that is reprinted from the original publication source. Each article is an exemplar of the research design covered in the chapter.

SUGGESTED STUDY STRATEGY

Examine the Book's Organization

Before reading the book, explore its layout: the table of contents, the list of reprinted articles, the organization of each chapter in the Detailed Contents, and the end matter (self-check test answers, appendixes, glossary, and name and subject indexes).

Start Each Chapter by Reading the Lists

Studying the lists of problems of practice, important ideas, and key terms will help you see what you already know about the chapter's topics and what will be new to you.

Read the Body of the Chapter

As you read the chapter, reflect on how the research techniques and examples relate to a problem of practice that is familiar to you or to a study that you might conduct.

Read the Full-Text Article(s)

As you read each reprinted research article, analyze how it employs the techniques described in the chapter. Also, consider how the findings of the study contribute to your understanding of problems of practice that you encounter in your work. If you come across an unfamiliar technical term in an article, you will most likely find it defined in the glossary. Another option is to look for it in the subject index, and then read the section of the book that explains it.

Check Your Mastery

After reading the chapter, return to the list of important ideas and see whether you can elaborate on them in your own words. Similarly, see if you can provide your own definition for each term in the list of key terms. If you come across a topic that you have not mastered, study the chapter further or use another resource, such as Google, which often yields informative websites. Then take the self-check test in the chapter, which includes multiple-choice items related to the chapter's important ideas. If you wish to expand your understanding of particular topics, you can read the resources for further study listed at the end of the chapter.

Prepare for Tests

You can prepare for the instructor's tests by reviewing the lists of important ideas and key terms, any chapter material that you highlighted, and your class notes. Another useful strategy is to hold a review session with one or more of you classmates. You can take turns acting as the instructor, making up questions about the chapter content and having classmates answer them.

Complete Homework Assignments

If your instructor gives you assignments that involve preparing a research proposal or conducting a study, you can refer to Chapter 2 and the guide in Appendix 1 to help you. If you are given assignments involving the preparation of a literature review, you can refer to the chapters in Part Two and Appendix 2.

If an assignment requires you to evaluate a full-text research article, you can refer to Appendix 3 (general criteria for evaluating quantitative research studies), Appendix 4 (general criteria for evaluating qualitative research studies), and Appendix 5 (evaluation criteria that are specific to a particular research design). Also, you can read about these evaluation criteria in the chapter where they are explained.

If you are asked to identify a problem of practice and explain how research might shed light on it, you will find it helpful to refer to the section titled *An Example of How [chapter topic] Can Help in Solving Problems of Practice* at the end of most chapters.

INSTRUCTOR'S MANUAL

The Instructor's Manual for the seventh edition of *Applying Educational Research* includes suggestions for designing an introductory research course for undergraduate or graduate students in education and related fields, teaching activities related to each chapter's content, and a test-item bank with both multiple-choice and short-answer items covering the content of each chapter.

ACKNOWLEDGMENTS

We thank our many colleagues who have shared with us their knowledge, insights, and experiences relating to educational research. In particular, we express our appreciation to the following reviewers for their helpful feedback about the sixth edition: Vikki K. Collins, Troy University; Ronald F. Dugan, College of Saint Rose; and Fred Jacobs, American University. We also wish to thank our copyeditor, Cassie Tuttle, for her careful review of the manuscript and helpful suggestions.

M. D. (Mark) Gall

Joyce P. (Joy) Gall

Brief Contents

Contents

PART FIVE COMBINING QUANTITATIVE AND QUALITATIVE METHODOLOGIES TO STUDY PROBLEMS OF PRACTICE

CHAPTER 17 MIXED-METHODS RESEARCH 474

PART SIX USING OTHER RESEARCH METHODOLOGIES TO STUDY PROBLEMS OF PRACTICE

CHAPTER 18 ACTION RESEARCH 503

Reprinted Articles

The following articles are reprinted exactly as they appeared in the original source, except that the format of the original articles (e.g., column layout) has been standardized for presentation in this text. Two exceptions are the reprinted case study in Chapter 13 and the reprinted article in Chapter 14, where several typographical errors in the original articles were corrected with the permission of the authors of these articles.

CHAPTER 1

Use of Research Evidence, p. 21

Willis, J. (2009). How students' sleepy brains fail them. *Kappa Delta Pi Record, 45*(4), 158–162.

CHAPTER 3

Professional Review, p. 71

Marzano, R. J., & Pickering, D. J. (2007). The case for and against homework. *Educational Leadership, 64*(6), 74–79.

Meta-Analysis, p. 76

Graham, S., & Sandmel, K. (2011). The process writing approach: A meta-analysis. *The Journal of Educational Research, 104*(6), 396–407.

CHAPTER 5

Quantitative Research Study, p. 132

Dickin, K. L., Lent, M., Lu, A. H., Sequeira, J., & Dollahite, J. S. (2012). Developing a measure of behavior change in a program to help low-income parents prevent unhealthful weight gain in children. *Journal of Nutrition Education and Behavior, 44*(1), 12–21.

CHAPTER 8

Practical Significance of Research Findings, p. 201

Popham, W. J. (2005). Can growth ever be beside the point? *Educational Leadership, 63*(3), 83–84.

CHAPTER 9

Descriptive Research Study, p. 222

Picciano, A. G., Seaman, J., Shea, P., & Swan, K. (2012). Examining the extent and nature of online learning in American K–12 education: The research initiatives of the Alfred P. Sloan Foundation. *Internet and Higher Education, 15*, 127–135.

CHAPTER 10

Group Comparison Research Study, p. 248

Al-Amoush, S. A., Abu-Hola, I., & Eilks, I. (2011). Jordanian prospective and experienced chemistry teachers' beliefs about teaching and learning and their potential for educational reform. *Science Education International, 22*(3), 185–201.

CHAPTER 11

Correlational Research Study, p. 284

Sperling, R. A., Richmond, A. S., Ramsay C. M., & Klapp, M. (2012). The measurement and predictive ability of metacognition in middle school learners. *Journal of Educational Research, 105*(1), 1–7.

CHAPTER 12

Group Experiment, p. 322

McDonald, L., Moberg, D. P., Brown, R., Rodriguez-Espiricueta, I., Flores, N. I., Burke, M. P., & Coover, G. (2006). After-school multifamily groups: A randomized controlled trial involving low-income, urban, Latino children. *Children & Schools, 28*(1), 25–34.

Single-Case Experiment, p. 332

Amato-Zech, N. A., Hoff, K. E., & Doepke, K. J. (2006). Increasing on-task behavior in the classroom: Extension of self-monitoring strategies. *Psychology in the Schools, 43*(2), 211–221.

CHAPTER 13

Case Story, p. 368

Sacks, A. (2007, September 11). Teaching secrets: Ask the kids! *Teacher Magazine.* Retrieved January 17, 2009 from www.teachermagazine.org/tm/articles/2007/09/11/03tln_sacks_web.h19.html

Case Study, p. 369

Açikalin, M. (2010). Exemplary social studies teachers' use of computer-supported instruction in the classroom. *TOJET: The Turkish Journal of Educational Technology, 9*(4), 66–82.

CHAPTER 14

Critical Ethnography, p. 410

Trafi-Prats, L (2009). Destination Raval Sud: A visual ethnography on pedagogy, aesthetics, and the spatial experience of growing up urban. *Studies in Art Education, 51*(1), 6–20.

CHAPTER 15

Narrative Research Study, p. 437

Pearce, J., & Morrison, C. (2011). Teacher identity and early career resilience: Exploring the links. *Australian Journal of Teacher Education, 36*(1), Article 4, 48–59.

CHAPTER 16

Historical Research Study, p. 462

Rousmaniere, K. (2007). Go to the principal's office: Toward a social history of the school principal in North America. *History of Education Quarterly, 47*(1), 1–22.

CHAPTER 17

Mixed-Methods Research Study, p. 494

Isernhagen, J. C. (2012). A portrait of administrator, teacher, and parent perceptions of Title I school improvement plans. *The Journal of At-Risk Issues, 17*(1), 1–7.

CHAPTER ONE

Using Research Evidence to Improve Educational Practice

PROBLEMS OF PRACTICE *in this chapter*

- How much emphasis should a language arts curriculum place on nonfiction works versus fiction?
- Is students' physical fitness important for their learning?
- Does the Internet support or hurt student learning?
- What criteria should be used to evaluate teacher performance?
- What can be done to improve high school graduation rates?
- How can educators help the many students who switch from one school district to another each year?
- What can be done to help elementary teachers place more emphasis on developing children's thinking skills?
- How much federal funding for education should be allocated for research?

IMPORTANT *Ideas*

1. Educational research is having an increasing impact on educational policy and practice.
2. Evidence-based practice is becoming more prevalent in medicine, psychology, education, and other professions.
3. Teachers' traditional motivations and workplace conditions have not been conducive to evidence-based practice.
4. Evidence-based practice in education has four key elements: (1) focus on problems of practice, (2) reliance on research evidence, (3) clinical expertise, and (4) respect for stakeholders' values.
5. An important impetus for improving education is heightened awareness of pressing problems of practice and a commitment to solve them.
6. Educators need to understand research methodology so they can evaluate the quality of others' research or conduct their own research.
7. Educators need to view research evidence from multiple ethical perspectives.
8. Educators can collaborate productively with researchers by participating in their research studies or by joining with them in shaping policy agendas to improve education.

9. Research differs from other forms of inquiry in its emphasis on (1) making direct observations of phenomena; (2) taking steps to eliminate, or make explicit, personal bias in data collection, analysis, and interpretation; and (3) carefully determining the generalizability of findings to individuals and situations other than those that were studied.

10. Research produces four types of knowledge: (1) descriptions, (2) predictions, (3) evidence about the effects of experimental interventions, and (4) explanations.

11. The purpose of basic research is to understand fundamental processes and structures that underlie observed behavior, whereas the purpose of applied research is to develop and validate interventions that can be used directly to improve practice.

12. Postmodernists believe that no one method of inquiry is inherently better than any other, whereas social scientists believe that their methods of inquiry have a special legitimacy and claim to authority, based on use of (1) explicitly defined concepts or procedures available for inspection by anyone; (2) replication studies to test the soundness of findings from a single study; (3) knowledge claims that can be tested, and possibly refuted, by empirical data; and (4) explicit procedures to minimize researcher errors and biases.

13. Quantitative and qualitative research differ in various ways, but chiefly in epistemology. Quantitative researchers assume an objective social reality that exists independently of observers and participants, whereas qualitative researchers assume that social reality is continuously constructed by observers and participants.

14. Mixed-methods research studies make use of both quantitative and qualitative research methods.

KEY TERMS

action research	epistemology	progressive discourse
APA Presidential Task Force on Evidence-Based Practice	evaluation research	qualitative research
	evidence-based practice	quantitative research
applied research	experimental method	reflexivity
basic research	interpretivism	refutation
clinical expertise	No Child Left Behind Act	replication
Cochrane Collaboration	positivism	theory
construct	postmodernism	triangulation
descriptive research	prediction research	What Works Clearinghouse
educational research		

Each of the principal authors of this book (Mark Gall and Joy Gall) has had a career in education spanning more than 40 years. Our experience leads us to stand in awe of the many educational practitioners (called *educators* in this book) who do such a remarkable job of teaching increasingly diverse students while also performing many other school functions, all in the face of ever-present budgetary challenges and shifting policy initiatives.

We also are impressed by the expansion of educational research over the past 40 years. An ever-growing network of researchers throughout the world has developed sophisticated methods for studying the educational enterprise, producing a substantial body of research knowledge and efficient electronic methods for accessing it.

Unfortunately, something is missing from this picture of progress. We have not yet witnessed a meaningful bridge between educational research and educational practice. Researchers and educators live mostly in separate worlds. They come together only occasionally in university courses, workshops, conferences, and journals that both groups read.

There are signs, though, that the two worlds—the world of educational practice and the world of educational research—are coming closer. The signs, mostly seen at the level of national legislation and policy making, point to a sea change in education. The findings of educational research are becoming increasingly influential in shaping national and state legislation about education, which in turn is compelling changes in educational practice.

If you are an educator, these changes mean that you will need to study research if you wish to enter into a dialogue with researchers and the policy makers who make decisions based on research findings. Otherwise, you and your colleagues might find yourselves in the uncomfortable position of trying to implement programs and policies that you did not have a voice in shaping.

In short, we claim that educational research is becoming too important for anyone interested in schooling to ignore. In the next sections, we make our case for the validity of this claim. We invite you to reflect on the soundness of the claim and, if you think it has merit, how you plan to respond in your role as an educator.

EVIDENCE-BASED PROFESSIONAL PRACTICE

The movement called **evidence-based practice** has created a remarkable change in the relationship between educational research and practice. This relatively new approach to professional decision making relies on rigorous research findings rather than custom, personal experience, or intuition. For example, suppose a teacher recommends that a student needs one-on-one tutoring to come up to grade level in writing skills. Suppose the parents ask whether tutoring is likely to help their child. A teacher who is well versed in evidence-based practice would be able to refer to research findings demonstrating the effectiveness of tutoring and then justify the applicability of this research to their child's needs.

Evidence-based practice is changing the foundations of various professions. We will consider two of these professions—medicine and clinical psychology—before discussing evidence-based practice in education. Perhaps you will agree with us that evidence-based practice is not just a passing fad, but rather a fundamental advance.

Evidence-Based Practice in Medicine

Suppose you have a heart problem and seek treatment for it. How do you decide on the best treatment? You might try to contact other patients with the same problem. Perhaps they will offer testimonials about some medicine or individual who helped them. Another option is to seek a professional opinion, probably by making an appointment to see a doctor with expertise, such as a board-certified doctor in cardiology.

Testimonials, case examples, and expert opinions can be worthwhile. On the other hand, they might lead you astray if they are based on untested beliefs, inaccurate observations, or reliance on outmoded research. Evidence-based practice in medicine represents an effort to avoid such pitfalls. It does so by basing treatment decisions on the best possible research evidence about a patient's condition (Straus et al., 2010).

Evidence-based medical practice has two significant features. The first involves the need to identify good research evidence. The fact that a research study has been published does not necessarily guarantee that its findings are sound. Professionals need to sift through research findings to determine which ones hold up well under critical scrutiny. Although researchers might be in the best position to do this screening, medical practitioners also need to understand research methodology to validate for themselves what others consider good research evidence for a particular treatment option. For example, medical practitioners need to understand that researchers use systematic procedures to synthesize evidence collected across research studies on a particular medical intervention, such as meta-analysis, which we describe in Chapter 4.

Several organizations coordinate and publish these research syntheses. Among the most prominent is the **Cochrane Collaboration**, whose website (cochrane.org) publishes reviews of research on interventions for various medical problems. For example, when we visited the site, we found featured reviews on the use of sound therapies for autism spectrum disorders, behavioral interventions to reduce the transmission of HIV infection, and the comparative effectiveness of computer-assisted and oral-and-written methods for recording the diet history of patients with diabetes.

The second feature of evidence-based medical practice is the use of clinical expertise in applying research evidence. A treatment option that is generally effective might be harmful for a particular patient. For this reason, the Cochrane Collaboration states: "Evidence-based medicine is the conscientious, explicit and judicious use of current best evidence in making decisions about the care of individual patients" (Cochrane Collaboration, n.d.). **Clinical expertise** is the ability to make informed ethical judgments about whether a particular professional intervention is both evidence-based and appropriate for the needs of an individual client.

We see then that evidence-based medicine does not seek to improve medical practice by research evidence alone or by clinical expertise alone. Both are necessary in order to create a sound bridge between medical research and medical practice.

Evidence-Based Practice in Psychology

Psychological practice to help clients with various emotional, cognitive, and medical problems has grown enormously over the past half-century. Recently, it has evolved into evidence-based practice. In 2005, the American Psychological Association (APA) commissioned the APA Presidential Task Force on Evidence-Based Practice (APA Task Force, 2006). The work of this task force should be of interest to educators because educational practice has been influenced greatly by psychology, especially in the areas of achievement testing, instructional design, and behavior management.

The APA Task Force defined evidence-based practice in psychology as "the integration of the best available research with clinical expertise in the context of patient characteristics, culture, and preferences" (APA Task Force 2006, p. 273). You will notice that this definition is similar to the Cochrane Collaboration's definition of evidence-based medicine, but with an even greater emphasis on the

importance of the client's individual characteristics in determining an effective intervention.

The Task Force concluded that a variety of research methods can generate evidence to guide psychological practice, among which are methods that are also commonly used in educational research. These methods are covered in different chapters of this book:

- Clinical observation, including individual case studies (Chapter 13)
- Single-case experimental designs (Chapter 12)
- Ethnographic research (Chapter 14)
- Experiments on treatment efficacy (Chapter 12)
- Meta-analysis to synthesize research results from multiple studies (Chapter 4)

Keep in mind, then, that learning about the methods of educational research described in this book has multiple benefits. Your learning will apply to education but also will generalize to research as it is conducted in other professions, including psychology, medicine, business, and technology development.

The Task Force analyzed eight components of clinical expertise in psychology. Struck by their applicability to clinical expertise in teaching, we list them in Figure 1.1. As you study the list, we invite you to draw parallels to the teaching process and to reflect on how it is possible to interweave clinical expertise and research evidence.

EVIDENCE-BASED PRACTICE IN EDUCATION

Robert Slavin (2002) provides us with a concise statement about the history of educational practice and its current status:

> At the dawn of the 21st century, education is finally being dragged, kicking and screaming, into the 20th century. The scientific revolution that utterly transformed medicine, agriculture, transportation, technology, and other fields early in the 20th century almost completely bypassed the field of education. If Rip Van Winkle had been a physician, a farmer, or an engineer, he would be unemployable if he awoke today. If he had been a good elementary school teacher in the 19th century, he would probably be a good elementary school teacher today. It is not

FIGURE 1.1 • Components of Clinical Expertise in Evidence-Based Psychological Practice

1. *Diagnostic judgment and treatment planning.* "The clinically expert psychologist is able to formulate clear and theoretically coherent case conceptualizations, assess patient pathology as well as clinically relevant strengths, understand complex patient presentations, and make accurate diagnostic judgments."

2. *Treatment implementation and monitoring.* "Clinical expertise entails the skillful and flexible delivery of treatment. Skill and flexibility require knowledge of and proficiency in delivering psychological interventions and the ability to adapt the treatment to the particular case."

3. *Interpersonal expertise.* "Central to clinical expertise is interpersonal skill, which is manifested in forming a therapeutic relationship, encoding and decoding verbal and nonverbal responses, creating realistic but positive expectations, and responding empathically to the patient's explicit and implicit experiences and concerns."

4. *Self-reflection and self-development.* "Clinical expertise requires the ability to reflect on one's own experience, knowledge, hypotheses, inferences, emotional reactions, and behaviors and to use that reflection to modify one's practices accordingly."

5. *Evaluation and application of research evidence.* "Clinical expertise in psychology includes scientific expertise. . . . An understanding of scientific method allows psychologists to consider evidence from a range of research designs, evaluate the internal and external validity of individual studies, evaluate the magnitude of effects across studies, and apply relevant research to individual cases."

6. *Sensitivity to individual differences.* "Clinical expertise requires an awareness of the individual, social, and cultural context of the patient, including but not limited to age and development, ethnicity, culture, race, gender, sexual orientation, religious commitments, and socioeconomic status."

7. *Willingness to draw on other resources.* "When research evidence indicates the value of adjunctive services or when patients are not making progress as expected, the psychologist may seek consultation or make a referral."

8. *Planning phase prior to treatment.* "Clinical expertise requires a planful approach to the treatment of psychological problems. . . . Psychologists rely on well-articulated case formulations, knowledge of relevant research, and the organization provided by theoretical conceptualizations and clinical experience to craft interventions designed to attain desired outcomes."

Source: Based on APA Presidential Task Force on Evidence-Based Practice (2006). Evidence-based practice in psychology. *American Psychologist 61*(4), 271–285.

that we have not learned anything since Rip Van Winkle's time. It is that applications of the findings of educational research remain haphazard, and that evidence is respected only occasionally, and only if it happens to correspond to current educational or political fashions. (p. 16)

We believe that Slavin's assessment is accurate. This leads us to ask, Why has education been so resistant to research?

Traditional Educational Practice

Most educators start their careers by preparing to be teachers. Their motivations often involve a love of children, personal gratification in seeing students learn and develop, a passion for particular subject areas (e.g., science, social studies, literature), and a desire to instill this passion in others.

Another motivating factor is that the teaching profession allows for independence and creative freedom; teachers typically have responsibility for their own classroom with minimal supervision by others. The desire to apply research to practice, if present, does not have nearly the same priority as these other motivations for entering the teaching profession.

Another attraction of teaching is that the professional preparation program is not as demanding as that for other professions such as medicine and psychology. In fact, in regions with teacher shortages, college graduates are typically able to begin teaching immediately if they agree to professional preparation, either concurrently or over several summers. There is relatively little opportunity for research training within the typical teacher preparation curriculum.

After becoming licensed and employed by a school system, teachers typically find that the work of a classroom teacher is time-consuming and often stressful. They also experience professional isolation because they and their colleagues are so busy meeting their students' needs. There is little free time to discuss issues and ideas or how to apply research evidence to problems of practice.

Many teachers are able to develop increasing expertise as their careers progress, but they have little opportunity to share it with others. They eventually retire and take their hard-won expertise with them. There is no system for recording that expertise, testing its validity through systematic research, and then making it available to novice teachers.

During their careers, some teachers earn additional licenses and degrees. With these credentials, they can assume positions as instructional specialists, school administrators, or education professors. Their basic outlook on education, however, continues to be shaped by their experiences as classroom teachers, not by their knowledge of research evidence.

Other roadblocks exist to building bridges between research and existing educational practice. Even if researchers have strong evidence to support a new instructional method, they lack authority to require its use. Also, researchers who ask educators to join in seeking legislation to fund educational research might find that educators' priority is to seek funding for their own pressing needs.

The Movement Toward Evidence-Based Education

As we noted above, the APA created an official definition of evidence-based practice in psychology. We have modified this description to define *evidence-based practice* in education as the art of solving problems of practice through the integration of the best available research combined with educators' clinical expertise and values. Clinical expertise involves the types of skills listed in Figure 1.1. Values, as we explain later in this chapter, govern the ethics of both research and practice.

The federal government has moved strongly in the direction of evidence-based education. The **No Child Left Behind Act** of 2001 (commonly referred to as NCLB) requires every state to specify standards of achievement in basic skills that all students in certain grades are expected to meet. Furthermore, educators are required to use scientifically

based research evidence in choosing programs and procedures to help students achieve those standards. NCLB administrators and many researchers believe that randomized experiments (see Chapter 12) produce the best possible research evidence for improving educational practice.

NCLB has been heavily criticized (e.g., Ravitch, 2011) for various reasons, such as imposing requirements on schools without providing adequate funding, focusing only on basic skills, forcing teachers to "teach to the test," and threatening public education by allowing parents with children in "failing" schools to transfer them to nonpublic schools.

We do not know at the present time whether NCLB will survive in the political arena. However, even if it is revoked, some elements of it are likely to continue, including a continued push to base educational practice on the best possible research evidence. Because medicine, psychology, and other professions appear to have made a long-term commitment to evidence-based practice, it will be difficult for education to stand alone against this movement.

Another sign of the movement toward evidence-based education is the establishment of the Institute of Education Sciences (IES) by the U.S. Department of Education in 2002. The mission of this institute is "to provide rigorous evidence on which to ground education practice and policy" (U.S. Department of Education, n.d.). IES currently includes four centers, all of which support scientifically based research to improve student learning outcomes.

IES also administers the **What Works Clearinghouse** (WWC), whose mission is "to promote informed education decision making through a set of easily accessible databases and user-friendly reports that provide education consumers with high-quality reviews of the effectiveness of replicable interventions (programs, products, practices, and policies) that intend to improve student outcomes" (Institute of Education Sciences, n.d.). WWC's syntheses of research on educational interventions are similar to those of the Cochrane Collaboration, described earlier in the section on evidence-based medicine. We describe WWC in more detail in Chapter 4.

Problems of Practice in Education

The greatest impetus for improving professional practice is the acknowledgement of problems. The medical profession is a good example of this principle. Disease and injuries, and the human suffering that accompanies them, are problems that cry out for solutions. For this reason, basic and applied medical research is heavily funded by governmental agencies and the private sector all over the world. New treatments that ameliorate a medical problem, even to a modest degree, gradually find their way into medical practice.

Serious problems also abound in education, and the news media continually bring them to the public's attention. Consider this statement by Dana Hawkins-Simons (2008) in *U.S. News & World Report:*

> Each week seems to bring more evidence of how the United States is losing step with the rest of the developed world when it comes to educating children. Seventy percent of eighth graders are not proficient in reading, over a million high schoolers drop out each year, and nearly one third of college freshmen must take remedial math or English courses. (p. 29)

If evidence-based programs and procedures are available to lessen the severity of these problems, the education profession has a moral imperative to examine them closely and to consider adopting them.

You can develop your own sensitivity to the problems that educators need to solve by reading various news sources, including daily newspapers. These news sources often publish articles about school incidents, academic achievement data, poll results, and policy debates that highlight problems of educational practice. In fact, some of the problems of practice that we present as features near the end of each chapter in this book (including this chapter) are drawn directly from news sources.

ASCD SmartBrief is a particularly informative news source about problems—and successes—that are likely to be of interest to educators. Each item in the newsletter summarizes a recent newspaper article, journal article, or institutional report that has educational relevance. Published by the Association for Supervision and Curriculum Development, one of the largest professional organizations for educators in the United States, it is available online (smartbrief.com/ascd).

We reviewed *SmartBrief* newsletter items from 2012 to identify which educational problems were the frequent subject of news reports. A sample of the problems revealed by our search is shown in Figure 1.2.

Individual teachers and school districts might try to solve problems like these on their own. However, their magnitude is so great that more systematic, well-funded efforts are necessary, involving the development of innovative programs and procedures whose effectiveness is tested by researchers. On the other hand, some problems require **basic research**, which seeks to go beyond the surface manifestations of a problem and study it at a more fundamental level to identify underlying processes and structures. Eventually, basic research should yield insights that have practical applications.

In summary, evidence-based practice that addresses compelling problems of teaching and learning probably is our best long-term approach to improving education. For this approach to work, every educator and policy maker will need to understand how research evidence is generated and the factors that differentiate high-quality research from weak research. The purpose of this book is to help you acquire this understanding, either for the purpose of doing your own research or for judging whether research done by others is sound and applicable to your own professional practice.

The Ethics of Educational Research and Practice

Ethical issues in research are of great concern to the general public and to the research community. These issues are two types: (1) issues involving the conduct and reporting of research studies and (2) issues involving the use of research findings. An example of the first type of issue is whether researchers have taken adequate steps to protect sensitive data (e.g., individual students' scores on high-stakes tests) from nonauthorized groups. Another example is whether researchers have obtained consent from individuals to participate in their studies.

In Chapter 2, we discuss these and many other issues that researchers must consider when undertaking a study. Here, we consider the second type of issue, that is, the ethical use of research findings. We start by noting that education is a thoroughly human enterprise. As humans, our values can, and should, influence our judgments and behavior. For example, researchers might identify an effective set of procedures for reducing the incidence of student misbehavior in school. However, the procedures

FIGURE 1.2 • Significant Problems of Practice in Education

Teacher expertise.

Data indicate that students with science degrees can earn thousands of dollars more annually by opting to go into fields other than teaching, writes Gerald F. Wheeler, the executive director of the National Science Teachers Association. Perhaps that's why nearly half of high school biology students and roughly two-thirds of chemistry and physics students are taught by teachers without majors or certification in the relevant field, he writes.

(*Education Week*, May 13, 2008)

Educating the talented and gifted.

Dalton Sargent's poor grades, despite his high IQ, are emblematic of the nation's failure to address the needs of the 3 million U.S. children identified as gifted and more who are never labeled, advocates say.

(*Los Angeles Times*, May 12, 2008)

Mathematics education.

California's requirement that each high school graduate pass algebra was meant to better prepare students for college, but instead, community colleges are finding more students lacking in both algebra and basic math skills. "It's the million-dollar question," said Mary Martin, who chairs the math department at a community college where nearly 52% of students require remedial math courses, up from 43% in 2003. "We are asking more of our high school students, so why isn't it transferring over to college?"

(*The Sacramento Bee*, May 12, 2008)

Fostering student creativity.

Many employers value workers with creative skills, yet new research suggests most high schools provide the problem-solving or artistic endeavors believed to foster creativity only on an elective basis. "The findings . . . present an opportunity for school systems and business leaders to further engage in a dialogue about how best to foster creativity among students, not only to produce a competitive workforce, but also to help all students succeed in life," said Paul D. Houston, executive director of the American Association of School Administrators.

(*eSchool News*, May 2, 2008)

Student boredom.

Teens capable of producing YouTube videos, publishing anime or podcasting are likely to be underwhelmed by school, researchers say. "Kids associate one word with school: 'boring,'" Deborah Stipek, a Stanford professor and dean of education, said, adding, "The question becomes what is the role of school in this larger environment."

(*CNET*, April 24, 2008)

Student bullying.

Students who self-report regular bullying behavior are more likely than their classmates to experience difficulty in relating to their friends or parents, are apt to associate with other bullies, display aggressive tendencies, and lack strong moral values, according to a study of 871 students, conducted by researchers at York University and Queens University.

(*ScienceDaily*, March 26, 2008)

Source: News items referenced in *ASCD SmartBrief*, a publication of the Association for Supervision and Curriculum Development

might have harmful effects on students' self-esteem, motivation, or respect for teachers. Other solutions that are effective for students and do not have negative side effects might be so expensive that they diminish the budget for other educational priorities.

Evidence-based practice, then, must not endorse blind use of research evidence, no matter how sound it is. For example, in medicine, doctors might have effective procedures for prolonging the life of a patient, but it may be at the cost of great suffering with only a small probability of a positive outcome. All stakeholders, therefore, including the patient and the patient's loved ones, need to weigh treatment effectiveness and values in reaching a decision. Some professionals, called medical ethicists, specialize in identifying and weighing the values that are an inextricable part of medical research and practice. Similarly in education, all stakeholders concerned about students' and educators' well-being need to examine research evidence from the perspective of their own personal values as well as the shared values of society.

Keep in mind, too, that the relationship between research and practice is a two-way street. Educators need to make value judgments about research evidence as it becomes available. However, they also need to realize that their willingness to support research and seek out research findings is itself a value judgment. Educators who prefer to rely only on their own beliefs and experiences, without considering research evidence, might be denying students access to more effective programs and procedures than they are providing. In other words, the dismissal of evidence-based practice is a value-laden decision that should not be made lightly.

The use of research findings is an ethical issue even in basic research. For example, a study about a bird flu virus became a major news item recently (Grady & McNeil, Jr., 2011). Researchers were experimenting with the deadly virus H5N1. The mutated airborne virus created by the researchers could infect many people quickly and cause a pandemic. Without mutation, though, the deadly virus's harm is limited because it only can be transmitted from one bird to another or, more seldom, from one human to another.

Some experts argued that the experiment should not have been done because the procedures used to create the mutated virus and the virus itself might somehow fall into the wrong hands, with deadly consequences. Other experts argued that the experiment was worthwhile because the mutation might occur naturally in birds. Research findings about the deadly consequences of the mutation would alert scientists worldwide to monitor the bird population. If they found the mutated virus, they would alert appropriate authorities to take immediate steps to kill infected birds before the virus spread.

This example shows how an apparently innocent basic research study raises difficult ethical issues. These issues are not limited to the physical sciences but also can arise in educational research. For example, Arthur Jensen (1973), an educational researcher, conducted studies to determine whether white and black students differed in intelligence. He reported racial differences favoring white students and subsequently came under attack by fellow researchers and community leaders. They believed that the findings lent themselves to several interpretations, not just a genetic explanation, and that racists could use the findings to create unjust discrimination against racial minorities. More recently, two researchers (Herrnstein & Murray, 1994) came to similar conclusions about race differences in IQ and created a national controversy with the publication of their book, *Bell Curve*.

Resolving the ethical issues raised by the bird virus and intelligence studies is by no means straightforward. The medical profession has created the role of medical ethicist to help doctors with these issues, but there currently is no such role in the education profession. Instead, we rely on professional educational organizations, such as the American Educational Research Association, to monitor and take positions on ethical issues in research as they arise. As an educator, you too should examine research findings that affect you and your profession from multiple perspectives, including the all-important ethical perspective.

THE PURPOSE OF EDUCATIONAL RESEARCH

Up to this point in the chapter, we have discussed the relationship between research and educational practice, showing how evidence-based education can bridge these two enterprises. We now turn our attention to the nature of educational research and how it differs from other forms of inquiry.

We start with a definition. **Educational research** is the systematic collection and analysis of empirical data in order to develop valid, generalizable knowledge in the form of (1) descriptions of educational phenomena, (2) predictions about future events or performance, (3) evidence about the effects of experimental interventions, and (4) explanations of the basic processes that underlie observed phenomena.

This definition will become clearer as you study the chapters of this book. For now, we wish to highlight the fact that research seeks to produce *valid* knowledge, meaning that it uses special methods to control for personal biases and confounding factors that might compromise the soundness of its findings. Also, research seeks to produce *generalizable* knowledge, meaning that it uses special methods to produce knowledge applicable to other situations besides the one that was investigated. Finally, research relies on *empirical data*, meaning that it uses special methods to make replicable observations of the phenomena being studied.

Other forms of inquiry, such as personal observations and intuitive thinking, can also result in useful knowledge. However, they do not employ the special methods of educational research.

Our definition of educational research asserts that it produces four types of knowledge: (1) descriptions, (2) predictions, (3) evidence about the effects of experimental interventions, and (4) explanations. In the next sections, we discuss how research produces each of these types of knowledge.

Descriptive Research

The purpose of **descriptive research** is to make careful, highly detailed observations of educational phenomena. For example, Marilyn Adams's monumental synthesis of research on learning to read includes findings about how an individual's eyes move while reading text (Adams, 1990). Contrary to popular belief, researchers have found that good readers process every word in the text rather than engage in selective scanning, a finding with important implications for teaching children to read.

Descriptive research is particularly good for discovering problems of practice. For example, Mary McCaslin and her colleagues (2006) observed 145 teachers' classrooms (grades 3–5) during 447 visits for 2,736 ten-minute intervals. Among their many research findings they discovered:

> the cognitive demands of most observed instructional opportunities were judged as only basic facts and skills content (37%) or a mixture of basic facts and skills, elaborations, and related thinking (37%). In comparison, 3% of the instructional opportunities were judged to involve students only in tasks that involved higher-order thinking/reasoning. (p. 324)

McCaslin and colleagues note that these observations of normative practice are discrepant from "best practice" recommendations of groups such as the National Association for the Education of Young Children and the National Council of Teachers of Mathematics. These groups recommend "considerably more opportunities for 'constructive' learners to think, reason, and construct personally meaningful learning than we observed" (McCaslin et al., 2006, p. 327).

This discrepancy between normative and best practice in elementary schools is a serious problem whose solution would greatly improve education. If individuals claim that the problem might exist elsewhere but not in their particular school system, we might reasonably ask them to present empirical data to back their claim.

You will study methods of descriptive research in Chapters 5 and 9 involving the collection of numerical data. Other types of descriptive research rely primarily on verbal data, such as interviews, historical records, or ethnographic data. This research approach—often called qualitative research—is explained in the chapters of Part Four.

Prediction Research

Prediction research seeks to determine whether data collected at one point in time can predict behavior or events that occur at a later point in time. This type of research can be helpful in solving problems of practice. For example, we know that a substantial percentage of students drop out of high school or have poor academic achievement. If we could identify these students at a younger age, we might be able to provide them with instruction and other interventions to prevent these problems. Prediction research can provide knowledge to guide this identification process.

Another example involves college administrators, who often face the problem of having more applicants than they can accept. Prediction research can be helpful in identifying characteristics of students who will do well academically and in other aspects of college life. Future applicants then can be assessed on these characteristics in order to select those most likely to be successful in a particular college.

Prediction studies typically involve the use of group comparison or correlational methods, which are explained in Chapters 10 and 11.

Experimental Research

Some research studies try to determine the effects of a particular intervention in a natural or laboratory setting. Studies of this type use what is commonly called the **experimental method**. For example, many researchers have conducted experiments to determine whether introducing cooperative learning into a classroom improves students' learning. Any observed improvement in student learning can be considered an effect of the intervention and therefore an indicator of the intervention's effectiveness.

The findings of experimental research are particularly important to educators. Virtually everything they do is an intervention of some sort. For example, teachers intervene in students' lives in order to facilitate their learning or to help them with their personal problems. Administrators intervene by engaging in leadership behavior that facilitates the work of other individuals in the organization or that solves workplace problems. Experiments can determine which types of interventions are most likely to be successful.

Methods of experimentation involving quantitative data are explained in Chapter 12. Some researchers study the effects of an intervention by in-depth exploration of its use in one or a few situations. This type of research involves the use of case study methodology, which we explain in Chapter 13.

Educators, either on their own or in groups, can do small-scale experiments to improve local practice. They can test locally developed programs, or they can determine whether evidence-based programs developed elsewhere are effective in their particular school system. This approach, called **action research**, is explained in Chapter 18.

Educators, working together or with a professional researcher, can do studies to determine not only the effects of an intervention but also the value or worth of the intervention. For example, they might wish to determine whether the intervention is cost effective, better than other possible interventions, or valued by the community. This type of investigation, called **evaluation research**, is explained in Chapter 19.

Explanatory Research

The purpose of some research studies is to explain individual or group behavior. Explanatory research, as we use the term here, involves statements about cause-and-effect relationships. For example, a common explanation of the finding that students in some schools do better than average on state or national tests is that they come from families with a high socioeconomic status. In other words, socioeconomic status (the cause) is invoked as an explanation of students' academic achievement (the effect).

All the research methods previously mentioned, with the exception of purely descriptive methods, can be used to investigate cause-and-effect

relationships. The researchers hypothesize that one or more factors are causes and one or more factors are effects. They then collect data to determine whether variations in the presumed cause (e.g., schools with high teacher morale versus schools with low teacher morale) are associated with variations in the presumed effect (e.g., high student attendance rate versus low student attendance rate).

Some researchers investigate cause-and-effect relationships to develop and test theories. Indeed, some researchers believe that the ultimate goal of educational research is to develop theories that explain various aspects of education. A **theory** is an explanation of particular phenomena in terms of a set of underlying constructs and principles that relate these constructs to each other. **Constructs** are structures or processes that are presumed to underlie observed phenomena.

Theories about brain structures and processes are currently of great interest to professionals in various disciplines, including education. If researchers can determine how the brain works to facilitate or hamper students' learning and motivation, this understanding might well lead to new solutions to problems of practice. The journal article reprinted at the end of this chapter presents brain theories that help us understand the effects of sleep on students' learning. It also includes suggestions about how to help students get sufficient sleep. The author of the article is a neurologist who became a classroom teacher.

Basic and Applied Research

Researchers do not use a single approach to inquiry. Some of their investigations can be characterized as basic research, whereas others can be characterized as applied research. The purpose of basic research, as previously noted, is to understand fundamental processes and structures that underlie observed behavior.

For example, we can observe teachers and students in a classroom as they engage in their activities. We might note that the teacher distributed a worksheet to the students and gave directions for completing it and that students took a writing instrument and made marks on their worksheet. These behavioral observations might be useful information, but they do not tell us what the teacher and students were thinking or what neural–chemical processes were activated in the students' brains as they learned new skills and concepts by completing the worksheet. The study of processes that underlie observed behavior is the province of **basic research**.

In contrast, the purpose of **applied research** is to develop and test interventions that can be used directly to improve practice. In education, the development and testing of a new method to help students engage in mathematical problem solving would be an example of applied research. The published research articles that are included in Chapters 12 (Experimental Research), 18 (Action Research), and 19 (Evaluation Research) are examples of applied research.

Some educators believe that applied research is more valuable as a guide to their work than basic research and that it should therefore have funding priority over basic research. A study of medical research by Julius Comroe and Robert Dripps (1976) raises doubts about this view. Comroe and Dripps studied the advances in research knowledge that were necessary for innovations in the treatment of cardiovascular and pulmonary disease (e.g., cardiac surgery and chemotherapy). Surprisingly, many more basic research studies were instrumental in the development of these innovations than were applied research studies. Basic research leads to theoretical understanding of underlying processes and structures, and this understanding is the best foundation for constructing interventions that are likely to be effective.

CHARACTERISTICS OF RESEARCH AS AN APPROACH TO INQUIRY

Some philosophers and social critics question the relevance of research to understanding human behavior and society. Their critique of social science has led to a movement called **postmodernism**. Postmodernists (e.g., Graham, Doherty, & Malek, 1992) acknowledge that science has contributed to an understanding and control of the physical world, but they argue that no one method of inquiry can claim to be true, or better than any other method, in developing knowledge about the human condition. For example, postmodernists would argue that the methods of social science inquiry are not superior to personal reflection or other forms of investigation, such as aesthetic and religious studies.

The postmodern critique of scientific inquiry has caused social science researchers (including educational researchers) to rethink their claims to authority in the pursuit of knowledge. They have identified several characteristics of research that they believe help to establish its claim to authority and that differentiate it from other forms of inquiry. We describe these characteristics in the following sections.

Use of Concepts and Procedures That Are Shared, Precise, and Accessible

Social science researchers have developed specialized concepts (e.g., test reliability), procedures (e.g., purposeful sampling), and carefully defined terminology. Their terminology, concepts, and procedures are explicit and accessible. Everyone is free to learn and use them. Indeed, most journals that publish research reports use a "blind" review procedure, meaning that reviewers do not have access to the authors' names or other identifying information.

Of course, there are power struggles in the arenas of funding and publicity for research findings, but it is highly unlikely that important theories or findings can be suppressed over the long term because researchers generally are committed to **progressive discourse** (Bereiter, 1994). Anyone at any time can offer a criticism about a particular research study or research methodology, and if it proves to have merit, that criticism is listened to and accommodated.

Many educators perform their work at a high level of excellence and have developed many insights from their personal inquiries. However, they lack carefully refined concepts and forums for making their ideas widely accessible. Hence, their knowledge cannot be publicly debated, and it generally disappears when they retire. By contrast, new researchers are able to learn from experienced researchers, and the results are available in research journals for all to study.

Replicability of Findings

For researchers to have their findings published, they must be willing to make public the procedures by which those findings were obtained. Because the procedures are public, other researchers can conduct similar studies to compare results. Called **replication** studies because they involve repetition of the original study under similar conditions but with a new sample of participants, such studies can provide additional confidence in the original findings, or refutation of them.

Individuals who engage in nonscientific inquiry might discover potentially important interventions and insights. However, their inquiries are of limited value because they do not make their procedures sufficiently explicit for others to replicate. Thus we have no way of knowing whether an individual's claimed findings and insights are unique to that individual or can inform the work of other individuals.

Refutability of Knowledge Claims

Karl Popper (1968) proposed a standard for testing knowledge claims that has won general acceptance among social science researchers. Popper argued that science advances through the process of **refutation**, which involves submitting knowledge claims (theories, predictions, hunches) to empirical tests that allow them to be challenged and disproved. If the data are inconsistent with the knowledge claim, we can say that it is refuted. The knowledge claim must then be abandoned or modified to accommodate the negative findings. If the data are consistent with the knowledge claim, we can conclude that it is supported, but not that it is correct. We can say only that the knowledge claim has not been refuted by any of the tests that have been made thus far.

Refutation tests knowledge claims more rigorously than we usually test everyday knowledge claims. For example, suppose a school administrator visits a teacher's classroom one day and discovers that (1) the teacher has attended a recent workshop on classroom management, and (2) the teacher's class is unusually quiet and orderly. The administrator might conclude that the workshop is effective and therefore mandate participation from all teachers. In effect, the administrator made an observation first and then formulated a broad knowledge claim. In contrast, researchers who follow Popper's logic make a knowledge claim first, perhaps based on a similar observation, and then test it by making further observations before reaching any conclusions.

Control for Researcher Errors and Biases

Researchers acknowledge the likelihood that their own errors and biases will affect their data collection. Therefore, they design research studies to minimize the influence of such factors. For example, in making observations, researchers often seek to reduce error by using multiple observers and training them beforehand in the system for collecting data on observational variables. In addition, they typically use statistical procedures to estimate the observers' level of agreement. While the observations of different observers rarely agree perfectly, a certain level of agreement must be achieved before the observational data are accepted as valid.

An approach often used in case study research is to validate findings by triangulation of data sources. **Triangulation** refers to researchers' attempts to corroborate data obtained by one method (e.g., observation of individuals) by using other methods (e.g., interviews of individuals or examination of documents).

Other research procedures described throughout this book are also intended to minimize various researcher errors and biases in data collection and analysis. We invite you to compare the rigor of these methods with the everyday methods that individuals use to arrive at and justify knowledge claims.

QUANTITATIVE AND QUALITATIVE RESEARCH

Educational research is not a unified enterprise. The approaches to research described in Part Three, called **quantitative research**, involve the study of samples and populations and rely heavily on numerical data and statistical analysis. In contrast, the research traditions described in Part Four, called **qualitative research**, rely on the study of individual cases and make little use of numbers or statistics, preferring instead verbal data and subjective analysis.

Why does educational research include such diverse approaches? To answer this question, we need to consider the different **epistemologies**— that is, the different views about the nature of knowledge—that guide educational researchers.

Some researchers assume that features of the human environment have an objective reality, meaning that they exist independently of the individuals who created them or are observing them. These researchers subscribe to a positivist epistemology. **Positivism** involves the belief that there is a real world "out there" available for study through scientific means similar to those developed in the physical sciences.

Most quantitative research is carried out by researchers who subscribe to the positivist epistemology. They define their topics of interest in terms of observable behavior (e.g., "feeling good about one's teacher" might become "students report positive attitudes"). They attempt to define that behavior in terms of the specific operations used to measure it (e.g., "students with positive attitudes gave average ratings of 3 or higher on 5-point scales"). They also are concerned about generalizing what they discover about a research sample to the larger population from which that sample was presumably drawn.

Other researchers take the epistemological position known as interpretivism (Erickson, 1986), believing that aspects of the human environment are constructed by the individuals who participate in that environment. **Interpretivism** involves the belief that social reality has no existence apart from the meanings that individuals construct for it. For example, a teacher might form the construction that the students in his first-period class are "13 boys and 16 girls," or "29 unique individuals, each with their own needs," or "easier to teach than students I've had other years," depending on when the teacher is thinking about them. If the principal steps into the teacher's classroom, her construction of the students in the class might vary depending on how they are behaving at the moment, how the principal is feeling, or many other factors.

Most qualitative research is carried out by individuals who subscribe to interpretivist epistemology. These researchers believe that scientific inquiry must focus on the study of the different social realities that different individuals in a social situation construct as they participate in it. Because of the complexity of these constructions, qualitative researchers usually study single individuals or situations, each of which is called a *case*. They determine the applicability of case findings to other situations mainly by comparing cases or suggesting that educators do this comparison with their own situation.

Qualitative researchers also acknowledge their own role in constructing the social realities that they describe in their research reports and thus often include their own experiences in their reports. This focus on the researcher as a constructor of social reality is called **reflexivity**.

While some scholars refer to positivism and interpretivism to distinguish these two approaches to research, the terms *quantitative research* and *qualitative research* are more commonly used, and we will use these terms in this book. The words *quantitative* and *qualitative* highlight the differences in the kinds of data that typically are collected by researchers and how these data are analyzed and interpreted. Table 1.1 provides a further elaboration of the distinguishing characteristics of quantitative and qualitative research.

Given that both quantitative and qualitative methods are used to study education, several questions arise. Is one approach better than the other? Do they complement each other in some way? Do they produce conflicting findings? We address these questions in Chapter 17. For now, we will observe that many researchers believe that the methods of qualitative research and quantitative research are complementary and that researchers who use a combination in mixed-methods research studies are in the best position to create a meaningful picture of educational practices and problems.

COLLABORATING WITH RESEARCHERS

In order for educational research to play a role in improving practice, educators need to participate in an ongoing dialogue with professional researchers. Maintaining a dialogue is no easy matter, though. One challenge is that researchers and educators tend to have very different views about knowledge and research. According to Lilian Katz and Dianne Rothenberg (1996), researchers' main interest in knowledge is scientific. When confronted with a problem, they seek to explore and discover the nature of the problem, no matter how long that might take. In contrast, educators' main interest in knowledge is clinical. When confronted with a problem, they seek information that will allow them to solve it, usually under the pressure of a time limit. Katz and Rothenberg also note that effective practice "depends to some extent on the

TABLE 1.1 • Differences Between Quantitative and Qualitative Research

Quantitative Researchers	Qualitative Researchers
Assume an objective social reality.	Assume that social reality is constructed by the participants in it.
Assume that social reality is relatively constant across time and settings.	Assume that social reality is continuously constructed in local situations.
View causal relationships among social phenomena from a mechanistic perspective.	Assign human intentions a major role in explaining causal relationships among social phenomena.
Take an objective, detached stance toward research participants and their setting.	Become personally involved with research participants, to the point of sharing perspectives and assuming a caring attitude.
Study populations or samples that represent populations.	Study cases.
Study behavior and other observable phenomena.	Study the meanings that individuals create and other internal phenomena.
Study human behavior in natural or contrived settings.	Study human actions in natural settings.
Analyze social reality into variables.	Make holistic observations of the total context within which social action occurs.
Use preconceived concepts and theories to determine what data will be collected.	Discover concepts and theories after data have been collected.
Generate numerical data to represent the social environment.	Generate verbal and pictorial data to represent the social environment.
Use statistical methods to analyze data.	Use analytic induction to analyze data.
Use statistical inference procedures to generalize findings from a sample to a defined population.	Generalize case findings by determining their applicability to other situations.
Prepare impersonal, objective reports of research findings.	Prepare interpretive reports that reflect researchers' constructions of the data and an awareness that readers will form their own constructions from what is reported.

Source: Gall, M. D., Gall, J. P., & Borg, W. R. (2007). *Educational research: An introduction* (8th ed.). Boston, MA: Pearson. Reprinted by permission of the publisher.

certainty with which the practitioner approaches his or her task. And by definition, the researcher's task is to prize doubt and uncertainty and be open to being wrong" (p. 8).

Nonetheless, researchers and educators have a shared desire to improve educational practice. Therefore, they should take steps to understand each other's needs and to communicate clearly with each other. For example, researchers can develop research agendas that are responsive to educators' needs. Also, they can write reports of their findings in nontechnical language and spell out their implications for practice. In turn, educators need to make an effort to understand the language and methods used by researchers. In addition to improving lines of communication, educators and researchers can strengthen the application of research to practice through collaboration, as described in the following sections.

Being a Research Participant

Researchers often ask educators to participate in their studies. The effort required might be minimal (e.g., filling out a questionnaire) or more extensive (e.g., volunteering your class to be part of the experimental group or control group in an experiment). By volunteering to participate, you might be eligible to receive special training, consultation, or free use of innovative curriculum materials. You also will have the opportunity to learn how research is actually done.

Participating in Program Evaluations

Educational institutions occasionally receive grants from private or government funding sources to implement experimental programs. These grants typically require the grantee to carry out an evaluation of the program. If your institution employs evaluation specialists, you can work alongside them to design an appropriate evaluation study. For this collaboration to happen, however, you need to be knowledgeable about evaluation research. If no evaluation specialists are available to help you in securing a grant and satisfying its criteria for evaluation, you will need to know even more about evaluation research to deal effectively with the grant's requirements.

Chapter 19 explains how to conduct an evaluation study and also how to decide whether you can apply the findings of an existing evaluation study to your own situation. Because evaluation research typically involves one or more of the research approaches described in Parts Three and Four of this book, study of those chapters will be helpful to you, too.

Influencing Policy Agendas for Education

Various policy-making bodies, ranging from national and state legislatures to the central offices of local school districts, are constantly proposing changes in educational practice that directly affect educators' work. We described one such change, the No Child Left Behind Act, earlier in the chapter.

Some policy-driven changes are sound, but others make little sense to the educators who must implement them. For example, many states have implemented or are considering mandatory achievement testing of all students in order to make educators accountable for student learning outcomes. Many teachers are concerned about the validity of these tests and whether they respect the huge individual differences in students' learning needs and family situations. However, without knowledge about research on achievement testing and student characteristics, teachers and other educators are handicapped in their ability to influence statewide testing programs.

Ill-considered policies perhaps could be avoided if educators and researchers would collaborate to make their views and knowledge known to policy makers. For this to happen, though, researchers and educators must be familiar with each other's knowledge, goals, and perspectives. One way to achieve this familiarity is to become a member of the American Educational Research Association, which is the primary organization for individuals interested in current trends and issues in educational research.

A PERSONAL NOTE: THE RESEARCH "SPARK"

We are well aware that some individuals do not have an interest in formal research methodology, which is what this book is primarily about. Those individuals might take great interest in new discoveries, such as breakthroughs in medicine or alternative sources of energy or how the brain affects our ability to learn, but not in the research processes that led to those discoveries. In fact, many adults have had little or no exposure to the kind of work that researchers do in creating new knowledge.

We believe that interest in research methodology and the desire to do one's own research are set off by some "spark" that differs among people. Since we (Mark and Joy Gall) know our own "sparks" best, we will recount them briefly here.

Mark Gall

I began my doctoral studies with the intention of becoming a clinical psychologist in private or group practice. Gradually, I began to wonder whether psychotherapy was actually as effective as was claimed. That was the "spark" that led to my interest in research; I wanted to know what researchers had learned about the effectiveness of different psychotherapeutic approaches (e.g., Freudian, Jungian, Adlerian) and how I could do my own research to determine their effectiveness.

Later in my career, after I became a teacher educator, I became interested in teacher enthusiasm, which some research studies had found to be positively associated with student learning. Several of my doctoral students wondered whether it was possible to train teachers to become more enthusiastic during classroom instruction. That question was the "spark" for a series of doctoral studies that I chaired. To do these studies, both the students and I needed to learn how to use particular research methods. In particular, we needed to study methods for conducting experiments (see Chapter 12), because each study involved training some teachers to use indicators of enthusiasm (the experimental group) but not others (the control group) and then observing the effects of this intervention on their instructional behavior and on their students' learning.

Joy Gall

I began my doctoral studies with an interest in social psychology and the ways in which groups such as families, work organizations, or schools shape individuals' thinking, emotions, and behavior. While doing my doctoral studies, I was hired by two psychology professors who had a funded grant to develop curriculum materials for young students based on the latest principles of scientific discovery. I developed materials that were designed to bring science alive for young learners. The work of developing curriculum or training materials based on the findings of research is known as research and development. My understanding of how research and practice could be connected began with this work.

During my career, I have continued to apply my psychological research and writing skills by developing research-based curriculum and training materials for educational administrators, teachers, and students. I also have addressed the learning needs of various community groups, including parents of students. My "spark" involves the desire to discover ways to help individuals understand and improve their social environment through individual and joint learning endeavors.

You

You might already have experienced your own "spark." Perhaps that spark is a desire to find answers to a question or problem that you can't stop thinking about. Perhaps it is a desire to test a personal theory about a better way to teach. If you have a research "spark" for this or another reason, you have the requisite motivation to study this book.

If your primary "spark" is a desire to get into schools and help students learn, we encourage you to be on the lookout for *what works* and also for *problems* that trouble you and your colleagues. You might find answers in the workplace, but we encourage you to look also at the research literature on education. You might find answers there, or at least new ways of thinking about what works, and what doesn't, in education. You might even find that you wish to do your own research project.

An example of
How Research Can Help in Solving Problems of Practice

Note to the reader. You will find features similar to this section in most of the other chapters of this book. We present a problem of practice that has reached public attention through newspapers or other media. Then we suggest how the research methodology described in the particular chapter can be used to design studies that address the problem.

These vignettes are designed to develop your understanding of the relationship between educational problems and educational research. We hope you will see that conventional wisdom and individual effort alone are insufficient to solve many of the pressing problems in education. Empirical knowledge generated by well-designed research studies also is necessary.

An editorial about the status of educational research in the United States appeared in November 2008 in *The Boston Globe*. The following excerpts are from the newspaper editorial:

> Grover Whitehurst, who heads the research arm of the U.S. Department of Education, says that the quality of education research today is the rough equivalent of medical research in the 1920s.
>
> [Whitehurst recommended] operating a national education department that spends just $575 million—1 percent of its budget—on research.

Editorial (2008, November 1). Healing America's schools. *The Boston Globe*. Retrieved from www.boston.com/bostonglobe.

A few years later, Michael McPherson, president of the Spencer Foundation, made a similar point at a briefing held on Capitol Hill on February 14, 2011. He stated that "we are a very impatient nation" and "we spend very little on education research" (AERA Highlights, 2011, p. 66).

Medical research has led to huge advancements in practice. Could research do the same for educational practice? Some educators, such as Grover Whitehurst and Michael McPherson, believe that research can accomplish this goal. Other educators, however, believe that federal monies are best used for direct service to students. A research study might help educators and their professional organizations decide what the priority should be.

A simple survey study should be sufficient to learn educators' views. For example, a sample of educators could be asked to read *The Boston Globe*'s editorial and then respond to a question such as: "Based on what you just read and what you know about research, do you think that the U.S. Department of Education should allocate 1 percent of its budget for research?"

In designing this study, we would need to pay particular attention to the sampling procedure. The population should be defined as all educators in the United States. A large random sample should be drawn from that population so that we have confidence that the survey results represent the views of educators in general, not just educators from one region or educators who volunteer to complete the survey.

SELF-CHECK TEST

1. Evidence-based practice requires that educators
   a. collect evidence on their own effectiveness as teachers.
   b. make use of relevant research findings in solving problems of practice.
   c. disregard stakeholders' values in decision making unless they are consistent with research evidence.
   d. use instructional programs and procedures that rely primarily on educators' clinical expertise.
2. The Institute of Education Sciences and the What Works Clearinghouse exemplify education's movement in the direction of
   a. basic research.
   b. qualitative research.
   c. postmodernism.
   d. evidence-based practice.
3. Assuming that policy agendas for education become more evidence-based, educators will most likely
   a. seek to develop a greater understanding of research concepts and procedures.
   b. use their professional organizations to resist such agendas.
   c. argue that education's problems are unique and cannot be solved by research.
   d. claim that evidence does not lead to improvement in professional practice.
4. Educational research emphasizes
   a. collection of empirical data.
   b. control for personal biases in collecting, analyzing, and interpreting empirical data.
   c. sample selection such that findings can be generalized to other individuals and situations.
   d. All of the above.
5. The role of theory in educational research is primarily to
   a. develop precise descriptions of educational phenomena.
   b. evaluate the effectiveness of specific instructional interventions.
   c. explain phenomena in terms of constructs and principles.
   d. provide a language that facilitates collaboration between researchers and educators.

6. Postmodernists argue that
   a. contemporary research methods have overcome serious deficiencies of research methods used in the first part of the 20th century.
   b. educational research is not superior to other forms of inquiry about problems of practice.
   c. basic research is ultimately more important than applied research in solving problems of practice.
   d. any knowledge claim can be refuted.
7. Triangulation is a method by which researchers
   a. look for explanations about why a finding from one research study fails to replicate in a subsequent study.
   b. obtain data from different sources in order to check for errors and biases in their findings.
   c. determine whether a problem of educational practice can be studied by collecting empirical data.
   d. collaborate with educators and policy makers in the design of an empirical study.
8. Positivist researchers
   a. subscribe to the belief that there is an objective reality that exists independently of the observer.
   b. believe that aspects of the human environment are constructed by the participants in the environment.
   c. emphasize description as the goal of scientific inquiry.
   d. disregard the possible effects of their own biases on research findings.
9. Qualitative researchers typically
   a. focus on making subjective judgments about the quality of educational programs and procedures.
   b. include quantitative measures to represent the qualities of each case they study.
   c. argue that the methods of social science inquiry are not superior to other forms of investigation.
   d. emphasize the study of individual cases of a phenomenon.
10. Mixed-methods research
   a. is designed to produce descriptive and predictive findings within a single study.
   b. was developed to speed up the transfer of research findings into educational practice.
   c. uses a combination of quantitative and qualitative research methods.
   d. uses theories from multiple disciplines to study problems of practice.

CHAPTER REFERENCES

Adams, M. J. (1990). *Beginning to read: Thinking and learning about print.* Cambridge, MA: MIT Press.

AERA Highlights. (2011). *Educational Researcher, 40*(65), 65–66.

APA Presidential Task Force on Evidence-Based Practice. (2006). Evidence-based practice in psychology. *American Psychologist, 61*(4), 271–285.

Bereiter, C. (1994). Implications of postmodernism for science, or, science as progressive discourse. *Educational Psychologist, 29*, 3–12.

Cochrane Collaboration. (n.d.). *Evidence-based health care and systematic reviews.* Retrieved from http://www.cochrane.org/docs/ebm.htm (updated August 10, 2013)

Comroe, J. H., Jr., & Dripps, R. D. (1976). Scientific basis for the support of biomedical science. *Science, 192*, 105–111.

Erickson, F. (1986). Qualitative methods in research on teaching. In M. C. Wittrock (Ed.), *Handbook of research on teaching* (3rd ed., pp. 119–161). New York, NY: Macmillan.

Grady, D., & McNeil, Jr., D. G. (2011, December 26). Debate persists on deadly flu made airborne. *The New York Times.* Retrieved from http://www.nytimes.com/2011/12/27/science/debate-persists-on-deadly-flu-made-airborne.html?pagewanted=all&_r=0

Graham, E., Doherty, J., & Malek, M. (1992). Introduction: The context and language of postmodernism. In J. Doherty, E. Graham, & M. Malek (Eds.), *Postmodernism and the social sciences* (pp. 1–23). Basingstoke, UK: Macmillan.

Hawkins-Simons, D. (2008, May 19). Not a primary concern. *U.S. News & World Report*, 29–31.

Herrnstein, R. J., & Murray, C. (1994). *Bell curve: Intelligence and class structure in American life*. New York, NY: Free Press.

Institute of Education Sciences. (n.d.). *What Works Clearinghouse*. Retrieved from http://ies.ed.gov/ncee/wwc/overview

Jensen, A. (1973). Race, intelligence and genetics: The differences are real. *Psychology Today, 7*(7), 80–84.

Katz, L. G., & Rothenberg, D. (1996). Issues in dissemination: An ERIC perspective. *ERIC Review, 5*, 2–9.

McCaslin, M., Good, T. L., Nichols, S., Zhang, J., Wiley, C. R., Bozack, A. R., Burross, H. L., & Cuizon-Garcia, R. (2006). Comprehensive school reform: An observational study of teaching in grades 3 through 5. *Elementary School Journal, 106*(4), 313–331.

Popper, K. (1968). *Conjectures and refutations*. New York, NY: Harper.

Ravitch, D. (2011). Dictating to the schools. *Education Digest, 76*(8), 4–9.

Slavin, R. E. (2002). Evidence-based education policies: Transforming educational practice and research. *Educational Researcher, 31*(7), 15–21.

Straus, S. E., Glasziou, P., Richardson, W. S., & Haynes, R. B. (2010). *Evidence-based medicine: How to practice and teach it* (4th ed.). London, UK: Churchill-Livingstone.

U.S. Department of Education. (n.d.). *About the Institute of Education Sciences*. Retrieved from http://www.ed.gov/about/offices/list/ies/index.html

RESOURCES FOR FURTHER STUDY

Moss, P. A. (Ed.). (2007). *Evidence and decision making* (106th Yearbook of the National Society for the Study of Education, Part I). Malden, MA: Blackwell.

The chapter authors examine the process by which educators use information to improve schools. They consider the use of quantitative and qualitative research evidence, standardized test scores, and survey and interview data. They also examine various materials, including samples of students' works. This book identifies the difficulties, but also the promise, of evidence-based practice in education.

Phillips, D. C., & Burbules, N. C. (2000). *Postpositivism and educational research*. New York, NY: Rowman & Littlefield.

Most of us understand something about how scientists, including educational researchers, work. However, few of us are aware of the fundamental assumptions that underlie scientific inquiry and also the ongoing controversies about these assumptions. If you wish to deepen your understanding of science, this book will enlighten you.

Taber, K. S. (2007). *Classroom-based research and evidence-based practice: A guide for teachers*. Los Angeles, CA: Sage.

This book is written for teachers who are interested in incorporating evidence-based practice into their instructional repertoires. The author describes skills needed to critically evaluate research reports and to carry out one's own school-based research.

How Students' Sleepy Brains Fail Them

Willis, J. (2009). How students' sleepy brains fail them. *Kappa Delta Pi Record, 45*(4), 158–162.

The author of the following journal article notes that many students, from kindergarten through high school, experience sleep deprivation. She cites research studies that have found serious decrements in student learning resulting from sleep deprivation.

In reading this article, you will see the importance of basic research in helping us understand the brain's role in the learning process. You also will see how applied research is used to document positive results from interventions designed to reduce sleep deprivation among students. The author of the article is both a board-certified neurologist and middle school teacher.

The article is reprinted here in its entirety, just as it appeared when originally published.

How Students' Sleepy Brains Fail Them

JUDY WILLIS
Santa Barbara Middle School, Santa Barbara, CA

Educators are barraged with information about the value of brain food, water, exercise, and vitamins on student learning. This information is often contradictory to and not substantiated by medical or cognitive research. As a neurologist and middle school teacher, I have found the evidence supporting the value of these factors limited, particularly when scrutinized through a medical lens.

One aspect of brain health that has been well examined through neuroimaging and cognitive testing is the influence of sleep on the brain. The findings are indeed a wake-up call with regard to the impact of sleep on focus, memory, test performance, mood, and high-risk behavior.

Sleep Tight

Nearly 40 percent of students in kindergarten through fourth grade have sleep disturbances, and those poor sleep habits in children carry into adolescence. Some sleep deprivation in children has been attributed to the rising use of computers, video games, iPODS®, and text messaging, as well as to the increased volume of homework compounded by earlier school start hours (Carskadon, Acebo, and Seifer 2001).

Sleep performs a restorative function for the body and the brain, and many brain functions become considerably less efficient after a sleepless night (Maquet 2001). Sleep-deprived children display lower brain activity while working on math problems than they do when rested, and they make more mistakes and omit more answers on tests (Drummond et al. 1999).

fMRI scans monitored activity in the brains of subjects performing simple verbal learning tasks. The temporal lobes—which are important for language processing—and the prefrontal cortex—which is active during coordinated attention and memory processing—were significantly more active during verbal learning in rested subjects than in sleep-deprived subjects. When two groups were tasked with memorizing short lists of words following either a full night's sleep or about 35 hours without sleep, word recall and recognition dropped sharply in the sleep-deprived group (Drummond et al. 2000).

Harvard researchers studied the brain's need for sleep to solidify the new information learned during the day. In a study test group of 60 students, each participant was asked to memorize 20 pairs of random words. Half were told to return 12 hours later, after a good night's rest. The other half were told not to sleep and to return in 12 hours. Seventy-six percent of the rested students correctly recalled all the words on a test, while only 32 percent of the sleepless students had all words correct (Ellenbogen 2005).

Rehearsals During Sleep

Sleep influences both the encoding and consolidating of memories, as well as the construction of new connections within networks that store the new memories. The sleeping brain is less distracted by the sensory input

Judy Willis, a neurologist and credentialed teacher at Santa Barbara Middle School in California, combines her training in neuroscience and neuroimaging with her teacher education training and years of classroom experience. She is an authority in the field of learning-centered brain research and teaching strategies derived from this research.

that bombards it all day, leaving a greater portion of its energy (metabolism) available for organizing and storing memories formed during the day. During sleep, when the prefrontal cortex receives less environmental sensory input, the executive functioning areas are less metabolically active. This reduced-activity brain state may provide the opportunity for recently learned material to be rehearsed, repeated (perhaps in dreams), and consolidated into long-term memory.

> "Sleep performs a restorative function for the body and the brain, and many brain functions become considerably less efficient after a sleepless night."

"Dream sleep" associated with rapid eye movement (REM) sleep may be the time of encoding and consolidating during which new information is reviewed and coded into relational memories. Non-REM sleep appears to be the time during which new connections in neural networks are constructed to store the new memories and existing connections are strengthened.

During late stages of REM sleep, memories may be rehearsed and strengthened. Human subjects performing difficult tasks tend to improve their scores between sessions on consecutive days, but not between sessions on the same day—implicating sleep in the learning process (Walker et al. 2002). Mice allowed to sleep after being trained "remembered" what they had learned (connecting a sound to an electric shock) better than those deprived of sleep when tested several hours after the conditioned learning took place (Graves 2003).

REM sleep and its dreams—as forms of replaying and rehearsing new information to consolidate it from short-term to long-term memory—is an area ripe for study in the neuroscience of learning. In one research project, rats were trained on a track to reach a food reward. Electrical activity in the "place cell" neurons reflected the same or very similar activity during sleep as these hippocampal and prefrontal cortex neurons displayed during the track running behavior; even specific patterns of activity based on the rats' location on the track could be identified both in waking and sleep. Researchers concluded that during sleep, the rats were reconstructing their movements through locations on the track that led them to the reward by reactivating their original memory tracts (Ji and Wilson 2007).

During REM sleep, the brain stem sends messages to the visual center of the cortex as it does during wakefulness (Dement 1960). Because the sleeping person cannot respond to these messages physically, dreams may be the response to these neural impulses. This neural processing during sleep, therefore, could come from internal sources rather than from the physical world, yet still serve to consolidate the memory through the restimulation of the memory network (Purves et al. 2004).

> "Increasing sleep time from six or less to eight hours can increase memory up to 25 percent."

Sleep Construction

The term *neuroplasticity* describes the brain's ability to change or increase the dendrite connections and synapses between neurons, and thereby impact memories stored in neural networks. It is during the later hours of REM and non-REM sleep that the brain converts the greatest amount of amino acids into the proteins that are the building blocks of neuron-to-neuron connections such as dendrites (Benington and Frank 2003).

To convert the circulating amino acids into the proteins from which new connections are constructed, the brain needs nerve growth hormones and neurotransmitters such as neurotrophic growth factor and serotonin. The levels of both of these chemicals are especially high during later stages of sleep, the period when most new dendrite branching takes place (Murck et al. 2001).

In animal experiments, memory consolidation is associated with the synthesis of new proteins in the hippocampus and subcortical frontal lobe memory storage areas. Dendrite growth and new synapse formation correlate with the levels of nerve growth factor BDNF, brain-derived neurotrophic factor protein (Lo 1995). The increased release of nerve growth factor and serotonin during the later REM and non-REM sleep states—after six to eight hours of sleep—appears to influence plasticity through chemical and physical changes (McAllister, Katz, and Lo 1996; Alsina, Vu, and Cohen-Cory 2001). In animals, increased brain oxygen use triggers the construction of proteins from amino acids. This increase is evident on their fMRI scans 24 hours after information is stored (Drummond et al. 2000).

The *More* One Knows, the Easier It Is to Learn *More*

According to neuroplasticity theory and animal research, these brain cell networks that form connections with increasing dendrites and synapses are the hard-wiring associating newly learned information with previously stored, related knowledge in permanent memories (Benington and Frank 2003). The brain cell networks grow when increasing numbers of dendrites branch out from the nerve cells and link more and more neurons together. A correlation appears to exist between the number of dendrites and the efficiency of the brain to recognize similarities between new experiences and already stored ones (patterning) and to link new information with existing categories of knowledge (encoding into the memory circuit) (Leutgeb et al. 2005).

Construction of neural networks takes time, as dendrite sprouts grow and new synapses form (Bennington and Frank 2003). This construction of memory storage appears most active during the longest periods of uninterrupted deep (non-REM) sleep that begin after six to eight hours of sleep. During these hours, the brain may construct the physical structures that represent the networks where the recent memories can, with further rehearsal (review and network restimulation), become long-term memories (Maquet 2001).

This sleep/memory research provides support for what many students have discovered through their own study habits: reviewing notes while still alert is more effective than reviewing right before falling asleep. The quality and quantity of retained memory is superior when students review their notes thoroughly, stop, and go to sleep when they begin to feel drowsy. Retained memory diminishes when students extend their review time any number of hours once they become drowsy and thereby reduce their sleep time to less than six or eight hours (Stickgold, James, and Hobson 2000). A study of students who received low grades (C and lower) reported sleeping an average of 20 minutes less and going to bed an average of 40 minutes later on school nights than students with higher grades. The recognition of the correlation between sleep and memory has led some researchers to test and confirm their predictions that increasing sleep time from six or less to eight hours can increase memory up to 25 percent (Frand 2000).

Sleep and Syn-*naps*

Nightly sleep is not the only way to maintain healthy brains and support learning and memory. Syn-*naps*, or brain breaks, are important throughout the day to keep neurons firing efficiently. Depending on students' ages and focus abilities, the number of syn-*naps* needed will vary. Syn-*naps* should take place before fatigue, boredom, distraction, and inattention set in. As a general rule, to keep children alert and engaged, syn-*naps* should be scheduled after 10 minutes of concentrated learning for elementary school and 15–30 minutes for middle and high school students (Willis 2006).

These three- to five-minute breaks do not need to disrupt the flow of learning. Simply stretching, drinking water, or moving to a different part of the room can provide a fresh outlook. A bit of physical activity, such as jumping jacks or singing a song can be revitalizing. During these breaks, the newly learned material has the opportunity to go from short-term to working memory while children relax and refresh their supply of neurotransmitters (the brain's chemical messengers). Physical movement during syn-*naps* increases blood flow to the cranial circulation, and the deep breathing of exercise increases the blood levels of oxygen.

Teens

Adolescents need up to two hours more sleep than when they were in elementary school for their brains to consolidate and cement new knowledge and experience into memory and avoid behaviors associated with sleep deprivation that interfere with cognitive and attention skills. This recommendation is in part attributed to the finding that, during sleep, teenagers start to secrete melatonin, a sleep promoting neurochemical, up to two hours later in their sleep cycle than when they were younger (Wurtman and Lieberman 1985). Yet, only 15 percent of adolescents reported sleeping 8 or more hours on school nights and the older teens reported an average of 7.7 hours of sleep a night, with 11 percent sleeping less than 6.5 hours a night (Javaheri et al. 2008).

A number of problems stem from sleep deprivation in adolescents. Auto accidents among teens are a prime example. Drowsy drivers are attributed with causing 100,000 auto accidents a year in the United States; drivers age 25 or under caused more than half of these crashes by falling asleep at the wheel (Wu and Yan-Go 2006).

Academic achievement also takes a hit by sleep deprivation. During the earliest classes in middle and high school, teachers notice a comparatively lower level of alertness in their students. Twenty percent of all high school students fall asleep in school, and more than 50 percent of students report being most alert after 3:00 p.m. High school students who sleep less than six hours a night generally have poorer grades even when they study the same reported number of hours as higher-achieving students (Wolfson and Carskadon 1998).

Sleep deprivation additionally reduces the body's supply of cortisone and growth hormone and disrupts hormones that regulate appetite. Teens who sleep less than 7 hours a night are more likely to be obese (Vgontzas et al. 1999) and have more than twice the risk of high blood pressure even when the data are adjusted for sex, weight, and socioeconomic status (Javaheri et al. 2008). With less than 7 hours of sleep, teens also have higher levels of stress, anxiety, and depression, and tend to take more unnecessary risks including drug and alcohol abuse, sexual promiscuity, and unsafe driving (Williamson and Feyer 2000).

Reports indicate that some high school students drink as many as five cans of "energy drinks" a day to combat sleep deprivation. The consumption of these drinks by teens compounds the problems associated with sleep deprivation. When teens mix these drinks with alcohol, the likelihood of them becoming victims or perpetrators of aggressive sexual behavior increases (Miller 2008).

Creating Sleep-Friendly Schools

School systems can help positively influence sleep patterns in several ways when educators, school health providers, and other school personnel are knowledgeable about sleep needs and patterns as well as the signs of sleep loss. Further benefits come from informing parents about the importance of optimizing sleep quality for their children with regular sleep and wake times and bedrooms that are kept quiet, dark, and conducive to sleep. Students need to be knowledgeable about the physiology and benefits of sleep and the consequences of sleep deprivation in their academic success and physical health and safety.

In 2004, Duke University stopped scheduling any 8 a.m. classes because students weren't getting enough sleep. "They're coming in to see us, and they're ragged," said Assistant Dean Ryan Lombardi. Duke also has offered students individual health assessments to help them learn what to eat and how many hours to sleep (Grace 2004).

Minneapolis Public Schools was the first major school district to change its starting times to meet adolescent sleep needs. During the 10-year period after this change, positive impacts were noted: improvements in attendance rates, less falling asleep in school, fewer incidents of misbehavior, and increased alertness in class (Wahlstrom et al. 2001). In addition, students reported that it was easier to stay awake when doing homework, and their moods improved as well as their grades (Kubow, Wahlstrom, and Bemis 1999; Wahlstrom 2000). Even parents reported better relationships with their children (Kubow et al. 1999).

Other school districts have adopted patterns similar to the Minneapolis schools, changing the start time for high school from 7:15 a.m. to 8:40 a.m., and middle school from 7:40 a.m. to 9:40 a.m. Among the sleep–sensitive schools with later start times are schools in Lynchburg, Virginia; West Des Moines, Iowa; and Orange County, Florida.

As sleep research has demonstrated, students from elementary school through college need an age-associated number of hours of sleep to learn effectively. Armed with this information, students can make more informed decisions. When students understand the physiology of sleep, they may realize that it's better to review their notes thoroughly and go to sleep for nine hours than to cram for an extra hour. Knowledge can help students make better decisions when they are faced with choices of an extra hour of sleep, an extra hour of study, or an hour spent playing video games and sending text messages.

REFERENCES

Alsina, B., T. Vu, and S. Cohen–Cory. 2001. Visualizing synapse formation in arborizing optic axons in vivo: Dynamics and modulation by BDNF. *Nature Neuroscience* 4(11): 1093–101.

Benington, J. H., and M. G. Frank. 2003. Cellular and molecular connections between sleep and synaptic plasticity. *Progress in Neurobiology* 69(2): 71–101.

Carskadon, M. A., C. Acebo, and R. Seifer. 2001. Extended nights, sleep loss, and recovery sleep in adolescents. *Archives of Italian Biology* 139(3): 301–12.

Dement, W. 1960. The effect of dream deprivation. *Science* 131(3415): 1705–07.

Drummond, S., G. Brown, J. Gillin, et al. 2000. Altered brain response to verbal learning following sleep deprivation. *Nature* 403(6770): 655–57.

Drummond, S. P., G. G. Brown, J. L. Stricker, et al. 1999. Sleep deprivation-induced reduction in cortical functional response to serial subtraction. *NeuroReport* 10(18): 3745–48.

Ellenbogen, J. M. 2005. Cognitive benefits of sleep and their loss due to sleep deprivation *Neurology* 64(7): E25–27.

Frand, J. L. L. 2000. The information-age mindset: Changes in students and implications for higher education. *Educause Review* 35(5): 15–24.

Grace, F. 2004. Help for sleep-deprived students: Duke eliminates 8 a.m. classes, tells students sleep is important. CBS News, April 19. Available at: *www.cbsnews.com/stories/2004/04/19/health/main612476.shtml.*

Graves, L. A., E. A. Heller, A. I. Pack, and T. Abel. 2003. Sleep deprivation selectively impairs memory consolidation for contextual fear conditioning. *Learning & Memory* 10(3): 168–76.

Javaheri, S., A. Storfer-lsser, C. L. Rosen, and S. Redline. 2008. Sleep quality and elevated blood pressure in adolescents. *Circulation* 118(10): 1034–40.

Ji, D., and M. Wilson. 2007. Coordinated memory replay in the visual cortex and hippocampus during sleep. *Nature Neuroscience* 10(1): 100–07.

Kubow, P. K., K. L. Wahlstrom, and A. E. Bemis. 1999. Starting time and school life: Reflections from educators and students. *Phi Delta Kappan* 80(5): 366–71.

Leutgeb, S., J. K. Leutgeb, M. B. Moser, and E. I. Moser. 2005. Place cells, spatial maps and the population code for memory. *Current Opinion in Neurobiology* 15(6): 738–46.

Lo, D. C. 1995. Neurotrophic factors and synaptic plasticity. *Neuron* 15(5): 979–81.

Maquet, P. 2001. The role of sleep in learning and memory. *Science* 294(5544): 1048–52.

McAllister, A. K., L. C. Katz, and D. C. Lo. 1996. Neurotrophin regulation of cortical dendritic growth requires activity. *Neuron* 17(6): 1057–64.

Miller, K. E. 2008. Wired: Energy drinks, jock identity, masculine norms, and risk taking. *Journal of American College Health* 56(5): 481–90.

Murck, H., R. M. Frieboes, I. A. Antonijevic, and A. Steiger. 2001. Distinct temporal pattern of the effects of the combined serotonin-reuptake inhibitor and 5-HT$_{IA}$ agonist EMD 68843 on the sleep EEG in healthy men. *Psychopharmocology* 155(2): 187–92.

Purves, D., et al., eds. 2004. *Neuroscience*, 3rd ed. Sunderland, MA: Sinauer Associates.

Stickgold, R., L. James, and J. A. Hobson. 2000. Visual discrimination learning requires sleep after training. *Nature Neuroscience* 3(12): 1237–38.

Vgontzas, A. N., et al. 1999. Sleep deprivation effects on the activity of the hypothalamic-pituitary-adrenal and growth axes: Potential clinical implications. *Clinical Endocrinology* 51(2): 205–15.

Wahlstrom, K. L. 2000. Sleep research warns: Don't start high school without the kids! *Education Digest* 66(1): 15–16.

Wahlstrom, K., M. Davison, J. Choi, and J. Ross. 2001. *School start time study: Executive summary.* Minneapolis, MN: Center for Applied Research and Educational Improvement. Available at: *http://cehd.umn.edu/CAREI/ Reports.*

Walker, M. P., T. Brakefield, A. Morgan, J. A. Hobson, and R. Stickgold. 2002. Practice with sleep makes perfect: Sleep-dependent motor skill learning. *Neuron* 35(1): 205–11.

Williamson, A. M., and A-M. Feyer. 2000. Moderate sleep deprivation produces impairments in cognitive and motor performance equivalent to legally prescribed levels of alcohol intoxication. *Occupational and Environmental Medicine* 57(10): 649–55.

Willis, J. 2006. *Research-based strategies to ignite student learning: Insights from a neurologist and classroom teacher.* Alexandria, VA: Association for Supervision and Curriculum Development.

Wolfson, A. R., and M. A. Carskadon. 1998. Sleep schedules and daytime functioning in adolescents. *Child Development* 69(4): 875–87.

Wu, H., and F. Yan-Go. 1996. Self-reported automobile accidents involving patients with obstructive sleep apnea. *Neurology* 46(5): 1254–57.

Wurtman, R. J., and H. R. Lieberman. 1985. Melatonin secretion as a mediator of circadian variations in sleep and sleepiness. *Journal of Pineal Research* 2(3): 301–03.

CHAPTER TWO

Doing Your Own Research: From Proposal to Final Report

PROBLEMS OF PRACTICE *in this chapter*

- Is it better to use symbolic representations or concrete examples in teaching math to children?
- Do kindergarten children's academic achievement, socioemotional status (hyperactivity, prosocial behavior, anxiety, depression), and attentiveness determine their academic performance and socioemotional status at subsequent grade levels?
- Does the effectiveness of college instruction affect students' decision to drop out or re-enroll?
- Is the program known as Project ALERT actually effective in achieving its goals of affecting adolescent students' intentions to use alcohol, cigarettes, and marijuana?
- Should teachers "teach to the test"?
- Do teachers in fact align their instruction and assessment with state curriculum standards and assessment?
- Do students perform better on their teachers' assessments and on statement assessments if their teachers improve their curriculum alignment?

IMPORTANT *Ideas*

1. Preparing a proposal for your research study increases the probability that all the subsequent steps of the research process will be successful.
2. A good way to start identifying a research problem to investigate is by reading literature reviews and articles in your areas of interest.
3. Replication of previous research findings is important for the advancement of research knowledge.
4. You are more likely to write a successful research proposal if you follow a standard proposal guide from your university or other authoritative source.

5. Test your understanding of your proposed research study by attempting to state its purpose in one or two sentences.

6. After stating the purpose of your study in general terms, you should make it more specific by formulating research questions or hypotheses and by identifying the variables (in quantitative research) or case features (in qualitative research) that you plan to study.

7. A systematic literature review will help you prepare a sound research proposal and solve problems of practice.

8. In preparing a research proposal, you need to decide on the research design that is most appropriate for answering your research questions or testing your hypotheses.

9. It usually is impossible to study everyone in the population that interests you, so you need to select a sample from that population and specify your sampling procedure in the research proposal.

10. Careful identification of variables or case features will make it easier to identify the measures or cases needed for your proposed study.

11. Specify your data analysis procedures in the research proposal to ensure that your eventual data can be analyzed appropriately.

12. You probably will need to submit your research proposal to an institutional review board, which will determine whether it adequately protects the research participants from certain risks.

13. In planning your research proposal, you need to think about the steps you will take to gain the cooperation of the research participants.

14. You should create a timeline for all the steps of your proposed study to ensure that there are no conflicts with your own time limitations or those of your research participants.

15. A pilot study of your measures and procedures, preferably completed as part of the proposal preparation process, helps to ensure that you will not encounter unexpected difficulties when you actually conduct the study.

16. Unexpected problems often arise while a study is being conducted, and you will need to find ways to solve them without compromising the integrity of the study.

17. To help in preparing the report of your completed research study, first read exemplary reports that are similar in format (e.g., dissertations, journal articles) to the one that you are writing.

KEY TERMS

construct	informed consent	search engine
database	institutional review board	theory
empirical data	*Publication Manual of the*	variable
human subjects	*American Psychological*	
review committee	*Association*	
hypothesis	replication research	

If you are enrolled in a university degree program, you might be required to complete a research project. It might consist of library research, meaning a literature review on a topic that you select. A step-by-step process for doing a literature review is presented in Chapter 3, with several of the steps explained in more detail in Chapters 3 and 4.

Another possible degree requirement is completion of your own research study, which is the subject of this chapter. In describing how to conduct a research study, we refer to concepts and procedures that we explain in depth in other chapters. We recommend that you read this chapter first, though, because it provides a framework for understanding the other chapters.

Doing a research study involves three major steps:

1. preparing a proposal that describes the study to be done and its significance;
2. collecting and analyzing data; and
3. writing a report of the completed study.

The first step, preparing the proposal, is the most crucial because it provides the foundation for the other two steps of the research process. Others can review the proposal for flaws and offer suggestions while there is still opportunity to benefit from them. Obviously, the reviewers can provide better feedback if the proposal has detailed specifications.

Another benefit of a well-prepared proposal is that it can serve as the basis for the final report and thereby speed up the process of writing it. For example, if your proposal contains a good literature review and descriptions of tests or other measures, you can incorporate them directly into the final report.

If you publish your completed study as a master's thesis or doctoral dissertation or present it at a professional conference, you will be required to submit the proposal, perhaps in modified form, to an institutional review board, which we describe later in the chapter. This board will determine whether you have included adequate procedures for protecting the rights of your research participants. If the board rejects your proposal, you will need to revise it. Revision will delay the start of data collection, which can be a serious problem for studies that are dependent on the schedule of schools or other organizations.

IDENTIFYING A RESEARCH PROBLEM

The critical first step in conducting a study is identifying a suitable problem to investigate. How you frame the problem determines everything that follows and often is the difference between a study that genuinely advances knowledge about education and one that does not. Therefore, we advise you to take your time with this step.

Novice researchers often attempt to identify a problem solely by reflecting on their experience as educators or by simply thinking about education in general. Reflection is fine, but it must be supplemented by reading the research literature in an area of interest to you. You can start by reading a published literature review in your area of interest (see Chapters 3 and 4 for guidance on locating a suitable review) or by reading research articles in a relevant journal. Before long, you should come across a research study or set of related studies that attract your interest. It is highly likely that you will be able to identify a research problem by building on this study or set of related studies.

Some educators think that this approach does not lead to an "original" study or that they are somehow "cheating" by building on the ideas of others. In fact, the goal of research in the physical and social sciences is to construct a cumulative body of knowledge and theory, not to create a series of original findings that are unrelated to each other.

It is legitimate and useful to pursue this goal by doing **replication research**, which is an investigation that uses the methods of a previous study to determine whether the same findings are repeated. The replication study does not need to copy the previous study's methods exactly, though. For example, it might include a sample drawn from a different population to determine whether the original study's findings are generalizable beyond the population the researchers studied. Another possibility is that the replication study uses different measures of the constructs that were administered in the original study, with the purpose being to determine whether the study's findings are affected by the use of particular measures.

If you examine the research literature in education, you will find some studies that are explicit replications, as exemplified by the use of the word "replication" in their title. Examples of such studies are presented in Figure 2.1. The abstracts shown in this figure are from the ERIC database (see Chapter 3). The studies demonstrate that replications are an integral part of the research literature in education and that they can make significant contributions to knowledge.

FIGURE 2.1 • Examples of Replication Studies in Education

De Bock, D., Deprez, J., Van Dooren, W., Roelens, M., & Verschaffel, L. (2011). Abstract or concrete examples in learning mathematics? A replication and elaboration of Kaminski, Sloutsky, and Heckler's study. *Journal for Research in Mathematics Education, 42*(2), 109–126.

Kaminski, Sloutsky, and Heckler (2008a) published in "Science" a study on "The advantage of abstract examples in learning math," in which they claim that students may benefit more from learning mathematics through a single abstract, symbolic representation than from multiple concrete examples. This publication elicited both enthusiastic and critical comments by mathematicians, mathematics educators, and policy-makers worldwide. The current empirical study involves a partial replication—but also an important validation and extension—of this widely noticed study. The study's results confirm Kaminski et al.'s findings, but the accompanying qualitative data raise serious questions about their interpretation of what students actually learned from the abstract concept exemplification. Moreover, whereas Kaminski et al. showed that abstract learners transferred what they had learned to a similar abstract context, this study shows also that students who learned from concrete examples transferred their knowledge to a similar concrete context.

Romano, E., Babchishin, L., Pagani, L. S., & Kohen, D. (2010). School readiness and later achievement: Replication and extension using a nationwide Canadian survey. *Developmental Psychology, 46*(5), 995–1007.

In this article we replicate and extend findings from Duncan et al. (2007). The 1st study used Canada-wide data on 1,521 children from the National Longitudinal Survey of Children and Youth (NLSCY) to examine the influence of kindergarten literacy and math skills, mother-reported attention, and mother-reported socioemotional behaviors on 3rd-grade math and reading outcomes. Similar to Duncan et al., (a) math skills were the strongest predictor of later achievement, (b) literacy and attention skills predicted later achievement, and (c) socioemotional behaviors did not significantly predict later school achievement. As part of extending the findings, we incorporated a multiple imputation approach to handle missing predictor variable data. Results paralleled those from the original study in that kindergarten math skills and Peabody Picture Vocabulary Test-Revised scores continued to predict later achievement. However, we also found that kindergarten socioemotional behaviors, specifically hyperactivity/impulsivity, prosocial behavior, and anxiety/depression, were significant predictors of 3rd-grade math and reading. In the 2nd study, we used data from the NLSCY and the Montreal Longitudinal-Experimental Preschool Study (MLEPS), which was included in Duncan et al., to extend previous findings by examining the influence of kindergarten achievement, attention, and socioemotional behaviors on 3rd-grade socioemotional outcomes. Both NLSCY and MLEPS findings indicated that kindergarten math significantly predicted socioemotional behaviors. There were also a number of significant relationships between early and later socioemotional behaviors. Findings support the importance of socioemotional behaviors both as predictors of later school success and as indicators of school success.

Pascarella, E. T., Salisbury, M. H., & Blaich, C. (2011). Exposure to effective instruction and college student persistence: A multi-institutional replication and extension. *Journal of College Student Development, 52*(1), 4–19.

This study analyzed a multi-institutional and longitudinal data set to determine the impact of exposure to effective instruction on first-year persistence—defined as reenrolling for the second year of college at the same institution. Net of important confounding influences, exposure to effective instruction significantly increased the likelihood that the student would reenroll for the second year of college. The effect was mediated primarily through student satisfaction with the quality of the overall educational experience at the institution. These findings have implications for the role of the classroom experience in student persistence in higher education.

Clark, H. K., Ringwait, C. L., Hanley, S., & Shamblen, S. R. (2010). "Project ALERT's" effects on adolescents' prodrug beliefs: A replication and extension. *Health Education & Behavior, 37*(3), 357–376.

This article represents a replication and extension of previous studies of the effects of "Project ALERT", a school-based substance use prevention program, on the prodrug beliefs of adolescents. Specifically, the authors' research examined "Project ALERT's" effects on adolescents' intentions to use substances in the future, beliefs about substance use consequences, normative beliefs, and resistance self-efficacy. In all,

(continued)

FIGURE 2.1 • Examples of Replication Studies in Education (*Continued*)

34 schools with Grades 6 to 8 completed this randomized controlled trial and 71 "Project ALERT" instructors taught 11 core lessons to 6th graders and 3 booster lessons to 7th graders (one grade level earlier than in previous studies). Students were assessed in 6th grade prior to the onset of the intervention, in 7th grade after the completion of the 2-year curriculum, and again 1 year later in 8th grade. The authors found no evidence to suggest that "Project ALERT" had a positive impact on any alcohol, cigarette, or marijuana prodrug beliefs. Implications for school-based substance use prevention are discussed.

Source: Abstracts in the ERIC database (eric.ed.gov).

Even a simple replication of a previous study can make an important contribution to knowledge about education. Anthony Kelly and Robert Yin (2007) make the point this way:

> A limitation of both qualitative and quantitative studies in education is that they are difficult to replicate, which has led to many one-time-only study reports in both genres. However, the findings from any single study cannot be the basis on which a practitioner or policymaker draws a conclusion about a phenomenon or takes action. The most responsible use of research articles follows an accumulation of knowledge across multiple research studies. (p. 133)

The phrase "accumulation of knowledge" in this statement expresses well the idea that one research study builds on another. In doing a research study, you should consider yourself a member of a community of fellow researchers, not a lone explorer.

The value of replication and knowledge accumulation is illustrated by research studies in the medical field (Tsouderos, 2011). Judy Mikovits and her research colleagues had reported in 2009 in the journal *Science* that a type of virus called XMRB appeared much more frequently in the blood of patients with chronic fatigue syndrome than in the blood of healthy peers. Many patients with this syndrome were greatly relieved to find that their symptoms had a medical basis and were not simply the product of their imagination. Some patients even began taking virus-fighting drugs to combat the syndrome.

Unfortunately, replication studies by independent researchers could not find the virus in patients with chronic fatigue syndrome or anyone else. These findings, plus flaws discovered in the study after it was published, led *Science* editors to retract the published paper. On the other hand, some chronic fatigue patients heaped praise on Mikovits and came to her defense when she ran into legal trouble.

We see, then, the necessity of replication to prevent the use of treatments, programs, or other interventions that initially appear to be helpful, but prove to be harmful or of no benefit. However, we should be careful to conclude that the story ends with a single replication attempt. It could be that Mikovits's findings are valid and that the replication researchers reached the wrong conclusions. Knowledge must be accumulated through a series of replication studies before we can have confidence that a particular study has yielded valid results.

We recommend that you read some research articles in refereed journals. In the vast majority of them, you will find statements that indicate how the researchers grounded their study in the existing literature on the problem being studied. Also, you will find statements about possible directions that future research might take in light of the research results that they reported.

To illustrate the process of identifying a research problem, we start with a newspaper article that was cited in the *ASCD SmartBrief*, an online newsletter published by the Association for Supervision and Curriculum Development (see Chapter 1). The article, which appeared in the *Christian Science Monitor* (April 17, 2008), has the provocative title, "Good Teachers Teach to the Test." The author, Walt Gardner, starts the article with this comment: "I have a confession to make. For the entire 28 years that I taught high school English, I taught to the test. And I'm proud to finally admit it." Gardner goes on to note that, for him, teaching to the test means teaching the body of skills and knowledge represented by the test, not teaching the exact test items.

Gardner proceeds to make this claim: "If we're being honest, teaching to the test is done by almost all other effective teachers." We think that this claim frames a good problem for a research study. The problem to be investigated is whether the claim is true. We might put the claim to an empirical test by determining whether effective teachers spend more of their instructional time "teaching to the test" (as defined by Gardner) than do ineffective teachers.

Of course, we could not investigate this problem without defining what we mean by "effective" and "ineffective" teachers. Most likely, we would define teacher effectiveness, as many other people do, as the teacher's ability to promote student learning. By this definition, students would learn more from a highly effective teacher than from a less effective teacher.

Teacher effectiveness could be defined differently. That is the researcher's choice. However, the researcher has the responsibility to provide an explicit definition and defend it. You might recall from Chapter 1 that the use of explicitly defined concepts and procedures is one of the hallmarks of scientific research.

At this point, our research problem is firmly grounded in practice because it is based on an assertion by a highly experienced teacher about his own teaching and that of his colleagues. Also, we know from reading newspapers and professional journals that many educators are critical of "teaching to the test," especially the high-stakes tests mandated by the federal No Child Left Behind Act. A common criticism is that preparing students for these tests takes too much time away from instruction. Another criticism is that the tests focus on certain learning outcomes while ignoring other important learning outcomes.

Our next step is to start reading the research literature. We want to know how researchers have conceptualized the problem and what they have learned about it. Exploring the literature, we find that researchers typically conceptualize the problem as a "curriculum alignment" issue. They have investigated the extent to which state tests are aligned with state curriculum standards and the extent to which teachers align their classroom instruction with their own tests as well as with state tests and curriculum standards.

The claim underlying much of this research is that aligning instruction with one's own tests, as well as with other tests required by government agencies, is part of good teaching. Similarly, Walt Gardner, the teacher whose article we cited above, claims that it is a good idea to "teach to the test," which can be rephrased as a claim that teachers should "align" their instruction with the test. Of course, this is just a claim until it is tested by research involving empirical data. The data either will support or reject the claim.

OUTLINING A RESEARCH PROPOSAL

The process of identifying an idea for a research study and developing it into a proposal is challenging, even for an experienced researcher. A research proposal includes many elements, each of which requires careful thought. For this reason, you will benefit from a guide that specifies each element of the proposal and the order in which it appears, as shown in Figure 2.2. The guide will help you organize your thinking and ensure that you have not overlooked any part of the process of getting the proposal approved, collecting and analyzing data, and writing the final report. Two sample proposals based on the guide in Figure 2.2 are presented at the end of the chapter.

The guide shown in Figure 2.2 organizes a research proposal into nine sections. Your university or other institution might require a different format for research proposals. It is unlikely, though, that their format differs markedly from the one shown in Figure 2.2. Also, most journals require or recommend that authors organize their research manuscripts into the sections stated in the **Publication Manual of the American Psychological Association** (APA) (American Psychological Association, 2010, p. 10):

- *introduction:* development of the problem under investigation, including its historical antecedents, and statement of the purpose of the investigation;
- *method:* description of the procedures used to conduct the investigation;
- *results:* report of the findings and analyses; and
- *discussion:* summary, interpretation, and implications of the results.

If you compare the APA guidelines and the proposal guide in Figure 2.2, you will see that they are similar. For this reason, following the proposal guide will facilitate not only the process of conducting

FIGURE 2.2 • Guide for Outlining a Quantitative or Qualitative Research Proposal

This form consists of a list of items in the form of questions and directions. By completing each item, you can create an outline of a research proposal. The outline then can be elaborated into a formal research proposal.

1. **Purpose of Study**
   A. The purpose of this study is to . . . (state the purpose succinctly in one or two sentences)
   B. What previous research is your study most directly based on? (select three to five publications that are absolutely central)
   C. How does your study build on previous research?
   D. How will your study contribute to educational research and practice?

2. **Research Questions, Hypotheses, Variables, and Case Delineation**
   A. List your research questions or hypotheses.
   B. If you propose to test hypotheses, describe briefly the theory from which the hypotheses were derived.
   C. If your study is quantitative in nature, list the variables that you will study. For each variable, indicate whether it is an independent variable, a dependent variable, or neither.
   D. If the study is qualitative in nature, describe the case features on which data collection and analysis will focus.

3. **Literature Search**
   A. List the search engines and indexes that you will use to identify relevant publications.
   B. List the keywords and descriptors that you will guide your use of search engines and indexes.
   C. Identify published literature reviews (if available) relating to your study.

4. **Research Design**
   A. Describe the research design that you selected for your study: descriptive, group comparison, correlational, experimental, qualitative (case study or specific qualitative research tradition), evaluative, mixed-method, or action research.
   B. If your study is quantitative in nature, what are the threats to the internal validity of your research design? (Internal validity means the extent to which extraneous variables are controlled, so that observed effects can be attributed solely to the independent variable.) What will you do to minimize or avoid these threats?
   C. If your study is quantitative in nature, what are the limitations to the generalizability (i.e.,

   external validity) of the findings that will result from your research design? What will you do to maximize the generalizability of your findings?
   D. If your study is qualitative in nature, what criteria do you consider to be relevant to judging the credibility and trustworthiness of the results that will be yielded by your research design?

5. **Sampling**
   A. If your study is quantitative in nature, describe the characteristics of the population that you will study.
   B. If your study is qualitative in nature, describe the phenomenon you wish to study and the cases that comprise instances of the phenomenon.
   C. Identify your sampling procedure and sampling unit.
   D. Indicate the size of your sample, and explain why that sample size is sufficient.
   E. Indicate whether the sample will be formed into subgroups and, if so, describe the characteristics of the subgroups.
   F. If your study will involve the use of volunteers, explain whether their characteristics will affect the generalizability of the research findings.

6. **Methods of Data Collection**
   A. For each of the variables that you plan to study (see 2.C), indicate whether you will measure it by a test, questionnaire, interview, observational procedure, or content analysis. Indicate whether the measure is already available or whether you will need to develop it.
   B. For each measure stated above, indicate which types of validity and reliability are relevant and how you will check them.
   C. If your study is qualitative in nature, indicate whether your data collection will focus on etic or emic perspectives or both; how you will collect data on each case feature that you have chosen for study (see 2.D); and the nature of your involvement in the data-collection process.

7. **Data-Analysis Procedures**
   A. What descriptive statistics and inferential statistics, if any, will you use to analyze your data for each of your research questions or hypotheses?

FIGURE 2.2 • Guide for Outlining a Quantitative or Qualitative Research Proposal (*Continued*)

B. If your study is qualitative in nature, indicate whether you will use an interpretational, structural, or reflective method of analysis.

8. Ethics and Human Relations
A. What risks, if any, does your study pose for research participants? What steps will you take to minimize these threats?
B. Will the study need to be approved by an institutional review board? If yes, describe the approval process.

C. How will you gain entry into your proposed research setting, and how will you gain the cooperation of your research participants?

9. Timeline
A. Create a timeline listing in order all the major steps of your study. Also indicate the approximate amount of time each step will take.

---

your study but also the preparation of a final report (e.g., a thesis or dissertation) and a manuscript submitted to a journal for publication.

The next sections of this chapter explain each section of the proposal guide and illustrate it by using the research problem about curriculum alignment that we introduced above.

You will note that the guide shown in Figure 2.2 specifies various ways in which a proposal for a quantitative research study differs from a proposal for a qualitative research study. We explain these differences in this chapter, and they are further elaborated in other chapters of the book.

Because we will continue to refer to Figure 2.2 throughout the book, we have helped you locate it easily by repeating it as Appendix 1.

Purpose of Study

A good self-check on whether you understand your proposed study is to see if you can state your research purpose in one or two sentences. Using our "teaching to the test" example, we might state our purpose in the following words:

> One purpose of my study is to determine the extent to which teachers design their classroom instruction and assessments so that they are aligned with state standards and assessments. The other purpose is to determine what school districts are doing to help teachers improve their instruction/assessment alignment with state standards and assessments.

This statement is brief but sufficiently detailed to give direction to the design of the study. Note that

we used the term *assessment* because it connotes a broader range of possible tests (e.g., projects, essays, class presentations) than the term *test*, which has more limited connotations (typically multiple-choice or brief-response items).

Before you can state your research purpose in such a concise form, you will need to review relevant educational literature, including articles and books written for practitioners and reports of research studies. You are likely to find many publications on important topics, but typically just a few that strongly influence the design of your study. You should discuss these publications in some depth to give the reader a sense of what is known about the topic and what you propose to study in order to advance knowledge about it.

We found a substantial number of research articles, opinion articles, and books about curriculum alignment in the literature. Several research articles and one book appeared to be particularly useful:

Kurz, A., Elliott, S. N., Wehby, J. H., & Smithson, J. L. (2010). Alignment of the intended, planned, and enacted curriculum in general and special education and its relation to student achievement. *Journal of Special Education, 44*(3), 131–145.

Paik, S., Zhang, M, Luneberg, M. A., Eberhardt, J., Shin, T. S., & Zhang, T. (2011). Supporting science teachers in alignment with state curriculum standards through professional development: Teachers' preparedness, expectations, and their fulfillment. *Journal of Science Education and Technology, 20*(4), 422–434.

Squires, D. A. (2008). *Curriculum alignment: Research-based strategies for increasing student achievement.* Thousand Oaks, CA: Corwin.

The studies included in these sources are relevant to our study's purpose and therefore would facilitate the preparation of our own literature review.

The study by Alexander Kurz and his colleagues found a low level of alignment between teachers' curriculum and state standards. They also found that the students of teachers with better curriculum alignment had better academic achievement than students of teachers with less curriculum alignment. These results support the importance of the proposed study because they demonstrate the importance of curriculum alignment and helping teachers improve it in their classrooms. The study by Sunhee Paik and colleagues is also relevant as it identified a professional development program that is effective in improving teachers' curriculum alignment. Our proposed study is significant in that its aim is to determine whether this or other types of professional development are occurring in school systems other than the one they studied.

The book by David Squires is useful because it provides a review of major studies of curriculum development and the efforts to improve it, both nationally and internationally. The author's knowledge and insights are likely to be valuable in helping us focus our study on key problems relating to the implementation of curriculum development.

Research Questions and Hypotheses

A purpose statement provides a general description of what you hope to learn by doing your research study. This statement then should be elaborated to make it more specific. Typically, specificity is achieved by preparing a set of research questions. The following research questions reflect the purpose statement in the previous section, with a specific focus on one aspect of the curriculum (science) and one age range of students (fourth-graders and sixth-graders):

1. To what extent are teachers' instructional activities in science aligned with state assessments in science that are administered to fourth-grade and sixth-grade students?
2. To what extent are teachers' classroom assessments in science aligned with state assessments that are administered to fourth-grade and sixth-grade students?

3. What professional development programs for science curriculum alignment do school systems make available to fourth-grade and sixth-grade teachers?

As we proceed to other sections of the research proposal, these questions will help us select appropriate procedures for data collection and data analysis. As we select each procedure, we will need to ask ourselves how appropriate the procedure is for answering our research questions.

The three questions above were written with the intent of doing a quantitative research study. Research questions for a qualitative research proposal typically will be written in a different style, because qualitative researchers do not dictate the specific direction of data collection and analysis in advance. They need to remain open to what they observe and what their research participants tell them; these observations and comments often open up new lines of inquiry within the study.

Now let us consider a possible qualitative research proposal. Suppose we find that a state is conducting professional development workshops to help teachers understand instruction–assessment alignment and incorporate it into their lesson planning. Further suppose that the purpose of our qualitative study is to learn about the benefits and drawbacks that teachers see in their state's alignment program (i.e., state standards and state assessments aligned to them) and the problems that they see in trying to alter their classroom teaching to accommodate the alignment program.

The following are examples of research questions that might follow from this purpose statement if we chose to make an intensive qualitative case study of professional development workshops in one school district:

1. What benefits and drawbacks about the state's alignment program and proposals for classroom implementation do each of the selected teachers mention as their professional development workshop proceeds?
2. How does curriculum alignment relate to each of the selected teachers' personal philosophy of teaching?
3. What problems and opportunities do each of the selected teachers experience when they return to their schools after the professional development workshop?

Note that these research questions do not restrict the kinds of data collection and analysis procedures that can be used.

Depending on the qualitative study's purpose, other research questions can be framed. For example, we might focus on just one school and pose research questions about how various stakeholders (e.g., teachers, administrators, specialists, students, parents) respond to the state's alignment program over a designated period of time.

In qualitative research, we typically avoid seeking to predict our findings (or even specify all our data-collection methods) in advance, but instead allow them to emerge. Therefore, we are unlikely to state research hypotheses in our proposal.

Returning to quantitative research study proposals, we might choose to state research hypotheses that will guide our study instead of framing research questions. In simple terms, a **hypothesis** in a research study is a prediction about expected findings. For example, we posed the following research question: "Do fourth-grade and sixth-grade students whose teachers align their classroom assessments to a greater extent with state assessments perform better on the state assessments than students whose teachers align their classroom assessments to a lesser extent?"

This question instead can be stated as a hypothesis: "Fourth-grade and sixth-grade students whose teachers use classroom assessments that are well aligned with state assessments will achieve higher scores on the state assessments than students whose teachers use poorly aligned classroom assessments."

Before you consider stating research hypotheses, you should be aware that hypotheses are a particular form of prediction in that they are explicitly derived from theories. As stated in Chapter 1, a **theory** specifies a set of **constructs** and how they relate to each other. We also stated that constructs are structures and processes that are believed to underlie observed events and behavior. For example, intelligence is a construct because many people believe that it is a real but unobservable structure that enables some students to learn better than others.

Hypotheses are more commonly used in basic research than in applied research because the main goal of basic research is to deepen our collective understanding of phenomena through the development of good theories. The soundness of a theory is determined by doing empirical tests of hypotheses derived from it. The following are titles of several recent studies that tested hypotheses derived from theories:

Barry, C. Y. H., & Okun, M. A. (2012). Application of investment theory to predicting maintenance of the intent to stay among freshmen. *Journal of College Student Retention: Research, Theory & Practice, 13*(1), 87–107.

Fitousi, D., & Wenger, M. J. (2011). Processing capacity under perceptual and cognitive load: A closer look at load theory. *Journal of Experimental Psychology: Human Perception and Performance, 37*(3), 781–798.

Sullivan, A. L., & Artiles, A. J. (2011). Theorizing racial inequity in special education: Applying structural inequity theory to disproportionality. *Urban Education, 46*(6), 1526–1552.

Each of these studies tested one or more hypotheses derived from the theory specified in the journal article's title. If you come across such a study in your literature review or wish to do such a study, you will need to develop a deep understanding about the theory of interest.

Quantitative Variables and Case Delineation

Once you have stated your research purpose and research questions or hypotheses (items 1.A and 2.A in Figure 2.2), the next step is to specify the variables (in quantitative research) or aspects of cases (in qualitative research) that you will study. If specification of variables or case aspects is too difficult, it probably means that you need to read and think about the existing research literature in more depth.

If you are planning a quantitative study, you will need to identify each variable that you intend to measure. We explain the importance and meaning of variables in Chapters 5 and 6. For now, you can think of **variables** as anything you wish to study that has some degree of variability. For example, if students vary in the scores they receive on a test, we can say that student test performance is a variable. If all students take the same test, the test itself has not varied. In this case, a researcher would say that the test is a "constant," not a variable.

Three main variables are expressed in the four research questions stated previously for the proposed quantitative study:

1. The degree of alignment of teachers' instructional activities with the state assessment in science.

(Instructional alignment can vary among teachers.)

2. The degree of alignment of teachers' classroom assessments with the state assessment in science. (Assessment alignment can vary among teachers.)

3. Type of professional development workshop. (The researcher can develop a typology of workshops and determine how many workshops experienced by the teachers are of each type.)

Each of these variables will be studied at two grade levels (fourth grade and sixth grade). Therefore, we have a total of six variables.

Qualitative researchers usually do not think in terms of variables. Instead, they select a case, or several cases, for intensive study. Then they think about which features of the case to study, because it is not practical to study everything about a case. Instead, we must focus our study by identifying a limited number of features of the case about which we will collect data. This process is explained in Chapter 13.

We stated three research questions for a proposed qualitative research study. Although a state curriculum alignment program involves many stakeholders, we limited our case study to the perspectives of teachers. We also delineated which features of their perspectives to study, choosing to examine their perceptions about two aspects of the program (benefits and drawbacks) and whether their general attitude is welcoming or resistant. Also, we might choose to collect data about their perspectives in two contexts: public workshops and confidential meetings.

The third research question implies an interest in personal characteristics and how they affect teachers' perceptions and attitudes. Therefore, we will need to decide which aspects of the teachers' personal characteristics to study. For example, we might study their personality patterns, upbringing, level of schooling, academic achievement, views about students, and political attitudes. As we start collecting data, we might find ourselves generating additional research questions, each of which will require us to consider the possibility of new cases, and new features of those cases, to study.

Literature Search

We stated earlier in the chapter that a good research study is built on a strong understanding of the existing literature on the problem that you wish to investigate. Chapters 3 and 4 will help you conduct a literature review to identify an interesting research problem and find what has been learned about it, as reported in books, journal articles, institutional reports, conference papers, and other publications.

We explain in those chapters that professional associations, governmental agencies, and commercial publishers create bibliographic citations for their publications, which other organizations incorporate into electronic **databases**. You can explore these databases using **search engines** and keywords. Most likely, you are already familiar with electronic databases, search engines, and keywords even if you have not studied research methodology. For example, you probably use Google, Yahoo!, or some similar search engine to look for information on the Internet.

We used a search engine and database for educators, ERIC (Education Resources Information Center), to look for studies relating to our research problem. We entered two phrases, "teaching to the test" and "curriculum alignment," in the ERIC search bar, which generated hundreds of relevant citations and brief summaries (called *abstracts*) that helped us develop an understanding of what is already known about our research problem.

Your ability to search the education literature will enhance your professional expertise, whether you are preparing a proposal for a research study or looking for ideas to solve a problem of practice.

Research Design

The fourth set of items in Figure 2.2 involves the design of your research study. Over time, researchers have developed standard methods of inquiry (called *designs*) for answering their questions or testing their hypotheses. In fact, much of this book is concerned with explaining commonly used research designs.

To illustrate how research designs can differ, consider the problem of investigating teachers' reactions to a state-mandated curriculum alignment program. We might use a case study design to study in depth a few teachers at one school. We could interview them extensively to learn what they think about the alignment program.

Alternatively, we could use an experimental design in which we compare two groups of teachers: one group participates in a workshop that attempts to help them develop positive attitudes toward instruction–assessment alignment; a control group of teachers does not participate in the program. We measure the attitudes of both groups of teachers by a quantitative scale before and after the workshop interval.

The case study design is not better or worse than the experimental design. Both are well-established research designs, and each has advantages depending on the researchers' preferences, needs, and constraints. Also, each is susceptible to different flaws. You need to be aware of these flaws and take steps to avoid them. That is why we explain not only the features of each research design in this book but also their potential weaknesses and how to minimize them.

Sampling

It is nearly impossible to study every instance of the phenomenon that interests you. For example, if you are interested in investigating teachers' reactions to state-mandated tests administered in their classroom, it simply would be too expensive and time consuming to survey the entire population of teachers in the United States or any other country. However, there are ways to select a sample that is representative of the population that interests you. By using an appropriate sampling procedure, you can generalize your findings from the sample to that population if you have done a quantitative research study. If you have done a qualitative research study involving one or several cases, you can consider the applicability of your findings to other cases.

The section on sampling in Figure 2.2 specifies various factors that you will need to consider in selecting a sample for your study. Sampling procedures in quantitative and qualitative research are described in Chapters 5 and 13, respectively.

Methods of Data Collection

Whatever research design you choose, you will be collecting empirical data. In fact, the collection of empirical data to answer questions or test hypotheses is the very essence of research. **Empirical data** are direct observations or other measurements of the phenomena that we are studying. By contrast, our beliefs and theories are claims about what we would find if we collected empirical data. The major

advances that we have seen over the past century in medicine, engineering, and other professions have come about, in large part, because researchers collected empirical data to make discoveries or to test their beliefs and theories.

Section 6 of the proposal guide in Figure 2.2 will help you think about the measures you will need for collecting empirical data and ensuring that they will hold up to critical scrutiny.

A complete listing of your variables or case features (Section 2 of Figure 2.2) will help you greatly in selecting methods of empirical data collection. If your list is complete, you will not find later on, to your dismay, that you failed to measure an important variable or case feature during the data-collection phase of your study.

Chapters 5 and 13 present a range of data-collection procedures used in quantitative and qualitative research, respectively. Other chapters describe measurement procedures specifically for use with particular research designs.

Data-Analysis Procedures

Raw data do not speak for themselves. They need to be analyzed and interpreted. Therefore, your research proposal should include a section on how you plan to analyze your data. Completing Section 7 of Figure 2.2 will help you determine whether your research design will generate data that are relevant to your research questions and hypotheses and can be analyzed by statistical or qualitative procedures.

The analysis of quantitative data involves the use of statistical techniques, which are described in the chapters in Part Three. Some qualitative data are also amenable to statistical analysis, but more likely you will use the analytical techniques described in the chapters in Part Four.

Ethics and Human Relations

The ethics of educational research has become an increasing focus of concern. The federal government has responded to this concern by requiring the establishment of **institutional review boards** (also called **human subjects review committees**). Their purpose is to ensure that research participants are protected from harm or risk of harm. For example, institutional review boards, commonly called IRBs, oversee medical research because the potential for physical or emotional harm to individuals is high. IRBs also oversee educational research because of the potential for harm to participants, especially young children and students with disabilities.

A guiding assumption of IRBs is that researchers have greater power than the participants in a research study. An obvious example is a survey study: the researcher collects questionnaire or interview data from participants, but participants do not have the authority to collect data from the researcher. Similarly, in experiments, the researcher tests the effects of an intervention (e.g., a teaching method) on participants, but the participants do not test the effects of an intervention on the researcher. In certain kinds of qualitative research, however, researchers and participants share power in studying a phenomenon of interest to both of them. Proposed studies of this type can be problematic for IRBs. We discuss this problem in Chapter 13.

Your university or school district most likely has an IRB to monitor research conducted under its auspices. You will need to submit your research proposal, and likely complete a questionnaire as well, to the IRB before undertaking your study. An exception might be a small research project that is done as a course project, with no possibility that the research results will be disseminated. In this

situation, the course instructor will need to consult with the IRB to ensure that the class projects do not require their review.

If you plan to do a research project because of personal interest, you still will need to have it approved by an IRB. You can search for an IRB that is located near you and ask whether it will undertake the approval process for you.

The American Educational Research Association (AERA) recently has published a code of ethics that you must follow as you plan a study, conduct it, and report its findings (American Educational Research Association, 2011). The approval process of IRBs likely incorporate most, if not all of AERA's code of ethics. We highly recommend that you study it before preparing the documentation required by your IRB.

An outline of the Code of Ethics is shown in Figure 2.3. The complete code of ethics is available online. You should study it as you prepare your research proposal to be sure that you will not unintentionally violate any of its ethical standards for research. Unless your adviser asks you to address each of the 22 standards, you can focus on those standards that pose a potential risk for your study in the Ethics and Human Relations section of your proposal.

FIGURE 2.3 • Code of Ethics, American Educational Research Association. Approved by the AERA Council February 2011

PREAMBLE

BACKGROUND

PRINCIPLES

Principle A: Professional Competence
Principle B: Integrity
Principle C: Professional, Scientific and Scholarly Responsibility
Principle D: Respect for People's Rights, Dignity, and Diversity
Principle E: Social Responsibility

ETHICAL STANDARDS

1. Scientific, Scholarly, and Professional Standards
2. Competence
3. Use and Misuse of Expertise
4. Fabrication, Falsification, and Plagiarism
5. Avoiding Harm
6. Nondiscrimination
7. Nonexploitation
8. Harassment
9. Employment Decisions
   9.01 *Fair Employment Practices*
   9.02 *Responsibilities of Employees*
10. Conflicts of Interest
    10.01 *Adherence to Professional Standards*
    10.02 *Disclosure*
    10.03 *Avoidance of Personal Gain*
    10.04 *Decision making in the Workplace*
    10.05 *Decision making Outside of the Workplace*
11. Public Communications
    11.01 *Researcher Communications*
    11.02 *Statements by Others*

FIGURE 2.3 • Code of Ethics, American Educational Research Association. Approved by the AERA Council February 2011 (*Continued*)

12. Confidentiality
  - 12.01 *Maintaining Confidentiality*
  - 12.02 *Limits of Confidentiality*
  - 12.03 *Discussing Confidentiality and Its Limits*
  - 12.04 *Anticipation of Possible Uses of Information*
  - 12.05 *Electronic Transmission and Storage of Confidential Information*
  - 12.06 *Anonymity of Sources*
  - 12.07 *Minimizing Intrusions on Privacy*
  - 12.08 *Preservation of Confidential Information*
13. Informed Consent
  - 13.01 *Scope of Informed Consent*
  - 13.02 *Informed Consent Process*
  - 13.03 *Informed Consent of Students and Subordinates*
  - 13.04 *Informed Consent With Children*
  - 13.05 *Use of Deception in Research*
  - 13.06 *Use of Recording Technology*
14. Research Planning, Implementation, and Dissemination
  - 14.01 *Planning and Implementation*
  - 14.02 *Dual Relationships*
  - 14.03 *Unanticipated Research Opportunities*
  - 14.04 *Offering Inducements for Research Participants*
  - 14.05 *Reporting on Research*
  - 14.06 *Data Sharing*
15. Authorship Credit
16. Publication Process
  - 16.01 *Submission of Manuscripts for Publication*
  - 16.02 *Duplicate Publication of Data*
  - 16.03 *Responsibilities of Editors*
17. Responsibilities of Reviewers
18. Teaching, Training, and Administering Education Programs
  - 18.01 *Teaching and Training*
  - 18.02 *Administering Education Programs*
19. Mentoring
20. Supervision
21. Contractual and Consulting Services
22. Adherence to the Ethical Standards of the American Educational Research Association
  - 22.01 *Familiarity With the Code of Ethics*
  - 22.02 *Confronting Ethical Issues*
  - 22.03 *Fair Treatment of Parties in Ethical Disputes*
  - 22.04 *Reporting Ethical Violations of Others*
  - 22.05 *Improper Complaints*
  - 22.06 *Cooperating With Ethics Committees*

Source: Copyright 2011 by the American Educational Research Association. Reproduced by permission of the publisher.

We comment below on standards that might not be obvious or that are particularly relevant to research studies that graduate students in education might do. In doing so, we wish to emphasize that our comments are no substitute for your own careful review of the entire Code of Ethics.

2. *Competence.* You should do research only on problems that you feel competent to investigate. An important aspect of competence is in-depth knowledge of the existing literature on your research problem.

3. *Use and Misuse of Expertise.* You should take care that your research study does not get co-opted by other individuals for their agenda.

For example, certain individuals might have a stake in a controversial program and wish you to demonstrate its effectiveness. In this case, you need to be assured that you have the authority to design your study independently of these individuals and that all stakeholders in your study have an opportunity to express possible concerns before it is conducted.

6. *Nondiscrimination.* In selecting a sample, you should consider carefully whether you are unwittingly excluding certain groups. For example, if you are studying classroom instruction, a school principal might give you a list of classes that does not include those for children with special needs. You need to take steps to ensure that the list is complete and that you have a sound research rationale for including or excluding particular classes.

7. *Nonexploitation.* A researcher might select a sample from his own school or school district because he has influence with a particular administrator or is himself an administrator. In this case, the sample might feel an element of coercion to participate in the study. The researcher needs to take steps to remove any element of coercion, perhaps by enabling potential participants to respond to an anonymous questionnaire asking their views about the value of the study and whether it will interfere with their duties or have potentially negative consequences for them.

10. *Conflicts of Interest.* Graduate students in education typically must complete a research project or dissertation in order to earn their master's or doctoral degree. Therefore, their study has a direct benefit for them. They cannot let this benefit interfere with the best interests of the individuals affected by their study. This problem usually can be avoided by being forthright in telling school officials or other individuals about this benefit and having an open discussion about it. Also, you should be able to state benefits that might accrue to the research participants and the education profession by agreeing to the study. If they see that the study has larger benefits, they are not likely to be concerned that the study is only being done to meet the graduate student's personal need.

12. *Confidentiality.* Researchers should consider all data collected from participants as private and potentially harmful to them if revealed. Therefore, you must take steps to preserve the confidentiality of your data. One way to do this is to assign each participant an identification code (e.g., a number) and then create a name-code list linking each individual's name with her code. If persons other than you need access to the data (e.g., a statistician or your research adviser), they should have access only to the codes, not the name-code list, unless there is a compelling reason to give it to them. Also, you will need to determine where to store the name-code list and the data and for how long a period of time before destroying them.

13. *Informed Consent.* A researcher must seek the informed consent of each individual that she wishes to include in her study. **Informed consent** means that individuals have been informed about all the possible risks and costs involved in participating in the research study and that no coercion has been used to obtain their consent, including threats of possible negative consequences if they decline to participate. If an individual cannot be expected to understand the informed consent process (e.g., a young child), permission must be obtained from the individual's parent or guardian. Informed consent is not necessary if data are to be collected in public places or if the researcher plans to use publicly available information. Waivers of consent can be requested from IRBs if the research involves minimal or no risk, or if informed consent would compromise the soundness of the research study.

15. *Authorship Credit.* Only the student is listed as the author of a master's thesis or doctoral dissertation. (There might be exceptions to this rule that we are not aware of.) Some students might report their findings in other forms as well, for example, as a conference presentation or journal article. In such cases, it is appropriate to include the student's adviser and other individuals who contributed substantially to the study (e.g., a statistician who provided extensive consultation on data analysis). For this reason, you will find that many studies in the literature have multiple authors. If you are the senior author of a publication, it by no means diminishes your stature by including, as authors, other individuals who contributed to your study.

16. *Publication Process.* You cannot submit a manuscript to multiple journals or book publishers at the same time, except with their permission. Also, once you have published your findings in a journal or book, you cannot publish them elsewhere unless you cite the source where they were first published.

22. *Adherence to the Ethical Standards of AERA.* If you plan to conduct an educational research study, you have an ethical obligation to be familiar with AERA's Code of Ethics, the requirements of IRB reviews, and other ethical standards and legal requirements that are specific to your study. If you have reason to believe that a researcher associated with your study or another study has violated an ethical code, you have an obligation to bring it to the attention of that researcher or to an appropriate authority.

In addition to ethical considerations, Section 8 of Figure 2.2 refers to human relations. You cannot take it for granted that your intended research participants will allow you to collect data from them directly or from their students or clients. Whether your participants are individuals in a professional role (e.g., school staff) or community representatives (e.g., residents of a household), they typically will want assurance that you are conducting a research study that has the seal of approval from an institution they respect. They also will want assurance that you are trustworthy and will treat participants and the data they provide with respect.

These assurances can come from the IRB, which typically has a standard form that indicates its approval of your research study. Assurances also can come from representatives of an institution that the research participants respect, possibly in the form of a letter on official letterhead, indicating that they have studied your proposal and approve of it. Ideally, the letter would also state what benefits are expected and who would benefit from the findings of your study.

Timeline

As you have seen above, a research study involves many steps. The process might seem overwhelming at first, but it won't be if you are systematic in your approach.

To be systematic, you need to analyze all the steps in your proposed study and estimate a completion date for each step. This process is particularly important if you plan to collect data in schools. For example, if you plan to collect data from teachers, you most likely will need to do it when school is in session. If you plan to collect data from students, you probably will need to do it on days when they are not involved in activities such as taking tests or going on field trips.

OTHER STEPS IN THE RESEARCH PROCESS

We believe that the intellectual exercise of preparing a detailed research proposal is at the heart of the research process. A detailed proposal greatly increases the likelihood of a successful study, and it also facilitates other steps in the research process, which we describe next.

Pilot Study

A pilot study of key measures and procedures helps to ensure the success of any research study. For example, if you plan to develop a questionnaire, test, or other data-collection instrument, it is helpful to try it out with a few research participants prior to formal data collection. You might discover that some of your questions and directions are unclear or require skills that data collectors or research participants do not possess. You can ask the pilot-study participants for guidance in revising the items and directions as needed.

The ideal situation is to conduct a pilot study of key measures and procedures before or during preparation of the research proposal. Reviewers of the proposal, including an IRB, will look at the proposal more favorably if you can state that your measures and procedures have been piloted and revised as needed.

If necessary, it might be possible to do a pilot study after the proposal has been reviewed and approved. However, you will probably need to submit to the IRB or review board any substantial changes made as a result of the pilot study.

Data Collection

The vast majority of research studies in education involve collecting data from humans, and there is always the possibility that your best-laid plans will go astray. For example, suppose your study involves administration of a test to a class of students. Some students might be absent on the day of testing. Makeup sessions are an option if they do not interfere with your research timeline.

Many other problems can occur during the data-collection phase of a research study. You will need to exercise judgment and ingenuity in dealing with them. More experienced researchers can help you devise the best solution for a particular situation. Most problems can be managed if you have designed the proposal well, pilot-tested key measures and procedures, and built good relations with all stakeholders involved with the study.

Writing a Research Report

Writing a research proposal that includes the items shown in Figure 2.2 will greatly facilitate the last step—writing your final report. The proposal is an outline, or framework, for the finished report, and most parts of a proposal are included in final reports, such as theses, dissertations, journal articles, and conference papers. If your university or other institution has a required format for writing a research report, you simply need to follow that format.

We find it particularly helpful to locate good examples of research reports and adopt their organization and style. If you are writing a course paper, master's thesis, or doctoral dissertation, you can ask your advisers to recommend completed papers, theses, or dissertations that they consider exemplary.

Another approach is to read articles in refereed journals that publish research studies similar to yours. After reading five or so articles, you will begin to develop a sense of the writing style and format that are appropriate for formal research reports.

Many universities require that their students in education and related disciplines follow the style specifications of the *Publication Manual of the American Psychological Association* (2010). We referred to this manual's specifications for the format of research reports earlier in this chapter. The manual contains many additional specifications related to such matters as language bias, statistical symbols, tables and figures, and bibliographic citations.

The APA manual is approximately 270 pages and can appear intimidating. We do not recommend that you study it page by page. Instead, review the table of contents to get a sense of the topics that it covers. Then, refer to it as you have questions about the preparation of your research report, such as how to construct a table or prepare a list of references that you have cited.

One of the most important features of a research report is the tables and figures that present the results of statistical analyses. A well-prepared table or figure can create a picture in the reader's mind that is more vivid than a written description of statistical findings. Standard procedures for creating tables and figures for different types of statistical analyses are available (Nicol & Pexman, 2010a, 2010b).

A Final Note about Using a Proposal Guide

This concludes our explanation of how to conduct a research study. As you read the remaining chapters of the book, each step of the process should become clearer to you.

If you are planning to do a research study, we recommend that you review the proposal guide in Figure 2.1 or another suitable guide as you read each chapter. After reading a chapter, determine how its content pertains to a particular section, or sections, of the guide. Then complete the sections if they are relevant to your proposed study. Over time, you will see your study gradually taking shape.

We recommend that you occasionally show your evolving proposal to your research adviser for feedback and assurance that you are on the right track. It is relatively easy to revise an outline for a proposal, or trash it and start over again. It is much more difficult and emotionally draining to write a complete, polished proposal only to learn that it must undergo extensive revision or be scrapped.

SELF-CHECK TEST

1. A study that seeks to replicate findings of previous research
   a. adds nothing of value to the research literature.
   b. is a worthwhile contribution to the research literature.
   c. should be conducted only by the researchers who reported the original findings.
   d. is important for theory building but not for an applied discipline like education.
2. Reviews of the research literature in your areas of interest
   a. should be read only after you have formulated your research questions.
   b. should be read only after you have formulated your research design.
   c. are most useful when you are attempting to interpret the results of your data analyses.
   d. are particularly useful for generating ideas for your own research project.
3. Hypotheses are
   a. predictions about what you expect to find when you analyze your research data.
   b. statements of the constructs that will best describe your research data.
   c. primarily useful when conducting a replication study.
   d. most useful in applied research.

4. Which of the following is the best example of a variable?
   a. All students in the research sample will read the same chapter in a history textbook.
   b. A researcher will study one teacher's written comments on students' essays over an entire school year.
   c. A researcher will measure individual differences in students' academic self-esteem.
   d. A researcher states a hypothesis about the relationship between class size and students' off-task behavior.

5. If a researcher is interested in how teachers view students with autism, case delineation would be particularly useful for
   a. determining which features of a teacher's views will be the focus for interviews and classroom observation.
   b. determining how many teachers to include in the study.
   c. eliminating teachers who have difficulty in reflecting on their instruction.
   d. all of the above.

6. Search engines, databases, and keywords are most useful for
   a. conducting complex data analyses.
   b. conducting a literature review.
   c. deciding whether quantitative or qualitative research is most relevant to answer your research questions.
   d. deciding which sampling procedure will yield the most appropriate sample size.

7. Procedures for data analysis
   a. should be specified in a research proposal only for a quantitative study.
   b. should be specified in a research proposal only for a qualitative study.
   c. are the only part of the research process that cannot be specified in a research proposal.
   d. can be specified in a research proposal, even if no data of any sort have been collected.

8. The main function of an IRB (institutional review board) is to determine whether the research proposal
   a. conforms in all respects to the *Publication Manual of the American Psychological Association*.
   b. follows all the specifications of the proposal guide published by the researcher's university or other source.
   c. includes procedures that will avoid or minimize harm to the research participants.
   d. includes procedures to ensure that students complete every item on each test that is administered.

9. Pilot studies and timeline specifications
   a. are best completed as part of the process of writing a research proposal.
   b. are not necessary for a research study that is intended as a replication of previous research findings.
   c. are always required by an IRB (institutional review board).
   d. are useful only for a study that will use quantitative research methodology.

10. The publication manual of the American Psychological Association
    a. is useful only for studies that measure psychological variables.
    b. is primarily useful for helping a researcher prepare a report for publication.
    c. needs to be supplemented by the use of other publication manuals if a research report contains tables and figures.
    d. is used by many universities to dictate the format for research reports prepared by students majoring in education.

CHAPTER REFERENCES

American Educational Research Association. (2011). AERA Code of Ethics: American Educational Research Association approved by the AERA Council February 2011. *Educational Researcher, 40*(3), 145–156.

American Psychological Association. (2010). *Publication manual of the American Psychological Association* (6th ed.). Washington, DC: Author.

Gardner, W. (2008). Good teachers teach to the test. *Christian Science Monitor*. Retrieved from http://www.csmonitor.com/Commentary/Opinion/2008/0417/p09s02-coop.html

Kelly, A. E., & Yin, R. K. (2007). Strengthening structured abstracts for education research: The need for claim-based structured abstracts. *Educational Researcher, 36*(3), 133–138.

Nicol, A. M., & Pexman, P. M. (2010a). *Displaying your findings: A practical guide for creating tables* (6th ed.). Washington, DC: American Psychological Association.

Nicol, A. M., & Pexman, P. M. (2010b). *Presenting your findings: A practical guide for creating figures, posters, and presentations.* Washington, DC: American Psychological Association.

Tsouderos, T. (2011, December 23). Science journal retracts controversial research paper. *Chicago Tribune.* Retrieved from http://www.chicagotribune.com/health/ct-met-science-journal-retraction-1223-20111223,0,6408682.story

RESOURCES FOR FURTHER STUDY

Bloomberg, L. D., & Volpe, M. F. (2012). *Completing your qualitative dissertation: A roadmap from beginning to end* (2nd ed.). Thousand Oaks, CA: Sage.

> As the title suggests, this book covers all phases of conducting a qualitative research study as either a master's thesis or doctoral dissertation. The authors discuss the elements both of a qualitative research proposal and the final report.

Cooper, H. (2011). *Reporting research in psychology: How to meet journal article reporting standards.* Washington, DC: American Psychological Association.

> This book explains and illustrates standards for reporting psychological research, but the standards apply equally to reports of educational research studies. The standards are designed to help readers understand a published study and to help researchers search for patterns of findings across related studies. If you are planning to prepare a report of your study for a research journal, you will find help in this book.

Henson, K. T. (2003). Writing for professional publication: Some myths and some truths. *Phi Delta Kappan, 84*(10), 788–791.

> The author provides advice about how to prepare a publishable manuscript and select an appropriate journal to which to submit it. The article includes an extensive list of education journals, with information about such matters as rejection rates and how to communicate with journal editors.

Krathwohl, D. R., & Smith, N. L. (2005). *How to prepare a dissertation proposal: Suggestions for students in education and the social and behavioral sciences.* Syracuse, NY: Syracuse University Press.

> This book is a revision of a classic text on preparing a dissertation proposal. Although intended for doctoral students, anyone who is preparing a research proposal of any type can benefit from it.

Sample Outline of a Quantitative Research Proposal

We created two proposal outlines to illustrate the process of using the proposal guide shown in Figure 2.2. The proposals are for a research study about curriculum alignment. They are similar in certain respects to the example already presented in this chapter.

The first outline is for a quantitative research study. If you are planning to do a quantitative study using one of the research designs presented in Part Three, this example will be helpful.

1. Purpose of Study

A. Purpose Statement

The purpose of this study is to learn how educators go about aligning curriculum content with instruction and test content under conditions involving a federal or state mandate to improve students' learning.

B. Relevant Previous Research

Among the studies we have identified in our literature review, the following three studies, all involving quantitative research designs, are particularly relevant to our research purpose. We provide the bibliographic citation and the abstract for each study as it appears in the ERIC database.

Paik, S., Zhang, M, Luneberg, M. A., Eberhardt, J., Shin, T. S., & Zhang, T. (2011). Supporting science teachers in alignment with state curriculum standards through professional development: Teachers' preparedness, expectations, and their fulfillment. *Journal of Science Education and Technology, 20*(4), 422–434.

ABSTRACT Since "A Nation at Risk" was released in the 1980s, standards-based reform has been the most dominant trend in American educational policy, and the No Child Left Behind Act pushed the trend further by requiring states to develop rigorous curriculum standards. Though much has been said about these new standards, less has been said about whether or how well professional development helps teachers link their instruction to these standards. This study examined the impact of a professional development program for K–12 science teachers in helping teachers meet state curriculum standards. Seventy-five science teachers in Michigan participated in a two-week summer workshop that used Problem-Based Learning for improving teachers' content knowledge and pedagogical content knowledge. Researchers surveyed participating teachers about the change of teachers' preparedness for standards-based teaching, their expectations to meet state curriculum standards, and whether their expectations were met. In addition, the usefulness of workshop activities was examined. Data analysis showed that to align teaching with state curriculum standards, participating teachers expected to learn instructional strategies and enhance science content knowledge through professional development, and by and large, their expectations were met. Collaboration with colleagues and facilitators helped teachers achieve their goals in terms of teaching within state curriculum standards. These findings have important implications for designing professional development to help teachers align instruction with curriculum standards.

Parke, C. S., & Lane, S. (2008). Examining alignment between state performance assessment and mathematics classroom activities. *Journal of Educational Research, 101*(3), 132–147. (ERIC Reference Number EJ787815)

ABSTRACT The authors describe research on the extent to which mathematics classroom activities in Maryland were aligned with Maryland learning outcomes and the Maryland School Performance Assessment Program (MSPAP; Maryland State Department of Education, 1995, 2000). The study was part of a larger research project (S. Lane, C. S. Parke, & C. A. Stone, 1999) that focused on the overall impact of MSPAP on schools, teachers, and students. The authors collected 3,948 instruction, assessment, and test-preparation activities from a statewide stratified random sample of 250 teachers in the tested grades (3, 5, and 8) and nontested grades (2, 4, and 7). The authors describe the methods used to collect, code, and analyze teachers' classroom activities concerning 7 components: (a) mathematics process outcomes; (b) mathematics content outcomes; (c) student response types; (d) interpretation of charts, tables, and graphs; (e) use of manipulatives and calculators; (f) integration with other subject areas; and (g) overall similarity to MSPAP. They also highlight results for overall degree of alignment as well as differences in alignment across grade levels and type of activity (instruction vs. assessment). Most classroom activities aligned with aspects of state assessment and standards. Only minimal differences occurred across grades. However, degree of alignment was higher for instruction than assessment activities. This research approach can be useful to other educators and researchers interested in studying alignment among standards, assessment, and instruction.

Roach, A. T., Niebling, B. C., & Kurz, A. (2008). Evaluating the alignment among curriculum, instruction, and assessments: Implications and applications for research and practice. *Psychology in the Schools, 45*(2), 158–167. (ERIC Reference Number EJ783243)

ABSTRACT   Alignment has been defined as the extent to which curricular expectations and assessments are in agreement and work together to provide guidance for educators' efforts to facilitate students' progress toward desired academic outcomes. The Council of Chief State School Officers has identified three preferred models as frameworks for evaluating alignment: Webb's alignment model, the Surveys of Enacted Curriculum model, and the Achieve model. Each model consists of a series of indices that summarize or describe the general match or coherence between state standards, large-scale assessments, and, in some cases, classroom instruction. This article provides an overview of these frameworks for evaluating alignment and their applications in educational practice and the research literature. After providing an introduction to the use of alignment to evaluate large-scale accountability systems, the article presents potential extensions of alignment for use with vulnerable populations (e.g., students with disabilities, preschoolers), individual students, and classroom teachers. These proposed applications can provide information for facilitating efforts to improve teachers' classroom instruction and students' educational achievement.

C. Building on Previous Research

Previous research has found promising evidence that alignment of curriculum with instruction and test content improves students' academic achievement (e.g., Paik et al., 2011, cited above). Also, some research studies have examined the existing degree of alignment among curriculum, instruction, and tests in schools (e.g., Parke & Lane, 2008, cited above). However, we could find no studies that examined the process used by schools to improve these alignments.

Our proposed study extends previous research by examining the alignment process.

D. Contribution to Educational Research and Practice

Research on other school improvement initiatives demonstrates that the reform process often is beset with problems and that educators' success in solving these problems affects how well the initiative is institutionalized and how much it benefits students. By examining the process of curriculum alignment at selected school sites, we hope to identify factors that facilitate or hinder the process.

Identification of these factors might help other schools plan their alignment process in ways that increase their likelihood of success in improving students' academic achievement.

The proposed study, once completed and reported, might stimulate other researchers to conduct additional studies on this particular approach to school improvement to identify how best to plan and conduct it.

2. Research Questions, Hypotheses, Variables, and Case Delineation

A. Research Questions

We have three research questions:

1. What percentage of schools in the state have engaged in professional development to improve their curriculum alignment?
2. For schools that have engaged in curriculum alignment, how many hours of professional development have teachers received?
3. What problems do professional development groups encounter as they engage in planning and conducting the alignment process?
4. What solutions do these groups attempt as they cope with problems in planning and conducting the alignment process?

B. Hypotheses

Not relevant to this study.

C. Variables

The questionnaire described in section 6.A below includes items asking about a school's involvement in a curriculum-instruction-test alignment process during the previous two years and about problems and solutions during the process. For now, we will assume that the items include three problems (A, B, C) and their corresponding solutions (A, B, C).

In this scenario, there are a total of 11 variables:

1. The presence or absence of a professional development program for a school's teachers to improve curriculum alignment.
2. For schools having a professional development program, how many hours did it involve for each participating teacher?
3. Occurrence of problem A (a yes-no scale)
4. Occurrence of problem B (a yes-no scale)
5. Occurrence of problem C (a yes-no scale)
6. Occurrence of solution A (a yes-no scale)
7. Occurrence of solution B (a yes-no scale)
8. Occurrence of solution C (a yes-no scale)
9. Usefulness of solution A (a 7-point scale)
10. Usefulness of solution B (a 7-point scale)
11. Usefulness of solution C (a 7-point scale)

In addition, we will include two open-ended items: (1) Did you encounter any other problems and (2) what solutions, if any, did you try in order to solve the problems? Each problem and solution mentioned by the participants will constitute an additional variable.

D. Case Delineation

Not relevant to this study.

3. Literature Search

A. Search Engines and Indexes

The ERIC search engine will be sufficient for our research purposes.

B. Keywords and Descriptors

Our preliminary use of ERIC suggests that the keywords "alignment" and "curriculum alignment" by themselves or combined with the ERIC descriptors "achievement gains" and "academic achievement" will identify studies relevant to our research purpose.

C. Published Literature Review

The following literature review appears pertinent to our research studies. It is an article in a journal's theme issue about how educators have developed and studied methodological procedures involved in curriculum alignment over the past decade.

Beck, M. D. (2007). Commentary: Review and other views—"Alignment" as a psychometric issue. *Applied Measurement in Education, 20*(1), 127–135.

4. Research Design

A. Type of Design

The research questions call for a descriptive research design using quantitative methodology. The first question requires us to determine the *percentage* of schools having a certain characteristic, namely, involvement in curriculum alignment. The other three questions require us to determine the *frequency of use* of various alignment procedures, the *frequency* of various problems that occur during the alignment process, and the *frequency* of various solutions to these problems.

B. Threats to Internal Validity

Not relevant to this study.

C. Threats to Generalizability

The study will include a random sample of schools drawn from one state. The results should generalize at least to other schools in this state and possibly to other states having similar characteristics.

D. Criteria for Judging Credibility and Trustworthiness of Results

Not relevant to this study.

5. Sampling

A. Population Characteristics

All school systems in the United States are experiencing the need to improve student learning because of the No Child Left Behind Act. Our resources do not enable us to study all 50 states and U.S. territories. Therefore, we will focus on the state in which we reside. In the future, we or other researchers can replicate our study in other states.

B. Cases and Phenomena

Not relevant to this study.

C. Sampling Procedure

We will obtain a list of all schools in our selected state from the state department of education. We then will draw three random samples of schools from this list. Specifically, we will draw a random sample of elementary schools, a random sample of middle schools, and a random sample of high schools. There will be an equal number of schools in each of these samples.

Our sampling unit is schools. The sampling procedure is stratified random sampling, because we are drawing random samples from three different types of schools.

D. Sample Size

We do not have sufficient resources to study every school in the state. However, we wish to be able to make reasonably accurate generalizations from our sample to the population (i.e., all schools in the state). We will consult with a statistician to determine a sample size that will yield an acceptable margin of error for our statistics.

E. Sampling Subgroups

As we stated in section 5.C above, the sample will include three subgroups: elementary schools, middle schools, and high schools.

F. Use of Volunteers

We hope to obtain the participation of all schools included in our random sample. If a school does not wish to participate, we will randomly draw another school of the same type (elementary, middle, high) from the list of all schools in the state.

We will keep track of the number of schools in the original sample that decline participation in the sample. We realize that each declining school creates a risk for the generalizability of our findings to the target population (i.e., all schools in the selected state).

6. Methods of Data Collection

A. Measures

We will use a questionnaire as our data-collection instrument. It will be mailed to the principal of each school unless the principal has been in this position at the school for less than two years. If that is the case, we will not include the school in the sample but will randomly draw another school from the list of all schools in the state.

The questionnaire will include a scale on which the principal will rate his school's involvement in a curriculum-instruction-test alignment process. The lowest point on the school indicates no involvement in this type of process. The highest point indicates a major change in the school's curriculum and instructional/testing practices as a result of an alignment process.

The questionnaire also will include a list of problems (e.g., school staff members who question the need for an alignment process) and solutions (e.g., recruiting an external consultant) that are commonly found in the literature on school improvement. The questionnaire will ask the principal to rate each problem on a scale from 0 (it did not occur) to 7 (it was a major stumbling block for the process). It also will ask the principal to indicate whether the solution was used and, if it was used, to rate its effectiveness on a scale from 0 (it was not useful) to 7 (it was a substantial aid in moving the alignment process forward).

The questionnaire also will include space for the principal to indicate problems and solutions not on the list and also to make comments about the alignment process.

B. Validity and Reliability

We will ask a small sample of principals not involved in the study to evaluate the questionnaire items for clarity and relevance to the alignment process. We will make changes to the questionnaire based on their feedback.

We will select a small group of principals in the research sample for a reliability check. We will ask each of these principals to nominate another educator in the school (e.g., a teacher or assistant principal) who is knowledgeable about the school's activities over the past year.

We will ask each of these nominated individuals to complete the same questionnaire. If the questionnaire is reliable, we should find a high level of agreement between the principal's responses and the other individual's responses.

C. Emic and Etic Perspective

Not relevant to this study.

7. Data-Analysis Procedures

A. Statistical Analysis

We will compute the percentage of schools that reported one of the three problems or three solutions listed in the questionnaire. Also, we will report the mean and standard deviation for each of the seven rating scales. We will do these analyses separately for each of the three subgroups: elementary, middle, and high schools.

We will do an analysis of variance for each of the rating scale scores to determine whether there is a significant difference in the ratings of the elementary, middle, and high schools. Also, we will do a chi-square analysis to determine whether the percentage of each of the problems and solutions differs significantly at each of these levels of schooling.

We will do a content analysis of the principal's comments about problems and solutions not included in our list. We will identify each problem and solution that was mentioned and then count the frequency with which each one was mentioned by each subgroup of principals (elementary, middle, and high school).

B. Qualitative Analysis

Not relevant to this study.

8. Ethics and Human Relations

A. Ethical Risks

Principals might feel that they are at risk if their ratings of the alignment process were revealed to school staff and other administrators. Therefore, we will state the procedures that we will use to ensure that their identities will be concealed in the data analyses and final report.

We will report demographic data about the schools included in the sample, but in a manner that makes it impossible to link demographic data about a particular school with the ratings of that school's principal.

B. Approval by an Institutional Review Board

The study will need to be reviewed by an institutional review board, especially because it poses risks for some participants. We will identify the appropriate board and follow its designated procedures.

C. Gaining Entry and Cooperation

We think that the proposed study will be of great interest to state departments of education that are concerned about improving student achievement because of federal and state legislative mandates. We will try to ask an official at the selected state department of education to write a letter endorsing our study and encouraging principals to complete the questionnaire. We propose to include the letter with the questionnaire.

9. Timeline

We would like to mail the questionnaire several months after the school year begins. Although principals are always busy, they are likely to be less busy at this time than at the start of the school year.

By mailing the questionnaire early rather than late in the school year, we will have sufficient time for several follow-up mailings in order to increase the response rate to the questionnaire.

Sample Outline of a Qualitative Research Proposal

The following proposal outline is for a qualitative research study. If you are planning to do a qualitative study using one of the research designs presented in Part Four, this example will be helpful.

1. Purpose

A. Purpose Statement

The purpose of this study is to learn how educators go about aligning curriculum content with instruction and test content under conditions involving a federal or state mandate to improve students' learning.

B. Relevant Previous Research

Among the studies identified in our literature review, three studies are particularly relevant to our research purpose.

Foley, E. M., Klinge, A., & Reisner, E. R. (2007). *Evaluation of New Century High Schools: Profile of an initiative to create and sustain small, successful high schools. Final report.* Policy Studies Associates, Inc. (ERIC Document Reproduction Service No. ED498781)

ABSTRACT   "The most important school-level influence on student performance, as measured by credit accrual, was 'the quality of instructional systems,' including measures of the perceived alignment of instruction with Regent standards. . . . Case studies in the 2005–06 school year and earlier evaluation findings illuminated the influence on student outcomes of conditions that were fairly uniform across NCHS schools. Influential factors included: (1) Small enrollments; (2) Close student-teacher relationships and adult mentoring of youth; (3) Extension of student learning outside the regular school setting and school day; and (4) Use of data to track student performance."

Larson, W., & Howley, A. (2006). *Leadership of mathematics reform: The role of high school principals in rural schools.* Appalachian Collaborative Center for Learning, Assessment, and Instruction in Mathematics. (ERIC Document Reproduction Service No. ED498435)

ABSTRACT   "This monograph presents the results of qualitative interviews of seven selected principals [in remote Appalachian schools]. . . . The principals' responses revealed six categories . . . [The second category is] Strategies: Two strategies were used by most schools: curriculum alignment and individualization."

Campbell, T. (2007). *The science laboratory experiences of Utah's high school students.* (ERIC Document Reproduction Service No. ED497728)

ABSTRACT   "This research investigated the extent to which science laboratory experiences encountered by Utah high school students aligned with reform efforts outlined in national standards documents. Through both quantitative and qualitative methods the findings revealed that while there were instances of alignment found between science laboratory experiences and national standards documents when considering scientific content emphasis, this same alignment was not found when considering whether the experiences emphasized scientific processes."

C. Building on Previous Research

Previous research has found promising evidence that aligning of curriculum with instruction and test content improves students' academic achievement. However, we could find no studies that examined the actual alignment process. Our proposed study extends previous research by looking at this process in depth.

D. Contribution to Educational Research and Practice

Research on other school improvement initiatives demonstrates that the reform process often is beset with problems and that educators' success in solving these problems affects how well the initiative is institutionalized and how much it benefits students. By examining the process of curriculum alignment at selected school sites, we hope to identify factors that facilitate or hinder the process.

Identification of these factors might help other schools plan their alignment process in ways that increase their likelihood of success in improving students' academic achievement.

The proposed study, once completed and reported, might stimulate other researchers to conduct additional studies on this particular approach to school improvement to identify how best to plan and conduct it.

2. Research Questions, Hypotheses, Variables, and Case Delineation

A. Research Questions

We have three research questions:

1. What procedures do administrators, teachers, and specialists use in planning and conducting a

process to align curriculum content with instruction and test content?

2. What problems do these groups encounter as they engage in planning and conducting the alignment process?

3. What are the solutions that these groups attempt as they cope with problems in planning and conducting the alignment process?

B. Hypotheses

Not relevant to this study.

C. Variables

Not relevant to this study.

D. Case Delineation

We plan to focus on (1) the problems that occur during the process and how those problems get resolved and (2) alignment procedures and products for which there is consensual agreement and those for which consensual agreement could not be reached.

3. Literature Search

A. Search Engines and Indexes

The ERIC website will be sufficient for our research purposes.

B. Keywords and Descriptors

Our preliminary use of ERIC suggests that the keywords "alignment" and "curriculum alignment," by themselves or combined with the ERIC descriptors "achievement gains" and "academic achievement," will identify studies relevant to our research purpose.

C. Published Literature Review

We have not yet identified a literature review on curriculum-instruction-test alignment.

4. Research Design

A. Type of Design

The research design is a case study. This choice is based on our desire to produce a thick description of the process of curriculum alignment. We wish to understand in depth the experiences of a few school sites from the perspective of those directly involved in the process, rather than to grasp at a surface level the experiences of many school sites.

B. Threats to Internal Validity

Not relevant to this study.

C. Threats to Generalizability

Our plan to use a volunteer sample might limit the applicability of our findings to other schools undergoing an alignment process. We will provide an intensive description of the school's characteristics to help readers of our final report decide whether our findings apply to their situation.

D. Criteria for Judging Credibility and Trustworthiness of Results

We will create a chain of evidence by making a record of all data collected in the study, the individuals involved in the data collection, and the dates of data collection. Constructs and themes identified in the data analysis will be related to specific examples of data sources from which they were inferred.

We will write detailed vignettes of critical incidents in the curriculum alignment process so that the process becomes clear and real for readers of the study. We will have several educational practitioners involved in the process read and evaluate the report in terms of its soundness and usefulness to them. Their feedback will be used to revise the report.

The primary methods of data collection will be interviews, direct observations of critical events, and inspection of documents generated as part of the curriculum alignment process. The collected data will be analyzed to determine whether they provide corroborative evidence for constructs and themes that we identify in the curriculum alignment process.

The soundness of data coding will be checked by having several researchers code samples of the data to determine whether they derive similar constructs and themes from the data.

The soundness of the interview data, observational data, and documents selected for analysis will be checked by having selected participants in the study check them for accuracy, bias, and completeness.

To ensure thoroughness of data collection, we will continually check with participants that we have identified all the individuals involved in the curriculum alignment process and that we have identified all relevant events leading up to initiation of the process and the process itself. The check will include a list of the individuals and events we have identified, showing the list to a sample of participants, and asking them whether any person or event is missing from the list.

5. Sampling

A. Population Characteristics

Not relevant to this study.

B. Cases and Phenomena

The phenomenon of interest to us is the process of curriculum alignment as enacted at the school level, although we realize that administrators at the district and state level also might influence it. Therefore, our case will comprise a school involved in this process.

C. Sampling Procedure

Because of the intensive data collection required by this study, we will select just one school (the case). The sampling strategy will be to select a typical case, which for us means a school that has a recent history of neither being a district leader in school change nor a reluctant participant.

We believe that this sampling strategy will enable us to identify typical (rather than atypical) problems, solutions, and products that result from a curriculum alignment process. To an extent, sampling also will involve a convenience strategy in that the school will be selected from a district that is near the researchers' work site. The proximity will permit the researchers to make frequent trips to the school to collect data and make validity checks.

D. Sample Size

We will select just one school for the case study. However, the sample will include anyone in the school, community, school district, or other agency who has an involvement in the alignment process within this school.

E. Sampling Subgroups

Participants in the study will be selected to represent all the stakeholders in the curriculum alignment process. The known stakeholders include district-level specialists, the principal, teachers on the alignment team, and teachers not on the team but affected by the alignment outcomes.

If additional stakeholders are identified as the study progresses, they will be invited to participate in the study. If the number of individuals in a stakeholder group is large, a purposeful sample of these individuals will be selected.

F. Use of Volunteers

We will need to identify a school that has a mandate to engage in a curriculum-instruction-test alignment process but has not yet started it. We will attempt to identify several schools that are near our work site and inquire about their willingness to volunteer as study participants.

The volunteer nature of the sample might limit its applicability to other schools undergoing an alignment process. We will provide an intensive description of the school's characteristics to help readers of our final report decide whether our findings apply to their situation.

6. Methods of Data Collection

A. Measures

The case study is exploratory, so we will use measures that capture a wide range of data.

We will observe and take notes on significant events in the process. These notes will provide the basis for interviewing event participants about their perceptions of specific incidents that occurred during an event.

If an upcoming event seems particularly significant, efforts will be made to videotape it. We will watch the video with the event participants to obtain their perceptions as the event unfolds.

Furthermore, we will interview stakeholders who were not directly involved in the event but who will be affected by it. We also will collect significant documents prepared by stakeholders during the alignment process.

B. Validity and Reliability

One researcher will be the primary observer and interviewer. However, another researcher occasionally will observe the same event as a check on inter-observer reliability. Also, another interviewer will interview research participants who have the same perspective (e.g., two teachers at the same grade level) to determine whether both interviewers ask designated questions and collect similar kinds of data.

C. Emic and Etic Perspective

The procedures for data collection will focus on an emic perspective, that is, the perspective of the stakeholders as they experience the curriculum alignment process.

The researchers who collect data will not participate in the alignment process. They will maintain a supportive perspective but will act primarily as observers. If asked their opinion or advice, they will defer from offering it.

7. Data-Analysis Procedures

A. Statistical Analysis

We do not anticipate that we will collect quantitative data.

We likely will report school-level results for standardized tests mandated by the school district or state. Those results would have been statistically analyzed by the agency.

B. Qualitative Analysis

An interpretational approach to data analysis will be used. The interview and observational data will be entered into computer files and analyzed using the software program Ethnograph to analyze qualitative data. We will focus on identifying constructs, themes, and patterns relating to problems and problem-resolution processes and also on alignment procedures and products.

8. Ethics and Human Relations

A. Ethical Risks

Some participants in the alignment process might feel that they will incur the displeasure of colleagues and administrators if they criticize the alignment process during the research interviews.

Another risk is that the presence of a researcher during meetings associated with the alignment process might influence what participants say and do.

We will try to minimize these risks by assuring participants that the identity of all participants will be concealed in the final report. Also, we will assure participants that any comment they make to us will not be passed on to anyone, except to researchers directly involved in the study.

B. Approval by an Institutional Review Board

The study will need to be reviewed by an institutional review board, especially because it poses risks for the participants. We will identify the appropriate board and follow its designated procedures.

C. Gaining Entry and Cooperation

We will meet initially with the school board, local school administrators, and representatives of the local teachers association. If they appreciate the benefits of the study and of the safeguards we describe to minimize risks to participants, their endorsement should help us gain the cooperation of teachers and others who are directly involved in the study.

Also, we will tell the participants that they can express concerns about data collection or other research matters at any time. We will inform them that we will make appropriate adjustments to the research design to the extent that doing so will not compromise the integrity and overall purpose of the study.

9. Timeline

We are particularly interested in the initial stages of a curriculum alignment process. The process generally occurs in the summer with workshops and meetings of planning groups. Therefore, we will need to have obtained all necessary permissions and specified our data-collection procedures prior to the summer.

Depending on our resources, we might need to limit data collection to the summer months. If resources permit, we will continue data collection into the start of the new school year until the winter break.

CHAPTER THREE

Conducting and Writing Your Own Literature Review

PROBLEMS OF PRACTICE *in this chapter*

- Is cyberbullying of students a serious problem?
- What features must a professional development school have in order to be effective?
- Do some students benefit more from computer-based learning environments than others?
- Is the method of instruction known as cooperative learning actually effective?
- Should teachers assign homework?
- Is the process writing approach actually effective in improving students' writing skills?

IMPORTANT *Ideas*

1. The quality of a research journal partly depends on whether it is peer reviewed and on the reputation of its editorial board.
2. A formal literature review can help you (1) develop expert knowledge about an educational topic or problem of practice, (2) select or develop methods for your own research study, and (3) identify a research problem that you can study with some assurance that it is considered significant by other researchers.
3. A professional literature review focuses on a particular problem of practice and is written in a style that will be comprehensible to readers who do not have a sophisticated understanding of research methodology.
4. Framing specific research questions or hypotheses relating to your research problem helps you focus your literature search and thereby reduce the risk of information overload.
5. Search engines, bibliographic indexes, and experts in your area of interest can help you greatly improve the efficiency and effectiveness of your literature search.
6. It is helpful first to read secondary source publications in order to acquire a broad understanding of existing research knowledge about a topic or problem of practice and then to read selected primary source publications to acquire deeper and more detailed knowledge.

7. One of the most convenient ways to obtain a copy of a publication is to download it from a publication reprint service linked to a search engine.

8. As you identify publications for your literature review, you should develop categories that will help you decide which publications to read first and how to synthesize their findings.

9. A report of a literature review typically has four sections: (1) introduction, (2) presentation of findings, (3) discussion, and (4) list of references.

10. The introductory section of a literature review should state the questions that guided the review.

11. Synthesizing findings across a set of quantitative research studies on the same problem can be done by the method of meta-analysis, which involves the calculation of effect sizes.

12. Synthesizing findings across a set of case studies about similar phenomena can be done by the exploratory case study method or meta-ethnography.

13. In writing a report of a literature review, you should make the findings section as objective as possible, but in the discussion section, you can provide your own interpretation of the findings and make your own recommendations for future research and practice.

14. If you are writing a literature review for a university or other institution, you will need to learn what bibliographic style it requires for the reference list.

KEY TERMS

bibliographic citation	Listserv	primary source
chart essay	meta-analysis	professional literature review
effect size	meta-ethnography	search engine
formal literature review	peer-reviewed journal	secondary source

In this and the next chapter, we describe a process for reviewing literature on educational topics and problems of practice. Also, we describe three types of literature reviews: (1) informal, (2) formal, and (3) professional.

We start by explaining what we mean by the term *literature*. Virtually any written document can be considered literature. In the context of educational research, though, literature has the connotation of being authoritative. We might view a journal article, newspaper article, or book as authoritative because the authors are considered by others to be experts on the subject about which they are writing.

Research articles generally are considered to be more authoritative if they are published in a **peer-reviewed journal**, a type of journal in which the peers are authorities who review the research manuscript and decide whether it merits publication. The reviewers might reject the manuscript

outright or accept it after it has been revised in accordance with the reviewers' criticisms and suggestions. Journals are considered to be more or less authoritative depending on the reputation of the journal editor and the editorial board. These individuals and their institutional affiliations typically are listed at the front of each issue.

You can use the procedures described in this chapter to search for any kind of publication. However, our emphasis is on publications that are authoritative in the sense that we just described.

INFORMAL LITERATURE REVIEWS

Literature searches can vary in purpose and depth. An **informal literature review** is one that satisfies a need for immediate information to get a quick overview of a problem of practice or an educational topic. For example, suppose you hear a news report about cyberbullying in schools, and it arouses your curiosity. You might ask yourself questions such as:

1. Exactly what is cyberbullying?
2. What are some instances of cyberbullying in schools?
3. Is it a problem in our local school district?

A quick way to satisfy your curiosity is to "google" the term *cyberbullying*, which we did by using the search engine Google on December 26, 2012. Google listed 9,550,000 websites that included the term *cyberbullying*. Next, we went to a website (http://en.wikipedia.org/wiki/Cyberbullying) that contained an encyclopedia entry about this topic.

This entry was sufficient to satisfy our immediate curiosity about the first two questions. To answer the third question, we most likely would need to talk to educators in our school district. However, we should also consider the possibility that, if cyberbullying is a problem in our district, the local newspaper might have run an article about it. To find out, we would need to search the newspaper literature. In fact, we did that, again using Google. We entered "Cyberbullying Eugene Register-Guard" (the *Register-Guard* is the name of our local newspaper). Google produced a list of 30,400,00 websites listed in order of relevance. Some of the first 30 or so websites were directly relevant to our third question.

FORMAL LITERATURE REVIEWS

An informal literature search, such as the one just described, is a quick and useful way to learn about many problems of practice. However, our primary focus in this and the next chapter is on **formal literature reviews**, which are systematic, thorough searches and syntheses of the literature on a problem of practice or educational topic. The Cochrane Collaboration and the What Works Clearinghouse, both of which we describe in Chapter 1, exemplify the production of systematic literature reviews on particular topics. They make explicit their procedures for doing a literature review, and they continually refine these procedures. For example, the What Works Clearinghouse has published a handbook describing its procedures for determining the quality of each research study that it reviews (What Works Clearinghouse, n.d).

Formal literature reviews are done for one of two main purposes. One purpose is to develop a personal understanding about what is known about a particular educational topic or problem of practice. You might do this type of literature review for self-education or to complete a course or degree requirement. We describe procedures that will enable you to do a high-quality literature review of this type.

The other purpose for conducting a formal review of the literature is to initiate planning for your own research study. If you think about it, the reason for doing any research study is to add to what is already known about a particular problem or topic. If you have no idea of what is already known about that problem or topic, you will be unable to determine whether you have contributed anything to research knowledge. Certainly, you want to avoid the embarrassment of claiming an original discovery in your research study, only to discover that the same findings have already been reported in the literature.

In addition to telling you what is already known about your problem or topic, a formal literature review will inform you about the research designs, sampling methods, and measures that other researchers have used. It is likely that you can adopt or adapt some of them for your study, thereby saving you the enormous amount of time often required to develop one's own procedures and materials from scratch. Moreover, researchers often discuss pitfalls and limitations of their investigations, which can be the stimulus for further research. You can address and solve such problems in your study and thereby make a significant contribution to research methodology for investigating the problem.

Last but not least, a formal literature review can help you identify a research topic worthy of study. In the discussion section of their reports, researchers often identify problems in need of further investigation. If you are just learning how to do research, reading the discussion section of recent research reports can get you off to a good start. You can learn from more experienced researchers about the problems that, if investigated, will advance research knowledge. If you investigate one of these problems, you have some assurance that your research journey will lead you to discoveries that contribute to the improvement of educational practice.

PROFESSIONAL LITERATURE REVIEWS

Professional literature reviews synthesize research findings but with much less technical detail than formal literature reviews, because their primary audience is educators, policy makers, and other stakeholders whose research expertise is limited. These reviews typically focus on a particular problem of practice, synthesize research knowledge and other literature about it, and, most important, draw implications for improving educational practice. The journal article about the effectiveness of homework reproduced at the end of this chapter is an example of a professional literature review.

Unless a professional review is recent, it might not provide a sound basis for making decisions about improving educational practice. Over time, new research knowledge and the changing conditions of educational practice might invalidate the reviewer's conclusions. Even so, a professional literature review can be useful as a reflection of the state of knowledge and practice that prevailed at the time it was prepared. You can supplement it by conducting your own literature search for publications that appeared subsequent to the review.

Professional reviews generally lack the rigor of a formal literature review, so you need to consider carefully whether the reviewer's conclusions and recommendations are warranted. Also, individuals with limited experience in conducting or interpreting research sometimes write a professional review. Therefore, you are advised to read for yourself some of the primary and secondary sources cited in a professional review before basing important educational decisions on the reviewer's conclusions.

A SYSTEMATIC PROCEDURE FOR DOING FORMAL LITERATURE REVIEWS

Preparing a good formal literature review is easier if you use a systematic procedure, such as the one we describe here. It has eight steps, which are summarized in Figure 3.1. Each step is described in this chapter, and occasional references are made to Chapter 4, where certain aspects of the steps are described in more depth.

Step 1: Framing Questions to Guide the Literature Search

It is easy to get lost in the information explosion that has occurred over the past half century. Even a simple Google search, such as the one relating to cyberbullying, yields information spread over millions of websites. To avoid information

---

FIGURE 3.1 • A Systematic Process for Conducting a Formal Review of the Research Literature

1. Frame the information you are seeking in your literature review as a set of questions.
2. Contact experts who can answer your research questions directly or guide you to relevant publications.
3. Select bibliographic indexes and search engines that will help you identify publications that are relevant to your research questions.
4. Read secondary sources (i.e., published literature reviews) to obtain an overview of relevant publications and to provide a foundation for doing your own literature review.
5. Read and evaluate primary sources that are relevant to your research questions.
6. Classify the publications that you have identified as relevant to your literature review into meaningful categories.
7. Analyze trends in research results across studies using a meta-analytical approach or a case-study synthesis approach.
8. Prepare a report of the findings of your literature review.

overload, you will need to focus your literature search. One way to do this is to reflect on your information needs and then frame them as a set of questions, as in the following examples.

■ An elementary school teacher is concerned about students fighting during and after school. She has heard that anger management and conflict resolution programs have been developed for schools and wants to learn about them. She formulates the following questions to guide her literature search: "What anger management and conflict resolution programs, if any, have been developed for use at the elementary school level? What are the characteristics of these programs? Is there any evidence that they are effective?"

■ A committee of school superintendents has met with officials from the state department of education to learn more about plans for statewide mandatory testing of student achievement at selected grade levels. The superintendents expressed several concerns about the testing program. State officials work with the superintendents to frame questions for which the state department agrees to seek answers. "What have other states with mandatory testing programs done to ensure that the tests accurately reflect the school curriculum? What have other states done to ensure that the tests are administered and scored fairly? What percentage of students fail to earn each state's criterion score on the tests? What remediation programs, if any, have these states developed to help students who fail to achieve the criterion score? How effective are these remediation programs?"

■ An educator from an Asian country is enrolled in a master's degree program at a U.S. university and wants to learn teaching methods that she can use in a private school she operates in her home country. In particular, she is interested in the latest methods for teaching English as a second language (ESL), which is the subject of her final master's degree project. She frames the following questions for this project: "What methods are currently used to teach ESL in U.S. schools? What is the theoretical basis, if any, for these methods? How effective are these methods? Are particular teaching resources needed in order to use these methods effectively?"

Framing questions to guide a literature search can be modified for different circumstances. For example, as you start reading publications identified through an initial literature search, you might generate new questions for which you would like answers. These questions can be added to those that you framed initially, and you can reorient your literature search accordingly.

Another possible goal is to find research evidence to support or refute a knowledge claim of interest to you. For example, you might be convinced that students would perform much better in college if they could take their course examinations without the pressure of time limits. In this case, the purpose of your literature search is to find evidence to support a belief rather than to answer a question.

Step 2: Consulting with Experts

Educators occasionally call on experts when they have a pressing need for information and advice. More than likely, they will pay a fee to the experts for their time. However, many experts are willing to help you as a professional courtesy without charge if your information need involves a research study and if the need is clearly defined. They often are willing, even eager, to tell you their ideas and can point you to the most important publications relating to your information needs. With their expert knowledge as an initial framework, you can carry out a literature search with greater confidence and efficiency.

Educators in your local community might know an expert in your area of interest or be able to refer you to someone who is likely to know of such an expert. For example, the principal of a high school in Portland, Oregon, was planning to switch to block scheduling. (In block scheduling, fewer classes are offered, but they meet for longer time periods than in conventional scheduling of classes.) He wanted information about how best to implement block scheduling so that teachers would buy into it and students' learning would be enhanced.

He mentioned his information need to a member of his teaching staff, who in turn called us. We are not experts in the practice of block scheduling, but we know a colleague who is. We referred the principal to our colleague, and he was able to obtain an orientation to block scheduling from her. Thus, he had a strong initial background of information prior to conducting his own search of the literature on this practice.

A good way to contact experts outside your geographic area is to send them an e-mail message. You can use various search engines (e.g., Yahoo!) to identify individuals who can be useful to you. If you know the individual's institutional affiliation, you often can get their contact information by going to the institution's website and searching for the individual there.

Educators have formed many computer networks through which members engage in discussions or post information or queries of various types, such as announcements of upcoming conferences and requests for members' opinions and experiences. Called *bulletin boards* or *discussion forums*, many of these Internet sites are managed by the computer software program **Listserv**. Some Listserv bulletin boards are moderated, meaning someone monitors the contributed messages and decides which ones will be posted.

Step 3: Using Bibliographic Indexes and Search Engines

The education literature consists of hundreds of thousands of publications—books, journal articles, technical reports, papers presented at professional conferences, curriculum guides, and so forth. Even if you limit your literature search to publications that have appeared in the past five or ten years, the number of retrieved publications can be overwhelming. For this reason, professional organizations and publishers have created bibliographic indexes and search engines to help you navigate the literature and retrieve citations only for the publications most relevant to your topic or research problem.

A **bibliographic index** is a list of publications on a particular topic, usually in alphabetical order by author or title. The index typically appears in book form or, increasingly, on a website. A **search engine** is software that looks for publications or other information in a database, based on user-defined criteria. Chapter 4 describes various bibliographic indexes and search engines that you can use to retrieve citations for relevant publications. They differ in their database of publications and in their procedure for retrieving relevant publications from the database.

Bibliographic indexes and search engines also differ in the amount of information about each publication in their database. This information about a publication usually is referred to as a **citation**. Most citations include the authors' names, title of the publication, publisher, and publication date. If the publication is a journal article, the page numbers of the article also will be included. Some **bibliographic citations** include an **abstract**, which is a brief summary (typically 100 words or less) of the information contained in the publication.

Bibliographic indexes and search engines generally include both secondary source and primary source publications. We describe each type of publication in the following sections.

Step 4: Reading Secondary Sources

Once you have identified the questions that you want to answer through a literature review, we recommend that you read several secondary sources in order to form a general picture of the research that has been done on your topic. A **secondary source** is a publication in which the author reviews research studies, theories, and educational practices and programs that others have generated about a particular problem or topic.

Some of the sources described in Chapter 4 are considered to be secondary sources and contain literature reviews on a wide variety of educational topics. The *Encyclopedia of American Education* is an example of this type of secondary source. Other secondary sources are more specialized. They focus on a single topic or a set of closely related topics. The *Handbook of Reading Disability Research* is an example of this type of secondary source.

Our discussion of secondary sources in Chapter 4 emphasizes published reviews of the research literature. However, we describe other types of secondary sources as well, such as published reviews of educational programs, curriculum guides and materials, tests, and measures.

Step 5: Reading Primary Sources

In contrast to secondary sources, a **primary source** is a publication written by the individual or individuals who actually conducted the work presented in that publication. Examples of primary sources include a journal article that reports a research study conducted by the author of the article, a curriculum guide prepared by the developers of the curriculum, a diary of reflections and experiences in the form in which its author prepared it, or a report describing the author's opinions about a particular educational phenomenon or practice.

In short, a secondary source is a publication that is written by author A about the writings of authors X, Y, and Z, whereas a primary source is the actual writings of authors X, Y, and Z.

It sometimes is necessary to read primary sources directly rather than to rely on the summary of the primary source contained in a secondary source. For example, if you conduct and report a research study, the report must include a review of relevant literature that, among other things, provides a detailed analysis of selected primary sources and their relationship to the problem you investigated.

Other situations also require you to read primary sources. Suppose you read a secondary source that reviews research evidence about a program you want your school or organization to consider adopting. This research evidence might play a critical role in convincing others to adopt the program. Therefore, you will want to read the actual primary sources that produced this evidence, not just the secondary source.

Similarly, you will want to read program materials and documents written by the program's developers (i.e., primary sources) rather than relying on others' description of them in secondary sources. The reason is that a secondary source almost inevitably gives a briefer treatment of the research or development process than a primary source does. Also, authors of secondary sources typically are less familiar with details of the program and so might skip or even misreport some of them.

Searching for a primary source in a library or ordering it through interlibrary loan can be time-consuming. Imagine, then, the frustration if you finally receive it and discover that it is irrelevant to your information needs. To avoid this problem, we recommend a careful study of the abstracts that often are included in bibliographic citations. An abstract usually contains sufficient information for you to decide whether the publication is relevant to your information needs.

If you plan to read a set of research studies, it is usually a good idea to start with the most recent studies. The reason is that these studies use earlier research as a foundation and thus are likely to help you understand what has already been learned about the problem under investigation. It then will be easier to read the older studies.

The organization of most reports of education research studies is based on the specifications of the *Publication Manual of the American Psychological Association* (American Psychological Association, 2010). Briefly stated, a research report includes four main sections: (1) introduction, (2) method, (3) results, and (4) discussion. The report concludes with citations for publications mentioned in the report, sometimes followed by a technical appendix expanding on some feature of the study's research methodology. Once you learn this reporting style, you will be able to read a research article more efficiently and find specific information within it more quickly.

Obtaining Copies of Primary and Secondary Sources

You might discover that a primary or secondary source you need is available only in a hard-copy format at the library or can be checked out from the library only for a short period of time. You can take notes on the source, and these notes possibly will be sufficient for your literature review and other uses. However, if the publication is important to your study, you should consider photocopying it. Copying costs money, but is probably less expensive than repeated trips to the library to study the publication for details on which you did not take notes the first time.

Another option is to scan the publication if you have a scanner, computer, and scanning software. However, scanning can be difficult or impossible if the publication is bound and the pages cannot be placed flat on the scanning surface.

The best option, if available, is to use a search engine linked to a publication reprint service. We describe this capability in Chapter 4. Briefly, it involves using a search engine to identify relevant publications and then following a link to a source where you can obtain an electronic copy at no or minimal cost.

Step 6: Classifying and Taking Notes on Publications

As you begin reading the publications identified in your literature search, you should start the process of developing categories to group them. For example, suppose you are reviewing the literature to help your school system plan an effective staff development program for its administrators. As you read the literature, you might observe that some publications concern school administrators specifically, whereas others concern administrators in business and industry or administrators generally.

This observation suggests grouping the publications into three thematic categories: (1) school administrators, (2) administrators in business and industry, and (3) administrators in general. You also might find that different publications concern different purposes of staff development, leading you to create the following subcategories under each of the three main categories: (a) staff development to help administrators improve staff morale, (b) staff development to help administrators lower their stress and maintain a healthy lifestyle, (c) staff development to help administrators improve client/student outcomes, and (d) staff development for other purposes.

This categorizing process will give you a sense of the diversity in the available literature on your problem of practice. It will also help you decide which types of studies to include in your review and which to exclude. At this point, too, you will have some sense of the content of the publications to be included in your review, and you can proceed to analyze them in depth. For each study you review, we suggest that you make notes about how it relates to each of your thematic categories.

In addition to these notes, it is helpful to make notes under the categories of: sample, measures, method, and results. Using our example of staff development, we will want to examine each publication and record the number of participants in the staff development program under the category of "sample." We might also want to record characteristics of the sample, such as school level (e.g., elementary, middle school, high school) and participants' years of administrative experience. This information will enable us to determine similarities and differences across studies and possibly whether studies with certain similarities have particular program outcomes.

Because our study is concerned with the effectiveness of staff development, we will want to create categories for the various outcomes (e.g., improvement in teacher morale, improvement in client/student outcomes) and how they were measured. Then, as we examine each study, we can code their outcomes and measures using our category system. Also, we will have a category for the

statistical or qualitative results reported in each study. Many of the studies are likely to be experiments, in which case we would record how well administrators assigned to the staff development program performed subsequently relative to administrators in the control condition (e.g., no opportunity to participate in staff development). If the researcher did case studies, we would take notes on participants' comments about the staff development program, perhaps classifying them as positive or negative about the program.

These categories and others that you choose to develop will help you focus your analysis of each study to be included in your literature review. They will also facilitate your note-taking for each study and enable you to search for similarities and differences across studies.

Step 7A: Analyzing Trends in Research Results across Quantitative Studies

As we explained in Chapter 1, research studies use either quantitative or qualitative methodology, or a combination of the two. The methods for examining trends in findings across studies are different for each of these methodologies. Literature reviews of quantitative studies often use the method of meta-analysis, whereas literature reviews of qualitative studies use the exploratory case study method or another method similar to it.

Meta-analysis

Many research studies are concerned with testing the effectiveness of a particular educational intervention. The researcher wants to know whether the intervention is better than existing practice. For example, a researcher might conduct an experiment to determine whether students in classrooms where class size has been reduced have better academic achievement than students in classrooms where no reduction has occurred. If there are many studies of this type, their results can be compared by using the method of meta-analysis.

Meta-analysis involves translating the statistical results from each of a set of research studies on the same problem into a statistic called an effect size. (We explain the statistical basis of effect sizes in depth in Chapter 8.) Suppose a literature reviewer identified research studies involving experiments to test the effectiveness of a particular educational program. In this situation, the **effect size** is a number that indicates the degree to which participants in the experimental group show superior performance compared to a comparison group, called the control group, that is in no educational program or is in an alternative program.

The effect size typically is computed by a simple formula. The numerator is the difference between the mean score of the experimental group and the mean score of the control group on a criterion measure (for example, an achievement test). The denominator can be computed various ways. For present purposes, you can think of it as the average of the two groups' standard deviations (a measure of score variability) on the criterion measure.

For example, imagine a study of the effect of small cash rewards on the achievement of students in an inner-city high school. For one school year, 100 experimental students receive cash rewards for passing weekly quizzes, and 100 control students receive no cash rewards. At the end of the year, both the experimental and control group students take the same standardized achievement test, which is the criterion measure. For the experimental group, the mean score is 46.2 and the standard deviation is 4.0. For the control group, the mean score is 41.2 and the standard deviation is 3.6.

The numerator for the effect size is 46.2 minus 41.2, which equals 5.0. The denominator is the average of the two standard deviations: (4.0 + 3.6) ÷ 2 = 3.8. Dividing the numerator (5.0) by the denominator (3.8) equals 1.32, which is the effect size.

The practical significance of an effect size of 1.32 usually is determined by making percentile comparisons. In our example, an effect size of 1.32 means that a student who scores at the 50th percentile in the experimental group has a score that is equivalent to a score at the 91st percentile in the control group.

This type of percentile comparison is explained in mathematical terms in Chapter 8. We can explain it more simply here by asking you to suppose that you typically score in the 50th percentile among your fellow students on achievement tests. Suppose that the incentive of cash rewards motivates you to study harder and learn more. An effect size of 1.32 predicts that you are likely to score at or around the 91st percentile among your fellow students on achievement tests. That is quite a jump in achievement for you.

Students who typically score somewhat lower or higher than the 50th percentile also are likely to make substantial percentile gains from the cash reward relative to students not receiving the incentive. The specific gain will depend on their beginning percentile and the distribution of scores on achievement tests among their fellow students.

In our experience, educational researchers believe that an effect size of 0.33 or larger has practical significance. An effect size of 0.33 indicates that a student in the experimental group whose score is at the 50th percentile would be at the 63rd percentile of the other group's score distribution.

The advantage of the effect size over other methods of comparing performance is that it transforms the results from various studies into a comparable unit of measure. It does not matter that one study used the XYZ Mathematics Test, on which scores can vary from 0 to 70, and that another study used the ABC History Test, on which scores can vary from 0 to 100. An effect size can be calculated for the results of both studies, and these effect sizes can be directly compared. An effect size of 1.00 is twice as large as an effect size of 0.50, regardless of the measures and scoring systems that were used.

Not all studies in the research literature report the means and standard deviations for calculating an effect size in the manner described above. However, procedures exist for estimating an effect size from virtually any statistical data reported in a research study.

The means of the effect sizes from different studies can be combined to determine the average effect that the experimental program or method produces relative to a comparison intervention across the studies. For example, suppose that you find seven research studies on the effects of class size. In each study, a sample of large classes was compared with a sample of small classes. Also in each study, data on all students' performance on an achievement test were collected at the end of the school year.

Each of the seven studies would yield one effect size. Each effect size has the same meaning no matter how large or small the sample size or the type of achievement test or other measure. Therefore, you can synthesize the results across the seven studies by calculating the mean of the seven effect sizes across the seven studies. The mean effect size is likely to give you a more valid estimate of the effects of class size than the effect size derived from a single research study.

Meta-analysis has become a popular method for synthesizing research findings in medicine, psychology, education, and other fields. We illustrate its use at the end of this chapter with a meta-analysis of research on the effectiveness of a method of writing instruction known as the process writing approach.

Meta-analysis is a powerful method of synthesizing quantitative studies for a literature review, but you must examine each meta-analysis that you read for potential limitations. In particular, you need to consider reviewer basis in deciding whether to include or exclude particular studies in a meta-analysis or a reviewer's failure to locate all relevant studies in the literature.

For example, Haller, Child, and Walberg (1988) conducted a meta-analysis of research on the effects of metacognitive instruction on reading comprehension. Metacognitive instruction involves teaching students how to regulate their own thinking and learning processes. Haller and her colleagues state that they examined 150 references but limited their analysis to 20 studies. These 20 studies met certain criteria: the use of metacognitive intervention, employment of a control group for comparison, and provision of statistical information necessary to compute effect sizes.

Gene Glass (1976), one of the primary developers of meta-analysis, would have advised Haller and her colleagues to include as many of the 150 original studies as possible in their analysis, even though some were methodologically more sound than others. Glass argues that either weaker studies will show the same results as stronger studies and thus should be included or that a truer picture will emerge if weak studies are also analyzed.

In contrast, Robert Slavin (1986) argues against including every possible study in a meta-analysis. Slavin examined eight meta-analyses conducted by six independent teams of reviewers and compared their procedures and conclusions against the studies they analyzed. Slavin reported that he found errors in all eight meta-analyses that were serious enough to invalidate or call into question one or more of the major conclusions of each study.

Therefore, Slavin recommends that a meta-analysis should include only research studies providing "best evidence," that is, studies that meet criteria such as methodological adequacy and relevance to the issue at hand. He also makes a strong case for calculating not only an overall mean effect size but also separate effect sizes for subsets of studies, for example, those that used the same measure of the dependent variable or those that studied a specific ethnic group.

Whether you agree with Glass or Slavin, we advise you not to accept an effect size in a meta-analysis at face value. At the least, you should examine several of the research studies that contributed statistical data for the calculation of the effect size. By taking this extra step, you can check how the literature reviewer synthesized these studies and judge the extent to which the studies actually investigated the particular educational practice or issue of interest to you.

Step 7B: Analyzing Trends in Research Results Across Qualitative Studies

In the preceding section, we considered procedures for reviewing research studies that involve quantitative methodology. As we explained in Chapter 1, qualitative research represents another approach to scientific inquiry. It involves the study of specific cases in an effort to understand the unique character and context of each case. If a sufficient number of case studies of a particular phenomenon have been completed, they can be synthesized by methods specifically developed for this purpose.

Ogawa and Malen (1991) suggested one such method, called the exploratory case study method, for this purpose. Reviewers who use the **exploratory case study method** provide a synthesis of case studies on the same topic by identifying concepts and principles that are present across cases, while also acknowledging the unique characteristics of each case. Although the primary focus is qualitative studies, Ogawa and Malen's method allows reviewers to include other kinds of writings (e.g., newspaper editorials or articles in journals for practicing educators) in their synthesis of the literature on a particular educational topic.

Meta-ethnography is a more recent method for synthesizing case studies. **Meta-ethnography** makes use of qualitative research techniques, such as induction and interpretation, to identify concepts and themes in the case studies being reviewed, to examine similarities and differences in concepts and themes across the case studies, and to develop a set of interpretive findings based on these analyses. Whereas a meta-analysis summarizes findings across studies, a meta-ethnography can create new findings based on the researchers' own interpretations and discoveries as they analyze a set of case studies on a particular phenomenon.

Meta-ethnography involves a seven-phase process, which is illustrated in a literature synthesis by Elizabeth Rice (2002). The first phase involved identifying the focus of her synthesis—professional development schools (PDS), particularly the nature of the collaboration process. A PDS is a collaboration between K–12 schools and university teacher education programs for the purpose of improving the quantity and quality of student teachers' field experiences. This phase and the other six phases are labeled in Table 3.1, together with a brief description of how they were implemented in the literature synthesis.

Rice identified 64 case studies in the literature, 20 of which satisfied criteria that were important to her (see Phase 2 in Table 3.1). She then used a coding process to identify themes that emerged from reading each study (Phase 3). The themes were "emergent" in that they evolved from the reviewer's interpretation of a reported finding rather than started with a prespecified set of themes and then determined whether they occurred, and how frequently, across the case studies. The emergent themes for each study were then compared and combined across studies (Phases 4 and 5).

The next phase of the meta-ethnography process involved looking for commonalities across themes and making sense of them (Phase 6). Rice drew on collaboration theories involving organizations to help her understand how certain emergent themes clustered together. For example, she found that some emergent themes related to the structural dimension of collaboration, which involves the various administrative agreements that define how partnership members relate to each other. In this case, the partners are the university teacher education program and the various schools providing field experiences for student teachers. Other emergent themes related to the relational dimension of collaboration, which involves how individuals in each partnership organization interact with each other, develop trust, and handle conflict.

Rice describes and discusses 12 emergent themes in the report of her study (Phase 7 in Table 3.1). They are briefly described in Table 3.2, which also includes the number of case studies (total N = 20) in which they were observed. Rice also drew recommendations from these themes that might help universities and

TABLE 3.1 • The Process of Completing a Meta-Ethnography

Phase	Title	Steps for This Study
Phase 1	Getting started	The area of interest is the professional development school (PDS) movement and the collaboration process in PDSs.
Phase 2	Deciding what is relevant to the researcher	Case studies that describe the collaboration process in PDSs are of interest. These case studies must be particularistic to collaboration, descriptive, capable of interpretation, and provide details. In addition, the case studies must have explicit research questions, describe data collection procedures, and provide adequate findings.
Phase 3	Reading the studies	Themes were collected while reading the case studies based on the researcher's interpretations of the data.
Phase 4	Determining how the studies are related	Themes were identified and compared while reading each case study.
Phase 5	Translating the studies into each other	Similarities, differences, and unusual information in the case studies were combined across case studies.
Phase 6	Synthesizing the translations	The commonalities of the themes were analyzed and synthesized. These themes were examined within the context of literature on interorganizational relationships, and the facilitators of and barriers to the collaboration process were identified.
Phase 7	Expressing the synthesis	The results of the analysis were written.

Source: Rice, E. H. (2002). The collaboration process in professional development schools: Results of a meta-ethnography, 1990–1998. *Journal of Teacher Education, 53*(1), 56–67.

TABLE 3.2 • Emergent Themes in a Meta-Ethnographic Synthesis of Case Studies of Professional Development Schools[1]

1. Some school and university faculty were unwilling to collaborate. (13)

2. Prior history between school and university faculty created positive or negative relationships and attitudes that affected PDS collaboration. (8)

3. The uncertainty of funding from one year to the next created strain for PDS participants. (13)

4. Some PDSs lacked a formal structure, creating strain on the participants. (8)

5. Some PDSs experienced a struggle for parity and control in decision making. (5)

6. The school principal was critical to the success of a PDS. (16)

7. PDSs experienced communication problems, including insufficient communication among participants and selective listening. (12)

8. Schools and universities experienced strain within their own organization, including tension between participating and nonparticipating teachers within a school and lack of commitment to the PDS by some university faculty. (8)

9. Conflicts arose from the different missions of participating universities (teacher preparation) and schools (student learning). (9)

10. There was initial distrust among participants and skepticism that the PDS collaboration would work. (13)

11. PDSs need key individuals who can facilitate communication and collaboration across the participating schools and university. (8)

12. Informal meetings, often with refreshments, were instrumental in developing trust and collaboration. (10)

Note 1. The number in parentheses after each theme is the number of case studies (total N = 20) in which the theme emerged from analysis of the case study.

Source: Rice, E. H. (2002). The collaboration process in professional development schools: Results of a meta-ethnography, 1990–1998. *Journal of Teacher Education, 53*(1), 56–67.

schools in starting a PDS or improving the effectiveness of an existing PDS. One of the recommendations is that PDS partnerships should be "voluntary endeavors" (p. 64); if university or school faculty are compelled to participate in a PDS, the collaboration process is likely to break down. Another recommendation is to create formal written policies and procedures to guide the transition process into a formal PDS structure. Perhaps most important, Rice found that most problems of practice in PDSs were created by poor interpersonal interactions between individuals within a PDS. She suggests that "most issues of parity, control, infighting, and conflicting goals would dissipate if members of the PDS were more aware of the skills of collaboration and cooperation" (p. 66).

Step 8: Preparing a Report of a Literature Review

The literature review in a typical journal article is generally brief, even though a great deal of

work might have gone into its preparation. Reading some articles in research journals will give you a sense of how literature reviews are written and how they fit into the overall organization of the article. Typically, key studies and trends in findings are reported in the introductory section. These topics are usually revisited in the discussion section, which considers how the study's findings contribute to what is already in the literature. Each of these sections is described in the next section.

PARTS AND PRESENTATION OF A STAND-ALONE LITERATURE REVIEW

Some university programs make the completion of a formal literature review a degree requirement. Also, a literature review by itself might constitute a thesis or dissertation, especially if it involves an exhaustive search for research evidence relating to a problem and if it uses a formal analytic process, such as meta-analysis. These literature reviews are "stand-alone" publications in that they are not part of a publication that also reports a research study conducted by the author. The typical sections of these stand-alone literature reviews are introduction, findings, discussion, and references.

Introductory Section

The introductory section of the report should state the research questions that motivated your literature review and the reasons you chose to investigate them (step 1 in Figure 3.1). For example, Daniel Moos and Roger Azevedo (2009) did a literature review to determine whether certain types of students benefited from computer-based learning environments (CBLEs). Specifically, they wanted to know whether students who were high in computer self-efficacy benefited more from CBLE than students with low computer self-efficacy. They defined computer self-efficacy as an individual's perception of his or her capabilities relating to computer skills and knowledge. They posed three questions to guide their literature review:

1. What is the relationship between computer self-efficacy and learning outcomes with CBLEs?
2. What factors are related to the development of computer self-efficacy?
3. What is the relationship between computer self-efficacy and learning processes with CBLEs?

The first question addresses a practical concern: Are computer-based learning environments best suited for a particular type of student? The other questions seek to understand how a particular student characteristic develops and how it is manifested in the learning process.

The introduction also should include a description of your literature search procedures, indicating the bibliographic indexes and search engines you consulted (step 3 in Figure 3.1), the years that were covered, the keywords that were used, and any special problems that the reviewer encountered. If you come across publications that provide a historical background or conceptual framework for your literature review, you can discuss them in the introduction.

Section on Findings

You can organize the findings of your literature review by the questions that guided your literature search (step 1 in Figure 3.1) or by the categories that you created to organize the publications identified in your search (step 6 in Figure 3.1). In the case of the review of literature on computer-based learning environments, the reviewers organized their findings by the three questions stated above.

You will need to decide on the order in which to present your questions or categories. Then for each question or category, you need to decide the order in which to present relevant research studies, theories, programs, methods, and opinions. By grouping closely related publications together, you can emphasize areas of agreement and disagreement that will be of interest to readers. A particular publication might be pertinent to several questions or categories and thus might be cited several times in your report.

Recommendations for writing the findings section of your report are presented in Figure 3.2. Also, this chapter includes two literature reviews, which will give you additional ideas for organizing the findings of your literature review. And, you can find examples of high-quality literature reviews in the journal, *Review of Educational Research*, which is published by the American Educational Research Association.

Discussion Section

When you write the findings section of the literature review, it is important to be objective and therefore fairly literal in presenting research findings, theories, program characteristics, and other types of information. In the discussion section, however, you are free to provide your own interpretation and assessment of this information.

A good procedure for writing the discussion section is to start by listing the main findings of your review. You can compile this list by asking yourself, "What did I learn from this review?" and then attempting to answer this question without looking at your report of the findings. By relying on memory, you are more likely to focus on the major findings than on a variety of specific details. If necessary, you then can check the findings against your discussion to be sure you did not miss any important findings.

FIGURE 3.2 • Recommendations for Writing a Report of a Literature Review

1. Use straightforward language that clearly expresses if you are reporting someone's research findings, theories, or opinions. For example, an author might have described a new program and its advantages but not reported any empirical evidence. In this case you might write, "Jiminez (1991) claims that . . ." If the author conducted a research study, you might write, "Jiminez (1991) found that . . ." If the author developed a theory or referred to another's theory, you might write, respectively, "Jiminez (1991) theorized that . . ." or "Jiminez (1991) referred to Piaget's theory of . . ."

2. Use frequent headings and subheadings to help the reader follow your sequence of topics more easily.

3. Describe the strengths and weaknesses of the methods used in important studies so that readers have sufficient information to weigh the results and draw their own conclusions.

4. Discuss major studies in detail, but devote relatively little space to minor studies. For example, you might first discuss the most noteworthy study in depth and then briefly cite others on the same topic: "Several other studies have reported similar results (Anderson, 1989; Flinders, 1991; Lamon, 1985; Moursund, 1990; Wolcott, 1990)."

5. Use varied words and phrases, such as: "Martinez found that . . .," "Smith studied . . .," "In Wychevsky's experiment, the control group performed better on . . .," "The investigation carried out by Singh and Yang showed that . . ."

6. Use a direct quotation only when it conveys an idea especially well or when it states a viewpoint that is particularly worth noting.

Now list the findings in order of importance, reflecting on each one. You might ask yourself questions such as these: "To what extent do I agree with the overall thrust of the research evidence, theories, descriptions, and expert opinions that I examined? Are alternative interpretations possible? How can I explain the contradictions in the literature, if any? What is the significance of a particular finding for the problem of practice I need to solve or the question I want to answer?"

The discussion also should contain your recommendations regarding the problem or questions that initiated your literature review. The recommendations should be stated clearly and, if possible, without qualification. If you are tentative or indirect, readers of your report will not know where you stand. They want to know your opinions and recommendations, because you were the one who did a review of the literature. Therefore, you are an expert compared to policy makers or colleagues who do not know the literature.

In the literature review on CBLEs, the authors noted recent studies that had questioned the effectiveness of CBLEs. They also noted that their findings suggest that students need to have both computer self-efficacy and self-regulated learning processes in order to benefit from CBLEs. They recommended further research to determine what these self-regulated learning processes might be and whether these processes are different for different kinds of CBLEs.

It might seem to you that this literature review raises more questions than it answers. This is often the case for literature reviews, because educational interventions sometimes vary in their effectiveness from study to study and because students differ so widely in their abilities and learning processes. Nonetheless, trends in findings are often found, and these trends can guide education professionals as they work in particular learning environments and with particular students. (You will note in Figure 3.3 that the findings of the literature review presented there are described as "trends" rather than as absolute truths.)

References

All of the publications you cite in your report should be included in a reference list at the end of the report. Conversely, the reference list should contain no publications not cited in the report. If you wish to provide non-cited publications for some reason, present them in a separate list, with a heading such as "Supplemental References" and an explanatory note about why they are being cited.

FIGURE 3.3 • Visual Presentation of Selected Findings from a Literature Review on Cooperative Learning

Research Question 1: How effective is cooperative learning relative to traditional instruction in fostering academic achievement?

In 60 studies, there were 68 comparisons of cooperative learning classes and traditional classes on an achievement measure. Achievement was:

significantly higher in the traditional classes in:	not significantly different in the cooperative learning and traditional classes in:	significantly higher in the cooperative learning classes in:
4% of the comparisons.	34% of the comparisons.	62% of the comparisons.

Research Question 2: How important is it that group goals and individual accountability both be present for cooperative learning to be effective?

Percentage of studies showing significantly positive achievement effects for cooperative learning when group goals and individual accountability are:

Present	Absent
80%	36%

Trends

Cooperative learning is more effective than traditional instruction in promoting student achievement.

Cooperative learning is most effective when it includes both group goals and individual accountability.

Source: Based on data from Slavin, R. (1992). Cooperative learning. In M. C. Alkin (Ed.), *Encyclopedia of educational research* (6th ed., vol. 1, pp. 235–238). New York, NY: Macmillan.

Citation styles might vary across bibliographic indexes and search engines, and across reference lists in primary and secondary sources. You will need to convert all of your citations to the same style, namely, the style required by your institution or the journal to which you submit the literature review.

If no particular style is required, we recommend that you use the citation style of the American Psychological Association (APA), because it is the most widely used style in educational and psychological journals. For example, the chapter references and list of resources for further study at the end of each chapter in this book are written in APA style. To learn APA style, obtain a copy of the sixth edition of the *Publication Manual of the American Psychological Association*. Various guides and other aids for writing bibliographic citations in APA style can be found on the Internet (http://apastyle.apa.org).

Preparing a Visual Presentation of a Literature Review

Suppose you have an opportunity to present your literature review to an audience that does not understand the technical aspects of research studies. In this situation, a chart essay or similar format is useful. A **chart essay**, such as the one shown in Figure 3.3, uses charts to focus the audience's attention on aspects of the literature review that will be interesting and comprehensible. The chart essay format was originally designed to summarize the findings of a single research study (Haensly, Lupkowski, & McNamara, 1987; Jones & Mitchell, 1990). Here, we have adapted it to illustrate the value of a visual format for presenting the findings of a literature review in a nontechnical form. The chart essay in Figure 3.3 is a graphic presentation of two findings from a literature review of research on cooperative learning (Slavin, 1992).

You can see that the chart poses one research question, immediately followed by the empirical research findings that pertain to it. The second research question is presented in similar fashion. The chart concludes with two trend statements, which are generalizations that can be inferred from the empirical findings. These statements are called *trends* because the evidence pertaining to each question was not perfectly consistent across studies but was sufficient to serve as a guide to improving educational practice.

The chart essay in Figure 3.3 is shown as a single chart. However, if you were to show the chart essay to an audience as a PowerPoint presentation or a set of overhead transparencies, you might want to use three charts—one for each of the research questions and a third for the trend statements.

SELF-CHECK TEST

1. Search engines
   a. are equivalent to bibliographic indexes in literature coverage and citation style.
   b. share a universal standard for bibliographic citation style.
   c. vary in the amount of information they provide about each publication in their database.
   d. provide less information about each publication in their database than does the typical bibliographic index.
2. A report of a research study written by the individuals who conducted the study is
   a. a primary source.
   b. a secondary source.
   c. both a primary and a secondary source.
   d. exempt from peer review when submitted to a journal for publication.
3. Most published reports of educational research follow the style specifications established by
   a. Google.
   b. the American Educational Research Association.
   c. the American Psychological Association.
   d. the most widely used bibliographic indexes and search engines.
4. The most useful system for classifying publications obtained through a review of the literature is likely to be one that sorts publications by
   a. year of publication.
   b. topics relevant to the research questions.
   c. magnitude of the statistical results.
   d. the search engines and bibliographic indexes by which they were identified.

5. The report of a literature review
   a. should include a description of your literature search procedures.
   b. should cite only primary sources.
   c. should emphasize findings that agree across studies rather than findings that disagree across studies.
   d. all of the above.
6. Meta-analysis
   a. is the standard procedure for synthesizing the findings of quantitative research studies.
   b. is the standard procedure for synthesizing the findings of qualitative research studies.
   c. avoids the need to compute an effect size for each research study included in a literature review.
   d. is used in systematic literature reviews to exclude studies with findings that are not statistically significant.
7. Effect sizes
   a. are calculated to determine whether the sample in a research study represents the population.
   b. cannot be used to make judgments about the practical significance of a research finding.
   c. provide information about the practical significance of a research finding.
   d. cannot be used to compare the findings of studies that investigated the same topic but used different measures.
8. There is general consensus among researchers that an effect size has practical significance if it has a value
   a. of 0.10 or larger.
   b. of 0.20 or larger.

c. of 0.33 or larger.

d. between −0.10 and 0.

9. Reviewers who use meta-ethnography as a method for synthesizing research results

a. limit their focus to the unique characteristics of each case in a set of qualitative research studies.

b. seek to identify concepts and principles that are present across cases in a set of qualitative research studies.

c. calculate effect sizes with a different formula than that used in reviews of quantitative research studies.

d. may include various types of publications in their review except online sources.

10. The primary advantage of a chart essay over a written report of a literature review is that a chart essay

a. identifies the particular studies on which the findings of the literature review are based.

b. focuses on the statistics that were used to test the significance of the research findings.

c. highlights the categories that were used to cluster the publications included in the review.

d. is easier to understand by individuals without sophisticated knowledge about research methodology.

CHAPTER REFERENCES

American Psychological Association. (2010). *Publication manual of the American Psychological Association* (6th ed.). Washington, DC: Author.

Glass, G. V (1976). Primary, secondary, and meta-analysis of research. *Educational Researcher, 5*(10), 3–8.

Haensly, P. A., Lupkowski, A. E., & McNamara, J. F. (1987). The chart essay: A strategy for communicating research findings to policy makers and practitioners. *Educational Evaluation and Policy Analysis, 9*, 63–75.

Haller, E. P., Child, D. A., & Walberg, H. J. (1988). Can comprehension be taught? A quantitative synthesis of "metacognitive" studies. *Educational Researcher, 17*(9), 5–8.

Jones, B. K., & Mitchell, N. (1990). Communicating evaluation findings: The use of a chart essay. *Educational Evaluation and Policy Analysis, 12*(4), 449–462.

Moos, D. C., & Azevedo, R. (2009). Learning with computer-based learning environments: A literature review of computer self-efficacy. *Review of Educational Research, 79*(2), 576–600.

Ogawa, R. T., & Malen, B. (1991). Towards rigor in reviews of multivocal literatures: Applying the exploratory case study method. *Review of Educational Research, 61*, 265–286.

Rice, E. H. (2002). The collaboration process in professional development schools: Results of a meta-ethnography, 1990–1998. *Journal of Teacher Education, 53*(1), 56–67.

Slavin, R. E. (1986). Best-evidence synthesis: An alternative to meta-analytic and traditional reviews. *Educational Researcher, 15*(9), 5–11.

Slavin, R. (1992). Cooperative learning. In M. C. Alkin (Ed.), *Encyclopedia of educational research* (6th ed., vol. 1, pp. 235–238). New York, NY: Macmillan.

What Works Clearinghouse (n.d.). *Procedures and standards handbook* (Version 2.1). Retrieved from http://ies.ed.gov/ncee/wwc/pdf/reference_resources/wwc_procedures_v2_1_standards_handbook.pdf

RESOURCES FOR FURTHER STUDY

Cooper, H. M. (2010). *Research synthesis and meta-analysis: A step-by-step approach* (4th ed.). Los Angeles, CA: Sage.

This book is helpful if you plan to do a literature review as your primary requirement for completion of a master's or doctoral degree and if the studies you review are primarily quantitative in design.

Dunkin, M. J. (1996). Types of errors in synthesizing research in education. *Review of Educational Research, 66*, 87–97.

The author identifies nine types of errors that occur in literature reviews. For example, reviewers might exclude relevant literature, report details of a study incorrectly, or draw unwarranted conclusions from the literature reviewed.

Randolph, J. J. (2009). A guide to writing the dissertation literature review. *Practical Assessment, Research & Evaluation, 14*(3), 1–13.

   The author elaborates on some of the steps in a literature review that we describe in this chapter.

Maxwell, J. A. (2006). Literature reviews of, and for, educational research: A commentary on Boote and Beile's "Scholars before Researchers." *Educational Researcher, 35*(9), 28–31.

   This article and an earlier article by Boote and Beile in the same journal list common flaws in published literature reviews. The authors present their views on the purpose of a literature review in a research study.

Sandelowski, M., & Barroso, J. (2007). *Handbook for synthesizing qualitative research*. New York, NY: Springer.

   This book will be useful if your literature review focuses primarily on qualitative research. The author presents procedures for planning the review, searching for qualitative research reports, evaluating the quality of the reports, synthesizing their findings, and writing the literature review report.

Sample Professional Review

The Case For and Against Homework

Marzano, R. J., & Pickering, D. J. (2007). The case for and against homework. *Educational Leadership*, *64*(6), 74–79. © 2007 by ASCD. Used with permission. Learn more about ASCD at www.ascd.org.

Arguments for and against homework occasionally appear in newspapers and magazines. Does homework take time away from students' pursuit of other important activities? Does homework help students reach a higher level of academic achievement, which could have long-term benefits?

These arguments are likely to confuse parents, students, educators, and others. The following journal article addresses the arguments by presenting a professional literature review about the effectiveness of homework. The authors refer to the results of research meta-analyses, but in a relatively nontechnical manner. They also make recommendations for professional practice.

The article is reprinted in its entirety, just as it appeared when originally published.

The Case For and Against Homework

ROBERT J. MARZANO AND DEBRA J. PICKERING

Robert J. Marzano *is a Senior Scholar at Mid-Continent Research for Education and Learning in Aurora, Colorado; an Associate Professor at Cardinal Stritch University in Milwaukee, Wisconsin; and President of Marzano & Associates consulting firm in Centennial, Colorado; robertjmarzano@aol.com.* Debra J. Pickering *is a private consultant and Director of Staff Development in Littleton Public Schools, Littleton, Colorado; djplearn@hotmail.com.*

Homework has been a perennial topic of debate in education, and attitudes toward it have been cyclical (Gill & Schlossman, 2000). Throughout the first few decades of the 20th century, educators commonly believed that homework helped create disciplined minds. By 1940, growing concern that homework interfered with other home activities sparked a reaction against it. This trend was reversed in the late 1950s when the Soviets' launch of *Sputnik* led to concern that U.S. education lacked rigor; schools viewed more rigorous homework as a partial solution to the problem. By 1980, the trend had reversed again, with some learning theorists claiming that homework could be detrimental to students' mental health. Since then, impassioned arguments for and against homework have continued to proliferate.

We now stand at an interesting intersection in the evolution of the homework debate. Arguments against homework are becoming louder and more popular, as evidenced by several recent books as well as an editorial in *Time* magazine (Wallis, 2006) that presented these arguments as truth without much discussion of alternative perspectives. At the same time, a number of studies have provided growing evidence of the usefulness of homework when employed effectively.

The Case For Homework

Homework is typically defined as any tasks "assigned to students by school teachers that are meant to be carried out during nonschool hours" (Cooper, 1989a, p. 7). A number of synthesis studies have been conducted on homework, spanning a broad range of methodologies and levels of specificity (see Figure 1). Some are quite general and mix the results from experimental studies with correlational studies.

Two meta-analyses by Cooper and colleagues (Cooper, 1989a; Cooper, Robinson, & Patall, 2006) are the most comprehensive and rigorous. The 1989 meta-analysis reviewed research dating as far back as the 1930s; the 2006 study reviewed research from 1987 to 2003. Commenting on studies that attempted to examine the causal relationship between homework and student achievement by comparing experimental (homework) and control (no homework) groups, Cooper, Robinson, and Patall (2006) noted,

> With only rare exceptions, the relationship between the amount of homework students do and their achievement outcomes was found to be positive and statistically significant. Therefore, we think it would not be imprudent, based on the evidence in hand, to conclude that doing homework causes improved academic achievement. (p. 48)

FIGURE 1 • Synthesis Studies on Homework

Synthesis Study	Focus	Number of Effect Sizes	Average	Percentile Gains
Graue, Weinstein, & Walberg, 1983[1]	General effects of homework	29	.49	19
Bloom, 1984	General effects of homework	—	.30	12
Paschal, Weinstein, & Walberg, 1984[2]	Homework versus no homework	47	.28	11
Cooper, 1989a	Homework versus no homework	20	.21	8
Hattie, 1992; Fraser, Walberg, Welch, & Hattie, 1987	General effects of homework	110	.43	17
Walberg, 1999	With teacher comments	2	.88	31
	Graded	5	.78	28
Cooper, Robinson, & Patall, 2006	Homework versus no homework	6	.60	23

Note: This figure describes the eight major research syntheses on the effects of homework published from 1983 to 2006 that provide the basis for the analysis in this article. The Cooper (1989a) study included more than 100 empirical research reports, and the Cooper, Robinson, and Patall (2006) study included about 50 empirical research reports. Figure 1 reports only those results from experimental/control comparisons for these two studies.

[1]Reported in Fraser, Walberg, Welch, & Hattie, 1987.

[2]Reported in Kavale, 1988.

The Case Against Homework

Although the research support for homework is compelling, the case against homework is popular. *The End of Homework: How Homework Disrupts Families, Overburdens Children, and Limits Learning* by Kralovec and Buell (2000), considered by many to be the first high-profile attack on homework, asserted that homework contributes to a corporate-style, competitive U.S. culture that overvalues work to the detriment of personal and familial well-being. The authors focused particularly on the harm to economically disadvantaged students, who are unintentionally penalized because their environments often make it almost impossible to complete assignments at home. The authors called for people to unite against homework and to lobby for an extended school day instead.

A similar call for action came from Bennett and Kalish (2006) in *The Case Against Homework: How Homework Is Hurting Our Children and What We Can Do About It*. These authors criticized both the quantity and quality of homework. They provided evidence that too much homework harms students' health and family time, and they asserted that teachers are not well trained in how to assign homework. The authors suggested that individuals and parent groups should insist that teachers reduce the amount of homework, design more

valuable assignments, and avoid homework altogether over breaks and holidays.

In a third book, *The Homework Myth: Why Our Kids Get Too Much of a Bad Thing* (2006a), Kohn took direct aim at the research on homework. In this book and in a recent article in *Phi Delta Kappan* (2006b), he became quite personal in his condemnation of researchers. For example, referring to Harris Cooper, the lead author of the two leading meta-analyses on homework, Kohn noted,

> A careful reading of Cooper's own studies . . . reveals further examples of his determination to massage the numbers until they yield something—anything—on which to construct a defense of homework for younger children. (2006a, p. 84)

He also attacked a section on homework in our book *Classroom Instruction That Works* (Marzano, Pickering, & Pollock, 2001).

Kohn concluded that research fails to demonstrate homework's effectiveness as an instructional tool and recommended changing the "default state" from an expectation that homework will be assigned to an expectation that homework will not be assigned. According to Kohn, teachers should only assign homework when they can justify that the assignments are "beneficial" (2006a,

p. 166)—ideally involving students in activities appropriate for the home, such as performing an experiment in the kitchen, cooking, doing crossword puzzles with the family, watching good TV shows, or reading. Finally, Kohn urged teachers to involve students in deciding what homework, and how much, they should do.

Some of Kohn's recommendations have merit. For example, it makes good sense to only assign homework that is beneficial to student learning instead of assigning homework as a matter of policy. Many of those who conduct research on homework explicitly or implicitly recommend this practice. However, his misunderstanding or misrepresentation of the research sends the inaccurate message that research does not support homework. As Figure 1 indicates, homework has decades of research supporting its effective use. Kohn's allegations that researchers are trying to mislead practitioners and the general public are unfounded and detract from a useful debate on effective practice.[1]

The Dangers of Ignoring the Research

Certainly, inappropriate homework may produce little or no benefit—it may even decrease student achievement. All three of the books criticizing homework provide compelling anecdotes to this effect. Schools should strengthen their policies to ensure that teachers use homework properly.

If a district or school discards homework altogether, however, it will be throwing away a powerful instructional tool. Cooper and colleagues' (2006) comparison of homework with no homework indicates that the average student in a class in which appropriate homework was assigned would score 23 percentile points higher on tests of the knowledge addressed in that class than the average student in a class in which homework was not assigned.

Perhaps the most important advantage of homework is that it can enhance achievement by extending learning beyond the school day. This characteristic is important because U.S. students spend much less time studying academic content than students in other countries do. A 1994 report examined the amount of time U.S. students spend studying core academic subjects compared with students in other countries that typically outperform the United States academically, such as Japan, Germany, and France. The study found that "students abroad are required to work on demanding subject matter at least twice as long" as are U.S. students (National Education Commission on Time and Learning, 1994, p. 25).

To drop the use of homework, then, a school or district would be obliged to identify a practice that produces

a similar effect within the confines of the school day without taking away or diminishing the benefits of other academic activities—no easy accomplishment. A better approach is to ensure that teachers use homework effectively. To enact effective homework policies, however, schools and districts must address the following issues.

Grade Level

Although teachers across the K–12 spectrum commonly assign homework, research has produced no clear-cut consensus on the benefits of homework at the early elementary grade levels. In his early meta-analysis, Cooper (1989a) reported the following effect sizes (p. 71):

- Grades 4–6: ES = .15 (Percentile gain = 6)
- Grades 7–9: ES = .31 (Percentile gain = 12)
- Grades 10–12: ES = .64 (Percentile gain = 24)

The pattern clearly indicates that homework has smaller effects at lower grade levels. Even so, Cooper (1989b) still recommended homework for elementary students because

> homework for young children should help them develop good study habits, foster positive attitudes toward school, and communicate to students the idea that learning takes work at home as well as at school. (p. 90)

The Cooper, Robinson, and Patall (2006) meta-analysis found the same pattern of stronger relationships at the secondary level but also identified a number of studies at grades 2, 3, and 4 demonstrating positive effects for homework. In *The Battle over Homework* (2007), Cooper noted that homework should have different purposes at different grade levels:

- For students in the *earliest grades*, it should foster positive attitudes, habits, and character traits; permit appropriate parent involvement; and reinforce learning of simple skills introduced in class.
- For students in *upper elementary grades*, it should play a more direct role in fostering improved school achievement.
- In *6th grade and beyond*, it should play an important role in improving standardized test scores and grades.

Time Spent on Homework

One of the more contentious issues in the homework debate is the amount of time students should spend on homework. The Cooper synthesis (1989a) reported that for junior high school students, the benefits increased as time increased, up to 1 to 2 hours of homework a night, and then decreased. The Cooper, Robinson, and Patall (2006) study reported similar findings: 7 to 12 hours of

---

[1]For a more detailed response to Kohn's views on homework, see Marzano & Pickering (2007) and Marzano & Pickering (in press).

homework per week produced the largest effect size for 12th grade students. The researchers suggested that for 12th graders the optimum amount of homework might lie between 1.5 and 2.5 hours per night, but they cautioned that no hard-and-fast rules are warranted. Still, researchers have offered various recommendations. For example, Good and Brophy (2003) cautioned that teachers must take care not to assign too much homework. They suggested that

> homework must be realistic in length and difficulty given the students' abilities to work independently. Thus, 5 to 10 minutes per subject might be appropriate for 4th graders, whereas 30 to 60 minutes might be appropriate for college-bound high school students. (p. 394)

Cooper, Robinson, and Patall (2006) also issued a strong warning about too much homework:

> Even for these oldest students, too much homework may diminish its effectiveness or even become counterproductive. (p. 53)

Cooper (2007) suggested that research findings support the common "10-minute rule" (p. 92), which states that all daily homework assignments combined should take about as long to complete as 10 minutes multiplied by the student's grade level. He added that when required reading is included as a type of homework, the 10-minute rule might be increased to 15 minutes.

Focusing on the amount of time students spend on homework, however, may miss the point. A significant proportion of the research on homework indicates that the positive effects of homework relate to the amount of homework that the student completes rather than the amount of time spent on homework or the amount of homework actually assigned. Thus, simply assigning homework may not produce the desired effect—in fact, ill-structured homework might even have a negative effect on student achievement. Teachers must carefully plan and assign homework in a way that maximizes the potential for student success (see Research-Based Homework Guidelines).

Parent Involvement

Another question regarding homework is the extent to which schools should involve parents. Some studies have reported minimal positive effects or even negative effects for parental involvement. In addition, many parents report that they feel unprepared to help their children with homework and that their efforts to help frequently cause stress (see Balli, 1998; Corno, 1996; Hoover-Dempsey, Bassler, & Burow, 1995; Perkins & Milgram, 1996).

Epstein and colleagues conducted a series of studies to identify the conditions under which parental involvement enhances homework (Epstein, 2001; Epstein & Becker, 1982; Van Voorhis, 2003). They recommended interactive homework in which

- Parents receive clear guidelines spelling out their role.
- Teachers do not expect parents to act as experts regarding content or to attempt to teach the content.
- Parents ask questions that help students clarify and summarize what they have learned.

Good and Brophy (2003) provided the following recommendations regarding parent involvement:

> Especially useful for parent-child relations purposes are assignments calling for students to show or explain their written work or other products completed at school to their parents and get their reactions (Epstein, 2001; Epstein, Simon, & Salinas, 1997) or to interview their parents to develop information about parental experiences or opinions relating to topics studied in social studies (Alleman & Brophy, 1998). Such assignments cause students and their parents or other family members to become engaged in conversations that relate to the academic curriculum and thus extend the students' learning. Furthermore, because these are likely to be genuine conversations rather than more formally structured teaching/learning tasks, both parents and children are likely to experience them as enjoyable rather than threatening. (p. 395)

Going Beyond the Research

Although research has established the overall viability of homework as a tool to enhance student achievement, for the most part the research does not provide recommendations that are specific enough to help busy practitioners. This is the nature of research—it errs on the side of assuming that something does not work until substantial evidence establishes that it does. The research community takes a long time to formulate firm conclusions on the basis of research. Homework is a perfect example: Figure 1 includes synthesis studies that go back as far as 60 years, yet all that research translates to a handful of recommendations articulated at a very general level.

In addition, research in a specific area, such as homework, sometimes contradicts research in related areas. For example, Cooper (2007) recommended on the basis of 60-plus years of homework research that teachers should not comment on or grade every homework assignment. But practitioners might draw a different conclusion from the research on providing feedback to students, which has found that providing "feedback coupled with remediation" (Hattie, 1992) or feedback on "testlike events" (Bangert-Drowns, Kulik, Kulik, & Morgan, 1991) positively affects achievement.

Riehl (2006) pointed out the similarity between education research and medical research. She commented,

> When reported in the popular media, medical research often appears as a blunt instrument, able to obliterate skeptics or opponents by the force of its evidence and arguments. . . . Yet repeated visits to the medical journals themselves can leave a much different impression. The serious medical journals convey the sense that medical research is an ongoing conversation and quest, punctuated occasionally by important findings that can and should alter practice, but more often characterized by continuing investigations. These investigations, taken cumulatively, can inform the work of practitioners who are building their own local knowledge bases on medical care. (pp. 27–28)

If relying solely on research is problematic, what are busy practitioners to do? The answer is certainly not to wait until research "proves" that a practice is effective. Instead, educators should combine research-based generalizations, research from related areas, and their own professional judgment based on firsthand experience to develop specific practices and make adjustments as necessary. Like medical practitioners, education practitioners must develop their own "local knowledge base" on homework and all other aspects of teaching. Educators can develop the most effective practices by observing changes in the achievement of the students with whom they work every day.

Research-Based Homework Guidelines

Research provides strong evidence that, when used appropriately, homework benefits student achievement. To make sure that homework is appropriate, teachers should follow these guidelines:

- Assign purposeful homework. Legitimate purposes for homework include introducing new content, practicing a skill or process that students can do independently but not fluently, elaborating on information that has been addressed in class to deepen students' knowledge, and providing opportunities for students to explore topics of their own interest.
- Design homework to maximize the chances that students will complete it. For example, ensure that homework is at the appropriate level of difficulty. Students should be able to complete homework assignments independently with relatively high success rates, but they should still find the assignments challenging enough to be interesting.
- Involve parents in appropriate ways (for example, as a sounding board to help students summarize what they learned from the homework) without requiring parents

to act as teachers or to police students' homework completion.
- Carefully monitor the amount of homework assigned so that it is appropriate to students' age levels and does not take too much time away from other home activities.

REFERENCES

Balli, S. J. (1998). When mom and dad help: Student reflections on parent involvement with homework. *Journal of Research and Development in Education, 31*(3), 142–148.

Bangert-Drowns, R. L., Kulik, C. C., Kulik, J. A., & Morgan, M. (1991). The instructional effects of feedback in test-like events. *Review of Educational Research, 61*(2), 213–238.

Bennett, S., & Kalish, N. (2006). *The case against homework: How homework is hurting our children and what we can do about it.* New York: Crown.

Bloom, B. S. (1984). The search for methods of group instruction as effective as one-to-one tutoring. *Educational Leadership, 41*(8), 4–18.

Cooper, H. (1989a). *Homework.* White Plains, NY: Longman.

Cooper, H. (1989b). Synthesis of research on homework. *Educational Leadership, 47*(3), 85–91.

Cooper, H. (2007). *The battle over homework* (3rd ed.). Thousand Oaks, CA: Corwin Press.

Cooper, H., Robinson, J. C., & Patall, E. A. (2006). Does homework improve academic achievement? A synthesis of research, 1987–2003. *Review of Educational Research, 76*(1), 1–62.

Corno, L. (1996). Homework is a complicated thing. *Educational Researcher, 25*(8), 27–30.

Epstein, J. (2001). *School, family, and community partnerships: Preparing educators and improving schools.* Boulder, CO: Westview.

Epstein, J. L., & Becker, H. J. (1982). Teachers' reported practices of parent involvement: Problems and possibilities. *Elementary School Journal, 83*, 103–113.

Fraser, B. J., Walberg, H. J., Welch, W. W., & Hattie, J. A. (1987). Synthesis of educational productivity research [Special issue]. *International Journal of Educational Research, 11*(2), 145–252.

Gill, B. P., & Schlossman, S. L. (2000). The lost cause of homework reform. *American Journal of Education, 109*, 27–62.

Good, T. L., & Brophy, J. E. (2003). *Looking in classrooms* (9th ed.). Boston: Allyn & Bacon.

Graue, M. E., Weinstein, T., & Walberg, H. J. (1983). School-based home instruction and learning: A quantitative synthesis. *Journal of Educational Research, 76*, 351–360.

Hattie, J. A. (1992). Measuring the effects of schooling. *Australian Journal of Education, 36*(1), 5–13.

Hoover-Dempsey, K. V., Bassler, O. C., & Burow, R. (1995). Parents' reported involvement in students' homework: Strategies and practices. *The Elementary School Journal, 95*(5), 435–450.

Kavale, K. A. (1988). Using meta-analyses to answer the question: What are the important influences on school learning? *School Psychology Review, 17*(4), 644–650.

Kohn, A. (2006a). *The homework myth: Why our kids get too much of a bad thing.* Cambridge, MA: Da Capo Press.

Kohn, A. (2006b). Abusing research: The study of homework and other examples. *Phi Delta Kappan, 88*(1), 9–22.

Kralovec, E., & Buell, J. (2000). *The end of homework: How homework disrupts families, overburdens children, and limits learning.* Boston: Beacon.

Marzano, R. J., & Pickering, D. J. (2007). *Response to Kohn's allegations.* Centennial, CO: Marzano & Associates. Available: http://marzanoandassociates.com/documents/KohnResponse.pdf

Marzano, R. J., & Pickering, D. J. (in press). *Errors and allegations about research on homework.* Phi Delta Kappan.

Marzano, R. J., Pickering, D. J., & Pollock, J. E. (2001). *Classroom instruction that works: Research-based strategies for increasing student achievement.* Alexandria, VA: ASCD.

National Education Commission on Time and Learning (1994). *Prisoners of time.* Washington, DC: U.S. Department of Education.

Paschal, R. A., Weinstein, T., & Walberg, H. J. (1984). The effects of homework on learning: A quantitative synthesis. *Journal of Educational Research, 78*, 97–104.

Perkins, P. G., & Milgram, R. B. (1996). Parental involvement in homework: A double-edge sword. *International Journal of Adolescence and Youth, 6*(3), 195–203.

Riehl, C. (2006). Feeling better: A comparison of medical research and education research. *Educational Researcher, 35*(5), 24–29.

Van Voorhis, F. (2003). Interactive homework in middle school: Effects on family involvement and science achievement. *Journal of Educational Research, 96*, 323–338.

Walberg, H. J. (1999). Productive teaching. In H. C. Waxman & H. J. Walberg (Eds.), *New directions for teaching practice research* (pp. 75–104). Berkeley, CA: McCutchen.

Wallis, C. (2006). Viewpoint: The myth about homework. *Time, 168*(10), 57.

 ## Sample Meta-Analysis

The Process Writing Approach: A Meta-analysis

Graham, S., & Sandmel, K. (2011). The process writing approach: A meta-analysis. *The Journal of Educational Research, 104*(6), 396–407.

This literature review provides a good illustration of how the statistical methods of meta-analysis can be used to synthesize the findings of a large number of studies on an important problem of practice in education.

The problem of practice concerns the effectiveness of a particular method of writing instruction—the process writing approach. The authors of the review explain the principles of this method and describe claims made by its proponents and criticisms stated by its opponents. The purpose of the meta-analysis is to determine which of these competing views is supported by research studies testing the effectiveness of the process writing approach. A total of 29 experiments reported in the literature were included in the meta-analysis.

The authors of the literature review report various research and statistical methods, some of which we describe in other chapters. They distinguish between experiments and quasi-experiments: Experiments include random assignment of students or classes to the experimental and control groups, whereas quasi-experiments do not have this feature (see Chapter 12). The authors refer extensively to effect sizes (described in this chapter) and confidence intervals (described in Chapter 7). Briefly, confidence intervals are statistics that are calculated to estimate whether the average of all of the effect sizes calculated for the studies included in the review is likely to approximate the effect size that we would find if experiments had been done for all students in the population, not just the samples included in the experiments. The authors employ several sophisticated statistical methods that you might not know, but they are not critical for your understanding of the major findings of the literature review.

The Process Writing Approach: A Meta-analysis

STEVE GRAHAM
KARIN SANDMEL
Vanderbilt University

ABSTRACT The process approach to writing instruction is one of the most popular methods for teaching writing. The authors conducted meta-analysis of 29 experimental and quasi-experimental studies conducted with students in Grades 1–12 to examine if process writing instruction improves the quality of students' writing and motivation to write. For students in general education classes, process writing instruction resulted in a statistically significant, but relatively modest improvement in the overall quality of writing (average weighted effect size [ES] = 0.34). Variation in ES was not related to grade, reliability of the writing quality measure, professional development, genre assessed, or quality of study. The process writing approach neither resulted in a statistically significant improvement in students' motivation nor enhanced the quality of struggling writers' compositions.

Keywords: meta-analysis, writing, writing process

According to findings from the 2007 National Assessment of Educational Progress (NAEP; Salahu-Din, Persky, & Miller, 2008), only 33% of eighth-grade and 24% of 12th-grade students perform at or above the proficient level in writing (defined as solid academic performance). Students who score below this level are classified as obtaining only partial mastery of the literacy skills needed at their respective grade. If partial mastery is interpreted as performing below grade level, then 67% of eighth-grade and 76% of 12th-grade students can be considered as writing below grade level. These and previously disappointing findings from past NAEP assessments (Greenwald, Persky, Ambell, & Mazzeo, 1999; Persky, Daane, & Jen, 2003) as well as concerns about students' readiness for the writing demands of college and the world of work (Achieve, Inc., 2005; Bates, Breslow, & Hupert, 2009; Greene, 2000) have led to calls to improve the teaching of writing in American schools (National Commission on Writing, 2003).

The call to reform writing instruction is based on the assumption that there are effective practices for teaching this complex skill. The results from several meta-analyses conducted during the last three decades supports this contention (Bangert-Drowns, 1993; Goldring, Russell, & Cook, 2003; Graham & Perin, 2007; Hillocks, 1986; Rogers & Graham, 2008). These reviews verified the effectiveness of a variety of writing methods, ranging from explicitly teaching strategies for planning, revising, paragraph and sentence construction, word processing as a tool for writing, and studying and emulating models of good writing.

The instructional method that is probably best situated to be implemented broadly in any effort to reform writing practices in the United States is the process writing approach (sometimes referred to as Writers' Workshop; Atwell, 1987; Calkins, 1983; Graves, 1983). A sizable minority of elementary and secondary teachers presently use this approach exclusively when teaching writing, with a majority of teachers combining process writing with other instructional procedures, such as more traditional writing skills instruction (Cutler & Graham, 2008; Kiuhara, Graham, & Hawken, 2009). Perhaps even more importantly, the National Writing Project (see Nagin, 2006) provides professional development in how to use the process writing approach to more than 100,000 teachers a year. No other instructional approach in writing comes close to having such an infrastructure for scaling up (see also commercial materials such as those produced by Calkins & Colleagues, 2008). If writing becomes a central element in the national reform movement, then the writing process approach is likely to play a major role in this effort.

Although there is no universally agreed-on definition for the process approach to writing, there are a number of underlying principles that are common to it (e.g., Graham & Perin, 2007; Nagin, 2006; Pritchard & Honeycutt, 2006). Students engage in cycles of planning (setting goals, generating ideas, organizing ideas), translating (putting a writing plan into action), and reviewing (evaluating, editing, revising). They write for real purposes and audiences, with some of their writing projects occurring over an extended period of time. Students' ownership of their writing is stressed, as is self-reflection and evaluation. Students work together collaboratively, and teachers create a supportive and nonthreatening writing environment. Personalized and individualized writing instruction is provided through minilessons, writing conferences, and teachable moments.

There are many potential advantages to the process writing approach (Graham & Harris, 1997). First, students

---

Address correspondence to Steve Graham, Vanderbilt University, Peabody College, Box 228, Nashville, TN 37023, USA. (E-mail: steve.graham@vanderbilt.edu)

are encouraged to plan, draft, and revise. The cognitive activities involved in these writing processes account for close to 80% of the variance in the quality of papers produced by adolescent writers (Breetvelt, Van den Bergh & Rijlaarsdam, 1994, 1996; Rijlaarsdam & Van den Bergh, 2006; Van den Bergh & Rijlaarsdam, 1996). Second, instruction in writing through minilessons, conferences, and teachable moments should result in improved quality of writing. These teaching tools also provide mechanisms for addressing the instructional needs of individual students. Third, motivation for writing should be enhanced as collaboration, personal responsibility, personal attention, and a positive learning environment are stressed. These types of activities are thought to facilitate the value that students place on specific academic tasks (Wigfield, 1994).

Despite possible advantages, the process approach to writing is not without its critics (e.g., Baines, Baines, Stanley, & Kunkel, 1999). Some have charged that the instruction provided in process writing classrooms is not powerful enough to ensure that students, especially students experiencing difficulty with writing, acquire needed writing skills and processes (for a discussion of potential strengths and weaknesses, see Graham & Harris, 1997). Critics argue that not enough attention is devoted to mastering foundational skills, such as handwriting, spelling, and sentence construction (although the National Writing Project does emphasize systematic sentence-combining instruction; Nagin, 2006). They also contend that very little time is devoted to explicitly teaching students strategies for carrying out basic writing processes such as planning and revising (for data consistent with this viewpoint, see Cutler & Graham, 2008).

Given the popularity of the process writing approach and the possibility that it may likely be applied even more broadly in the future, it is important to determine its effectiveness. Two previous meta-analyses have addressed this issue, with varying degrees of success. First, a seminal meta-analysis of writing intervention research conducted by Hillocks (1986) examined the effectiveness of the natural process mode in nine studies with students in Grade 6 through freshman year in college. Hillocks defined this approach as involving general objectives for writing, free writing using self-selected topics, writing for and receiving generally positive feedback from peers, opportunities to revise written work, and high levels of student interactions. Although the natural process mode and process writing as described previously share a number of commonalities (e.g., student revising and high levels of student interaction), they are not identical. For example, free writing (Fox & Suhor, 1986) and teacher as facilitator (Stotsky, 1988) received more emphasis in Hillocks's natural process mode than is typical in most process-oriented approaches. Although Hillocks's review included studies compatible with our previous characterization of the process writing approach (e.g., Alloway et al., 1979), this was not the case in all instances (e.g., Wienke, 1981). In addition, the two studies with the weakest effects involved college students (average effect size [ES] = −0.14). As a result, the relatively small average ES of 0.18 for writing quality reported by Hillocks may not provide a true estimate of the impact of process writing for children in Grades 1–12.

Second, a larger average weighted ES of 0.32 for writing quality was reported for the process approach in a meta-analysis of the writing intervention literature with students in Grades 4–12 (Graham & Perin, 2007). Because there was considerable variability in ES, moderate analyses were undertaken to determine if specific study features were associated with the obtained ES. Graham and Perin found that when teachers received professional development in applying the process approach model (most often provided through the NWP) effects were larger (ES = 0.46) than when teachers were not provided with such preparation (ES = 0.03). However, in a follow-up analysis involving studies in which teachers did not receive professional development (considerable variability in ES still existed in these studies), the process writing approach had a positive and statistically significant impact on writing quality for students in Grades 4–12 (ES = 0.27), but not for students in Grades 7–12 (ES = −0.05).

Although Graham and Perin (2007) selected studies that met the description of process writing presented previously, their review excluded studies conducted with younger students (Grades 1–3) as well as studies in which the reliability of the outcome measure (i.e., writing quality) was not established. Moreover, in four of the 21 studies reviewed, the process approach to writing was compared to strategy instruction in which students were taught strategies for carrying out specific writing processes, such as planning (Moye, 1993; Troia & Graham, 2002) or planning and revising (Gamelin, 1996; Yeh, 1998). In each of these studies, strategy instruction was the treatment condition and process writing was the control condition.

In this article, we report the findings of a new meta-analysis examining the effectiveness of the process approach to writing. Similar to Graham and Perin (2007) and Hillocks (1986), we limited our review to experimental and quasi-experimental research. Such designs include mechanisms for eliminating alternative explanations for the claim that treatment was responsible for observed changes in behavior (Phye, Robinson, & Levin, 2005). However, it is important to note that we extend the two previous reviews in six important ways.

First, younger students were not included in the two previous meta-analyses. For example, Graham and Perin (2007) limited their review to studies conducted only with students in Grades 4–12. It is possible that their analyses underestimated the effects of process writing on school-age students in general. They found that ES for younger students (Grades 4–6) were larger than ES for older ones (Grades 7–12). Thus, it is possible that the inclusion of studies conducted with primary-grade children (Grades 1–3) may increase the average ES for all process writing studies. It is also possible that differences in the effectiveness of process writing between younger and older students are accentuated by the inclusion of studies conducted with primary-grade children. Consequently, in this review we examine the effectiveness of process writing from Grades 1–12.

Second, similar to Graham and Perin (2007) and Hillocks (1986), we were interested in the impact of the process writing approach on the overall quality of students' writing. However, we did not limit our analyses just to studies where scoring reliability was established, as was done in the two previous meta-analyses. The assumption underlying this decision was that the assessment of writing quality involves some degree of subjectivity, making it important to consider reliability of scoring procedures (Graham & Perin, 2007). Although we do not disagree with the subjectivity assumption, there are two ways to approach the problem. One is to exclude studies where scoring reliability is not demonstrated, and the other is to include all studies and determine if scoring reliability is related to variation in ES. We chose the latter approach, as the exclusion of studies can bias analysis and limit inference (Herbison, Hay-Smith, & Gillespie, 2006).

Third, in contrast with Graham and Perin (2007), we did not calculate ES for studies that compared the process writing approach to strategy instruction for planning, revising, or both (such studies were not reviewed by Hillocks [1986]). Pritchard and Honeycutt (2006) placed strategy instruction under the process approach umbrella, arguing that process writing includes direct instruction in writing strategies. As a result, we decided to limit the comparison condition in the studies we reviewed to more traditional writing instruction (e.g., teaching writing skills). Process writing developed, in part, as a reaction and alternative to such instruction (Nagin, 2006). Nevertheless, we did not treat strategy instruction as synonymous with process writing instruction for two reasons. First, the level of systematic and explicit instruction provided in strategy instructional studies exceeds what is evident in the programs developed by process advocates (e.g., Atwell, 1987; Calkins, 1983; Graves, 1983). Second, strategy instruction, unlike the process writing approach, does not constitute a full writing program, and many studies investigating its effectiveness concentrate on teaching strategies for a restricted range of processes, such as planning (see Graham & Perin, 2007; Rogers & Graham, 2008).

Fourth, Graham and Perin (2007) and Hillocks (1986) did not examine the effects of the process writing approach on students' motivation. Proponents of the process approach contend that this method of teaching enhances developing writers' attitudes toward writing (e.g., Pritchard & Honeycutt, 2006). Consequently, writing quality and motivation served as outcome measures in this review. Based on the findings from the previous reviews, we anticipated that process writing would have a positive impact on writing quality. We also based this prediction on the emphasis this approach places on critical writing processes such as planning and revising as well as the inclusion of instructional components (e.g., minilessons) aimed at improving students' writing skills. It was further expected the process writing would enhance motivation because it includes instructional components, such as a positive learning environment, peer collaboration, and personal attention, theorists contend heighten the value students place on academic tasks (Maehr & Midgley, 1991; Wigfield, 1994).

Fifth, in contrast with Graham and Perin (2007) and Hillocks (1986), ES for quasi-experimental studies in this meta-analysis were adjusted for possible pretest differences between the process writing group and comparison group. Because students were not randomly assigned to conditions in such studies, their performance may not be equivalent at the start of the investigation, biasing the obtained outcomes.

Last, we examined if the process writing approach had a positive impact on improving writing quality for struggling or at-risk writers. This analysis was done separately from our analysis with more typical students, whereas such an analysis was not undertaken by Graham and Perin (2007) or Hillocks (1986). We decided to compute a separate average weighted ES for struggling writers because of critics' concerns that the process writing approach is not powerful enough for these students (see Graham & Harris, 1997). However, we did not make a prediction concerning the effects of process writing for these students. It is possible that this approach to writing enhances these students' performance because of its emphasis on the processes of writing (planning, translating, and reviewing), the inclusion of instructional components designed to enhance writing skills (e.g., minilessons and writing conferences), and methods for fostering motivation (e.g., collaboration and positive learning environment). In addition, several case studies (Cousin, Aragon, & Rojas, 1993; Foulger & Jimenez-Silva, 2007; Zaragoza & Vaughn, 1992; Zucker, 1993) reported that the process writing approach had a positive impact on struggling writers, including students with learning disabilities (LD) and English language learners (ELL). Nevertheless, it is possible that this approach is not effective with these students, as not enough attention and intensity is directed at teaching basic text transcription skills, sentence construction skills, or strategies for planning and revising. Struggling writers typically have difficulty in one or more of these areas (Graham, 2006).

Similar to Graham and Perin (2007), we tested if professional development, type of genre assessed, and quality of the study was associated with higher ES for process writing instruction. We expected that training would mediate the impact of this approach to writing, as it is a complex intervention. As noted previously, Graham and Perin reported that process writing studies that involved professional development had a larger average effect than studies in which no training was provided. We did not anticipate that genre would be associated with magnitude of ES. Graham and Perin did not find such a relationship, and there is no evident reason why process writing should be more effective with one genre than another. Likewise, we did not expect that study quality would be associated with writing quality, as Graham and Perin did not find a statistically significant association between magnitude of ES and study quality for the broader writing intervention literature.

In summary, this meta-analysis addressed the following questions:

Research Question 1: Does the process approach to writing improve the quality of students' writing in general education classrooms in Grades 1–12?

Research Question 2: Does this approach improve the quality of writing produced by struggling or at-risk writers in Grades 1–12?

Research Question 3: Are effects for writing quality related to grade, reliability of the outcome measure, professional development, genre assessed, or study quality?

Research Question 4: Does this approach enhance student motivation?

Method

Selection of Studies

The search for articles in this meta-analysis was influenced by seven factors. First, only studies examining the effectiveness of the process writing approach were included. We applied Graham and Perin's (2007) definition of the process writing approach, and it involved the following elements: extended opportunities for writing; writing for real audiences and purposes; emphasis on the cyclical nature of writing, including planning, translating, and revising; student ownership of written compositions; interactions around writing between peers as well as teacher and students; a supportive writing environment; and students self-reflection and evaluation of their writing and the writing process. If a process intervention focused on just one component of the process writing approach (e.g., planning or revising), the study was excluded.

Second, only studies that employed an experimental or quasi-experimental design were included. Studies that employed a correlational, descriptive, single-subject, or qualitative design were excluded. Thus, all selected studies had to include a process writing treatment group and a control or comparison group. Acceptable control or comparison conditions included traditional skills instruction (e.g., grammar-based instruction) or a district or school writing curriculum (as long as it was not a process writing program). Studies were excluded when the comparison condition was another form of process writing instruction. We also excluded studies in which the comparison condition involved strategy instruction in one or more writing processes. If a study compared process writing and process writing plus an additional component to a comparison group, then only the process writing condition and control group were compared. For example, if a study compared process writing instruction and process writing instruction plus word processing to a control condition, we only compared the process writing approach alone to the control, as word processing is not commonly used in writing programs at either the elementary or secondary levels (Cutler & Graham, 2008; Kiuhara et al., 2009).

Third, only quasi-experimental studies that collected data at pretest and posttest were included. The pretest data had to measure the same construct as the posttest measure. This allowed us to adjust for possible pretest differences. A pretest was not required for experimental studies, as random assignment is designed to ensure that students in different groups are equivalent at the start of a study.

Fourth, only studies that measured writing quality, motivation, or both were included. Writing quality is based on readers' judgment of the overall merit of a paper, taking into account factors such as ideation, organization, vocabulary, sentence structure, and tone. These attributes are assessed singularly (analytic scale) or together (holistic scale) on a numerical Likert-type rating scale (Diederich, 1966). We also considered scores from norm-referenced writing tests, such as the Test of Written Language–3 (TOWL-3; Hammill & Larsen, 1996), as a measure of overall quality, as long as the score was based on a sample of students' writing. Measures of motivation involved self-report measures where students quantified their attitudes on Likert-type scales.

Fifth, a study was only included if it contained sufficient information to calculate an ES (Lipsey & Wilson, 2001). Sixth, studies that were conducted with students in Grades 1–12 were included, whereas studies involving kindergarten or college students were excluded. Seventh, studies conducted with students attending regular public or private schools were included. We did not include studies delivered in special schools for children with deafness, autism, severe emotional disturbance, and so forth. Although we believe that writing instruction is an important part of the curriculum for these students (and that they should be educated in their neighborhood schools whenever possible), the purpose of this review was to draw recommendations on the effectiveness of the process writing approach within regular school settings. This included studies conducted with students with disabilities or ELL in separate settings, as long as instruction occurred in regular school settings.

Strategies for Identifying Appropriate Studies

Four specific techniques were used to locate possible studies for inclusion in this review. First, an extensive search of published and unpublished studies was conducted using the following five databases: ERIC (Education Resources Information Center), Education Abstracts (Education Full Text), Dissertation Abstracts, PsycINFO, and ProQuest. The initial search included the following terms: *free writing, free writing and elementary, free writing and middle school, free writing and high school, process approach to writing, process approach to writing and elementary, process approach to writing and middle school, process approach to writing and high school, national writing project, national writing project and elementary, national writing project and middle school, national writing project and high school, process writing, process writing and elementary, process writing and middle school, process writing and high school, writing process approach, writing process approach and elementary, writing process approach and middle school, writing process approach and high school, writer's workshop, writer's workshop and elementary, writer's workshop and middle school, writer's workshop and high school, attitude and writing, self-efficacy and writing, belief and writing, and perception and writing.* The ending date for these searches was August 2009.

Second, reference lists of previous meta-analyses of the writing intervention literature (Graham & Perin, 2007; Hillocks, 1986) were examined to identify potentially appropriate studies. Third, a hand search of *Research in the Teaching of English* and *Written Communication* was conducted from 1986 to 2009. In addition, *Research in the Teaching of English* periodically publishes bibliographies of scholarly papers in the area of composition studies, and these sources were also examined to identify possible studies. Last, the reference lists in all collected studies were examined to locate additional articles and papers.

Once all studies were collected, each was read and assessed by Karin Sandmel to determine if it was appropriate for inclusion in this review, using the seven criteria reviewed in the previous section. These were treatment involved the process writing approach as defined; study was an experimental or quasi-experimental design; quasi-experimental design study included a pretest; control condition was appropriate as defined; writing quality, motivation, or both were outcome measures; subjects were in Grades 1–12 in a regular school setting; and an ES could be computed. To be included in the present review, a study had to meet all of these criteria.

A random sample of one third of all collected studies were independently rescored by a second rater to establish reliability of the study inclusion procedures. Reliability was calculated by determining the number of agreements (accepts or rejects) between the two raters and dividing by total number of agreements plus disagreements. Reliability was .93. If a disagreement occurred, the study was reviewed a second time to determine if it should be included in the review.

Coding the Studies

Each study included in this review was coded for eight descriptive and eight indicators of study quality. The descriptive variables scored were: (a) publication type (e.g., journal article, dissertation, other), (b) professional development versus no professional development, (c) the length of professional development in days when professional development was provided, (d) length of treatment in weeks, (e) grade level of students (elementary school, middle school, high school, or a combination), (f) student type (general education population including students with disabilities or ELLs, general education population excluding students with disabilities or ELLs, only students with disabilities, or only ELLs), (g) genre of writing (narrative, expository, persuasive, combination of writing genre or student choice, and nonidentifiable), and (h) environment in which treatment was delivered (general education classroom, self-contained special education classroom—students spend more than 60% of the day in the classroom, pull-out, or resource classroom—student spends less than 60% of the day in the classroom, or classroom for ELLs).

The eight study quality indicators (taken from Gersten et al., 2005) were (a) type of experimental design (experiment with random assignment and correct unit of analysis = score of 1.0; experiment with random assignment and incorrect unit of analysis = score of .75; quasi-experiment with correct unit of analysis = score of .50; or quasi-experiment with incorrect unit of analysis = score of .25), (b) ceiling or floor effects for measures (if the mean for a measure for any condition was more than one standard deviation away from the highest score of the measure and less than one standard deviation away from the lowest score possible = score of 1.0; if these conditions were not met = score of 0), (c) description of the control group (traditional approach or a district or school curriculum described and applied = score of 1.0; activities not described = score of 0), (d) attrition (90% or more of students who began the study completed it = score of 1.0; if this condition was not met = score of 0), (e) equivalent attrition (if overall attrition 10% or less and attrition equivalent across conditions = score of 1.0; if these conditions were not met = score of 0), (f) treatment integrity (data showing that at least 70% or more of the treatment delivered as intended = score of 1.0; lack of such data = score of 0), (g) teacher effects were controlled (teachers randomly assigned to conditions, teachers taught both conditions, or researchers matched the teachers = score of 1.0; no control for teacher effects = score of 0), and (h) reliability of writing quality measure (reliability was reported at .60 or higher = score of 1.0; no reliability score or score below .60 = 0). A total quality score was computed by summing the separate scores for the eight indicators.

Karin Sandmel coded each study for the descriptive and study quality indicators. A trained second rater independently scored a random sample of 33% of all studies. Interrater reliability between the two coders was .91.

Calculating Effect Sizes

For experimental studies, an ES was calculated for writing quality, motivation, or both by calculating the mean difference between the process writing and the control group (i.e., $\bar{Y}_{tx} - \bar{Y}_{ctrl}$) and dividing by the pooled standard deviation (i.e., d). For quasi-experimental studies, d was calculated by determining the mean difference between the treatment and control group (i.e., $\bar{Y}_{tx} - \bar{Y}_{ctrl}$) after first adjusting for pretest differences by subtracting the mean difference at pretest from posttest or estimating the posttest mean-difference statistic from covariate-adjusted posttest means. The adjusted posttest mean difference was standardized by the reported or estimated posttest standard deviation (What Works Clearinghouse, 2007). If standard deviations were not reported, they were estimated from summary statistics or by estimating residual sums of squares to compute a root mean squared error (RMSE; Shadish, Robinson, & Congxiao, 1999; Smith, Glass, & Miller, 1980). All computed effects were adjusted for small-sample size bias (Hedges, 1982).

As noted previously, measures of writing quality take into account factors such as ideation, organization, vocabulary, sentence structure, and voice. For holistic measures, all of these factors are considered simultaneously when assigning a single score. For analytic measures, a score is assigned to each factor separately. If a holistic score was available, we calculated the ES with this measure. If holistic and analytic scores were available, only the holistic score was used. If just an analytic scale was available, we first calculated an ES for each attribute separately, and then averaged these separate ES to obtain a global measure of writing quality (similar to a holistic score). For the most part, the holistic and analytic measures used in the studies reviewed here concentrated on the attributes of writing quality described previously.

For two studies (Gauntlett, 1978; Pritchard & Marshall, 1994), the population samples were large and could potentially influence the direction of the average ES. These two population samples were winsorized using the Tukey method. A box plot was created to look at the distribution of the ES. The interquartile range was calculated by subtracting the 25th percentile value from the 75th percentile value. This interquartile range was then multiplied by 1.5. If an ES was greater than 1.5 times the interquartile range plus the 75th percentile value or less than 1.5 times the interquartile range subtracted from the 25th percentile value, the ES was winsorized so that it was equivalent to the one of the two obtained values just described (i.e., the value it was closest to). In addition, the ES for writing quality for one study (Kelley, 1984) was almost 5 times the size of the interquartile range. Consequently, this ES was winsorized using the previous formula. All ES were calculated separately by Steve Graham and Karin Sandmel. Any disagreements between the two scorers were resolved. This was only necessary in 12% of the cases ($n = 4$).

Statistical Analysis for Effect Sizes

Our meta-analysis employed a weighted random-effects model. A separate weighted effect and confidence interval was calculated for writing quality for students in general education classrooms as well as struggling or at-risk writers. A separate weighted effect and confidence interval was also calculated for motivation. Weighted ES were computed by multiplying each ES by its inverse variance. It should be noted that when a confidence interval does not intersect zero, then the average weighted ES is significantly greater than no effect. A random-effects model was applied, as it allows generalizability to studies not included in this meta-analysis (Lipsey & Wilson, 2001). Although great care was undertaken to locate all studies, it was possible that some studies were missed, making a random-effects model preferable.

For each average weighted ES calculated, we conducted a test of homogeneity (using a fixed-effects model) to determine if the various ES weighted and averaged together in a treatment estimated the same population ES. We further conducted a moderator analyses with writing quality for students in the general education setting (there were not enough ES for writing quality for students who struggle with writing or the motivation measure to do this) to determine if variability in effects were related to identifiable differences between studies (e.g., grade level). Using a random-effects model (Lipsey & Wilson, 2002), ES were grouped into two mutually exclusive categories (i.e., ES calculated from studies where professional development was provided vs. studies where no training was provided), and the homogeneity of ES within each category was tested, as was the difference between the levels of the two mutually exclusive categories (i.e., the independent variable). Preplanned contrasts focused on grade, reliability of the writing quality measure, professional development, genre tested, and study quality. The statistical package used to conduct these analyses was MetaWin (Version 2; Rosenberg, Adams, & Gurevitch, 2000).

Results

Description and Quality of Studies

We located 29 studies that met our inclusion criteria (see Table 1). Most of these studies ($n = 24$) were conducted with typical students in general education classes (7,865 students). All but one of these studies assessed the impact of the process writing approach on quality of writing, with six studies assessing its effect on motivation. An additional five studies were conducted with struggling or at-risk writers (285 students). This included four studies that involved students with disabilities (Clippard & Nicaise, 1998; Croes, 1990; Curry, 1997; Weiss, 1992) and one investigation with ELL students (Green, 1991). All of these studies assessed writing quality, and one of them also assessed motivation (Clippard & Nicaise, 1998).

Almost one half of the studies were conducted exclusively with elementary students ($n = 14$), 21% with high school students ($n = 6$), 14% with middle school students ($m = 4$), and 17% with students at multiple levels ($n = 5$). All of the studies conducted with struggling or at-risk writers ($n = 5$) involved children in the elementary grades (see Table 1). In 55% of the studies, teachers were taught how to apply the process writing

Table 1

Studies, Population, Grades, Sample Size (SS), Genre, Professional Development, Publication Type, Quality, and Attitude Effect Sizes (ESs)

Study	SS	Grades	n	Genre	Professional Development	Publication	ES Quality	ES Attitude
Adams, 1971	GE	hs	135	?	N	D	0.45	−0.27
Alloway, 1979	GE	ms/hs	225	?	Y	C	0.57	—
Beachem, 1984	GE	ele	87	C/SC	N	D	0.62	—
Clippard, 1998	SE	ele	27	C/SC	Y	J	0.39	0.86
Croes, 1990	SE	ele	157	N	Y	D	0.34	—
Curry, 1997	SE	ele	45	N	Y	D	0.41	—
Dougans, 1993	GE	ele	86	E	N	D	0.25	—
Eads, 1989	GE	ele/ms/hs	502	C/SC	Y	D	0.22	—
Ewing, 1992	GE	ms	235	P	Y	D	−0.04	—
Fleury, 1988	GE	es	74	?	Y	D	0.34	—
Ganong, 1974	GE	hs	135	?	N	D	0.06	—
Gauntlett, 1978	GE	hs	791	?	N	D	0.05	—
Green, 1991	ELL	ele	32	E	N	D	−0.54	—
Hamilton, 1992	GE	ele	124	N	N	D	0.77	—
Hansen, 1985	GE	ele	205	C/SC	N	D	0.82	—
Hayes, 1984	GE	ms	70	C/SC	N	D	0.11	—
Kelley, 1984	GE	ms	101	N	N	D	1.04	—
Marker, 2000	GE	ele	46	?	Y	D	0.09	—
Moore, 1983	GE	hs	40	C/SC	N	D	0.28	—
Olson & DiStefano, 1980	GE	ms	201	E	Y	J	0.40	—
Pantier, 1999	GE	ele	29	N	N	D	−0.24	0.17
Pollington, 1999	GE	ele	130		Y	D	—	0.37
Pritchard, 1987	GE	ele/ms/hs	383	?	Y	J	0.38	—
Pritchard & Marshall, 1994	GE	ele/ms/hs	3919	E	Y	J	0.45	—
Reimer, 2001	GE	hs	60	E	Y	D	−0.09	—
Roberts, 2002	GE	ele/ms/hs	132	E	Y	D	0.37	0.16
Scannella, 1982	GE	hs	95	E	Y	D	0.35	0.27
Umbach, 1990	GE	ele	60	C/SC	Y	D	0.07	—
Weiss, 1992	SE	ele	24	?	N	D	0.89	—

Note. GE = general education; SE = special education; ELL = English language learners; ele = elementary school; ms = middle school; hs = high school; C/SC = combination of genres or student choice; E = expository writing; N = narrative writing; P = persuasive writing; ? = unknown genre; Y = yes, participated in professional development; N = no, did not participate in professional development; D = dissertation; J = journal article.

approach ($n = 16$), with relatively similar percentages for students in general classes and for struggling or at-risk writers. When researchers reported length of professional development ($n = 9$), it ranged from 2 to 40 days. Length of the process writing treatment for students ranged from 3 to 45 weeks in general education, and from 8 to 40 weeks for struggling or at-risk writers. Writing genres emphasized in treatment varied from 25% of studies in which a combination of genres or self-selection were emphasized ($n = 7$), 25% of studies focusing on expository writing ($n = 7$), 18% concentrating on narrative ($n = 5$), and 4% on persuasive writing ($n = 1$). Writing genre was not identified in 29% of the investigations ($n = 8$).

All of the studies included in this meta-analysis were selected so that the following quality indicator was present: Students in the process writing condition were compared to students in a control or comparison condition. Only three studies involved random assignment, with the researchers conducting statistical analysis using the correct unit of assignment. In three additional studies, teachers were randomly assigned to treatments, but student-level data were analyzed. Thus, 90% of all studies were quasi-experimental.

Overall, the quality of studies was not strong, but also not that dissimilar from the quality of writing intervention studies reviewed by Graham and Perin (2007). For the eight quality indicators assessed (see Table 2), only 45% were evident for studies involving students in general education classes (quality score range = 1.25–7.25), whereas 58% were met for studies with struggling or at-risk writers (quality score range = 2.5–6.25). For all 29 studies, four of the quality indicators were met in the typical study: writing quality was reliably assessed (72% of studies; $n = 21$); attrition was equivalent across groups (62% of studies; $n = 20$), control condition was described (62% of studies; $n = 20$); attrition was less than 10% (62% of studies; $n = 18$), and no ceiling or floor effects for measures were evident (52% of studies;

$n = 15$). However, teacher effects were controlled in only 34% of studies ($n = 10$), random assignment with the correct unit of analysis occurred in just 10% of studies ($n = 3$), and researchers provided evidence that the treatment was delivered as intended in just 7% of all studies ($n = 2$).

Does Process Writing Improve Writing Quality for Students in General Education Classes?

As expected, the process approach to writing instruction improved the overall quality of writing produced by students in general education classes. The mean average weighted ES computed with a random-effects model was 0.34. This was statistically different than no effect, as the confidence interval did not cross zero (confidence interval ranged from .22 to .47). Eighty-three percent of the comparisons resulted in a positive effect for the process writing approach. ES varied substantially, $Q(22) = 87.90$, $p < .001$, indicating that the studies were not from a single population of studies (see Table 1 for specific ES).

Does Process Writing Improve Writing Quality for Struggling and At-Risk Writers?

The process approach to writing instruction did not improve struggling or at-risk students' overall writing quality. Although the average weighted ES was 0.29, this average weighted effect did not statistically differ from no effect, as the confidence interval crossed zero (the confidence interval ranged from –0.24 to 0.81). Nevertheless, the ES appeared to be from a single population, as the test for homogeneity was not statistically significant, $Q(4) = 7.62$, $p = .11$.

Is Variation in Writing Quality Effects Related to Professional Development, Grade, Scoring Reliability, Genre Assessed, or Study Quality?

As noted previously, ES for writing quality varied considerably for students in general education classes. Consequently, we examined if specific study features moderated

Table 2

Total Quality Score and Percentage of Studies in Which Quality Indicator Was Present, by Treatment

Treatment	Total Quality Score			Assignment (Random) (%)	Attrition Above 90% (%)	Mortality Equivalent (%)	Ceiling or Floor (%)	Control Type (%)	Treatment Fidelity (%)	Teacher Effects (%)	Interrater Reliability (%)
	M	*SD*	*n*								
Process writing (general classes)	3.95	1.64	24	12.5	58.3	66.7	45.8	62.5	04.2	33.3	75.0
Process writing (struggling or at-risk writers)	4.70	1.59	5	0.0	80.0	80.0	80.0	100.0	20.0	40.0	60.0

average weighted ES and accounted for excess variability. None of the preplanned comparisons was statistically significant. Grade level did not moderate ES (Grades 1–6 ES = 0.37; Grades 7–12 ES = 0.31), Q(between) = 0.31, p = .58; nor did the establishment of scoring reliability for the quality measure (reliability established ES = .36; reliability not established ES = .26), Q(between) = 0.43, p = .51; nor did professional development (professional development ES = .28; no professional development ES = .42), Q(between) = 1.05, p = .31. We also examined if type of writing moderated ES. This involved four categories of writing: expository (expository or persuasive; n = 6), combination of genres or self-selection (n = 6), narrative (n = 3), and writing genre not specified (n = 7). Genre of writing did not account for excess variability in ES (expository ES = 0.24; combination or self-selection ES = 0.37; narrative ES = 0.73; not specified ES = 0.27), Q(between) = 7.29, p = .06.

It is interesting to note that studies of the highest quality yielded a slightly lower average weighted ES than did studies of lower quality. For the three experimental studies (i.e., random assignment with the correct unit of analysis), the average weighted ES was 0.29, whereas it was 0.35 for the 20 quasi-experimental studies. Likewise, for the 11 studies that met one half or more of the quality indicators, the average weighted ES was 0.33. For the remaining 12 studies, it was 0.35. Study quality did not moderate ES for writing quality; the Q statistic for the regression model was .08 and not statistically significant, $Q(1)$ = 0.08, $\chi^2(23)$ = 0.78, p = ns.

Does Process Writing Enhance Motivation?

Contrary to expectations, the process writing approach did not enhance students' motivation. The average weighted ES was 0.19, and it was not statistically different from no effect, as the confidence interval crossed zero (the confidence interval ranged from −.16 to .53). In addition, the ES appeared to be from a single population, as the test for homogeneity was not statistically significant, $Q(5)$ = 10.35, p = .07.

Discussion

The primary purpose of this meta-analysis was to determine if the process approach to writing is an effective method for teaching writing to students in Grades 1–12. This is an especially important question, as the process writing approach is likely to play a prominent role in any efforts to reform writing instruction in the United States. It is already a relatively popular approach to writing instruction (Cutler & Graham, 2008; Kiuhara et al., 2009), with a substantial infrastructure for making it even more widely available, ranging from the work of the National Writing Project (Nagin, 2006) to commercial materials developed by advocates such as Lucy Calkins (e.g., Calkins & Colleagues, 2008). Moreover, the findings from two previous meta-analyses of experimental and quasi-experimental research (Graham & Perin, 2007; Hillocks, 1986) provided evidence that this approach improves the writing of students in Grades 4–12.

This review builds on the two previous meta-analyses by extending the range of studies analyzed. This includes studies conducted with primary-grade children (Grades 1–3), investigations with struggling or at-risk writers at any grade level, and studies assessing the impact of process writing on student motivation. In contrast with prior reviews, studies did not have to establish reliability of outcome measures to be included, but a pretest was required for all quasi-experimental studies. This allowed us to provide a more general and less biased answer to the previous question.

Based on the available scientific evidence from experimental and quasi-experimental intervention studies, the answer to our question about the effectiveness of the process writing approach depends on who is assessed and on what outcome. As expected, when studies were conducted in general education classrooms, students receiving process writing instruction were better writers at the end of the experiment than were students in the control condition. The average weighted ES of 0.34 for writing quality in 24 studies was statistically greater than no effect. This was almost identical to the ES of 0.32 reported by Graham and Perin (2007), even though there was only a 59% overlap in the studies used to compute these two summary statistics. This was due to us including nine investigations not analyzed in prior reviews (e.g., ones without established reliability), and excluding seven studies from it (e.g., no pretest provided for quasi-experimental studies).

Interpretation of this positive effect must be tempered by five factors. First, the obtained effect is based on comparisons to classes in which students were mainly taught writing skills or the writing instruction received by control students was not described (39%). Thus, no claims can be made about the effectiveness of process writing in comparison to other types of writing treatments. Second, definitions of process writing have changed over time (Stotsky, 1988), and there is presently some disagreement as to what constitutes a process approach (see Pritchard & Honeycutt, 2006). We applied the same definition as Graham and Perin (2007), and any conclusions about the effectiveness of process writing must be made in reference to this characterization.

Third, the obtained ES may be inflated due to Hawthorne effects. For example, professional development was provided to process writing teachers in 12 of the 23 studies (52%). Such training was not provided to teachers in the control classrooms. It is possible that process writing teachers in these studies were made to feel special, enhancing their effort and performance. However, it is worth noting that the data from this review are not consistent with this hypothesis, as the average weighted ES for studies with and without professional development did not differ statistically. Fourth, the overall quality of these 24 studies was not strong. On average, each study met slightly less than one half (45%) of the eight quality indicators assessed. This raises concerns about the confidence that can be placed in the claim that the process writing approach improves the writing of students in typical classrooms. These concerns are alleviated somewhat by the finding that the average weighted ES for higher quality studies was generally similar to the average weighted ES for lower quality studies.

The fifth factor that must be taken into consideration when interpreting the obtained effect is magnitude. A widely used rule of thumb is that an ES between 0.20 and 0.49 is a positive but small effect. Lipsey and Wilson (2001) argued against using such a formulaic approach, as it is important to interpret an ES within the context of a given field. This better contextualizes the magnitude of an ES.

To contextualize the findings from the present study, we draw on Graham and Perin (2007). They obtained average weighted ES for writing quality for 10 other practices for teaching writing, with average weighted ES for practices ranging from −.32 to .82. Within this context, the magnitude of the average weighted ES for the process writing approach fares relatively well when considered against teaching writing through inquiry (ES = 0.32), using prewriting strategies to gain and organize ideas for writing (ES = 0.32), and studying and emulating models of writing (ES = 0.25) or traditional grammar instruction (ES = −0.32). However, it fares less well when considered against strategy instruction (ES = 0.82); summary writing instruction (ES = 0.82); collaborative planning, drafting, and revising (ES = 0.75); goal setting (ES = 0.70); word processing (ES = 0.50); and sentence combining (ES = 0.50). Viewed within this context, the process approach to writing instruction is an effective, but not particularly powerful approach for teaching writing to students in general education classrooms.

When the focus of the analysis narrows to just weaker writers, the evidence from this meta-analysis does not support the claim that the process writing approach is an effective method for improving quality of writing. The average weighted ES in five studies was 0.29, and not statistically different than zero. This finding is at odds with several case studies (Cousin et al., 1993; Foulger & Jimenez-Silva, 2007; Zaragoza & Vaughn, 1992; Zucker, 1993), where the process writing approach reportedly improved struggling writers' compositions. Additional research is needed to more fully examine if process writing is an effective approach to teaching weaker writers. This research needs to expand the age and type of writers tested. The five studies analyzed here concentrated just on elementary grade students, and participants were either students with learning disabilities (four studies) or ELLs (one study).

The findings from this meta-analysis were also not supportive of the process writing approach when the focus shifted from writing quality to motivation. The average weighted ES for motivation in six studies was 0.19, and this was not statistically different from zero. Thus, the available evidence from experimental and quasi-experimental research does not support the contention that the process approach to writing enhances students' motivation, at least when compared with more traditional and undefined writing interventions. We anticipated positive motivational effects, as this approach includes a variety of instructional components thought to enhance motivation (Wigfield, 1994), including peer collaboration, personal responsibility, and creation of a positive learning environment. It should be noted that motivation is difficult to measure, and the methods used to assess it differed from one study to the next. This may have contributed to the obtained outcome. Additional research is needed to assess possible motivational effects of process writing.

Contrary to expectations, we did not find a statistically significant relationship between variability in writing quality ES and study characteristics, such as receiving professional development, grade level of students (1–6 vs. 7–12), or establishing reliability of the outcome measure. Likewise, genre assessed and study quality did not account for excess variability in ES (as predicted). The finding that scoring reliability was not associated with magnitude of ES provides some support for our decision to include studies where reliability for writing quality was and was not established. Previous reviews (Graham & Perim, 2007; Hillocks, 1986) excluded studies when reliability was absent. However, the first two findings were unanticipated, as each (professional development and grade) had accounted for significant variance in process writing effects in Graham and Perin (2007). The reasons for the obtained differences between this meta-analysis and the previous one are unclear, but it is likely due, at least in part, to differences in the criteria for including and excluding studies.

We indicated previously that the process writing approach is likely to play a significant role in any serious effort to reform writing instruction in the United States. Even if writing remains mostly absent from national reform efforts, it is likely that this approach will continue to play a key role in how writing is taught due to its popularity and the available infrastructure for promoting its implementation and continued use. If this is the case, this review raises an important concern. Although the process approach is effective in improving the writing of typical students, it is not a particularly powerful approach relative to other writing treatments, and its impact with those that are most vulnerable educationally, ELLs and children with learning disabilities, are unproven outside of a few case studies. Unfortunately, case studies do not provide the strongest evidence for establishing the value of an instructional practice, as the data presented is often selective and no attempt is usually made to rule out competing explanations (Graham, 2010).

We are not suggesting that the process approach to writing as it was characterized in this review be abandoned. First, we think that this is unlikely to happen. Second, there is much to like about the process approach. This includes its emphasis on the critical role of process in writing, collaboration, personal responsibility, authentic writing tasks, and a supportive learning environment. Instead, we suggest that advocates of process writing instruction integrate other effective writing practices into this approach. There is some empirical evidence that this is a fruitful avenue to pursue. For example, impressive improvements in the writing of average and struggling writers were obtained when the amount of explicit and systematic instruction provided in process writing classrooms was increased (Curry, 1997; Danoff, Graham, & Harris, 1993; MacArthur, Schwartz, & Graham, 1991). These studies involved teaching strategies for planning and revising. Other studies are needed to determine if incorporating other evidence-based practices, such as sentence combining (Graham & Perin, 2007) or spelling and handwriting instruction (Graham, 2010), into the process writing instruction further enhances the power of this approach.

Our recommendation that the process writing approach needs to undergo experimentation and change is not a radical idea. In fact, process writing has evolved since the 1980s, when pioneers such as Graves (1983) and Calkins (1983) began promoting this method for teaching writing (Pritchard & Honeycutt, 2006) .Groups such as the National Writing Project have also taken a flexible stance over time, recommending the use of evidence-based practices such as inquiry learning and sentence combining (Hillocks, 1986) as part of the process writing approach (Nagin, 2006). Perhaps the greatest experimentation takes place in schools, where more teachers combine process writing and traditional skills instruction together than just teach the process writing approach alone (Cutler & Graham, 2008; Graham, Harris, Fink, & MacArthur, 2002). High-quality research is needed to examine the effectiveness of the most promising hybrids.

REFERENCES

References marked with an asterisk (*) indicate studies included in the meta-analysis

Achieve, Inc. (2005). *Rising to the challenge: Are high school graduates prepared for college and work?* Washington, DC: Author.

*Adams, V. A. (1971). *A study of the effects of two methods of teaching composition to twelfth graders* (Unpublished doctoral dissertation). University of Illinois, Champaign-Urbana, IL.

*Alloway, E., Carroll, J., Emig, J., King, B., Marcotrigiano, I., Smith, J., & Spicer, W. (1979). *The New Jersey Writing Project*. New Brunswick, NJ: Rutgers University, Educational Testing Program Service, and Nineteen New Jersey Public School Districts.

Atwell, N. (1987). *In the middle: Reading, writing, and learning from adolescents.* Portsmouth, NH: Heinemann.

Baines, L., Baines, C., Stanley, G., & Kunkel, A. (1999). Losing the product in the process. *English Journal, 88*, 67–72.

Bangert-Drowns, R. (1993). The word processor as an instructional tool: A meta-analysis of word processing in writing instruction. *Review of Educational Research, 63*, 69–93.

Bates, L., Breslow, N., & Hupert, N. (2009). *Five states' efforts to improve adolescent literacy.* Washington, DC: Institute of Education Sciences.

*Beachem, M. T. (1984). *An investigation of two writing process interventions on the rhetorical effectiveness of sixth grade writers* (Unpublished doctoral dissertation). Rutgers, the State University of New Jersey, New Brunswick, NJ.

Breetvelt, I., Van den Bergh, H., & Rijlaarsdam, G. (1994). Relations between writing processes and text quality: When and how. *Cognition and Instruction, 12*, 103–123.

Breetvelt, I., Van den Bergh, H., & Rijlaarsdam, G. (1996). Rereading and generating and their relation to text quality: An application of mutilevel analysis on writing process data. In G. Rijlaarsdam, H. Van den Bergh, & M. Couzjin (Eds.), *Theories, models and methodologies on writing research* (pp. 10–21). Amsterdam, The Netherlands: Amsterdam University Press.

Calkins, L. (1983). *Lesson from a child: On the teaching and learning of writing.* Portsmouth, NH: Heinemann.

Calkins, L., & Colleagues (2008). *Units of study for primary writing: A yearlong curriculum (K–2).* Portsmouth, NH: Heinemann.

*Clippard, D., & Nicaise, M. (1998). Efficacy of writers' workshop for students with significant writing deficits. *Journal of Research in Childhood Education, 13*, 7–26.

Cousin, P., Aragon, E., & Rojas, R. (1993). Creating new conversations about literacy: Working with special needs students in a middle-school classroom. *Learning Disability Quarterly, 16*, 282–298.

*Croes, M. J. (1990). *The efficacy of employing a writing process approach for the instruction of language arts with learning disabled elementary students* (Unpublished doctoral dissertation). Baylor University, Waco, TX.

*Curry, K. A. (1997). *A comparison of the writing products of students with learning disabilities in inclusive and resource room settings using different writing approaches* (Unpublished doctoral dissertation). Florida Atlantic University, Boca Raton, FL.

Cutler, L., & Graham, S. (2008). Primary grade writing instruction: A national survey. *Journal of Educational Psychology, 100*, 907–919.

Danoff, B., Harris, K. R., & Graham, S. (1993). Incorporating strategy instruction within the writing process in the regular classroom: Effects on the writing of students with and without learning disabilities. *Journal of Reading Behavior, 25*, 295–322.

Diederich, P. (1966). How to measure growth in writing ability. *English Journal, 55*, 435–449.

*Dougans, J. Y. (1993). *Teaching writing to fifth-grade children: The process/conference approach versus the traditional method* (Unpublished doctoral dissertation). Temple University, Philadelphia, PA.

*Eads, V. A. (1989). *A study of the effects of teacher training in writing on students' writing abilities* (Unpublished doctoral dissertation). Baylor University, Waco, TX.

*Ewing, S. C. (1992). *The effects of time and instruction on writing performance of eighth-grade students in writing assessment situations* (Unpublished doctoral dissertation). Purdue University, West Lafayette, IN.

*Fleury, B. (1988). *Cumulative editing writing instruction: Implications for staff development* (Unpublished doctoral dissertation). Northern Arizona University, Flagstaff, AZ.

Foulger, T., & Jimenez-Silva, M. (2007). Enhancing the writing development of English language learners: Teacher perceptions of common technology in project-based learning. *Journal of Research in Childhood Education, 22*, 109–124.

Fox, D., & Suhor, C. (1986). Limitations of free writing. *English Journal, 75*, 34–36.

Gamelin, Y. M. A. (1996). *The effects of Cognitive Strategy Instruction in Writing (CSIW) on the writing skills of severely learning disabled students and their peers in an inclusive classroom* (Unpublished master's thesis). Simon Fraser University, Burnaby, British Columbia, Canada.

*Ganong, F. L. (1974). *Teaching writing through the use of a program based on the work of Donald M. Murray* (Unpublished doctoral dissertation). Boston University, Boston, MA.

*Gauntlett, J. F. (1978). *Project WRITE and its effect on the writing of high school students* (Unpublished doctoral dissertation). Northern Arizona University, Flagstaff, AZ.

Gersten, R., Fuchs, L., Compton, D., Coyne, M., Greenwood, C., & Innocenti, M. (2005). Quality indications for group experimental and quasi-experimental research in special education. *Exceptional Children, 71*, 149–164.

Goldring, A., Russell, M., & Cook, A. (2003). The effects of computers on student writing: A meta-analysis of studies from 1992–2002. *Journal of Technology, Learning, and Assessment, 2*, 1–51.

Graham, S. (2006). Writing. In P. Alexander & P. Winne (Eds.), *Handbook of Educational psychology* (pp. 457–478). Mahwah, NJ: Earlbaum.

Graham, S. (2010). Teaching writing. In P. Hogan (Ed.), *Cambridge encyclopedia of language sciences* (pp. 848–851). Cambridge, UK: Cambridge University Press.

Graham, S., & Harris, K. R. (1997). Whole language and process writing: Does one approach fit all? In J. Lloyd, E. Kameenui, & D. Chard (Eds.), *Issues in educating students with disabilities* (pp. 239–258). Hillsdale, NJ: Erlbaum.

Graham, S., Harris, K. R., Fink, B., & MacArthur, C. (2002). Primary grade teachers' theoretical orientations concerning writing instruction: Construct validation and a nationwide survey. *Contemporary Educational Psychology, 27*, 147–166.

Graham, S., & Perin, D. (2007). A meta-analysis of writing instruction for adolescent students. *Journal of Educational Psychology, 99*, 445–476.

Graves, D. (1983). *Writing: Teachers and children at work.* Exeter, NH: Heinemann.

*Green, L. C. (1991). *The effects of word processing and a process approach to writing on the reading and writing achievement, revision and editing strategies, and attitudes towards writing of third-grade Mexican American students* (Unpublished doctoral dissertation). University of Texas at Austin, Austin, TX.

Greene, J. (2000). *The cost of remedial education: How much Michigan pays when students fail to learn basic skills.* Midland, MI: Mackinac Center for Public Policy.

Greenwald, E., Persky, H., Ambell, J., & Mazzeo, J. (1999). *National assessment of Educational progress: 1998 report card for the nation and the states.* Washington, DC: U.S. Department of Education.

*Hamilton, A. C. (1992). *Performance assessment of personal correspondence on the development of written language use and functions in traditional and process writing second-grade classrooms* (Unpublished doctoral dissertation). University of Alabama, Birmingham, AL.

Hammill, D. D., & Larsen, S. (1996). *Test of written language–3.* Austin, TX: Pro-Ed.

*Hansen, T. L. (1989). *A comparison of the effects of two process writing programs and a traditional program on the writing development of first-grade children* (Unpublished doctoral dissertation). University of South Dakota, Vermillion, SD.

*Hayes, B. L. (1984). *The effects of implementing process writing into a seventh grade English curriculum*

(Unpublished doctoral dissertation). Delta State University, Cleveland, MS.

Hedges, L. V. (1982). Estimation of effect size from a series of independent experiments. *Psychological Bulletin, 92,* 490–499.

Herbison, P., Hay-Smith, J., & Gillespie, W. (2006). Adjustment of meta-analyses on the basis of quality scores should be abandoned. *Journal of Clinical Epidemiology, 59,* 1249–1256.

Hillocks, G. (1986). *Research on written composition: New directions for teaching.* Urbana, IL: National Council of Teachers of English.

*Kelley, K. R. (1984) *The effect of writing instruction on reading comprehension and story writing ability* (Unpublished doctoral dissertation). University of Pittsburgh, Pittsburgh, PA.

Kiuhara, S., Graham, S., & Hawken, L. (2009). Teaching writing to high school students: A national survey. *Journal of Educational Psychology, 101,* 136–160.

Lipsey, M., & Wilson, D. (2001). *Practical meta-analysis.* Thousand Oaks, CA: Sage.

MacArthur, C., Schwartz, S., & Graham, S. (1991). Effects of a reciprocal peer revision strategy in special education classrooms. *Learning Disability Research and Practice, 6,* 201–210.

Maehr, M., & Midgley, C. (1991). Enhancing student motivation: A schoolwide approach. *Educational Psychologist, 26,* 399–427.

*Marker, E. S. (2000). *The impact of the writer's conference on the writing achievement of at-risk fourth-grade students* (Unpublished doctoral dissertation). Widener University, Chester, PA.

*Moore, M. A. (1987). *The effect of word processing technology in a developmental writing program on writing quality, attitude towards composing, and revision strategies of fourth and fifth grade students* (Unpublished doctoral dissertation). University of South Florida, Tampa, FL.

Moye, M. J. (1993). *The impact of a cognitive strategy on students' composing skills* (Unpublished doctoral dissertation). College of William and Mary, Williamsburg, VA.

Nagin, C. (2006). *Because writing matters: Improving student writing in our schools.* San Francisco, CA: Jossey-Bass.

National Commission on Writing. (2003). *The neglected R: The need for a writing revolution.* New York, NY: CollegeBoard.

*Olson, M. C., & DiStefano, P. (1980). Describing and testing the effectiveness of a contemporary model for in-service education in teaching composition. *Engineering Education, 12,* 69–76.

*Pantier, T. F. (1999). *A comparison of writing performance of fifth-grade students using the process writing approach and the Shurley method* (Unpublished

doctoral dissertation). Oklahoma State University, Stillwater, OK.

Persky, H. R., Daane, M. C., & Jin, Y. (2003). *The nation's report card: Writing 2002* (NCES 2003-529). Washington, DC: U.S. Department of Education, Institute of Education Sciences, National Center for Education Statistics.

Phye, G., Robinson, D., & Levin, J. (Eds.). (2005). *Empirical methods for evaluating educational interventions.* San Diego, CA: Elsevier.

*Pollington, M. F. (1999). *Intermediate grade writers self-perception: A comparison of the effects of writing workshop and traditional instruction* (Unpublished doctoral dissertation). Brigham Young University, Provo, UT.

*Pritchard, R. J. (1987). Effects on student writing of teacher training in the National Writing Project Model. *Written Communication, 4,* 51–67.

Pritchard, R. J., & Honeycutt, J. (2006). Process writing. In C. MacArthur, S. Graham, & J. Fitzgerald (Eds.), *Handbook of Writing Research* (pp. 275–290). New York, NY: Guilford.

*Pritchard, R. J., & Marshall, J. C. (1994). Evaluation of a tiered model for staff development in writing. *Research in the Teaching of English, 28,* 259–285.

*Reimer, M. (2001). *The effect of a traditional, a process writing, and a combined talking and writing instructional approach on the quality of secondary English students' written response* (Unpublished master's thesis). University of Manitoba, Winnipeg, Manitoba, Canada.

Rijlaarsdam, G., & Van den Bergh, H. (2006). Writing process theory: A functional dynamic approach. In C. MacArthur, S. Graham, & J. Fitzgerald (Eds.), *Handbook of writing research* (pp. 41–53). New York, NY: Guilford.

*Roberts, C. A. (2002). *The influence of teachers' professional development at the Tampa Bay Area Writing Project on student writing performance* (Unpublished doctoral dissertation). University of South Florida, Tampa, FL.

Rogers, L., & Graham, S. (2008). A meta-analysis of single subject design writing intervention research. *Journal of Educational Psychology, 100,* 879–906.

Rosenberg, M., Adams, D., & Gurevitch, J. (2000). *MetaWin: Statistical software for meta-analysis* (Version 2). Sunderland, MA: Sinauer Ass.

Salahu-Din, D., Persky, H., & Miller, J. (2008). *The Nation's Report Card: Writing 2007* (NCES 2008–468). Washington, DC: U.S. Department of Education, Institute of Education Science, National Center for Education Statistics.

*Scannella, A. M. (1982). *A writing-as-process model as a means for improving compositions and attitudes toward composition in the high school* (Unpublished doctoral dissertation). Rutgers, the State University of New Jersey, New Brunswick, NJ.

Shadish, W. R., Robinson, L., & Congxiao, L. (1999). *ES: A computer program for effect size calculation.* Memphis, TN: University of Memphis.

Smith, M. L., Glass, G. V., & Miller, T. I. (1980). *The benefits of psychotherapy.* Baltimore, MD: Johns Hopkins University Press.

Stotsky, S. G. (1988). Commentary. *Research in the Teaching of English, 22,* 89–99.

Troia, G., & Graham, S. (2002). The effectiveness of a highly explicit, teacher-directed strategy instruction routine: Changing the writing performance of students with learning disabilities. *Journal of Learning Disabilities, 35,* 290–305.

*Umbach, B. T. (1990). *A comparison of two methods of teaching written language to low-performing fourth graders in two rural schools* (Unpublished doctoral dissertation). Auburn University, Auburn, AL.

Van den Bergh, H., & Rijlaarsdam, G. (1996). The dynamics of composing: Modeling writing process data. In C. Levy & S. Ransdell (Eds.), *The science of writing* (pp. 207–232). Mahwah, NJ: Erbaum.

*Weiss, D. H. (1992). *The effects of writing process instruction on the writing and reading performance of students with learning disabilities* (Unpublished doctoral dissertation). Florida International University, Miami, FL.

What Works Clearinghouse. (2007). *Technical details of WWC-conducted computations.* Retrieved from http://www.whatworks.ed.gov/reviewprocess/conducted_computations.pdf

Wienke, J. W. (1981). *Strategies for improving elementary school students' writing skills.* Retrieved from ERIC database. (ED209679)

Wigfield, A. (1994). The role of children's achievement values in the self-regulation of their learning outcomes. In. D. Schunk & B. Zimmerman (Eds.), *Self-regulation of learning and performance: Issues and educational applications* (pp. 101–124). Hillsdale, NJ: LEA.

Yeh, S. (1998). Empowering education: Teaching argumentative writing to cultural minority middle-school students. *Research in the Teaching of English, 33,* 49–48.

Zaragoza, N., & Vaughn, S. (1992). The effects of process writing instruction on three 2nd-grade students with different achievement profiles. *Learning Disabilities Research and Practice, 7,* 184–193.

Zucker, C. (1993). Using whole language with students who have language and learning disabilities. *Reading Teacher, 46,* 660–670.

AUTHORS NOTE

Steve Graham is the Currey-Ingram Professor of Special Education and Literacy at Vanderbilt University. His research interests include writing development, writing instruction, and writing-to-reading connections.

Karin Sandmel is a doctoral student at Vanderbilt University in the Department of Special Education. Her interests involve writing and students who are second-language learners.

CHAPTER FOUR

Using Search Engines and Available Literature Reviews

PROBLEMS OF PRACTICE *in this chapter*

- Are charter schools more effective than regular public schools?
- What can be done to help disadvantaged students graduate from high school and enroll in college?
- What can be done to help students who are aggressive or antisocial?
- How can mathematics be taught using online instruction?
- Is it beneficial to give students tangible rewards for good grades?

IMPORTANT *Ideas*

1. A search engine typically includes thousands of bibliographic citations in its database and has features that make it easy for you to identify the citations most relevant to your research problem or problem of practice.
2. Several search engines are comprehensive, free of charge, and useful to educators: Google (for websites), ERIC (for any type of educational publication), and the Library of Congress Online Catalog (for books).
3. Many search engines are designed to help educators locate particular types of publications: bibliographies, book reviews, books, dissertations and theses, journal articles, and magazine and newspaper articles.
4. Maintaining a log of your search engine use will help you avoid repeating a search needlessly and enable you to accurately describe your search process when reporting your literature review.
5. You can save relevant bibliographic citations by using features that the search engine provides or by using a citation manager.
6. Search engines like ERIC provide information about how to obtain copies of the actual publications that you have identified as relevant to your needs.
7. Free online journals about education are increasingly available.
8. You can use search engines to look for published literature reviews.
9. Published literature reviews can be found in encyclopedias, handbooks, yearbooks, journals, and periodic reports.

10. You cannot accept the findings of a published literature review at face value, but instead, you must evaluate the reviewer's credentials and search procedures, the quality of research evidence used to support each conclusion, and the process used to resolve inconsistent findings across the studies included in the review.

KEY TERMS

bibliographic citation

bibliographic index

citation manager

DOI

ERIC (Education Resources
 Information Center)

fugitive literature

keyword

online journal

search engine

THE PURPOSE OF SEARCH ENGINES

In Chapters 2 and 3, we introduced search engines and bibliographic databases as important aids in conducting a literature review. In this chapter, we explain how to use these resources. Also, we describe how you can search for literature reviews that are available on problems of practice of interest to you. An available literature review might be adequate for your needs, thereby saving you the time required to do your own.

The education literature is large. One of the main guides to this literature, called **ERIC (Education Resources Information Center)**, included 1.4 million bibliographic citations in its database as of early 2012. If you wish to conduct an efficient, effective search of this literature, you will need to learn a systematic search strategy.

A good starting point is to consider what is meant by the term *publication*. Books and journal articles clearly are publications, but how about newspaper articles, government reports, curriculum guides, test manuals, tables of statistical data about education, conference papers, and websites? In this chapter, we consider all of them to be publications that you might wish to identify for your literature review. The term *publication* conveys one of their important features, namely, that they are publicly available to various extents.

A published book from a large publisher that is available from a bookstore or website such as Amazon.com is clearly "publicly available." Other publications, such as out-of-print books that were published decades ago and in small quantities are still likely to be publicly available but more difficult to locate. Even a paper that was presented at a conference that did not publish its proceedings is potentially publicly available—if you can locate the authors and if they are willing to send you a copy. Publications like these are sometimes called **fugitive literature** because while they are not widely disseminated or easily obtained, they still exist and are part of the professional literature.

In this chapter, we explain how to search for publications of many different types and degrees of availability. We make reference to specific publications and also to bibliographic citations. A **bibliographic citation** consists of information about a particular publication, such as its author, title, year of publication, and an abstract summarizing the information in it. If you wish to examine the actual publication, the bibliographic citation might provide information about how to locate it.

Bibliographic Indexes and Search Engines

Until computers became widely available, **bibliographic indexes** (sometimes called *guides* or *indexes*) to the professional literature at a specific location, such as a library or archive, were available in the form of library card catalogs, books, or periodicals. They sometimes are called *hard-copy indexes*, because they have a physical entity.

Most hard-copy indexes have disappeared, and the information in them has been converted to electronic databases and search engines. As we explained in Chapter 3, a **search engine** is computer software that includes a list of entries (e.g., bibliographic citations, websites, addresses) and tools for searching through the entries to identify those that are relevant to the user. In this chapter, we are primarily concerned with search engines that have databases of bibliographic citations for publications relevant to education. Search engines typically are time-sensitive, meaning that there is only a short time lag, perhaps a few months or less, between the appearance of the publication and its incorporation into the search engine's database.

It is worth taking a moment to reflect on the wonderful nature of search engines and electronic databases. They enable us to identify relevant publications in a matter of minutes. Prior to their development, you would have to travel to a university library and spend many hours going through card catalogs and hard-copy indexes to find relevant publications, and you would be likely to miss some of them. Also, it would take many hours to find journals on bookshelves and make notes on relevant articles or make photocopies of them. Now, many journal articles can be obtained online in a few minutes, and, if you wish, you can get hard copies of them using a printer.

The skills that you acquire in using search engines and databases will serve you throughout your professional career, not just in completing a research project or a literature review. For example, if you are teaching and want to know how you might use tablet computers (e.g., the iPad) in your classroom, a search engine can help you find relevant information quickly.

In the following sections, we describe procedures for selecting and using a search engine. By following these procedures, you will be able to compile a list of publications that will provide a good foundation for your literature review.

SELECTING A USEFUL SEARCH ENGINE

ERIC might well be the only search engine you need to identify publications for your literature review. We make this statement because ERIC's home page (eric.ed.gov) describes ERIC as "the world's largest digital library of education literature." It is a free service funded by the U.S. government that can be easily accessed by your web browser (e.g., Internet Explorer, Safari, Firefox).

If you are not familiar with ERIC, we recommend that you take a few minutes to access the website and perform a basic search by entering any term of interest to you (e.g., "educational leadership," "classroom management"). Doing so will help you understand other sections of this chapter. Note that enclosing your ordered search terms in quotations marks ensures that your exact keyword phrase will be searched for as a whole and not picked apart by the search engine.

Before ERIC created its search engine, it indexed educational publications in hard-copy format. The indexes were updated periodically during the year and then cumulated into an annual volume. The indexes were of two types. Journal articles were indexed in *Current Index to Journals in Education* (*CIJE*), and all other reports were indexed in *Resources in Education* (*RIE*). You might still find these indexes on the shelves of some university libraries and school offices. However, all of the citations in these indexes, extending back to ERIC's inception in 1966, are now electronically filed in the ERIC database, which is much easier to use than the hard-copy indexes.

Some search engines require a subscription or fee. However, university libraries typically have a website that includes free access to a set of commercial search engines for their students, faculty, staff, and others. These search engines might be maintained by a commercial service, which organizes the search engines, including ERIC, in a particular way. Therefore, you might find some differences between a commercial search engine that you access directly through the company's website and the same search engine that you access through a university library or other service. Generally, the differences are minor.

In this chapter, we describe search engines in each of the following categories: (1) comprehensive; (2) bibliographies; (3) books; (4) dissertations and theses; (5) journal articles, papers, and reports; and (6) magazines and newspapers. Most of the citations in these lists generally are not for the search engines but rather for their website home pages. You will need to determine whether your university or other institution has access to the actual search engine. Additional search engines are described in two other chapters of this book: search engines for tests and measures in Chapter 5 and search engines for historical publications in Chapter 16.

With experience, you will identify the search engines that are most relevant to your professional needs. For us, personally, we rely most often on four search engines: Google (to identify relevant websites), ERIC (to identify a wide range of relevant publications, including journal articles), PsycINFO (to identify education publications in journals and other sources not included in ERIC's database), and the Library of Congress Online Catalog (to identify relevant books). With the exception of PsycINFO, these are free search engines, accessible via the Internet.

Comprehensive Search Engines for Websites

Google, Yahoo!, AltaVista, HotBot, MetaCrawler, and AOL Search are among the comprehensive search engines whose databases include a great many of the world's websites. You can use these search engines to identify websites that include databases of education literature by entering "literature review" and your topic as the keywords.

A **keyword** is a word or phrase that you enter in the appropriate search engine window to identify all citation entries (e.g., books, journals, websites) in its database containing that word or phrase. If you type quotation marks around a particular phrase (e.g., "literature search"), you will retrieve only citation entries that contain those two words together, in that order. You need to choose your keywords carefully because the search engine will only identify citation entries with that exact keyword. It will not identify citation entries that use synonyms or related terms for the keyword.

We used a combination of two keyword phrases—"educational technology" and "literature search"—to see which websites Google would retrieve from its database. It retrieved 290,000 websites, including the following:

- The Center for Comprehensive School Reform and Improvement (centerforcsri.org). We entered "technology" in its search window and obtained a list of 48 publications.
- Evaluation of Evidence-Based Practices in Online Learning: A Meta-Analysis and Review of Online Learning Studies (ed.gov/rschstat/eval/tech/evidence-based-practices/finalreport.pdf). The entire publication is available at the website and includes an extensive review of

the literature on online learning, including a recent meta-analysis of research studies comparing online instruction and face-to-face instruction.

Websites such as these two provide a good initial overview of publications and other resources in the field of educational technology.

Search Engine for Bibliographies

Researchers sometimes compile bibliographies on specialized topics in education. They can provide a good starting point for your own literature review. *Bibliographic Index Plus* was a search engine designed to help researchers find bibliographies, but it was discontinued in 2011. In its place, you can use a search engine like Google. Enter the topic of interest followed by the word "bibliography." This will help you identify bibliographies that are relevant to your research problem or problem of practice.

Search Engines for Book Reviews

Some of the publications you identify in your literature review are likely to be books. A review of a particular book can help you decide whether it is sufficiently relevant to take on the task of obtaining a copy. The following search engines are designed to help you determine whether reviews of your book are available.

- Book Review Index Online Plus. This database includes more than 5 million reviews of several million books. See gale.cengage.com/BRIOnline/ for more information.
- Education Review (edrev.asu.edu). This multilingual online journal contains reviews of books relating to educational research and practice. It is a free service.
- PsycCritiques (apa.org/psyccritiques). This full-text database includes reviews of books, films, videos, and software about psychology. Many of the reviews are about education-related publications.

Search Engines for Books

Books about education generally do not report original research, except for those that present extensive case studies, historical studies, and ethnographies (see Part Four). However, many education books are about research methodology and problems of practice in education. Also, many handbooks and encyclopedias include chapters synthesizing what is known about particular topics. The following search engines can help you identify these books.

- Books in Print. This search engine includes bibliographic data about more than four million books, audios, and videos. If you go to the home page of its publisher (bowker.com), you will find information about it and also more specialized search engines and hard-copy indexes, such as *El-Hi Textbooks and Serials in Print* and *Children's Books in Print*.
- Library of Congress Online Catalog (catalog2.loc.gov/). This website contains a comprehensive, searchable database of books, recordings, maps, and manuscripts. It is a free service of the U.S. government.

Search Engine for Dissertations and Theses

Reports of research studies conducted for a doctoral degree are called *dissertations*. At the master's degree level, these reports usually are called *theses*. Some students rewrite their dissertation or thesis for journal publication, but many do not. If you want to do a comprehensive review of the literature, you should consider searching for relevant dissertations. An exhaustive review would include theses as well. The following search engine or its hard-copy indexes can be used for this purpose.

- Proquest Dissertations & Theses (proquest.com). This database includes bibliographic citations for more than 2 million dissertations and theses from around the world. The vast majority of these citations also include a full-text version of the dissertation or thesis. The following are hard-copy indexes of various subsets of the Proquest database: *Dissertation Abstracts International*, *Masters Abstracts International*, and *American Doctoral Dissertations*.

Search Engines for Journal Articles, Papers, and Reports

Some search engines are designed to help you identify relevant journal articles, conference proceedings, agency reports, position papers on educational policy, descriptions of best practices, and statistical summaries. The following are search engines with large, general databases.

- Education Index Retrospective: 1929–1983 (ebscohost.com/public/education-index-retrospective). This search engine encompasses older education literature not included in ERIC, which extends back only to 1966. Related search engines produced by EBSCO in collaboration with H. W. Wilson are *Education Research Complete* and *Education Source*. Other search engines maintained by these publishers can be found at ebscohost.com/promoMaterials/Flyer_Education-2013.pdf.
- ERIC (eric.ed.gov). This undoubtedly is the most frequently used search engine by educational researchers and educators. We explain its various features in Appendix 2.
- Google Scholar (scholar.google.com). The database for this search engine includes publications from many disciplines. Therefore, you might find relevant publications in it that are not included in education-specific search engines.
- National Center for Education Statistics (nces.ed.gov). This government website includes a search engine and many publications and statistical tables pertaining to the demographics and performance outcomes of public and private K–12 schools, school districts, and postsecondary education. We recommend that you explore its resources by going to the list under "Most Viewed NCES Sites" on the NCES home page. Among them are Nation's Report Card, Digest of Education Statistics, and Data Tools.
- PsycINFO (apa.org/psycinfo). This website is maintained by the American Psychological Association. Its publications database includes more than 2.4 million sources in more than 2,000 journals and other sources extending back to the 1800s. Its comprehensiveness might help you identify relevant publications

not found using education-specific search engines.

■ Web of Science (thomsonreuters.com/web-of-science/). This search engine has a special feature. Suppose you identify a journal article that is critical to your research problem or problem of practice. You want to know whether other publications have referenced this article, because if they did, these publications also are likely to be relevant for your purposes. By using Web of Science, you can identify the journal article of interest and then search for other publications that have cited it.

Other search engines and a few hard-copy indexes are listed in Figure 4.1. The list is not exhaustive because education includes so many specialties, and new databases continue to be developed.

Search Engines for Magazine and Newspaper Articles

Articles in magazines and newspapers are good sources for identifying problems of practice and how educators, the community, and public officials are addressing them. The following search engines can help identify relevant articles.

■ MagPortal (magportal.com). This search engine enables you to find online magazine articles on a wide range of topics, including education.

FIGURE 4.1 • Examples of Search Engines and Bibliographic Indexes for Specific Education Topics

- Catalog of U.S. Government Publications (catalog.gpo.gov/). A free search engine for U.S. government publications.
- Chicano Database (ebscohost.com/academic/chicano-database). A search engine for approximately 60,000 publications about Chicanos, Puerto Ricans, Cuban Americans, and Central American immigrants.
- CSA Sociological Abstracts (csa.com). A search engine for publications relating to various aspects of sociology, including culture and social structure, evaluation research, management and complex organizations, sociology of education, and substance abuse and prevention.
- Education Policy Alliance (nepc.colorado.edu/publications). A free search engine for locating policy research on many problems of practice in education. The research reports come from 33 leading university centers in 23 states.
- Educational Administration Abstracts (ebscohost.com/academic/educational-administration-abstracts). A database for locating publications about various aspects of educational administration.
- Family Studies Abstracts (ebscohost.com/academic/family-studies-abstracts). A database of publications about various aspects of family studies, such as family services, reproduction issues, courtship, and marriage.
- GPO Access—Catalog of U.S. Government Publications (catalog.gpo.gov). A free search engine for a wide range of information products produced by the U.S. government.
- International Index to Black Periodicals Full Text (iibp.chadwyck.com). A search engine for more than 150 international periodicals relating to African American studies.
- JSTOR (jstor.org). A search engine for important scholarly journals in various disciplines as they were originally designed, printed, and illustrated.
- PubMed (ncbi.nlm.nih.gov/pubmed/). A free search engine maintained by the U.S. National Library of Medicine (nlm.nih.gov/). It includes over 17 million citations from the PubMed/MEDLINE database and other life science journals.
- SPORTDiscus (ebscohost.com/academic/sportdiscus). A search engine for publications relating to sports, health, fitness, and sports medicine.
- Women's Studies International (ebscohost.com/academic/womens-studies-international). A database of sources about women's studies, including such topics as feminist studies, psychology and body image, women and the media, reproductive rights, and racial/ethnic studies.

- Newspaper Source (ebscohost.com/public/newspaper-source). This search engine includes full-text coverage for almost 400 newspapers, newswires, and other sources dating from the 1990s to the present.
- Ulrich's Periodicals Directory. This is a comprehensive international search engine for journals, magazines, and newspapers. Ulrich's also publishes a hard-copy version of the directory.

USING SEARCH ENGINES

You probably have had the experience of entering a word or phrase (e.g., "no child left behind act"—note that your search can ignore upper and lower case letters) in a search engine like Google. Almost immediately, you get a list containing thousands, or even millions, of websites. Google helps you by listing what it thinks are the most relevant websites first. Relevance is decided by a sophisticated algorithm developed by Google.

Some of the search engines described above or listed in Figure 4.1 are different in that they provide options to help you establish criteria of relevance *prior* to the search. You probably are familiar with these options from your previous coursework in college or graduate school. If not, you can find a discussion and illustration of these options in our description of ERIC in Appendix 2. You will learn how to focus your literature search by using such techniques as wildcards, truncation, connectors, specification of publication types and education levels, and citation pearl growing.

We chose ERIC as our example in Appendix 2 for several reasons. First, it is the search engine most widely used by educational researchers and practitioners. Second, the use of ERIC is free. Third, the search options are similar to those available for other well-developed search engines, such as PsycINFO.

As you search for relevant publications for your literature review, you are likely to experiment with different search engines, different keywords, and different search-engine features. We recommend that you keep a log of each search. The log will help you from needlessly repeating a search and in writing up your search procedures in your literature review.

Citation Managers

A **citation manager** is software that makes it possible to store bibliographic citations so that they can be retrieved easily and systematically. For example, the results of a literature search using ERIC or another search engine can be stored in a citation manager. You can classify each citation with your own list of descriptors and later retrieve all of the citations that have the specified descriptor. You also can integrate a citation manager with your word processing software so that as you write a paper, its reference section is automatically prepared as you refer to particular citations within the body of the paper.

Two of the more commonly used citation managers in education are Endnote and ProCite. You can go to their websites (endnote.com and procite.com) to learn their specific capabilities. A comprehensive list of citation managers is available in the online encyclopedia Wikipedia. Go to its home page (en.wikipedia.org) and enter "comparison of reference management software" in the search window. You will be taken to another Wikipedia page, "Comparison of Reference Management Software," that identifies various software (with embedded links to those software companies' websites). Most of this software is free.

It might not be worthwhile to purchase a citation manager if you plan to use it only for a single project, such as a master's thesis. However, a citation manager can serve you well over the course of your career as a researcher or educator. From time to time, you are likely to come across publications that you find relevant to your work. You can jot a citation on a note card or piece of paper, but such items are easily misplaced over time. A citation manager, by contrast, will store your "library" of citations on your computer, and your reference citations will then be as close at hand as your computer is. You can add new citations whenever you wish, and they are easily retrieved whenever you need them.

OBTAINING A PUBLICATION AFTER A LITERATURE SEARCH

A search engine provides a bibliographic citation for each relevant publication and perhaps the publication itself. Citations typically include an abstract of the publication's content, which can help you avoid the effort of obtaining publications that are not relevant to your literature review. If the citation is relevant, the abstract might provide sufficient information so that you will not need to search for the actual publication.

If you need the actual publication, you might be able to obtain the full text directly from the Internet, typically in the form of a pdf file or from a website such as JSTOR, though there may be a charge for it. If the article you want is not available on the Internet, your best resource for obtaining a copy is a university library. They most likely will have a web-based catalog of their books and other holdings, so you can determine whether your library has a copy of the book or journal containing the article you want. If a university library does not have the publication, a librarian might be able to obtain it by interlibrary loan. Also, the library is likely to have subscriptions to services that allow you to download journal articles and other publications without charge. Before you begin a literature review, then, you should contact your library to determine the extent of its holdings and its electronic resources for literature searching.

An increasing number of professional journals are moving toward online publication of their articles. An **online journal** is a periodic publication (typically monthly or quarterly) that is available via the Internet. Some journals are available both in hard-copy format and online. Many online journals charge no fee for simply viewing articles on your computer, saving them as electronic files, or printing them. You can obtain a list of current peer-reviewed electronic journals in education by going to the Directory of Open Access Scholarly Journals in Education (ergobservatory.info/ejdirectory.html).

If a journal article is available online, the citation should include the publication's Internet address. Also, research publications increasingly include a DOI, which might be incorporated into the citation. A **DOI**, which is an acronym for *digital object identifier*, is a permanent link to the publication's location on the Internet. Even if the publication moves to a new Internet address and you have only the former address, you can still locate the publication using its DOI. The use of DOIs in citations and as a method for accessing publications on the Internet is described in the publication manual of the American Psychological Association (2010).

LOCATING PUBLISHED LITERATURE REVIEWS

Up to this point, we have focused on search engines and websites with searchable databases, and using them to find general types of publications, such as bibliographies, book reviews, dissertations, and journal articles. Now we turn our attention to methods for finding a specific type of publication, namely, formal and professional literature reviews. (The distinction between formal and professional literature reviews is discussed in Chapter 3.) These methods include the use of search engines, encyclopedias, handbooks, yearbooks, journals, and periodic reports. Each source of literature reviews is described in the next sections.

Search Engines

We recommend search engines as the first resource to use when attempting to locate published literature reviews in your area of interest. We described these resources earlier in the chapter. Also, ERIC, the principal search engine for educators, is described in Appendix 2.

One way to use ERIC and similar search engines to identify literature reviews on a topic of interest is simply to enter "literature reviews" as a descriptor or keyword and your topic as another descriptor or keyword. Suppose that we are interested in literature reviews about charter schools, which have become a major movement in the past decade. Advocates of charter schools make various claims about their effectiveness in improving student achievement, but critics questions these claims. What does the research evidence tell us? Going to the ERIC website (eric.ed.gov), we use the advanced search feature and enter "charter schools" as one descriptor (found in the ERIC thesaurus) and "literature reviews" (also found in the ERIC thesaurus) as another descriptor. (It is necessary to put quote marks around both terms.) The results of this search yielded 34 citations, each involving some aspect, or aspects, of charter schools. For example, consider the ERIC abstract for this literature review, which is available in its entirety by clicking on the "Download full text" button adjacent to the citation:

Di Carlo, M. (2011). The evidence on charter schools and test scores. Policy brief. Washington, DC: Albert Shanker Institute. Abstract retrieved from http://www.eric.ed.gov. (Accession No. ED528633)

The public debate about the success and expansion of charter schools often seems to gravitate toward a tiny handful of empirical studies, when there is, in fact, a relatively well-developed literature focused on whether these schools generate larger testing gains among their students relative to their counterparts in comparable regular public schools. This brief reviews this body of evidence, with a focus on high-quality state- and district-level analyses that address, directly or indirectly, three questions: (1) Do charter schools produce larger testing gains overall?; (2) What policies and practices seem to be associated with better performance? and (3) Can charter schools expand successfully within the same location?

Another search option is to use "meta-analysis" as a descriptor, especially if you are searching for a review of quantitative research studies that relies on this approach. We repeated our search for literature reviews on charter schools using "charter schools" as one descriptor and "meta analysis" as another descriptor (the ERIC Thesaurus spells it as two words with no hyphen). The search yielded four citations. The following is one of them (the abstract is slightly abbreviated here):

Betts, J. R., & Tang, Y. E. (2011). The effect of charter schools on student achievement: A meta-analysis of the literature. Abstract retrieved from http://www.eric.ed.gov. (Accession No. ED526353)

Charter schools are largely viewed as a major innovation in the public school landscape, as they receive more independence from state laws and regulations than do traditional public schools, and are therefore more able to experiment with alternative curricula, pedagogical methods, and different ways of hiring and training teachers. Unlike traditional public schools, charters may be shut down by their authorizers for poor performance. But how is charter school performance measured? What are the effects of charter schools on student achievement? Assessing literature that uses either experimental (lottery) or student-level growth-based methods, this analysis infers the causal impact of attending a charter school on student performance. Focusing on math and reading scores, the authors find compelling evidence that charters underperform traditional public schools in some locations, grades, and subjects, and out-perform traditional public schools in other locations,

grades, and subjects. However, important exceptions include elementary school reading and middle school math and reading, where evidence suggests no negative effects of charter schools and, in some cases, evidence of positive effects. Meta-analytic methods are used to obtain overall estimates on the effect of charter schools on reading and math achievement. The authors find an overall effect size for elementary school reading and math of 0.02 and 0.05, respectively, and for middle school math of 0.055. Effects are not statistically meaningful for middle school reading and for high school math and reading. Studies that focus on urban areas tend to find larger effects than do studies that examine wider areas. Studies of KIPP charter middle schools suggest positive effects of 0.096 and 0.223 for reading and math respectively. New York City and Boston charter schools also appeared to deliver achievement gains larger than charter schools in most other locations. A lack of rigorous studies in many parts of the nation limits the ability to extrapolate.

The full text for this study is available by simply clicking on the "Download full text" button adjacent to the citation. Reading this meta-analysis and the literature review by Di Carlo would teach you a lot in a relatively short period of time about the effectiveness of charter schools and how they differ from conventional schools. After reading these reviews, you can read individual studies mentioned in them that are of particular interest to you.

Another option is to use "meta-ethnography" as a descriptor to search for reviews of qualitative studies. Meta-ethnography is not an ERIC descriptor, so we entered it into the search bar as a keyword and also entered "charter schools" as a descriptor. ERIC identified no relevant citations. We then entered "meta-ethnography" alone as a keyword, and the search yielded 28 citations, eight of which are meta-ethnographies on different problems of educational practice. The other citations involved methodological issues in reviewing a set of qualitative studies.

This finding does not mean that qualitative studies are overlooked in published literature reviews. Rather, they often are considered in general literature reviews that also examine quantitative studies. Using "literature reviews" as a descriptor in an ERIC search should be sufficient to identify these general literature reviews.

Encyclopedias

Many literature reviews are published in encyclopedias, which contain articles (also called *entries*) on a wide range of topics, but the articles typically are short, ranging from a few paragraphs to a few pages in length. However, they are useful in providing an overview on what is known about a particular topic.

A good way to identify encyclopedias about education is to use a search engine for books.

The Library of Congress online catalog (catalog2.loc.gov/) is particularly helpful because it is comprehensive and free. Using its advanced search feature, we looked for encyclopedias by using "encyclopedia" as a keyword, AND as a connector, and "education" as another keyword. Instead of "education," you could use your particular topic (e.g., "history education") as the keyword. We limited our search to encyclopedias published from 2005 through 2013.

Table 4.1 contains a partial list of general and subject-specific encyclopedias resulting from our

---

TABLE 4.1 • Examples of Encyclopedias Containing Literature Reviews

Comprehensive Encyclopedias

McCulloch, G., & Crook, D. (Eds.). (2008). *The Routledge international encyclopedia of education.* London & New York: Routledge.

Mohr, C. L. (Ed.). (2011). *Education.* Chapel Hill: University of North Carolina Press.

Unger, H. G. (Ed.). (2007). *Encyclopedia of American Education* (3rd ed.). New York: Facts on File.

Specialized Encyclopedias

Anfara, V. A., Jr., Andrews, G., & Mertens, S. B. (Eds.). (2005). *The encyclopedia of middle grades education.* Greenwich, CT: IAP-Information Age.

Bajaj, M. (Ed.). (2008). *Encyclopedia of peace education.* Charlotte, NC: Information Age.

Banks, J. A. (Ed.). (2012). *Encyclopedia of diversity in education.* Thousand Oaks, CA: Sage.

Cenoz, J., & Hornberger, N. H. (Eds.) (2008). *Knowledge about language* (2nd ed.). New York: Springer.

English, L. M. (Ed.). (2005). *International encyclopedia of adult education.* New York: Palgrave Macmillan.

Feinstein, S. (Ed.). (2013). *From the brain to the classroom: The encyclopedia of learning.* Thousand Oaks, CA: Greenwood.

González, J. M. (Ed.). (2008). *Encyclopedia of bilingual education.* Los Angeles: Sage.

Kerr, B. (Ed.). (2009). *Encyclopedia of giftedness, creativity, and talent.* Thousand Oaks, CA: Sage.

Klein, B. T. (Ed.). (2007). *Reference encyclopedia of the American Indian* (13th ed.). Boca Raton, FL: Todd.

Lomotey, K. (Ed.). (2010). *Encyclopedia of African American education.* Los Angeles: Sage.

Martin-Jones, M., De Mejia, A., & Hornberger, N. H. (Eds.). (2008). *Discourse and education* (2nd ed.). New York: Springer.

Ness, D., & Lin, C. (Eds.). (2013). *International education: An encyclopedia of contemporary issues and systems.* Armonk, NY: M. E. Sharpe.

New, R. S., & Cochran, M. (Eds.). (2007). *Early childhood education. An international encyclopedia.* Westport, CT: Praeger.

Provenzo, E. F., Jr., & Renaud, J. P. (Eds.). (2009). *Encyclopedia of the social and cultural foundations of education.* Thousand Oaks, CA.

Reynolds, C. R., Vannest, K. J., & Fletcher-Janzen, E. (Eds.). (2013). *Encyclopedia of special education* (4th ed.). Hoboken, NJ: Wiley.

Rogers, P. L., Berg, G. A., Boettcher, J., Howard, C, Justice, L., & Schenk, K. D. (Eds.). (2009). *Encyclopedia of distance learning* (2nd ed.). Hershey, PA: Information Science Reference.

Russo, B. L. (Ed.). (2011). *Encyclopedia of teaching and teacher research.* New York: Nova Science Publishers.

Russo, C. J. (Ed.). (2008). *Encyclopedia of education law.* Thousand Oaks, CA: Sage.

Turkington, C., & Harris, J. R. (Eds.). (2006). *The encyclopedia of learning disabilities* (2nd ed.). New York: Facts on File.

search. The list illustrates the range of encyclopedias containing literature reviews. The entries in them will give you a quick overview of the literature in your field of interest. This overview might be sufficient for your needs or a starting point for a more detailed literature review.

Handbooks

Whereas encyclopedias typically include short entries on a large number of topics, handbooks cover a smaller number of topics, each in a separate chapter. The chapter might be a literature review or include a literature review as part of a discussion of an issue of educational practice. A handbook has one or more general editors who oversee the design of the chapters and the authorities who write them.

An effective way to search for a handbook on your topic of interest is to use the Library of Congress Online Catalog as your search engine. Using the advanced search feature, we entered "handbook" as a keyword, AND as a connector, and "education" as another keyword. We limited our search to handbooks published in English from 2005 to the end of 2013. The search yielded more than 850 citations. Table 4.2 illustrates the range of educational domains for which handbooks are available. When doing your own search, we recommend that you enter your topic in its least restrictive form (e.g., "writing" instead of "writing instruction") to increase your likelihood of identifying a relevant handbook.

Yearbooks, Journals, and Periodic Reports

Several organizations publish yearbooks, journals, and reports that are primarily reviews of the education literature, usually with a focus on topics of current interest to educators.

TABLE 4.2 • Examples of Handbooks Containing Literature Reviews about a Particular Domain of Education

Bhatia, T. K., & Ritchie, W. C. (Eds.). (2013). *The handbook of bilingual and multilingualism* (2nd ed.). Malden, MA: Wiley-Blackwell.

Felicia, P. (Ed.). (2011). *Handbook of research on improving learning and motivation through educational games: Multidisciplinary approaches.* Hershey, PA: Information Science Reference.

Fraser, B. J., Tobin, K., & McRobbie, C. (Eds.). (2010). *Second international handbook of science education.* Dordrecht, NY: Springer.

Haumann, R., & Zimmer, G. (Eds.). (2013). *Handbook of academic performance: Predictors, learning strategies and influences of gender.* Hauppauge, NY: Nova Science.

Lester, F. K. (Ed.). (2010). *Second handbook of research on mathematics teaching and learning.* Charlotte, NC: Information Age Publishing.

Lovat, T., Toomey, R., & Clement, N. (Eds.). (2010). *International research handbook on values education and student wellbeing.* New York: Springer.

Lynn, M., & Dixson, A. D. (Eds.). (2013). *Handbook of critical theory in education.* New York, NY: Routledge.

Mayer, R. E., & Alexander, P. A. (Eds.). (2011). *Handbook of research on learning and instruction.* New York: Routledge.

McGill-Franzen, A., & Allington, R. L. (Eds.). (2010). *Handbook of reading disability research.* New York: Routledge.

Pianta, R. C., Barnett, W. S., Justice, L. M., & Sheridan, S. M. (Eds.). (2012). *Handbook of early childhood education.* New York: Guilford Press.

Tozer, S. E., Gallegos, B. P., & Henry, A. M. (Eds.). (2010). *Handbook of research in the social foundations of education.* New York: Routledge.

Pelech, J. (Ed.). (2010). *The comprehensive handbook of constructivist teaching: From theory to practice.* Charlotte, NC: Information Age Publishing.

Sharpes, D. K. (Ed.) (2010). *Handbook on international studies in education.* Charlotte, NC: Information Age Publishing.

Smart, J. C., & Paulsen, M. B. (Eds.). (2012). *Higher education: Handbook of theory and research.* New York: Springer.

NSSE Yearbooks

The NSSE Yearbooks are sponsored by the National Society for the Study of Education. They are listed on NSSE's website (nsse-chicago.org/). Each yearbook covers recent research, theory, and commentary related to a major educational theme. In recent years, the themes have included

- A moral critique of contemporary education (2013)
- Design-based implementation research (2013)
- The place of music in the 21st century: A global view (2012)
- Organization and effectiveness of induction programs for new teachers (2012)
- Rethinking identity and literacy education in the 21st century (2011)
- Taking stock of professional development schools: What's needed now (2011)
- Learning research as a human science (2010)
- Education, immigrant students, refugee students, and English learners (2010)

Each of these themes reflects problems of practice that are currently of great interest to educators.

Publications of the American Educational Research Association

The *Review of Research in Education* is a yearbook published by the American Educational Research Association (AERA). Each volume contains chapters written by leading educational researchers who provide critical surveys of research on important problems and trends in education. For example, Volume 36, published in 2012, focuses on the theme of education, democracy, and the public good. It includes 12 chapters on such topics as Latino education, citizenship education, social justice, and charter schools.

Review of Educational Research, also published by AERA, is a journal consisting entirely of reviews of research literature on educational topics. It is published quarterly, and each issue typically contains four to seven reviews.

What Works Clearinghouse

The Institute of Education Sciences, a branch of the U.S. Department of Education, sponsors the What Works Clearinghouse (WWC). WWC (ies.ed.gov/ncee/wwc) publishes periodic reports that review the scientific evidence for various educational programs and practices. The purpose of these reports is to help educators and policy makers choose those programs and practices that are most likely to improve student outcomes.

WWC currently focuses on reviewing research about interventions in the areas of academic achievement, dropout prevention, language development, mathematics/science, personal/social development, and reading/writing. If you click on "Intervention reports guide evidence-based decisions" on WWC's home page, you will find an archive of its reports. Most of them present a synthesis of research on a particular intervention or a set of related interventions. The following interventions have been the subject of recent reports:

- Intervention: Reading Mastery (November 2013). A program designed to provide systematic instruction in reading to students in grades K–6.
- Intervention: Saxon Math (May 2013). A textbook series covering grades K–12 based on incremental development and continual review of mathematical concepts to give students time to learn and practice concepts throughout the year.
- Intervention: Talent Development Middle Grades Program (January 2013). A whole school reform approach for large middle schools that face serious problems with student attendance, discipline, and academic achievement.

Reports on these and other interventions provide a rigorous review of the research evidence to help educators decide whether to adopt them for their own schools or organizations.

CRITERIA FOR EVALUATING PUBLISHED LITERATURE REVIEWS

The following criteria can help you judge the merits of published literature reviews in your area of interest.

1. *Reviewer's credentials.* The reviewer's reputation and experience with the topic are factors to consider when reading a literature review. One way to determine these characteristics about the

reviewer is to examine the reference list at the end of the source to see whether the reviewer has done research on the topic and, if so, where and when it was published. You can also check for information in the article itself about the author's affiliation, title, and experience related to the topic.

2. *Search procedures.* In older published reviews, the reviewers usually did not specify their search procedures, so we cannot tell whether the search was comprehensive or cursory. Now it is customary for reviewers to identify the search engines and bibliographic indexes they examined, the keywords they used, and the years they covered. This is more likely to be the case in a systematic literature review than in a professional literature review.

3. *Breadth of the search.* Research reviews vary widely in their breadth, from an exhaustive search for all primary sources on a topic to a highly selective search. The advantage of a comprehensive search is that you have some assurance that no significant research evidence or theoretical framework has been overlooked. A narrower search might be just as useful for your purposes, but in this case, knowing how the reviewer selected the publications included in the review is even more important. The following dimensions reflect the breadth of the reviewer's search of the literature.

a. Period of time covered by the search. The publication dates of the most recent and oldest sources provide an indication of this time period. Keep in mind, though, that the time period might span beyond these dates if the reviewer's search did not yield older or more recent publications that were relevant to the topic.

b. Types of publications reviewed. As an example, the literature review might include only published journal articles, or it also might include dissertations and so-called fugitive literature, such as technical reports produced by a research team for its funding agency.

c. Geographical scope of the search. Some reviewers examine only studies carried out in the United States, whereas others also include studies conducted in other countries.

d. Range of grade levels and types of students, teachers, educational institutions, or other entities that were included in the literature review.

e. Range of theoretical and ideological perspectives on the topic. For example, did the reviewer consider both studies based on behavioral theory and studies based on cognitive theory? Were different ideological perspectives considered, such as critical theory (see Chapter 14) and the accountability movement?

f. Use of criteria to exclude any of the reports that were initially examined. The reviewer might choose to exclude research studies that involved atypical students or experiments that did not employ random assignment procedures. (Random assignment is explained in Chapter 12.)

4. *Amount of information provided about the studies included in the literature review.* Reviewers have the challenging task of summarizing findings of a large number of studies briefly so as to be readable yet in sufficient detail that the basis for the reviewer's conclusions and interpretations is reasonably clear. Simply including a citation or two in parentheses after making a sweeping generalization does not accomplish this goal. Many systematic literature reviews often include a table listing each study and information such as sample size, research design, measures, and key statistics.

5. *Exercise of critical judgment.* Research reviews range from those that reflect uncritical acceptance of research findings to those in which the reviewer finds flaws in every research study and asserts that no conclusions can be drawn from them. Neither extreme is likely to be justified for topics that have been extensively researched. Another aspect of critical judgment is whether the reviewer tended to lump studies together or discriminated among studies that appeared to deal with the same question but were substantially different in design or purpose. The latter approach generally reflects better critical judgment.

6. *Resolution of inconsistent findings.* Nearly every research review will reveal that the results obtained in some studies do not agree with those found in other studies. You should examine carefully how the reviewer dealt with these inconsistencies.

An example of
How Literature Reviews Can Help in Solving Problems of Practice

We occasionally read articles about the idea of giving students tangible rewards for good grades. The idea is controversial, with stakeholders providing arguments for and against the practice. Washington, DC, experimented with this practice, and a retired teacher, Kathy Megyeri, wrote an article in the *Washington Post* about it. Based on her 34 years as an English teacher, she claimed that "little trinkets, treats and rewards" worked very well for her. She wondered whether cash payments would be any more effective than her small rewards. Megyeri observed positive effects of these small rewards on her students:

> My giving of those small prizes enhanced the cooperative atmosphere of learning, sharing and doing well in class, especially for students who did not usually succeed in school or are from impoverished homes.

Immediately after this comment, she stated:

> Thus, I was shocked when my school's assistant principal called me in to complain that I "bribed" my students and complained

that there was a plethora of research and literature that condemned this practice.

> Megyeri, K. A. (November 6, 2008). Like Wall Street bonuses for doing well. *Washington Post*. Retrieved November 23, 2008, www.washingtonpost.com

Is there, in fact, a substantial body of research evidence demonstrating negative effects resulting from small rewards?

One way to respond to this question—and to the complaint of Megyeri's assistant principal—is to look for literature reviews that summarize the research evidence. Literature reviews are particularly helpful if you do not have time to review individual studies directly.

We did a quick search of the literature using ERIC as our search engine. We used "literature reviews" and "rewards" in one search and "literature reviews" and "extrinsic motivation" in another search. We found a few literature reviews, with each summarizing a small body of studies. In general, the research evidence is inconclusive and does not allow one to strongly endorse or condemn the use of small rewards, including cash. However, Megyeri's observations are compelling, and they lead us to recommend either formal experiments (see Chapter 12) or action research (see Chapter 18) to study this problem of practice.

SELF-CHECK TEST

1. Publications are considered fugitive literature if they are
   a. only included in ERIC's database.
   b. are professional literature, but not easily obtained.
   c. are in the form of internal memos of a school organization.
   d. classified as pertaining to matters affecting national security.

2. Search engines for literature reviews typically
   a. include procedures for converting citations to the style format of the *APA Publication Manual*.
   b. include a collection of bibliographic citations and procedures for searching through them.

   c. include an option for direct purchase of a publication in hard-copy format.
   d. typically have a time lag of two years between the publication of a journal article and its appearance in the search engine.

3. If you enter a keyword in a search engine, you will
   a. retrieve all citations that include the keyword.
   b. not retrieve any citations unless you put quotation marks around the keyword.
   c. retrieve citations only for publications that include the keyword.
   d. not be able to retrieve citations for meta-analyses and meta-ethnographies.

4. Search engines can be used to identify bibliographic citations for
   a. dissertations.
   b. book reviews.
   c. newspaper articles.
   d. all of the above.
5. The most widely used search engine by educational researchers is
   a. PsycINFO.
   b. PsycCritiques.
   c. ERIC.
   d. Education Review.
6. If an educator is interested in the demographic characteristics of American schools and the academic achievement of its students, the most relevant search engine would be
   a. the National Center of Education Statistics.
   b. Google Scholar.
   c. Google.
   d. PsycINFO.
7. Citation managers
   a. provide a way to store bibliographic citations from search engines.
   b. enable you to classify bibliographic citations with your own descriptors.
   c. can be used to integrate bibliographic citations with word processing software.
   d. all of the above.
8. Online journals in education and other professions currently
   a. are very few in number.
   b. have increased in number over time.
   c. can be accessed only by using the ERIC search engine.
   d. are not peer reviewed and are thus of lower quality than hard-copy journals.
9. Published literature reviews in education
   a. are not included in the databases of search engines.
   b. can be found in encyclopedias and handbooks.
   c. appear only in publications of the American Educational Research Association.
   d. are required to limit their scope to journal articles with publication dates no earlier than a decade prior to the year in which the review was done.
10. In evaluating a published literature review, one should
   a. expect to see a discussion of the literature search procedures that were used.
   b. be concerned if the authors include research studies in which they participated.
   c. be concerned if the author includes not only journal articles but also dissertations in the literature review.
   d. give more weight to the older studies that were reviewed.

CHAPTER REFERENCE

American Psychological Association. (2010). *Publication manual of the American Psychological Association* (6th ed.). Washington, DC: Author.

RESOURCES FOR FURTHER STUDY

Ahn, S., Ames, A. J., & Myers, N. D. (2012). A review of meta-analyses in education: Methodological strengths and weaknesses. *Review of Educational Research, 82*(4), 436–476.

The authors review 56 meta-analyses in education and examine their strengths and weaknesses. They make recommendations for future meta-analyses based on their systematic review of these existing meta-analyses.

Cooper, H. M., Hedges, L. V., & Valentine, J. C. (Eds.). (2009). *The handbook of research synthesis and meta-analysis* (2nd ed.). New York, NY: Russell Sage Foundation.

The chapters are written by experts on such topics as using reference databases, judging the quality of research studies to be included in a literature review, computing effect sizes and combining them across studies, selecting a reporting format, and using literature reviews in public policy making.

Lather, P. (1999). To be of use: The work of reviewing. *Review of Educational Research, 69*, 2–7.

This article will help you understand how published literature reviews reflect to some extent the biases, values, and agendas of the reviewer.

Sandelowski, M., & Barroso, J. (2006). *Handbook for synthesizing qualitative research*. New York, NY: Springer.

Although written for health disciplines, this handbook will also be helpful to educators interested in synthesizing qualitative research related to educational topics. The authors describe all aspects of the literature review process, from identifying relevant studies to synthesizing them, drawing valid conclusions, and writing a report of the review.

Schlosser, R. W., Wendt, O., Bhavnani, S., & Nail-Chiwetalu, B. (2006). Use of information-seeking strategies for developing systematic reviews and engaging in evidence-based practice: The application of traditional and comprehensive pearl-growing—A review. *International Journal of Language and Communication Disorders, 41*(5), 567–582.

The authors explain search engines and various kinds of pearl growing (see Appendix 2) that can be used to search for relevant publications. They illustrate pearl growing with examples from research and practice involving individuals with speech and language disabilities.

CHAPTER FIVE

Analyzing and Evaluating Reports of Quantitative Research Studies

PROBLEMS OF PRACTICE *in this chapter*

- How can we help teachers feel confident that they can engage all students in the learning process, even those who are unmotivated?
- How can we determine whether a test or attitude scale is valid and reliable?
- Can item response theory be used to create better tests than those now available?
- Where can we find information about tests and other measures that we might want to use?
- What can be done to increase the currently small percentage of women who take courses and pursue careers in STEM disciplines (science, technology, engineering, math)?
- What can be done to prevent students from becoming overweight?

IMPORTANT *Ideas*

1. Most reports of quantitative research in the field of education follow the style specified in the *Publication Manual of the American Psychological Association*.
2. In reading research reports, you should identify the researcher's constructs because these constructs determined which phenomena the researchers selected for study, how they measured those phenomena, and how they interpreted their data.
3. Constructs can be thought of as variables, meaning that research participants can differ from each other to measurable degrees. If the participants do not differ from each other, the construct is considered to be a constant.
4. You should look for explicit research hypotheses, questions, or objectives in the introductory section of a research report because you will judge the quality of the study by how well the hypotheses were tested, the research questions were answered, or the research objectives were achieved.

5. Space limitations in research journals do not allow for extensive literature reviews, but the authors should at least discuss the previous studies most relevant to their own study.

6. The authors of a research report should state whether they studied the entire population of interest or a sample from either the target population or the accessible population.

7. The authors of a research report should state whether they used stratified random sampling or proportional random sampling to ensure that subgroups in the population of interest were adequately represented in their sample.

8. Educational researchers typically study volunteer samples because the legal requirements of informed consent allow individuals to refuse to participate in a study if they wish.

9. To determine whether findings for the research sample that was studied are generalizable to the target population, the accessible population, or your local setting, you need to compare them to the sample on important characteristics, such as socioeconomic status, age, gender, and ethnicity.

10. The authors of a research report should specify each variable and whether it was measured by a test, scale, questionnaire, interview, direct observation, content analysis, or other approach.

11. If a questionnaire was used in a quantitative research study, you should check to see whether it was pretested, whether it included leading or psychologically threatening questions, and whether the research respondents could reasonably be expected to have the information that it requested.

12. If an interview was used in a quantitative research study, you should check to see whether it was pretested, whether the interviewers were trained properly, whether it included leading or psychologically threatening questions, and how the interview data were recorded for subsequent analysis.

13. If direct observation was used in a quantitative research study, you should check to determine whether the observed variables were high-inference or low-inference, whether the observers were adequately trained, whether a standard observation form was used, whether the observation period was of sufficient duration, and how conspicuous the observers were to the research participants.

14. If content analysis was used in a quantitative research study, you should ascertain whether the content categories were well defined, whether the procedure for selecting a sample of documents was sound, and whether the observers who content-analyzed each document generated reliable data.

15. A test described in a research report is valid to the extent that interpretations of scores earned by the test takers are supported by various types of evidence: content-related evidence, predictive evidence, convergent evidence, concurrent evidence, response-process evidence, and consequential evidence.

16. A test described in a research report is reliable to the extent that it is free of measurement error, as determined by the consistency of its items, its stability across time, its standard error of measurement, and the consistency with which it can be administered and scored.

17. A test that is developed by the methods of item response theory consists of items that are ordered on a difficulty scale such that an individual with a given amount of the ability measured by the test will be able to answer most of the items below a certain point on the scale and few or no items above that point.

18. Search engines and bibliographic indexes are available to help you locate or evaluate available tests and other measures described in a research report.

19. The methods section of a quantitative research report should explain details of the research design in sufficient detail that a reader can judge whether it satisfies commonly accepted standards for that kind of design.

20. The results section of a quantitative research report is an objective presentation of the statistical findings, without interpretation.

21. The discussion section of a quantitative research report provides an opportunity for the researchers' own interpretation of the results, evaluation of the study's methodology, and discussion of the significance of the study's findings for future research, theory development, and improvement of professional practice.

KEY TERMS

abstract
accessible population
closed-ended item
cluster sampling
concurrent evidence of test validity
consequential evidence of test validity
constant
construct
content analysis
content-related evidence of test validity
convergent evidence of test validity
Cronbach's alpha
direct observation
face validity
high-inference variable
high-stakes test
hypothesis

inter-rater reliability
interview
item consistency
item response theory
Kuder-Richardson Formula 20
Likert-type scale item
low-inference variable
measurement error
observer bias
open-ended item
parameter
performance measure
population validity
predictive evidence of test validity
proportional random sampling
Publication Manual of the American Psychological Association
quantitative research
questionnaire

reliability
reliability coefficient
response-process evidence of test validity
sample
sampling error
scale
simple random sampling
standard error of measurement
Standards for Educational and Psychological Testing
stratified random sampling
target population
test
test-retest reliability
test stability
test validity
true score
variable
volunteer sample

ORGANIZATION OF A QUANTITATIVE RESEARCH REPORT

Chapter 1 describes quantitative research and qualitative research as two different approaches to scientific inquiry in education. Among the primary characteristics of **quantitative research** are an epistemological belief in an objective reality, the analysis of reality into measurable variables, the

creation of generalizable knowledge through the study of samples that accurately represent a defined population, and reliance on statistical methods to analyze data.

In this part of the book, you will read several reprinted articles reporting quantitative research studies, and in this chapter, we describe how to read such articles analytically and critically.

Most reports of quantitative research studies are organized similarly because many researchers follow the style guidelines in the ***Publication Manual of the American Psychological Association*** (2010). These follow the manuscript style guidelines in Chapter 2 of the publication as follows:

Abstract
Introduction
Methods
    Sampling Procedures
    Measures (or Materials)
    Research Design and Procedures
Results
Discussion

Each of these sections is explained in this chapter.

The ability to comprehend a quantitative research report is important, but you also must be able to evaluate the soundness of the study that it reports. Therefore, as we describe each section of a report, we also explain how to judge whether its content is sound or flawed.

To make these judgments, it is helpful to ask yourself questions as you read each section of the report. A set of questions for this purpose is presented in list form in Appendix 3. Another list of questions, intended for specific research designs, is presented in Appendix 5.

ABSTRACT AND INTRODUCTION

A research report begins with an **abstract**, which is a brief summary of the report's content (typically about 100 words). Reading the abstract first will give you an idea of the purpose of the study, its methods of inquiry, and its major findings. With this overview in mind, you will find it easier to comprehend the many details included in the full report.

The following is an abstract for a research study (Karimi, 2011) that was published in the *Australian Journal of Teacher Education*.

Despite the importance of teacher efficacy, there has been little research on the effects of interventions intended to increase it. Thus, the present study considered the potential of Professional Development (PD) in enhancing teachers' beliefs about their teaching ability. The study was quantitative in nature and utilized the reliable survey instrument known as "Teacher Sense of Efficacy Scale." Two groups of English as a Foreign Language (EFL) teachers (an experimental group and a convenience sample of control teachers) were surveyed in the study in a Pre-test Post-test (and delayed Post-test) Control Group Design. After administering a Pre-test on self-efficacy which indicated no significant difference between the two groups, the treatment teachers received three 16-session courses during which they were provided with opportunities for PD using five PD models including In-service Training, Fellow Observation/Assessment, Development/Improvement Process, Mentoring, and Study Groups. The two groups were then compared on the post- and delayed post-tests which showed that the treatment teachers obtained significantly higher efficacy scores than the control group of teachers. (p. 50)

This abstract concisely states the purpose of the study and its key findings. In the next sections of this chapter, we will use this same study to illustrate other features of a research report. It is worth noting that the study was conducted by a professor at Tarbiat Moallem University in Iran and published in an Australian research journal. Educational research is thriving in countries around the world, and so we have much to learn about educational problems of practice by examining relevant research, wherever it was conducted.

The introductory section of a quantitative research report comes immediately after the abstract. It describes the purpose of the study, relevant constructs and variables, and the specific hypotheses, questions, and objectives that guided the study. In addition, the introductory section includes a review of previous research findings and other information that is relevant to the study. We explain these features of a research report in the sections that follow.

Constructs and Variables

The introductory section of a research report should identify and describe each of the concepts that was studied. Examples of concepts studied by educational researchers are learning style, aptitude, academic achievement, intrinsic motivation, school leadership, and curriculum standards. Researchers typically refer to these concepts as constructs or variables.

A **construct** is a structure or process that is inferred from observed behavior. For example, psychologists have observed that some individuals tend to speak about themselves in consistent ways, such as "I'm very good at sports," "I am ambitious," or "I don't like to draw attention to myself." The consistency of these self-perceptions over time and situations has led social psychologists to infer that individuals have a psychological structure that they call *self-concept*. Self-concept, then, is a construct inferred from observed behavior; it cannot be observed directly. Other related constructs have been inferred as well, such as self-esteem, self-determination, and self-efficacy.

Some constructs are tied to a particular theory. For example, logical operations and sensorimotor intelligence are key constructs in Piaget's theory of human development. Metacognition, short-term memory, and long-term memory are key constructs in certain cognitive theories. Oppression and voice are key constructs in critical research (see Chapter 14).

Constructs are extremely important in all types of educational research. They determine how researchers view reality, the phenomena they study, their procedures for measuring these phenomena, and their interpretations of empirical findings. If you do not accept a researcher's definition of a construct, this would be a basis for rejecting the study and its findings.

In Karimi's study of teacher education (introduced in the preceding section), the two key constructs are (1) teacher efficacy and (2) professional development. The value of the study to you and others depends on how the researchers defined these two constructs. Karimi used a definition of teacher efficacy developed by two other researchers: it is "a teacher's judgment of his or her capabilities to bring about desired outcomes of student engagement and learning, even among those students who may be difficult or unmotivated" (Tschannen-Moran & Hoy, 2001). The construct of professional development is more complex. Karimi reviewed seven models of professional development proposed by other researchers and chose five as an intervention to improve teachers' efficacy. Each model is a separate construct and therefore requires a definition, which is included in the journal article. For example, observation/assessment is one of the models, and it is defined as a process that "involves colleagues who provide feedback based on observations about the

performance of fellow educators" (p. 55). Development/improvement process is another model, and it is defined as a process "in which the participant teachers are called together to make decisions and changes in organizational plans, procedures and activities" (p. 55).

In reading the journal article, you need to decide whether you agree with the researcher's definitions of these constructs. You also need to decide whether you agree with the goal of the professional development process—improvement of teachers' efficacy. This goal might or might not be a priority for the problem of practice that is of concern to you.

Variables and Constants

Quantitative researchers typically use the term *variable* rather than *construct* when conceptualizing their studies and writing their reports. A **variable** expresses a construct as a range of quantitative values. For example, we can think of the construct of self-concept as ranging from highly negative (-5) to neutral (0) to highly positive ($+5$).

Variables usually are measured in terms of scores on a measure, such as an achievement test or attitude scale. Variables also can take the form of categories, for example, tall versus short, public schools versus private schools, or authoritarian versus democratic versus laissez-faire styles of leadership.

If a construct is part of the design of a research study but does not vary, it is called a **constant**. For example, suppose a researcher conducts an experiment to compare the effectiveness of teaching method A and teaching method B for community college students. The educational level of the students (that is, community college) is a constant because no other educational level is included in the research design. Suppose, however, that the experiment compares the effectiveness of the two teaching methods to see which is most effective for community college students and which is most effective for high school students. In this experiment, educational level is a variable because it takes on two values: community college and high school.

In reviewing a research report, you should examine carefully how each construct is defined, how it is treated as a variable, and how that variable is measured. If the definitions are unclear or nonexistent, the significance of the research results is cast into doubt. More doubts arise if the definitions of the constructs are inconsistent with the methods used to measure them.

In Karimi's teacher efficacy study, professional development is a variable having two categories: implementation of a particular professional development program and nonimplementation of the program. These two categories of the variable were represented in the research study by having one group of teachers participate in the professional development program and another group not receive any professional development. Additional categories can be imagined. For example, the professional development program included five models. Karimi could have included another group in the research study that participated in three of the models, or perhaps in only one of them.

All of the outcome constructs in this study are variables that can be measured by interval scales (explained in Chapter 6). Possible scores on the test of professional teaching knowledge range from 0 to 38. The other outcome measures are rating scales that range from 0 to 18 (quality of lesson plan), 0 to 22 (teaching performance), and 0 to 9 (postlesson reflection). Different researchers might consider other options. For example, a researcher might view the construct "quality of lesson plan" as a variable having three possible values: excellent, adequate, and not acceptable.

Research Hypotheses, Questions, and Objectives

A **hypothesis** in a research study is a reasoned speculation or prediction about how two or more variables are related to each other. For example, researchers might hypothesize that children's order of birth in their family relative to their siblings is linked to their level of leadership in school activities or that method A is more effective than method B in promoting the academic achievement of students involved in distance education. After formulating a hypothesis, researchers collect data to test that hypothesis and then examine the data to decide whether or not to reject it. Hypotheses usually are formulated on the basis of theory and previous research findings.

If theory or previous research does not provide an adequate basis for formulating hypotheses,

researchers instead can formulate questions or objectives to guide their investigation. Karimi chose to state three questions for his study:

1. Does participation in effective professional development activities significantly affect teachers' efficacy beliefs about their ability to engage students?
2. Does participation in effective professional development activities significantly affect teachers' efficacy beliefs about their ability to implement appropriate teaching strategies?
3. Does participation in effective professional development activities significantly affect teachers' efficacy beliefs about their ability to manage students?

Karimi instead could have stated objectives. For example, one objective of this study was to determine whether professional development activities affect teachers' efficacy beliefs about their ability to engage students. The choice of research questions or objectives is generally a matter of personal preference. In our experience, journal articles more commonly state research questions.

The formulation of hypotheses, questions, or objectives provides a foundation for the other phases of a quantitative research study. Therefore, you should look for hypotheses, questions, or objectives in the introductory section of the report. If they are not stated or if no rationale for them is provided, you have reason for concern about the quality of the study and the validity of its findings. You also should be concerned that the hypotheses, questions, or objectives are not addressed directly in the research design and statistical analyses.

Literature Review

If you do a comprehensive literature review on a particular problem, you will soon notice that a few key studies are cited in many of the research reports. If these key studies are not reviewed in a particular research report, it might indicate that the researchers were careless in reviewing the literature. If important studies that disagree with the researchers' findings are omitted, bias might be involved.

Most research journals allow researchers limited space for reviewing previous research, so you should not expect detailed reviews. However, the five to ten most relevant previous studies should be discussed, even if only briefly. Significant syntheses of the literature also merit discussion in a research report. Research reports not appearing in journals, such as doctoral dissertations, usually provide much more detailed literature reviews because they are not subject to space limitations.

The report of the teacher efficacy study included 45 references. The majority of them involved research articles about teacher efficacy or professional development, or the relationship between these two concepts.

The Researchers' Qualifications

Because quantitative researchers strive to be objective, they generally reveal little or nothing about themselves in their reports. Each author's institutional affiliation typically is listed beneath the author's name at the start of the report, and there might be a note indicating the author's job title. The literature review might refer to reports of other studies or scholarly work that the authors have written.

Knowledge about the researchers can raise questions about whether their study is biased. For example, some research studies involve experimental tests of the effectiveness of an educational program or method. If we know that the researchers have a stake in the program or method (which is often the case), we should be on the alert for any indications that the design of the experiment was slanted to support its effectiveness.

Whenever researchers have reason for wanting their research to support a particular viewpoint, the likelihood of bias is greatly increased. Occasionally, the bias becomes so great that the researchers slant their findings or even structure their research design to produce a predetermined result. A famous case of researcher bias involved the study of twins by Sir Cyril Burt. It appears that Burt was so intent on proving that intelligence is inherited that he incorrectly analyzed, or even fabricated, research data to support his hypothesis (Evans, 1976).

METHOD SECTION: SAMPLING PROCEDURES

Researchers ideally would investigate all of the individuals to whom they wish to generalize their findings. These individuals constitute the **target population**, meaning that they comprise the entire group of individuals (or organizations, events, objects, etc.) having the characteristics that interest the researchers. Because of the great expense involved in studying most populations of interest, researchers are limited to studying a sample of individuals who represent the population.

For example, suppose researchers wish to study the effect of a new reading program on the reading comprehension of visually impaired children in U.S. elementary schools but lack the resources to try it out with the entire population of such children. Therefore, they must first define an accessible population and then select a sample from this population. The **accessible population** is the entire group of individuals (or other entities) that can feasibly be included in the research sample. For example, the researchers might define the accessible population as all of the students within a certain region of the state in which they work. They would then select a sample from this accessible population. A **sample** is the actual group of research participants (or some other entity such as textbooks or school buildings) that is included in a research study and is intended to represent the target population.

The researchers now have solved the problem of making the study feasible, but they have created a different problem, namely, whether they can generalize their findings from a limited sample drawn from the accessible population to the entire population of visually impaired children in U.S. elementary schools. As we explain below, researchers can use various sampling procedures to increase the likelihood that their findings have valid generalizability.

Samples seldom have the exact characteristics as the populations from which they are drawn. For example, suppose that you randomly select three male students from each class in a large high school and measure their height. Because each member of the population has an equal and independent chance of being included in the sample, your sampling procedure is random. Nonetheless, it is unlikely that the mean height of this sample will turn out to be identical to the mean height of all male students in the school (defined to be the target population in this example).

The difference between the mean height of this random sample and the population's mean height is a sampling error. In technical terms, a **sampling error** is the difference between (1) a statistic (e.g., a mean score) for a sample and (2) the same statistic for the population. The technical term for a statistic derived from measuring the entire population is a **parameter**.

Sampling errors are likely to occur even when the sample is randomly drawn from the population. The size of the errors tends to become smaller as we select a larger random sample. For this reason, we can be more confident in generalizing results from studies with a large random sample than studies with a small random sample. We describe the effects of sampling error in more detail in Chapter 7.

Despite the advantages of a random sample, researchers often must study nonrandom samples. Unfortunately, sampling errors in nonrandom samples cannot be estimated by mathematical procedures. Therefore, generalizations about populations based on nonrandom samples need to be viewed as tentative. If the research findings have important implications for educational theory or practice, researchers are likely to do replication studies with other samples to confirm or refute the generalizability of the original findings to the target population.

Types of Sampling

Researchers have developed various techniques for drawing random samples from a target population. Two of the most common methods are simple random sampling and stratified random sampling, which we describe here. Additional sampling techniques, intended specifically for longitudinal research, are described in Chapter 9.

Simple Random Sampling

In **simple random sampling**, all of the individuals in the defined population have an equal and independent chance of being selected as a member of the sample. By *independent*, we mean that the selection of one individual does not affect in any way the chances of selection of any other individual into the sample.

Various methods can be used to select a simple random sample. For example, the researchers might assign a number to each individual in the population and use a computer-based random number generator or hard-copy table of random numbers to select the needed number of individuals.

Simple random sampling is most feasible in survey research. For example, if researchers wish to know the opinion of psychologists on some educational issue, they might be able to obtain a directory of psychologists from a national organization such as the American Psychological Association. They can then draw a simple random sample of psychologists from the directory list and request the sample group to complete an online questionnaire or telephone interview.

Not everyone in the sample is likely to agree to participate. In this case, the resulting sample of participants is no longer a random sample. If the response rate to the questionnaire or telephone interview falls below 70 percent, you should be concerned about the randomness of the sample.

Cluster Sampling

In **cluster sampling**, researchers select naturally occurring groups, rather than individuals, as the sampling unit. For example, suppose we wish to know how high school seniors perform on a new test of reading comprehension. We only have resources to administer the test to a sample of students in a school district. It would be difficult to select a random sample of students and find a way to administer the test to each of them individually. The task is much easier if we use a naturally occurring group in schools, such as a class of students taking a particular course. For example, we might identify a course that all high school seniors take and then randomly select some of those classes for our sample. We could test all of the students efficiently because they are assembled together in convenient clusters.

Stratified Random Sampling

Stratified random sampling is a procedure for ensuring that individuals in the population who have certain characteristics are represented in the sample. For example, suppose that researchers are interested in whether boys and girls from four different home environments (single parent, mother; single parent, father; both parents together; guardians) have different attitudes toward mathematics.

If the researchers draw a simple random sample from a school district's list of students, they possibly will get few or no students in one of these eight classifications: (1) boys with single parent, mother; (2) girls with single parent, mother; (3) boys with single parent, father; (4) girls with single parent, father; (5) boys with both parents together;

(6) girls with both parents together; (7) boys with one or more guardians; and (8) girls with one or more guardians.

To ensure that all eight groups are represented in the sample, the researchers can use stratified random sampling. They would consider each of these groups (called *strata* or *levels* in sampling terminology) as a separate population. They then would draw a random sample of a given size from each group, thereby ensuring that each population is represented adequately in the sample.

Another option is to draw random samples of different sizes (but each size being an adequate number) so that the proportion of students in each group in the sample is the same as their proportion in the population. This procedure is called **proportional random sampling**.

Volunteer Samples

Educational research usually requires face-to-face interaction with individuals, as when a researcher needs to administer tests under standardized conditions or try out a new instructional method. It is expensive, though, to define a target or accessible population that covers an extensive geographical area, randomly select a sample from it, and then travel to the individuals in the sample to collect the necessary data. Therefore, researchers often work with nonrandom samples.

Sampling is further complicated by the fact that researchers are legally and ethically required to obtain informed consent from individuals or their guardians before involving them in a research project. An individual can refuse to participate for any reason. As a result, many studies involve **volunteer samples**, that is, samples based on individuals' expression of willingness to participate in a research study rather than on systematic sampling strategies. Samples of this type sometimes are called *convenience samples*.

In the teacher efficacy study, Mohammad Karimi relied on two volunteer samples, which he labeled as convenience samples. The treatment sample participated in the professional development program, and the control sample did not:

> The teachers in the treatment group were a convenience sample of 30 teachers accepted in the Ilam Province Teacher Training Center. The teachers assigned to the control group were a purposefully selected sample of 30 teachers in the junior high schools of Ilam and Kermanshah. For the control group, attempts were made to choose teachers with characteristics similar to those in the treatment group. Thus, the equivalency of the teachers in the two groups in terms of length of service, age range, and number of male and female teachers was confirmed prior to pre-testing them on self-efficacy. (p. 56)

You will note that the control group was not entirely a convenience sample. Karimi needed to select teachers who matched the treatment group on certain characteristics in order to be included in the sample. The success of the matching is demonstrated by statistics in the article showing the similarity of the control group to the treatment group in length of service, age range, and percentage of male and female teachers.

Population Validity

The primary difficulty with volunteer samples is that they might have characteristics that differ from the population they are intended to represent. If the differences are large, the sample is said to have low population validity. The term **population validity** refers to the degree to which the sample of individuals in the study is representative of the population from which it was selected. Population validity is important because it tells us how generalizable the results of a particular study are.

Population validity is established in part by demonstrating that the selected sample is similar to the accessible population, which is the immediate population from which the researchers drew their sample. The researchers also must demonstrate that the accessible population is similar to the target population, which is the population to which the researchers wish to generalize or apply their research findings.

For example, if researchers are interested in investigating career planning among high school seniors, the target population could be defined as all seniors in U.S. public and private high schools. This target population most likely would be too large from which to draw a sample. The researchers might then limit themselves to their local community—let's say, Denver, Colorado. In this case, Denver high school seniors would be the accessible population from which the sample would be drawn.

To establish population validity, the researchers need to demonstrate similarity on variables that are relevant to their research problem among (1) the sample, (2) the accessible population (Denver high school seniors), and (3) the target population (all U.S. high school seniors). For example, it seems reasonable to expect that career planning would vary by students' gender, socioeconomic status, and grade point average. Therefore, the researchers should determine the extent to which their sample, the accessible population, and the target population are similar on these variables. Evidence of similarity helps to establish the population validity of the sample.

It also is important to determine the degree to which students, teachers, or other groups in the research sample are similar to the groups in the local setting to which you wish to apply the research findings. As the similarity between the research sample and the local group decreases, the generalizability of the research results becomes more uncertain.

Comparison of the research sample with your local group is sometimes a difficult task for several reasons. First, research reports may include very little information about the sample and the accessible population from which it was drawn. Second, local educational organizations often can provide only limited information about the characteristics of the local group that is of interest to you. Third, it might be difficult to decide which differences between the research sample and the local group might actually affect the applicability of the research findings.

Given these problems, the best test of population validity might be to check research-validated educational practices and other research findings by collecting local data. Action research, which we describe in Chapter 18, is often useful for this purpose.

METHOD SECTION: MEASURES

Research data are only as sound as the measures used to obtain them. Therefore, the research report should include information about each measure that was used: the construct being measured, the scoring procedures for the measure, and evidence of the measure's validity and reliability. You should be able to obtain this information by using one of the search engines or bibliographic indexes described later in the chapter.

Another good way to learn about a measure used in a research study is to examine a copy of it. Some school systems and universities maintain collections of commonly used tests and the manuals that accompany them. Otherwise, you might be able to order a copy from the publisher. If the measure was developed specifically for the research study, you can write to the researchers and request a copy. They should be willing to send you a copy if you state a reasonable purpose for your request and if you provide assurances that you will maintain the confidentiality of the measure.

Types of Measures

Four types of measures are commonly used in quantitative research studies: (1) paper-and-pencil tests and scales, (2) questionnaires, (3) interviews, and (4) direct observation. Each type is described in the following sections.

Tests, Scales, and Performance Measures

Tests (commonly called *achievement tests*) measure an individual's knowledge, skills, or depth of understanding within one or more curriculum domains. They typically yield a total score, based on the number of items answered correctly. In recent decades, achievement tests have been used to make high-stakes decisions about schools, teachers, and students. In this context, they are called **high-stakes tests** because they hold schools, teachers, or students to particular accountability standards, which, if not met, can have adverse consequences for them. For example, influential groups in recent years have recommended that decisions about retaining or firing teachers should be based on their students' performance on achievement tests.

Scales measure an individual's attitudes, personality characteristics, emotional states, interests, values, and related factors. They typically yield a total score, which is the sum of the individual's responses to item scales. For example, a **Likert-type scale item** typically has five response options (such as 5 points for "strongly agree" to 1 point for "strongly disagree"). This was the type of measure used in Mohammed Karimi's professional development study, the purpose of which was to determine whether a particular type of professional development would enhance teachers' self-efficacy.

Karimi used a previously developed scale, the Teacher Sense of Efficacy Scale, to measure this outcome. It has 24 items, each of which is responded to on a 9-point scale, with anchors at 1 (nothing), 3 (very little), 5 (some influence),

7 (quite a bit), and 9 (a great deal). The following are three sample items:

How much can you do to get through to the most difficult students?

To what extent can you craft good questions for your students?

How well can you establish routines to keep activities running smoothly?

In addition to a total score for the 24 items, the measure can be scored on three 8-item subscales: Efficacy for Instructional Strategies, Efficacy for Classroom Management, and Efficacy for Student Engagement.

Many tests and scales are designed to fit on standard-size (8½" × 11") sheets of paper. Individuals can write their responses directly on the test sheets or on an answer sheet with a pen or pencil. For these reasons, measures of this type traditionally have been called *paper-and-pencil measures*. Now that computers are commonly available, test-and-scale items often are displayed on computer screens, and research participants can enter their responses using the computer keypad.

Performance measures involve the evaluation of individuals as they carry out a complex real-life task. A driving test is an example of a performance measure because the test requires that you drive a car while being evaluated by an examiner. These measures typically must be individually administered. They are used much less than paper-and-pencil or computer-administered measures in research studies because they typically cost more and are more time-consuming.

Paper-and-pencil or computer-administered tests and scales have certain limitations, however. First, most of them require that the research participant be able to read and write. Thus, individuals who lack these skills will be unable to show what they know or think about the constructs measured by such tests and scales. Another limitation is that they rely on self-report. This is not a serious problem when measuring academic achievement, but in attitude measurement, for example, individuals might wish to hide their true attitude in order to produce a socially acceptable response. The third limitation is that many tests and scales are group-administered. Thus, it is difficult for the researcher to determine the physical and mental state of the persons being assessed.

If they happen to be ill, tired, or emotionally upset, they are likely to perform atypically on the measure.

In educational practice, teacher grades at the end of a school term or grading period are the most common type of student assessment. Their use in educational research, however, is problematic. Different teachers might look at different components of students' academic achievement and classroom behavior in assigning grades, and they might place different weights on these components. For example, Hunter Brimi (2011) conducted a study of high school teachers' grading of students' writing performance. Seventy-three high school teachers were asked to grade the same student paper on a 100-point scale. Their scores ranged from 50 to 96, suggesting wide variability among teachers in what they looked for as elements of a good student paper and how much weight to place on each element. This finding is all the more remarkable because the teachers had been trained to use the same scoring system, called a rubric. It is no wonder, then, that teachers' grades are not commonly used as measures in educational research.

Questionnaires

A paper-and-pencil test or scale usually measures one or two variables, such as knowledge of vocabulary or attitude toward school. In contrast, a **questionnaire** is a set of questions in paper-and-pencil or computer format that typically measures many variables. For example, a questionnaire might ask respondents about the type of computer they have, the software programs they use, the frequency of use of each program, their previous training in computers, and their intentions to expand their use of computers in the future. The response to each question constitutes a separate variable in the research study.

Questionnaires might include **open-ended items**, which require individuals to write responses in their own words. For example, an item might ask the sample participants to describe their main uses of the computer. Questionnaires also might include **closed-ended items**, which require individuals to make a choice among options. For example, an item might include 10 common uses of a computer and ask sample participants to check each use that applies to them. Information about the construction of questionnaires is provided in Chapter 9.

In evaluating a research questionnaire, we recommend that you ask yourself the following questions.

1. *Was the questionnaire pretested?* A research participant might interpret a questionnaire item differently than intended by the researcher. Therefore, the researcher should pilot-test (i.e., try out) the questionnaire on a small sample of individuals prior to the main study. Analysis of their responses should be used to refine the questionnaire. If a pilot study has been done, you can have more confidence that the findings reported in the main study are valid.

2. *Does the questionnaire include leading questions?* If a copy of the questionnaire is included in the research report, check it for leading questions. These are questions framed in such a way that individuals are given hints about the kind of response that is expected. Results obtained from leading questions are likely to be biased, so they should be interpreted with caution.

3. *Does the questionnaire include psychologically threatening questions?* The researcher should avoid questionnaire items that might be psychologically threatening. For example, a questionnaire sent to school principals concerning the morale of their teachers would be threatening to some principals because low morale suggests that they are failing in part of their job. If they feel threatened, the principals probably will not complete and return the questionnaire. If they do return it, little confidence can be placed in the accuracy of their responses because of their ego involvement in the situation.

4. *Do the individuals who received the questionnaire have the requested information?* Researchers inadvertently might send a questionnaire to a sample that does not have the desired information. If this happens, the sample will provide inaccurate information or simply not complete the questionnaire.

Interviews

Unlike paper-and-pencil tests, scales, and questionnaires, **interviews** involve the collection of verbal—and sometimes nonverbal—data through direct interaction between the researcher and the individuals being studied. One of their main advantages is adaptability to the situation. The researcher typically creates a schedule of interview questions beforehand but allows the interviewers to ask additional questions in order to produce a full picture of the respondents' opinions and feelings.

The major disadvantage of interviews is that the direct interaction between researcher and interviewee makes it easy for subjectivity and bias to occur. Research participants might be eager to please their interviewer or might, on the other hand, develop a vague antagonism toward the interviewer because of the constant stream of questions. Another concern is that interviewers might seek out answers that support their preconceived notions.

The following questions will help you evaluate research studies that use interviews to collect data.

1. *How well were the interviewers trained?* The level of training required for interviewers is directly related to the type of information being collected. Less training is required for structured interviews because the interviewer asks specific questions from an interview schedule and does not deviate from them. More training is required for semistructured and unstructured interviews because the interviewer does not employ a detailed interview guide. Instead, the interviewer has a general plan and decides, as the interview progresses, what questions and comments to use in order to lead the interviewee toward the interviewer's objectives. Information on the training that interviewers received should be included in the research report.

2. *How was information recorded?* Audio recording is the most accurate method of recording interview information. If interviewers take notes instead of audio recording the interview, they might overlook important information or take biased notes. If the situation permits, video recording can yield even more information.

3. *Were the interview procedures pilot-tested before the study began?* Because interviewing tends to be highly subjective, the researcher must employ various safeguards to obtain objective data. A pilot study should be done to develop these safeguards before data for the main study are collected.

4. *Were leading or psychologically threatening questions asked?* As with questionnaires, leading and psychologically threatening questions can invalidate interview data.

If an interview was a primary measure in a research study, the report should include at least the main questions that were asked. You should study these questions for signs of bias. More information about the construction of interviews is provided in Chapter 9.

Direct Observation

Direct observation involves an observer collecting data while an individual is engaged in some form of behavior or while an event is unfolding. The observer generally uses a standard observation form that defines each variable and provides directions for recording each observed occurrence of it.

Direct observation yields more accurate data about particular variables than questionnaires or interviews because questionnaires and interviews rely on self-reporting, which is more susceptible to distortion and error than direct, impartial observation. However, a disadvantage of direct observation is that it tends to be time-consuming. Also, the observer might change the situation being observed, albeit unintentionally. Another possible problem is **observer bias**, which is the tendency to perceive an event in such a way that relevant aspects of the event are overlooked, distorted, or falsified.

In evaluating the use of observational procedures in a research study, you should consider the following questions.

1. *Were high-inference or low-inference variables observed?* Observational variables differ in the amount of inference required by the observer. A **high-inference variable** requires the observer to examine a behavior and then think carefully about whether it is the result of an underlying cognitive or an emotional process. A **low-inference variable** requires the observer only to examine a behavior and then decide whether it is an instance of a behavioral construct. The validity of the observer's data will be more of an issue if the observational variables are high-inference than if they are low-inference.

For example, an observer will need to engage in a greater degree of inference to decide how much enthusiasm a teacher is exhibiting during a lesson than to decide how many verbal praise statements the teacher makes. Enthusiasm is a cognitive and emotional construct that underlies and motivates behavior. A verbal praise statement is a construct that can be defined in terms of the language that a person uses. It does not require inferences about the individual's underlying cognitions and emotions.

2. *Were observers trained to identify the variables to be observed?* The researcher should describe the extent and type of training provided for the observers.

3. *How long was the observation period?* The observation period should be of sufficient duration to obtain a representative sample of the behaviors being studied. Otherwise the observation data could yield atypical results. The necessary period of observation will depend on such factors as the nature of the behaviors being observed, the circumstances under which the behavior occurs, and the frequency of occurrence.

4. *How conspicuous were the observers?* For ethical reasons, observers in most research studies need to be visible to the research participants. Consequently, the observers are likely to have some impact on the participants. This problem can be overcome to a certain extent if the observers do not record any observational data initially. In classrooms, for example, students usually will become accustomed to observers after a while and will engage in their customary behavior. You should examine the research report to determine whether the researchers were sensitive to the possibility of observer effects and took steps to minimize them.

In the study of professional development that we are using as an example, teachers in the experimental group participated in three 16-session courses about language teaching that made use of five professional development models. The researcher colleted attendance data to ensure that the teachers participated in each session. This is a form of indirect observation. The researcher also might have considered directly observing some of the sessions to determine how well they followed the intended professional development model. If a model was not followed according to a set of specifications, this information would be useful in itself and also might explain failures to improve teacher self-efficacy if such failures were found.

Content Analysis

Researchers sometimes focus their observations on documents produced or used by research participants. The investigation of data derived from documents is called **content analysis**. For example, researchers might study how males and females are portrayed in textbooks or the issues that are mentioned in the minutes of school board meetings.

Content analysis involves the development of categories and then a frequency account of the occurrence of each category in the document. For example, a researcher might establish the following categories for the analysis of elementary school mathematics textbooks: calculation problems involving only numbers, word problems involving situations that children are likely to encounter, and word problems involving situations that children are not likely to encounter. The researcher might collect data about the frequency and percentage of each type of problem in different textbook series.

In evaluating the soundness of a content analysis, you should look for evidence that (1) the categories are clearly defined and worthy of study, (2) the procedure for selecting a sample of documents is sound, and (3) different observers are able to use the categories reliably.

Validity of Measures

The definitive guide for determining the quality of tests and other measures is *Standards for Educational and Psychological Testing* (American Educational Research Association, American Psychological Association, & National Council on Measurement in Education, 1999). We refer to this book hereafter as the *Standards*. According to the *Standards*, a good test is one that yields reliable test scores from which we can make interpretations that have strong validity.

The key concepts in this view of test quality are validity and reliability. We discuss validity in this section of the chapter and reliability in the next.

Test validity refers to the "degree to which evidence and theory support the interpretation of test scores entailed by proposed uses of tests" (*Standards*, p. 9). For example, if we administer a science achievement test to a group of students, each student earns a score on the test. We would interpret this score as a representation of how much each student has learned about science relative to other students. It is helpful to think about this interpretation as a *claim* that we make about the scores on this test.

Note that, according to the *Standards*, a test is neither valid nor invalid. Furthermore, the scores earned by individuals who take the test are neither valid nor invalid. Rather, it is our interpretations of the test scores—or, in other words, the claims that we make about the test scores—that are valid or invalid. Test developers and test users need to provide empirical evidence that their claims are valid. We might find that one claim about the test scores is valid, but that another claim about the same test scores is invalid.

Five types of evidence and theory can be used to demonstrate the validity of the claims we might make from individuals' scores on a test or other measure:

1. Evidence from test content
2. Evidence from internal structure
3. Evidence from relationship to other variables
4. Evidence from response processes
5. Evidence from consequences of testing

Some of these types of evidence might be more important than others for judging the validity of a particular test used in a research study. To make this judgment, you need to be familiar with all five types. Also, you should be aware that authors of older research reports used different terms to refer to these types of evidence. The terms used in the 1999 edition of the *Standards* are intended to convey the fact that there are not different types of test validity. Rather, there are only different types of evidence to support test validity, which is a unitary construct.

Evidence from Test Content

Content-related evidence of test validity involves a demonstration that the content of the test's items matches the content that it is designed to measure. For example, researchers might claim that the XYZ Test is a valid measure of how much students have learned about algebra in high school. To support their claim, they might argue that the test has **face validity**, which involves the degree to which the test *appears* to measure what it claims to measure. For example, we might examine the items of the XYZ Test and conclude that the test is valid because the items correspond to our view of what high school students typically are taught in an algebra course.

The evidence for test validity would be much stronger if we went beyond appearance (i.e., the "face" of the test) by systematically comparing the test content with course content. This comparison is time-consuming because we need to analyze in minute detail the textbooks, lesson plans, hand-outs, classroom assignments, and teacher-made tests as well as each item on the XYZ Test.

Content-related evidence of test validity is particularly important in research on how different teaching methods affect students' learning. The test of learning should measure as precisely as possible the curriculum content that was taught in the methods under investigation.

The Ohio State Teacher Efficacy Scale was used in Karimi's study of professional development. If we wanted, we could obtain a copy of this measure and examine the content of each item to determine whether it corresponded to the concept of teacher efficacy, either as we conceptualize it or as it was conceptualized by the developers of the measure.

Evidence from Internal Structure

Nearly all tests and other measures have multiple items. These items and their relationship to each other constitute the internal structure of the test. An examination of a test's internal structure can provide evidence about its validity.

Suppose that researchers claim that a particular test, which has 10 items, measures a teacher's desire to engage in continuous professional development. If this claim is true, each of the 10 items should measure this variable. This means that if a teacher responded to an item in a certain way, we would predict a similar response to all of the other items; conversely, a teacher who responded to the item in a different way should respond to the other items the same way. This prediction can be tested by the use of correlational statistics (see Chapters 6 and 11).

Evidence from Relationship to Other Variables

The *Standards* describes several types of validity evidence that have a common feature, namely, the degree of relationship between (1) individuals' scores on the test and (2) their scores on another measure. These types of validity evidence include predictive evidence, convergent evidence, and concurrent evidence.

Predictive evidence of test validity involves a demonstration that (1) individuals' scores on the test predict (2) their future performance on

another test or measure. For example, suppose that the developers of a test claim that it measures skill in reading comprehension among students in the upper grades. If the test in fact measures reading comprehension, it is reasonable to predict that eighth-grade students who earn higher scores on it will also earn higher grades in their high school courses because good reading comprehension is necessary for success in these courses. The researchers can collect empirical data to test this hypothesis. If the results support the hypothesis, they can serve as evidence of the test's validity.

Convergent evidence of test validity involves a demonstration that (1) individuals' scores on the test are related to (2) their scores on another test or measure of the same variable. Mohammad Karimi, the researcher who used the Ohio State Teacher Efficacy Scale, referred to evidence of this type to support his contention that the measure was valid. He cited research studies demonstrating that teachers who score high on the Ohio State Teacher Efficacy Scale are likely to score high on these two other measures of the same concept.

Some tests are rather long, so developers create a shorter version as an alternative option. Evidence supporting the validity of the longer test might be strong, but this does not mean that the shorter version also has validity. To demonstrate the validity of the shorter version, the developers need to do studies in which a sample of individuals take both versions. If individuals who earn higher scores on the longer version also earn higher scores on the shorter version, this serves as evidence of the shorter test's validity. This type of evidence, based on administration of two versions of the same test within a brief time interval, is called **concurrent evidence of test validity** in the *Standards*.

Evidence from Response Processes

As we take a test, we engage in particular cognitive processes. Some of these processes might be consistent with the variable that the test is designed to measure, but other processes might not be. **Response-process evidence of test validity** involves a demonstration that the processes used by individuals in taking the test are consistent with the particular variable that the test presumably measures.

For example, a test of critical thinking might be designed to engage students' higher-order reasoning processes to solve certain types of mathematical problems. Suppose, however, that some students obtain high scores on the test because they had received extensive instruction on these problem types and therefore were able to solve them by applying memorized algorithms rather than using higher-order reasoning processes. In this case, the validity of the claim that the test scores reflect higher-order reasoning would be compromised.

Evidence from Consequences of Testing

Individuals' scores on a test can have consequences for them. **Consequential evidence of test validity** is the extent to which the values implicit in the variables measured by a test and in the intended uses of the test are consistent with the values of test-takers, those who will use the test results to make decisions, and other stakeholders.

For example, students who get low scores on a standardized achievement test might face the consequence of being denied admission to the college of their choice. Children's scores on a test battery might have the consequence of labeling them as having a learning disability, with the further consequence that they might be assigned to special education teachers. In each of these examples, we need to determine whether the test was developed with these consequences in mind.

These two examples illustrate the direct consequences for individuals that can result from interpretations of their test scores by others. At a more general level, policies about testing also have consequences. For example, some policy makers argue that preservice teachers should take and pass competency tests in order to obtain a teaching license, claiming that this requirement will result in a more effective teacher workforce (Mitchell, Robinson, Plake, & Knowles, 2001). Evidence relating to this claimed consequence of tests of teacher competency should be collected. This evidence can be used to judge the validity of the competency tests for their intended use by policy makers.

Karimi did not explicitly discuss the consequential validity of the Ohio State Teacher Efficacy Scale. However, he cites research evidence that enhanced teacher efficacy has positive effects on teachers' instructional success, commitment to teaching, and adoption of innovative teaching strategies. To the extent that we value these outcomes, we can say

that the measure has sound consequential validity. However, some teacher educators might argue that other professional development programs focus on more important teacher characteristics and outcomes. From their perspective, the Ohio State Teacher Efficacy Scale has undesirable consequential validity.

Reliability of Measures

A test or other measure is considered to have **reliability** to the extent that it is free of measurement error. In classical test theory, **measurement error** is construed as the difference between the scores that individuals actually obtain on a test and their true scores.

A **true score** is the score that an individual would receive if it were possible to obtain a perfect measure of the construct. For example, if two individuals score a student's test and obtain different total scores, measurement error has occurred. Because there is only one true score that a student can earn on the test, the assumption is that at least one of the scorers has miscalculated.

Less obviously, suppose a student takes the same achievement test on two different days and obtains two different scores. These different results also constitute measurement error. They are not errors in the usual sense of the word, that is, mistakes resulting from the student's lack of skill. Instead, they reflect shortcomings in the test's ability to measure the student's performance in a stable manner. Because an individual can have only one true score on a test, the assumption is that at least one of the test administrations on the two days has a measurement error.

A variety of factors can create measurement error. Possible factors are differences in the skill of those who administer the measure, changes in the conditions of test administration from one day to the next, temporary fluctuations in how individuals respond to the measurement situation, and features of the measure's items that affect different individuals differently. It is virtually impossible to eliminate all of these sources of error from a test or other measure.

If a test or other measure has very low reliability, it will produce large errors of measurement. These errors will obscure the effects of methods and programs or the magnitude of a relationship between variables. This problem can be understood by considering the case of a completely unreliable test. After the test is administered, the resulting scores will consist entirely of measurement error, meaning that they are essentially random numbers. Random numbers obviously cannot reveal the true effects of educational programs or the true relationships between variables. For this reason, you need to check how reliable a measure is before you reach conclusions about research findings based on its use.

The degree of reliability of an educational measure is usually expressed by a **reliability coefficient**. A reliability coefficient is a type of correlation coefficient, which we explain in Chapters 6 and 11. For now, it is sufficient for you to know that reliability coefficients range from .00, which indicates no reliability, to 1.00, which indicates perfect reliability. In other words, a reliability coefficient of .00 signifies that the test scores are meaningless because they consist entirely of measurement error; in contrast, a reliability coefficient of 1.00 means that the measure has absolutely no measurement error. As a rule of thumb, a measure is considered reliable for most research and practical purposes if its reliability coefficient is .80 or higher. In the case of the Ohio State Teacher Efficacy Scale, Karimi cites evidence from other studies that reliability coefficients for the entire scale have ranged from .92 to .95 and that reliability coefficients for the three subscales have ranged from .86 to .90.

Procedures have been developed to estimate the magnitude of the different types of measurement errors in a test. We describe four of these procedures in the next sections. In doing so, we use *test* as a generic term to refer to various forms of measurement, such as achievement tests, attitude scales, observational scales, and frequency counts of content analysis categories.

Item Consistency

One type of measurement error is caused by inconsistencies in the items that make up the test. For example, if a test of visual creativity contains some items that measure one variable and other items that measure a somewhat different variable, the total score will be an inaccurate indicator of visual creativity. Therefore, test developers strive for **item consistency**, that is, a test in which all of the items measure the same construct. In other words, they want the items to be consistent. If the items are perfectly consistent, individuals who score one way on an item should score the same way on all of the remaining items.

Cronbach's alpha is a reliability coefficient that is commonly used to quantify the extent to which an individual's scores across different items on a test are consistent with each other. This coefficient is commonly used to test the internal consistency of attitude scales. If the items are dichotomous, as is the case with most achievement tests (1 = correct, 0 = incorrect), the internal consistency of the measure is determined by the **Kuder-Richardson Formula 20**. It is seldom the case that all items on an achievement test are equally difficult, but if they are, the Kuder Richardson Formula 21 is used instead.

Stability of Measurement

Measurement error often occurs when individuals take the same test on several different occasions. These variations can occur for several reasons. For example, an individual might be fatigued on one testing occasion and rested on the next. Or an individual might have reviewed a relevant item of information just before one testing occasion, but not just before the next.

If a test is free of this type of measurement error, individuals should earn the same score on each testing occasion. To determine the extent to which this is the case, researchers administer the test to a sample of individuals, and after a delay of several days or more, they administer the same test again to the same sample. Scores obtained from the two administrations are correlated to determine their reliability or, in other words, their consistency across time. This type of reliability is called **test-retest reliability** or **test stability**.

Consistency of Administration and Scoring

Individuals who administer or score tests can create measurement errors because of absentmindedness, not knowing the correct procedures, or other reason. Measures with highly objective scores, such as multiple-choice tests, tend to be free of this type of measurement error. However, even test-scoring machines have been known to make scoring mistakes because of mechanical defects. Measures with less objective scores, such as individually administered intelligence tests, personality tests, or high-inference observational scales, are more subject to administration and scoring errors.

Test administration errors can be identified by having several individuals administer the same test to the same sample. Similarly, scoring errors can be identified by having several individuals or machines score the same set of tests. A reliability coefficient is calculated for the sets of scores to determine how well they agree. The degree of reliability among the individuals who administer or score measures usually is called **inter-rater reliability**.

Standard Error of Measurement

Another approach to expressing the magnitude of a test's reliability is to calculate the standard error of measurement. This reliability statistic is based on the assumption that each individual's score on a test has two components: the individual's true score and the measurement error.

Suppose that the test measures knowledge of vocabulary. The individual's true score would be a perfect measure of the amount of this ability that the individual actually possesses. The difference between the individual's obtained score on the test and the individual's true score is the measurement error. Although we cannot know the individual's true score (except on a perfectly reliable test), the **standard error of measurement** is an estimate of the probable range of scores within which the individual's true score falls.

The calculation procedures and rationale for the standard error of measurement are fairly sophisticated. For present purposes, it is sufficient to know that the calculation of a standard error of measurement enables the researcher to make a statement like: "The chances are about 95 in 100 that this sample's true score on the test lies between 12.75 and 16.63." It is advantageous for researchers to use a highly reliable test because it reduces the range of values likely to contain the true score.

Evaluating Researchers' Determination of Reliability

We have described four procedures for estimating a test's reliability: calculation of item consistency, stability of measurement, consistency of test administration and scoring, and the standard error of measurement. It is unlikely that researchers will determine all of these types of reliability for each measure used in a study. Depending on the measure involved and the research situation, one of these types of reliability usually is of most concern.

Item Response Theory

It is difficult to develop a test that is reliable for all individuals. For example, consider the measurement of mathematical problem-solving ability. This ability varies across a long continuum, from none at all to the ability to solve the types of mathematical problems taught in school, and ultimately to the ability to solve complex problems in theoretical mathematics.

A test that contained primarily items in the mid-range of this ability would be unsuitable for estimating the true score of individuals having the most rudimentary problem-solving skills in mathematics or the true score of individuals with highly sophisticated problem-solving skills. Also, even for individuals in the mid-range of this ability, the test might have satisfactory reliability for individuals at some points in this mid-range but not for individuals at other points.

These problems can be overcome to a large extent by developing tests based on item response theory (IRT). **Item response theory** is based on the assumption that individuals with different amounts of an ability will perform differently on the items measuring that ability. For example, suppose we have a large sample of items that represents the entire continuum of mathematical problem-solving ability and a large sample of individuals who also represent the entire continuum of this ability. Most of the individuals will be able to answer the simplest items. As the items become more difficult, fewer individuals—the ones with more problem-solving ability—will be able to answer them.

By using individuals' item responses and IRT statistical procedures, test developers can order the items by difficulty level so that they can determine the level at which a particular individual "tests out." By this we mean that the test items are placed in order such that a particular individual is able to answer most of the items below that difficulty level and few or no items above that difficulty level. Once we find the difficulty level at which the individual tests out, we can administer more items at that difficulty level in order to improve the reliability of measurement.

Test development using IRT procedures is complex and expensive. Also, test administration typically requires a computer that presents items one at a time while also adjusting item difficulty based on the individual's responses to preceding items.

However, because of the superior reliability of tests based on IRT, this approach is being used increasingly to develop high-stakes tests, such as those used to assess students' academic achievement or potential for success in university studies and different occupations. Scores from such test administrations are likely to be used increasingly in educational practice and research.

Limitations to Tests of Validity and Reliability

Researchers sometimes determine the validity and reliability of their measures by using evidence from other studies. If these studies involve a different population from the one used in the researcher's study, the validity and reliability evidence might not be applicable. In other words, a measure might be valid and reliable for one population but not another. Therefore, you need to check the source of the validity and reliability evidence that is presented in a research report.

Another problem found in some research reports is that the researchers develop their own measure but do not adequately check its validity and reliability. A common reason for not making these checks is that they are time-consuming and expensive.

Rather than developing new measures, many researchers choose well-developed existing measures. If you are planning to do a quantitative research study, consider whether you can frame your research problem in such a way that you can rely on existing measures of your variables rather than having to develop new ones.

Sources of Information about Established Measures

Thousands of measures have been developed for use in educational research and related disciplines. They measure a wide range of individual characteristics, including academic achievement, academic aptitude, learning styles, personality traits, self-concept, attitudes, and vocational interests.

As stated above, before developing your own measure for research or practice, you should consider searching for a suitable measure that has already been developed. The search engines and publications described in Chapter 4 are helpful for this purpose. Consider, too, search engines and publications specifically designed to index measures of various types. Some of the more widely used ones are listed in Figure 5.1.

These resources can help you identify measures for your study and also help you evaluate the validity and reliability of measures that you encounter in research reports or educational practice. Manuals for widely used measures, particularly aptitude and achievement tests, also provide this type of information. In addition, you can inspect the measure itself and make judgments about its soundness and applicability to your needs.

Developing a Measure

Developing a measure is a complex process. This is particularly true for achievement tests, attitude scales, and personality scales. The development steps include the following.

- Define the construct that is to be measured, and show how it relates to similar but different constructs. Justify the importance of the construct.
- Define the population for whom the construct and the measure are appropriate.
- Review related measures that have already been developed. Explain why your new measure is needed.
- Develop a prototype of the measure. Write an adequate number of items, with attention to the relationship of each item to the construct and to the other items in the measure. Write the items so that they will be comprehensible for the intended audience.
- Conduct a field test of the measure. Collect adequate data for an analysis of each item.
- Revise the measure based on the field results. Continue the cycle of field testing and revision until the measure has achieved accepted standards for validity, reliability, and usability by those who will administer it to individuals and samples in the target population.

This list of steps reveals that developing a measure requires expertise and time. In fact, some researchers conduct studies whose only purpose is to determine the validity and reliability of measures that they or others have developed. The

FIGURE 5.1 • Sources of Information about Measures Used in Education

BEHAVIORAL ASSESSMENT

Herson, M., & Bellack, A. S. (2002). *Dictionary of behavioral assessment techniques*. Clinton Corners, NY: Percheron.

EXCEPTIONAL STUDENTS

Taylor, R. L. (2009). *Assessment of exceptional students: Educational and psychological procedures* (8th ed.). Upper Saddle River, NJ: Pearson.

FAMILY PROCESSES

Touliatos, J., Perlmutter, B. F., Straus, M. A., & Holden, G. W. (Eds.). (2001). *Handbook of family measurement techniques* (Vols. 1–3). Thousand Oaks, CA: Sage.

GENERAL

Educational Testing Service (n.d.). *Test Link*. Retrieved from http://www.ets.org/test_link/find_tests/ This website contains a database of information about more than 25,000 tests. Some of the tests can be obtained on the website.

MENTAL MEASUREMENT

Spies, R. A., Carlson, J. F., & Geisinger, K. F. (Eds.). (2010). *Mental measurements yearbook* (18th ed.). Lincoln, NE: Buros Institute of Mental Measurements.

Continually updated to include new tests, revised tests, and frequently referenced tests. The online version of these yearbooks is *Test Reviews Online* (see below). Another relevant resource is *Tests in Print*, which is a hard-copy index, updated periodically, to all the Yearbooks.

Buros Center for Testing (n.d.) *Test reviews online*. Retrieved from http://buros.unl.edu/buros/jsp/search.jsp

This resource is a web-based version of the *Mental Measurements Yearbook*, providing information on nearly 4,000 tests and critical reviews for many of them. The test information is free, but the critical reviews are fee-based.

PSYCHOLOGICAL ASSESSMENT

Hersen, M. (Ed.). (2004). *Comprehensive handbook of psychological assessment* (Vols. 1–4). Hoboken, NJ: Wiley.

Each volume covers tests for a particular purpose: intellectual and neuropsychological assessment, personality assessment, behavioral assessment, and industrial and organizational assessment.

American Psychological Association (n.d.). *PsycTESTS*. Retrieved from http://www.apa.org/pubs/databases/psyctests/

This website contains a database of information about psychological tests and other types of measures. The focus is on unpublished measures that have been used in research.

SOCIAL PROCESSES

Kempf-Leonard, K. (Ed.). (2004). *Encyclopedia of social measurement* (Vols. 1–3). Washington, DC: American Psychological Association.

---

journal article reprinted at the end of this chapter illustrates this kind of study, as do the following citations:

Garmy, P., Jakobsson, U., & Nyberg, P. (2012). Development and psychometric evaluation of a new instrument for measuring sleep length and television and computer habits of Swedish school-age children. *Journal of School Nursing, 28*(2), 138–143.

Kim, J., & Craig, D. A. (2012). Validation of a video-conferenced speaking test. *Computer Assisted Language Learning, 25*(3), 257–275.

Sandholtz, J. H., & Shea, L. M. (2012). Predicting performance: A comparison of university supervisors' predictions and teacher candidates' scores on a teaching performance assessment. *Journal of Teacher Education, 63*(1), 39–50.

Weiland, C., Wolfe, C. B., Hurwitz, M. D., Clements, D. H., Sarama, J. H., & Yoshikawa, H. (2012). Early mathematics assessment: Validation of the short form of a prekindergarten and kindergarten mathematics measure. *Educational Psychology, 32*(3), 311–333.

If you are planning to conduct your own research study, you should consider searching for well-developed measures for your variables. Otherwise, you will need to acquire expertise in measurement and extend the time line for your study to include measure development.

Method Section: Research Design and Procedures

Research reports should describe the research design that was used to obtain the data needed to test the hypotheses, answer the questions, or achieve the objectives of the research study. Chapters 9 through 12 explain how quantitative studies vary in their research design.

As a simple illustration, consider this research question: Do students in small classes learn more than students in large classes? One research design for answering this question would be to find existing classes that are large and small, but that all have students at the same grade level learning the same curriculum subject. We can compare the two groups of classes on an achievement test administered after a certain period of instructional time has elapsed.

Another research design would be to start with a sample of teachers and randomly assign one group to teach a large class and one group to teach a small class. This is a classic experimental design because it involves manipulating a situation rather than studying a situation that is already in place. As in the research design described in the preceding paragraph, we can compare the two groups of classes on an achievement test after a certain period of instructional time has elapsed.

This illustration demonstrates that the same research question can be answered by two different research designs. The designs have advantages and disadvantages relative to each other—a matter that is discussed in subsequent chapters.

The descriptions of procedures in research reports vary in length. Because descriptive research designs (see Chapter 9) generally are simple, the researchers might find it sufficient to explain how

and when the measures were administered. If descriptive data were collected periodically, as in longitudinal research, the time intervals should be specified.

Other research designs, especially experimental designs (see Chapter 12), require more detailed explanations. For example, the report should indicate the time line of the experiment so that readers know when the various measures and treatments were administered. Also, each of the experimental treatments (for example, a new teaching method) should be described so that other researchers could implement them as intended if they wish to replicate the study.

You will need a basic understanding of various research designs in order to evaluate the adequacy of the research design used in a particular quantitative research study. Chapters 9 through 12 are intended to help you develop this understanding. In addition to explaining each design, we present a report of an actual research study that used it.

Results Section

The results section of a quantitative research report presents the results of statistical analyses of the data collected from the measures that were administered to the sample. Interpretation of the results is left to the final section of the report, namely, the discussion section.

In Karimi's study of professional development for teachers, the statistical analyses focused on comparisons of the treatment and control group on the measure of teacher self-efficacy. These comparisons are shown in Table 5.1 in the form of two descriptive statistics—the mean and standard deviation (SD). These statistics show that the treatment

TABLE 5.1 • Comparison of the Treatment and Control Groups on the Test of Teacher Efficacy in a Professional Development Study

Group	Pretest Means (SD)	Posttest Means (SD)	3-Month Delayed Posttest Means (SD)
Treatment (N = 30)	105.53 (31.54)	120.36 (27.33)	120.36 (27.68)
Control (N = 30)	102.86 (31.68)	103.26 (31.65)	103.20 (31.76)

Based on Karimi, M. N. (2011). The effects of professional development initiatives on EFL teachers' degree of self efficacy. *Australian Journal of Teacher Education, 36*(4), 50–62. Reprinted by permission of the Australian Journal of Teacher Education.

and control groups were very similar in self-efficacy prior to professional development for the treatment group. However, the treatment group made substantial gains in self-efficacy after participating in professional development, while the control group remained at its pretest level. The treatment group maintained its gains in self-efficacy three months after the professional development group ended.

Karimi also tested the statistical significance of the difference between the mean scores of the treatment and control groups at each of the three administrations of the teacher self-efficacy scale. The difference was not statistically significant for the pretest comparison, but it was for the posttest and delayed posttest comparisons. We explain descriptive statistics in Chapter 6 and tests of statistical significance in Chapter 7. Then, in Chapters 9 through 12, we explain how these statistical techniques are used in conjunction with particular quantitative research designs.

If you are planning to do a quantitative research study, you might find that reading these chapters is sufficient for your professional needs. However, depending on your degree or licensing program, you might be required to take courses on research statistics and test development. These courses will enhance your capacity to do your own research or interpret research findings in the literature.

Discussion Section

The final substantive section of a quantitative research report is the discussion (sometimes called *conclusions*). Following the discussion section is a list of bibliographic citations for the publications mentioned in the body of the report. Next, there might be one or more appendices, such as a supplemental statistical analysis or a copy of a measure used in the study.

The discussion section gives researchers the opportunity to express their own interpretations of the results, evaluate shortcomings in the design and execution of the study, draw conclusions about the practical and theoretical significance of the results, and make recommendations for further research.

In evaluating the discussion section, you must decide whether you agree with the researchers' judgments about how the results should be interpreted and their implications for theory and professional practice. The most critical factor in this evaluation is whether you think the researchers'

judgments are supported by their empirical findings and the findings of previous research studies that they cited. Your ability to make this evaluation will improve as you develop your understanding of research methodology and knowledge of the research literature to which a particular study contributes.

In the professional development study, Mohammad Karimi reflected on his statistical results and the findings of previous related research and concluded: "The results of the study proved a significant effect of PD [professional development] initiatives on enhancing EFL [English as a foreign language] teachers' sense of efficacy in teaching" (p. 59). As an educator, you might be called on to make a judgment about whether this conclusion is sufficiently compelling to warrant the expense of instituting the type of professional development that was tested in the researcher's study. Also, you might be asked to defend teacher self-efficacy as an important goal for professional development.

After reading the study, you might decide that its findings and the findings of related research are promising, but not sufficiently compelling to warrant changes in current professional development policies. If so, you will need to identify and explain the shortcomings of this and related studies to your colleagues. You also might be called upon to recommend a study, or group of studies, that would lead to conclusive results.

This situation illustrates the high stakes involved in conducting and interpreting research. If you wish to make a contribution to the improvement of education, you will need to learn all you can about research methodology. Otherwise, you and your colleagues might institute changes in practice that have no actual evidence to support them or, conversely, fail to make changes that would lead to genuine, demonstrable improvement of practice.

An example of
How Quantitative Research Can Help in Solving Problems of Practice

The June 27, 2012, issue of the *Christian Science Monitor* (Robelen, 2012) reported that girls are underrepresented in STEM (science, technology, engineering, and mathematics) courses and careers. For example, only 20 percent of the students who took the Advanced Placement (AP) test in computer science were female. Also, recent government statistics show that females represent only 25 percent of the workforce in STEM careers.

What can educators do to solve this problem of practice? One approach is to continue doing the kind of quantitative research that yields the statistics cited in the article. We need to know how large the gender gap in STEM coursework and careers is and whether it is diminishing or increasing over time. If the gap remains large, these statistics might galvanize educators and policy makers to create initiatives that will reduce, or even eliminate, the gap.

The article mentioned several such initiatives that were identified by Linda Rosen, the chief executive officer of Change the Equation, an alliance of business executives who promote STEM education:

> Promising examples she cited include the National Girls Collaborative Project, an effort that has received funding from the National Science Foundation to promote STEM for girls, and GirlStart, which provides

STEM-focused after-school programs and summer camps.

We need to ask whether these initiatives are producing the desired results. Quantitative research studies can provide the answer. For example, experiments can be done in which girls are randomly assigned to participate in GirlStart and a no-intervention control group. Researchers can follow both groups over time and do statistical analyses to see whether a larger percentage of the GirlStart participants take STEM courses and AP tests in STEM subjects. Researchers also can collect the participants' STEM course grades and AP test scores and do statistical analyses to compare their grades and scores with those of boys taking the same courses and tests.

Without this type of quantitative research, we have no reliable way of knowing whether interventions can effectively reduce STEM gender inequity. The statistical data yielded by quantitative research might seem cold and impersonal, but in fact, they touch on students' lives in a very real and personal way if properly used by educators and policy makers.

SELF-CHECK TEST

1. Reports of quantitative research studies typically
   a. are written in a more personal style than are reports of qualitative research studies.
   b. follow the style guidelines of the American Psychological Association.
   c. do not include an abstract.
   d. begin with a description of the research design that was employed.

2. Many research studies in education are designed to test the effectiveness of different instructional methods. In this kind of research, the instructional methods being studied constitute a
   a. constant.
   b. scale.
   c. variable.
   d. research hypothesis.

3. In simple random sampling, researchers
   a. select a sample of individuals who are easily accessible in the target population.
   b. identify sample populations and randomly select one of them to be studied.
   c. ensure that each individual in the population has an equal chance of being in the sample.
   d. all of the above.

4. To evaluate population validity, researchers must analyze
   a. the selected sample, the accessible population, and the target population.
   b. the selected sample and the target population.
   c. the accessible population and the target population.
   d. the membership list used to define the target population.

5. A research questionnaire ideally should
   a. include several leading questions to put the respondent at ease.
   b. measure only one variable.
   c. be used instead of an interview to collect psychologically threatening information.
   d. undergo pretesting before being used with the actual research sample.

6. In a study that involves direct observation of classroom instruction, the best example of a low-inference observational variable would be
   a. teacher enthusiasm.
   b. amount of time allocated for seatwork.
   c. students' on-task behavior during seatwork.
   d. the cognitive level of students' responses to teacher questions.

7. If researchers want to develop a test whose items are ordered on a scale of difficulty, they will find it useful to
   a. do a content analysis to identify the constructs being measured.
   b. follow the procedures specified by item response theory.
   c. focus on collecting concurrent evidence of test validity.
   d. focus on collecting consequential evidence of test validity.

8. If a measure has high reliability, it means that it
   a. is relatively free of measurement error.
   b. can be understood and completed by most students.
   c. will yield valid results for most users.
   d. has a low Cronbach's alpha value.

9. All of the following typically appear in the discussion section of a quantitative research report, except
   a. the statistical results.
   b. an interpretation of the statistical results.
   c. speculations about the practical significance of the results.
   d. recommendations for further research.

10. Shortcomings in the design and execution of a study typically are analyzed
   a. by a peer reviewer in a separate section of the report.
   b. at the beginning of the report.
   c. in the discussion section of the report.
   d. in the methodology section of the report.

CHAPTER REFERENCES

American Educational Research Association, American Psychological Association, & National Council on Measurement in Education. (1999). *Standards for educational and psychological testing.* Washington, DC: American Educational Research Association.

American Psychological Association. (2010). *Publication manual of the American Psychological Association* (6th ed.). Washington, DC: Author.

Brimi, H. M. (2011). Reliability of grading high school work in English. *Practical Assessment, Research & Evaluation, 16*(17), 1–12. Retrieved from http://pareonline.net/pdf/v16n17.pdf

Evans, P. (1976). The Burt affair: Sleuthing in science. *APA Monitor, 12*, 1, 4.

Karimi, M. N. (2011). The effects of professional development initiatives on EFL teachers' degree of self efficacy. *Australian Journal of Teacher Education, 36*(6), 50–62.

Mitchell, K. J., Robinson, D. Z., Plake, B. S., and Knowles, K. T. (Eds.). (2001) *Testing teacher candidates: The role of licensure tests in improving teacher quality.* Washington, DC: National Academy Press.

Robelen, E. W. (2012, June 27). Girls in science: Gender gaps still persist in STEM subjects. *The Christian Science Monitor.* Retrieved from http://www.csmonitor.com/layout/set/r14/The-Culture/Family/2012/0627/Girls-in-science-Gender-gaps-still-persist-in-STEM-subjects

Tschannen-Moran, M., & Hoy, A. W. (2001). Teacher efficacy: Capturing an elusive construct. *Teaching and Teacher Education, 17*, 783–805.

RESOURCES FOR FURTHER STUDY

Bovaird, J. A., Geisinger, K. F., & Buckendahl, C. W. (Eds.). (2011). High-stakes testing in education: Science and practice in K–12 settings. Washington, DC: American Psychological Association.

This book provides a discussion of important issues involved in the development and use of high-stakes tests in local and state assessments, accountability systems, and the assessment of special populations and students applying to colleges or other institutions having entrance requirements.

Downing, S. M., & Haladyna, T. M. (Eds.). (2006). *Handbook of test development*. Mahwah, NJ: Lawrence Erlbaum.

The 32 chapters of this book cover all aspects of test development and use, including an extensive treatment of the kinds of evidence that can be used to establish a test's validity.

Fowler, F. J. (2008). *Survey research methods* (4th ed.). Thousand Oaks, CA: Sage.

This book provides a basic guide for designing and conducting research surveys involving questionnaires and interviews. Among the topics covered are methods for constructing survey questions, methods for obtaining high response rates, and the use of computers, the Internet, landline phones, and cell phones to collect and analyze data.

Gall, M. D., Gall, J. P., & Borg, W. R. (2007). *Educational research* (8th ed.). Boston, MA: Allyn & Bacon.

This book is intended for individuals who want to develop a deeper understanding of each of the topics covered in this chapter.

Green, J. L., Camilli, G., & Elmore, P. B. (Eds.). (2006). *Handbook of complementary methods in education research*. Mahwah, NJ: Lawrence Erlbaum.

The chapters in this book are written by experts in research methodology. Some of them cover topics that we discuss in this chapter, including direct observation, interviewing, measurement, item response theory, and survey research.

Krippendorff, K. H. (2012). *Content analysis: An introduction to its methodology* (3rd ed.). Thousand Oaks, CA: Sage.

This book explains conceptual bases for content analysis, procedures for conducting a content analysis, and methods for evaluating the validity and reliability of a content analysis.

Waxman, H. C., Tharp, R. G., & Hilberg, R. S. (Eds.). (2004). *Observational research in U.S. classrooms: New approaches for understanding cultural and linguistic diversity*. Cambridge, UK: Cambridge University.

This book describe various observational measures and how they can be used in both research and the improvement of educational practice.

Developing a Measure of Behavior Change in a Program to Help Low-Income Parents Prevent Unhealthful Weight Gain in Children

Dickin, K. L., Lent, M., Lu, A. H., Sequeira, J., & Dollahite, J. S. (2012). Developing a measure of behavior change in a program to help low-income parents prevent unhealthful weight gain in children. *Journal of Nutrition Education and Behavior, 44*(1), 12–21.

The following journal article illustrates the process of developing a measure. The authors describe the development of the HCHF Behavior Checklist. You will note that the researchers took particular care that the wording of the scale items was comprehensible to the intended audience. They also checked the reliability and validity of the scales using procedures described in this chapter.

The authors used a particular type of statistic, the correlation coefficient, in checking the reliability and validity of the HCHF Behavior Checklist. This statistic is explained in Chapter 11. In simple terms, a correlation coefficient tells us the extent to which individuals' scores on one measure predict their scores on another measure. A positive correlation coefficient (e.g., .33) tells us that our predictions will be better than random guesses, but not perfect. The highest possible correlation coefficient (1.00) tells us that we can make perfect predictions.

Developing a Measure of Behavior Change in a Program to Help Low-Income Parents Prevent Unhealthful Weight Gain in Children

KATHERINE L. DICKIN, PhD[1]; MEGAN LENT, BS[1]; ANGELA H. LU, MS, RD[1]; JORAN SEQUEIRA, BS[2]; JAMIE S. DOLLAHITE, PhD, RD[1]

ABSTRACT

Objective: To develop and test a brief measure of changes in eating, active play, and parenting practices after an intervention to help parents shape children's choices and home environments.

Design: Sequential phases of development and testing: expert panel review, cognitive testing interviews, field testing, test-retest study, and assessment of convergence with detailed previously validated instruments.

Setting and Participants: Expanded Food and Nutrition Education Program (EFNEP), New York State. Low-income parents of 3- to 11-year-old children; Cooperative Extension nutrition and parenting educators.

Main Outcome Measures: Questionnaire reliability, validity, respondent comprehension, and feasibility of use in program contexts.

Analysis: Qualitative analysis of item comprehension. Correlational analysis of test-retest reliability and convergent validity.

Results: A behavior checklist was developed to assess change in parent-reported family eating, physical activity, and parenting practices addressed by an intervention. The checklist was feasible for use in EFNEP and questions were understood as intended. Test-retest reliability was good ($r = 0.83$) and scores correlated significantly (range, 0.25 to −0.60; $P < .05$) with detailed measures of dietary habits, parental modeling, physical activity, and home environment.

Conclusions and Implications: Development and testing in a program context produced a tool community nutritionists can use to evaluate educational interventions aimed at helping parents promote healthful eating and activity.

Key Words: nutrition education, parenting practices, program evaluation, child overweight, low-income population (*J Nutr Educ Behav.* 2012;44:12–21.)

[1]Division of Nutritional Sciences, Cornell University, Ithaca NY

[2]New York Medical College, Valhalla, NY

Address for correspondence: Katherine L. Dickin, PhD, 348 MVR Hall, Division of Nutritional Sciences, Cornell University, Ithaca, NY 14853; Phone: (607) 255-7297; Fax: (607) 255-0027; E-mail: kld12@cornell.edu

doi:10.1016/j.jneb.2011.02.015

Introduction

Translational research and evaluation of nutrition education programs to help families prevent unhealthful weight gain in children require brief, high-quality tools to measure behavioral outcomes in program contexts. Despite extensive research on how parents shape children's eating and activity habits, there is a shortage of data on the effectiveness of obesity-prevention efforts targeting parents.[1] Discussing barriers to the translation of public health research into action, Glasgow and Emmons[2] emphasize the need for practical behavioral trials in actual program contexts. Integrating evaluation into program processes is a sustainable and cost-effective way to gather data needed to inform program decisions.[3] This type of integrated evaluation calls for measurement tools that ensure trustworthy data, yet are simply worded and have low respondent burdens feasible for program use.[4]

The Expanded Food and Nutrition Education Program[5] (EFNEP) is a large-scale program that conducts continuous evaluation of outcomes to complement but not replace more controlled, external evaluations. EFNEP's internal evaluation system collects pre- and posteducation self-report data on key behaviors[6] and was recognized by the United States Government Accountability Office as having many strengths, including assessing behavioral change during intermediate periods, a set of core items against which all programs report, and flexibility to fit local programming.[7] In addition to 10 required items on primary EFNEP objectives, items can be added to assess behaviors targeted by particular curricula.

This article describes the development and testing of a measure of behavior change for a new, behaviorally based EFNEP curriculum called "Healthy Children, Healthy Families: Parents Making a Difference!" (HCHF).[8] This curriculum integrates nutrition, active play, and parenting education in an 8-session workshop series for parents or caregivers of 3- to 11-year-old children in EFNEP's low-income audience. The HCHF workshops are part of the Collaboration for Health, Activity and Nutrition in Children's Environments (CHANCE), a multicomponent childhood obesity prevention initiative in EFNEP in New York State.[9] The CHANCE initiative is based on the socioecological model, recognizing that health behaviors are influenced by physical, cultural, and socioeconomic environments that must be considered in programs promoting behavior change.[10] For example, to make healthful choices easier for children, parents can create home environments in which healthful foods are available and their consumption is modeled.[9]

The HCHF workshops focus on eating and physical activity behaviors that help prevent unhealthful weight gain in children and on effective parenting practices for promoting healthful habits.[8] Concurrent with the development of HCHF, a tool was created to monitor change over time in specific behaviors promoted in the intervention. To fit within program setting and timing, the pre-post questionnaire had to be simple and short enough for self-administration by participants of various literacy skills.[4] For evaluation purposes, the measure had to be detailed enough to capture change in key behaviors and tested to ensure validity and reliability. Balancing the sometimes conflicting priorities of programming and evaluation is an unavoidable challenge of translational research.

The research objectives were to (1) develop an easily-administered tool assessing change in nutrition, active play, and parenting behaviors between initial and final sessions of HCHF; (2) ensure that items were interpreted as intended, covered key learning objectives of HCHF, and were feasible for use in usual programming; and (3) assess the scale's test-retest reliability and convergent validity.

Methods

The HCHF Behavior Checklist (BC) was developed in an iterative process from selection and review of items through several phases of testing (Table 1). Demographic information, including age, education, race, ethnicity, and number and ages of children, was collected in all phases and research respondents were representative of the HCHF audience. No incentives were paid to HCHF program participants, but respondents participating in testing outside the program received a modest cash incentive ($15–$25). All protocols were approved by the Cornell University institutional review board. Written informed consent was obtained from all respondents.

HCHF Behavioral Objectives

Items were developed to measure, by parental report, the current frequency of the food, activity, and parenting practices promoted by the curriculum.[8] Minimal time is available for collecting data in program settings, so BC length was limited by reviewing and reducing HCHF behavioral objectives to those with the highest priority and relevance. The BC was developed in tandem with the curriculum, so efforts to refine behavioral objectives contributed to both endeavors.

Selection of HCHF nutrition and physical activity behavioral objectives was based on research evidence demonstrating relevance for preventing unhealthful weight gain in children and reducing risk of chronic disease.[11-14] Nutrition objectives were that parents and children increase consumption of vegetables and fruits, drink low- or nonfat milk and water instead of sweetened beverages, reduce consumption of energy-dense foods (eg, high-fat or high-sugar snacks and convenience foods), and eat "sensible servings" by starting with small amounts and attending to hunger and satiety. Desired physical activity behaviors included limiting

Table 1

Summary of the Process of Behavior Checklist Development and Revision

Method	Purpose	Version
Development of items, expert panel review, internal review	Content validity/behavioral objectives Brevity/clear language	Reviewed 36 items; revised and selected items for version 1
Field testing: round 1	Feasibility Distribution of entry scores	Version 1 (14 items)
Cognitive testing	Clarity/interpretation of items Ease of understanding and responding	Version 1 plus alternate wording options
Field testing: round 2	Feasibility Variability of entry scores	Version 2 (16 items)
Test-retest assessment	Temporal stability	Version 2
Comparison with detailed instruments	Convergent validity	Version 2, slightly revised

television, computer, and video screen time to no more than 2 hours per day; 60 minutes of active play most days for children, and 30 minutes of moderate physical activity most days for adults. Parenting practices promoted as ways to achieve these food and activity goals were characteristic of authoritative parenting and feeding styles,[15–17] including role modeling, being supportive, offering choices within limits, and shaping home (and other) environments. Parental food choices were viewed as affecting parents' health directly and influencing children via modeling.

Initial Item Development

Item format conformed to the EFNEP behavioral checklist,[6] assessing the frequency of behaviors with 5 response options representing increasing levels of frequency. To capture expected ranges in frequency before and after HCHF, response options varied by question to include the likely *current* frequencies of behaviors for most participants and also the *recommended* frequencies. For example, parents were asked, "How often do you eat together with your child at least 1 meal a day?" and the responses were almost never, 1 to 2 days each week, 3 to 4 days each week, 5 to 6 days each week, or every day. Review of existing items in the federal EFNEP database and other questionnaires did not identify sufficient items on HCHF behavioral objectives with low-literacy wording and formatting to assess frequency, so new items were developed.

Expert Panel

An expert panel of 5 nutrition and 2 parenting Cooperative Extension professionals in counties collaborating on HCHF reviewed items for the BC to enhance content validity.[18] The panel reviewed 36 items, rating item clarity, suitability for program audience, and relevance to HCHF on 3-point scales ("poor" to "good"). According

to this input, 22 items were selected and revised. Further internal review by the researchers resulted in the initial 14-item version 1 of the BC (Table 2).

Cognitive Testing

Interviews were conducted in 3 communities to investigate whether respondents understood the BC items as intended and to assess ease of answering.[19–21] Each respondent participated in a 1-hour audiorecorded interview. The interviewer read and showed each item to respondents, asked them to "think aloud" as they answered, and used verbal probes (eg, "What does 'regular soda' mean to you?" "How did you count up the number of servings of vegetables you ate?") to elicit specific information or clarify responses.[20] Response options (eg, "once a week") were tested similarly. Three rounds of interviews, alternating with qualitative analysis and item revision, were conducted. Data were analyzed by summarizing respondents' comments, understanding and interpretation of terms (eg, snacks, moderate physical activity), ease of responding, and suggestions for improvement. Common themes and conflicting responses were identified[19] and summarized across participants for each item.[22] Peer debriefing[23] after each round guided scale revision.

Field Testing

The BC was field tested in the program, with usual staff and participants, to assess feasibility of use and variability of responses. Version 1 was used from January to September 2007 and version 2 was used from September 2007 to October 2008 (Table 2). Both versions were translated into Spanish (and backtranslated) and field tested in English and Spanish. As is usual practice in EFNEP in New York, program educators collected demographic and BC data from all participants at program entry. Analysis of BC items assessed the distribution of entry scores for all participants

Table 2

Behavior Checklist Items and Comparison of Wording in Versions Used in Field Tests

Version 1	Version 2	Item[a]
	How many days each week do you usually eat fruit (including fresh, dried, frozen, and canned)?	1
	How many days each week do you usually eat vegetables (including fresh, frozen, and canned)?	2
How often do you drink regular soda or sugary drinks (juice drinks, sports drinks, energy drinks, etc)?	How often do you drink regular (NOT diet) soda?	3
How often do you use either low-fat (1%) or nonfat (skim) milk?	How often do you use 1% or skim milk?	4
How often do you participate in at least 30 minutes of moderate physical activity each day? This includes brisk walking, gardening, and biking.	How often are you moderately physically active for at least 30 minutes a day? This includes brisk walking, dancing, playing actively with kids, and vacuuming.	5
How often do you offer fruits to your children?	How many days each week do your children usually eat fruit (including fresh, dried, frozen, and canned)?	6
How often do you offer vegetables to your children?	How many days each week do your children usually eat vegetables (including fresh, frozen, and canned)?	7
How often can your children have regular soda or sugary drinks (juice drinks, sports drinks, energy drinks, etc)?	How often do your children drink regular (NOT diet) soda?	8
How often do your children have low-fat dairy products (milk, yogurt, etc)?	How often do your children have 1% milk, skim milk, or low-fat yogurt?	9
How often do you let your child decide how much food to eat?	How often do you let your children decide how much food to eat?	10
How much time does your child spend watching TV, using the computer, or playing video games?	How much time do your children spend watching TV, using the computer, or playing video games?	11
How often does your child (children) play actively for at least 60 minutes a day?	How often do your children play actively for at least 60 minutes a day?	12
How often do you eat with your children in a fast food restaurant?	How often do your children usually eat take out, delivery, or fast foods (such as burgers, fried chicken, pizza, Chinese food)?	13
How often do you eat at least 1 meal with your children each day?	How often do you eat together with your children at least 1 meal a day?	14
When shopping for snacks, how often do you buy foods like cookies, potato chips, candy, etc?	How often are high-fat or high-sugar snacks available at home for your children to eat? This includes chips, candy, cookies, and sweets.	15
How often do you offer fruits or vegetables to your children as snacks?	How often are fruits available at home for your children to eat?	16

[a]Item number in version 2. Order of version 1 adjusted for comparison of wording of similar items.
Note: Version 1 did not ask about adult consumption of fruit or vegetables.

who answered an item, even if data were missing on other items, so sample size varied by item.

Test-Retest Reliability

Temporal stability, or the consistency of scores over time,[18] was assessed as test-retest reliability.[24] The BC was administered twice, about 2 weeks apart, to eligible parents who had not participated in HCHF but were in groups similar to the program setting. Pearson correlation coefficients assessed within-person correlation of scores on the overall BC at the 2 time points.

Convergent Validity

To determine how well this brief scale measured the underlying constructs it targeted, convergent validity was assessed as the scale's correlation with other measures of related constructs.[24] In 45- to 60-minute sessions, respondents who were eligible for but had not participated in HCHF completed the BC plus comparison instruments measuring domains of behavior similar to the BC, but in greater depth. As described below and in Table 3, comparison instruments were selected according to previous validation, psychometric properties, and appropriateness for the HCHF audience.

The Food Behavior Checklist (FBC), developed for a program context similar to that of HCHF, includes pictures to aid comprehension[25] and was previously validated against 24-hour recall data and serum carotenoid values.[26] The Child Food Frequency Questionnaire on parent report of child intake of fruits, vegetables, soda, and sweets has been validated by comparison with a 3-day food diary.[27] The Parental Dietary Modeling Scale assesses parental modeling of healthful eating and was previously found to correlate with reported parent eating patterns and fat, fruit, and vegetable intake.[28] The Family Eating and Activity Habits Questionnaire (FEAHQ) differentiated between families of overweight and normal-weight children and includes multiple subscales on adult and child behaviors and home environments.[29] The Sports, Play, and Active Recreation for Kids (SPARK) Parent Survey[30] was the best available parental-report measure of adult and child physical activity and parental support of child activity. Published information on the validity of the overall scale is lacking, but the adult physical activity items have been tested for reliability and validity.[31] The Caregiver Feeding Style Questionnaire

Table 3

Subscales of Behavior Checklist and Instruments Used to Assess Convergent Validity

Scale Description and Reference	Subscales	Items
HCHF BC (family eating, activity, and parenting practices covered in HCHF curriculum)	Fruits and vegetables	5
	Low-fat dairy foods	2
	Soda	2
	Energy-dense foods	2
	Physical activity	3
	Parenting practices	2
FBC[26] (adult dietary patterns)	Fruits and vegetables	7
	Milk	2
	Fat and cholesterol	2
	Dietary quality	4
	Food security	1
PDMS[28]	NA	6
CFFQ[27]	NA	4
SPARK Parent Survey[30] (child and parent physical activity)	Child MET	18
	Parent MET	3
	Barriers and supports for child activity	7
FEAHQ[29] (home environment and family habits)	Hunger cues	4
	Family rites (meal routines)	4
	Parent FEAHQ (eating and activity)	24
	Child FEAHQ (eating and activity)	24
CFSQ[17,32]	Demandingness	19
	Responsiveness (ratio of 7/19 items)	26

BC indicates Behavior Checklist; CFFQ, Child Food Frequency Questionnaire; CFSQ, Caregiver Feeding Style Questionnaire; FBC, Food Behavior Checklist; FEAHQ, Family Eating and Activity Habits Questionnaire; HCHF, Healthy Children, Healthy Families; MET, metabolic equivalent task; NA, not applicable; PDMS, Parental Dietary Modeling Scale; SPARK, Sports, Play, and Active Recreation for Kids.

has been validated against measures of parenting and feeding and found to predict child body mass index.[17,32] Its responsiveness score (the ratio of "child-centered" to "demanding" subscale scores) assesses authoritative parenting style and is therefore relevant to the practices promoted in HCHF.

The BC (version 2 in Table 2) was divided into subscales: vegetables and fruits (items 1, 2, 6, 7, and 16), low-fat dairy (items 4 and 9), soda (items 3 and 8), physical activity (items 5, 11, and 12), energy-dense foods or sweets and fats (items 13 and 15), and parenting (items 10 and 14). Subscales varied in focus on individual parent or child behaviors or actions to shape home environments. Convergent validity of the BC and its subscales with relevant comparison instruments was assessed with Pearson correlation coefficients.

Results

All respondents in each phase were responsible for the care of a 3- to 11-year-old child (96%–100% were parents) and had low income, and the majority of respondents were women (Table 4). The majority (71%–85%) had 1 to 2 children. The field-test sample, consisting of actual HCHF participants, included higher proportions of Latinos and non-high school graduates compared with the samples of other phases (Table 4).

Cognitive Testing

Interviews were conducted with 13 respondents typical of HCHF participants. Problems identified included

finding simple wording that conveyed intended meanings clearly to all respondents, given the diversity of families and age range of children, and capturing the frequencies of parenting practices with brief items. Although it is not possible to report all of the qualitative results and the basis for all revisions, key themes that emerged in multiple interviews or across items are summarized below.

Use of Examples. Examples clarified meanings. Respondents strongly favored items on fruits or vegetables that listed "fresh, dried, frozen, and canned" to remind them to consider all these forms. Otherwise, some underestimated intake. Similarly "chips, candy, cookies, and sweets" were relevant examples of high-fat, high-sugar snacks. For physical activity, "gardening" and "biking" were replaced with "dancing" and "playing actively with kids," both more relevant to the audience and the curriculum.

Multiple Categories. Mentioning more than one category of food in an item was problematic because consumption patterns often differed for each category. When intake of a food type was low, parents tended to disregard this food, answering in relation to other foods. Hence, fruits and vegetables had to be separated. The item on high-fat, high-sugar snacks was well understood, ie, if chips were never available, responses still reflected the other high-fat, high-sugar snacks that were available.

Portion, Frequency, and Variety. Previous researchers have assessed frequency of consumption "in the past week."[33] To increase accuracy of recall, items on intake

Table 4

Description of Samples for Each Phase of Testing, n (%)

Demographic Variables	Cognitive Testing (n = 13)	Test-Retest Reliability (n = 38)	Convergent Validity (n = 62)	Field Testing (n = 308)
Respondent age, y				
< 30	23.1 (3)	39.5 (15)	30.7 (19)	36.0 (111)
30–39	53.8 (7)	28.9 (11)	45.2 (28)	41.6 (128)
40–50	23.1 (3)	21.1 (8)	22.6 (14)	14.6 (45)
> 50	0.0 (0)	7.9 (3)	1.6 (1)	7.8 (24)
Female	100.0 (13)	94.7 (36)	90.3 (56)	92.5 (285)
Education				
< High school graduate	23.1 (3)	10.5 (4)	27.4 (17)	42.9 (132)
≥ High school graduate (or passed the General Educational Development test)	76.9 (10)	89.5 (34)	72.6 (45)	57.1 (176)
Race				
Latino	0.0 (0)	5.3 (2)	27.4 (17)	52.6 (162)
White	53.8 (7)	81.6 (31)	50.8 (31)	32.8 (101)
Black or African American	46.2 (6)	10.5 (4)	29.5 (18)	12.0 (37)
Other	0.0 (0)	5.3 (2)	19.7 (12)	2.6 (8)

were tested with this wording, but consumption varied widely week to week because of fluctuating household food resources and infrequent food shopping. When "in the past week" was dropped, respondents did not have difficulty answering items on usual frequency of intake, eg, "How many days each week do you usually eat __?" Items such as "How many vegetables do you usually eat in a day?" were eliminated because of pervasive confusion about whether to answer in terms of quantity, frequency, or variety.

Labels for Categories of Foods and Activity. Several words and phrases used to label types of food or activity were tested for understanding. "High-fat, high-sugar" was a well-understood description of energy-dense foods. "Regular soda" was sometimes interpreted as cola or caffeinated soda, but "non-diet" was not conventional usage and respondents misread "non-diet" as "diet" or focused more on "soda," answering differently than they did once the intended meaning was explained. A revised item referring to "regular (NOT diet) soda" was well understood. Another unfamiliar term was "moderate physical activity." Interpretations ranged from "work out in the gym" to "just from time to time." Some interpreted moderate as length of time rather than intensity. Revision of "How often do you participate in at least 30 minutes of moderate physical activity each day?" to "How often are you moderately physically active for at least 30 minutes?" with relevant examples clarified this item.

Parenting and Home Food Environment. Asking how often parents offer children vegetables and fruits was problematic because some children had free access, which parents did not perceive as "offering" the foods, so responses underestimated child access. Interpretations of items asking "How often can your child...?" or "How often do you allow...?" ranged from the amount a child ate to how a parent responded to child requests, so results were not consistent. The focus of these items was changed from parenting practice to child dietary behavior (eg, frequency of drinking soda, eating vegetables). This improved clarity but reduced the ability to measure parenting practices.

An item on serving fruits or vegetables as snacks confused parents who viewed fruits, vegetables, and snacks as 3 separate food types consumed in different quantities and frequencies. Some regarded "snacks" as sweets or chips. This item was revised to address the food environment, with fruits and vegetables separated into 2 questions. "How often are fruits available at home for your children to eat?" was easily answered. However, the same item addressing vegetable availability was eliminated because it was too difficult to distinguish between simple availability (ie, in the home but not ready to eat) vs preparing and serving vegetables to children.

An item on frequency of family meals was revised repeatedly because of multiple and conflicting interpretations. "How often do you sit with your children to eat at least one meal a day?" was often interpreted as a sit-down dinner with all family members. The intended focus of this item was the parent-child dyad, so it was revised to "How often do you eat together with your children at least one meal a day?" which parents answered without difficulty. An item on allowing children to decide how much food to eat was readily understood and did not need revision.

Finally, response categories that included specific frequencies such as 1 to 3 times per week were better understood than "sometimes" or "usually." In some families, consumption of fast foods was infrequent, so response categories on frequencies per month rather than per week were more appropriate and sensitive to change. Interviews also provided insights about why less change may occur in certain behaviors or families. For example, some parents reported that after buying 2% milk for a toddler, they could not afford to also buy low-fat milk for other family members.

The outcome of cognitive testing was the 16-item BC version 2. Overall, the interviews and revisions demonstrated that BC items were appropriate and well understood by low-income parents but also indicated some limits in the types of behavior that can be measured with this format.

Field Testing

Paraprofessional EFNEP educators successfully collected BC data at the start and end of HCHF series within the workshop setting and timing. In discussions and interviews, educators said it was feasible to use the BC and took about 5 to 10 minutes, no more than the usual EFNEP measure. During field testing, 308 participants provided BC data at program entry, 264 (85.7%) answered all questions, and the remaining 44 missed from 1 to 9 items. This indicates that most participants found the items acceptable and not difficult to answer. Mean BC entry score was 3.64 (SD 0.54). Except for 5 items, mean entry scores by item were in the middle of the 5-point scale, ranging from 2.58 (SD 1.53; n = 291) for adult intake of low-fat dairy products to 3.86 (SD 1.19; n = 296) for fruit availability. The 5 items with entry scores from 4.0 to 4.4 were child and adult soda intake, child physical activity, fast food and take out, and eating together with children. These entry scores leave little room for improvement but do identify areas in which the program audience may already be doing well, needing only reinforcement. Feedback from staff confirmed positive practices among many participating families. Even on these items, however, a substantial subset of people had low entry scores, and overall, scores were sufficiently variable to capture behavior change post-intervention.

Test-Retest Reliability

A sample of 38 respondents completed the BC twice, with no intervening nutrition or parenting education. The average interval between administrations was 18.9 days, with a range of 14 to 28 days. The BC had good test-retest reliability,[24] with a Pearson correlation coefficient of 0.83 ($P < .001$) of scores at time 1 and time 2 (within person).

Convergent Validity

Respondents were 62 parents or caregivers in 6 sites, ranging from small towns to urban areas. Most (84%) were parents who lived with their child all or most of the time; others were with the child for part of each week. Results of correlational analysis are presented below and in Table 5.

Overall BC Scores. Overall BC scores correlated significantly with the FBC and its subscales on fruit and vegetable intake, diet quality, and food security (Table 5). The correlation was surprisingly high, given that FBC assesses only adult practices. The correlation with FBC food security score has implications for families' ability to adopt recommended practices if food insecure (food security score was 3.15 of 5). Overall BC score also correlated with parental modeling and child food frequency scales, both of which relate to parents' child feeding practices. In sum, the BC score converged with more detailed and validated assessments of adult and child dietary intake, particularly fruits and vegetables, and parental feeding practices.

BC Subscale Scores. The BC vegetable and fruit subscale correlated with the FBC and its fruit and vegetable, fat, and food security subscales and also with the child food frequency scales, showing convergence with a validated measure of adult fruit and vegetable intake and with measures of child intake. More surprising, it also correlated with parental role modeling and fat intake, but not with the FEAHQ measures of home environment and eating practices.

The BC subscale on adult and child intake of low-fat dairy foods correlated with the FBC milk subscale (assessing adult dairy intake but not specifying low fat). No other scales directly assessed dairy intake. This BC subscale also correlated with FBC food security score, again suggesting the salience of economic barriers for families trying to make healthful food choices.

Table 5

Summary of Correlations[a] of Behavior Checklist (BC) and Subscales with Variables Assessed Using Other Instruments (n = 62 unless otherwise indicated)

Instrument	BC Overall	Fruit and Vegetable	Dairy	Soda	Sweets and Fats	Physical Activity	Parenting
FBC[26]	0.48***	0.44***	0.16	0.31*	0.09	—	0.32*
Fruit/vegetable	0.41***	0.46***	0.05	0.09	0.11	—	0.32*
Milk	0.22	0.00	0.28*	0.24	−0.13	—	0.10
Fat	0.21	0.25*	0.11	0.08	−0.14	—	0.20
Diet quality	0.27*	0.20	0.05	0.36**	0.18	—	0.17
Food security	0.31*	0.28*	0.26*	0.17	−0.11	—	0.03
Child Food Frequency[27]	0.52***	0.35**	0.19	0.41***	0.41***	—	0.06
Parental Modeling[28]	0.56***	0.39**	0.14	0.26*	0.08	0.43***	0.42***
SPARK[30] Survey[b]	0.08	—	—	—	—	0.44***	—
Child activity (n = 61)	0.07	—	—	—	—	0.36**	—
Parent activity	0.03	—	—	—	—	0.39**	—
Parent Eating and Activity Habits[29]	−0.10	0.06	0.16	−0.31*	−0.24	0.08	−0.07
Child Eating and Activity Habits[29]	−0.19	0.03	−0.10	−0.29*	−0.09	−0.10	−0.03

FBC indicates Food Behavior Checklist; SPARK, Sports, Play, and Active Recreation for Kids;—, comparison not tested because of lack of conceptual overlap in behavioral domains.

*$P < .05$; **$P < .01$; ***$P < .001$; [a]Pearson correlation coefficients; [b]SPARK parent survey on parent and child activity (metabolic equivalent task units) and parental support.

The BC subscale assessing adult and child soda intake was convergent with many other instruments, including FBC total and diet quality subscale, child food frequency, modeling, SPARK subscale on child physical activity, and FEAHQ total scores for parent and child. It also correlated with FEAHQ subscales on parent eating situation (-0.38; $P < .01$), child eating situation (-0.33; $P < .01$), and family rites or eating together (-0.25; $P < .05$). The negative correlation with the FBC milk subscale approached significance. BC soda intake seemed to be a marker for many practices measured by these more comprehensive instruments, even though not all of them directly assessed soda intake.

The BC subscale on energy-dense food correlated with the child food frequency score and the FEAHQ total score for parents. Convergence was particularly strong with FEAHQ parent (-0.55; $P < .001$) and child (-0.60; $P < .001$) home environment subscales, which assess types of and child access to sweets and snack foods in the home. Even with only 2 items, this BC subscale was an adequate proxy measure for access to a range of energy-dense foods.

The BC physical activity subscale correlated with the overall SPARK and its child and parent activity subscales. It also correlated with the FEAHQ home environment subscales for parents (0.26; $P < .05$) and children (0.31; $P < .05$), but not with the FEAHQ parent or child leisure subscales (which included activities not relevant to low-income parents and young children). There was also a significant positive correlation between this BC subscale and the parental dietary modeling scale.

The BC parenting subscale correlated with the parental dietary modeling score and the FBC total and fruit and vegetable scores but not with the FEAHQ family rites subscale that compiles more detailed information on adults eating with children at each daily meal and snack. The BC family meal item asked about eating together at least 1 meal per day because many children eat breakfast, lunch, and snacks at school. This difference in focus may underlie the lack of convergence with the FEAHQ subscale. Although focused on parenting around food, the BC parenting subscale also correlated with the SPARK subscale on parental support for child physical activity (0.33; $P = .009$).

A key goal of HCHF is to promote responsive parenting, so it was valuable to compare the BC with the CSFQ, a detailed measure of parental feeding styles, but it was not expected that the BC would converge highly with the CSFQ because of lack of overlap in the behaviors measured. The positive correlation between the CSFQ responsiveness and overall BC scores reached borderline significance ($r = 0.23$; $P = .08$; n = 61) and there was similar convergence with the BC parenting subscale ($r = 0.22$; $P < .10$), trends suggesting that the BC measured constructs related to parental feeding styles.

Discussion

Assessing intervention effectiveness in program contexts is needed to translate research into practice[2] and requires measures that fit program objectives, audience, and time constraints.[34] It may seem simple to devise a short questionnaire, but takes effort to ensure that it is well understood, is reliable, and collects data relevant to program objectives.[35] Particular challenges included adequately assessing parenting practices with a frequency scale, measuring both child and adult practices through parental report, and assessing many dietary behaviors in a brief format. The BC, by virtue of its brevity and simplicity, has limitations but also important strengths for monitoring program success.

The results of this research indicate that although cognitive testing can be time consuming, it should be considered an essential step in tool development. BC items that appeared well-worded to researchers and the expert panel were in fact open to multiple conflicting interpretations by parents. Items were improved through revision, but it remains the case that no simple sentence is likely to have the same meaning to everyone. Training should ensure that staff conducting outcome assessments can clarify the meaning of items to improve data quality. Cognitive testing was conducted only in English, and further work is needed to test comprehension and ease of use of the BC with diverse audiences.

Field testing demonstrated the feasibility and acceptability of using this measure in program contexts to monitor participant outcomes. Revisions to achieve lower mean entry scores could enhance the tool's sensitivity to behavior change. Test-retest reliability was good, with most people answering consistently during a period of about 2 weeks, enhancing confidence that variation in scores reflects change in the underlying construct of interest rather than random measurement error.[36]

The BC scores correlated with detailed measures of healthful eating, activity, and parenting. This convergent validity shows that BC data parallel data obtained by using instruments with greater breadth and depth but also greater response burden. In particular, convergence of BC scores with a fruit and vegetable subscale previously validated against serum carotenoids[26] strengthens the credibility of BC data. Convergence of the BC soda subscale with multiple instruments merits further investigation of soda intake as a marker of families in which a constellation of behaviors puts children at risk. This is particularly interesting in light of strong evidence linking soda consumption and unhealthful weight gain in children.[14,33] Correlation of the BC with parental dietary modeling was promising, given that helping parents to model healthful choices was a key objective of HCHF.

Convergent validity strengthens the conclusions that can be drawn from BC data on outcomes and supports use of the BC as a proxy indicator of the broader range of behaviors covered by HCHF or similar curricula. However, the BC has not yet been validated against actual behavior or biological markers, and this remains an important goal for future research. Internal reliability was not assessed in the BC because the focus was on breadth of practices covered and simplicity to facilitate program use. Although internal reliability is a desirable attribute of longer scales that contain multiple items to measure a common underlying construct,[18] the need for brevity in the BC meant that most items measured discrete behaviors and it was not meaningful to assess interitem correlation.

Implications for Research and Practice

Development and testing in a program context produced a tool community nutrition educators can use to evaluate educational interventions aimed at helping parents promote children's healthful eating and activity habits. After field testing, when HCHF was integrated into usual EFNEP in New York, version 2 of the BC was reduced to 15 items to fit with EFNEP procedures.[6] Testing did not indicate any particular item that was not performing well, but there were 3 items on fruit, so it was decided that dropping one (item 6) would have minimal influence on the breadth of behaviors assessed.

Appropriate programmatic evaluation tools are essential to ensure an emphasis on quality and attention to participant outcomes. This research demonstrated how such a tool can be created as an integral part of developing a new educational intervention. Feasibility and fit with intervention objectives are important for programmatic measures and often take priority over other considerations, but it is also important to ensure that evaluation tools are valid and reliable. This takes additional effort but can be accomplished with fairly limited resources and will strongly enhance the meaningfulness of the data. The HCHF BC is reliable, valid, easy to understand and administer, and brief enough for program use. Although no simple questionnaire can capture all the benefits of an educational program and no self-reported data collected by program staff can take the place of rigorous external evaluation, a tool such as the BC is invaluable for monitoring outcomes, identifying areas for improvement, and providing staff and agencies with feedback on the effect of their work.

Acknowledgments

This research was supported by Cornell University Agricultural Experiment Station federal formula funds, Project No. NYC-399412, Cooperative State Research, Education and Extension Service, United States Department of Agriculture. Any opinions, findings, or conclusions expressed in this publication are those of the authors and do not necessarily reflect the view of the United States Department of Agriculture. We acknowledge the staff and participants who made this research possible. Tisa Fontaine Hill and Dr Wendy Wolfe helped develop HCHF and Michelle Scott-Pierce assisted with data analysis.

REFERENCES

1. Lindsay A, Sussner K, Kim J, Gortmaker S. The role of parents in preventing childhood obesity. *The Future of Children*. 2006;16:169–186. http://www.princeton.edu/futureofchildren/publications/journals/article/index.xml?journalid=36&articleid=100. Accessed September 23, 2011.

2. Glasgow RE, Emmons KM. How can we increase translation of research into practice? types of evidence needed. *Annu Rev Public Health*. 2007;28:413–433.

3. Patton MQ. *Utilization-Focused Evaluation*. 3rd ed. Thousand Oaks, CA: Sage Publications; 1997.

4. Townsend MS, Kaiser LL, Allen LH, Joy AB, Murphy SP. Selecting items for a food behavior checklist for a limited-resource audience. *J Nutr Educ Behav*. 2003;35:69–82.

5. National Institute of Food and Agriculture. Expanded Food and Nutrition Education Program (EFNEP). US Department of Agriculture Web site. http://www.csrees.usda.gov/nea/food/efnep/efnep.html. Updated September 15, 2010. Accessed June 28, 2011.

6. National Institute of Food and Agriculture. Nutrition Education Evaluation and Reporting System (NEERS5). US Department of Agriculture Web site. http://www.csrees.usda.gov/nea/food/efnep/neers5/neers5.html. Updated March 18, 2011. Accessed June 28, 2011.

7. US Government Accountability Office. *Nutrition Education: USDA Provides Services Through Multiple Programs, But Stronger Linkages Among Efforts Are Needed*. Washington, DC: Government Accountability Office; 2004.

8. Lent M, Hill TF, Dollahite JS, Wolfe WS, Dickin KL. Healthy Children, Healthy Families: Parents Making a Difference! A curriculum integrating key nutrition, physical activity, and parenting practices to help prevent childhood obesity [published online ahead of print September 5, 2011]. *J Nutr Educ Behav*. doi: 10.1016/j.jneb.2011.02.011.

9. Collaboration for Health, Activity, and Nutrition in Children's Environments. Food and Nutrition Education in Communities, Cornell University Web site. http://www.fnec.cornell.edu/Our_Initiatives/CHANCE.cfm. Updated February 7, 2011. Accessed July 7, 2011.

10. Sallis J, Owen N. Ecological models. In: Glanz K, Lewis FM, Rimer BK, eds. *Health Behavior and Health Education: Theory, Research, and Practice*. San Francisco, CA: Jossey-Bass; 1997:403–424.

11. Institute of Medicine. *Preventing Childhood Obesity: Health in the Balance*. Washington, DC: Institute of Medicine of the National Academies; 2004.

12. Whitaker RC. *A Review of Household Behaviors for Preventing Obesity in Children.* Princeton, NJ: Mathematica Policy Research, Inc; 2004.

13. Woodward-Lopez G, Ritchie LD, Gerstein DE, Crawford PB. *Obesity: Dietary and Developmental Influences.* Boca Raton, FL: CRC Press; 2006.

14. Davis MM, Gance-Cleveland B, Hassink S, Johnson R, Paradis G, Resnicow K. Recommendations for prevention of childhood obesity. *Pediatrics.* 2007;120(suppl 4):S229–S253.

15. Patrick H, Nicklas TA, Hughes SO, Morales M. The benefits of authoritative feeding style: caregiver feeding styles and children's food consumption patterns. *Appetite.* 2005;44:243–249.

16. Baumrind D. Current patterns of parental authority. *Dev Psychol.* 1971;4:1–103.

17. Hughes SO, Power TG. Orlet Fisher J, Mueller S, Nicklas TA. Revisiting a neglected construct: parenting styles in a child-feeding context. *Appetite.* 2005;44:83–92.

18. DeVellis RF. *Scale Development: Theory and Applications.* Thousand Oaks, CA: Sage; 2003.

19. Alaimo K, Olson CM, Frongillo EA. Importance of cognitive testing for survey items: an example from food security questionnaires. *J Nutr Educ.* 1999;31:269–275.

20. Willis GB, Royston P, Bercini D. The use of verbal report methods in the development and testing of survey questionnaires. *Appl Cogn Psychol.* 1991;5:251–267.

21. Altschuler A, Picchi T, Nelson M, Rogers JD, Hart J, Sternfeld B. Physical activity questionnaire comprehension: lessons from cognitive interviews. *Med Sci Sports Exerc.* 2009;41:336–343.

22. Willis GB. Cognitive Interviewing: A "How To" Guide. http://appliedresearch.cancer.gov/areas/cognitive/interview.pdf. Published 1999. Accessed July 18, 2011.

23. Miles M, Huberman M. *Qualitative Data Analysis: A Sourcebook of New Methods.* Beverly Hills, CA: Sage Publications; 1984.

24. Mahoney CA, Thombs DL, Howe CZ. The art and science of scale development in health education research. *Health Educ Res.* 1995;10:1–10.

25. Townsend MS, Sylva K, Martin A, Metz D, Wooten-Swanson P. Improving readability of an evaluation tool for low-income clients using visual information processing theories. *J Nutr Educ Behav.* 2008;40:181–186.

26. Murphy SP, Kaiser LL, Townsend MS, Allen LH. Evaluation of validity of items for a food behavior checklist. *J Am Diet Assoc.* 2001;101:751–756, 761.

27. Vereecken CA, Keukelier E, Maes L. Influence of mother's educational level on food parenting practices and food habits of young children. *Appetite.* 2004;43:93–103.

28. Tibbs T, Haire-Joshu D, Schechtman K, et al. The relationship between parental modeling, eating patterns, and dietary intake among African-American parents. *J Am Diet Assoc.* 2001;101:535–541.

29. Golan M, Weizman A. Reliability and validity of the Family Eating and Activity Habits Questionnaire. *Eur J Clin Nutr.* 1998;52:771–777.

30. Sallis J, Alcaraz J, McKenzie T, Hovell M, Kolody B, Nader P. Parental behavior in relation to physical activity and fitness in 9-year-old children. *Am J Dis Child.* 1992;146:1383–1388.

31. Godin G, Shephard RJ. A simple method to assess exercise behavior in the community. *Can J Appl Sport Sci.* 1985;10:141–146.

32. Hughes SO, Anderson CB, Power TG, Micheli N, Jaramillo S, Nicklas TA. Measuring feeding in low-income African-American and Hispanic parents. *Appetite.* 2006;46: 215–223.

33. Dubois L, Farmer A, Girard M, Peterson K. Regular sugar-sweetened beverage consumption between meals increases risk of overweight among preschool-aged children. *J Am Diet Assoc.* 2007;107:924–934.

34. Contento IR, Randell JS, Basch CE. Review and analysis of evaluation measures used in nutrition education intervention research. *J Nutr Educ Behav.* 2002;34:2–25.

35. Townsend MS. Evaluating food stamp nutrition education: process for development and validation of evaluation measures. *J Nutr Educ Behav.* 2006;38:18–24.

36. Netemeyer RG, Bearden WO, Sharma S. *Scaling Procedures: Issues and Applications.* Thousand Oaks, CA: Sage; 2003.

CHAPTER SIX

Using Descriptive Statistics to Study Problems of Practice

PROBLEMS OF PRACTICE *in this chapter*

- Is the number of homeless children and youth sufficiently large to be a matter of serious concern?
- What can be done about the persistent achievement gap between Hispanic and white students?
- Are teacher salaries adequate for the contribution they make to society?
- What types of educational technology will prove to be most useful?
- How do we encourage teachers to make use of educational technology?

IMPORTANT *Ideas*

1. Quantitative data play an important role in improving educational practice.
2. A measure of a construct is not synonymous with the construct. It is possible to have different measures of the same construct, with each measure having particular strengths and weaknesses.
3. A construct can be represented as a variable, which represents how individuals differ with respect to the construct.
4. Quantitative research and statistical analysis are largely about the study of the variations between individuals in important characteristics and achievements.
5. Nominal scales, ordinal scales, interval scales, and ratio scales differ from one another in terms of whether their values have orderable magnitude, equal distance between any two sets of adjacent values, and a true zero point.
6. A sample statistic or population parameter becomes meaningful only when we examine the construct, variable, measurement scale, and group of scores from which it was derived.
7. The mean, median, and mode are different ways of representing the point around which a distribution of scores is centered.
8. The standard deviation provides useful information about whether a distribution of scores varies widely or narrowly around its mean.
9. If a set of scores is normally distributed, standard deviation units enable us to estimate the percentage of the sample that has earned scores within a particular interval of scores.

10. Variability in the distribution of a set of scores can be displayed graphically by histogram, bar graphs, and pie charts.
11. Researchers can determine the strength of the relationship between one distribution of scores and another distribution by doing a correlational analysis or by making group comparisons.
12. Researchers increasingly favor the use of correlational analysis because it provides a more mathematically precise representation of the strength of the relationship between two or more score distributions.

KEY TERMS

bar graph	mean	rank
bell-shaped curve	mean absolute deviation	ratio scale
categorical scale	median	scale
central tendency	mode	scattergram
construct	multivariate descriptive statistics	scatter plot
correlation coefficient	nominal scale	skewness
correlational analysis	normal curve	standard deviation
dependent variable	normal probability distribution	statistic
descriptive statistics	ordinal scale	sum of squares
Excel	outlier	value
histogram	parameter	variable
independent variable	pie chart	variance
interval scale	range	

Individuals generally enter the education profession primarily because they are interested in helping others—children, adolescents, young adults, lifelong learners. They do not go into education because they want to work primarily with numerical data. Yet, as we will show in this chapter, numerical data and statistics have much to do with real people, and they are essential to identifying and solving problems of practice in education.

Some educators are concerned that numbers, such as IQ and GPA (grade point average), stereotype students in ways that negatively affect their self-concept as learners or block their access to certain educational opportunities. They also are concerned about the type of school "report cards" now required by the No Child Left Behind Act that hold educators accountable for student learning (Ravitch, 2011). They claim that these number-based report cards ignore certain factors that affect student learning but are beyond educators' control.

Given these concerns, can a case be made for the benefits of numbers and statistics in education?

To answer this question, consider an example from medicine, described in an article that appeared in the *New York Times* (Abelson, 2007). It concerns the efforts of Cincinnati Children's Hospital to become a national center of excellence in pediatric medicine. The article states: "Cincinnati Children's is among the relatively few medical centers that meticulously collect a wide range of data, to let the hospital see whether patients are getting good, effective care—and to look for ways to improve." As an example, the hospital was able to reduce the number of surgical infections from 95 in 2005 to 42 in 2006; this is nearly a 50 percent improvement. This achievement required the hospital staff to collect quantitative data, identify it as representing a problem of practice, and use the data as a marker for determining whether improvement efforts were working.

The article cites other areas of improvement in the treatment of serious children's diseases. For example, through careful monitoring of quantitative data, hospital staff have helped children with cystic fibrosis improve their lung function, ward off infection through flu shots, and avoid being seriously underweight through good nutrition.

Can quantitative data be of similar help to educators? To answer this question, consider an article in the newspaper *The Oregonian* that reported there are 15,517 homeless children and youth in Oregon, 18 percent more than the previous year and 37 percent more than two years before (Hammond, 2007). Furthermore, 2,500 of the 15,517 homeless children and youth lacked not only a home but also a parent or guardian. Clearly, this situation posed a problem of practice for educators and the community. Had this problem not been quantified, it might have gone unnoticed or underappreciated in terms of its severity.

Other serious problems of practice, such as the achievement gap between white students and ethnic-minority students, similarly might not have come to our attention if the achievement gap had not been quantified. An example of this type of quantification is illustrated in Figure 6.1, which

shows score comparisons on the mathematics test of the National Assessment of Educational Progress for White and Hispanic students in the eighth grade from 1990 to 2009 (Hemphill, Vanneman, & Rahman, 2011). The achievement gap has not been narrowed for Hispanic students, even though they are a significant ethnic group in the United States. In fact, the population of U.S. Hispanics increased by 15 million from 2000 to 2010, accounting for more than half of the total population increase in the United States during this period of time (Humes, Jones, & Ramirez, 2011). Looking at these statistics, educators, policy makers, and others are compelled to see this achievement gap as a significant problem of practice that needs to be solved.

If you are persuaded by the argument that quantitative data can play an important role in education and other professions, your next step is to learn the characteristics of such data, how they are used in research, and how they are subjected to statistical analysis. That is the purpose of this

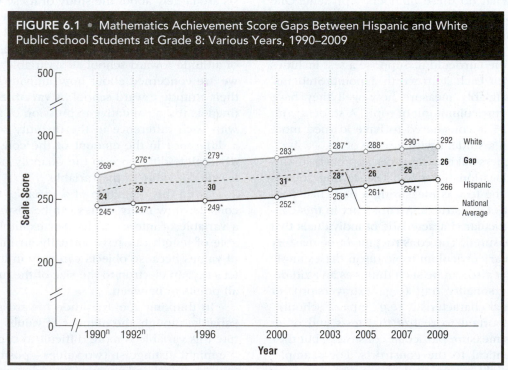

FIGURE 6.1 • Mathematics Achievement Score Gaps Between Hispanic and White Public School Students at Grade 8: Various Years, 1990–2009

[n]Accommodations were not permitted for this assessment.
[*]Significantly different (p<.05) from 2009.
Note: Score gaps are calculated based on differences between unrounded average scores.
Source: Hemphill, F. C., Vanneman, A., & Rahman, T. (2011). Achievement gaps: How Hispanic and white students in public schools perform in mathematics and reading on the National Assessment of Educational Progress (NCES 2011-459). Washington, DC: National Center for Education Statistics, Institute of Education Sciences. Retrieved from http://www.edpubs.gov/document/ed005240p.pdf?ck=520

chapter. Our focus is on quantitative data and statistical analysis in research studies, but much of the discussion applies as well to quantitative data and statistical analysis in educational practice.

CONSTRUCTS, VARIABLES, AND MEASUREMENT SCALES

Most of us experience tests, attitude scales, and other measures only in their final form. We read the title of the measure, perhaps some of its items, and a summary of a sample's scores on it. There is much more to the story, though. Measurement has a logic of its own. To understand measurement, we need to study its logic. We start by examining what it is we measure. Our discussion builds on ideas introduced in the previous chapter.

Constructs

By definition, quantitative data take the form of numbers. What do these numbers represent? One way to answer this question is to consider classroom tests. They typically measure how well students have mastered the facts, concepts, and skills covered in the curriculum. Suppose a test includes 30 items with each item worth 1 point. Students' scores presumably measure how well they have mastered a curriculum unit or topic. A student with a score of 25 is considered to have learned more content than a student with a score of 18.

Researchers take a rigorous approach to this common educational practice. The starting point is to think of the test as measuring a particular construct or set of constructs. A **construct** in this context is a particular characteristic of individuals that is being measured. The construct might be mastery of a particular curriculum topic (as in the example above), but it also can be such things as an attitude, aptitude, personality trait (e.g., extraversion), or organizational characteristic (e.g., type of school).

It is important to realize that tests and other instruments measure particular constructs, but they are not identical to the constructs. For example, a teacher might assign students to write an essay (the measurement device) to demonstrate their understanding of freedom (the construct). However, the teacher could create other measures of this construct, such as a multiple-choice test or an oral presentation. In other words, constructs are not directly measurable, but instead manifest themselves in forms of behavior that are measurable, such as students' performance on tests and essays.

A measure might have a label indicating the construct it was designed to assess, but this is no guarantee that the measure is valid. For example, intelligence tests were developed more than a century ago, but there is still controversy over whether they actually measure intelligence (White, 2005).

Variables

If all individuals were the same, quantitative analysis would be simple. For example, if we were interested in the construct "attitude toward school," we could develop a measure of the construct and administer it to one individual. We then would know how well all other individuals would rate their attitude toward school. In reality, though, individuals vary, often greatly, on nearly any construct we can imagine. Quantitative research and statistical analysis are largely about the study of these variations.

When our interest is in how individuals vary with respect to a construct, it is useful to think of the construct as a variable. For example, if we think of attitude toward school as a variable, this means we are concerned about how individuals differ in their attitude toward school. A **variable** can be defined as the quantitative expression of a construct, with each difference in the quantity representing a difference in the amount of the construct. Each discernible difference in the quantity of a variable is called a **value** of the variable.

Given this definition of a variable, we need to consider how many values can be distinguished in a variable of interest to us. For example, the variable of length can have virtually an infinite range of values because objects can vary in length from, let's say, an electron to the size of the universe and all points in between.

In thinking about attitude toward school as a variable, though, the number of values that constitute this variable is more difficult to conceptualize. We might distinguish two values—positive attitude toward school and negative attitude toward school. Or we might distinguish four values—very positive attitude, positive attitude, negative attitude, very negative attitude. Even more values of this attitude can be distinguished, but there is most likely an upper level. Individuals probably can distinguish where their attitude toward school falls on a continuum of 6 values (e.g., 6 points on a rating scale), but it is unlikely that they can do so on a continuum of 20 values.

The values of a variable can be expressed as numbers on a scale. For example, some school report cards use a 100-point scale, with 100 being perfect academic performance and some other point (perhaps 60) representing failing performance. In other situations, the values of a variable are represented by a symbol rather than a number. For example, some report cards use letters of the alphabet to represent academic performance (e.g., A+, A, A−, B+, B, and so forth). These are symbols, but they can be converted to numbers if one wishes.

Types of Measurement Scales

We stated above that a variable can have different values, each of which is expressed by a different number. These numbers are organized into scales for the purpose of measuring a construct. A **scale** is a set of numbers that represents the range of values of a variable. For example, currency in the United States is measured by a scale that represents money as a set of numbers that increase in value by one-penny intervals. (In some uses of currency, the values, called *mills*, are even smaller.)

In the following sections, we describe four types of scales used in educational research. Each type yields data that are amenable to different kinds of statistical analysis.

Nominal Scales

A **nominal scale** is a set of numbers that represent a variable whose values are categories that have the properties of being mutually exclusive and not orderable. Marital status is a good example of a nominal scale. An individual can be married or not married, but not both. Also, a married individual is neither more nor less than a nonmarried individual. We can assign numbers to married and nonmarried individuals, such as a 1 to represent married individuals and 2 to represent nonmarried individuals. This numbering is arbitrary but useful for entering information about a research sample into a database for statistical analysis.

Nominal scales sometimes are called **categorical scales** because each number on the scale represents a different category. In a research study involving a variable that is measured on a nominal scale, researchers typically will report a frequency count of the number of individuals or objects that are members of each category. For example, researchers might be asked to determine the number of teachers in each of the 50 states and commonwealths. Each state and commonwealth is a separate category.

Ordinal Scales

An **ordinal scale** is a set of numbers that represent a variable whose different values can be placed in order of magnitude, but the difference between any two sets of adjacent values might differ. The values often are called **ranks** (or rankings). We commonly see ordinal scales in sports. For example, in a golf tournament, the person with the best score occupies first place, the next best scorer occupies second place, and so forth. Each "place" represents a different rank.

One of the most widely cited ordinal scales is found in national rankings of colleges and universities, such as those reported in *U.S. News & World Report*. For example, law schools might be rated by various groups on different scales; then these scales are summated in some manner to yield a total score. If there are, let's say, 50 law schools in the survey, the top-scoring law school is ranked first, and the lowest-ranking law school is ranked 50th.

An important limitation of ordinal scales is that they yield numerical data in the form of ranks, but the ranks do not necessarily represent equal differences from one rank to the next. For example, suppose the top-ranked student in a class has a GPA of 3.98. The second-ranked student might have a GPA of 3.97 or 3.85 or 3.62. In other words, the second-place ranking indicates only that the student has the next-lower GPA than the student with the first-place ranking, but it does not indicate how much lower the GPA is.

Despite this limitation, the rankings produced by ordinal scales often are meaningful and important to various constituencies. For example, scholarships might be awarded to the top five students in a class, irrespective of how much or how little they differ on the criteria used to determine the rankings. In selecting candidates for a job, the search committee might select the top three candidates, as determined by their scores on rating scales, for an interview—no matter how much their scale scores differ among each other and no matter how close the fourth-ranked candidate's scores on the scales are to the third-ranked candidate's scores.

Interval and Ratio Scales

An **interval scale** is a set of numbers that represent a variable whose different values can be placed in order of magnitude, with an equal interval between any two adjacent values. An easy way to understand this type of scale is to think of an ordinary ruler. The distance between the 1-inch point and the 2-inch point is equal to the distance between the 5-inch point and the 6-inch point; the distance between the 17.4-inch point and the 17.8-inch point is equal to the distance between the 11.4-inch point and the 11.8-inch point; and so forth.

Interval scales are commonly found in measurement instruments used in the physical sciences and related professions. It is questionable whether any of the measures used in education, such as achievement and attitude scales, represent an interval scale. For example, the amount of learning needed to go from a score of 5 to a score of 10 on a 50-item achievement test is probably less than the amount of learning needed to go from a score of 45 to 50. For this reason, some researchers justifiably view educational tests and other measures as ordinal scales, which do not assume equal intervals between any two adjacent scores. However, for purposes of statistical analysis, these tests and measures usually are treated as if they were interval scales.

The reason is that the statistical procedures described in the next sections assume an interval scale of measurement. This assumption usually is not a problem so long as one is cautious in drawing conclusions about such matters as achievement gains. For example, one student might show more gain than another student on an achievement test when it is readministered after remedial instruction, but the amount of gain might mean something different for the two students if their initial scores on the achievement test were different.

A **ratio scale** has the same characteristics as an interval scale—the values of the variable can be ordered, and the interval between any two adjacent values is equal—plus it has a true zero point. For example, currencies are ratio scales: a person can be in the position of having zero dollars, euros, shekels, or other currency.

Ratio scales are commonly found in the physical sciences and related professions, but not in education and related fields. As we indicated, a ratio scale has all the properties of an interval scale, and these properties are difficult to achieve in education. However, some educational constructs have a true zero point. For example, some individuals might have absolutely zero knowledge about a particular language, country, or academic discipline.

STATISTICAL ANALYSIS OF DATA

A **statistic** is a number that describes some characteristic of quantitative data collected from a sample. The data take the form of a group's scores on a scale, or scales, and the scales represent measures of variables such as academic achievement and attitudes.

The calculation of a statistic, then, is one step in a chain of events. First, the researchers define a construct that is of interest to them. Second, they think about how individuals differ with respect to the construct, and that leads them to think of the construct as a variable. The third step is to develop a measure of the variable that will yield scores on a suitable scale (nominal, ordinal, interval, ratio). Next, they administer the measure to a sample, and each member of the sample receives a score on the measure. At this point, researchers can begin the process of statistical analysis to determine certain features of the collection of scores.

We see, then, that a statistical analysis is not a stand-alone procedure. Its quality depends on the soundness of the steps leading up to it.

Statistics and Parameters

The focus of statistics is on a sample's distribution of scores on a measure, not on individual scores. To interpret a statistic, then, we need to understand the nature of samples. Chapter 5 explains samples and sampling procedures in quantitative research. For the purposes of this chapter, it is sufficient to understand that a sample is a group of individuals who share a common characteristic. For example, the students in Mr. Smith's math class would be a sample; their common characteristic is that they are enrolled in that class. All the students in all the classes taught by Mr. Smith also would be a sample; their common characteristic is that they are taught by Mr. Smith.

A **parameter** is similar to a statistic except that the numbers describe some characteristic of a population's scores on a scale or scales. Determining whether a group of individuals constitutes a sample or a population is a matter of perspective. If we are interested only in Mr. Smith's students, they would constitute the population. However, if Mr. Smith is a math teacher, and we are interested in learning how math teachers generally work with students, he and his students would be considered a sample that represents, in some manner, all math teachers.

The distinction between statistics (based on samples) and parameters (based on populations) affects the process of statistical analysis in various ways. It especially affects inferential statistics, which we discuss in Chapter 7.

DESCRIPTIVE STATISTICS

Descriptive statistics are numerical summaries of a sample's distribution of scores on a scale, or scales. Suppose we ask a teacher how her class of 30 students did on a homework assignment. The teacher might say that the students did quite well, OK, or poorly. That is a descriptive summary. Descriptive statistics, used properly, would provide a fuller and more quantitatively precise description of the meaning conveyed by phrases like "quite well," "OK," and "poorly."

To illustrate descriptive statistics, we will consider teacher salaries in U.S. schools. We chose this variable because we consider it a problem of practice if teachers are not adequately compensated for their contributions to society in teaching students. Salaries that are too low might have an adverse effect on teachers' morale, and they might be a deterrent to attracting talented individuals to the teaching profession.

In this example, we view the underlying construct as financial compensation for full-time teaching. This construct can be refined further. We need to consider whether financial compensation will be defined just as regular salary or whether it also will include extra-duty pay and employer contributions to pension plans and health insurance.

Table 6.1 shows the salary statistics for U.S. teachers for the 2010–2011 school year. The salary statistics for several states (e.g., Georgia and Oklahoma) include these salary supplements, but it is not clear whether other states pay for these supplements or whether they were reported. Nonetheless, the statistics shown in the table likely provide a fairly valid description of teacher salaries for the particular year (2010–2011) in which data were collected. The sources for this table use the label *statistic* rather than *parameter*, so it might be the case that the numbers in Table 6.1 represent a random sample from the population of teachers in each state rather than each and every teacher in the population.

The table shows that teacher salaries vary, so we can view the construct of salary as a variable that will have many values. We can measure the variable of salary as U.S. currency, which is a ratio scale because the interval between any two equal ranges—for example, $30,000 to $32,000 and $47,000 to $49,000—is identical and because there is an absolute zero (theoretically, a teacher could work for free and earn zero dollars).

Measurement of the variable of teacher salary can be done in several ways, such as asking each teacher to state his or her salary or examining salary reports generated by a school's business office. The measurement procedure used to generate salary statistics in Table 6.1 are not specified by the National Education Association (NEA), which reported them. NEA only states that the salary statistics are based on data collected primarily by state departments of education and other governmental agencies.

Measures of Central Tendency

Some descriptive statistics are intended to identify the central tendency of a sample's scores on a measure. **Central tendency** can be defined as a point in the distribution of scores around which a distribution of scores is centered. The most common measure of central tendency is the mean, but the median and the mode are also reported in certain situations.

Mean

The **mean** is a measure of central tendency that is calculated by summing the individual scores of the sample and then dividing the total sum by the number of individuals in the sample. For example, if the ratings for four people on a scale are 1, 2, 4, and 4, the mean is 2.75 (1 + 2 + 4 + 4 = 11; 11 ÷ 4 = 2.75). The statistics reported in Table 6.1 are labeled as *averages*, a term that almost always refers to means.

TABLE 6.1 • Descriptive Statistics for Teacher Salaries and Household Incomes in Each State

State	Teachers' Average Salary in 2010–2011 School Year	Deviations from the Mean ($52,770)	Squares for the Deviations from the Mean	Mean Household Income in 2010
Alabama	$47,803	4,967	24,671,089	$55,778
Alaska	$62,918	−10,148	102,981,904	$81,290
Arizona	$47,553	5,217	27,217,089	$62,838
Arkansas	$46,500	6,270	39,312,900	$52,382
California	$67,871	−15,101	228,040,201	$79,465
Colorado	$49,228	3,542	12,545,764	$72,423
Connecticut	$69,165	−16,395	268,796,025	$90,074
Delaware	$57,934	−5,164	26,666,896	$72,550
Florida	$45,732	7,038	49,533,444	$61,877
Georgia	$52,815	−45	2,025	$62,967
Hawaii	$55,063	−2,293	5,257,849	$79,560
Idaho	$47,416	5,354	28,665,316	$56,086
Illinois	$64,509	−11,739	137,804,121	$72,022
Indiana	$50,801	1,969	3,876,961	$58,451
Iowa	$49,844	2,926	8,561,476	$60,901
Kansas	$46,598	6,172	38,093,584	$63,094
Kentucky	$48,908	3,862	14,915,044	$54,320
Louisiana	$49,006	3,764	14,167,696	$59,116
Maine	$47,182	5,588	31,225,744	$59,300
Maryland	$63,960	−11,190	125,216,100	$89,563
Massachusetts	$70,752	−17,982	323,352,324	$84,005
Michigan	$63,940	−11,170	124,768,900	$59,772
Minnesota	$53,680	−910	828,100	$71,345
Mississippi	$41,975	10,795	116,532,025	$50,591
Missouri	$45,321	7,449	55,487,601	$59,525
Montana	$47,132	5,638	31,787,044	$56,266
Nebraska	$47,368	5,402	29,181,604	$61,630
Nevada	$53,023	−253	64,009	$66,630
New Hampshire	$52,792	−22	484	$77,323
New Jersey	$66,612	−13,842	191,600,964	$90,882
New Mexico	$46,888	5,882	34,597,924	$57,655
New York	$72,708	−19,938	397,523,844	$78,726
North Carolina	$46,605	6,165	38,007,225	$59,053
North Dakota	$44,807	7,963	63,409,369	$61,289
Ohio	$56,715	−3,945	15,563,025	$59,654
Oklahoma	$44,343	8,427	71,014,329	$56,533
Oregon	$56,503	−3,733	13,935,289	$61,552

TABLE 6.1 • Descriptive Statistics for Teacher Salaries and Household Incomes in Each State (*Continued*)

State	Teachers' Average Salary in 2010–2011 School Year	Deviations from the Mean ($52,770)	Squares for the Deviations from the Mean	Mean Household Income in 2010
Pennsylvania	$60,760	−7,990	63,840,100	$65,878
Rhode Island	$60,923	−8,153	66,471,409	$69,840
South Carolina	$47,050	5,720	32,718,400	$56,365
South Dakota	$39,850	12,920	166,926,400	$59,391
Tennessee	$45,891	6,879	47,320,641	$56,835
Texas	$48,638	4,132	17,073,424	$66,756
Utah	$47,033	5,737	32,913,169	$68,176
Vermont	$50,141	2,629	6,911,641	$63,768
Virginia	$48,761	4,009	16,072,081	$81,608
Washington	$52,926	−156	24,336	$71,739
West Virginia	$44,260	8,510	72,420,100	$50,574
Wisconsin	$54,195	−1,425	2,030,625	$62,376
Wyoming	$56,100	−3,330	11,088,900	$66,710
Mean Teacher Salary	$52,770			
Mean Absolute Deviation	$6,591			
Sum of Squares	3,231,016,514			
Variance	65,939,113			
Standard Deviation	8,120			
Mean Household Income	$65,930			
Correlation between teacher salaries and household income	$r = .59$			

Source: Teacher salary statistics from Rankings of States and Estimates of School Statistics: 2012–2013 Rankings & Estimates. Retrieved from http://www.nea.org/home/44479.htm. Household income statistics retrieved from http://factfinder2.census.com.

You will note that the descriptive statistic for the teachers in each state is their average salary, namely, the sum of all of the teachers' salaries in that state divided by the number of teachers. In addition, Table 6.1 reports the average of the averages, which is $52,770. This is the average salary for all teachers in the United States. However, $52,770 is only an approximation of the average salary for U.S. teachers. This is because our calculation gives the same weight to the average salary for each state. For example, California has many more teachers than North Dakota, but our computation of the U.S. average salary does not take this fact into account. To get a more precise estimate, we would need to multiply the average salary for California teachers by the number of teachers in that state and do the same for all of the other states. Then we would sum the numbers resulting from the multiplication process and divide that result by the total number of teachers across the 50 states.

Median

The **median** is the middle score in the distribution of scores. If there were 51 states, the median would be the average teacher salary for the state that ranked 26th in the distribution of states; half of the states would have a higher average salary than the median, and half would have a lower average salary than the median.

In reality, there are 50 states, so we cannot determine an exact middle score. In this situation, the usual procedure for determining the median is to use the two scores in the middle of the distribution and calculate the average of those two scores. In Table 6.1, Vermont ranks 25th (average salary is $50,141), and Indiana ranks 26th (average salary is $50,801). Summing these two salary averages and dividing by 2 yields a median salary of $50,471. This statistic indicates that almost half the states have a salary higher than $50,471, and almost half have a salary lower than that.

The mean is much more commonly reported than the median in educational research. One reason for preferring the mean is that it has desirable mathematical properties for calculating other statistics, including those discussed below. The other is that the mean is the most stable of the measures of central tendency presented here. This means that if you drew repeated random samples from a population, there would be less variation between the means than between other measures of central tendency.

In some situations, though, the median is a useful measure of central tendency. For example, real estate professionals often report the median price of houses in a particular city. The reason is that the median price provides useful information to house hunters. If their financial status enables them to buy a house in the $200,000 range, then knowing that the median price of houses in their city is $190,000 tells them that they will be able to find a lot of affordable houses.

Calculation of both the mean and the median sometimes provides interesting results. For example, in the report that we examined in Table 6.1 for salary statistics for teachers, we also examined household income; the table includes the mean household income. In nearly every state, the mean household income is substantially higher than the median household income. For example, in Alabama, the median household income is $40,474, but the mean household income is $55,778. This difference indicates that some households in the upper half of the distribution have very large incomes, thereby pulling the mean upward.

To understand how this effect occurs, suppose that we have 11 households, each earning $40,000. The mean income and the median income is $40,000. Now suppose one household has an income of $200,000. The median remains the same ($40,000), but the mean shoots upward. Summing the incomes yields $600,000, and dividing that number by 11 (the number of households) equals $54,545. We see, then, that a small percentage of households with very large incomes can create a substantial difference between the mean and the median.

Mode

The **mode** is the most frequently occurring score in the distribution of a sample's scores on a particular measure. It is seldom used in educational research as a measure of central tendency. The reason is that there is so much variation in scores on most measures that no single score stands out as representative of the central tendency of a score distribution. For example, all of the state teacher salaries in Table 6.1 differ. In other words, they all occur with the same frequency, and so there is no modal salary. If there were multiple instances of a particular salary, this salary would constitute the mode, but we would not know where in the salary distribution it was located. Therefore, we would not know whether this modal salary was representative of all of the state salaries.

It is possible to imagine situations where the mode would be a useful measure of central tendency. For example, suppose that educators are working with architects to design a new high school. They do a survey of class sizes in existing high schools in their region and find that classes of 26 students are most prevalent. This finding informs educators and architects that they should design an ample number of classrooms to accommodate classes with that number of students. They could examine the next most frequently occurring class size and make corresponding design decisions. This statistical approach is likely to be more informative than calculating the mean class size or median class size for all classrooms in the sample.

Outliers

Some samples include **outliers**, that is, individuals who have an extremely high or low score on a measure. The presence of a few outliers in a sample can distort a measure of central tendency and lead to misinterpretations.

To illustrate this principle, suppose that California, Connecticut, Massachusetts, and New York had an unusually large number of highly experienced teachers and that these teachers were at the top end of the salary scale. Let's say their average salary is $10,000 higher than that shown in Table 6.1. California's would be $77,871, Connecticut's would be $79,165, Massachusetts's would be $80,752, and New York's would be $82,808. They are outliers because their average salary is $10,000 higher than the next highest state, New Jersey.

Now let's compute the mean salary for the 50 states with these four outliers included in the sample. The mean salary would be $53,570, which is $800 higher than the actual mean salary ($52,770). The presence of just four outliers inflates the mean salary for all 50 states by nearly $1,000.

The presence of outliers could be a concern if a national or state mandate required educators to test all students in each class for accountability purposes. A teacher might have one or two students who score unusually low on the test for reasons beyond the teacher's control. Another teacher might not have such students, and the class's mean score would be higher for that reason alone.

This example does not imply that some students should be excluded from testing simply because they are potential outliers. Rather, it makes a case for not relying on the mean as the sole measure of central tendency. The entire score distribution should be examined for outliers and other anomalies in order to develop a valid picture of how a class, school, district, or other grouping of students performed on the test.

Nominal Scale Data

We explained above that the values of a nominal scale—called *categories*—are not orderable. Therefore, it is not meaningful to use a measure of central tendency to determine a representative score for the score distribution of nominal scale data. Instead, researchers would calculate the number of individuals in a sample who fit into each category of the nominal scale. For example, marital status is a nominal scale. Categories typically used as values of the scale are: never married, married, divorced, and widowed. The categories are not orderable, meaning that none of the categories is "more" or "less" than the other categories.

Suppose a sample includes 200 individuals, and the marital status of each individual is known. This information could be summarized as frequencies or percentages. Suppose the results are 70 never-married individuals, 100 married, 20 divorced, and 10 widowed. These frequency counts provide a meaningful summary of the data. Another meaningful summary would be a conversion of the frequency counts to percentages: 35 percent never married, 50 percent married, 10 percent divorced, and 5 percent widowed.

Measures of Variability

A measure of central tendency provides useful information, but the variability in a group's scores on a measure is of most interest in identifying and studying problems of practice. To understand why this is true, let's examine Table 6.1. It shows that the mean state salary for teachers is $52,770. Suppose that all of the states clustered tightly around this mean. For example, suppose that no state's teachers' salary was more than $1,000 above or below this mean. This low variability probably would attract no attention. However, the actual variability is substantial. The highest state salary, $72,708 (New York), is more than $32,000 greater than the lowest state salary, $39,850 (South Dakota).

That is a lot of money, and it raises concerns. Does the salary variability mean that some states value their teachers much more than other states do? Does it mean that higher-salary states attract better teachers than other states, and therefore the children in higher-salary states receive a better education? If true, is this fair? Should students' learning and potential be limited by the state in which they happen to reside?

Perhaps there is a more benign explanation. It might be that the variability in teacher salaries simply reflects the different cost of living in each state. Perhaps the cost of living is much greater in Connecticut than in South Dakota. If so, the differences in state teachers' salaries might simply reflect this economic reality and have no effect on teacher quality or morale or on students' opportunity to learn.

We see, then, that variability is an important aspect of a sample's scores on a measure. In the following sections, we present several descriptive statistics that are designed to represent this variability. Each of them assumes that the scores have the key property of an interval or ratio scale, namely, an equal interval between any two adjacent scores on the scale. Thus, these measures of variability are not appropriate for categorical or rank data.

Range

The **range** is the largest score in the sample's score distribution minus the smallest score. In Table 6.1, the largest salary ($72,708) minus the smallest salary ($39,850) equals $32,358. The range, then, is $32,358. This is a useful indicator of the amount of variability in a score distribution.

A disadvantage of the range is that it can be distorted by an outlier at either end of the score distribution. If the highest salary ($72,708) was $10,000 greater or the lowest salary ($39,850) was $10,000 lower, the range would increase dramatically to $42,358. This large value for the range ignores the fact that the variability among the other 49 states did not change at all. Other measures of variability, described below, are much less susceptible to this type of distortion.

Mean Absolute Deviation

The **mean absolute deviation** is the mean of all of the amounts by which each score deviates from the actual mean of the scores, ignoring whether the deviation from the mean is positive (i.e., a score greater than the mean) or negative (i.e., a score lower than the mean).

As an illustration of mean absolute deviations, Table 6.1 includes a column labeled "Deviations from Mean ($52,770)." The number in each row is the state's average salary minus the mean salary for all states, which is $52,770. For example, teachers' average salary in Alabama is $38,186, which "deviates" from the mean salary for all states by $4,967. The mean absolute deviation, which is labeled on a separate row near the bottom of Table 6.1, is $6,591.

The mean absolute deviation provides a simple, clear measure of how much variability there is in a set of scores. In the case of teacher salaries, the mean deviation of $6,591 indicates a fair amount of variability across states. The typical state is either approximately $6,500 higher or lower than the mean of all states ($52,770).

Sum of Squares

The standard deviation is a more stable and mathematically useful measure of the variability of scores around the mean than the mean absolute deviation. To explain the meaning of a standard deviation, we must first introduce two other measures of variability: the sum of squares and variance.

Looking at Table 6.1, we see that Alabama's deviation from the mean is $4,967. The next column to the right (labeled "Squares for the Deviations from the Mean") shows the square of that deviation, which is 24,671,089. The same column also shows the square of the deviation for the other 49 states. The sum of all of the squared deviations for a set of scores for a sample is called the **sum of squares**. This statistic, as shown in Table 6.1, is 3,231,016,514.

The sum of squares is one of the most important statistics used in statistical analysis. In simple terms, the sum of squares represents the total amount of variability in a set of scores. The purpose of many statistical analyses—for example, correlation, the *t* test, analysis of variance, multiple regression—is to determine whether other variables measured in a research study "explain" the variability that is expressed by the sum of squares.

Variance

The variance is another measure of the variability of scores around the mean. It sometimes is calculated as part of a statistical analysis. The **variance** is simply the sum of squares divided by the sample size minus one ($n - 1$). In other words, it is the average of the squared deviations from the mean. If the data to be analyzed represent an entire population, the equation stated above is modified slightly: The sum of squares is divided by the population size (in this case, the 50 states); it is not necessary to subtract 1 from 50.

For our purposes here, we will assume that the National Education Association obtained salary data on a sample of teachers, albeit a very large sample. If you examine Table 6.1, you will see the variance on a separate line of the table (variance = 65,939,113). That number is the sum of squares (3,231,016,514) divided by the sample size minus 1 (50 − 1 = 49).

Standard Deviation

The **standard deviation** is the square root of the variance of a sample's scores on a measure. In Table 6.1, the standard deviation of state teacher salaries is 8,120, which is the square root of the variance. You will note that the mean absolute deviation shown in Table 6.1 (6,591) is not much different in magnitude from the standard deviation (8,120), but the standard deviation is used because it has several desirable statistical properties. The standard deviation is the most commonly used measure of variability of a sample's scores in educational research. The term *standard deviation* is commonly abbreviated as SD in research reports. We follow this convention in the following sections of the chapter.

Normal Curve

The standard deviation is a particularly useful statistic if the individual scores on the measure form a normal probability distribution, which is shown in Figure 6.2. To understand this figure, suppose that a large number of individuals are measured on a particular variable. The height of the curve at any point along the vertical line (i.e., the *y* axis) indicates the total number of individuals who obtained the score represented by that point. If the sample's scores are normally distributed, more individuals will obtain the mean score than any other score in the distribution of scores. The mean is represented on the *x* axis by the number 0 because the mean has a standard deviation of zero.

Examining Figure 6.2 will help you understand that a **normal probability distribution** is a set of scores that are clustered around each side of the mean in a symmetrical pattern known as the **normal curve** or **bell-shaped curve**.

Note, too, that actual scores for a measure are not shown in Figure 6.2. Instead, the scores are represented immediately below the curve as standard deviation units (-3, -2, -1, etc.). To understand what these units mean, let's assume that we have a set of scores on a measure for a particular sample. The mean of these scores is 34.15, and the SD is 7.32. If an individual scored 1 standard deviation unit above the mean, it indicates that he or she obtained a score of 41, that is, $34.15 + 7.32 = 41.47$, rounded to the whole number of 41. This score corresponds to the $+1$ in Figure 6.2. Individuals who score 1 standard deviation unit below the mean score would obtain a score of 27, that is, $34.15 - 7.32 = 26.83$. This score corresponds to the -1 in Figure 6.2.

Now consider the case of an individual who scores 2 standard deviations above the mean, that is, $7.32 \times 2 = 14.64$. That individual's score would be 49, that is, $34.15 + 14.64 = 48.79$. This score corresponds to the $+2$ in Figure 6.2.

The standard deviation units immediately beneath the normal curve shown in Figure 6.2 include a zero (0). The zero is the mean of the raw scores of the sample or population. If you think about it, there is no deviation of a mean score from itself. Therefore, it has a value of zero when expressed in standard deviation units.

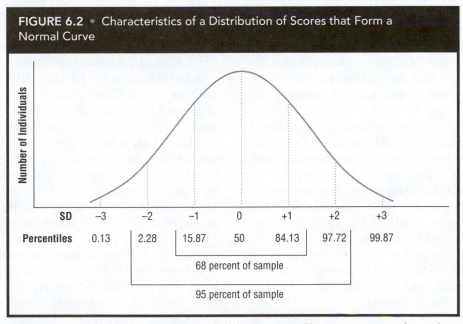

FIGURE 6.2 • Characteristics of a Distribution of Scores that Form a Normal Curve

SD	−3	−2	−1	0	+1	+2	+3
Percentiles	0.13	2.28	15.87	50	84.13	97.72	99.87

68 percent of sample

95 percent of sample

Note: The *x* axis in this figure represents standard deviation units. The *y* axis represents the number of individuals in a sample or population whose score on a measure has a particular SD/unit value on the *x* axis.

The advantage of the standard deviation units shown in Figure 6.2 is that the raw scores for any measure can be represented by them, assuming that the scores are normally distributed. It does not matter whether one measure has 100 possible points and another has 20 possible points, or whether one measure employs an interval scale and another measure employs a ratio scale. The standard deviation units for each measure have the same meaning with respect to the normal curve.

The normal curve is helpful in interpreting the results of research studies. If you know the mean and standard deviation for the scores on a measure, you can use these two bits of information to determine the amount of variability in the scores (assuming the scores are normally distributed). Referring to Figure 6.2, you will see that scores 1 standard deviation below the mean are at approximately the 16th percentile, and scores 1 standard deviation above the mean are at approximately the 84th percentile. Thus, approximately 68 percent of the sample (84 − 16) will earn scores between +1 and −1 standard deviation. By a similar procedure, we can determine that approximately 96 percent of the sample (97.72 − 2.28) will earn scores between +2 and −2 standard deviations.

Suppose that for a particular sample the mean of their scores on a measure that has 50 possible points is 25 and the standard deviation is 2. Assuming the scores form a normal curve, we can conclude that most of the sample (approximately 96 percent) earned scores between 21 (−2 SD units) and 29 (+2 SD units). In other words, the scores are clustered tightly around the mean score, and so the mean is a good representation of the performance of the entire sample.

Suppose that for another sample the mean is again 25 but the standard deviation is 10. The variation in scores is quite large. If we consider only those individuals who scored within the range of +1 and −1 standard deviation units (approximately 68 percent of the sample), their scores are expected to vary from 15 (25 − 10) to 35 (25 + 10) if the distribution of scores follows the normal curve. In interpreting the research results, we need to keep in mind that the individuals in this research example are more different than alike with respect to the variable that was measured.

Standard deviation units also provide useful information about individual members of a sample. The row of percentiles in Figure 6.2 indicates each member's approximate percentile in the sample, based on his or her score. For example, an individual whose score places her 2 standard deviations above the mean would be at approximately the 98th percentile (97.72) relative to the rest of the sample. Statistics books contain tables that show percentiles for each standard deviation unit, usually to two decimal places (e.g., −1.37 SD units).

The mean and standard deviation are mathematically elegant because these two statistics together provide a succinct summary of a sample's scores on a measure. Even if the sample includes 1,000 individuals, we can learn a lot about how they performed on a measure just by calculating the mean and standard deviation of their scores on the measure.

Skewness

Many of the variables measured by researchers and educators yield score distributions that follow a normal curve. However, some do not. In fact, this is the case with the teacher salary data in Table 6.1. The approximate shape of the distribution is illustrated in Figure 6.3.

If teacher average salaries across states were normally distributed, we would expect an approximately equal number of states above and below the overall mean, which is $52,770. However, as shown in Figure 6.3, there are 17 states above the range of salaries ($51,000–$53,999) that contains this mean and 28 states below it.

If the distribution of average state teacher salaries followed a normal curve, the salary range that contains the mean ($52,770) would have the largest number of states in it. This is clearly not the case, as we see in Figure 6.3. Only five states are in the salary range that contains the mean.

The kind of score distribution shown in Figure 6.3 exhibits a substantial degree of **skewness**, which is the tendency for a majority of scores to be bunched on one side of the mean and for the other scores to tail off on the other side of the mean. In the case of teacher salaries, most are on the left side of Figure 6.3, with a small number trailing to the right side. Skewness is neither good nor bad but is simply a feature of some score distributions. In fact, it is a research finding in its own right. One might wonder why so many states have salaries in the $39,000–$56,000 range, while a smaller number have average salaries of $57,000 or more.

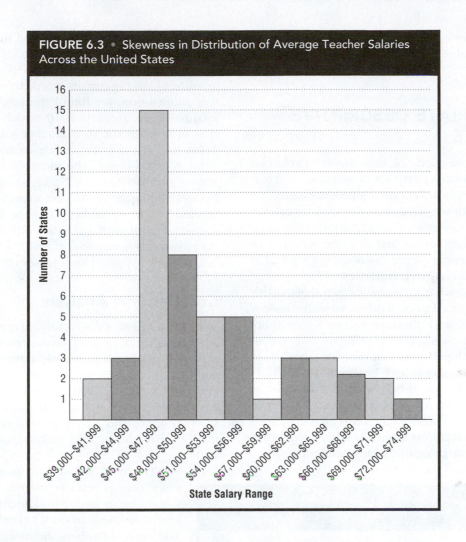

FIGURE 6.3 • Skewness in Distribution of Average Teacher Salaries Across the United States

Graphical Displays of Variability

The skewness in teacher salaries is demonstrated graphically in Figure 6.3. This pictorial device, called a **histogram**, is a set of rectangles, one side of which represents a range of values for a particular variable and the other side of which represents the number of cases in the sample or population that has these values. In Figure 6.3, the horizontal side of the rectangle represents a range of state teacher salaries, and the vertical side represents the number of states that fall within this range of salaries.

A **bar graph** is similar to a histogram, but one side of the rectangle is a discrete value of the variable, not a range of values. Figure 9.3 in Chapter 9 is an example of a bar gram, because each type of effort is a separate value of the variable "types of efforts for improving academic achievement." The discreteness of the values is represented graphically by creating a space between each rectangle. In contrast, the rectangles in Figure 6.3 are immediately adjacent to each other.

Pie charts are another way to graphically display variability in a sample's scores on a variable. A **pie chart** is a circle that is divided into sections, each of which is proportional to the percentage of the sample or population having a particular value of the variable. In effect, a pie chart displays variability in percentages. For example, we might define five ethnic groups (e.g., black, white, Asian, Hispanic, other) and create a pie chart for a school district in which each section of the pie represents the percentage of students of a particular ethnicity. Pie charts are best suited for variables having a small number of values. For variables having more than four or five values, a bar graph or histogram provides a better graphical display of the variability of scores or values on variables for the research sample.

MULTIVARIATE DESCRIPTIVE STATISTICS

The preceding sections of this chapter explained the use of descriptive statistics to reveal several features of a sample's scores on a single measure. We now move to descriptive statistics that reveal the relationship between score distributions on two or more measures. Statistics that describe this type of relationship between score distributions are called **multivariate descriptive statistics**.

To illustrate what it means for two score distributions to be related to each other, we will consider the question of why there is so much variability among states in average teacher salary. We speculated earlier in the chapter that perhaps some states value education more and compensate teachers accordingly. This would be a matter of concern as educators undoubtedly expect all communities in all states to place high value on their work. Perhaps, though, variations in state teacher salaries are a reflection of variations in state economies.

Let's suppose that household income is an indicator of a state's economy: The amount of money that a state's economy generates is reflected in the amount of money that its residents earn. Acting on this supposition, we found the median household income for each state in 2010, which is the same period of time for the state teacher salaries shown in Table 6.1. These statistics are shown in a separate column in Table 6.1. The mean household income across all 50 states is $65,930, as shown near the bottom of the table. If you examine the column labeled "Mean Household Income in 2010," there is considerable variability around this mean. The range extends from a low of $50,574 (West Virginia) to a high of $90,882 (New Jersey).

Correlational Analysis

We wish to answer the following question: Is there a relationship between a state's teacher compensation and its overall economic status? To answer it, we need to view these two constructs as variables and then measure them on scales. Teacher compensation can be measured by salary, which is an interval scale, and states' economic status can be measured by household income, also an interval scale.

The next step is to determine whether variations in teacher salaries are related to variations in household income. More precisely, we wish to do a **correlational analysis**, which involves determining the extent to which variations in scores on one variable are related to variations in scores on one or more other variables. In our example, a correlational analysis is done to determine whether the distribution of teacher salaries (a variable) is related to the distribution of household incomes (another variable).

A simple way to do a correlational analysis is to create a **scattergram** (also called a **scatter plot**), which is a chart having (1) two axes (*x* and *y*) representing the two scales and (2) a set of points, each of which represents a sample member's score on the two scales.

Figure 6.4 is an example of a scattergram. The horizontal (*x*) axis is a scale representing a range of teacher salaries, and the vertical (*y*) axis is a scale representing a range of household incomes. Each point

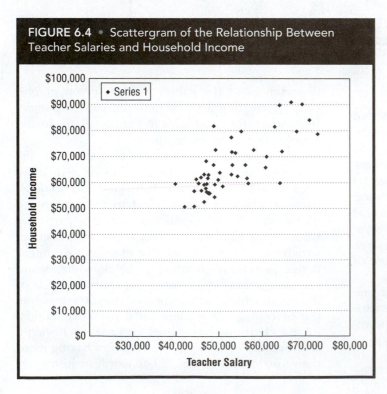

FIGURE 6.4 • Scattergram of the Relationship Between Teacher Salaries and Household Income

in the scattergram is data for an individual state. Looking down from the point, we see the state's average teacher salary, and looking to the left of each point, we see the state's average household income.

Inspection of the scattergram reveals a clear relationship between state teacher salaries and household incomes. States with higher household incomes are likely to have higher teacher salaries. The degree of this relationship can be mathematically described by a statistic called a **correlation coefficient**, which is explained in Chapter 11. The correlation coefficient, represented by the symbol r, for the relationship between state teacher salaries and household incomes is shown in Table 6.1. The r value of .59 is moderately high, meaning that if we know a state's household income, we can make a fairly good prediction about its teachers' average salary.

A closer inspection of Figure 6.4 indicates that there is more to the story than the finding that the strength of a state's economy is associated with teacher salaries. There are exceptions to this finding. Some states have similar household incomes but different state salaries. For example, looking back at Table 6.1, we find that Michigan and South Dakota have similar household incomes ($59,772 and $59,391, respectively), but their average teacher salaries are quite different ($63,940 and $39,850, respectively). Another example is Illinois and Colorado. Their average household incomes are similar ($72,022 and $72,423, respectively), but their average teacher salaries are quite different ($64,509 and $49,228, respectively).

These examples indicate that other variables besides the strength of a state's economy are creating variations in state teacher salaries. Perhaps some states have stronger teacher unions or teachers with more experience or credentials, all of which might increase teacher salaries beyond the effect of the state's economy. Correlational techniques, described in Chapter 11, can tease out the relationship between these other variables and teacher salaries.

The study of teacher salaries becomes more complex—and interesting—when we investigate not only which factors determine variations in teacher salaries but also how these variations possibly affect student learning. For example, suppose our research question is, "do teachers who are paid higher salaries produce more student learning?"

This question can be answered by measuring each variable and using correlational analysis to examine whether scores on one measure are related to scores on the other measure. In this case, teacher salaries are the **independent variable** (i.e., the hypothesized cause), and student learning is the **dependent variable** (i.e., the hypothesized effect). In the previous example, the strength of the state economy, as measured by average household income, was the independent variable (the hypothesized cause), and teacher salary was the dependent variable (the hypothesized effect).

Group Comparisons

Correlational analysis is one way to describe the relationship between distributions of scores on two (and sometimes more) measures. Another approach is to consider scores on one of the measures as categorical, form groups based on those categories, and then compare these groups with respect to their scores on the other measure.

To illustrate this approach, we grouped states into two categories: high household income and low household income, depending on whether the state's household income is above or below the median. Table 6.2 shows the two types of states (high and low household incomes) and the average teacher salary in each state.

We then computed the average teacher salary across the 25 states of each type. As shown at the bottom of Table 6.2, we found that the mean teacher salary in high-household-income states is $57,299, and the mean teacher salary in low-household-income states is $48,184. These descriptive statistics make it easy to see that the salaries of teachers depend heavily on whether they teach in a high-household-income state or a low-household-income state.

An analysis using correlational statistics, as shown in Figure 6.4 (with the r value in Table 6.1), would yield a similar finding. Does it have any advantage over the group comparison shown in Table 6.2? The answer is that a correlational analysis using the r statistic provides a mathematically more precise description of the relationship between two or more score distributions than that provided by a group comparison. Also,

TABLE 6.2 • Comparison of Teacher Salaries in High-Income and Low-Income States

Average Teacher Salaries in States with High Household Incomes		Average Teacher Salaries in States with Low Household Incomes	
New Jersey	$66,612	Wisconsin	$56,100
Connecticut	$69,165	Florida	$45,732
Maryland	$63,960	Nebraska	$47,368
Massachusetts	$70,752	Oregon	$56,503
Virginia	$48,761	North Dakota	$44,807
Alaska	$62,918	Iowa	$49,844
Hawaii	$55,063	Michigan	$63,940
California	$67,871	Ohio	$56,715
New York	$72,708	Missouri	$41,975
New Hampshire	$52,792	South Dakota	$39,850
Delaware	$57,934	Maine	$47,182
Colorado	$49,228	Louisiana	$49,006
Illinois	$64,509	North Carolina	$46,605
Washington	$52,926	Indiana	$50,801
Minnesota	$53,680	New Mexico	$46,888
Rhode Island	$60,923	Tennessee	$45,891
Utah	$47,033	Oklahoma	$44,343
Texas	$48,638	South Carolina	$47,050
Wyoming	$56,100	Montana	$47,132
Nevada	$53,023	Idaho	$47,416
Pennsylvania	$60,760	Alabama	$47,803
Vermont	$50,141	Kentucky	$48,908
Kansas	$46,598	Arkansas	$46,500
Georgia	$52,815	Mississippi	$41,975
Arizona	$47,553	West Virginia	$44,260
	$M = \$57,299$		$M = \$48,184$
	$SD = \$8,134$		$SD = \$5,303$

correlational analysis using r statistics makes it easier to look for relationships among multiple variables. For these two reasons, many educational researchers prefer correlational analysis to group comparisons.

Of course, readers of the research report will need to understand correlational statistics in order to interpret the results of this type of analysis.

That is why reports written for a general audience often present statistics based on group comparisons. Most people find these statistics easier to understand.

Chapter 10 presents research designs based on group comparisons. Chapter 11 presents research designs based on correlational analysis. The designs use very different statistics to analyze data, but they are similar in their purpose, which is to investigate relationships between variables.

CALCULATING DESCRIPTIVE STATISTICS

The calculations needed to generate a descriptive statistic for a set of scores can be done by hand, especially if the data set is small. Some handheld calculators can do these analyses. All you need to do is enter the data and then press the appropriate function key.

We find that the Microsoft software program **Excel** works quite well for calculating descriptive statistics. If you have Microsoft Office for Windows or Mac installed on your computer, you most likely have Excel included as part of Office. You can enter your data on an Excel spreadsheet and then use the Data Analysis feature in the Tools drop-down menu. We were able to generate the tables in this chapter, including the descriptive statistics shown in them, using only Excel. The Chart function under the Insert menu can create scattergrams, score distribution graphs, and other pictorial displays.

Helpful tutorials for generating statistics with Excel can be found on the Internet. Simply enter the statistic you wish to compute followed by Excel, for example, "standard deviation Excel." You should be able to find useful websites, including YouTube videos, that illustrate each step of the process.

More complicated statistical analyses require software that is run on a personal computer or workstation. The Statistical Package for the Social Sciences (IBM SPSS, available at spss.com) is an example. SPSS enables you to do any of the statistical analyses described in this book. Because of its widespread use, you should be able to find someone in your local research community who can help you learn how to use SPSS if needed. Another option is the Statistical Analysis System (see Products and Solutions at the SAS Institute website, available at sas. com). SAS products are more difficult to use than SPSS but have more capabilities.

Errors can easily occur while conducting a statistical analysis. Therefore, you should run checks on your data entry and software operations. One helpful check is to do a few statistical analyses by hand and compare the results with those generated by your statistical software.

An example of
How Descriptive Statistics Can Help in Solving Problems of Practice

Many educators believe that schools are in the midst of a revolution involving ever-larger use of technology in instruction. This revolution raises two problems of practice: What types of educational technology will prove to be most effective? And how do we encourage teachers to make use of educational technology?

Tim Brady, a technology entrepreneur, addressed these questions in an online article (Brady, 2012). He identifies four types of technology that can improve education: (1) tools that automate teachers' clerical work; (2) instructional websites as exemplified by the Khan Academy; (3) more teacher input in the selection of instructional technology; and (4) online assessments based on the Common Core curriculum that can be used by teachers, parents, and students. Researchers can provide a valuable service by collecting survey data and analyzing them by descriptive statistics that tell us which of these technological innovations are being adopted, at what rate, and by whom. If the surveys also measure attitudes about these innovations, we can analyze them by descriptive statistics that will tell us whether educators, students, and parents have a negative, neutral, or positive attitude about them.

Brady predicts that web-based technology products will no longer be marketed to school administrators but will be marketed directly to teachers. Teachers will be given a free version of these products and invited to use them:

> When dozens of teachers in a school district are using the free version . . ., it is clear that the product is effective and necessary. . . . Superintendents no longer have to investigate what teachers want, nor do they have to "sell it internally" once it is purchased. . . . The best products, rather than the best sales forces, will begin to win the day.

Brady's prediction, if true, will require the use of descriptive statistics to determine the extent of use of free versions of educational technology. Teachers, administrators, and school boards will need to know how to interpret these statistics in order to make sound purchase decisions.

On another matter, Brady cites a statistic from the National Center for Education Information that 30 percent of teachers are under the age of 30. These young teachers grew up with personal computers, the Internet, and other technology tools. He predicts that these teachers will be early adopters of new educational technology. But what about older teachers? Brady does not speculate about this population, but one might wonder whether they will resist the adoption of new, increasingly sophisticated technology. Research is needed to determine whether younger and older teachers have different patterns of adoption of new technology and also whether their attitudes toward new technology differs. Researchers can analyze their data by computing descriptive statistics: the percentage of teachers in each group who adopt each new technology product and the mean and standard deviation of the distribution of their scores on an attitude scale.

Without systematic data collection and descriptive statistics, the adoption of educational technology will be guesswork and subject to the whims of particular decision makers. Descriptive statistics on important variables such as frequency of use and attitudes can provide a level of objectivity that results in better decision making.

SELF-CHECK TEST

1. Quantitative data
   a. are useful only in basic educational research.
   b. are useful in identifying problems of practice.
   c. are not useful in identifying problems of practice.
   d. have been found to be useful in educational research but not in medical research.
2. An educational construct
   a. can only be measured by one instrument.
   b. cannot be represented as a variable.
   c. is a constant that does not vary across members of a sample.
   d. can be conceptualized as a variable on which members of a sample can differ.
3. An ordinal scale consists of
   a. categories that are not orderable.
   b. values that can be placed in order of magnitude but without an equal magnitude between any two adjacent values.
   c. values that can be placed in order of magnitude with an equal magnitude between any two adjacent values.
   d. values that can placed in order of magnitude with an equal magnitude between any two adjacent values and a true zero point.

4. An interval scale consists of
   a. categories that are not orderable.
   b. values that can be placed in order of magnitude but without an equal magnitude between any two adjacent values.
   c. values that can be placed in order of magnitude with an equal magnitude between any two adjacent values.
   d. values that can placed in order of magnitude with an equal magnitude between any two adjacent values and a true zero point.
5. A statistic is different from a parameter because it
   a. represents a sample, whereas a parameter represents a population.
   b. represents a population, whereas a parameter represents a sample.
   c. is derived from a random sample, whereas a parameter is derived from a nonrandom sample.
   d. is derived from a nonrandom sample, whereas a parameter is derived from a random sample.
6. As a measure of central tendency,
   a. the mode is more stable across samples drawn randomly from a population than is the median.

b. the mean is more stable across samples drawn randomly from a population than is the median.

c. the mode is more likely than the median to detect outliers in the sample.

d. the mode is most favored by researchers when analyzing the results of an experiment.

7. The sum of squares is

a. the mean of all of the amounts by which each score deviates from the actual mean of the scores.

b. the square root of the variance.

c. the total of all of a sample's scores on a measure after each score has been squared.

d. the total of all the squared deviations of each score from the sample mean.

8. If a distribution of scores is normally distributed, scores that are between +1 and −1 standard deviation unit would include

a. 68 percent of the members of the sample.

b. 98 percent of the members of the sample.

c. fewer than 10 percent of the members of the sample.

d. the top 10 percent of the members of the sample.

9. If the distribution of scores for a sample is skewed, we can infer that

a. the sample was not randomly drawn from a population.

b. a ratio scale was used to measure the variable.

c. the majority of the scores are clustered to one side of the mean.

d. the scores include no outliers.

10. A scattergram is used primarily to determine whether

a. the standard deviations of two distributions of scores are similar.

b. the means of two distributions of scores are similar.

c. there is skewness in one or both of two distributions of scores.

d. there is a relationship between two distributions of scores.

CHAPTER REFERENCES

Abelson, R. (2007, September 15). Managing outcomes helps a children's hospital climb in renown. *New York Times.* Retrieved from http://www.nytimes.com/2007/09/15/business/15child.html?pagewanted=all&_r=0

Brady, T. (2012, July 24). What will the ed tech revolution look like? Retrieved from www.fastcoexist.com/1680231

Hammond, B. (2007). More kids have a school but not a home. *The Oregonian.* Retrieved from www.oregonlive.com

Hemphill, F. C., Vanneman, A., & Rahman, T. (2011). Achievement gaps: How Hispanic and white students in public schools perform in mathematics and reading on the National Assessment of Educational Progress (NCES 2011-459). Washington, DC: National Center for Education Statistics, Institute of Education Sciences. Retrieved from http://www.edpubs.gov/document/ed005240p.pdf?ck=520

Humes, K. R., Jones, N. A., & Ramirez, R. R. (2011). *Overview of race and Hispanic origin: 2010* (C2010BR-02). Retrieved from U. S. Census Bureau website: http://www.census.gov/prod/cen2010/briefs/c2010br-02.pdf

Ravitch, D. (2011). *The death and life of the great American school system: How testing and choice are undermining education.* New York, NY: Basic Books.

White, J. (2005). Puritan intelligence: The ideological background to IQ. *Oxford Review of Education, 31*(3), 423–442.

RESOURCES FOR FURTHER STUDY

Leech, N. L., Barrett, K. C., & Morgan, G. A. (2007). *SPSS for introductory and intermediate statistics: Use and interpretation* (4th ed.). Mahwah, NJ: Lawrence Erlbaum.

The authors describe the capabilities and procedures of SPSS, one of the most commonly used statistical software packages. Even if you turn your data over to an SPSS expert, this book will help understand SPSS so that you can consult with the expert about the statistical analyses you want done.

Salkind, N. J. (2010). *Excel statistics: A quick guide.* Thousand Oaks, CA: Sage.

The author describes how to use the capabilities of Microsoft's Excel software program to compute various kinds of descriptive statistics and create graphical charts for a set of research data.

Smith, L. D., Best, L. A., Stubbs, D. A., Archibald, A. B., & Roberson-Nay, R. (2002). Constructing knowledge: The role of graphs and tables in hard and soft psychology. *American Psychologist, 57*(10), 749–761.

The authors discuss the various descriptive statistics presented in this chapter. They demonstrate the importance of these statistics not only in the social sciences but also in the physical sciences. The article illustrates how even simple statistical analyses can reveal important insights about the phenomena being studied.

Vogt, W. P., & Johnson, R. B. (2011). *Dictionary of statistics and methodology: A nontechnical guide for the social sciences* (4th ed.). Thousand Oaks, CA: Sage.

This dictionary provides definitions of approximately 2,000 terms. Its comprehensive nature means that you are likely to find a definition of any statistical or methodological term that you encounter in reading research reports.

CHAPTER SEVEN

Tests of Statistical Significance

PROBLEMS OF PRACTICE *in this chapter*

- What countries have a poorly educated citizenry, and what can be done to improve educational opportunities for their citizens?
- Would students learn more if the school year was extended to 190 days or longer?

IMPORTANT *Ideas*

1. Tests of statistical significance are used to make inferences about a population's scores on a measure when all that is available are the scores of a sample that is drawn, randomly if possible, from that population.
2. Confidence intervals around a sample statistic (e.g., the mean) enable us to estimate a range of values that are likely to include the actual population parameter for that statistic.
3. The null hypothesis is a prediction about population parameters from data collected on a sample, and a test of statistical significance is done to determine the likelihood that the prediction is correct.
4. A test of statistical significance is more likely to reject the null hypothesis when the sample is large or when there is a substantial real difference in the parameters of the populations that the samples represent.
5. Every test of statistical significance is susceptible to a Type I error and a Type II error. Generally, Type I errors are more acceptable than Type II errors.
6. The statistical power of a test of statistical significance is dependent on four factors: sample size, the designated p value, directionality of the hypothesis, and effect size.
7. There are many tests of statistical significance, each intended for a different type of null hypothesis or directional hypothesis. The t test, analysis of variance, and analysis of covariance are among the more commonly used tests of statistical significance.
8. Parametric tests of statistical significance make assumptions about a sample's score distribution and the scale properties of measures, whereas nonparametric tests do not make these assumptions.

9. Tests of statistical significance continue to be widely used in educational research, but they are problematic. These tests assume that the samples are randomly drawn from a defined population, but that is seldom true of actual educational research studies.

10. Education is a "people profession," and therefore it is easy to dismiss the seemingly "cold" numbers that statistics provide. However, statistics have an essential role to play in improving education.

KEY TERMS

analysis of covariance (ANCOVA)
analysis of variance (ANOVA)
chi-square test
confidence interval
confidence limit
directional hypothesis
F value
inferential statistics
interaction effect
margin of error

nonparametric test of statistical significance
null hypothesis
one-tailed test of statistical significance
parametric test of statistical significance
population
p value
random sample
Scheffé's test

statistical power
statistical significance
test of statistical significance
t test for correlation coefficients
t test for independent means
t test for related means
Tukey's test
two-tailed test of statistical significance
Type I error
Type II error

THE LOGIC OF STATISTICAL SIGNIFICANCE AND CONFIDENCE INTERVALS

Many reports of quantitative research studies include tests of statistical significance and mathematical expressions such as "$p < .05$." For this reason, you need to develop an understanding of what these tests and expressions mean. Our explanation of tests of statistical significance focuses on their underlying logic and meaning rather than computational procedures. Hopefully, our nontechnical explanations and illustrations will help you understand statistics textbooks that present computational procedures for these tests and the mathematical reasoning that underlies them.

The concepts of practical significance and statistical significance are similar terms, but they have different purposes. Indicators of practical significance (e.g., gain scores and effect sizes) help us determine how important a statistical result is for educational practice. Practical significance is the subject of Chapter 8.

In contrast, tests of statistical significance help us to make inferences about a population's scores on a measure when we only have the scores of a sample that presumably is representative of the population. Because the focus is on making inferences from a sample to a population, tests of statistical significance often are called *inferential statistics*. The process by which these inferences are made is explained in the following sections.

Population Data and Sample Data

To illustrate population data, we will use a data set created by the National Bureau of Economic Research (NBER). Robert Barro and Jong-Wha Lee, two of its researchers, determined the average number of years of schooling for citizens of 146 countries for the year 2010. For our purposes, we will consider these countries the population of interest. A **population** is the complete set of individuals, groups, events, or other entity that is of interest in a research study.

As a side note, other sources, such as the website About.com, state that the world actually contains 196 independent countries. We assume that NBER included a smaller number of countries as their population because of difficulty in accessing relevant, current data from all countries.

The NBER researchers determined the average number of years of schooling completed by each country's citizens, age 25 and older. Years of schooling is an important variable for educators and policy makers because it has an important influence on individuals' lives and nations' economic, political, and social well-being. A country with a poorly educated citizenry represents a problem of practice that should be addressed by both that country and the world community.

Table 7.1 shows the mean number of years of schooling for each of the 146 countries that constitute the population studied by the NBER researchers. You will note considerable variation in years of schooling, ranging from a low of 1.21 years (Mozambique) to a high of 13.27 years (United States). As shown near the bottom of the table, the mean (*M*) number of years of schooling for all 146 countries is 7.84, and the standard deviation is 2.84.

As was explained in Chapter 6, the mean and standard deviation for these data are called *parameters* because they refer to characteristics of the entire population of countries studied by the researchers. If we compute the mean and standard deviation for a sample of countries in this population, they are called *statistics*.

Drawing Random Samples from a Population

Suppose no one had collected data on years of schooling for the world's nations. Further suppose that we wished to have this information, but our funding for collecting it is limited. Faced with this situation, a good decision would be to study a random sample of the countries. A **random sample** is a group in which each member of the group is chosen entirely by chance from the population. The size of the random sample would be as large as our budget allowed.

This approach raises an important question: How well will the sample statistics match the actual population parameters? We answered this question by drawing random samples from this population and determining how well the sample statistics estimated the population of all 146 countries.

Our first step was to randomly select a sample of five countries, determine their years of schooling using the data shown in Table 7.1, and compute the mean and SD for these data. The results are shown in the row of the first and third data columns of Table 7.2 under the heading, "Five Random Samples (*N* = 5 for Each Sample)." The sample mean is 7.99, which overestimates the population mean (7.84) by .15 years, as shown in the column "Deviation from Population Mean (7.84)."

Our next step was to draw four more samples of five countries to see what would happen. We used a table of random numbers to select our samples. (See *Resources for Further Study* at the end of this chapter for a web-based random-number generator.) As shown in the first column of Table 7.2, none of the sample means matched the actual population mean, although the first one came very close. However, another randomly drawn sample substantially underestimated the population mean; its mean was 5.06. Their average deviation from the population mean was 1.12, as shown in Table 7.2.

The SD for each of the five random samples is also shown in the same section of Table 7.2. None of them matched the population SD (2.84). On average, they deviated from the population SD by 0.67 schooling years.

What happens if we double the size of the random sample (*N* = 10)? The second section of Table 7.2 shows the mean and SD for five samples, each including 10 countries that we drew randomly from the population of 146 countries. If you look at Table 7.2, you will see that none of the sample means and SDs matched the population mean and SD, but their deviations from these parameters were, on average, smaller when *N* = 10 than when *N* = 5. The average deviation from the population mean was 0.71, and the average deviation from the population SD was 0.32.

What happens if we increase the size of the random sample to 20 countries? The bottom section of Table 7.2 shows what happened when we did this five times. You can see that four of the five sample means were good estimates of the population mean; just one of them (9.08) deviated substantially from the population mean, but less so than the worst estimate for the random samples with *N* = 5 (5.06) or with *N* = 10 (9.19). Also, the mean deviation for the sample SDs (0.29) was smaller than the corresponding number for random samples of *N* = 5 and *N* = 10.

TABLE 7.1 • Average Years of Schooling for the World's Countries (*N* = 146) as of 2009

Afghanistan	3.14	Fiji	9.58
Albania	10.38	Finland	10.29
Algeria	7.61	France	8.37
Argentina	9.28	Gabon	7.50
Armenia	10.79	Gambia	2.79
Australia	12.04	Germany	12.21
Austria	9.76	Ghana	7.00
Bahrain	9.42	Greece	10.50
Bangladesh	4.78	Guatemala	4.07
Barbados	9.34	Guyana	8.53
Belgium	10.57	Haiti	4.90
Belize	9.18	Honduras	6.50
Benin	3.23	Hong Kong	10.02
Bolivia	9.21	Hungary	11.67
Botswana	8.86	Iceland	10.41
Brazil	7.18	India	4.41
Brunei	8.37	Indonesia	5.82
Bulgaria	9.95	Iran	7.84
Burundi	2.69	Iraq	5.56
Cambodia	5.77	Ireland	11.61
Cameroon	5.91	Israel	11.91
Canada	12.26	Italy	9.30
Central African Republic	3.54	Jamaica	9.63
Chile	9.74	Japan	11.48
China	7.55	Jordan	8.65
Colombia	7.34	Kazakhstan	10.37
Congo	5.89	Kenya	6.95
Costa Rica	9.00	Korea	11.46
Cote d'Ivoire	8.35	Kuwait	6.10
Croatia	8.98	Kyrgyzstan	9.27
Cuba	10.20	Laos	4.58
Cyprus	9.75	Latvia	10.42
Czech Republic	12.32	Lesotho	5.78
Democratic Republic of the Congo	3.47	Liberia	3.93
Denmark	10.27	Libya	7.26
Dominican Republic	6.91	Lithuania	9.30
Ecuador	7.59	Luxemburg	10.09
Egypt	6.40	Macau	7.42
El Salvador	7.54	Malawi	4.24
Estonia	12.01	Malaysia	9.53

TABLE 7.1 • Average Years of Schooling for the World's Countries (*N* = 146) as of 2009   *(Continued)*

Maldives	4.38	Serbia	9.55
Mali	1.38	Sierra Leone	3.26
Malta	9.93	Singapore	8.83
Mauritania	3.74	Slovakia	11.56
Mauritius	7.18	Slovenia	11.71
Mexico	8.52	South Africa	8.21
Moldova	9.68	Spain	10.35
Mongolia	8.31	Sri Lanka	10.80
Morocco	4.37	Sudan	3.14
Mozambique	1.21	Swaziland	7.12
Myanmar (Burma)	3.88	Sweden	11.62
Namibia	6.19	Switzerland	10.26
Nepal	3.24	Syria	4.88
Netherlands	11.17	Taiwan	11.03
New Zealand	12.50	Tajikistan	9.82
Nicaragua	5.77	Tanzania	5.11
Niger	1.44	Thailand	6.56
Norway	12.63	Togo	5.27
Pakistan	4.87	Tonga	9.36
Panama	9.39	Trinidad & Tobago	9.24
Papua New Guinea	3.91	Tunisia	6.48
Paraguay	7.70	Turkey	6.48
Peru	8.66	Uganda	2.95
Philippines	8.66	Ukraine	11.28
Poland	9.95	United Arab Emirates	8.86
Portugal	7.73	United Kingdom	9.42
Qatar	7.28	United States	13.27
Reunion	7.12	Uruguay	8.41
Romania	10.44	Venezuela	6.19
Russian Federation	11.73	Vietnam	5.49
Rwanda	3.35	Yemen	2.50
Saudi Arabia	7.78	Zambia	6.70
Senegal	4.45	Zimbabwe	7.25
		M = 7.84 (SD = 2.84)	

Source: Barro, R. J., & Lee, J. (2010). *A new set of educational attainment in the world, 1950–2010.* Retrieved from the Barro-Lee Educational Attainment Dataset website: www.barrolee.com

These data analyses demonstrate that increases in sample size increase the likelihood of obtaining good estimates of the population parameters. Another conclusion is that even a random sample of 20 countries, which is just a small fraction of the total number of countries (*N* = 146), is likely to yield a good estimate of population parameters. Thus, random sampling is a good option

TABLE 7.2 • Years of Schooling Based on Random Samples of Different Sizes from the Defined Population of 146 Countries

5 Random Samples (N = 5 for Each Sample)				
Sample M	Deviation from Population Mean (7.84)	Sample SD	Deviation from Population SD (2.84)	Confidence Interval
7.99	0.15	3.98	1.14	4.01–11.97
7.23	0.61	2.64	0.2	4.92–9.54
5.06	2.78	1.50	1.34	3.56–6.56
8.40	0.56	3.26	0.42	5.54–11.26
6.36	1.48	2.57	0.27	4.88–7.84
	M = 1.12		M = .67	
5 Random Samples (N = 10 for Each Sample)				
Sample M	Deviation from Population Mean (7.84)	Sample SD	Deviation from Population SD (2.84)	Confidence Interval
8.73	0.89	2.61	0.23	7.15–10.35
7.12	0.72	3.02	0.18	5.25–8.99
8.40	0.56	2.74	0.10	6.70–10.10
9.19	1.35	1.86	0.98	8.04–10.24
7.80	0.04	2.73	0.11	5.07–10.53
	M = 0.71		M = .32	
5 Random Samples (N = 20 for Each Sample)				
Sample M	Deviation from Population Mean (7.84)	Sample SD	Deviation from Population SD (2.84)	Confidence Interval
7.35	0.49	2.99	0.15	6.04–8.66
9.08	1.24	2.27	0.57	8.09–10.07
7.92	0.08	2.91	0.07	6.64–9.20
8.37	0.53	2.58	0.26	7.24–9.50
8.22	0.38	2.46	0.38	7.14–9.30
M = 8.19	M = .54		M = .29	

when funds are insufficient to study an entire population.

Survey studies of the U.S. population rely on these principles when trying to determine demographic characteristics (e.g., family size per household) or opinions about education and other matters. It is too expensive to collect data from every individual in the population, but a random sample can yield very good estimates of the population parameters.

Confidence Intervals

In the preceding section, we had available to us both the population parameters (i.e., the population mean and standard deviation) and the sample statistics (i.e., the sample mean and standard deviation). Suppose we did not know the population parameters but had available the sample statistics for one of the random samples of 20 countries. Can we use these statistical results to say anything about the population parameters?

In fact, statisticians have developed mathematical equations that allow us to use our sample statistics to determine a range of means that *probably* includes the actual population mean. The equations make use of the sample mean and SD, and they construct an interval around the sample mean that is likely to include the population mean. This interval, called a **confidence interval**, is a range of values derived from known characteristics of a random sample (mean, SD, and sample size) that is likely to include a population parameter.

For a mean of 7.99 and an SD of 1.14 (the first random sample of $N = 5$ in Table 7.2), the confidence interval is 4.01 and 11.97. In simple terms, the confidence interval tells us that there is a high likelihood that the actual population mean lies somewhere between 4.01 and 11.97. More exactly, the confidence interval tells us that if we took 100 random samples with $N = 5$ from a population, 95 of those samples would have a confidence interval that includes the actual population mean. Thus, it is likely that our sample is one of the 95 samples whose confidence interval includes the population mean.

As it happens, one of our randomly drawn samples of five countries ($M = 5.06$) yielded a confidence interval (3.56–6.66) that did not include the population mean by a substantial margin. It also happens that one of the samples of 10 countries ($M = 9.19$) and 20 countries ($M = 9.08$) had confidence intervals outside the population mean, but barely so. These examples illustrate that the confidence interval is often, but not always, an indicator of the range of values that includes the population value.

In Table 7.2, you will see columns of confidence intervals that estimate the population mean. It is also possible to compute a confidence interval for the population standard deviation or other parameter, such as a correlation coefficient (see Chapter 11).

If researchers wish to be more certain that their sample includes the population interval, they will compute confidence intervals that contain the population parameter of interest for 99 of every 100 hundred samples randomly drawn from the population. The trade-off for this greater level of certainty is a larger, and therefore less precise, confidence interval.

Another way to understand the concept of confidence intervals is to consider a random sample whose mean score on a variable is 7.99 (the first mean shown in Table 7.2). Even if we do not know the population mean for this variable, it is easy to realize that the population mean is very unlikely to be, let's say, 50. A population with a mean of 50 might have some scores of 7 or lower, but it is extremely improbable that we would draw a random sample that would consist of such low scores.

It is similarly improbable that a population whose mean is 30 would include sufficient low scores that we could draw a random sample and obtain a sample mean of 7.36. However, it is reasonable to imagine that a population whose mean score is 7.84 might yield a sample whose mean is 5.06 or 9.19, which are the lowest and highest sample means across all 15 samples in Table 7.2.

Statisticians use the term **confidence limit** to label the upper or lower value of a confidence interval. For example, the confidence limits for our sample mean of 7.99 are 4.01 and 11.97. A population whose mean is above or below the confidence limits is highly unlikely to generate the mean that we obtained for our sample.

You are likely to find confidence intervals in reports or recent educational research studies. The *American Psychological Association Publication Manual* (American Psychological Association, 2010), which is the standard style reference for educational researchers, states:

> The inclusion of confidence intervals [in research papers] can be an extremely effective way of reporting results. . . . As a rule, it is best to use a single confidence interval specified on an a priori basis (e.g., a 95% or 99% confidence interval), throughout the manuscript. (p. 34)

Confidence intervals serve as a reminder that the mean or other statistic for a sample is only an estimate of the corresponding population parameter.

Margin of Error

You probably have come across the term *margin of error* in popular media, such as newspapers. This term is often used in connection with political polls. For example, *The Boston Globe*, among many other newspapers, reported that, in a poll of likely Republican voters in New Hampshire leading up to the 2008 presidential election, Mitt Romney had the support of 28 percent of these voters, and John McCain had the support of 25 percent. *The Boston Globe* also reported that the poll "has a margin of error . . . of plus or minus 4.9 percent" (Helman, 2007).

A **margin of error** has the same meaning as a confidence interval. It is a range of values derived from known characteristics of a random sample (mean, SD, and sample size) that is likely to include a population parameter. The margin of error is typically set at 95 percent. In the case of the New Hampshire poll, this margin of error means that there is a strong likelihood that Romney's level of support was between 23.10 percent (28 − 4.9) and 32.9 (28 + 4.9). The margin of error also tells us that McCain's level of support was probably between 20.1 (25 − 4.9) and 29.90 (25 + 4.9).

This information leads us to the conclusion that in the actual population of likely Republican voters in New Hampshire (not the sample that was polled), there is a small probability that Romney's actual level of support might have been as low as 23.10 (or even lower) and McCain's level of support might have been as high as 29.90 (or even higher). Therefore, it might be that McCain actually had more support than Romney, even though the poll found the opposite to be the case. The safest conclusion, based on the survey results and margin of error, is that Romney's and McCain's levels of support were approximately the same at that period of time.

More certainty about the voters' preferences could be obtained if the pollsters surveyed every likely voter or increased their sample size to lower the margin of error. However, as the sample size increases, so does the cost of the poll. In general, a margin of error that yields a small 95 percent confidence level is considered cost-effective. The poll is affordable, and the level of certainty is acceptable for those who want the survey information.

The preceding example comes from the world of politics, but polls are commonly done in education as well. For example, school districts regularly survey members of the community on issues such as the need for new school bonds and whether schools are adequately serving students with various characteristics. The cost of these surveys usually comes out of the district budget, so administrators need to select a sample size that is affordable yet likely to yield results that accurately reflect the total community.

INFERENTIAL STATISTICS

As we explained above, confidence intervals are useful because they enable us to estimate a population parameter based on a sample statistic. Another relationship between samples and populations is of great interest to researchers. It is the subject of the following sections of this chapter.

We start by considering the statistics shown in Table 7.2. Each of the sample means for the variable "years of schooling" was computed by drawing a random sample of a given size from a known population of 146 countries. Looking at the five random samples where $N = 20$, we see that the means fluctuate: 7.35, 9.08, 7.92, 8.37, and 8.22. These fluctuations are to be expected whenever we draw random samples from a population.

Although the means fluctuate and none of them are exactly the same as the population mean, we know one thing for certain: All five samples were drawn from the same population. Suppose, however, that we know the sample means but not the population mean. For example, suppose one researcher had studied 20 countries below the equator and found a mean of 7.35 years of schooling, and another researcher had studied 20 countries above the equator and found a mean of 9.08 years of schooling. (These are the first two means in Table 7.2 for samples where $N = 20$.)

It is possible to make one of two inferences from these sample means. One inference is that the mean number of years of schooling for the two samples are chance fluctuations from two populations (countries above and below the equator) that have identical means and score distributions. This is an entirely reasonable inference because, as shown in Table 7.2, fluctuations in means occur for samples drawn from exactly the same population.

The other inference is that the two sample means differ because they were drawn from two different populations having different means. It is possible, for example, that the population of all countries below the equator has a lower average number of years of schooling, causing the obtained mean (7.35) to be lower than that for countries above the equator (9.08).

Which is the correct inference? Does the difference in the two sample means reflect chance fluctuations from identical populations? Or does it reflect a real difference between the two populations that the two samples were selected to represent?

An entire branch of statistics has been developed to answer these and similar questions that arise when researchers have collected data only on samples. This branch of statistics, sometimes called **inferential statistics**, involves statistical procedures for making *inferences* about characteristics of populations based on data collected from samples that were selected to represent those populations.

The Null Hypothesis

Inferential statistics follow a particular logic. In the case of two sample means, they test the validity of one of two possible inferences, namely, (1) that the samples come from identical populations or (2) that the samples come from different populations having different means. The first inference is called the null hypothesis. In the case of comparisons involving two samples, we can define the **null hypothesis** as a prediction that there is no difference between the populations that the two samples are designed to represent; stated another way, it is a prediction that the two samples come from the same population.

A statistical procedure, called a test of statistical significance, is used to determine how likely it is that the null hypothesis is true. If the statistical test finds that the null hypothesis is unlikely to be true, we then make the opposite inference: We infer that the two samples come from different populations having different means. We do not know exactly what those means are or how different they are, but we can estimate them by computing confidence intervals.

The Meaning of *p* Values and Statistical Significance

In the case of comparisons involving two samples, a **p value**, in which *p* stands for probability, refers to the percentage of occasions that a chance difference between mean scores of a certain magnitude will occur when the population means are identical. The lower the *p* value, the less often a chance difference of a given magnitude will occur; therefore, the more likely it is that the null hypothesis is false.

For example, a *p* value of .001 indicates that it is much more likely that the null hypothesis is false than does a *p* value of .01. A *p* value of .001 indicates that a mean score difference between two groups as large as the mean score difference that was found in the research study would occur only once in 1,000 drawings of two random samples from identical populations. A *p* value of .01 indicates that a mean score difference as large as the obtained mean score difference would occur only once in 100 drawings.

In educational research, a *p* value of .05 is generally considered sufficient to reject the null hypothesis. This high a *p* value makes it fairly easy to reject the null hypothesis, because the observed difference between mean scores does not need to be large.

It is possible to reject the null hypothesis when it is true. In other words, we might conclude that the difference between the mean scores of two random samples occurred because they came from two populations with different mean scores when, in fact, they came from identical populations. This false rejection of the null hypothesis is more likely to occur when $p = .05$ than when $p = .01$. For this reason, you should be cautious about generalizing results from a sample to a population if the *p* value is .05 or higher (e.g., .10). You have less need for caution, though, if other research studies in the literature report findings similar to those that you obtain.

Some researchers will report *p* as less than .05 ($< .05$) rather than equal to .05 ($= .05$). Usually, the *p* value is not exactly .05 but rather some value less than that. The symbol $<$ (meaning "less than") is a shorthand way of expressing this information.

If a *p* value reaches the desired level to reject the null hypothesis, researchers state that the difference between the two sample means is statistically significant. Otherwise, the result is not statistically significant. We can define **statistical significance** as a designation that an observed difference between two sample means is large enough to reject the null hypothesis.

The procedure used to determine whether an observed difference is statistically significant is called a **test of statistical significance**. A better label might be *test of the null hypothesis*, because that is the purpose of the procedure—to determine whether the null hypothesis should be accepted or rejected.

Type I and Type II Errors

Keep in mind that tests of statistical significance are not perfect. They are educated guesses, based on mathematical logic, for estimating population means (or other parameters) from sample statistics. Therefore, erroneous inferences are possible. One kind of error, called a **Type I error**, involves rejection of the null hypothesis when it is actually true. Another kind of error, called a **Type II error**, involves acceptance of the null hypothesis when it is actually false.

Researchers can lower the risk of making a Type I error, but it is at the expense of increasing the risk of a Type II error. In medical research, the better risk usually is a Type I error. For example, suppose researchers are testing a new drug with an experimental group of patients (they get the new drug) and a control group of patients (they get the conventional drug). If the researchers reject the null hypothesis that the two drugs are equally effective and conclude that the new drug is more effective, the typical result will be more testing of the new drug. These additional tests should reveal whether the new drug truly is more effective or whether the initial test resulted in a chance difference between the two groups.

Consider now the case of a Type II error, that is, an acceptance of the null hypothesis when it is actually false. In this situation, the new drug is more effective than the conventional drug, but the null hypothesis of no difference between the two drugs' effectiveness is accepted. This incorrect inference from the test of statistical significance might lead the researchers to conclude that the new drug is a blind alley, and, as a result, they and other researchers might decide to abandon it. This is indeed an unfortunate error because a new drug has been abandoned even though it is effective and would likely have been found to be effective with further testing.

Similarly, in educational research, it is better to make the error of concluding that an ineffective new practice is effective than the error of concluding that an effective new practice is ineffective. Further research should eventually correct the error. Researchers do not want to waste valuable resources going down blind alleys, but neither do they want to prematurely abandon promising new practices. Therefore, the trade-offs between Type I and Type II errors in tests of statistical significance need to be carefully considered.

Directional Hypotheses

As we stated above, a null hypothesis predicts that there is *no* difference between the parameters of the populations that the samples represent. Most research studies test null hypotheses. However, in some studies, researchers predict that there actually is a difference between the populations that the samples represent. Furthermore, they predict the direction of the difference.

A prediction of this type is called a directional hypothesis. A **directional hypothesis** involves the assumption that a difference exists between the parameters of the populations represented by the samples and that the difference is in a specific direction, that is, that one population will have a higher mean score than the other.

For example, researchers might predict that Population *A*, which is represented by sample *A* in their study, will have a higher mean score on a particular test than Population *B*, which is represented by sample *B* in their study. In order to specify a directional hypothesis rather than a null hypothesis, the researcher needs to justify it on the basis of theory or the findings of previous research studies.

The advantage of a directional hypothesis is that the test of statistical significance makes it easier to obtain findings that lead to acceptance of the directional hypothesis. Stated another way, the test of statistical significance makes it more difficult to reject the directional hypothesis. This is a desirable situation because researchers typically do studies in order to find a difference (e.g., the innovative teaching method is better than the conventional teaching method) rather than to find no difference.

When possibilities of a difference in either direction are tested, the test is called a **two-tailed test of statistical significance**. When only a possibility of a difference in one direction is tested, as is the case with a directional hypothesis, the test is called a **one-tailed test of statistical significance**.

Statistical Power

The preceding discussion of inferential statistics leads us to the conclusion that there is no absolute test of statistical significance. For example, a researcher can set the *p* values at different levels and can do a statistical significance for either a directional or nondirectional hypothesis. These and other factors determine the likelihood of rejecting the null hypothesis. Analysis of these factors enables a researcher to determine the statistical power of a test of the null hypothesis. **Statistical power** is the probability that a particular test of statistical significance will lead to the rejection of a false null hypothesis. Four factors determine this probability.

1. *Sample size.* We demonstrated earlier in the chapter that larger samples provide better estimates of population parameters than smaller samples. Tests of statistical significance take this fact into account. Suppose our hypothesis is that students from higher-income households demonstrate better academic achievement than do students from lower-income households, and suppose that this hypothesis is correct. (In fact, a considerable body of research supports this hypothesis.) If we draw a small sample of, let's say, 10 students from each population, we might find by chance that the sample means on a test of academic achievement do not differ or that the lower-income students have better achievement. This type of finding is less likely to occur with larger samples of, let's say, 50 students in each group. Tests of statistical significance take this fact in account. It will be more difficult to reject the null hypothesis with a smaller sample than with a larger sample.

2. *Level of significance.* As we explained above, it is easier to reject the null hypothesis when the p value is set at a high level (e.g., .10) than when it is set at a low level (e.g., .01). A lower p value has more statistical power because it is more likely to reject a null hypothesis that is actually false. In the case of our example of low-income and high-income students, our sample data is more likely to lead us to reject our null hypothesis of no difference between the two populations when we set our p value at .10 than when it is at .001. However, we can be more certain that our null hypothesis of no difference is false when we set p at .001.

3. *Directionality.* In our discussion of directional hypotheses, we noted that it is easier to support a directional hypothesis than it is to reject a null hypothesis. In our example, this means that if we test the directional hypothesis that students from high-income households will have better academic achievement than students from low-income households, our test of statistical significance will have good statistical power to accept the hypothesis if in fact it is true. Our test of statistical significance will have less statistical power to reject the corresponding null hypothesis, which is that there is no difference between the two populations.

4. *Effect size.* We discuss effect size in the next chapter, but for now, we can define effect size as the magnitude of the difference between two populations on a particular variable. If the magnitude of the difference is large, the test of statistical significance will have power to reject the null hypothesis. In our example, the difference between the academic achievement of high-income and low-income students in the population is substantial, so it is likely that we can reject the null hypothesis of no difference between the two populations even if we draw small samples from them. On the other hand, suppose that a new reading program improves students' reading achievement, but only by a small amount. We will need larger samples of students in the experimental condition (the new reading program) and control group (the regular reading program) in order to have some assurance of rejecting the null hypothesis that there is no difference between the two groups.

TESTS OF STATISTICAL SIGNIFICANCE

The following chapters present different quantitative research designs. These designs require different types of null hypotheses, each of which is accepted or rejected by a different test of statistical significance. We explain the more commonly used tests of statistical significance below. Table 7.3 lists these tests, the type of statistical value that each test yields, and the null hypothesis tested by each test of statistical significance.

Comparison of Two Sample Means

Many research studies involve the selection of two samples, each one being a group that represents a different population. For example, we might want to know whether U.S. males and females differ in their average years of schooling. Our resources

TABLE 7.3 • Commonly Used Tests of Statistical Significance and Their Null Hypotheses

Test of Statistical Significance	Value	Description of Null Hypothesis Tested
t test for independent means	t	The observed difference between the mean scores of two samples are chance fluctuations between populations having identical mean scores.
t test for related means	t	The observed difference between the mean scores of two samples that are correlated with each other are chance fluctuations between populations having identical mean scores.
analysis of variance (ANOVA)	F	The observed difference between the mean scores of three or more samples are chance fluctuations between populations having identical means. Follow-up tests can be done to determine whether the mean scores of any two of the samples are chance fluctuations between populations having identical mean scores. ANOVA also can be used to determine whether the interaction between a level of one factor and a level of another factor is a chance fluctuation between populations having identical mean scores on the specified level of one factor and the specified level of the other factor.
analysis of covariance (ANCOVA)	F	Used to test the same null hypotheses as ANOVA except that the different sample means are more or less equated on a pretest measure on which they might differ.
chi-square test	χ^2	The observed difference between the frequency counts on a nominal scale for two samples are chance fluctuations between populations having identical frequency counts on the nominal scale.
t test for correlation coefficients	T	The observed correlation coefficient for a sample is a random fluctuation for a population having a correlation coefficient of 0.00. Another null hypothesis that can be tested by t is that the difference between the correlation coefficients for two samples is a random fluctuation between populations having identical correlation coefficients.

might allow us to collect data only on 100 males and 100 females, who will represent the total populations of U.S. males and females, respectively.

The **t test for independent means** is used to determine whether to accept or reject the null hypothesis that two populations, each represented by a sample (in this case, males and females) have identical means on a variable (in this case, years of schooling). The t test is given that label because it yields a value called t. The mathematical basis of t is beyond the scope of this book, but it can be found in statistics textbooks. For present purposes, though, you should know that the t value can be converted to a p value. It is the p value that is used to decide whether to accept or reject the null hypothesis.

In some research studies, the scores of the two samples representing the two populations of interest are related to each other. For example, suppose we administer a scale that measures interest in politics to a sample of high school seniors before and after they view a video about the importance

of voting in a democracy. Prior to the video, the sample represents the population of all high school seniors who have not seen the film. After viewing the video, the sample represents the population of all high school seniors who have seen the video. Because the same group of individuals is in both samples, the **t test for related means** (also called the "t test for correlated means" or the "t test for dependent means") is used.

Comparison of More Than Two Sample Means

Some research studies involve more than two samples, each representing a different population. For example, suppose we want to compare the grade point average (GPA) for four different types of college students: (1) students living in a college dormitory, (2) students living in a fraternity or sorority, (3) students living with other students off-campus, and (4) students living alone off-campus. Our null hypothesis is that the mean GPA for the four populations represented by these four groups is identical. The appropriate test of statistical significance would be **analysis of variance (ANOVA)**. Analysis of variance is generally used to test differences when more than two means are being compared.

Analysis of variance yields an *F* value. You can consult a statistical table, found in most statistics textbooks, that converts *F* to a *p* value. If only two sample means are being compared, the *F* value and the *t* value (resulting from use of the *t* test) will be identical.

If the analysis of variance leads to the rejection of the null hypothesis, this result does not necessarily imply that all four populations represented by the four samples have different GPA means. It is possible that two of the populations have different GPA means (e.g., the groups designated "1" and "3" differ from each other). The null hypothesis for each pair of samples representing different populations can be tested with a special form of the *t* test, usually **Tukey's test** or **Scheffé's test**.

Comparisons of Sample Means in Complex Data Sets

Analysis of variance is a versatile statistical procedure because it can test several null hypotheses for a complex data set. To illustrate its versatility, we constructed data for a hypothetical experiment comparing two types of text. Two groups of students were formed prior to the experiment: students with high reading ability and students with low reading ability.

Students within each of these two groups were randomly assigned to experimental and control conditions. Students in the experimental condition read a text passage with inserted questions inviting them to relate the information being presented to something they already knew. Students in the control treatment read the same text passage but with no inserted questions. A multiple-choice test covering the content of the text passage was administered a day before students read the passage (the pretest) and a day after (the posttest).

The top part of Table 7.4 shows descriptive statistics for each subgroup on the posttest. The bottom part of the table shows descriptive statistics for combinations of subgroups on the posttest, for example, the mean score (*M*) and standard deviation for all experimental group students, whether they have high or low reading ability.

Many comparisons are possible for the mean scores shown in Table 7.4—for example, all experimental group students versus all control group students; high-ability students versus low-ability students in the experimental group; high-ability students in the experimental group versus high-ability students in the control group. One could do *t* tests for all of these comparisons. However, not only is this procedure tedious, but as the number of comparisons increases, so does the likelihood of false conclusions. (It can be shown mathematically that, as the frequency of inferential statistics calculated for a set of data increases, so does the likelihood of falsely rejecting one of the null hypotheses.)

Analysis of variance is a more elegant and accurate method of making all of the comparisons at once to determine which ones are likely to be chance differences. Table 7.5 shows a summary of the *F* values generated by the analysis of variance of the data presented in Table 7.4 and whether each *F* value is statistically significant ($p = .05$ or less). The first line of results shows the *F* value (49.88) for the comparison of all experimental group students ($M = 16.30$) and all control group students ($M = 8.55$) on the posttest, ignoring whether the students have high or low reading ability. This *F* value is statistically significant ($p < .001$), meaning that the difference is generalizable to the populations represented by the samples.

The second line shows the *F* value (25.58) for the comparison of all high-reading-ability students ($M = 15.20$) and all low-reading-ability students ($M = 9.65$) on the posttest. This *F* value, too, is statistically significant ($p < .001$).

Interaction Effects

The next line of Table 7.5 shows an *F* value of 6.28 ($p < .05$) for the interaction effect. In many educational experiments, including our example, an **interaction effect** involves a finding that an intervention has a different effect on some members of the experimental group than it does on others. In statistics, an interaction effect is said to have occurred when the difference between two groups on variable *B* varies according to the value of variable *A*.

To understand what an interaction effect means, consider the research results shown in Table 7.4. For students with low reading ability (one level of variable *B*), the difference in the posttest mean

TABLE 7.4 • Posttest Scores for Students Classified by Reading Ability and Experimental Group or Control Group Assignment in a Hypothetical Experiment on Inserted Questions in Text

| Experimental Group | | Control Group | |
High Reading Ability	Low Reading Ability	High Reading Ability	Low Reading Ability
23	18	19	3
14	17	12	7
16	9	16	1
18	10	14	6
16	17	7	4
17	19	8	7
19	8	13	6
20	20	10	5
17	15	19	3
17	16	9	2
$M = 17.70$	$M = 14.90$	$M = 12.70$	$M = 4.40$
$SD = 2.50$	$SD = 4.33$	$SD = 4.32$	$SD = 2.12$

| | Subgroup Statistics | | |
Subgroup	N	M	SD
Experimental Group	20	16.30	3.73
Control Group	20	8.55	5.39
High-Reading-Ability Group	20	15.20	4.29
Low-Reading-Ability Group	20	9.65	6.33

scores of the experimental and control groups (variable A) is substantial (14.90 − 4.40 = 10.50 points). For students with high reading ability (the other level of treatment variable B), the difference in the posttest mean scores of the experimental and control students (variable A) is much smaller (17.70 − 12.70 = 5 points).

TABLE 7.5 • Summary of Analysis of Variance for Posttest Scores in a Hypothetical Experiment on Inserted Questions in Text

Source	F	p
Treatment (T)	49.88	< .001
Reading Ability (R)	25.58	< .001
$T \times R$ Reaction	6.28	< .051

This analysis reveals that the experimental text passage helped poor readers much more than it helped good readers. The significant F value for this interaction effect suggests that it is a real difference between the populations represented by the samples in the experiment.

Analysis of Covariance

We have not yet addressed the pretest results for our hypothetical experiment. The pretest was administered in order to determine how much students knew about the text passage content prior to the experiment. The pretest mean scores for each group are shown in Table 7.6. These results complicate our interpretation of the posttest results because they show that the experimental group had higher scores on the pretest than did the

TABLE 7.6 • Pretest Means for Students in a Hypothetical Experiment on Inserted Questions in Text

	Experimental Group M	Control Group M
High-Ability Readers	10.10	7.70
Low-Ability Readers	4.30	2.90

control group. The experimental group's superior knowledge of the text passage content beforehand, rather than the inserted questions in the text passage, might be responsible for its higher score on the posttest.

We could eliminate superior pretest knowledge as an explanation for the results by doing another experiment in which the students selected for the experimental and control groups were equivalent on the pretest. This solution, however, is time-consuming and expensive. Another solution is to use gain scores, which are computed by subtracting the pretest score from the posttest score for each student in the experiment. However, gain scores have several limitations, so they are seldom used to analyze experimental data.

The best solution to the problem is to make the groups equivalent on the pretest by applying a statistical technique known as **analysis of covariance (ANCOVA)**. ANCOVA adjusts each research participant's posttest score, either up or down, to take into account his pretest score. Analysis of covariance yields F values similar in meaning to those described for analysis of variance.

The procedure used in analysis of covariance is similar in principle to the handicapping procedure used in sports such as golf. Poor golf players can compete with good golf players by being assigned a handicap based on their past performance. Each golf player's score in a tournament is determined by how much better or worse she does than her handicap (that is, her previous performance).

Comparisons Between Sample Frequencies

The tests of statistical significance described in the preceding sections involve comparisons of samples with respect to the mean of their scores on a particular measure. However, some measures yield frequency counts because they constitute nominal scales. (We explained nominal scales in Chapter 6.) The **chi-square test** is the appropriate test for deciding whether to accept or reject null hypotheses that involve frequency data on nominal scales.

To illustrate the use of the chi-square test, suppose that we want to determine whether urban school districts are more likely to employ female school superintendents than are rural school districts. A random sample of 100 urban school districts and 100 rural school districts is drawn from a population of school districts. The gender of each district's superintendent is determined.

The two variables involved in this study are gender (male versus female) and type of school district (urban versus rural). Both variables are categorical because they cannot be ordered on a continuum. For example, a rural district is neither "more" nor "less" than an urban district.

Table 7.7 shows hypothetical data relating to our research question. The descriptive statistics are in the form of frequencies, with each frequency being the number of superintendents in each gender category for a particular type of district. Table 7.7 shows that the distributions of male and female superintendents vary across districts. We need to determine whether these differences occurred by chance or are characteristic of the populations represented by the random samples.

The chi-square test is used to make this determination. It yields an inferential statistic known as *chi*, which is squared and represented by the symbol χ^2. Statisticians have created tables that convert χ^2 to p values. The χ^2 value for the distributions shown in Table 7.7 was calculated to be 7.42. This value is associated with a p value that is less than .01. Therefore, we reject the null hypothesis that these results occurred by chance. Instead, we conclude that there are real differences in the proportion of male and female superintendents in the populations of districts represented by the two random samples.

TABLE 7.7 • Hypothetical Distribution of Male and Female Superintendents in Urban and Rural School Districts

	Urban	Rural
Males	65	82
Females	35	18

Comparisons Between Correlation Coefficients

The use of correlation coefficients in educational research is described at length in Chapter 11. We mention them here only to note that tests of statistical significance are available to accept or reject null hypotheses involving correlation coefficients. The most common null hypothesis is that the obtained correlation coefficient for a sample is a chance fluctuation from a correlation coefficient of zero ($r = .00$) for the population represented by the sample. A zero correlation coefficient means that there is no relationship between the two sets of scores. Therefore, an individual's score on one measure has no value in predicting his or her score on the other measure.

Even if the correlation coefficient for the population is zero, random samples drawn from that population might produce correlation coefficients that differ from zero. Some of these coefficients might be small; others might be large. Some of the coefficients might be positive, indicating that high scores on one measure are associated with high scores on the other measure. Other coefficients might be negative, indicating that high scores on one measure are associated with low scores on the other measure.

A test of statistical significance can be done to help us decide whether to accept the null hypothesis, namely, that the correlation coefficient for our sample is a chance deviation from a population coefficient that is zero. If the test yields a statistically significant result, we reject the null hypothesis and conclude that the correlation coefficient for the population represented by the sample is not zero. The test does not tell us what the correlation coefficient for the population is, but constructing confidence intervals (described earlier in the chapter) around the sample correlation coefficient can give us a range of correlation coefficients that are likely to include the population correlation coefficient.

Parametric Versus Nonparametric Tests of Statistical Significance

All of the tests of statistical significance described above, with the exception of the chi-square test, are **parametric tests of statistical significance**, meaning that they make several assumptions about the measures being used and the populations that are represented by the research samples. These assumptions are that (1) there are equal intervals between the scores on the measures, (2) the scores are normally distributed about the mean score, and (3) the scores of the different comparison groups have equal variances.

Suppose the assumptions underlying parametric tests, especially the assumption of equal intervals, cannot be satisfied. In this case, researchers might use a parametric test anyway, if the assumptions are not violated seriously. Otherwise, they will use a **nonparametric test of statistical significance**, which makes no assumptions about the measures being used and the populations that are represented by the research samples. The chi-square test is the most commonly used nonparametric test, because many variables are in the form of categories, which do not form an interval scale.

Cautions in Interpreting Tests of Statistical Significance

It is easy to be misled by certain phrases in research reports such as, "the difference between the experimental and control group was statistically significant." The word *significant* might suggest that the research result is important. In fact, as we explained above, statistical significance means only that the null hypothesis or directional hypothesis can be rejected. Even then, a statistically significant result is subject to a Type I or Type II error.

Probably the most serious problem with tests of statistical significance is that educational researchers seldom have the opportunity to work with random samples drawn from a defined population. This is unfortunate, because random sampling is essential to the mathematical logic of tests of statistical significance and, for that matter, to the logic of confidence intervals.

Instead of working with random samples, educational researchers typically work with volunteer samples, also called convenience samples. A volunteer sample is a group of individuals that happens to be accessible to the researchers. (We explain volunteer samples in Chapter 5.) Volunteer samples might have characteristics that are representative of the population that interests the researchers, but they also might have distinctive characteristics.

For these and other reasons, research methodologists (e.g., Harlow, Mulaik, & Steiger, 1997) have expressed concerns about the appropriateness of tests of statistical significance in research about education and related professions. Our recommendation is that you view a statistically significant result as a tentative finding. Similarly, if the statistically significant result involves a positive difference favoring an innovative program or technique, we recommend that you look at the result as a promising finding that is reason for cautious optimism.

The critical next step is attempting to replicate the finding. Indeed, carefully designed replications are the most powerful way to determine whether a research finding has narrow generalizability or whether it applies to the entire population of interest. Different researchers should attempt to replicate the original study elsewhere with different samples (including volunteer samples) and with different measures of the same variables, if possible.

Over time, the results of different studies can be accumulated and analyzed to determine the features of the population to which the research result applies and the populations to which the research result does not apply. This accumulation and analysis is done most effectively by meta-analysis, which we explain in Chapter 3.

Jacob Cohen (1990), a statistician, succinctly explains both the limitations of tests of statistical significance and the superiority of replication research:

> The prevailing yes-no decision at the magic .05 level from a single research study is a far cry from the use of informed judgment. Science simply doesn't work that way. A successful piece of research doesn't conclusively settle an issue, it just makes some theoretical proposition to some degree more likely. Only successful future replication in the same and different settings (as might be found through meta-analysis) provides an approach to settling the issue. (p. 1311)

Cohen's recommendation echoes our own statements about replication as a research strategy in Chapter 1 and in other parts of this book. If you are just learning how to do research, you can advance the field of research knowledge about education by replicating and extending previous research. This is a surer path to developing research expertise and making a research contribution than striking off in a new direction to study a problem about which little is known and for which measures and procedures are either unavailable or uncertain.

CALCULATING STATISTICS

In Chapter 6, we note that Excel is standard software on most computers and that it is an effective tool for calculating many statistics. You need only to enter the raw scores, double-check them for accuracy, and then use the appropriate Excel function. The Data Analysis function under the Tools menu can calculate descriptive statistics and some of the tests of statistical significance described in this chapter.

More complicated statistical analyses require software that is run on a personal computer or workstation. We described two of these software programs (SPSS and SAS) in Chapter 6.

In our experience, large data sets involving many variables and samples or populations require the services of expert statisticians and data managers. For example, if large groups of students have taken a standardized test, they typically record their response to each item on a sheet that can be optically scanned. The scanning process is complex, as is the process of transferring the scanning results into a data set that can be analyzed by statistical software. Each step in the process requires expert skill and judgment.

If your skills lie more in professional practice, you probably will find it best to consult statisticians and data managers who are trained to work with large data sets and to conduct tests of statistical significance. It would be a mistake, though, to simply turn over the data to experts. It is best to work alongside them so that both you and they have the same understanding of the data and the goals of the statistical analyses. This approach also will help you answer questions raised by your colleagues and other stakeholders rather than having to plead ignorance and refer them to the experts. Also, you can help the experts identify possible errors that can creep in at each stage of data entry and analysis. (Just think of the errors that can creep into your checkbook entries and calculations.)

USING STATISTICS TO IMPROVE PROFESSIONAL PRACTICE

Most of us enter the education profession because we wish to work with people, not numbers. Education is first and foremost a "people profession." The quality of the interpersonal relations that teachers develop with students and parents and with their colleagues is critical to helping students learn. In contrast, statistical analysis deals with numbers and relies on mathematical logic, which can seem remote and arcane for those of us who do not have a strong background in mathematics.

Nonetheless, statistical analysis is an essential tool for improving educational practice. The history of educational research shows that it is possible to develop valid quantitative measures of learning, motivation, attitudes, interests, teaching behavior, and other constructs that are central to educational practice. These measures can be used to collect data that give us a reasonably objective picture of what actually occurs in schools. We can examine this objective picture to see how well it corresponds to ideal practice. Discrepancies between the actual and the ideal can and should be the stimulus for improving practice so that all students have the best opportunity to learn.

Moreover, quantitative data collection and statistical analysis can be used to identify whether promising innovations actually do improve learning, teacher morale, community support of schools, and other important educational outcomes. Statistical evidence of these improvements can provide the necessary leverage to obtain funding to disseminate and implement these innovations.

For these reasons and others, it is important for professional educators to learn the statistical concepts and procedures presented in this chapter. Statistical analysis is not an end in itself (except possibly for theoretical statisticians), but it is an important means to an end, namely, the improvement of educational practice.

An example of
How Tests of Statistical Significance Can Help in Solving Problems of Practice

According to the National Center on Time and Learning, a nonprofit research group in Boston, about 170 schools—more than 140 of them charter schools—across the country have extended their calendars in recent years to 190 days or longer. . . . [But] critics say that with so many schools already failing,

giving them more time would do little to help students.

Rich, M. (2012, August 5). To increase learning time, some schools add days to academic year. *New York Times.* Retrieved from http://www.nytimes.com/2012/08/06/education/some-schools-adopting-longer-years-to-improve-learning.html

It should be good news when we learn about a new approach to help schools whose students are lagging behind expectations for academic achievement. Extending the school year seems like a good approach, and there is some groundswell of support for it. One can argue that extending the school year will prevent students from forgetting what they learned during the traditional school year, and it will create opportunities for enrichment activities such as art and music. However, some critics claim that this approach is costly and will not improve students' learning because teachers will not use the additional time effectively.

Research can help us determine whether the advocates or the critics of an extended school year are correct. We might consider a research study using schools that already have an extended school year and compare them with a control group of schools that have a traditional school year on measures of academic achievement. This type of study has several flaws, though, one of them being that schools that already have an extended school year might be unlike other schools in certain ways. Suppose the study finds that these schools have superior student achievement compared to traditional schools. We cannot conclude that an extended school year will help schools in general, because they might not have the other characteristics of schools with an extended school year already in place.

It is critical that the study involve a national random sample of schools that represents a defined population because a random sample provides a sound basis for generalizing the results beyond the sample to the population that it represents. The random sample would be divided into two groups: a group of schools that implements an extended school year and a control group of schools that continues their traditional school year. A test of statistical significance can be done on the students' achievement test scores at the end of the school year to determine the probability that any observed differences between the two groups are due to chance (the null hypothesis) or to real differences in the populations represented by the two samples. Statistical adjustments (perhaps analysis of covariance) should be made to account for possible differences in achievement scores between the two groups at the beginning of the school year.

Suppose the test of statistical significance leads to the rejection of the null hypothesis, and we find that the difference on the achievement test favors the schools with an extended school year. These results might not allow us to conclude that the intervention will work in every school. However, the results do allow us to reach tentative conclusions about the percentage of schools in the population that will benefit from the intervention and by how much. These conclusions provide a better basis for deciding whether to promote the widespread adoption of this approach to improving schools or to take seriously the claims of its critics.

SELF-CHECK TEST

1. The purpose of inferential statistics is to determine whether
   a. a set of scores forms a normal distribution.
   b. the sample size is sufficiently large to detect real differences between the experimental and control group.
   c. an observed statistical result for a sample randomly drawn from a population is a chance finding.
   d. the results of one study constitute a non-chance replication of the results of another study.

2. As the size of a research sample increases, the confidence interval
   a. around the mean score of a measure administered to the sample is likely to increase.
   b. around the mean score of a measure administered to the sample is likely to decrease.
   c. is less likely to include the population parameter.
   d. becomes more similar to the standard deviation of the population.

3. Researchers use the p value in a test of statistical significance to
   a. decide whether it is best to state a null hypothesis or a directional hypothesis.
   b. determine whether a Type I or Type II error has occurred.
   c. decide whether to accept or reject the null hypothesis.
   d. determine whether the sample size was sufficiently large.

4. The likelihood that the null hypothesis is false is greatest when the p value is
   a. .001.
   b. .01.
   c. .10.
   d. 1.00.

5. A Type I error means that the researcher has
   a. rejected the null hypothesis when it is actually true.
   b. accepted the null hypothesis when it is actually false.
   c. used the wrong test of statistical significance.
   d. used a volunteer sample rather than a random sample.

6. Suppose that researchers have administered a measure of open-mindedness to a sample of students at the start (pretest) and end (posttest) of their college careers. They should test the statistical significance of the difference between the pretest and posttest means on this measure by doing
   a. an analysis of covariance.
   b. an analysis of variance.
   c. the t test for related means.
   d. the t test for correlated means.

7. If the pretest scores of two groups in an experiment differ, researchers can try to compensate for this problem by
   a. using analysis of covariance.
   b. computing confidence intervals around the pretest mean scores.
   c. converting the pretest and posttest scores to gain scores.
   d. using a nonparametric test of statistical significance.
8. Researchers would conclude that an interaction effect occurred in an analysis of variance if they found that
   a. boys and girls had different pretest means on a measure of mathematics achievement.
   b. the experimental group performed better than the control group on the posttest.
   c. discovery learning was more effective for high-achieving students than low-achieving students.

d. the pretest affected the research participants' response to the intervention.
9. Nonparametric tests of statistical significance
   a. assume that the scores to be analyzed form an interval scale.
   b. do not assume that the scores to be analyzed form an interval scale.
   c. must be used even if the scores constitute a minor violation of the assumptions underlying analysis of variance.
   d. can be used only with continuous scores.
10. The most serious problem with tests of statistical significance is
   a. the prevalence of Type I errors.
   b. the prevalence of Type II errors.
   c. that educational researchers usually can collect only data that form a nominal scale.
   d. that educational researchers usually must work with volunteer samples rather than random samples.

CHAPTER REFERENCES

American Psychological Association. (2010). *Publication manual of the American Psychological Association* (6th ed.). Washington, DC: Author.

Cohen, J. (1990). Things I have learned (so far). *American Psychologist, 45*, 1304–1312.

Harlow, L. L., Mulaik, S. A., & Steiger, J. H. (Eds.). (1997). *What if there were no significance tests?* Mahwah, NJ: Lawrence Erlbaum.

Helman, S. (2007, December 23). McCain closing gap with Romney. *The Boston Globe*. Retrieved from www.boston.com

RESOURCES FOR FURTHER STUDY

Fidler, F., & Cumming, G. (2007). Lessons learned from statistical reform efforts in other disciplines. *Psychology in the Schools, 44*(5), 441–449.

The authors claim that tests of statistical significance have limited value, especially for the improvement of professional practice. They argue that effect sizes and confidence intervals provide stronger evidence for judging the practical significance of statistical results.

Stat Trek (n.d.). *Random number generator.* Retrieved from the Stat Trek website: http://stattrek.com/statistics/random-number-generator.aspx.

We used this websites to generate random numbers for the statistics in Table 7.2. Similar websites can be identified by searching "random number generator" on the Internet.

Thompson, B. (2008). *Foundations of behavioral statistics.* New York, NY: Guilford.

Many books about statistics are available. This one provides in-depth coverage of statistical significance and related topics.

Vickers, A. J. (2009). *What is a p-value anyway? 34 stories to help you actually understand statistics.* Boston, MA: Addison Wesley.

This is one of various books that explain statistical concepts in a nontechnical manner. Among the topics covered are hypothesis testing, *p* values, and confidence intervals.

CHAPTER EIGHT

The Practical Significance of Statistical Results

PROBLEMS OF PRACTICE *in this chapter*

- What are ideal standards for public education?
- How large is the racial gap in students' science achievement, and what can be done to reduce it?
- Is the National Assessment of Educational Progress a worthwhile approach to conceptualizing, measuring, and reporting student achievement?
- Do tables of norms, such as those for SAT subject tests, provide useful information about student achievement?
- Is the Adequate Yearly Progress requirement of the No Child Left Behind Act an effective way to stimulate teachers to improve students' academic achievement?
- What is the best way to determine whether schools are making continual improvements in their mission to foster students' academic achievement?

IMPORTANT *Ideas*

1. A statistical result has practical significance if the result has important consequences for individuals for whom the result is relevant.
2. Statistical results can have practical significance when compared against personal standards, organizational standards, or curriculum standards.
3. A distribution of scores sometimes is converted into rank scores in order to determine prizes or awards, which often have practical significance for the winners.
4. Tables of norms based on grade equivalents, age equivalents, or percentile ranks have practical significance because they inform educators whether an individual student or group of students is performing well or poorly relative to a norming group that the educators view as important.
5. Converting raw scores on a test or other measure into z-scores is helpful for interpreting how an individual compares with other individuals on a measure, how an individual's performance varies across different measures, or how one group compares with other groups on a measure.

6. The most common type of standard score is z, but some test developers convert raw scores on their measures to other types of standard scores.

7. An effect size is a useful statistic because it provides a quantitative index of how much two groups differ on a measure or the strength of the relationship between two variables.

8. Gain scores and percentage increases or decreases are useful because they provide a quantitative index of how much an individual or group has changed over time as a result of instruction, maturation, or other factors.

9. In response to federal demands for school accountability, educators increasingly are using growth models as evidence of year-to-year improvement in student academic achievement.

10. The practical significance of statistical results can be quantified to an extent, but educators also must rely on their own expertise and judgment to determine whether statistical results indicate problems of practice and solutions to these problems.

KEY TERMS

Adequate Yearly Progress (AYP)	Nation's Report Card	*Publication Manual of the American Psychological Association*
age equivalent	No Child Left Behind Act (NCLB)	
ceiling effect		
Cohen's *d*	normal curve	ranking
effect size	normal curve area	raw score
gain score	norming group	standard score
Glass's Δ	norm-referenced test	status model
grade equivalent	percentile rank	table of norms
growth model	practical significance	*z*-score
National Assessment of Educational Progress (NAEP)		

THE PRACTICAL SIGNIFICANCE OF STATISTICAL RESULTS

In Chapter 6, we present various statistics that can describe a distribution of scores on a measure. These statistics include the mean, median, mode, and standard deviation. We also explained statistics that describe relationships between two or more distributions of scores, such as a correlation coefficient or comparison of groups.

These statistics on their own have little meaning for professional practice. We need judgment and expertise to interpret the meaning of statistical results and their value, if any, for professional practice. If a group (e.g., educators, students, parents, policy makers) decides that a statistical result has value for understanding or improving professional practice, we can say that it has **practical significance** for that group.

Determining the practical significance of a statistical result often involves transforming raw scores on a test or other measure into another type of scale. For example, on a multiple-choice test, each item typically is scored 1 (correct) or 0 (incorrect), and all of the item scores are summed to yield a total score on the test. This is the individual's **raw score** for the test. As you read this chapter, you will learn various ways in which these raw scores can be transformed into other types of scales, such as grade equivalents or rankings, to make them more useful to educators and other groups.

COMPARISONS WITH PERSONAL AND ORGANIZATIONAL STANDARDS

In Chapter 6, we use teacher salaries to illustrate descriptive statistics. The average teacher salary in each of the 50 states is shown in Table 6.1. Suppose you are an individual living in the state of Arizona, and you find that the average teacher salary there is $47,553. If you reside in Arizona and are thinking about teaching as a career, you might look at that salary and conclude that (1) this salary will support the lifestyle I desire, (2) this salary will not support my desired lifestyle, or (3) I want to learn more about the variability around this average salary to determine whether some teaching specialties have a higher-than-average salary that will support my desired lifestyle.

In each case, you are judging the statistical result (i.e., the state's average teacher salary) against a standard, namely, the salary needed to support your desired lifestyle. Thus, the statistical result has practical significance for making decisions about your choice of career. The statistical result also would have practical significance for anyone else for whom salary is a factor in making a decision about career choice.

Policy makers in various organizations (e.g., school boards, state legislatures, teachers unions) also might find that the statistical results in Table 6.1 have practical consequences for them. For example, suppose that school administrators are experiencing difficulty in recruiting and retaining teachers in their state, and they find that one of the main reasons is that their teacher salaries are insufficient. The teacher salary and household income statistics shown in Table 6.1, combined with other statistical data, can help them decide what level of salary increase might be necessary to improve teacher recruitment and retention. The enhanced salary becomes the standard against which existing salaries are compared and also the standard that policy makers will need to justify in order to win taxpayers' support.

COMPARISONS WITH IDEAL STANDARDS

Achieving consensus on a standard for teacher salaries might be difficult, but there is near universal agreement on standards that represent ideal conditions for educational practice. For example, it is difficult to imagine anyone who would disagree with the following standards: Schools should strive for a school dropout rate of 0 percent; school violence and vandalism should be nonexistent; all students should be physically fit; there should be a 100 percent rate of high school

completion. Identifying and promoting ideal standards of this type is a problem of practice that educators, the community, and policy makers need to contemplate.

Descriptive statistics on actual rates of a phenomenon have practical significance when judged against the standard of the ideal rate. For example, if we find a school system with a dropout rate of 30 percent, we know that the system has a serious problem that needs to be addressed. In other words, the statistical result (30%) has practical results. Also, statistical results from research studies have practical significance if they identify variables that affect dropout rates or experimental interventions that change the dropout rate in the desired direction.

COMPARISONS WITH CURRICULUM STANDARDS

In recent years, educators have seen the development of new curriculum standards for various school subjects. National commissions formed by federal agencies and education organizations as well as state departments of education have been involved in this work. Their standards, often accompanied by the development of tests keyed to the standards, can be used to judge the practical significance of statistical results.

The **National Assessment of Educational Progress (NAEP)** is a major ongoing activity of the National Center for Education Statistics. The NAEP governing board and staff have been at the forefront of this focus on creating curriculum standards and tests to measure them. NAEP standards and test results periodically are written up as a **Nation's Report Card**, the purpose of which is to inform various constituencies, including educators and policy makers, about the academic achievement of elementary and secondary students in the United States. NAEP issues these report cards periodically on various subjects, particularly reading, mathematics, and science. An important feature of the report cards is that they provide comparisons with the results of previous test administrations so that we can determine whether students' academic achievement is improving across time.

Consider, for example, NAEP's identification of a curriculum standard for science achievement

FIGURE 8.1 • NAEP's Science Curriculum Standards and Achievement Test for Eighth-Grade Science for the Year 2011

At grade 8, 144 assessment questions were developed to test for students' mastery of three types of science content: physical science, life science, and earth and space sciences. Students' scores for each type of content were converted to a scale ranging from 1 to 300. Also, three levels of achievement (basic, proficient, and advanced) were identified for each type of content. To illustrate, the following are descriptions of the achievement levels for life science and the lower end of the score range that students would need to attain to be considered competent at that achievement level.

Basic (141): Eighth-grade students performing at the Basic level "should be able to identify levels of organization within cells, multicellular organisms, and ecosystems; describe how changes in an environment relate to an organism's survival; describe types of interdependence in ecosystems; identify related organisms based on hereditary traits; discuss the needs of animals and plants to support growth and metabolism; and analyze and display data showing simple patterns in population growth."

Proficient (170): Eighth-grade students performing at the Proficient level "should be able to explain metabolism, growth, and reproduction at multiple levels of living systems: cells, multicellular organisms, and ecosystems; predict the effects of heredity and environment on an organism's characteristics and survival; use sampling strategies to estimate population sizes in ecosystems; and suggest examples of sustainable systems for multiple organisms."

Advanced (215): Eighth-grade students performing at the Advanced level "should be able to explain movement and transformations of matter and energy in living systems at cellular, organismal, and ecosystem levels; predict changes in populations through natural selection and reproduction; and describe an ecosystem's populations and propose an analysis for changes based on energy flow through the system."

Source: National Center for Education Statistics. (2012). *The nation's report card: Science 2011* (NCES 2012-465), pp. 14–15. Retrieved from http://nces.ed.gov/nationsreportcard/pdf/main2011/2012465.pdf

for eighth-grade students. NAEP identified separate standards for three types of science content: physical sciences, life sciences, and earth and space sciences. We will consider life sciences here. The standard for this scientific content identifies three levels of proficiency, as shown in Figure 8.1. NAEP developed a test keyed to the standard and cut-off scores for each level of science performance, as shown in the figure.

Table 8.1 shows statistical results for a national sample of 122,000 eighth-grade students from 7,290 schools who took the life science test in 2011. The table includes the percentage of students at each level of science proficiency for the total sample and also for five racial/ethnic groups.

The first data column shows the average score of each group on the science test. What do these scores mean, and what is their practical significance? Elsewhere on the website containing these data, we find that the test is a scale whose scores range from 0 to 300. This information gives us only a limited understanding of what the scores mean and what their significance is.

The other data columns are much more informative. The statistics are the percentage of students who have achieved each level of proficiency in the life sciences. For example, we find in Table 8.1 that 80 percent of white students meet at least the basic standard of proficiency in the life sciences. Looking at Figure 8.1, we can read descriptions of the life sciences standard represented by each level to determine the life sciences skills that all these students have. We also can look at Figure 8.1 to determine the life sciences skills that the 43 percent of students who score at or above the proficient standard have.

The statistics for ethnic-minority students are also easy to interpret. We find, for example, that there is an achievement gap for all ethnic-minority groups except for Asian/Pacific Island students: a substantial percentage of students in these groups lack basic proficiency in life sciences skills, as defined in Figure 8.1.

The fact that the statistics (in this case, percentages) are tied to defined curriculum standards makes it possible for educators to frame problems

TABLE 8.1 • Performance on the NAEP Life Science Test Taken by a National Sample of Eighth-Grade Students in 2011

Group	Average Scale Score	Percentage of Students Below Basic Level	Percentage of Students at or above Basic Level	Percentage of Students at or above Proficient Level	Percentage of Students at Advanced Level
White Students	163	20	80	43	2
Black Students	129	63	37	10	<1
Hispanic Students	137	52	48	16	<1
Asian/Pacific Island Students	159	26	74	20	5
American Indian/Alaska Native Students	141	49	51	20	1
Two or More Races	156	31	69	35	2

Source: Nation's Report Card. Retrieved from http://nationsreportcard.gov/science_2011/g8_nat.aspx?tab_id=tab2&subtab_id=Tab_3#chart

of practice and to set goals for addressing them. In other words, the statistics have practical significance. Looking at the statistics in Table 8.1, educators might decide that the achievement gap between white students and other racial/ethnic groups in basic life sciences proficiency is a serious problem and that resource allocation to reduce this gap should be a high priority. Another priority might be to increase the percentage of students, irrespective of their racial/ethnic status, who can meet the standard of proficiency, as defined in Figure 8.1.

Tests and other measures that are keyed to curriculum standards are not commonly used in educational research. However, as standards and standards-based measures become part of the mainstream of educational practice, perhaps they will become a central focus of educational research methodology. If this happens, educators would pay more attention to statistical results involving curriculum-based achievement tests because of their practical significance.

COMPARISONS BASED ON RANKINGS

A **ranking** expresses the position of an individual on a measure relative to the positions held by other individuals. Educators use rankings for various purposes. For example, a school might rank the students at a particular grade level with respect to academic achievement, or athletes might be ranked with respect to performance in a sports contest (e.g., first place, second place, and third place). These ranks can have important consequences for students' self-esteem and eligibility for future opportunities to learn and perform. Because of their significance, rankings sometimes are collected and analyzed by educational researchers.

Rankings typically have unequal intervals. For example, in one classroom, there might be very little difference in academic achievement between the first-ranked and second-ranked students. In another classroom, however, these two rankings might reflect substantial differences in academic achievement. You should keep this limitation of rankings in mind when interpreting statistical results based on this type of scale.

COMPARISONS INVOLVING TABLES OF NORMS

You are probably familiar with the height and weight chart found in some doctors' offices. The chart shows the average height and weight for children at many age levels starting in infancy (e.g., 6 months old, 6 years old, 6 years 1 month old,

6 years 2 months old). The chart is constructed by gathering a large sample of children at different age levels who are representative of the general population. Using children at each age level, the researchers compute their mean height and weight.

When parents take their child to a doctor's office, someone measures the child's height and weight. The doctor then uses these data to determine whether the child is above or below the mean height or weight of other children the same age. This comparison can have diagnostic value, especially if it is found that the child deviates markedly from the mean.

In this example, the large sample used to represent the general population's scores on a test or other measure is called the **norming group**. The chart of mean heights and weights for different age groups is typically called a **table of norms**. Commercial tests intended for wide use often have tables of norms so that local users can compare their students' scores with those of students in the general population who are at the same age or grade level. Tests that include tables of norms that are of practical use to educators for comparing their students' scores with a norming group often are called **norm-referenced tests**.

Norms can be of various types. The above example involving a doctor's office involved norms relating to height and weight. The following sections describe several types of norms commonly used in educational research and practice.

Grade Equivalents

Grade equivalents are a type of norm in which a student's score on a test is interpreted in terms of the grade level of other students whose mean score is the same as the student's score. For example, consider the Iowa Test of Basic Skills (ITBS), a widely used battery of tests of students' achievement in four school subjects—language arts, math, social studies, and science. Because the ITBS creates norms based on national samples of students, the grade equivalents are called national grade equivalents (NGE). The website for the ITBS explains what these national grade equivalents mean:

> A grade equivalent is a score that describes your student's achievement on a grade level scale. The NGE is a decimal number that describes academic performance in terms of grade level and

month. For example, if your student (as a 3rd grade student) receives a NGE of 4.2 on the third grade Reading Test, this means your student scored as well as a fourth grade student in the second month of the school year if given the same third grade Reading Test. ("Interpreting results from the Iowa Assessments," http://itp.education. uiowa.edu/ia/documents/IA_Interpreting_Results. pdf.)

The table of norms is created by administering a test each month of the school year to nationally representative samples of students at each grade level. The mean of the scores of each group (e.g., all students in the fourth month of the eighth grade) is computed, and this mean is considered the norm for that group.

These norms have practical significance for teaching students because they tell educators whether a particular student or group of students is at, below, or above grade level. Of course, one would need to know what it means to have, let's say, the reading skills of a typical third-grader in order to understand the actual meaning of a grade equivalent. The ITBS website provides reading standards for various grade levels to help us understand what these reading skills are. (For example, see "Iowa Testing Programs," https://itp.education.uiowa.edu/ia/ContentOverviewWebinarsWithAudio.aspx.)

Age Equivalents

Age equivalents are similar to grade equivalents except that a student's score on a test is interpreted as the average age of students in the norming sample who earned that score. The average age is the mean of the ages of the students who earned the score. The table of norms, then, would include a list of possible scores on the test, and next to each score would be the average age of students who earned that score. If we know a student's age, we can say whether she is performing at the same level as her peer group (i.e., students of the same age) or at the level of older or younger students.

Percentile Ranks

Percentile ranks specify the percentage of students in a sample or population whose scores on a test are at or below a particular score. For example, if a research sample's mean on a test translates into a percentile of 72 in a table of norms, we can say that the sample's mean is at the 72nd percentile of students in the norming group.

Calculation of percentile ranks is especially appropriate if the test is designed for a particular age group or grade level. Students in the norming group would be approximately the same age, and all would be in the same grade, so tables of age norms or grade norms would not make sense. However, calculation of percentile ranks makes it possible to determine the cumulative percentage of students who earned each possible score on the test, starting with the lowest score.

By consulting a table of norms based on these cumulative percentages, we can determine what percentage of students in the norming group earned the same score as a research sample or other group. Knowledge about how well a research sample performed relative to a peer group might have practical significance. For example, if the research sample has a low percentile rank, educators who serve students similar to the research sample might decide that special interventions should be put in place to help these students.

A table of norms based on percentile ranks is shown in Table 8.2. This table is for one of the SAT Subject Tests, which are used nationally and internationally for college admissions. The tests are developed by the Educational Testing Service (ets.org) and administered by the College Board (collegeboard.com).

The norming group for the percentile ranks was a large national sample of 120,004 of college-bound seniors who took the test in 2011. To illustrate use of the table, suppose that a student earned a score of 600 on the literature test. That would place the student in the 55th percentile of the norming group on the test. This means that the student performed better on the test than the bottom half of the norming

TABLE 8.2 • SAT Percentile Ranks for Literature Subject Test for Year 2011

Score	Literature	Score	Literature	Score	Literature	Score	Literature
800	99	630	63	460	16	290	1–
790	99	620	60	450	14	280	1–
780	98	610	57	440	13	270	1–
770	97	600	55	430	11	260	1–
760	96	590	52	420	9	250	1–
750	94	580	48	410	7	240	–
740	92	570	45	400	6	230	–
730	91	560	43	390	5	220	–
720	89	550	40	380	4	210	–
710	87	540	36	370	2	200	–
700	83	530	33	360	2		
690	81	520	31	350	1		
680	78	510	29	340	1		
670	75	500	26	330	1–		
660	73	490	24	320	1–		
650	69	480	22	310	1–		
640	66	470	19	300	1–		

Source: "SAT Subject Tests Percentile Ranks: 2011 College-Bound Seniors," © Copyright 2011. The College Board. www.collegeboard.org. Reproduced with permission.

group. It also means that 45 percent of the norming group performed better than the student did.

In a preceding section, we described the use of rankings to determine the practical significance of a group's scores on a measure. Percentile ranks are similar except that they rank individuals in terms of percentiles rather than numbers. For example, we could say that a student's grade point average placed him in the 85th percentile of his class, or that he ranked third in his class in grade point average.

COMPARISONS INVOLVING STANDARD SCORES

In the preceding sections, we described how tables of norms can be used to understand the practical significance of raw scores on a test or other measure. In the next sections, we describe an approach to interpreting raw scores in terms of the score distribution itself. This approach involves the conversion of raw scores into standard scores. A **standard score** is a score that involves a transformation of an individual's raw score on a test or other measure by using the standard deviation of the score distribution. One advantage of standard scores is that they enable direct comparison of a student's performance across a range of measures.

The Most Common Standard Score: The z-Score

To explain standard scores, we need to refer to the concept of a **normal curve**, which we explain in Chapter 6. We displayed a normal curve distribution of scores in Figure 6.2. For the sake of convenience, we show the same normal curve again in Figure 8.2.

If the scores for a sample of individuals approximate a normal curve, the mean and standard deviation of the raw scores can be used to transform them into standard scores. The process is fairly simple. We simply subtract the sample mean from the individual's raw score and divide that result by the standard deviation of the sample.

For example, suppose that a sample's mean score is 20 and the standard deviation is 5. If an individual in the sample earned a raw score of 20, we would subtract that score from 20, which is zero. Dividing zero by the standard deviation (5) equals zero. Therefore, the individual's standard score is zero. Looking at Figure 8.2, we see that a standard score of zero puts the individual at zero on the normal curve, which is the mean (20) and also the 50th percentile of the score distribution. Stated another way, a standard score of zero is zero standard deviation units (the x axis in Figure 8.2) away from the mean.

Taking another example, suppose the individual's raw score is 25. Subtraction of the mean (20) from the raw score equals 5. Dividing 5 by the standard deviation (5) equals a standard score of 1.0. Looking at Figure 8.2, we see that a raw score of 25, which equals a standard score of 1.0, places the individual at approximately the 84th percentile of the score distribution. Stated another way, a standard score of 1 is one standard deviation unit (the x axis in Figure 8.2) away from the mean.

Some standard scores have a negative value. Suppose the individual's raw score is 15. Subtraction of

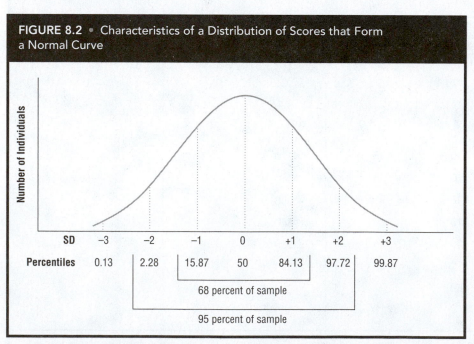

FIGURE 8.2 • Characteristics of a Distribution of Scores that Form a Normal Curve

SD	−3	−2	−1	0	+1	+2	+3
Percentiles	0.13	2.28	15.87	50	84.13	97.72	99.87

68 percent of sample

95 percent of sample

Note: The x axis in this figure represents standard deviation units. The y axis represents the number of individuals in a sample or population whose score or a measure is a particular SD unit value on the x axis.

the mean (20) from 15 equals −5. Dividing −5 by the standard deviation (5) equals a standard score of −1.0. Looking at Figure 8.2, we see that a raw score of 15, which equals a standard score of −1.0, places the individual at approximately the 16th percentile of the score distribution.

In the preceding paragraphs, we referred to three standard scores: 0, 1.0, and −1.0. Another name for these standard scores is z-scores. A **z-score** is the expression of a raw score in terms of another type of score, namely, a standard score that is based on the standard deviation of the score distribution. In a subsequent section of this chapter, we describe several other types of standard scores.

As we explained, we can use z-scores to indicate an individual's percentile rank within the sample or population. For example, looking at Figure 8.2, we see that an individual whose raw score translates into a z-score of +2 is at approximately the 98th percentile of the score distribution. The 98th percentile means that 98 percent of the sample or population have earned z-scores that are at or below a z-score of +2.

Another way of stating this information is to think of the normal curve as containing a certain area. Segments within this total area consist of all the area between one of the curved lines and the vertical line that can be drawn at any point on the x axis. If the normal curve can be divided into areas, what does the 98th percentile mean? It means that 98 percent of the area of the normal curve lies below the z-score of +2. Conversely, we can interpret the 98th percentile to mean that 2 percent of the area of the normal curve lies above the z-score of +2.

As another example, consider a z-score of −1. If we examine the normal curve in Figure 8.2, we can interpret this z-score to mean that approximately 16 percent of the area of the normal curve falls below a z-score of −1, and approximately 84 percent of the area is above −1.

The Presentation of z-Scores in Table Form

The normal curve shown in Figure 8.2 includes only a small number of benchmark z-scores (−3, −2, −1, 0, +1, +2, +3). Statisticians have constructed tables that include a much larger number of units on an interval scale, usually to three or four decimal places. (An example of such a chart is available at regentsprep.org/Regents/

math/algtrig/ATS7/ZChart.htm.) Table 8.3 presents a small number of z-scores to illustrate what these tables look like.

You will note that the table has a column that shows z-scores and a column that shows their corresponding normal curve area. The **normal curve area** is the amount of area from the leftmost of the normal curve to the z-score of interest to us. In Table 8.3, a z-score of −3.00 covers only .001 of a normal curve area. An individual whose z-score on a measure was −3.00 would be below the 1st percentile of the group on which the normal curve was based. In contrast, a z-score of +3.00 covers almost the entire area of the normal curve (.999), so an individual with that z-score would be at the 99th percentile.

The Practical Significance of z-Scores

An individual's raw score on a test or other measure generally is not of much use to educators. A low score might indicate low achievement or a negative attitude, but perhaps that is typical of others in the same group who took the test or other measure. If we convert the raw score to a z-score, however, we now have information about where that individual stands relative to this group. The z-score tells us whether this individual is typical of others (low positive or negative z-scores) or whether he is atypical (high positive or negative z-scores).

The use of z-scores has another important application. Suppose that students have taken achievement tests in several subjects, such as chemistry,

TABLE 8.3 • Examples of z-Scores and Normal Curve Areas

Normal Curve (examples of negative z-scores)		Normal Curve (examples of positive z-scores)	
z-Score	Area	z-Score	Area
−3.00	.001	0.00	.500
−2.50	.005	+0.50	.692
−2.00	.018	+1.00	.841
−1.50	.056	+1.50	.933
−1.00	.138	+2.00	.978
−0.50	.278	+2.50	.994
		+3.00	.999

physics, and mathematics. Further suppose that each test has a different number of items. Raw scores, then, will have different meanings from one test to another. However, z-scores will have the same meaning across tests. For example, suppose that a student has a high z-score in mathematics and physics but a low z-score in chemistry. Educators might use this information to recommend that the student take more advanced coursework in mathematics and physics but do remedial study of chemistry before attempting advanced coursework in that subject.

Still another use of z-scores can be found when making group comparisons on a test or other measure. Suppose two groups, such as males and females, take the same test. We then calculate the mean score for each group and find that that they are different. Should we interpret the difference as trivial or sufficiently large to warrant further inquiry?

One way to answer this question is to first plot the score distribution for, let's say, females, so that it looks something like the normal curve shown in Figure 8.2. Next, we determine the average score (i.e., the mean) of the male group. Now we can ask the question: If a female had earned that score, where would that place her in the distribution of scores for the female group? To answer this question, we can convert the raw score to a z-score, calculated by using the mean and standard deviation of the females' scores.

If we find that the z-score is +1, this would mean that the average male is at the 84th percentile of the females' score distribution. If we find that the z-score is −1, the average male is at the 16th percentile of the females' score distribution. Depending on the actual percentile, educators might decide whether there is a gender gap and whether it is sufficiently large, in percentile terms, to constitute a problem of practice that needs to be addressed.

In general, educators do not use z-scores in their work. Instead, they rely on students' actual test scores or grades, with occasional use of ranks. However, z-scores to compare groups is important in educational research. The calculations that we describe are the basis for calculating effect sizes, which we explain later in the chapter.

TYPES OF STANDARD SCORES

We explained in the preceding section that z-scores are a distribution of raw scores that have been converted into standard scores having a mean of zero and a standard deviation of 1. Some test developers use a different type of standard score to represent the raw scores yielded by their measure. For example, raw scores on intelligence tests such as the Stanford-Binet Intelligence Scale and the Wechsler Adult Intelligence Scale are expressed as standard scores having a mean of 100 and a standard deviation of 16. An individual's standard score on these tests is commonly referred to as their IQ, which stands for intelligence quotient. An adult with an IQ of 100 is at the 50th percentile of the norming sample used to represent the population of U.S. adults. A person with an IQ of 116 would be approximately at the 84th percentile of the norming sample.

The College Board at the Educational Testing Service (ETS) has developed some of the most widely used tests in education—the SAT Reasoning and Subject Tests for college admission; the Test of English as a Foreign Language (TOEFL) to determine English language proficiency (often administered to international students seeking admission to U.S. universities); the Graduate Records Examination (GRE) for admission to graduate programs; and the Praxis tests administered to teacher education candidates.

Raw scores on these tests are converted to standard scores that can range between 200 and 800. The mean and standard deviation of the standard scores for each test can vary, so you need to obtain information for the test that is of interest to you. For example, you can access a website containing standard score distributions, percentiles, means, and standard deviations for SAT Subject Tests for the 2012 test administration (http://media.collegeboard.com/digitalServices/pdf/research/SAT-Subject-Tests-Percentile-Ranks-2012.pdf).

EFFECT SIZES

Imagine a research study designed to investigate the effect of small cash rewards on the achievement of high school students. For one school year, experimental students receive cash rewards for passing weekly quizzes, and control students receive no rewards. At the end of the year, both the experimental and control group students take the XYZ Mathematics Test, which is the criterion measure. The mean score for the experimental group is 46.2, and its standard deviation is 4.0. The mean score for the control group is 41.2, and its standard deviation is 3.8.

This hypothetical experiment demonstrates that cash rewards have a positive effect on student learning because the experimental group scored

5 points higher than the control group on the math test. But just how large is a 5-point difference? And does it have practical significance?

Researchers typically answer these questions by calculating a statistic known as an effect size. An **effect size** is a statistic that quantifies the magnitude of the difference between two groups or, more generally, the magnitude of the relationship between two variables. Several measures of effect size are available. Perhaps the most popular is **Cohen's d**, which is a measure of effect size calculated by subtracting the mean score of Group 1 from the mean score of Group 2 and then dividing this difference by the standard deviation (SD) of the scores of the combined groups. If the research data are from an experiment with a control group, Glass's delta statistic (symbolized by Δ) might be calculated instead. **Glass's Δ** is a measure of effect size calculated by subtracting the mean score of the control group from the mean score of the experimental group and then dividing this difference by the standard deviation of the control group. To illustrate this calculation procedure, consider the preceding experiment.

1. Subtract the control group mean (41.2) from the experimental group mean (46.2). The result is 5.0.
2. Divide 5.0 by 3.8, which is the control group's SD. The result is 1.32. This number (1.32) is the effect size.

The next task is to interpret the significance of this effect size (1.32). It is very close in meaning to z-scores, explained earlier. The standard score for an individual in a sample involves subtracting his score from the sample mean and dividing that result by the sample's SD. We follow the same procedure in computing an effect size, except that we subtract one group's mean from the other group's mean, and we divide the result by the control group's SD.

Referring to Table 8.3, we see that an effect size of 1.32 (viewed as a z-score) covers a point between .841 ($z = +1.00$) and .933 ($z = .933$) of the area of a normal curve. In other words, an effect size of 1.32 lies somewhere between the 84th and 93rd percentile. Using a more detailed table of values for z, we find that an effect size of 1.32 is at the 91st percentile.

To interpret this result, consider experimental group students who earned the mean math test score ($M = 46.2$) at the end of the school year.

These students would be in the 50th percentile of the experimental group score distribution but in the 91st percentile of the control group's score distribution. This is because students in the control group who have a score of 46.2 on the math test are at the 91st percentile relative to other students in their control group.

Of course, it is not only experimental group students with an average math test score (46.2) who made greater gains relative to the control group students. The entire score distribution of the experimental group moved up relative to the score distribution of the control group. In other words, most students who received cash rewards, no matter what their achievement test score was, performed better than if they had been in the control group.

Educators who are concerned about improving the mathematics achievement of high school students should take an effect size this large seriously. Of course, they also need to reflect on ethical concerns about giving cash rewards for learning. Statistical results have practical significance, but they should not be the sole determinant of decision making in education.

Educational researchers generally consider an effect size of 0.33 or larger to have practical significance. An effect size of 0.33 indicates that a student in the group with a higher mean score whose score is at the 50th percentile would be at the 63rd percentile of the other group's score distribution.

Suppose that two research studies investigated the same variables but used different statistical analyses. For example, in Chapter 6, we showed how the relationship between a state's average teacher salary and its average household income can be analyzed using group comparisons or correlation. One researcher might investigate this relationship by making group comparisons, and another researcher might investigate this relationship by correlational analysis.

An advantage of effect size statistics is that the results of these two studies, each involving a different statistical approach, can be converted to a common metric, namely, an effect size. Readers of the two research reports can determine whether the observed relationship between teacher salaries and household income is similar in the two studies simply by comparing the two effect sizes.

Meta-analysis of research results across studies, which we explained in Chapter 3, relies on the effect size metric. Researchers can synthesize the findings of many studies by converting the results of diverse statistical analyses into effect sizes. It does not matter if different studies measured the same variables using different measures. All of the findings can be converted to the effect size metric.

Furthermore, suppose that the studies examined the effect of the same independent variable on different outcome variables. No matter what the outcome variable is or how it was measured, the statistical results can be converted to a single metric, namely, effect size. The individual doing a meta-analysis need only convert each finding of each study to an effect size, then convert to group effect sizes according to the outcome variable that was measured, and finally determine whether the independent variable (e.g., an experimental intervention) had a different effect on different outcome variables.

Effect sizes commonly appear in reports of quantitative research, especially in recent years. In part, this is because the ***Publication Manual of the American Psychological Association*** (American Psychological Association, 2010) strongly recommends them: "For the reader to appreciate the magnitude or importance of a study's findings, it is almost always necessary to include some measure of effect size in the Results section" (p. 34). The manual also includes a recommendation to report the confidence interval for effect sizes. (We discuss confidence intervals in Chapter 7.) Most educational journals follow APA publication guidelines, and therefore journal editors are likely to require authors to adhere to this recommendation.

GAIN SCORES

Educators' fundamental mission is to promote the learning and personal development of their students. Researchers think of these two concepts—learning and development—as a series of changes that occur in students across time. They can detect these changes by administering the same measure to individuals at two or more points in time. The amount of change can be quantified by computing a **gain score**, which is simply the difference in an individual's score on the measure from one time to the next. Gain scores are often positive, but they can also be negative, as when a student forgets information learned earlier.

Researchers sometimes include gain scores in their reports, but you should view them with caution. For example, they are subject to the **ceiling effect**, which occurs when a student's academic achievement exceeds the highest achievement measured by the test. To understand this effect, suppose that a student scores 95 out of 100 possible points on initial testing. The student can improve by a maximum of only 5 points on this test when it is readministered. This 5-point range might be inadequate to measure all of the new information or skills that the student has learned during the intervening time. In other words, the ceiling (100 possible points) is too low.

Another limitation of gain scores is that most tests are not true interval scales, meaning that they do not have equal intervals. For example, suppose a test has 50 items, with each correctly answered item earning a score of 1. Further suppose that the items vary in difficulty. Now consider the case of two students who earn the same gain score of 5. But one goes from a raw score of 10 to a raw score of 15, whereas the other goes from a raw score of 40 to a raw score of 45. It probably is more difficult for the second student to make a gain score of 5 than it is for the first student because the second student will need to correctly answer test items that are more difficult. If this is true, the same gain score does not have the same meaning for both students.

Still another problem is that most tests contain different types of items. For example, suppose that two students earn the same gain score on a subtraction test, but they do it by making gains on different types of subtraction items. Once again, the gain score is the same, but it does not have the same meaning for the two students.

Percentage Gains and Losses

Gains and losses occasionally are expressed in terms of percentages. For example, we might read that there has been a 50 percent increase in the number of students in a school who report being the victim of cyberbullying from one school year to the next. This statistic suggests a problem of practice that should be addressed. But exactly how big a problem is it?

The calculation procedure involves (1) subtracting the frequency of cyberbullying in Year 1 from the frequency in Year 2, (2) dividing that result by the frequency in Year 1, and (3) expressing that result in percentage form. To illustrate, suppose the frequency of cyberbullying in Year 1 is 100 in a particular school district, and the frequency in Year 2 is 150. Subtracting 100 from 150 equals 50. Dividing 50 by 100 equals 1/2, and 1/2 expressed in decimal form is 0.50. In percentage form, 0.50 is 50 percent.

If only percentage increases or decreases are reported, faulty interpretations can result. In the example just reported, a 50 percent increase in cyberbullying appears ominous because it represents 50 more students who report being cyberbullied. However, suppose the number of students who report being the victim of cyberbullying in Year 1 is 4, and the number in Year 2 is 6. The percentage increase is 50 percent ([6 − 4] ÷ 4 = 2/4), which equals 0.50, or 50 percent.

In both examples, the percentage increase is 50 percent. However, in the second example, the increase is only 2 students, which might indicate a much less serious problem of practice for educators than an increase of 50 students, which was the case in the first example.

This illustration indicates the need to know not only the percentage of increase or decrease but also the actual frequencies that are involved. Because of this need, some researchers and educators report ratios instead. For example, we found these statistics in a Wikipedia article about autism:

> Attention has been focused on whether the prevalence of autism is increasing with time. Earlier prevalence estimates were lower, centering at about 0.5 per 1,000 for autism during the 1960s and 1970s and about 1 per 1,000 in the 1980s, as opposed to today's 1–2 per 1,000. (Wikipedia, n.d., citing Newschaffer et al., 2007)

In this example, the authors present the incidence of autism as a ratio. We can see that there has been an increase in the autism rate, but the prevalence at the present time (1 or 2 per 1,000 children) is still very low. From a human perspective, of course, even if one more child is diagnosed with autism from one year to the next, that is a great personal problem for the child, his parents, and the community.

Status Models and Growth Models for School Accountability

Policy makers are increasingly interested in collecting and analyzing gain scores for the purpose of holding schools accountable for student learning (Goldschmidt et al., 2005). To understand the reasons for this trend, we need to examine the accountability standards of the federal government's **No Child Left Behind Act (NCLB)**, which we discuss in Chapter 1 and elsewhere.

Among other things, the NCLB Act requires that all students achieve proficiency in mathematics and reading by the 2013–2014 school year. To determine whether schools are making adequate gains toward this goal, educators must demonstrate that the percentage of students who achieve proficiency in mathematics and reading increases each year. This type of requirement for improvement in student achievement, as measured by students' performance on standardized tests, is called **Adequate Yearly Progress (AYP)** in the NCLB statute.

This approach to school accountability sometimes is referred to as a status model. In a **status model**, students at a particular grade level are tested each year, and the achievement test scores of students at that grade level in year X are compared with the scores of students at the same grade level in year Y. For example, if 60 percent of fifth-graders in a particular school achieved proficiency in reading in the 2008–2009 school year, then the children who are in fifth grade the next school year (2009–2010) must exceed that percentage (60%) by a particular amount. If the annual target is 10 percent improvement, educators will be expected to have 66 percent of the 2009–2010 fifth-graders achieving proficiency in reading. The Adequate Yearly Progress requirement of the NCLB Act is based on the status model.

This way of measuring gain has several problems. One is that the fifth-graders in the 2008–2009 school year might have substantially different characteristics (e.g., male–female ratio) than fifth-graders in the 2009–2010 school year. If so, we are measuring gain using two different types of students, and therefore the amount of gain or loss might be impossible to interpret. Another problem is that the statistical results do not provide any information about the amount of gain that fifth-graders in the 2008–2009 school year made during the 2009–2010 school year when they were sixth-graders.

A particularly serious problem with the status model occurs if students are assessed with respect to standards of performance, such as Below Basic, Basic, Proficient, and Advanced. (These standards are used by the National Assessment of Educational Progress, which we discussed earlier in the chapter.) Under the NCLB Act, educators must bring all students up to the Proficient level within a certain number of years.

Suppose that 40 percent of students in a school are Below Basic, 30 percent are Basic, and 30 percent are Proficient in the 2008–2009 school year. Suppose further that educators work intensively to improve students' learning the following school year, with these results: Only 10 percent of the students score at the Below Basic level; 60 percent score at the

Basic level; and 30 percent score at the Proficient level. Student learning in this school has improved tremendously, but the statistical results show no gain in the percentage of students who score at the Proficient level. In both years, it is 30 percent.

In reality, many schools have had great difficulty in meeting Adequate Yearly Progress requirements. For example, more than 50 percent of the schools in some states failed to make adequate yearly progress in 2011 (McNeil, 2011). For this reason and others, legislators are rewriting NCLB requirements so that schools will still be required to improve student achievement, but without the constraints of the Adequate Yearly Progress model in the original NCLB statute.

Because of these and other problems with the status model for measuring gain, researchers and assessment experts have proposed using growth models instead. **Growth models** use tests to measure the same students' learning over time. For example, researchers and educators might administer a test to fourth-graders at the end of the school year, administer it again to the same students when they have completed fifth grade, and still again when these same students have completed sixth grade. Statistical analyses would focus on how much gain these students make on the test as they progress across different grade levels.

One of the main advantages of growth models is that they provide relatively clear statistics describing whether a group of students is learning as they progress through school and whether each new cohort of students enrolled at the school learns more than previous cohorts. Among the disadvantages of growth models are that they require a lot of student testing and data analysis and the development of tests that measure a span of curriculum content sufficiently wide to include several grade levels.

PRACTICAL SIGNIFICANCE AS AN INTERPRETIVE PROCESS

Statistical results do not speak for themselves. Means, standard deviations, ranges, correlation coefficients, and score distributions are not a direct guide to practice or to the development of theories that might affect practice. Educators and researchers must always use their expertise and apply judgment to determine whether a specific statistical result has practical significance.

In particular, they need to consider the variables to which the statistical results pertain. For example, we primarily used examples in this chapter that refer to students' scores on academic achievement tests. Educators value what these tests measure, but they are interested in other academic outcomes, too, such as helping students develop creativity, improving students' self-esteem, eliminating school violence and bullying, helping students develop habits that maintain physical health, and promoting good citizenship. A small effect size for one of these outcome variables might be more valued, and therefore have more practical significance, than a larger effect size for an outcome variable that is less valued.

An example of
How Determining the Practical Significance of Statistical Results Can Help in Solving Problems of Practice

Educators often find that some students have personal problems that interfere with their learning. Some of these problems involve physical illness. Educators need to understand such illnesses, how they affect students, and what remedies are available.

One such illness is asthma. A review of research about this disease, reported in the medical journal *BMC Family Practice*, was made available to the general public by various news services, including Reuters. The news item indicated that the researchers who did the literature review found that exercise can improve aerobic fitness and psychological well-being in asthmatic children. However, the researchers also found that children and young people with asthma "tend to be less active than their peers without the disease [and] that many young people with asthma didn't think they were able to fully participate in sports and physical activities." (Reuters, 2008)

The article states that asthmatic children and young people are "less active" than their peers. However, the article does not specify what "less active" means in quantitative terms. Thus, we do not know how serious a problem this is.

We can gain insight into the seriousness of the problem by obtaining a copy of the research team's literature review. Hopefully, the review contains effect sizes that can be analyzed to determine the percentile of the average asthmatic child's exercise level relative to the distribution of exercise levels for nonasthmatic children. If the average asthmatic child is at the 40th percentile, this suggests a less serious problem than if the average asthmatic child is at the 20th percentile.

The phrase "many young people with asthma" poses a similar problem. What does "many" mean? It would be helpful to compute percentages so that we know exactly what percentage of young people with asthma have negative beliefs about their ability to participate in physical activities.

By precise quantification of "less active" and "many young people," we can develop a better understanding of the magnitude of the problem. If the effect sizes and percentages indicate a serious problem, these statistical findings could spur policy makers and educators to institute programs that better meet the needs of asthmatic children. The programs might pay dividends by improving the health of these children and decreasing their absence from school because of illness.

SELF-CHECK TEST

1. Curriculum standards are
   a. not available for any school subject at the national level.
   b. useful for formulating research hypotheses.
   c. useful for judging the practical significance of statistical results.
   d. useful for developing tests but minimally useful for developing curriculum.
2. A norming group represents
   a. the entire population for whom a test was developed.
   b. a random sample of the population for whom a test was developed.
   c. the portion of the sample who fall between the 25th and 75th percentile in a table of norms.
   d. the sample or population used to create a table of norms for a test.
3. A grade equivalent for a test indicates
   a. the grade level of the average student who earned a particular raw score on a test.
   b. the grade level for which a test is most appropriate.
   c. whether a status model or growth model should be used to measure students' achievement gain over the course of a school year.
   d. the accuracy with which a particular test predicts the grades of a sample of students randomly selected from a population of students.

4. A standard score represents an individual's raw score in relation to
   a. the standard deviation of the score distribution.
   b. grade equivalents or age equivalents.
   c. percentile ranks based on a table of norms.
   d. all of the above.
5. If a group of individuals takes the same test, those with a z-score of +1.0 are
   a. one standard deviation below the group mean.
   b. one standard deviation above the group mean.
   c. at the 18th percentile of the score distribution.
   d. at the 99th percentile of the score distribution.
6. The z-score
   a. is not a type of standard score.
   b. is equivalent to an effect size.
   c. can be used to compare an individual's scores on different tests that vary in number of items.
   d. can be used to compare an individual's scores on different tests only if the number of items is constant across the tests.
7. The results of intelligence tests and SAT Subject Tests are commonly reported in terms of
   a. raw scores.
   b. standard scores.
   c. effect sizes.
   d. rank scores.

8. An effect size
  a. compares the standard deviation of Group A and Group B.
  b. compares the mean scores of Group A and Group B using a table of norms.
  c. compares the score distributions of Group A and Group B to the score distribution for a norming group.
  d. compares the mean scores of Group A and Group B in relation to the score distribution of Group B or the score distributions of the two groups.
9. The interpretation of gain scores can be difficult because
  a. of the possibility of a ceiling effect.
  b. most tests tend to have unequal intervals between the points on the scale.
  c. a test usually includes items measuring different types of academic achievement.
  d. all of the above.
10. The status model for school accountability is illustrated by
  a. selecting a group of students in fifth grade and tracking their learning for several years.
  b. selecting students who are in fifth grade in 2012 and comparing their learning with that of students who enter the fifth grade in 2013 at the same school.
  c. selecting fifth-grade classes of students across a sample of schools in 2012 and comparing them using a table of norms based on grade equivalents.
  d. selecting a sample of students at different grade levels in 2012 and comparing their test performance by calculating effect sizes.

CHAPTER REFERENCES

American Psychological Association. (2010). *Publication manual of the American Psychological Association* (6th ed.). Washington, DC: Author.

Goldschmidt, P., Roschewski, P., Choi, K., Auty, W., Hebbler, S., Blank, R., & Williams, A. (2005). *Policymakers' guide to growth models for school accountability: How do accountability models differ?* Washington, DC: Council of Chief State School Officers. Retrieved from http://www.ccsso.org/Documents/2005/Policymakers_Guide_To_Growth_2005.pdf

McNeil, M. (2011, August 3). Are 82% of schools "failing" under NCLB, as Duncan warned? *Education Week*. Retrieved from http://www.edweek.org

Newschaffer, C. J., Croen, L. A., Daniels, J., Giarelli, E., Grether, J. K., Levy, S. E., Mandell, D. S., Miller, L. A., Pinto-Martin, J., Reaven, J., Reynolds, A. M., Rice, C. E., Schendel, D., & Windham, G. C. (2007). The epidemiology of autism spectrum disorders. *Annual Review of Public Health, 28*(2), 235–258.

Reuters. (2008, July 31) Asthmatic kids face obstacles to getting fit. *Reuters*. Retrieved from http://www.reuters.com/article/healthNews/idUSGOR18144620080731

Wikipedia. (n.d.). Epidemiology of autism. *Wikipedia*. Retrieved from http://en.wikipedia.org/wiki/Epidemiology_of_autism

RESOURCES FOR FURTHER STUDY

Bracey, G. (2006). *Reading educational research: How to avoid getting statistically snookered*. Portsmouth, NH: Heinemann.

  The author provides a list of 32 guidelines for avoiding being misled by statistical results presented in reports of educational research. The author presents many examples to illustrate how statistical results can be manipulated to support the biases and political agendas of researchers and funding agencies.

Sun, S., Pan, W., & Wang, L. L. (2010). A comprehensive review of effect size reporting and interpreting practices in academic journals in education and psychology. *Journal of Educational Psychology, 102*(4), 989–1004.

  The authors provide a comprehensive overview of effect sizes as a measure of practical significance and as a method for accumulating knowledge across studies of a particular problem of practice. Also, they review the use of effect sizes in published research studies, and they illustrate what they consider to be good reporting of effect sizes.

Yell, M. L., & Dragsow, E. (2009). *No Child Left Behind: A guide for professionals* (2nd ed.). Boston, MA: Pearson.

  The No Child Left Behind Act is undergoing legislative change in the current decade. To understand proposed changes, it is helpful to know the original intents of the NCLB Act, especially its requirements for Adequate Yearly Progress. The authors explain these requirements and other aspects of the NCLB Act. They also explore the effects of the NCLB Act on the American educational system.

Can Growth Ever Be Beside the Point?

Popham, W. J. (2005). Can growth ever be beside the point? *Educational Leadership, 63*(3), 83–84.

The following article describes current statistical methods that are being recommended for determining whether schools are making year-to-year improvements in student achievement. Even though the author does not offer a solution to avoiding the flaws in such statistical methods, he performs a service to the education profession by identifying them.

The article demonstrates why educators and policy makers need to understand the practical significance of statistical results. Without this understanding, they might adopt a method that produces statistical results that hamper, rather than improve, educational practice.

The article is reprinted in its entirety, just as it appeared when originally published.

All About Accountability: Can Growth Ever Be Beside the Point?

W. JAMES POPHAM
UCLA Graduate School of Education and Information Studies

A school is supposed to nurture children's intellectual growth—that is, to promote students' increasing command of significant bodies of knowledge and key cognitive skills. Consequently, if a school *does* promote greater intellectual growth in its students each year, you would think that any annual evaluation of the school's effectiveness would reflect that growth.

Although the architects of No Child Left Behind (NCLB) clearly wanted U.S. schools to foster gobs of student growth, this law's evaluative requirements currently don't function that way. Each state's success or failure under NCLB hinges on the particular cut score that a state's officials have selected, often arbitrarily, to determine whether a student's performance on a state accountability test classifies that student as proficient. On the basis of that cut score, a state identifies its students as either "not proficient" or "proficient or above." For simplicity's sake, I'll call this cut score the *proficiency point*. A state's proficiency point on each of its standardized tests becomes the most significant factor—by far—in determining how many schools will stumble during that state's annual NCLB sweepstakes.

If a designated percentage of a school's students don't earn proficiency on the state-mandated tests, that school is classified as having failed to make adequate yearly progress (AYP). Yet as odd as it may sound, such

AYP failure can occur despite the fact that the school has promoted substantial overall growth in its students' achievement levels.

I can illustrate the absurdity of this situation with a fictitious school I'll call Pretend Prep. Let's locate Pretend Prep in a state that uses four levels of NCLB-determined proficiency—below basic, basic, proficient, and advanced. Two years ago, 50 percent of Pretend Prep's students earned such low scores on their state's standardized NCLB tests that they were classified as below basic. The other 50 percent of this imaginary school's students, because of their higher test scores, were classified as proficient.

However, because of an intense, yearlong instructional effort on the part of Pretend Prep teachers, last year all the below-basic students scored well enough on the tests to move up one level to the basic category. Moreover, all the school's proficient students improved their scores so that they, too, jumped up one category to the advanced classification. This represents astonishing academic growth on the part of the school's students. However, because NCLB success is *only* determined by the percentage of students who score at or above the state's proficiency point, Pretend Prep has shown no AYP-related progress. Despite the blatant evidence of remarkable growth in student achievement, 50 percent of the students remained below the proficiency point, and 50 percent remained above.

Although my example is both fictitious and extreme, it illustrates an important point: In real-world school evaluations, students will often improve on state-mandated tests, sometimes dramatically, but the improved scores will not influence a school's AYP status because those students' scores don't cross the proficiency point.

The major drawback of a school evaluation system that doesn't take growth into account is that it encourages teachers to focus excessive instructional attention on students who are at the cusp of proficiency—just above or below a test's proficiency point. Because students who are well above or well below that proficiency point won't affect a school's evaluation, teachers may be tempted to neglect those two categories of students.

Although I am urging the adoption of a growth-based approach to NCLB school evaluation, I am not advocating the adoption of "value-added" evaluative models, such as those first used in Tennessee but now adopted by a number of other states. These value-added models are explicitly designed to monitor individual students' grade-to-grade achievement growth. By following individual students' growth across grade levels, value-added models can circumvent NCLB's "cross-sectional" analyses whereby test scores of this year's crop of 4th graders, for example, are compared with the test scores of last year's crop of 4th graders. Because of the sometimes considerable disparities in the abilities of different grade-level groups, any evaluative approach that doesn't depend on cross-sectional analyses has great appeal.

For Tennessee's version of the value-added method to work properly, however, student test scores must be statistically converted to a special kind of analytic scale so that student achievement gains in particular content areas represent the same amount of growth at different grade levels. Thus, an analytic scale must be generated so that a 6th grader's 10 percent improvement in mastering 6th grade math content, for example, will be equivalent to a 5th grader's 10 percent improvement in mastering 5th grade math content. Without such analytic scales, most value-added approaches just won't work.

These kinds of analytic scales are difficult to create, however. That's because substantial curricular variation exists between grades, even in the same content area. Moreover, children have an annoying habit of developing cognitively and emotionally in different ways at different times. Accordingly, the only statistically defensible analytic scales for value-added models are excessively general ones, such as scales measuring a student's "quantitative competence" or "language arts mastery."

But these overly general analytic scales supply teachers with no diagnostically useful information about *which* skills or bodies of knowledge a student has or hasn't mastered. Consequently, any useful diagnostic information instantly evaporates with the installation of value-added approaches. Regrettably, value-added methods sacrifice effective instructional diagnoses on the altar of statistical precision. We need to find better ways of measuring students' growth for our AYP analyses.

Fortunately, the U.S. Department of Education has appointed a number of study groups to advise Secretary of Education Margaret Spellings about how best to incorporate growth models into NCLB's accountability requirements. I'm hopeful that these advisory groups can come up with reasonable ways to incorporate growth into NCLB's school evaluations and that Secretary Spellings will heed their advice. Although advocates of a value-added strategy sure know how to belt out an alluring siren song, I suggest we all steer clear of that approach.

W. James Popham is Emeritus Professor in the UCLA Graduate School of Education and Information Studies; wpopham@ucla.edu.

CHAPTER NINE

Descriptive Research

PROBLEMS OF PRACTICE *in this chapter*

- What can teachers do to engage their students in learning?
- How good are teacher evaluation systems and how can they be improved?
- How important is it to prepare students to acquire financial literacy?
- Why has the reading performance of 17-year-olds not improved over the past four decades?
- What do Americans consider to be the biggest problems facing their schools?
- What changes to the American school system are most likely to improve students' academic achievement?
- Why are few states approving curriculum materials aligned to Common Core Standards and requiring their use?
- Should educators adopt online learning courses for their students as an alternative to regular classroom instruction?
- Is an online course sufficient, or does it need to be blended with some form of classroom instruction?

IMPORTANT *Ideas*

1. Descriptive research provides knowledge about the status quo, which is often the first step in improving educational practice.
2. Descriptive research designs identify characteristics of a group at one point in time or changes in such characteristics across time, but they do not explore cause-and-effect relationships involving these characteristics.
3. The Gallup Poll, the National Assessment of Educational Progress, and other organizations regularly collect descriptive data about various aspects of education.
4. Panel studies, trend studies, and cross-sectional studies use different sampling procedures to study human development or changes in a group over a period of years.
5. Tests, questionnaires, observation schedules, interview guides, and other measurement methods can be used to collect data in a descriptive research study.

6. Researchers commonly analyze descriptive data to determine the central tendency and variability of score descriptions.
7. The findings of descriptive research studies can reveal the prevalence of problems, opinions, academic achievement, and other phenomena across an entire defined population.

KEY TERMS

cohort study
confidence interval
cross-sectional study
descriptive research
Guttman scale
Likert item

Likert scale
longitudinal research
margin of error
National Assessment of
    Educational Progress (NAEP)
panel study

Phi Delta Kappa/Gallup Polls
survey research
trend study

THE RELEVANCE OF DESCRIPTIVE RESEARCH TO EDUCATIONAL PRACTICE

Educators and researchers are curious about what is happening in schools. Are teachers using research-based methods of instruction? How safe are schools? Are ethnic-minority students respected and supported? What problems do teachers face in their work? How does the public feel about school vouchers and charter schools?

We can answer these questions by drawing on our own experience and the experience of those around us. For example, Heather Wolpert-Gawron (2012), a middle school teacher, reported the results of a questionnaire that she gave to her eighth-graders. The question she asked them was: "What engages students?" The results are summarized in Figure 9.1.

The results of this student survey have the ring of truth, but one might ask whether the students' responses are unique to this teacher or whether they are more widely applicable. To answer this question, we need the scientific approach of descriptive research, which relies on valid measures, representative samples, and sound statistical analyses. The knowledge gained by this type of research is often the first step in launching efforts to improve education. For example, knowledge about problems and successful practices in one school district can help educators in other school districts. Conversely, knowledge about problems and successful practices across many school districts can help educators in a particular school district.

The value of large-scale descriptive research is illustrated in the medical profession by a problem involving artificial joints (Meier, 2008). An American surgeon discovered that several of his patients suffered greatly after being implanted with a metal hip socket called the Durom cup, manufactured by Zimmer Holdings. He alerted colleagues in a professional association and found that some of them had also found problems with this hip socket. Sales of the device were suspended until the problem was solved. Meier notes that the patients' suffering might have been averted:

> If those patients lived in other countries where artificial joints were tracked by national databases—including Australia, Britain, Norway and Sweden—many might have been spared that risk. And Zimmer might have suspended sales of the cup months ago. Unfortunately, the United States lacks such a national database, called a joint registry, that tracks how patients with artificial hips and knees fare. The risk in the United States that a patient will need a replacement procedure because of a flawed product or technique can be double the risk of countries with databases, according to Dr. Henrik Malchau of Massachusetts General Hospital.

Educators often find that the most useful thing about conferences and workshops is the opportunity to share their local problems and practices

FIGURE 9.1 • Eighth-Graders' Responses to the Question, "What Engages Students?"

1. **Working with their peers.** Students want to interact with each other and engage in discussion.
2. **Working with technology.** Students live in a digital age, and they want to use video, computers, social networks such as Facebook and Twitter, and other technology to help them learn.
3. **Connecting the real world to the work we do in class.** Students want to engage in projects and discussion that take them beyond the textbook into current reality and their own interests.
4. **Clearly love what you do.** Teachers should teach with passion and enthusiasm.
5. **Get me out of my seat!** Students in this age group want activities that get them standing and moving about the classroom.
6. **Bring in visuals.** Students enjoy visual images that help them understand the content they are learning.
7. **Student choice.** Students want the freedom to choose their own projects so that they can follow their own interests and work at a level that is consistent with their abilities.
8. **Understand your clients—the kids.** Students want teachers who can see things from their perspective and who create a partnership with students to facilitate the learning process.
9. **Mix it up!** Students want a variety of learning activities, including games.
10. **Be human.** Students want teachers who engage with them on a human level, such as by asking students what interests them rather than making assumptions.

Source: Wolpert-Gawron, H. (2012, April 26). Kids speak out on student engagement. *Edutopia.* Retrieved from http://www.edutopia.org/blog/student-engagement-stories-heather-wolpert-gawron

with other educators. This sharing is undoubtedly useful, but educators also need to consider the value of national-level descriptive data about problems and practices. In this chapter, we consider how descriptive research can produce this type of knowledge, either for the nation as a whole or for particular defined populations within it. You will find that many descriptive research studies involve surveys using questionnaires or interviews, but other methods of data collection can be used as well.

EXAMPLES OF DESCRIPTIVE RESEARCH

The results of descriptive research about education are published in scholarly journals but also in popular media and reports issued by public and private institutes. Let's consider some examples.

Descriptive Research in Popular Media

Christian Science Monitor, a weekly news magazine, published an article about procedures for assessing teacher evaluation (Paulson, 2012). It cited a study

by the New Teacher Project (TNTP), a national center whose mission is to end the injustice of educational inequality:

> A landmark study of 12 districts in four states by TNTP found that more than 99 percent of teachers were rated satisfactory. The study confirmed what many in the education field already knew. Traditional "evaluations" gave very little feedback to teachers and their administrators.

This finding from a descriptive research study highlights a problem of practice and brings it to the attention of the general public. In some cases, this attention results in action to find solutions to the problem. The article presents one such solution—the Measures of Effective Teaching (MET) research sponsored by the Gates Foundation. Their research has identified three key features of an effective teacher evaluation system: detailed classroom observation using standard evaluation criteria; measurement of student achievement growth; and student surveys that rate teachers' classroom performance.

A story about the financial literacy of adults and students appeared in the daily newspaper, the *Wall Street Journal* (Coombes, 2012). The author of the article, Andrea Coombes, cites Professor Michael Finke, who claims that it is becoming increasingly difficult for adults to function effectively in the United States without being financially literate. Coombes also reports research findings that schools are not doing an adequate job of developing this kind of literacy in their students:

> While 46 states include personal-finance education in state standards, just 36 require those standards to be implemented, and only 13 require students to take a personal-finance course in high school, according to a 2011 study by the Council for Economic Education, a nonprofit that aims to promote financial literacy through teacher training and other means.

Coombes also cites a study by the National Endowment for Financial Education, which found that only 20 percent of teachers and student teachers felt prepared to teach the basics of personal finance.

Stories and statistics such as these are regularly reported in newspapers and other mass media. Success stories are reported, but stories of problems and failings seem to be more common. As an educator, you will want to take note of these reports as they shape public opinion about schools generally and, fairly or not, about local schools.

Descriptive Research Conducted by Public and Private Institutes

In the previous sections, each of our examples of popular media cited descriptive research conducted by institutes (also called foundations, centers, endowments, and similar terms). The institutes might be funded by the government, professional organizations, or private individuals. You can find their reports by going directly to their websites or by using a search engine (see Chapter 4). The following are examples of descriptive research conducted by these institutes.

National Assessment of Educational Progress

Many public and private organizations conduct descriptive research on problems of practice in education. One of the most important such organization is the **National Assessment of Educational Progress (NAEP)**. NAEP is a congressionally mandated project of the National Center for Education Statistics (ed.gov/programs/naep). It has been assessing U.S. students' performance since 1969 to determine how well students are learning school subjects such

as reading, mathematics, science, writing, history, and geography.

NAEP publishes many reports about the academic achievement of current students and changes in academic achievement levels across time. For example, we discussed NAEP's descriptive study of American students' level of proficiency in the life sciences in Chapter 8. That survey was limited to students' academic achievement in 2011. Another NAEP descriptive study reported on changes in students' reading achievement over an extended period of time—from 1971 to 2008. Some of the results of that study are shown in Figure 9.2.

We see that 9-year-olds and 13-year-olds had a higher level of reading achievement in 2008 than in 2004 or in 1971. Seventeen-year-olds also had a higher level of reading achievement in 2008 than in 2004, but it was only one point higher than it was in 1971, and lower than it was throughout the 1990s. These findings reveal at least two important problems of practice: Why has the reading performance of 17-year-olds not improved over a substantial period of time, and how can we raise their level of reading performance along the 500-point scale that is used to measure this aspect of academic achievement?

The Gallup Polls

You probably are familiar with the Gallup polls, as their findings are widely disseminated by the mass media and various publications. The general purpose of Gallup polls is to serve as a barometer of public opinion about various matters of interest to society.

One of the Gallup polls should be of particular interest to educators. It is the annual **Phi Delta Kappa/Gallup Poll** of the Public's Attitudes Toward the Public Schools. At their website (pdkintl.org/poll/index.htm), you can find the results of the most current annual poll and all other annual polls back to the first, which was conducted in 1969.

We refer here to PDK/Gallup Poll 44, conducted in 2012 (Bushaw & Lopez, 2012). The report includes 45 tables containing statistics that describe the public's opinions about such matters as school governance, testing, the achievement gap, curriculum, teachers, the No Child Left Behind Act, and Common Core Standards. One of the tables from this poll is shown in Table 9.1, both because it is

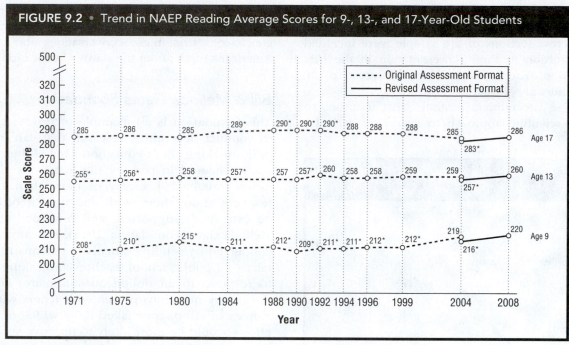

FIGURE 9.2 • Trend in NAEP Reading Average Scores for 9-, 13-, and 17-Year-Old Students

*Significantly different (p < .05) from 2008.
Source: Institute of Education Sciences, National Center for Education Statistics. (2009). *NAEP 2008 Trends in Academic Progress* (NCES 2009-479). Retrieved from p. 3 of http://nces.ed.gov/nationsreportcard/pdf/main2008/2009479_1.pdf

representative of most of the tables and because it highlights problems of practice in education. The problems identified through this type of descriptive research could shape future priorities for school improvement, research funding, and governmental intervention.

TABLE 9.1 • Phi Delta Kappa/Gallup Poll: Question about Problems of Practice

	National Totals		Public School Parents '12 (%)
	'12 (%)	'02 (%)	
Lack of financial support	35	23	43
Lack of discipline	8	17	3
Overcrowded schools	5	17	6
Fighting/gang violence	4	9	5
Drugs	2	13	2

Source: Bushaw, W. J., & Lopez, S. J. (2012). Public education in the United States: A nation divided: The 44th annual Phi Delta Kappa/Gallup poll of the public's attitudes toward the public schools. *Phi Delta Kappan, 94*(1), 8–25. Reprinted with permission of Phi Delta Kappa International. www.pdkintl.org. All Rights Reserved.

The PDK/Gallup polls are a form of survey research. We define **survey research** as the systematic collection of data about participants' beliefs, attitudes, interests, and behavior using standardized measures such as questionnaires, interviews, and tests. The measures are standardized in that each participant receives the same measure, administered in the same manner. The data typically are summarized in the form of descriptive statistics. (Descriptive statistics are explained in this chapter and in Chapter 6.)

The value of survey research, or any kind of descriptive research, depends on the sample from which data are collected. If the PDK/Gallup poll reflected only the views of local educators and parents or people who were approached by data collectors in local public settings, the usefulness and meaning of the results would be much different than if they represented the entire U.S. population.

In fact, the researchers who conducted Gallup Poll 44 wanted to represent the entire U.S. population, and so they used a systematic approach to achieve this goal. They completed 1,002 interviews from May 7 to June 10, 2012, using random-digit telephone dialing so that households with unlisted telephone numbers were as likely to be included in the sample as households with listed telephone numbers. They also took steps to ensure that different cross-sections of the sample were included in proportion to their representation in the U.S. population. The cross-sections of interest to the researchers are shown in Table 9.2.

These procedures illustrate what it means to take a scientific approach to surveying. It is far different from, for example, talking to one's circle of friends and neighbors about education and drawing conclusions from these conversations about what Americans think about the status of education.

Bill & Melinda Gates Foundation

This foundation is an example of private efforts to conduct descriptive research that can inform policy making about education. One of their studies, sponsored in part by the Scholastic Corporation, involved a survey of more than 10,000 teachers about their work and how it best can be evaluated, supported, and rewarded (Bill & Melinda Gates Foundation, 2012). The survey was conducted by sending e-mails to persons in a database of public school teachers and asking them to respond to an online questionnaire. One of the survey questions presented teachers with examples of efforts and asked them which of those efforts would be most likely to improve students' academic achievement. Teachers responded to each effort on a four-point scale: very strong impact; strong impact; moderate impact; no impact at all. The efforts listed in the questionnaire and the percentage of teachers who thought a particular effort would have a very strong or moderate impact are shown in Figure 9.3.

We find it interesting that the majority of teachers believe that a longer school year and a longer school day are not likely to improve student achievement. Yet some states and school districts currently are in the process of experimenting with these changes. The survey results could be helpful to educators and policy makers in rethinking these initiatives and considering whether the teachers' top priority (improving family involvement and support) should be adopted instead.

In considering these options, educators and policy makers would be well advised to review the research literature on each initiative to see whether there is evidence to support one over the other. In fact, teachers' top priority, family involvement and support, has been validated by research evidence. William Jeynes (2012) reviewed 51 studies of the relationship between various kinds of parental involvement programs and the academic achievement of students at different grade levels, from prekindergarten through 12th grade. Some of the programs emphasized shared reading between parents and their children, whereas others involved

TABLE 9.2 • Phi Delta Kappa/Gallup Poll: Cross-Sections of the Sample	
Adults	**%**
No children in school	67
Public school parents	27
Nonpublic school parents	4
Age	**%**
Over 40	67
40 and under	32
Gender	**%**
Male	49
Female	51
Region	**%**
East	18
Midwest	23
South	36
West	23
Political Party	**%**
Republican	28
Democrat	36
Independent	35
Undesignated	1
Education	**%**
Total college	62
Total high school	38

'Percentages may not add up to 100% due to weighted samples and rounding.
Source: Bushaw, W. J., & Lopez, S. J. (2012). Public education in the United States: A nation divided: The 44th annual Phi Delta Kappa/Gallup poll of the public's attitudes toward the public schools. *Phi Delta Kappan, 94* (1), 8–25. Reprinted by permission of Phi Delta Kappa International, www.pdkintl.org. All Rights Reserved.

FIGURE 9.3 • The Percentage of Teachers Who Believe that a Particular Effort Will Have a Very Strong or Strong Impact on Students' Academic Achievement

Change Effort	Percentage of Teachers
Family involvement and support	98%
High expectations for all students	96%
Effective and engaged principals and building-level leaders	91%
Fewer students in each class	90%
Learning experiences that provide students with 21st-century skills	89%
Curriculum that goes beyond what is tested on standardized tests	89%
Teaching resources to help differentiate instruction	88%
Up-to-date technology that is well integrated into the classroom	87%
Professional development for teachers that is relevant to personal and school goals	85%
Curriculum that clearly lays out the scope and sequence of what should be taught	79%
In-school teaching mentors/coaches for first three years of teaching	72%
Paraprofessionals/teacher assistants in the classroom	70%
In-school behavioral support from therapists and psychologists	69%
Common standards across all of the states	64%
In-school career and college counselors	58%
Teachers receiving real-time, technology-based feedback while teaching	54%
Common assessments across all states	49%
A longer school year	21%
Monetary rewards for teachers based on their individual performance	26%
Monetary rewards for teachers based on the performance of the entire school	25%
A longer school day	22%

Source: Based on *Primary sources: 2012. America's teachers on the teaching profession.* Retrieved from http://www.scholastic.com/primarysources/pdfs/Gates2012_full.pdf

partnerships between parents and teachers and parental checking of their children's homework. All of these types of programs had a positive effect on students' academic achievement, thus supporting the survey result in the study conducted by the Bill & Melinda Gates Foundation.

Descriptive Research in Academic and Professional Journals

Many descriptive studies are published in academic and practitioner journals. One example is a study by Mary McCaslin and her colleagues (2006). They used a structured observation instrument to create a picture of how elementary teachers in low-income schools provide literacy and mathematics instruction to third-, fourth-, and fifth-grade students. The schools were selected because they were receiving supplemental funds from the Comprehensive School Reform Demonstration Act "to adopt research-based, comprehensive whole-school improvement plans to enhance student achievement" (p. 314).

The researchers collected observational data on a total of 145 teachers for 2,736 ten-minute intervals over the course of 447 classroom visits. Their data analyses led them to conclude that, by and large, the teachers were not engaged in "best practice" based on research about effective literacy and mathematics instruction. The challenge

TABLE 9.3 • Summary of Observations of Elementary Students' Behavior in Low-Income Schools

Variable	Time-Sampled Intervals	
	Number	Percent
Student on task:		
1 = not evident/can't tell	12	.42
2 = 25% or fewer	34	1.20
3 = 25%–75%	351	12.36
4 = 75% or more	2,438	85.88
Level of productivity:		
1 = not evident/can't tell	132	4.65
2 = not productive	292	10.29
3 = productive	2,400	54.54
Student questions:		
1 = none	1,825	64.58
2 = task management	488	17.27
3 = task management and corrections	152	5.38
4 = correctness	268	9.48
5 = thinking included	93	3.29
Disruptions (coming/going):		
1 = none	2,504	88.20
2 = a few	304	10.71
3 = many	31	1.09
Disruptions (from main office):		
1 = none	2,670	94.21
2 = yes	164	5.78

Source: McCaslin, M., et al. (2006). Comprehensive school reform: An observational study of teaching in grades 3 through 5. *Elementary School Journal, 106* (4), 313–331. Reprinted by permission of the University of Chicago Press.

for educators then is how to provide "best-practice" instruction to the children who most need it.

An interesting feature of this descriptive research study is that it corrects misperceptions that some individuals might have about the classroom behavior of low-income children. Table 9.3 provides a summary of trained observers' data about the children's activity patterns during class. One of the results is particularly striking. During 86 percent of the observed 10-minute intervals, at least 75 percent of the children were on task. Furthermore, students' on-task behavior was productive during 85 percent of the intervals.

McCaslin and her colleagues concluded from these results that: "Contrary to the stereotypes of disruptive and disinterested students who attend high-poverty schools, the students in our study contributed to an orderly, safe, and predictable classroom" (p. 326). This finding reminds us that, although we emphasize the use of descriptive research to discover and document problems of practice, it can also be used to identify and report successes in educational practice.

FEATURES OF A DESCRIPTIVE RESEARCH REPORT

What do the descriptive research studies discussed above have in common? First, all of them create a *quantitative* representation of behavior, opinions, or other educational phenomena. Second, they

TABLE 9.4 • Typical Features of a Descriptive Research Report

Section	Content
Introduction	Hypotheses, questions, or objectives are stated. A review of relevant literature is presented. A common purpose is to study a problem of practice to determine its prevalence and severity.
Research design	The researchers select a sample that has the characteristic or problem of interest to them. The sample typically is studied at one point in time or at several predetermined points in time. The variables that are to be studied are specified in advance of data collection.
Sampling procedure	The researchers ideally select a sample that is representative of the population to which they wish to generalize their findings.
Measures	Virtually any kind of measure can be selected for data collection. Questionnaires, tests, and structured interviews are commonly used.
Data analysis	Descriptive statistics are computed and commonly presented in tables or graphs.
Discussion	The main findings are summarized. Flaws and limitations of the study are noted. Implications of the findings for further research and professional practice are discussed.

focus on representative samples or entire populations in order to draw conclusions about what is generally true rather than what is true of one individual, one group, or one institution. Third, the researchers specify the particular characteristics (technically, the variables) they wish to study in advance of data collection.

Given these three features, we can define **descriptive research** as the collection and analysis of quantitative data in order to develop a generalizable, statistical representation of a sample's behavior or personal characteristics with respect to predetermined variables. Other quantitative research designs (group comparison research, correlational research, and experiments) also describe behavior and personal characteristics, but their primary purpose is to identify cause-and-effect relationships involving behavior and personal characteristics.

Another comparison is between descriptive research and the qualitative research designs discussed later in the book. These designs emphasize description, but much less is specified in advance of data collection. Rather, they are voyages of discovery where the focus and methods of data collection can change as the researcher's questions and interests change over the course of the study.

Table 9.4 presents typical features of descriptive research studies that are reported in education journals, technical papers, or other formats. We discuss each of these features in the following sections.

Introduction

The introduction of a descriptive research report defines the problem and the particular aspects of the problem that will be investigated. Each aspect is a separate variable. For example, the NAEP study presented earlier in the chapter has three variables, as shown in Figure 9.2. One variable is the year in which the reading assessment occurred. Because 12 separate years are included, this variable has 12 values. Another variable is reading proficiency, which has a continuous range of values from 0 to 500. The third variable is age level, which has three values (9, 13, 17). Researchers should state why they chose the particular variables to be studied. They also should provide a literature review that describes, among other things, what is already known about these variables.

Literature reviews and the measurement of variables are time-consuming, so it is better to study a few variables in depth than many variables superficially. To understand this point, think of educators you know who have become experts on a certain subject, such as multicultural education or classroom management. They could not have become experts without thoroughly studying the literature on their subject area, practicing the skills that the subject area involves, and observing various field settings in which the skills are relevant. Similarly, researchers tend to focus their investigations on a few central variables related to a problem of practice or theoretical framework so that they become recognized experts in them.

Research Design

The researchers should explain why they chose to use a descriptive research design to investigate the problems of interest to them. Typically, a descriptive research design is chosen because the educational phenomena that will be studied can be quantified and measured with a degree of objectivity.

Sampling Procedure

The soundness and utility of a descriptive research study are greatly affected by the procedure used to select a sample. Guidelines for good sampling were presented in Chapter 5.

If you are doing a descriptive research study, your primary concern will be to select a sample that is representative of the population of interest to you. If you are reading a descriptive research report, your primary concern will be to determine whether the sample selected by the researchers represents the individuals or groups of interest to you.

Sampling in Longitudinal Research

Longitudinal research involves the collection of data about changes in a population's characteristics over a specified period of time. Sample selection in this type of research is more complex than a descriptive study that examines a problem or phenomenon at one point in time.

Suppose we wish to study a sample of talented middle school students to determine how they develop their talents over a period of five years. This is called a **panel study**, which is a research study that surveys the same sample at each data-collection point. In contrast, a **cohort study** follows the same group over time, but not necessarily the same members of the group at each data-collection point. For example, we might identify a population of 1,000 talented students and draw a random sample from this population for each of the five years in which we collect data.

Another strategy for studying longitudinal changes is to conduct a trend study. **Trend studies** are research studies that describe change by selecting a different sample at each data-collection point from a population that does not remain constant. For example, suppose the researchers define a population of 1,000 talented students in Year 1 and

randomly select a sample of 100 of them to study each year. In Year 2, they find that have lost contact with 75 students in the population, and so they must select 100 students from a slightly different population.

One of the most common sampling strategies in longitudinal research is to select samples that represent different stages of development and study all of the samples at the same point in time. Longitudinal studies of this type are called **cross-sectional studies**. For example, Marilyn Nippold and her colleagues (2005) wished to study how syntactic complexity develops as children mature into adulthood.

Syntactic complexity involves such language factors as sentence length and frequency of subordinate clauses attached to the main clause of a sentence. Research knowledge about syntactic complexity can help educators in various ways, such as providing them with the ability to determine whether a child's use of language is developing in a typical manner or is better or worse than the norm.

Nippold and her colleagues studied syntactic complexity at six different age levels: 8, 11, 13, 17, 25, and 44. If she and her colleagues had started with a sample of 8-year-olds, they would have needed to follow them for 36 years until they reached the age of 44. Of course, this approach is not feasible, except in the case of large-scale, heavily funded longitudinal research. Lewis Terman's famous studies of gifted individuals who were followed from childhood into adulthood (e.g., Terman & Oden, 1959) are examples of that type of research.

Nippold and her colleagues solved the problem of sample selection by using cross-sectional sampling. They selected samples of individuals who represented each of the six age groups. This selection process probably required just a few weeks of the researchers' time, not the 36 years required for a panel sample.

The downside of cross-sectional sampling is that the different age levels might represent different populations. For example, 44-year-olds might have had less opportunity to develop their language skills (e.g., less or no exposure to television, computers, and other media) than the current generation of 8-year-olds. In reading the report, we found that these researchers did not consider the possibility of population differences as a threat to their goal of describing how syntactic complexity develops as individuals in our society mature.

Measures

The variables studied in descriptive research can be measured by any of the approaches described in Chapter 5: tests, scales, questionnaires, interviews, and direct observation. For example, the PDK/Gallup polls, which we described above, collect opinions using attitude scales administered by telephone. The National Assessment of Educational Progress, also described above, relies heavily on standardized tests of academic achievement for its research data.

Construction of Questionnaires and Interviews

Many novice researchers choose to conduct surveys using questionnaires or interviews because these measures appear simple to construct and administer. In fact, it might be relatively easy to develop questionnaire and interview items, but the collection of evidence to demonstrate the measure's validity and reliability requires expertise and resources. (We discuss measurement validity and reliability in Chapter 5.) Without this evidence, we cannot determine the soundness of research findings obtained by using the measure. We recommend that, whenever possible, you select a well-developed questionnaire or interview for use in your research study. By doing so, you will save the time required to develop and validate your own measure.

If you choose to develop your own questionnaire or interview, we describe several of the steps in the following sections. (The resources at the end of the chapter provide a more detailed description of the development process.) Our example is a questionnaire, the Stages of Concern Questionnaire (SoC), which has been widely used in educational research and practice since the 1970s. The measure, its administration procedures, and evidence for its validity and reliability are freely available by finding the citation (Hall, George, & Rutherford, 1977) in ERIC and then using ERIC's full-text feature.

Identification of Constructs

You will need to identify the constructs that you wish to measure in your questionnaire or interview. (Constructs are explained in Chapter 5.) For example, the Stages of Concern Questionnaire (SoC) was designed to measure seven hypothesized stages of concern that educators go through when considering whether to adopt an educational innovation in their local setting. Gene Hall and his colleagues did a literature review and found that concern is an important construct in educational practice. For example, researchers have found that teachers have many concerns about their instruction and that these concerns change in type and severity as their careers progress.

Hall and his colleagues (hereafter "the SoC developers") wondered whether educators had other concerns, such as concerns about an innovation (e.g., a new organizational structure, program, textbook series, or teaching method) being considered for adoption in their schools. They defined the construct of concern as "the composite representation of the feelings, preoccupation, thought, and consideration given to a particular issue or task" (p. 5).

The SoC developers refined the construct of concern about an innovation into seven stages, each of which is a separate construct:

1. *Adoption*. Little concern about or involvement with the innovation.
2. *Informational*. General awareness of the innovation and interest in learning more about it.
3. *Personal*. Uncertainty about the demands of the innovation, one's adequacy to meet those demands, and what one's role will be if the innovation is adopted.
4. *Management*. Concerns about the efficiency, organizing, managing, scheduling, and time demands of the innovation.
5. *Consequence*. Concerns about the impact of the innovation on students within one's sphere of influence.
6. *Collaboration*. Concerns about coordinating and cooperating with others in using the innovation.
7. *Refocusing*. Exploration of more universal benefits from the innovation and concerns about whether a more powerful alternative to the innovation is possible.

The SoC developers hypothesized that each of these stages of concern must be resolved or lessened before the next stage could become the focus of the educator's attention.

It is common to include demographic questions in questionnaires and interviews. Demographic questions are queries about characteristics of the sample or population that readers of the research report would consider important or interesting. The following demographic questions were included in the questionnaire that also contained the SoC:

- What percent of your job is: teaching __% administration __% other (specify) __%
- Do you work: full time __ part time __
- Female __ Male __
- Total years teaching: __
- Number of years at present school: __ (Hall, George, & Rutherford, 1977, p. 69)

Each of these demographic characteristics is itself a construct that requires careful analysis. If you ask research participants to reveal information about personal characteristics, such as age, you should be able to justify the request. Researchers generally do not consider it ethical to ask participants to provide information unless it is relevant to the objectives of the research study.

In the case of the SoC, its developers asked these and other demographic questions to determine whether individuals' personal characteristics had an influence on their expressed concerns about an educational innovation. They report their findings as follows:

> It has been of interest to us, in our research to date, that there have been no outstanding relationships between standard demographic variables and concerns data. Rather, as our research unfolds, there is increasing support for the hypothesis that "interventions" and "conditions" associated with the implementation effort are more critical variables than age, sex, teaching experience, etc. (Hall, George, & Rutherford, 1977, p. 62)

We see then that including demographic variables in the questionnaire yielded a useful finding. The research results suggest that educators who attempt to introduce an intervention into a school system should focus more on creating conditions that facilitate its adoption than on the personal characteristics of those who are part of the adoption and implementation process.

Writing Questionnaire and Interview Items

Research methodologists have developed many guidelines for the writing of questionnaire and interview items. Items that are poorly written can create a negative impression on research participants, causing them to complete the items haphazardly or not respond at all. The following guidelines for writing questionnaire items are also applicable to writing interview items:

- Begin with a few interesting and nonthreatening items.
- Put threatening or difficult items near the end of the questionnaire.
- Include examples of how to respond to items that might be confusing or difficult to understand.
- Avoid terms like *several*, *most*, and *usually*, which have no precise meaning.
- Avoid negatively stated items because they are likely to be misread by respondents.
- Avoid "double-barreled" items that require the participant to respond to two separate ideas with a single answer. For example, "do you favor abstinence education and drug education?" is double-barreled because it asks about two different types of education but only allows a single answer.
- Avoid biased questions, such as, "what do you see as the benefits of requiring all students to learn algebra in the eighth grade?" This question assumes that the respondent sees benefits when, in fact, they may not.

With the advent of Internet surveys, additional guidelines have been developed to accommodate the capabilities and limitations of this electronic medium. These guidelines are described in publications listed in the resource section at the end of this chapter.

Attitude scales are different from other types of questionnaire and interview items in that they typically take the form of a Likert scale, which consists of a series of Likert items. In responding to a **Likert item**, respondents read a statement, sometimes called the *item stem*, and then express the intensity of their feeling about the statement by responding to a horizontal line that typically has 5 points on it:

1. Strongly disagree
2. Disagree
3. Neither agree nor disagree
4. Agree
5. Strongly agree

If several items are used to measure the item, they collectively are called a **Likert scale**. The items typically are summed to yield a total score, but alternatively, they can be averaged to yield a mean score. If individuals have limited reading ability, such as young children, the items can be read aloud. The respondents can express their attitude by pointing to or circling one of a series of pictures (e.g., smiling faces) that represent different levels of feeling about the person, concept, or thing being measured (Reynolds-Keefer & Johnson, 2011).

Some attitude measures take the form of a Guttman scale. A **Guttman scale** measures an attitude that is conceptualized to have one dimension and a set of items in a sequence such that an individual who agrees with a specific question in the sequence will also agree with all previous questions in the sequence. For example, consider the following items.

1. I would welcome a charter school in our community.
2. I believe that our state's legislature should pass a statute allowing school districts to authorize the establishment of charter schools.
3. I believe that charter schools will improve education in the United States.

It seems likely that an individual who agrees with item 3 also would agree with items 2 and 1, and that an individual who disagrees with item 3 also would disagree with items 2 and 1. These assumptions need to be empirically tested with a sample, and if the data support the assumed response pattern, we can conclude that the items form a Guttman scale. In practice, developers of a Guttman scale to measure a particular attitude would construct many items and test their ordering by a statistical method called scalogram analysis.

The SoC developers prepared an initial set of 544 items that they thought would measure the seven stages of concern in adopting an innovation. They submitted these items to various groups for their appraisal and also performed statistical analyses on them. They gradually whittled the 544 items to a 35-item questionnaire. Their item development process was unusually extensive, but even a more modest development process requires considerable effort.

Each of the 35 items asks the respondent to circle a number on an 8-point scale. A respondent circles one of the low numbers (0, 1, 2) if the concern is "not true of me now." The respondent circles one of the middle numbers (3, 4, 5) if the concern is "somewhat true of me now" and one of the high numbers (6, 7) if the concern is "very true of me now."

The following are seven of the items in the 35-item questionnaire. Each item represents a different level of concern, shown in parentheses.

1. I don't even know what the innovation is. (Awareness)
2. I would like to know what resources are available if we decide to adopt this innovation. (Informational)
3. I am concerned about my inability to manage everything the innovation requires. (Personal)
4. I would like to know who will make the decisions in the new system. (Management)
5. I am concerned about how the innovation affects students. (Consequence)
6. I would like to coordinate my effort with others to maximize the innovation's effects. (Collaboration)
7. I would like to modify our use of the innovation based on the experience of our students. (Refocusing) (Hall, George, & Rutherford, 1977, pp. 65–66)

Note that each item is simply worded and directly relevant to the construct it was designed to measure. This simplicity and relevance are among the reasons that the SoC questionnaire has been widely used by researchers and educators.

At the time it was developed, the SoC questionnaire was administered as a paper-and-pencil measure. Now that the Internet has become universally available, questionnaires like this are increasingly administered online. There are three main types of Internet-based research surveys.

1. Researchers can send an e-mail message to prospective survey respondents with the survey embedded as a part of the message. Respondents can then reply to the message with their answers to the survey items.
2. Researchers can send an e-mail message with a file attachment containing the survey. Respondents can then open the attachment, answer the questions, and return them as an attachment to an e-mail message addressed to the researchers.
3. Researchers can send an e-mail message with a direct link to an Internet website containing the survey, which has been designed using a web-based software program. As the respondent replies to each item, the answer is transmitted directly back to the researchers

via the Internet. Some software programs have the capacity to analyze the data and record which respondents in the sample have completed the survey. Two of the more popular web-based survey services are eSurveyspro (esurveyspro.com) and SurveyMonkey (surveymonkey.com).

The decision about which of these options to use depends on the respondents and the characteristics of the survey, such as its length. The third option (web-based surveys) probably is now the most widely used in educational research studies. The reason is that the populations of interest to educational researchers generally have access to both the Internet and e-mail and also the ability to follow the directions presented in web-based software programs.

Evidence of Validity and Reliability

Validity and reliability are often associated with achievement tests because many of them are high-stakes measures. However, validity and reliability should be of equal concern when considering the soundness of questionnaires and interviews. For example, consider a questionnaire item that asks respondents to report age or occupation. How do we know that their responses are valid? A respondent might choose to report inaccurate information for various reasons. Therefore, the developers should consider a validity check to corroborate the self-report information with other data, if possible. This type of validity check is especially important when the item asks for sensitive information.

The SoC developers provide various types of validity and reliability evidence for their measure in the accompanying manual (Hall et al., 1977). For example, they found that teachers' scores on the SoC questionnaire were related to their expressed concerns about an innovation in an interview setting. They also found that, as predicted, teachers' concerns moved along the seven stages of the scale over a two-year period from when an innovation was first introduced to them to its subsequent adoption and implementation in their school.

Results

The procedures used to analyze descriptive research data tend to be fairly simple. The distribution of the sample's scores on each measured variable are analyzed for their central tendency and variability. The mean and standard deviation are the most commonly used statistics for this purpose (see Chapter 6.)

Figures and graphs can be helpful in presenting statistical results, especially for audiences who are not experienced in reading dense statistical tables.

An example of a figure taken from the study by Marilyn Nippold and her colleagues is shown in Figure 9.4.

The horizontal line (the *x* axis) at the bottom of the figure represents the six age levels that were studied. The vertical line on the left side of the figure (the *y* axis) is the mean number of T-units in each age group's discourse. A T-unit is an occurrence of an independent clause and its accompanying subordinate clauses, if any, while talking to another person (labeled *discourse* in the research report). A T-unit typically consists of one complete sentence.

The frequency of T-units was computed for two types of discourse with each participant for five to eight minutes: (1) conversation about common topics such as school, family, and friends, and (2) expository discourse (labeled *explanation* in Figure 9.4) in

FIGURE 9.4 • Language Output (Total T-Units Produced) for Conversational and Expository Discourse for Each Age Group

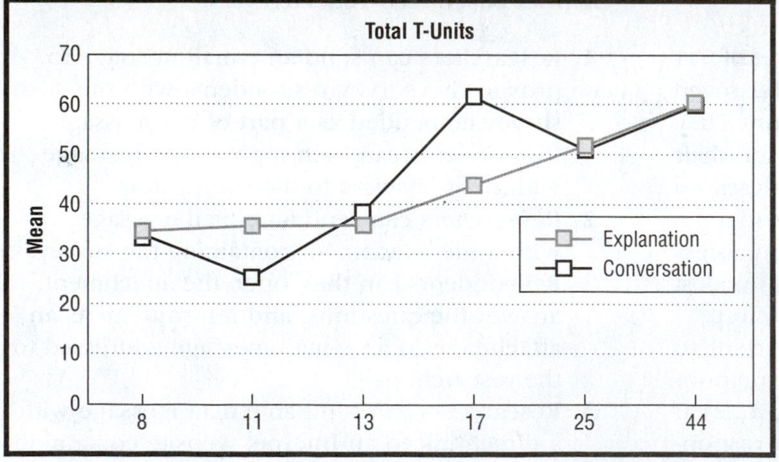

Source: Nippold, M. A., Hesketh, L. J., Duthie, J. K., & Mansfield, T. C. (2005). Conversational versus expository discourse: A study of syntactic development in children, adolescents, and adults. *Journal of Speech, Language, and Hearing Research, 48,* 1048–1064 (Figure 1 on p. 1054). Copyright © 2005 by American Speech-Language-Hearing Association. All rights reserved. Reprinted by permission.

which the participant explained the rules and strategies of a favorite game or sport.

Figure 9.4 makes it easy to comprehend the results. Individuals' language output during expository discourse (explanation) remains fairly steady until age 13, at which point it steadily increases into adulthood. Language output in conversation is more uneven, with a drop at age 11 and a large spike at age 17. Interestingly, this type of syntactic complexity is no greater at age 44 than at age 17. The same results could be shown in statistical tables, but tables generally are not as easy to grasp as graphs.

Some descriptive studies involve surveys using questionnaires or brief structured interviews. Because these measures are easy to administer and score, researchers sometimes can form a truly random sample from a defined population. If this is the case, it is appropriate to compute confidence intervals around the sample mean or other descriptive statistic. **Confidence intervals** (also called *margins of error*) provide information about how likely it is that the range of numerical values in the confidence interval contain the actual population parameter. (We explain confidence intervals more fully in Chapter 7.)

Discussion

According to the *Publication Manual of the American Psychological Association* (2010), the discussion section of a research report includes a summary of the results for each research question or hypothesis and also an explanation for unexpected results and analysis of whether the results were consistent with the findings of other studies. The discussion section also provides an analysis of flaws and problems in the design and execution of the study and limits to the generalizability of the findings. Additionally, the authors should explore the theoretical or practical implications of the study and provide suggestions for further research. The authors can express a personal point of view that generally would not be appropriate in other sections of the report.

We illustrate several of these features of the discussion section of a research report by using two of the studies discussed earlier in the chapter.

The 44th PDK/Gallup Poll. This poll, which involves survey-type descriptive research, presents a large number of findings reflecting many aspects of education. The authors of the report, William Bushaw and Shane Lopez, conclude the report with this statement:

> We confess that as coauthors of this poll, **we are optimists**. We believe we will attract and keep high-quality teachers who are rigorously prepared and that we can create a stronger curriculum, more engaging instructional approaches, and better techniques to assess student learning. We believe we will increase the number of students who graduate from high school and that they will be better prepared for college and careers. And we believe we will steadily close the achievement gap, providing opportunities for all young Americans to be successful. . . . Come to think of it, many of these changes are already under way, and according to these poll findings, these efforts have the complete support of the American public (Bushaw & Lopez, 2012, p. 24).

This type of statement should not appear in the results section of a descriptive research report, but it is appropriate to include in the discussion section.

Quality of Teaching in Low-Income Schools. Mary McCaslin and her colleagues did not find "best practices" for literacy instruction in their observational study of low-income schools. The discussion section of their report interprets this finding:

> "Best practices" teaching does not occur in many schools, however. And maybe that is, however unfortunately, appropriate. Developmental differences in childhood and the realities of the current era of high-stakes testing and accountability may undermine [best practices] recommendations for exploration and discovery opportunities, which also can be time consuming. (pp. 327–328)

We see in this example that the researchers do not merely report their findings but also try to interpret their meaning and possible implications for schooling.

Longitudinal Study of Syntactic Development. Marilyn Nippold and colleagues reported that, "As predicted, expository discourse elicited greater syntactic complexity than conversational" (2005, p. 1057). But they also noted that one of their predictions was not supported:

> Although we predicted that expository discourse might undergo a longer developmental time course than conversational discourse, there was no evidence for continued growth beyond early adulthood in either genre. (p. 1057)

This unexpected finding might stimulate researchers to explore why syntactic complexity does not develop beyond early adulthood.

EVALUATING A DESCRIPTIVE RESEARCH STUDY

The questions stated in Appendix 3 can be used to evaluate a descriptive research study. They can be supplemented by the following questions.

■ Did the researchers develop their questionnaire, interview, or observation schedule by doing a pilot study?

   Construction of measures is more difficult than it may seem. Therefore, look for indications that the researchers developed an initial version of their measure, pilot-tested it, and then revised it. The mention of pilot testing suggests that a measure is likely to have some level of validity and reliability.

■ Are the items in the measure of good quality?

   Writing good items is difficult, whether it be for questionnaires, interviews, or observation schedules. If the research report includes the items, examine them for clarity and relevance. If they are questionnaire items, you can apply the criteria for writing them that we presented earlier in this chapter.

An example of

How Descriptive Research Can Help in Solving Problems of Practice

The most substantial reform movement in American education in the past decade is probably the initiative to create Common Core State Standards in literacy and mathematics so that K–12 students are adequately prepared for college and careers. The National Governors Association and the Council of Chief State School Officers have been the primary sponsors of this initiative. These associations, together with corporate leaders, support Achieve, an independent, bipartisan, nonprofit organization, one of whose activities is to conduct an annual survey of all 50 states and the District of Columbia to determine

their progress in adopting Common Core Standards.

Among the findings of the survey are these:

All 50 states and the District of Columbia have adopted English language arts/literacy and mathematics standards that reflect the knowledge and skills colleges and employers demand of high school graduates. . . . Nearly all states are supporting districts and schools by *providing guidance*, such as high-quality processes and exemplars, and *developing curricular and supplemental materials* aligned to the standards for voluntary use. Far fewer states are *approving/certifying lists of approved materials*, and even fewer are *requiring districts and schools to use materials aligned to the standards*.

(Achieve, 2012, p. 3)

It is one thing to adopt curriculum standards and materials. It is quite another matter to implement them at the classroom level. The Achieve survey results for 2012 indicate that the development of curriculum standards and materials has advanced greatly, but not the mandate to use them. This finding raises several questions. Will the number of states that create and mandate the use of standards-aligned materials increase in coming years? If not, what are the obstacles that prevent them from doing so? Are some school districts, schools, and teachers using these materials on a voluntary basis despite the lack of a mandate? How satisfied are teachers with the use of standards-aligned materials?

Researchers can answer these questions by continuing to conduct descriptive research using the survey questions developed by Achieve. On the matter of obstacles to mandates involving standards-aligned materials, though, interviews might be necessary. Researchers will need to identify key decision makers in all states, or a sample of states, and use closed-ended and open-ended interview items that encourage them to express obstacles to these mandates. Because these obstacles might be political in nature, interviewers will need to gain the decision makers' trust and ensure the anonymity of their responses.

Researchers can conduct descriptive research, perhaps using a combination of questionnaires and interviews, to determine teachers' satisfaction in using standards-aligned curriculum materials. If teachers find that the materials are difficult to use, this can be a major problem in the adoption of nationwide Common Core Standards. It is a long distance from policy-making boards, such as those that guide Achieve, to the classroom teacher who is asked to put their mandates into practice. Descriptive research at each stage of the process can help determine progress and obstacles and also suggest better practices than those being implemented. The Stages of Concern model (Hall et al., 1977) described in this chapter might be helpful for conceptualizing this process.

SELF-CHECK TEST

1. The primary purpose of the National Assessment of Educational Progress is to
   a. collect periodic data about the public's perceptions of the quality of public schools.
   b. collect ideas from educators about how schools in their district can be improved.
   c. determine how well American students are learning selected school subjects.
   d. all of the above.
2. A major feature of descriptive research studies is that
   a. the focus is on discovering cause-and-effect relationships between variables.
   b. the focus is on intensive study of individual cases of a phenomenon.
   c. the variables of interest are identified prior to data collection.
   d. the variables of interest are identified after data collection has been completed.
3. In a cross-sectional longitudinal study, the researchers
   a. select samples that represent different age levels and study all of the samples at the same point in time.
   b. select different samples at different times from a population that does not remain constant.
   c. select a sample and follow it across time.
   d. stratify a population so that the subgroups of interest are well represented across different points in time.
4. In a panel study, the researchers
   a. select samples that represent different age levels and study all of the samples at the same point in time.
   b. select different samples at different times from a population that does not remain constant.

c. select a sample and follow it across time.
   d. stratify a population so that the subgroups of interest are well represented across different points in time.
5. In a trend study, the researchers
   a. select samples that represent different age levels and study all of the samples at the same point in time.
   b. select different samples at different times from a population that does not remain constant.
   c. select a sample and follow it across time.
   d. stratify a population so that the subgroups of interest are well represented across different points in time.
6. The terms *confidence interval* and *margin of error* refer to
   a. a situation in which 10 percent or more of a sample fail to take the research survey.
   b. a range of values of a sample statistic that is likely to include the population parameter.
   c. a range of values of a sample statistic that is not likely to include the population parameter.
   d. a situation in which the mean, median, and mode for a sample differ significantly from each other.
7. Descriptive research
   a. is limited to the use of survey questionnaires.
   b. is limited to the use of standardized achievement tests.
   c. can make use of any measure that yields quantifiable data.
   d. differs from other types of quantitative research in that validity and reliability of measurement are not matters of concern.

8. Questionnaires require
   a. validity evidence but not reliability evidence.
   b. reliability evidence but not validity evidence.
   c. both reliability and validity evidence.
   d. the use of demographic items.
9. Questionnaire items
   a. should not be written prior to specification of the constructs that are to be measured.
   b. should be ordered so that difficult items appear last.

   c. can be used to determine the respondents' demographic characteristics.
   d. all of the above.
10. The soundness of an interview is judged
    a. on evidence of both its validity and reliability.
    b. only on evidence of its validity.
    c. only on evidence of its reliability.
    d. primarily by evidence that the interview items were clearly understood by the respondents.

CHAPTER REFERENCES

Achieve (2012). *Closing the expectations gap: 50-state progress report on the alignment of K–12 policies and practice with the demands of college and careers*. Washington, DC: American Diploma Project Network. Retrieved from http://www.achieve.org/files/Achieve201250StateReport.pdf

American Psychological Association. (2010). *Publication manual of the American Psychological Association* (6th ed.). Washington, DC: Author.

Bill & Melinda Gates Foundation. (2012). *Primary sources: 2012. America's teachers on the teaching profession*. Retrieved from http://www.scholastic.com/primarysources/pdfs/Gates2012_full.pdf

Bushaw, W. J., & Lopez, S. J. (2012). Public education in the United States; A nation divided: The 44th annual Phi Delta Kappa/Gallup poll of the public's attitudes toward the public schools. *Phi Delta Kappan, 94*(1), 8–25.

Coombes, A. (2012, September 4). True or false: Many Americans don't understand the basics of investing. *Wall Street Journal*. Retrieved from http://online.wsj.com/article/SB10000872396390444812704577605232303164416.html

Hall, G. E., George, A. A., & Rutherford, W. L. (1977). *Measuring stages of concern about the innovation: A manual for the use of the SoC Questionnaire*. Austin, TX: University of Texas Research and Development Center for Teacher Education. (ED147342).

Jeynes, W. (2012). A meta-analysis of the efficacy of different types of parental involvement program for urban students. *Urban Education, 47*(4), 706–742.

McCaslin, M., Good, T. L., Nichols, S., Zhang, J., Wiley, C. R. H., Bozack, A. R., Burross, H. L., & Cuizon-Garcia, R. (2006). Comprehensive school reform: An observational study of teaching in grades 3 through 5. *Elementary School Journal, 106*(4), 313–331.

Meier, B. (2008, July 29). The evidence gap: A call for a warning system on artificial joints. *New York Times*. Retrieved from www.nytimes.com

Nippold, M. A., Hesketh, L. J., Duthie, J. K., & Mansfield, T. C. (2005). Conversational versus expository discourse: A study of syntactic development in children, adolescents, and adults. *Journal of Speech, Language, and Hearing Research, 48*, 1048–1064.

Paulson, A. (2012, August 12). Back to school: How to measure a good teacher. *Christian Science Monitor*. Retrieved from http://www.csmonitor.com/USA/Education/2012/0812/Back-to-school-How-to-measure-a-good-teacher

Reynolds-Keefer, L., & Johnson, R. (2011). Is a picture worth a thousand words? Creating effective questionnaires with pictures. *Practical Assessment, Research & Evaluation, 16*(8). Retrieved from http://pareonline.net/pdf/v16n8.pdf

Terman, L. M., & Oden, M. M. (1959). *The gifted group at midlife* (Vol. 5). Stanford, CA: Stanford University Press.

Wolpert-Gawron, H. (2012, April 26). Kids speak out on student engagement. *Edutopia*. Retrieved from http://www.edutopia.org/blog/student-engagement-stories-heather-wolpert-gawron

RESOURCES FOR FURTHER STUDY

Berends, M. (2006). Survey methods in educational research. In J. L. Green, G. Camilli, & P. B. Elmore (Eds.), *Handbook of complementary methods in education research* (3rd ed.) (pp. 623–640). Mahwah, NJ: Lawrence Erlbaum.

The author provides a brief overview of survey methods commonly used in educational research.

Groves, R. M., Fowler, F. J., Jr., Couper, M. P., Lepkowski, J. M., Singer, E., & Tourangeau, R. (2009). *Survey methodology* (2nd ed.). Hoboken, NJ: Wiley.

The authors provide a comprehensive description of all phases of a survey study, including sampling procedures, nonresponse issues, the design of interview and questionnaire items, the analysis of survey data, and ethical considerations.

Sue, V. M., & Ritter, L. A. (2007). *Conducting online surveys.* Thousand Oaks, CA: Sage.

This book provides extensive coverage of the methodology involved in designing and conducting Internet surveys.

Stewart, C. J., & Cash, W. B., Jr. (2010). *Interviewing: Principles and practices* (13th ed.). Boston, MA: McGraw-Hill.

This book provides extensive coverage of the practical aspects of interviewing and also the theoretical underpinnings of this research methodology.

Examining the Extent and Nature of Online Learning in American K-12 Education: The Research Initiatives of the Alfred P. Sloan Foundation

Picciano, A. G., Seaman, J., Shea, P., & Swan, K. (2012). Examining the extent and nature of online learning in American K-12 education: The research initiatives of the Alfred P. Sloan Foundation. *Internet and Higher Education, 15*, 127–135.

The following journal article involves a descriptive research study that seeks to understand how online learning is being used in schools. The question of central interest is whether online learning can be used to satisfy student needs and interests that currently cannot be met within the constraints of conventional classroom instruction. The survey results address this question and also inform us about the extent to which online learning resources are being used in schools nationwide. As you read the article, you can consider the extent to which online learning, whether by itself or in combination with classroom instruction, can solve existing problems of practice and provide new opportunities for students.

This research study examines trends in the use of online learning, but only for two school years, 2005–2006 and 2007–2008. Ongoing research is needed to determine whether the observed trends reflect an accelerating use of online learning or whether its use has leveled off.

The methodology of the two surveys reported in the journal article is briefly described. More detail about the methodology is available in two reports (Picciano & Seaman, 2007; Picciano & Seaman, 2009) that can be accessed on the Internet.

The article is reprinted in its entirety, just as it appeared when originally published.

Examining the Extent and Nature of Online Learning in American K-12 Education: The Research Initiatives of the Alfred P. Sloan Foundation

ANTHONY G. PICCIANO[a, *], JEFF SEAMAN[b], PETER SHEA[c], KAREN SWAN[d]

ARTICLE INFO   Available online 3 August 2011

Keywords: Online learning, Distance learning, Blended learning, Distance education, Asynchronous learning, Primary education, Secondary education, K-12, Survey research

[a]Program in Urban Education, Graduate Center, City University of New York, United States
[b]Babson Survey Research Group, Babson College, United States
[c]Educational Theory and Practice & College of Computing and Information, University at Albany, State University of New York, Albany, United States
[d]Stukel Distinguished Professor of Education Leadership, University of Illinois, Springfield, United States
*Corresponding author. Tel.: +1 212 87 8281.
E-mail addresses: apicciano@gc.cuny.edu (A.G. Picciano), jseaman@seagullhaven.com (J. Seaman), PShea@uamail.albany.edu (P. Shea), kswan4@uis.edu (K. Swan).

1096-7516/$ - see front matter © 2011 Elsevier Inc. All rights reserved.
doi:10.1016/j.iheduc.2011.07.004

ABSTRACT   In 1992, the Alfred P. Sloan Foundation began its *Anytime, Anyplace Learning Program*, the purpose of which was to explore educational alternatives for people who wanted to pursue an education via Internet technology. Part of this grant activity was a research award to the Babson College Survey Research Group to examine online learning in American K-12 education. Three studies were conducted based on national surveys of school district and/or high school administrators. The focus of these studies was twofold: one, to examine the extent and nature of online learning in K-12 school districts; second, to examine the role of online learning in high school reform initiatives. The purpose of this article is to share the findings from these studies and to look critically at what they mean for the future of online learning in American K-12 schools.

© 2011 Elsevier Inc. All rights reserved.

1. Introduction

In 1992, the Alfred P. Sloan Foundation began its *Anytime, Anyplace Learning Program*, the purpose of which was to explore educational alternatives for people who wanted to pursue an education via Internet technology.

This exploration resulted in a promulgation of a major development in pedagogical practice commonly referred to as the asynchronous learning network or ALN. To date, more than 350 grants totaling $70 million dollars have been awarded by the Foundation mostly to American colleges and universities. Part of this grant activity was a research award to the Babson College Survey Research Group to examine online learning in American K-12 education. Three studies were conducted based on national surveys of school district and/or high school administrators (Picciano & Seaman, 2007, 2009, 2010). The focus of these studies was twofold: one, to examine the extent and nature of online learning in K-12 school districts (Picciano & Seaman, 2007, 2009); second, to examine the role of online learning in high school reform initiatives (Picciano & Seaman, 2010). These studies have been widely cited and are evolving into a well-respected body of research on this topic. The purpose of this symposium is to share the findings from these studies and to look critically at what they mean for the future of online learning in American K-12 schools. The purpose of this article is to share the findings from these studies and to look critically at what they mean for the future of online learning in American K-12 schools. The research issues discussed in this article relate to K-12 online learning including student access to educational opportunities, faculty attitudes, high school graduation rates, credit-recovery programs, financial considerations and state and local policies.

2. The Studies

In March 2007, the Alfred P. Sloan Foundation issued its first report on the extent and nature of online learning in K-12 schools (Picciano & Seaman, 2007). Entitled, *K-12 Online Learning: A Survey of U.S. School District Administrators*, this report was welcomed by professional organizations and the popular media interested in the use of online technology for instruction in the public schools. The report was based on a national survey of American public school district chief administrators (N = 366) conducted for the 2005–2006 academic year. It was one of the first studies to collect data on and compare fully online and blended learning (part online and part traditional face-to-face instruction) in K-12 schools. Since its publication in 2007, several hundred articles, news reports, and other media have cited the report's findings (e.g., Christensen, Horn, & Johnson, 2008; Davis, 2009; Means, Toyama, Murphy, Baka, & Jones, 2009; U.S. Department of Education, 2007). In this study, the number of students enrolled in at least one online or blended course in American K-12 schools was estimated at 700,000. In a 2009 follow-up study, *K-12 Online Learning: A 2008 Follow Up of the Survey of U.S. School District Administrators*, based on data collected for the 2007–2008 academic year (N = 867), the number of students enrolled in at

least one online or blended course was estimated at 1,030,000, which represented 2% of the total K-12 population. (Picciano & Seaman, 2009). Of these estimates, 70% of the students were enrolled at the secondary level. In examining and sharing the results of the findings from these studies, an issue or need arose regarding the role of online learning related to reform efforts seeking to improve the quality and experiences of students in American high schools. The need centered on informing education policymakers at federal, state, and local governing agencies who were considering how to expand the use of this technology to improve instruction at the secondary level. In 2010, a third study, *Class Connections: High School Reform and the role of Online Learning*, based on a national survey of American high school principals for the 2008–2009 academic year (N = 441), was published that looked at issues related to online learning and high school reform initiatives. For the purposes of these studies the following definitions were used:

> Fully online course—a course where most or all of the content is delivered online, and typically has no face-to-face meetings. Blended/hybrid course—a course that blends online and face-to-face delivery, and where a substantial proportion of the content is delivered online, sometimes uses online discussions and typically has few face-to-face meetings.

3. The Extent and Nature of Online Learning in American K-12 Schools

Earlier in this article, it was mentioned that in a 2007 national study of school district administrators, the number of students enrolled in at least one online or blended courses in American K-12 schools was estimated at 700,000. In a 2009 follow-up study, the estimate was 1,030,000. These enrollments are the result of students taking either online or blended courses in three quarters of all the school districts (74.8%) in the United States. Approximately another 15% of the districts were planning to introduce them over the next 3 years. Respondents in this study anticipated that the number of students taking online courses will grow by 22.8% and that those taking blended courses will grow even more over the next 2 years. It also appeared that the number of school districts offering online courses is accelerating.

One of the questions asked in the 2009 follow-up study of respondents who were offering online or blended learning courses, was: In what year did any student in your district *first* take a fully online or blended/hybrid course? Figures 1 and 2 provide bar graphs illustrating the responses to this question. They show that online and blended learning were on an upward trend for the previous 8 years. The data in these charts supported the upward growth estimates discussed above. In the 2007 study, it was predicted that over the subsequent 5 or

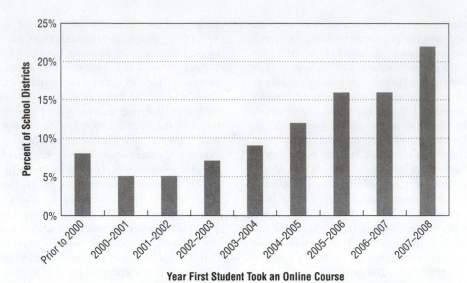

Figure 1 School districts reporting year in which the first student took a fully online course.

6 years, the K-12 enrollment in online courses would easily approach several million students.

3.1. Why Online and Blended Learning in K-12 Schools?

Figure 3 illustrates that school district administrators saw a real value in online and blended learning in their schools. The basic reason K-12 school districts were offering online and blended learning was to meet the special needs of a variety of students and to allow them to take courses that otherwise would not have been available. Large percentages of respondents, in excess of 60 to 70%, perceived the importance of online learning as related to:

1. Offering courses not otherwise available at the school.
2. Meeting the needs of specific groups of students.
3. Offering Advanced Placement or college-level courses.
4. Permitting students who failed a course to take it again (e.g., credit recovery).
5. Reducing scheduling conflicts for students.

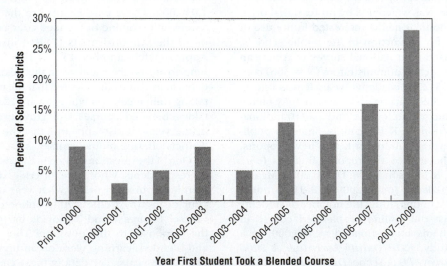

Figure 2 School districts reporting year in which the first student took a blended course.

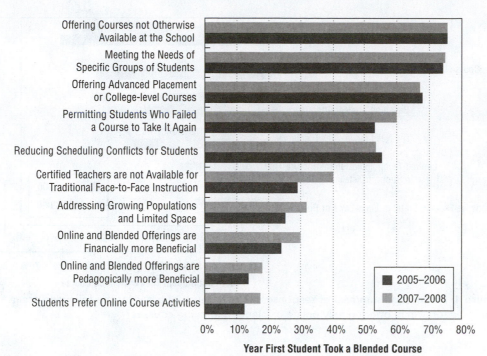

Year First Student Took a Blended Course

Figure 3 Summary of school district responses to: How important do you believe the following reasons are for a school district to offer fully online or blended learning?

The data presented in Figure 3 were collected from school district administrators reporting on their K-12 system in 2005–2006 and again in 2007–2008.

3.2. Barriers

Figure 4 provides data on barriers school district administrators faced in developing and offering online and blended learning in their schools. The most significant barrier was concern about course quality. In addition, concerns about funding, state attendance policies, and the need for teacher training were prominent

3.3. The Future of Online Learning in K-12 Schools

In 2008, Clayton Christensen, Michael Horn, and Curtis Johnson published a book entitled *Disrupting Class: How Innovation Will Change the Way the World Learns* (2008). Christensen is a professor at the Harvard Business School and the best-selling author of *The Innovator's Dilemma*. In *Disrupting Class . . .*, Christensen et al. present a compelling rationale for changing education in a way that makes far greater use of online technology to provide more student-centered and individualized instruction. The book's call for change was cited as something policymakers needed to consider in looking at the future of American education. Among the most provocative aspects of this book were predictions that by the year 2016 about one-quarter of all high school

courses will be online and that by the year 2019 about one-half of all high school courses will be online. In Chapter 4, Christensen et al. provided the bases for their prediction and among other citations, referred twice to our original study published in 2007. While we are not making the same predictions as Christensen et al., the data collected in our 2007 and 2009 studies indicate that online learning is spreading throughout K-12 education and specifically in secondary education.

As indicated earlier, in the 2007 study, the number of students enrolled in online courses was estimated at 700,000. In the 2009 follow-up study, it was estimated at 1,030,000, a 47% increase in 2 years. This is quite a substantial increase. Furthermore, these figures do not derive from a few highly-successful large virtual schools or the distance learning needs of rural school districts. They are the result of students taking either online or blended courses in three quarters of all districts (74.8%) with approximately another 15.0% of the districts planning to introduce them over the next 3 years. Furthermore, online learning in K-12 education is in its nascent stages and significant growth is yet to come. A majority of the respondents in the 2009 study anticipated that the number of students taking online courses will grow by more than 20% and that those taking blended courses will grow even faster over the next 2 years. It also appeared that the number of school districts offering online courses was accelerating. In the 2007 study,

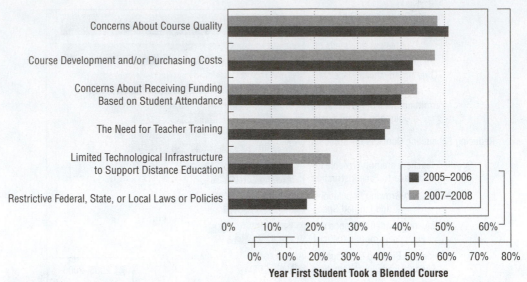

Figure 4 Percentage summary of responses to: How much of a barrier the following areas would be (or are) in offering fully online or blended learning courses?

a prediction was made that over the subsequent 5 or 6 years, the K-12 enrollment in online courses would approach 3–4 million students. The data collected in 2009 study suggested that this prediction be revised upwards. It is conceivable that by 2016, online enrollments could reach approximately 5 million K-12 (mostly high school) students.

4. The Role of Online Learning in American High School Reform

Increasingly, the American high school is becoming a major concern for policymakers across the spectrum of education in the United States. Research points to a number of issues, with the most serious being persistently low graduation rates from American high schools. A report published by the Center for Labor Market Studies (2009) characterizes the high school dropout problem as a crisis that has life-long economic impacts on individuals as well as the American society at large. Barack Obama, in his first major address on American education after assuming the presidency, pleaded with American youth that:

> "dropping out of high school is no longer an option. It's not just quitting on yourself, it's quitting on your country; and this country needs and values the talents of every American." (Obama, 2009)

There is also interest in the role that online learning can play in high school reform especially with regard to improving graduation rates, building connections for high school students to college careers, differentiating instruction, and supporting cost-efficiency for instruction. The data collected from the third (Picciano & Seaman, 2010) of the three studies discussed in this paper will be presented specifically looking at the role of online learning in high school reform initiatives.

4.1. Why Online and Blended Learning in the High Schools?

Perhaps one of the most important questions posed in the study of online learning in American high schools was "why are high schools offering online and blended learning courses to their students?" Based on data collected from a survey of high school principals in 2008–2009, Figure 5 provides a bar chart showing the percentage of responses given by those respondents offering online or blended learning courses for each of the thirteen options provided in the survey for the question: Regardless of whether your school is currently offering online or blended/hybrid courses, how important do you believe each of the following items would be in offering or potentially offering online and blended/hybrid courses? The options receiving the greatest responses were:

1. Provide courses that otherwise were not available (79%).
2. Permit students who failed a course to take it again— credit recovery (73%).
3. Provide additional Advanced Placement Courses (61%).
4. Provide for the needs of specific students (60%).

These responses represented the significance of online learning in meeting a variety of student needs whether taking advanced placement or making up

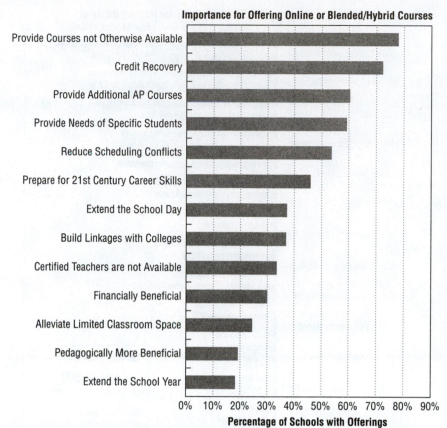

Importance for Offering Online or Blended/Hybrid Courses

Provide Courses not Otherwise Available
Credit Recovery
Provide Additional AP Courses
Provide Needs of Specific Students
Reduce Scheduling Conflicts
Prepare for 21st Century Career Skills
Extend the School Day
Build Linkages with Colleges
Certified Teachers are not Available
Financially Beneficial
Alleviate Limited Classroom Space
Pedagogically More Beneficial
Extend the School Year

0% 10% 20% 30% 40% 50% 60% 70% 80% 90%
Percentage of Schools with Offerings

Figure 5 Summary of responses to: How important do you believe each of the following items would be in offering or potentially offering online and blended/hybrid courses?

courses (e.g., credit recovery). Meeting needs related to basic school issues such as finances, classroom space, and extending the school year were perceived as of less importance.

Figures 6 and 7 present the perceived importance of data shown in Figure 5 cross tabulated by size of school and locale. In Figure 6, a clear pattern presents itself showing that the smaller the school, the greater the importance of "providing courses not otherwise available". Figure 7 shows that rural schools perceive online and blended courses as more important in the five leading categories than do schools in other locations and especially those in urban settings.

A specific question was included in the survey to detail the types of courses being offered online or in blended modes (see Figures 8 and 9). These data show a somewhat different pattern between online and blended courses. Credit recovery is the most popular type of course offered in online mode whereas elective courses are the most popular type in blended courses. While it is difficult to determine exactly why this is so, speculation is that there are several successful, for-profit entities

that provide fully online credit recovery courses to the schools. These courses are generally self-contained, programmed-instruction courses. The importance of online credit recovery courses is a relatively recent phenomenon but one that has gained considerable popularity among high school administrators. This appears to be particularly true in urban high schools (see Figure 10).

The major purpose of the 2010 study was to examine the role that online learning was playing in addressing concerns and issues facing the American high school. In examining the findings, it was determined that there are certain initiatives involving online learning that directly address large school reform issues such as improving graduation rates, credit recovery, building connections for students to their future college careers, and differentiating instruction.

4.2. Improving Graduation Rates and Credit Recovery

Improving the graduation rate is perhaps the most important aspect of many high school reform initiatives. While this study did not collect data on the graduation rates

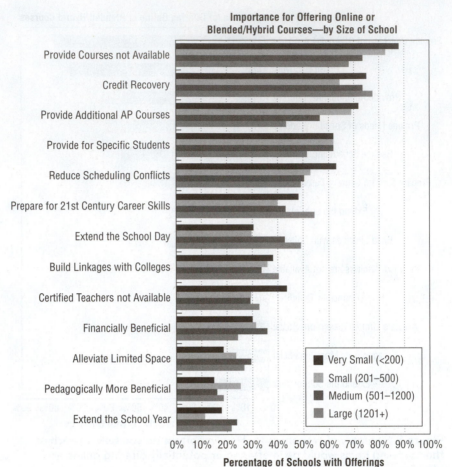

Importance for Offering Online or Blended/Hybrid Courses—by Size of School

Provide Courses not Available
Credit Recovery
Provide Additional AP Courses
Provide for Specific Students
Reduce Scheduling Conflicts
Prepare for 21st Century Career Skills
Extend the School Day
Build Linkages with Colleges
Certified Teachers not Available
Financially Beneficial
Alleviate Limited Space
Pedagogically More Beneficial
Extend the School Year

■ Very Small (<200)
■ Small (201–500)
■ Medium (501–1200)
■ Large (1201+)

0% 10% 20% 30% 40% 50% 60% 70% 80% 90% 100%

Percentage of Schools with Offerings

Figure 6 Summary of responses to: How important do you believe each of the following items would be in offering or potentially offering online and blended/hybrid courses? cross tabulated by size of the school.

per se, it did specifically collect data on how online and blended learning were being used in providing options to students in enrolling in and completing coursework. The term "credit recovery" refers to courses that students take to make up for courses that they need to graduate. The need for these courses varies but relates to students having not completed required coursework earlier in their high school careers due to illness, scheduling conflicts, academic failure, etc. Students needing such courses make up a significant portion of the high school student population that subsequently drops out or is late in graduating. The findings indicate that credit recovery has evolved into the most popular type of online course being offered at the secondary level. A relatively new phenomenon, online credit recovery courses were practically non-existent a few years ago and have now become a dominant form of online course offerings in many high schools. What is particularly interesting is that urban high schools, which historically have the lowest graduation

rates of any schools in the country, appear to be embracing online credit recovery as a basic part of their academic offerings (Balfanz & Legters, 2004). This finding is collaborated by reports from several providers of online courses that are seeing significant increases in demand for credit recovery courses. Gregg Levin, vice president for sales for Aventa Learning, a for-profit provider of online services to K-12 schools, in a recent article said that demand for online credit recovery courses had increased "eight-fold between 2005 and 2008" (Zehr, 2010). Many high schools have been forced to find solutions to their high school drop-out problems due to pressure from state education departments and the federal *No Child Left Behind* mandates to improve student outcomes. Online credit recovery appears to be an integral part of the solutions for many of these schools.

While it would be easy to state that the advance of online credit recovery is a positive finding in the 2010 study, it should be taken with some caution. The data in

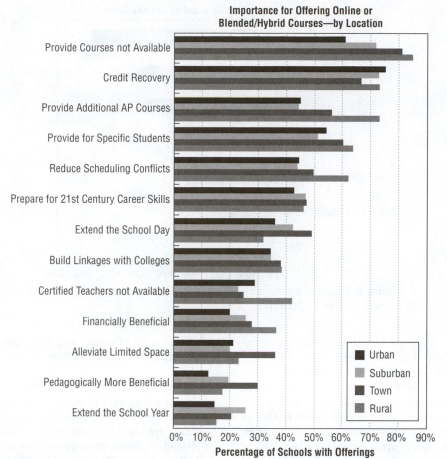

Importance for Offering Online or Blended/Hybrid Courses—by Location

Provide Courses not Available
Credit Recovery
Provide Additional AP Courses
Provide for Specific Students
Reduce Scheduling Conflicts
Prepare for 21st Century Career Skills
Extend the School Day
Build Linkages with Colleges
Certified Teachers not Available
Financially Beneficial
Alleviate Limited Space
Pedagogically More Beneficial
Extend the School Year

Legend: Urban, Suburban, Town, Rural

0% 10% 20% 30% 40% 50% 60% 70% 80% 90%
Percentage of Schools with Offerings

Figure 7 Summary of responses to: How important do you believe each of the following items would be in offering or potentially offering online and blended/hybrid courses? cross tabulated by the location of the school.

this study suggested that while high school administrators were providing more opportunities for students to enroll in online courses, they also had concerns about the quality of online courses and indicated that students need maturity, self-discipline, and a certain command of basic skills (reading and mathematics) in order to succeed in these courses. Many of the students who need to recover credits are those who may not have these characteristics. There have also been concerns that some school districts might be using credit-recovery, whether online or face-to-face, as a quick, convenient way to move students through to graduation. As an example, a *New York Times* article raised concerns by teachers and others that some New York City public schools were "taking shortcuts" and "gaming the system" to move students through to graduation with questionable practices related to weak credit recovery programs (Gootman and Coutts, 2008). Nevertheless, credit recovery has become a major aspect of many high school academic programs and the online versions of these are proving to be especially popular. A

prime area for future research would be the study of the quality and effectiveness of these programs.

4.3. Building Bridges to College Careers

An important aspect of the high school reform dialog has centered on the importance of advising students to stay in school and move onto a college career upon graduation. Students who have set the goals of attending college for themselves are more likely to do well in school and graduate. Rather than waiting for graduation, educators have been developing programs to bridge the high school and college experiences at an earlier time. Whether through advanced placement or registration in college courses as electives, there has been a growing population of high school educators seeking to expand the opportunities for their students to start their college careers while still in high school. While many models for this exist, there have always been logistical issues with regards to transporting students to colleges, training high school teachers to teach college-level courses, articulating

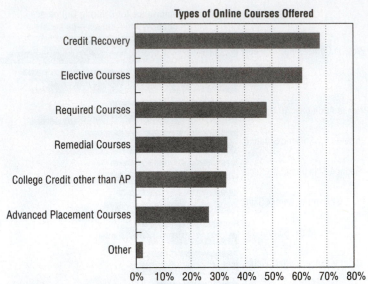

Figure 8 Types of online courses offered by percentage of the schools with the offerings.

courses taken in high school for college credit, etc. It appears from this study that online and blended learning courses are increasingly being used to overcome these logistical issues. By enrolling in online and blended learning courses, high school students no longer need to be transported to a college campus, can enroll in college courses taught by college professors, and can be given college credit immediately upon completing and passing their coursework. Data from this study indicate that high school administrators see online elective college-level courses as an effective way for some of the more able students to begin their college careers.

4.4. Differentiating Instruction

Christensen et al. (2008) referenced earlier, see online learning as an integral part of high school reform specifically by allowing high schools to customize instruction and to differentiate course offerings to meet a wide variety of student needs. However, while offering a wide breadth of courses is most desirable, doing so

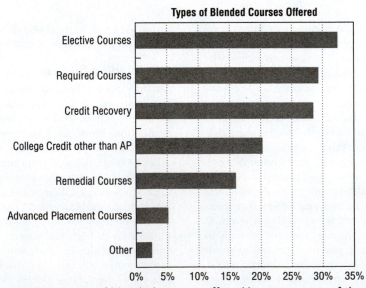

Figure 9 Types of blended courses offered by percentage of the schools with the offerings.

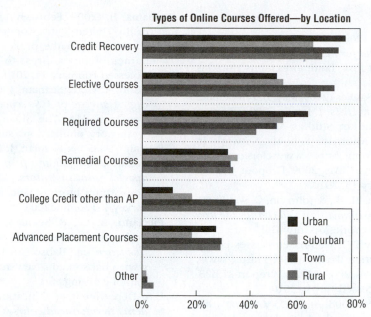

Figure 10 Types of online courses offered by percentage of the schools with the offerings cross tabulated by location.

in face-to-face mode can be quite expensive. Offering online courses to students allow for greater breadth of course offerings without necessarily incurring the costs for offering entire courses face-to-face. For example, to offer a face-to-face elective course generally requires that there be a certain amount of student interest and enrollment for the course in order to make it cost effective. A student interested in taking elective coursework in chemistry might not be interested in taking an advanced foreign language course and vice versa. To meet the needs of both students, high school schedulers would have to offer both an advanced chemistry and a foreign language course and then hope that there are enough students registered to make them cost-effective. Online and blended courses, on the other hand, can be made available for just a single student and only incur the cost for that one student. The data consistently indicate that high school administrators see online learning as meeting the diverse needs of their students whether through advanced placement, elective college courses, or credit recovery. Indeed, the data indicate that the major reason for offering online and blended courses is to offer courses that otherwise would not be available. This supports strongly the concept promulgated by Christensen, Horn, and Johnson of the role that online technology can play in differentiating instruction and providing more choices for high school administrators in developing their academic programs.

5. Conclusion

The purpose of the above research was to examine the role that online learning was playing in American K-12 education. It is our conclusion that online and blended learning are making inroads into K-12 academic programs and most significantly at the secondary level. Furthermore, and perhaps more importantly, online and blended learning grew by 47% between 2005–2006 and 2007–2008. Every indication is that this growth will continue in the foreseeable future. If K-12 follows the pattern of enrollment growth in higher education, it is quite possible that online learning will emerge as a substantial component of all learning at the secondary level.

The American high school has been characterized as an institution in crisis and the call for reform has been loud and strong. The results of the 2010 study indicated that online and blended learning are becoming integral to a number of high school reform efforts, especially with regard to improving graduation rates, credit recovery, building connections for students to their future college careers, differentiating instruction, and supporting cost-efficiency for instruction. However, while high schools are depending upon online and blended learning for many of their programs, concerns remain among educators. The issue of the quality of online instruction persists. There is a continuing need to establish and update state and local policies for funding, attendance requirements, and other issues related to online instruction. Careful evaluation needs to be undertaken for relatively new online programs such as credit recovery. The benefits, concerns, and costs related to online and blended learning are prime areas for future research as they increasingly become a topic of focus in the national dialog on improving American education.

REFERENCES

Balfanz, R., & Legters, N. (2004). *Locating the dropout crisis. Report of the Center for Research on the Education of Students Placed At Risk*. Baltimore: Johns Hopkins University Press.

Center for Labor Market Studies (2009, May 5). Left behind: The nation's drop-out crisis. (May 5, 2009). Boston: Center for Labor Market Studies at Northeastern University and the Alternate Schools Network in Chicago. Retrieved from: http://www.clms.neu.edu/publication/documents/CLMS_2009_Dropout_Report.pdf Accessed February 15, 2010.

Christensen, C. M., Horn, M. B., & Johnson, C. W. (2008). *Disrupting class: How innovation will change the way the world learns*. New York: McGraw-Hill.

Davis, M. (2009, January 27). Web-based classes booming in schools. *Education Week, 28*(19), 5 http://www.edweek.org/ew/articles/2009/01/28/19report-s1.h28.html?qs=picciano Accessed July 9, 2010.

Gootman, E., & Coutts, S. (2008, April 11). *Lacking credits, some students learn a shortcut*. Retrieved from:. *New York Times* http://www.nytimes.com/2008/04/ll/education/11graduation.html?pagewanted=print Accessed: June 26, 2010.

Means, B., Toyama, Y., Murphy, R., Baka, M., & Jones, K. (2009). *Evaluation of evidence-based practices in online learning: A meta-analysis and review of online learning studies*. Washington, D.C.: U.S. Department of Education.

Obama, B. (2009, February). Address to a joint session of the United States Congress. Retrieved from: www.whitehouse.gov/the_press_office/remarks-of-president-barack-obama-address-to-joint-session-of-congress Accessed February 14, 2010.

Picciano, A. G., & Seaman, J. (2007). *K-12 online learning: A survey of U.S. school district administrators*. Needham, MA: The Sloan Consortium http://www.sloan-c.org/publications/survey/K-12_06.asp

Picciano, A. G., & Seaman, J. (2009). *K-12 online learning: A 2008 follow up of the survey of U.S. school district administrators*. Needham. MA: The Sloan Consortium http://sloanconsortium.org/publications/survey/k-12online2008

Picciano, A. G., & Seaman, J. (2010). *The American high school: High school reform and the role of online learning*.: Babson Survey Research Group http://www3.babson.edu/Newsroom/Releases/online-high-school-learning.cfm

U.S. Department of Education (2007). *Connecting students to advanced courses online*. Washington, D.C.: Office of Innovation and Improvement.

Zehr, M. A. (2010, June 21). District embracing online credit recovery options. Retrieved from:. *Education Week* http://www.edweek.org/ew/articles/2010/06/21/36credit.h29.html?tkn=XVRFzKWhrHlYcunWSbGvc0q7fz4fNNfYiEcG&cmp=clp-edweek Accessed: June 21, 2010.

CHAPTER TEN

Group Comparison Research

PROBLEMS OF PRACTICE *in this chapter*

- What can be done to increase the percentage of rural students who enroll in college and earn a college degree?
- How prevalent is student truancy and residential mobility, and should it be a matter of concern to educators?
- What symptoms should teachers and parents look for in considering whether a child has autism spectrum disorder, and are these symptoms the same for boys and girls?
- Should educators adopt block-based school schedules if they wish to support standards-based instruction?
- Should students be encouraged to take advanced placement (AP) courses in high school even if those courses challenge the limits of their abilities?
- Can we rely on chemistry teachers developing beliefs about classroom instruction that are consistent with best practices as they move from student teaching to experienced-teacher status?

IMPORTANT *Ideas*

1. The improvement of education depends greatly on our ability to discover the causes of problems in educational practice and also the harmful effects that can occur if the problems of practice are not solved.
2. The independent variable is not manipulated in group comparison and correlational research studies.
3. The introductory section of a report of a group comparison study should explain (1) why the study is important, (2) the study's specific purposes, (3) the variables that were investigated, and (4) the findings from a literature review.
4. A group comparison research design can include multiple independent variables and multiple dependent variables.
5. In an ideal group comparison research design, the sample would be randomly selected from a defined population.
6. A group comparison research design does not impose any restrictions on the instruments that can be used to measure the independent and dependent variables.

7. Commonly used tests of statistical significance in group comparison research include the *t* test, analysis of variance, and their nonparametric counterparts (the Mann-Whitney *U* test, the Wilcoxon signed-rank test, the Kruskal-Wallis test, and the chi-square test).

8. The practical significance of statistical results obtained in group comparison research can be determined by computing effect sizes.

9. In the discussion section of a report of a group comparison study, the researchers should (1) summarize the study's findings, (2) consider flaws in the design and execution of the study, and (3) state implications of the study for subsequent research and improvement of professional practice.

KEY TERMS

analysis of variance
causal relationship
dependent variable
effect size
fixed variable
group comparison
    research
independent variable
interaction effect

Kruskal-Wallis test of statistical
    significance
Mann-Whitney *U* test of statistical
    significance
matching procedure
nonparametric test of statistical
    significance
parametric test of statistical
    significance

test of statistical significance
t test
variable
Wilcoxon signed-rank test of
    statistical significance
x variable
y variable

CLASSIFICATION OF QUANTITATIVE RESEARCH DESIGNS

The literature on research methodology does not have consistent terminology for classifying different types of quantitative research designs. This is particularly true of the research designs that we explain in this chapter and the next. Therefore, we start this chapter with a discussion of research designs and our choice of terminology to classify them.

Our starting point is the variables that researchers choose to study. We explain in Chapter 5 that a **variable** is a quantitative expression of a construct that can vary. For example, the construct of self-esteem can be viewed as a variable because we can imagine variations in this construct. People have different levels of self-esteem, ranging from high to low.

In descriptive research (see Chapter 9), the variables refer to characteristics of the sample—for example, academic achievement, years of education,

socioeconomic status, and attitudes. Descriptive research studies do not attempt to determine whether these variables have a causal influence on other variables.

All other quantitative research designs, either explicitly or implicitly, conceptualize variables as reflecting a **causal relationship** to each other. If the research study involves two variables, for example, one is usually conceptualized as the cause and the other is conceptualized as the effect. It is common practice among researchers to label the "cause" variable as the **independent variable** and the "effect" variable as the **dependent variable**. In statistics, the "cause" variable sometimes is labeled the **x variable**, and the "effect" variable is labeled the **y variable**.

In experimental research designs, the intervention, typically an educational program or teaching technique, is the independent variable. The intervention is introduced into an existing situation to determine what effect, or effects, it might have. These effects are the dependent variables.

The labels *descriptive research* and *experimental research* are straightforward and are used consistently by researchers. The one exception is that descriptive research is sometimes called *survey research*. However, in some studies, researchers collect data about variables that they have conceptualized to be in a causal relationship to each other, but there is no intervention. Their research designs are neither descriptive nor experimental. They involve two other types of research design, which are the subjects of this chapter and the next.

Nonexperimental Research Involving Causal Relationships

Studies that explore cause-and-effect relationships between variables, but without using the experimental method, have been given various labels in education and other disciplines, including *causal-comparative research*, *correlational research*, *ex post facto research*, *group comparison research*, and *relational research*. Burke Johnson (2001) noted the confusion created by these terms and suggested two new terms—*predictive nonexperimental research* and *explanatory nonexperimental research*. Each of these terms has merit. We mention them here so that you are aware of them should you come across them in reading research reports. Our preference is to distinguish between two types of research designs, both of which are nonexperimental and both of which are used to explore causal relationships between variables.

One type of design involves group comparisons (e.g., comparing the mean scores of two groups on a particular measure), so we label it *group comparison research*. The other type of design involves the use of correlational statistics, and so we label it *correlational research*.

In previous editions of this book, we used the label *causal-comparative research* instead of *group comparison research* because the former was commonly used in the research literature. However, Johnson and others criticize the use of this label because it implies that causal-comparative research can be used to explore causal relationships whereas correlational research cannot be similarly used.

As you will see, both of these types of nonexperimental research designs—group comparison research and correlational research—are useful for exploring causal relationships even though they cannot confirm results to the degree that experimental research can.

THE RELEVANCE OF GROUP COMPARISON RESEARCH TO EDUCATIONAL PRACTICE

If you reflect on your concerns about educational practice, you are likely to realize that many of them involve cause-and-effect relationships. For example, consider phenomena that currently alarm many educators and other groups—the increasing frequency of obesity among youth, the rising incidence of autism in children, the persistent achievement gap between white students and students of other ethnicities, and the prevalence of bullying behavior on school grounds.

These problems raise a question about cause and effect. Why do these problems occur? Note that this question is based on the premise that the effect (e.g., autism) has already occurred, and now we are looking to the past to determine its cause. In other words, the focus of the research is on explanation. We observe a certain phenomenon and seek to explain what caused it. In the language of research, the effect is the dependent variable, and the cause is the independent variable.

In addition to searching for causes, educators are concerned with prediction. For example, teacher educators and school officials wish to select the best candidates for a teacher education program or teaching position. They ask such questions as, "if we select this individual for a teaching vacancy, how likely is she to be an effective teacher in the future?"

Elected officials and the general public are also concerned about matters involving prediction. How likely is it that low-achieving students will drop out of school? Will learning-disabled students who are mainstreamed into regular classrooms be successful? As classroom size increases because of budget cuts, will students' academic achievement suffer? If we analyze the process of prediction, we realize that it too involves the study of cause and effect, but with a focus on future rather than past occurrences. The cause is a particular action or event (e.g., increasing a school budget), and the consequence of that action is the effect. In the language of research, the cause is the independent variable, and the effect is the dependent variable.

Group comparison research is commonly used to explore possible cause-and-effect relationships such as those just described. We define **group comparison research** as empirical, quantitative studies that explore cause-and-effect relationships either (1) by comparing groups that differ on the independent variable to determine whether they also differ on the dependent variable or (2) by comparing groups that differ on the dependent variable to determine whether they also differ on the independent variable.

If the comparison groups differ on the independent variable (e.g., high school graduates vs. dropouts), the purpose of the study will be to predict how they differ on variables that will occur at a later point in time. If the comparison groups differ on the dependent variable (e.g., high school graduates vs. dropouts), the purpose of the study will be to explain these differences in terms of variables that occurred at an earlier time.

EXAMPLES OF GROUP COMPARISON RESEARCH

The following are examples of group comparison studies and the problems of practice for which they are relevant. In presenting each example, we label which variables were treated as independent and which were treated as dependent.

Comparison of Rural, Suburban, and Urban Students

Byun, S., Meece, J. L., & Irvin, M. J. (2012). Rural-nonrural disparities in postsecondary educational attainment revisited. *American Educational Research Journal, 49*(3), 412–437.

The purpose of this study was to determine whether students from rural communities have a different percentage of college enrollment and completion than do students from urban and suburban communities. The researchers found substantial differences in their sample: 84% of the urban students and 82% of the suburban students enrolled in college, compared with 74% of the rural students. Also, the rural students had the lowest percentage of college degrees or higher (30%), compared with 40% of the suburban students and 43% of the urban students.

In this study, students' community is the independent variable, and college enrollment and completion are the dependent variables. The reason is that the community in which students grew up occurred prior in time to their decisions about college.

The researchers also examined other factors that might affect students' college decisions. Among the factors were the following: parental level of education, parental involvement in their children's academic work, community social resources, and the rigor of the students' high school courses. These factors are independent variables because they occurred prior in time to the two dependent variables—college enrollment and college completion.

The researchers do not recommend steps that can be taken to increase rural students' enrollment in college and completion of a college degree. However, their study does point to a problem of practice for educators in rural communities.

Comparison of Girls and Boys Who Have Autism Spectrum Disorder

Mandy, W., Chilvers, R., Chowdhury, U., Salter, G., Seigal, A., & Skuse, D. (2012). Sex differences in autism spectrum disorder: Evidence from a large sample of children and adolescents. *Journal of Autism and Developmental Disorders, 42*(7), 1304–1313.

The researchers note that autism spectrum disorder (ASD) is much more common among males than females: one female for every four males. Therefore, it is difficult to obtain adequate samples of females with ASD to determine whether they differ in significant ways from boys with ASD and whether the differences vary by age.

Working with a larger sample than those in previous studies, the researchers found no gender differences in verbal or performance IQ, problems in reciprocal social interaction and communication, visual-spatial or motor impairment, feeding difficulties, and sensitivity to sound. Younger boys and girls with ASD did not differ in motor skills, but older girls had fewer motor difficulties than their male counterparts. Parents of girls with ASD reported more emotional difficulties than parents of boys with ASD, and teachers reported that boys with ASD had more problems with hyperactivity, attention, and prosocial behavior than girls with ASD. Teachers and parents both reported that boys with ASD were more likely to exhibit certain repetitive and stereotyped behaviors than girls with ASD.

These gender differences led the researchers to conclude that girls with ASD are less likely to receive this diagnosis than boys because certain ASD behaviors are not as prevalent. In particular, girls are less likely to exhibit repetitive and stereotyped behaviors, which are becoming increasingly important in making an ASD diagnosis. Therefore, a girl might have ASD, but not receive this diagnosis and therefore not receive appropriate health care and educational resources.

Comparison of Students with Good School Attendance and a Stable Residence and Students with Poor School Attendance and a Nonstable Residence

Parke, C. S., & Kanyongo, G. Y. (2012). Student attendance, mobility, and mathematics achievement in an urban school district. *Journal of Educational Research, 105*(3), 161–175.

The authors cite evidence that student mobility, defined as a change in residence, and student nonattendance at school are prevalent in American schools. For example, they cite U.S. Census Bureau data indicating that 4.3 million Americans moved between March 1999 and March 2000. In another study involving Ohio schools, the rate of attendance varied from 85 percent to 99 percent across schools.

Their study had several purposes, one of which was to determine the effects of student mobility and nonattendance on mathematics achievement. They formed four groups of students: (1) stable attenders—students who remained in the same school for the entire school year and were absent less than 5 percent of the school year, (2) stable nonattenders—students who did not move but were absent more than 5 percent of the school year; (3) mobile attenders—students who moved but were absent less than 5 percent of the school year; and (4) mobile nonattenders—students who both moved and were absent more than 5 percent of the school year. They examined eighth-graders and eleventh-graders in each of these four groups. For both eighth-graders and eleventh-graders, they found that stable attenders had significantly better mathematics achievement than the other three groups. Mobile nonattenders at each grade level had the lowest mathematics achievement of the four groups.

Student mobility and student attendance are the independent variables, and mathematics achievement is the dependent variable in this study. This is because mobility and attendance were events that occurred prior in time to the administration of the mathematics achievement test.

The researchers made several recommendations based on these findings, one of them being that school districts should monitor the mobility and attendance of each of their students. They also cited interventions that some school districts have made to increase student attendance, such as appointing one teacher in each school to be a parent liaison who works with parents and community services to help students with poor school attendance. Concerning mobility, the researchers suggest that educators should study the support structures that Department of Defense schools have established to help military families who move frequently.

FEATURES OF A GROUP COMPARISON RESEARCH REPORT

Table 10.1 presents typical features of a group comparison research report. In the following sections, we explain each feature and illustrate it with a research study about a type of school scheduling known as block scheduling. At the end of the chapter, you will find another group comparison study investigating whether student teachers who plan to teach chemistry have the same beliefs as experienced teachers of this subject, and also whether the beliefs of each group are consistent with what is considered best practice.

Introduction

The introductory section of a report of a group comparison study should explain (1) why the study is important, (2) its specific purposes, (3) the variables that were investigated, and (4) the findings of the authors' literature review.

Consider the study of block scheduling conducted by Leslie Flynn, Frances Lawrenz, and Matthew Schultz (2005). They started their report by noting that the traditional school schedule in middle schools and high schools includes six or seven time periods. This schedule typically allocates 40 or 50 minutes for each subject. In contrast, block scheduling has fewer time periods so that each subject can be taught for 85 to 100 minutes. The researchers also noted recent national mandates for standards-based instruction, which, among other things, require that teachers develop students' problem-solving and higher-order thinking skills.

TABLE 10.1 • Typical Sections of a Group Comparison Research Report

Section	Content
Introduction	Hypotheses, questions, or objectives are stated. A review of relevant literature is reported. The independent and dependent variables are described.
Research design	Two or more groups of research participants are specified. If the study examines the factors that caused the groups to be different, the variable on which the groups differ is the dependent variable, and the factors (i.e., the presumed causes) are the independent variables. If the study involves prediction, the groups will differ on the independent variable, and the variables that are measured subsequently are the dependent variables (i.e., the effects).
Sampling procedure	The researchers attempt to select groups of research participants who differ significantly on the independent or dependent variable but are similar in all other respects. Ideally, the groups are randomly drawn from a defined population.
Measures	Virtually any kind of measure can be used to collect data on the independent and dependent variables.
Data analysis	Descriptive statistics for the independent and dependent variables are computed. Commonly used tests of statistical significance for the observed differences between the different groups of research participants are the *t* test, analysis of variance, analysis of covariance, and the chi-square test.
Discussion	The main findings of the study are summarized. Flaws and limitations of the study are considered. Implications of the findings for further research and professional practice are considered.

The researchers hypothesized that "[b]ecause many standards-based instructional practices call for in-depth investigations, discussions, and reflections, extended periods associated with block scheduling may act as a catalyst for standards-based teaching techniques that have been neglected in the traditional school schedule" (Flynn et al., 2005, p. 15). Their study was designed to test this hypothesis.

Another intent of the study was to help educators address a problem of practice. The researchers noted that educators currently are being held accountable for student learning and adherence to curriculum standards. The question is whether block scheduling can help educators meet these accountability requirements. As the researchers put it: "The present study provides additional data for school administrators to use in making decisions about school scheduling options" (Flynn et al., 2005, p. 16).

The independent variable in the study (i.e., the presumed cause) was school schedule, which had two values: (1) block scheduling and (2) traditional scheduling. The dependent variable (i.e., the presumed effect) was mathematics teachers' use of 17 standards-based "minds-on" activities reflecting current national standards for mathematics instruction.

Research Design

Researchers typically use a group comparison research design when they are not able to manipulate the independent variable. In the study we are examining, it is difficult to imagine that the researchers could obtain school administrators' permission to select a sample of their traditional schedule schools and randomly assign them to either continue with traditional scheduling or to adopt block scheduling. School systems are not accustomed to this level of experimentation, nor do they have the resources for it.

The alternative is to look for "natural" experiments in which school systems or other agencies, on their own initiative, have instituted the education practices of interest to the researchers. This was the case with the block-scheduling study. The researchers selected schools that had adopted block scheduling and compared them to schools that had retained traditional scheduling.

A group comparison research design is also used when the independent variable involves a personal or group characteristic that cannot be manipulated. Some researchers refer to these variables as **fixed variables**, because they cannot be changed by the researchers or other groups. For example, ethnicity is intrinsic to individuals. Similarly, other characteristics, such as family composition (e.g., two parents, one parent, multigenerational) are determined by factors that are beyond manipulation by an external agency.

The study we are examining here involves one independent variable, school schedule. This basic group comparison research design could be modified to include additional independent variables. For example, all of the schools in the sample were middle schools. If the researchers had included high schools with traditional schedules and block schedules, school level would be another independent variable.

The addition of the variable of school level would enable the researchers to determine the effects of time schedule (an independent variable) and school level (another independent variable) on teacher instruction (the dependent variable). Also, the researchers could investigate whether the effects of school schedule varied by school level. For example, they might find that block scheduling affects the instruction of middle school teachers but not the instruction of high school teachers.

A group comparison research design also can include multiple dependent variables. For example, the researchers could examine the effects of block scheduling on such dependent variables as teacher lesson planning, teacher stress level, student attitude toward school, and student academic achievement.

Sampling Procedure

As in any quantitative research study, researchers who do a group comparison study should select a sample that is representative of the population to which they wish to generalize their results. To achieve this goal, they need to identify the population and randomly select a sample from it.

Typically, researchers lack the resources to define a population and then randomly select participants from it. This is particularly true if the population is distributed across a wide region and if data collection requires direct contact with the sample. Therefore, researchers compromise by selecting an available volunteer sample and describing its characteristics in detail. Readers of the report can study these characteristics and make their own determination of the population to which the results might generalize.

In the school schedule study, the researchers' sample included schools from three states. They comment, "Although the sample was not drawn randomly and, therefore, is not necessarily representative of all schools across the three states, it contains a broad range of teachers', principals', and school characteristics" (Flynn et al., 2005, p. 17).

Ideally, the comparison groups should represent different values of the independent variable but be identical in all other respects. Otherwise, we do not know for certain whether observed differences between the comparison groups on the dependent variables are the result of the independent variable or of other variables on which the groups differ.

In the school schedule study, the researchers compared the traditional schedule schools and the block schedule schools on various characteristics. They found that a higher percentage of the traditional schedule schools had small enrollments and more students from poor families. Teachers in both types of schools had a similar amount of teaching experience and professional preparation. However, a significantly greater percentage of teachers in the block schedule schools had earned a degree with a major in mathematics (75 percent versus 51 percent of the traditional schedule teachers).

One way to make the comparison groups more similar, so as to rule out the possible influence of extraneous independent variables, is to link each research participant in one comparison group with a research participant in the other comparison group who has similar characteristics. This linking procedure, in which one research participant is paired with another because they share a common characteristic, is called a **matching procedure**. It is used occasionally in research, but it has several potential drawbacks. It might result in elimination of some research participants, and it does not ensure that the resulting comparison groups are similar in characteristics that were not matched by the researchers.

Another way to make the comparison groups more similar is to use statistical techniques such as analysis of covariance (see Chapter 7) or multiple regression (see Chapter 11). These techniques are imperfect, but they enable the researchers to estimate whether a specific independent variable has an effect on the dependent variable apart from the effect of other independent variables that were measured.

In the case of the school schedule study, it might have been possible for the researchers to use analysis of covariance to determine the effect of such independent variables as school size and teachers' mathematics training on teachers' instruction (the dependent variable) and also to factor out these effects in determining the effect of school scheduling on teachers' instruction. Stated differently, analysis of covariance provides an estimate of how much school scheduling variations would affect teachers' instruction if the schools and teachers in the two comparison groups were truly similar with respect to school size and teachers' preparation in mathematics.

Measures

The variables studied in a group comparison study can be measured by any of the approaches described in Chapter 5: tests, scales, questionnaires, interviews, and direct observation.

In the block scheduling study, the researchers did not administer their own measures but instead relied on measures and data available from a large multistate study funded by the National Science Foundation. In that study, school principals completed a questionnaire about school characteristics, and teachers completed a questionnaire in which they reported on their classroom activities and use of time during mathematics instruction. The 17 classroom activities are shown in Table 10.2, and the use-of-time variables are shown in Table 10.3. The scales used to measure each variable are described in a note below each table.

Results

The usual first step in data analysis for a group comparison study is to compute descriptive statistics, most likely, the mean and standard deviation. Descriptive statistics for the block scheduling study are shown in Tables 10.2 and 10.3.

Much can be learned by carefully inspecting the descriptive statistics. Our review of the two tables leads us to conclude that mathematics teachers in block schedule schools provide similar instruction to that provided by mathematics teachers in traditional schedule schools. Differences between means are found for some of the scales, and these indicate that block schedule teachers use standards-based instructional practices slightly more than traditional schedule teachers.

The next step is to determine whether the observed difference between means for the two groups is statistically significant. **Tests of statistical significance** are explained in Chapter 7. Commonly used tests of statistical significance in group comparison research are shown in Table 10.4. Some of these

statistical tests can be done by the Data Analysis feature in Excel (under the Tools pull-down menu). Other tests can be done by using statistical software such as SPSS or by following the computational steps specified in some statistics textbooks (see the resource section at the end of the chapter).

The t Test in Group Comparison Research

In the school schedule study, the researchers used a **t test** to determine whether each pair of means differed significantly from each other (see Tables 10.2 and 10.3). We explain the t test in Chapter 7. Only two of the comparisons were statistically significant: (1) use of calculators or computers and (2) writing of reflections.

As the number of group comparisons increases, so does the likelihood of finding a statistically significant difference by chance. In other words, if this research study were repeated, it is possible that a comparison of two means that was statistically significant in the first study might not be statistically significant in the replication study. However, the fact that there is a consistent trend across all comparisons for block schedule teachers to make more use of standards-based instructional practices than the traditional schedule teachers suggests that the populations represented by these two groups actually differ, albeit slightly, in this respect.

The t test also can be used to determine whether the variability of scores for two groups is statistically significant. The typical statistic used to describe variability is the standard deviation (SD). If we examine the student activity "Use calculators or computers to solve mathematical problems" in Table 10.2, we see that the SD for the block schedule teachers is 0.90, whereas the SD for the traditional schedule teachers is 1.30.

The SDs are different, but how likely are they to have occurred by chance if, in fact, the block schedule teachers and traditional schedule teachers are two samples drawn from two identical populations? The t test for variances can answer this question.

Effect Sizes in Group Comparison Research

The t test is used to determine whether the difference between the means or variances of two groups is statistically significant. However, the t test does

TABLE 10.2 • Student Classroom Activities in Traditional and Block Schedule Schools

Student Activity	Schedule	N	Mean	SD	p
Use calculators or computers to solve mathematical problems	Block	69	4.07	0.90	.04*
	Traditional	79	3.70	1.30	
Work on solving real-world problems	Block	70	3.94	1.10	.91
	Traditional	79	3.82	0.97	
Participate in discussions to deepen mathematics understanding	Block	69	3.59	1.02	.07
	Traditional	79	3.24	1.35	
Share ideas or solve problems with each other in small groups	Block	69	3.45	1.08	.49
	Traditional	79	3.32	1.24	
Document and evaluate their own mathematics work	Block	69	3.19	1.36	.34
	Traditional	79	2.96	1.52	
Read from a mathematics textbook in class	Block	70	3.11	1.52	.61
	Traditional	79	3.24	1.48	
Describe what they know about a topic before it is taught	Block	70	2.84	1.19	.32
	Traditional	79	2.65	1.23	
Participate in student-led discussions	Block	69	2.81	1.48	.22
	Traditional	77	2.51	1.48	
Engage in hands-on mathematics activities	Block	70	2.69	0.93	.54
	Traditional	79	2.58	1.12	
Record, represent, and/or analyze data	Block	70	2.64	0.96	.93
	Traditional	79	2.68	1.15	
Complete worksheets that emphasize mastery of essential skills	Block	70	2.50	1.03	.48
	Traditional	79	2.62	0.93	
Write reflections in a notebook or journal	Block	70	2.19	1.38	.00*
	Traditional	79	1.59	1.10	
Model or work on simulations	Block	70	2.07	1.07	.96
	Traditional	79	2.08	1.20	
Read other (nontextbook) mathematics-related materials in class	Block	69	1.91	1.09	.96
	Traditional	79	1.92	1.30	
Make formal presentations in class	Block	69	1.48	0.82	.96
	Traditional	79	1.48	0.89	
Use community resources in the classroom (museums, business people)	Block	69	1.35	0.64	.76
	Traditional	79	1.32	0.63	
Prepare written mathematics reports of at least three pages in length	Block	70	1.07	0.26	.82
	Traditional	79	1.08	0.31	

Note: Means based on 5-point scale: 1 = rarely or never, 2 = once a month, 3 = once a week, 4 = 2–3 times a week, and 5 = daily.

Source: Flynn, L., Lawrenz, F., & Schultz, M. J. (2005). Block scheduling and mathematics: Enhancing standards-based instruction? *NASSP Bulletin, 89*(642), 14–23.

TABLE 10.3 • Use of Time in Classroom

Activity	Schedule	N	Mean	SD	p
Teacher instructs the class as a whole	Block	70	3.96	0.98	.91
	Traditional	81	3.96	1.02	
Students work individually	Block	68	3.22	0.86	.12
	Traditional	81	3.47	1.05	
Students work in small groups	Block	69	3.14	0.88	.16
	Traditional	78	2.91	1.08	

Note: Means are the percentage of class time based on a 6-point scale: 1 = 0%, 2 = 1–10%, 3 = 11–30%, 4 = 31–50%, 5 = 51–70%, and 6 = 71–100%.

Source: Flynn, L., Lawrenz, F., & Schultz, M. J. (2005). Block scheduling and mathematics: Enhancing standards-based instruction? *NASSP Bulletin, 89*(642), 14–23.

not provide information relating to two important questions: How large is the difference and does the difference have practical significance?

Effect sizes can be calculated to answer these questions. (We explain effect sizes in Chapter 8.) They are not reported in the school schedule study, but you can calculate them on your own if the research report includes the means and standard deviations of the two groups.

To illustrate, consider the first variable in Table 10.2 ("Use calculators or computers to solve mathematical problems"). The first step in calculating an effect size is to subtract one group mean from the other. We are interested in knowing how much better block scheduling is than traditional scheduling, so we will subtract the traditional schedule mean (3.70) from the block schedule mean (4.07). The difference is 0.37, which is the numerator in the effect size equation.

TABLE 10.4 • Statistical Techniques Used to Analyze Group Comparison Research Data

Test of Statistical Significance	Purpose
Parametric	
t test	Used primarily to determine whether two means differ significantly from each other; also used to determine whether a single mean differs significantly from a specified population value.
Analysis of variance	Used to determine whether group means on one or more variables differ significantly from each other and whether differences between group means reflect significant interaction effects.
Analysis of covariance	Similar to analysis of variance but permits adjustments to the post-treatment mean scores of different groups on the dependent variable to compensate for initial group differences on variables related to the dependent variable.
Nonparametric	
Mann-Whitney U test	Used to determine whether two uncorrelated means differ significantly from each other.
Wilcoxon signed-rank test	Used to determine whether two correlated means differ significantly from each other.
Kruskal-Wallis test	Used to determine whether the mean scores of three or more groups on a variable differ significantly from one another.
Chi-square test	Used to determine whether the frequency distributions or scores for two or more groups differ significantly from each other.

The second step is to determine the standard deviation, which is the denominator in the effect size equation. The calculation can be done in several different ways. Our choice is to use the standard deviation of the scores of the traditional schedule teachers on this measure (1.30).

Dividing 0.37 by 1.30 yields an effect size of 0.28. This means that the average teacher in the block schedule schools uses calculators or computers during math class at a level that would place him or her at the 61st percentile among teachers in traditional schedule schools. Experts in professional development probably would consider a move from the 50th to the 61st percentile a worthwhile incremental gain in teaching skill.

Analysis of Variance in Group Comparison Research

Analysis of variance is commonly used in group comparison research, so we will explain its features here by using the school schedule study. (Analysis of variance is also discussed in Chapter 7.) Suppose we hypothesize that teachers who have substantial expertise in mathematics will be able to take advantage of block scheduling to use standards-based instructional activities, whereas teachers who lack this expertise will not be able to take advantage of block scheduling in this way. Furthermore, we hypothesize that traditional scheduling hinders both expert and nonexpert teachers, so neither group has the opportunity to make much use of standards-based activities.

Table 10.5 shows hypothetical data for the activity "Writes reflections in a notebook or journal" to illustrate the type of data analyses that would be done to test these hypotheses. Looking at the row means in Table 10.5, we see that expert teachers make greater use of reflection writing ($M = 2.6$) than nonexpert teachers ($M = 1.8$), ignoring the type of school in which they teach. Analysis of variance can determine whether the difference between these means is statistically significant.

Looking at the column means, we see that there is more writing of reflections in block schedule schools ($M = 2.7$) than in traditional schedule schools ($M = 2.0$), ignoring variations in teacher expertise. Analysis of variance can determine whether the difference between these means is statistically significant.

Finally, we see an **interaction effect**, meaning that there is a relationship between two variables, but only under a certain condition. In the hypothetical study we are discussing, there is more writing of reflections in block schedule schools, but only if the teacher has expertise in mathematics. Furthermore, we do not find that expert teachers assign more writing of reflections irrespective of setting; it depends on whether they are teaching in a block or traditional schedule school. Analysis of variance can test whether this interaction effect is statistically significant.

Note that the preceding discussion does not refer to three separate analyses of variance. Rather, one analysis of variance does all three tests of statistical significance and can provide support, or refutation, for the two hypotheses stated above.

The addition of teacher expertise or other factors as an independent variable would complicate the school schedule study and would require a more complex test of statistical significance (analysis of variance) than the t test. However, it might better represent the complexities of education and yield more insights into the causal relationships that operate within it.

As a research strategy, though, it is sometimes desirable to study intensively the effects of one independent variable, as was done in the study by Flynn and colleagues. If interesting findings are obtained, subsequent studies can look for more complex causal relationships, as in our hypothetical study involving block scheduling and teacher expertise.

TABLE 10.5 • Hypothetical Data for the Activity "Writes Reflections in a Notebook or Journal"

Teacher Expertise	Block Schedule School	Traditional Schedule School	Row Means
Expert teachers	3.4	1.8	2.6
Nonexpert teachers	1.8	1.8	1.8
Column means	2.7	2.0	

Nonparametric Tests of Statistical Significance

As we explain in Chapter 7, the *t* test and analysis of variance are parametric tests of statistical significance. A **parametric test of statistical significance** makes several assumptions about the scores of the population represented by the sample used in a research study. One key assumption is that the scores of the populations being compared are normally distributed. Another key assumption is that the variances of the scores in the populations being compared are equal.

Researchers typically use a parametric test if these assumptions are not grossly violated. Otherwise, they use a nonparametric counterpart of a parametric test of statistical significance. **Nonparametric tests of statistical significance** do not require satisfaction of the assumptions of a parametric test. The more common nonparametric tests are listed and briefly described in Table 10.4.

Discussion: Implications for Practice

The discussion section of a group comparison research report typically includes a summary of the main findings and analysis of possible flaws in the design and execution of the study. It is particularly important for the researcher to note the inherent limitations of this type of research in demonstrating cause-and-effect relationships. In the school schedule study, for example, the researchers did not manipulate the independent variable by assigning some schools to retain the traditional schedule and others to institute a block schedule. Therefore, we cannot be certain that the finding of a slightly greater use of standards-based class activities was caused by block scheduling or some other factor. We need to be particularly cautious, because the two types of schools differed in other respects besides scheduling. Most notably, the block schedule schools have a higher percentage of teachers who earned a degree with a major in mathematics.

The discussion section usually contains researcher comments about the implications of the findings for practice. For example, the report of the school-schedule study contains the following statement:

> Simply changing the structure of the school schedule cannot act as the sole catalyst for instructional change. Teachers in block-schedule settings may need to be provided with ongoing professional development to optimize the benefits of the extended period schedule. (Flynn et al., 2005, p. 21)

This recommendation seems reasonable. It also illustrates the point that one research study is rarely definitive. Additional research is needed to ensure that block scheduling, rather than some other factor associated with block scheduling, improves teachers' instruction. Then, a research and development process (see Chapter 19) can be employed to create a professional development program to optimize block scheduling and demonstrate its effectiveness.

EVALUATING A GROUP COMPARISON RESEARCH STUDY

The questions stated in Appendix 3 are relevant to evaluating a group comparison research study. The following additional criteria, stated in question-and-answer format, can be used to judge whether a study was weakened by specific problems that can arise in group comparison research.

- Did the researchers specify a cause-and-effect model that links the variables that were studied?

  A group comparison design is used to explore possible causal relationships. Therefore, check whether the researchers clearly specified which variables are the presumed causes and which variables are the presumed effects. Also, examine whether the researchers provided a rationale to justify their cause-and-effect model.

- Are the comparison groups similar in all respects except for the variable on which they were selected to differ?

  It is difficult to select two comparison groups that differ only on the variable of interest. Look for evidence of similarity between the two groups on other variables that might have an influence on the cause-and-effect relationship. Also, look for the use of statistical procedures, such as analysis of covariance, to statistically equate the comparison groups on these variables.

- Did the researchers draw tentative, rather than definitive, conclusions about whether observed relationships between independent and dependents are causal in nature?

Group comparison studies can explore causal relationships, but they cannot demonstrate definitively that variable *A* was influenced by variable *B* or that variable *A* has an effect on variable *C*. Check that the researchers did not use their findings to make a causal claim, for example, a claim that if educators manipulate variable *A* (e.g., implement a procedure such as block scheduling), changes in variable *C* (e.g., improved student learning) will occur.

An example of

How Group Comparison Research Can Help in Solving Problems of Practice

Advanced placement (AP) courses are available in many high schools, particularly those located in affluent neighborhoods. Completion of AP courses and good test scores on AP tests administered by the Educational Testing Service can improve students' chances of college admission and also earn college credit. The following news item describes a recent trend to make AP courses available to students in lower-income neighborhoods and students who ordinarily would not take these courses.

Meg Wiggins' fifth-period Advanced Placement Biology class was standing-room-only one recent morning as 27 students crowded around lab tables to study sample sizes. If that seems like a large group, consider that Wiggins' second-period class has 30 students.

She knows the work pushes the limit of a few students' abilities—about one in three are sophomores, who rarely take the course this early in their high school career. And enrolling so many kids in advanced science will likely bring down Woodside High School's average score on the big end-of-year exam, with more 1s and 2s on the five-point scale—a 3 or higher is considered a passing grade and eligible for college credit. But she and her colleagues have decided it's worth the cost.

"People need to strive to do things that are meaningful and good and *hard*," she said.

"The more kids you can convince to do tougher things, the better off your society will be."

Toppo, G. (2012, October 1). More students enrolling in AP math, science. *USA Today*. Retrieved from http://www.usatoday.com/story/news/nation/2012/10/01/teaching-for-the-future-access-ap-classes-widens/1601237/

You might wonder, as we do, whether students who enroll in an AP course have different characteristics than students who enroll in a non-AP version of the course and also whether students who earn 1s and 2s on the AP test subsequent to the AP course have different characteristics than students who earn 3, 4, or 5 on the AP test. You also might wonder about the future academic and occupational careers of these three groups.

Researchers can answer these questions by selecting a sample of low-income high schools that have instituted an AP initiative similar to the high school described in the *USA Today* article. (The high school is located in Newport, VA.) Using a group comparison research design, researchers would define three groups of students: those who take an AP course on a particular subject and earn a score of 3 to 5; those who take the same course and earn a score of 1 to 2; and students who take a non-AP course on the same subject. Prior to the course, the researchers would collect data on factors that they think might explain their AP test scores, for example, their grade point average, level of interest in the course's subject matter, study habits, and level of aspiration. Then they would conduct statistical analyses to determine whether the three groups differed on these factors and by how much. Because the comparisons involve three groups, analysis of variance would be the appropriate statistical procedure.

The same group comparison design also would be well suited for a prediction study. The researchers would follow the three groups through high school and collect data on each student's decision to apply for college and the type and reputation of the college to which they applied. With sufficient resources, the researchers could follow the students for a period of years after high school and collect data on the grades and coursework selection of those who attended college and on the career choices for all the students in the sample.

This example illustrates the versatility of group comparison research for studying causal relationships. In the first study we described, the purpose is to discover factors (the causes) that influence students' decisions to take AP courses (an effect) and their performance on the AP test (another effect). In the second study, the purpose is to discover outcomes in later years (the effects) that appear to result from the students'

decisions to take AP courses (one causal factor) and their AP test scores (another causal factor).

Both types of group comparison research have the potential to contribute to our knowledge about providing opportunities for disadvantaged students to take AP courses. The findings might provide a basis for policy makers to allocate funds so that these courses are more widely available. Also, the findings might provide the basis for encouraging certain students to take an AP course and for providing supports for students who might otherwise struggle while taking the course.

SELF-CHECK TEST

1. Prediction research
   a. does not involve the study of causal relationships.
   b. can involve the study of causal relationships.
   c. involves the manipulation of independent variables.
   d. involves only the study of dependent variables.
2. A variable is characterized as "independent" if it
   a. is not measured at the time of data collection.
   b. has been measured by individuals not associated with the research study.
   c. is hypothesized to be the effect of particular causes.
   d. is hypothesized to be the cause of particular effects.
3. In a research study that investigates the effects of school budget and instructional use of technology on students' academic achievement,
   a. school budget is the independent variable.
   b. school budget is the dependent variable.
   c. technology use is the independent variable.
   d. both school budget and technology use are independent variables.
4. In order to infer that two variables are causally related to each other, it is necessary to establish that
   a. both variables represent characteristics of the sample at the same point in time.
   b. the independent variable has an empirical association with more than one dependent variable.

   c. the independent variable occurred prior in time to the dependent variable.
   d. the dependent variable occurred prior in time to the independent variable.
5. A group comparison research design
   a. cannot be used to explore the effects of multiple hypothesized independent variables.
   b. can be used to explore the effects of multiple hypothesized independent variables.
   c. assumes that a single independent variable has a single effect.
   d. assumes that a single independent variable has multiple effects.
6. Researchers typically decide to use a group comparison research design when
   a. there are more than three independent variables.
   b. their primary purpose is to describe research participants' scores on variables measured at the same point in time.
   c. their primary purpose is to compare research participants' scores on a measure administered at two different points in time.
   d. they wish to study independent variables that are difficult or impossible to manipulate.
7. The ideal situation in group comparison research is to
   a. select comparison groups that differ on the independent variable but are identical in all other respects.

    b. use a matching procedure to pair each participant in one comparison group with a participant in another comparison group.

    c. use analysis of covariance to equate comparison groups on extraneous variables on which they differ.

    d. select comparison groups that differ on the dependent variable being studied but that are identical on other dependent variables.

8. When used to analyze data in a group comparison study, the *t* test and analysis of variance differ from each other in that only

    a. the *t* test can be used to compare differences between group means.

    b. the *t* test can be used to determine whether the comparison groups differ on more than one dependent variable.

    c. analysis of variance can be used to search for interaction effects.

    d. analysis of variance is considered a parametric test of statistical significance.

9. The practical significance of a statistical result in a group comparison study is best determined by

    a. the effect size statistic.

    b. the *t* test.

    c. analysis of variance.

    d. nonparametric tests of statistical significance.

10. The findings of a group comparison research study

    a. have only theoretical significance.

    b. are of no value unless they are supported by another study that exactly replicates it.

    c. are of tentative value for solving problems of practice.

    d. are educators' best basis for solving problems of practice.

CHAPTER REFERENCES

Flynn, L., Lawrenz, F., & Schultz, M. J. (2005). Block scheduling and mathematics: Enhancing standards-based instruction? *NASSP Bulletin, 89*(642), 14–23.

Johnson, B. (2001). Toward a new classification of non-experimental quantitative research. *Educational Researcher, 30*(2), 3–13.

RESOURCES FOR FURTHER STUDY

Bruning, J. L., & Kintz, B. L. (1997). *Computational handbook of statistics* (4th ed.). New York, NY: Longman.

    The authors use sample data sets to illustrate step-by-step procedures for computing the statistical procedures described in this chapter. Even if you use statistical software such as Excel or SPSS, you can improve your understanding of how the software is analyzing your data by studying these step-by-step procedures.

Gall, M. D., Gall, J. P., & Borg, W. R. (2007). *Educational research: An introduction* (8th ed.). Boston, MA: Allyn & Bacon.

    In Chapter 10 of this book, the authors provide an advanced treatment of factors that should be considered in designing a group comparison research study. (In the book the authors describe such research as causal-comparative research.)

Johnson, B. (2001). Toward a new classification of non-experimental quantitative research. *Educational Researcher, 30*(2), 3–13.

    The author explains the essential similarities between group comparison research designs (explained in this chapter), correlational research designs (explained in Chapter 11), and descriptive research designs (explained in Chapter 9). The author also discusses the difficulties that researchers face in demonstrating that two variables are causally related.

Shaw, S. M., Walls, S. M., Dacy, B. S., Levin, J. R., & Robinson, D. H. (2010). A follow-up note on prescriptive statements in nonintervention research studies. *Journal of Educational Psychology, 102*(4), 982–988.

    This study examined journal articles that reported the findings of studies that used nonintervention designs, such as the group comparison design. Many of these studies and subsequent studies that cited them included prescriptive, cause-and-effect statements. The authors explain that nonintervention research can be used to explore cause-and-effect relationships but cannot be used to make statements of the type, "If you do X, Y will result."

Jordanian Prospective and Experienced Chemistry Teachers' Beliefs about Teaching and Learning and Their Potential Role for Educational Reform

Al-Amoush, S. A., Markic, S., Abu-Hola, I., & Eilks, I. (2011). Jordanian prospective and experienced chemistry teachers' beliefs about teaching and learning and their potential role for educational reform. *Science Education International, 22*(3), 185–201.

Teachers traditionally have had a substantial amount of discretion in the content of what they teach and in their instructional style. The research study reported here raises the question of whether teachers' discretionary choices are consistent with what is considered best practice. This study also raises the question of whether teachers' beliefs about classroom instruction become more consistent with best practice as they move from student teaching to experienced-teacher status. The researchers use a group comparison design to contrast the beliefs of student teachers and experienced teachers.

The study involved teachers in Jordan, and it was conducted by a researcher in Jordan in collaboration with two researchers in Germany. International studies of this type are increasingly common. They might be published in an American journal, an international journal, or a foreign journal. If you conduct a literature search on a particular educational problem, you are likely to find articles of all three types in a database such as ERIC (see Chapter 4).

The study reprinted below was conducted with Jordanian teachers, so you will need to decide whether the results are applicable to American teachers or to teachers in another country. If you think the findings are important, you might consider at least a small-scale study to determine whether they are applicable to your situation. Also, you might find that studies on a particular problem of practice have been done in various countries. If you find similar results across countries, you might conclude that the problem of practice is universal and so the findings can be widely generalized. In fact, the literature review in the journal article that we present below cites a substantial body of previous research conducted in various countries. This body of research suggests that the discrepancy between teachers' beliefs about classroom instruction and what is considered best practice is a universal concern.

The article is reprinted in its entirety, just as it appeared when originally published.

Jordanian Prospective and Experienced Chemistry Teachers' Beliefs about Teaching and Learning and Their Potential Role for Educational Reform

SIHAM A. AL-AMOUSH,
SILVIJA MARKIC
University of Bremen, Germany

IMFADI ABU-HOLA
University of Jordan, Jordan

INGO EILKS
University of Bremen, Germany

ABSTRACT   This paper presents an exploratory study of Jordanian chemistry student teachers' and experienced teachers' beliefs about teaching and learning. Different instruments were used, focusing on different aspects of teaching and learning. The first instrument is based on teachers' and students' drawings of teaching situations. It includes open questions evaluated by a grid describing teachers' Beliefs about Classroom Organization, Beliefs about Teaching Objectives and Epistemological Beliefs. A second evaluation using the same data source is made by applying the 'Draw-A-Science-Teacher-Teaching'-Checklist (DASTT-C), which shows the teacher-or student-centeredness of teachers' beliefs concerning science teaching. A third approach is composed of a Likert-questionnaire examining teachers' beliefs about what constitutes good education in general. The results indicate that both above-mentioned groups hold quite traditional beliefs, which are teacher- and purely content-centered when it comes to chemistry teaching practices. Student teachers profess ideas which are even more pronouncedly traditional. Nevertheless, the general educational beliefs are more open and promising. Implications for chemistry teacher education and educational reform in Jordan are also addressed.

Keywords: Chemistry education, chemistry teacher education, (student) teachers' beliefs, educational reform

Introduction

Teachers' beliefs have recently gained increased attention in both general educational research (Munby, Russell & Martin, 2001) and in the field of science education (Abell, 2007; De Jong, 2007). The latter field is expanding, with studies focusing on both in-service teachers (Smith, 1993; Woolley, Benjamin, & Woolley, 2004) and student teachers (Abed, 2009; Bryan, 2003; Foss & Kleinsasser, 1996; Haritos, 2004; Richardson, 2003). Research on (student) teachers' beliefs has become an active field, since such studies provide promising approaches to better understanding teachers' learning processes and behavior in the classroom (Fenstermacher & Soltis, 1986; Nespor, 1987). Evidence of student teachers' beliefs is also valuable for teacher trainers, who can map out currently-held ideas about teaching and learning, then see how they can be applied and/or changed (Nisbett, 1980). Such knowledge also shows potential for improving university teacher education programs in order to better facilitate candidates' personal learning and professional development (Bryan, 2003). Finally, research on beliefs is seen as useful for curriculum innovators and planners, who can more effectively implement curriculum changes by taking existing teachers' beliefs into consideration (De Jong, Veal & Van Driel, 2002; Eilks, Markic, Valanides, Pilot & Ralle, 2006; Justi & Van Driel, 2006).

In Pajares' (1992) research review, the author argued that teachers' beliefs are a long-neglected field of educational research. He stated that they should, however, be developed into a proper construct for investigating and improving teacher education and classroom practices. One example of the link between teachers' beliefs and changes within teacher training programs was presented in the study published by Haritos (2004). Haritos examined the relationship between teacher concerns and personal beliefs about one's own role in teaching. The results revealed three areas of concern which a teacher must overcome: concern about pupils, issues dealing with the teaching situation itself, and survival concerns. Such research offers focal points for training measures (pre- and in-service), including making teacher educators explicitly aware of these areas so they can address them during teacher training.

Becoming aware of one's own beliefs about teaching and learning is an important first step. Self-reflection on one's actions in the classroom is very necessary, because personal beliefs act as filters for interpreting new experiences, selecting new information, and choosing innovative instructional approaches (e.g. Goodman, 1988; Nespor, 1987; Pajares, 1992; Putnam & Borko, 1997).

Bandura (1997) defined beliefs as the best indicator of why people make specific decisions throughout their lifetimes and how they will act in a given situation. This is also the case for teachers when it comes to their decisions and actions in the classroom. It is also why paying increased attention to both teachers' beliefs and their effects may potentially enhance educational effectiveness through a better understanding of teachers' conceptual frameworks, beliefs, and belief systems (Brophy, 1988). Tobin, Tippins and Gallard (1994) have also recognized the importance of knowledge about teachers' beliefs with respect to science education. They recommended that further research should not only expose relevant beliefs, but also enrich our understanding of the relationship between beliefs and their impact on educational reform in science education. Their argument is that successful reforms must take teachers' beliefs into account if they aim at overall change in classroom practices (Lumpe, Haney & Czerniak, 2000). Furthermore, Trigwell, Prosser & Taylor. (1994) point out that educational reform is doomed to failure if it limits its emphasis to the development of specific skills without taking teachers' beliefs, intentions and attitudes into account. For instance, many innovations are viewed as impractical by teachers, since these changes are unrelated to familiar routines and also do not fit with teachers' personal beliefs about educational goals (Brown & McIntyre, 1993). Van Driel, Bulte and Verloop (2007) have already emphasized that addressing teachers' beliefs must be the first step when planning and changing teaching practice.

From previous research we know that different factors influence and shape existing teachers' beliefs. These include a teacher's own learning experiences in school, his/her educational background, the quality of pre-service experiences in the classroom, opportunities for self-reflection (or the lack thereof) during pre-service training, and the influence of discipline-related and domain-specific subject matter training (Bean & Zulich, 1992; Cherland, 1989; Goodman, 1988; Markic & Eilks, 2008). The larger context of national policies and the context of cultural norms and values also play an important role in affecting teachers' beliefs (Isikoglu, Basturk & Karaca, 2009). Markic and Eilks (2008) have demonstrated the influence of educational domain and the level of education on the formation of educational beliefs. In their study of freshman student teachers in Germany, primary school science and secondary biology teacher trainees showed themselves to be very student-centered in their views and approaches. Their colleagues with a comparable educational and cultural background preparing to teach secondary school chemistry and physics proved to be much more teacher-centered, holding extremely content structure-driven beliefs where the learning of facts is the central focus while the facts are detached from their scientific origin and not connected to potential applications in relevant contexts.

Increasing numbers of studies about teachers' beliefs are now being published. Starting from trainees' general educational beliefs, Van Driel et al. (2007) were able to distinguish between two different ideologies which form a continuous dimension visible within various belief studies. These ideologies occur as a common feature repeated in various studies. The first system has been called teacher-centered (Bramald, Hardman, & Leat, 1995) or, alternately, subject-matter oriented (Billig et al., 1988). On the opposite end of the spectrum we find the personal (Shen, 1997), also called student-supported (Samuelowicz & Bain, 1992; Trigwell et.al., 1994) or learner-centered (Bramald et al., 1995) learning. Markic and Eilks (2008) suggest viewing this spectrum as a range between traditional beliefs (transmission-oriented beliefs of learning with a focus on pure subject-matter knowledge) and modern beliefs (beliefs based on constructivistic learning, student-oriented classroom structures, and an orientation on more general educational skills, including Scientific Literacy for all). This dichotomy is in line with other studies, e.g. Thomas, Pederson and Finson (2001). It also parallels discussions about educational reform and differences between traditional practices and the reform movement in science education in general (see Van Driel et al., 2007), including the present situation in Jordan (Qablan, Jaradat, & Al-Momani, 2010) what is the background of this study.

In addition to these two orientations themselves, the relationship linking them together is also of great importance. Do these viewpoints represent the opposite extremes of a continuous scale with intermediate ideologies between them as suggested by Van Driel et al. (2007)? Can individuals hold different beliefs with respect to different subtopics or domains? Do these beliefs always have to be coherent within themselves? Minor, Onwuegbuzie, Witcher, and James (2002) described pre-service teachers' beliefs as representing a seemingly contradictory mix of ideas. In their study, some student teachers supported both transmissive and constructivistic beliefs of teaching simultaneously. Although such beliefs about teaching and learning appear to be contradictory and dichotomous (Chai, Hong, & Teo, 2009), the presence of both beliefs might be understood as a continuum of positions, thus allowing teachers to adapt to a situation depending on both the content and their view of the context (Samuelowicz & Bain, 1992). However, it also has become clear that beliefs can be changed by educational programs, thus moving candidates away from more teacher- and purely content-structured beliefs to more open, student-orientated contexts and methods (Luft, 2009; Markic & Eilks, 2011a).

The timeframe in which pre- and in-service teachers' beliefs are recorded also seems to be of particular relevance. Luft (2009) considered the first year of practical teaching as the most difficult period for a teacher and therefore crucial for more detailed research efforts. This study went on to describe the effect of induction programs on the professional development process of first year teachers in the US. Analysis of the results revealed that teachers participating in science-specific induction programs significantly abandoned their teacher-centered beliefs and practices in favor of more student-supportive ones. Jordan has outlined a similar system for preparing teachers using post-Bachelor's training. Nevertheless, the influence of training in Jordan seems to be more restricted or at the least less clear, as Qablan et al. (2010) described for primary science teachers. Nevertheless, Alqaderee (2009) concluded that various effects are possible. Changes concerning teachers' epistemological beliefs on the learning of scientific concepts were described for a course on science curricula and methodologies. This observation shows that such courses can be both effective and potentially advantageous for improving teachers' epistemological perceptions. But questions about the depth, penetration and sustainability of changes in teachers' beliefs and knowledge base remain open.

In the case of Germany, Markic and Eilks (2011a) compared student teachers' beliefs at different stages of their pre-service teacher training. The German system is based on a bottom-up teacher training style, where courses on education and domain-specific learning accompany a five year university program, including school internships. Three different groups of chemistry student teachers were studied. A substantial change in candidates' beliefs about teaching and learning was indicated as a result of the teacher training program. The data showed that student teachers' beliefs swung dramatically during their university education from very traditional, teacher-centered beliefs in the beginning to more modern, learner-oriented educational beliefs based on constructivistic theories of learning by the end.

Observing the present situation, it is clear that research on science teachers' beliefs is an expanding field. The growing body of research has shed light on many aspects of science teachers' beliefs. Nevertheless, beliefs are context-bound and thus related to the educational and cultural circumstances in which teachers live, the institutions in which they were educated, and the places where they currently work (Alexander, 2001; Woolfolk-Hoy, Davis, & Pape, 2006). In the case of Jordan, evidence concerning secondary chemistry (student) teachers' beliefs about teaching and learning is relatively scarce in the literature. Unfortunately, research in this area remains underdeveloped and is currently lagging behind. Despite this fact, educational innovations are being planned and implemented in Jordan. Currently, the country is going to great efforts to develop and expand its educational system (Jordan Ministry of Education, 2010). Many reforms have already been elaborated upon and tested (early childhood education, school to career measures, etc.). However, teachers' beliefs are not included in the focus of these innovations, whose implementation remains unsatisfactory as recently described in the case of primary school teachers (Qablan et al. 2010). The purpose of the current study was, therefore, to investigate different aspects of (student) teachers' beliefs about secondary chemistry in order to pinpoint any differences between Jordanian in-service and pre-service teachers. The focal points selected were quite general. They dealt primarily with achieving a general overview of chemistry teachers' beliefs about teaching and learning, the aims and objectives of chemistry lessons, and classroom culture and activities.

This study attempts to answer the following questions:

1. What beliefs do Jordanian teacher trainees and in-service teachers hold regarding chemistry teaching and learning, including student- and teacher-centeredness, overall teaching objectives, understanding the learning process, and the nature of good education?
2. What are the similarities and/or differences in beliefs about teaching and learning for these two groups regarding the above-mentioned fields?

Background and Sample

Where in some countries teacher studies are a self-standing program on its own right with integrating content learning, pedagogical seminars and school placements during a the whole university studies, e.g. in Germany, Jordan's teacher education system uses a layered model. The teacher training begins with students completing a Bachelor's degree in the subject to be taught. Students can decide to whether continue science studies after the Bachelor's degree or to move into science teaching. In the later case, the university studies are extended pedagogical workshops during the first active year of teaching after the Bachelor's for getting a full secondary science teacher qualification. Trainers for the pedagogical seminars must possess a Master's degree.

Also some teachers also obtained a Master's level of education before entering science education practice and the accompanying one-year pedagogical seminars (e.g. Qablan et al., 2010). The pedagogical workshops accompanying the initial stage of a teacher's career concentrate on teaching methodology, different types of assessment, performing experiments within the educational context, and other educational issues. These workshops are conducted once a week for five hours. Additionally, a computer workshop focuses on the use of information technology in education. The International Computer Driver's License (ICDL) and Intel for the future are among the things learned (Alhawari, 2008; Jordan Ministry of Education, 2010). Jordan started offering its science teachers manuals for improving their practices and methodology in a 2003 reform project called "Educational Reform for Knowledge Economy" (ERFKE, 2008). Some chemistry teachers also have the chance to continue postgraduate studies in the field of science education, however, this is not an obligatory component.

The sample in this study consists of two groups: Jordanian chemistry student teachers (N = 23) and in-service chemistry teachers (N = 44). A second group (N = 35) of teacher trainees was added to the quantitative part of the study to better support the findings (see description below). The student teachers all attended different government universities with secondary school programs, but had not yet completed their Bachelor's degree. They had not had any courses related to teaching and learning prior to this study. This meant that they had not yet been influenced by the teacher training program normally given to teachers during the first year of their teaching career. The in-service chemistry teachers sample consisted of teachers from various schools in Jordan. All of these teachers possess at least a Bachelor's degree and have completed the workshop-based training unit. Eight of these forty-four teachers had finished a Master's of Education program. Some of the characteristics of both groups are presented in Table 1.

Table 1

Characteristics of the Sample

Characteristic		Student Teachers (N = 23)		Teachers (N = 44)	
		Number	Percentage	Number	Percentage
Gender	Female	13	56	25	57
	Male	10	44	19	43
Age	19–25	11	48	4	9
	26–36	11	48	20	45
	37–47	1	4	17	39
	48–58	0	0	3	7

Table 2

An Overview of the Scales in the Qualitative Part of the Study (Markic & Eilks, 2008)

	Traditional Beliefs		Modern Beliefs
Beliefs About Classroom Organization	Classroom activities are mostly teacher-centered, -directed, -controlled and dominated by the teacher.	↔ −2, −1, 0, 1, 2	Classes are dominated by student activity and students are (at least partially) able to choose and control their activities.
Beliefs About Teaching Objectives	Teaching focuses more-or-less exclusively on content learning. Facts are learned detached from their origin and potential contexts of application.	↔ −2, −1, 0, 1, 2	Learning of competencies, problem solving or thinking in relevant contexts are the main focus of teaching.
Epistemological Beliefs	Learning is passive, top-down and controlled by the dissemination of knowledge.	↔ −2, −1, 0, 1, 2	Learning is a constructivistic, autonomous and self-directed activity.

However, this kind of knowledge is not the same as a list of disconnected facts but organised around core concepts or "big ideas" that guide their thinking about their domains

Methods

Traditional vs. Modern Beliefs on Chemistry Education. The first part of the study is qualitative in nature and is based on a modified version of the "Draw-A-Science-Teacher-Test Checklist" (DASTT-C). The original DASTT-C (Thomas, Pedersen & Finson, 2000; 2001) requests the participant to draw him/herself and learners in a typical classroom situation. The drawing is followed up by two open-ended questions asking about the activities of teacher and students. Markic, Eilks, and Valanides (2008) added another two open-ended questions to this to gain a more detailed overview of the situation. The added questions inquire into the teaching and learning objectives of the situation depicted and the approach chosen towards the drawn situation. An evaluation grid was also developed (Markic et al., 2008) based on Grounded Theory. This grid categorizes a range stretching from traditional beliefs to more modern beliefs in line with current educational theory. Traditional beliefs are characterized by teacher-centered classroom organization, strong orientation on the structure of the subject matter, and transmission-oriented beliefs about teaching and learning. Conversely, modern beliefs are characterized by student-oriented classroom organization, an orientation on problem-solving and scientific literacy objectives, and constructivistic learning theories. The evaluation pattern analyzes participants' beliefs in three qualitative categories: 1) Beliefs About Classroom Organization, 2) Beliefs about Teaching Objectives, and 3) Epistemological Beliefs. Each category was evaluated using a range from −2 to +2 to describe beliefs in the above-mentioned dimensions along an ordinary, but non-linear scale. An overview of the categories is presented in Table 2. A full description of the categories can be found in Markic et al. (2008).

Data was encoded by two independent raters. Inter-rater reliability was calculated by the agreement rate. Following Marques & McCall (2005) there is no commonly accepted threshold for the agreement rate. Anyhow, most papers on qualitative and phenomenological studies suggest rates above 66,7% or 80% for considering the agreement rate as being acceptable. This part of our study uses qualitative data which evaluated by a non-linear scale of potential interpretation. Therefore the discussion of Marques and McCall (2005) might provide a framework for reflecting our agreement rate which we remained continuously remaining above 80%. Thus we consider the agreement as being acceptable. Anyhow, in those cases of disagreement, joint rating was carried out by searching for inter-subjective agreement to get a mostly complete evaluation of the data (Swanborn, 1996).

Beliefs about Teacher- and Student-Centeredness

The second focus of this study applied the original evaluation pattern from the "Draw-A-Science-Teacher-Test Checklist" (DASTT-C) by Thomas et al. (2000; 2001). In DASTT-C, (student) teachers' drawings and the open-ended questions about the activities of teacher and learners (see above) are evaluated using a checklist. The total score depends on the presence or absence of thirteen attributes in three main areas: the teacher, the students, and the environment. The complete checklist can be found in Thomas et al. (2000). The accompanying questions in our case are only used to better understand the drawings. The presence of any of the thirteen attributes within a section is scored with a "1", an absence with "0".

Table 3

Distribution of Traditional vs. Modern Beliefs about Chemistry Education

		Student Teachers (N = 23)		Teachers (N = 44)	
		Frequency	Percent	Frequency	Percent
Beliefs About Classroom Organization	−2	13	62	12	27
	−1	7	33	23	51
	0	0	0	8	18
	1	1	5	2	4
	2	0	0	0	0
	not coded	2	9	0	0
Beliefs About Teaching Objectives	−2	14	67	21	47
	−1	2	9	13	29
	0	0	0	9	20
	1	3	14	2	4
	2	0	0	0	0
	not coded	2	9	0	0
Epistemological Beliefs	−2	14	67	13	29
	−1	6	28	25	56
	0	1	5	5	11
	1	0	0	2	4
	2	0	0	0	0
	not coded	2	9	0	0

Thus, the total score can fall between 0 and 13. Scores of 0-4 indicate student-centered teaching, while values between 7 and 13 represent teacher-centeredness. For scores of 5 or 6 no decision can be made (Thomas et al., 2000). The data was rated by two independent raters according to the checklist; inter-rater reliability was tested by Cohen's Kappa. With Landis and Koch (1977) inter-rater reliability was moderately high with $\kappa = 0.74$ for teachers and $\kappa = 0.76$ for student teachers.

Beliefs about Good Education

A third source of information is provided by a Likert questionnaire on (student) teachers' beliefs about the nature of good education. The questionnaire asks about how teaching practices should be organized (Hermans, Van Braak, & Van Keer, 2008). It consists of eighteen Likert items describing two dimensions: Transmissive Beliefs (TD) and Developmental Beliefs (DB). Transmissive Beliefs cover ideas that education satisfies external goals which can be met using closed, curriculum-oriented outcomes. The extent of knowledge acquisition can be viewed as being achieved through transmission. Developmental Beliefs identifies education as oriented toward individual development within an open curriculum, including to what degree knowledge should be acquired through constructivistic means. The core concept of this dimension is the presence of students as active participants in the education process (Smith, 1997). In our study, we evaluated both dimensions using a six-point Likert scale ranging from 1 (strongly disagree) to 6 (strongly agree). Data was interpreted by calculating mean scores, standard deviations and missing values. Pearson correlations and *t*-tests between the scales and between the two groups were also explored. Cronbach's alpha for both scales (seven developmental items, and nine transmissive items) was between 0.50-0.74 (see Table 4) and thus can be considered acceptable (Hatcher & Stephanski, 1994).

Results and Discussion

Traditional vs. Modern Beliefs in Science Education. The three categories in this part of the study were interpreted along the traditional-modern spectrum on the basis of current educational theory (Markic & Eilks 2008). The results are presented in Table 3 and Figure 1. We can see that the Jordanian chemistry teachers in this

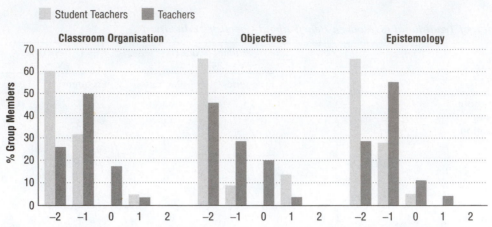

Figure 1 Distribution of traditional vs. modern beliefs about chemistry education

sample hold a wide variety of beliefs concerning teaching and learning. Nevertheless, clear tendencies can also be recognized.

In the category Beliefs about Classroom Organization strong tendencies towards teacher-centered beliefs can be recognized in both groups. Over 90% of the student teachers and almost 80% of experienced teachers described a classroom dominated by the teacher, where student activity plays only a minor role and is completely dominated by the teacher. The same can be said for Beliefs about Teaching Objectives. A dominant majority (about 80%) of student teachers expressed traditional beliefs about the objectives of chemistry lessons. The more-or-less exclusive goal of chemistry lessons in their estimation is the learning of subject-matter content where in the pedagogy the content is detached from its scientific origin and potential student-relevant contexts of application. This is in line with Qablan et al. (2010), whose findings described Jordanian primary school teachers' attitudes towards educational reform. These teachers discussed reforms primarily by referring to developments in more effective methods of pure knowledge transfer. The same can be said for the group of in-service chemistry teachers, by the number are being a bit less extreme but the tendency towards the most strongly traditional beliefs was more pronounced. For Epistemological Beliefs both groups draw situations with chemistry teaching being quite strongly as a transmission of knowledge organized by the teacher (scores "−2" and "−1"). About 70% of the student teachers expressed strong traditional beliefs about teaching (score "−2"). The in-service teachers were not as traditional as the student teachers in this regard. The majority received a score of "−1" in this category, which can be interpreted as being "rather transmission-oriented". No student teacher professed beliefs which could be rated as either modern or quite modern; even among experienced teachers there were only about 5%

(scores "2" and "1") of participants who expressed relatively modern ideas.

Markic and Eilks (2008) suggest that the interdependence of the three categories is important. If a teacher has similar replies in each of the three categories, the combination of codes will appear on or near the diagonal stretching from (−2/−2/−2) to (2/2/2). Placement of (student) teachers' replies within the respective 3D-diagram using this system of evaluation allows us an overall consideration of the data. The closer a given code combination comes to the upper, right, back part of the 3D-diagram, the closer these beliefs are to modern educational theory. Conversely, code combinations appearing in the lower, left, front part of a 3D-diagram represent more traditional beliefs. Figure 2 gives the code combinations for all of the participants. Most Jordanian teachers' code combinations appear close to the 3D diagonal, thus supporting Markic and Eilks' (2008) interpretation. Beliefs about teaching, learning, and teaching objectives are also interdependent upon one another in both samples. Figure 2 reveals that Jordanian student teachers in general hold beliefs which can be considered very traditional. The ideas expressed by experienced, in-service chemistry teachers show more scattering, but also evidence a tendency towards more traditional beliefs. Both groups professed more-or-less strongly teacher-centered, content-structure, and transmission-oriented beliefs when it comes to teaching and learning, with student teachers being pronouncedly stronger in their convictions than the experienced teachers.

Beliefs about Teacher- and Student-Centeredness

Two examples from the sample are given in Figure 3 (see also Markic & Eilks, 2008). Figure 3a represents an example of teacher-centered beliefs, whereas Figure 3b gives a student-centered viewpoint. The teacher in Figure 3a appears in the center of classroom activity. The students

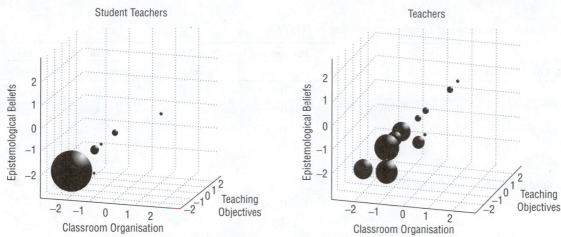

Figure 2 Results of Jordanian educators with respect to traditional vs. modern beliefs about chemistry education

are either responding to the teacher by answering his questions or simply listening to him; the blackboard is the focus of all student attention. This classroom is a traditional one without any indicators of student activity (experimental equipment, etc.). The drawing in Figure 3b shows students in the lab performing an experiment. Typical teacher-centered indicators are not present, for example, the teacher standing in the center of the classroom or media centralizing the students' attention.

Table 4 and Figure 4 present the results of DASTT-C. The data show that Jordanian chemistry teachers and teacher trainees both hold predominantly teacher-centered beliefs. According to the categories defined by Thomas et al. (2001) we see that 87% of student teachers fall into the teacher-centered area (a score of 7–13). The majority of experienced teachers also achieved scores of 7–13, but this group is 70% smaller than that of the student

teachers. Only 4% of student teachers and 16% of the in-service teachers attained a score which showed them to be student-centered.

Beliefs about the Nature of Good Education

Table 5 documents the results of Jordanian teachers' beliefs about the nature of good education. On the transmissive scale, both groups supported the idea that education serves external goals and is outcome oriented within a closed curriculum. Student teachers, however, expressed this beliefs more strongly (mean 4,76) than in-service teachers (mean 4,53). Stronger support by both groups appeared on the more modern dimension of Developmental Beliefs than it did on the transmissive scale. In both groups are these differences statistical significant on a 1% level (2-tailed). This area states that education should be oriented towards broad and

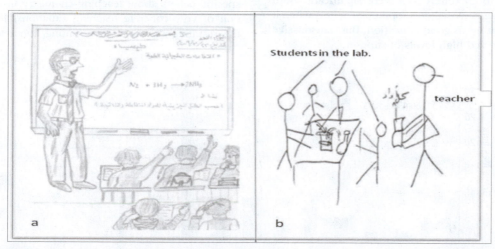

Figure 3 Drawings of two Jordanian teachers of a typical chemistry lesson, (a) traditional/teacher-centered and (b) modern/student-centered

Table 4

The Number and Percentage of Teachers According to DASTT-C

DASTT-C Checklist Score	Student teachers (N = 23)		Teachers (N = 44)	
	Frequency	Percent	Frequency	Percent
0	0	0	0	0
1	0	0	1	2
2	0	0	1	2
3	0	0	2	5
4	1	4	3	7
Subtotal: Student-centered scores (0-4)	1	4	7	16
5	0	0	2	5
6	2	9	4	9
Subtotal: Neither student-centered nor teacher-centered scores (5-6)	2	9	6	14
7	3	13	4	9
8	6	26	13	29
9	5	22	4	9
10	5	22	4	9
11	1	4	6	14
12	0	0	0	0
13	0	0	0	0
Subtotal: .Teacher-centered scores (7-13)	20	87	31	70
Sum	23		44	

individual development, be process oriented within an open curriculum, and that knowledge should be largely acquired through constructivistic means. Expanding the sample of student teachers by another 35 participants confirmed that both differences were significant. Both groups of teachers favored developmental beliefs when it comes to the nature of good education. But transmissive beliefs also received high levels of support.

Interpretation and Conclusions

This study describes the beliefs of Jordanian student teachers and teachers about chemistry teaching and learning. The first two parts of the study investigated domain-specific beliefs about teaching chemistry in the imagination of very concrete teaching situations. Judging from the resulting drawings representing concrete classroom

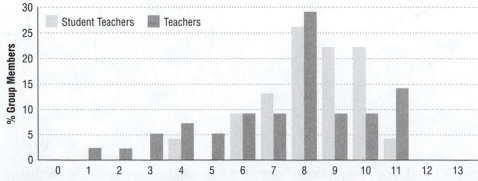

Figure 4 Distribution of student and in-service teachers according to DASTT-C

Table 5

Mean Scores, Standard Deviation and Scale Homogeneity for Beliefs about the Nature of Good Education

		Developmental Beliefs	Transmissive Beliefs
Student teachers[+]	M	5,06	4,76
	SD	0,33	0,28
	α	.50	.74
Teachers	M	4,92	4,53
	SD	0,242	0,15
	α	.56	.74

[+]Differences for the original sample of student teachers (N = 23) were not statistically significant. The results presented here use an expanded sample (N = 58).

practices, we can conclude that both Jordanian in-service teachers and student teachers hold very traditional beliefs when it comes to teaching and learning chemistry. Such traditional beliefs can be characterized by high levels of teacher-centeredness, a transmission-oriented understanding of learning, and a strong focus on the pure learning of subject-matter. On the other hand, the third part of the study reveals that both groups of teachers value more modern beliefs when it comes to teaching and learning in general. It seems that the teachers instinctively understand that learning is far more than rote memorization and that learning is a developmental process. Unfortunately, it seems that such positive beliefs about developmentally-oriented teaching and learning are forgotten as soon as teachers are asked to picture concrete situations in their chemistry classrooms. Most probably the teachers imagination does not last enough, because own experiences in a different style of learning are as well missing as the repertoire of student-activating teaching methods might be.

A second observation is that student teachers' beliefs tend to be much more traditional than those of experienced teachers. This might stem from the fact that Jordanian chemistry teachers attend a workshop-based training program, which encompasses various educational courses. Nevertheless, beliefs and ideas expressed about chemistry teaching practice still remain very traditional. Only in rare instances are they connected with modern, theory-driven characteristics of chemistry education. Reasons for this might include the lack of appropriate in-service training in Jordan, the content level of courses offered, the amount of total training available and an extremely short training duration of only one year. Strongly bottom-up teacher training programs, e.g. those found in Germany, have already shown that substantial and sustainable changes are possible in the long run by combining educational courses with domain-specific education (Markic & Eilks, 2011a). Another important consideration is the fact that nearly all of the student teachers expressed very strong, traditional beliefs. These

beliefs have mainly been constructed due to their previous experience as learners in school—and possibly at the university. This interpretation yields a picture of the prevalent practices in the Jordanian educational system which demands more self-reflection on these practices using the lens of modern educational theory.

However, the structure of chemistry teacher education in Jordan in general also requires further scrutiny. Jordanian teachers are prepared to become a scientist first and a chemistry teacher only secondarily. The special focus on learning about education and the pedagogy of chemistry teaching is limited to only some seminars accompanying the initial year of being a teacher in practice. Changes in such fundamental areas as beliefs about teaching styles and ideas about learning theories is difficult and will not occur overnight (Oliamat, 2009). The inclusion of a limited number of workshops during the initial phase of active teaching may not be enough to lead to substantial, sustainable changes away from transmission-oriented styles of teaching and learning. This is i.e. relevant, because one can assume that most teachers and student teachers have probably experienced exactly such teaching styles themselves in school and at university. Perhaps offering additional courses and expanding the initial teacher training over a longer period of time in the beginning phase of working as a teacher might be of greater potential for provoking the process of long-term, far-ranging changes in prospective teachers' beliefs. But, one can also think of another solution. Maybe a better approach would be to start earlier. From recent studies in Germany (Markic & Eilks, 2011a) we know that educational seminars and school placements during the university training program do have great potential for substantial change in the student teachers' beliefs. Change took place from very traditional towards modern, student-centered and theory driven beliefs. Also the structure of the introductory educational seminars should be reflected. This is not only a question of duration. Evidence from research says that effective in-service teacher training asks for long-term cooperation, external support and structured connectedness towards own experiences and reflection. Using these principles Continuous Professional Development (CPD) of teachers can substantially change their beliefs and knowledge (e.g. Eilks, Markic & Witteck, 2009; Markic & Eilks, 2011b). Obviously, the most potential strategy is to refer all three points of potential action (I) allowing prospective teachers learn about their later profession of being a chemistry teacher from the beginning of their university studies, (II) re-organize the introductory seminars in the initial phase of teaching towards more connectedness with experience and reflection, and (III) establish long-term CPD programmes based e.g. on teacher collaboration, interactive workshops, or action research based innovations (e.g. Mamlok-Naaman & Eilks, 2011).

In any case, the situation described here demands new innovations in teacher training. This falls in line with Oliamat (2009), who recommended a more thorough concentration on the elaboration of teacher training programs to develop both teachers' pedagogical knowledge and teaching practices. Furthermore, Luehmann (2007) found out in her study that there is also a need for creation of a safe place and scaffolding ways for beginning science teachers to try on and develop their identities as reform-minded science teachers. Systems and structures are notoriously hard to change. Perhaps it would be easier and more effective to simply change the content within already existing courses. Teaching workshops should include self-reflection (Luehmann, 2007). The workshops should be optimized to more thoroughly present prospective teachers with concrete student-active methods, instructional tools and illustrating examples for the domain-specific learning environments they later on will work in. But the teachers and student teachers also need tools and competencies to reflect upon teaching objectives in the sense of scientific literacy, or different approaches to constructivistic learning. This is in line with Al-Doulat and Abu Hola (2009), who recommend that science teacher education programs should be developed and improved in Jordan. From our own experience, a promising starting point might be an initial reflection upon one's a priori beliefs and prevalent ideas about teaching and learning. A self-reflection session focussing on the question of teacher- or student-centeredness often helps to plant the seeds of change. As suggested by Markic and Eilks (2008), tools like DASTT-C (or its modified version) can readily and easily applied for this purpose, especially for science education programs in which the initial stage of teacher training is over.

REFERENCES

Abed, O. (2009). Class teacher students' efficacy beliefs regarding science teaching and its relation to their understanding level of scientific concepts. *Jordan Journal of Educational Sciences, 5*, 187–199.

Abell, S. K. (2007). Research on science teacher knowledge. In S. K. Abell & N. G. Lederman (Eds.), *Research on science education* (pp. 1105-1150). Mahwah: Lawrence Erlbaum.

Al-Doulat, A., & Abu-Hola, I. R. (2009). Science teachers' perceptions about Learning. theories and its relation with their teaching practices. *Journal of the Associate of Arab Universities, 52*, 159–211.

Alhawari, A., & Audeh, A. (2008). Psychometric properties for selected forms of International Computer Driving Licence Tests in Jordan, and equating their scores. *Jordan Journal of Educational Sciences, 4*, 297–319.

Alqaderee, S. (2009). The effects of the science curricula and teaching methods course in improving the epistemological views of learning scientific concepts of students in the class teacher program at Al al- Bayt University. *Jordan Journal of Educational Sciences, 5*, 277–291.

Alexander, R. J. (2001). *Culture and pedagogy: International comparisons in primary education.* Oxford: Wiley-Blackwell.

Bean. T.W., & Zulich. J. (1992). A case study of three pre-service teachers' beliefs about content area reading through the window of students-professor dialogue journals. In C. K. Kinzer & D. J. Leu (eds.). *Literacy research, theory, and practice: Views from many perspectives* (*p.* 463–474). The National Reading Conference. Inc.

Billig, M., Condor, S., Edwards, D., Gane, M., Middleton, D., & Rad, E. (1988). *Ideological dilemmas: a social psychology of everyday thinking.* London, Sage.

Bramald, R., Hardman, F., & Leat, D. (1995). Initial teacher trainees and their views of teaching and learning. *Teaching and Teacher Education, 11*, 23–31.

Brophy, J. (1988). Research linking teacher behavior to student achievement: Potential implications for instruction of Chapter 1 students. *Educational Psychologist, 23*, 235–286.

Brown, S., & McIntyre, D. (1993). *Making sense of teaching*: Milton Keynes: Open University.

Bryan, L. (2003). Nestedness of beliefs: Examining a prospective elementary teacher's belief system about science teaching and learning. *Journal of Research in Science Teaching, 40*, 835–868.

Chai, C. S., Hong, H. Y., & Teo, T. (2009). Singaporean and Taiwanese pre-service teachers' beliefs and their attitude towards ICT use: A comparative study. *The Asia-Pacific Education Researcher, 18*, 117.

Cherland, M. R. (1989). The teacher educator and the teacher: When theory and practice conflict. *Journal of Reading, 32*, 409–413.

De Jong, O. (2007). Trends in western science curricula and science education research: A bird's eye view. *Journal of Baltic Science Education, 6*, 15–22.

De Jong O., Veal W. R., & Van Driel J. H. (2002). Exploring chemistry teachers' knowledge base. In J. K. Gilbert, O. de Jong, R. Justi, D. F. Treagust & J. H. Van Driel (Eds.): *Chemical Education: Towards Research-based Practice* (pp. 369–390), Dordrecht: Kluwer.

Eilks I., Ralle B., Markic S., Pilot A., & Valanides N, (2006), *Ways towards research-based science teacher education*. In I. Eilks and B. Ralle (Eds.), *Towards research-based science teacher education* (pp. 179–184). Aachen: Shaker.

ERFKE (2008). *EQUIP2/Jordan program of support for the education reform for the knowledge economy (ERfKE) intiative*. Retrieved February 01, 2011, from www.equip123.net.

Fenstermacher, G. D., & Soltis, J. F. (1986). *Approaches to teaching*. New York: Teachers College Press.

Foss, D., & Kleinsasser, R. (1996). Preservice elementary teachers' views of pedagogical and mathematical content knowledge. *Teaching and Teacher Education, 12*, 429–442.

Goodman J., (1988), Constructing a practical philosophy of teaching: A study of pre-service teachers' professional perspectives, *Teaching and Teacher Education, 4*, 121–137.

Haritos, C. (2004). Understanding teaching through the minds of teacher candidates: a curious blend of realism and idealism. *Teaching and Teacher Education, 20*, 637–654.

Hatcher, L., & Stephanski, E. J. (1994.). *A step-by-step approach to using the SAS1 system for univariate and multivariate statistics*: Cary: SAS Institute.

Hermans, R., Van Braak, J., & Van Keer, H. (2008). Development of the beliefs about primary education scale: Distinguishing a developmental and transmissive dimension. *Teaching and Teacher Education, 24*, 127–139.

Isikoglu, N., Basturk, R., & Karaca, F. (2009). Assessing in-service teachers' instructional beliefs about student-centered education: A Turkish perspective. *Teaching and Teacher Education, 25*, 350–356.

Jordan Ministry of Education (2010). Retrieved, November 20, 2010, from http://www.moe.gov.jo/Projects/ProjectMenuDetails.aspx?MenuID=1&ProiectID=2

Justi R., & Van Driel J. H. (2006). The use of the Interconnected Model of Teacher Professional Growth for understanding the development of science teachers' knowledge on models and modelling. *Teaching & Teacher Education, 22*, 437–450.

Luehmann, A. L. (2007). Identity development as a lens to science teacher preparation. *Science Education, 91*, 822–839.

Luft, J. (2009). Beginning secondary science teachers in different induction programs: The first year of teaching. *International Journal of Science Education, 31*, 2355–2384.

Lumpe, A. T., Haney, J. J., & Czerniak, C. M. (2000). Assessing teachers' beliefs about their science teaching context. *Journal of Research in Science Teaching, 37*, 275–292.

Mamlok-Naaman, R., & Eilks, I. (2011). Action research to promote chemistry teachers' professional development—Cases and experiences from Israel and Germany. *International Journal of Mathematics and Science Education* published online first July 01, 2011.

Markic, S., & Eilks, I. (2008). A case study on German first year chemistry student teachers beliefs about chemistry teaching, and their comparison with student teachers from other science teaching domains. *Chemistry Education Research and Practice, 9*, 25–34.

Markic, S., & Eilks, I. (2011a). Die Veränderung fachbezogener Vorstellungen angehender Chemielehrkräfte über Unterricht während der Ausbildung—eine Cross Level Studie [The change in domain-specific beliefs about teaching and learning of prospective chemistry teachers during their teacher education—a cross level study]. *Chemie konkret, 18*, 14–19.

Markic, S., & Eilks, I. (2011b). Effects of a long-term Participatory Action Research project on science teachers' professional development. *Eurasia Journal of Mathematics, Science and Technology Education* in print.

Markic, S., Eilks, I., & Valanides, N. (2008). Developing a tool to evaluate differences in beliefs about science teaching and learning among freshman science student teachers from different science teaching domains: a case study. *Eurasia Journal of Mathematics, Science and technology Education, 4*, 109–120.

Marques, J. F., & McCall, C. (2005). The application of interrater reliability as a solidification instrument in a phenomenological study. *The Qualitative Report, 10*, 439–462.

Minor, L. C., Onwuegbuzie, A. J., Witcher, A. E., & James, T. L. (2002). Preservice teachers' educational beliefs and their perceptions of characteristics of effective teachers. *The Journal of Educational Research, 96*, 116–127.

Munby, H., Russel, T., & Martin, A.K. (2001). Teachers' knowledge and how it develops. In V. Richardson (Ed.), *Handbook of research on teaching* (pp. 877–904). Washington: AERA.

Nespor, J. (1987). The role of beliefs in the practice of teaching. *Journal of Curriculum Studies, 19*, 317–328.

Nisbett, R. & Ross, L. (1980). *Human Interferences: Strategies and Shortcomings of Social Judgement:* Englewood Cliffs: Prentice-Hall.

Landis, J. R., & Koch, G. G. (1977). The measurement of observer agreement for categorical data. *Biometrics. 33*, 159–174.

Oliamat, M. (2009). Science teachers' perceptions about their pedagogical knowledge and its relation with their teaching practices in the Basic Stage, *http://www.damascusuniversity.edu.sy/faculties/edu/images/stories/news/t/35.doc.*

Pajares M. F., (1992), Teachers' beliefs and educational research: cleaning up a messy construct, *Reviews in Educational Research*, 62, 307–332.

Putnam, R., & Borko, H. (1997). Teacher learning: Implications of new views of cognition. In B. J. Biddle, T. L. Good & 1. F. Goodson (eds.), *International handbook of teachers and teaching* (S. 1223–1296). Dordrecht: Kluwer.

Qablan, A., Juradat, S., & Al-Momani, I. (2010). Elementary science teachers' perceptions of educational reform in relation to science teaching in Jordan. *Jordanian Journal of Educational Sciences*, 6, 161–173.

Richardson, V. (2003). Preservice teachers' beliefs. In J. Raths (ed.), *Teacher beliefs and classroom performance: The impact of teacher education* (pp. 1–22). Greenwich, Connecticut: Information Age Publishing.

Samuelowicz, K., & Bain, J. (1992), Conceptions of teaching held by academic teachers. *Higher Education, 24*, 93–111.

Shen, J. (1997). Structure of the theoretical concept of educational goals: A test of factorial validity. *Journal of Experimental Education, 65*, 342–352.

Smith, K. (1993). Development of the primary teacher questionnaire. *The Journal of Educational Research, 87*, 23–29.

Smith, K. E. (1997). Student teachers' beliefs about developmentally appropriate practice: Pattern, stability, and the influence of locus of control. *Early Childhood Research Quarterly, 12*, 221–243.

Swanborn, P. G. (1996). A common base for quality control criteria in quantitative and qualitative research. *Quality and Quantity, 30*, 19–35.

Thomas, J. A., Pederson, J. E., & Finson, K. (2000). *Validating the draw-a-science-teacher-test Checklist (DASTT-C): From images to beliefs.* Paper presented at the annual meeting of the Association for the Education of Teachers of Science, Akron, US.

Thomas, J. A., Pedersen, J. E., & Finson, K. (2001). Validating the draw-a-science-teacher-test checklist (DASTT-C): exploring mental models and teacher beliefs. *Journal of Science Teacher Education, 12*, 295–310.

Tobin, K., Tippins, D. J., & Gallard, A. J. (1994). Research on instructional strategies for teaching science. In D. L. Gabel (ed.), *Handbook of research on science teaching and learning* (pp. 45–93). New York: Macmillan.

Trigwell, K., Prosser, M., & Taylor, P. (1994). Qualitative differences in approaches to teaching first year university science. *Higher Education, 27*, 75–84.

Van Driel, J., Bulte, A., & Verloop, N. (2007). The relationships between teachers' general beliefs about teaching and learning and their domain specific curricular beliefs. *Learning and Instruction, 17*, 156–171.

Woolfolk Hoy, A., Davis, H. & Pape, S. J. (2006). Teacher knowledge and beliefs. In P. A. Alexander & P. H. Winne (eds.), *Handbook of educational psychology* (pp. 715–737). Mahwah: Lawrence Erlbaum.

Woolley, S. L., Benjamin, W. J. J., & Woolley, A. W. (2004). Construct validity of a self-report measure of teacher beliefs related to constructivist and traditional approaches to teaching and learning. *Educational and Psychological Measurement, 64*, 319.

CHAPTER ELEVEN

Correlational Research

PROBLEMS OF PRACTICE *in this chapter*

- What can be done about the high rate at which teachers leave the profession within their first five years of teaching?
- What can be done to help high school students improve their ability to cope with stress in their lives?
- What should be taught in parent education programs?
- Why does a family's poverty affect how well its children do in school?
- What is the optimal amount of control that parents should exert over their children's behavior?
- How can we make an early identification of students who will struggle in learning to read so that they can receive timely instructional support?
- Can social networking websites such as Twitter enhance the quality of classroom instruction?
- Is students' ability to reflect on their learning processes important to their academic success?

IMPORTANT *Ideas*

1. Correlational research designs and group comparison research designs have the same purpose but involve different types of statistical analysis.
2. Correlational research takes into account all of the values of at least one of the variables that have been measured in a research study.
3. Correlation coefficients and scattergrams provide information about both the direction and degree of relationship between a sample's scores on two or more measures.
4. The direction of relationship between two variables can be positive, negative, nonlinear, or zero.
5. The larger the value of a correlation coefficient, the more accurate we can be in using an individual's score on one measure to predict his score on another measure.
6. To determine the statistical significance of a correlation coefficient, researchers typically test the null hypothesis that the correlation coefficient

between two variables in the entire population represented by the sample is zero.

7. Multivariate correlational techniques show how three or more variables relate to each other, for the purpose of either explanation or prediction.

8. The introduction of a correlational research report should explain the importance of the study, its research questions or hypotheses, the variables of interest, and a review of relevant literature.

9. Correlational research differs from experimental research in that the researchers do not manipulate the independent variable.

10. In correlational research, the researchers should attempt to select a sample that is representative of the population to which they wish to generalize their results.

11. In the discussion section of a report of a correlational study, the researchers should summarize the study's findings, consider flaws in the design and execution of the study, and state implications of the study for subsequent research and improvement of professional practice.

KEY TERMS

artificial dichotomy
bivariate correlational statistics
canonical correlation
continuous variable
correlational research
correlation coefficient
correlation matrix
criterion variable
curvilinear correlation
dependent variable
dichotomous variable
differential analysis
discrete variable
discriminant analysis

effect size
factor analysis
hierarchical linear modeling
    (HLM)
independent variable
linear correlation
line of best fit
logistic regression analysis
moderator variable
multiple regression
multivariate correlation
negative correlation
nesting
nonlinear correlation

path analysis
Pearson product-moment
    correlation coefficient (*r*)
positive correlation
prediction research
predictor variable
r
scattergram
scatter plot
statistical significance
structural equation modeling
tetrachoric correlation
    coefficient
true dichotomy

COMPARISON OF CORRELATIONAL AND GROUP COMPARISON RESEARCH DESIGNS

Chapter 10 is about group comparison research designs. In this chapter you will find that those research designs and the other research designs presented in this chapter have the same purpose—either to explain why things are a certain way or to predict how things will be in the future. Also, both have the same limitation, namely, that they can explore causal relationships but not prove them. Only experimental research

designs, which we discuss in the next chapter, allow for strong conclusions about whether variations in one variable have a direct causal effect on another variable. The reason is that experiments directly manipulate one variable to see if it creates an effect on another variable.

As an illustration, suppose we observe that students with better sleep habits earn better grades in school. It might be that good sleep habits directly affect students' grades, but it also might be that students with better sleep habits have other characteristics, such as good study skills, that actually determine their ability to earn good grades. Only an experiment can determine whether sleep habits actually affect students' grades. In an experiment, we would directly manipulate sleep habits, perhaps by taking a group of students with poor sleep habits, and randomly assign half of them to a program that improves their sleep habits. If students who participate in the program then earn better grades relative to the nonparticipants, we have a much stronger basis for asserting that sleep habits have a direct, causative effect on students' grades.

As we did in Chapter 10, we will refer here to the presumed cause in a causal relationship as the **independent variable**. We will refer to the presumed effect as the **dependent variable**.

In group comparison studies, groups are formed to represent the independent variable, dependent variable, or both. For example, consider the group comparison studies that we presented in the first part of Chapter 10. The first study investigated the relationship between the community in which students lived and their college enrollment and degree completion. The research design was based on a comparison of three groups of students: those who lived in rural communities, those who lived in suburban communities, and those who lived in urban communities.

The second study investigated the relationship between the gender of children who have autism spectrum disorder and their cognitive and behavioral functioning. The research design was based on a comparison of two groups: boys and girls.

The third study investigated the relationship between students' residential mobility and their mathematics achievement and also the relationship between their rate of school attendance and their mathematics achievement. The research design was based on a comparison of four groups: students with a stable residence and an absenteeism rate of less than 5 percent; students with a stable residence and an absenteeism rate of more than 5 percent; students who moved and had an absenteeism rate of less than 5 percent; and students who moved and had an absenteeism rate of more than 5 percent.

If you think about it, you will realize that some of these group comparisons involve only a few of the possible ranges of values for the variable of interest. For example, consider the first study, which involved a comparison of students in different kinds of communities: rural, suburban, and urban. In reality, though, there are differences within each type of community. For example, rural communities vary in size. A **correlational research** design could involve forming a sample of rural schools and using their population size as one of the variables rather than artificially putting all rural students into one category. A similar correlational research design could be used to determine the effect of variations in population size within suburban communities and within urban communities.

As another example, consider the research study on student mobility and attendance rate. Each student's attendance rate was calculated and then sorted into just two categories: absenteeism rate of less than 5 percent and absenteeism rate of greater than 5 percent. In this group comparison design, we are not able to determine whether students with perfect attendance have better mathematics achievement than students with a 1 percent absenteeism rate, whether students with a 1 percent absenteeism rate do better than those with a 2 percent absenteeism rate, and so on through all the different levels of absenteeism in the sample. A correlational research design is capable of considering all of the values of absenteeism and include them in the statistical analysis.

In this chapter, we will use the term **continuous variable** to denote a variable all of whose values have been measured and used by the researchers. We need to note, however, that this term has a more limited meaning in mathematics. In that context, a continuous variable is one that can assume different values between each point. For example, height is a continuous variable because a person can be 65 inches tall or 66 inches tall, but can also be 65.1 inches tall, 65.13 inches tall, and so forth. In contrast, **discrete variables** have fixed values. For example, a family can have 2 children or 3 children, but not 2.4 children. For the sake of simplicity, we refer to the variables used in correlational research design as continuous, although some of them might in fact yield discrete values.

EXAMPLES OF CORRELATIONAL RESEARCH

The following studies illustrate the relevance of correlational research to problems of practice. In each study, we identify which variables are independent and which are dependent.

Factors Associated with Teachers' Job Satisfaction

Skaalvik, E. M, & Skaalvik, S. (2011). Teacher job satisfaction and motivation to leave the teaching profession: Relations with school context, feeling of belonging, and emotional exhaustion. *Teaching and Teacher Education, 27*(6), 1029–1038.

The researchers cite previous research findings that 25 percent of teachers in the United States leave the teaching profession before their third year of teaching, and almost 40 percent leave within five years. Similar statistics have been observed in Norway, where they conducted their study of teachers in grades 1–10. They did not study teacher attrition directly, but rather two factors that are related to assumed antecedents of teacher attrition—teacher job satisfaction and motivation to leave the profession.

The researchers found that teachers were less satisfied with their jobs and were motivated to leave the profession (the dependent variables) under the following antecedent conditions (the independent variables): their values were inconsistent with those of the school; they felt a lack of support from their supervisors, fellow teachers, and their students' parents; they experienced time pressure; and they had disruptive students in their classroom.

The researchers state that their findings have implications for school administrators if they wish to retain teachers in the teaching profession: "It seems important to create a supportive school environment, to clarify and develop mutual goals and values, to reduce time pressure on teachers, and to establish school-based directions for student behavior" (p. 1037).

Factors Associated with High School Students' Grades, Feelings about School, and Satisfaction with Their Life

MacCann, C., Lipnevich, A. A., Burrus, J., & Roberts, R. D. (2012). The best years of our lives? Coping with stress predicts school grades, life satisfaction, and feelings about high school. *Learning and Individual Differences, 22*(2), 235–241.

The researchers wished to study how students' ability to cope with stress affects their grades, feelings about participating in school life (after-school activities, homework, work in class, and tests), and life satisfaction (e.g., whether they feel that their life is going well and whether they are getting what they want from life). Drawing on previous research findings, they distinguished between three types of coping with school-related stressors: (1) problem-based

coping, which involves trying to resolve whatever is causing the stress; (2) emotion-based coping, which involves efforts to handle one's emotional response to stressors; and (3) avoidant coping, which involves efforts to avoid the stressor. These coping processes are the independent variables, because presumably they occur prior in time to students' grades and affect students' grades, feelings about participating in school life, and life satisfaction.

The researchers measured these variables in a representative sample of American high schools. They found that students who relied on problem-based coping had better school grades, whereas students who relied on emotion-based coping and avoidance-based coping had worse school grades. Students who relied on problem-based coping also had greater life satisfaction and more positive feelings about school. Students who relied on emotion-based coping had less life satisfaction and more negative feelings about school. Students who relied on avoidant coping had both more positive and more negative feelings about school.

One implication of this study for improving educational practice is that educators should consider developing and implementing programs that help students improve the way they cope with stressors in their school life and life outside of school.

Factors Associated with Parental Competence and Children's Emotional and Behavioral Problems

Winter, L., Morawska, A., & Sanders, M. (2012). The Knowledge of Effective Parenting Scale (KEPS): A tool for public health approaches to universal parenting programs. *Journal of Primary Prevention, 33*(2–3), 85–97.

Parent education programs are widely advocated, but it is not clear what knowledge should be taught in these programs. For example, the Knowledge of Infant Development Inventory (KIDI) assesses knowledge about parenting practices, developmental processes, health and safety guidelines, and norms and milestones in child development. In contrast, the Knowledge of Effective Parenting Scale (KEPS) assesses knowledge about how to promote healthy child development (e.g., how to encourage desirable behavior), principles of effective parenting (e.g., ensuring a safe and engaging environment), use of assertive discipline, and causes of behavior problems.

The researchers conducted a study of Australian parents of children between the ages of 2 and 3 to determine which type of knowledge (as measured by the KIDI and KEPS) was most closely associated with paper-and-pencil measures of emotional and behavioral problems in the parents' children; dysfunctional discipline styles (laxness, authoritarian discipline, and hostility); parenting style (responsive, coercive, and psychologically controlling); parental nurturance; parental self-efficacy in dealing with difficult child behavior; and parental depression and anxiety. The researchers also assessed parenting competence by in-home observations. In this study, knowledge is the independent variable, because it is presumed to have an effect on the variables relating to parenting styles, presence of problems in parents' children, parents' mental health, and parenting competence. Because these variables are presumed to be influenced by parental knowledge, they are the dependent variables.

The researchers found that parents' scores on the KEPS were significantly correlated with the majority of the dependent variables—dysfunctional parenting, children's emotional and behavioral problems, parental anxiety, and parenting competence. Parents' scores on the KIDI were not significantly correlated with any of the dependent variables. The implication for educational practice is that parent education programs should focus more on the types of knowledge emphasized on the KEPS measure (effective parenting strategies) than on the knowledge emphasized on the KIDI measure (child development processes, norms, and milestones). These programs could be offered through community outreach or as a class in high school or college.

CORRELATION BETWEEN TWO VARIABLES

Correlational research is based on a particular type of statistical analysis that yields what are known as correlation coefficients. A **correlation coefficient** is a mathematical expression that provides information about the direction and magnitude of the relationship between a sample's scores on measures of two or more variables. Correlation coefficients can range in value from -1.00 to $+1.00$.

Statistics courses and textbooks explain the mathematic logic, equations, and calculations for correlation coefficients. Our goal here is different. We seek to help you develop an intuitive understanding of correlation coefficients and correlational research designs by providing simple examples without formal mathematical equations. If you have correlational data that can be entered into an Excel spreadsheet, you can compute correlation coefficients and other types of correlational outputs (scatter plots and regression equations) using the Data Analysis option under Excel's Tool drop-down menu. Otherwise, you can use statistical software such as SPSS and SAS.

The Advantages of Continuous Variables

The principal advantage of correlational research is that it provides more information about the sample's scores (or values) on the measured variable than is typically possible with group comparison research. For example, suppose we want to know whether there is a relationship between family poverty and school persistence. Our concern is whether individuals whose families are living in poverty are more likely to give up on school and remain unemployed or settle into low-wage jobs, thereby perpetuating the poverty cycle.

The National Center for Education Statistics has collected data that allow us to test part of the causal relationship that concerns us, namely, the relationship between poverty and school completion. The data are shown in Table 11.1. The first column lists states; the second column lists the percentage of individuals in each state who were below the government's defined poverty level between 2002 and 2004; and the third column lists the percentage of individuals aged 18 years and older in that state who had completed high school in 2000.

The bottom of Table 11.1 (below the state of Wyoming) shows that the mean poverty percentage for the 50 states plus the District of Columbia is 12.4. We decided to group the states into two categories: (1) high poverty if the percentage is 12 or higher, and (2) low poverty if the percentage is 11 or lower. We find that that the average percentage of individuals who have graduated from high school in low-poverty states is 85 percent. In high-poverty states, the average is 79 percent.

This result supports our theory that poverty affects school persistence. However, it leaves some questions unanswered. For example, we might

TABLE 11.1 • State Comparison of Percentage of Poverty-Level Residents and Percentage of High School Completers

States and District of Columbia	Percentage below Poverty Level	Percentage High School Completion or Higher	States and District of Columbia	Percentage below Poverty Level	Percentage High School Completion or Higher
Alabama	16	75	Montana	15	87
Alaska	9	88	Nebraska	10	87
Arizona	14	81	Nevada	11	81
Arkansas	16	75	New Hampshire	7	87
California	14	77	New Jersey	9	82
Colorado	9	87	New Mexico	18	79
Connecticut	8	84	New York	15	79
Delaware	9	83	North Carolina	12	78
District of Columbia	20	78	North Dakota	12	84
Florida	13	80	Ohio	11	83
Georgia	13	79	Oklahoma	15	81
Hawaii	11	85	Oregon	12	85
Idaho	12	85	Pennsylvania	11	82
Illinois	11	81	Rhode Island	12	78
Indiana	10	82	South Carolina	14	76
Iowa	9	86	South Dakota	13	85
Kansas	10	86	Tennessee	14	76
Kentucky	16	74	Texas	15	76
Louisiana	20	75	Utah	9	88
Maine	11	85	Vermont	9	86
Maryland	9	84	Virginia	10	82
Massachusetts	9	85	Washington	11	87
Michigan	11	83	West Virginia	18	75
Minnesota	8	88	Wisconsin	9	85
Mississippi	20	73	Wyoming	11	88
Missouri	12	81	Mean for all states and District of Columbia	12.4	80.4

Source: Based on http://nces.ed.gov/programs/digest/d05/tables/dt05_011.asp; http://nces.ed.gov/programs/digest/d06/tables/dt06_020.asp

wonder whether poverty affects school persistence only if it reaches a certain level. Examining Table 11.1, we see that four states (Louisiana, Mississippi, New Mexico, and West Virginia) and the District of Columbia have very high poverty rates (18 percent or more). Perhaps poverty exerts an influence on school persistence within a state only when it is at this high a level. At lower levels, perhaps the effect of poverty is diminished or nonexistent.

Because we looked only at two levels of poverty (low and high) and ignored differences within levels, we cannot test these possibilities. Suppose, however, that we consider poverty as a continuous variable and use statistics that are appropriate for such variables. Then we can examine the effect of poverty on school persistence across all levels of poverty that exist in the 50 states and the District of Columbia. In the following section, you will see how a particular type of visual display, called a scattergram, facilitates this type of examination.

Using Scattergrams to Represent Correlation

A **scattergram** is a graph of the relationship between two variables, such that the scores of individuals on one variable are plotted on the *x* (horizontal) axis of the graph and the scores of the same individuals on another variable are plotted on the *y* (vertical) axis. A scattergram is sometimes called a **scatter plot**.

Note that in the previous paragraph, we used the term *relationship* in defining a scattergram. Instead, we could substitute the word *co-relationship* or, more simply, *correlation*. Hereafter, we will use the word *correlation* because that is the term used by statisticians and researchers.

Scattergrams are useful because they provide a simple, clear picture of the correlation between a group's scores on two variables. Figure 11.1 shows a scattergram of the relationship between two variables: (1) the percentage of individuals below the poverty level in each state and (2) the percentage of individuals who earned a high school diploma or higher degree in each state.

You can see that the data in Figure 11.1 for each state and the District of Columbia are represented in the scattergram by a single point. For example, the leftmost point in Figure 11.1 is New Hampshire. This state has the lowest poverty level (7 percent), so its point is at the lowest end of the *x* (horizontal) axis of the scattergram; it has nearly the highest graduation rate (87 percent), so its point is also at the top end of the *y* (vertical) axis.

Negative Correlational Patterns in Scattergrams

Inspection of the scattergram in Figure 11.1 reveals a *negative* correlation between poverty level and school graduation rate. In other words, as the poverty level increases (going from left to right on the *x* axis), the graduation rate decreases (going from top to bottom on the *y* axis). There is no leveling off of the effect of poverty across the continuum of the 50 states and the District of Columbia. With each increase in the poverty level, there is, with a few exceptions, a decrease in the school graduation rate.

This example illustrates the definition of **negative correlation** as any situation in which higher scores on a measure of one variable are linked to lower scores on a measure of the other variable.

Positive Correlational Patterns in Scattergrams

As you might imagine, a **positive correlation** occurs when higher scores on a measure of one variable are associated with higher scores on a measure of the other variable. For example, if there had been a positive correlation between poverty level and school graduation rate, higher levels of poverty would be accompanied by higher school graduation rates.

If you examine Figure 11.1, you see that the data points slope down from the left side to the right side of the scattergram. That is the hallmark of a negative correlation. If the data points slope up from the left to the right side of a scattergram, that indicates a positive correlation.

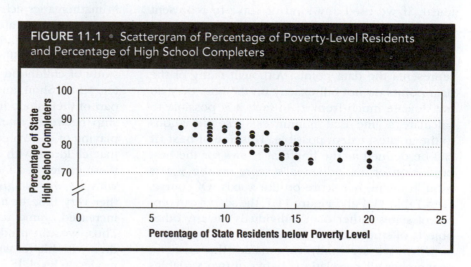

FIGURE 11.1 • Scattergram of Percentage of Poverty-Level Residents and Percentage of High School Completers

Positive correlations are often found in educational research. For example, in the study of high school students' ability to cope with stress described earlier in the chapter, the researchers found that increases in students' scores on a measure of problem-based coping were accompanied by increases in scores on school grades and measures of life satisfaction and positive feelings about school.

Linear and Nonlinear Correlational Patterns in Scattergrams

Most correlational statistics are based on the assumption that if two variables are correlated with each other, the correlation is linear in nature. If the **linear correlation** is perfect and positive in a sample of individuals having scores on two variables, each increase in the score on one variable will be accompanied by an increase in the score of the other variable. Conversely, if the linear correlation is perfect and negative, each increase in the score on one variable will be accompanied by a decrease in the score of the other variable.

For example, consider the scattergram in Figure 11.1. Visualize a line that runs through all of the data points. One end of the line touches the leftmost data point, which represents New Hampshire, the state with the lowest poverty level (7%) and one of the highest school completion rates (87%). The line gradually slopes down to touch the three states with the highest poverty level (20%) and that are among the three highest poverty levels.

You will see that most of the data points cluster around this straight line. For this reason, we say that the correlation between the two variables is linear. If we used any kind of curve to represent the relationship, it would not show the correlation nearly as well.

In this example, we estimated the line that best represents the data points. Although many of the data points do not fall exactly on the line, they do not deviate much from it. In fact, it is possible to calculate a line that minimizes these deviations to the greatest extent possible. This **line of best fit** can be defined as the line that allows for the best prediction of an individual's score on the y axis from knowing her score on the x axis. Of course, as in Table 11.1 and Figure 11.1, the scores can represent states rather than individuals (or any other objects of study).

Now we are ready to consider the question of whether all correlations between two variables are best represented by a straight line. In fact, some relationships between variables are characterized by a **nonlinear correlation**, meaning that the variables are correlated with each other, but not in a linear manner. For example, consider physical strength and chronological age. As individuals grow from infancy to adulthood, most will get progressively stronger. As they continue to age, however, their strength will decline. In other words, the correlation between age and strength is positive up to a point, and after that point, the correlation is negative. This particular type of relationship between variables is called **curvilinear correlation**, because the line of best fit forms a curve, such that low values of variable A are associated with low values of variable B, medium values of variable A are associated with high values of variable B, and high values of variable A are associated with low values of variable B.

Nonlinear relationships between variables have been found in some research studies. For example, Casey Knifsend and Sandra Graham (2012) found a curvilinear relationship between high school students' grade point average and their participation in four types of extracurricular activities (academic/leadership groups, art activities, clubs, sports). Students who had a moderate amount of extracurricular activity (i.e., they participated in two of the types) earned a higher grade point average than students who had a higher or lower amount of extracurricular activity. In another study, Jacob Werblow and Luke Duesbery (2009) found that students in very small high schools (fewer than 674 students) and very large high schools (more than 2,592 students) demonstrated greater growth in mathematics achievement than students in high schools of moderate size.

Nonlinear relationships between variables are not always curvilinear. For example, consider a study of childhood obesity by Elizabeth Vandewater, Misuk Shim, and Allison Caplovitz (2004). One part of their study involved examining the relationship between young children's weight and their playing of electronic games. The researchers found that children with a higher weight status played these games at a moderate level, whereas children with a lower weight status played these games either very little or a lot. In other words, as weight increased, game usage did not increase linearly. Thus, we can predict from the findings that children with higher weight status will play games at a moderate level. If a child has a lower weight status, we cannot make a prediction. The child might play electronic games either a lot or a little.

Absence of a Correlational Pattern in Scattergrams

We now have considered correlations between two variables that are positive, negative, or nonlinear. Suppose, though, that the correlation is zero or nearly so, meaning that scores on one variable are useless in predicting scores on the other variable.

An example of a zero correlation is shown in Figure 11.2. We generated the scattergram by using a set of values between 1 and 9 in a table of random numbers to represent the *x* variable and another set of such values to represent the *y* variable. In effect, we correlated two random sets of numbers with each other. In examining the scattergram, you will observe that the data points do not slope upward or downward or form a nonlinear pattern. If you drew a line representing the midpoint of each set of *y* values for a given *x* value, the line would be horizontal, or nearly so.

The Meaning of Correlation Coefficients for Two Variables

Earlier in the chapter, we stated that correlation coefficients can range between +1.00 and −1.00. Now we will examine this idea more closely by referring to the scattergrams presented above.

In one of our examples, we explored the hypothesis that poverty may correlate with lack of school persistence. The scattergram shown in Figure 11.1 supports the hypothesis, because it shows that higher poverty levels are associated with lower school completion percentages.

Table 11.2 shows the same data as in Table 11.1, but rearranged so that for each poverty level, we see the school completion percentage for all states having that poverty level. Let's examine the range of school completion percentages within each state, shown in the third column of Table 11.2. For example, of the six states having a poverty rate of 12 percent, the lowest school

completion rate is 78 percent, and the highest rate is 85 percent. The range of percentages then is 7 (85 − 78 = 7). Now let's examine the range of school completion rates for all states, irrespective of poverty level. The total range is 14 and extends from 74 to 88 (see bottom of Table 11.2).

If we did not know a state's poverty level, we could say only that its school completion rate is somewhere between 74 and 88. However, by knowing the state's poverty level, we can predict its school completion rate within a much narrower range. The mean of all of the ranges for each poverty level, as shown in Table 11.2, is 5 (the precise mean is 4.92). Thus, for most poverty levels, we can use that information to predict a state's school completion rates typically within 5 percentage points.

The preceding analysis can help us understand what a correlation coefficient means. The question that we wish to answer is: if the total range of school completion rates is 14 and if the range of rates averages 4.92 when we know a state's poverty level, how does 4.92 compare to 14? The answer is that 4.92 is 35 percent of 14 (4.92 ÷ 14 = 0.35).

The final step of the analysis is to consider what 35 percent means. The average range of state school completion rates, when we know a state's poverty level, is 4.92. The total range, when we don't know a state's poverty level, is 14. This means

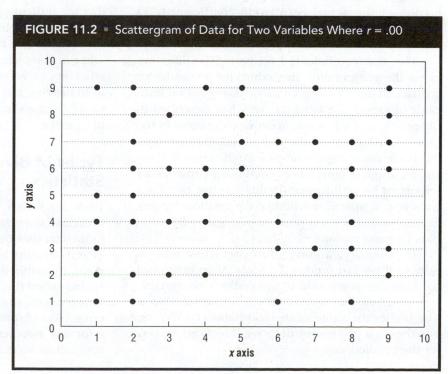

FIGURE 11.2 • Scattergram of Data for Two Variables Where *r* = .00

TABLE 11.2 • School Completion Percentages for All States with Same Poverty Level

State Poverty Levels (Percentage)	Percentage High School Completion or More	Range of School Completion Percentages	Number of Percentage Points in Range
7	87	87–87	0
8	84, 88	84–88	4
9	82, 83, 84, 85, 85, 86, 87, 88, 88	82–88	6
10	82, 82, 86, 87	82–87	5
11	81, 81, 82, 83, 83, 85, 85, 87, 88	81–88	7
12	78, 78, 81, 84, 85, 85	78–85	7
13	79, 80, 85	79–85	6
14	76, 76, 77, 81	76–81	5
15	76, 79, 81, 87	76–87	11
16	74, 75, 75	74–75	1
17			
18	75, 79	75–79	4
19			
20	73, 75, 78	73–78	5
	Total range	74–88	14
	Mean of ranges		4.92

Source: Based on http://nces.ed.gov/programs/digest/d05/tables/dt05_011.asp.

that we have reduced the range by 65 percent $(1 - 0.35 = 0.65)$. This number (.65) is an approximation of the actual correlation coefficient (.77) for the relationship between states' combined poverty level and school completion rate.

The two coefficients (.65 and .77) differ because the computation procedure for a correlation coefficient uses a more mathematically sound indicator of range (the variance, which is described in Chapter 6) and takes into account differences in the score distributions of the two variables. However, the basic meaning of the two coefficients is similar, although a correlation coefficient provides an important bit of information that our use of ranges does not. It specifies whether the relationship between two variables is positive or negative by using plus (+) and minus (−) signs.

In summary, a correlation coefficient tells us how well we can predict the score of an individual (or state, or some other aggregation) on variable y if we know that individual's score on variable x. The higher the value of the correlation coefficient, whether in a positive or negative direction, the better the prediction.

Keep in mind that prediction is closely related to the idea of causal relationships. If we can predict an individual's score on variable y from her score on variable x, it is probably possible to do so because the two variables are related to each other in some causal manner. Thus, correlation coefficients serve us well whether we are interested in improving our predictions or in trying to detect possible causal relationships involved in a problem of practice.

Types of Bivariate Correlational Statistics

Table 11.3 lists the most widely used types of **bivariate correlational statistics**. *Bivariate* refers to the fact that the statistic indicates the magnitude of relationship between two, and only two, variables. Probably the best known of these statistics is r, also called the **Pearson product-moment correlation coefficient**. Because r has a small sampling error (see Chapter 6), researchers often compute r for any two sets of scores, even if they are not continuous scores. The other bivariate correlational

TABLE 11.3 • Bivariate Correlational Techniques for Different Forms of Variables

Technique	Symbol	Variable 1	Variable 2	Remarks
Product-moment correlation	r	Continuous	Continuous	The most stable technique, i.e., smallest standard error
Rank-difference correlation (*rho*)	ρ	Ranks	Ranks	A special form of product-moment correlation, used when the number of cases is under 30
Kendall's *tau*	τ	Ranks	Ranks	Preferable to *rho* for numbers under 10
Biserial correlation	r_{bis}	Artificial dichotomy	Continuous	Values can exceed 1 and have a larger standard error than *r*; commonly used in item analysis
Widespread biserial correlation	r_{wbis}	Widespread artificial dichotomy	Continuous	Used when researchers are interested in individuals at the extremes on the dichotomized variable
Point-biserial correlation	r_{pbis}	True dichotomy	Continuous	Yields a lower correlation than r_{bis}
Tetrachoric correlation	r_t	Artificial dichotomy	Artificial dichotomy	Used when both variables can be split at critical points
Phi coefficient	ϕ	True dichotomy	True dichotomy	Used in calculating inter-item correlations
Contingency coefficient	c	Two or more categories	Two or more categories	Comparable to r_t under certain conditions; closely related to chi-square
Correlation ratio, *eta*	η	Continuous	Continuous	Used to detect nonlinear relationships

Source: Based on Gall, M. D., Gall, J. P. & Borg, W. R. (2007). Educational research: An introduction, 8th Ed. Upper Saddle River, NJ: Pearson. Reprinted by permission of the publisher.

statistics in Table 11.3 are used less frequently because they are more appropriate only under the conditions listed in the "Remarks" column.

You will note in Table 11.3 that some of the correlational statistics refer to dichotomous variables. A **dichotomous variable** can have only two values. If the variable expresses a **true dichotomy**, it has only two possible values in reality. For example, high school graduation is a true dichotomy because it only has two values: graduated and not graduated.

In contrast, an **artificial dichotomy** has only two values because they have been created by researchers or others. For example, Table 11.1 shows that the percentage of poverty across states has many values, ranging from 7 to 20. However, if we wish, we can artificially reduce the range of possibilities to just two values: high-poverty states and low-poverty states.

Table 11.3 shows that we can calculate a **tetrachoric correlation coefficient** to determine whether the two values of poverty level (high and low) are related to scores on another measured variable. Another option is to think of high-poverty states and low-poverty states as two groups and compare them on another measured variable by doing a *t* test of statistical significance, which we explained in Chapter 10. In doing this, we in fact are using a group comparison research design.

This example illustrates the point that group comparison research designs and correlational research designs generate data that can be analyzed by correlational statistics or group comparison statistics, such as the *t* test and analysis of variance. In practice, researchers increasingly are using correlational statistics to analyze data that involve a group comparison design, because these statistics provide a more precise representation of the relationship between variables. This same trend is evident even in experimental research (see Chapter 12), which typically involves comparing two groups (an experimental group and a control group) on one or more outcome variables.

Statistical Significance and Effect Size for Bivariate Correlational Statistics

As we explained in Chapter 7, a **test of statistical significance** indicates the likelihood that the statistical results obtained from the research sample are chance deviations from the results (the technical term is parameters) that would have been obtained if the researchers had studied the entire population that the sample represents.

In the case of correlation coefficients, researchers typically test the null hypothesis that the correlation coefficient for the entire population represented by the sample is zero. If the test of statistical significance leads to the rejection of the null hypothesis, researchers conclude, with some level of confidence, that their obtained correlation coefficient reflects a real relationship between the two variables in the population represented by the sample.

In Chapter 8, we explained that **effect sizes** are helpful in determining the practical significance of statistical results. It is possible to convert a correlation coefficient to an effect size. The larger the correlation coefficient, the larger the effect size will be.

CORRELATION INVOLVING MORE THAN TWO VARIABLES

In the preceding sections of this chapter, we focused on the correlation between two variables. We now proceed to consider **multivariate correlation**, which involves a statistical analysis of the relationship between three or more variables.

Research findings for multiple correlation can have significant implications for solving problems of practice. For example, researchers sometimes find that a particular instructional method (variable *A*) improves academic achievement (variable *B*), but not for all students. It might be that it works well for students who have a high level of a certain characteristic (variable *C*), but not for students having a low level of that characteristic. Knowledge about the three variables in combination can help educators decide whether to use the new method and for which students.

Various correlational statistics have been developed for situations such as these. We summarize the more commonly used statistics of this type in Table 11.4 and explain them in the next sections.

TABLE 11.4 • Types of Correlational Statistics Involving More Than Two Variables

Statistic	Purpose
Canonical correlation	To determine the amount of relationship between a set of predictor variables and a set of criterion variables
Differential analysis	To determine whether the amount of relationship between two or more variables is the same for groups having different characteristics
Discriminant analysis	To determine the amount of relationship between a set of predictor variables and a criterion variable whose measurement yields categorical scores
Factor analysis	To determine whether a sample's scores on measures of multiple variables reflect a smaller number of underlying factors
Hierarchical linear regression	To determine whether the amount of relationship between two or more variables is the same at different levels of nesting, for example, individual teachers versus teachers grouped according to the school in which they teach
Logistic regression	To determine the amount of relationship between a set of predictor variables and a criterion variable whose measurement yields dichotomous scores
Multiple linear regression	To determine the amount of relationship between a set of predictor variables and a criterion variable, with the assumption that if there is a relationship, it is linear
Path analysis	To determine whether a set of variables are related to each other in the manner predicted by a theory that hypothesizes causal links between the variables
Structural equation modeling	Has the same purpose as path analysis, but some or all of the variables are measured by two or more tests, scales, or other instruments

Multiple Regression

Earlier in the chapter, we considered the hypothesis that poverty has an influence on school persistence. Using data from the National Center for Education Statistics, we found strong support for the hypothesis. The correlation coefficient between these two variables is .77, but it is not perfect. A perfect correlation coefficient (r) is either $+1.00$ or -1.00.

The fact that poverty is not a perfect predictor of school persistence is illustrated by the scattergram in Figure 11.1. The points for most values on the x axis are tightly clustered, but they are not identical. Thus, if we know a state's poverty level, we can predict its percentage of high school completers, but not perfectly.

This lack of perfect predictability indicates that other factors besides poverty have an influence on school completion. Therefore, researchers need to consider other factors if they wish to improve their ability to predict an outcome such as completion of high school. The technique of multiple regression enables us to determine whether these other factors, combined with the poverty data, improve the prediction of high school completion. Defined more generally, **multiple regression** is a mathematical technique that enables researchers to determine (1) how well the scores for *each* of a set of measured independent variables predict the scores on the measured dependent variable and (2) how well the *combination* of scores for all the measured independent variables predict the scores on the measured variables.

The mathematics used in multiple regression is complex and requires advanced study of statistics. However, we can provide a brief nontechnical explanation here by referring to the data shown in Table 11.2. Look at the school completion rate for states whose poverty level is 9. There are nine such states, and their school completion rates vary between 82 and 88. If we used the median rate (85 percent) to predict the rate for a particular state, our prediction would either be correct (the rate for two of the states is 85 percent) or we would be off by just a few points in either direction.

Suppose, though, that we found that another factor—for example, state investment in dropout prevention programs—is positively correlated with school completion rates. Also suppose that this investment improves the school completion rate for all states, regardless of poverty level. To simplify the explanation, we will classify the state investment as high (1) or low (2) rather than use the actual investment amount in dollars.

In this situation, if we know that the state's poverty level is 9, we can predict that its school completion rate is between 82 and 88 percent, and if we know that the state's investment in dropout prevention programs is high, we might be able to make a more precise prediction, for example, that its school completion rate is between 86 and 88 percent. Similarly, if we know that a state's poverty level is 12 percent, we can predict that its school completion rate is between 78 and 85 percent; and if we also know that its investment in dropout prevention programs is low (0), we might be able to make a more precise prediction, for example, that its completion rate is between 78 and 81 percent.

These examples illustrate the point that multiple independent variables have the potential to improve the precision with which we can predict scores on the dependent variable. Multiple regression is a powerful statistical procedure for determining which combination of independent variables, if any, lead to better predictions than any single independent variable. Also, keep in mind that if an independent variable, or combination of such variables, predicts the dependent variable, a likely reason for this finding is that the independent and dependent variables have a causal relationship with each other.

Discriminant Analysis and Logistic Regression

Multiple regression is used when the scores on the dependent variable are continuous. There are situations, though, when the measure of the dependent variable yields categorical scores. For example, suppose that the scores on the dependent variable consist of three categories indicating whether parents enroll their child in a regular public school, private school, or public charter school.

Now suppose we have identified several independent variables that we think might predict the category in which each child will fall. The appropriate statistical technique for testing these predictions is discriminant analysis. **Discriminant analysis** is a type of multiple regression that enables researchers to determine how well scores on several independent variables predict scores on a dependent variable when those scores are in the form of categories.

Logistic regression analysis also can be used for this purpose, but it is more commonly used when the dependent variable is dichotomous. Examples of dichotomous variables that might be of interest to educators include the following: enrolled in school, not enrolled in school; will be promoted to the next grade, will be held back a grade; has attention deficit disorder, does not have attention deficit disorder.

Canonical Correlation

Canonical correlation is a specialized type of multiple regression used when there are multiple dependent variables that can be viewed as different facets of an underlying factor. For example, suppose that we wish to predict students' attitudes toward school. We might administer separate measures to predict, let's say, their attitude toward their teacher, their program of studies, their homework, and the assessment methods used by the teacher.

One option would be to do separate multiple regression analyses to determine how well the independent variables predict the scores on each attitude measure. However, suppose that bivariate correlational statistics show that scores on each of these attitude measures are correlated with each other. We might conclude, then, that these different attitudes are different manifestations of one attitude, namely a general positive or negative attitude toward school.

In this case, we can do a single canonical correlation analysis whose purpose is to determine whether the independent variables predict a composite score that represents the factor underlying the different attitudes. This factor is similar in meaning to the type of factors identified by factor analysis, which we explain in a subsequent section.

Hierarchical Linear Modeling

Suppose we wish to investigate the relationship between the poverty level of students' families and their scores on state-mandated tests of social studies achievement. Further suppose that we have data on these two variables for a random sample of 25 school districts in the state, all 150 high schools within the selected school districts, and all 4,700 ninth-grade students enrolled in the 400 ninth-grade social studies classes in the selected high schools.

Analyzing this situation, we see that (1) each student in this sample has a particular social studies teacher, (2) each social studies teacher works within a particular school, and (3) each school is located in a particular school district. How then should we analyze the relationship between the students' poverty status and their social studies achievement?

We could simply compute a correlation coefficient for the two variables (poverty level and academic achievement) for all 4,700 students in the sample, ignoring the fact that they have different teachers, go to different schools, and reside in different school districts. Or we could compute the average poverty level and average score for each ninth-grade social studies class. Because there are 400 such classrooms, we would compute 400 correlation coefficients. However, this procedure ignores the fact that the classrooms are located in different schools and different school districts. Or we could compute 150 correlation coefficients (one for each of the 150 schools), but this procedure ignores the fact that the schools are located in different school districts.

Which data analysis is correct? In fact, all of the analyses have merit. We might want to know whether the correlation between students' poverty status and their social studies achievement varies across social studies teachers. If it does, this finding would suggest that some teachers are doing something in their instruction to either mitigate or worsen the effect of students' poverty status on their achievement. Similarly, we might want to know whether the correlation between students' poverty status and social studies achievement varies across schools within a district. If it does, this finding would suggest that certain schools are doing something to either mitigate or worsen the effect of students' poverty status on their achievement.

Researchers conceptualize these complex data sets in terms of **nesting**, which is a situation in which a variable exists at several levels of an organizational structure. They think of students being "nested" in a classroom, meaning that each student is affected by the teacher's behavior and by the other students' behavior. Teachers are "nested" in schools, meaning that they are affected by the behavior of other teachers and staff in the building. Schools are "nested" in districts, meaning that they are affected by the staff of other schools and central offices in the district.

Hierarchical linear modeling (often abbreviated as **HLM**) is a sophisticated statistical technique that enables researchers to determine how the correlation between two variables is affected by different levels of nesting. If no nesting effects are detected, this finding would suggest that the correlation between the variables is robust in the sense that it is not affected by the organizational structure of the learning environment. If a nesting effect is found, it indicates that the correlation between two variables is different across different settings.

Larger data sets that include multiple levels of nesting are becoming more common in education. For this reason, there is increasing use of HLM to analyze correlational data.

Path Analysis and Structural Equation Modeling

Path analysis and **structural equation modeling** are sophisticated multivariate techniques for testing causal links among the different variables that have been measured. For example, suppose that researchers hypothesize that, among teachers, (1) childhood travel experiences lead to (2) tolerance for ambiguity and (3) desire for travel as an adult, and that (2) and (3) make it more likely that a teacher will (4) seek an overseas teaching position and (5) adapt well to the position.

Path analysis and structural equation modeling are methods for testing the validity of the hypothesized causal links involving these five factors. They differ primarily in that structural equation modeling yields more valid and reliable measures of some or all of the factors. Both approaches are similar, though, in that their goal is to help researchers understand causal relationships rather than to maximize prediction of a criterion variable from some combination of independent variables.

Differential Analysis

Used sometimes in prediction research, **differential analysis** is the technique of using moderator variables to form subgroups when examining the relationship between two other variables. For example, suppose that we have reason to believe that self-esteem has more effect on school performance for students of lower socioeconomic status (SES) than for students of higher SES. Socioeconomic status, then, is a third variable that is thought

to mediate the relationship between the first two variables. This third variable is called a **moderator variable** because it is presumed to affect the strength or direction, or both, of the correlation between the other two variables. It is similar in meaning to the interaction effects sometimes found in analysis of variance (see Chapter 10).

Let's suppose that the correlation coefficient for the relationship between self-esteem and school performance is .40 for low-SES students and .25 for high-SES students. These results demonstrate that SES moderates the strength of the relationship between self-esteem and school performance.

Factor Analysis

The multivariate correlational techniques that we described in preceding sections have a similar purpose, namely, to examine the strength of the relationship between one or more independent variables and one or more dependent variables.

Factor analysis also examines the strength of the relationship between multiple variables, but it does not classify them as independent and dependent. Instead, the purpose of **factor analysis** is to determine whether a set of variables reflects a smaller number of underlying factors.

For example, suppose that researchers have developed measures of eight study skills: (1) organizing one's study materials, (2) time management, (3) classroom listening, (4) classroom note-taking, (5) planning for assigned papers, (6) writing assigned papers, (7) preparing for tests, and (8) taking tests. The researchers wonder whether these are related skills, meaning that students who are strong in one skill are likely to be strong in all or some subset of the other skills.

Factor analysis examines the sample's scores on all eight variables and determines whether they cluster into a smaller number of factors based on high correlations among the variables within each cluster. Suppose we hypothesize that the eight study skills reflect three underlying factors: (1) skills that involve writing, (2) skills that involve planning, and (3) skills that involve recall of learned information. Factor analysis would reveal this underlying structure of factors, if indeed it exists. This is useful research knowledge in its own right. Another benefit is that if a substantial number of measures can be reduced to several factors, subsequent statistical analyses can be simplified.

FEATURES OF A CORRELATIONAL RESEARCH REPORT

Table 11.5 presents typical features of a correlational study report. In the following sections, we discuss each feature and illustrate it with a research study about the validity of an oral reading fluency measure in predicting young children's subsequent reading achievement. Also, at the end of the chapter, you will find a journal article that reports a correlational research study on the relationship between students' metacognitive ability (i.e., their ability to monitor their own learning) and their academic achievement.

Introduction

The introductory section of a correlational research report should explain the importance of the study, the research questions to be answered or hypotheses to be tested, and the variables of interest. It also should include a review of relevant literature so that the reader can understand how the study is attempting to build on existing knowledge.

As an example, we consider a prediction research study conducted by Stephen Schilling, Joanne Carlisle, Sarah Scott, and Ji Zeng (2007). **Prediction research** is a type of investigation that involves the use of data collected at one point in time to predict future behavior or events. The researchers start their report by noting that the No Child Left Behind Act mandates that states, districts, schools, and teachers should be held accountable for students' reading achievement. They then state a problem of practice, namely that educators need to have valid measures to identify students who are not making adequate progress in reading so that these students can receive timely instructional support.

Drawing on their review of the literature, the researchers identified a promising measure for this purpose. Called DIBELS (Dynamic Indicators of Basic Early Literacy Skills), this measure assesses oral reading fluency and accuracy. The theory underlying DIBELS is that if students have mastered lower-order

TABLE 11.5 • Typical Sections of a Correlational Research Report

Section	Content
Introduction	Hypotheses, questions, or objectives are stated. A review of relevant literature is reported. The purpose of the study usually is to explicitly or implicitly study the factors that affect a problem of practice or the consequences resulting from a problem of practice.
Research design	If the study is designed to investigate cause-and-effect relationships, at least one variable is designated as the independent variable (i.e., the presumed cause). At least one other variable is designated as the dependent variable (i.e., the presumed effect). If the study focuses on prediction, at least one variable is designated as the predictor variable (also called the independent variable). At least one other variable is designated as the criterion variable (also called the outcome variable or dependent variable). The independent variable must have occurred prior in time to the dependent variable. Typically, at least one of the variables is conceptualized as continuous.
Sampling procedure	The researcher selects a sample of research participants who have the characteristics that are represented by the independent and dependent variables.
Measures	Virtually any kind of measure can be used to collect data on the independent and dependent variables.
Data analysis	Descriptive statistics for the independent and dependent variables are computed. Bivariate correlational statistics are used if the purpose is to determine the relationship between two variables. Multivariate correlational statistics, such as multiple regression, are used if the combined relationship among three or more variables is of interest.
Discussion	The main findings of the study are summarized. Flaws and limitations of the study are considered. Implications of the findings for further research and for professional practice are considered.

reading skills, such as word decoding, they can devote their cognitive resources to mastering higher-order skills involved in reading comprehension.

A major purpose of the study stated by the researchers was "to examine the effectiveness and trustworthiness of DIBELS fluency-based measures as predictors of year-end reading achievement" (Schilling et al., 2007, pp. 430–431). Another purpose was to determine whether certain cutoff scores on DIBELS measures can be used to identify students who will have low scores on subsequent tests of reading achievement if they do not receive special intervention. Oral reading fluency and accuracy are **predictor variables**, which are variables that are measured at one point in time and then correlated with a criterion variable. Reading achievement is a **criterion variable** because it is measured at a subsequent point in time and because it is the outcome that researchers are attempting to predict.

Research Design

As with group comparison research, a correlational design usually is chosen because the researchers cannot manipulate the independent variable. In the prediction study we are using as an example, it would not be ethical for the researchers to withhold instruction in oral reading fluency from some children and offer it to others. Therefore, Schilling and his colleagues examined naturally occurring variations among children in their oral reading fluency and accuracy and determined whether these variations predicted their subsequent reading achievement.

As we explained earlier in the chapter, prediction research often is based on hypothesized causal relationships. Predictor variables (also called independent variables) are the presumed causes, and criterion variables (also called dependent variables) are the presumed effects.

In the prediction study we are examining, the predictor variables were measured by a set of DIBELS tests: (1) letter-naming fluency; (2) phoneme-segmentation fluency, which involves asking students to identify separate phonemes in spoken words; (3) nonsense word fluency, which involves asking students to decode three-letter nonsense words; (4) word usage, which involves giving students a word and asking them to use it in a sentence; (5) and oral reading fluency. The researchers studied children in grades 1 to 3, and different groups of these five tests were administered

depending on the children's grade level. Also, the DIBELS tests were administered at three points in the school year—fall, winter, and spring.

The criterion variables were measured by subtests of the Iowa Test of Basic Skills (ITBS): (1) vocabulary, (2) ability to analyze word structure, (3) ability to understand words and phrases presented orally, (4) grammatical knowledge and spelling, (5) reading comprehension, and (6) total reading ability, which is a composite of students' scores on the six subtests.

Sampling Procedure

In doing correlational studies, researchers should select a sample that is representative of the population to which they wish to generalize their results. Ideally, the sample should be randomly drawn from the defined population.

The sample in the reading study consisted of students in districts or local education agencies in the state of Michigan that received Reading First funds during the 2002–2003 school year. Reading First was a federal program that provided resources to high-poverty, low-achieving schools to help students become successful readers. This sample is appropriate for the purposes of the study because many students in Reading First schools are particularly at risk for reading failure, and therefore it is important to identify these students as soon as possible so they can receive reading interventions that will prevent failure.

A correlational study might include several samples representing different populations. The reading study included samples of children in grade 1, grade 2, and grade 3, which enabled the researchers to determine whether different predictor variables are effective at each grade level. For example, it might be that vocabulary knowledge is a good predictor of reading achievement at the end of grade 1, but not at the end of grade 2.

Measures

As with other quantitative research designs, the independent and dependent variables can be measured by any of the methods described in Chapter 5. These methods include tests, attitude scales, questionnaires, interviews, and direct observation.

The reading study by Schilling et al. relied on the two tests, DIBELS and ITBS, described above. In addition, Schilling and his colleagues collected demographic data about the students' ethnicity and risk category (economic disadvantage, limited English proficiency, disability status). The methods for collecting these data are not described in the journal article.

Results

Schilling and his colleagues conducted various analyses of their data using correlational statistics. One analysis involved correlating students' scores on the DIBELS measure of oral reading fluency (ORF), administered three times during the school year, with their scores on the ITBS subtests and total test, administered near the end of the school year. The ORF measure involves having each student read aloud three passages. The number of words read correctly in one minute on the middle passage constitutes the student's ORF score.

Table 11.6 shows the result of this correlational analysis. We find that ORF scores correlate fairly highly (usually .50 or above) with all of the ITBS subtest scores and total test scores. Correlational statistics on the order of .50 or higher mean that students' ORF scores are good predictors of their

ITBS scores. This finding generalizes across grades 2 and 3.

Each correlation coefficient in Table 11.6 involves two variables, making them bivariate coefficients. The specific type of coefficient (see the list in Table 11.3) is not stated in the report. In all likelihood, though, they are product-moment correlation coefficients because both variables yield continuous scores. Also, product-moment correlation coefficients are so prevalent in research reports that they are rarely identified by name. If researchers use another type of bivariate correlation, they typically label it.

Table 11.6 presents a partial correlation matrix. A complete **correlation matrix** is one that shows the correlation coefficient for all pairs of variables that were measured. The correlation matrix in Table 11.6 is partial because it shows the correlation coefficient for all pairs of ORF variables and ITBS variables, but it does not show the correlation coefficients for each pair of ITBS variables (e.g., the correlation between ITBS Vocabulary and ITBS Word Analysis). This is an acceptable procedure because the correlation between ITBS variables

TABLE 11.6 • Correlation of DIBELS Oral Reading Fluency and Spring ITBS Subjects for Second and Third Grade

ITBS Subtest	DIBELS Oral Reading Fluency		
	Fall	Winter	Spring
Grade 2:			
Vocabulary	.61	.65	.64
Word analysis	.59	.63	.62
Listening	.29	.33	.33
Language	.59	.65	.64
Reading comprehension	.68	.75	.75
Reading total	.69	.75	.75
Grade 3:			
Vocabulary	.57	.58	.56
Word analysis	.63	.68	.63
Listening	.36	.37	.37
Language	.67	.69	.68
Reading comprehension	.63	.65	.63
Reading total	.65	.67	.65

Note: All $p < .001$.
Source: Schilling, S. G., Carlisle, J. F., Scott, S. E., & Zeng, J. (2007). Are fluency measures accurate predictors of reading achievement? *Elementary School Journal, 107*(5), 429–448. Reprinted by permission of the University of Chicago Press.

TABLE 11.7 • Fall DIBELS Subtests Predicting ITBS Reading Total

Fluency Variable	Partial R^2	Model R^2	F Value*
Oral reading fluency	.475	.475	1,949.64
Word usage	.014	.488	57.76
Nonsense word	.005	.493	19.58

Note: First grade n = 2,231 for fall, n = 2,369 for winter. Second grade n = 2,156 for fall.
*All p < .001.
Source: Based on Schilling, S. G., Carlisle, J. F., Scott, S. E., & Zeng, J. (2007). Are fluency measures accurate predictors of reading achievement? *Elementary School Journal, 107*(5), 429–448. Reprinted by permission of the University of Chicago Press.

was not a question of interest in this study. Also, the matrix does not show the correlations between the students' scores for the three administrations of the ORF measure.

The researchers used multiple regression to determine whether students' scores on a combination of DIBELS measures predicts their ITBS scores better than any one of them alone. One of these analyses is shown in Table 11.7. We see that, for second-graders, ORF scores in the fall are the best predictors of their ITBS reading scores in the winter (R^2 = .475). R^2 is simply the square of the correlation coefficient r. It is used to represent the results of a multiple regression analysis because it has desirable mathematical properties.

Looking at Table 11.7, we see that students' word usage scores improve the prediction of their ITBS scores. Combined with the ORF scores, R^2 increases to .488. Adding scores on one more measure (nonsense word fluency) increases the R^2 to .493. Thus, we find that ORF scores are a good predictor of students' ITBS scores, but a combination

of scores on several DIBELS measures (see the column labeled "Model R^2") improves the prediction, albeit slightly.

Schilling and his colleagues did additional analyses to demonstrate more concretely how the best predictor measure, ORF, can help teachers identify students early in the year who are at risk of reading failure in the spring. One of these analyses, for second-graders, is shown in Table 11.8. ORF scores are divided into three categories. For example, students who accurately read 26 words or fewer per minute were classified as at risk; students who read accurately at faster rates were classified as some risk or low risk.

Now suppose the second-grade data shown in Table 11.8 had been collected in one school year and we wished to apply it to the following school year. Also assume that the same instructional conditions and student population remained constant across the two years. What would be our best prediction of whether a particular student would experience reading failure, which we will define as reading

TABLE 11.8 • Prediction of ITBS Scores of Second-Graders Above and Below the 25th Percentile from ORF Fall Status

	Fall DIBELS Oral Reading Fluency			
ITBS Reading Total	At Risk (< 26 wpm)	Some Risk (26–43 wpm)	Low Risk (> 43 wpm)	Total ITBS
Number of students below 25th percentile	692	177	37	906
Number of students at or above 25th percentile	224	430	599	1,253
Total number of students	916	607	636	2,159

Source: Based on Schilling, S. G., Carlisle, J. F., Scott, S. E., & Zeng, J. (2007). Are fluency measures accurate predictors of reading achievement? *Elementary School Journal, 107*(5), 429–448. Reprinted by permission of the University of Chicago Press.

below the 25th percentile on the ITBS, or have at least some reading success, which we will define as reading at or above the 25th percentile on the ITBS?

Without any predictive information, our best forecast is that all 2,159 students in the sample will be reading successes. This is because 1,253 students were reading successes. We would be correct for 58 percent of the students (1,253 ÷ 2,159 = 58%). If we predicted instead that all students would be reading failures, we would be correct only for 42 percent of the students (906 ÷ 2,159 = 42%).

Now let's use students' ORF scores in the fall to predict their reading success or failure in the spring. Suppose we know that a student was at risk based on her ORF score. If we predict that the student will be a reading failure, we would be correct for 75 percent of the at-risk students (692 ÷ 916 = 75%).

Suppose we know that a student was at some risk based on his ORF score. If we predict that the student will be a reading success, we would be correct for 70 percent of students at some risk (430 ÷ 607 = 70%). Finally, suppose we know that a student was low risk based on the ORF score. If we predict that the student will be a reading success, we would be correct for 94 percent of low-risk students (599 ÷ 636 = 94%).

This example illustrates the value of correlational research for the purpose of predicting reading failure. The empirical findings reveal that the use of ORF results in better predictions (75%, 70%, and 94%) than if we had no predictive information at all (42%). If resources for intensive reading instruction are limited, educators might be better advised to focus on students classified by their ORF score as at risk than to distribute the resources equally—and consequently, less intensively—to all students.

Discussion: Implications for Practice

The discussion section of a correlational research report typically includes a summary of the main findings and analysis of limitations and flaws in the design and execution of the study. For example, Schilling and his colleagues (2007) made the following observation:

> In interpreting these results, the reader should also keep in mind that during the year of this study teachers were encouraged to use DIBELS results to make decisions about reading instruction. (p. 442)

It might be, then, that some students who would have been classified by ORF as at risk or as reading failures at the end of the school year in actuality became reading successes as a result of teachers' interventions. If this were true, it would have the effect of underestimating the predictive validity of ORF. Without teacher intervention, these students would have increased the number of reading failures, thereby increasing the power of low ORF scores to predict low ITBS scores.

The discussion section of a correlational research report sometimes includes comments about implications of the study's findings for practice. For example, in the discussion section of their report, Schilling and his colleagues recommend that teachers use the at-risk category of ORF scores to identify students who are likely to be below the 25th percentile on ITBS at the end of the school year. The ORF assessment is relatively simple to administer and score, but it yields valuable information that can help educators pay special attention to students who do not respond well to regular classroom instruction and therefore end the year as poor readers.

EVALUATING A CORRELATIONAL RESEARCH STUDY

The questions stated in Appendix 3 are relevant to evaluating a correlational research study. The following additional criteria, stated in question-and-answer format, are useful for evaluating the quality of correlational research studies.

■ Did the researchers specify a cause-and-effect model that links their variables?

A correlational research design is used to search for causal relationships, whether for the purpose of explanation or of prediction. Therefore, make sure the researchers clearly specified which variables are the presumed causes and which variables are the presumed effects. Also, examine whether the researchers provided a rationale that explains why one variable is hypothesized to have an effect on another variable.

■ Did the researchers express appropriate tentativeness in making causal inferences from their results?

Correlational research studies can explore causal relationships, but they cannot demonstrate definitively that variable *A* has an effect on variable *B*. Check the report for statements indicating that the researchers avoided drawing strong conclusions of this type or claims that if educators manipulate variable *A* (e.g., implement a new procedure), changes in variable *B* (e.g., improved student learning) will occur.

An example of
How Correlational Research Can Help in Solving Problems of Practice

The following is a problem of practice involving the use of computers to enhance classroom instruction.

Twitter is an online social networking service that individuals can use to send and read "tweets," which are text-based messages of up to 140 characters. An education professor, Christine Greenhow, has been experimenting with the use of Twitter in her college classes. In an article about her work (United Press International, 2012), she reports that, "College students who tweet on the social network as part of their class instruction are more engaged with the course content and with the teacher and other students and achieve higher grades." She also states, "The students get more engaged because they feel it is connected to something real, that it's not just learning for the sake of learning. . . . It feels authentic to them."

UPI.com (2012, October 17). Twitter said to improve student learning. Retrieved from http://www.upi.com/Science_News/Technology/2012/Twitter-said-to-improve-student-learning/UPI-91031350502916/

Greenhow's use of Twitter is promising, but we need to ask whether Twitter lives up to the claim that it improves learning. One research question we can pose is whether students who make more use of Twitter (i.e., generate more tweets) in a course earn better grades and find the course more relevant than students who make less use of Twitter. Another question is why some students are

more motivated to use Twitter in a course than other types of students. Correlational research can help to answer these questions.

Tweets are publicly available, at least within a course, so we can count the number of tweets that each student generated in the course. It is a simple matter, then, to correlate students' frequency of tweets with their course grades and possibly also with their grades on individual assignments within the course. In this example, tweet frequency would be the independent variable because it is presumed to have a causal effect on grades, which is the dependent variable.

We should be able to find a questionnaire with good validity and reliability that students can use to rate the course content on dimensions mentioned by Greenhow—authenticity and engagement. Students' ratings of these course dimensions, and perhaps others as well, can be correlated with their tweet frequency. Authenticity and engagement would be the dependent variables because the assumption is that tweeting (the independent variable) enhances students' perceptions of the course's value to them.

Regarding the question of why some students are more motivated to use Twitter, we can hypothesize reasons by reviewing the research literature on students' use of computers for learning and by making our own speculations. For example, we might hypothesize that students who regularly use texting, Facebook, Twitter, and other social networking services in their daily lives are more likely to generate tweets in a course of the type that Greenhow describes than students who seldom use these services or not at all. To test this hypothesis, we would create a measure that asks students to rate their frequency of use of these services in their daily life. Then we would correlate the students' ratings with their frequency of tweets in a course setting. In this study, students' use of social networking services is the independent variable because it is thought to have a causal influence on their frequency of tweets.

SELF-CHECK TEST

1. Correlational research
   a. can be used to explore causal relationships.
   b. can be used to provide conclusive confirmation of causal relationships.
   c. can be used to study causal relationships, whereas group comparison research cannot be used for this purpose.
   d. involves the manipulation of the independent variable, whereas group comparison research does not involve this kind of manipulation.

2. Correlational research is primarily intended for determining
   a. which of two variables is the independent variable.
   b. how variations in a sample's scores on one measure are related to variations in their scores on one or more other variables.
   c. whether a sample's scores on two or more measures have the same distributions.
   d. whether a sample's scores on each measure constitute categorical or interval scales.

3. A correlation coefficient provides information about
   a. the magnitude of the relationship between two variables but not the direction of the relationship.
   b. the direction of the relationship between two variables but not its magnitude.
   c. the linearity of the relationship between two variables.
   d. the magnitude and direction of the relationship between two variables but not its linearity.

4. Inspection of a scattergram provides information about whether
   a. data from a sufficient number of research participants are available for exploring a causal relationship.
   b. the correlation between two variables is linear or nonlinear.
   c. the variable on the x axis is the cause or the effect of the variable on the y axis.
   d. all of the above.

5. As a correlation coefficient increases in size, it means that
   a. the direction of the causal relationship between two variables is more uncertain.
   b. the two variables being correlated are more likely to have a nonlinear relationship to each other.
   c. the relationship between the two variables being correlated is more likely to have a negative slope.
   d. scores on one variable are better able to predict scores on the other variable.

6. The null hypothesis in a typical correlational study states that
   a. the true correlation coefficient in the population represented by the research sample has a positive value.
   b. the true correlation coefficient in the population represented by the research sample is zero.
   c. the correlation between the independent variable and the dependent variable is statistically significant.
   d. the effect size for the correlation coefficient is 0.33 or greater.

7. If researchers wish to determine the influence of multiple independent variables on a single dependent variable, the appropriate statistical technique would be
   a. hierarchical linear modeling.
   b. path analysis.
   c. multiple regression.
   d. factor analysis.

8. If researchers wish to determine whether the correlation between two variables is affected by different levels of "nesting," the appropriate statistical technique would be
   a. factor analysis.
   b. hierarchical linear modeling.
   c. discriminant analysis.
   d. canonical correlation.

9. A correlational research design can include
   a. multiple predictor variables.
   b. only one predictor variable.
   c. only predictor and outcome variables that are negatively related to each other.

d. only predictor and outcome variables that are positively related to each other.

10. In their report of a correlational study, the researchers should

    a. put greater emphasis on the implications of their findings for theory than for practice.

b. identify and discuss flaws in the study.

c. not speculate about whether the observed relationships between variables reflect causality.

d. not present the corresponding effect sizes for correlation coefficients.

CHAPTER REFERENCES

Knifsend, C. A., & Graham, S. (2012). Too much of a good thing? How breadth of extracurricular participation relates to school-related affect and academic outcomes during adolescence. *Journal of Youth and Adolescence, 41*(3), 379–389.

Schilling, S. G., Carlisle, J. F., Scott, S. E., & Zeng, J. (2007). Are fluency measures accurate predictors of reading achievement? *Elementary School Journal, 107*(5), 429–448.

Vandewater, E. A., Shim, M., & Caplovitz, A. G. (2004). Linking obesity and activity level with children's television and video game use. *Journal of Adolescence, 27*(1), 71–85.

Werblow, J., & Duesbery, L. (2009). The impact of high school size on math achievement and dropout rate. *High School Journal, 92*(3), 14–23.

RESOURCES FOR FURTHER STUDY

Harrison, D. M., & Raudenbush, S. W. (2006). Linear regression and hierarchical linear models. In J. L. Green, G. Camilli, & P. B. Elmore (Eds.), *Handbook of complementary methods in education research* (pp. 411–426). Mahwah, NJ: Lawrence Erlbaum.

    The authors explain two of the multivariate correlational techniques described in this chapter by addressing an illustrative research question. The question concerns whether there is a relationship between the socioeconomic status of students' families and their academic achievement.

Meyers, L. S., Gamst, G. C., & Guarino, A. J. (2012). *Applied multivariate research: Design and interpretation* (2nd ed.). Thousand Oaks, CA: Sage.

    The authors explain several of the correlational statistical techniques in this chapter: bivariate correlation, multiple regression, hierarchical linear regression, logistic regression, discriminant analysis, canonical correlation, factor analysis, and structural equation modeling.

Wainer, H., & Velleman, P. F. (2006). Statistical graphics: A guidepost for scientific discovery. In J. L. Green, G. Camilli, & P. B. Elmore (Eds.), *Handbook of complementary methods in education research* (pp. 605–621). Mahwah, NJ: Lawrence Erlbaum.

    The authors show how various types of graphs, including scattergrams, help to clarify characteristics of observed relationships between variables.

The Measurement and Predictive Ability of Metacognition in Middle School Learners

Sperling, R. A., Richmond, A. S., Ramsay C. M., & Klapp, M. (2012). The measurement and predictive ability of metacognition in middle school learners. *Journal of Educational Research, 105*(1), 1–7.

Many students develop the ability to reflect on their learning processes as they engage in studying. For example, a student might be reading a section of text and realize, "I don't understand what this means." Or a student might say to herself, "I'm going to need to review this material before the test." These and other self-reflections on one's learning are called metacognition.

In the following study, the researchers wanted to determine whether students who have more developed metacognitive processes earn a higher science grade point average (GPA) and overall GPA than students whose metacognitive processes are less developed. They used three different measures to assess students' metacognitive ability. In their results section, they display a correlation matrix showing the correlation betweens students' scores on each of these metacognition measures and each of the GPA scores. Also, they conducted a particular type of correlational analysis—multiple regression—to determine whether two of the measures of metacognition predicted GPA better than either one alone.

The article is reprinted in its entirety, just as it appeared when originally published.

The Measurement and Predictive Ability of Metacognition in Middle School Learners

RAYNE A. SPERLING
The Pennsylvania State University

CRYSTAL M. RAMSAY
The Pennsylvania State University

AARON S. RICHMOND
Metropolitan State College of Denver

MICHAEL KLAPP
Washoe County School District

ABSTRACT The authors examined relations among components of metacognition from varying theoretical perspectives, explored the psychometric characteristics of known measures of metacognition, and examined the predictive strength of measures of metacognition for both science and overall academic achievement in 97 seventh-grade students. Findings indicated expected significant correlations between 2 measures of metacognition, the Junior Metacognitive Awareness Inventory (Sperling, Howard, Miller, & Murphy, 2002) and an open-ended version of Swanson's (1990) metacognition measure and a significant correlation between the Swanson measure and general science teacher ratings of students' metacognition. Student measures demonstrated sound psychometric properties and both were significant predictors of science achievement. Additional analyses, recommendations for future research, and suggestions for practitioners and educators interested in measuring and promoting metacognition are provided.

Keywords: measurement, metacognition, self-regulation

Practitioners and researchers often hold intuitive conceptual understandings of metacognition as an important learning construct. Metacognition is casually referred to as an individual's thinking about thinking or knowing about knowing (e.g., Metcalfe & Shimamura, 1994). Despite these casual definitions, most researchers and practitioners recognize that metacognition certainly must play a critical role in students' memory, learning, and achievement. Research supports this intuition, as hundreds of studies over the last three decades have demonstrated that metacognition is a key variable in students' development and also their academic success (e.g., Winne & Nesbit, 2010). Of additional emphasis in present research and practice is the recognition of the important role metacognition plays in students' self-regulation (e.g., Abar & Loken, 2010; Lee, Lim, & Grabowski, 2009). For example, metacognitive learners are able to recognize when they are effectively learning and when they are struggling and therefore must employ the use of additional strategies or control and monitor their motivation (e.g., Alexander, 2008).

Many years of previous research has established the critical role of metacognition. However, many questions regarding learners' metacognition as a self-regulatory construct remain and, as evidenced by recent theoretical discussions and numerous current studies, research into metacognition continues (e.g., Annevirta & Vauras, 2006; Desoete, 2008; Greene & Azevedo, 2009; Hadwin, Nesbit, Jamieson-Noel, Code, & Winne, 2007; Huff & Nietfeld, 2009; Kung & Linder, 2007; Roll, Aleven, McLaren, & Koedinger, 2007; Zohar & David, 2008).

The focus of present metacognitive research is distributed across numerous disciplines, content areas, and contexts (e.g., Karpicke, 2009; Waters & Schnieder, 2010). However, much of the recent theoretical developments and research focus on metacognition in science, technology, engineering, and mathematics (STEM) learning and problem solving (e.g., Desoete, 2008; Desoete, Roeyers, & De Clercq, 2003; Greene & Azevedo, 2009; Moos & Azevedo, 2008a, 2000b; Schwartz, Andersen, Hong, Howard, & McGee, 2004; White & Frederiksen, 2005).

This study extends the existing knowledge base with intent to contribute to the broader understanding of the nature of metacognition and focus additional attention on the effective measurement of metacognition. One purpose of this focus is to provide better information for researchers, designers, and practitioners interested in promoting and measuring metacognition in school and other learning environments. For this work we drew from a long line of existing metacognition research and the considerable recent attention that has focused on the role of metacognition and self-regulation within content domains. This research includes focus on, among other areas, reading and writing (e.g., Waters & Schnieder, 2010; Yau, 2009); mathematics (e.g., Perels, Dignath, & Schmitz, 2009); and many science content areas such as biological systems (e.g., Greene & Azevedo, 2009; Moos & Azevedo, 2008a, 2008b), environmental and physical sciences (e.g., Graesser, Wiley, Goldman, O'Reilly, Jeon, & McDaniel, 2007; Schwartz et al., 2004), physics (e.g., Kung & Linder, 2007; Nielsen, Nashon, & Anderson, 2009), and science systems (e.g., Manlove, Lazonder, & de Jong, 2007).

Researchers and practitioners emphasize metacognition as an independent construct (e.g., Waters & Schnieder, 2010) as well as one situated within self-regulation (e.g., Zimmerman, 2002). Foundational metacognition research is rooted in one of two theoretical perspectives that emerged several decades ago (e.g., Brown, 1978; Flavell, 1979). Brown's (1978) framework emphasizes knowledge of cognition and regulation of cognition, whereas Flavell's (1979) framework

emphasizes the person, task, and strategy components of metacognitive knowledge and goals and strategies. These two perspectives continue to be the foundation for most of the present research on metacognitive processing with some recent views including metacognitive knowledge, regulation, and experiences (e.g., Nussinson & Korait, 2008; Zohar & David, 2008).

Many researchers have extended Brown's (1978) framework and consider subprocesses for both knowledge of cognition and regulation of cognition. For example, Schraw and Dennison (1994) explored subprocesses that included declarative, conditional, and procedural knowledge of cognition, and numerous studies have focused on subcomponents of regulation of cognition including planning, monitoring, and evaluation (e.g., Ariel, Dunlosky, & Bailey, 2009; Huff & Nietfeld 2009; Moos & Azevedo, 2009).

Flavell's (1979) framework has also been extended and applied in clinical and educational contexts (e.g., Cross & Paris, 1998; Peverly, Brobst, & Morris, 2002; Swanson, 1990; Veenman & Spaans, 2005). In this framework, under metacognitive knowledge, person variables include an individual's knowledge of his or her own and others' cognitions. The task variables include information available about a given task and the perceived task demands. Strategy variables include knowledge about the viability of given strategies. In addition to these and related metacognitive knowledge variables, theoretically, Flavell also proposed that metacognitive experiences, which can occur before, during, or after a task interact with knowledge and metacognitive knowledge.

On the surface, the constructs and processes presented in these two foundational metacognition frameworks may seem distinct. However, on closer examination, as most researchers and practitioners would attest, there is significant overlap between the two approaches. For example, among some of the similarities, both recognize the (a) importance of an individual's awareness and understanding of an individual's cognition, (b) the contextualized nature of metacognition, and (c) the importance of metacognition for regulation of an individual's thinking and actions.

We used measures of metacognition rooted in each of these two foundational perspectives, but consistent with present theoretical additions (e.g., Hacker, Dunlosky, & Graesser, 1998; Schraw & Moshman, 1995), and explored the relations among the components of metacognition across these perspectives. We expected moderate significant correlations among measures of metacognition developed from these two perspectives.

One of the challenges that those who study metacognition as well as those who scaffold supports for metacognition continue to face is the effective measurement of metacognitive constructs. Metacognition has been measured through a variety of strategies including

Address correspondence to Rayne A. Sperling, The Pennsylvania State University, ESPSE, 232 CEDAR, University Park, PA 16802, USA. (E-mail: rsd7@psu.edu)

discrepancy indices such as calibration techniques (e.g., Hacker, Bol, & Bahbahani, 2008; Nietfeld, Cao, & Osborne, 2006; Schraw, 2009), think-aloud protocols (e.g., Armstrong, Wallace, & Chang, 2008; Greene & Azevedo, 2009; Moos & Azevedo, 2008a, 2008b), and structured interviews (e.g., Swanson, 1990, 1993; Zimmerman & Martinez-Pons, 1986, 1988). Traces of students' learning have also been analyzed for students' metacognitive processing (e.g., Hadwin et al., 2007; Perry & Winne, 2006). Several self-report inventories are also often-used measures (e.g., Duncan & McKeachie, 2005; Pintrich, Smith, Garcia, & McKeachie, 1991; Schraw & Dennison, 1994; Schwartz et al., 2004; Sperling, Howard, Miller, & Murphy, 2002; Sperling, Howard, Staley, & DuBois, 2004). Further, some researchers have also included teachers' ratings of their students' metacognition as a dependent measure (e.g., Desoete, 2008; Sperling et al., 2002). However, relatively little is known regarding the construct validity and other psychometric properties of the measures of metacognition. As Muis, Winne, and Jamieson-Noel (2007) recently noted regarding self-report measures of older learners' metacognition, not all existing measures similarly assess metacognitive processes.

In this work we further examine metacognition as a theoretical construct that supports academic success. Theoretically, metacognition should be a predictor of academic performance. However, many studies report little relation between metacognition and achievement or aptitude in children (e.g., Allon, Gutkin, & Bruning, 1994; Sperling et al., 2002; Swanson, 1990). However, there has been some evidence clearly linking achievement to metacognition (e.g., Otero, Campanario, & Hopkins, 1992; Taraban, Rynearson, & Kerr, 2000; Tobias, Everson, & Laitusis, 1999). Therefore, we expected measures of metacognition to be moderate but significant predictors of achievement as measured by students' science grade point average (GPA) and overall GPA.

In an effort to further examine metacognition as a critical variable in achievement and to provide additional information regarding effective and efficient measures of metacognition to practitioners and researchers, we examined the metacognition of early adolescents in science classrooms with three primary purposes. The first was to examine the relations among components of metacognition from two traditionally separate, but not divergent, theoretical perspectives of metacognition. The second was to examine the strengths and weaknesses in the psychometric characteristics of known measures of metacognition for school-aged children. The reliability and the construct validity of these instruments as indicated by relations among teacher ratings of metacognition and both measures in conjunction with measures of academic achievement in science and overall was addressed. The third was to consider the predictive

strength of metacognition for academic performance in science and overall academic performance.

Method

Participants

Participants were 107 seventh-grade students enrolled in general science classes at a large suburban middle school. The sample was 48.6% Hispanic, 32.7% Caucasian, 2.8% Asian, 2.8% Native American, and 2.8% African American, with 10.3% claiming other ethnicity. Approximately 45% of students in the school qualified for free and reduced-price lunch. Some of the sampled students failed to answer one or more items. For consistency across participants, no missing data strategy was imposed but instead data from any student participants who missed even one item on either of the metacognitive measures were discarded. The resulting sample consisted of 97 students.

Measures and Procedures

Students provided demographic information and were administered the Junior Metacognitive Awareness Inventory (Jr. MAI; Sperling et al., 2002) and the Swanson Metacognitive Questionnaire (SMQ; Swanson, 1990). Administration of these inventories was counterbalanced. Teachers' ratings of students' metacognition, students' science GPA, and students' overall GPA completed the data set. Independent samples t tests indicated no order effects for either instrument order, for Jr. MAI, $t(95) = -0.81$, $p > .05$; and for the SMQ, $t(95) = -0.38$, $p > .05$.

Sperling et al. (2002) published the Jr. MAI as a measure of metacognitive knowledge and regulation. The Jr. MAI was developed from an adult measure of metacognition, the MAI (Schraw & Dennison, 1994) and is grounded in Brown's (1978) theoretical framework. In addition to numerous publications that have used the original MAI (e.g., Muis et al., 2007; Sperling et al., 2004), the Jr. MAI has been administered in several published studies with school-aged American students (e.g., Schwartz et al., 2004) as well as with international students (e.g., Karakelle & Sarac, 2007). The 18-item Jr. MAI was used in this study. The instrument includes equal number of items ($n = 9$) identified as regulation of cognition and knowledge of cognition. Example items from the Jr. MAI include "I learn best when I already know about the topic" and "I ask myself if there is an easier way to do things when I am done with a task." Previous studies reported strong internal consistency reliability (e.g., Howard, 1998; Schraw Olafson, Weibel, & Sewing, 2010; Sperling et al., 2002). For example, Sperling et al. (2002, Experiment 2) reported an internal consistency reliability of .82 for the overall scale. In the present study internal consistency reliability (Cronbach's α) was .76 for the scale that included the items identified as knowledge of cognition items and .80 for the items identified as regulation of cognition items by Sperling et al. (2002). Using procedures recommended Onwuegbuzie and Daniel (2000, 2002) the upper confidence interval was calculated for each of these coefficients. Results illustrate an upper confidence of .91 for the reliability of the full scale and .83 and .86 for the knowledge and regulation scales, respectively.

Students also completed a measure developed by Swanson (1990, 1993) that was adapted from Kreutzer, Leonard, and Flavell (1975) and Myers and Paris (1978). In previous research the measure was administered as a structured interview with younger children. In the present study students independently completed the SMQ. We sought information regarding the viability of using this measure in an alternative manner, as we recognize the benefit of alternative measures of metacognition (e.g., Winne & Perry, 2000). Due both to potential developmental differences in our sample participants when compared with previous research and the alternative format of the measure used in this study, we anticipated some differences between our findings and previous research. In the present study a 15-item version of the open-response instrument was administered. Consistent with the scoring previously used with the interview measure, students' responses were rated on an established 6-point scoring scheme that provides a unique rubric for each item. Although in independent ratings interrater reliability reached greater than 90% for sampled responses, two researchers rated and reached consensus on all students' responses. We reported total scores across items on the scale as the measure of metacognition. Example items included "How do children figure out things, like how to do something?" Internal consistency, as measured by Cronbach's alpha, was lower (.60) with an upper confidence interval of .69, likely due in part to item format and the breadth of the instrument, but nonetheless met standards for "a rating of sufficient" given present use as a test intended for research at a group level (Evers, 2001, p.172). Previous researchers had not used this scale as it was used in the present study, so previous reliability estimates were unavailable. The items on this scale were

derived from metacognitive theory but items did not directly map back to specific subconstructs of metacognition. Therefore, scale scores were not computed.

Consistent with use in previous research (Sperling et al., 2002), a teacher was provided five behavioral descriptors each for high and low student metacognition and rated each child. These descriptors targeted student behaviors of directed attention, purposive studying, planning, monitoring, and evaluation components. These behaviors are representative of those found in metacognitve students. The science teacher provided students' metacognition ratings and science GPA. The overall GPA for each student was obtained from the school administration.

Results

First, we examined the relations among components of metacognition from two traditionally separate, but not contradictory, theoretical perspectives of metacognition. To do this, we examined two measures grounded in varying theoretical and conceptual frameworks. Due to these differences, as noted, we expected unique information regarding students' metacognition to be captured by each of these measures but still expected moderate relations among them. Table 1 presents relevant descriptive statistics for the variables, and Table 2 provides a correlation matrix for these variables. As noted in Table 2, a significant moderate correlation ($r = .30$, $p = .003$) was indicated between the Jr. MAI, a measure grounded in Brown's (1978) theoretical framework, and our administration of the SMQ, a measure grounded in Flavell's (1979) perspective of metacognition. Second, we examined strengths and weaknesses in the psychometric characteristics of the measures of metacognition for school-aged children used in this study. First, although Swanson's (1990) structured interview was previously used with fourth- and fifth-grade learners, we explored its use as an open-ended self-report measure with slightly older learners. Table 3 presents item-level data for the present sample for the Jr. MAI and the SMQ. In this sample, using the alternative administration, the SMQ demonstrated sound item-level variance, and no items demonstrated floor or ceiling effects.

Table 1

Descriptive Statistics for Critical Variables

Variable	n	Range	Min	Max	M	SD
Jr. MAI total	97	49.00	35.00	84.00	63.44	10.32
SMQ	97	43.00	11.00	54.00	37.29	7.23
Teacher rating	97	5.00	1.00	6.00	3.70	1.36
Science GPA	96	4.00	0.00	4.00	3.07	0.98
Overall GPA	97	3.00	1.00	4.00	3.12	0.76

Note: Jr. MAI = Junior Metacognitive Awareness Inventory; SMQ = Swanson Metacognitive Questionnaire; GPA = grade point average.

Table 2

Correlations Among Measures

Scale	1	2	3	4	5
1. SMQ	—	.30**	.47**	.35**	.26**
2. Jr. MAI		—	.12	.32**	.25*
3. Teacher rating			—	.65**	.58**
4. Science GPA				—	.81**
5. Overall GPA					—

Note: SMQ = Swanson Metacognitive Questionnaire; Jr. MAI = Junior Metacognitive Awareness Inventory; GPA = grade point average.
*p < .05.
**p < .01.

Next, the Jr. MAI scores were examined. The sample in this study was more diverse than some previous American samples, and so the high internal consistency reliability (Cronbach's α = .87) in this sample contributes to existing literature that suggests that the measure is reliable (Schraw et al., 2010; Schwartz et al., 2004). Item-level characteristics in this sample were similar to those published in previous research (e.g., Sperling et al., 2002).

We next addressed the teacher ratings of students' metacognition. Consistent with previous administrations, teachers' ratings were relatively high in this sample. In this sample the mean teachers' ratings of students' metacognition based upon a 6-point scale was 3.70 (*SD* = 3.85) as compared with a mean of 3.85 in Sperling et al.'s (2002) study.

Correlations among measures of metacognition administered in this study also provide support for their

Table 3

Item-Level Means and Standard Deviations for Student Measures

Item	Jr. MAI		SMQ	
	M	SD	M	SD
1	3.90	0.76	3.93	1.08
2	3.95	0.89	2.38	1.43
3	3.43	1.12	1.93	1.00
4	4.26	0.99	2.09	0.81
5	4.32	0.79	2.58	1.37
6	2.56	1.14	2.76	1.30
7	2.31	1.06	1.44	1.61
8	3.41	1.13	1.86	1.05
9	3.16	1.30	3.57	1.08
10	2.93	1.22	1.88	1.06
11	4.06	0.90	2.58	1.04
12	4.59	0.73	2.11	1.54
13	3.29	1.01	2.36	1.24
14	3.29	1.06	2.17	0.75
15	3.82	1.09	3.76	1.69
16	3.22	1.07		
17	3.23	1.18		
18	3.79	1.17		

Note: Jr. MAI = Junior Metacognitive Awareness Inventory; SMQ = Swanson Metacognitive Questionnaire.

construct properties. As noted in Table 2, the SMQ scores were significantly correlated with the Jr. MAI scores and the teacher ratings of students' metacognition. The correlation between the teacher ratings and the Jr. MAI scores was not significant. However, the correlation was higher than reported in previous research that administered both measures (Sperling et al., 2002). As in previous research (e.g., Sperling et al., 2002) teacher ratings of students' metacognition were more strongly correlated with achievement measures than they were with students' self-reported metacognition.

Third, we considered the predictive strength of the two student measures of metacognition for science and overall academic performance. When both measures were simultaneously entered into regression models, both were significant predictors for science GPA and overall GPA. In the first model, overall GPA was regressed on the SMQ and the Jr. MAI. These two predictors accounted for 10% of the variance in overall GPA ($R^2 = .10$), which was significant in the model, $F(2, 94) = 5.15$, $p = .008$. The SMQ ($\beta = .21$, $p = .05$) demonstrated significant effects on the achievement scores whereas the Jr. MAI contribution was limited ($\beta = .18$, $p = .08$). In the second model, the SMQ and the Jr. MAI accounted for a significant 17% of the variance in science GPA, $F(2, 95) = 9.83$, $p < .001$. The SMQ ($\beta = .29$, $p = .005$) and the Jr. MAI ($\beta = .23$, $p = .02$) contributed significantly to the model. In both models the SMQ was a better predictor variable. However, additional variance was accounted for by the addition of the related Jr. MAI score.

Discussion

As evidenced by present research and practice, many researchers continue to be interested in the role that metacognition and related self-regulatory constructs can play in academic success. In recognition of the importance of metacognition, present research continues to explore the benefits of instructional mechanisms such as training programs, prompts, and scaffolds for promoting successful metacognitive processing (e.g., Azevedo, 2005; Dignath & Buttner, 2008; Stark & Krause, 2009). Further, researchers and practitioners are keenly interested in the characteristics, reliability, and validity of tools available to measure metacognition as a critical variable in students' learning. Researchers who study mechanisms to benefit and increase students' metacognition continue to be challenged and constrained by a lack of accessible instruments designed to effectively measure metacognition. In this work we contribute to our understanding regarding potential tools for future research studies and practitioners. Such work is necessary for those interested in metacognition from theoretical and practical perspectives.

Given the areas of metacognition research in learning, our data illustrate consistency and divergence in metacognition as conceptualized from two theoretical frameworks. The consistency lends additional support for metacognition as a construct, and the divergence supports that researchers and practitioners continue to explore the use of multiple measures of metacognition and self-regulation (e.g., Winne & Perry, 2000). Consistent with research that examines the role of metacognition in science learning, our findings indicated metacognition is a significant predictor in science achievement and overall achievement as measured by GPA.

Further, the study contributes to the knowledge regarding the psychometric properties of the measures of metacognition examined. Researchers, designers, and practitioners interested in studying the effects of metacognition as well as those interested in assessing the benefits of interventions need tools known to have sound psychometric properties. In this work, additional empirical support was indicated for the reliability and validity of the Jr. MAI, a student self-report Likert-type scale measure. Further, our findings indicated empirical support for administration of Swanson's (1990) structured interview protocol as an open-ended instrument. Although the instrument demonstrated less reliability than was ideal, the trade-off of the possibility that an alternative open-ended measure can account for additional metacognitive information as well as significant variance in achievement, future research with this measure is warranted. Taken together, these two student-level measures provide related but independent information regarding students' reported metacognition and regulation.

As in previous research (e.g., Desoete, 2008; Sperling et al., 2002; Zimmerman, 1988), we used teacher ratings of students' metacognition. In our data, teacher ratings were found to correlate to students' science and overall achievement, but not to student self-ratings of metacognition. Consistent with these findings, teacher ratings also were correlated with achievement in previous research (e.g., Sperling et al., 2002). Thus, of interest for additional research is the degree to which achievement outcomes may directly influence teachers' ratings of students' metacognition. It may be challenging for teachers to separate achievement from student regulation, as metacognition is difficult to observe. Data gleaned from traces of student learning as a measure of metacognition (e.g., Perry & Winne, 2006) may contribute meaningfully to future predictive models that explore the contribution of metacognition and related regulation in achievement and learning outcomes.

Future researchers may find the use of the measures targeted in this study (the Jr. MAI, the SMQ, and teacher ratings) to be of benefit as they examine the role of metacognition in learning and achievement outcomes, as well as when they measure the effects of interventions and instructional support mechanisms designed to promote metacognition. Both student-level measures provide information in addition to that provided by teachers' ratings of students' metacognition. Some researchers may find that the ease of use and time necessary to administer and score the self-report Jr. MAI measure, coupled with strong reliability, compelling for use over the open-ended SMQ. However, for trained practitioners as supported by the data in this study, each may provide important unique information regarding learners' metacognition; taken together, these measures account for informative variance in student achievement outcomes.

REFERENCES

Abar, B., & Loken, E. (2010). Self-regulated learning and self-directed study in a pre-college sample. *Learning and Individual Differences, 20*, 25–29.

Alexander, P. A. (2008). Why this and why now? Introduction to the special issue on metacognition, self-regulation, and self-regulated learning. *Educational Psychology Review, 20*, 369–372.

Allon, M., Gutkin, T. B., & Bruning, R. (1994). The relationship between metacognition and intelligence in normal adolescents: Some tentative but surprising findings. *Psychology in the Schools, 31*, 93–96.

Annevirta, T., & Vauras, M. (2006). Developmental changes of metacognitive skill in elementary school children. *Journal of Experimental Education, 74*, 197–225.

Ariel, R., Dunlosky, J., & Bailey, H. (2009). Agenda-based regulation of study-time allocation: When agendas override item-based monitoring. *Journal of Experimental Psychology: General, 138*, 432–447.

Armstrong, N. A., Wallace, C. S., & Chang, S. (2008). Learning from writing in college biology. *Research in Science Education, 38*, 483–499.

Azevedo, R. (2005). Using hypermedia as a metacognitive tool for enhancing student learning? The role of self-regulated learning. *Educational Psychologist, 40*, 199–209.

Brown, A. L. (1978). Knowing when, where, and how to remember: A problem of metacognition. In R. Glaser (Ed.), *Advances in instructional psychology* (pp. 367–406). New York, NY: Halsted Press.

Cross, D. R., & Paris, S. G. (1988). Developmental and instructional analyses of children's metacognition and reading comprehension. *Journal of Educational Psychology, 80*, 131–142.

Desoete, A. (2008). Multi-method assessment of metacognitive skills in elementary school children: How you test is what you get. *Metacognition and Learning, 3*, 189–206.

Desoete, A., Roeyers, H., & De Clercq, A. (2003). Can offline metacognition enhance mathematical problem solving? *Journal of Educational Psychology, 95*, 188–200.

Dignath, C., & Buttner, G. (2008). Components of fostering self-regulated learning among students: A meta-analysis on intervention studies at primary and secondary school level. *Metacognition and Learning, 3*, 231–264.

Duncan, T. G., & McKeachie, W. J. (2005). The making of the motivated strategies for learning questionnaire. *Educational Psychologist, 40*, 117–128.

Evers, A. (2001). The revised Dutch rating scale for test quality. *The International Journal of Testing, 1*, 155–182.

Flavell, J. H. (1979). Metacognition and cognitive monitoring: A new area of cognitive-developmental inquiry. *American Psychologist, 34*, 906–911.

Graesser, A. C., Wiley, J., Goldman, S. R., O'Reilly, T., Jeon, M., & McDaniel, B. (2007). SEEK Web tutor: Fostering a critical stance while exploring the causes of volcanic eruption. *Metacognition and Learning, 2*, 89–105.

Greene, J. A., & Azevedo, R. (2009). A macro-level analysis of SRL processes and their relations to the acquisition of a sophisticated mental model of a complex system. *Contemporary Educational Psychology, 34*, 18–29.

Hacker, D. J., Bol, L., & Bahbahani, K. (2008). Explaining calibration accuracy in classroom contexts: The effects of incentives, reflection, and explanatory style. *Metacognition and Learning, 3*, 101–121.

Hacker, D. J., Dunlosky, J., & Graesser, A. C. (Eds.). (1998). *Metacognition in educational theory and practice.* Mahwah, NJ: Erlbaum.

Hadwin, A. F., Nesbit, J. C., Jamieson-Noel, D., Code, J., & Winne, P. H. (2007). Examining trace data to explore self-regulated learning. *Metacognition and Learning, 2*, 107–124.

Howard, B. C. (1998). *Metacognitive awareness inventories: NASA COTF research results* (Technical Report). Wheeling, WV: NASA Classroom of the Future.

Huff, J. D., & Nietfeld, J. L. (2009). Using strategy instruction and confidence judgments to improve metacognitive monitoring. *Metacognition and Learning, 4*, 161–176.

Karakelle, S., & Saraç, S. (2007). Validity and factor structure of Turkish versions of the metacognitive awareness inventory for children (Jr. MAI)—A and B forms. *Türk Psikoloji Yazilari, 10*(20), 87–103.

Karpicke, J. D. (2009). Metacognitive control and strategy selection: Deciding to practice retrieval during learning. *Journal of Experimental Psychology: General, 138*, 469–486.

Kreutzer, M. A., Leonard, C., & Flavell, J. H. (1975). An interview study of children's knowledge about memory. *Monographs of the Society for Research in Child Development, 40*, 1–60.

Kung, R. L., & Linder, C. (2007). Metacognitive activity in the physics student laboratory: Is increased metacognition necessarily better? *Metacognition and Learning, 2*, 41–56.

Lee, H. W., Lim, K. Y., & Grabowski, B. (2009). Generative learning strategies and metacognitive feedback to facilitate comprehension of complex science topics and self-regulation. *Journal of Educational Media and Hypermedia, 18*(1), 5–25.

Manlove, S., Lazonder, A. W., & de Jong, T. (2007). Software scaffolds to promote regulation during scientific inquiry learning. *Metacognition and Learning, 2*, 141–155.

Metcalfe, J., & Shimamura, A. P. (1994). *Metacognition: Knowing about knowing.* Cambridge, MA: MIT Press.

Moos, D. C., & Azevedo, R. (2008a). Exploring the fluctuation of motivation and use of self-regulatory processes during learning with hypermedia, *Instructional Science: An International Journal of the Learning Sciences, 36*, 203–231.

Moos, D. C., & Azevedo, R. (2008b). Monitoring, planning, and self-efficacy during learning with hypermedia: The impact of conceptual scaffolds. *Computers in Human Behavior, 24*, 1686–1706.

Moos, D. C., & Azevedo, R. (2009). Self-efficacy and prior domain knowledge: To what extent does monitoring mediate their relationship with hypermedia learning? *Metacognition and Learning, 4*, 197–216.

Muis, K. R., Winne, P. H., & Jamieson-Noel, D. (2007). Using a multitrait-multimethod analysis to examine conceptual similarities of three self-regulated learning inventories. *British Journal of Educational Psychology, 77*, 177–195.

Myers, M., & Paris, S. G. (1978). Children's megacognitive knowledge about reading. *Journal of Educational Psychology, 70*, 680–690.

Nielsen, W. S., Nashon, S., & Anderson, D. (2009). Metacognitive engagement during field-trip experiences: A case study of students in an amusement park physics program. *Journal of Research in Science Teaching, 46*, 265–288.

Nietfeld, J. L., Cao, L., & Osborne, J. W. (2006). The effect of distributed monitoring exercises and feedback on performance, monitoring accuracy, and self-efficacy. *Metacognition and Learning, 1*, 159–179.

Nussinson, R., & Koriat, A. (2008). Correcting experience-based judgments: The perseverance of subjective experience in the face of the correction of judgment. *Metacognition and Learning, 3*, 159–174.

Onwuegbuzie, A. J., & Daniel, L. G. (2000, November). *Reliabilty generalization: The importance of considering sample specificity, confidence intervals, and subgroup differences.* Paper presented at the annual meeting of the Mid-South Educational Research Association, Bowling Green, KY.

Onwuegbuzie, A. J., & Daniel, L.G. (2002). A framework for reporting and interpreting internal consistency reliability estimates. *Measurement and Evaluation in Counseling and Development, 35*, 89–103.

Otero, J., Campanario, J. M., & Hopkins, K. D. (1992). The relationship between academic achievement and metacognitive comprehension monitoring ability of Spanish secondary school students. *Educational and Psychological Measurement, 52*, 419–430.

Perels, F., Dignath, C., & Schmitz, B. (2009). Is it possible to improve mathematical achievement by means of self-regulation strategies? Evaluation of an intervention in regular math classes. *European Journal of Psychology of Education, 24*, 17–31.

Perry, N. E., & Winne, P. H. (2006). Learning from learning kits: GStudy traces of students' self-regulated engagements with computerized content. *Educational Psychology Review, 18*, 211–228.

Peverly, S. T., Brobst, K. E., & Morris, K. S. (2002). The contribution of reading comprehension ability and meta-cognitive control to the development of studying in adolescence. *Journal of Research in Reading, 25*, 203–216.

Pintrich, P. R., Smith, D. A. F., Garcia, T., & McKeachie, W. J. (1991). *A manual for the use of the Motivated Strategies for Learning Questionnaire (MSLQ).* Ann Arbor, MI: University of Michigan, National Center for Research to improve Postsecondary Teaching and Learning.

Roll, I., Aleven, V., McLaren, B. M., & Koedinger, K. R. (2007). Designing for metacognition applying cognitive tutor principles to the tutoring of help seeking. *Metacognition and Learning, 2*, 125–140.

Schraw, G. (2009). A conceptual analysis of five measures of metacognitive monitoring. *Metacognition and Learning, 4*, 33–45.

Schraw, G., & Dennison, R. S. (1994). Assessing metacognitive awareness. *Contemporary Educational Psychology, 17*, 460–475.

Schraw, G., & Moshman, D. (1995). Metacognitive theories. *Educational Psychology Review, 7*, 351–371.

Schraw, G., Olafson, L., Weibel, M., & Sewing, D. (2010). *Metacognitive knowledge and field-based science learning in an outdoor environmental education program.* Manuscript submitted for publication.

Schwartz, N. H., Andersen, C., Hong, N., Howard, B., & McGee, S. (2004). The influence of metacognitive skills on learners' memory information in a hypermedia environment. *Journal of Educational Computing Research, 31*, 77–93.

Sperling, R. A., Howard, B. C., Miller, L. A., & Murphy, C. (2002). Measures of children's knowledge and regulation of cognition. *Contemporary Educational Psychology, 27*(1), 51–79.

Sperling, R. A., Howard, B. C., Staley, R., & DuBois, N. (2004). Metacognition and self-regulated learning constructs. *Educational Research and Evaluation, 10*, 117–139.

Stark, R., & Krause, U. (2009). Effects of reflection prompts on learning outcomes and learning behaviour in statistics education. *Learning Environments Research, 12*, 209–223.

Swanson, H. L. (1990). Influence of metacognitive knowledge and aptitude on problem solving. *Journal of Educational Psychology, 82*, 306–314.

Swanson, H. L. (1993). An information processing analysis of learning disabled children's problem solving. *American Educational Research Journal, 30*, 867–893.

Taraban, R., Rynearson, K., & Kerr, M. S. (2000). Metacognition and freshman academic performance. *Journal of Developmental Education, 24*(1), 12–26.

Tobias, S., Everson, H. T., & Laitusis, V. (1999, April). *Towards a performance based measure of metacognitive knowledge monitoring: Relationships with self-reports and behavior ratings.* Paper presented at the annual meeting of the American Educational Research Association, Montreal, Quebec, Canada.

Veenman, M. V. J., & Spaans, M. A. (2005). Relation between intellectual and metacognitive skills: Age and task differences. *Learning and Individual Differences, 15*, 159–176.

Waters, H. S., & Schneider, W. (Eds.). (2010). *Metacognition, strategy use, and instruction.* New York, NY: Guilford Press.

White, B., & Frederiksen, J. (2005). A theoretical framework and approach for fostering metacognitive development. *Educational Psychologist, 40*, 211–223.

Winne, P. H., & Nesbit, J. C. (2010). The psychology of academic achievement. *Annual Review of Psychology, 61*, 653–678.

Winne, P. H., & Perry, N. E. (2000). Measuring self-regulated learning. In M. Boekaerts, P. R. Pintrich, & M. Zeidner (Eds.), *Handbook of self-regulation* (pp. 532–564). San Diego, CA: Academic Press.

Yau, J. C. (2009). Reading characteristics of Chinese-English adolescents: Knowledge and application of strategic reading. *Metacognition and Learning, 4*, 217–235.

Zimmerman, B. J. (2002). Becoming a self-regulated learner: An overview. *Theory into Practice, 41*, 64–72.

Zimmerman, B. J., & Martinez-Pons, M. (1986). Development of a structured interview for assessing student use of self-regulated learning strategies. *American Educational Research Journal, 23*, 614–628.

Zimmerman, B. J., & Martinez-Pons, M. (1988). Construct validation of a strategy model of self-regulated learning. *Journal of Educational Psychology, 80*, 284–290.

Zohar, A., & David, A. B. (2008). Explicit teaching of meta-strategic knowledge in authentic classroom situations. *Metacognition and Learning, 3*, 59–82.

AUTHORS NOTE

Rayne A. Sperling is an Associate Professor in the Educational Psychology Program at The Pennsylvania State University. Much of her primary research addresses learners' variables such as metacognition and self-regulation while reading and solving problems. She also often examines instructional mechanisms to support learners' higher-order processing and self-regulation.

Aaron S. Richmond is an Associate Professor at the Metropolitan State College of Denver. His primary research interests include defining the processes involved in mnemonic and strategic development, addressing transfer and retentional issues in cognitive and learning strategies, investigating moral reasoning and its role in teacher and adolescent education, and studying different pedagogical approaches to online instruction.

Crystal M. Ramsay is a Research Associate and Instructional Consultant with the Schreyer Institute for Teaching Excellence at The Pennsylvania State University. Her research interests include classroom assessment strategies in higher education, the impact of instructional interventions on disciplinary learning, reading in the disciplines, and the roles of interest and motivational constructs in learning.

Michael Klapp is a science teacher at Kendyl Depoali Middle School in Washoe County School District, Nevada. In his classes he engages his students with numerous hands-on and inquiry science activities.

CHAPTER TWELVE

Experimental Research

PROBLEMS OF PRACTICE *in this chapter*

- Is it feasible and effective to offer an online version of an algebra course for eighth-grade students who otherwise would not be able to study this subject?
- Teachers believe that they can be more effective if they have smaller classes, but do student in smaller classes actually achieve more than students in larger classes?
- Does a program like Opportunity NYC-Family Rewards, which provides cash incentives to poor families, have the intended positive effects on parental behavior and the behavior of their children?
- Is it possible to improve on traditional instruction by using an innovative teaching method called QER, which involves a graphic organizer with questions on it and teacher-student collaboration to answer the questions?
- What can be done to improve middle-school students' life skills, especially avoidance of harmful drugs?
- What can be done to improve the performance of students with autism spectrum disorder and moderate mental retardation?
- What is flipped instruction, and does it have advantages over traditional instruction?
- What can be done to improve the low academic performance and high dropout rate of Latino students?
- Can an electronic beeper improve students' on-task behavior in class?

IMPORTANT *Ideas*

1. Educational fads perhaps would be less prevalent if we required rigorous experiments testing their effectiveness before putting them into practice.
2. The essential feature of an experiment is an intervention by researchers and collaborators in a particular setting.
3. Experiments typically have four phases: (1) formation of experimental and control groups, (2) initial administration of a measure of the outcome variable, (3) an intervention for the experimental group for a period of time, and (4) second administration of a measure of the outcome variable.

4. The introductory section of a report of an experiment should state its importance, purposes, and variables and also provide a review of relevant literature.

5. A pretest-posttest control-group experiment with randomization has three features: (1) at least two groups with each one receiving different interventions or one receiving no intervention, (2) random assignment of individuals in the sample to the different intervention or no-intervention conditions, and (3) administration of one or more pretests and posttests.

6. In a pretest-posttest control-group experiment, it is possible for both the experimental intervention and other variables to have a causal influence on the outcome variables.

7. If the experimental data satisfy certain conditions, statistical adjustments (e.g., analysis of covariance) can be made to control for preexisting differences between the experimental and control groups on pretest measures.

8. Of the various quantitative research designs, experiments have the strongest implications for practice, especially if they are conducted in a real-life setting.

9. If random assignment is not possible, a quasi-experiment is a viable option, especially if the experimental and control groups can be matched on critical variables that might affect the posttest variables.

10. Factorial experiments enable researchers to determine whether each of several independent variables has an effect on the dependent variable and also whether a particular independent variable has an effect only under certain conditions.

11. An experiment is internally valid to the extent that extraneous factors can be ruled out as possible causes of observed differences between the experimental and control groups on an outcome variable.

12. The extraneous factors commonly considered to be threats to the internal validity of an experiment in education are history, maturation, testing, instrumentation, statistical regression, differential selection, selection-maturation interaction, and experimental mortality.

13. An experiment loses value if treatment fidelity departs from the researchers' specifications for each treatment condition or if the treatment lacks sufficient potency.

14. An experiment is externally valid to the extent that the results of an experiment can be generalized to other individuals, settings, and time periods.

15. Single-case experiments involve the application of an intervention to a single individual or a few individuals, whereas group experiments involve the application of an intervention to a substantial sample of individuals or groups.

16. Typical features of a single-case experiment are baseline and treatment conditions, behavior analysis, focus on low-incidence populations, detailed description of each research participant, repeated administration of one measure, and graphical presentation of data.

KEY TERMS

A-B-A-B research design	baseline condition	control condition
A-B-A research design	behavior analysis	dependent variable
attrition	behavior modification	differential-selection effect

ecological validity
experiment
experimental condition
experimental mortality
external validity
extraneous variable
factor
factorial experiment
group experiment
Hawthorne effect
history effect
independent variable
instrumentation effect
interaction effect
internal validity
maturation effect

multiple-baseline research design
one-group pretest-posttest study
one-shot case study
population validity
posttest
posttest-only control-group
    design with randomization
posttest-only control-group
    design without randomization
pretest
pretest-posttest control-
    group experiment with
    randomization
pretest-posttest control-group
    experiment without
    randomization

quasi-experiment
random assignment
randomized control trial
randomized trial
reversal phase
selection-maturation interaction
    effect
single-case experiment
Solomon four-group experiment
statistical regression
testing effect
treatment condition
treatment fidelity
two-factor experiment
What Works Clearinghouse

THE RELEVANCE OF EXPERIMENTAL RESEARCH TO EDUCATIONAL PRACTICE

Richard Snow, an educational researcher, once described educational innovations as a "garden of panaceas" (Fletcher, Tobias, & Wisher, 2007). Others see educational innovations as fads that come and go. When an innovation is brought into a school district, veteran teachers have been heard to say, "We tried this before and it didn't work. Why are we trying it again?"

Among the innovations currently in vogue are the conversion of a large school into small schools on the same campus, new computer hardware and instructional software, brain-based teaching and learning, teaching to students' different learning styles, charter schools and voucher systems, and summer school and special tutoring for students who are failing to make adequate progress. Each of these innovations has its advocates but also its critics. Even if an innovation takes hold here or there, there is little assurance that it will become institutionalized and improve education over the long term.

What can we do to solve the problem of faddism in educational practice? From a research perspective, two steps are necessary. First, we must support rigorous experiments to determine whether the claims for a particular innovation are valid. Second, we must determine the necessary "buy-ins," pitfalls, and unintended side effects when moving from experimentation to full-scale implementation and adoption by educators.

In this chapter, we consider what counts as a rigorous experiment. In the chapter on program evaluation (Chapter 19), we consider how researchers go about determining what needs to happen for a particular innovation to become part of the complex world of education practice.

Rigorous experiments in education have now entered the realm of federal policy. In 2005, the U.S. Department of Education issued new regulations that give priority to researchers who propose to conduct rigorous experiments (Glenn, 2005). The **What Works Clearinghouse (WWC)** was instituted in 2002 by the federal government (see Chapters 1 and 4) to highlight innovative programs whose effectiveness has been demonstrated by rigorous experiments. You can obtain e-mail updates from WWC about evidence from experiments on innovative educational programs by enrolling in its free subscription service.

An example of a WWC review of an experiment is shown in Figure 12.1. You will note that the brief review of the experiment has a download feature that allows you to access the full report of the experiment (called a randomized, controlled trial in Figure 12.1).

Of course, experimental evidence alone is not sufficient to improve practice. Educators' advocacy, visionary leadership, clinical skills, and ability to secure financial resources are equally essential.

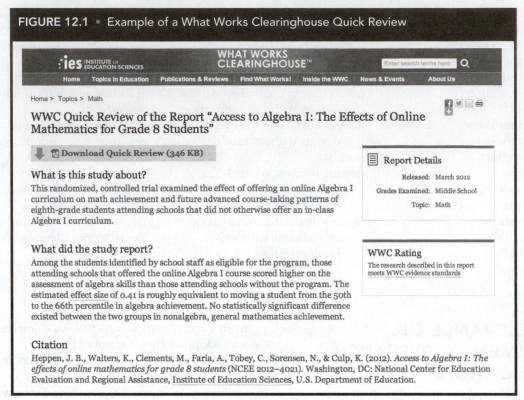

FIGURE 12.1 • Example of a What Works Clearinghouse Quick Review

Source: What Works Clearinghouse (2012, March). *WWC quick review of the report "Access to algebra I: The effects of online mathematics for grade 8 students."* Retrieved from http://ies.ed.gov/ncee/wwc/quickreviewsum.aspx?sid=198.

However, in the absence of empirical evidence, these professional skills, even if well intentioned, can lead down fruitless paths.

CHARACTERISTICS OF EXPERIMENTS

An **experiment** is an empirical study in which researchers manipulate one variable (e.g., a teaching technique) to determine its effect on another variable (e.g., students' on-task behavior in class). If the experiment is well done, the researchers can conclude that the first variable caused or did not cause a change in the second variable. No other type of quantitative research design (descriptive, correlational, or group comparison) is as powerful in demonstrating causal relationships among variables as an experiment.

The essential feature of experiments, as described in the previous paragraph, is manipulation.

Experimenters enter a situation and change (i.e., manipulate) some parts of it either themselves or through collaborators. The collaborators might be specially trained research assistants or professional educators.

Another way of describing experimental manipulation is to say that the researcher introduces an intervention into a situation. For example, the researcher might intervene in classroom teachers' regular instruction—with their permission, of course—by having them use an experimental curriculum or teaching method.

Interventions sometimes are called *conditions*, *experimental conditions*, *treatment conditions*, or *independent variables* in research reports. For example, the research report might state that the participants were assigned to different experimental conditions. Each **experimental condition** is a situation where a group of research participants receives an intervention to determine its effect on the dependent variable. One of the conditions might be a **control condition**, which is a situation where a group of research participants receives no intervention or an alternative intervention, against whose performance the experimental group's performance is compared.

Some experiments in education are called **randomized trials** or **randomized control trials**. Randomized trials are experiments, but unlike small-scale experiments conducted under laboratory-like conditions, they typically are large-scale, well funded, and conducted in real-life settings. They also involve an intervention addressing outcomes that are important to the general public and random assignment of individuals or groups to the experimental and control conditions. (We discuss random assignment later in the chapter.)

Randomized trials are widely used in medicine to test the effectiveness of new drugs and medical procedures before they are released for national or international use. In education, randomized trials typically are used to test the effectiveness of new programs that address important educational outcomes. Randomized trials often are called the "gold standard" of research studies because the rigor of their designs allows for strong cause-and-effect conclusions between a program or other intervention (the cause) and the measured outcomes (the effects) that the intervention is designed to address.

Group comparison and correlational research do not rely on interventions but rather on naturally occurring variations. For example, some classes have fewer students than others—not because of a researcher's intervention but because of school policy, scheduling procedures, or other factors. Researchers have discovered that these variations in class size are correlated with student academic achievement; students generally learn more in small classes. A meta-analysis of their research studies was conducted by Mary Lee Smith and Gene Glass (1980).

This finding, while intriguing, does not prove that if we reduce class size in a school district, student learning will necessarily improve. Other classroom features might be associated with smaller class size (e.g., more experienced teachers might have priority assignment to smaller classes), and these might be the actual features that cause improvement in student learning.

In an experiment, however, researchers do not rely on naturally occurring variations; instead, they manipulate the situation. In our example, they might make one group of classes smaller while keeping another group of classes at their current size. Moreover, they would try to hold all other factors constant between the two groups of classes. Thus, they can attribute any observed differences in student learning to this intervention. Educators then can have confidence that if they manipulate their own situation in the same manner, they will observe the same effects the researchers observed.

PHASES OF AN EXPERIMENT

After research participants have been selected, an experiment typically involves four phases:

1. A sample of research participants is randomly assigned to either the experimental group or the control group. **Random assignment** means that each participant has an equal chance of being in either group. Thus, previously existing group differences are unlikely to be the cause of observed differences in the outcome variable. For example, if the sample includes a certain percentage of males, random assignment makes it likely that a similar percentage of males will be in the experimental and control groups.

2. Both groups are administered a measure, usually called a **pretest**, which is the same as that administered in phase 4 (the *posttest*). The pretest is a measure that is used to determine whether the experimental and control groups are similar on the variable that the intervention is designed to affect. Also, it can be readministered at the conclusion of the intervention to determine the amount of change created by the intervention relative to the control condition.

3. The experimental group is exposed to an intervention, while the control group either receives an alternative intervention or no intervention.

4. The experimental and control groups are compared with respect to their scores on the measured variable that the experiment is designed to affect. This variable is called the **dependent variable** (sometimes called

the *criterion variable* or *outcome variable*), because participants' scores on a measure of this variable are presumed to be dependent on the intervention introduced by the researchers. The dependent variable is measured by a **posttest**, which is a measure that is administered at the conclusion of the intervention and that is typically the same measure as the pretest.

The majority of this chapter, starting with the next section, is about **group experiments**, that is, experiments that involve samples of research participants, typically 10 or more participants in each experimental condition. In the last part of this chapter, we consider single-case experiments, which involve an intervention with a single research participant or a few participants.

EXAMPLES OF EXPERIMENTAL RESEARCH

The following studies illustrate the relevance of experimental research to problems of practice. In each study, we identify the randomization procedure and the independent and dependent variables.

Effects of Different Class Sizes

Finn, J. D., & Achilles, C. M. (1990). Answers and questions about class size: A statewide experiment. *American Educational Research Journal, 27*(3), 557–577.

One of the most important experiments in education in the past 25 years involved class size (the independent variable). The rigorously designed, large-scale experiment was conducted in actual classrooms. Funded by the Tennessee legislature and commonly known as Project STAR (Student/Teacher Achievement Ratio), this experiment since its publication has served as a model for other experiments funded at the federal and state levels.

Primary school students were randomly assigned to three experimental conditions: (1) one certified teacher and more than 20 students; (2) supplemented classes (one certified teacher, a full-time noncertified teacher's aide, and a class of

more than 20 students); and (3) small classes (one certified teacher and approximately 15 students). The students stayed in their assigned condition for up to four years—from kindergarten through third grade. Because new students enter a school each year, some students stayed in their experimental condition for four years, while students entering later were in their experimental condition for one, two, or three years.

The dependent variables were achievement in reading, word study, and mathematics, measured at the end of each school year by the Stanford Achievement Test.

Biddle and Berliner (2002) summarized findings for the dependent variable of reading achievement in a graph, shown in Figure 12.2. If you examine the figure, you will see that children in small classes made greater gains in reading achievement than children in the other experimental conditions at each grade level. For example, kindergartners in small classes were half a month ahead of children in large classes by the end of the school year. After four years of small classes, the children were 7.1 months ahead of children in large classes.

Another finding shown in Figure 12.2 is that length of time in small classes makes a difference in reading achievement. For example, students who were in small classes for only two years (i.e., students who entered the experimental condition in second grade) were 3.3 months ahead in reading achievement, relative to students in large classes, at the end of third grade. However, their classmates who had experienced small classes since kindergarten were 7.1 months ahead.

Follow-up research was done to determine the academic achievement of children in the experimental group when they entered standard-sized classes after the end of the third grade, which was the conclusion of the experimental intervention. The follow-up studies indicated that these students had greater academic achievement than other students all the way through high school.

As we stated earlier in the chapter, experimental findings do not necessarily lead directly to improvement in educational practice. Although reduction of class size is demonstrably effective, it is also expensive. Smaller classes require more teachers and more classrooms, both of which are very costly. It is necessary, then, for policy makers and the general public to weigh costs

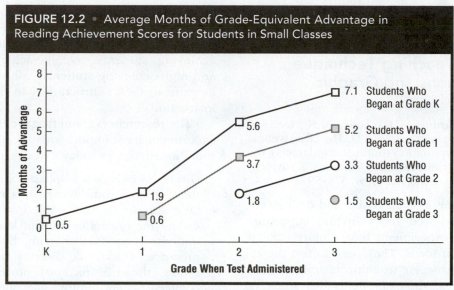

FIGURE 12.2 • Average Months of Grade-Equivalent Advantage in Reading Achievement Scores for Students in Small Classes

Source: Biddle, B. J., & Berliner, D. C. (2002). Small class size and its effects. *Educational Leadership,* *59*(5), 12–23. Reprinted by permission of the author.

against benefits and the value they ascribe to those benefits.

Effects of Cash Incentives to Poor Families

Morris, P, Aber, J. L., Wolf, S., & Berg, J. (2012). Using incentives to change how teenagers spend their time: The effects of New York City's Conditional Cash Transfer Program. Retrieved from MDRC website: http://www.mdrc.org/publication/using-incentives-change-how-teenagers-spend-their-time

MDRC, a nonprofit research organization, conducted a randomized trial to test the effectiveness of the Opportunity NYC-Family Rewards program in New York City. This program, designed for low-income families, uses cash incentives tied to improvements in children's education, preventive health procedures, and parental employment. The randomized trial found that the program produced the following outcomes:

■ Changed how teenagers spent their time. For the subgroup of academically proficient teenagers, it increased the proportion of those who engaged primarily in academic activities and reduced the proportion who engaged primarily in social activities;

■ Increased parents' spending on school-related and leisure expenses and increased the proportion of parents who saved for their children's future education;

■ Had no effects on parents' monitoring of their teenage children's activities or behavior and did not increase parent-teenager conflict or teenagers' depression or anxiety;

■ Had no effects on teenagers' sense of academic competence or their engagement in school but substantially reduced their problem behavior, such as aggression and substance use;

■ Did not reduce teenagers' intrinsic motivation by paying them rewards for school attendance and academic achievement.

These findings reveal that the program had a positive effect on some outcomes but no effect on others. The program's developers could use these findings as feedback to improve the program and then test it again in another randomized trial. Because the program is expensive and its intended outcomes are very important, randomized trials are fully justified. Social and educational agencies would not want to find themselves in the position of allocating their resources to a program that looked promising but whose effectiveness was uncertain.

Effects of a Teaching Technique Using Questions and Graphic Organizers

Bulgren, J. A., Marquis, J. G., Lenz, B. K., Deshler, D. D., & Schumaker, J. B. (2011). The effectiveness of a question-exploration routine for enhancing the content learning of secondary students. *Journal of Educational Psychology, 103*(3), 578–593.

The experiments on class size and cash incentives that we reviewed above involve large-scale programs. Other experiments have a much smaller but still important focus. They seek to test the effectiveness of particular teaching techniques and learning strategies. An example is this study of a question-exploration routine (QER). It involved a social studies teacher, a science teacher, and their middle-school students whose parents signed consent forms allowing them to participate in the experiment.

The QER teaching method has three instructional phases. In the first phase, the teacher introduces a lesson topic and gives students a graphic organizer with questions on it and space to take notes. Among the questions are a key question that requires students to think, a question that requires students to identify key terms and their definitions, and questions that ask students to apply the curriculum content to the real world and other situations. In the second phase, the teacher and students work together to answer these questions; and in the third phase, they review the questions and answers covered in the graphic organizer and the process they used to answer the key question. This experimental method was compared with a control condition involving traditional instruction: distribution of a note-taking sheet, teacher presentation of information on which students were to take notes and information on an overhead transparency that students copied directly onto their note-taking sheet. Each student received both QER instruction and traditional instruction but with different curriculum content for each method.

The researchers found that students earned much higher scores on tests that measured lower-cognitive and higher-cognitive learning when they received QER instruction than when they received traditional instruction. Furthermore, when the data were analyzed separately for different sub-groups of students (students with disabilities, low-achieving students; average-achieving students, and high-achieving students), all of them learned more from QER instruction than from traditional instruction.

The researchers claim that the findings of their experiment have implications for improving classroom instruction in today's world:

> Given the increased emphasis on higher order thinking in outcome assessments in schools, the QER appears to be a viable instructional procedure for promoting student knowledge and understanding. Further, with the pronounced presence of academic diversity in most classrooms, these instructional procedures could commensurately improve the outcomes of all student subgroups.
>
> Bulgren et al., p. 591

A small-scale experiment such as this one is unlikely to produce large-scale improvements in education. However, it can stimulate follow-up experiments to determine whether the findings are replicable across different settings, students, and curriculum content. If the QER method proves to be robust, developers can produce materials to facilitate its use and a professional development program to help teachers learn it. Then educators can go about the process of disseminating the materials and program on a large scale. This is not a simple process, but it is one that is used in other professions, especially medicine.

FEATURES OF A REPORT OF A PRETEST-POSTTEST CONTROL-GROUP EXPERIMENT WITH RANDOMIZATION

Table 12.1 presents the typical features in a report of an experimental study. In the following sections, we discuss each feature and illustrate it with an experiment involving a program that was designed to teach life skills and drug-avoidance skills to middle school students. The experiment was conducted by Marvin Eisen, Gail Zellman, and David Murray (2003).

TABLE 12.1 • Typical Features of an Experimental Research Report

Feature	Experimental Research
Introduction	Hypotheses, questions, or objectives are stated. A review of relevant literature is reported. There is a statement of purpose, which typically involves the desirability of instituting an experimental program and determining its effects, typically in comparison to one or more control conditions.
Research design	Typically, the section on research design involves a description of the experimental and control groups, whether random sampling was used, and the schedule for administering pretests and posttests.
Sampling procedure	The sample is described, and differences between the experimental and control groups, if any, are noted.
Measures	The measures used to collect data on the independent and dependent variables are described, together with evidence relating to their validity and reliability.
Data analysis	This section typically presents descriptive statistics for the pretest and posttest measures. Tests of statistical significance, effect sizes, and statistical procedures to control for initial differences between the experimental and control groups on the posttests are also presented.
Discussion	The main findings of the study are summarized. Flaws and limitations of the study are considered as are implications of the findings for further research and for professional practice.

Of the various available experimental designs, this study employed the one that researchers view as most valid.

Introduction

The researchers started their report by noting the seriousness of substance abuse among teenagers. For example, they cited research findings that 15 percent of eighth-graders had smoked cigarettes and 14 percent had engaged in binge drinking during the month before they were surveyed. The researchers also noted that several substance abuse prevention programs for middle school students have been developed but have not been demonstrated as effective. The purpose of their experiment was to evaluate the effectiveness of another program, Skills for Adolescence (SFA), which more than 50,000 trained teachers and other school personnel had used by the end of the 1990s.

Research Design

The key features of a **pretest-posttest control-group experiment with randomization** are contained in its name. You might come across this term in a research report or alternative terms such as *randomized trial*, *randomized field trial*, or *true experiment*.

Inclusion of a Control Group

The study that we are describing was a control-group experiment because it included at least two groups of research participants: the group that received the intervention of primary interest and a control group that received another kind of intervention. Another possible arrangement might have been for one group to receive the full program while another group received a scaled-down version of the program and still another group continued with its usual activities.

In the experiment on substance abuse prevention, the experimental group participated in the SFA program. According to the researchers, this program includes processes that "utilize social influence and social cognitive approaches to teach cognitive-behavioral skills for building self-esteem and personal responsibility, communicating effectively, making better decisions, resisting social influences and asserting rights, and increasing drug use knowledge and consequences" (Eisen, Zellman, & Murray, 2003, p. 887). Students in the control condition received drug education, the elements of which were generally left to the discretion of their teachers and school administrators.

Random Assignment of Research Participants

The second feature of this experimental design is that the research participants are randomly assigned to the experimental and control conditions. Random assignment should not be confused with random selection, which involves procedures to ensure that all individuals in a defined population have an equal chance of being selected for participation in the research study.

Various procedures can be used to achieve random assignment. For example, we can make a list of the names of all of the research participants. Then we pick an arbitrary starting point in a table of random numbers. The first listed participant is assigned the starting number, the second participant is assigned the random number just below it, and so on. Then we place the list of names in numerical order using the random numbers assigned to each name. Finally, we assign the first name in the list to, let's say, the experimental condition. We assign the second name to the control condition, the third name to the experimental condition, and so on.

Random assignment does not guarantee that the experimental and control conditions will be equivalent in all possible ways. For example, by chance, a substantially higher percentage of males might end up in one condition or the other. This is more likely to happen if the total pool of research participants is small. Randomization ensures only that there is no systematic bias in the assignment of participants to the experimental and control groups. If the randomization procedure results in a substantial disparity between groups on an important variable, the researcher should consider repeating the randomization procedure.

In the case of the SFA experiment, middle schools in 4 of the 10 largest metropolitan areas in the United States were recruited. Those that agreed to the conditions of the experiment were randomly assigned to the experimental and control conditions. Thus, teachers in each school used either the SFA

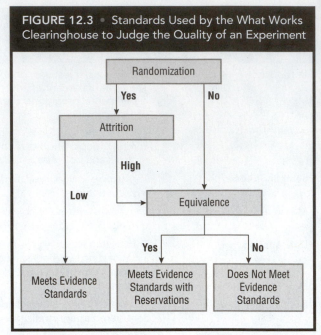

FIGURE 12.3 • Standards Used by the What Works Clearinghouse to Judge the Quality of an Experiment

Source: What Works Clearinghouse (2011, September). *Procedures and standards handbook* (Version 2.1). Retrieved from http://ies.ed.gov/ncee/wwc/pdf/reference_resources/wwc_procedures_v2_1_standards_handbook.pdf

program or their regular substance abuse prevention program.

This research design satisfies strong evidence standards, as specified by the What Works Clearinghouse. The primary evidence standards are shown in Figure 12.3. The figure shows that the primary standard is randomization (i.e., random assignment of individuals or groups to the experimental and control conditions). Without randomization, the best an experiment can do is to meet evidence standards with reservations. If randomization is present, the next relevant standard is attrition. If there is too much attrition of the sample during the experiment's duration or if there is too much differential attrition of participants in the experimental and control groups, the experiment is considered to have met the evidence standards with reservations.

Administration of Pretests and Posttests

The third feature of a pretest-posttest control-group experiment with randomization is the administration of at least one pretest and one posttest to the participants in the experimental and control conditions. This feature enables researchers to determine the extent of change or gain created by the experimental condition compared to the control condition.

Scores on the pretest measure also can be used to make a statistical adjustment that equalizes, to a degree, the experimental and control groups on that measure, even though their mean scores are different. If the statistical adjustment works, any observed difference between the two groups on the posttest measure can be attributed to the experimental intervention rather than to preexisting differences on the pretest measure. This statistical adjustment is typically accomplished by analysis of covariance (see Chapter 7) or multiple regression (see Chapter 11).

Variables measured by pretests are considered independent variables because they measure individual characteristics (e.g., academic achievement, attitudes, self-esteem) that exist prior to the beginning of the experimental and control conditions. Variables measured by posttests are considered dependent variables because they measure individual characteristics following the conclusion of the experimental and control conditions.

In terms of cause and effect, the experimental intervention and control conditions are the causes, and the posttest variables are the effects. Pretest variables also might be causes of these effects. For example, students who score high on a pretest measure of reading are likely to score high on a posttest using the same measure, regardless of whether they are in the treatment or control condition.

Sampling Procedure

As with any research design, researchers should select a sample that is representative of the population to which they wish to generalize their results. The researchers who conducted the SFA experiment reported, "Teenage drug usage remains a serious problem in the U.S., despite efforts by policymakers, health officials, educators, and prevention scientists to reduce it" (p. 884). The prevalence of drug use in this population justifies the researchers' decision to select a sample consisting of teenagers, specifically seventh-graders at the time they participated in the SFA program or control condition.

The researchers needed to obtain active parental consent for their children to participate in the experiment. Consent was obtained for 71 percent of the students in the participating schools.

The pretests were administered while the sample group was in the sixth grade. The experimental and control conditions occurred during the seventh grade, and a first set of posttests was administered at the end of this grade. Another publication reported the effects of the SFA program on this set of posttests (Eisen, Zellman, Massett, & Murray, 2002). The posttests were readministered at the end of eighth grade to determine the persistence of SFA effects one year later. These are the posttests that we are describing here.

As one might expect, sample attrition occurred from the time of the sixth-grade pretests to the end-of-eighth-grade posttests. The group that took the eighth-grade posttests included 87 percent of those students who completed the seventh-grade posttests.

Measures

The pretests and posttests used in an experimental design can include any of the measurement methods described in Chapter 5—tests, questionnaires, interviews, and direct observation. In the substance abuse prevention experiment, the pretests and posttests consisted of questionnaires. English and Spanish versions were created, and students could choose the version they preferred to complete. The primary variables measured by the questionnaires were self-reported use of alcohol, cigarettes, marijuana, cocaine/crack, and any other illicit drug during their lifetime and over the 30-day period prior to completing the questionnaire.

In addition, students completed questionnaire items that measured other variables: intent to use drugs in the next three months, beliefs about drug abuse held by their friends and peer group, beliefs about whether drug use would make it easier to fit in with others, perceptions concerning harmful effects of drugs, sense of self-efficacy about refusing drugs in various situations, perceived parental monitoring of their whereabouts after school, propensity for sensation seeking, and various demographic characteristics such as gender, family composition, and race/ethnicity.

Results

Analysis of variance (see Chapter 7) can be used to analyze experimental data. In analysis of variance, the two posttest means are compared to determine whether the posttest mean of the experimental condition is significantly greater or less than the posttest mean of the control group.

Analysis of covariance (see Chapter 7) is also used frequently. This statistical technique determines whether the posttest means differ significantly from each other after adjusting for possible differences in the pretest means of the two groups.

Multiple regression is another method for analyzing experimental data (see Chapter 11). In the substance abuse prevention experiment, the experimental condition (SFA versus the school's regular substance abuse prevention program) constitutes one variable. It is a dichotomous variable because it has only two values: each participating school is coded as SFA or non-SFA. SFA can be given a value of 1, and non-SFA can be given a value of 0, or vice versa. Another variable is the sample's posttest scores on each posttest measure. If SFA is coded as 1 and non-SFA is coded as 0, a positive correlation coefficient would mean that the students who participated in the SFA program had a higher posttest mean than students who participated in their school's regular substance abuse prevention program. Additional variables (e.g., pretest variables) can be examined to determine whether they predict the sample's posttest scores either independently or in relation to other variables that have been entered into the multiple regression equation.

Our explanations of analysis of variance, analysis of covariance, and multiple regression simplify their use in experiments. Understanding how they actually work requires extensive study of statistics. If you have not yet engaged in such studies, you can still learn a lot about the results of an experiment simply by examining the researchers' presentation of descriptive statistics, typically the means and standard deviations.

Eisen and his colleagues (2003) analyzed their data primarily by comparing the percentage of students in the SFA group and control group who engaged in substance use. They adjusted these percentages to account for group differences in substance use prior to the SFA program. The differences were generally small. For example, 22.85 percent of the SFA group consumed alcohol over a 30-day period compared to 23.18 percent of the control group; 11.32 percent of the SFA group smoked marijuana over a 30-day period compared to 13.79 percent of the control group.

Another finding is that substance use increased significantly from the time the students were in the sixth grade to the time they were in the eighth grade. For instance, the researchers found that 3.5 percent of the combined groups smoked cigarettes over a 30-day period in the sixth grade, but 12.47 percent of the SFA group and 11.48 percent of the control group smoked cigarettes over a 30-day period when they were surveyed in the eighth grade.

One other statistically significant difference was reported by the researchers. They found that, among students who reported on the pretest questionnaire that they were binge drinkers, a lower percentage (27 percent) who had participated in the SFA program reported binge drinking on the posttest questionnaire than students who had participated in their school's regular substance abuse prevention program (37 percent). For students who did not report binge drinking on the pretest, there was no difference in the percentage who reported binge drinking on the posttest (SFA group = 12 percent; control group = 12 percent).

Discussion: Implications for Practice

The discussion section of an experimental research report typically includes a summary of the main findings and an analysis of the study's limitations. Among the limitations described by the researchers who conducted the substance abuse prevention experiment was this: "Those students whose parents failed to return the consent form or denied consent cannot be assumed to be the same as those students with more compliant parents" (Eisen et al., 2003, p. 896). This is a legitimate concern because, as we indicated in the section on sampling above, only 71 percent of the parent sample gave consent.

The researchers' report provides various explanations for nonreturn of the parent consent form, such as a student not giving the form to a parent or a parent not being available to read and sign the form. These explanations, among others, suggest that the students who did not return the form have different characteristics than those who did, and these characteristics might have made them more, or less, receptive to the SFA substance abuse prevention program.

Of the various quantitative research designs, experiments typically have the most implications for practice, particularly if they yield positive results for students, educators, or other groups. The reason is that the researchers actually intervened in a situation and improved it. It seems likely then that educators might obtain similar benefits if they replicated the procedures used by the researchers in their own settings. The likelihood of replication of benefits is increased if the experiment is conducted in a real-life setting (e.g., a school) rather than in a laboratory-like situation.

The researchers who conducted the SFA experiment made the following claim based on their findings: "To our knowledge, these results provide the first tangible evidence that elements of a commercially available and widely used prevention program can delay regular marijuana use and reduce binge drinking among early onset drinkers for at least a 1-year post intervention period" (Eisen et al., 2003, p. 896).

Our own speculation is that the SFA program would have been even more beneficial for teenagers if it had been extended over several years rather than being used as a one-year intervention in the seventh grade. Of course, this remains only a speculation until tested by more experiments.

OTHER GROUP EXPERIMENT DESIGNS

A pretest-posttest control-group experiment with randomization, as described above, is almost always the preferred experimental design. Other experimental designs are available for special purposes or because of constraints imposed by administrators in the setting where the experiment is to bee conducted.

Table 12.2 lists experimental designs from which researchers typically choose when planning an experiment. We discuss two of them in the following sections. Other designs not listed in the table generally are extensions of them. The most common extension is the incorporation of additional comparison groups into the experimental design. For example, the experimental substance abuse education program was conducted while the students were in seventh grade; the control program was the school's regular substance abuse prevention program. This design could have been extended, let's say, by including an experimental condition in which some of the students participated in the experimental program in the seventh grade and received additional education about substance abuse

in the eighth grade. The statistical analysis, then, would have involved comparison of the posttest means for three groups, not two.

Quasi-Experiments

Randomization is fairly easy to achieve under laboratory-like conditions. For example, many experiments about learning processes are conducted with college students, often students enrolled in psychology or education classes. They are asked to come to a special room (a "laboratory" of sorts) and participate in the experimental condition to which they have been randomly assigned. The intervention typically lasts less than an hour. Students might receive grade points or some other reward for their participation.

Experiments in real-life school settings (often called *field settings*), especially if they are of extended duration, place many more demands on school personnel. Random assignment of students or classrooms to different experimental conditions can be disruptive to regular school routines. For this reason, school personnel and parents might refuse to consent to this design feature of an experiment.

The alternatives left to the researchers are either to abandon the experiment or to design it without randomization. If the experimental program or intervention seems promising, it does not make sense to abandon efforts to test its effectiveness. Therefore, researchers might choose the other option, a **quasi-experiment**, which is an experiment with experimental and control groups but without random assignment of participants to these groups. This label has negative connotations, but in fact, a quasi-experiment can yield much useful knowledge if steps are taken to make the groups as equivalent as possible when they are selected for participation in the experiment.

The customary procedure is for the researchers to work together with school personnel to select schools and teachers where the experimental program or intervention can be tried. For example, in the substance abuse education experiment, the researchers could search for schools willing to try the SFA program. Once those schools are identified, the researchers and school personnel can form a control group by identifying other schools with characteristics similar to those of the experimental-condition schools. This procedure provides some

TABLE 12.2 • Types of Experimental Designs

Type of Experimental Design	Comments
Single-Group Designs	
One-shot case study	Weakest design. No way to determine amount of change resulting from the intervention.
X O	
One-group pretest-posttest design	Weak design. Can be used as an exploratory experiment, particularly if researchers can estimate expected pretest-posttest change in the research participants if they had not received the experimental intervention.
O X O	
Control-Group Designs	
Pretest-posttest control-group design with randomization	Strong design. The substance abuse education experiment described in this chapter is an example.
R O X O	
R O Y O	
Pretest-posttest control-group design without randomization	Moderately strong design. Sometimes called a quasi-experiment. Because random assignment is lacking, it can be difficult to determine whether differences in pretest-posttest change are due to the experimental condition or to initial differences between the groups.
O X O	
O Y O	
Posttest-only control-group design with randomization	Moderately strong design. Its use is recommended when there is reason to believe that administration of a pretest would raise the possibility that posttest differences could be attributed, in whole or in part, to the pretest rather than solely to the experimental intervention.
R X O	
R Y O	
Posttest-only control-group design without randomization	Very weak design. Change from pretest to posttest cannot be determined because no pretest is administered, and it is not possible to determine whether differences on the posttest are due to the experimental intervention or initial differences between the groups.
X O	
Y O	
Factorial Designs	
Two-factor experiments	Strong design. Its purpose is to determine the simultaneous effects of several interventions or participant characteristics on pretest-posttest change. The two-factor design can be extended to include three or more factors.
R O $X_1 Y_1$ O	
R O $X_1 Y_2$ O	
R O $X_2 Y_1$ O	
R O $X_2 Y_2$ O	
Solomon four-group experiment	Strong design. It is similar to the posttest-only control-group design with randomization except that it enables the researcher to determine whether administration of a pretest affects participants' posttest scores and also whether the pretest administration interacts with the experimental or control condition to affect the posttest scores.
R O X O	
R X O	
R O Y O	
R Y O	

R = research participants are randomly assigned to the experimental or control condition
O = observation, either a pretest or posttest
X = experimental condition
Y = control or comparison condition

assurance that any observed differences between the experimental and control groups on the post-test are due to the experimental program, not to preexisting differences in characteristics of concern to the researchers.

Factorial Experimental Designs

In experiments, the term **factor** has the same meaning as the term **independent variable**. Each factor is viewed as an independent variable that exists prior to the dependent variable measured by the posttest and therefore possibly having a causal influence on that variable. The term **factorial experiment** is used to refer to an experiment having more than one factor (i.e., independent variable).

In the substance abuse prevention experiment, teachers, counselors, and other school personnel delivered the SFA program. Suppose we hypothesized that counselors might make the best program instructors because of their specialized training in students' emotional and behavioral problems. To test this hypothesis, we could design an experiment with two factors: type of program and type of instructor, as depicted in the following table:

Type of Instructor	Type of Program	
	SFA Program	School's Regular Program
Teachers	Cell 1	Cell 2
Counselors	Cell 3	Cell 4

You can see that the experimental program has four cells, each of which includes a different program and type of instructor. If we had 40 participating teachers, we ideally would randomly assign them to cells 1 and 2; and if we had 40 participating counselors, we ideally would randomly assign them to cells 3 and 4.

We can use analysis of variance or analysis of covariance to address several questions about the data resulting from this factorial design. First, we can determine whether one type of instructor produces better student outcomes (i.e., less substance abuse at the end of eighth grade) than the other, irrespective of which program she or he taught. Second, we can determine whether one program produces better student outcomes than the other, irrespective of who taught it.

Third, we can examine the possible occurrence of program-by-instructor interactions. An **interaction effect** means that an independent variable has an effect on the dependent variable, but only under certain conditions in the experimental design. For example, it might be that counselors are more effective than teachers for the SFA program but that counselors and teachers are equally effective when delivering the school's regular program. If we obtained this finding, we would say that an interaction effect occurred.

The factorial design that we are describing has two factors. It also is possible to create experimental designs with three or more factors.

THREATS TO THE INTERNAL VALIDITY OF EXPERIMENTS

Program adoption decisions increasingly are made on the basis of evidence from experiments. Therefore, educators need to understand how to determine whether the evidence is sound. In particular, educators need to be able to judge whether the observed results were caused by the experimental intervention or by one or more extraneous factors.

An **extraneous variable** is a factor other than the treatment variable that might have an effect on the outcome variables. If extraneous variables are present, the researchers will find it difficult to determine the extent to which an observed difference between the experimental and control groups on the dependent variable is caused by the intervention or by one or more extraneous variables.

For example, suppose that, by chance, a higher percentage of male students are in the school's regular substance abuse program than in the SFA (Skills for Adolescence) program. Suppose, too, that male students have a higher rate of substance abuse than female students.

Now suppose that we discover the students in the SFA program have better results on the outcome variables than students in the school's regular program. One explanation for this finding is that the SFA program is more effective. Another explanation, equally plausible, is that the SFA program was not more effective, but it produced better outcomes because it had fewer male participants than the regular substance abuse prevention program. The extraneous variable of gender has made it difficult, if not impossible, to determine the actual impact of the SFA program on the outcome variables.

Ideally, an experiment would have no extraneous factors. Such an experiment would be said to have high **internal validity**, meaning that observed differences between experimental and control groups on an outcome variable are solely attributable to the treatment variable. If an experiment has low internal validity, it means that observed differences between experimental groups on an outcome variable can be attributed to the treatment variable or to extraneous factors.

Donald Campbell and Julian Stanley (1963) identified eight types of extraneous variables that can affect the internal validity of experiments. Other extraneous variables have been identified, but these eight extraneous variables reflect common challenges to researchers in designing and conducting experiments.

History Effect

If an experimental intervention extends over a substantial period of time, there is opportunity for other events to have an effect on the outcome variables. If these other events influence the outcome variables, researchers say that a **history effect** occurred.

In the substance abuse education experiment, the SFA program lasted for a substantial part of the students' seventh grade of school. During this time and the follow-up period (students were not given the posttest until the end of eighth grade), many other events could have occurred to affect students' substance abuse. However, the experiment included a randomly assigned control group, which presumably would have experienced similar events.

The statistical analysis compared the experimental group relative to the control group, so observed posttest differences would reflect the SFA program's effectiveness over and above the effects of history. Thus, history can be ruled out as an extraneous variable.

Maturation Effect

While an experimental treatment is in progress, certain developmental processes occur in the research participants. For example, participants become older and therefore might experience increased physical fitness, optimism, or some other emotional or physical change, all of which are forms of maturation as defined by Campbell and Stanley (1963). If these developmental changes affect the outcome variables in an experiment, researchers say that a **maturation effect** has occurred.

In the experiment we have been analyzing, the SFA program was compared to a randomly formed control group, which had equal time for maturation. Thus, the extraneous variable of maturation was controlled.

Testing Effect

In many educational experiments, a pretest is administered, followed by the treatment and control conditions and concluding with a posttest. If the pretest and posttest are similar or are administered close together in time, research participants might show an improvement on the posttest simply as a result of their experience with the pretest. In other words, they have become test wise. These possible threats to the internal validity of an experiment can be assessed by doing a **Solomon four-group experiment** (see Table 12.2). If administration of a pretest affects posttest scores, the two groups that took the pretest but did not participate in the experimental or control condition will show a significant change from their pretest scores to their posttest scores.

It is also possible that administration of a pretest enhances or other otherwise affects the treatment condition. For example, the pretest might sensitize participants to the content of the experimental condition, and therefore they learn more from the experimental condition than if they had not taken the pretest. Because the design of the experiment includes the experimental condition both with and without a pretest, this type of pretest sensitization can be detected. The only drawback is that the Solomon four-group design can be difficult to implement. The researcher needs to recruit a substantial number of participants and gain their cooperation in being assigned to one of four experimental conditions.

If repeated administration of a test affects the outcome variable, researchers say that a **testing effect** has occurred. It is unlikely that this extraneous variable was operating in the substance abuse education experiment because the interval between the pretest and posttest was nearly two years.

Instrumentation Effect

An apparent learning gain from the pretest to the posttest might occur if a different measure was used each time. For example, suppose the pretest in the substance abuse prevention experiment involved interview questions, and the posttest involved the same questions but in a questionnaire format. This procedure would make it nearly impossible to determine whether observed pretest-posttest differences in the experimental group and control group were due to the intervention or to the change in testing procedure. If changes in the measuring instrument affect the results of an experiment, researchers say that an **instrumentation effect** has occurred.

Statistical Regression

Whenever a pretest-posttest procedure is used to assess learning in an experiment, the individuals scoring very high or very low on the pretest will tend to have scores somewhat closer to the mean on the posttest. This phenomenon is known as **statistical regression**.

For example, suppose that the average pretest score of students in the experimental group was at the 15th percentile on national norms for the test. When this group of students takes the test again (i.e., the posttest), they are likely to earn a higher mean score, with or without any intervening experimental treatment. The reason for this phenomenon is that the students' low initial scores likely result not only from lower ability but also from chance factors. Perhaps they were feeling ill on the day of the test, or maybe they made unlucky guesses on some test items.

On retesting, these chance factors are unlikely to be present again. Consequently, their test scores will improve independently of the effect of the experimental intervention. Similarly, due to chance factors, when students with very high pretest scores are retested, their scores also are likely to regress, that is, move downward toward the mean.

The possibility of statistical regression needs to be considered if all, or most, of the research participants are very high or very low on a key variable in the experiment. For example, an experiment involving highly talented youth might be susceptible to statistical regression on a pretest-posttest measure of achievement. This problem can be avoided if the pretest and posttest are sufficiently difficult that the majority of the research participants do not earn very high scores on them.

Differential Selection

In quasi-experiments, described previously, participants are selected for the experimental and control groups by a procedure other than random assignment. Because the participants in the two groups have been differentially selected, the groups might have different initial characteristics that affect the posttest variable.

If the different initial characteristics of the selected groups affect the outcome variables, researchers say that a **differential selection effect** has occurred. The presence of this effect makes it difficult to determine the extent to which observed differences between the experimental and control groups on the posttest are caused by the experimental intervention or by differences in the groups' initial characteristics. Quasi-experiments are particularly susceptible to this problem because the sample is not randomly assigned to the experimental and control groups. However, the threat of a differential-selection effect can be mitigated by making an effort to select control-group participants who are similar to the experimental-group participants on crucial initial characteristics.

Selection-Maturation Interaction

This extraneous variable is similar to differential selection except that maturation is the specific confounding variable. Suppose that first-grade students from a single school district are selected to receive instruction in a new reading program, whereas the control group is drawn from the population of first-grade students in another school district. Because of different admissions policies in the two school districts, the mean age of students in the control group is six months higher than the mean age of students in the experimental group.

Suppose we find that the experimental group made significantly greater achievement gains than the control group. Do these results reflect the greater effectiveness of the experimental treatment or the effects of maturation? Due to differential selection of students into the experimental and control groups, the researchers would not be able to answer this question with any confidence. This situation is called a **selection-maturation interaction effect** because the experimental and control groups contain participants who are at different developmental levels.

Experimental Mortality

Experimental mortality, more commonly called **attrition**, involves the loss of research participants over the course of the experimental treatment. Attrition can make it difficult to interpret the data if the participants who drop out in the experimental group and control group have different characteristics.

For example, analysis of attrition data in the substance abuse prevention experiment revealed that 37 percent of the students who reported in the pretest questionnaire that they had used marijuana recently failed to complete the eighth-grade posttest questionnaire. In contrast, only 23 percent of the students who did not report using marijuana recently failed to complete this questionnaire. Because of this differential attrition, we cannot be certain of the effectiveness of the SFA program relative to the control condition in helping students avoid marijuana one year after completing the program.

THREATS DIRECTLY INVOLVING THE EXPERIMENTAL INTERVENTION

Educators know that different teachers are likely to implement the same curriculum differently. For example, the essentials of the curriculum might be present in all teachers' classrooms, but some teachers might place more emphasis on certain topics, and other teachers might include topics not in the curriculum. In an experiment, however, all participants need to implement the experimental program as it was designed. Otherwise, the program might be found to be ineffective simply because it was implemented haphazardly. If so, the program might be added to the list of failed innovations even though it actually might be effective if implemented as intended by its developers. Research reports should include information about this feature of experiments, called **treatment fidelity** and defined as the extent to which the experimental intervention is implemented according to the specifications of the researchers or program developers.

In the substance abuse education experiment, the SFA program included 40 sessions, each lasting 35 to 45 minutes. However, the experimenters found variations among teachers. The mean number of sessions, based on teacher self-report, was 32.74, with some teachers conducting more sessions and others conducting fewer. This flaw in treatment fidelity might have weakened the program's effectiveness.

Another threat relating to experimental programs is the potency of the intervention. A program might be strong or weak in various dimensions, such as duration, intensity, quality of instructional design, and skill of the individuals delivering the program. In medicine, for example, researchers often need to experiment with the proper dosage of a new drug. The drug might be effective, but not if too little or too much is administered or if it is administered for too brief a period of time.

In the substance abuse education experiment, the teachers who delivered the SFA program attended a three-day workshop conducted by certified SFA trainers. Was this a sufficient amount of training? This question was not addressed in the report. However, the fact that program effects on the posttest were found suggests that the amount of training was at least minimally adequate.

The posttest results from the study by Eisen and his colleagues (2003) indicate that the SFA students had better outcomes than the control-group students on several of the variables. However, in our view, the rate of substance abuse in both groups is alarming. It seems that a much stronger program than that tested in the researchers' experiment is necessary to substantially lower the rates of substance use or bring them to a "zero tolerance" level.

Another kind of threat relating to the experimental intervention is the **Hawthorne effect**. In an experiment, the intervention is thought to be whatever procedures are specified for the experimental group. However, it is also the case that the research sample has an awareness that they are participating in an experiment and are receiving special attention from the researchers. This awareness can give rise to what is known as the **Hawthorne effect**, which is an improvement in the experimental group's performance because of the special attention that they have received from the researchers. Of course, improvement in the experimental group's performance might be a function of both the Hawthorne effect and the power of the experimental intervention.

The possibility of the Hawthorne effect in a particular experiment can be tested by interviewing a sample of the research participants at the conclusion of the experimental period. The participants might say that their performance improved for various reasons, such as enjoying the attention of the researchers (the Hawthorne effect) or feeling that the experiment brought them into a more collaborative arrangement with colleagues or fellow students. These interviews can be formalized by using a mixed-methods research design, which we discuss in Chapter 17.

THREATS TO THE EXTERNAL VALIDITY OF EXPERIMENTS

Experiments often are expensive to conduct, and therefore the experimental intervention is limited to a relatively small sample in one setting within a limited time frame. If the intervention proves to be effective, though, educators will want to know whether it will work as well in other settings with other individuals. In researchers' terminology, this is a matter of external validity. Experiments have **external validity** to the extent to which their results can be generalized to other individuals, settings, and time periods. Bracht and Glass (1968) analyzed experiments and concluded that they are vulnerable to three threats to external validity: population validity, personological variables, and ecological validity.

Population Validity

In Chapter 5, we defined **population validity** as the degree to which the results of a research study can be generalized from the specific sample that was studied to the population from which the sample was drawn. To determine population validity, one must assess the degree of similarity among the research sample that was used in the study, the accessible population from which the research sample was drawn, and the larger target population to which the research results are to be generalized.

The more evidence the researcher provides to establish links between the sample, the accessible population, and the target population, the more confident you can be in generalizing the research findings to the target population. The lack of such evidence acts as a threat to the external validity of the experiment.

Educators usually are not as interested in the similarity between the research sample and the target population as in the similarity between the research sample and the individuals in their local setting. To determine this type of similarity, educators

should note all relevant information in the research report about the sample, such as age, gender, academic aptitude, ethnicity, socioeconomic status, and the characteristics of the communities in which they live. They can compare the resulting profile with information about the local setting to which they wish to apply the research findings.

Personological Variables

Another factor affecting external validity is the possibility that various personal characteristics of the research sample interact with the experimental intervention. An interaction is present if the experimental results apply to research participants with certain characteristics (e.g., those who have low test anxiety) but not to those with other characteristics (e.g., those who have high test anxiety). If this type of interaction is thought to be likely and important, a factorial experiment (described previously in this chapter) can be conducted to verify its existence and magnitude.

If an experiment has high external validity, the results of the experiment should apply to all kinds of individuals, not just to individuals having a certain characteristic. Of course, if researchers find that the results apply only to a population having a certain characteristic, we can say at least that the experiment has external validity for that population.

Ecological Validity

Ecological validity is the degree to which an experimental result can be generalized to settings other than the one that was studied. To determine ecological validity for a particular setting, you need to determine whether its critical features, such as grade level, type of school, and type of community, are similar to the situation in which the experiment was conducted.

SINGLE-CASE EXPERIMENTS

A **single-case experiment** (also called a *single-subject experiment* or a *time-series experiment*) is a research study in which the effect of an intervention on a dependent variable is determined by applying that intervention to a single individual or more than one individual treated as a single group. Researchers favor single-case experiments over group experiments when they wish to observe the effects of interventions on specific behaviors and skills of individuals or a single group.

For example, researchers might wish to diagnose a dyslexic student's reading problem, devise an individualized strategy to solve it, and then conduct a single-case experiment to rigorously test the effectiveness of the strategy through repeated phases of data collection. No matter how uncommon the individual's problem, a single-case experiment can be designed to investigate it. There is no need to search through a large population for a sufficient number of individuals who can participate in a conventional experiment with experimental and control groups.

Some researchers view single-case experiments as watered-down versions of one of the group-experiment designs presented earlier in this chapter. In fact, single-case experiments are rigorous and time-consuming, and often they involve as much data collection as a design involving experimental and control groups. Furthermore, researchers who conduct single-case experiments are just as concerned about issues of internal and external validity as researchers who conduct group experiments.

The treatment condition in a single-case experiment often involves some form of behavior analysis and behavior modification. **Behavior analysis** involves careful observation of an individual in a setting, determination of dysfunctional behaviors in that setting, and specification of desired behaviors. **Behavior modification** involves techniques such as reinforcement, modeling, and discrimination training to increase or decrease the frequency of specified behaviors.

The purpose of single-case experiments in these situations is to determine whether a particular type of behavior analysis and behavior modification is effective for individuals with a certain type of problem. Therefore, single-case experiments have direct implications for the improvement of professional practice. The titles of the following journal articles illustrate the range of problems that single-case experiments can address:

Blood, E., Johnson, J. W., Ridenour, L., Simmons, K., & Crouch, S. (2011). Using an iPod Touch to teach social and self-management skills to an elementary student with emotional/behavioral disorders. *Education and Treatment of Children, 34*(3), 299–321.

Faul, A., Stepensky, K., & Simonsen, B. (2012). The effects of prompting appropriate behavior on the off-task behavior of two middle school students. *Journal of Positive Behavior Interventions, 14*(1), 47–55.

Legutko, R. S., & Trissle, T. T. (2012). The effects of background music on learning disabled elementary school students' performance in writing. *Current Issues in Education, 15*(1).

Patterson, S. Y., Smith, V., & Mirenda, P. (2012). A systematic review of training programs for parents with autism spectrum disorders: Single subject contributions. *Autism: The International Journal of Research and Practice, 16*(5), 498–522.

In the next sections, we illustrate the features of a single-case experiment by Linda Mechling, David Gast, and Beth Cronin (2006) to test the effectiveness of an intervention to improve the task performance of two middle school students with a diagnosis of moderate mental retardation and autism spectrum disorder (ASD).

Although an increasing number of children are being diagnosed as autistic, its incidence in the population is still low. Therefore, it would be difficult to form a research sample of sufficient size for one of the group-experiment designs described in the first part of the chapter. Moreover, the intervention in the experiment by Mechling and colleagues was designed to change specific behaviors, as determined by a careful behavioral analysis of particular autistic students' needs. Single-case experiments are especially appropriate under these conditions.

FEATURES OF A REPORT OF A SINGLE-CASE EXPERIMENT

Table 12.3 presents typical features of a report of a single-case experiment. We describe each of these features in the following sections.

Introduction

The introductory section of the report should demonstrate the significance of the single-case experiment, its specific purposes, and the major variables of interest. It also should include a literature review so that the reader understands how the present study intends to contribute to research knowledge.

In the autism experiment, the researchers reviewed research findings on the kinds of reinforcers that are effective for autistic children. (*Reinforcer* is a technical term in behavioral theory, similar in meaning to *reward*.) They found that these children

TABLE 12.3 • Typical Features of a Research Report for a Single-Case Experiment

Feature	Experimental Research
Introduction	Hypotheses, questions, or objectives are stated. A review of relevant literature is reported. There is a statement of purpose, which usually is to test the effectiveness of an intervention on one or a few individuals.
Research design	Description of the research design refers to several phases: one or more phases are baseline conditions in which the intervention is absent, and one or more phases are treatment conditions in which the intervention is present.
Sampling procedure	Description of the sample usually refers to one or a few individuals who have a particular problem. The problem typically has behavioral manifestations and a low incidence in the general population.
Measures	The report typically refers to an observational scale for counting the frequency of one or more specific behaviors. Trained observers report data on the scale at several fixed intervals during each phase (baseline and treatment) during the course of the experiment.
Data analysis	The report typically includes a graph, the y axis of which represents the frequency of a specific behavior and the x axis of which represents the points in time that the behavior was observed.
Discussion	The main findings of the study are summarized. Flaws and limitations of the study are considered. Implications of the findings for further research and for professional practice are considered.

like stimuli that are not of interest to nonautistic children and also that they like to have choices of rewards. However, their review also discovered that specific reinforcers may lose their effectiveness over time and also that some reinforcers for autistic children are not readily available.

On the basis of this research knowledge, Mechling and her colleagues formulated the purpose for their experiment: "Faced with the need to (a) provide reinforcers to motivate children with ASD and (b) prevent satiation through the use of novel or different stimuli, the current study evaluated the use of video technology as an alternative means for providing choice and access to high-preference items to increase motivation" (p. 8).

Research Design

Single-case experiments can vary in design, but all share two elements: a baseline condition and a treatment condition. A **baseline condition** is the set of typical conditions under which the research participant behaves; it typically is designated as "A." A **treatment condition** is the set of conditions that represent the experimental intervention; it typically is designated as "B." Thus, in an **A-B-A**

research design, the experiment includes an initial period of time during which the research participant is observed under typical conditions. Next follows the experimental intervention and observation of the research participant under those conditions. Finally, there is a period of time in which the research participant is once again observed under typical conditions.

The autism experiment involved an **A-B-A-B research design**. This design is similar to the A-B-A design just described except that it involves one more phase, namely, reinstatement of the experimental intervention. If the intervention is effective, we would expect to see

- the desired change in the research participant's behavior occur after the intervention (B) is introduced
- a return of the research participant's behavior to its original state (A) after the intervention is stopped
- the desired change in the research participant's behavior recur after the intervention (B) is once again introduced

The A-B-A-B design has strong internal validity because it includes a **reversal phase**, which involves a second A condition to demonstrate active control of the target behavior by removing the intervention that is hypothesized to have caused the initial change (the initial B condition). Reinstatement of the treatment (the second B condition) provides additional evidence of the intervention effect.

Some behaviors might not reasonably be expected to revert to their original state after the intervention is removed. Also, there might be ethical prohibitions about reinstating the conditions that existed prior to the intervention. For example, suppose a researcher wished to evaluate a counseling intervention designed to reduce a research participant's anxiety level. If the participant's anxiety level was lowered during the course of the intervention, the researcher could not ethically withdraw the successful intervention in order to observe whether the client's anxiety level returned to its pretreatment level.

In these situations, researchers would use a **multiple-baseline research design**, which includes situations other than the naturally occurring condition as a control for determining the presence of intervention effects. For example, the researcher might select three different behaviors that the intervention is hypothesized to improve. If the intervention is applied to the first behavior and it improves while the other two behaviors remain unchanged, this is evidence that the intervention has an effect not attributable to other factors.

The next step is to apply the intervention to the second behavior. If this behavior improves and the third behavior does not, this is more evidence that the intervention is having an effect. Finally, the intervention is applied to the third behavior, and if it too improves, this finding adds to the weight of evidence supporting the effectiveness of the intervention.

In the autism experiment, the two participating students (Donald and Jackson) completed their usual independent work sessions, which were scheduled one or two times per day for 30 minutes each. The work session included three learning tasks, such as reading simple directions, answering "wh-" questions from a story, and using a written menu to order food. Upon completion of their learning tasks, the students had 10 minutes to engage with a preselected reinforcing material or activity.

In the baseline condition (A), the students spent their 10 minutes with one of two reinforcers selected by the teacher. (In the journal article, they are called "tangible reinforcers.") These reinforcers had been previously chosen by the students as their most preferred stimuli. For Donald, the two reinforcers were Dr. Seuss books and sitting inside a tent. For Jackson, they were a pinball game and listening to music.

In the treatment condition (B), the reinforcers were more varied, but all involved viewing minute-long computer-based videos. Some of the videos showed the student (Donald or Jackson) interacting with one or the other of his previously chosen preferred stimuli. Others showed the student interacting with a preferred stimulus not available in the classroom setting. For Donald, the preferred stimuli were holiday scenes in the community and expressions of familiar adults. For Jackson, the preferred stimuli were community choirs and his own participation singing in a choir.

During the 10-minute reinforcement period, the student was shown three photos on the computer screen, each representing a preferred stimulus. The student chose one of the photos and then viewed the corresponding one-minute video. This process was repeated nine more times during the reinforcement period, with an equal number of opportunities to choose each photo.

Sampling Procedure

Single-case experiments typically test the effectiveness of interventions that will be delivered individually to persons with special needs that have a low population incidence (e.g., autism). Therefore, random selection of a sample from a defined population, although a powerful sampling method, is seldom possible.

Instead, the researcher typically prepares a detailed description of each participant's characteristics so that educators can decide whether the students whom they are trying to help have similar characteristics. Also, the researcher might replicate the research design with several similar individuals to determine whether the intervention effects recur. If the replication is successful, this finding should increase educators' confidence that the intervention will be effective with students who are similar to those who participated in the experiment.

In the report of the autism experiment, Mechling and her colleagues included two research participants, each of whom completed the experiment independently of the other. Also, they provided a detailed description of each participant. Among other findings, we learn that one of them, Jackson, age 13 years 2 months at the time of the experiment, had been diagnosed with autism at age 6 by a professional psychologist and that he was found to have mild mental retardation based on two assessment measures. The other student, Donald, age 14 years 4 months, was diagnosed with autism at age 4 by a licensed psychologist and was found to have moderate mental retardation based on two assessment measures. In addition to providing this information, the researchers described the students' intellectual capabilities and learning needs in some detail.

Measures

Single-case experiments generally do not have pretests and posttests, as is typical of group experiments. Instead, one measure is administered repeatedly to determine whether performance on the measure changes from one condition (baseline or treatment) to another. Most often, the measurement is based on direct observation of the frequency or duration of the behavior that is targeted for change. If the target variable is a learning outcome, a brief test that can be administered repeatedly will be used. If the target variable is an emotional state such as anxiety, a brief paper-and-pencil scale can be administered.

In the autism experiment, the target behavior was the amount of time it took Daniel and Jackson to complete the three learning tasks in a work session, which was designed to last approximately 30 minutes. An observer recorded the duration of work sessions in the baseline and treatment conditions.

The observational data would be invalid, of course, if the observer did not record duration times accurately. Therefore, the observer's measurements were checked for reliability by videotaping a third of the work sessions. An independent observer viewed the tapes and recorded work-session durations. This observer's data were found to be highly similar to the data collected by the person who directly observed the two students' behavior.

Results

The results of the autism experiment are shown in Figure 12.4, a form of graphical representation that is standard in reports of single-case experiments. Figure 12.4 contains two graphs, one for each student. The dotted vertical lines in each graph indicate the transition point from one condition (baseline or treatment) to the other. Each data point is the number of minutes it took for Donald or Jackson to complete all of the learning tasks in a work session.

Inspection of each graph shows clearly that both boys completed their tasks in much less time when their reinforcer consisted of an opportunity to choose a video and then to watch it. The use of a tangible reinforcer was much less effective.

As with group experiments, various factors can threaten the validity of causal interpretations made on the basis of statistical results from single-case experiments. In the case of the autism experiment, we need to consider the possibility that a factor other than the video-and-choice reinforcer caused Donald and Jackson to complete their learning tasks much more quickly.

The A-B-A-B design used in the experiment and the results shown in Figure 12.4 provide a strong basis for ruling out other factors as possible causal agents. If the availability of a reinforcer, regardless of type, was the causal agent, the duration of the work sessions would be relatively constant across the baseline and treatment conditions. Figure 12.4 rules out this explanation because the data points vary dramatically across the two conditions.

The timing of the baseline and treatment conditions provides another possible interpretation of cause and effect. The video-and-choice condition came after the tangible reinforcer condition, so one could argue that, by the time it ended, the students had become familiar with the observer and the work session procedures; therefore, they executed the tasks more quickly in the next condition (video and choice).

However, the A-B-A-B design includes two more conditions. When the tangible reinforcer was reintroduced, the students' duration time increased once again. This result rules out familiarity with the observer and procedure as causes of the observed effects.

Descriptive statistics can be computed for data generated in a single-case experiment. For example, the researchers reported that Donald's mean task-completion time across sessions for the first baseline condition (tangible reinforcers) was 27.8 minutes, and the mean task-completion time across sessions for the first video-and-choice condition was 11 minutes. These descriptive statistics are helpful supplements to the information gained from visual inspection of the graphs.

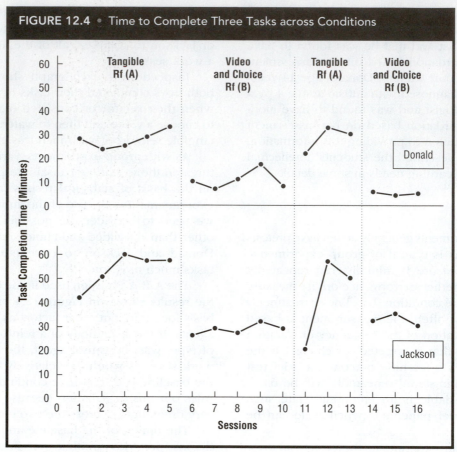

FIGURE 12.4 • Time to Complete Three Tasks across Conditions

Note: Rf = reinforcement

Source: Mechling, L. C., Gast, D. L., & Cronin, B. A. (2006). The effects of presenting high-performance items, paired with choice, via computer-based video programming on task completion of students with autism. *Focus on Autism and Other Developmental Disabilities, 21*(1), 7–13. Copyright © 2006 by Sage Publications. Reprinted by permission of Sage Publications.

Discussion: Implications for Practice

The discussion section of a report of a single-case experiment typically includes a summary of the main findings, analysis of the study's limitations, and recommendations for further research. For example, in the autism experiment, Mechling and her colleagues noted that the tangible reinforcement condition did not allow the students to choose a reinforcer, whereas the video reinforcement condition did. Therefore, we do not know whether it was (1) the opportunity to make choices, (2) the viewing of videos, or (3) a combination of choice and videos that produced superior results relative to the tangible reinforcement condition. The researchers recommended further study to determine which of

these three possibilities made the video reinforcement condition an effective intervention.

Researchers also use the discussion section to consider implications of their findings for professional practice. In the autism experiment, for example, the researchers stated that "results of the current study indicate that providing students the opportunity to view high-preference items and activities via video technology may be a viable means of providing novel, meaningful, and highly preferred stimuli that can function as positive reinforcement" (Mechling et al., 2006, p. 12).

The discovery of this "viable" procedure is likely to be welcomed by parents and teachers of autistic children. It is one more method that they can try out as they strive to promote the learning of this special and increasingly prevalent population. Furthermore, the findings might stimulate the development of new techniques for other groups, including students in the regular school population so that they, too, learn more effectively.

EVALUATING AN EXPERIMENTAL RESEARCH STUDY

The questions stated in Appendix 3 are relevant to evaluating an experimental research study. The following additional questions can help you judge whether a group experiment was weakened by specific problems that can arise in descriptive research.

■ Did the researchers randomly assign the sample to the experimental and control conditions?

Check the report to determine how the researchers assigned the sample to the different conditions. Randomization procedures do not necessarily result in similar groups, so check whether the researchers compared the randomly assigned groups on demographic variables and other relevant variables. If randomization procedures were not used, it is especially important to check whether the researchers compared the groups to determine how similar they were to each other.

■ Did the researchers check for threats to the internal and external validity of the experiment?

Check the report to determine whether the internal validity of the experiment was subject to any of the eight threats described in this chapter. Similarly, check for any of the three threats to the external validity of an experiment described in the chapter.

■ Did the research participants follow the researchers' specifications for the experimental intervention or control conditions?

Check the report to determine whether the researchers collected data to determine how well the research participants, which might include both teachers and students, adhered to the intervention or control conditions.

■ Was the intervention sufficiently strong?

Make a judgment about how strong the intervention would need to be in order to have an effect on the dependent variables

in the experiment. Then check the report to determine whether the strength of the intervention is consistent with your judgment.

Single-case experiments can also be evaluated using the questions in Appendix 3. In addition, consider the following questions.

■ Did the experiment contain sufficient data points?

The dependent variable should have been measured sufficiently often that you can see a clear trend during each of the intervention and control conditions. You can check whether the trends are clear and convincing by examining the graphs that typically are included in reports of this type of research.

■ Did the experiment include a control condition?

Check the report to determine whether the control condition provided an appropriate contrast to the experimental condition. The results for the two conditions should be sufficiently different to convince you that the experimental intervention actually had an effect. If there was an effect, make a judgment about whether it was substantially better than any effect produced by the control condition.

The What Works Clearinghouse (2011) has developed additional criteria for evaluating the quality of single-subject experiments. If you are planning to review or conduct single-subject experiments, we recommend that you study these criteria, which are presented in Appendix F of the What Works Clearinghouse handbook. The criteria involve the internal validity of these experiments, their design, evidence of a causal relationship between the intervention and outcome variables, and visual analysis of data points presented in graphical form.

An example of

How Experimental Research Can Help in Solving Problems of Practice

Educators are constantly developing new methods to improve their students' learning. One method that has become popular is flipped instruction. Basically, flipped instruction involves students watching a video lecture or other presentation of a lesson's content for homework and then using class time to apply what they have learned by solving problems in small groups or by engaging in projects, with the teacher playing a facilitating and tutoring role. In contrast, traditional instruction involves the teacher introducing curriculum content by lecture or other presentation method during class time and then assigning problems or other activities for students to do as homework.

The newspaper, *The Dallas Morning News*, printed an article describing two teachers who experimented with flipped instruction:

> Like most teachers, Cristi Derow and Jennifer Bradley have spent most of their careers giving classroom lectures to students who sat passively in their seats.
>
> The Lewisville school district teachers were keenly aware that the hours they spent preparing lessons were wasted on many students.
>
> "We thought we were making them interesting," said Derow, who co-teaches history classes with Bradley. "But we were losing half the class. They were looking at us. But they weren't listening."
>
> So these teachers at Forestwood Middle School in Flower Mound did something radical.
>
> "We've completely done away with our lectures," Derow said.
>
> And homework assignments "are all done in class," Bradley said.
>
> Derow and Bradley are part of a growing number of teachers who have embraced the "flipped classroom" method of instruction that's turning the traditional teaching model on its head at schools in North Texas and throughout the country.
>
> With the flipped concept, a student's typical homework assignment is to watch recorded lectures on their computers or smartphones.
>
> They walk into class ready to discuss the topic, collaborate with other students and work on assignments based on what they learned from the videos.
>
> Freed from lecturing, teachers say they can use class time to delve deeper into the subject, focus on difficult concepts and work individually with students.
>
> Hundley, W. (2012, September 27). 'Flipped classrooms' in North Texas turn traditional

teaching on its head. *The Dallas Morning News*. Retrieved from http://www.dallasnews.com/news/education/headlines/20120927-flipped-classrooms-in-north-texas-turn-traditional-teaching-on-its-head.ece

Flipped instruction looks as if it should be effective, and in fact, the two teachers mentioned in the Dallas newspaper article claim that their students are now more actively engaged in class work and have improved their test scores. But would flipped instruction work for other teachers, for other grade levels, and for other school subjects? This question is best answered by experiments, such as the one described next.

Researchers might start by selecting a subject and a grade level for which a curriculum based on flipped instruction could be developed without too much difficulty. Next, they would recruit a group of teachers who relied on traditional instructional methods (lecture, seatwork, homework) and randomly select half of them to be trained in this curriculum and use it in at least one of their classes. The other half would be assigned to the control condition, which would involve them continuing to use traditional instruction.

Some teachers assigned to the experimental condition might decline the invitation, in which case the researchers would note their characteristics (e.g., age, years of teaching experience) and check whether they differ from the characteristics of teachers who accepted the invitation. This information has implications for the external validity of the experiment: it would help educators know what to expect if they wished to recruit teachers for professional development in flipped instruction outside the experimental setting.

The next steps would be to develop procedures for training the experimental group in the flipped-instruction curriculum and to select or develop outcome measures for such variables as student engagement in the learning process, attitudes toward the course, and achievement of the course's learning objectives. Teachers in the control group would need to have access to these learning objectives, so that they could incorporate them into their course while still using traditional instructional methods. Next, the researchers would train teachers in the flipped-instruction curriculum and check their proficiency in implementing it.

The experiment ideally would use a pretest-posttest control-group design with randomization. Therefore, the researchers would need to administer the outcome measures at the beginning of the term that the course was offered. The experimental and control courses would be offered the same term in order to control for several threats to the internal validity of the experiment, primarily history and maturation effects. As the course progressed, the researchers would do occasional classroom observations to ensure that there is adequate treatment fidelity in both the experimental and control conditions. Finally, the outcome measures would be administered as posttests at the end of the course. The data would be analyzed to determine whether students in the experimental group performed better on the outcome measures than students in the control group.

An experiment of this type, like most randomized trials of educational programs and methods, would be expensive and time-consuming to conduct. However, the costs would be justified if the experiment demonstrated that flipped instruction was superior to traditional instruction. If follow-up trials yielded similar results for flipped instruction at other grade levels and for other school subjects and for students with different ability levels, these findings would make a powerful argument for creating a fundamental change in classroom instruction nationally and internationally. On the other hand, if the experiments showed no advantage for flipped instruction (and perhaps demonstrated some disadvantages), teachers would be spared the frustration of being encouraged, or forced, to adopt an innovation only to find that it is an ineffective fad that gradually disappears.

SELF-CHECK TEST

1. Unlike group comparison and correlational research designs, experiments
   a. rely on observations under naturally occurring conditions.
   b. study naturally occurring changes in an experimental group and control group.
   c. introduce an intervention into a laboratory or real-life situation.
   d. have few implications for the improvement of educational practice.

2. The pretest-posttest control-group experiment with randomization
   a. is easy to conduct but has weak internal validity.
   b. is not considered as effective as a quasi-experiment.
   c. is generally regarded as the most powerful of the experimental designs.
   d. uses randomization procedures to select research participants from a defined population.

3. In a pretest-posttest control-group experiment with randomization,
   a. the variable measured by the pretest is the only independent variable.
   b. the variable measured by the pretest is the dependent variable.
   c. the variables measured by the pretest and the experimental intervention are independent variables.
   d. the experimental intervention is the dependent variable.

4. The statistical significance of group differences found in a pretest-posttest control-group experiment with randomization can be determined by
   a. analysis of variance.
   b. analysis of covariance.
   c. multiple regression.
   d. all of the above.

5. A quasi-experimental research design does not include
   a. random assignment of research participants to the experimental and control conditions.
   b. pretests.
   c. posttests.
   d. manipulation of the independent variable.

6. Statistical regression is likely to occur if
   a. the pretest and posttest are administered close together in time.
   b. the research participants score very high or low on the pretest.
   c. the pretest and posttest involve the use of different measuring instruments.
   d. all of the above.

7. An experiment has treatment fidelity if
   a. the experimental treatment is not affected by personal characteristics of the research participants.
   b. the research participants for the experimental and control groups are selected by the same procedure.
   c. the experimental treatment controls for all of the extraneous variables to which experiments are susceptible.
   d. the experimental treatment is implemented according to its developers' specifications.

8. All of the following are threats to the external validity of experiments except
   a. lack of population validity.
   b. lack of ecological validity.
   c. selection-maturation interactions.
   d. interactions between personal characteristics of the research sample and the experimental intervention.

9. The baseline condition in a single-case experiment
   a. is the set of typical conditions under which a research participant behaves.
   b. is the set of conditions represented by the experimental intervention.
   c. is not required if an A-B-A-B design is used.
   d. has the same purpose as random assignment of research participants in a group experiment.

10. A typical single-case experiment
    a. has multiple posttests, each measuring a different dependent variable.
    b. has multiple administrations of the same measure, each measuring the same dependent variable.
    c. has two different measures, one measuring the independent variable and the other measuring the dependent variable.
    d. has only one baseline condition.

CHAPTER REFERENCES

Biddle, B. J., & Berliner, D. C. (2002). Small class size and its effects. *Educational Leadership, 59*(5), 12–23.

Bracht, G. H., & Glass, G. V (1968). The external validity of experiments. *American Educational Research Journal, 5*, 437–474.

Bulgren, J. A., Marquis, J. G., Lenz, B. K., Deshler, D. D., & Schumaker, J. B. (2011). The effectiveness of a question-exploration routine for enhancing the content learning of secondary students. *Journal of Educational Psychology, 103*(3), 578–593.

Campbell, D. T., & Stanley, J. C. (1963). Experimental and quasi-experimental designs for research on teaching. In N. L. Gage (Ed.), *Handbook of research on teaching* (pp. 171–246). Chicago, IL: Rand McNally.

Eisen, M., Zellman, G., Massett, H., & Murray, D. (2002). Evaluating the Lions-Quest "Skills for Adolescence" drug education program: First-year behavior outcomes. *Addictive Behaviors, 27*(4), 619–632.

Eisen, M., Zellman, G. L., & Murray, D. M. (2003). Evaluating the Lions-Quest "Skills for Adolescence" drug education program: Second-year behavior outcomes. *Addictive Behaviors, 28*(5), 883–897.

Fletcher, J. D., Tobias, S., & Wisher, R. A. (2007). Learning anytime, anywhere: Advanced distributed learning and the changing face of education. *Educational Researcher, 36*(2), 96–102.

Glenn, D. (2005, March 11). New federal policy favors randomized trials in education research. *Chronicle of Higher Education*, p. 16.

Mechling, L. C., Gast, D. L., & Cronin, B. A. (2006). The effects of presenting high-preference items, paired with choice, via computer-based video programming on task completion of students with autism. *Focus on Autism and Other Developmental Disabilities, 21*(1), 7–13.

Morris, P, Aber, J. L., Wolf, S., & Berg, J. (2012). Using incentives to change how teenagers spend their time:

The effects of New York City's Conditional Cash Transfer Program. Retrieved from MDRC website: http://www.mdrc.org/publication/using-incentives-change-how-teenagers-spend-their-time

Smith, M. L., & Glass, G. V (1980). Meta-analysis of research on class size and its relationship to attitudes and instruction. *American Educational Research Journal, 17*(4), 19–33.

What Works Clearinghouse (2011, September). *Procedures and standards handbook* (Version 2.1). Retrieved from http://ies.ed.gov/ncee/wwc/pdf/reference_resources/wwc_procedures_v2_1_standards_handbook.pdf

RESOURCES FOR FURTHER STUDY

Cook, T., & Sinha, V. (2006). Randomized experiments in educational research. In J. L. Green, G. Camilli, & P. B. Elmore (Eds.), *Handbook of complementary methods in education research* (pp. 551–566). Mahwah, NJ: Lawrence Erlbaum.

> The authors review the fundamentals of experiments and consider the current role of experiments in advancing knowledge about education. They review arguments for and against experiments and make a case for the usefulness of experiments, especially if complemented by the use of other research methods.

Gast, D. L., & Ledford, J. (Eds.). (2009). *Single subject research methodology in behavior sciences*. New York, NY: Routledge.

> The contributors to this book provide a comprehensive discussion of all facets of single-subject research design, data analysis, and data interpretation.

Murnane, R. J., & Willet, J. B. (2010). *Methods matter: Improving causal inference in educational and social science research*. New York, NY: Oxford University Press.

> This book provides an advanced discussion of several topics in this chapter. In particular, the authors observe that experiments do not demonstrate causality between independent and dependent variables as clearly as is sometimes portrayed in the literature. Interpretation of causal effects is partly science, but also partly judgment.

Wendt, O., & Miller, B. (2012). Quality appraisal of single-subject experimental designs: An overview and comparison of different appraisal tools. *Education and Treatment of Children, 35*(2), 235–268.

> The authors discuss various approaches that have been developed for judging the soundness of a single-case experiment.

After-School Multifamily Groups: A Randomized Controlled Trial Involving Low-Income, Urban, Latino Children

McDonald, L., Moberg, D. P., Brown, R., Rodriguez-Espiricueta, I., Flores, N. I., Burke, M. P., & Coover, G. (2006). After-school multifamily groups: A randomized controlled trial involving low-income, urban, Latino children. *Children & Schools, 28*(1), 25–34.

The problem of practice addressed in this experiment is the low academic performance and high dropout rate of Latino students. The purpose of the researchers' experiment was to determine whether a specific program to increase Latino parent involvement in their children's education has desirable effects on their academic performance and classroom behavior. The name of the program is FAST: Families and Schools Together.

The literature review in the article includes references to two prior experiments on the effectiveness of FAST. Since the article appeared, the results of several other experiments have been published:

Gamoran, A., Turley, R. N. L., & Fish, R. (2012). Differences between Hispanic and non-Hispanic families in social capital and child development: First-year findings from an experimental study. *Social Stratification and Mobility, 30*(1), 97–112.

Crozier, M., Rokutani, L., Russett, J. L., Godwin, E., & Banks, G. E. (2010). A multisite program evaluation of Families and Schools Together (FAST): Continued evidence of a successful multifamily community based prevention program. *School Community Journal, 20*(1), 187–207.

Kratochwill, T. R., McDonald, L., Levin, J. R., Scalia, P. A., & Coover, G. (2009). Families and Schools Together: An experimental study of multi-family support groups for children at risk. *Journal of School Psychology, 47*(4), 245–265.

The results of a single experiment should not be taken as conclusive. A series of experiments, especially well-controlled experiments with randomization, provides a body of replicated knowledge that enables informed judgments about the effectiveness and generalizability of an intervention such as FAST.

The descriptive statistics in the article are easy to understand. Another set of statistical analyses, reported in Table 3 of the article, involves hierarchical regression modeling (see Chapter 11). It provides a more detailed analysis of the effects of the experimental treatment relative to the control condition. The results of the hierarchical regression modeling are fairly consistent with the descriptive statistics in Table 2 and Figure 1 in the article, so an understanding of Table 3, while helpful, is not essential to comprehending the main findings of the experiment.

The article is reprinted in its entirety, just as it appeared when originally published.

After-School Multifamily Groups: A Randomized Controlled Trial Involving Low-Income, Urban, Latino Children

Lynn McDonald, D. Paul Moberg, Roger Brown, Ismael Rodriguez-Espiricueta, Nydia I. Flores, Melissa P. Burke, and Gail Coover

ABSTRACT This randomized controlled trial evaluated a culturally representative parent engagement strategy with Latino parents of elementary school children. Ten urban schools serving low-income children from mixed cultural backgrounds participated in a large study. Classrooms were randomly assigned either to an after-school, multifamily support group (FAST: Families and Schools Together) or to receive eight behavioral parenting pamphlets with active follow-up (FAME: Family Education). Of 180 Latino parents assigned to FAST, 90 percent came once and 85 percent graduated. Two-year follow-up teacher data were collected for 130 Latino children. The teachers, blind to condition, evaluated the children's classroom functioning. Data were analyzed with hierarchical linear modeling, using a conservative, intent-to-treat model. On standardized mental health instruments (Teacher's Report Form of the Child Behavior Checklist; Social Skills Rating System), statistically significant differences favored assignment to FAST rather than to FAME on academic performance and classroom behaviors, including aggression and social skills.

Keywords: Hispanics; immigrants; parent involvement; protective factors; social inclusion

A *USA Today* headline reported: "Hispanic population gains fail to translate in classroom . . . Hispanic children face a bleak educational future" (p. A14). Factors cited as relevant to the Latino school dropout rate were poor research, weak accountability, low expectations, and bad communication between Latino parents and schools (Hispanic Population Gains Fail, 2003). The National Center for Education Statistics reported on dropout rates in the United States: "73 percent of all Latino youth graduated from high school compared with 92% [of] white students" (National Center for Education Statistics, 2003, p. 42). This statistic must be considered in a social context: although 9 percent of white children reside in poverty, 27 percent of Hispanic children reside in poverty in the United States (Suarez-Orosco, Suarez-Orosco, & Doucet, 2003). Almost all growth in the number of U.S. youths over the next 20 years will be among Hispanics (Fry, 2003). Schools need evidence-based approaches to improve communication between Latino parents and schools and address the achievement gap.

The No Child Left Behind Act of 2001 (P.L. 107-110) mandates the achievement of all children and considers parents as critical to achieving successful schools (http://www.ed.gov/print/nclb/overview). Title I specifies that 1 percent of the federal funds going to school districts to serve low-income children must be used for parent involvement. Research linking parent engagement with student outcomes supports these federal policies. Henderson and Mapp's (2002) review shows that parent involvement is positively correlated with school success, but rather than being linear, it is a complex relationship and manifests in various forms. Similarly, Christenson and colleagues' (1992) and Christenson's (2003) research describes the impact of systemic approaches to family, school, and community, which are based on relationships across systems, rather than any one specific form of parent–teacher communication. Epstein's (1991) conceptual framework on parent involvement with schools refers to six forms: parenting, communicating, supporting school, learning at home, decision making, and collaborating with the community (Epstein & Sanders, 2000).

Principals, teachers, and social workers are committed to parent involvement but are frustrated with unsuccessful

efforts to achieve this involvement (Allen-Meares, Washington, & Welsh, 1996; Kurtz & Barth, 1989). Parents may be seen as not caring about their child's schooling, rather than as impeded by economic and social policy obstacles (Hewlett & West, 1997; Pena, 2000). Social stressors of poor housing, dangerous neighborhoods, poor transportation, and lack of "living wage" employment, interfere with parental participation in parent–teacher conferences (Garbarino, 1995; Shumow, Vandell, & Posner, 1999). Although parent involvement is supported by federal policies, few strategies have been tested with randomized controlled trials in urban communities.

Evidence-Based Practices

Educational policy is shifting toward funding evidence-based approaches—that is, tested with randomized controlled trials. The Substance Abuse and Mental Health Services Administration (SAMHSA), U.S. Department of Health and Human Services, funded the National Registry of Prevention Programs and Practices to rigorously assess 1,000 programs with peer reviews, regional technical assistance structures, and state implementation of evidence-based models. Only 54 programs met the criteria for being an evidence-based "model" (Schinke, Brounstein, & Gardner, 2003). Half of the models involved schools; only a few were tested with Latino youths (www.samhsamodels.org). We describe a randomized controlled trial with Latino children of a SAMHSA model, an after-school, multifamily support group model.

Families and Schools Together (FAST): An Evidence-Based SAMHSA Model

Families and Schools Together (FAST) is an after-school, multifamily support group to increase parent involvement in schools and improve children's well-being (McDonald, Coe-Braddish, Billingham, Dibble, & Rice, 1991; McDonald, Billingham, Conrad, Morgan, & Payton, 1997). A collaborative, culturally representative, team of parents and professionals facilitates the multifamily group to engage parents into building social networks through the schools. These relationships act as protective factors at several levels of the child's social ecology (Bronfenbrenner, 1979). Teams provide home visits and lead eight weekly multifamily sessions (with five to 15 families); then for two years, parent graduates lead monthly sessions.

There is no formal curriculum or instruction at FAST. Instead, the team leads a structured package of interactive processes at the group sessions to enhance relationships. The activities are based on theory and research: family stress theory (Boyd-Franklin & Bry, 2000; Hill, 1958; McCubbin, Thompson, Thompson, & Fromer, 1998); family systems theory (Alexander & Parsons, 1982; Minuchin, 1974; Rutter, 1999; Satir, 1983); parent-led play

McDonald, L., Moberg, D. P., Brown, R., Rodriguez-Espiricueta, I., Flores, N. I., Burke, M. P., & Coover, G. (2006). After-school multifamily groups: A randomized controlled trial involving low-income, urban, Latino children. *Children & Schools, 28*(1), 25–34. Copyright 2006, National Association of Social Workers, Inc., Children & Schools.

therapy (Kogan, 1978; Kumpfer, Molgaard, & Spoth, 1996; Webster-Stratton, 1985); group work (Gitterman & Shulman, 1994); and adult education and community development (Alinsky, 1971; Freire, 1997). Based on experiential learning principles, the repeated encounters build trusting, reciprocal relationships, called "social capital" (Bryk & Schneider, 2002; Putnam, 2000), which are then maintained at monthly groups. McDonald and Sayger (1998) summarize the linkages between these theories and the FAST structured activities.

For the first hour of each FAST session, parents lead communication at their family table, while sharing a meal, singing group songs, and playing family games. The child repeatedly experiences parental hierarchy, embedded compliance requests, and family cohesion, and has fun with his family while at the school. In the second hour, participants separate into peer groups: The children play, and parents meet to talk in small groups, without assigned topics. The groups provide parents with an opportunity to build social connections and a shared identity. The next activity is 15 minutes of cross-generational, dyadic time, when a parent and her child engage in uninterrupted play, in an adaptation of play therapy, with no teaching, bossing, or directing. At the parent-planned graduation, the principal congratulates the parents for their involvement, and the team members present behaviorally specific affirmations to each parent.

These group activities support parents to help their child connect the cultures of home and school (Valenzuela & Dornbusch, 1994). In the school, with school personnel present, the parents lead the table-based, family activities; without lectures or reading requirements, participants at all levels of English literacy are equally competent. Each FAST team implements the core components (40 percent) while adapting the processes (60 percent) to fit cultural preferences. An example of a core component is "shared governance," whereby the team must represent the social ecology of a child's life, including the culture and language of the neighborhood (Szapocznik & Kurtines, 1993). In addition, a parent with a child at that school partners with professionals from community agencies and the school on the FAST team.

Since its development in 1988, FAST has been implemented, with on-site training and evaluation of child and family outcomes by a national, non-profit organization (www.fastnational.org) at more than 800 schools in 45 states and five countries. Thousands of primarily low—income parents from diverse backgrounds have increased their involvement in schools through FAST: 51 percent white, 23 percent Latino, 20 percent African American, and 1 percent Asian American/Native American. On average, nationally, 80 percent of parents who attend the first session return and graduate from FAST (McDonald & Frey, 1999). In a randomized controlled trial in inner-city New Orleans, parents assigned to FAST compared with parents in the comparison condition were significantly more likely at one-year follow-up to report increased parent involvement in their communities, and to report their children as having decreased aggression and increased social skills (Abt Associates, 2001). Another randomized controlled trial of FAST was conducted in collaboration with three Indian Nations and rural American Indian families; one-year follow-up teacher data showed behavioral outcomes favoring FAST rather than control children (Kratochwill, McDonald, Levin, Young Bear-Tibbetts, & Demaray, 2004).

Method

Research Design
Classrooms in 10 urban, elementary schools were randomly assigned to either the treatment (FAST) or the comparison Family Education (FAME) condition. A universal recruitment strategy was used. All families with children in the treatment or comparison condition classrooms were recruited for the study. After exposure to the program, first- and second-year follow-up data were collected for both conditions. This article presents data on the subsample of Latino children. (For complete information about the larger study, see Moberg, McDonald, Brown, & Burke, 2003).

Latino Subsample Characteristics
A total of 473 Milwaukee study children and their families were involved at the baseline data collection of the larger study (FAST = 272 and FAME = 201). Of the original 180 Latino families who participated in this research study, 87 percent of the parents were successfully followed up two years later. Teacher reports could only be collected with specific release forms from the parents interviewed at the two-year point. The Latino subsample with two-year follow-up data by teachers (n = 130, with 80 assigned to FAST, 50 assigned to FAME), was similar to the original sample of 180 Latino children at baseline except on gender and grade. More boys were assigned to FAST (54 percent) compared with FAME (28 percent) and more third-graders were in FAST (51 percent) compared with FAME (38 percent) .These group differences were adjusted for in the multivariate analysis described later.

One of the sociodemographic strengths of the subsample of 130 self-identified Latino families was having married parents. More than 70 percent lived in intact family homes (Table 1). The Latino families lived in a relatively stable part of the urban community, and most of their children remained in their original schools over the two years of the study. The Latino families, however, struggled with extremely low incomes: More than 70 percent had annual incomes of less than $20,000, and a third of the families reported incomes less than $10,000. The parents had relatively low educational attainment:

Table 1

Baseline Demographics of Children and Families

Demographics	FAST (Treatment) ($n = 80$) (%)	FAME (Comparison) ($n = 50$) (%)
Household Income		
Less than $10,000	37	33
$10,000 or less than $20,000	33	33
$20,000 or less than $30,000	24	22
$30,000 or more	7	13
Parent education		
Less than high school	46	49
High school grad or GED	32	33
Some college or tech school	17	13
College graduate or more	5	4
Marital status		
Married	70	69
Divorced/separated/widowed	14	10
Never married/unmarried couple	16	20
Child's gender*		
Male	54	28
Female	46	72
Child's grade		
First	13	4
Second	27	54
Third	51	38
Fourth	9	4

Notes: FAME = Family Education, FAST = Families and Schools Together.

Percentages may not add to 100 due to rounding.

*Groups differ significantly at $p < .95$. Only self-identified Latino families in the larger study, with two-year follow-up teacher data, are included.

Almost half of the parents reported that they had not completed high school, and only 20 percent had more than a high school education. Length of residence in the United States and country of origin were not assessed, although anecdotally most families were of Mexican origin. The average age for the Latino children at baseline was seven years, and slightly more than half were girls.

Procedure

The FAST research project was presented to all elementary school principals in Milwaukee, and they were invited to participate in the study. The 10 schools selected served high rates of Title I-eligible children and served students who were primarily African American (4), Latino (4), and mixed heritage (2). The six schools that served Latino students implemented 12 multifamily group sessions from 1997 to 1999: Four were in Spanish and English, four were in Spanish only, and four were in English (with translators). Program manuals for the team members and all evaluation materials were translated into Spanish; adaptations of activities were planned by each local team.

To recruit families into the study, teachers at each school agreed to offer either program to all children in their classrooms. Classrooms were matched by grade and then randomly assigned to either condition: FAST (intervention) or FAME (comparison). Teachers distributed cards to children to take home to obtain parental consent to being contacted about the study. If parents agreed to participate, there were four in-home interviews: preintervention, postintervention, one year post, and two years post. In addition, parents were paid $25 for each interview. (If not enough parents responded in a school, first- or third-grade classrooms were also recruited). At the two-year postprogram interview, parents were asked to provide releases so that teachers could be contacted for follow-up evaluation. Teachers were generally unaware of the condition of the participating students.

Because randomization was of whole classrooms, parents were assigned to FAST or FAME before the home visits. As discussed in a previous section, families recruited to the FAST condition were offered eight weekly, culturally representative, team led, after-school, multifamily group sessions and parent graduate-led monthly meetings for two years. The comparison condition families were sent eight weekly mailings of behaviorally oriented parenting skills booklets in English or Spanish (see Channing L. Bete Company, 1997), with follow-up phone calls to see whether they had read the booklets, and an invitation to a formal lecture on "parenting." To engage families in the research study for two years and maintain their addresses over time, both groups of families were mailed regular FAME or FAST newsletters and sent birthday cards from FAME or FAST coordinators.

Measures

Teachers evaluated the children's socioemotional functioning and academic performance by completing two forms that have been used with Latino populations and have been translated into Spanish: (1) the Teacher's Report Form (TRF) of the Child Behavior Checklist (CBCL) (Achenbach, 1991) and (2) the Social Skills Rating System (SSRS) (Gresham & Elliott, 1990). The TRF is a widely used, broad-based, standardized rating scale instrument for socioemotional problems, in the child mental health field, with 120 items that measure problem behaviors on a scale ranging from 1 = never to 3 = often. The TRF, with established validity and reliability, is used to screen children in schools for emotional disturbance. The standardized scores mean that the average level of functioning is 50; at risk is 53 to 56; high risk is 57 to 60; and higher than 60 is clinical. The primary scales are Externalizing (delinquent and aggressive behaviors) and Internalizing (withdrawal, somatic complaints, anxiety, and depression). The TRF Academic Performance scale asks the teacher to assess a child on specific academic skills, including reading, writing, and math, relative to other children at the same grade level.

The SSRS is also a standardized, widely used, multi-rater instrument, with established validity and reliability. Teachers complete 57 items, including the Academic Competence subscale, which contains nine items that require comparing the child being rated to other students in that specific classroom. The Academic Competence scale includes reading, mathematics, motivation, parental encouragement, and intellectual functioning. The SSRS assesses problem behaviors in the classroom (not used in this study), but its main emphasis is on the child's social skills in the classroom. Questions are about positive behaviors scored with reference to domains of assertiveness, cooperation, and self-control. It has a three-point rating scale (0 = never, 1 = sometimes, 2 = often), indicating the extent to which each item describes a child's behavior.

Data Analysis

An intent-to-treat model was used, which means that families who agreed to be in the study and were assigned to the treatment group condition but did not actually come to any FAST sessions were included in the analysis as part of the treatment group. The classroom teachers of the focal child in either condition completed evaluation forms at pretest, at posttest about three months later, and after two years. Two years later the focal child's current teacher, who was blind to the child's condition, completed the forms. These data are the focus of this article.

Hierarchical repeated measures regression models were used to estimate the net effects of the FAST program after two years, on a range of relevant precursors of substance abuse and on child behavior outcomes based on teacher reports (Moberg et al., 2003). Twelve multifamily group cycles included Latino families, and because the families were assigned to a condition (treatment or comparison), this formed distinctive groupings. A multilevel regression model explicitly models the manner in which families are grouped within cycles and has several advantages. It enables researchers to obtain statistically efficient estimates. By using the clustering information, it provides correct standard errors, confidence intervals, and significance tests, which generally are more conservative than the traditional analyses; and by allowing the use of covariates, it can measure at any level of the hierarchy.

Results

The first key outcome of this study concerns parent engagement. Of the 80 Latino families who agreed to be study participants from classrooms assigned to the FAST condition, 90 percent went once to the after school family support group; of these, 85 percent returned for at least five sessions and graduated. In addition, the FAST families attended an average of 9.9 parent-led family support groups over the next two years. In contrast, of the 50 Latino families who agreed to be study participants from classrooms assigned to FAME, 100 percent were contacted with mailed behavioral parenting booklets, and through mailed newsletters and phone calls; however, only 4 percent attended the FAME formal lecture on parenting.

Did increased parent involvement and participation in FAST affect the Latino children's school performance as assessed by their teacher two years later? To answer this question, we compared results for students in FAST and FAME, using hierarchical linear modeling (HLM) and intent-to-treat analyses. Although the students assigned to FAST had a slightly higher rate of completion of teacher forms than did the control condition (76 percent compared with 67 percent) at two years, this difference was not significant. The teachers were blind to condition—that is, student assignment in the study, and [were] asked to assess the child's academic performance, social skills, and behavior problems. Means and standard deviations for teachers' ratings of students on both the TRF and the SSRS instruments at baseline and at two-year follow-up show that the children assigned to FAST tended to improve their mean scores from pretest to follow-up, whereas FAME students tended to have more negative means from pretest to follow-up (Table 2). Of most note at two-year follow-up, the means of the students assigned to FAST on the academic performance scale of the TRF were significantly higher ($p = .03$) than the means for students assigned to the comparison condition.

At the outset, the two groups were similar at baseline on four of the five teacher evaluation measures. One-way ANOVAs comparing the groups found significant baseline differences: FAME students scored higher on the SSRS at baseline than did the FAST students ($p = .054$). Note that at two-year follow-up, the scores on social skills in the classroom were reversed: FAST students scored significantly higher (meaning that their social skills were better) than those in FAME, who were not exposed to the after-school multifamily groups.

Within[-]group analysis using paired t tests indicated that FAME comparison group students' scores were significantly less favorable than at baseline on each of the five measures analyzed. For those students assigned to FAST, two of the five domain means showed improvement (including the TRF Externalizing scale), two showed no change, and one showed less favorable scores (the TRF Internalizing scale). The ratings were provided independently by different teachers at baseline and at two-year follow-up, but all measures for both groups were significantly correlated over time.

For a more rigorous statistical analysis, these data were analyzed with hierarchical regression models. Table 3 provides the results from the essential data analyses from complex hierarchical regression models. The models take account of the random effect of assignment to FAST or FAME cycle (the grouping variable in the design that controls for cluster rather than random assignment to condition) as well as a number of other covariates. Coefficients are provided for fixed effects of the FAST condition from hierarchical regression models. Random effects of family/student are nested within [the]

Table 2

Teacher Evaluations on Classroom Behavior Scales

	Baseline		Two-Year Follow-Up	
Teacher's Report Form (TRF)	*M*	*SD*	*M*	*SD*
Child Internalizing (anxiety)				
FAME	47.6	8.9	52.0	10.8
FAST	47.5	10.2	51.9	10.5
Child Externalizing (aggression)				
FAME	49.1	8.4	53.5	9.8
FAST	50.1	9.7	51.2	7.9
Academic Performance				
FAME	47.5	9.8	43.6	8.0
FAST	45.8	6.9	46.6	7.8
Social Skills Rating System (SSRS)				
Social Skills				
FAME	104.2	17.4	100.3	16.2
FAST	97.4	17.7	102.4	14.9
Academic Competence				
FAME	95.9	13.8	92.3	13.0
FAST	95.5	11.2	95.0	11.8

FAST ($n = 80$); FAME ($n = 50$)

Note: FAME = Family Education; FAST = Families and Schools Together.

Table 3

Fixed Effects of FAST Condition Based on Hierarchical Regression Modeling

| Classroom Behavior Scales | Two-Year Follow-Up Teacher Evaluations | |
	Coefficient*	SD
TRF Child Internalizing	−0.92	(2.22)
TRF Child Externalizing	−4.68**	(1.57)
TRF Academic Performance	3.06*	(1.50)
SSRS Child Social Skills	4.45*	(2.12)
SSRS Academic Competence	2.48	(1.64)

Note: TRF = Teacher's Report Form of Achenbach's Child Behavior Checklist (CBCL). SSRS = Gresham and Elliot's Social Skills Rating System. FAST = Families and Schools Together. FAME = Family Education. FAST (*n* = 80), FAME (*n* = 50).

*Coefficients provided for fixed effects of FAST condition using hierarchical regression models. Random effects of FAST family/student are nested within cycle of FAST implementation. Models have been adjusted for baseline value of dependent measure, for family income, parent education, parent marital status, student sex and grade in school, and student baseline overall CBCL risk level.
*$p < .05$, **$p < .001$.

cycle of FAST implementation. Models have been adjusted for baseline value of dependent measure, family income, parent education, parent marital status, student sex and grade in school, and student baseline CBCL risk level. The hierarchical regression models indicate a statistically significant program effect of FAST on three of the five teacher variables measured, two years after the intervention (Figure 1). Specifically, on the TRF-CBCL Externalizing Scale (largely due to the aggressive

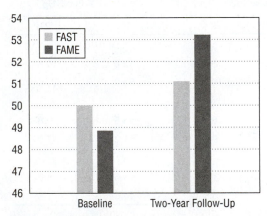

Figure 1 Teacher Reports of Children's Classroom Aggression (TRF Externalizing)

Notes: TRF = Teacher's Report Form of Achenbach's Child Behavior Checklist. FAST = Families and Schools Together. FAME = Family Education. FAST (*n* = 80), FAME (*n* = 50)

Only cases with data at both points were included: teachers at two years were not aware of the condition to which the Latino child was assigned. Between group differences were not significant. Baseline to two-year paired *t* tests were significant at $p < .001$ for FAME. Hierarchical regression models showed significant effect of FAST condition.

behavior subscale), on the SSRS Total Overall social skills rating, and on the academic performance subscale of the TRF-CBCL. The effect size of these differences is approximately .25 standard deviation units, a moderate effect. Thus, two years after the family support groups, teachers rated Latino students assigned to FAST as having significantly more social skills, less aggressive behavior in the classroom, and better academic skills than those assigned to FAME.

Discussion

High engagement and retention rates reflect a possible compatibility of this multifamily group model with the cultural norms of the Latino community. Researchers consistently report on the primacy of the extended family across Latino communities from Latin America, including Mexico, Cuba, and Puerto Rico (Frauenglass, Routh, Pantin, & Mason, 1997; Perez, Pinzon, & Garza, 1997; Santiago-Rivera, Arredondo, & Gallardo-Cooper, 2002; Zambrana, 1995). The FAST process engages everyone in the family and values their perspective on the primacy of the family, which includes the nuclear and extended family, for example, fathers, mothers, siblings, aunts, uncles, grandparents, and so forth. Personally inviting the whole family to school functions may be particularly effective for Latino families rather than invitations, usually sent home on fliers, issued only to parents. For a school to take the trouble and expend the funds to make a home visit, and host family meals and group activities after school shows the community a respect for the importance of the whole family to be involved for the child's success in school.

Parent participation in after school activities is voluntary, and so attendance alone can be considered to be an objective measure of a program's acceptability in a particular community. Latino parent involvement in these elementary schools increased for parents who participated in FAST. Principals and other school personnel at the six schools serving Latino children reported being pleased with the increased parent involvement and reported increased parent engagement over time at school functions.

The school-based, culturally representative FAST team is trained with role play to show respect both nonverbally and verbally to low-income, ethnic minority parents, and to help children at FAST meetings be respectful to their parents. Respect for the parents as partners in the process of supporting the child to succeed in school is fundamental to FAST. The Latino child observes the school staff being respectful towards his or her parents who might have minimal English language skills or a minimal educational background; this observation supports the child's respect for his or her own parents. This respect for parents is congruent with the reported values of immigrants from Mexico and other Latin American countries (Brown, 1981; Stanton-Salazar, 2001).

FAST offered a structure for meeting other parents and building reciprocal relationships, when other community societal structures are often not available to immigrant parents. FAST team members go to the home and invite families to come to the school for repeated meetings, with time in the evening to network together. Researchers report that the Latino cultures recognize the importance of consistently nourishing support networks by patterns of exchange within one's local community (that is, the social importance of groups) (Gutiérrez & Ortega, 1991; Vega & Kolody, 1985). The mobility of immigration interrupts the familiar extended family and the local networks. Informal, trusted, friendship networks are critical to the survival of ethnic minority families in a majority dominant culture, particularly when struggling with economic hardship.

Chrispeels and Rivero (2000) identified five clarifications that effectively increased Latino parent engagement in schools: (1) actual and perceived school invitations and opportunities to be involved, (2) parents' sense of place in their child's education, (3) parents' knowledge and skills about how to be involved, (4) parents' concept of parenting, (5) parents' aspirations and love for their child. FAST addresses each of these five processes, thereby "helping Latino parents to shift their parenting styles and their engagement with the school, especially with the teacher, when given information and an opportunity to explore how their attitudes and practices affect their children" (Henderson & Mapp, 2002, p. 95).

In addition to effectively engaging Latino parents and increasing their involvement in schools, the teacher evaluations two years later showed that assignment to FAST resulted in significantly better academic performance, decreased problems of aggressive behaviors in the classroom, and increased social skills in the classroom compared with FAME students. The follow-up data showed positive effect[s] in three distinct areas, suggesting that multisystemic, relationship building, multifamily groups are effective with low-income Latino children in school over time.

However, the direction of the change was troubling: By teacher report, the differences between the two conditions were significant because of worsening ratings of the comparison group. This pattern held across all three domains of functioning in the classroom: social skills, classroom aggression, and academic performance. At two years, the FAME students showed decreased academic performance and social skills and increased classroom aggression. Protective factors of multiple relationships across systems of families, schools, and communities may act to shield the FAST Latino child from some of the stresses of racism, poverty, and toxic urban environments.

Study Limitations

The first limitation of this study concerns the comparability of the two study conditions: FAST and FAME. As described earlier, FAME was created as a comparison condition for the FAST intervention. However, a recent study shows that behavioral parenting pamphlets are effective interventions, particularly with active follow-up (Montgomery, Stores, & Wiggs, 2004). The FAME comparison condition of receiving the eight parenting booklets with the active tracking of the families over time may have functioned as an intervention with effects on the children and families. This would suggest that the impact of FAST may actually be considerably stronger than these data show, because the comparison group received a kind of intervention (behavioral parenting pamphlets) rather than treatment as usual or no treatment.

A second limitation of the study was the unknown generalizability of these classroom results to all Latino immigrant populations. A weakness of the study was our lack of specification of the country of origin of the Latino sample and our failure to determine first, second, or third generational status in the United States. In addition, the distribution of the Latino subsample was across six schools serving low-income populations. Of the 12 multifamily group cycles, one-third were in mixed cultural schools, and two-thirds were in monocultural schools. Our sample size and the nonrandom assignment of families to these school settings prevents us from investigating the impact of the language and culture setting on parent involvement rates and classroom impact rates. This should be pursued in future research.

Another limitation was the attrition of the Latino parents over the two-year period, resulting in loss of data on 50 families from the original sample of 180 Latino students at pretest evaluations. This was partly due to family attrition and partly due to failure of some teachers to provide data even when parental release was obtained. Another issue concerns the disproportionate number of boys in the experimental condition compared with the comparison condition. This difference was controlled for in the hierarchical regression.

Although three of the five teacher-reported measures showed significant outcomes, two did not show significant differences: the TRF Internalizing Scale (depression, anxiety) and the SSRS Academic Competence Scale. The implications of the same teachers assessing the same children on two different measures of academic functioning with different results remain unclear.

Implications

The findings from this study suggest that after-school, multifamily groups can increase parent involvement and may help address the achievement gap. However, the lasting effectiveness of the evidence-based intervention is contingent on successful parent engagement and social inclusion. An evidence-based model that builds relationships across systems—the family, the school, and the community—can significantly change outcomes for low-income, culturally marginalized families. This change was achieved in this study through respectful inclusion of the parents in the after-school program, and cultural representation of the child's social ecology in the implementation team. If schools serving Latino students take responsibility for providing evidence-based parent involvement practices, they can support the federal goals of improved academic achievement for all students.

REFERENCES

Abt Associates. (2001). *National evaluation of family support programs: Volume B. Research studies: Final report.* Cambridge, MA: Author. Retrieved July 10, 2003, from http://www.abtassoc.com/reports/NEFSP-VolB.pdf

Achenbach, T. M. (1991). *Manual for the Child Behavior Checklist and 1991 Profile.* Burlington: University of Vermont, Department of Psychiatry.

Alexander, J. E., & Parsons, B. V. (1982). *Functional family therapy.* Monterey, CA: Brooks/Cole.

Alinsky, S. D. (1971). *Rules for radicals: A programmatic primer for realistic radicals.* New York: Random House.

Allen-Meares, P., Washington, R. Q., & Welsh, B. L. (1996). *Social work services in schools* (2nd ed.). Boston: Allyn & Bacon.

Boyd-Franklin, N., & Bry, B. H. (2000). *Reaching out in family therapy: Home-based, school, and community interventions.* New York: Guilford Press.

Bronfenbrenner, U. (1979). *The ecology of human development: Experiments by nature and design.* Cambridge, MA: Harvard University Press.

Brown, J. A. (1981). Parent education groups for Mexican—Americans. *Social Work in Education, 3,* 22–31.

Bryk, A. S., & Schneider, B. L. (2002). *Trust in schools: A core resource for improvement.* New York: Russell Sage Foundation.

Channing L. Bete Company. (1997). *Scriptographic parenting booklet series.* South Deerfield, MA: Author.

Chrispeels, J., & Rivero, E. (2000, April). *Engaging Latino families for student success—Understanding the process and impact of providing training to parents.* Presentation at the annual meeting of the American Educational Research Association, New Orleans.

Christenson, S. L. (2003).The family-school partnership: An opportunity to promote the learning competence of all students. *School Psychology Quarterly, 18,* 454–482.

Christenson, S. L., Rounds, T., & Gorney, D. (1992). Family factors and student achievement: An avenue to increase students' success. *School Psychology Quarterly, 7,* 178–206.

Epstein, J. (1991). School and family partnerships. In M. Alkin (Ed.), *Encyclopedia of educational research* (6th ed., pp. 1139–1151). New York: Macmillan.

Epstein, J. L., & Sanders, M. G. (2000). Connecting home, school, and community: New directions for social research. In M. T. Hallinan (Ed.), *Handbook of the sociology of education* (pp. 285–306). New York: Kluwer Academic/Plenum Press.

Frauenglass, S., Routh, D., Pantin, H., & Mason, C. (1997). Family support decreases influence of deviant peers on Hispanic adolescents substance use. *Journal of Clinical Child Psychology, 26*(1), 15–23.

Freire, P. (1997). *Pedagogy of the oppressed.* New York: Continuum.

Fry, R. (2003). *Hispanic youth dropping out of US schools: Measuring the challenge.* Washington, DC: Pew Hispanic Center.

Garbarino, J. (1995). *Raising children in a socially toxic environment.* San Francisco: Jossey-Bass.

Gitterman, A., & Shulman, L. (Eds.). (1994). *Mutual aid groups, vulnerable populations, and the life cycle.* New York: Columbia University Press.

Gresham, F. M., & Elliott, S. N. (1990). *Social Skills Rating System.* Circle Pines, MN: American Guidance Service.

Gutirrez, L. M., & Ortega, R. (1991). Developing methods to empower Latinos: The importance of groups. *Social Work with Groups, 14*(2), 23–42.

Henderson, A. T., & Mapp, K. L. (2002). *A new wave of evidence: The impact of school, family, and community connections on student achievement.* Austin, TX: Southwest Educational Development Lab.

Hewlett, S., & West, C. (1997). *War against parents.* Cambridge, MA: Harvard University Press.

Hill, R. (1958). Social stresses on the family: Generic features of families under stress. *Social Casework, 39,* 139–150.

Hispanic population gains fail to translate in classroom. (2003, January 31). *USA Today,* p. A14.

Kogan, K. L. (1978). Help-seeking mothers and their children. *Child Psychology and Human Development, 8,* 204–218.

Kratochwill, T. R., McDonald, L., Levin, J. R., Young Bear-Tibbetts, H., & Demaray, M. K. (2004). Families and schools together: An experimental analysis of a parent-mediated multi-family group intervention program for American Indian children. *Journal of School Psychology, 42,* 359–383.

Kumpfer, K. L., Molgaard, V., & Spoth, R. (1996). The Strengthening Families Program for the prevention of delinquency and drug use. In R. D. Peters & R. J. McMahon (Eds.), *Preventing childhood disorders, substance abuse, and delinquency* (pp. 241–267). Thousand Oaks, CA: Sage Publications.

Kurtz, D. P., & Earth, R. P. (1989). Parent involvement: Cornerstone of school social work practice. *Social Work, 34,* 407–420.

McCubbin, H. I., Thompson, E. A., Thompson, A. I., & Fromer, J. E. (Eds.). (1998). *Resiliency in Native American and immigrant families.* Thousand Oaks, CA: Sage Publications.

McDonald, L., Billingham, S., Conrad, T., Morgan, A. O. N., & Payton, E. (1997). Families and Schools Together (FAST): Integrating community development with clinical strategy. *Families in Society, 78,* 140–155.

McDonald, L., Coe-Braddish, D., Billingham, S., Dibble, N., & Rice, C. (1991). Families and Schools Together: An innovative substance abuse prevention program. *Social Work in Education, 13,* 118–128.

McDonald, L., & Frey, H. E. (1999). Families and Schools Together: Building relationships [*OJJDP Bulletin*]. Washington, DC: U.S. Department of Justice, Office of Justice Programs, Office of Juvenile Justice and Delinquency Prevention.

McDonald, L., & Sayger, T. V. (1998). Impact of a family and school based prevention program on protective factors for high risk youth: Issues in evaluation. *Drugs and Society, 12,* 61–85.

Minuchin, S. (1974). *Families and family therapy.* Cambridge, MA: Harvard University Press.

Moberg, D. P., McDonald, L. W., Brown, R., & Burke, M. (2003, June). *Randomized trial of Families and Schools Together (FAST).* Paper presented at the Society for Prevention Research 11th Annual Meeting, Washington, DC.

Montgomery, P., Stores, G., & Wiggs, L. (2004). The relative efficacy of two brief treatments for sleep problems in young learning disabled (mentally retarded) children: A randomized controlled trial. *Archives of Diseases of Childhood, 89,* 125–130.

National Center for Education Statistics. (2003). *The condition of education 2003* (NCES 2003-067). Washington, DC: U.S. Government Printing Office.

No Child Left Behind Act of 2001, P.L. 107-110, 115 Stat. 1425 (2002).

Pena, D. C. (2000). Parent involvement: Influencing factors and implications. *Journal of Educational Research, 94*(1), 42–54.

Perez, M. A., Pinzon, H. L., & Garza R. D. (1997). Latino families: Partners for success in school settings. *Journal for School Health, 67,* 182–184.

Putnam, R. (2000). *Bowling alone: The disappearance of civic America.* Cambridge, MA: Harvard University Press.

Rutter, M. (1999). Resilience concepts and findings: Implications for family therapy, *Journal of Family Therapy, 21,* 119–144.

Santiago-Rivera, L., Arredondo, P., & Gallardo-Cooper, M. (2002). *Counseling Latinos and la familia: A practical guide.* Thousand Oaks, CA: Sage Publications.

Satir, V. (1983). *Conjoint family therapy* (3rd ed.). Palo Alto, CA: Science and Behavior Books.

Schinke, S., Brounstein, P., & Gardner, S. (2003). *Science-based prevention programs and principles 2002: Effective substance abuse and mental health programs for every community* (DHHS Publication No. 03-3764). Rockville, MD: U.S. Department of Health and Human Services, Substance Abuse and Mental Health Services Administration, Center for Substance Abuse Prevention.

Shumow, L., Vandell, D. L., & Posner, J. (1999). Risk and resilience in the urban neighborhood: Predictors of academic performance among low-income elementary school children. *Merrill-Palmer Quarterly, 45,* 309–331.

Stanton-Salazar, R. (2001). *Manufacturing hope and despair: The school and kin support networks of U.S.–Mexican youth.* New York: Teachers College Press.

Suarez-Orosco, C., Suarez-Orosco, M., & Doucet, F. (2003). The academic engagement and achievement of Latino youth. In J. Banks & C. McGee-Banks (Eds.), *Handbook of research on multicultural education* (2nd ed., pp. 420–437). San Francisco: Jossey-Bass.

Szapocznik J., & Kurtines, W. M. (1993). Family psychology and cultural diversity: Opportunities for theory, research, and application. *American Psychologist, 48,* 400–407.

Valenzuela, A., & Dornbusch, S. (1994). Familism and social capital in the academic achievement of Mexican origin and Anglo adolescents. *Social Science Quarterly, 75,* 18–36.

Vega, W., & Kolody, B. (1985). The meaning of social support and the mediation of stress across cultures. In W. Vega & M. Mirand (Eds.), *Stress and Hispanic mental health: Relating research to service delivery* (DHHS Publication No. 85-1410, pp. 48–75). Washington, DC: U.S. Government Printing Office.

Webster-Stratton, C. (1985). Predictors of treatment outcome in parent training for conduct disordered children. *Behavior Therapy, 16,* 223–243.

Zambrana, R. E. (Ed.). (1995). *Understanding Latino families: Scholarship, policy, and practice.* Thousand Oaks, CA: Sage Publications.

ABOUT THE AUTHORS

Lynn McDonald, PhD, MSW, is senior scientist, Wisconsin Center for Education Research, University of Wisconsin-Madison, 1025 West Johnson Street, Madison, WI 53706; e-mail: mrmcdona@wisc.edu. D. Paul Moberg, PhD, is deputy director, Population Health Institute, University of Wisconsin-Madison. Roger Brown, PhD, is professor of research methodology, School of Nursing and Medicine, University of Wisconsin-Madison. Ismael Rodriguez-Espiricueta, MA, is director, Student Support Services, Central Texas College, Killeen, TX. Nydia I. Flores, MS, is bilingual school psychologist, Allen-Field Elementary School, Milwaukee Public Schools. Melissa P. Burke, BS, is research specialist, Center for Health Policy and Program Evaluation, University of Wisconsin-Madison. Gail Coover, PhD, is research manager, FAST Project, Wisconsin Center for Education Research, University of Wisconsin-Madison. This study was supported by grant DA10067 from the National Institute of Drug Abuse. For more information about FAST, see: www.fastprogram.org.

 Sample Single-Case Experiment

Increasing On-Task Behavior in the Classroom: Extension of Self-Monitoring Strategies

Amato-Zech, N. A., Hoff, K. E., & Doepke, K. J. (2006). Increasing on-task behavior in the classroom: Extension of self-monitoring strategies. *Psychology in the Schools, 43*(2), 211–220.

Many students have difficulty staying on-task during classroom instruction. This is a problem because if students are not on-task, their learning suffers.

The following article describes a single-case experiment to test the effectiveness of a new device, called the MotivAider, to solve this problem. The MotivAider is designed to prompt students to self-monitor their on-task behavior, with the ultimate goal of having students internalize self-monitoring without need for the device.

The article is reprinted in its entirety, just as it appeared when originally published.

Increasing On-Task Behavior in the Classroom: Extension of Self-Monitoring Strategies

NATALIE A. AMATO-ZECH
Community Consolidated School District 59

KATHRYN E. HOFF AND KARLA J. DOEPKE
Illinois State University

ABSTRACT   We examined the effectiveness of a tactile self-monitoring prompt to increase on-task behaviors among 3 elementary-aged students in a special education classroom. Students were taught to self-monitor their attention by using the MotivAider (MotivAider, 2000), an electronic beeper that vibrates to provide a tactile cue to self-monitor. An ABAB reversal design was used for each participant. Results indicated that upon implementation of the self-monitoring intervention, students increased on-task behavior from a mean of 55% to more than 90% of the intervals observed. Additionally, teachers and students provided high ratings of treatment acceptability of this self-monitoring intervention. Limitations, implications, and future directions of these findings are discussed.

S elf-monitoring among children has been examined extensively as a way to improve attention, academic productivity, and decrease off-task behavior in the classroom (Cole, Marder, & McCann, 2000; Shapiro & Cole, 1994). Self-monitoring involves two processes: self-observation and self-recording. Self-observation requires students to pay attention to a specific aspect of behavior, and discriminate whether the behavior being monitored has occurred. For example, students may be taught to ask themselves "Am I paying attention?" in response to a specific prompt (e.g., when a prerecorded tone sounds). Next, the student records whether the behavior being monitored has occurred (Nelson & Hayes, 1981).

Self-monitoring is an appealing strategy for promoting behavior change. Researchers have demonstrated that students with and without disabilities can learn to use self-monitoring to regulate their own behavior and enhance independent activity (McDougall & Brady, 1998; Shapiro & Cole, 1994). Self-monitoring procedures can decrease reliance on external agents (e.g., teachers, parents, peers) for behavior change, thus facilitating generalization to untrained settings and maintenance of acquired skills (McLaughlin, Krappman, & Welsh, 1985). Further, self-monitoring interventions are easy to use and can be implemented with minimal demands on teacher time or curricular modifications, making them optimal for use in schools (Shimabukuro, Prater, Jenkins, & Edelen-Smith, 1999).

Numerous investigations demonstrate the effectiveness of school-based self-monitoring interventions (Gardner & Cole, 1988; Hughes, Korinek, & Gorman, 1991; McDougall, Farrell, & Hoff, 2004; Shapiro & Cole, 1994). The majority of this research has focused on self-monitoring of attention-to-task, and demonstrates that self-monitoring of attention is effective in decreasing disruptive behavior (e.g., Lam, Cole, Shapiro, & Bambara, 1994) and increasing on-task behavior (e.g., Dalton, Martella, & Marchand-Martella, 1999; Dunlap et. al., 1995; Reid, 1996). Collateral effects of self-monitoring of attention also are apparent, in that self-monitoring of attention is associated with positive changes in academic performance such as academic productivity and academic accuracy (e.g., Harris, Graham, Reid, McElroy, & Hamby, 1994; Maag, Reid, & DiGangi, 1993). Finally, self-monitoring procedures are effective across diverse populations and settings. In particular, research supports the use of self-monitoring for students with emotional and behavioral disorders (Edwards, Salant, Howard, Brougher, & McLaughlin, 1995; McDougall & Brady, 1995; Moore, Cartledge, & Heckaman, 1995; Nelson, Smith, Young, & Dodd, 1991), learning disabilities (Hallahan, Marshall, & Lloyd, 1981; Prater, Hogan, & Miller, 1992; Prater, Joy, Chilman, Temple, & Miller, 1991; Rooney, Hallahan, & Lloyd, 1984), autism (Callahan & Rademacher, 1999; Harrower & Dunlap, 2001; Mancina, Tankersley, Kamps, Kravits, & Parrett, 2004), and mild to severe cognitive impairments (Alberto, Tabs, & Frederick, 1999; Briggs et al., 1990; Gilberts, Agran, Hughes, and Wehmeyer, 2001; Hughes et al., 2002). Further, self-monitoring interventions have proven effective in self-contained resource rooms and general education classroom settings (Dalton et al., 1999; Hughes & Hendrickson, 1987; Moore, Prebble, Robertson, Waetford, & Anderson, 2001; Reid, 1996).

Although research clearly supports the effectiveness of self-monitoring interventions, self-monitoring procedures can be impractical, infeasible, or disruptive in certain classroom settings. To date, the majority of self-monitoring interventions have relied on overt audio cues to prompt students to self-monitor their behavior (McDougall et al., 2004). For example, a tape recorder emits a prerecorded tone and this audible cue prompts a student to record whether they were paying attention (Hallahan et al., 1981). Other audible methods of prompting students in self-monitoring procedures include using a tape recorder with headphones for students to hear the cue, a kitchen timer, or verbal prompts from the teacher (Cole & Bambara, 2000). Although effective, these audible prompts have some potential disadvantages. Noticeable cues (e.g., wearing headphones or audible cues which others can hear) may be perceived as stigmatizing or aversive to the target student participating in the intervention and might be distracting to other students in the classroom who are not directed to self-monitor. Similarly, verbal prompts from a teacher can prove distracting, and requires the teacher to interrupt his or her lesson to provide the prompt. Self-monitoring methods that are perceived as aversive by students or difficult or distracting for teachers (i.e., low social validity) may reduce the chance that self-monitoring methods will be employed in the classroom (Reid, 1996). Finally, the use of a more stationary self-monitoring prompt may not be portable outside of the classroom (e.g., recess), thus limiting the situations in which the prompt can be used.

Recently, an alternative self-monitoring procedure has emerged that is less intrusive and may prove more practical and feasible for classroom use than traditional aural or verbal prompts. The MotivAider (MotivAider, 2000) is an electronic beeper that vibrates to provide a tactile prompt to self-monitor. The MotivAider attaches to the student's waistband and can be programmed to emit a cue for any desired length of time and on a continuous or intermittent schedule. Although self-monitoring procedures using the MotivAider are promising and have high intuitive appeal, research has not evaluated the efficacy of using the MotivAider for self-monitoring. As such, this is the first known study to analyze the effectiveness of the MotivAider for increasing on-task behavior in the classroom. We sought to extend the self-management literature by examining the use of a tactile self-monitoring cue and contribute to the applied knowledge base by exploring an alternative self-monitoring strategy for the classroom.

Method

Participants

Participant selection was based on teacher referral of students with low levels of on-task behavior. Prior to inclusion in the project, these reports were confirmed by the researchers through direct observations in the

Amato-Zech, N. A., Hoff, K. E., & Doepke, K. J. (2006). Increasing on-task behavior in the classroom: Extension of self-monitoring strategies. *Psychology in the Schools, 43*(2), 211–220. Copyright © 2006 by John Wiley & Sons. Reprinted with permission of John Wiley & Sons, Inc.

classroom, with observations indicating that levels of on-task behavior occurred on less than 55% of the intervals observed for all participants.

Three fifth graders participated in this study. Jack and David were both 11-year-old boys who had been given multiple diagnoses of speech and language impairment and specific learning disabilities. Allison was an 11-year-old girl who had been given a diagnosis of emotionally disturbed and speech and language impairment. Each of the students was enrolled in the same self-contained special education classroom.

Setting

The study took place at an elementary school located in the Midwest United States. The classroom was a self-contained, multi-age classroom that included seven students: three third graders and four fifth graders. This self-contained program was a new addition to the continuum of services that existed within the district and was in its first year of implementation. A teacher and a full-time teacher assistant initially staffed the classroom; however, a long-term substitute replaced the teacher midway through the project (i.e., the fifth session of the return to baseline phase for all participants).

Experimental sessions were conducted during a regularly scheduled 45-min period in Reasoning and Writing. Instruction in Reasoning and Writing consisted of direct instruction on language reasoning skills and writing skills and independent seatwork on related materials. The length of time students spent in direct instruction and independent seatwork was consistent throughout the study. During the initial baseline phase and the initial intervention phase, all students received Instruction in Reasoning and Writing at a round table. During the return to baseline phase and throughout the rest of the study, students were sitting at desks during instruction.

Materials

The MotivAider was used for the cue to self-monitor throughout the intervention phase. The MotivAider looks like a pager and attaches to a belt or a waistband. It emits a pulsing vibration, which was used as the cue for participants to self-monitor their behavior. In addition to the MotivAider, all participants used a paper-and-pencil recording system to record whether they were paying attention at the time the MotivAider vibrated.

Measures

On-Task Behavior. Direct observation data were collected for on- and off-task behavior using categories from the *Behavioral Observation of the Students in Schools* (BOSS) structured observational code (Shapiro, 1996). On-task behavior was defined as the student actively or passively attending to instruction or assigned work and the absence of off-task behavior during the observed interval. Three possible categories of off-task behavior were recorded: off-task motor, off-task verbal, and off-task passive behaviors. Off-task motor behaviors were defined as any motoric movement that occurred that was not associated with the academic task at hand (e.g., randomly flipping pages in a textbook or out of seat). Off-task verbal behaviors were coded whenever the student made any audible verbalizations that were not relevant to the assigned task or not permitted during the assigned task (e.g., talking to peers, humming, or calling out answers). Off-task passive behaviors occurred whenever there was passive disengagement for a period of at least 3 consecutive seconds (e.g., looking away from assigned material).

Data were collected using a 15-s partial interval recording system. If the student engaged in off-task behavior at any time during the interval, the student's behavior was recorded as off-task rather than on-task for that interval. Direct observations were conducted for 15 min per day, two to three times per week for each student. The first author served as the primary data collector, and the teacher's assistant collected interobserver agreement data.

Interobserver agreement data were collected for 18% of the total sessions observed. Interobserver agreement was calculated by dividing total interval agreements by total intervals observed (Kazdin, 1982). The mean percentage of overall agreement was 96% (range = 92–100%). Additionally, occurrence agreements were calculated on an interval-by-interval basis by dividing the agreements by the total number [of] agreements and disagreements and multiplying by 100. The mean interobserver reliability for the occurrence of off-task behavior was 81% [range = 0 (which occurred when there was only one off-task behavior observed during the session and agreement was not reached)–100%].

Treatment Integrity. Treatment integrity was assessed with a five-item checklist detailing specific steps of the intervention. The primary investigator conducted measures of treatment integrity for 46% of the intervention sessions. Adherence to all steps in the intervention occurred 100% of the time.

Treatment Acceptability. Questionnaires were completed at the end of the study to assess treatment acceptability and feasibility of the self-monitoring intervention using the MotivAider. The classroom teacher, the teacher's assistant, and the long-term substitute completed the later Intervention Rating Profile-20 (IRP-20; Witt & Martens, 1983). This questionnaire consists of 20 items rated on a Likert scale ranging from 0 (*strongly disagree*) to 6 (*strongly agree*). Students were administered a seven-item questionnaire adapted from the Children's Intervention Rating Profile (Turco & Elliot, 1986). This questionnaire consists of seven items rated on a Likert scale of 1 (indicating that the student disagrees with the statement) to 6 (indicating agreement).

Experimental Design and Procedures

An ABAB reversal design was used for each participant in the study, with an extended baseline for the third participant. The specific experimental phases are described next.

Baseline. Initial baseline observations of student behavior were conducted in Reasoning and Writing as well as Math settings. During baseline, self-monitoring procedures were not in place, and teachers were instructed to use their typical procedures for classroom management (e.g., praising appropriate behavior and redirecting off-task behavior). Additionally, all students in the class participated in a classroom-wide point system, which was in place throughout the study. With this system, each child earned stamps throughout the day for working on his or her personal behavioral goal, and exchanged the stamp sheets at the end of the week for a small incentive. This system was used throughout the course of the study and, was not linked to the self-management procedures.

Student Training. Participants were trained to observe and record (i.e., self-monitor) their on-task behavior during two group-training sessions and two practice sessions in the classroom. The training sessions were 30 min in length, and were conducted by the first teacher in her office at the school. During student training, students were taught to identify on- and off-task behaviors using the SLANT strategy (Ellis, 1991). SLANT is an acronym that stands for Sit up, Look at the person talking, Activate thinking, Note key information, and Track the talker. Off-task behavior was defined as the absence of one or more SLANT behaviors. Next, within the training session, students practiced self-monitoring of their on-task behavior, first with an overt audio cue (to ensure they were self-recording accurately and to better provide performance feedback) and then using the MotivAider. Following the two student-training sessions, each student practiced using the MotivAider in the classroom during the 45-min Reasoning and Writing instruction period until they could use the self-monitoring procedures without assistance, as demonstrated by self-recording at the end of each 2-min interval for one entire class session. On the second day of training, all participants were able to self-monitor their on-task behavior and to begin intervention implementation.

Self-Monitoring Intervention. All participants self-monitored their on- and off-task behavior during Reasoning and Writing instruction. Students wore the MotivAider, which elicited electronic vibrations to cue self-monitoring. When the MotivAider vibrated, students recorded whether they were paying attention at that moment in time by checking "yes, I was paying attention" or "no, I was not paying attention" on a self-monitoring form. After each session, the students returned their completed self-monitoring forms and MotivAider to the classroom teacher. The self-monitoring forms were collected on a weekly basis. After the initial student-training

sessions, the classroom teacher was responsible for managing the intervention (i.e., distribution of MotivAiders and self-monitoring forms).

For all participants, the MotivAider was set at 1-min fixed intervals for the first week of the intervention phase; however, at the beginning of the second week of the intervention, the classroom teacher expressed a concern stating that she felt the 1-min cue was too intrusive. After consultation with the teacher about an acceptable cueing interval, the MotivAider was programmed to emit a vibration every 3 min throughout the duration of the study (i.e., the remaining intervention phase and final return to the second intervention phase).

Generalization. Generalization probes were conducted for 10% to 12% of the sessions (i.e., once during each experiment phase). Generalization probes were conducted in a second academic setting (Math) identified by the teacher. The MotivAider was not used in the generalization setting. A direct instruction curriculum (Connecting Math Concepts) was used during this class period.

Results

On-Task Behavior

Figure 1 displays the percentage of intervals of on-task behavior far the three participants. In general, similar results were obtained for each participant in the study. During initial baseline observation, Jack, David, and Allison displayed low levels of on-task behavior (i.e., less than 60% of intervals observed). During the initial intervention phase, participants' on-task behavior increased and reached above 90% at the end of the phase. When the intervention was discontinued (i.e., return to baseline conditions), there was a steady decrease in on-task behavior. Upon reinstatement of the intervention, on-task behavior immediately improved to more than 90% of the intervals observed and remained stable. Specific results of participants are described next.

Jack. Jack's mean percentage of on-task behavior during baseline occurred for 53% of the intervals (range = 47–61%). His on-task behavior showed a slight increasing trend during baseline; however, the final 3 points in baseline were stable. During the self-monitoring phase, Jack's on-task behavior increased to a mean of 79% of intervals observed (range = 65–95%). When the intervention was discontinued, Jack's on-task behavior displayed a decreasing trend and a mean of 74% of intervals observed (range = 65–81%). When the intervention was reintroduced, Jack's rate of on-task behavior quickly improved to a mean occurrence of 91% intervals observed (range = 85–100%).

The percentage of nonoverlapping data points was calculated to summarize intervention effects. Results indicated that the percentages of nonoverlapping data points between the initial baseline phase and the initial

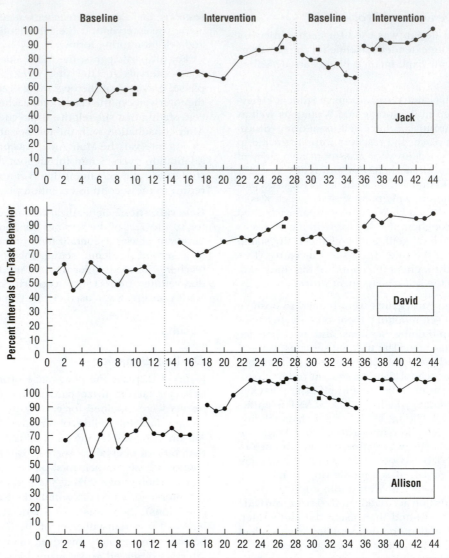

Figure 1 Percentages of Intervals of On-Task Behavior for Jack, David, and Allison

intervention phase, as well as the initial baseline phase and the return to intervention phase, was 100%, suggesting the intervention was consistently associated with behavior change. The percentage of nonoverlapping data points between the initial intervention phase and the return to baseline phase was 54%. The overlapping points between the return to baseline phase and the initial intervention phase consist of the first few data points collected during the intervention, suggesting the intervention did not have an immediate dramatic effect on behavior. Finally, the percentage of nonoverlapping data points between the return to baseline phase and the return to intervention phase was 100%.

Generalization data for Jack indicate his on-task behavior occurred for 55% of the intervals observed during

the initial baseline phase. During the self-monitoring phase, Jack's off-task behavior in Math increased to 87% of intervals observed. When the intervention was returned to baseline, Jack's on-task behaviors in Math remained stable, occurring for 85% of the intervals observed. Upon reintroduction of the intervention, Jack's off-task behaviors again remained stable at 85% of the intervals observed.

David. Results indicate that David's on-task behavior during baseline occurred an average of 55% of intervals observed (range = 43–62%). When the self-monitoring intervention was introduced, his on-task behavior showed an increasing trend with a mean of 79% intervals observed (range = 68–93%). When the intervention was discontinued, David's on-task behavior decreased to a mean of 76% intervals observed (range = 70–80%). Upon reinstatement of the intervention, David's on-task behavior increased to an average of 93% of the intervals observed (range = 87–97%).

The percentage of nonoverlapping data points between the initial baseline phase and the initial intervention phase was 100% for David, as well as for the initial baseline phase and the return to intervention phase. The percentage of nonoverlapping data points between the initial intervention phase and the return to baseline phase was 22%, suggesting that the intervention did not have an immediate effect on on-task behavior but instead led to a gradual decease in on-task behavior. Finally, the percentage of nonoverlapping data points between the return to baseline phase and the return to intervention phase was 100%.

Generalization data for David indicate that David's on-task behavior in Math during the initial baseline phase, intervention phase, return to baseline phase, and reimplementation of the intervention occurred for 60, 88, 70, and 90% of the intervals, respectively.

Allison. During the initial baseline phase, Allison's on-task behavior occurred at a mean rate of 56% of the intervals observed (range = 45–67%) and displayed a flat trend. Upon introduction of the self-monitoring intervention, Allison's on-task behavior increased to a mean of 89% of the intervals observed (range = 73–98% of the intervals observed). When the intervention was discontinued, Allison's on-task behavior displayed a steady decreasing trend with a mean of 84% intervals observed (range = 75–91%). When the intervention was reintroduced, Allison's on-task behavior immediately increased to a mean rate of 96% of intervals observed (range = 88–98%).

The percentage of nonoverlapping data points between the initial baseline phase and the initial intervention phase was 100%, as well as for the initial baseline phase and the return to intervention phase. The percentage of non-overlapping data points between the initial intervention phase and the return to baseline phase was 60%, suggesting that the intervention had a gradual impact on increasing levels of on-task behavior. Finally, the percentage of nonoverlapping data points between the return to baseline phase and the return to intervention phase was 88%. When examining the overlapping data points, there was a single dip in Allison's level of on-task behavior during one intervention session that accounts for the overlap.

Generalization data for Allison indicate that for on-task behavior in Math during the initial baseline phase, intervention phase, return to baseline phase, and re-implementation of the intervention occurred for 67, 95, 83, and 90% of the intervals, respectively.

Treatment Acceptability

Result of the treatment acceptability ratings by classroom personnel were high. The classroom teacher, the teacher's assistant, and the long-term substitute reported total acceptability scores of 115, 102, and 98, respectively, where 120 of 120 indicates the most acceptable score possible. Specifically, results indicated that all teachers strongly agreed on factors such as intervention procedures being beneficial to the student (i.e., two ratings of 5 and one rating of 6), intervention procedures being easy to implement without a lot of training (i.e., two ratings of 6 and one rating of 5), and that overall, the teachers would be willing to use the self-monitoring intervention in the classroom setting (i.e., two ratings of 5 and one rating of 6).

Total acceptability scores on the Children's Intervention Rating Profile for Jack, David, and Allison were 33, 31, and 36 of 42, respectively, where 42 of 42 indicates the most acceptable score possible. All students strongly agreed that they liked the intervention (i.e., three ratings of 6), felt that the intervention would help them in school (i.e., two ratings of 6 and one rating of 5), and did not think there were better ways to help their inattentive behavior (i.e., three ratings of 6).

Discussion

This is the first known investigation of the use of self-monitoring with the MotivAider for increasing the on-task behaviors of elementary-aged students in a special education classroom. Upon implementation of the self-monitoring intervention, students increased levels of on-task behavior from a mean of 55% to more than 90% of the intervals observed. These findings are consistent with prior self-monitoring literature and provide additional empirical support of the effectiveness and acceptability of self-monitoring in the classroom. The data also demonstrate that students with learning and behavioral challenges can effectively use a tactile self-monitoring prompt for behavior change.

The results of this study have several practical implications for use in schools. First, self-monitoring using the MotivAider was easy and relatively time effective. Because the students were responsible for monitoring and recording their own behavior, the intervention was easy to implement and placed few demands on the teachers' time. These are important factors to consider, as interventions requiring low amounts of teacher time are likely to lead to increased follow-through and higher rates of treatment acceptability compared to time-intensive interventions or interventions that take away from classroom instruction (Frith & Armstrong, 1986). Second, students' on-task behaviors increased despite the absence of tangible rewards for doing so (i.e., no complex reinforcement program was required). These results are similar to prior research findings indicating that self-monitoring can produce positive gains without backup consequences (Hallahan & Sapona, 1983; Shimabukuro et al., 1999). These results also are consistent with prior theories indicating that self-monitoring leads to heightened awareness of a target behavior and subsequent behavior change (i.e., reactivity; Kanfer, 1970) and that self-monitoring appropriate behavior can take on motivational properties, providing reinforcement for behavior change (Nelson & Hayes, 1981). The absence of an external reinforcement program can make this intervention more acceptable and less intrusive in the classroom as well as facilitate generalization to untrained settings and skills (McLaughlin et al., 1985). Although these preliminary findings are promising, further research is necessary to explore whether the positive results would maintain over time without additional reinforcement.

Also encouraging were the high intervention acceptability ratings provided by the teachers and the students. Teachers indicated that the intervention was highly acceptable and easy to implement, and responded that they would use the self-monitoring intervention again for a similar problem. Likewise, high ratings of student acceptability revealed that students viewed the MotivAider as a tool to help them stay on task, did not feel the intervention was intrusive in the classroom, and reported that wearing the MotivAider was "cool."

Limitations

Although we obtained positive results using the MotivAider, there are several limitations to this study worth noting. First, we did not see incomplete return to initial baseline levels when the MotivAider was removed. One possible explanation of this observation is that students were learning to self-manage their behavior; if this were the case, we would not expect a reversal to baseline conditions. Nonetheless, data for all participants clearly demonstrated a decreasing trend of on-task behavior once the MotivAider was removed. Thus, it would appear that students still relied on the MotivAider for behavior change to some extent. It remains to be explored empirically if over time, students can control on-task behavior on their own, without reliance on external prompts, or whether the reactive effects of self-monitoring are more short term and disappear when self-monitoring is discontinued (Nelson, 1977).

Finally, our generalization data must be interpreted with caution, as only one observation per phase was conducted. When examining these limited data, however, it is surprising to note that for two participants, Allison and David, the generalization probes verbally correspond with the data collected during each phase of the study. For example, during the initial baseline phase, Allison's on-task behaviors in Reasoning and Writing occurred for a mean of 55% of the intervals observed and for 67% of the intervals in the generalization setting (Math). Upon implementation of the intervention, Allison's on-task behaviors increased in the intervention setting and generalization setting where the MotivAider

was not being used. It would be interesting to explore whether generalization data collected on a more consistent basis would yield the same results.

Future Directions

As this is the first published study that has explored the use of the MotivAider for self-monitoring, future research should include attempts to replicate the results obtained with the use of the MotivAider. Additionally, issues related to long-term use of self-monitoring, such as generalization and maintenance of self-monitoring with the MotivAider across settings and over time, warrant further investigation. Research examining what age ranges and for what behaviors the MotivAider might be most useful would add to the current knowledge base. Finally, future research should explore commensurate changes in academic performance and social acceptance of children using the MotivAider.

In conclusion, self-monitoring using the MotivAider appears to be an effective and practical intervention for increasing on-task behavior for students with learning difficulties and behavioral challenges. Additional research is needed to replicate and extend the findings of this study and to explore ways for students to become an active participant for behavior change.

REFERENCES

Alberto, P. A., Taber, T. A., & Fredrick, L. D. (1999). Use of self-operated auditory prompts to decrease aberrant behaviors in students with moderate mental retardation. Research in Developmental Disabilities, 20, 429–439.

Briggs, A., Alberto, P., Sharpton, W., Berlin, K., McKinley, C., & Ritts, C. (1990). Generalized use of a self-operated audio prompt system. Education and Training in Mental Retardation, 25, 381–389.

Callahan, K., & Rademacher, J. A. (1999). Using self-management strategies to increase the on-task behavior of a student with autism. Journal of Positive Behavior Interventions, 1, 117–122.

Cole, C. L., & Bambara, L. M. (2000). Self-monitoring: Theory and practice. In E. S. Shapiro & T. R. Kratochwill (Eds.), Behavioral assessment in schools: Theory, research, and clinical foundations (pp. 202–232). New York: Guilford Press.

Cole, C. L., Marder, T., & McCann, L. (2000). Self-monitoring. In E. S. Shapiro & T. R. Kratochwill (Eds.), Conducting school-based assessment of child and adolescent behavior (pp. 121–149). New York: Guilford Press.

Dalton, T., Martella, R. C., & Marchand-Martella, N. E. (1999). The effects of a self-management program in reducing off-task behavior. Journal of Behavioral Education, 9, 157–176.

Dunlap, G., Clarke, S., Jackson, M., Wright, S., Ramos, H., & Brinson, S. (1995). Self-monitoring of classroom behaviors with students exhibiting emotional and behavioral challenges. School Psychology Quarterly, 10, 165–177.

Edwards, L., Salent, V., Howard, V. F., Brougher, J., & McLaughlin, T. F. (1995). Effectiveness of self-management on attentional behavior and reading comprehension for children with attention deficit disorder. Child & Family Behavior Therapy, 17, 1–17.

Ellis, E. S. (1991). SLANT: A starter strategy for class participation. Lawrence, KS: Edge Enterprises, Inc.

Frith, G. H., & Armstrong, S. W. (1986). Self-monitoring for behavioral disordered students. Teaching Exceptional Children, 18(Winter), 144–148.

Gardner, W. I., & Cole, C. L. (1988). Self-monitoring procedures. In E. S. Shapiro & T. R. Kratochwill (Eds.), *Behavioral assessment in schools: Conceptual foundations and practical applications* (pp. 106–146). New York: Guilford Press.

Gilberts, G. H., Agran, M., Hughes, C., & Wehmeyer, M. (2001). The effects of peer delivered self-monitoring strategies on participation of students with severe disabilities in general education classrooms. Journal of the Association for Persons with Severe Handicaps, 26, 25–36.

Hallahan, D., Marshall, K., & Lloyd, J. (1981). Self-recording during group instruction: Effects on attention to task. Learning Disability Quarterly, 4, 407–413.

Hallahan, D., & Sapora, R. (1983). Self-monitoring of attention with learning-disabled children: Past research and current issues. Journal of Learning Disabilities, 16, 616–621.

Harris, K. R., Graham, S., Reid, R., McElroy, K., & Hamby, R. S. (1994). Self-monitoring of attention versus self-monitoring of performance: Replication and cross-task comparison studies. Learning Disability Quarterly, 17, 121–139.

Harrower, J. K., & Dunlap, G. (2001). Including children with autism in general education classrooms: A review of effective strategies. Behavior Modification, 25, 762–784.

Hughes, C., Copeland, S. R., Agran, M., Wehmeyer, M. L., Rodi, M. S., & Pressley, J. A. (2002). Using self-monitoring to improve performance in general education high school classes. Education and Training in Mental Retardation and Developmental Disabilities, 37, 262–272.

Hughes, C., & Hendrickson, J. (1987). Self-monitoring with at-risk students in the regular class setting. Education and Treatment of Children, 10, 225–236.

Hughes, C. A., Korinek, L., & Gorman, J. (1991). Self-management for students with mental retardation in public school settings: A research review. Education and Training in Mental Retardation, 26, 271–291.

Kanfer, F. H. (1970). Self-monitoring: Methodological limitations and clinical applications. Journal of Consulting and Clinical Psychology, 35, 148–152.

Kazdin, A. E. (1982). Single case research designs: Methods for clinical and applied settings. New York: Oxford University Press.

Lam, A. L., Cole, C. L., Shapiro, E. S., & Bambara, L. M. (1994). Relative effects of self-monitoring on-task behavior, academic accuracy, and disruptive behavior in students with behavior disorders. School Psychology Review, 23, 44–58.

Maag, J. W., Reid, R., & DiGangi, S. A. (1993). Differential effects of self-monitoring attention, accuracy, and productivity. Journal of Applied Behavioral Analysis, 26, 329–344.

Mancina, C., Tankersley, M., Kamps, D., Kravits, T., & Parrett, J. (2000). Reduction of inappropriate vocalizations for a child with autism using a self-management treatment program. Journal of Autism & Developmental Disorders, 30, 599–606.

McDougall, D., & Brady, M. P. (1995). Using audio-cued self-monitoring for students with severe behavior disorders. Journal of Educational Research, 88, 309–318.

McDougall, D., & Brady, M. P. (1998). Initiating and fading self-management interventions to increase math fluency in general education classes. Exceptional Children, 64, 151–166.

McLaughlin, T. F., Krappman, V. F., Welsh, J. M. (1985). The effects of self-recording for on-task behavior of behaviorally disordered special education students. Remedial and Special Education, 6, 42–45.

Moore, D. W., Prebble, S., Robertson, J., Waetford, R., & Anderson, A. (2001). Self-recording with goal setting: A self-management programme for the classroom. Educational Psychology, 21, 255–265.

Moore, R. J., Cartledge, G., & Heckaman, K. (1995). The effects of social skill instruction and self-monitoring on game-related behaviors of adolescents with emotional or behavioral disorders. Behavioral Disorders, 20, 253–266.

MotivAider. (2000). Thief River Falls, MA: Behavioral Dynamics.

Nelson, R. O. (1977). Assessment and therapeutic functions of self-monitoring. In M. Herson, R. M. Eisler, & P. M. Miller (Eds.), Progress in behavior modification (Vol. 5, pp. 263–308). New York: Academic Press.

Nelson, R. O., & Hayes, S. (1981). Theoretical explanations for reactivity in self-monitoring. Behavior Modification, 5, 3–14.

Nelson, J. R., Smith, D. J., Young, R. K., & Dodd, J. M. (1991). A review of self-management outcome research conducted with students who exhibit behavior disorders. Behavioral Disorders, 16, 169–179.

Prater, M. A., Hogan, S., & Miller, S. R. (1992). Using self-monitoring to improve on-task behavior and academic skills of an adolescent with mild handicaps across special and regular education settings. Education and Treatment of Children, 15, 43–55.

Prater, M. A., Joy, R., Chilman, B., Temple, J., & Miller, S. R. (1991). Self-monitoring of on-task behavior by adolescents with learning disabilities. Learning Disabilities Quarterly, 14, 164–177.

Reid, R. (1996). Research in self-monitoring with students with learning disabilities: The present, the prospects, the pitfalls. Journal of Learning Disabilities, 29, 317–331.

Rooney, K. J., Hallahan, D. P., & Lloyd, J. W. (1984). Self-recording of attention by learning disabled students in the regular classroom. Journal of Learning Disabilities, 17, 360–364.

Shapiro, E. S. (1996). Academic skills problems workbook. New York: Guilford Press.

Shapiro, E. S., & Cole, C. (1994). Behavior change in the classroom: Self-management interventions. New York: Guilford Press.

Shimabukuro, S. M., Prater, M. A., Jenkins, A., & Edelen-Smith, P. (1999). The effects of self-monitoring of academic performance on students with learning disabilities and ADD/ADHD. Education and Treatment of Children, 22, 397–414.

Turco, T., & Elliot, S. (1986). Assessment of students' acceptability ratings of teacher initiated interventions for classroom misbehavior. Journal of School Psychology, 24, 277–283.

Witt, J., & Martens, B. (1983). Assessing the acceptability of behavioral interventions used in classrooms. Psychology in the Schools, 20, 510–517.

CHAPTER THIRTEEN

Case Studies in Qualitative Research

PROBLEMS OF PRACTICE *in this chapter*

- How do case stories and case studies differ in their ability to help educators solve problems of practice?
- What are the advantages and disadvantages of teaching bilingual education in a segregated bilingual high school rather than an integrated comprehensive high school?
- How can an elementary teacher improve class discussions to foster students' inquiry-based learning of mathematics?
- What competencies and work structures facilitate efforts by instructional technologists to improve district-level curriculum and instruction?
- What are significant trends in the privatization of public schools, and are they creating worthwhile school reform?
- Can an innovative program for teaching ethnic-minority high school students improve their retention as college students?
- Can fathers learn a more satisfying way to foster their children's development?
- What can we learn about the benefits of online learning from intensive study of one parent and her child as they engage with an online learning environment?
- What types of computer-supported instruction do exemplary social studies teachers most commonly use in teaching junior high and high school students, and what unique approaches do they also use?

IMPORTANT *Ideas*

1. Unlike case stories in magazines or professional publications for educators, case studies in our context are systematic investigations that attempt to satisfy research standards for validity and reliability.
2. Qualitative research case studies involve in-depth inquiry into particular instances of a phenomenon in its natural context, from both the researchers' (etic) and the research participants' (emic) perspective.
3. Qualitative case studies reflect the interpretivist view, which sees reality not as objective but rather as subjectively constructed by each individual.

4. The introductory section of a qualitative case study report typically states questions to be answered, issues to be addressed, or purposes to be achieved.

5. The purpose of qualitative research case studies is usually description, evaluation, or explanation of particular phenomena.

6. Selection of qualitative research cases typically is based on purposeful sampling, which involves a search for instances of a phenomenon that are information-rich.

7. Because construction, meaning making, and interpretation are central in qualitative research, the researcher typically is the primary instrument of data collection.

8. Qualitative researchers often practice reflexivity, engaging in self-reflection to identify, communicate, and attempt to reduce the effects of their personal biases with respect to the phenomena being studied.

9. The most common forms of data collection in qualitative research case studies are individual or focus group interviews, participant observation, analysis of documents and media, and use of paper-and-pencil measures.

10. Case study researchers typically begin data analysis while still engaged in data collection, and continue data collection until additional data contribute nothing new about the phenomenon being studied.

11. Interpretational analysis of case study data is based on the principles of grounded theory, which involve coding data segments into categories and grouping them to identify different levels of information that give meaning to the data.

12. Case study researchers sometimes analyze their data through reflective analysis, relying on their own intuition and personal judgment.

13. Case study researchers reflect on the applicability of their findings to other settings and provide thick descriptions of their cases to help readers make their own judgments of applicability.

14. A variety of evaluative strategies are available to case study researchers to demonstrate the credibility and trustworthiness of their findings, including usefulness, participant involvement, inclusion of quantitative data, long-term observation, coding checks, member checking, triangulation, and contextual completeness.

15. Qualitative researchers have developed qualitative research traditions over time. These traditions draw on general principles of qualitative research methodology, but they focus on different types of phenomena and use specialized research techniques to study them.

KEY TERMS

applicability	constant comparison	grounded theory
audit trail	construct	in-depth study
case	criterion sampling	insider
case focus	critical research	interpretational analysis
case story	crystallization	interpretivism
case study	emic perspective	key informant
causal pattern	etic perspective	member checking
chain of evidence	fieldwork	multivocality
coding check	focus group	outsider

participant observer
pattern
performance ethnography
phenomenon
positivism
purposeful sampling

qualitative research tradition
reflective analysis
reflexivity
relational pattern
snowball sampling
tacit knowledge

theme
theoretical saturation
thick description
triangulation

HOW QUALITATIVE CASE STUDY RESEARCH CAN HELP EDUCATORS SOLVE PROBLEMS OF PRACTICE

In sharing what they know about education, most educators tell stories. They have stories about their own experience as students, often going back to childhood. They have joyful stories about their own successes with particular students and sad stories about others. Many educators can quickly relate insightful, moving descriptions as to why a student like Jimmie or Chaneva or Oliver probably will, or won't, do well in school this year. They often tell ongoing stories about new programs being implemented in their schools.

Many individuals who are preparing to become teachers have told us that they found greater value in their field experience than in their teacher education coursework. Perhaps one reason is that in the field, their learning is based more on stories from their fellow student teachers, supervising teachers, and others as well as from their own and other students' experience. Many of these stories convey to new teachers messages about "the way we do things here" and "what you need to do if you want to get—and keep—a job in this school district."

Example of a Case Story

Bruce Biddle and Donald S. Anderson (1986) argued that some published qualitative research studies would be better described as case stories than case studies. To illustrate the difference, we present at the end of this chapter a case story that appeared in *Teacher Magazine*. We recommend that you read it now. A **case story** describes a series of related events in an interesting manner, but it provides little evidence for judging the validity

of the events described or their applicability to other contexts. Nonetheless, this and other case stories are enlightening and interesting, and they give teachers ideas about ways to improve their classroom instruction.

To what extent are case stories like this a sound guide for other educators' practice? This question cannot be answered with any certainty because the article in *Teacher Magazine* does not present evidence to validate the author's assertions that her students "worked more productively" and "were surprisingly responsible about their use of time." In the words of Biddle and Anderson, a case story "is designed to illustrate conclusions to which the author is already committed" (p. 239). These conclusions might well be valid, but we cannot know for certain.

In contrast, a **case study** is a systematic qualitative research investigation. It involves in-depth study of instances of a phenomenon in its natural context while conveying both the researchers' and the participants' perspectives and using procedures that test the validity and applicability of its findings. It would be possible for researchers to take the insights of the case story in *Teacher Magazine* and test them by rigorous case studies or other research methods.

KEY CHARACTERISTICS OF CASE STUDIES

The methodology of case study research derives primarily from ethnography, which is one of the earliest forms of qualitative research. Ethnography was initially carried out by anthropologists who immersed themselves in a different culture and made holistic studies of cultural behavior, beliefs, and artifacts. (We discuss the method of ethnography in Chapter 14.)

In the next sections, we describe four key characteristics of a qualitative research case study, using as an example a case study about bilingual education reported by Ofelia García and Lesley Bartlett (2007).

Study of Particular Instances of a Phenomenon

A case study is conducted to shed light on a particular **phenomenon**—that is, a set of processes, events, individuals, programs, or any other events or circumstances of interest to researchers. Examples of educational phenomena are daily life in a school's computer lab, a particular curriculum, school staff with similar work responsibilities, or school events such as meetings of the district's school board. Typically, case study researchers first specify the broader phenomenon, which they hope to clarify through doing their case study, and then describe the **case** they selected for intensive study, which is the specific instance of the phenomenon, bounded in time and place.

García and Bartlett's case study involved analysis of a particular institution that provides bilingual education, which is the phenomenon of interest. A phenomenon has many aspects, so researchers must select a focus for their investigation. A **case focus** represents those aspects of the phenomenon on which the researchers concentrate their data collection and analysis.

In our example, the researchers wished to study a model of bilingual education different from those currently found in most bilingual schools. The specific case that they studied as an instance of this phenomenon is Gregorio Luperón High School, a segregated bilingual high school for Latino newcomers in a suburban New York community. Of its 350 students, 85 percent are from the Dominican Republic, and 82 percent have been in the United States three years or less. The researchers' primary focus for data collection and analysis was the strengths and drawbacks of this type of bilingual high school.

In-Depth Study of the Case

A case study ideally involves **in-depth study** of the phenomenon, meaning that a substantial amount of data are collected about the specific case or cases selected to represent the phenomenon. The data primarily are verbal statements, images, or physical objects, but some quantitative data also might be collected.

The data typically are collected over an extended time period, with several methods of data collection. In our example, the researchers collected data in a variety of ways:

1. Weekly participant observation for a nine-month period in lower-level English as a second language (ESL) and Spanish classes and other content-area classes.
2. Seven focus groups conducted in Spanish with newly arrived students enrolled in ESL 1 and 2. (As we explain below, focus groups are a form of group interview in which a number of people participate in a discussion guided by a skilled interviewer.)
3. Individual interviews with five teachers and two administrators of the school.
4. A focus group conducted with some ESL teachers and another with the Spanish teachers.
5. Recordings of monthly staff development sessions that were coordinated by the authors during the first year of the study.

The researchers also collected data on their own experience with the school's bilingual program, as well as the research participants' experience. Data collection continued for more than a year.

This extensive process of data collection exemplifies what it means to do an in-depth study of a case. The depth in this case was made possible by the researchers' strategic decision to study one school as a specific instance of the phenomenon of interest rather than a sample of schools, as would be done in a typical quantitative research study. The authors concluded that the "anachronistic educational model" of a segregated bilingual high school was successful because it viewed second language acquisition "not just as the individual psycholinguistic process of students" but also "as a social process building on the speech community itself" (Garcia & Bartlett, p. 1).

Study of a Phenomenon in Its Natural Context

Jerome Kirk and Marc Miller (1986) define qualitative research as an approach to social science research that involves "watching people in their own territory and interacting with them in their own language, on their own terms" (p. 9). This approach to research typically involves **fieldwork**, a process in which researchers interact with participants in the field, meaning in their natural settings rather than in a setting established primarily for research purposes.

In education, fieldwork settings typically are schools or other educational institutions, because that is where the research participants of interest to educational researchers often are found. However, we need to remember that students, teachers, and other school participants also have active lives outside of these institutional contexts. Thus, you should examine case studies (or any type of research) in education to see whether the researchers conducted fieldwork in other natural sites of teaching and learning, such as the home.

In the bilingual education study, it appears that all data were collected in the school. García and Bartlett state that "most of the teachers are Dominicans, and most of these are immigrants themselves. The principal of the school . . . is also a Dominican" (p. 7). Consistent with its staff and student population and its unique model of bilingual education, "Gregorio Luperón simply teaches most content in Spanish" (p. 17).

Representation of Both the Emic and Etic Perspectives

Case study researchers must come to understand a phenomenon from the research participants' point of view while also maintaining their own point of view. The participants' viewpoint about the phenomenon under study is called the **emic perspective**. Typically, researchers obtain the emic perspective through informal conversations with the case study participants and by observing their natural behavior in the field.

At the same time, the researchers maintain their own perspective as investigators of the phenomenon. Their viewpoint of the phenomenon under study as outsiders, which is called the **etic perspective**, helps them make conceptual and theoretical sense of the case and to report the findings so that their contribution to the literature is clear to other researchers.

In the case study of bilingual education, the researchers convey the emic perspective of the participants in varied ways. They include detailed quotations, in both Spanish and English, reflecting students' and teachers' views on various issues, such as the necessity of learning English and the value of students' bilingualism in fostering their achievement. In their acknowledgements, the researchers note three research participants who read a first draft of the case study report.

The two researchers, both affiliated with the Teachers College of Columbia University, make their etic perspective apparent in several ways. Their study includes a review of bilingual education from the 1960s on, citing political and legislative milestones and describing various models of bilingual education. The researchers discuss the strengths of the model of bilingual education practiced at the Gregorio Luperón High School for Math & Science, as perceived by the research participants. In addition, they provide their own perspective by discussing the model's limitations, including the social isolation fostered by the school's homogeneous student population. The researchers express their concern that this model for bilingual education might hinder the ability of Dominican students to function effectively beyond their immediate community.

Ethical Issues in Qualitative Research

Students' qualitative research proposals generally require review by an Institutional Review Board (IRB), described in Chapter 2. Here, we focus on perspectives toward such a review held by prominent qualitative researchers and the primary ethical issues that they highlight as important to address in qualitative research, whether it must undergo IRB review or not.

The history of scientific research includes many instances of individuals being unknowingly subjected to such treatment as the administration of dangerous drugs or infectious substances, or psychological endeavors to get people to behave in a manner contrary to their normal behavior (Patton, 2002, p. 271). The movement to protect human "subjects" (many qualitative researchers prefer the term *participants*) originated to prevent research of this type and to alert all researchers to the need to address ethical issues involved in all research.

Research in anthropology, the field in which qualitative research first became prominent, "was commissioned and used by colonial administrators to maintain control over indigenous peoples" (Patton, 2002, p. 271). Today, qualitative researchers tend to study groups of individuals from non-Western cultures or economically and ethnically diverse cultures within their own society that are different from their own. Researchers must avoid assumptions about the meaning and value of research to those they desire to be participants in their research.

Some qualitative research authors argue against the operation of IRBs generally, claiming that they favor, or even exclusively define, research from a positivist orientation. Gaile Cannella and Yvonna Lincoln (2013) argue that

the dominant (non-critical) research community and the institutions that support research are not critical and tend to support modernist forms of governmentality. Ethics are likely to be legislated or constructed by individual researchers from within value structures that either maintain that science can solve all problems, therefore legitimating intervention into the lives of others in the name of science, or that free-market capitalism will improve life conditions for all, also used as the ethical justification for research

choices and actions. These conceptualizations of ethics . . . remain modernist, male-oriented, and imperialist. (p. 178)

Cannella and Lincoln suggest that qualitative researchers consider research ethics in relation to such questions as: "How are forms of exclusion being produced? Is transformative and liberatory research possible that also examines its own will to emancipate? . . . How does the practice of research reinscribe our own privilege?" (Cannella & Lincoln, 2007, p. 321).

For students who need a thorough guide to addressing the ethical issues involved in a specific research proposal, Patton (2002) provides an ethical issues checklist. In Table 13.1, we reproduce the 10 topics and some of the questions found in the checklist. These questions cover most of the issues of primary concern to an IRB but also help the qualitative researcher think through the issues from a personal and critical perspective. While designed for use in qualitative interviewing, we see it as relevant to other forms of data collection used by qualitative researchers. It also reflects the emergent nature of qualitative research, meaning that new research questions can be framed as data collection occurs. Table 13.1 also reflects the practice in some qualitative studies of involving participants as active reviewers or coauthors of the research study.

TABLE 13.1 • Summary of Questions in Michael Patton's Ethical Issues Checklist

1. *Explaining purpose.* How will you explain the purpose of the inquiry and methods to be used in ways that are accurate and understandable?

2. *Promises and reciprocity.* What's in it for the interviewer?

3. *Risk assessment.* In what ways, if any, will conducting the interview put people at risk?

4. *Confidentiality.* What are reasonable promises of confidentiality that can be fully honored? Know the difference between confidentiality and anonymity.

5. *Informed consent.* What kind of informed consent, if any, is necessary for mutual protection?

6. *Data access and ownership.* Who will have access to the data? For what purposes?

7. *Interviewers' mental health.* How will you and other interviewers likely be affected by conducting the interviews?

8. *Advice.* Who will be the researcher's confidante and counselor on matters of ethics during the study?

9. *Data collection boundaries.* How hard will you push for data?

10. *Ethical versus legal.* What ethical framework and philosophy informs your work and ensures respect and sensitivity for those you study, beyond whatever may be required by law?

Source: Excerpt from Exhibit 7.6 in Patton, M. Q. (2002). Qualitative research and evaluation methods (3rd ed.) Thousand Oaks, CA: Sage. Exhibit 7.6 provides an expanded list of questions beyond those listed here.

EXAMPLES OF CASE STUDIES

Case studies, and qualitative research generally, are a rich source of knowledge that educators draw on to identify, explore, and solve their problems of practice. The following three case studies illustrate the varied kinds of phenomena that case studies address and the approaches used to explore them.

A Case Study of Teacher Development

A researcher (Roza Leikin) and a teacher (Shelly Rota) conducted a collaborative practitioner-oriented study to explore how teachers learn through the process of teaching and reflection (Leikin & Rota, 2006). Rota, an elementary teacher of mathematics, was both the subject and coauthor of the study. The study focused on the teacher's management of whole-class discussion during inquiry-based mathematics instruction in one of her mathematics classrooms. The purpose of the study was to analyze the effects of changes in classroom instruction and classroom discourse.

Rota had several reasons for initiating inquiry-based instruction, which assumes that knowledge is constructed by the learner rather than acquired directly from teachers and other sources. First, she wanted to improve her students' class contributions during instruction and also their learning outcomes. Second, she and Leikin sought to clarify how she and other teachers could teach mathematics with less stress and more confidence. Third, they wanted to discover how teachers can encourage students' exploration and understanding of mathematics as opposed to rote learning of mathematical concepts.

Their study analyzed the teacher's change in two aspects of instruction. The first, discussion structure, involves changes in teaching that occur in class discussion as the nature of the mathematical task shifts toward exploration and away from stating facts or seeking to give correct answers. The second, lesson organization, involves changes in how a teacher structures the elements of a lesson.

Leikin and Rota intermittently videotaped 15 months of Rota's lessons and then analyzed the videotaped lessons. The categories for analyzing lesson organization were drawn from previous research. To analyze discussion structure, the researchers developed themes based on **grounded theory**, meaning that they developed theory inductively by examining their data directly without external influence (Corbin & Strauss, 2007). Three lessons, each representing a different point in Rota's development, were the focus of intensive analysis.

Based on their generation of timeline diagrams, Leikin and Rota found that the second and third lessons were better organized than the first lesson "and revealed sharp boundaries between different activities and a clear correspondence between the actual and the intended lesson organization" (p. 51). For example, they found that the teacher needed to reintroduce the task four times during the first lesson because her initial introduction was confusing, whereas "in the second and the third lessons new tasks were presented . . . with a clear connection to relevant learning materials studied earlier" (p. 52).

With respect to classroom discourse, student participation became more active, and the teacher's participation became more responsive as the lessons proceeded. The researchers identified four discussion themes: stimulating initiation, stimulating reply, summary reply, and listening and watching. Within the first three themes, they defined six categories of discussion actions: questioning, translating a representation, exact repetition of students' utterances, constructing a logical chain, stating a fact, and providing feedback. Leikin and Rota concluded from their data analysis that:

> [O]bserved changes in lesson organization, in discussion structure, and in the quality of the discussion actions indicate the development of Shelly's proficiency in managing the inquiry-based lesson. . . . Shelly became more flexible . . . and more able to show trust. (2006, p. 61)

This analysis also led them to suggest a model of teacher discussion activity that "is useful for diagnostic purposes" (p. 64) in analyzing teacher proficiency: "For example, the model reveals that the more proficient teacher performs more actions of the stimulated reply type, connected to student conjectures, designing the actual learning trajectory based on student ideas" (p. 64). A similar analysis of student discussion activities also reveals important changes, including taking a more active part in whole-class discussion and becoming more likely to "construct a logical chain" rather than merely "stating a fact" in their statements (p. 62).

Leikin and Rota caution that while teaching actions are teachable, they "are of a heuristic nature, that is, they are not describable by algorithm" (p. 64). In other words, no simplistic formula will help teachers develop proficiency, but rather they must construct their teaching actions flexibly based on a clear conception of their subject, their students, and their own role in the teaching-learning process.

A Case Study of Instructional Technologists' Work

A case study by Leigh Ausband (2006) examined the involvement of district-level instructional technology (IT) specialists in the curriculum work of one school district. The cases were one former and three current IT specialists in a district in central South Carolina comprising 48 schools. Ausband, previously an IT specialist in this district, was most concerned by this problem of practice: How should school districts define and organize the work of these specialists to increase their impact on curriculum work and thereby on classroom teaching and learning?

Ausband drew on themes and categories generated by previous researchers to describe various aspects of curriculum work on a district level and also various aspects of IT specialists' work. He identified five themes that characterized the district's curriculum work: (1) curriculum and instruction, (2) technical expertise, (3) program management, (4) program coordination, and (5) communication among school staff. He then generated a table comparing the categories of curriculum work and IT work, showing similarities and differences. He used that table as a framework for analysis of documents, observations of each research participant, and development of questions for individual interviews and a focus group interview. He coded interview transcripts and other data, a methodological procedure discussed in greater depth later in the chapter.

Ausband found that IT specialists' work had evolved to include three additional functions: improving and changing curriculum, evaluating instruction, and evaluating programs and research. These new functions reflect the specialists' perceptions that information technology fully corresponds to curriculum work. In the words of one specialist, "I don't think today you can have curriculum without technology. . . . We can't teach today without including technology" (2006, p. 12).

The IT specialists described their actual job responsibilities as including

working with teachers to help them integrate technology into the curriculum through teaching courses and workshops, helping teachers develop lesson plans that utilized technology, and supporting teachers as they developed their technology portfolios. . . . Through their membership on district-level curriculum committees and the Joint Department Leadership Team, the instructional technology specialists were involved in goal-setting, improving curriculum, planning, evaluating, and updating policies and procedures, dealing with problems, and program management. (Ausband, 2006, p. 13)

Ausband found that IT specialists were concerned about several barriers that they felt limited their contributions to curriculum work: exclusion from decision making; lack of time to spend working in schools; and communication, relationship, and leadership issues. For example, Ausband states that the IT specialists

felt the district's curriculum specialists had not changed their focus on curriculum to include technology . . . [and that they] were more curriculum workers than the curriculum specialists themselves because most of the curriculum specialists don't have a clue about technology and don't see it as part of the curriculum. (2006, p. 14)

Drawing on these case study findings, Ausband recommends that IT specialists and curriculum specialists be physically located in the same department within the district organization to facilitate greater cooperation and coordination of their functions. Ausband also suggests the combination of their functions into one IT-curriculum specialist role.

A Case Study of Educational Privatization

Patricia Burch (2006) did a case study to describe the fundamental shifts occurring in K–12 educational privatization in the United States. Educational privatization involves schools contracting with outside firms to carry out essential operations, ranging from specific services to the takeover of entire school systems. Until recently, research on this phenomenon reflected two opposing perspectives: (1) arguments by proponents that contracting public education services to nongovernmental parties can improve quality and reduce costs and (2) arguments by opponents that privatization is part of a larger threat to public education, which aggravates existing inequities among students based on their ethnicity, social class, and geographic location.

Burch (2006) argues that these perspectives ignore new realities pushing for increased privatization. She draws on organizational field theory—which was developed by sociologists—to understand these new realities. Burch contends that institutions representing three types of organizations (local education agencies, nonprofit and for-profit nongovernmental agencies, and the federal government) all can be considered part of the same organizational field. Interactions across all of these organizations was the primary focus of her case study.

Burch used several forms of data collection and analysis in her case study. Examining annual reports and other documents involving the contracting of educational services by government over the past 20 years, she identified four dominant domains of contracting now occurring in the K–12 education sector. She then analyzed policy documents of 10 large school districts, available on the Internet, to examine their contracting activities and also the impact of regulations in the No Child Left Behind Act of 2001.

Burch found that in the past, vendors' primary role was "creating the content of tests and materials designed to increase students' test performance" (2006, p. 2589). The vendors' role now has expanded to include aligning tests with other aspects of district reform agendas. She concludes that vendors "have expanded their role from designers of assessments to designers of systems for monitoring compliance with standards and designers of prepackaged interventions" (2006, p. 2590).

Her analysis revealed an increase from 40 to 70 percent in private companies' annual reported revenues in test development and preparation; from 19 to 46 percent in data management and reporting; from 86 to 300 percent in remedial services; and from 20 to 150 percent in curriculum-specific programming. Burch also found that

> sales of printed materials related to standardized tests nearly tripled between 1992 and 2003, jumping from $211 million to $592 million. . . .

One of the four largest companies in the area of test development and preparation generated sales of $4.4 billion and a profit of $560 million in 2003. (2006, p. 2589)

To situate the new educational privatization in local reform efforts, Burch carried out a three-year qualitative research project in three school districts that reported relying on contracts with vendors in their efforts to implement local reform. She also did an intensive case study of one of the districts.

In her case study, Burch found that reform efforts from 2000 to 2004 continued a prior emphasis on assessment, but "the work moved from a tri-part focus on standardized tests, district-wide performance assessments, and classroom-based assessments to a more exclusive focus on norm-referenced standardized tests" (2006, p. 2598). Burch attributes this shift to "anticipation of the high-stakes accountability reforms legislated under the No Child Left Behind Act" (2006, p. 2598).

The school district that she studied began to spend significantly more money on the purchase of outside products and services. It contracted with a company that initially was local but was bought by a large national firm. Burch reports that interactions with the national firm were much less personal and less responsive to the school district's needs than the school district's interactions had been with the local company.

In the discussion section of her report, Burch speculated that the influence of federal policy contradicts the view of educational privatization as a move away from government regulation and centralized governance. Instead, the expanded federal role in education has shaped the form and level of privatization now occurring. Also, her study shows the diversion of huge amounts of funds away from the public sector in its established role of educating students and administering educational decision making toward the private sector as a silent partner in the most basic educational endeavors.

THE NATURE OF QUALITATIVE RESEARCH

We have now explained the basic characteristics of case studies and presented three examples. Later in the chapter, we describe the specific design elements typically included in a report of a case study.

To lay the foundation for our description, we first briefly review the nature of qualitative research.

As we explain in Chapter 1, much of qualitative research is based on a philosophy of epistemology known as interpretivism. According to **interpretivism**, reality is constructed by the individuals who participate in it. Therefore, one can only understand reality and its meaning from the viewpoint of specific individuals, based on their subjective consciousness of experience from moment to moment. Thus, any phenomenon or event—a book, a mountain, a high school football game—is not seen as having an existence independent of its participants.

A major purpose of qualitative research is to discover the nature of the meanings associated with social phenomena. Case study, the basic method of qualitative research, involves in-depth investigation of the meanings that individuals ascribe to particular instances of a phenomenon, known as cases, in their natural setting.

By contrast, the philosophy of epistemology that characterized most prior investigation in philosophy and science until late in the 20th century, called **positivism**, assumes that there is a real world "out there," which can be known by using quantitative research strategies similar to those that guide the physical sciences and professions such as medicine and engineering. We suggest that you review Table 1.1 in Chapter 1, which summarizes other ways in which qualitative and quantitative researchers differ in their approach to investigating educational and social phenomena.

Qualitative research sometimes is called case study research because of its focus on cases. However, some case studies are carried out based on the positivist orientation typical of quantitative researchers (Yin, 2008). In addition, one form of experimental research (see Chapter 12) involves single-case experiments, which also focus on specific cases. Therefore, we do not refer to qualitative research in general as case study research. We focus in this chapter on case studies reflecting an interpretivist orientation.

QUALITATIVE RESEARCH TRADITIONS

Early in this chapter, we noted that qualitative research includes a wide variety of research traditions. Each of them involves a community of researchers who have an expressed interest in particular phenomena and agreed methods for studying them. Various researchers (e.g., Gall, Gall, & Borg, 2007; Jacob, 1987; Lancy, 1993; Patton, 2002; Tesch, 1990) have attempted to identify and classify these **qualitative research traditions**. All of these classification systems have merit. We selected one of them to present here. Table 13.2 is a list of theoretical traditions in qualitative research created by Michael Quinn Patton (2002, p. 132). The list shows the primary disciplinary roots of each perspective and the central questions that it seeks to answer. It thus provides a good starting point for exploring particular types of qualitative research that might appeal to you.

You should keep in mind that qualitative researchers tend to combine and differentiate these traditions over time. For example, Table 13.2 lists two ethnographic approaches: ethnography (sometimes called *holistic ethnography*) and autoethnography. The *Sage Handbook of Qualitative Research* (Denzin & Lincoln, 2011) includes five chapters with the word *ethnography* in their titles: (1) performance ethnography, (2) narrative ethnography, (3) online ethnography, (4) performance autoethnography, and (5) refunctioned ethnography. These chapters reflect the ways in which a qualitative research tradition can morph or expand into various other forms.

While Patton's (2002) list is fairly comprehensive, it does not include some forms of qualitative research that we think can be considered traditions, namely, action research and historical research. Although these forms of qualitative research are among the most general in terms of possible topics, they are very specific in their approach to research.

In the following chapters, we cover five qualitative research traditions that have had a strong influence in education: ethnography and critical research in Chapter 14; narrative research in Chapter 15; historical research in Chapter 16; and action research in Chapter 18. We also include two chapters that involve distinctive uses of qualitative research: mixed-methods research (Chapter 17), which combines quantitative and qualitative research methodologies, and evaluation research (Chapter 19), which can draw on qualitative or quantitative methodology, or both.

TABLE 13.2 • Variety in Qualitative Theoretical Traditions

Perspective	Disciplinary Roots	Central Questions
1. Ethnography	Anthropology	What is the culture of this group of people?
2. Autoethnography	Literary arts	How does my own experience of this culture connect with and offer insights about this culture, situation, event, and/or way of life?
3. Reality testing: Positivist and realist approaches	Philosophy, social sciences, and evaluation	What's really going on in the real world? What can we establish with some degree of certainty? What are plausible explanations for verifiable patterns? What's the truth insofar as we can get at it? How can we study a phenomenon so that our findings correspond, as much as possible, to the real world?
4. Constructionism/ constructivism	Sociology	How have the people in this setting constructed reality? What are their reported perceptions, "truths," explanations, beliefs, and world view? What are the consequences of their constructions for their behaviors and for those with whom they interact?
5. Phenomenology	Philosophy	What is the meaning, structure, and essence of the lived experience of this phenomenon for this person or group of people?
6. Heuristic inquiry	Humanistic psychology	What is my experience of this phenomenon and the essential experience of others who also experience this phenomenon intensely?
7. Ethnomethodology	Sociology	How do people make sense of their everyday activities so as to behave in socially acceptable ways?
8. Symbolic interaction	Social psychology	What common set of symbols and understandings has emerged to give meaning to people's interactions?
9. Semiotics	Linguistics	How do signs (words, symbols) carry and convey meaning in particular contexts?
10. Hermeneutics	Linguistics, philosophy, literary criticism, theology	What are the conditions under which a human act took place or a product was produced that makes it possible to interpret its meanings?
11. Narratology/narrative analysis	Social sciences (interpretive): Literary criticism, literary nonfiction	What does this narrative or story reveal about the person and world from which it came? How can this narrative be interpreted to understand and illuminate the life and culture that created it?
12. Ecological psychology	Ecology, psychology	How do individuals attempt to accomplish their goals through specific behaviors in specific environments?
13. Systems theory	Interdisciplinary	How and why does this system as a whole function as it does?
14. Chaos theory: Nonlinear dynamics	Theoretical physics, natural sciences	What is the underlying order, if any, of disorderly phenomena?
15. Grounded theory	Social sciences, methodology	What theory emerges from systematic comparative analysis and is grounded in fieldwork so as to explain what has been and is observed?
16. Orientational: Feminist inquiry, critical theory, queer theory, among others	Ideologies: Political, cultural, and economic	How is X perspective manifest in this phenomenon?

Source: Patton, M. Q. (2003). *Qualitative research & evaluation methods* (3rd ed.). Thousand Oaks, CA: Sage.

FEATURES OF A CASE STUDY REPORT

The basic features of a report of a case study are shown in Table 13.3. In explaining these features in the following sections of the chapter, we will use an illustrative case study conducted by David Emiliano Zapata Maldonado, Robert Rhoads, and Tracy Lachica Buenavista (2005). The purpose of the case study was to examine an innovative program to improve the retention of ethnic-minority students once they have entered college.

Introduction

In the introductory section of a case study report, researchers usually do not state hypotheses, but they often indicate questions they hope to answer or issues they wish to address. The introduction also presents the general purpose of the case study, which is to describe, explain, or evaluate particular educational phenomena, as explained below.

Description

The purpose of many case studies is to depict and conceptualize an educational phenomenon clearly. These case studies usually provide a **thick description** of the phenomenon, that is, a set of statements that recreate the situation and its context and give readers a sense of the meanings and intentions that its participants ascribe to it. The term *thick description* originated in anthropology but is now widely used throughout qualitative research.

Evaluation

Case study researchers have developed several qualitative approaches to evaluation (see Chapter 19). In each approach, researchers conduct a case study about certain phenomena and make judgments about those phenomena. For example, a historical case study carried out by Larry Cuban (1997) bears a title reflecting the case study's evaluative purpose: "Change without Reform: The Case of Stanford University School of Medicine, 1908–1990."

Explanation

Some case studies seek to explain particular phenomena. The researchers look for relationships among phenomena within a case or across cases. For example, researchers might observe that American teachers in international schools vary (1) in their perceptions of teaching in such schools and (2) in their perceptions of the local culture. Suppose that the researchers find that the teachers' perceptions of teaching are related to their perceptions

Section	Content
TABLE 13.3 • Typical Sections of a Case Study Report	
Introduction	Hypotheses, questions, or objectives are stated. Relevant literature is reviewed. The purpose of the study usually is to describe, explain, or evaluate phenomena relating to a problem of practice.
Research design	The researcher describes the specific cases and aspects of the cases that will be studied. The researcher also describes the context surrounding the case and whether the case will be studied from an emic or etic perspective, or both. If the case study is grounded in a particular qualitative research tradition, it, too, is specified.
Sampling procedure	The researcher describes the purposeful sampling strategy that was used in the study and explains why that particular strategy was chosen.
Measures	Case studies typically rely on interviews and observation for data collection. Other measures, including quantitative paper-and-pencil measures, can be used as well.
Data analysis	The researcher describes how interpretational analysis (usually based on grounded theory principles) or reflective analysis was used to make sense of the case study data. The researcher also describes the themes and patterns that were identified as a result of the data analyses.
Discussion	The main findings of the study are summarized. Flaws and limitations of the study are considered. Implications of the findings for further research, theory development, and professional practice are considered.

of the culture. They can therefore say that they have discovered a **pattern**, that is, a systematic relationship between two or more phenomena within a case or across cases. If a systematic relationship is found but no cause is specified, this is called a **relational pattern**. If one variation appears to have a causal effect on others, it is referred to as a **causal pattern**.

The researchers state their intention to develop a new theory of the best approach to promote retention of students of color in higher education institutions. They note that for the past 20 years "few higher education topics have drawn more attention than student retention" (Maldonado et al., 2005, p. 605) and that universities are now stressing the need to graduate admitted students within a reasonable time frame, adding that "this is especially true in the case of students of color, who tend to leave colleges and universities at higher-than-average rates" (2005, p. 606). Previous retention efforts have met with limited success, so there is a need to look for new approaches.

They then introduce the phenomenon of interest in their research, namely, a student-initiated retention project (SIRP). They explain that "SIRPs represent a unified effort among student organizations to develop programs and support structures that are, in significant ways, *student organized, student run, and student funded* and that primarily serve students of color" (Maldonado et al., 2005, p. 606, italics in original). Such efforts, which have become major programs at many large public universities, aim to increase the retention and academic success of students of color.

Maldonado and colleagues state the following objectives for their research: (1) raising critical questions about dominant retention theories in higher education, (2) developing a new conceptual framework by combining knowledge from a critique of these theories with their own experience working with SIRPs, and (3) explaining the findings of a case study of the SIRPs at two major universities by applying their conceptual framework. We see, then, that the case study focuses on explanation.

Their conceptual framework involves examining how students' college experience is shaped by, and shapes, the four key concepts of cultural capital, social capital, collectivism, and social praxis. These concepts concern students' individual and organizational power in situating themselves in the college experience and working collectively to transform their higher education experience. A key source in the researchers' literature review for these concepts is Paulo Freire's (1970) critique of the "banking method of education" (p. 613). The "banking method" conception of education is based on the implicit but all-too-common presumption among teachers that the teacher is the all-knowing keeper of knowledge and students are passively situated, empty receptacles to be filled with facts and information by the teacher.

Research Design

The design of a basic qualitative case study involves the four key characteristics described earlier in the chapter (see pp. 344–345). Our example of case study research involves an examination of SIRPs, considering specific instances at the University of California at Berkeley and another at the University of Wisconsin at Madison. The phenomenon was investigated in its natural context, that is, on the campus of each institution where students of color lived, studied, and participated in their institution's SIRP. An in-depth study was made of these two cases, and the researchers sought to represent both their own (etic) perspective and the student (emic) perspective.

Maldonado and his colleagues (2005) state that their case study of SIRPs builds on the qualitative research tradition of critical theory research. Such research, also known as **critical research**, involves an examination of "the ways that the economy, matters of race, class, and gender, ideologies, discourses, education, religion and other social institutions and cultural dynamics interact to construct a social system" (Kincheloe & McLaren, 2000, p. 281). Critical research is focused on how injustice and subjugation, propagated by members of a society who have power, shape the world view of everyone in the society. Critical researchers strive to engage research participants in efforts to emancipate and empower themselves. See Chapter 14 for further discussion of critical research.

Sampling Procedure

The selection of cases in qualitative research involves **purposeful sampling**, meaning that the researchers rely on their judgment to select instances that are information-rich with respect to the phenomenon being studied.

Michael Patton (2002) identified 16 purposeful sampling strategies that case study researchers can use. Many involve selection of cases that represent a characteristic of interest to the researchers to different degrees. For example, a homogeneous sample of students based on math ability might include only students of average math ability, excluding students with high or low math ability. Other strategies reflect a conceptual rationale for selecting cases, such as cases that are well known or politically important.

Maldonado and his colleagues "selected the SIRPs at Berkeley and Madison because of previous knowledge we had about the size and scope of their operations" (2005, p. 616). In our view, this sampling strategy represents what Patton (2002) calls **criterion sampling**, with the criterion being the comprehensiveness of the SIRPs at the two chosen universities.

Maldonado and his colleagues (2005) focused their sampling of research participants on student organizers within each SIRP. Interviews were conducted with 45 student organizers, 34 of whom served SIRP-related functions at the time of the study and 11 of whom had previously worked on SIRP projects.

Key informants or other research participants currently at the universities identified these former organizers. **Key informants** are individuals who have special knowledge or status, and so their emic perspective of the phenomenon being studied is likely to yield worthwhile data. Selection of student organizers also involved the use of another sampling strategy, **snowball sampling**, in which cases are recommended by individuals who know other individuals likely to yield relevant, information-rich data. In addition to sampling student organizers, Maldonado and his colleagues (2005) interviewed six full-time professional staff members with knowledge of the SIRPs at their institutions. Including these individuals in the research sample helped the researchers create an even thicker description of the SIRPs.

Data-Collection Procedures

It has been said that the primary instrument of data collection in qualitative research is the researcher himself or herself (Lincoln & Guba, 2011). This view of data collection reflects the centrality of construction, making of meaning, and interpretation in qualitative research.

Case study researchers use any methods of data collection that are appropriate to their purpose. They might begin a case study with one method of data collection and gradually shift to, or add, other methods. The purpose for this data-collection strategy is **triangulation**, also known as **crystallization** (Richardson & St. Pierre, 2005), which involves the use of multiple methods to collect data about the same phenomenon in order to confirm research findings or to resolve discrepant findings. It can also involve the use of different data sources, methods of analysis, or theories to check case study findings. In the next sections, we describe the methods of data collection most often used in case studies.

Interviews

Researchers often conduct interviews with field participants. They typically use open-ended questions to which the research participants can respond freely in their own terms rather than selecting from a fixed set of responses. The interviews can be informal, occurring in the natural course of conversation. If many respondents are being interviewed, or if more than one interviewer is involved, the researchers might choose to use an interview guide that outlines a set of topics to be explored with each respondent.

Focus groups are a form of group interview in which a number of people participate in a discussion guided by a skilled interviewer. Because the respondents can talk to and hear each other, they are likely to express feelings or opinions that might not emerge if they were interviewed individually.

Observation

Case study researchers often observe individuals in their natural settings over an extensive period of time. They might videotape their observations and make handwritten or tape-recorded notes. Many researchers strive to become **participant observers**, meaning that they interact personally with participants during activities in the natural setting in order to build empathy and trust and to further their understanding of the phenomenon. They generally take notes on their observations only after they have left the field.

Case study researchers might also make observations of material culture. For example, Peter Manning and Betsy Cullum-Swan (1994) did a case study of McDonald's restaurants using the qualitative research tradition of semiotics, which investigates how both verbal and configural sign systems convey meaning. They studied the meaning of McDonald's sign systems as conveyed by such elements as the design of the menu board, lighting, outdoor playgrounds, food containers and utensils, and the use of the prefix *Mc-* to label food items.

Document and Media Analysis

Case study researchers often study written communications that are found in field settings. In accord with interpretivist epistemology, these researchers believe that the meaning of a text varies depending on the reader, the time period, the context in which the text appears, and so forth. For example, G. Genevieve Patthey-Chavez (1993) did a document analysis in her case study of the cultural conflict between Latino students and their mainstream teachers in a Los Angeles high school. She interpreted a local newspaper article as revealing the school's mission to assimilate immigrant students into the mainstream, whether the students wanted to be assimilated or not.

Paper-and-Pencil Measures

In some case studies, research participants are asked to fill out questionnaires, tests, or other self-report measures. Researchers typically use questionnaires when extensive contact with every research participant is not feasible and the desired information is not deeply personal. If well designed, a questionnaire can elicit in-depth information, as illustrated in a study by Ismail Yahya and Gary Moore (1985). These researchers designed a questionnaire with open-ended questions calling for lengthy replies. They sent the respondents an audiotape with the questionnaire, asking respondents to record their responses on the tape.

Tests are commonly used in quantitative research, but they also can be useful in qualitative case studies. For example, in a case study of the mismatch between a teacher's expectations and the actual reading achievement of two of her first-grade students, Claude Goldenberg (1992) combined qualitative and quantitative methods of data collection. He made qualitative observations of each child's classroom behaviors and administered two standardized tests of reading achievement to each child. Goldenberg found that the child with the lower reading achievement score actually improved in reading, probably due to the teacher's greater involvement with that child, whereas the child with a higher reading achievement score remained in a low reading group.

Data Collection in the Student Retention Study

In the SIRP study, Maldonado and his colleagues conducted interviews and observations and gathered relevant documents at each site. They made three two-day visits to the Berkeley site and one four-day visit to Madison. Formal structured interviews with each of the 45 research participants, from one to two hours long, were tape recorded and transcribed verbatim.

At Berkeley, the researchers observed the SIRP organizers while they were in their office engaging in such activities as planning events and meeting with staff of the recruitment and retention center. At Madison, researchers observed organizers in various informal settings and at their off-campus work site.

Maldonado and his colleagues mention in their report that two of them were at one time organizers working for SIRPs and that they thus could be viewed as insiders rather than outsiders. In case study research, an **insider** typically is a practitioner who has an internal, or local, perspective on the problems of practice being studied. By contrast, an **outsider** is an individual who has an external perspective on the problems of practice being studied (Kemmis & McTaggart, 2000).

Having some insider experience undoubtedly gave the researchers credibility and facilitated their entry to the research sites. However, no mention is made in the case study report of any efforts by the researchers to practice **reflexivity**, which is a process of self-reflection that case study researchers use to identify their biases and attempt to control for them as they engage in data collection and interpretation.

Data Analysis

In case study research, researchers typically begin to analyze data while they are still engaged in data collection. They seek to discover what types of findings are emerging and to modify their data-collection procedures to shed further light on the phenomenon of interest. They continue this process until they have reached **theoretical saturation**, which refers to a point in the process of comparing theoretical constructs and empirical indicators of their meaning when additional data collection and analysis no longer contribute new understanding about the phenomenon under investigation. At that point, the researchers conclude their analysis.

Interpretational Analysis

Case study researchers often use interpretational analysis (Miles & Huberman, 1984) to analyze their data. **Interpretational analysis** is the process of closely examining and grouping elements in case study data in order to identify constructs, themes, and patterns that make sense of the data.

Constructs are concepts that are inferred from commonalities among observed phenomena and that are presumed to explain or shed light on the meaning of those phenomena. For example, in Ms. Jones's fifth-grade class, many of the teacher's acts and statements appear to be aimed at keeping order among students. An important construct that might be inferred from observation of Ms. Jones's class is that of classroom management.

In contrast, a **theme** is a salient, recurring feature of a case. For example, suppose that when Ms. Jones begins presenting on a topic, many students begin making jokes, calling out to classmates, or moving around the room. Such behavioral incidents suggest a theme characteristic of the class, namely, students actively seeking to interrupt Ms. Jones's teaching activities. **Patterns** represent systematic relationships between two or more phenomena within a case or across cases. If Ms. Jones repeatedly responds to student interruptions by attempting to ignore them and continue her presentation, researchers might presume a causal pattern between her behavior (ignoring interruptions) and students' behavior (continuing interruptions).

A classic model of interpretational analysis is based on grounded theory (Strauss & Corbin, 1990). **Grounded theory** involves the principle that qualitative researchers should *discover* theory that is grounded in the data. They do this by examining data inductively rather than using the deductive approach of posing a theory or hypotheses in advance to explain what they are studying.

The grounded theory procedure involves (1) recording the data (usually text obtained from interviews or observations), (2) breaking the text into segments (e.g., sentences or lines), (3) defining specific categories to reflect each important conceptual or structural element that appears in the text, and (4) coding each segment for all of the categories that apply to that segment. Once all data segments have been coded into categories, the researchers then refine the set of categories through constant comparison, an essential element of grounded theory. **Constant comparison** is a process of comparing instances of each code across segments in order to discover commonalities in the data that reflect the underlying meaning of, and relationships among, the coding categories. It depends not merely on frequency counts but also on the researchers' effort to interpret, that is, give meaning to, the data.

The researchers who studied SIRPs state that they "followed both deductive and inductive strategies" (Maldonado et al., 2005, p. 618) of data analysis. At the beginning of their study, they generated hypotheses involving a critique of the traditional views of retention that seek to promote social integration and multiculturalism. Their hypotheses involved efforts to understand the effectiveness of SIRPs from the standpoint of the "conceptual points" of cultural capital, social capital, collectivism, and social praxis (p. 609). As described in the section on findings, the researchers identified three general themes in their data that corresponded closely with these conceptual points from their original research hypotheses. They are thus based on the researchers' deductive approach rather than an inductive approach consistent with grounded theory.

The SIRP researchers indicated, however, that they also used an inductive approach to identify the particular processes associated with successful development and implementation of SIRPs. They generated coding categories by searching through the data for regularities, patterns, and topics that reflected key discoveries about how the student organizers affected, and were affected by, the SIRP at their institution. Through this approach, they discovered "unanticipated concerns or areas of understanding in which we had such minimal knowledge that meaningful theories and hypotheses could not be generated a priori" (Maldonado et al., 2005, p. 618). In the findings section, they provide examples of the specific patterns that were inductively discovered in the data. The researchers also measured the degree to which two of them agreed in their coding of SIRP data, which, at 85 percent, was considered satisfactory.

Computer Software for Analyzing Qualitative Data

Like the SIRP study, many published case studies rely on a manual approach, using 3 × 5 cards, to sort data segments into categories. However, when case study data involve various forms of media, when the amount of data is large, or when complex forms of analysis are desired, a computer software program can speed up the process of data analysis. Consider, for example, four currently available computer software programs for qualitative data analysis.

DataSense markets NVivo, with versions 7, 8, 9, and 10 currently available for the Microsoft Windows platform and Mac OS X version 10.6. The program is described as being good for managing complex, unstructured, or multimedia information like field notes, videos, transcripts, and audio recordings. These versions supercede previous versions of QSR International software, including earlier NVivo versions and the NUD*IST (Nonnumerical, Unstructured, Data: Indexing, Searching, and Theorising) software program versions 4, 5, and 6.

Qualis Research markets *Ethnograph 6.0*, a software program originally developed for use in ethnographic research, available at qualisresearch.com. The website provides a quick online tour showing the basics of creating projects and coding data files.

ResearchWare markets *HyperRESEARCH* through the website researchware.com. This advanced software program allows qualitative researchers to analyze text, graphic, audio, and video data sources. An online tutorial and a free limited edition of HyperRESEARCH are available. A software program called *HyperTRANSCRIBE* is available; it allows users to open and play audio/video formats and to export text to other forms.

Atlast.ti markets *Atlas.ti 7* through its website (atlasti.com). This software program has similar features to those described above.

Reflective Analysis

As described above, interpretational analysis involves an explicit category coding system. By contrast, **reflective analysis** requires case study researchers to rely mainly on their own intuition and personal judgment to analyze their data. The resulting findings are thus reflective both in the sense that they mirror the conceptual framework of the particular researcher who did the analysis and in the sense that they result from a deep and deeply personal process of pondering a phenomenon.

Reflective analysis can be compared with artistic endeavors, because visual artists reflect on phenomena that they experience and then portray them to reveal both their surface features and essences. Similarly, expert critics and connoisseurs study a piece of art both to appreciate its aesthetic elements and "message" and to make critical judgments about its artistic merit.

Many case study researchers engage in similar reflections and portrayals. For example, some case studies involving evaluation (see Chapter 19) follow a process of reflective analysis known as educational connoisseurship and criticism. Evaluators using reflective analysis attempt to describe the features and purposes of educational programs, but they also help educators to appreciate the strengths and weaknesses of these programs Just as an art or literary critic develops reflective ability with experience, an educational evaluator must build up a store of experience in order to use reflective analysis wisely.

Reflective analysis appears to be the primary way in which findings are generated in creative forms of case study research or qualitative research more generally. Such forms include **performance ethnography**, which involves staged reenactments of the cultural phenomena observed by ethnographers (Alexander, 2005). For example, Joni Jones (2002) staged a production, *Searching for Osun*, that focused on aspects of the deity Osun in Yoruba, a Nigerian culture "that moved [her] most—dance, music, divination, Osun's relationship to children, 'women's work,' and food preparation" (p. 1). The performers assumed archetypal characters in Yoruba life, and the invited audience entered the performance space as participants, engaging in dance, dining rituals, and other performances characteristic of Yoruba life.

Other forms of reflective analysis result in poetry, oral readings, comedy, satire, and visual social science (Harper, 2005). In qualitative research using these methods, it can be difficult to distinguish between the process of data analysis and the reporting of findings, because the form of reporting itself reflects the manner in which the researchers have analyzed their data.

Laura Richardson (1992) observed that qualitative researchers who use reflective analysis typically have a postmodern sensibility. As we explain in Chapter 1, postmodernism questions all claims to authoritative methods of analysis and reporting, including mainstream scientific reports. A postmodernist would view poetry or street art as just as legitimate a form of case study reporting as more standard forms involving text, quotations, and observation.

Findings

As is typical in case study research, Maldonado and his colleagues (2005) presented their findings as themes derived from verbal data (e.g., field notes, transcripts of interviews, and videotapes). By contrast, quantitative researchers present their findings as statistics and generalizations derived from numerical data.

The primary findings from the SIRP researchers' deductive approach to data analysis involved identification of three themes relating to the collective strategies used in student-initiated retention programs. They are described below, along with findings from the researchers' inductive analysis of the data they collected about the SIRPs and from SIRP student organizers.

Theme 1: Developing Necessary Knowledge, Skills, and Social Networks

Maldonado and his colleagues (2005) tied this theme to the conceptual points of cultural capital and social capital from their original hypotheses. The activities that the SIRPs provided to advance students' academic success, for example, included tutorial programs, study groups, organized study halls, mentoring programs, and direct efforts to assist students of color in interacting with faculty and instructors. As an example, Susan, a Laotian student organizer at Berkeley, learned that questioning her teachers was an acceptable and useful practice, and she credited her involvement in a SIRP with encouragement to "don't just accept knowledge uncritically" (Maldonado et al., 2005, p. 621).

Another inductive finding related to this theme is that SIRPs helped student organizers develop knowledge of both the dominant culture and their own cultural identity while expanding their capacity to balance participation in each. Additionally, SIRPs developed students' skills in public speaking, leadership, organization, and critical thinking, and also provided a social network that gave ongoing support and resources for dealing with personal issues.

Theme 2: Building a Sense of Students' Commitment to Particular Communities, Including Ethnic/Racial Communities

This theme was tied back to the researchers' conceptual point of collectivism. Based on their inductive analysis, the researchers found that SIRPs "seek to enhance students' commitment to their cultural heritage" (Maldonado et al., 2005, p. 623), which gives students a better understanding of the needs of each ethnic community and their role in helping to meet such needs. The SIRPs also built bridges across particular racial/ethnic communities "for the sake of organizing a united community of color" (p. 624).

Theme 3: Challenging Oppressive Social and Institutional Norms

The researchers tied this theme to the conceptual point of social praxis from their deductive analysis. Findings from their inductive analysis showed that the SIRPs engaged students in efforts to promote improved education, protest for change, work institutionally, challenge racism, and serve their racial/ethnic communities. They found that these efforts challenged social and institutional norms that "discourage greater participation by people of color in higher education" (Maldonado et al., 2005, p. 625).

The findings also indicated that SIRP organizers aim to reconstruct the universities "on the basis of cultural norms more consistent with those of their own racial/ethnic communities" (Maldonado et al., 2005, p. 625) and, as a result, ultimately improve the retention of students of color. The researchers reported that student organizers and SIRP students engaged in active challenges to racist practices in classrooms and the university as a whole. For example, they worked institutionally to influence university decisions through participation in student government.

The researchers concluded that the vast majority of SIRP programs and activities do resist an assimilationist position, consistent with one of their hypotheses. In other words, the philosophy that guides SIRPs does not emphasize assimilation of students of color to the mainstream culture, but rather it promotes students' intellectual and social development within their own racial/ethnic and collective communities. Because the researchers were committed to a critical research orientation, with the goal of empowerment, their report promoted this mission of student-initiated retention projects.

A Hierarchical Approach to Interpretational Analysis

Coding qualitative data is a common procedure in qualitative data analysis, although the coding process and the resulting levels of coding are not consistently named or carried out across research studies. While not explicitly hierarchical, the process of coding qualitative data into categories typically appears to produce a set of statements that fall into several levels and thus constitute a hierarchy.

To illustrate the levels of a hierarchical coding system, we describe research findings from a study of Haitian Christian fathers by Carl Auerbach and Louise Silverstein (2003), based on a theory about the transformation of fathering in U.S. culture. One of their findings is that "Haitian Christian fathers have constructed a new definition of fatherhood which is more socially progressive and more personally satisfying than the traditional Haitian fathering role" (p. 141).

Auerbach and Silverstein's approach to coding and data analysis involves generating three levels of data, described below and illustrated in Table 13.4.

Level 1: Text-Based Categories.   Researchers begin data analysis by selecting segments of text that they see as relevant to the basic concerns of the study. They then develop a set of low-inference

TABLE 13.4 • Example of Theoretical Constructs, Sensitizing Concepts, and Text-Based Categories from Research on Haitian American Fathers

I. Bicultural gender role strain	
A. Praising aspects of the traditional Haitian father	50%
1. My dream was to look like my father.	
2. There is no inch of laziness in my father.	
3. I love the way my father treated my mother.	
B. Dissatisfactions with aspects of traditional Haitian fatherhood	60%
4. My father never said I love you.	
5. Adults do not play.	
6. When they say your father is coming you run inside.	
7. My father took care of other children and didn't care much for me.	
II. Constructing a more gratifying definition of fatherhood	
A. Definition of a "good" father	100%
8. My job is to look over the family.	
9. You're not a boss for the children, you're more like a friend.	
10. You have to be there whenever the child needs you.	
11. You call your kid and say I love you.	
12. Jesus was my role model.	
B. An enhanced sense of self	75%
13. It has changed you, it has reconstructed you.	
14. You're looking at the children growing it is beautiful	
III. A facilitating ideology	
A. God makes all things possible	75%
15. We are co-workers in the field of God.	
16. It won't be your doing, it will be God's doing.	

Note: N = 20. The percentages refer to the percentage of fathers in the sample who used each of the sensitizing concepts.
Source: Based on Auerbach, C. F., & Silverstein, L. B. (2003), *Qualitative data: An introduction to coding and analysis.* New York, NY: New York University Press.

text-based categories that paraphrase or generalize those text segments. An example of a text-based category from Table 13.4 is "1. My dream was to look like my father." The table shows 16 numbered text-based categories.

Level 2: Sensitizing Concepts.

The researchers then organize the text-based categories into clusters of middle-level sensitizing concepts. These concepts reflect tacit or explicit themes that the text categories represent. An example of a sensitizing concept from Table 13.4 is "A. Praising aspects of the traditional Haitian father." The table shows five such concepts, each preceded by a capital letter.

Level 3: Theoretical Constructs.

Finally, the researchers group the sensitizing concepts into high-level theoretical constructs. These theoretical constructs provide the "big picture," or theoretical interpretation, of what the researchers learned from analysis of their data. The following three theoretical constructs are shown in Table 13.4, each preceded by a Roman numeral: "I. Bicultural gender role strain," "II. Constructing a more gratifying definition of fatherhood," and "III. A facilitating ideology."

From the data shown in Table 13.4, we can trace the coding process used by the researchers. For example, the five numbered statements under the Sensitizing Concept "A. Definition of a 'good' father" are all text-based categories that describe specifics of good fathering, from "8. My job is to look over the family" to "12. Jesus was my role model."

In turn, the sensitizing concepts "A. Definition of a 'good' father" and "B. An enhanced sense of self" both represent the theoretical construct "II. Constructing a more gratifying definition of fatherhood." At the highest level of analysis, we see the three related theoretical constructs noted above.

In summary, Auerbach and Silverstein's research on Haitian American fathers shows how data from a case study can be coded into three hierarchical levels: text-based categories, sensitizing concepts, and theoretical constructs. This approach to interpretational analysis appears easy to learn and promising for studying problems of practice.

Discussion

The discussion section of a case study report typically includes a summary of the research findings, recommendations for practice and future research, and limitations of the study and suggestions for how these could be overcome in future research.

In the discussion section of their report, Maldonado and his colleagues detail some of the proactive efforts made by students involved in the SIRPs to create change. They conclude that these efforts are "consistent with the view of transformative education advanced by Freire (1970)" (2005, p. 633). They also conclude that the SIRP is a better model of student retention than any other described in the literature. Finally, they assert that the student organizers' vision of social change and their contributions to democracy "should extend well beyond simply the scope of their collegiate careers" (2005, p. 634).

These conclusions reflect the researchers' use of critical research as a framework for understanding society and individuals within it. Their endorsement of student-initiated retention projects as essential to the emancipation and empowerment of college students of color is entirely consistent with critical theorists' agenda for research and practice.

CHECKING THE APPLICABILITY OF CASE STUDY FINDINGS

Quantitative researchers are concerned with whether their findings generalize to samples or populations other than those who participated in a particular research study. Qualitative researchers have a related but different concern: How can educators determine whether the findings of a specific case study are applicable to their own workplace? In general terms, **applicability** refers to an individual's judgment that the findings of a case study can be used to inform a problem of practice in other settings or to serve as evidence for or against a theory of interest.

Case study findings depend on an ongoing interaction between the data and the researchers' creative processes of analysis and interpretation. Therefore, one might argue that the findings are unique to the case that was studied. However, most qualitative researchers believe that case study findings can be applied to other settings.

One approach to determining the applicability of case study findings is to consider the sampling strategy that the researchers used to select the case. If the researchers studied a typical or extreme case, the results should be applicable to other similar cases. Researchers who use a multiple-case design usually conduct a cross-case generalizability analysis to help readers determine whether the findings are similar across cases. Demonstration of similarity suggests that the findings will also be applicable to other situations and individuals similar to those studied by the researchers.

Another view about applicability is that readers of the case study findings are responsible for making this judgment. In this view, the readers, not the researchers, need to determine whether the cases that were studied are similar to the situation of interest to the readers. Researchers can help readers make this determination by providing a thick description of the participants and contexts that comprise the case.

Still another view of applicability is that case studies resemble stories in works of literature or "human interest" news accounts. Reading such case studies can deepen your understanding of educational phenomena that interest or concern you. Also, researchers' insights and speculations can help you develop the capacity to explore and refine your educational practice.

EVALUATING THE QUALITY AND RIGOR OF A CASE STUDY

The case studies described in this chapter reflect an interpretivist view of reality. This view rejects the notion of an external reality that can be discovered through objective means. Interpretivists instead believe that each researcher, research participant, and reader of a case study report will have his or her own unique interpretation of the meaning and value of the case study. Nonetheless, qualitative researchers have developed various evaluative strategies to demonstrate the credibility and trustworthiness of their findings and methods. These strategies typically are designed to ensure (1) that the research study has been carefully designed, (2) that sufficient data have been collected to provide rich information about the phenomenon of interest, and (3) that readers will be able to determine whether and how the results can be applied to their own settings.

We describe ten of these strategies in the next sections. They are listed in Table 13.5, together with questions you can ask yourself as you evaluate a case study. We also suggest that you examine Appendix 4, which contains a list of questions to consider when evaluating qualitative research reports.

TABLE 13.5 • Evaluative Strategies Framed as Questions to Ask in Evaluating the Quality and Rigor of a Case Study

Evaluative Strategies	Question
1. Assessment of usefulness	Is the study useful in the sense of being relevant to problems of practice?
2. Participant involvement	Is the emic perspective of the research participants represented in the report?
3. Inclusion of quantitative data	Are quantitative data used, when relevant, to support qualitative observations?
4. Long-term observation	Did the researchers observe the case over a sufficiently long period of time?
5. Coding checks	If data were coded, did the researchers check the reliability of the coding?
6. Member checks	Did the research participants check the report for accuracy and completeness?
7. Triangulation	Did the researchers check whether the findings were supported by different data collection methods, data sources, analysts, and theories?
8. Assessment of contextual completeness	Did the researcher provide an in-depth description of the history, setting, participants, and culture within which the case was situated?
9. Assessment of chain of evidence	Are the research questions, data, data analyses, and findings clearly and meaningfully related to each other?
10. Researcher reflections	Do the researchers state personal assumptions, values, theoretical orientations, and biases that influenced their approach to the case study?

Assessment of Usefulness

The most useful case studies focus on topics that are relevant to readers and that provide helpful information for solving problems of practice. We selected the case studies described in this chapter with usefulness to educators as a criterion. For example, the case study about teacher learning through teaching inquiry-based math classes (Leikin & Rota, 2006) appears useful to teachers in considering how to assess and improve their skills in guiding student learning. Ausband's (2006) study of instructional technology is useful to educators in considering how to organize and guide the work of instructional specialists in school districts for the greatest impact on teaching and learning.

Participant Involvement

Some case studies involve research participants in all phases of the research, from conceptualization of the study to writing the final report. This strategy increases researchers' understanding of participants' emic perspective and their ability to convey it clearly to readers.

Carl Auerbach and Louise Silverstein (2003) note that participant involvement improves the opportunity for case study research to contribute to a social-action agenda. Participatory research focuses on participants' voices and acknowledges that individuals' life experience is not standard but varies from one person to the next. It involves designing research in which researchers examine their own biases and address issues that help improve participants' lives.

Leikin and Rota's (2006) case study of a teacher learning through her own teaching experience reflects this strategy. Rota, the subject of the research and also the report's coauthor, participated fully as a researcher. Chapter 18 on action research further explores research in which practitioners participate as researchers.

Inclusion of Quantitative Data

Case study researchers can supplement their findings by doing simple quantitative analyses—whether specific findings are typical, rare, or extreme. For example, Burch's case study (2006) about the trend toward educational privatization included budgetary statistics to reveal the huge increases in funding to vendors for managing aspects of schools' operations since the passage of the No Child Left Behind Act of 2001.

In another case study, Leikin and Rota (2006) presented statistics about the amount of time a teacher spent on various teaching activities during three lessons at different points in the school year. The observed changes in the teacher's time allocations revealed her growing proficiency in teaching inquiry-based math.

Long-Term Observation

Case study researchers often observe a phenomenon over a substantial period of time. This strategy enables them to study a phenomenon in depth and determine whether certain features of it are consistent over time.

In their study of a high school using bilingual education, García and Bartlett (2007) made weekly observations in classes for nine months and participated for a full year in monthly staff development sessions. In their study, Leikin and Rota (2006) intermittently videotaped 15 months of the teacher's math inquiry lessons from which the three lessons described in the case study were selected. Burch's study of educational privatization (2006) included a three-year qualitative research project, during which more than 250 research participants were interviewed.

Coding Checks

In their case study of student-initiated retention projects (SIRPs), Maldonado and his colleagues (2005) did a coding check of their categories. The purpose of a **coding check** is to determine the degree to which different researchers agree in their classification of qualitative data into pre-specified categories. Two researchers had assigned the same category to 85 percent of a sample of data segments, which is a high, though not perfect level of agreement. The researchers then discussed the discrepancies in their coding in order to improve the level of agreement in subsequent coding.

Member Checks

Maldonado and his colleagues (2005) used member checking to increase the authenticity of their findings. **Member checking** is the process of having field participants review research procedures and statements in the research report for accuracy and completeness. They carried out member checking "by sharing interview transcripts with all of the research participants and by sharing early drafts of this article with several volunteer readers from 'bridges' and the MCSC" (p. 619). The researchers also stated that the article was created "in a dialogical manner" (p. 633) with the student activists they studied. These procedures helped to ensure that not only the researchers' etic perspective but also the emic perspective of the research participants were included in the case study.

Triangulation

Case study researchers seek to achieve triangulation by using different data collection methods, data sources, analysts, and theories to check their findings. This process might produce convergence, or it might clarify the reasons for apparent contradictions among findings about the same phenomenon. For example, in studies of controversial or stressful phenomena, research participants' self-report data might be inconsistent with data resulting from more direct methods of data collection such as observation or document analysis.

Most of the case studies discussed in this chapter used a range of data collection methods and strategies to strengthen triangulation. For example, in his study of instructional technology, Ausband (2006) analyzed documents, observed three research participants, interviewed each participant individually, and conducted a focus group interview of the three participants.

Maldonado and his colleagues (2005) sought to develop a thick description of each SIRP based on the varied perspectives of those involved in it. Therefore, they conducted in-depth interviews and observations of 45 student organizers and 6 professional staff members associated with the SIRP at their institution. They also read documents from each site and engaged in various SIRP events.

Contextual Completeness

An important strategy to help readers fully understand a case study involves describing the context in which the case study took place: its history, physical setting, cultural characteristics, social rules, and other features that characterize the setting.

Because participants do not speak with a unified voice in such settings, researchers need to be sensitive to a setting's **multivocality**, that is, the likelihood that research participants do not speak with a unified voice but instead express diverse interests and viewpoints. They also need to incorporate **tacit knowledge**, the nonverbal cues that convey "the largely unarticulated, contextual understanding that is often manifested in nods, silences, humor, and naughty nuances" (Altheide & Johnson, 1998, p. 492).

García and Bartlett's study (2007) of a segregated bilingual high school in New York included a description of the setting and quotations from students and teachers, reflecting the researchers' concern about providing contextual completeness for the phenomena that they studied.

Chain of Evidence

A description of a case study's design and findings ideally would include a **chain of evidence**, which involves demonstrating how the research questions, raw data, data analysis procedures, and findings are linked to each other in a meaningful manner. The chain of evidence typically takes the form of an **audit trail**, which is a written record that documents the researchers' procedures for data collection and analysis. This feature makes it possible for other researchers to check the soundness of the study's methodology and to use a similar audit trail in subsequent research designed to replicate or extend the original case study. Case studies tend to be long and journals impose length limits, so discussion of the chain of evidence is brief or absent in many case study articles.

Researcher Reflections

Because researchers are the primary "measuring instrument" in case studies, they can be a major source of bias or error. To address this problem, case study researchers should engage in researcher reflection, also known as reflexivity, a process in which researchers ponder their role in the research setting and their assumptions, world view, and personal and theoretical orientation toward the phenomenon being studied. This process helps both to clarify the basis for their etic perspective and, to the extent possible, remove any unintended bias or error based on such factors.

All of the case study researchers whose work we have described in this chapter obviously had personal and professional experience that affected their decision to study the particular phenomena they studied. However, their case study reports typically give minimal detail about whether researcher reflection occurred. In such situations, readers should use their own reflective processes to determine whether bias might have occurred at various points in the research process.

An example of

How Case Study Research Can Help in Solving Problems of Practice

One of the Gallup Polls (see Chapter 9) is an annual survey of American students. A report of recent surveys (Gallup Student Poll, 2012) presented these findings: 8 in 10 elementary students are engaged with their schooling, but only 6 in 10 middle school students feel engaged, and even fewer high school students (4 in 10) feel engaged. In blogging about this finding, Ellen Wexler (2013) refers to a comment by the executive director of Gallup Education: "The drop in student engagement for each year students are in school is our monumental, collective national failure."

Wexler and individuals who commented on her blog suggest several reasons for this drop in engagement with schooling as students progress from elementary school to high school. Among them are the emphasis on standardized testing, the standardization of the curriculum through common core standards, lack of experiential and project-based learning for students who are not college-bound, and the inability of students with poor reading skills to access the curriculum.

Research sometimes is stimulated by the simple question, "What is going on here?" This question certainly comes to mind when faced with such overwhelmingly negative statistical findings about student engagement. Case studies are well suited to addressing the question because they are open-ended and flexible and not limited by predetermined variables.

One possible case study would be to focus on a few disengaged high school students—students who are bored by their classes, are frequently off task in the classroom, and have a poor record of completing homework assignments. We might select four students—a male and female who have the academic skills to succeed in high school but who are disengaged and a male and female who have poor academic skills and are disengaged.

Our case focus will be what these students find boring/disengaging/irrelevant and what they find interesting/involving/relevant during their entire day. This means that we will need to collect data about each student's activities not only in school but also in their other ecological environments, such as their home, friend's homes, public spaces, and, if they have a job, their workplace. We will need to collect data throughout the week because the students' environments might change from one day to the next.

Participant observation would be one good method of data collection. Where this is not feasible, we could interview students periodically and ask them about events in and out of school during the preceding day. We might also ask the participants to keep a diary or perhaps give them an audiotaping device into which they can speak when they wish to make a comment that is relevant to the study's purposes.

The data would be analyzed by interpretational analysis, specifically by the use of grounded theory, because our goal is to understand the student's world from his or her perspective—not from our own perspective or an established theory of motivation or other such construct.

A study of this type raises various ethical concerns. Among other things, we will need to assure students that their data will be kept confidential, that we will not enter any of their ecological environments except with permission, and that we will report findings in such a way that their anonymity is not compromised.

This case study should have value not only for its findings but also for bringing the student's voices to one of the most serious problems of practice facing American schools today, namely, students' increasing disengagement as they progress from elementary school through high school.

SELF-CHECK TEST

1. In a case study, the researchers strive to do all of the following except
   a. conduct an in-depth study of the phenomenon.
   b. study the phenomenon in its natural context.
   c. maintain an objective perspective on the phenomenon.
   d. reflect the research participants' perspective on the phenomenon being studied.

2. Looking for causal patterns in a case study reflects the goal of _____ a phenomenon.
   a. describing
   b. explaining
   c. evaluating
   d. generalizing

3. Qualitative researchers use purposeful sampling in order to
   a. reduce the chances of selecting atypical cases of the phenomenon to be studied.
   b. eliminate the need to study more than one case.
   c. select cases that are the most convenient for in-depth study.
   d. select cases that are information-rich with respect to the purposes of the study.

4. In qualitative research, the primary instrument of data collection typically is
   a. a questionnaire or other self-report measure used to collect data.
   b. audio or video recordings of field events.
   c. the researchers themselves.
   d. researchers' key informants.

5. In interpretational data analysis, researchers
   a. search for constructs, themes, and patterns inherent in the data.
   b. impose theory-based constructs to find meaning in the data.
   c. search for naturally occurring segments in the data.
   d. use categories developed by other researchers.

6. Researchers who wish to rely on their own intuition and judgment in analyzing case study data will most likely use _____ analysis.
   a. interpretational
   b. structural
   c. reflective
   d. narrative

7. Reflective reporting of a case study tends to involve
   a. an objective writing style.
   b. computer analysis of the data.
   c. a conventional organization of topics.
   d. the strong presence of the researchers' voice.

8. Qualitative researchers believe that the best approach to minimizing bias in case studies is
   a. honest exploration of the researcher's identity and beliefs as possible biasing factors.
   b. comparison of qualitative data with quantitative data.
   c. having the data collected by individuals who are similar to the field participants.
   d. studying phenomena in which one has a minimal stake.

9. If researchers want to increase the applicability of their case study findings to other settings, it is not advisable to
   a. study an atypical case.
   b. study more than one case.
   c. compare their case to similar cases studied by other researchers.
   d. provide a thick description of their case.

10. Qualitative research traditions typically
   a. do not use methods associated with case study research to investigate phenomena.
   b. are grounded in positivism.
   c. use the research methods of various academic disciplines in the study of phenomena.
   d. are based primarily on models from the physical sciences.

CHAPTER REFERENCES

Alexander, B. K. (2005). Performance ethnography: The reenacting and inciting of culture. In N. K. Denzin & Y. S. Lincoln (Eds.), *The Sage handbook of qualitative research* (3rd ed., pp. 411–442). Thousand Oaks, CA: Sage.

Altheide, D. L., & Johnson, J. M. (1998). Criteria for assessing interpretive validity in qualitative research. In N. K. Denzin & Y. S. Lincoln (Eds.), *Handbook of qualitative research* (pp. 485–499). Thousand Oaks, CA: Sage.

Auerbach, C. F., & Silverstein, L. B. (2003). *Qualitative data: An introduction to coding and analysis.* New York, NY: New York University Press.

Ausband, L. T. (2006). Instructional technology specialists and curriculum work. *Journal of Research on Technology in Education, 39*(1), 1–21.

Biddle, B. J., & Anderson, D. S. (1986). Theory, methods, knowledge, and research on teaching. In M. C. Wittrock (Ed.), *Handbook of research on teaching* (3rd ed., pp. 230–252). New York, NY: Macmillan.

Burch, P. E. (2006). The new educational privatization: Educational contracting and high stakes accountability. *Teachers College Record, 108*(12), 2582–2610.

Cannella, G. S., & Lincoln, Y. S. (2007). Predatory v. dialogic ethics: Constructing an illusion or ethical practice as the core or research methods. *Qualitative Inquiry, 13*(3), 315–335.

Cannella, G. S., & Lincoln, Y. S. (2013). Ethics, research regulations, and critical social science. In Denzin, N. K., & Lincoln, Y. S. (Eds.), *The landscape of qualitative research* (4th ed., pp. 169–187). Thousand Oaks, CA: Sage.

Corbin, J., & Strauss, A. L. (2007). *Basics of qualitative research: Techniques and procedures for developing grounded theory* (3rd ed.). Newbury Park, CA: Sage.

Cuban, L. (1997). Change without reform: The case of Stanford University school of medicine, 1908–1990. *American Educational Research Journal, 34*, 83–122.

Denzin, N. K., & Lincoln, Y. S. (Eds.). (2011). *The Sage handbook of qualitative research* (4th ed.). Thousand Oaks, CA: Sage.

Freire, P. (1970). *Pedagogy of the oppressed.* (M. B. Ramos, Trans.). New York, NY: Grove Press.

Gall, M. D., Gall, J. P., & Borg, W. R. (2007). *Educational research: An introduction* (8th ed.). Boston, MA: Pearson.

Gallup Student Poll. (2012). *Gallup student poll overall scorecard fall 2012.* Retrieved from http://www.gallupstudentpoll.com/159221/gallup-student-poll-overall-scorecard-fall-2012.aspx

García, O., & Bartlett, L. (2007). A speech community model of bilingual education: Educating Latino newcomers in the USA. *The International Journal of Bilingual Education and Bilingualism, 10*(1), 1–25.

Goldenberg, C. (1992). The limits of expectations: A case for case knowledge about teacher expectancy effects. *American Educational Research Journal, 29*, 517–544.

Harper, D. (2005). What's new visually? In N. K. Denzin & Y. S. Lincoln (Eds.), *The Sage handbook of qualitative research* (3rd ed., pp. 747–762). Thousand Oaks, CA: Sage.

Jacob, E. (1987). Qualitative research traditions: A review. *Review of Educational Research, 57*, 1–50.

Jones, J. (2002). Performance ethnography: The role of embodiment in cultural authenticity. *Theatre Topics, 12*(1), 1–15.

Kemmis, S., & McTaggart, R. (2000). Participatory action research: Communicative action and the public sphere. In N. K. Denzin & Y. S. Lincoln (Eds.), *The Sage handbook of qualitative research* (2nd ed., pp. 567–605). Thousand Oaks, CA: Sage.

Kincheloe, J. L., & McLaren, P. (2000). Rethinking critical theory and qualitative research. In N. K. Denzin & Y. S. Lincoln (Eds.), *Handbook of qualitative research* (2nd ed., pp. 279–313). Thousand Oaks, CA: Sage.

Kirk, J., & Miller, M. L. (1986). *Reliability and validity in qualitative research.* Beverly Hills, CA: Sage.

Lancy, D. F. (1993). *Qualitative research in education: An introduction to the major traditions.* New York, NY: Longman.

Leikin, R., & Rota, S. (2006). Learning through teaching: A case study on the development of a mathematics teacher's proficiency in managing an inquiry-based classroom. *Mathematics Education Research Journal, 18*(3), 44–68.

Lincoln, Y., & Guba, E. (2011). *The SAGE handbook of qualitative research.* Beverly Hills, CA: Sage.

Maldonado, D. E. Z., Rhoads, R., & Buenavista, T. L. (2005). The student-initiated retention project: Theoretical contributions and the role of self-empowerment. *American Educational Research Journal, 42*(4), 605–638.

Manning, P. K., & Cullum-Swan, B. (1994). Narrative, content, and semiotic analysis. In N. K. Denzin & Y. S. Lincoln (Eds.), *Handbook of qualitative research* (pp. 463–477). Thousand Oaks, CA: Sage.

Miles, M. B., & Huberman, A. M. (1984). *Qualitative data analysis: An expanded sourcebook* (2nd ed.). Beverly Hills, CA: Sage.

Patthey-Chavez, G. G. (1993). High school as an arena for cultural conflict and acculturation for Latino Angelinos. *Anthropology and Education Quarterly, 24,* 33–60.

Patton, M. Q. (2002). *Qualitative evaluation & research methods* (3rd ed.). Thousand Oaks, CA: Sage.

Richardson, L. (1992). The consequences of poetic representation: Writing the other, rewriting the self. In C. Ellis & M. G. Flaherty (Eds.), *Investigating subjectivity: Research on lived experience* (pp. 125–140). Newbury Park, CA: Sage.

Richardson, L., & St. Pierre, E. A. (2005). Writing: A method of inquiry. In N. K. Denzin & Y. S. Lincoln (Eds.), *The Sage handbook of qualitative research* (3rd ed., pp. 959–978). Thousand Oaks, CA: Sage.

Strauss, A., & Corbin, J. (1990). *Basics of qualitative research: Grounded theory procedures and techniques.* Newbury Park, CA: Sage.

Tesch, R. (1990). *Qualitative research: Analysis types & software tools.* Philadelphia, PA: RoutledgeFalmer.

Wexler, E. (2013, January 14). Gallup: Student engagement drops with each grade. *Education Week Teacher.* Retrieved from http://blogs.edweek.org/teachers/teaching_now/2013/01/gallup_student_engagement_drops_with_each_grade.html

Yahya, I. B., & Moore, G. E. (1985, March). On research methodology: The cassette tape as a data collection medium. ERIC Document Reference No. ED262098.

Yin, R. K. (2008). Case study research: Design and methods (4th ed.). Los Angeles, CA: Sage.

RESOURCES FOR FURTHER STUDY

Denzin, N. K., & Lincoln, Y. S. (Eds.) (2013). *The landscape of qualitative research* (4th ed.). Thousand Oaks, CA: Sage.

> The contributors to this book discuss important contemporary issues and agendas in qualitative research, including critical theory, feminist research, queer theory (which involves questioning and deconstructing the concept of a unified sexual subject), disability communities, and Asian epistemologies.

Gorlewski, J. A., & Gorlewski, D. A. (2012). *Making it real: Case stories for secondary teachers.* Rotterdam, Netherlands: Sense Publishers.

> Designed for teachers facing evaluation of their teaching in relation to the current educational reform movement toward standards and standardization. Based on a model of core teaching standards, this book presents a systematic approach to teachers' analysis of their case stories. We include it as a resource to help teachers consider how to transform case stories into case studies in their classrooms.

Hancock, D. R., & Algozzine, B. (2011). *Doing case study research: A practical guide for beginning researchers* (2nd ed.). New York, NY: Teachers College Press.

> Designed for beginning researchers, this book includes tools for planning and implementing case studies. The author includes procedures for evaluating case studies and information on nonstandard forms of research dissemination such as blogs and editorials.

Liu, X. (2008). *Great ideas in science education: Case studies of noted living science educators.* Rotterdam, Netherlands: Sense Publishers.

> The author presents case studies of eight living educators who have made significant contributions to the field of science education. The book illustrates how relevant case studies can help educators address the problem of improving teaching and learning in specific education fields.

Merriam, S. B. (2009). *Qualitative research: A guide to design and implementation.* San Francisco, CA: Jossey-Bass.

> The author explains all phases of research design in a case study, with detailed descriptions of actual case studies of adult learners in various contexts.

Seidman, I. (2012). *Interviewing as qualitative research: A guide for researchers in education & the social sciences* (4th ed.). New York, NY: Teachers College Press.

> The author provides step-by-step guidance in the design and use of interviewing techniques and the connection of interviewing to broader issues of qualitative research. Among the topics discussed are long-distance interviewing, computer-assisted qualitative data analysis software, and the ethics of interviewing.

Soldaña, J. (2013). *The coding manual for qualitative researchers* (2nd ed.) Thousand Oaks, CA: Sage.

> The author presents 32 methods for coding qualitative data. Many of the methods are designed for specific qualitative research traditions, including case studies based on grounded theory, phenomenology, and narrative inquiry. Each coding method is illustrated with an example.

Teaching Secrets: Ask the Kids!

Sacks, A. (2007, September 11). Teaching secrets: Ask the kids! *Teacher Magazine*. Retrieved from www.teachermagazine.org/tm/articles/2007/09/11/03tln_sacks_web.h19.html

Teachers are always looking for new techniques to improve their classroom management. The following article is a case story about one teacher's discovery of a technique that made a difference in her classroom.

After reading this article, we recommend that you read the next article, which reports a case study. By doing so, you can see for yourself the differences between case stories and case studies in purpose and presentation of evidence to support their conclusions.

The article is reprinted in its entirety, just as it appeared when originally published.

Teaching Secrets: Ask the Kids!

ARIEL SACKS

It was the middle of my second year of teaching in a high-needs New York City public school. I was finally planning successful lessons and my class of 8th grade transitional English—language learners had become enthusiastic readers of whole novels in English.

So it took me by surprise when, around February, I noticed these same students yawning, poking one another, throwing paper balls, and complaining during class. I bristled at their displays of frustration and heard myself snapping back at them. I was becoming that cranky teacher I vowed never to be.

After weeks of such behavior, I began to get nervous every time this class would enter my room. I tried to make the work more exciting, but nothing seemed to change. Finally, one afternoon, I couldn't take it any longer. My students entered my room and sat down as usual in the U-shaped configuration of benches called the meeting area. Our agenda was on the board, and I was about to run through it. I had gotten in the habit of doing this as quickly as possible, in my most energetic tone, while I still had the illusion of my students' attention.

But that day I thought to myself, *Why do I keep pretending this is working? Something is wrong.*

"You know what?" I said to the class. "I'm really stressed out. I don't even want to go through the agenda today. Is anyone else feeling stressed?"

My students responded with a resounding, "Yeeessss!" For the first time in weeks, I had everyone's attention.

"Wow," I said. "Let's go around and hear from everyone. Say anything you want. How are you feeling today about school, life—anything?"

I was amazed when one of our school's most academically motivated students, Ana, started us off. "I feel that school is so boring now," she said. "All we want is to talk with our friends."

"Yeah," added Litzabet. "We are so stressed, because of all the tests. One test finishes and you have a test or a project due the next day. We don't get a break! We are, like, oppressed people." ("Oppression" was a literary theme we'd been discussing.)

José said, straight-faced, "Sometimes we just want to have fun."

Suddenly, the whole class was talking at once. I had to remind them to take turns and let everyone be heard. They did, because they really wanted to hear what others thought.

Comments I might have laughed off as adolescent whining on another day, I decided to take seriously. "You never give us popcorn anymore" and "We never watch movies" took on new meaning. The students' pleas for more time to socialize struck me as particularly important in a school that offered no recess, no advisory, and gym and art only once a week. The students' developmental needs were not being met by the school. I would have to do something differently if I expected any real change in my classroom.

We began negotiating. I wrote on the board, "Social time, popcorn, movies, fun." I thanked the students for being honest with me and told them I was willing to make changes to satisfy each one of these requests.

Sacks, A. (2007). Teaching secrets: Ask the kids! *Teacher Magazine,* September 11. Retrieved from www.teachermagazine.org/tm/articles/2007/09/11/03tln_sacks_web.h19.html

I offered to give them the first five minutes of class for social time. There would be rules, but this would be strictly free time. They could walk around, talk with one another, play cards, etc. But they were not permitted to run, throw, play-fight, use cell phones, or allow the volume in the room to get so loud that they couldn't hear the Tibetan meditation bell that always signals the end of break. They had to come immediately to the meeting area at the sound of the bell. We would then assess how the break went before moving into our agenda for the day.

I never knew so much relief could come from five minutes of freedom! We also decided that if the class worked well Monday through Thursday, we would have popcorn and fun on Friday. We watched movies that related to our literature studies, or we played games. Other times, we needed Fridays to finish work. I found that, when I opened it up for negotiation, the students were surprisingly responsible about that use of time.

Despite some difficult conditions, the rest of the year was a joy. My students and I battled burnout through honest dialogue, and they worked more productively than I had imagined possible. I'll never forget that class for helping me to develop routines I still use—and for showing me what students are capable of when we take time to listen and include them in the decisions of our classrooms.

ABOUT THE AUTHOR

Ariel Sacks was beginning her fourth year of teaching in the New York City schools.

 # Sample Case Study

Exemplary Social Studies Teachers' Use of Computer-Supported Instruction in the Classroom

Açikalin, M. (2010). Exemplary social studies teachers' use of computer-supported instruction in the classroom. *TOJET: The Turkish Journal of Educational Technology, 9*(4), 66–82.

Computer technology is gradually transforming the process of teaching and learning in nearly every content area of school curriculum. Social studies is of special interest, because it provides unique opportunities for incorporating computer software and hardware into the curriculum. The case study presented here explores how four exemplary social studies instructors at the middle school and high school level each used computer-supported instruction in teaching their students. The study includes samples from teacher interviews and the researcher's observations in each classroom. It summarizes common and unique ways in which these teachers incorporated student use of the Internet, computer programs for teacher and student class presentations, and software for note-taking, editing, and other strategies to make student work in the social studies more efficient and of better quality.

Exemplary Social Studies Teachers' Use of Computer-Supported Instruction in the Classroom

MEHMET AÇIKALIN
Istanbul University, TURKEY
acikalin@istanbul.edu.tr

ABSTRACT Educators increasingly support the use of computer-supported instruction in social studies education. However, few studies have been conducted to study teacher use of computer-supported instruction in social studies education. This study was therefore designed to examine the use of exemplary social studies teachers' computer-supported instruction in the classroom. Case study methodological approach was used for this study. Four exemplary social studies teachers who use computer-supported instruction in their teaching practices were selected as participants. The data were collected from interviews and classroom observations. The data analysis indicated that all of the participants agreed that the computer is a powerful research tool which facilitates students' work and makes the work faster and easier for the students. The participants used various types of computer-supported instruction in their classrooms. The use of the Internet and software programs such as Microsoft Power Point, Microsoft Word, and Excel were the most common use of computer-supported instruction in the classrooms observed.

Keywords: Computer-supported instruction, Social studies, In-service teachers

Introduction

Major developments in computer and Internet technologies have increased the availability of computer and Internet access in schools. According to data from the National Center for Education Statistics (NCES, 2003), computers have been widely introduced into schools in recent years. In 2002, the average public school contained 131 instructional computers, and 99% of schools had access to the Internet in the United States. Like other disciplines, these developments in computer hardware and software in the last decades have increased computer integration in social studies education (Açıkalın, 2006; Açıkalın & Duru, 2005; Berson & Balyta, 2004; Nickell, Field, & Roach, 2001; Rose & Fernlund, 1997; VanHover, Berson, Mason-Bolick, & Owings-Swan, 2004; White, 1997; Whitworth & Berson, 2003).

These substantial developments in computer and Internet technologies and the growing availability of computer and Internet access in schools have brought such terms as "Computer-Based Training" (CBT), "Computer-Based Instruction" (CBI), and Computer-Assisted/Aided Instruction" (CAI) (see Kausar, Choudhry, & Gujjar, 2008; Yusuf & Afolabi, 2010) into the field of education. These terms are frequently used interchangeably to refer to virtually any kind of computer use for training and instruction (see Freedman, 2001, p. 116, 171; Margolis, 1999, p. 77-78). Nevertheless, there are important differences between these terms that should be maintained. The phrase "Computer-Based" refers to the computer as a central part of instruction, which I believe is far beyond the utility of the computer in education. On the other hand, "Computer-Assisted/Aided Instruction (CAI)" is almost exclusively associated with computer programs such as drills and practice, tutorials, and simulations (see Jonassen, 2000, p. 4; Kleinedler et al., 2001, p. 39; Plaffenberger, 2001, p. 86) that limit the scope of computer utilization in education. I therefore have preferred to use the term "Computer-Supported Instruction (CSI)" as a reference to all aspects of computer use in the instructional context in order to help teach any kind of knowledge and skills to individuals. This includes the uses of any types of software (i.e. MS Word, Excel, PowerPoint), games, simulations, Internet searches, any sorts of online communications (i.e. e-mail exchanges, blogs, forums), virtual field trips and Webpage developments for instructional purposes (Açıkalın, 2006).

Literature Review/Purpose of The Study

Social studies is the integrated study of the social sciences such as history, geography, economy, sociology, anthropology, psychology, philosophy, political science, law, and civic education (Milli Eğitim Bakanlığı Talim Terbiye Kurulu Başkanlığı [TTKB] 2009a, 2009b; National Council for Social Studies [NCSS], 1994). Many scholars point out that the disciplines of social studies are intended to develop effective citizens who possess critical thinking, problem-solving, and decision-making skills (Berson, 1996; Engle & Ochoa, 1988; Newmann, 1991; VanSickle & Hoge, 1991).

Likewise, many researchers in the field of social studies education highlight the role of computers in engaging students in critical thinking, problem-solving, and decision-making (see Açıkalın & Duru, 2005; Bennett & Pye, 1999; Berson, 1996; Berson & Balyta, 2004; Casutto, 2000; Dils, 2000; Fontana, 1997; Hicks, Tlou, Lee, Parry, & Doolittle, 2002; Larson, 1999; Rice & Wilson, 1999; Rose & Ferlund, 1997; Saye & Brush, 1999; Whitworth & Berson, 2003; Zukas, 2000). According to Berson (1996), "Computer-based learning has the potential to facilitate development of students' decision-making and problem-solving skills, data-processing skills, and communication capabilities. By using the computer, students can gain access to expansive knowledge links and broaden their exposure to diverse people and perspectives" (p. 486). Likewise, educational organizations such as the National Council for Social Studies, the College and University Faculty Assembly (CUFA), and the International Society for Technology Information (ISTE) recognize the potential of computer integration to transform learning in social studies (Hicks, Doolittle, & Lee, 2004; NCSS, 1994; Mason et al., 2000; VanHover et al., 2004).

While the computer integration in social studies education has been increasing, not much research has been done about the level of use of computer-supported instruction in the social studies classroom. Prior studies indicated that word processing, simulation, drill and practice and tutorials were listed as the most common computer applications used by social studies teachers (Northup & Rooze, 1990; Pye & Sullivan, 2001). On the other hand, database exploration and problem-solving were less common strategies compared to the previous four categories (Northup & Rooze, 1990; Pye & Sullivan, 2001).

Nevertheless, a number of studies showed that "Internet use" and "accessing information from the Web" have become the most common use of computers in social studies education (Whitworth & Berson, 2003; see also Pye & Sullivan, 2001; Vanfossen, 2000, 2001).

370

This change might be explained by the rapid new developments and innovations in computer and Internet technologies. However, the common findings of these studies were that social studies teachers use the Internet for personal purposes, and to gather background information for planning rather than for teaching and learning activities in the classroom (Gibson & Nocente, 1999; Keiper, Harwood, & Larson, 2000; Sunal, Smith, Sunal, & Britt, 1998; Vanfossen, 2000, 2001).

On the other hand, an increasing body of research emphasizes the crucial role of the Internet in providing information to students about multiple perspectives, cultures, and real-world issues (see Bennett & Pye, 1999; Cassutto, 2000; Dils, 2000; Hicks et al., 2002; Hicks & Ewing, 2003; Larson, 1999; Risinger, 1996, 1998, 2000, 2001, 2003; Shiveley & VanFossen, 1999; Zukas, 2000).

Despite the increasing availability of the computer and Internet access in schools (NCES, 2003), there are still common barriers keeping social studies teachers from employing computer-supported instruction more frequently. The most extensively cited barriers are (a) lack of availability of computers and problems with Internet access (Gibson & Nocente, 1999; Keiper et al., 2000; Sunal et al., 1998; VanFossen, 2000, 2001); (b) lack of training in how to apply computer- and Internet-supported instruction in the classroom (Rice, Wilson, & Bagley, 2001; VanFossen, 2000, 2001); (c) lack of time (Sunal et al., 1998; Rice et al., 2001); and (d) lack of funding (Rice et al., 2001).

In summary, the review of the literature revealed that few studies have been conducted to study teacher use of computer-supported instruction in the social studies classroom. Despite the extensive support for integrating computers into the social studies curriculum, further research regarding the effectiveness of computer integration and its impact on student learning and the classroom environment in social studies education is still needed (Berson & Balyta, 2004; Diem, 2000; Martorella, 1999; Nickell et al., 2001; Shaver, 1999; Whitworth & Berson, 2003). Therefore, there is a need to examine the use of computer-supported instruction in the social studies classroom. It is also important to investigate the exemplary use of computer-supported instruction in the social studies classroom in order to reveal current and good examples of the uses of computer-supported instruction. Thus, this study may provide valuable views and ideas for social studies teachers and educators about the use of computer-supported instruction and may inspire them to apply this sort of instruction in their classrooms. In order to investigate exemplary teachers' use of computer-supported instruction in the social studies classroom, the following research questions were generated for this research:

1. How do exemplary social studies teachers view the computer as an instructional tool?

2. What are the current computer-supported instructional applications used by exemplary teachers in their classrooms?
3. How do exemplary social studies teachers use computer-supported instruction in their classrooms?

This study was designed with the intention of analyzing the exemplary use of computer-supported instruction in social studies education so that the findings from the study may be helpful for discussion and new directions about more effective computer use in social studies education.

Methodology

Design of the Study: Qualitative Case Studies

Case study design (Bogdan & Biklen, 1998; Merriam, 1998) is employed for this study to gain an in-depth description, understanding and interpretation of a situation. Moreover, in order to collect data from different perspectives and be able to compare the findings from different settings, I chose to use a "multi-case studies" approach that involved more than one subject and setting in the research process (Bogdan & Biklen, 1998; Merriam, 1998; Yin, 2003).

Settings and Participants

Participants and sites were selected based on a "purposeful sampling" approach in which "researchers intentionally select individuals and sites to learn or understand the central phenomenon" (Creswell, 2005, p. 204; see also Ritchie, Lewis, & Elam, 2003). In this approach, samples are chosen based on a set of criteria because they have particular features or characteristics that enable detailed exploration and understanding of a central phenomenon or puzzle which the researcher wishes to study (Ritchie et al., 2003). Thus, the following criteria were developed for the selection of the participant teachers. The participant teachers should be (a) experienced secondary social studies teachers; (b) knowledgeable in computer-supported instruction; and (c) using computer-supported instruction frequently.

Along with these criteria, the "heterogeneous samples" (Ritchie et al., 2003) or "maximum variation sampling" (Patton, 2002) method was taken under consideration for this study to ensure diversity among participants and settings so that participants' perspectives, ideas, and classroom practices can be compared within the various contexts.

According to these criteria, four participants were located by means of a nomination process. Two of the participants (Mike: Pseudonym, David: Pseudonym) were nominated by the social studies education faculty from a Midwestern University in the U. S. Initially I had planned to work with four participants, so I continued to search for social studies teachers who met my selection criteria. I was able to locate two more social studies

Table 1

Demographic Information of the Participants

Name (Pseudonym)	Age	Race	Gender	Years of Teaching	Educational Background	Major	School Context
David	47	White	Male	25	B.S., M.A. and Ph.D. work	Social Studies	Public Middle
Bill	52	White	Male	22	B.A., M.A. and Ph.D. work	Social Studies	Private Middle
Mike	43	African American	Male	19	B.A.	Social Studies	Public High
Kate	46	White	Female	24	B.A., M.Ed.	History	Public Middle

teachers. One of them was nominated by a parent who was a doctoral student in the field of education at that time (Bill: Pscudonym) and the other participant (Kate: Pseudonym) was nominated by one of the district administrators in her school district. Therefore, the nomination process for the study was completed by means of three different sources: the social studies education faculty members, one school administrator, and one parent.

As can be seen from Table 1, two of the selected participant teachers were White males, one of them was an African American male, and the other was a White female. This variety in the teacher's gender and race provided different perspectives and ideas about the use of computer-supported instruction in the social studies classroom. Also, one of the teachers was teaching in a private school whereas the other three were teaching in public schools, which contributed to heterogeneous sampling and provided diverse data about private and public school settings. In addition to that, as Table 1 shows all participant teachers were very experienced. All of them had almost or more than 20 years of experience. Another important factor about the participants was their academic backgrounds. As can be seen from Table 1, the variety in academic background of the participants

was also a contributing factor to the heterogeneity of the sample.

Data Collection

Interviews. The four participants were interviewed twice during the data collection period. The first set of interviews was done in one-on-one and in-depth (unstructured) form (Creswell, 2005). This set of interviews served an exploratory purpose, to understand the participants' computer use in the classroom. The second set of interviews was conducted in a structured format, and the interview questions were developed by the researcher after analyzing the transcriptions of the first interviews. All interview sessions were audio taped and transcribed. Table 2 shows the dates, duration, and location of the first and second interview of each social studies teacher.

Classroom Observations. The purpose of observation sessions was to monitor the way the participant teachers employ computer-supported instruction and to explore some hints and evidences about the influence of computer-supported instruction on student learning. Therefore, field notes were taken during the classroom observations. Many things were recorded during classroom observations, such as the length of time students

Table 2

Interview Chart

Name (Pseudonym)	Interview Date–Time	Duration	Place
David	Nov. 10, 05–3:45 pm	46 minutes	In school
Bill	Dec. 06, 05–12:30 pm	33 minutes	In school
Mike	Dec. 14, 05–11:25 am	20 minutes	In school
Bill	Jan. 12, 06–12:45 pm	26 minutes	In school
Mike	Jan. 19, 06–9:30 am	10 minutes	In school
David	Jan. 24, 06–3:10 pm	39 minutes	In school
Kate	Jan. 30, 06–8: 00 am	13 minutes	In school
Kate	Feb. 15, 06–10:30 am	24 minutes	In school

worked on the computers; the names of the computer-supported instructional applications or software that were used; and even sometimes the Web sites visited by the students. Notes of informal discussions with teachers during these visits were also taken. These conversations were not audio taped, but summaries of each discussion were written after the classroom observations.

Although initially it had been planned to observe each classroom at least for five sessions, the total number of actual classroom observations was around one hundred. As Charmaz (2000) pointed out, the researcher should keep collecting data until the saturation point is reached. Therefore, I increased the number of classroom observations until finding the same data pattern in each individual case. The number of classroom observations in each teacher's class ranged from 7 to 31, based on the participant's frequency of computer use and the length of the instructional units in which the computer was integrated.

Data Analysis

All audio taped interview sessions were transcribed and classroom observation notes were typed as Word documents. Using the NVivo (QSR International, 2002) software program, the data were coded and the codes were grouped into similar codes to construct general themes that represent the pattern of the data.

A multi-case studies approach (Bogdan & Biklen, 1998; Merriam, 1998; Yin, 2003) was used for this study, and every single case was comprehensively analyzed independently. Once within-case analysis is complete, cross-case analysis begins. In a cross-case analysis, the researcher attempts "to build a general explanation that fits each of the individual cases, even though the cases will vary in their details" (Yin, 2003, p. 121). Therefore, after I describe the contextual variables and data findings for each case individually, I will apply the technique of cross-case analysis and compare all cases to find some patterns and build abstractions that apply across all the cases (Merriam, 1998).

Findings

Case # 1: David (Pseudonym)

Background Information about David and the School Setting. David is a 47-year-old White male social studies teacher with 25 years of teaching experience. He completed his bachelor's degree at a Midwestern university in the field of secondary social studies education. He also earned a Master of Arts degree in the field of social studies from a large Midwestern university, and at the time of the study he was a doctoral candidate in the social studies program at the same institution.

The school was a suburban middle school in a Midwestern state. The class was a seventh grade social studies class with 12 boys and 8 girls, all of whom were White. There were three desktop computers in the classroom for instructional purposes. There was one computer lab in the school building, consisting of 30 Macintosh desktop computers and a laser printer. Also there was one mobile lab station with 25 Macintosh laptop computers and one printer. The class was observed by the researcher for 31 class periods. David complained about computer availability and inadequacy of the software programs in his school.

David's Use of Computer-supported Instruction. David believed that the computer was a great instructional tool which enabled easier and faster access to different perspectives and provided opportunities for students to improve their work. While David acknowledged the great benefits of computer technologies, he did not differentiate the computer from any other instructional tools in the classroom. He used the computer when it provided "a faster and deeper connection" (Nov. 10, 05) to information and points of view that could not be found in traditional library or text materials. This next excerpt summarizes David's view about the computer ". . . Is it [computer] a panacea to everything? 'No'. Is it another helpful tool? 'Yeah'" (Nov. 10, 05). According to David, there were three main ways to use computer technology in the classroom: (a) information gathering; (b) use in the classroom (presentation tool); and (c) manipulated by students (use of students) (Informal discussion: Nov 28, 05).

The interviews and classroom observations indicated that David integrated the computer in his teaching or ". . . have the kids working directly on a computer as a part of the class . . . five or six times a month" (Nov. 10, 05). David used a wide range of computer-supported instruction in his teaching. When he was asked about the most commonly used instructional applications in his classroom he replied "The most common use for me would be the Internet, word processing. It would be for research. It is the vast majority how I use the computer" (Nov. 10, 05). Furthermore, he cited database development, web page development, and use of software programs such as Microsoft Excel, Power Point, and Hyperstudio as other sorts of computer-supported instruction in his classroom. In addition, he mentioned a tele-collaboration activity he had been involved in, in which his students got connected with their counterparts in Ukraine, Poland, and Russia. Although David had experiences with a broad range of computer-supported instructional strategies, only some of them were observed during the classroom observations within "The Historical Figure" project. In the next section, the project and the observed computer-supported instructional activities will be discussed.

The Historical Figure Project. In this project students were to do research on a historical figure and discover three positive character traits they have in common. The requirements were to have at least two Internet sources and one print source to complete the research. Another source of information was the personal interviews. In order to complete the assignment, the students were supposed to write an essay in which they compared themselves to the historical figures. Another part of the assignment was to present their findings in a secondary way beyond the essay. For this part, students created projects in which they compared themselves to the historical figures. The type of project was optional. Students were given a choice of doing either a computer-supported project or another traditional type of project.

The students used the computer lab for Internet search and the school library for print resources in order to find information for their essays and projects. Students used the computer lab for 8 class periods and spent a total of 12 class periods to complete the project.

Internet Search. The interviews and classroom observations showed that Internet search was the most common use of the computer in David's classroom. He used the Internet mostly for its reference materials in presenting students with different points of view and ideas. The following excerpt shows how David viewed the role of the Internet in terms of having students exploring diverse perspectives.

> It's [Internet] nice reference area and a good way to look at different points of view and to look at different ideas and I want them to have enough sources that messes their whole idea up because they're going to find sources disagree with one another. (Jan. 24, 06)

During the classroom observations students used the Internet for a minimum of eight class periods for this project. The Google search engine was the most common search engine used among the students. Students found text resources about historical figures that they had chosen. They used that information to write their essay as well as create their project. Many of the students searched on the Internet for pictures of their historical figure. As David pointed out during the Internet search, students encountered many resources that provided different points of view about the historical figures they had chosen.

Word Processing. During the classroom observation Microsoft Word was used extensively among the students. Many students used the program during Internet searches. The Word program was used by students as a notebook for note taking. Most of the students used copy and paste features of the program when they got information from Internet resources. Even URL's were copied on Word documents by some students. They used those documents like "scratch paper" while searching and finding information from the Internet. They put any information relevant to their projects into these Word documents. Then, they read, filtered, and edited the information before they wrote their essays and created their projects.

Students also typed their reference lists for this project using Microsoft Word. They were supposed to create a reference list for the project and David was very strict about the format they were using. He gave them a sheet that showed how references were supposed to be written in the reference list and cited in papers. Students had to use the editing features of the program many times as they corrected their reference lists.

Computer as a Presentation Tool. David rarely used the computer for presentation purposes during the classroom observations. He usually preferred to use the overhead projector with transparencies for that purpose. However, one time he used the computer for a presentation for this project. He used the computer in order to show the students how to write a reference list based on the format he had given them. He used one of the student's reference lists as an example and projected it onto the wall. It was a Microsoft Word document and he corrected the mistakes on the paper using the computer and this software program so that students could see the proper format for the references. Although in the interview he mentioned that he used "it [computer] for instruction through PowerPoint presentations" (Nov. 10, 05) he did not use it with PowerPoint during the classroom observations.

PowerPoint. PowerPoint was another software program used in David's classroom. Almost half of the students preferred to do PowerPoint presentations for this project. The presentations were mostly 4 to 6 slides. The first slide was the title page. The second and third slide were about the historical figures they studied and the following slide was about themselves. The next slide was a comparison of themselves with the historical figures, and the final slide was the bibliography, which had been created based on the format given them by David. When students created the slides they used the information they had gathered through Internet searches, print sources, and the personal interviews. Most of them used the notes they took on Microsoft Word documents from Internet searches.

Case # 2: Bill (Pseudonym)

Background Information about Bill and the School Setting. Bill is a 52 years old White male social studies teacher with 22 years teaching experience. He completed his Bachelor's and Master of Arts degrees at a large Midwestern university in the field of social studies education. The school was a private school located in a large city in a Midwestern state. The class was a seventh grade American History class with a population of 10 boys and 9 girls. There were 12 White and seven African American students.

There were four desktop computers in the classroom for the use of the students. Also there was one laptop computer connected to the Smart Board for instructional purposes. There was one DVD player which connected to the Smart Board. Also, there were 20 PC desktop computers in the computer lab. This class was observed by the researcher for 28 class periods. According to Bill, computers and software programs are sufficient in his school, but it would be better if they were improved.

Bill's Use of Computer-supported Instruction. Bill considered the computer as one of the instructional tools that could be used in the classroom. In both interviews he pointed out this view a number of times. He acknowledged the great benefits of using computer in the classroom in terms of gathering information and reviewing different resources. He stated that

> I use the computer as a tool. A tool that enables to the students . . . okay . . . to become more responsible for gathering information for themselves . . . rather than, myself, being the sole source of information for the students and rather than the textbook being the sole source of information . . . okay? The computer opens up a whole new world of resources. (Dec. 06, 05)

He also highlighted the advantages of using computers as contributing to the students' project and helping them to work more effectively and easily to accomplish their tasks. He stated that ". . . projects are made okay, much more effective, or are . . . frankly made much easier by using the computer" (Dec. 06, 05). According to Bill, "the computer allows kids to do so much" and creates more opportunities for them through the information accessed to be able construct knowledge.

Although Bill recognized the effectiveness of computer use in the classroom in terms of helping students to create and construct, he clearly drew a line between computer use and the purpose of tasks or projects that students were assigned to do. On the one hand, he acknowledged the extreme importance of computer use in the classroom; on the other hand, he definitely did not put the computer in the center of his instruction. This statement from the first interview showed his view about the computer as an instructional tool.

> . . . the computer is not the center of what I do. The computer is just a means . . . for accomplishing the task. So, the role of the computer . . . again it's extremely important because it allows so much . . . to be done. But, the other side of it is I would do the same thing, if I did not have a computer. (Dec. 06, 05)

The classroom observations and the interview sessions indicated that Bill used computers very frequently in his teaching. He stated that

> In one form or another I use the computer everyday. So . . . whether it is in a form of project such as the kids have just completed or whether simply to put . . . notes on . . . the Smart Board, the computer is used everyday in my class. (Dec. 06, 05)

As he reported, the most commonly used instructional applications in Bill's classroom were the Smart Board, Internet search, and use of software programs such as Microsoft Word and PowerPoint. However, during the classroom observation periods, there was not an assignment that required a PowerPoint presentation. The other computer-supported instructional applications were observed in Bill's classroom through "The Colonial Newspaper Project."

The Colonial Newspaper Project. In this project, students were supposed to produce a newspaper that was set in the colonial period just prior to the American Revolution. The newspaper had to have the following sections: an editorial page, classified section, international news section, entertainment section, and at least one cartoon. Students were given a handout that explained the project through the whole process. In this handout, it was highlighted that students were supposed to give "clear expression of the viewpoints of both Patriots and Loyalists". The second handout about the project was the list of events that had to be covered in the newspaper. Another handout given by Bill was a list of some Internet sources about the Colonial Era. The project was a set up as a group project and students were assigned to the groups by Bill.

Smart Board as a Presentation Tool. As Bill pointed out, using the Smart Board as a presentation tool was the most common use of the computer in his classroom. The next excerpt shows how Bill utilized the Smart Board in his classroom. "Using the computer as a means of activating the Smart Board, placing . . . information notes onto the Smart Board which are then saved . . . and are downloaded to a web site that the students can access later" (Dec. 06, 05).

The classroom observations also showed that Bill used the Smart Board in a variety of ways, such as introducing students to the project and showing them some useful web sites and sources from the Internet. During the classroom observations, another use of the Smart Board was to use its screen to show students some documentary films. Bill showed the students a set of documentary films about the American Revolution for 10 class periods. The film set was in DVD format and therefore sound and visual effects of the films were of a very high quality.

Internet Search. The interviews and the classroom observations indicated that Internet search was one of the most common types of computer-supported instruction used in Bill's classroom. During the classroom observations, students were sent to the computer lab to do Internet searches at least for 10 class periods to find resources and information for their newspapers.

While Bill considered the Internet as another important source of information, he did not completely rely on it, and wanted his students to seek other sources of information as well, such as textbooks or other print materials. Bill also emphasized the issue of the validity of the information gathered through Internet sources. He stated that ". . . we constantly have to remind them [students] . . . that simply because it is there, it doesn't mean that it is valid in itself" (Dec. 06, 05). In order to make sure his students check the validity of the information that they gathered from the Internet, Bill suggested that they use multiple sources of information. Bill stated that

> What we need to do, though, is to constantly remind them that they need to be able to find multiple sources. They have to confirm information from more than one source before they can begin to consider whether or not is valid. (Jan. 12, 06)

During the colonial newspaper project Bill reminded students several times to check the validity of the information. He asked them to confirm what they have with other sources on the Internet as well as print sources such as their textbooks.

Word Processing. Some of the conventional software programs such as Microsoft Word were also among the frequently used programs in Bill's classroom. In the first interview Bill pointed out that writing papers was another common use of the computer in his classroom. He stated that ". . . Actually the students would write papers . . . as a part of it as well. . . . But I have my students . . . Sixth and seventh grade type most of the formal papers that they do for me" (Dec. 06, 05).

Also the classroom observation notes showed that students used the computer extensively to type their articles and other sections for the newspaper project. Students used several features of the program such as copying and pasting information from the Internet to the Word documents. In the documents students were able to edit the information, rewrite their sections, and use various types of fonts and colors that resembled an authentic Colonial Era newspaper.

Case # 3: Mike (Pseudonym)

Background Information about Mike and the School Setting. Mike is a 43 year old African American male social studies teacher with 19 years of teaching experience. He completed his bachelor's degree in a Midwestern university in the field of social studies education. The school was a suburban high school in a Midwestern state.

Mike's two different classes were observed in the same classroom. The first class was 12th grade American Government and the second one was 10th grade American History. There were 12 boys and 12 girls (21 White and three African American) in the American Government class. This class was observed by the researcher for 19 class periods. There were 12 boys and 11 girls (18 White, four African American, and one Hispanic) in the American History class, and it was observed for 11 class periods.

There were 6 desktop and 12 laptop computers in the classroom for Mike and his students to use. During the classroom observations neither of the classes used the computer lab in the school. Although the number of computers seemed to be adequate, students complained about the availability of computers on a couple of occasions during the classroom observation. When each student wanted to work individually on the computer, some of the students could not find an available computer because the number of computers is less than the number of students in each class. Likewise, Mike complained about the inadequacy of the computers and lack of software programs.

Mike's Use of Computer-supported Instruction. Mike believed that "the computer just another tool that allows students to go in depth with their learning; allowing students to be in charge of their own learning; allowing them to experiment and to be more creative" (Dec. 14, 05). Mike believed that computer use in the classroom promoted the creativity of the students, and he also mentioned that sometimes the computer makes it easier to ". . . reach students . . . especially students who are . . . visual learners" (Dec. 14, 05).

Mike also mentioned another great advantage of computer technology over traditional methods. According to Mike, computer technology provided students with the ability to edit and read not only textual information but also visual and audio features of their projects. However, it would not be possible for them to edit and read their work if they used traditional types of materials. According to Mike, this feature of computer technology allowed students to do a better job on their projects.

Mike integrated the computer in his teaching frequently. He pointed out that he used the computer on average three times a week. His most common uses of computer-supported instructional applications can be listed as Internet search, web page development, and use of software programs such as Microsoft Word, PowerPoint and Movie Maker (Microsoft Corporation, 2004). During the classroom observation most of these software programs were used extensively by the students, especially PowerPoint and Movie Maker, which allowed students to create their own videos through the student projects in both classes. As Mike's two different classes were observed, there were two different projects in which computer-supported instruction had been used.

The Projects. The first project was "The City Planning" project (12th grade American Government). This was a group project. Each group consisted of three to five students, and students were free to select their group members. Every group was supposed to create a city on their own. One part of the project was to submit a written report about the city, including history, landmarks, maps, zoning (laws), economics, schools, and other public buildings. The second part was creating a ten-minute video that introduced the city. Students were allowed to use Internet sources not only to gather information for the written part, but also to find appropriate sound and visual effects for their videos.

The second project was "The World War I (WWI) Project" (10th grade American History). There were three options for this project: writing a diary, creating a newspaper, or creating a PowerPoint presentation. Except for the newspaper projects, students worked individually. Students or groups were assigned to topics related to WWI by Mike. Students were allowed to use the Internet sources not only to gather information, but also to find appropriate sound and visual effects and even historical videos for their projects.

Internet Search. The Internet was being used in Mike's classroom primarily for finding information. While he used the Internet to find primary sources and web sites for students, he also had the students search on the Internet to find text and visual materials such as images and videos for their projects. Mike gave special attention to the visual and audio materials on the Internet as he believed, "the American public are mostly visual learners" (Jan. 19, 06). Therefore, he liked to have his students use more visual materials in the classroom. All projects in this class were created based on information acquired from the Internet.

Computer as a Presentation Tool. The interviews and classroom observation indicated that Mike used the computer as a presentation tool. He usually used web sites and reflected them on the wall to support his lectures. He stated that

> . . . Not only can students listen to what I am saying but also they can actually see an example of what I am talking about. If I were talking about a general in World War I, then I'd try to find a visual of that person. (Dec. 14, 05)

During the classroom observations, Mike used the computer as a presentation tool a number of times, especially in the 12th grade American Government class. He reflected on the wall the official web site of the county, city, and their school districts to show students how the local government works and to introduce the city and county officials, such as mayors, governors, or other official figures like board members of their school district.

Software—Multimedia. Utilizing multimedia types of software was one of the most common instructional strategies in Mike's classroom. He cited a number of times that his major focus was on multimedia-related software programs. He stated that

> I think right now, my most common use of multimedia is bringing video in the classroom and integrating it with a lesson enhancing a lecture. This type of presentation is working because kids today are more visual learners because they're of the TV generation. (Dec. 14, 05)

As indicated in the quotation, the reason why Mike used multimedia types of software in his teaching was his belief that contemporary American students were mostly visual learners. The Movie Maker program was used for the "The City Planning Project" in the American Government class during the classroom observations. Students used the Movie Maker software program to edit, add sounds, and other visual effects to their introductory movies about their cities after they had filmed them around town.

Word Processing—Excel. Microsoft Word and Excel were the most common software programs were used in Mike's classroom. The Word program mostly was used for note-taking purposes during Internet searches. In both classes Internet searches were a big part of the projects. Students did Internet searches in both classes and as they found sources they copied and pasted information into Microsoft Word documents. Then they processed the information and used it for their projects. In both classes, students typed necessary parts of the projects into the Word documents.

In the American Government class, along with the Word program, Microsoft Excel was also commonly used for projects. In order to complete the written part of the "City Planning" project students were supposed to come up with some statistics about the city such as population, religions, and economics for the city. Therefore, this program was used frequently among the groups in order to create bar charts or pie charts that represented the city statistics.

PowerPoint. PowerPoint was another frequently used software program in Mike's classroom. In the American History class, eight students did PowerPoint projects, as they had an option to choose the format of the project. There were a wide variety of topics such as "WWI Tanks", "WWI Weapons", "WWI Personalities" and "Battles of WWI". Students used information and images they had found from Internet sources. There were many images in the presentations, such as tanks, weapons and aircraft that had been used in the war. The students added sound and texts to the video, which made it stand on it own. Most of the PowerPoint projects were high quality and met Mike's expectations.

Case 4: Kate (Pseudonym)

Background Information about Kate and the School Setting. Kate is s a 46 year old, White, female social studies teacher with 24 years of teaching experience. She completed her bachelor's degree in a Midwestern university in K-8 teacher education program. She received a Master of Education degree in the field of Curriculum & Instruction with emphasis on social studies education from another Midwestern university.

The school was a suburban middle school in a Midwestern state. The class was the eighth grade American History class with 10 boys and 11 girls (19 White and two African American). There were four desktop computers in the classroom for the use of the students and one for Kate's use. There were three laptop stations in the school for classroom use. Each station consisted of 25 laptop computers and one printer. Kate complained about the limited availability of these stations. The class was observed by the researcher for seven class periods. Fewer classroom observations were conducted in Kate's classroom due to limited computer availability in her school. She was only allowed to use computers in her classroom five days a month.

Kate's Use of Computer-supported Instruction. Kate considered the computer an aid for instruction. Kate thought that the computer was a powerful tool that helped students gain access to a lot of information. According to her, text materials cannot cover entire topics thoroughly and provide information on many issues related to the course of study. She stated that "I just think it is the only way to really get a lot of information . . . the Internet is important in getting some expanded knowledge for the students. So, you have to have that" (Feb. 15, 06). She believed that computer technologies gave students alternative "opportunities to go as wide as and as deep as they want to go" (Feb. 15, 06). Along with that, Kate pointed out the importance of computer technologies in providing more advanced presentation tools for students.

Kate's computer integration was less frequent compared to other participants due to the computer unavailability. She stated that "I try to use them [computers] once a nine week in terms of some sort of research" (Jan. 30, 06). Her main computer use with the students was to utilize the computer as a research tool. She also used the computer herself to update the school web page with student homework and grades. Internet searches and PowerPoint presentations were the most common uses among the students in her classroom. Likewise, students used these two software programs when they created their projects, which are explained in the next section.

The "War of 1812" Project. During the classroom observation periods, students were working on the "War of 1812 Project". The project was designed as a group project, and each group consisted of two or three students. There were 12 topics stated by Kate in the project handout, usually individual battles in the War of 1812. Students were assigned to the topics based on their choices. Students were supposed to do Internet searches to find information for their projects and create a project, either computer-supported such as Power Point or a traditional type of project such as a poster presentation.

Internet Search. Internet search was the most common use of the computer in Kate's classroom. The following excerpt was a summary of how she used the Internet in the classroom. ". . . like for 'the war of 1812' project, each student had a topic. They would go in detail about their topic and find not only just information but pictures that would represent that time period any primary sources . . ." (Jan. 30, 06).

As Kate pointed out during the "the War of 1812" project, students searched the Internet to find information about their projects. They were looking for not only textual information but also for pictures and images that could be used for their projects. Students used search engines, mostly the Goggle search engine, and typed keywords related to their project to find relevant sources of information. So, the Internet was used by students to create a base of information for their projects.

Kate preferred to use primary sources from the Internet rather than go and spend time on opinion resources. Therefore, she usually limited students to specific websites which consisted of primary sources such as, The Smithsonian or The National Archives. She stated that ". . . I try to keep with those more than getting into an opinion kind of thing" (Feb. 15, 06).

Word Processing. The Microsoft Word program was the second most common computer use in Kate's classroom. During the project, students used this program every day. Most of the students were using the copy and paste features of the program in order to take notes for their project. They were copying and pasting some texts they had found from the Internet and also some pictures and images of the people about which they were searching.

Students who did PowerPoint projects usually used the Word program to edit and adjust the textual information on the documents before transferring their work to a PowerPoint file. Yet, students who did not have computer-supported projects also used the program for note taking, and print functions in order to put them on poster board.

Computer as a Presentation Tool. Kate used the computer as a presentation tool in the classroom. She used a number of features of the presentation system, such as connecting it to the Internet, and showed the whole class websites rather than have them search information by themselves. Another feature she used was presenting information through this device, such as handouts or other types of documents concerning the instructional unit. She emphasized that it was a great feature of computer technology to allow all students to follow lessons. She stated that "It's kind of a nice way for everybody to be on the same page, so to speak. You know, which is pretty big in the middle school because they don't always want to be on the same page" (Feb. 15, 06).

PowerPoint. Although the PowerPoint software program was not Kate's favorite program, it was used a lot by her students. According to Kate, mostly students cut textual information from the Internet and tended to put long text into their PowerPoint presentation without editing the information (Informal discussion: Feb. 16, 06). Yet, PowerPoint seemed to be students' favorite software. Kate stated that

> . . . They [students] love doing PowerPoint. I think it's because it is easy. 'Cut and paste; next screen; cut paste; put a figure in.' . . . I don't think they utilize much . . . creativity. I mean you can pick the slide you want; you type your title; you type, you know. (Feb. 15, 06)

As Kate pointed out many students used PowerPoint for their projects during the classroom observations. The problem she indicated was visible on most Power-Point presentations. Students usually used long textual information on the slides. Even some of the text was not legible. It was clear that they did not do much editing of the information they had retrieved from the Internet. On the other hand, there were a couple of projects that were designed very well. One of them was a recreation of a battle, and the students who did the project added sound and animated images to simulate the battle strategy.

Cross-Case Analysis and Discussions of Research Questions

Research Question 1: How Do Exemplary Social Studies Teachers View the Computer as an Instructional Tool?

The data analysis indicated that all participants viewed the computer as an instructional tool that facilitates teaching and learning in multiple ways. David mentioned that the computer was a great instructional tool which enabled easier and faster access to different perspectives and provided opportunities for students to improve their work. Bill considered the computer one of the instructional tools that could be used in the classroom. Mike stressed that the computer was just another tool that can promote the creativity of the students. Kate considered the computer as an aid for instruction. Kate thought that the computer was a powerful tool that helped students gain access to a lot of information.

While all participants saw the computer as another instructional tool and acknowledged its great benefits, especially David and Bill specifically stated that they do not put the computer in the center of their instruction.

They were aware that it is only another tool and they only used it when it was necessary for their instructional design. David stated that he only used the computer when he "could not teach a unit in any other way" (Nov. 10, 05).

While the computer is seen as any other instructional tool by the participants, all of them agreed that it is a valuable research tool that can provide a wide variety of sources and information for the students to help them improve their work. The classroom observations also indicated that students used the computer as a research tool extensively to complete their projects. The students searched on the Internet for visual and textual sources to build various parts of their projects.

Research Question 2: What are the Current Computer-supported Instructional Activities Used by Exemplary Teachers in Their Classrooms?

The interviews and classroom observations showed that the participant teachers used a number of computer-supported instructional applications in their classrooms. As Table 3 shows, use of the Internet and of software programs such as Microsoft Power Point, Word, and Excel were the most common types of computer-supported instruction in the classrooms observed. In addition, computers were used as presentation tools frequently in these classrooms. Multimedia software was used by only one teacher during the classroom observations. Other strategies listed in the table were not observed during the data collection period, although the participant teachers reported they had had experiences with these applications.

The Internet was the most common computer use in the observed classrooms. All participants used the Internet because it provided fast and easy access to a vast amount of resources and information. Along with its fast and easy access to information, most of the participant teachers valued the Internet for its ability to provide global and multiple perspectives to students.

The computer was also frequently used as a presentation tool in the observed classrooms, either by students or by the teachers. All participant teachers used the computer to show websites and handouts related to student's projects during the classroom observations. Another form of computer use was to present students' projects. All participant teachers stated that computers were frequently used in their classes for student presentations. There were many PowerPoint projects presented during the classroom observations in all classrooms observed.

Although computers were used as presentation tools frequently by both teachers and students, not much has been written in the literature on this subject. Nevertheless, it seems that there are a number of benefits of using computers as presentation tools. The data showed that when a computer was used as a presentation tool, it not

Table 3

Self-Reported Use of Computer-Supported Instruction by the Participants in Their Classrooms

	David	Bill	Mike	Kate
Internet	X	X	X	X
Presentation Tool	X	X	X	X
PowerPoint	X	X	X	X
MS Word Excel	X	X	X	X
Multimedia Software	X		X	
Games Simulations				X
Databases	X			
Web Quest				
Web Page Development	X		X	
Tele-collaboration	X			
Virtual Field Trip		X		

only improved the quality of the presentation's visuals and sound, it also gave the teachers flexibility to use other types of tools with the computer, such as connecting to the Internet or to a DVD player. Clearly, it is not possible to have such flexibility and ease in transferring to another presentation tool with a traditional overhead projector.

Another common type of computer use by the participant teachers was the use of software programs. Only conventional software programs such as Microsoft Word, Excel, and PowerPoint were commonly used in the observed classrooms. The data in this study showed that newly developed software programs were rarely used in the observed classrooms. There are a number of reasons for that situation.

The data indicated that a number of factors influenced social studies teachers' computer use in their classrooms. The first factor was the limited availability of computers and computer software in the schools. The data showed that in three of the observed schools, computer availability was a factor that kept the teachers from integrating computers more with their teaching, even though data from the National Center for Education Statistics (NCES, 2003) showed a rapid increase in the number of instructional computers (an average of 131 instructional computers per school) in American schools.

In addition, the lack of software was a problem in some of the observed classrooms, and it kept at least one participant from using computer-supported instruction more frequently. Nevertheless, most of the participant teachers were not seeking new computer software programs that could be used in the social studies classroom. In fact, due to administrative processes, the teachers did not have much responsibility for choosing software programs or even much input on which programs were

chosen. Another factor influencing social studies teachers' use of computers in their classrooms could be related to lack of time due to curriculum requirements. Two of the participant teachers complained about the time limit and curriculum requirements.

In conclusion, the limited availability of computers and software and time issues related to the curriculum seem to be the major problems that prevent exemplary social studies teachers from using computer-supported instruction more frequently.

Research Question 3: How Do Exemplary Social Studies Teachers Use Computer-supported Instruction in Their Classrooms?

The study revealed that all four participants cited Internet search among the most common strategies they used in their classrooms. In the interviews all participants stated a number of times how frequently they used the Internet as a research tool. The classroom observations also showed that using the Internet for research was the most common strategy in the classrooms observed. Generally, the teachers had students use the Internet as a research tool to find textual and visual information for their projects.

Teachers' focuses within the strategy of using the Internet for research varied to some degree, yet most of them acknowledged the crucial role of the Internet in terms of providing information to students about multiple perspectives, cultures, and real-world issues. Only Kate wanted to keep her students from sources that represented opinions; she preferred them to use sources that represent "facts and events."

All participant teachers used computers as presentation tools in their classrooms, although how and how often they used them varied. Among all participants,

Bill used the computer for presentation purposes most frequently. He cited the Smart Board as the most common use of computers in his classroom. On the other hand, David rarely used the computer for presentation purposes. He generally preferred to use an overhead projector.

Computers were also used to present students' projects. All participant teachers stated that computers were used frequently in their classes for student presentations. Most of these presentations were made with Microsoft PowerPoint. It was one of the most frequently used programs in the classrooms observed. There were not many differences between classrooms in how this software program was used. Students did Internet searches and copied information from the Internet to Word documents so that they could evaluate information, analyze it, and edit it before creating their final PowerPoint projects. Many PowerPoint projects were presented during the classroom observations in all classrooms observed.

In addition, Microsoft Word was one of the most common software programs used in all classrooms. In all classrooms, students used Word documents to type their papers and also as "scratch paper" to take notes, evaluate and analyze information, and edit the information before they created their final projects. The editing feature of the software program was cited by all participant teachers as a great advantage for the students, as it freed them from needing to retype, consequently saving time and thereby helping to improve students' work. According to Mike, this feature of computer technology allowed students to do better work on their projects. He stated that "The computer allows students to correct . . . those mistakes; to retype a paragraph; to go back and look at their work . . . so what you get is better work from students." (Jan. 19, 06)

In addition, Microsoft Excel was also used by students in the classrooms observed. Although it was not used as frequently as Microsoft Word or PowerPoint, students used Excel to create databases, tables, and charts for their projects. The data indicated that other software programs were rarely used in the classroom. Mike was the only teacher who used a software program different from those just mentioned. He had students create videos using Windows Movie Maker.

Conclusion and Discussion

The analysis of the data indicated that all participants had similar views about the computer, as they did not differentiae it from any other instructional tool. Nevertheless, all of them agreed that the computer is a powerful research tool that facilitates students' work and makes doing the work faster and easier for students.

The participants used the computer in their classrooms in many ways and integrated the computer-supported instruction to the units they taught. The use of the Internet for research purposes was the most common type of computer-supported instruction in the classrooms observed. This finding is consistent with the recent literature. A number of studies showed that "Internet use" and "accessing information from the Web" were the most common use of computers in social studies education (Whitworth & Berson, 2003; see also Pye & Sullivan, 2001; Vanfossen, 2000, 2001). Most of the participant teachers valued the Internet for its ability to provide global and multiple perspectives to students. This finding also is consistent with current literature in the field. A number of studies emphasize the crucial role of the Internet in providing information to students about multiple perspectives, cultures, and real-world issues (see Bennett & Pye, 1999; Cassutto, 2000; Dils, 2000; Hicks et al., 2002; Hicks & Ewing, 2003; Larson, 1999; Risinger, 1996, 1998, 2000, 2001, 2003; Shiveley & VanFossen, 1999, Zukas, 2000).

The computer was also frequently used as a presentation tool in the observed classrooms, either by students or by the teachers. All participant teachers used the computer to show Web sites and handouts related to student's projects during the classroom observations. Another form of computer use was to present students' projects. All participant teachers stated that computers were frequently used in their classes for student presentations. There were many PowerPoint projects presented during the classroom observations in all classrooms observed. Although computers were used as presentation tools frequently by both teachers and students, not much has been written in the literature on this subject. The research focuses on the effectiveness of PowerPoint presentations in undergraduate courses (DenBeste, 2003; see also Bartsch & Cobern, 2003; Frey & Birnbaum, 2002; Susskind, 2005) rather than in K-12 educational settings. Therefore, it is clear that there is a need for more empirical research to investigate the role and effectiveness of the computer as a presentation tool and the use of PowerPoint in the social studies classroom.

The use of software programs such as Microsoft Word, and Excel was the other common type of computer-supported instruction in the classrooms observed. In all classrooms, students used Word documents to type their papers and also as "scratch paper" to take notes, evaluate and analyze information, and edit the information before creating their final projects. In addition, Microsoft Excel was also used by students in the classrooms observed. Although it was not used as frequently as Microsoft Word or PowerPoint, students used Excel to create databases, tables, and charts for their projects. However, there is not much research in the literature about the use of these applications in the classroom. There are few studies on the effectiveness of computer-supported writing activities in social studies (see Berson, 1996). Therefore, it is clear that there is a need for more empirical research to investigate the role of Microsoft Word in preparing student projects in the social studies classroom.

Multimedia software was used by only one teacher during the classroom observations. The data in this study showed that software programs other than Microsoft Word, Excel, and Power Point were rarely used in the observed classrooms. As the data showed there are a number of reasons for that including the lack of computer and software programs, curriculum requirements, and administrative issues. Likewise, the current literature indicated the following barriers which are keeping teachers from not using computer-supported instruction: (a) lack of availability of computers and problems with Internet access; (b) lack of training in how to apply the computer- and Internet-supported instruction in the classroom; (c) lack of time; and (d) lack of funding (Gibson & Nocente, 1999; Keiper et al., 2000; Sunal et al., 1998; VanFossen, 2000, 2001).

It is also important to investigate the influence of outside-classroom factors on computer integration in the social studies classroom. Administrative issues regarding computer and software use in schools can have significant influences on teachers' use of computer-supported instruction. It is very crucial whether school and district administrators support the use of computer-supported instruction in the classroom. Thus, further studies could be done to investigate school and district administrators' views and attitudes toward computer integration in the classroom.

Finally, both qualitative and quantitative studies could be done to examine effectiveness of a particular computer-supported instructional application such as Web Quest, PowerPoint, or the use of another type of software. Focusing on a particular computer-supported instructional application would provide more in-depth findings to help to examine the effectiveness of these strategies individually. Of course, the findings from that type of research would be more valuable if students were active participants in those studies.

REFERENCES

Açıkalın, M. (2006). *The influence of computer-supported instruction (CSI) on the principles of constructivist pedagogy in the social studies curriculum.* Unpublished doctoral dissertation, The Ohio State University.

Açıkalın, M., & Duru, E. (2005). The use of computer technologies in the social studies classroom. *Turkish Online Journal of Educational Technology, 4*(2), 18–26. Retrieved July 26, 2010 from http://www.tojet.net/volumes/v4i2.pdf

Bartsch, R. A., & Cobern, K. M. (2003). Effectiveness of PowerPoint presentations in lectures [Electronic version]. *Computers & Education, 41*, 77–86.

Bennett, L., & Pye, J. (1999). Instructional technology as a medium for learning world history. *International Journal of Social Education, 14*(1), 111–117.

Berson, M. J. (1996). Effectiveness of computer technology in the social studies: A review of the literature. *Journal of Research on Computing in Education, 2*(4), 486–499.

Berson, M. J., & Balyta, P. (2004). Technological thinking and practice in the social studies: Transcending the tumultuous adolescence of reform. *Journal of Computing in Teacher Education, 20*(4), 141–150.

Bogdan, R. C., & Biklen, S. K. (1998). *Qualitative research for education: An introductory to theory and methods* (3rd ed.). Boston: Allyn and Bacon.

Cassutto, G. (2000). Social studies and the World Wide Web. *International Journal of Social Education, 15*(1), 94–101.

Charmaz, K. (2000). Grounded theory: Objectivist and constructivist methods. In N. K. Denzin & Y. N. Lincoln (Eds.), *Handbook of qualitative research* (2nd ed., pp. 509–535). Thousand Oaks, CA: Sage.

Creswell, J. W. (2005). *Educational research: Planning, conducting, and evaluating quantitative and qualitative research* (2nd ed.). Upper Saddle River, NJ: Merrill.

DenBeste, M. (2003). PowerPoint, technology and the web: More than just an overhead projector for the new century? [Electronic version]. *The History Teacher, 36*(4), 491–504.

Diem, R. A. (2000). Can it make difference? Technology and the social studies. *Theory and Research in Social Education, 28*(4), 493–501.

Dils, A. K. (2000). Using technology in a middle school social studies classroom. *International Journal of Social Education, 15*(1), 102–112.

Freedman, A. (Ed.). (2001). *Computer desktop encyclopedia* (9th ed.) San Francisco: Osborne/McGraw-Hill.

Engle, S. H., & Ochoa, A. S. (1988). *Education for democratic citizenship: Decision making in the social studies.* New York: Teachers College Press.

Fontana, L. A. (1997). Online learning communities: Implications for the social studies. In P. H. Martorella (Ed.), *Interactive Technologies and the Social Studies* (pp. 1–25). Albany, NY: State University of New York Press.

Frey, B. A., & Birnbaum, D. J. (2002). *Learners' perceptions on the value of PowerPoint in lectures.* Pittsburgh: University Pittsburgh (ERIC Document Reproduction Service No. ED 467192).

Gibson, S., & Nocente, N. (1999). Computers in social studies education: A report of teachers' perspectives and students' attitudes. *Computers in the Schools, 15*(2), 73–81.

Hicks, D., Doolittle, P., & Lee, J. K. (2004). Social studies teachers' use of classroom-based and web-based historical primary sources. *Theory and Research in Social Education, 32*(2), 213–247.

Hicks, D., Ewing, E. T. (2003). Bringing the World into the classroom with online global newspaper. *Social Education, 67*(3), 134–139.

Hicks, D., Tlou, J., Lee. J. K., Parry, L., & Doolittle, P. (2002). Global connections: Using the Internet to support citizenship education. *International Journal of Social Education, 17*(1), 93–102.

Jonassen, D. H. (2000). *Computers as mindtools for schools: Engaging critical thinking* (2nd ed.). Upper Saddle River, NJ: Prentice-Hall.

Kausar, T., Choudhry, B. N., & Gujjar, A. A. (2008). A comparative study to evaluate the effectiveness of computer assisted instruction (cai) versus class room lecture (crl) for computer science at ics level. *Turkish Online Journal of Educational Technology, 7*(4), 19–29. Retrieved July 26, 2010 from http://www.tojet.net/volumes/v7i4.pdf

Keiper, T., Harwood, A., Larson, B. E. (2000). Preservice teachers' perceptions of infusing computer technology into social studies instruction. *Theory and Research in Social Education, 28*(4), 566–579.

Kleinedler, S., et al. (Eds.) (2001). *Dictionary of computer and Internet words*. Boston: Houghton Mifflin.

Larson, B. E. (1999). Current events and the Internet: Connecting "headline news" to perennial issues. *Social Studies and the Young Learner, 12*(1), 25–28.

Martorella, P. H. (1999). Technology and the social studies-or which way to the sleeping giant? *Theory and Research in Social Education, 25*(4), 511–514.

Margolis, P. E. (Ed.). (1999). *Random House Webster's computer and Internet dictionary* (3rd ed.). New York: Random House.

Mason, C., Berson, M., Diem, R., Hicks, D., Lee, J., & Dralle, T. (2000). Guidelines for using technology to prepare social studies teachers. *Contemporary Issues in Technology and Teacher Education* [Online serial], *1*(1). Retrieved October 28, 2004 from http://www.citejournal.org/vol1/iss1/currentissues/socialstudies/article1.htm

Merriam, S. B. (1998). *Qualitative research and case study applications in education: Revised and expanded from case study research in education*. San Francisco: Jossey-Bass.

Milli Eğitim Bakanlığı Talim Terbiye Kurulu Başkanlığı [TTKB]. 2009a. *Sosyal bilgiler 4. - 5. sınıf programı [Social studies curriculum: Grades 4-5]*. Ankara: author. Retrieved November 12, 2009 from http://ttkb.meb.gov.tr/ogretmen/modules.php?name=Downloads&d_op=viewdownload&cid=74&min=10&orderby=titleA&show=10

Milli Eğitim Bakanlığı Talim Terbiye Kurulu Başkanlığı [TTKB]. 2009b. *Sosyal bilgiler 6. - 7. sınıf programı [Social studies curriculum: Grades 6-7]*. Ankara: author. Retrieved November 12, 2009 from http://ttkb.meb.gov.tr/ogretmen/modules.php?name=Downloads&d_op=viewdownload&cid=74&min=20&orderby=titleA&show=10

National Center for Educational Statistics. (2003). *Digest of education statistics*. Washington DC: U.S. Department of Education, Retrieved 14 September, 2005, from http://nces.ed.gov/programs/digest/d03/ch_7.asp

National Council for the Social Studies. (1994). *Expectations of excellence: Curriculum standards for social studies*. Washington D.C.: National Council for the Social Studies.

Newmann. F. M. (1991). Promoting higher order thinking in social studies: Overview of a study of 16 high school departments. *Theory and Research in Social Education, 19*(4), 324–340.

Nickell, P., Field, S. L., & Roach, P. (2001). Trends, issues, and gaps, in technology for elementary social studies. *International Journal of Social Education, 15*(2), 76–91.

Northup, T., & Rooze, G. E. (1990). Are social studies teachers using computers?: A national survey. *Social Education, 54*(4), 212–214.

Patton, M. Q. (2002). *Qualitative research and evaluation methods* (3rd ed.). Thousand Oaks, CA: Sage.

Plaffenberger, B. (2001). *Webster's new world computer dictionary* (9th ed.). New York: Hungry Minds.

Pye, J., & Sullivan, J. (2001). Use of computer-based instruction in teaching middle school social studies. *The International Journal of Social Education, 15*(2), 92–102.

QSR International (2002). NVivo (Version 2.0) [Computer Software]. Doncaster, Victoria, Australia: Author.

Rice, M. L., & Wilson, E. K. (1999). How technology aids constructivism in the social studies classroom. *The Social Studies, 90*(1), 28–33.

Rice, M. L., Wilson, E. K., & Bagley, W. (2001). Transforming learning with technology: Lessons from field. *Journal of Technology and Teacher Education, 9*(2), 211–230.

Risinger, C. F. (1996). Global and international education on the World Wide Web. *Social Education, 60*(7), 447–448.

Risinger, C. F. (1998). Global education and the World Wide Web. *Social Education, 62*(5), 276–277.

Risinger, C. F. (2000). Teaching social issues using the Internet. *Social Education, 64*(7), 455–457.

Risinger, C. F. (2001). Teaching about terrorism, Islam, and tolerance with the Internet. *Social Education, 65*(7), 426–427.

Risinger, C. F. (2003). Teaching about war and peace with the Internet. *Social Education, 67*(3), 175–176.

Ritchie, J., Lewis, J., & Elam, G. (2003). Designing and selecting samples. In J. Ritchie & J. Lewis (Eds.), *Qualitative research practice: A guide for social science students and researchers* (pp. 77–108). Thousands Oaks, CA: Sage.

Rose, S. A., & Fernlund, P. M. (1997). Using technology for powerful social studies learning. *Social Education, 61*(3), 160–166.

Saye, J. W., & Brush, T. (1999). Student engagement with social issues in a multimedia supported learning environment. *Theory and Research in Social Education, 27*(4), 472–504.

Shaver, J. P. (1999). Electronic technologies and the future of social studies in elementary and secondary schools. *Journal of Education, 181*(3), 13–40.

Shiveley, J. M., & VanFossen, P. J. (1999). Critical thinking and the Internet: Opportunities for the social studies classroom. *The Social Studies, 90*(1), 42–46.

Sunal, C. S., Smith, C., Sunal, D. W., & Britt, J. (1998). Using the Internet to create meaningful instruction. *The Social Studies, 89*(1), 13–17.

Susskind, J. E. (2005). PowerPoint's power in the classroom: Enhancing students' self efficacy and attitudes [Electronic version]. *Computer & Education, 45,* 203–215.

VanFossen, P. J. (2000). An analysis of the use of the Internet and world wide web by secondary social studies teachers in Indiana. *International Journal of Social Education, 14*(2), 89–109.

VanFossen, P. J. (2001). Degree of Internet/www use and barriers to use among secondary social studies teachers [Electronic Version], *International Journal of Instructional Media, 28*(1), 57–74.

VanHover, S. D., Berson, M. J., Mason-Bolick, C., & Owings-Swan, K. (2004). Implications of ubiquitous computing for the social studies curriculum. *Journal of Computing in Teacher Education, 20*(3), 107–111.

VanSickle, R. L., & Hoge, J. D. (1991). Higher cognitive thinking skills in social studies: Concepts and Critiques. *Theory and Research in Social Education, 19*(2), 152–172.

White, C. (1997). Technology and social studies: An Introduction. *Social Education, 61,* 147–148.

Whitworth, S., & Berson, M. J. (2003). Computer technology in the social studies: An examination of the effectiveness literature (1996–2001). *Contemporary Issues in Technology and Teacher Education, 2*(4), 472–509.

Yin, R. K. (2003). *Case study research: Design and Methods* (3rd ed.). Thousand Oaks, CA: Sage.

Yusuf, M. O., & Afolabi, A. O. (2010). Effects of computer assisted instruction (cai) on secondary school students' performance in biology. *Turkish Online Journal of Educational Technology, 9*(1), 62–69. Retrieved July 26, 2010 from http://www.tojet.net/volumes/v9i1.pdf

Zukas, A. (2000). Active learning, world history, and the Internet: Creating knowledge in the classroom. *International Journal of Social Education, 15*(1), 62–79.

CHAPTER FOURTEEN

Ethnography and Critical Research

PROBLEMS OF PRACTICE *in this chapter*

- If the cultural norms of conventional classroom instruction hinder the teaching of the scientific method, what can be done to change those norms?
- Why does racism continue to be an ongoing problem in American culture, and what can be done to eliminate it?
- Does culture play a role in creating the achievement gap between white students and students of other races and ethnicities?
- Do school reform efforts like No Child Left Behind actually address the learning needs of struggling students?
- How can YouTube and other social networking websites help us understand students' interests and perspectives related to the world around them?
- Do certain students live in a state of internalized oppression, and, if so, what can be done to help them develop self-empowerment?
- Do standardized curriculum and tests favor certain cultural groups and oppress others?
- Does corporate culture have a positive or negative effect on students' learning?
- Can critical pedagogy improve the quality of school curriculum and instruction?
- Are pull-out programs like Project TRUST effective in helping students become less disruptive in class, learn conflict resolution skills, and develop self-esteem?

IMPORTANT *Ideas*

1. Ethnography involves in-depth study of a cultural entity in its natural context, from both the researchers' (etic) and research participants' (emic) perspective.
2. Culture, the central focus of ethnography, is what makes human beings unique as a species.
3. Culture is the pattern of traditions, symbols, rituals, and artifacts that characterize a particular society or group of individuals.

4. Ethnographers explain cultural phenomena by revealing aspects of the culture that are so central that most members of the culture appear to be almost unaware of them.

5. Educational ethnographers study the process of both cultural acquisition (how individuals learn to function in the culture) and cultural transmission (how a culture passes on its characteristics to new members).

6. Technology has created new opportunities for participant observation and thick description, two of the main characteristics of ethnographic research.

7. Critical research focuses on the negative effects of unequal power relationships found in most cultures and on the reasons for and means to reverse them.

8. Critical researchers have a value orientation aimed at highlighting and reversing oppressive cultural practices that are taken for granted by most mainstream researchers.

9. Critical research in education draws on several research and theoretical traditions, particularly cultural studies and critical pedagogy.

10. Critical ethnography is a qualitative research tradition that combines ethnography, which is the earliest qualitative research tradition, and critical research, a more recent tradition.

11. Critical ethnography uses various ethnographic methods to explore unequal power relationships in educational settings and their meaning to research participants and to researchers themselves.

12. Compared to other qualitative research approaches, critical ethnography puts particular emphasis on research strategies designed to validate various types of truth claims of researchers and research participants.

13. Critical ethnographers seek to shed light on the culture of the specific sites that they study, to clarify system relationships common to those and similar sites studied by other researchers, and to pose theoretical explanations of such relationships.

KEY TERMS

agency

anti-oppressive
    education

border pedagogy

conscientization

critical ethnography

critical pedagogy

critical research

critical theory

criticalist

cultural acquisition

cultural studies

cultural transmission

culture

deconstruction

dialogical data generation

emancipation

emic perspective

epistemology

ethnography

ethnology

etic perspective

feminisms

hegemony

hermeneutic circle

hermeneutics

holistic ethnography

instrumental rationality

internalized oppression

meaning fields

microethnography

monological data
    collection

normative-evaluative
    truth claims

norms

objective truth claims

participant observation

performance ethnography

postmodernism

praxis

privilege

reconstructive analysis

reproduction

subjective truth claims

text

thick description

troubling

voice

THE USE OF ETHNOGRAPHY AND CRITICAL RESEARCH TO STUDY PROBLEMS OF PRACTICE IN EDUCATION

This chapter first describes ethnography, one of the oldest traditions within qualitative research, and critical research, a relatively new qualitative research tradition. We then discuss critical ethnography, showing how it builds on these historical roots and how it has been applied to problems of practice in education.

THE CHARACTERISTICS OF ETHNOGRAPHIC RESEARCH

Ethnography is the firsthand, intensive study of the features of a specific culture and the patterns in those features. Reports of ethnographic research help readers develop an understanding of their own culture and of cultures much different from their own. Ethnography began in the field of anthropology, and many of its design features resemble those of qualitative case studies. (See Chapter 13.) In fact, David Lancy (1993) claims that ethnography is "the prototype for the qualitative method" (p. 66).

The case or cases studied in ethnography can range from a single individual to an entire community, society, or institution. In ethnographic research, as in qualitative case study research, the researcher

- studies particular instances of a phenomenon (in ethnographic research, the case is a culture or some aspect of culture).
- makes an in-depth study of the phenomenon of interest.
- studies the phenomenon in its natural context.
- represents both the field participants' (emic) and the researchers' (etic) perspectives.

Focus on Culture or Aspects of Culture

Culture is the central concept in ethnographic research. **Culture** can be defined as the pattern of traditions, symbols, rituals, and artifacts that characterize a particular society or group of individuals. Many early ethnographers lived in non-Western societies for an extended time period. They often examined specific phenomena, such as religious ceremonies, marriage, and kinship, that appeared to be ritualized in such societies. They believed that study of those phenomena in so-called "primitive" cultures might reveal universal patterns in the development of such phenomena.

Early ethnographers sought to provide a holistic description, which is a comprehensive analysis and description of the unique cultural patterns of a group of people who live close together in a specific geographical region. Their work represents the research tradition called **holistic ethnography**. The studies of Margaret Mead (1930) and Bronislaw Malinowski (1922) are widely known examples of such research.

Ethnographers believe that the influence of culture in human beings' lives is what makes us unique as a species. Culture allows a particular group of people to live together and thrive through a system of shared meanings and values. On the other hand, that same system also involves opposition to or oppression of groups whose cultures represent different shared meanings and values. Investigating the process of cultural oppression is central to critical ethnography, which we discuss later in the chapter.

Individuals display beliefs and behaviors that reflect the various cultures of which they are members, for example, their racial group, age group, religious affiliation, and occupation. Researchers have found that certain aspects of culture have a particularly strong influence on individual and group life, including family structure, socialization processes, religious affiliations, leisure activities, and ceremonial behavior. For example, ethnographers investigating education might focus on rituals marking transitional events in the lives of students in school, such as entry into kindergarten, receipt of report cards, summer vacation, the beginning and end of the school term, and school graduation.

These cultural influences on individual and group life are changing rapidly in the modern era. Lancy (1993) notes that today's world is becoming increasingly homogeneous with respect to culture. He argues that wealth, rather than influences unique to geographic location, is now the principal factor that differentiates the lifestyles of particular cultural groups.

Ethnographies have revealed that the culture of a given society or social group is not a consistent whole but more closely resembles what Murray

Wax (1993) called "a thing of shreds and patches" (p. 101). Each ethnographic study contributes a limited body of knowledge about certain aspects. This patchwork development of knowledge means that certain aspects of the culture are better understood than others. For example, in U.S. schools, more research exists about teacher culture than about the culture of school leaders, perhaps because groups in power are less inclined to reveal characteristics of their culture to outsiders. This research focus on a particular aspect of culture within a specific cultural group or society, rather than on the culture as a whole, is sometimes referred to as **microethnography**.

An ethnography by Kathleen Hogan and Catherine Corey (2001) exemplifies this focused approach. The researchers became guest science teacher-researchers in one fifth-grade classroom to observe "what happens as teachers work to create a scientific culture in their classrooms" (p. 215). The class was instructed to follow the norms of experimental science (such as rigor, control, and collaboration) in testing plant growth in the classroom. Students were guided to plan an experiment to compare different compost mixtures in stimulating plant growth. Students also reviewed their classmates' plans for conducting the experiment.

The researchers found that in designing their experiments and in giving peer feedback, students expressed the individualistic goals typical in most classrooms, not those consistent with scientific norms about how best to support knowledge claims. For example, most students wanted to have their own plants to control, and they expressed criticism rather than supportive comments of others' plans. Hogan and Corey's ethnography suggests that teachers can improve the way they guide students' learning of science by considering not only students' knowledge about scientific concepts but also the cultural norms and values that students bring to such learning endeavors.

Naturalistic Study of Individuals in the Field

Many ethnographers today study subcultures in their own geographic vicinity, carrying out data collection in the natural setting of the members of the culture. They rely on unobtrusive data collection methods, like informal observations and conversations, that will be comfortable to field participants.

Also, they seek to immerse themselves in the setting, both to gain participants' trust and to deepen their own understanding of cultural phenomena.

Making the Familiar Strange

Traditionally, ethnographers have sought to "make the familiar strange" (Spindler & Spindler, 1992). This goal involves analyzing a cultural phenomenon from the researcher's **etic perspective**, which is the perspective of an outsider to whom the phenomenon is strange, while also seeking to understand it from the participants' **emic perspective**, which is the perspective of an insider, to whom it is familiar.

Ethnographers can make the familiar strange in at least three ways. First, they can immerse themselves in a culture far different from their own. Second, they can study a subculture within their own community with which they are unfamiliar. Third, they can investigate a subculture with which they are familiar but look at it from the perspective of another subculture rather than from their own subculture's perspective.

Exemplifying this third approach, African American professor D. Soyini Madison (2005) describes her participation in street performance ethnography in Ghana to protest the killing of a young African American man, Amadou Diallo, by four New York police officers. **Performance ethnography** is a type of critical ethnography in which the researchers both (1) study cultural phenomena that can be considered performances (e.g., school plays and school marching bands) and (2) create reports that serve as the basis for staged reenactments that highlight their findings, especially those that concern oppression.

Diallo found that racism "is alive and still hurting people" both in "the home of my heart, Africa" (p. 539) and in the "the home of my birth, the United States" (p. 539). She cites three verbatim exchanges nearly three years after the shooting from a website celebrating Diallo's shooting and exulting White Power, Hitler, and white people.

Another way an ethnographer can make the familiar strange is to highlight the particular phenomena of which members of a culture are seemingly unaware because they appear to take them for granted. For example, an ethnographer studying the culture of college sports teams might notice patterns of acceptable and unacceptable behavior beyond those contained in the game rules, such as differences in how starters and bench players cluster around the coach during time-outs.

Thick Description

In writing their research reports, ethnographers typically generate a thick description of the cultural phenomenon they are studying. A **thick description** describes the field setting in great detail and uses extensive quotations from field participants. It is intended to bring the culture alive for the reader. Early ethnographers often wrote their descriptions in the present tense, which creates an exaggerated impression of the permanence, or even universality, of what is being described. Such ethnographic reports tend to promote the sense that the description applies not just to the specific cases that were studied but also to similar cases that might have been studied.

DIFFERENCES BETWEEN ETHNOGRAPHIES AND BASIC CASE STUDIES

Ethnographies have special characteristics beyond those of basic qualitative research case studies (see Chapter 13). They usually involve a longer, more in-depth period of data collection than a typical case study. Also, ethnographers often make a comparative study of a particular phenomenon as it manifests itself in different cultures, which is called **ethnology**. By contrast, case study researchers usually limit themselves to a single cultural context. Most important, while educational case studies can focus on any aspect of education, educational ethnographies focus specifically on aspects of culture that influence schooling or the teaching-learning process.

Educational ethnographers have done considerable research on learning as a cultural process. They have addressed the issue of whether learning is primarily a process of cultural acquisition or of cultural transmission. **Cultural acquisition** refers to the process by which individuals seek to acquire or, in some cases, avoid acquiring the concepts, values, skills, and behaviors that are reflected in the common culture. By contrast, **cultural transmission** is the process by which the larger social structure intentionally intervenes in the lives of new members of the culture in order to promote or, sometimes discourage, the learning of particular concepts, values, skills, or behaviors that are reflected in the common culture.

The relative importance of cultural acquisition and cultural transmission plays a central role in ethnographers' efforts to understand the achievement gap among students. The achievement gap refers to persistent differences in the levels of educational achievement and retention that have been documented for members of various cultural groups, as defined by race and ethnicity. Among the ethnographic studies focused on this problem are those conducted primarily between 1960 and 1980, exploring adaptation to public schooling by young people whose cultures were in transition. The cultures that were studied included villages in Africa and Papua New Guinea as well as Native American and Black communities in the United States.

Lancy (1993) reviewed these studies and concluded:

> All [of the studies] document persistent "failure" in the sense that one sees little pleasure in either the teaching staff or the children. There is no evidence that students are making satisfactory academic progress, enabling them to "climb out of the ghetto," "leave the reservation," or "become self-sufficient." Increasingly, anthropologists who study minority education now take student failure as their point of departure. (p. 41)

Lancy's review leads him to question a frequent assumption of critical researchers that "minority student failure can inevitably be traced to the fact that children who are poor, don't speak English, or are culturally different are inevitably given prejudicial treatment by public schools" (p. 50). He cites his own study of the U.S. Agency for International Development's effort to build rural schools in Liberia in the 1960s:

> The informal, casual nature of instruction, characteristic of the village, no longer applies in school. Now, in a relatively short period of time . . . students must master whole volumes of new information in a foreign language. The result . . . was "indoctrination without education." Students become indoctrinated with Western values and aspirations, reject the traditional values of the village, but the quality of instruction is so poor, they don't learn enough to succeed at increasingly higher levels in the education system. (1993, pp. 39–40)

This ethnographic finding suggests that at least One cause of the achievement gap is a disconnect between students' everyday culture and the culture of conventional schooling.

In seeking the cause of many U.S. minority students' lower level of academic success compared to that of students in the mainstream culture, the African American scholar John Ogbu conducted research based on a theoretical model of education and caste focused on learning as cultural acquisition (Foster, 2004). Ogbu claims that native-born members of minority groups who have suffered a long history of economic discrimination withhold their investment in education because they do not perceive it as having any economic payoff.

Other qualitative researchers interested in cultural acquisition have studied how individuals' sense of agency is formed. **Agency** refers to individuals' assumed ability to shape the conditions of their lives, whatever their cultural situation. Ethnographers George Spindler and Louise Spindler (1992) have questioned whether this focus on cultural acquisition as the primary explanation of the achievement gap makes it easy to slip into a "blame-the-victim" interpretation of individuals' learning problems. They argue that ethnography can best contribute to the understanding of learning by showing how societies use their cultural resources to organize the conditions and purposes of learning. Their research thus focuses on cultural transmission, that is, how schools and other agents facilitate or hinder specific types of learning by individuals from various cultures. We return to the topic of the achievement gap in our discussion of critical research.

EXAMPLES OF ETHNOGRAPHIC RESEARCH

The following two examples of research represent contemporary uses of ethnography to understand problems of practice in education.

An Ethnography of Government-Mandated After-School Tutoring

Koyama, J. (2011). Principals, power, and policy: Enacting "Supplemental Educational Services." *Anthropology & Education Quarterly, 42*(1), 20–36.

The No Child Left Behind (NCLB) Act is intended to reduce the achievement gap between white students and students of various racial minorities. One provision of NCLB is provision of out-of-school tutoring for failing schools through Supplemental Educational Services (SES), provided by state-approved companies, the majority of which are private enterprises. Schools are considered to be failing if students do not make adequate yearly progress for three consecutive years. (See Chapter 8 for an explanation of adequate yearly progress.)

On the face of it, NCLB and the SES programs appear worthwhile and in the best interests of students. However, Jill Koyama's ethnographic study found that the policies specified by NCLB and SES can become transformed, not necessarily for the better, when enacted by school principals and their various partners—federal education agencies, for-profit SESs, and various school reform boards and panels—all constituting different cultures. As is typical of ethnographic research, Koyama studied these cultures intensively. Her data collection extended over a three-year period and included analysis of many documents, hundreds of formal and informal interviews, and observations in various settings, including SES school sites, government meetings, teacher-training sessions, and community assemblies.

One of Koyama's findings is that school principals did not follow the SES mandates exactly, but in fact made their own demands of SES providers in their schools, "often persuading them to dramatically modify their preapproved programs" (pp. 27–28). In some cases, principals under-enrolled eligible students so that they could use SES monies for other purposes. Other principals enrolled all eligible students but managed to modify the SES curriculum to fit the existing school curriculum.

SES personnel also construed the SES mandates to suit their capabilities and needs. At one school site, an SES provider fabricated testing data to satisfy the principal's demands for "increased test scores across all grades" (p. 30). Koyama found that at least one SES provider took responsibility for collecting student test scores as part of its program but did not see that it had a responsibility for using the scores to diagnose student needs and inform instruction.

Koyama concluded from her findings that NCLB and SES programs focus on imposing accountability and testing requirements on schools rather than on actually improving student learning. The creation of SES programs, many of them run by private companies, create power conflicts between SES administrators and school principals that are not in students' best interests. The overarching problem, according to Koyama, is that NCLB, SES, and other governmental reform efforts are "conceived at a distance . . . from educators responsible for implementing them" (p. 33).

This ethnographic study, like many qualitative studies, draws attention to a problem of practice instead of solving it. However, the ethnographer's "thick description" of the problem helps us understand the problem better and might keep policy makers and educators from repeating solutions that have failed in the past. Ideally, ethnographic findings will point the way to more nuanced solutions and interventions that respect the complexity of the many cultures that exist within the education enterprise.

An Ethnography of Video Blogging

Young, J. R. (2007, May). An anthropologist explores the culture of video blogging. *Chronicle of Higher Education, 53*(36), A42.

This article describes the work of Michael Wesch, an assistant professor of cultural anthropology at Kansas State University, who began a collaborative ethnography of the online community with nine of his undergraduate students.

Calling themselves the Digital Ethnography Working Group, Wesch and his students undertook a study of the culture of YouTube, a website to which millions of people have posted videos that they recorded themselves. The working group uploaded a video about social networking and other interactive tools known as Web 2.0 to YouTube. Their online reports, available on the group's website (http://mediatedcultures.net), focus on video bloggers, including both Wesch's students and other people who responded with their own videos.

One group video of the Digital Ethnography Working Group, titled "A Vision of Students Today" (youtube.com/watch?v=dGCJ46vyR9o), shows a large university lecture hall, at first empty and then filled with hundreds of students. One at a time, students hold up diary-like signs describing the disconnects in their experience of learning in the university context versus in the world as a whole, as in the following examples:

- 18% of my teachers know my name.
- I will be $20,000 in *debt* after graduation!
- Over 1 billion people make less than $1 a day.
- I did not create the problems.
- But they are *my* problems.

Since its posting, hundreds of people have responded to that video with their own video blogs, or *vlogs*, as they have become known.

This study involves **participant observation**, which we defined in Chapter 13 as a process in which researchers assume a meaningful identity within the group being studied while maintaining their role as researchers collecting data. The making and sharing of videos online is a perfect medium for carrying out participation observation locally or worldwide. Videos like this might encourage teachers and students to use YouTube or other online sites to investigate their own and other students' perspectives about social issues. They could also examine how the learning process is affected by students who have access to video blogs as opposed to only lectures or written material. Recent ethnographies, in fact, have emphasized visual modes of data collection (e.g., photographs, visual art, video recordings) in contrast to the textual or verbal modes typical of early ethnographies (Reavey, 2011).

CRITICAL RESEARCH AS A FIELD OF INQUIRY AND PRACTICE

We turn now to an examination of critical research and its contributions to the study of education. **Critical research** (sometimes called **critical theory**, based on its strong theoretical orientation) involves a broad range of methods designed to uncover and help remedy the negative effects of unequal power relationships that prevail in the global community and in most cultures within it.

Researchers who carry out critical research are sometimes called **criticalists** because they specialize in critical inquiry and praxis. In qualitative research, **praxis** is a form of practical activity aimed at "doing the right thing and doing it well in interactions with fellow humans" (Schwandt, 2001, p. 207).

The concern for improving education through research is not unique to critical researchers, of course. Much existing educational research, whether qualitative or quantitative, also aims to improve the learning and opportunities of nonprivileged groups. However, critical research differs from other forms of research because of its specific focus on social justice and its efforts to highlight (through research and theory) and reverse (through praxis) causes of cultural inequities.

Examples of Issues Studied by Criticalists

Not a day goes by without claims by television news, magazines, and online news sources that political interests have dominated, distorted, or fabricated the information people receive about issues central to their own and others' social well-being. For example, the Associated Press featured a story about a report released in June 2008 by the office of the inspector general of the National Aeronautics and Space Administration (NASA). The report stated that NASA had "marginalized or mischaracterized" studies on global warming between 2004 and 2006 and had canceled a press conference on ozone pollution because it was too close to the 2004 presidential election (Borenstein, 2008). The belief or disbelief in global warming of various political leaders continues, often suggesting the bias of various power groups rather than a dispassionate review of scientific evidence.

News media increasingly include stories about personal economic and health disasters that individuals are experiencing. For example, the Associated Press reported that throughout the United States, food banks were finding more clients but receiving fewer donations to meet their needs (Nieves, 2008):

> April saw the biggest jump in food prices in 18 years, according to the Labor Department. At the same time, workers' average weekly earnings, adjusted for inflation, dropped for the seventh straight month. . . . In Baton Rouge, La., the public school system has found students hoarding their free and reduced-price lunches so they can bring them home to eat at night. (p. A-5)

A recent United Press poll also illustrates the continuing prevalence of racial prejudice as a force operating in U.S. culture. The poll found that racial attitudes had not improved in the four years after the United States elected its first Black president. In fact, the percentage of Americans polled who expressed explicit anti-Black attitudes had increased since a 2008 survey. Most Americans also expressed anti-Hispanic sentiments, in an AP survey done in 2011 (Ross & Agiesta, 2012). To the extent that these negative attitudes affect students' educational experience and their life opportunities, they are a continuing concern for educators.

Problems such as these have continued to worsen and affect more and more people. Critical research goes beyond standard reports of such events in an effort to understand and challenge the underlying political and economic forces that produce and maintain these problems. Indeed, critical research in education can be regarded as one form of anti-oppressive education. According to Kevin Kumashiro (2002), **anti-oppressive education** "involves constantly *looking beyond* what we teach and learn" (p. 6) for the critical purpose of "troubling" education and educational research. **Troubling** means exposing the assumptions underlying widely accepted but oppressive cultural practices that traditional educational practices help maintain.

Some criticalists have challenged the claims of quantitative research as being far more rigorous, objective, and hence more valid than qualitative research. Among them is Phil Carspecken (1996), who developed a methodological theory for conducting critical social research using methods of research design and interpretation that can withstand rigorous tests of validation. His research shares the value orientation of critical research, seeking to address what is hidden or concealed by the dominant or mainstream powers operating in education. Carspecken's model of critical ethnography, discussed later in this chapter, is critical both in its value orientation and its epistemological orientation and corresponding research methods of validation.

Two criticalists, Joe Kincheloe and Peter McLaren (1994), have described the main assumptions held by critical researchers. We have grouped their assumptions into two categories—those reflecting criticalists' value orientation and those reflecting their epistemological orientation. We describe the assumptions in the next sections.

The Value Orientation of Critical Research

Critical researchers make four assumptions about society. These assumptions, described next, reflect the high value they place on social justice.

The Tendency to Privilege and Oppress

Criticalists argue that every society systematically privileges certain cultural groups and oppresses other cultural groups. **Privilege** is the disproportionate power, resources, and life opportunities held by members of culturally dominant groups in society. It is reinforced by the wider society through **hegemony**, which refers to the ways in which privileged cultural groups maintain domination over other groups through various cultural agencies that exert power.

According to Peter McLaren (2003), the political, criminal justice, and educational systems are the three cultural agencies that most clearly reflect and promote hegemonic interests. The privileged always have an interest in preserving the status quo in order to protect their advantages. Critical research seeks to disclose the true interests (i.e., the needs, concerns, and advantages) of different groups and individuals, including both those who are privileged and those who are oppressed.

The Maintenance of Low Privilege

Criticalists believe that privilege is maintained in part through **internalized oppression**, which is the process by which individuals unwittingly maintain their lack of privilege through thoughts and actions consistent with a lesser social status. Through this process, **reproduction** of their oppression occurs, meaning that new members who are born to or join the culture accept, and behave consistently with, hegemony. In McLaren's terms, hegemony involves "a struggle in which the powerful win the consent of those who are oppressed, with the oppressed unknowingly participating in their own oppression" (1998, p. 182).

Critical research strives to highlight the factors that lead nonprivileged individuals to behave consistently with their lesser social status. Critical researchers use interviews and examine narratives to convey the sense of frustration and powerlessness that accompanies many individuals' awareness of the entrenched limits on their opportunities to realize their potential. Perhaps most important, such research directly seeks to provide insights to guide oppressed groups toward greater autonomy and, ultimately, **emancipation**, which can be defined as the actions and changes in consciousness of and toward the members of oppressed cultural groups that help free them from oppression.

The Multifaceted Nature of Oppression

Criticalists argue that the tendency to focus on one type of oppression (for example, racism) obscures the connections among forms of oppression and the weight of their joint operation in a given individual's life. To understand and combat oppression, they believe it is necessary to identify all of the cultural categories that operate to separate and oppress people and to examine their joint effects.

Kevin Kumashiro (2002) used this approach in eliciting the stories of queer activists. He interviewed them to "read" their multiple identities, cultures, and experiences of oppression. Kumashiro includes a poem about Pab, a teenage lesbian activist born in Nepal and then living in the United States. Through the poem, Kumashiro demonstrates the "impossibility of identity" experienced by gay Asian American women who are caught up in the conflicting cultural expectations involving Asian, Asian American, female, and heterosexual identities. Pab, like other Asian American women who are lesbians, is "often invisible both in Asian-American communities and mainstream society" (p. 95).

The Role of Mainstream Research in Maintaining Oppression

Critical researchers believe that mainstream research practices help reproduce systems of oppression that are based on class, race, gender, and other cultural categories. They observe that, despite a gradual increase in academic diversity, the majority of educational research is still based on positivist epistemology (see Chapter 1) and carried out by middle- or upper-class white males. This research rests on assumptions about science, truth, and good that such researchers accept as universal.

Critical researchers particularly oppose educational research that focuses on prediction and control for the purpose of maximizing educational productivity. In their view, such research reflects the operation of **instrumental rationality**, which is a cultural preoccupation with means over ends or purposes. Rex Gibson (1986) views the IQ testing movement as a key example of the shortcomings and injustices resulting from this preoccupation:

Instrumental rationality is the cast of thought which seeks to dominate others, which assumes its own rightness to do so, and which exercises its power to serve its own interests. Coldly following its narrow principle of efficiency and applying a crude economic yardstick, its results are all too obvious . . . the interests least served are those of comprehensive schools and pupils from working class homes. (pp. 8–9)

Critical theorists would likely view the current reliance on standardized testing to evaluate and enforce standards of student achievement as a manifestation of educational systems' preoccupation with instrumental rationality.

The Epistemological Orientation of Critical Research

Epistemology is a branch of philosophy devoted to the study of the nature of knowledge and the process by which knowledge is acquired and validated. Critical researchers make epistemological assumptions in their methods of acquiring knowledge, as we describe below.

Power Relationships That Underlie Knowledge

Criticalists assume that all thought is mediated by socially and historically constructed power relations. This assumption implies that the beliefs and knowledge of students, teachers, and other groups involved in education are inevitably affected by their experiences with power and dominance, both within and outside the educational system. As a result, their beliefs and knowledge can be understood only in reference to the unique context in which they are expressed.

For example, suppose that a student ignores a teacher's command to stop talking. Depending on classmates' views of the teacher, their history of experience with that student, and what else is occurring in the classroom when the teacher utters his command, some students might regard the talking student as a troublemaker, while others might see him as a buddy or hero or make no judgment at all.

According to criticalists, any educational phenomenon can be subjected to contextual analysis to determine how it reflects power relations. For example, Peter McLaren (2003) argues that multiculturalism—a movement aimed at improving relationships among students of different cultures and increasing their conformance to society's educational expectations—is still largely a mainstream, progressive agenda, exceedingly important but conceptually and politically compromised from the start.

A critical ethnography by Joan Parker-Webster (2001) illustrates the problems that educators can encounter in their attempts to implement multicultural themes in reading and language arts curricula.

Parker-Webster found vastly different understandings between white and African American teachers in a staff development program about what themes should be incorporated into the curricula. For example, she quotes a white teacher, Sandra: "So, anything that's different than what you live normally would mean multicultural. You know, just like, you know, the um, homosexual thing" (p. 44). Parker-Webster comments: "This response reflects the tension between Sandra's outwardly liberal stance that embraces differences, and her deep-seated belief that emphasizes sameness" (p. 44) as the core of what multiculturalism should be about.

The Value-Laden Nature of Knowledge

Criticalists believe that facts can never be isolated from the domain of values and prevailing assumptions about what is valued. Thus, they reject the notion that research about teaching and learning can ever be a neutral or value-free process. Indeed, critical researchers question the notion of objective reality itself. Like other qualitative researchers, critical researchers believe that all so-called facts about human nature and behavior are socially constructed and thus are open to many interpretations and modifiable through human action.

Critical research is sometimes associated with postmodernism. In Chapter 1 we explain that **postmodernism** is a philosophy based on the assertion that no one approach to developing knowledge about the human world is privileged over (that is, better than) any other. Consistent with this view, critical researchers are skeptical of any theory or method that claims to have timeless or universal application to understanding or improving the human condition. However, they remain committed to forms of social inquiry and action that promote the emancipation of nonprivileged individuals and groups, thereby affirming what Kincheloe and McLaren (1994) call "resistance postmodernism" (p. 144).

Critical researchers also argue that ideas about teaching and learning always involve preformed systems of values and beliefs, which usually reinforce the power of dominant groups in society. Some critical researchers (Apple, 2003) claim that even the most seemingly "common-sense" educational concepts, such as achievement, reform, innovation, and standards, are categories constructed by, and serving the interests of, privileged groups in the educational hierarchy.

The Role of Capitalist Culture in Framing Knowledge

Criticalists believe that every human "text" can be interpreted in relation to the cultural context of capitalist production and consumption. In critical research, the term **text** refers to any object, event, or instance of discourse that possesses communicative value. For a criticalist, the form and content of most texts reflect the values of the dominant culture and therefore are consistent with standards derived from a capitalist value framework.

Viewing most texts in education and research as problematic (that is, tending to misrepresent an individual's lived experience), criticalists subject such texts to deconstruction. **Deconstruction** is the critical analysis of texts based on the assumption that a text has no fixed meaning and that unrestricted efforts to interpret a text can yield multiple and often contradictory meanings. In deconstructing a teacher's letter to her students' parents, for example, a critical researcher would examine possible connotations of each term, opening the text to multiple interpretations, with none privileged over any other.

Consider professional sports as an example of a cultural text to be deconstructed. Most people regard football games and golf tournaments on television as a form of entertainment and a road to riches for a few outstanding athletes. Now consider the following deconstruction (Bourdieu, 1991):

> More than by the encouragement it gives to chauvinism and sexism, it is undoubtedly through the division it makes between professionals, the virtuosi of an esoteric technique, and laymen, reduced to the role of mere consumers, a division that tends to become a deep structure of the collective consciousness, that sport produces its most decisive political effects. (p. 364)

For criticalists, professional sports also highlight numerous issues of oppression that need much further examination—such as the extent of violence both during games and in the personal lives of some athletes, physical ailments that may arise for athletes in later life, and the difficulty for the average fan to afford a ticket to a professional sporting event.

Critical researchers are at the forefront in investigating educational influences in society beyond those of schools, particularly the products of popular corporate culture. Increasingly, the common discourse and interests of young people (and perhaps most people) lie in what is loosely called the "entertainment media," including movies, songs, advertising, videos, and blogs all made even more accessible with computers and tablets. In *Kinderculture: The Corporate Construction of Childhood*, Shirley Steinberg and Joe Kincheloe (1997) argue that the prevailing economic and technological climate in the United States has created a crisis of childhood through the increasing role of corporations as educators of young people and the growing presence of corporate products, images, and messages within as well as outside of schools.

Steinberg and Kincheloe make a strong case that the impact of corporate culture on education requires a new response from educators who have embraced traditional forms of cultural transmission. Paolo Freire (1974) refers to these traditional forms as the banking model of learning, in which knowledge is "deposited" into passive students' minds and then is expected to be displayed, or "withdrawn," at the teacher's request. Freire, who educated and encouraged the activism of laborers in his native Brazil, "created a notion of teaching as mining where first and foremost the teachers [sic] responsibility is to pull knowledge out—to build upon the knowledge students bring to the pedagogical situation" (Hughes, 2008, p. 249).

Like the signs described in Michael Wesch's video "A Vision of Students Today" (discussed earlier in the chapter), criticalists have found that factors like debt, poverty, and huge impersonal lecture classes are central to the educational experience of many students in today's institutions of higher learning (Young, 2007). They believe that educators at every level need to examine and address how these factors might hamper students' motivation and learning.

The Role of Cultural Texts in Maintaining Privilege

Cultural texts (including but not limited to language) are probably the most powerful means of expressing and maintaining differences in privilege. Criticalists view any discourse, object, or event as having communicative value and thus as being able to be analyzed as a text.

Criticalists claim that individuals' awareness can be expanded or constrained by the texts they experience and use to encode their experience. The formal and informal language in classrooms (including body language, gestures, or the absence of response) and instructional programs involving different forms of discourse (such as bilingual education or whole-language instruction) are examples of how educators use different forms of text to maintain or contest hegemony.

Critical researchers use the concept of *voice* to study texts that express domination or oppression in the educational system (Giroux, 1992). **Voice** refers to the degree to which the communications of individuals occupying particular social identities are privileged, silenced, muted, or empowered through discourses that maintain or contest dominant and subordinate cultures in a society.

In her book on critical pedagogy, Joan Wink (2000) uses the concept of conscientization to suggest how marginalized voices can be brought to the forefront of public discourse. **Conscientization**, a term coined by Paolo Freire in his book *Pedagogy of the Oppressed* (1974), is a process by which individuals come to understand their role in maintaining cultural processes that are not consistent with their basic values and subsequently to find voice to question and change their role.

Wink uses an example of conscientization about family involvement to illustrate teachers' need to have "voice and the courage to question ourselves and the role we are playing in maintaining educational processes that we do not value" (p. 37). Rainey and Carmen, two teachers in a school with a high proportion of Latino students, were discussing what their students' families needed. Rainey was a new teacher who had never been around Mexican children before but really wanted to help them learn. Carmen taught in Spanish and had been around Mexican children all her life. During their talk, Rainey said she could do a computer search of the university's library holdings to identify what Latino families need. Carmen nodded and then added, "Or, we could ask the families" (p. 41). At the next family meeting, the teachers asked, and the families told them their needs.

In our view, this example of exploring family needs does not discount research. Rather, it expresses the importance of teachers doing research directly with the parents and students who are their clients instead of relying solely on knowledge available in mainstream research literature. (This type of research, called action research, is discussed

in Chapter 18.) Wink's book gives numerous examples of how teachers' actions, particularly their use of language in interactions with students, can empower or disempower specific individuals every day.

The Contribution of Criticalist Thinking to Research

The eight assumptions presented above reveal how criticalists think about the purpose of research. On the one hand, they assume that cultural oppression has widespread effects on society, including the broader research community. On the other hand, they seek to balance their criticism with a deep hope and belief that the emancipation of nonprivileged groups will improve the lives of all groups and individuals. Critical researchers also question the authority of their own emancipatory agenda by deconstructing their statements expressing that agenda. They emphasize that no issue has one essential, universal answer, but that a key role of education is to encourage continual questioning and discussion of the meaning and impact of each issue.

Some individuals denounce critical research as promoting a negative view of capitalism, of the worldwide spread of the market culture, and of the politics of the United States and other Western societies. Although it shares with Marxism a critique of the inequities of the capitalist system, critical research promotes democratic principles as the best way to discover and correct these inequities, standing "in opposition to crude material or economic determinism" (Seymour-Smith, 1986, p. 59).

FOUNDATIONS OF CRITICAL RESEARCH IN EDUCATION

We now move to a discussion of the major foundations, theoretical orientations, and design characteristics of critical research in education. We start by describing two bodies of inquiry within the critical research tradition that have had a significant impact on education—cultural studies and critical pedagogy. Then we briefly consider the central role of theory in critical research. The rest of the chapter presents the qualitative research tradition of critical ethnography, which represents a blending of the traditions of ethnography and critical research.

Cultural Studies

Cultural studies involves the exploration of the economic, legal, political, and other socially constructed underpinnings of cultural phenomena (Nelson, Treichler, & Grossberg, 1992) while deconstructing many aspects of capitalist culture. Cultural studies pays particular attention to works of literature, art, and history as sources to be examined.

Many of the writings of cultural studies researchers are quite abstract and do not appear to involve fieldwork. However, cultural studies has direct relevance to educational practice. Their analyses often include critiques of the settings (e.g., schools, universities) and genres (e.g., conferences, journals) in which educators carry out their work.

The cultural categories of gender and race are specialized fields of study within cultural studies. Feminist research, sometimes called **feminisms** to reflect its diverse foci and methods, involves the study of how the cultural meanings that circulate through females' everyday lives shape their lived cultures and experiences (Olesen, 1994). Some critical feminists have identified and deconstructed cultural texts, such as films and popular literature, that depict women mainly as (1) sexual objects for men but also (2) responsible for domesticity, housework, child rearing, and care giving while still being considered (3) the weaker or secondary sex and (4) normally as well as normatively heterosexual (Agger, 1992). Later in the chapter, we discuss an example of critical feminist research concerning the depiction of young women's sexuality in an educational context.

With respect to race, cultural studies researchers have carried out research on each of the commonly identified racial or ethnic groups. Though members of the cultural groups being studied have conducted some of this research, white researchers have conducted the majority. According to African American scholar John Stanfield II (1994), the dominance of what he calls "mainstream researchers" in this line of investigation have tended to misinterpret their findings and to conceal, rather than highlight, the contributions of nonwhite racial and ethnic groups to society. Stanfield argues that mainstream researchers have sought to fit their analyses of African American culture into "the more orthodox norms of social scientific communities" (p. 177) and thus have "ignored, marginalized, or reinterpreted" (p. 177) the very aspects of African American intellectuals' lives that are the most empowering and normative.

The **norms** to which Stanfield refers can be defined as unstated sets of rules and assumptions that guide individuals' beliefs and social acts, in this case, those of mainstream (that is, white) intellectuals. Stanfield urges divergence away from those norms, including previous mainstream forms of investigation, and toward the use of indigenous qualitative methods that draw from the cosmos of people of color. For example, he recommends "the collection of oral histories that allow the examined people of color to articulate holistic explanations about how they construct their realities" (p. 185). He also urges researchers engaged in such research to discard their own notions of time, space, and spirituality in order to grasp the meaning of indigenous people's stories.

A new thread of cultural studies, initiated by the U.S. Army during the Iraq War, also has educational implications. This research is intended to improve U.S. military personnel's understanding of, and hence their effectiveness in working with, individuals and cultural groups in countries where U.S. troops are deployed. According to Anna Mulrine (2008), the University of Foreign Military and Cultural Studies at Fort Leavenworth installed its first team of graduates (nicknamed the Red Team) in Baghdad. Mulrine reports:

> The Red Teamers' job . . . involves questioning prevailing assumptions to avoid "getting sucked into that groupthink" . . . having someone inside that says, "Wait a minute, not so fast." (p. 30)

For example, the Red Teamers investigated the impact of using dogs in U.S. military operations in Iraq, a culture in which citizens generally regard dogs as unclean and, occasionally, evil. Another task involved identifying what Iraqis considered to be their own "greatest generation," similar to how people in the United States tend to regard its World War II veterans.

Lt. Col. Ragland, the Red Team commander, reported that he got little support when he proposed employing 12-year-old Iraqis to do odd jobs, "a practice contrary to U.S. child labor laws" (Mulrine, 2008, p. 32). He continues:

> We have a preconceived image of an American 12-year-old. But in Iraq, they may be, in everything but age, the head of the household—engrossed in the economy, governance, day-to-day life. . . . We've mirror-imaged it. (p. 32)

According to Mulrine, the policy of not hiring 12-year-olds "perhaps ceded some chance to help and influence everyday Iraqis" (p. 32).

This example illustrates some of the issues that cultural studies researchers face and how their learning helps them confront and attempt to resolve different values and biases within their own culture and other cultures.

Critical Pedagogy

Because of its commitment to foster emancipation from oppression, critical research in education is closely connected to educational practice. Here, we define **critical pedagogy** as teaching practices that are based on critical research and that include the use of various methods to empower students and help them understand freedom, authoritarianism, the connection between knowledge and power, and the value of social justice.

One example of critical pedagogy is the work of the James and Grace Lee Boggs Center in Detroit (boggscenter.org). According to the center directors, their form of critical pedagogy is appropriate for most types of educational institutions. One focus of their critical pedagogy is the sponsorship of community-building activities designed to motivate all of the community's children to learn and at the same time reverse the physical deterioration of its neighborhoods. These efforts include community gardening, mural painting programs, and other ways to build a foundation for systems change.

An activist for over 60 years, Grace Lee Boggs (1998) finds hope in her observation that "the new generation, which is beginning to discover its mission, is more open than the generation that led the movement in the 1960s" (p. 272). In another publication, Boggs (2003) argues that we must be the change that we want to see in the world:

> Children need to be given a sense of the unique capacity of human beings to shape and create reality in accordance with conscious purposes and plans. Learning . . . is not something you can make people do in their heads with the perspective that years from now they will be able to get a good job and make a lot of money. (p. 5)

Boggs continues to promote critical pedagogy through the center and her worldwide networking efforts. A recent article in the *Christian Science Monitor* about the numerous community programs building gardens in Detroit's vacant land parcels gives credit to the Boggs Center for beginning the urban garden movement (Bonfiglio, 2008).

THE ROLE OF THEORY IN CRITICAL RESEARCH

Critical research emphasizes theory to explain society and explore approaches to foster the emancipation of oppressed groups. For example, Henry Giroux (1988) developed a body of critical theory that can be applied to education in the United States and other Western cultures. Giroux's theory begins with the assumption that U.S. public education is in crisis. He sees this condition reflected most clearly in the contrast between hegemonic rhetoric that equates U.S. culture with democracy in its ultimate form and increasing indicators of the falsity of this rhetoric. As examples, he cites decreasing voter participation (though this trend was reversed in the 2008 presidential election), rising illiteracy rates among the general population, and a growing opinion among U.S. citizens that social criticism and social change are irrelevant to the maintenance of U.S. democracy.

Giroux seeks to replace the "politics of difference" that he views as characteristic of most standard dialogue about educational problems and solutions. In his view, standard educational dialogue favors a focus on the "democratic" treatment of difference. As a result, it can exhibit one of two oppressive tendencies. The first tendency involves the implication that individuals in certain cultural categories are superior to others—for example, old to young, heterosexual to homosexual, or able to disabled—because of inherent cultural or individual factors that presumably demonstrate and justify their supposed superiority.

The second tendency encourages students to buy into the notion of sameness—that cultural differences are irrelevant and thus should be ignored (as in the old notion of "color blindness") or actively eliminated. This second tendency promotes the view that school, and American society overall, is basically a "melting pot," in which cultural differences should be erased over time in the interests of promoting social harmony.

By contrast, Giroux proposes a postmodern, liberatory theory of critical pedagogy termed **border**

pedagogy. Consistent with the term *border*, this pedagogy reflects the theory that cultural differences between individuals and groups are permeable and changing, not captured in the rigid either-or nature of conventional social categories. Thus, in exploring cultural phenomena, this theory rejects both the concepts of better-worse and of sameness as the basis for describing or valuing the cultural characteristics of different individuals or cultural groups.

Giroux contends that "the struggle over public schools cannot be separated from the social problems currently facing this society. These problems are not only political in nature but are pedagogical as well" (1992, p. 199). He advocates that schools and pedagogy would be organized around a sense of purpose that makes the centrality of difference a critical notion of citizenship and democratic public life. In the pedagogy envisioned by this theory, educators at all levels of schooling would engage in redefining the nature of intellectual work and inquiry itself. The goal would be for educators and their students to "become knowledgeable and committed actors in the world" (1988, p. 208).

Giroux argues that if his theory were seriously applied in schools, students would no longer study unified subjects like reading, language arts, or science. Instead, they would explore the "borderlands" between diverse cultural histories as sites for critical analysis, experimentation, creativity, and possibility. Students would explicitly study the sources and effects of power in their own experience, seeking to understand how forms of domination are historically and socially constructed. Teachers would explore the ways in which they can use their authority to aid students' emancipation from internalized oppression and external sources of domination. Finally, students would be educated to read critically the ways in which various forms of discourse regulate the cultural texts that they encounter as learners and to see the different ideological interests that such texts express.

The work of Grace Lee Boggs, Henry Giroux, Anna Mulrine, and John Stanfield II are important contributions to the field of critical pedagogy. Other critical theorists whose work was reviewed by Wink (2000) also have contributed to the development of critical pedagogy as a focus for research and as an approach to solving problems of practice in education.

FEATURES OF A CRITICAL ETHNOGRAPHIC RESEARCH REPORT

Critical ethnography is a structured approach to critical research in which the research methods of ethnography are used to study power relationships and forms of oppression within particular cultures. We illustrate these research methods by describing a research study conducted by Phil Carspecken (1996). He evaluated Project TRUST, a school extraction program (also known as a pull-out program) for low-achieving students exhibiting a high level of school mobility. Project TRUST was established by Robert, one of Carspecken's former students in the school where Robert then served as vice principal.

Carspecken's description of Project TRUST includes all of the stages in his model of critical ethnography, and it describes problems that are still characteristic of many schools today. More recent critical ethnographies, generally less comprehensive in their design, have been carried out by Carspecken's students (Carspecken & Walford, 2001).

Introduction

Carspecken's report begins with a description of West Forest School (a pseudonym), an elementary school serving a low-income neighborhood in Houston that had previously served white middle-class families. After a severe downturn in the local economy, this school absorbed a large number of impoverished minority students who showed a high mobility rate from one school to another.

Robert, the school's vice principal, set up an extraction program that pulled the low-income students out of class to reduce the frequency of classroom disruptions. Carspecken commented:

> Robert was well aware of the fact that extraction policies often damage students through stigmatization, but he thought this risk could be ameliorated by keeping the TRUST students up-to-date on their academic programs and returning them to the normal classrooms as soon as possible. (p. 32)

Robert also wanted to raise the students' self-awareness and self-esteem and improve their conflict resolution skills while they were in the extraction program.

Carspecken claims that such programs usually seek to *control* disruptive students more than they actually *help* them. He wanted to see if that generalization applied to Project TRUST, but also "to understand more about the effects of extraction as well as refine our present understanding of power, culture, identity, and social reproduction" (p. 28). The school administration saw Carspecken's role as simple—"to find out whether or not TRUST worked" (p. 33). Carspecken viewed his role as more complex: to determine if disruption rates were in fact curbed by TRUST and if conflict resolution skills and self-esteem were higher after students' participation in TRUST.

Before entering the field, critical ethnographers specify their research questions. They also explore their value orientations so that they can make their biases explicit and consider how to counter them. Carspecken sought to formulate general, flexible questions while being fairly comprehensive. He listed the topics in which he was interested: the procedure for assigning students to Project TRUST; what was taught and learned in the TRUST classroom; and the project's relationship to the school, the neighborhood, and broader socioeconomic forces. His report focuses on using the Project TRUST research findings to illustrate his recommendations for carrying out the various design elements of a critical ethnography.

Research Design, Sampling, Measures, and Results

Carspecken's (1996) methodology for a critical ethnography involves five stages.

Stage One: Monological Data Collection

Monological data collection means that only the researcher "speaks" at this stage, writing the primary record from the etic perspective of a relatively uninvolved observer. The record comprises a thick description of field participants' verbal and nonverbal behavior.

The researcher thereby seeks to produce objective data that are similar to what other observers would likely obtain if they carried out the same study. Such data are intended to support **objective truth claims**, which are assertions that the researcher considers to be valid. The claims are open to multiple access, meaning that they can be understood and tested for validity by other observers.

To produce this type of data during Stage One, the researcher uses low-inference vocabulary, frequent time notations, occasional bracketed observer comments, context information, and italics for verbatim speech acts. These data enable the researcher to compare information obtained from the researcher's (etic) perspective during Stage One with data obtained during Stage Three, which seeks the participants' (emic) perspective.

Carspecken provides a rich introduction to Project TRUST, describing the crumbling neighborhood surrounding the school and the idealism and commitment he observed in a white teacher named Alfred. Carspecken's thick description of the Project TRUST classroom includes a diagram of the room's arrangement and detailed notes on student interactions that he observed.

Carspecken also provides monological data based on a detailed account of the interaction between Samuel, a student of mixed African American and white ethnicity, and the teacher, Alfred, at a point when the class was supposed to begin taking a test. The following description lists several highlights from the account:

- descriptions of participants' actions (e.g., "Samuel throws test on the floor. Hums a cheerful song." (p. 53)
- student and teacher comments in italics (e.g., from Alfred, "*We're at a critical point.*") and the researcher's low-inference descriptions (e.g., for Alfred, "Tone still calm.") (p. 54)
- two observer comments noting the researcher's interpretations of specific statements from participants (e.g., for Alfred, "As if, 'You know what is going on as well as I do, you are just refusing to talk about it. But I am patient.") (p. 54)

These excerpts represent the researcher's efforts to describe expressions of power as the teacher and student argue about taking the test.

Stage Two: Preliminary Reconstructive Analysis

Critical ethnographers next analyze the primary record to determine interaction patterns and their apparent meanings. **Reconstructive analysis** is the process of coding **meaning fields**, which are the possible intended meanings of participants' statements or nonverbal behavior that others in the setting might themselves infer. Coding begins at a low level of inference, as in the following example: "Reasons for not doing class work: (a) Sick, (b) 'Having a bad day,' (c) 'It's too hard'" (Carspecken, 1996, p. 148). Coding then moves to higher levels of inference: "Student conflicts: (a) Student reprimanding other student, (b) 'Your mama'" (p. 148). These codes clarify cultural themes and system factors that are derived from the primary record but that research participants rarely mention directly. Carspecken believes that the researcher "must become a 'virtual participant' in order to articulate the meaning fields" (p. 98).

Below is a segment of Carspecken's initial meaning reconstructions for the interaction between Samuel and Alfred referred to previously. The notation *A* designates the teacher Alfred, who is the subject of the entry; *OC* designates an observer's comment by the researcher; *MF* conveys the meaning field, which is the researcher's interpretation of possible meanings of the previous statement with (*OR*) used to indicate an alternate possible meaning.

A: Alfred looks up in Samuel's direction with placid, smooth facial features [OC: as if bland, nonchalant, "no big deal"].

A: *Samuel let's go now and take that test.* [OC: Addresses Samuel in matter-of-fact way, as if "no big deal, time to take the test, as we both know."]

[MF: *Alfred conveys social distance in his behavior; no greeting, no smile. He looks at papers first, then mentions the test implying that the test and his relationship with Samuel are just one of many things now on his mind. (OR) Alfred's actions indicate controlled nervousness. He is leery of beginning a conflict with Samuel and delays by looking at the papers*]. (p. 97)

During Stage Two, researchers also speculate about participants' **subjective truth claims**. These are the researcher's inferences about what an individual research participant would claim to be his or her specific thoughts and feelings.

During this stage, researchers also ask participants to generate positions that allow the researchers to infer participants' **normative-evaluative truth claims**, which are assertions about the social rightness, goodness, and appropriateness of various types of activities. During this stage, participants often express new or unanticipated comments compared to their comments during Stage One.

To illustrate Stage Two data, Carspecken presents a conversation between Alfred and Samuel about Samuel's home and family situation, involving questions about whether his mother was at home the previous night, where she went, and Samuel's beliefs and feelings about her possible actions while she was out. Examples of the truth claims that the researcher inferred from Alfred's comments in talking with Samuel are shown, in the format that the researcher depicted them.

Possible subjective claims

Foregrounded, Immediate
   "I care about you," "I want to understand you," "I want to help you cope with your problems"
Less Foregrounded, Less Immediate
   "I am a kind and caring teacher" (identity claim), "I am sincere"

Possible objective claims

Quite Foregrounded, Quite Immediate
   "Events are occurring in your home that many children would report as upsetting"
Highly Backgrounded, Remote, Taken-for-Granted
   "You live in a home," "You live with other people—mother and grandmother" (OR— just possible) "Black families have many domestic problems"

Possible normative-evaluative claims

Quite Foregrounded, Quite Immediate
   "It is good to talk about feelings"
Less Foregrounded, Less Immediate
   (OR) "Your mother's behavior is bad" (Carspecken, 1996, p. 112).

Inferring meaning involves **hermeneutics**, which is the study of how people interpret written texts and oral and nonverbal communication. Given the above interaction as an illustration, each specific comment by Alfred represents a part, and all of Alfred's comments and nonverbal behavior during the recorded episode represent the whole.

Carspecken (1996) describes the entire process of interpretation of the meaning of a text as the **hermeneutic circle**. This process includes five features that "raise awareness of an inference process we all employ tacitly in everyday life" (p. 102).

These features are explained from the researcher's perspective in the following list.

1. Taking the position of the participant, by imagining oneself in the participant's situation and "occupying virtually the positions of the others in the setting" (p. 99) in order to interpret the meaning of the situation.

2. Becoming culturally familiar with different research participants so as to be able to recognize specific statements as culturally typical or "uniquely constructed from culturally typical interactions" (p. 99).

3. Reflecting on the cultural norms the researcher employs in efforts to define the typical cultural representations of research participants. As an example, Alfred remains silent when Samuel does not begin taking the test after Alfred's second comment. Carspecken speculates that Alfred's silence means either that he is uncertain what to do next or that he wants Samuel to sense that he needs to respond or that he wants Samuel to understand that a sanction will occur unless he responds. Then the researcher tests these possible cultural norms by examining previous data involving the same research participants or collecting additional data on them.

4. Making tacit comparisons between the norms that the researcher claims as valid and those that individual research participants apparently claim as valid. For example, Alfred tends to wait longer to respond than Carspecken considers to be the norm. The researcher would need to make repeated observations of Alfred to confirm or disconfirm this inference.

5. Distinguishing between the effects of individual personality patterns (e.g., vocal tones and facial expressions) and culturally determined patterns in the observed behaviors of specific research participants.

Stage Three: Dialogical Data Generation

At Stage Three, researchers begin **dialogical data generation**, which is the process of creating a dialogue in which researchers help participants explore issues using their own vocabulary, metaphors, and ideas. These dialogical data are used to test the validity of the subjective and normative-evaluative truth claims that the researcher has posited to be characteristic of particular research participants.

Researchers need to specify interview questions for each topic area of interest, including (1) "lead-off questions, each designed to open up a topic domain" (Carspecken, 1996, p. 157), (2) "covert" questions that researchers do not want to ask explicitly because they could lead the interview too much but that they want the interviewee to address, and (3) possible follow-up questions, to ensure that the research participant has said enough about each topic area.

Researchers' responses to participants' statements can range on a 6-point scale from "1. bland encouragement" to "6. high-inference paraphrasing." The higher the number, the less often the researcher should use that response. The resulting data often challenge information from previous stages and give the participants more control over the research process, as Carspecken emphasizes:

> Interviews and group discussions produce many subjective truth claims: claims that people believe, feel, intend, value, and experience various things within a realm closed off to others . . . the realm of privileged access. We depend on honest and accurate self-reports to learn about the subjective states of others. (1996, p. 165)

Carspecken lists procedures for strengthening Stage Three claims: (1) checking whether the individual was consistent in comments made during recorded interviews, (2) interviewing the same individuals repeatedly, (3) engaging in member checks (see Chapter 13), and (4) using nonleading interview techniques.

The process of giving individuals a strong voice in this research process can be challenging for researchers. For this reason, Carspecken believes that researchers must remain open to being "wounded" through fieldwork, because what one learns "is going to effect [sic] you existentially" (p. 169). He adds:

> The more we reduce those modes of power that prevent all people from having an equal voice, the more open we must be to existential threats. But being "wounded" through conducting research with integrity is ultimately going to be more empowering for us because it will change us, broaden our horizons, help us grow as human beings. (1996, p . 170)

In this approach to critical ethnography, then, the researchers, in addition to the participants, have opportunities to experience personal growth and empowerment.

Stage Four: Discovering System Relationships

Carspecken's description of the Project TRUST research findings is not confined to a particular stage of his model. Here we give a brief summary.

With respect to reducing classroom disruptions, Project TRUST appears to have had some success. Two field journal entries from Carspecken's primary record during Stage One state: "Last year at this same date Robert had 600 referrals, this year he has had only half that number" (1996, p. 51). "Those present commented that disruption referrals have gone down since TRUST began because it is viewed as a stigma to go there" (p. 51).

One of the goals that school administrators had for Project TRUST was for students to learn conflict resolution skills. Carspecken provides some affirmative evidence. Specifically, he observed some teacher-student interactions in which "conflicts were resolved noncoercively" (p. 152). He also found evidence that students "had actually internalized covert messages about self and choice" (p. 152), based on observations of student-student interactions "when students used expressions in nonclassroom contexts that I had seen Alfred teach them" (p. 152).

We found no specific discussion of changes in students' self-esteem based on their participation in Project TRUST.

During Stage Four, researchers compare the findings from the specific site being investigated with findings from other sites involving a similar research focus. In this manner, they discover system relationships, that is, broad similarities that reveal common cultural features in the behavior of participants across different sites. Such system relationships appear similar to cross-case generalizability (see Chapter 13) because they allow readers to determine the extent to which the findings from one site are applicable to other sites.

In Project TRUST, one system relationship is how individual students sought to renegotiate stressful classroom settings by their expressed dominance of, or subordination to, other students. For example, the behavior in school of Samuel, a mixed-race student living with a white mother and white grandmother, was characterized by a system relationship that Carspecken calls *cultural isomorphisms*. As reflected in Project TRUST, cultural isomorphisms involved research participants'

efforts to change the interactive pattern of the school setting to more closely resemble the outside culture in which they felt more comfortable. For example, according to Carspecken, Samuel "frequently employed themes learned from home to defend himself from feelings of low self-respect in school" (p. 198). When attempting to renegotiate stressful classroom settings, such as teacher efforts to explain academic concepts, "Samuel would often bid for a session of chit-chat on themes that were rewarding for him at home . . . where the rules for a positive identity were under his control" (p. 198).

In analyzing the system relationships found in the Project TRUST research, Carspecken refers to Paul Willis's classic study (1977) of working-class "lads," one of the first critical ethnographies ever conducted. Willis discovered correspondences, which he termed *reproductive loops*, between the lads' behavior in three different social sites—school, home, and job setting. He found that the lads sought to avoid activities in school (e.g., doing the assigned work) that could conceivably help them move out of the working class into the middle class but which the lads viewed as a rejection of their home-based culture. Willis also observed that all of the lads' fathers had stayed within the working class in seeking work, and then the lads, in turn, moved into jobs involving physical labor when they left school.

Stage Five: Seeking Explanations of the Findings through Social-Theoretical Models

At this stage, the level of inference rises as the researcher explores how the interests and power relations discovered at Stage Four can serve as explanatory factors. In the Project TRUST research, Carspecken discovered parallels between Willis's study and the efforts of TRUST participants to negotiate their cultural heritage in a way that provided some opportunity to maintain dignity and self-respect. For example, Carspecken reports that Project TRUST students favored video games, TV shows, and types of popular music depicting violence, race relations, and traditional gender stereotypes. Carspecken interprets the themes of these media elements as reflecting the harsh living conditions of most families in Park Forest and the surrounding community. He notes the efforts of the TRUST students to challenge those conditions by talking tough and tending to glamorize violence, which in

effect duplicate the very conditions they are seeking to challenge.

Carspecken ties these themes and insights together by Willis's theoretical construct of reproduction. In this context, reproduction means that
individuals act in a manner consistent with broadly
distributed conditions, particularly the existing
long-term social systems of which they are a part.
Thus, the Project TRUST findings show how the
students accept, and behave consistently with, the
oppressive cultural patterns of their society.

In Willis's study, the history of family employment experienced by the parents of the lads was part
of a social system that the lads reproduced through
their behavior during and after their schooling.
Social systems are thus human activities, like work,
that have become patterned and continue to exist
because they are continuously reproduced. Despite
some positive results of Project TRUST, Carspecken
found that the Project TRUST students, like Willis's
working class lads, largely reproduced the social
conditions that surrounded them.

Conclusion

Carspecken (1996) summarizes the cultural conditions characteristic of children from Project TRUST
as follows:

- having to grow up fast and to continually
  defend themselves physically
- school as a place they had to go to but not a
  place around which their plans could revolve
- school as a place dominated by others of
  different racial and class categories who sought
  to impose authority on students
- home as a source of harsh discipline,
  accompanied by parents' resistance to any efforts
  of others to dominate them

Carspecken also describes the effects of these
conditions:

> Thus these children negotiated for harsh author-
> ity relations at school (the only form of authority
> they respected) while simultaneously resisting
> vigorously any form of authority. The culture of
> the neighborhood was not conducive to success
> at school. School work was rarely supported
> in the home, and few adults known by these
> children owed anything to past schooling for
> whatever life successes they displayed. In the
> school, teachers like Alfred strived hard to help

these children but found their hands tied in
many ways. (p. 206)

Carspecken then depicts the circumstances of West
Forest even more broadly as tied to "the economic
system of the United States, the economic circumstances of Houston, the conjuncture of race and
class categories within our society, and the political power of the middle and upper-middle classes
to establish educational policies in their interests"
(p. 206).

Carspecken notes that during periods of economic decline, typically, lower-class people lose
jobs in large numbers and then are reabsorbed
into menial positions when the economy picks
up. He notes that state laws controlling curriculum
and pedagogy limit the school system's efforts to
prepare all students for well-paying jobs. He concludes: "Schools end up keeping children like those
in the TRUST study off the streets, but the students
[are] ill prepared to do anything but unskilled labor"
(p. 206).

EVALUATING ETHNOGRAPHIES AND CRITICAL ETHNOGRAPHIES

Research conducted by ethnographers and criticalists is grounded in qualitative methods of inquiry.
Therefore, you can evaluate their research studies
using the questions in Appendix 3.

Ethnographers and criticalists typically focus
on selected cases as they seek to understand a
culture or the power relationships within a society.
Therefore, you can evaluate their case research by
using the strategies to evaluate the quality and rigor
of a case study described in Chapter 13.

The distinction between the emic and etic perspectives is particularly important in ethnographies
and critical ethnographies. Therefore, you should
evaluate how well these perspectives were represented during data collection and analysis. The following are several questions for you to consider as
you read research reports of this type.

- Does the report include an emic perspective?

  Examine the report for evidence that
  researchers took care to collect data about the
  participants' view of their own culture and
  their role in it. Examples of such evidence
  are quoted statements from participants, their
  writings and other forms of communication,
  and logs of their activities.

■ Does the report include an etic perspective? Examine the report for evidence that the researchers engaged in self-reflection about their personal values and beliefs concerning the phenomena being studied. The researchers also should try to identify personal biases that might distort their data collection and analysis. These reflections should occur during all phases of the study and especially when the phenomena are controversial or markedly different from the researchers' own background and experiences.

An example of
How Ethnography and Critical Research Can Help in Solving Problems of Practice

Many school districts allow high school students to take courses at a nearby community college or university if the high school does not offer the course and the student is capable of doing the work. A school district in North Carolina has taken this practice to a new level by opening a school within a community college for selected high school students. The local newspaper describes the experience of one student in the program:

> Antonio Hernandez-Blanco was doing well at Phillip O. Berry Academy of Technology, a magnet school with academic admission standards. But when he seized the chance to move to Cato Middle College High as a junior, he found himself in a whole new environment.
>
> Now he's among 200 high school students, all capable of doing college-level work, who share classrooms with older students at Central Piedmont Community College. It's exciting and a bit humbling, says Antonio, a 17-year-old senior.

> Helms, A. D. (2013, February 14). CMS finds success with blend of high school, college. *The Charlotte Observer*. Retrieved from http://www.charlotteobserver.com/2013/02/11/3842303/cms-finds-success-with-blend-of.html

From an ethnographic perspective, this type of school is interesting because it positions high school students within two different cultures—a community college and the school (called Cato Middle College) located within the community college. The high schoolers mingle with their peers but also with traditional community college students.

How well is this arrangement working? What problems, if any, arise? These questions can be addressed by different research designs, including ethnography, as we explain below.

The focus of our ethnography will be on various types of interactions: within the group of high schoolers; between the high schoolers and their community college classmates; between the high schoolers and their instructors; and between the Cato Middle College administrators and the community college administrators and instructors. We want to know whether these interactions reflect shared norms and values. We also wish to know whether power conflicts arise between these different groups and whether there is a shared vision about what is best for the students.

We might choose to select a cohort of students starting their first term at Cato Middle College and follow them for one or two terms of study. We could consider taking on the participant-observer role of a community college student, taking the same classes as some of the high schoolers. We would observe their behavior and conversations among themselves and with other groups. We would interview them periodically, with an emphasis on eliciting positive features of their community college experience and conflicts, if any, as they arise. We also would conduct periodic interviews with administrators and instructors involved in their studies. We would inquire about the scheduling of formal meetings to discuss the administration of Cato Middle College, and we would seek permission to attend these meetings and make field notes.

Analysis of the data could be done by one of the methods used in qualitative research, for example, interpretational analysis or reflective analysis. The resulting ethnography should result in a thick description of the experiences of this special group of high school students. If power conflicts or other issues are discovered, the findings could help administrators improve the program. If all of the involved groups find value in Cato Middle College, our thick description of it can serve as the basis for developing a formal model of this type of schooling. The model can be used as is or adapted by other school districts around the United States to provide an enriched learning experience for students who can benefit from it.

SELF-CHECK TEST

1. Ethnographers focus on the study of culture because they believe that
   a. the influence of culture on human beings is what makes them unique as a species.
   b. the study of primitive cultures can show how Western cultures evolved.
   c. an increasing number of distinct cultures are emerging in the world.
   d. the similarities observed between people from different parts of the world are best explained in terms of cultural factors.
2. In providing a description of a cultural phenomenon, ethnographers generally seek to
   a. examine the phenomenon in more than one culture.
   b. emphasize the perspective of high-status members of the culture.
   c. use their own perspective to reconcile conflicting views of the phenomenon.
   d. balance emic and etic perspectives.
3. Some educational ethnographers view the typically lower academic performance of students from certain ethnic groups as being due to their tendency to withhold investment in education because they do not perceive it as having any economic payoff. This explanation views student performance as being determined primarily by
   a. cultural acquisition.
   b. cultural assimilation.
   c. school organization.
   d. teacher bias.
4. In the view of critical researchers, mainstream research practices have maintained cultural oppression primarily by
   a. neglecting the study of racial and ethnic minorities.
   b. upholding hegemonic assumptions about truth, science, and good.
   c. questioning the meaning of all texts.
   d. not distinguishing between the effects of class, race, and gender on individuals' cultural attainments.
5. Criticalists refer to the tendency of certain researchers to become preoccupied with means over ends or purposes as
   a. instrumental rationality.
   b. voice.
   c. cultural assimilation.
   d. deconstruction.
6. Hegemony refers to
   a. emancipatory methods as conceptualized by criticalists.
   b. a conception of social justice advocated by criticalists.
   c. differences among the emic perspectives of the members of a nonprivileged cultural group.
   d. the domination of nonprivileged cultural groups by privileged cultural groups.
7. Deconstruction of a text involves
   a. rephrasing it in language that culturally oppressed groups can understand.
   b. specifying the cultural themes and system factors reflected in it.
   c. asking the members of the culturally dominant group to clarify its meaning.
   d. examining its connotations and various possible meanings.
8. In critical ethnography, it is desirable to
   a. involve field participants in all phases of data collection.
   b. demonstrate consistency between the data collected through passive observation and

the data collected through dialogue with field participants.

c. analyze the findings from the specific research site in terms of existing or emergent theory about system relationships.

d. primarily collect data that meet objective truth claims.

9. A criticalist's deconstruction of a chapter of a high school textbook on U.S. history would most likely result in

a. identification of the actual meaning of the text.

b. identification of multiple, often contradictory, meanings of the text.

c. an interpretation consistent with mainstream views of U.S. history.

d. all of the above.

10. Conscientization is a process designed to

a. improve students' classroom behavior.

b. encourage individuals to question and change oppressive cultural practices.

c. promote more classroom activities involving multicultural themes.

d. all of the above.

CHAPTER REFERENCES

Agger, B. (1992). *Cultural studies as critical theory.* Washington, DC: Falmer.

Apple, M. W. (2003). *The state and the politics of knowledge.* New York, NY: RoutledgeFalmer.

Boggs, G. L. (1998). *Living for change: An autobiography.* Minneapolis, MN: University of Minnesota Press.

Boggs, G. L. (2003, January). *We must be the change.* Paper based on a presentation at the University of Michigan, 2003 Martin Luther King Symposium, Ann Arbor, MI. Retrieved from http://www.boggscenter.org

Bonfiglio, O. (2008, August 21). Detroit grows green. *Christian Science Monitor,* p. 17.

Borenstein, S. (2008, June 2). NASA's own watchdog: Agency misled on global warming. *Associated Press.* Retrieved from http://www.foxnews.com/wires/2008 Jun02/0,4670,NASACensor,00.html

Bourdieu, P. (1991). Sport and social class. In C. Mukerji & M. Schudson (Eds.), *Rethinking popular culture: Contemporary perspectives in cultural studies* (pp. 357–373). Berkeley, CA: University of California Press.

Carspecken, P. F. (1996). *Critical ethnography in educational research: A theoretical and practical guide.* New York, NY: Routledge.

Carspecken, P. F., & Walford, G. (Eds.). (2001). *Critical ethnography and education.* Oxford, UK: Elsevier Science.

Foster, K. M. (2004). Coming to terms: A discussion of John Ogbu's cultural-ecological theory of minority academic achievement. *Intercultural Education, 15*(4), 369–384.

Freire, P. (1974). *Pedagogy of the oppressed.* New York, NY: Seabury.

Gibson, R. (1986). *Critical theory and education.* London, UK: Hodder & Stoughton.

Giroux, H. A. (1988). Critical theory and the politics of culture and voice: Rethinking the discourse of educational research. In R. R. Sherman & R. B. Webb (Eds.), *Qualitative research in education: Focus and methods* (pp. 190–210). New York, NY: Falmer.

Giroux, H. A. (1992). Resisting difference: Cultural studies and the discourse of critical pedagogy. In L. Grossberg, C. Nelson, & P. A. Treichler (Eds.), *Cultural studies* (pp. 199–212). New York, NY: Routledge.

Hogan, K., & Corey, C. (2001). Viewing classrooms as cultural contexts for fostering scientific literacy. *Anthropology and Education Quarterly, 32,* 214–243.

Hughes, S. A. (2008). Teaching theory as "other" to white urban practitioners: Mining and priming Freirean critical pedagogy in resistant bodies. In J. Diem & R. J. Helfenbein (Eds.), *Unsettling beliefs: Teaching theory to teachers* (pp. 245–271). Charlotte, NC: Information Age.

Kincheloe, J., & McLaren, P. (1994). Rethinking critical theory and qualitative research. In N. K. Denzin & Y. S. Lincoln (Eds.), *Handbook of qualitative research* (pp. 138–157). Thousand Oaks, CA: Sage.

Kumashiro, K. (2002). *Troubling education: Queer activism and anti-oppressive pedagogy.* New York, NY: RoutledgeFalmer.

Lancy, D. F. (1993). *Qualitative research in education: An introduction to the major traditions.* White Plains, NY: Longman.

Madison, D. S. (2005). Critical ethnography as street performance: Reflections of home, race, murder, and justice. In N. K. Denzin & Y. S. Lincoln (Eds.), *The Sage handbook of qualitative research* (3rd ed., pp. 537–546). Thousand Oaks, CA: Sage.

Malinowski, B. (1922). *Argonauts of the Western Pacific.* New York, NY: Dutton.

McLaren, P. (1998). *Life in schools: An introduction to critical pedagogy in the foundations of education* (3rd ed.). New York, NY: Longman.

McLaren, P. (2003, February). Critical pedagogy in the age of neoliberal globalization: The domestication of political agency and the struggle for socialist futures. Paper presented at the workshop *Transnationalism, ethnicity, and the public sphere* at the Center for Critical Theory and Transnational Studies, University of Oregon, Eugene, OR.

Mead, M. (1930). *Growing up in New Guinea: A comparative study of primitive education.* New York, NY: William Morrow.

Mulrine, A. (2008, May 26). To battle groupthink, the army trains a skeptics corps. *U.S. News & World Report*, pp. 30, 32.

Nelson, C., Treichler, P. A., & Grossberg, L. (1992). Cultural studies: An introduction. In L. Grossberg, C. Nelson, & P. A. Treichler (Eds.), *Cultural studies* (pp. 1–22). New York, NY: Routledge.

Nieves, E. (2008, May 27). Food banks finding more clients, fewer donations. Mobile, AL: *Register-Guard*, pp. A-1, A-5.

Olesen, V. (1994). Feminisms and models of qualitative research. In N. K. Denzin & Y. S. Lincoln (Eds.), *Handbook of qualitative research* (pp. 158–174). Thousand Oaks, CA: Sage.

Parker-Webster, J. (2001). In P. F. Carspecken & G. Walford (Eds.), *Critical ethnography and education* (pp. 27–60). Oxford, UK: Elsevier Science.

Reavey, P. (Ed.). (2011). *Visual methods in psychology: Using and interpreting images in qualitative research.* New York, NY: Routledge.

Ross, S., & Agiesta, J. (2012, October 27). AP poll: Majority harbor prejudice against Blacks. *Associated Press.* Retrieved from http://bigstory.ap.org/article/ap-poll-majority-harbor-prejudice-against-blacks

Schwandt, T. A. (2001). *Dictionary of qualitative inquiry* (2nd ed.). Thousand Oaks, CA: Sage.

Seymour-Smith, C. (Ed.). (1986). *Dictionary of anthropology.* Boston. MA: G. K. Hall.

Spindler, G., & Spindler, L. (1992). Cultural process and ethnography: An anthropological perspective. In M. D. LeCompte, W. L. Millroy, & J. Preissle (Eds.), *Handbook of qualitative research in education* (pp. 53–92). San Diego, CA: Academic Press.

Stanfield, J. H. II (1994). Ethnic modeling in qualitative research. In N. K. Denzin & Y. S. Lincoln (Eds.), *Handbook of qualitative research* (pp. 175–188). Thousand Oaks, CA: Sage.

Steinberg, S., & Kincheloe, J. (1997). *Kinderculture: The corporate construction of childhood.* Boulder, CO: Westview.

Wax, M. (1993). How culture misdirects multiculturalism. *Anthropology and Education Quarterly, 24*, 99–115.

Willis, P. (1977). *Learning to labour: How working class kids get working class jobs.* London, UK: Gower.

Wink, J. (2000). *Critical pedagogy: Notes from the real world* (2nd ed.) Boston, MA: Addison-Wesley Longman.

Young, J. R. (2007). An anthropologist explores the culture of video blogging. *Chronicle of Higher Education, 53*(36).

RESOURCES FOR FURTHER STUDY

Anderson-Levitt, K. M. (Ed.). (2012). *Anthropologies of education: A global guide to ethnographic studies of learning and schooling.* New York, NY: Berghahn Books.

This book provides a "world tour" of ethnographic research about education as practiced in different parts of the world. The author discusses some surprises, disagreements, and deficiencies readers may encounter as they learn how scholars have adopted ethnographic inquiry to a wide range of political, historical, and cultural contexts. For example, one scholar critiques U.S.-based anthropology of education as overly focused on school failure among ethnic and racial minorities to the neglect of other important topics. This book will help broaden the perspective both of American and international ethnographers.

Anderson-Levitt, K. M. (2006). Ethnography. In J. L. Green, G. Camilli, & P. B. Elmore (Eds.), *Handbook of complementary methods in education research* (pp. 279–295). Mahwah, NJ: Lawrence Erlbaum.

The author provides a clear summary of the purpose and methods of ethnography and its history in education. The author discusses the ethnographer's responsibility to research participants and gives a brief overview of research design and analysis in ethnography.

Angrosino, M. V. (2005). Recontextualizing observation: Ethnography, pedagogy, and the prospects for a progressive political agenda. In N. K. Denzin & Y. S. Lincoln (Eds.), *The Sage handbook of qualitative research* (3rd ed., pp. 729–745). Thousand Oaks, CA: Sage.

The author analyzes the central and evolving role of observation in ethnographic research, its relevance to service learning as a pedagogy for social justice, and current postmodernist, ethical, and epistemological issues related to observational research.

Madison, D. S. (2012). *Critical ethnography: Method, ethics, and performance* (2nd ed.). Thousand Oaks, CA: Sage.

The author explains the purpose of critical ethnographies, methods for doing them, and ethical issues that must be considered. Extensive descriptions of actual critical ethnographies are used to illustrate these methods and issues. Also included are chapters on a specialized type of critical ethnography known as performance ethnography.

Vavrus, F., & Bartlett, L. (2009). *Critical approaches to comparative education: Vertical case studies from Africa, Europe, the Middle East, and the Americas.* New York, NY: Palgrave Macmillan.

Using multi-sited ethnographic approaches, scholars examine linkages among local, national, and international levels of educational policy and practice. Topics include participatory development, the politics of culture and language, neoliberal educational reforms, and education in post-conflict settings. The book reflects the need for a world-wide perspective to understand and practice educational ethnography.

Wink, J. (2011). *Critical pedagogy: Notes from the real world* (4th ed.). Boston: Pearson.

An academic who draws heavily on her own and other teachers' K–12 teaching experiences, the author provides a clear analysis of critical research applied to teaching and other aspects of educational practice. She explains the language of critical pedagogy and discusses the work of various scholars in the critical theory tradition. She also suggests many classroom activities to foster teachers' and students' empowerment.

Wolcott, H. F. (2010). Ethnography lessons: A primer. Walnut Creek, CA: Left Coast Press.

One of the pioneers of educational ethnography, the author systematically lays out essential lessons he has learned from decades of ethnographic research in many cultures. The book is packed with personal anecdotes and practical ideas for both the novice and experienced ethnographer.

Destination Raval Sud: A Visual Ethnography on Pedagogy, Aesthetics, and the Spatial Experience of Growing Up Urban

Trafí-Prats, L. (2009). Destination Raval Sud: A visual ethnography on pedagogy, aesthetics, and the spatial experience of growing up urban. *Studies in Art Education, 51*(1), 6–20. Available at http://eric.ed.gov/?id=EJ868008.

The study presented here represents a blend of visual ethnography and critical research. It presents and analyzes photographs taken by and of sixth-grade students as they explore the urban neighborhood in which their school, in Barcelona, Spain, is located. The research seeks to expand both students' and readers' understanding of the culture in which these students live and its relationship to their lives. The article includes narrative statements made by the students and the adult workers whom they encountered during their field trips around the city. The researcher seeks to engage her students in imaginative actions that cultivate forms of aesthetic relationality between children and the urbanized spaces within which they live, spaces that are being increasingly constrained by corporate privatization.

Destination Raval Sud: A Visual Ethnography on Pedagogy, Aesthetics, and the Spatial Experience of Growing Up Urban

LAURA TRAFÍ-PRATS
University of Wisconsin-Milwaukee
Peck School of the Arts
P.O. Box 413
Milwaukee, WI 53201
trafipra@uwm.edu
(414) 690 8963

ABSTRACT The article focuses on issues of childhood identity and urban environment. It discusses how a performance art pedagogy inspired by nomadic and relational aesthetics can provide a framework to promote creative learning experiences that address migratory conditions and forms of public alienation lived by young people today. As Lefebvre (1991) suggests, a group only can be recognized as distinctive from others when they have the capacity to generate space. Taking this idea as a starting point, this article holds an interdisciplinary perspective and connects ideas from fields outside art education including reconstructionist studies of childhood, contemporary aesthetics, and critical pedagogy. It studies how public places and spaces are imagined and transformed from a child-sensitive perspective, and how children are public cultural agents and creators of visual culture. This theoretical discussion is projected into the interpretation of a visual ethnographic study centered on visual strategies, field narratives, and outcomes of migrant children documenting their urban environment, El Raval Sud, an intercultural neighborhood situated in Barcelona's downtown.

Introduction

This article discusses the role of art education in enhancing aesthetic and social interconnections between urban children and contemporary urban environments. As Greene (1995) affirms, it requires imaginative actions to teach children who see different from their teachers because they have been reared in poverty or have come from distant places. Both the critical re-viewing of the knowledge that we conceive to be foundational to our discipline, and the involvement in interdisciplinary endeavors are prerequisites for these imaginative actions. Following this direction, the article interweaves a network of ideas inspired by reconstructionist studies of childhood, nomadic and relational aesthetics, and performance art pedagogy. The aim of this interdisciplinarity is to serve a pedagogy centered on producing knowledge in action, avoiding mystification, and opening new beginnings in relation to which young people feel valued as participants in dialogs, and other instances of public knowledge.

The article follows and extends Duncum's (2002) statement that art education should include more consistent and realistic views of children. Art education should engage in more significant ways in current sociological and humanistic debates on childhood identity. Art education needs further experimentation with pedagogies that overcome modernist ideas, like seeing children as abstract and universal projects of development towards adulthood, to understand them instead as individual agents who create and modify cultural meaning.

The article is also inspired by ideas of environmental education, and the role of the arts in teaching responsive and transformative pedagogies that enhance the relationships between subjects and their local environments (e.g., McFee and Deggee, 1980; Blandy & Hoffman, 1993; Congdon, 2004). Followers of this perspective maintain that art education has a social responsibility in bettering the quality of shared environment and to educate children with different cultural backgrounds to creatively cope with the complexities of today's changing and fast-evolving societies (McFee and Degee, 1980). In this respect, place-based art pedagogies support all kinds of people's creative, affective and aesthetic practices of place-making and spatial appropriation (Blandy 2008), even when those practices challenge acquired ideas about what counts as art in modern and contemporary history (Blandy & Congdom, 1998). They concentrate on local forms of knowledge, art and aesthetics rather than on models of globalized and standardized curriculum decided elsewhere (Graham, 2007).

The Spatiality of Growing Up

Reconstructionist studies of childhood emerged as a response to the multiple dissonances existing between the material experiences of being a child in the actual world and the institutional forms and discourses framing childhood. Theorists working in reconstructive practices of history, sociology, psychology, and pedagogy agree there exists not only one form of childhood, but different childhoods and children, existing as specifically located socio-constructions, and subject positions (Aries, 1962; Jencks, 1996; Cannella, 1997; Duncum, 2002; Cannella, Kincheloe & Anijar, 2002). "Biological facts of infancy are but the raw material upon which cultures work to fashion a particular version of being a child" (Jencks, 1996, p. 20). For this reason, reconstructionist studies contest language and images that naturalize, generalize and globalize a dominant Western understanding of childhood as an innocent adult-protected experience. This is a discourse that emerged in the eighteenth century and progressed through the later development of disciplines like pediatrics, psychology and pedagogy, which centered on the creation of a distinct type of specialized knowledge about children. In this history what stands for adult protection sometimes can be better re-named as regulation or control. While children are given rights and duties, they are also emptied of all responsibility, political agency or autonomy. Often children are spoken through the voices of their parents, teachers, doctors and other adult representatives, while their own voices are rarely heard.

Reconstructionist studies of childhood instead see children as competent agents and active creators of their own lives (Rassmussen & Smidt, 2003). They call for an increased reflexivity between adult researchers and pedagogues and younger participants. This reflexivity aims to displace the control of adults upon childhood's knowledge by envisioning ways to collaborate with children, that acknowledge children's different views and that help researchers and pedagogues to find new forms of knowledge and representation that help us speak on behalf of young people without manipulating their voices (Aitken, 2001).

In postindustrial metropolis organized through capitalist hierarchies, cities function as landscapes of power (Matthews, 2003), where public spaces are designed for the comfort and use of middle class adult professionals. Life is spatially separated between production (work) and reproduction (home). Children are either kept at home or sheltered in specifically designed spaces-for-childhood. Children in the street are barely understood anymore as a community of risk, they are otherwise represented as the risk itself. This representation especially affects working class and/or ethnically and sexually diverse childhoods.

The city as a landscape of power operates through a fragmentation of space and time. Children grow up learning to organize and manage the time-space itineraries that set the separated spheres of production and reproduction. Since in globalized capitalism the times of production are becoming more and more flexible, the time to come back home to the rituals of reproduction has been increasingly delayed. Families are obliged to buy private services, where institutionalized others cover parcels of the time for care and play. Consequently, families and children devote an important part of their lives commuting between disconnected islands where supposedly safe activities for children take place. How families and children decide on these itineraries and places, and how children enjoy more or less freedom of movement and decision to organize their leisure determines spatial conceptions that will become relevant for the rest of the child's life and will shape his/her own desire to find a way into his/her own places (Zeiher, 2003; Aitken, 2001).

Reconstructionist studies of childhood advocate that forms of spatial occupation of the street, including the performance of usual itineraries and social encounters in the neighborhood, is an essential element for the growth of children's social identity, and their senses of location and sociability (Christensen & O'Brien, 2003). Streets are liminal places to explore the spaces of growing up, to negotiate hybrid identities, to experiment ambivalence, and set a public identity (Matthew, 2003). In order to make urban knowledge, representation, and change to be child-sensitive, researchers and pedagogues are collaborating with children to gain knowledge and include them as co-authors of their studies.

Nomadic and Relational Aesthetics

It makes sense to interconnect contemporary issues about childhood and spatiality with theories of nomadic and relational aesthetics because both encompass critical reconsiderations of modernist notions of belonging, emplacement, movement, and identities and can support the transition from a universal idea of the child to situated and evolving conceptions of childhood.

Nomadic aesthetics are concerned with creative juxtapositions, unexpected encounters and forms of parody that open intermediate spaces within dominant cultures. They constitute a creative space to be strangers to ourselves, and a practice of healthy skepticism towards mother tongues, and permanent identities or places of origin and adscription. Nomadic aesthetics encompass a critical, anti-capitalist idea of movement and spatial occupation that gives visibility to marginal identities and practices (Braidotti, 1994).

In the age of globalization and digital technologies, space-time distances may have shrunk but current imperial politics make evident that freedom of movement is a privilege not a choice, which does not belong to everyone equally (Kwon, 2004). Subjects and communities from different parts of the world are displaced against their will, or are kept in walled territories, refugee camps or prisons with no possibility of movement (Durrant & Lord, 2007). Nomadic artists experiment with narrative as a vehicle for weaving stories of fragmentation, representing paradoxes like the desire to access specific places and the impossibility of entering or inhabiting them (Saoul, 2007). It seems that the experience of growing up in cities with limited or very controlled experiences of movement and transition contains many similarities with other geopolitical forms of spatial control. While the voices of children who are shaped by migratory experiences or who suffer social alienation are not heard in large public forums, they do have the need to express and connect contradictory, complex and disjoined experiences.

Nomadic aesthetics favor spatial metaphors like tracing and mapping that entail reflective and alternative practices of movement and transition. Space in nomadic aesthetics is a relational specificity made of dialogical tensions between different spatial experiences. It is about the subjective negotiation of the possibilities opened by new fluidities together with the ruptures and disconnections that those provoke (Kwon, 2004). Artists interested in the representation of this form of spatiality recreate localities "shaped by global dynamics, operating in different domains, so that every location must be understood as the provisional effect of its relation with other locations, and with the global processes linking them" (Hoving, 2007, p.179).

Nomadic aesthetics and relational aesthetics have points of connection because both envision alternative spatial and social relations. Relational aesthetics are a political project that "draws inspiration from the flexible processes governing ordinary life" (Bourriaud, 2002, p. 47). Relational aesthetics change modernist notions of value associated with the object and the hermeneutical mastery of the artist and the critic to focus on relational, durational, and cumulative processes of exchange and dialogue. This seems consistent with a model of research centered on the representation of urban space and life that incorporates forms of doing based on conversation, negotiation, and collaboration between adults and children. Here adult researchers, like the artists working on relational projects, might need to give up on their gained expertise and professional technique to engage with other forms of representation and world-making that are more child-sensitive.

Relational aesthetics are more concerned with *formations* than with forms. In this sense, artists working with relational art projects are not only drawing inspiration from the world of art and its traditional disciplines, but from models that come from the social fabric and its ways of making. As Bourriaud (2002) affirms, "[Art] refers to values that can be transposed into society" (p. 18). Relational aesthetics bring the opportunity to see children as social actors whose cultural production does not belong to a lower cultural rank (child art). Instead, young people collaborate with adults artists/teachers/researchers to bring emancipatory insights into productions of art and urban space.

Performance Art Pedagogy

Both Nomadic and relational aesthetics can be connected to what Garoian (1999) calls *performance art pedagogy*, that concentrates on "the transformation of the artist/teacher and spectator/student from the object to the subject of cultural history [through] . . . liberatory forms of action" (p. 57). Garoian's performance art pedagogy challenges the mono-culturality, standardization and prescription that characterizes the places and spaces where learning takes place, like the school or the museum. He considers that the primary source of pedagogy comes from students' lives and cultural perspectives. Bringing non-academic, non-dominant intercultural and cross-disciplinary ideas into these two institutional contexts is a way of disrupting their pre-assumed purposes. Garoian views pedagogy as a collaborative construction of public discourse and practical democracy in which cultural agency and memory cannot be sacrificed for art's sake, curriculum standards or disciplinary traditions. In this sense, pedagogical practice is made of participation, interculturality, and cross-disciplinary dialogs. This inter-social transformative quality connects performance art pedagogy with relational aesthetics.

Performance art pedagogy situates the presentness of the living body as a site where cultural codes are inscribed, lived, and can be transformed through the language of culturally responsive and relational actions. Knowledge does not precede the learning actions, but knowledge happens in-the-making and by learning to think experimentally about important cultural transformations (Ellsworth, 2005). Performance art pedagogy embraces the indeterminacy of learning outcomes, and considers that interpretation is a non-fixed, situated practice of meaning production (Garoian 1999). Learning is not only or mainly about cognitive levels or patterns, but about sensational and affective knowledge made of felt experiences happening in transitional spaces and times between knowing and not-knowing (Ellsworth, 2005). It is in relation to the refusal of dichotomous thinking and the acknowledgement that learning is not only based upon logical statements but non-logical, indeterminate, undecidable, contradictory, unfinished experiences that performance art pedagogy links with nomadic aesthetics, and its pedagogical use of art as a site of productive disjunctions, paradoxes, and moving identities.

A Visual Ethnography Centered on Childhoods, Migration, and Urban Space

Inspired by the framework of social, aesthetic and pedagogical ideas discussed above, the second part of the article presents a visual ethnography done with two classes of 6th-grade children (40 children with five working groups per class) attending a urban intercultural school, an art specialist, two course tutors, and two researchers from Universitat Autònoma de Barcelona. The author of this article is one of the two researchers. In this study, the street becomes a pedagogical site and a place of transition, occupation, cultural encounter, visual representation and sensational pedagogy. These actions challenge modernist binary divisions between childhood and adulthood by situating young people as the central subjects of symbolic and spatial production.

Socio-Historical Context of the Research. The scenario of this case study is an elementary school located in the core of El Raval Sud, a historical neighborhood in Barcelona's old downtown. Barcelona is well-known for its modern architecture with its bohemian bourgeoisie flare that attracts many across Europe and the world. However, the modern history of the city is also represented by its growing industry and the massive migration of rural population to the metropolis at the turn of the last century. This working class migration became key in the transformation of Barcelona in as a cosmopolitan European center.

With the massive arrival of the newcomers, working class neighborhoods expanded in the city. El Raval Sud was one of them. Its landscape was a peculiar combination of very poorly designed residential buildings for the urban proletariat, artisan workshops, hostels, charity hospitals, orphanages, clandestine brothels and religious churches and convents constructed in earlier periods. Its location within the perimeter of the old medieval walls made El Raval Sud a narrow, dark, damp and often unhealthy living space for the urban poor. Although the economical conditions have improved since then, and urban reformation has affected large sections, El Raval Sud still shows many characteristics of this early working class urban structure (Villar, 1997).

During the last 30 years, El Raval Sud, like many other metropolitan centers in Europe, has become the site of arrival and the home to international immigrants coming from Magreb, Sub-Saharan countries, the Hindu peninsula, and South America. These irregular and regular citizens are the new occupants of the old working class apartments, coexisting now with new building constructions for an emerging creative class and liberal middle class professionals. While some see this heterogeneity and hybridization as quintessential elements that define cosmopolitism, others interpret this as a process of gentrification whose goal is to keep El Raval Sud with a tolerable and appealing level of cultural diversity (Goytisolo, 2004). In this context, *immigrant* is a political and social construction that does not apply to all travelers setting foot in a new land, or other bodies in transition, but those coming from the so called Third World countries, who enter through the back door, with no visa, a lack of skills, and barely any money in their pockets. They are the most vulnerable in the whole social structure (Delgado, 2008). The public school where this visual ethnographic study took place has 96% of students connected to this recent migratory history, and 4% of students who live with enduring forms of social disadvantage that are a product of earlier histories of marginality in El Raval Sud.

Goals of the Research. The goals of the research are:

■ To create a social and relational space of artistic production and interpretation that connects the classroom with the neighborhood and the street. The research draws inspiration from a model of performance art pedagogy based on rethinking

413

how we (children and adults) relate with ourselves, others, art, and the public world and to engage with anything and anyone that is different from ourselves (Garoian, 1999; Ellsworth, 2005).

■ To experiment with a model of curriculum that alters the linearity of the times and places of learning, as well as the disciplinal departmentalization of knowledge, and promote a model of learning based on connecting art with other forms of knowledge and with the real world experiences of children. This is also a model of curriculum that defies the standardization and globalization of knowledge and focus on local webs of relations (Graham, 2007).

■ To produce visual-ethnographic knowledge that narrates the process and outcomes of a nomadic/relational aesthetic that challenges modernist and canonic approaches to art and artists and avoids representing children as mere depositories of artistic content (Kester, 2004) by setting art in a long-term dialog with current social issues and formations connected to the lives and interests of young people (Bourriaud, 2002).

Visual Ethnography

The methodology used in this research is a reflective approach to visual ethnography. According to MacDougall (1997), visual ethnography rethinks anthropology's orientation as a discipline dominantly conducted by words to consider other forms of anthropological knowledge. In this sense, visual ethnography is not a copy, substitute, or complement to written ethnography but an alternate form of representation that focuses on those parts of culture that cannot be accessed by just the use of words (Pink, 2002). As Berger (1977) affirms: "Seeing comes before words . . . and establishes our place in the surrounding world (p.7). Therefore, the research uses the conceptual and analytic possibilities of visual texts to elaborate critical insight on the cultural relations between childhood, relational aesthetics, nomadic identities, and metropolitan conditions of life in El Raval Sud. This critical insight relies on the capacity of visual images "to reveal what is hidden in the inner mechanisms of the ordinary and the taken for granted, [as well as] the connections between things of different scope and scale" (Knowles & Sweetman, 2004, p. 7), like children's cultures and their urban imaginaries.

According to Pink (2002), visual ethnographic narratives aim to represent how participants construct different meanings at different points of the ethnographic research, analysis, and representations. Following this idea, the research concentrates on three different types of visual ethnographic narratives:

1. *The archive of visual strategies: Robert Frank as a case for relational aesthetics:* This ethnographic narrative reconstructs how the researchers produced meanings about Robert Frank's photographs that connected with children's lives and memories of migration. They produced this narrative through conversations and collaborative research at the exhibition and the library before the field experience. The visual ethnographic narrative expanded during the field experience through conversations with 6th-grade students both at the museum and the classroom.

2. *A video-narrative of knowledge-in-the-making as a shared cultural process between children and adults:* This narrative intended to capture the process of knowledge in-the-making during the interventions in the field (the museum, the classroom and the streets). The outcome is a 10-minute video-documentary. Figure 1 shows a linear arrangement of selected stills from this video.

3. *The montage of the images and texts produced by two groups of 6th-grade students:* This is a collection and connection of children's texts and images that represent multiple and dissonant points of views concerning the urban themes that children documented.

The following two sections discuss narratives #1 and #3 in more detail. Aspects of narrative #2 are incorporated within these two sections.

Frank's Relational Archive of Visual Strategies

At the time when the fieldwork of this case study was developed, Barcelona's Museum of Contemporary Art (MACBA), located in El Raval Nord, was showing Robert Frank Storylines. This exhibition presented "the creative journey taken by this artist from the 1940s to the present day" (Todolí & Brookman, 2008). We constructed an alternative non-linear, non-chronological journey to the exhibition by focusing on specific visual strategies present in Frank's work. Knwoles and Sweetman (2004), define visual strategies as the uses that the image can be put to both represent and construct realities.

The focus on visual strategies had a double intent: First, we wanted to produce a relational space between Robert Frank's biography and how this affected his own view of public life in a foreign country, the U.S., and children's life experiences of migration and urbanity in El Raval Sud. And second, we expected that those concepts and practices emerged and discussed during the looking and talking at the museum would transfer and affect children's photographic practices in the street (see Figure 1). The itinerary concentrated in the exploration of the following two visual strategies: The migratory point of view, and the motion picture.

The Migratory Point of View. Migration is considered an essential visual strategy shaping Frank's point of view and picture-making. For instance, Mitchell (2005) has interpreted *The Americans* (1958), Frank's most celebrated piece of work, as the traumatic view of an immigrant "experiencing his newly adopted homeland as an alien civilization" (p. 278). The personal and contextual forces that propelled Frank to travel across different countries in Europe, Peru and finally the United States, his new homeland, were implicitly presented in the exhibition narrative. We decided to concentrate the itinerary on creating a relational space centered on discussing how Frank produced images that showed a migratory point of view. As Garoian (1999) affirms, the rationale was to deconstruct and recompose art in ways that the expressive character of Frank's photos and his personal concerns as an artist found a parallel with the lives, desires, and imaginaries of our children in order they could see their own migratory experience "within a context of history" (p. 198).

The Motion Picture. Differing from earlier photo-documentalists like Cartier-Bresson who centered on the capture of decisive moments that summarized a totality within one sole image, Frank opposed the idea that one single instant could represent the complexity of life. Focusing on different examples through the exhibition, we observed how Frank worked with highly orchestrated sequences of images "that collapsed or even subverted time, to present multiple and layered meanings, to elicit numerous and conflicting emotional responses" (Greenough, 1994). Children were asked to capture public life in El Raval Sud also in terms of narratives and sequences of images showing contrasts and differences that were meaningful to them (see Figure 1, video stills E, F, G, and H).

Like other photographers of the late '40s and '50s, Frank experimented with the *motion picture* and the idea that the point of view can move with the flow of cosmopolitan life, having as a result an embodied representation of the ephemeral, random, and transitional character of urbanity (Kozloff, 2002). The motion picture style allowed children to experiment with movable and volatile points of view while they occupied and transited city itineraries that were familiar and attractive to them.

Raval's Montage of Images

The two montages presented in this final section account for the multiplicity of readings and views that acted together in the final outcomes of children's selected urban themes, photographs and writings (see Figures 2 and 3, below).

The analytical perspective in reading these two montages is inspired by Rassmussen and Smidt (2003), who affirm that in analyzing children's photographs of their

Figure 1 Video stills representing aspects of the field process; conversations in the museum (stills A, B, C, and D), actions of photo-documentation in public spaces (stills E, F, G, and H), and selection of images in the classroom (stills I and J).

neighborhoods one can gain three different types of knowledge: visual, physical, and narrative. The visual concerns the photograph and what it is shown and how it is shown. The physical knowledge shows the embodied and lived perception of the photographed reality. The narrative knowledge is related to the statements, anecdotes, and stories that children project into these photographs.

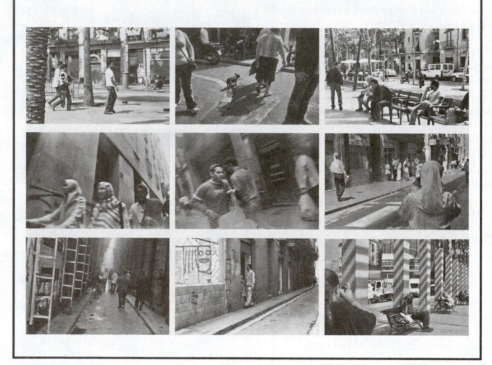

> I do not like dirty streets. I do not like narrow streets. You can see more people and more happiness in the wider streets… (Yuni)

> Raval is a really big barrio. It is kind of dirty because people dump garbage in the street, and also some men sleep outside… (Maribel)

> The people who live in el Raval is different. They are from different countries Morocco, Pakistan, Rumania, Spain, the South and East of Africa, England and India. Also many tourists from different countries come to visit the city. (Abdelnor)

> There is an enormous iron cat in La Rambla del Raval. The people who live there have a great time because the bigger parties always take place there (Laura)

Figure 2 Montage #1: Places of work along Calle Sant Pau. 6th grade students class 2005, Escola Collaso i Gil.

Montage #1: Places of Work Along Calle Sant Pau. During the field trip to Robert Frank's exhibition children were attracted to the series of images presented in the section named *Detroit 1957*, which showed the life in and around a Ford Motor factory. While looking at those images, we read a paragraph from a short story depicting working and living spaces in El Raval Sud, and we discussed possible correspondences between the pictures and the narrative. These conversations seemed to have had an impact on one of the working groups that selected "Working spaces in Calle Sant Pau" as their theme for the photo documentation of public life in El Raval Sud.

Children in this group were interested in representing the actions of people while they work. They came into different businesses, and negotiated the possibility of taking pictures. Children asked the workers who agreed to participate not to look at the camera and act as if they were doing their jobs. Days later when the group had the opportunity to look at the resulting photo-contacts, different members had varied opinions on how

416

People work constructing new streets and buildings. They also work in stores, bars, calling centers, hotels. Many workers are from other countries. People also come from other countries to take photos of Raval (Alex)

In Raval you can find many restaurants that sell shawarma. There is a sandwich store called Atlas, where they cook very tasty stuff. There are many stores selling phones, and also many bars (Kaula)

Most of the stores are from Pakistan or Morocco (Ghizlane)

Figure 3 Montage #2: Representing transitions and situations

to organize their visual sequences (see Figure 1, video Stills I and J). Some of the children in the group were especially interested in putting together linear series of images showing the different moments of a work action. Some others preferred to show situations that were fun and worth remembering. Some others wanted to put together sequences of places where they go to eat or buy regularly, connecting existing social bonds to their invented theme.

Physical Knowledge. From a physical perspective, children used play and fun to create an alternative mapping/ itinerary of Calle Sant Pau. Taking pictures of all these different work places along the street that they walk everyday at different times was a practice of seeing this space differently and of making childhood culture visible in the public realm.

Visual Knowledge. From a visual point of view that concentrates on what is shown in the photographs, we can see that the children's focus on the theme of work demonstrates that children negotiate their social identities by not only relating to childhood culture and children acquaintances, but by experiencing from their own point of view

417

the realities defining the world of adults (Mathews, 2003). The photographs in Figure 2 show in a concrete manner how children gained knowledge of these different places by exploring given environments, items, persons that were interesting to them. It is difficult to separate the visuality of these images from their physicality.

The frames in Figure 2 show specific senses of belonging, transition, occupation, and proximity. Some were taken from outside of the store, because their owners or employees decided not to participate (see photos of Raval Döner restaurant and butchery shop in Figure 2). These certainly differ from images that were taken inside with the consent of the owners. In these images you could see the proximity and the comfort both of adults and children interacting together in these places. See in Figure 2 the three images in the hair salon that intend to show the process of cutting hair. This is a transcription of what happened in the field:

(A group of children enter the barber's shop.)

ISRAEL: Hi, we are from the school. We would like to take some photos.

ASSISTANT: Of my face or of the place?

YUNAIDA: Of you working.

(Assistant laughs while owner walks in.)

ASSISTANT: Juri they want to take some photos, it's for schoolwork.

(Owner receives a phone call. Children wait grouped in front of him. Owner looks at the children while he is talking over the phone.)

FABIO: Can I sit there?

(Fabio points at the chair in front of the mirror. Israel also addresses the owner.)

ISRAEL: You can do like you are fixing his hair.

(Before the owner takes a decision, Yunaida sits in the chair. Owner hangs up and walks towards the chair, and puts a robe on Yunaida. He starts combing her hair. Owner smiles.)

YUNAIDA: Please, do not cut my hair!

OWNER: Nooo.

The rest of the children take lots of shots of the situation (Rifà & Trafí-Prats, 2005).

Narrative Knowledge. From a narrative point of view we can see how Alex's statement focuses on the experience of taking the photos, the things that can be photographed in Calle Sant Pau, and the different people, like tourists, that take photographs in el Raval. Kaula's statement concentrates on the things represented in the photographs that she likes, and more specifically food. Ghizlane's statement about the fact that many businesses

are owned by individuals from the Hindu peninsula and the Magreb region is more a re-affirmation of the intercultural character of the neighborhood, where different ethnic communities are associated with different types of jobs and forms of public life, than a negative remark or complaint. (Read all these statements in Figure 2.) The different characters appearing in these pictures are not shown as aliens or immigrants, they are represented as dignified individuals performing ordinary tasks in the daily life of their neighborhood. Most often urban experiences and social interconnections in the metropolis defy this fixed and monolithic model of identity associated with a place of origin to favor instead hybridized cultural experiences and nomadic and evolving models of identity.

Montage #2: Representing Transitions and Situations. During the field trip to Robert Frank's exhibition, we spent time observing and discussing the series named *From the Bus* (1958). In this particular series, Frank uses the camera as a device to capture different situations while traveling in a New York bus. The results are an evidence of flying situations and moving sights and bodies.

When looking at these images, children showed interest in knowing how the images were done. They discussed if they were real or fake situations while performing the possible situations and actions that the photographer did to take those (see Figure 1, video stills C and D).

Physical Knowledge. One of the working groups decided to base their photo-documentation on people walking and doing things in the street (see Figure 3). The idea of capturing fragments of situations, and moving realities is very perceptible in these images. The different points show what the very focus of the image is. When this focus is a tiny dog, children cropped the heads of the people to locate the dog and the street floor in the center of the image. When children represent someone walking through a street, they situate themselves as followers or crossers.

Visual Knowledge. The photos demonstrate that children are using Frank's moving picture strategy. Some photos show dynamic framings and moving subjects because children took the images while walking and following people. They used Frank's aesthetics in relational ways to experiment with new ways of viewing and representing what is familiar to them. Some other images show forms of occupying the space and actions that happen in the street like sleeping outside, doing construction work, meeting with others, and so forth.

Narrative Knowledge. Children's statements show different feelings, narratives and anecdotes about sociability and coexistence in El Raval Sud. Some are more positive than others, and we can see how children worry about poverty, public behavior and healthy spaces, but also feel part of a community to which specific spaces contribute to that feeling. All statements show that children care about the spaces where they live and that those spaces affect who they are.

Photographs and texts in these two montages have a highly experiential content. They are a proof of the different and specific perspectives, points of view, and body perceptions through which children show that the neighborhood is a "sensed, perceived, and experienced reality that it is stored within the child's body (. . .) The body and its movements are vital building blocks in making meaning of the environment. The creation of meaning is basically a physical manifestation" (Rassmussen & Smidt, 2003).

Conclusions

Interdisciplinary efforts are needed to construct a model of art education centered on relations and transformative actions with young people growing up in changing and challenging urban environments. The knowledge that we often consider foundational for art education needs to be transformed to adopt a pedagogical perspective centered on the cultures, memories and interests of young people whose social, cultural and geographical biographies significantly differ from the ones of their adult caregivers.

In this sense, it is urgent that art education participates more actively in contemporary discussions about childhood occurring in the sociological, pedagogical, anthropological, historical fields. The actualities of contemporary children, their visual culture experiences, and the geopolitical complexity of the world where they grow up are forcing us to review beheld conceptions of universalism, ethnocentrism, innocence, dependence, or spatial-temporal unity, through which modern disciplines, like art education, have conceived childhood. A defining trait of the new world order is that the commonality of public space is being challenged by corporate privatization. As a result of this movement, children are pushed out the streets and shuttled to different private realms of activity. A situation that contrasts with the reality that year after year more children move to metropolitan centers. Currently a 75% of the world's population of children lives in urban environments. Art educators interested in social justice and visual culture need to engage in imaginative actions that cultivate forms of aesthetic relationality between children and the spaces where they chose to live. Among these imaginative actions is the use of contemporary art, collaborative research practices, and visual narratives as a way of participation, exploration and transformation of art, adult-children relations, and urban realities.

REFERENCES

Aitken, S. C. (2001). *Geographies of young people. The morally contested spaces of identity*. London: Routledge.

Aries, P. (1962). *Centuries of childhood*. London: Jonathan Cape.

Blandy, D. (2008). Memory, loss and neighborhood schools. *Studies in Art Education, 49* (2), 83–86.

Blandy, D. & Congdon, K. G. (1998). Community-based aesthetics as an exhibition catalyst and a foundation for community involvement. *Studies in Art Education 29*(4), 6–14.

Blandy, D. & Hoffman, E. (1993). Toward an art education of place. *Studies in Art Education, 35*(1), 22–33.

Berger, J. (1977). *Ways of seeing*. London: Penguin.

Bourriaud, N. (2002). *Relational aesthetics*. Dijon: Les presses du réel.

Braidotti, R. (1994). *Nomadic subjects*. New York: Columbia University.

Cannella, G. S. (1997). *Deconstructing Early Childhood Education: Social Justice and Revolution*. New York: Peter Lang.

Cannella, G. S., Kincheloe, J. & Anijar, K. (Eds.) (2002). *Kidworld: Childhood studies, global perspectives and education*. New York: Peter Lang.

Christensen, P. & O'Brien, M. (2003). Children in the city: introducing new perspectives. In P. Christensen & M. O'Brien (Eds.), *Children in the city. Home, neighbourhood and community* (pp. 1–12). London & New York: RoutledgeFalmer.

Congdon, K. G. (2004). *Community art in action*. Worcester, MA: Davis.

Delgado, M. (2008). Qui pot ser immigrant a la ciutat? Retrieved September 26, 2008 from http://www.xcosta.arq.br/atlas/debate/immigracio_frames.htm.

Duncum, P. (2002). Children never were what they were: Perspectives on childhood. In Y. Gaudelius & P. Speirs (Eds.), *Contemporary issues in art education* (pp. 97–107). Upper Saddle River, NJ: Pearson Education.

Durrant, S. & Lord, C. M. (2007). Introduction: Essays in migratory aesthetics: Cultural practices between migration and art-making. S. Durrant & C. M. Lord (Eds.), *Essays in migratory aesthetics* (pp. 11–19). New York: Rodopi.

Ellsworth, E. (2005). *Places of learning. Media, architecture, pedagogy*. New York: RoutledgeFalmer.

Garoian, C. (1999). *Performing pedagogy. Toward an art of politics*. Albany, NY: State University of New York.

Graham, M. A. (2007). Art, ecology and art Education: Locating art education in a critical place-based pedagogy. *Studies in Art Education, 48*(4), 375–391.

Greene, M. (1995). *Releasing the imagination. Essays on education, the arts and social change*. San Francisco: John Wiley & sons.

Greenough, S. (1994). Fragments that make a whole: Meaning in photographic sequences. In S. Greenough & P. Brookman (Eds.) *Robert Frank. Moving out* (pp. 96–141). Washington: National Gallery of Art.

Goytisolo, J. (2004, September, 24). Metáforas de la migración. *El País*, p. 13.

Hoving, I. (2007). Between relation and the bare facts: The migratory imagination and relationality. In S. Durrant & C. M. Lord (Eds.), *Essays in migratory aesthetics* (pp. 179–190). New York: Rodopi.

Jenks, C. (1996). *Childhood*. London: Routledge.

Kerster, G. H. (2004). *Conversation pieces. Community + communication in modern art*. Berkeley: University of California Press.

Kozloff, M. (2002). *New York: Capital of Photography*. New York: The Jewish Museum & Yale University.

Knowles, C. & Sweetman, P. (Eds.) (2004). *Picturing the social landscape: Visual methods and the sociological imagination*. London: Routledge.

Kwon, M. (2004). *One place after another. Site-specific art and locational identity*. Cambridge, MA: MIT.

Lefebvre, H. (1991). *The production of space*. Oxford: Blackwell.

MacDougall, D. (1995). The subjective voice in ethnographic film. In L. Devereaux & R. Hillman (Eds.), *Fields of vision: Essays in film studies, visual anthropology and photography*. (pp. 217–255). Berkeley. University of California.

Matthews, H. (2003). The street as a liminal space: The barbed spaces of childhood. In P. Christensen & M. O'Brien (Eds.), *Children in the city. Home, neighbourhood and community* (pp. 101–117). London & New York: RoutledgeFalmer.

McFee, J. K. & Degge, R. (1980). *Art, culture, and environment. A catalyst for teaching*. Dubuque, IA: Kendall/Hunt.

Mitchell, W. J. T. (2005). The ends of American photography: Robert Frank as national medium. In *What do picture want?* (pp. 272–293). Chicago: University of Chicago.

Pink, S. (2002). *Doing visual ethnography*. London: Sage.

Rasmussen, K. & Smidt, S. (2003). Children in the neighbourhood: the neighbourhood in the children. In P. Christensen & M. O'Brien (Eds.), *Children in the city. Home, neighbourhood and community* (pp. 82–100). London & New York: RoutledgeFalmer.

Rifà, M. & Trafí-Prats, L. (2005). [Transcription of video excerpt of fieldwork]. Unpublished raw data.

Saloul, I. (2007). "Exilic Narrativity": The invisibility of home in Palestinian exile. In S. Durrant & C. M. Lord (Eds.), *Essays in migratory aesthetics* (pp. 111–128). New York: Rodopi.

Todolí, V. & Brookman, P. (2005). Robert Frank Storylines 09/02/2005–08/05/2005 MACBA. Retrieved September 24, 2008 from http://www.macba.es/controller.php?p_action=show_page&pagina_id=34&inst_id=19980

Vilar, P. (1997). *Historia y leyenda del Barrio Chino. 1900–1992 Crónica y documentos de los bajos fondos de Barcelona*. Barcelona: La Campana.

Zeiher, H. (2003). Shaping daily life in urban environments. In P. Christensen & M. O'Brien (Eds.), *Children in the city. Home, neighbourhood and community* (pp. 66–81). London & New York: RoutledgeFalmer.

AUTHOR NOTE

The research project discussed in this article was funded by the Vice-Rector of Research at the Universitat Autònoma de Barcelona in academic year 2005. My acknowledgement here is for my colleague Montserrat Rifà, the teachers at Escola Collasso i Gil, and Xavier Giménez, their art educator.

CHAPTER FIFTEEN

Narrative Research

PROBLEMS OF PRACTICE *in this chapter*

- Is it important to pay attention to the quality of an infant's attachment to his or her primary caregiver?
- What can be done when there is a discrepancy between textbook narratives of a nation's policies and students' own narratives about these policies?
- Why do some stories of efforts to institute school reforms paint a negative picture of these efforts, and what can be done to rectify the problem?
- What can be done to place more value on the role that mothers of disabled children can and should play in their children's education?
- How can educators foster students' creativity so that it has a positive effect on their careers and personal lives?
- How can a combination of online and in-person mentoring foster the development of both mentors and the students they are mentoring?
- What can be done to help beginning teachers develop a positive and resilient professional identity?

IMPORTANT *Ideas*

1. Narrative research involves the systematic study of stories.
2. Narratives are a rich source of data because people have many stories to tell about themselves and their society.
3. Individuals' stories often focus on disruptions, that is, unexpected, difficult, or disturbing occurrences.
4. Narrative researchers can study many types of stories, including those of groups, individuals, or the researchers themselves; preexisting stories and stories generated during the research process; historical and current stories; and stories that are written, spoken, or performed.
5. Narrative research obtains data from research participants that reflect their natural thinking, speaking, and emotionality.
6. Stories are a common form of communication among teachers and other educators to describe their students, educational practices, and work settings.

7. The primary design for narrative research is for researchers to elicit an individual's story and then "retell" it in order to clarify its sequence, structure, and meaning.

8. Data collection in narrative research relies primarily on interviews, supplemented by other types of data such as memos, photographs, and minutes of meetings.

9. Data analysis in narrative research involves identifying key events in an individual's story, organizing those events into a meaningful temporal structure, and then connecting the events and structure to a theoretical framework.

10. Narrative researchers sometimes involve research participants collaboratively in analyzing narrative data.

11. Interpretations derived from research participants' stories help educators make sense of their own stories and the stories of the students and colleagues with whom they work.

KEY TERMS

coding frame	narrative	restorying
commitment script	narrative identity	snowball sampling
dialectic	narrative research	stable story structure
disruption	progressive story structure	story
internal narrative	regressive story structure	
log	research narrative	

NARRATIVES AS A FOCUS FOR RESEARCH

In Chapter 13, we introduced you to case study research, which is the most common and basic type of qualitative research. We included a typical case story from *Teacher Magazine*. We noted that, by contrast with case studies, case stories do not constitute research because they do not involve the use of accepted research techniques for data collection and analysis or give readers a sound basis for judging their possible theoretical meaning and value in addressing problems of practice.

The fact that case stories do not constitute research does not mean that stories are unimportant. In fact, stories play an important role in people's lives. For this reason, the study of people's stories has become increasingly popular among researchers in education and the social sciences. This chapter will help you understand how researchers who study stories go about it. **Narrative research**, which is sometimes called *narrative inquiry*, is the systematic study and interpretation of stories of life experiences and the reporting of such research.

Livia Polanyi (1985) drew a distinction between a story and a narrative. A **story** is the original account of specific events that occurred at specific times in the past. A **narrative**, by contrast, is a later account in which a precise timeline, made up of discrete moments when the events took place, is established.

A **research narrative** can be defined as an organized interpretation of the events depicted in a narrative. Each part of this definition has significance. First, note that a research narrative is organized. Suppose we ask an individual to recount her experiences as a student teacher. Her story might jump from event to event, going from an experience at her school to one in a university seminar. Some events are simultaneous, some are sequential, and some go back to a previous point in time. The researcher's first task is to organize these accounts into a meaningful temporal sequence.

According to our definition, a research narrative not only recounts the events in the research participant's story but also interprets them. For example, the student teacher might recount experiences of being criticized by the cooperating teacher in whose classroom she is doing her student teaching. Depending on the story of how she reacted to these experiences, the student teacher might be inferred to be demonstrating increasing self-efficacy, which is regarded as a desirable result of student teaching. Then the researcher might draw on previous research and theory on self-efficacy (Skaalvik & Skaalvik, 2007) for an interpretive framework applicable to student teaching in general.

Perhaps in her story, the student teacher blames others for her teaching problems but attributes successes to her own efforts. Her comments might lead the researcher to an interpretation that emphasizes the attributions made by student teachers as they experience problems over the course of their student teaching experience. If so, the researcher might draw on attribution theory (Lam & Law, 2008) for an interpretive framework that can be used to explain this student teacher's experience or student teaching in general.

Our definition of a research narrative indicates that it is about events. In other words, the narrative states that *A* happened, and then *B* happened, continuing on until the last event has been recounted. Of course, a story also involves people, settings, emotions, thoughts, and other phenomena. However, these elements of the story are not meaningful in and of themselves. Rather, they acquire meaning as they relate to events in the story. For example, a new teacher might emphasize the emotional highs and lows of her student teaching experience. These emotional fluctuations take on meaning in a research narrative as they become tied to specific events in the teacher's story.

The Difference between Narrative Research and Case Study Research

The main difference between case studies and narrative research is that case studies seek to investigate a phenomenon in its natural context, whereas narrative research has a more limited focus, namely, making interpretations of a story. To illustrate, suppose a researcher is interested in investigating the student teaching experience. The researcher interviews and observes a student teacher (the research participant) over time and

finds that the student teacher makes comments about the cooperating teacher's words or actions, finding some helpful and others irrelevant or even harmful.

Given these data, the case study researcher might identify this theme—the manner in which a cooperating teacher facilitates or inhibits a student teacher's acquisition of instructional expertise. The researcher might want to study other cases (i.e., other new teachers who recently completed student teaching) and focus interviews and observations on this theme. He might even interview and observe some cooperating teachers to obtain their perspective on facilitating student teachers' acquisition of expertise.

By contrast, the research participant's story—either in its totality or about certain events within the story—is always the central element in a narrative study. The researcher might make particular note about the cooperating teacher's facilitation or inhibition of the student teacher's expertise, but only in the context of the student teacher's story. Narrative research is thus a specialized type of qualitative research in which the focus of inquiry is the research participants' stories.

Types of Narratives and Narrative Identities

Stories constitute much of the natural or enacted dialogue between people in most, if not all, cultures: "She said _____ and I said _____ and then she said _____ and then I said _____ . . ." You likely have heard people telling stories about personal experience that fit this structure, and you have probably told them yourself many times. Stories can occur in various types of communication, including conversation or presentations to a group, and in written form, such as e-mails, personal journals, and literary compositions.

Probably even more universal are **internal narratives**, that is, the ongoing stream of thought and self-talk that most individuals engage in during many of their waking moments, whether they are aware of it or not. Narrative researchers seek to document the ways in which we engage in these ongoing internal narratives as we move through our daily life, and they also study how these internal narratives affect our life. They have found that people tend to engage in narrative particularly when they experience a **disruption**, that is, an unexpected, difficult, or disturbing occurrence in life.

Individuals' ongoing narratives, both shared and internal, bring order and meaning to everyday life. Narratives also provide structure to individuals' very sense of selfhood, or what can be called their **narrative identity**. Because individuals operate in many different social environments and continually experience life changes, it can be argued that they have many narrative identities. In addition to individual narratives, groups, communities, and societies create narratives about their current and past histories. Through narratives, individuals and groups define themselves and clarify the continuity in their life experience. They also create narratives that express their shared aspirations.

Psychologists have found that individuals' narrative identity relates closely to their personal level of well being. Glenn Reisman (2007) studied young adults' stories about the degree of security they felt in their attachment to their primary caregiver beginning in infancy. Reisman found that narratives showing high attachment security during early childhood predicted the observed quality of young adults' romantic relationships and general interpersonal interactions. Reisman concluded that "developing a coherent narrative about early life events serves as a key psychological resource for successfully engaging adult relationships" (p. 4).

EXAMPLES OF NARRATIVE RESEARCH IN EDUCATION

Much narrative research in education has involved the analysis of teachers' stories. This emphasis reflects the central role of storytelling in teachers' work lives. Teachers frequently tell stories to help students learn and also to shape students' attitudes and behavior. Also, they share stories with other teachers as part of collegial information sharing and to indoctrinate new teachers into the school culture.

Other narrative studies have focused on the stories of students. Student narratives are often generated from writing assignments like essays or journal entries. Teachers study student narratives both to understand students' life experiences and also to analyze their ability to understand and generate language (Conle, 2003). Beyond such intentional uses, teachers also encounter students'

stories in informal conversations before, during, and after class or in chance meetings outside of school.

Narrative researchers also have studied the stories of stakeholder groups in education, including parents and community members. Some of their stories do not involve written communication but are represented in art and song.

The following are examples of narrative research whose findings are relevant to problems of educational practice.

State-Sanctioned Narratives and Student Narratives

Tsafrir Goldberg, Dan Porat, and Baruch Schwarz (2006) analyzed the narrative characteristics of brief essays written by 12th-grade students in response to questions regarding the Melting Pot policy in Israel. This policy concerns Israel's official stance toward the mass immigration of Jews from other nations to Israel in the 1950s. It is based on the Israeli government's intention to create a new nation through the assimilation of Jewish immigrants from other countries with Israel's existing population.

The students, who had not yet formally studied the Melting Pot policy as part of their school's curriculum, were asked to write an essay about (1) what they knew about the policy, (2) whether immigrants were helped or harmed by it, and (3) whether its implementation was essential to the construction of the state of Israel or a destructive political undertaking.

Of the 105 student participants, about half were descendants of Jewish immigrants from Moslem countries (the Mizrahi), and the other half were Jewish immigrants, or their descendants, from Christian countries (the Ashkenazi). The researchers analyzed students' narratives individually and then according to their ethnic group (Mizrahi or Ashkenazi) to identify cultural patterns and the level of agreement between the official state narrative of the mass immigration period and student narratives.

The researchers analyzed the student texts both quantitatively and qualitatively. Quantitative analysis was used to determine the percentage of students expressing various viewpoints. Qualitative analysis was used to identify patterns within the students' stories. The researchers drew on sociocultural theory to explain students' use of social representations of the past as a cultural tool for understanding their present life in Israel.

The researchers found that students' stories often diverged from the official Zionist narrative contained in school textbooks. This narrative emphasizes the "ordeal of redemption," which portrays the mass immigration policy as necessary and even heroic, and its accompanying difficulties as inevitable. By contrast, students' stories showed more differentiated narrative schemes, including "senseless sacrifice" (found in 46 percent of the students' essays), the "tragedy of errors" (in 27 percent of the essays), and the "ordeal of redemption" entwined with suffering and sacrifice (in 25 percent of the essays).

Only the third scheme, with its focus on redemption, resembles the official Zionist narrative. To illustrate the scheme of "senseless sacrifice," the researchers quote Giora, a member of a well-established Ashkenazi family, who summed up the whole immigration-absorption process in six words: "contributed residents, harmed immigrants, a destructive step" (Goldberg et al., 2006, p. 333). The researchers report: "At the other end of the spectrum we find complex accounts such as Alon's, whose father, from a Mizrahi family, immigrated to Israel in a perilous foot trip from Syria" (p. 333):

> The melting pot educational strategy was harmful and discriminated against the immigrants because on the whole it was the long-time residents who set the rules and decided on the education and the immigrants didn't have a say . . . immigrants came with their own knowledge which may have suited the state from which they came but wasn't enough for the state of Israel . . . from that moment the rift began between cultures and classes, that is whoever didn't fit the melting pot belonged "down-there." (p. 333)

Overall, 70 percent of the students expressed critical attitudes toward the Melting Pot policy, and only 18 percent expressed a positive stance. The researchers interpret their findings as reflecting a critical counter-narrative of the immigration era, emphasizing Mizrahi immigrants' suppression and "collective amnesia" about the difficulties endured by Ashkenazi immigrants. They attribute students' largely pessimistic view "as an attempt to account for the current social situation as they perceived it, and to establish a horizon of identity and responsibility (or irresponsibility) with respect to it" (Goldberg et al., 2006, p. 344).

This study is useful because it increases educators' understanding of problems of practice that can arise in multicultural education. It helps educators develop sensitivity to the ways in which students make sense of the past and accept or reject the historical narratives conveyed in textbooks. It also can help teachers understand why students from different cultural groups respond differently to historical and current narratives presented in the curriculum. Finally, this narrative research study suggests how essays and other student writings can be used as a resource for exploring students' attitudes toward individuals from other cultures.

A Teacher's Career Progression

Cheryl Craig (2006) conducted an extended self-narrative inquiry into two career dilemmas she experienced—first when she was a K–12 teacher and second when she was a tenured full professor involved in a local evaluation of a national school reform program. With respect to the reform program, five school principals in a mid-southern state had asked Craig to "join their campuses in this important school reform proposition in the nebulous role as a planning and formative evaluation consultant" (p. 1168). A recent U.S. immigrant from Canada and relatively new to the nearby university where she was a professor, Craig accepted the offer. With the principals, she deliberately negotiated her consulting role to be

> neither of the schools nor of the school districts, neither of the local reform movement nor of the national reform movement, neither a university employee nor a freelance consultant. In this intermediary zone, I was [to be] positioned "betwixt and between" all of these groups. (p. 1169)

In her research report, Craig focuses on the conflicting stories surrounding the reform effort. For example, she tells of the political shifts surrounding the local reform effort. They included major disagreements about the role of teachers and changes in leadership when existing leaders became frustrated with the degree to which "highly conservative forces rallied . . . to snuff out the change effort that was challenging, even disturbing, the status quo way of being in the mid-southern state" (2006, p. 1170). She also expresses her concern—her sense of disruption—in seeing how the local reform effort reproduced the standard educational hierarchy in which university academics were treated as higher in status and power than the school teachers with whom they were committed to collaborating.

Craig's own "flesh-and-blood dilemma" (2006, p. 1173) involved her discovery that she alone among the planning and evaluation consultants at the eleven case study sites was evaluated in the publicly distributed school reports, despite prior assurances that "as a matter of professional courtesy" (p. 1171), no one would be individually identified in the reports.

In her efforts to sort out and explain the serious problems that arose in her work on this reform effort, Craig admits that she "did not consciously adjust my way of being to fit the ideologically conservative milieu in which I found my work situated" (2006, p. 1172). She notes that she missed cues about adjustments that might have been appropriate.

Craig concludes her research report by noting the similarity between this dilemma and the earlier one she experienced as a K–12 teacher years before. In the earlier dilemma, she reports finding that

> other teachers' and my practical work with K–12 students [were] reduced in importance to test scores from which sweeping generalizations were produced and circulated about all students' performances and all teachers' practices. (2006, p. 1173)

She also notes an important lesson she learned about the phenomenon of educational evaluation:

> [I]f the underpinnings of the sacred story of evaluation do not change, it does not matter if the participating evaluators are quantitative researchers or qualitative researchers, or if the evaluated are teachers or planning and evaluation consultants, the hegemonies built into the educational enterprise will continue to play out the same—until the conduct of evaluators and the process of evaluation are themselves reformed alongside the roles and work of those being evaluated. (2006, p. 1174)

The findings of this narrative research study provide a cautionary lesson for school reformers who seek to solve problems of practice. Specifically, we learn that school reform programs, and the program evaluations often tied to them, can themselves become problematic. By reading Craig's narrative, school reform leaders and those involved in program evaluation (see Chapter 19) can glean insights that help them navigate their way among competing stakeholders in the change process.

Theatrical Performance Based on Narratives from Mothers of Children with Disabilities

Educators often complain that students, both young and old, appear more attracted to movies, art, and music than to the teaching and learning activities of most classrooms. Narrative researchers are finding creative ways to transform and extend research findings into creative performance modes that enliven audiences, including both educators and the countless others affected by education practice.

Jan Valle (2009), an education professor, conducted narrative research through the M.O.M. Project (*Mothers on Mothering: Narratives of Disability*), collecting oral narratives from 15 mothers of children with disabilities. Using the theoretical perspective of disability studies in education, Valle and her co-researcher, David Connor, did a follow-up study based on these narratives (Valle & Connor, 2012). They observed that:

> As former special education teachers, we both worked closely with parents of children with disabilities in accessing their rights under special education law . . . and routinely observed how the knowledge of mothers, in particular, became downplayed within conversation or entirely dismissed by professionals . . . parents [were] excluded from the decision making process, despite their legal right to participate.

Valle and Connor designed and publicly presented an ethnodrama, that is, a theatrical and visual staging of Valle's narrative research, to shed light on mothers' experiences with the special educators responsible for fostering their children's learning. Combined with the second author's visual art, this ethnodrama was intended to engage a wider audience in their research study and promote change in special education practice. They claimed that, in contrast to the positivist framing of statistical analysis more typical in special education research,

> [a]rts-based research has the capacity to transform consciousness, refine the senses, promote

autonomy, raise awareness, and express the complex feeling-based aspects of social life (p. 6).

A script was developed entirely from the 15 mother's interview comments. The narratives were collapsed into six roles embodying women of the varying social classes, residential contexts, ages, and ethnicities represented in the original sample. The resulting ethnodrama was presented in the researchers' college campus theater by an all-professional cast gathered from New York City's theatrical community. The director was a student in Valle's course at The City College of New York (CCNY) in which she had presented her narrative research. The audience of about 100 people represented many different constituents within the local community.

The researchers highlighted three themes that emerged from the script and that were elaborated upon by Connor's drawings: (1) Under the Microscope, in which parents complain that they were critically examined by special education professionals and ultimately blamed for their children's disabilities; (2) Meetings, describing how mothers in particular were largely dictated to and dismissed by the education professionals who were required to have periodic Individualized Education Plan (IEP) meetings with parents; and (3) Men, illustrating how these education professionals were more respectful, even deferent, to fathers when they attended the meetings.

Samples of the narratives as they appeared in the script follow to illustrate each theme:

1. Under the Microscope
   Linda: "What was the most odd, from the very start, from the very beginning of testing, the assumption was that the parents were doing something wrong to have caused these problems."
   Janene (an administrator): "Is there violence in your home that would be causing this child to have these problems?"
2. Meetings
   Kim: "What the hell am I doing here? I don't know what they are talking about!"
   Marie: "I remember when I came in with my notes. They wanted nothing to do with it."
3. Men
   Mimi: "We walk in and yes, [my husband] Mark is the man. 'Hello, Mr. Strauss.

Can I get you coffee?' All these women who are administrators and teachers and psychologists and this and they're acting like gofers for my husband."
Janene: [as administrator]: "Well, John, what do you think?"
Marie: "I was a little perturbed to say the least. But fortunately, he learned to say, 'What *she* said!'" [laughter]

Figure 15.1 shows the artist's drawing to illustrate the mothers' experience of their meetings with special education personnel (Theme 2). In the performance ethnodrama, this image, in turn with other drawings by the artist, were projected on a screen behind the actors corresponding with their place in the script.

Following the theatrical performance, the audience, cast, director, the two researchers, and two of the mothers whose stories appear in the script held a post-performance discussion. They talked about the impact of the performance on those in

FIGURE 15.1 • Artist's Portrayal of the Theme of Meetings as a Difficulty Faced by Mothers of Children with Disabilities

Source: Valle, J. W., and Connor, D. J. (2012). Becoming theatrical: Performing narrative research, staging visual representation. *International Journal of Education & the Arts,* 13 (Lived Aesthetic Inquiry), 1–28. Reprinted with Permission

attendance and made many suggestions for dissemination of the piece. Reflecting on these events, Valle and Connor commented:

> If the work we do as researchers is to matter in the world, it must reach and move the audience for whom we write. . . . The collective experience of an audience's response to theatrical and visual representations creates a natural context within which dialogic exchanges can take place—the kind of dialogue that has the potential to inspire action (p. 23)

This study illustrates how narrative research can combine with other types of qualitative inquiry, such as art and theatrical performance, to inform educators and others, ideally leading to a change in their beliefs and solutions to problems of educational practice.

FEATURES OF A NARRATIVE RESEARCH REPORT

Narrative research about education has become increasingly varied in design, focus, and application. It has no standard methodology. We describe features mentioned in some narrative research literature, but the possibilities extend beyond our description. Common features of a narrative research report are summarized in Table 15.1.

Introduction

The introductory section of a narrative research report includes a statement of its purpose, questions or hypotheses, and a review of relevant literature. For example, Dan McAdams and Regina Logan (2006) conducted research on the creation of self in narrative. They described the purpose of their study as an exploration of the life stories of individual university professors. In an exploration of the development of narrative identity, they wanted to find patterns that link the creative work and personal lives of professors. The researchers sought to articulate a model of creative work among professors, looking for "parallels between work and love" in their careers (p. 106).

A major purpose of any narrative research study is description, and the researchers' report describes what happened in each professor's story. As we stated earlier in the chapter, the participants' stories need to be "restoried" as a narrative so that they relate an organized series of events, settings, characters, thoughts, and emotions. **Restorying** is a

TABLE 15.1 • Typical Sections of a Narrative Research Report	
Section	Content
Introduction	Questions or objectives are stated. A review of relevant literature is reviewed. The purpose of the study usually is to describe, explain, or evaluate phenomena relating to a problem of practice.
Research design	The typical narrative research study has two main phases: (1) eliciting stories from the research participants that are relevant to the study's purposes and (2) retelling each story as an organized interpretation of the story's events.
Sampling procedure	The researcher describes the purposeful sampling strategy that was used in the study and explains why that particular strategy was chosen.
Measures	Narrative research studies typically rely on the use of interviews to solicit the participants' stories. Other measures, including quantitative measures, can be used as well.
Data analysis	The data analysis will vary, depending on whether the purpose of the study is description, explanation, or evaluation. The analysis results in an organized retelling of the story that includes relevant events and the context surrounding each event. Story structures that are in the existing literature on narrative research methodology, or a structure created by the researcher, can be used to interpret the research participants' stories.
Discussion	The main findings of the study are summarized. Flaws and limitations of the study are considered. Also, implications of the findings for further research, theory development, and professional practice are explored.

process used in narrative research to convert a story told by an individual, or group of individuals, into a research narrative.

Another purpose of narrative research is to search for causal patterns within the story. For example, if the story contains a disruption, the researcher might inquire about factors that caused the disruption to occur and also about its consequences. Researchers can look for explanations within the story itself or draw on theories that appear relevant to the story.

Narrative research studies generally do not seek to predict future outcomes beyond the end of a study. However, it is appropriate for researchers to ask participants what they think is likely to happen beyond the story's ending. Indeed, it might be of value to do a subsequent narrative research study to see how a story continued to unfold beyond the period of the initial study.

A narrative research study might also have an evaluative purpose, with participants making their own evaluations or the researcher making evaluative comments, both of which characterize Valle and Connor's (2012) study of the narratives of mothers' experiences with special education.

Research Design

The design of a narrative research study includes two phases. In the first phase, the researcher elicits a story from the participant that includes phenomena of interest to the researcher. In the second phase, the researcher "retells" the story by systematically interpreting and organizing the events recounted by the participant.

In their narrative study of university professors, McAdams and Logan (2006) started by eliciting stories that would clarify their focus of inquiry, namely the interplay between educators' creative work and their personal lives. They collected a sample of stories and then, in the second phase, analyzed them for insights into the interplay between these two arenas of lived experience.

Sampling Procedure

Any of the types of purposeful sampling used in case study research (see Chapter 13) are appropriate for a narrative research study. In their narrative research study, McAdams and Logan (2006) interviewed 15 professors, sampling individuals in the sciences, engineering, and the humanities. They selected professors whom their colleagues regarded as unusually creative and productive in scholarly endeavors. This sampling approach represents what Michael Patton (2002) calls **snowball sampling**, in which cases are recommended by individuals who know other individuals likely to yield relevant, information-rich data.

McAdams and Logan then focused their narrative analysis on two men and two women: a professor of computer science at a major research university, a professor of literature at a small liberal arts college, a professor of romance languages at a large public university, and a history professor who returned to the university after a successful business career.

Data-Collection Procedures

One approach to narrative research is to generate a self-narrative, as in the research study by Cheryl Craig (2006), described in a previous section, about her dilemmas in crossing the boundaries between K–12 and higher education. However, interviewing is the primary data-collection procedure in narrative research. Researchers have found that most participants will spend ample time and provide personal details about their lives when invited to tell their stories to a respectful listener. Participants appreciate the opportunity to have researchers help them understand their significant life events, although researchers sometimes need to meet with some participants several times to win their confidence and help them adopt a reflective frame of mind about their life experiences.

Researchers should also collect background information and personal information from each participant, which often proves to be useful during the data-analysis phase. Other kinds of data are often collected in narrative research to enrich and supplement interview data. For example, researchers can encourage participants to keep a personal journal, provide photographs depicting significant life experiences, or make video recordings in which they, and perhaps significant other persons in their life, recount their stories.

McAdams and Logan (2006) conducted individual interviews with each professor in their sample. They asked participants to describe the overall trajectory of their scholarly lives and then to focus on four particular scenes that stand out in their story: (1) an opening scene that reveals how the individual's interest in that specific area of scholarship originated, (2) a professional high point, (3) a low point, and (4) a turning point. The focus of the interviews was on individuals' scholarly lives and the extent to which they dovetail with or conflict with their personal lives.

In conducting interviews, researchers need to consider their position with respect to controlling the narrative. They might choose to remain neutral and minimize their own talk during the interview in order to foster free-flowing talk by the research participants. On the other hand, they might wish to structure their interview to shape the participants' responses in particular ways. They also need to consider what types of probes to use in following up on ambiguous or interesting points.

Instead of interviewing individuals, researchers can conduct focus groups with groups of research participants (see Chapter 13). Focus groups are particularly useful for developing a collective or group narrative.

Whether the interviews are conducted with individuals or groups, researchers typically record them and later have them transcribed into written form. Verbatim transcripts are valuable because they accurately capture what participants say, and a researcher or team of researchers can review them repeatedly. Also, the transcripts facilitate data analysis.

Some researchers use existing narratives, as in the study we described earlier about student essays on the great immigration to Israel in the 1950s. Memoirs, films, and other media also provide existing narratives for analysis. For example, Jennifer Terry (2007) did a narrative analysis titled "Buried perspectives: Narratives of landscape in Toni Morrison's *Song of Solomon*." Terry's narrative analysis traces how the author Toni Morrison shaped "her own potent narrative act" (p. 93) in her fourth novel, *Song of Solomon*. Terry explains how Morrison shaped her narrative in order to give voice to African American experience and cultural identity and to craft a counter-narrative that challenges traditional descriptions of historical structures of power in the United States.

Data Analysis

Data analysis begins at the point where the researcher becomes familiar with the narratives she has generated or selected for study. For example, if narratives are obtained from interviews, researchers often prepare a log of each interview shortly after concluding it. A **log** is a record of the topics covered in a specific interview, along with notations of any interesting occurrences (especially disruptions) and how they were handled. The log helps researchers highlight important aspects of the narrative—for example, nonverbal features such as facial expressions or laughter that might provide keys to the meaning of particular comments. Also, the interviewer can note her own thoughts and emotional reactions in a log during the interview. The researcher's thoughts and reactions are important data because the narrative that is reported is a joint production of the research participant and the researcher.

Table 15.2 provides an example of a log generated by one of the authors in an unpublished narrative study of a student's experience with an online education program.

TABLE 15.2 • Log from a Narrative Study of a Gifted Student's Online Learning Experience

Topics covered in Interview, 3/17/06

1. Reasons for choosing an online program to complete her master's degree

   a. Advantages to being in an online program

   Note: The student had high hopes that the online program would be more manageable for her; given her neurological disability, she wouldn't need to travel to a class (drive, park, walk).

   b. Disadvantages of being in an online program

   Note: The student realized that the online program was not designed for advanced research scholars such as she desired to be, and to be with colleagues.

The interpretive phase of data analysis can take various forms, depending on whether the researcher's purpose is description, explanation, or evaluation. If the purpose is description, the researcher will need to organize the data into a coherent story. This task requires interpretive skill, as the data might include one or more interviews and the researcher's later reactions to the participant's responses, as well as supplementary information from memos, documents, and other artifacts related to the story. Also, the researcher will need to depict the context for each event, which might include its setting, the individuals who played a role in the event, and their behavior, thoughts, and emotions.

In reading across their summaries of each narrative, researchers begin to get an idea of the main issues that have been raised. They can then develop a coding frame that can be applied to the various narratives. A **coding frame** is an analytic framework designed to capture the overall meaning of the narratives and the particular issues raised in them.

If the interpretive phase of data analysis focuses on explanation, the researcher will need to weave the events of the story into a structure that reveals causal relationships. Ken Gergen and Mary Gergen (1984) identified three structures that represent typical causal relationships in people's life stories. The first, a **progressive story structure**, conveys events to demonstrate progress toward a goal. The second, a **regressive story structure**, presents events as obstacles to achieving a goal or as a defeat leading to abandonment of the goal. The third is a **stable story structure**, in which events lead to little or no change in the individual's circumstances.

These three structures each organize the events of a story, and each can be elaborated on to explain how one event led to another. For example, the researcher might view the participants as active agents who try to control their own destiny, which would include self-determined goals. If the story has regressive elements, the researcher can analyze the obstacles that the participant encounters, the strategies used in an effort to overcome them, and the participant's reactions to the success or failure of the strategy.

If the interpretive phase of data analysis focuses on evaluation, the researcher will want to analyze the data for the participants' evaluation of programs, individuals, and other phenomena that form the content of the story. The researcher will seek to interpret why the individual made these evaluations and the consequences of doing so.

The purpose of data analysis in the study by McAdams and Logan (2006) was explanatory. They wanted to understand how professors' creative work and personal lives mutually affected each other. Their analysis of the stories that they elicited from the professors, supplemented by their previous study of highly creative individuals such as Darwin, led them to generate the following theoretical analysis:

> In sum, the narratives illustrate how the protagonist (a) encounters an early question or problem in childhood or adolescence that drives intellectual work thereafter; how the question (b) suggests an idealized image of something or someone in the world that (c) illuminates or embodies a personal aesthetic; how the question/image/aesthetic (d) sets up a corresponding dialectic, pitting contrasting proclivities or trends in life sharply against each other; and how this dialectic, which operates to organize one's story of creative work, may (e) play itself out in the personal realm as well, sometimes organizing certain aspects of one's story of love, family, and personal relationships. (p. 93)

The key construct in this theoretical model is the concept of the dialectic. A **dialectic** is an oppositional relationship between an important value or perspective in an individual's life story and a countervailing, equally powerful value or perspective.

For example, the life narrative of the professor of literature in McAdams and Logan's narrative research is strongly centered on her religious conversion to Christianity and her study of medieval religion. McAdams and Logan (2006) found that the central dialectic in her life was the choice "between unity and disintegration" (p. 100). Her conversion and decision to focus her academic career on a specific period of religion represent the perspective of unity in her story. It is opposed by the perspective of "disintegration," a term the professor used to characterize her previous life during which she had felt "in exile" (p. 96) from the "inner spiritual, intellectual, emotional sense" (p. 96) of grounding that she was led to following her conversion.

The use of the concept of dialectic to explain a life story is also illustrated in McAdams and Logan's analysis of stories involving Jerry Dennett (a pseudonym), a professor of computer science at a major U.S. research university. He teaches courses on robotics, computer programming, and artificial intelligence (AI). Since the sixth grade, Dennett has wanted to build the perfect robot, and he still does. He is interested in how the mind works and aims to build systems that can interact with an unpredictable environment and respond appropriately. Robots are systems that must "see" the physical environment, perform tasks, and move in an efficient, goal-directed manner, avoiding collisions. In short, they need to be self-regulating, just like the people they are meant to imitate—or replace.

McAdams and Logan found that "problems involving collisions and self-regulation are front and center in Dennett's life story" (2006, p. 91). Since graduate school, he has had five serious romantic relationships with women, including one whom he married and then divorced. In the narrative interview, he described each of his relationships as having characteristics he longed to have, but, as was the case with his father's relationships, each was out of his control. The narrative describes Dennett as still trying to "design" the perfect self-regulated companion.

McAdams and Logan characterize the dialectic in Dennett's life this way: "Dennett's image of the perfect robot and the aesthetic it illustrates set up a powerful dialectic in his narrative identity. . . . [A] signal opposition is that between the self-regulated and graceful movements of the perfect robot . . . and the chaotic, clumsy, and unpredictable actions" (McAdams & Logan, 2006, p. 95), which he has observed not only in some robots but also in the closest people in his life.

McAdams and Logan interpret Dennett's life story as a commitment script, which they explain as follows:

> The gifted protagonist enjoys a special advantage early in life, commits the self to realizing the potentials that come from that advantage, and continues to persevere through difficult times, believing that suffering will ultimately be redeemed. (2006, p. 94)

A **commitment script** can be defined then as an early decision to focus one's life in a particular direction that appears to offer a unique advantage for the individual, the pursuit of which the individual regards as worth whatever obstacles might arise along the way. In our view, a commitment script is similar to the concept of a progressive story structure, which we explained earlier.

In Dennett's case, the commitment script began when Dennett showed precocious skills in his sixth-grade class in computer programming. Prior to that, he had been an underperforming student, but his grades soon improved, and he started researching computers and robots at the local Radio Shack. From that point on, the robot became "the idealized image of Dennett's professional life story. It is a picture of what he wants to make or achieve" (McAdams & Logan, 2006, pp. 93–94). This goal has enabled him "to persevere through difficult times, believing that suffering will ultimately be redeemed" (p. 94).

Discussion

The discussion section of a narrative research report is similar to that of a case study report (see Chapter 13). The main findings of the study are summarized, flaws and limitations of the study are considered, and implications of the findings for practice and further research are explored. The criteria for determining the applicability and quality of a case study are equally appropriate for narrative studies.

Narrative accounts, such as those presented in the study by McAdams and Logan (2006), contain truths that may apply to individuals in your own life. For example, they can help you understand how particular students or colleagues develop particular interests and how those interests affect, or are affected by, their personal lives. In particular, the study can develop your sensitivity to conflicts (or dialectics) that students and colleagues must strive to resolve in order to achieve a sense of identity and self-fulfillment.

EVALUATING A NARRATIVE RESEARCH STUDY

Narrative research is grounded in qualitative methods of inquiry. Therefore, you can evaluate these research studies using Appendix 4. The following are two additional questions that will help you evaluate the quality of a narrative research study.

- Did the researcher elicit sufficient detail about the participants' stories?

  Participants might recount their stories in a superficial way, focusing primarily on the who, what, and where of events. In a good narrative study, the researcher will probe the participants' statements to determine how they felt about these events, their inner motivations, and their explanations about why events unfolded as they did.

- Does the researcher provide a credible interpretation of the story?

  A report of a narrative research study must include an interpretation of the participants' stories. You will need to judge whether the interpretation is justified by the empirical data, namely, the story details that are included in the report.

An example of
How Narrative Research Can Help in Solving Problems of Practice

Many high school students can benefit from having a mentor, and many professionals would like to be their mentor. The question is how to create a mentoring program that works for both groups. Big Brothers Big Sisters in the Dallas-Fort Worth area believes that it has created such a program, as described in the local newspaper:

> Life moves so fast nowadays. Sometimes you want to help others, but you just don't have the time.
>
> Trina George was like that. A manager for Allstate Insurance in Irving, she had her own kids to raise and higher education to pursue. How could she possibly have time to mentor anyone?
>
> Mentor 2.0, a program from Big Brothers, uses technology to power online-based relationships. [This program] now oversees about 300 partnerships at five high schools in the Dallas-Fort Worth area, with plans to expand to Houston.
>
> Students and mentors trade monitored emails weekly, prompted by questions about college or workforce readiness. Every six weeks, students and mentors meet at large face-to-face gatherings. . . .

Ramirez, M. (2013, February 19). E-mentoring links professionals with Dallas-Fort Worth high schoolers. *The Dallas Morning News*. Retrieved from http://www.dallasnews.com/news/ community-news/dallas/headlines/20130219- e-mentoring-links-professionals-with-dallas- fort-worth-high-schoolers.ece

A quantitative research study could be done to determine the effectiveness of this mentoring program by comparing outcomes (e.g., school grades, self-concept, level of aspiration) for mentored and nonmentored students. However, this type of study would not help us understand the experiences of mentors and students as they engaged in the mentoring process. What do mentors and students see as the high points of mentoring? Do disruptions occur? What did they do to make the relationship productive? How did the mentoring relationship develop over time? How has it affected their lives? Questions such as these might be addressed most effectively by a narrative research study.

The researchers could select a sample of mentors and students by talking to the Big Brothers Big Sisters administrators. As a start, they might ask the administrators to select mentoring relationships that were working well. Then they would ask those mentors and students for permission to include them as participants in their research study.

The primary method of data collection would be interviews. They might ask each mentor and student simply to tell the story of their relationship. How did it start? What were high points and roadblocks along the way? Where is the relationship now, and where is it heading? The researchers then could "retell" their stories by creating narratives that put events in chronological order and in context. They might analyze the narratives to look for the structures identified by Ken and Mary Gergen (1984): progressive story structure, regressive story structure, and stable story structure. Also, they might find it productive to compare the narratives of each member of the mentoring relationship to determine how the stories of each mentor and his or her student converged and diverged.

A follow-up study could be done to collect the stories of mentors and students involved in less productive relationships. The focus here would be to identify elements that are present in productive mentoring relationships and absent in nonproductive mentoring relationships. It would be of particular interest to find out whether characteristics of the mentors or characteristics of the students are most crucial to fostering a positive mentoring relationship.

Knowledge gained from these narrative research studies could be helpful to mentor administrators, mentors, and students. For example, they might learn ways to improve the electronic components of the mentoring process and the pairing of mentors and students. They might even use some of the stories recorded by the narrative researchers to promote the mentoring program among students and professionals in the community.

SELF-CHECK TEST

1. The difference between stories and research narratives is that
   a. stories have a timeline, but research narratives do not.
   b. stories involve interpretation, but research narratives provide an objective account of events with a minimum of interpretation.
   c. research narratives emphasize the researcher's interpretation of the events that comprise a story.
   d. the sequence of events is important in storytelling but not in research narratives.

2. Internal narratives consist of
   a. individuals' self-talk and thoughts during their waking hours.
   b. individuals' dreams.
   c. stories that are at the core of a society's culture.
   d. stories that have only meaning for a clique or other small, cohesive group.

3. Narrative research and case study research are
   a. similar in that both study stories within the larger context of people's lives.
   b. similar in that both rely exclusively on snowball sampling for selecting a sample.
   c. different in that narrative research examines stories exactly as told, whereas case studies "retell" the story so that it can be coded and analyzed.
   d. different in that narrative research focuses only on stories, whereas case studies focus on a variety of phenomena, all within their natural context.

4. Data collection in narrative research involves
   a. interviewing research participants to elicit their stories about events in their life.
   b. interviewing research participants to elicit patterns of self-talk during their waking hours.
   c. collecting research participants' personal journals and photos.
   d. all of the above.

5. Focus groups are primarily used in narrative research to
   a. obtain self-narratives from individual research participants.

b. make validity checks of an individual's story by using the accounts of witnesses to the events recounted in the story.

c. develop a collective or group narrative of particular events.

d. compare the stories of similar events as experienced by different cultural groups.

6. Making a log of a narrative interview helps researchers
   a. highlight important aspects of a story.
   b. note nonverbal expressions that occur as a research participants tells a story.
   c. keep track of their own reactions to a story as it is being told.
   d. all of the above.

7. Researchers develop a coding frame of a narrative primarily to
   a. break down the narrative into themes.
   b. interpret the narrative in relation to a theoretical framework.
   c. specify the issues raised in the narrative.
   d. put the events covered by the narrative into temporal order.

8. Story structures (progressive, regressive, and stable) are used to
   a. reveal causal relationships within a story.
   b. "retell" the story by organizing events according to time, place, or the individuals who were present.
   c. evaluate the individual's story by using cultural norms for success.

d. select events within a story that most contribute to the narrative identity of the storyteller.

9. In narrative research, a dialectic is
   a. the researcher's testing of which theory best describes a research participant's narrative.
   b. a coding check to determine whether a research narrative best fits a progressive, regressive, or stable story structure.
   c. a reliability check to determine whether a researcher not involved in the data collection creates the same narrative ordering of events from a research participant's stories as the researcher who collected the data.
   d. a conflict between two or more values that are central to a research participant's life story.

10. In narrative research, a commitment script involves
    a. a narrative reflecting an individual's perseverance in pursuing an early life goal.
    b. a verbal protocol researchers use to ensure that all interview topics are covered.
    c. a conflict between an individual research participant's personal and professional goals.
    d. a theory that helps researchers interpret the meaning of individual narratives.

CHAPTER REFERENCES

Conle, C. (2003). An anatomy of narrative curricula. *Educational Researcher, 32*(3), 3–15.

Craig, C. J. (2006). Dilemmas in crossing the boundaries: From K–12 to higher education and back again. *Teaching and Teacher Education, 23*(7), 1165–1176.

Gergen, K. J., & Gergen, M. M. (1984). The social construction of narrative accounts. In K. J. Gergen & M. M. Gergen (Eds.), *Historical social psychology* (pp. 173–190). Hillsdale, NJ: Lawrence Erlbaum.

Goldberg, T., Porat, D., & Schwarz, B. B. (2006). "Here started the rift we see today": Student and textbook narratives between official and counter memory. *Narrative Inquiry, 16*(2), 319–347.

Labov, W. (1972). *Language in the inner city: Studies in the Black English vernacular*. Philadelphia, PA: University of Pennsylvania Press.

Lam, S., & Law, Y. (2008). Open attitudes, attribution beliefs, and knowledge of Hong Kong teacher interns in an era of education reform. *Asia Pacific Journal of Education, 28*(2), 177–187.

McAdams, D. P., & Logan, R. L. (2006). Creative work, love, and the dialectic in selected life stories of academics. In D. P. McAdams, R. Josselson, & A. Lieblich (Eds.), *Identity and story: Creating self in narrative* (pp. 89–108). Washington, DC: American Psychological Association.

Patton, M. Q. (2002). *Qualitative research and evaluation methods* (3rd ed.). Thousand Oaks, CA: Sage.

Polanyi, L. (1985). *Telling the American story: A structural and cultural analysis of conversational storytelling*. Norwood, NJ: Ablex.

Reisman, G. I. (2007, Fall). The legacy of early experience: Prospective and retrospective evidence for enduring effects. *Psychology Times, 1*, 4.

Skaalvik, E. M., & Skaalvik, S. (2007). Dimensions of teacher self-efficacy and relations with strain factors, perceived collective teacher efficacy, and teacher burnout. *Journal of Educational Psychology, 99*(3), 611–625.

Terry, J. (2007). Buried perspectives: Narratives of landscape in Toni Morrison's *Song of Solomon. Narrative Inquiry, 17*(1), 93–118.

Valle, J. W. (2009). *What mothers say about special education: From the 1960s to the present.* New York, NY: Palgrave.

Valle, J. W., & Connor, D. J. (2012). Becoming theatrical: Performing narrative research, staging visual representation. *International Journal of Education & the Arts, 13* (Lived Aesthetic Inquiry), 1.

RESOURCES FOR FURTHER STUDY

Andrews, M., Squire, C., & Tamboukou, M. (Eds.). (2008). *Doing narrative research.* Thousand Oaks, CA: Sage.

> The contributors to this book discuss various approaches for creating narratives from stories and for analyzing the narratives. One of the chapters focuses on the politics and ethics of narrative research.

Chase, S. E. (2011). Narrative inquiry: Still a field in the making. In N. K. Denzin & Y. S. Lincoln (Eds.), *Sage handbook of qualitative research* (4th ed., pp. 421–434). Thousand Oaks, CA: Sage.

> A sociology and women's studies professor, Chase analyzes the forms of narrative research and issues facing narrative researchers and refers to her own research on the narratives of women school superintendents. The chapter gives a good picture of the complexities and varieties of narrative inquiry and its value in shedding light on the lives of those involved in educational endeavors.

Connelly, F. M., & Clandinin, D. J. (2006). Narrative inquiry. In J. L. Green, G. Camilli, & P. B. Elmore (Eds.), *Handbook of complementary methods in education research* (pp. 477–487). Mahwah, NJ: Lawrence Erlbaum.

> The authors lay out starting points for narrative inquiry; explain three commonplaces of this approach, namely temporality, sociality, and place; describe considerations in designing a narrative inquiry; and provide guidelines on moving from the original field text to a research text.

Freidus, H. (2002). Narrative research in teacher education: New questions, new practices. In N. Lyons & V. K. LaBoskey (Eds.), *Narrative inquiry in practice: Advancing the knowledge of teaching* (pp. 160–172). New York, NY: Teachers College Press.

> The author summarizes a three-year study in which researchers sought to provide professional development to experienced teachers implementing an instructional program involving promotion of student literacy. Through focus groups and interviews as exemplars of narrative research practice, teachers' perceptions of validation, community, and professional growth emerged as themes.

Sample Narrative Research Study

Teacher Identity and Early Career Resilience: Exploring the Links

Pearce, J., & Morrison, C. (2011). Teacher identity and early career resilience: Exploring the links. *Australian Journal of Teacher Education, 36*(1), Article 4, 48–59. Available at http://ro.ecu.edu.au/cgi/viewcontent.cgi?article=1513&context=ajte

The researchers address this problem of practice: the growing difficulty of attracting and retaining early career teachers. They conducted narrative research to explore factors that sustain new teachers as they form and practice their teacher identity, which includes resilience. In this article, they develop a portrait of Norah based on interviews during her first year of teaching. Norah's previous positive experience in working with people with disabilities and as a teacher assistant led her to undertake university preparation as a teacher. In her first term, she decided she would do what *she* wanted to do, not what everyone else expected. Combating her early identity formation as "dumb," and dissonance between her preferred ways of teaching and those of her teaching colleagues, Norah has continued to develop a resilient identity as a teacher based on the positive responses of parents and students in her social environment.

Teacher Identity and Early Career Resilience: Exploring the Links

JANE PEARCE
Murdoch University
J.Pearce@murdoch.edu.au

CHAD MORRISON
University of South Australia

ABSTRACT A collaborative research project that explored the impact of professional, individual and relational conditions on the resilience of early career teachers revealed the importance of understanding how they engage in the formation of professional identities. Drawing on the traditions of narrative enquiry and critical ethnography, this article focuses on the story of Norah, one of sixty beginning teachers interviewed for this study, as she experienced becoming a teacher. Norah's story provides an insight into how early career teachers engage in shaping a professional identity, and leads us to suggest that resilience may be enhanced when early career teachers engage consciously and in relationship with others in this process.

Introduction

The phenomenon of teacher shortage has become a focus of attention in many Western countries, with the difficulties of attracting and retaining early career teachers adding to the extent of the problem (Moon, 2007). Early career teachers undoubtedly experience particularly high levels of individual stress and burnout, leading to unacceptably high levels of attrition and teacher shortages (Howard & Johnson, 2004). This article explores some initial insights from a collaborative research project that aims to better understand the experiences of early career teachers and to investigate new ways in which teacher attrition can be addressed. The project involved three Australian universities and a group of eight industry partners. The research uses the lens of early career teacher resilience as a means of gaining an in-depth understanding of the interplay of personal and contextual conditions in early career teachers' experiences (Johnson et al., 2009).

As a starting point the research team adopted a definition of resilience as 'the process of, capacity for, or outcome of successful adaptation despite challenging or threatening circumstances' (Masten, Best & Garmezy, 1990, p. 425). Focusing on resilience not only as an outcome but also as a process enabled the team to go beyond the more traditional, individualistic explanations to explore the interactions between early career teachers and the social, cultural, political and relational contexts of their new profession. On the basis of the preliminary analysis of interviews with 60 early career teachers, we identified and developed five themes or 'domains'

RECOMMENDED CITATION

Pearce, Jane and Morrison, Chad (2011) "Teacher Identity and Early Career Resilience: Exploring the Links," *Australian Journal of Teacher Education*: Vol. 36: Iss. 1, Article 4. Available at: http://ro.ecu.edu.au/ajte/vol36/iss1/4

This Journal Article is posted at Research Online. http://ro.ecu.edu.au/ajte/vol36/iss1/4

in the form of a profile of contextual conditions that appear to support teacher resilience (Johnson et al., 2010). Teacher identity has emerged from this preliminary analysis as a major 'domain' in the framework of conditions that appear to enhance early career teacher resilience. In this article we focus on the story of Norah, one of sixty beginning teachers interviewed for this study, as she experienced becoming a teacher. Norah's story provides an insight into how early career teachers engage in identity work, and leads us to consider whether early career teacher resilience may be enhanced when teachers engage consciously in the construction of their professional identities.

Teacher Identity

Contemporary theory about identity has replaced the notion of a stable, unified identity with the notion of a self that is constantly being re-constituted (Holstein & Gubrium, 2000; Zembylas, 2003). This self is 'a practical discursive accomplishment 'in which individuals 'constitute and reconstitute each other' (Holstein & Gubrium, 2000, p. 70). While both personal and public identities are shaped discursively, the two are clearly distinct. Personal identity is a continuing feature of our point of view in the world and is connected to our sense of personal agency. Our public identities are those we present to the numerous different contexts in which we engage with the everyday world and behind which our personal identity 'persists' (Harre & van Langenhove, 1999, in Bullough, 2005, p. 239). Bullough's use of the terms 'core' identity and 'situational' identity are useful in clarifying the distinction between these two forms of identity (Bullough, 2005).

For teachers, situational identities are 'made available by the specific cultural and institutional contexts of schooling' (Bullough, 2005, p. 240). Institutions like schools tend to prefer and support the formation of certain kinds of professional identities above others, both limiting and enabling identity formations (Bullough, 2005). Beyond schools, identity is also subject to social and historical practices, including discourses around work and teaching. In this sense identity may be likened to *habitus*, since it is at once individual and social (Bourdieu, 1977, 1999, 2004; Maton, 2008).

Early career teachers often experience a mismatch or dissonance between idealism and reality (Abbott-Chapman, 2005). This points to the struggle that teachers experience at this stage of their careers when they are in the process of moving between 'communities of practice' (Wenger, 1998). Bullough frames his own experiences of this as having a 'double-identification and membership,' and describes the experience of living through the transition as a painful struggle: 'I was deeply and profoundly conflicted' (Bullough, 2005, pp. 246–247).

Given the difficult nature of this transition, understanding how early career teachers shape their new professional identities while at the same time enabling their personal selves to persist and remain coherent would seem to be an important part of understanding resilience. The conflicts or dissonance experienced at such moments might have negative consequences, leading to people leaving the profession, but might also have positive consequences such as new learning or motivation for change (Galman, 2009).

Alsup (2006), in her study of the intersection between personal and professional identity in preservice teachers, also explores the idea of 'situated identities', and demonstrates the complexity of the process of professional identity development. Several types of discourse intersect as part of the process of professional identity development, including the early professional identities that emerge during teacher preparation courses (Alsup, 2006). These 'borderland discourses' that describe 'attempts at connecting the multiple subjectivities or understandings of self' (Alsup, 2006, p. 55) enable teachers to build bridges between the discourses of their university courses and the new discourses of their profession. We see later how Norah experienced the difficulties of negotiating between these different discourses.

Methodology

This article draws on the traditions of narrative enquiry to develop a portrait of Norah. The portrait is based on interview data collected during term two and again at the end of term four of Norah's first year of teaching.

Narrative enquiry is a particularly appropriate approach to exploring identity formation, since personal narratives can be seen as a version of a person's identity work (Taylor & Littleton, 2006). Narratives are continuously under construction, and reflective of the changing social contexts in which they are created. They are produced for particular and prevailing ideologies within the individual's social environments (Taylor & Littleton, 2006, p. 23) and reflect the individual's motivations (Baumeister & Newman, 1994). Individuals are actively engaged in this identity work as the language, meanings and identity positions of their society continue, are negotiated and change. Furthermore, as socially constructed meanings change, the identities of individuals are dynamic, responsive and negotiated (Taylor & Littleton, 2006).

Personal narratives also incorporate the histories and experiences of the individual, scripting the biographies that are told through narrative. Importantly, personal narratives 'give voice' to those who are often silenced (Wink, 2005). Furthermore, narratives are shaped by and reflective of previous retellings of these stories that change through subsequent identity work (Zembylas,

2003). In many ways the retelling of narratives—the re-structuring of stories to incorporate the moulding of self in relation to social and/or institutional constructions—is identity work in itself, since the forming of stories to justify the reshaping at the same time further contributes to the reshaping of identities. In this sense, 'identities are the result of the inescapable and ongoing process of discussion, explanation, negotiation, argumentation and justification that partly comprises teachers' lives and practices' (Clarke, 2009, p. 187). Marsh (2003, p. 8) further states that 'we are continually in the process of fashioning and refashioning our identities by patching together fragments of the discourses to which we are exposed'. Narrative allows for this patching together of experience, incorporating its contradictory and ambiguous nature while building a richness and continuity of self that may otherwise be lost or overlooked (Baumeister & Newman, 1994). Consequently, narrative allows us to simultaneously analyse the individual and the narrative itself (Riessman & Speedy, 2007).

Norah's story provides an insight into how, as an early career teacher, she engages in this kind of identity work through constructing a narrative about her experiences of teaching. Her narrative includes reflections on her personal identity, a statement of her teaching philosophy, and accounts of interactions with significant others in her professional life (students, colleagues and parents). In the process of becoming a teacher, Norah experiences the complex interplay between personal and professional identities as she struggles to keep 'that little bit of me' in the classroom. Her story leads us to consider whether early career teacher resilience may be enhanced when they engage consciously in the construction of their professional identities.

Norah's Story

Norah is an early childhood teacher in her first year of teaching. At the time of the first interview she was based in a large primary (elementary) school and employed on a one-year contract. The school is situated in a low socioeconomic status, outer metropolitan suburb, and hers is a class of 22 five- and six- year olds. The older children are in their first year of compulsory schooling while the younger ones are in the 'pre-primary' phase: in other words, in the year prior to the first year of compulsory schooling. She first spoke about her experiences after two terms of teaching.

As a girl, Norah said, she had not wanted to be a teacher. She 'dropped out' in her final year of school, deciding she 'wasn't cut out for university', and went instead to a vocational education college to gain a qualification to work with people with disabilities. She did this for a while and then worked in a special school as an assistant to the teacher. There, others began to comment that she was a lot more confident when working with the children than the teacher was. 'Everyone used to joke and say I might as well be the teacher, including the teacher, because I'd sort of take control.' So Norah thought, 'Why not actually be the teacher?' This reframing of her identity led her to university.

University was a wonderful experience for Norah. She learnt a lot about herself in the four years of her degree, particularly that she could do well in an academic setting. As a child she had thought that she was the 'dumb one' in her family, the odd one out because her brother, sister and both parents were all 'really into reading' books while she was content to read comics. However, getting top marks for her work at university showed her that if she really put her mind to it she could achieve academically. Her success at university gave her a huge confidence boost.

At the end of her final year Norah applied to teach in a number of remote schools in the north of Australia, but when the principal of the school where she did her final pre-service teaching placement phoned to offer her a one-year teaching contract, she accepted.

In the first interview Norah spoke about her teaching philosophy. She believes strongly in the value of play-based education for young children. She feels passionate about this. She thinks a lot of people undervalue play and don't understand that children actually are learning when they are playing. She also likes having hands-on activities, and to display the individual things that the children have made. In this she is unlike the teachers in surrounding classrooms, where artwork 'such as 20 identical rabbits' is displayed 'just to make the classroom look attractive'. She also likes using the natural world as the basis for her teaching and is trying to explore that as much as possible by taking her class outside and planning learning based on the things to be found in the areas of bush around the school. At the time of the interview she was worried about plans to cut down some of the trees in the playground, because they are 'too annoying'. Her goal is to be the most effective teacher she can be.

The school where she works is broken down into small teaching teams of teachers and teacher assistants who work in adjacent classrooms teaching children in the same age group. The teachers who work alongside Norah do not share many of her views about teaching and learning, such as the value of play in the curriculum. This has made her feel rather alone in the school, as she has no one to talk to about how to develop as the kind of teacher she would like to become. She would like to have an ally on the staff who thinks the way she does. However, despite her professional isolation, Norah's approach seems to be working with the children and their parents. She hasn't had any 'major dramas' here, and her relationships with her students and their parents are going well.

Norah's most memorable teaching experience in her first term was when she decided she would do what *she* wanted to do, not what everyone else expected. She and her class played with ice. The original focus was reading, and the children were learning the letter 'i'. But the lesson turned into a science experiment when Norah let the class direct the learning themselves. Students talked excitedly about why the ice was melting and then timed how long it took to melt. Norah was able to sit and observe and interact with the students, and record what the children were saying so she could use it to inform her planning. This example shows the satisfaction Norah gained when she was able to teach in the way she believed was best for students' learning. The lesson showed so well how simple play could support 'all that learning'.

When we picked up Norah's story again at the end of term four she had just discovered that her contract was to be renewed for another year. Although she felt a sense of satisfaction about this she was not sure whether she would accept another contract. Since the earlier interview things had 'gone downhill fairly quickly' as she continued to struggle with the different opinions about teaching that she has found amongst her colleagues. She had 'sort of given up on a lot of things' that she would have liked to do, and it has been 'just too difficult' to work in the ways she would have liked to. The sense of isolation she described in the first interview has remained, despite her attempts to offer to share resources and ideas with her colleagues. She began to discover that her colleagues were making decisions that affected her when she was not there, and she has found it difficult to 'break in'. In the second interview she described how she has started to think about finding another job outside teaching. She came across an advertisement for a job as machine operator at a mine site, and thought, 'pushing buttons sounds good right now'. 'Will I do this [teach] forever?' she asked herself.

Identity Formation in Norah's Story

Norah's story reveals how she engages with becoming a teacher, and her story speaks of processes of identity formation. Identity formation involves a 'reflexive awareness' of a self, constituted in relation to others (Giddens, 1991, p. 52). Individual identity is only meaningful in relation to 'the social world of other people' (Jenkins, 1996, p. 20), and hence an important aspect of understanding identity is understanding where one 'fits' in relation to other people. For early career teachers like Norah, their colleagues, their students, the students' families and the local community all help to provide the relational boundaries within which they form new professional identities. It is also important to understand that Norah's identity formation began long before our research interest in her and will continue on long after our research interest has shifted (Riessman & Speedy, 2007).

Throughout her childhood, Norah's early identity formation framed her as 'dumb' in relation to her siblings and parents. This identity was later reinforced by her schooling experiences and led to her dropping out of school. However, once she began to work in classrooms her emerging identity as a teacher was confirmed by everyone around her and led to her pursuit of a teaching degree. Not only is she now a fully qualified teacher, but someone with a very clear view about the kind of teacher she wants to be and someone whose sense of professional identity is becoming coherent. But this may be fragile while she does not feel she has teaching colleagues who think the same as her.

A coherent sense of identity is characterised by an individual's ability to integrate experiences in the outside world into an 'ongoing 'story' about the self' (Giddens, 1991, p. 52). This process of integrating new experiences into a 'story of self' would seem to be a key aspect of the experiences of early career teachers as they explore new identities alongside the exploration of new professional roles. Norah is intent on sustaining her professional self despite her new experiences of an absence of affirmation by others and a limited sense of belonging.

The conviction with which Norah speaks of her goals and successes in teaching indicates that as an undergraduate she found a professional space within a set of guiding principles about pedagogy (based on play and student self-direction) that resonates with her. Her identity thus encompasses her beliefs about how children learn and about the role of the teacher in supporting learning, and is underpinned by her values such as what is worth knowing and the importance of recognising each child's individual achievement. Like all new teachers Norah is now operating in a particular professional space in which social interactions are vital in shaping her teacher identity (McLeod, 2001; Forde, McMahon, McPhee & Patrick, 2006) and not all of Norah's beliefs will be supported within this space. In Norah's case, her social interactions work against her developing the particular identity she seeks and hence she is left with feelings of isolation and dissonance, to the extent that after one year in teaching she is considering leaving. Her description of the wonderful day when she stepped back to allow the children to explore ice, when she decided she would just do what *she* wanted to do and not what everyone else was expecting her to do, shows that this experience took place in spite of, not because of, the existence of a professional space for this kind of work to happen. The fact that by the end of the year she has 'given up on a lot of things' is evidence of how hard it has been to continue to learn and grow in a situation of professional conflict.

Dissonance and Habitus: Their Potential for Learning and Growth

Cognitive dissonance occurs when 'two things occur together . . . [but] they do not belong together' (Festinger,

1958, p. 63). Cognitive dissonance can be thought of as the 'product of conflict between one or more opposing thoughts' (Galman, 2009, p. 471). For example, such dissonance may be the product of the difference between how individuals see themselves and how others perceive them (Raffo & Hall, 2006); the result of differences between the individuals' beliefs, values and expectations of teaching and the realities of the profession (Galman, 2009; Raffo & Hall, 2006); or teaching contexts that contrast with those previously experienced (Raffo & Hall, 2006).

In experiencing conflict between her own preferred ways of teaching and those of other teachers in the school, Norah could be said to be experiencing all of these types of cognitive dissonance (Galman, 2009). Cognitive dissonance is relevant to Norah's experiences as her current narrative reveals tensions between what she believes are important understandings about teaching, derived from and shaped by the formation of her habitus (Bourdieu, 1998, 2004), and the different realities of how teaching is structured by others around her. The experience of dissonance is not necessarily benign and leads in some instances to feelings of stress and depression (Anderson et al., 2010) that in turn are likely to compromise a person's resilience. Yet dissonance also brings with it the potential for growth, learning and transformation (Mezirow, 2000). For Norah and other early career teachers like her it will be important to ensure that their experiences of dissonance lead to positive outcomes, including the enhanced resilience that comes with the construction of professional identities that are 'in tune' with their personal identities.

For Norah, her continued experiences of failure and lack of enjoyment of school as a student contributed to her decision to leave early. As a teacher at the start of her career, it will be important to ensure that similar negative experiences do not once again contribute to a decision to leave the field. Norah continues to believe in herself as a teacher and in the philosophies that she has about teaching and learning, but also acknowledges the challenges to both that are present in the realities of her professional setting. The narratives that she constructs reveal this dissonance, but also show the subtle ways in which she is trying to establish congruence by consciously going against the grain and appealing to the positive feedback from students and parents to support her professional decisions. While at the time of the interview dissonance was acting as a motivator for Norah, the possibility remains that ultimately this dissonance will become an inhibitor that will lead her once again to make the decision to leave.

Raffo & Hall (2006) describe the type of positioning that Norah is engaged in as reflective of 'habitus' (Bourdieu, 1977, 1999, 2004). Bourdieu (1998, 2004) uses the concept to describe the way in which individuals behave and how they structure and live their daily lives. Habitus appears to be common sense and natural; it is of individuals' own making, but in many ways is made unselfconsciously. Habitus is intimately connected with the experiences that are the result of individuals' engagements with the external world.

Habitus is important in interpreting Norah's narratives—of self-as-other-than-teacher and eventually of self-as-teacher—as these reflect the systems, beliefs and structures that exist within her and her lived and experienced world (Bourdieu, 1998, 2004). Norah's history, prior values, dispositions, behaviours and orientations influenced her initially to believe that she could go to university. Later, she constructed new narratives that enabled her to envisage a different future as a teacher. These decisions reflect Norah's ability to capitalise on her cultural and material resources (Bourdieu, 1998), while attempting to reduce or eliminate cognitive dissonance (Festinger, 1958). Here, habitus provides the lens for viewing the structures and guiding framework for choice, while dissonance emerges as a force for action.

How are Identity Formation and Resilience Connected?

We note the perception that 'reduction of dissonance is rewarding, in the same sense that eating when hungry is rewarding' (Festinger, 1958, p. 63). While it would be a misapprehension, in our view, to limit the explanation of Norah's identity formation to a superficial view of the rewards of reducing dissonance, it is in the processes of coming to terms with dissonance that Norah reveals herself working to develop her professional identity. By attempting to overcome this dissonance, Norah is fashioning a sense of self that reflects the social and institutional expectations of the profession while also enabling her personal self to remain coherent. The extent to which she is successful may have a bearing on her capacity to be resilient.

Norah positioned herself early in life as someone who, because of her perceived academic limitations, lacked the potential to become a teacher. Later, as the result of new experiences and her different readings of how she was positioned in relation to the social, professional and learning spaces she inhabited, she opted into the teaching profession. Understandings of the rewards available to her (Bourdieu, 1977) throughout her undergraduate preparation contributed to the rewriting of stories that suited her needs. But this does not mean that her original position was one of a lack of resilience. While her experiences and sense of self are now telling her a new story of self-as-teacher, this does not then mean that teachers (pre-service, early career or experienced) tell themselves stories to keep themselves in the profession simply because it suits them to reaffirm those stories. The function of these stories may be to maintain a person's role and status as a teacher, to overcome dissonance (to learn, grow or be 'resilient') or to position themselves to make the most of their cultural capital within the field (Bourdieu, 1998), in this case the field of teachers' work.

We argue that resilience is about more than assuring positive outcomes for individual teachers in terms of the development of pedagogical effectiveness, the acquisition of a professional knowledge and skills base, and the achievement of professional acceptance and belonging. If Norah cannot reconcile her struggles to acknowledge where she falls outside of the boundaries of the field, from her colleagues' perspectives, her capacity to remain engaged in her profession is compromised. We suggest that if she is to be resilient and remain engaged in her profession it will be important for her to use her own beliefs about teaching and learning to author a new script that allows her to capitalise on her investments in becoming a teacher.

The stories that Norah constructs affirm the emergence of a secondary habitus (Bourdieu, 1977)—that of a teacher—and justify her place within the profession through the social responses of parents and students within her social environment. In this sense, Norah's story falls into what Alsup (2006) describes as 'borderland discourse', which involves becoming conscious of how one's thoughts and actions can 'incorporate the personal as well as the professional' (Alsup, 2006, p. 125). Engaging in such discourse involves honouring one's personal beliefs and experiences while at the same time acting in ways that are recognisably professional. Norah's experiences, in which she is not only trying to incorporate the personal as well as the professional but also having to choose between different ways of being professional, suggest that this process is not clear cut. Importantly, successful engagement in such work results in the development of a 'personal pedagogy' that incorporates both personal beliefs and ideologies and educational theory as a philosophical basis for decision making in the classroom (Alsup, 2006, p. 127).

Identity formation is the product of interaction with others, since 'identity is at once a complex matter of the social and the individual' (Clarke, 2009, p. 189). Such interactions, which may include the conversations teachers have about teaching, the emails they send to friends where they reconstitute events of the day, the seeking of support from critical friends about their practice and the myriad of other interchanges between teachers, we suggest when taken together constitute practices that result in identity formation. Through these exchanges teachers are modelling and shaping the self—the language, meanings and structuring of self go hand-in-hand with the formation of professional identities. We suggest that this means that the shaping of a professional identity takes place during teachers' social exchanges and as a result of interactions within other members of the school community such as students and parents. Evidence of this work

is embedded in Norah's story. For example, Norah's recognition that she *is* creating positive opportunities for students is likely to contribute to a different construction of herself as a teacher than if she were to incorporate her colleagues' counter perspectives to judge the quality of her teaching. The shaping of her professional identity involves reconciling the dissonance she has experienced when at the centre of these different social exchanges.

Whether Norah continues to make a success of this process as she makes her way through the difficult early years of teaching remains to be seen. It has been suggested that commonly occurring perceptions of teacher identities (such as a teaching 'personality', a disposition to care and the ability to teach a curriculum) may no longer 'fit the school contexts in which teachers operate' (Sugrue, 1997, p. 222). In Norah's story, there is a suggestion that normalised discourses about teaching in that particular school threaten to overshadow more individualistic expressions of identity such as those found in her story. In such a case, there is a risk that an impoverished view of the teacher's role will form the dominant narrative of what it is to be a teacher, with diminishing possibilities for behaving differently. However, '[e]ven in the face of strong "enculturation" individuals have choice about the positions they adopt in relation to the workplace, what they learn and how they identify with it' (Shreeve, 2009, p. 152). To ensure that Norah's experience of dissonance leads to growth and a desire to remain in the profession, it may be essential that she be supported in engaging in social exchanges with colleagues that enable her to consciously exercise this choice.

Conclusion

Identity formation is a discursive process, taking place as a result of interactions with others and developing as part of a narrative of the self (Giddens, 1991; Danielewicz, 2001; Sfard & Prusak, 2005; Alsup, 2006). Such identity formation may be seen as a constitution of oneself within a range of possibilities and meanings (Zembylas, 2003, p. 107). For teachers at the beginning of their career, interactions with colleagues (teaching and non-teaching), students and students' families are all crucial to this construction of self. Successful engagement in the construction of the new self seems to be assisted in professional contexts where new and different ways of thinking can be accommodated, both by teachers at the start of their careers and by more experienced colleagues. While Norah's interactions with others have at times led to experiencing dissonance that made her question her decision to become a teacher, her desire to 'have that little bit of me in there' remains a resource that helps her to engage productively with the challenges she faces. This realisation of her identity results in a sense of agency, 'of empowerment to move ideas forward, to reach goals, or even to transform the context' (Beauchamp & Thomas, 2009, p. 183), and in turn contributes to her becoming resilient through strengthening her ability to cope with negative experiences such as her sense of being isolated in the school. The experience of 'being disconnected from our own truth, from the passions that took us into teaching' has been described as 'painful' (Palmer, 1998, p. 21). Norah's story is indicative of the power of this assertion, and hints at the central importance for Norah of hanging on to fragments of her 'own truth' about the kind of teacher she wants to be as she grapples with what it means to be a teacher.

REFERENCES

Abbott-Chapman, J. (2005). Let's keep our beginning teachers! *Principal Matters*. Summer 2005, 2–4.

Alsup, J. (2006). *Teacher identity discourses: Negotiating personal and professional spaces*. Mahwah, NJ: Lawrence Erlbaum Associates.

Anderson, J., Reimer, J., Khan, K., Simich, L., Neufeld, A., Stewart, M. & Makwarimba, E. (2010). Narratives of 'dissonance' and 'repositioning' through the lens of critical humanism. *Advances in Nursing Science*, 33(2), 101–112.

Baumeister, R. & Newman, L. (1994). How stories make sense of personal experiences: Motives that shape autobiographical narratives, *Personality and Social Psychology Bulletin*, 20(6), 676–690.

Beauchamp, C. & Thomas, L. (2009). Understanding teacher identity: An overview of issues in the literature and implications for teacher education, *Cambridge Journal of Education*, 39(2), 175–189.

Bullough, R. J. (2005). The quest for identity in teaching and teacher education. In G. Hoban (Ed.) *The missing links in teacher education design* (pp. 237–258). Dordrecht: Springer.

Bourdieu, P. (1977). *Outline of a theory of practice*. Cambridge: Cambridge University Press.

Bourdieu, P. (1998). The new capital. In P. Bourdieu (Ed.), *Practical reason*. Stanford, CA: Stanford University Press.

Bourdieu, P. (1999). *The weight of the world: Social suffering in contemporary society*. Oxford: Polity Press.

Bourdieu, P. (2004). The forms of capital. In S. Ball (Ed.), *The RoutledgeFalmer reader in sociology of education*. Oxford: RoutledgeFalmer.

Clarke, M. (2009). The ethico-politics of teacher identity. *Educational Philosophy and Theory*, 41(2), 185–200.

Danielewicz, J. (2001). *Teaching selves: Identity, pedagogy and teacher education*. Albany, New York: State University of New York Press.

Festinger, L. (1958). The motivating effect of cognitive dissonance. In G. Lindsey (Ed.), *Assessment of human motives*. New York: Holt, Rinehart & Winston.

Forde, C., McMahon, M., McPhee, A. and Patrick, F. (2006). *Professional development, reflection and enquiry*. London: Paul Chapman.

Galman, S. (2009). Doth the lady protest too much? Pre-service teachers and the experience of dissonance as a catalyst for development. *Teaching and Teacher Education*, 25(3), 468–481.

Giddens, A. (1991). *Modernity and self-identity: Self and society in the late modern age*. Stanford, CA: Stanford University Press.

Holstein, J. and Gubrium, J. (2000). *The self we live by: Narrative identity in a postmodern world*. Oxford: Oxford University Press.

Howard, S., & Johnson, B. (2004). Resilient teachers: Resisting stress and burnout. *Social Psychology of Education*, 7(3), 399–420.

Jenkins, R. (1996). *Social identity*. London: Routledge.

Johnson, B., Le Cornu, R., Down, B., Sullivan, A., Peters, J., Pearce, J. and Hunter, J. (2009). Examining early career teacher resilience: Insights from an Australian study. *British Educational Research Association Annual Conference*, Manchester, UK 2–5 September.

Johnson, B., Down, B., Le Cornu, R., Peters, J. Sullivan, A., Pearce, J. and Hunter, J. (2010). Conditions that support early career teacher resilience. Refereed paper presented at the *Australian Teacher Education Association Conference*, Townsville, Queensland, 4–7 July.

Maton, K. (2008). Habitus. In M. Grenfell (Ed.), *Pierre Bourdieu: Key concepts*. Stocksfield: Acumen.

McLeod, J. (2001). *Teacher working knowledge: The value of lived experience*. Retrieved 28.08.09 from: http://ultibase.rmit.edu.au/Articles/nov01/mcleod1.htm

Marsh, M. (2003). *The social fashioning of teacher identities*. New York: Peter Lang.

Masten, A., Best, K. & Garmezy, N. (1990). Resilience and development: Contributions from the study of children who overcome adversity. *Development and Psychopathology*, 2, 425–444.

Mezirow, J. (2000). *Learning as transformation: Critical perspectives on a theory in progress*. San Francisco, CA: John Wiley.

Moon, B. (2007). *Research analysis: Attracting, developing and retaining effective teachers—a global overview of current policies and practices*. Paris, France: UNESCO.

Palmer, P.J. (1998). *The courage to teach: Exploring the inner landscape of a teacher's life*. San Francisco, CA: Jossey Bass.

Raffo, C. and Hall, D. (2006). Transitions to becoming a teacher on an initial teacher education and training programme. *British Journal of Sociology of Education*, 27(1), 53–66.

Riessman, C. Kohler and Speedy, J. (2007). Narrative inquiry in the psychotherapy professions: a critical review. In D. Jean Clandinin (Ed.) *Handbook of narrative inquiry: mapping a methodology*. Thousand Oaks, CA: Sage Publications.

Sfard, A. and Prusak, A. (2005). Telling identities: In search of an analytic tool for investigating learning, *Educational Researcher*, 34(4), 14–22.

Shreeve, A. (2009). 'I'd rather be seen as a practitioner, come in to teach my subject': Identity work in part-time art and design tutors. *International Journal of Art & Design Education*, 28(2), 151–159.

Sugrue, C. (1997). Student teachers' lay theories and teaching identities: Their implications for professional development. *European Journal of Teacher Education*, 20(3), 213–225.

Taylor, S., and Littleton, K. (2006). Biographies in talk: a narrative-discursive research approach. *Qualitative Sociology Review*, 2(1), 22–38.

Wenger, E. (1998). *Communities of practice: Learning, meaning and identity.* Cambridge: Cambridge University Press.

Wink, J. (2005). *Critical pedagogy: Notes from the real world* (3rd ed.) Boston, MA: Pearson Education.

Zembylas, M. (2003). Interrogating 'Teacher identity': Emotion, resistance and self-formation, *Educational Theory*, 53(1), 107–127.

ACKNOWLEDGEMENTS

This article is an outcome of a collaborative research project, funded by the Australian Research Council, between the University of South Australia, Murdoch University, Edith Cowan University and eight education sector organisations in South Australia and Western Australia. The research team also includes Professor Bruce Johnson, Professor Barry Down, Dr Anna Sullivan, Dr Rosie Le Cornu, Dr Judith Peters and Ms Janet Hunter.

CHAPTER SIXTEEN

Historical Research

PROBLEMS OF PRACTICE *in this chapter*

- How can female educators succeed in their quest for equal career opportunities and equal pay?
- Why was the practice of separate schooling for Mexican American children so prevalent in the Southwest for the first half of the 20th century?
- Why was social justice in education not a priority in the past, and what can be done to promote it?
- Why was school attendance not a priority in the past? How did the movement for compulsory school attendance come about?
- How serious was the problem of inequality between rural and urban school districts in the past, and what was done to address it?
- What foreign languages should be taught in schools?
- What is the proper role of the school principal?

IMPORTANT *Ideas*

1. Historical research relies primarily on qualitative approaches to data collection and analysis.
2. Historical research is relevant to educators as a basis for understanding current practices and policies and as a resource for planning the improvement of education.
3. Historians find data about the past by consulting search engines and bibliographic indexes to find secondary and primary sources and by collecting oral histories.
4. The past is preserved in various forms, including documents, records, photographs and other visual media, relics, census data, and stories continually retold within a society's oral traditions.
5. The authenticity and validity of historical data is established through a process of external criticism and internal criticism.
6. Historians continually reconstruct the past as their interests and questions change.

7. Historians use concepts and causal inference to interpret their data about the past.
8. As in other forms of research, historians need to take care in generalizing their findings beyond the persons and settings they have directly studied.
9. Quantitative data can strengthen the generalizability of historical interpretations and provide a common-man perspective on the time period being studied.
10. Unlike other types of research reports, historical reports usually present findings in the form of a story, organized around key time periods that have thematic significance for the historian.

KEY TERMS

archive	historical research	reconstructionist
artifact	internal criticism	record
bias	oral history	relic
document	presentism	repository
external criticism	primary source	revisionist historian
forgery	quantitative historical materials	search engine
futurology	quantitative history	secondary source

THE NATURE OF HISTORICAL RESEARCH

Nearly everyone reads histories—histories of countries, of wars, of organizations, of people, and of many other subjects. They watch histories on television, such as Ken Burns's series on the history of the Civil War, Prohibition, and baseball. Many movies also base their drama on events of historical significance—*Titanic*, *The Queen*, and *United 93* come to mind.

In this chapter, we examine the research process used to produce a history. **Historical research** is the process of systematically searching for and organizing data to better understand past phenomena and their likely causes and consequences.

Contemporary historians tend to dismiss most histories written by scholars of bygone eras as mere chronicles of events and lives. Their own writings generally are shorter, subordinating historical facts to an interpretive framework within which those facts are given meaning and significance. In this chapter, we treat historical research as a qualitative research tradition because of its reliance on, although not exclusive use of, qualitative approaches to data collection and analysis.

The types of research that we describe in other chapters of this book involve the creation of data. For example, researchers create data when they make observations or administer tests to determine the effectiveness of an instructional program. In contrast, historical researchers primarily discover data that already exist in such sources as diaries, official documents, and relics. On occasion, though, historical researchers interview individuals to gather their recollections of past events. This form of historical research, called **oral history**, does involve data creation.

THE ROLE OF HISTORICAL RESEARCH IN EDUCATION

Many journal articles and books about the history of education are published each year. The following list illustrates the range of possible topics.

Caruso, M. P. (2012). *When the sisters said farewell: The transition of leadership in Catholic elementary schools.* Lanham, MD: Rowman & Littlefield Publishers.

Gasman, M., & Geiger, R. L. (Eds.). (2012). *Higher education for African Americans before the Civil Rights era, 1900–1964.* New Brunswick, NJ: Transaction Publishers.

Gidney, R. D. (2012). *How schools worked: Public education in English Canada, 1900–1940.* Montreal, QC: McGill-Queen's University Press.

Kohlstedt, S. G. (2008). "A better crop of boys and girls": The school gardening movement, 1890–1920. *History of Education Quarterly, 48*(1), 58–93.

Spillman, S. (2012). Institutional limits: Christine Ladd-Franklin, fellowships, and American women's academic careers, 1880–1920. *History of Education Quarterly, 52*(2), 196–221.

Woyshner, C. (2011). School desegregation and civil society: The unification of Alabama's black and white parent-teacher associations, 1954–1971. *History of Education Quarterly, 51*(1), 49–76.

Why would anyone wish to study these past events when there are so many current problems in education to be solved? One answer to this question is the truism, "Those who ignore the lessons of the past are doomed to repeat them."

Another answer is that studying the past helps us understand why things are the way they are today. Powerful forces have shaped our current education system, and they continue to keep it in place. For example, several of the historical studies cited above concern the influence of conservative groups and radical reformers on educational practice. An understanding of those forces might help us to understand, for example, whether current educational reforms will take hold, be modified, or disappear.

Some historical studies trace the growth of an educational practice and identify key figures in that growth. The study of Christine Ladd-Franklin cited above (Spillman, 2012) serves that purpose. The researcher identifies her seminal contribution to equal opportunity and equal pay for female educators. Ladd-Franklin became one of the best-educated women in the latter part of the 1800s and then devoted her career to creating fellowship programs to enable women to have the same opportunities as men for careers in higher education. By showing that female professors could perform at the same level as male professors, she helped to change the way that female professors and school teachers were perceived, and this change in turn paved the way for equal pay for women in these careers. As professionals, we need real-life heroes to inspire us and demonstrate that improvement of educational practice actually can happen.

Before reading the history of the school gardening movement cited above (Kohlstedt, 2008), we did not realize that there once was such a movement. This historical study is interesting in its own right, but it also serves another purpose. It motivates educators to think about the implications of the school gardening movement for present-day schooling, nearly a century after it came and went. For example, the study suggests how the school curriculum might play a role in addressing current concerns about the health of the natural environment.

In short, historical research gives us a way to engage in a continuing dialogue with the past. What we know about past events changes as we ask new questions. What we learn about the past gives us new ways of thinking about the present and stimulates our thinking on how to improve the practice of education.

REVISIONIST HISTORY

Some historical researchers, generally called **revisionist historians** or **reconstructionists**, conduct research to point out aspects of a phenomenon that they believe were missed or distorted in previous historical accounts. Their studies are informed by critical theory (also called critical research), which we discuss in Chapter 14. The larger goal of revisionist history is to sensitize educators to past practices that appear to have had unjust aims and effects but have continued into the present and thus require reform. For example, a study of educational innovation in mid-19th-century Massachusetts demonstrated how it functioned to serve dominant economic interests and thwart many people's democratic aspirations (Katz, 1968).

As another example, a study of schooling in the Southwest in the first half of the 20th century (Gonzalez, 2013) found a widespread practice of separate schooling for Mexican American children. Gilbert Gonzalez concluded that this practice was encouraged by the economic interests of white communities in this part of the United States. These studies alert educators to the possibility of similar problems with current educational practices and innovations so that they can be avoided or corrected.

An example of revisionist history can be found in the study of the role of public school administrators. Catherine Lugg and Alan Shoho (2006) examined the life and influence of George Counts, who, in 1932, gave an influential speech, "Dare the School Build a New Social Order?" He and his followers called upon school administrators to advocate for social justice within their schools and to take on a political role within their community to advocate for this goal. This historical view of the school administrator's role contrasts with the historical approach in the reprinted article at the end of this chapter, which emphasizes the emergence of the school principal's role as bureaucratic manager and the conflicts that arose in deciding who was qualified to fill this role.

There is debate about whether and how educational historians should raise findings such as these in the arena of educational policy making. Some historians believe they should influence policy making directly, whereas others believe that historians might corrupt the integrity of their discipline by becoming too closely involved with the policy-making process. Ruben Donato and Marvin Lazerson (2000) reviewed these differing views and made their own recommendation:

> [E]ducational policies are proposed and implemented in the context of historical moments. Invariably, the policies rest on assumptions about the past; they rest on the stories people believe about the past. Educational historians have an obligation to thrust their stories into the policy arena for if they do not, the stories that become the common view will be told by others who often have little stake in the integrity of historical scholarship. Or, even worse, their stories will go unnoticed altogether. (p. 10)

Another viewpoint, which we espouse, is that educators and policy makers should search for all relevant evidence, including revisionist histories, when thinking about how to best solve a problem of practice.

FUTUROLOGY

A type of research called **futurology** specifically examines what the future is likely to be. Some futurology studies are based on surveys of current

trends, while others use simulation and gaming involving various imagined future scenarios. The predictions are based largely on statistical logic or rational reasoning derived from the study of past events.

Another purpose of historical research, then, is to assist educators in defining and evaluating alternative future scenarios involving a particular educational phenomenon. If we know how certain individuals or groups have acted in the past, we can predict with a certain degree of confidence how they will act in the future. For example, we can make a good prediction of how specific legislators will vote on an upcoming education bill by researching their past voting records.

METHODS OF HISTORICAL RESEARCH

In the next sections of this chapter, we describe the process of historical research as a series of steps: (1) identifying historical sources, (2) validating historical evidence, and (3) interpreting historical data. Keep in mind, though, that many researchers skip back and forth among these steps. For example, consider the research process used by the historian Edward Carr (1967):

> For myself, as soon as I have got going on a few of what I take to be the capital sources, the itch becomes too strong and I begin to write—not necessarily at the beginning, but somewhere, anywhere. Thereafter, reading and writing go on simultaneously. The writing is added to, subtracted from, re-shaped, cancelled, as I go on reading. The reading is guided and directed and made fruitful by the writing: the more I write, the more I know what I am looking for, the better I understand the significance and relevance of what I find. (pp. 32–33)

Carr's process might remind you of processes found in case study research (see Chapter 13). There is an initial research plan, but as data are collected and analyzed, new research questions can be framed, new research participants can be added, and new sources of data can be identified.

IDENTIFYING HISTORICAL SOURCES

As we explained above, historians primarily seek to discover rather than create data that are relevant to their research problems. Those data are available in various sources, which historians identify by reflecting on the types of sources likely to exist, which individuals or institutions are likely to have produced them, and where they are likely to be stored. These reflections are the basis for an initial search plan. As their interpretive framework develops, or as their sources point them toward new sources, historians can revise their tentative search plan.

Historians generally use the types of sources that we describe in Chapter 4—search engines and bibliographic indexes to find secondary and primary sources.

Search Engines and Bibliographic Indexes

A literature search for historical research studies usually begins with the use of a search engine. You will recall from Chapter 4 that a **search engine** is software that enables you to search through a database of publications to identify those relevant to your research topic. Hard-copy bibliographic indexes also are sources that can be used for this purpose.

Many of the general search engines and bibliographic indexes that we describe in Chapter 4 are useful for doing a search of historical literature. In addition, you might want to make use of these resources to identify researchers who have conducted historical studies in your area of interest. Figure 16.1 lists search engines and bibliographic indexes that you might find particularly useful.

Secondary Sources

A **secondary source** in historical research is a document or other record in which the author describes events not from direct witnesses but from descriptions generated by other individuals who witnessed or participated in them. Many newspaper articles and television news broadcasts are secondary sources, because the reporters rely on interviews with eyewitnesses to obtain the information. Annual reports of educational programs and school operations also are secondary sources if they are prepared by individuals who rely on data collected from other individuals, such as school administrators and teachers.

Most historians read a substantial number of secondary sources early in the research process in order to clarify their research problem and determine the types of primary sources that are relevant. Sometimes they decide just to accept the information in a secondary source about a relevant primary source rather than tracking down the primary source itself. In other cases, historians might decide they need to examine the primary source directly. In making this decision, they consider the reputation of the author of the secondary source, the degree of compatibility between that author's interpretive framework and their own, and the feasibility of gaining access to the primary source.

Primary Sources

A **primary source** in historical research is any document or other record (e.g., a diary, the minutes of a meeting, a map, a set of test scores, or physical objects) preserved from the past or created to document a past phenomenon by someone who witnessed or participated in it. Historians rely on four main types of primary sources: (1) text and other media, (2) oral history, (3) relics, and (4) quantitative materials. We describe each of these types of primary sources in the following sections.

Text and Other Media

Text materials, whether written or printed, are the most common primary source for historical research. Yvonna Lincoln and Egon Guba (1985) classify such materials as either a **document**, which is prepared for personal use only (e.g., a letter to a friend or a private diary), or a **record**, which has an official purpose (e.g., a legal contract, a will, or a newspaper article). Documents and records might contain handwritten, typed, or computer-generated text. They can be published or unpublished and represent various genres (e.g., newspaper articles, poetry, or novels).

The text materials examined by historians might include materials intentionally written to serve as a record of the past, such as a memoir or a school yearbook. Other text materials might be prepared only to serve an immediate purpose (e.g., school memos or teacher-prepared tests), with no expectation of any later use as a historical source.

FIGURE 16.1 • Search Engines and Hard-Copy Indexes for Historical Research

America: History and life. Retrieved from ebscohost.com/academic/america-history-and-life
   A search engine for identifying journal articles about U.S. and Canadian history from prehistory to the present.

Biography and genealogy master index. Retrieved from gale.cengage.com
   A hard-copy and electronic index to biographical sketches of several million contemporary and historical figures from around the world. Updated annually.

Biography reference bank. Retrieved from ebscohost.com/us-high-schools/biography-reference-bank
   A search engine for identifying biographical information, photos, and articles about more than 600,000 individuals.

Carson, D. C. (2012). *Directory of genealogical and historical libraries, archives and collections in the US and Canada.* Boulder, CO: Iron Gate.
   A two-volume, hard-copy index of genealogical and historical materials located in over 40,000 societies, periodicals libraries, archives, and collections.

Carter, S. B., Gartner, S. S., Haines, M. R., Olmstead, A. L., Sutch, R., & Wright, G. (Eds.). (2006). *Historical statistics of the United States.* Cambridge, UK: Cambridge University Press.
   A comprehensive source of quantitative data relating to American history. The data are organized into five categories: population; work and welfare; economic structure and performance; economic sectors; and governance and international relations. Available in electronic and hard-copy formats.

Fritze, R. H., Coutts, B. E., & Vyhnanek, L. A. (2004). *Reference sources in history: An introductory guide* (2nd ed.). Santa Barbara, CA: ABC-CLIO.
   A comprehensive guide to sources of historical information: national bibliographies and libraries, book reviews, periodicals and journals, dissertations, government publications and legal sources, biographies, dictionaries and encyclopedias, geographical and statistical sources, and archives.

National Union Catalog of Manuscript Collections. Retrieved from loc.gov/coll/nucmc/
   A search engine sponsored by the Library of Congress for identifying and cataloging nearly 1.5 million historical documents and archives of national interest.

United States Newspaper Program. Retrieved from loc.gov/rr/news/usnp/usnpp.html
   Sponsored by the National Endowment for the Humanities, the program maintains a microfilm collection of newspapers published in the United States from the 18th century to the present. The program also maintains an electronic database of newspapers.

Increasingly, visual media are used to store and communicate information—for example, television, film, CDs, DVDs, digital photos, and web-based streaming videos. Ian Grosvenor and Martin Lawn (2001) claim that these media can yield important evidence about historical events and practices in education.

Oral History

Many cultures use ballads, tales, and other forms of spoken language to preserve a record of past events for posterity. Historical researchers can make recordings of these oral accounts and use them as primary sources. Another possibility is to interview individuals who witnessed or participated in events of potential historical significance, recording and transcribing the interviews to produce a written record. The use of existing oral accounts of the past, or the collection of these oral accounts, constitutes what is commonly called **oral history**.

An example of oral history is *Missing Stories*, a book by Leslie Kelen and Eileen Stone (1996) about eight cultural communities in the state of Utah. These researchers conducted lengthy interviews with 352 individuals, taped the interviews, and transcribed them. The book presents the stories of 88 of the individuals, who share recollections of their past as it relates to their particular community.

For example, the epilogue to the chapter on the Chicano-Hispano community is the story of a Chicano woman who is an assistant principal of an intermediate school. She describes her father's struggle to get an education and become a teacher and how she, as an educator, continues his commitment to "reject rejection," despite living in an environment still tempered with racial stereotypes.

Relics

A **relic** is any object that provides information about the past. (In some historical writings, the term **artifact** is used instead of *relic*.) School supplies, computers, and blueprints of school buildings are examples of relics. Objects such as textbooks, worksheets, and instructional games can be viewed as relics if the focus of study is their material properties rather than the content of the text. For example, some material properties of textbooks are their cover (hardbound or soft cover), print color (one color or multicolor text); text augmentation (e.g., use of tables, figures, and photos); and format (hard copy or electronic file, or both). Helen Sheumaker and Shirley Wajda (2007) compiled an encyclopedia of such objects as well as other aspects of material culture that reveal glimpses of past periods in the United States.

Quantitative Historical Materials

Quantitative historical materials provide numerical information about educational phenomena and are another important primary source in historical research. Like documents and records, they are recorded and preserved in some form of print or as computer files. Census records, school budgets, school attendance records, teachers' grade sheets, test scores, and other compilations of numerical data can provide useful data for historians. Later in the chapter, we discuss the interpretive uses of quantitative materials in historical research.

Primary sources such as diaries, manuscripts, or school records and relics such as old photographs or classroom paraphernalia might be found in regional museums or archives. **Archives**, also known as **repositories**, are special locations for storing primary sources, particularly very old or rare primary sources, in order to preserve them in good condition and control access to them. Historians often must follow particular procedures to gain access to primary sources in an archive. They might be asked to indicate the length of time they will need the records, how they will record information, and how they plan to use the information in their research.

VALIDATING HISTORICAL EVIDENCE

Educators who wish to apply the findings of historical research need assurance that the historical sources on which historians have based their interpretations are valid. Otherwise, their views of present practices will be distorted by incorrect accounts of past events. The disturbances in contemporary society created by Holocaust denial stories, presumably based on "sound" historical evidence, provide a cautionary tale about the need for strong validation procedures in historical research. Historical sources are valid to the extent they are authentic and contain accurate information. In the sections that follow, we describe procedures for validating historical sources against these criteria.

In recent decades, historians and others who have been influenced by postmodernism (see Chapter 1) and deconstructionism (see Chapter 14) have questioned the validity of historical evidence. Taken to an extreme, these philosophical movements would lead one to conclude that a historical narrative and a novel are no different. Neither describes a reality beyond the text, because the only thing that can be known is the text (e.g., letters, recorded speeches, laws and regulation). Georg Iggers (2005) observed that contemporary historians generally reject this extreme view, but they accept the centrality of the language of the text in understanding the past. This view is sometimes called the "language turn" in historical research.

> The central element of this "turn" consists in the recognition of the importance of language or discourse in the constitution of societies. The social structures and processes that were seen as the determinants of a society and culture are now increasingly viewed rather as products of culture understood as a communicative community. This centrality of language has entered into a good deal of recent scholarship in political, social, cultural, and intellectual history." (Iggers, 2005, p. 123)

This view of historical research does not preclude the necessity of examining the validity of texts. It does reinforce the need for understanding the language of a text from the perspective of the culture and period of time during which it was created. Otherwise, the historian can fall into the trap of presentism, which we discuss later in the chapter.

Procedures for Determining the Authenticity of Historical Sources

Determining the authenticity of primary sources in historical research is called **external criticism**. The process of external criticism is concerned not with the content of the primary source but with whether the apparent or claimed origin of the source corresponds to its actual origin. The term *origin* refers to such matters as author, place where the source was prepared, date of publication, and publisher or sponsoring institution, all of which are usually found in the citation for a primary source.

Bibliographic citations, such as those found at the end of each chapter in this book, might look authoritative, but they are susceptible to error. For example, a researcher can make typing errors while copying a citation from another source, such as from the ERIC database or a journal article. Some primary sources, such as recorded speeches, are ghostwritten by someone other than the individual identified as the author. In other cases, authors use pseudonyms to conceal their identity. If a primary source lists multiple authors, it might be impossible to determine who wrote the parts relevant to a historical research problem. There is also the possibility of **forgery**, a fabrication claiming to be genuine, such as a famous document like the Declaration of Independence, reproduced at a later time by someone who wishes it to be taken as one of the original copies.

The place of origin of a primary source often is apparent from where it is stored or from indications in the source itself. The date of origin might be more difficult to ascertain. If no date is given, it might be possible to infer the date from references in the primary source or from other indicators such as its sequential location in a file cabinet. Dates on primary sources should be viewed critically, because people sometimes make errors. For example, at the start of a new year, it is not uncommon for someone to make the mistake of recording the previous year.

To determine the authenticity of a primary source, historians generate and test alternative hypotheses about each aspect of its reputed origin. For example, they might hypothesize that a subordinate in an organization wrote a particular primary source rather than the person designated as the author. If they collect information showing that this and other alternative hypotheses are untenable, they increase the probability, although never to the point of absolute certainty,

that the source is genuine. Any doubts that a historian has about the authenticity of a source should be noted in the research report.

Procedures for Determining the Accuracy of Historical Sources

The process of determining the accuracy of information in a primary historical source is called **internal criticism**. In doing internal criticism, researchers ask questions about the information. Is it likely that people would act in the way the writer described? Is it physically possible for the events described to have occurred this close together in time? Do the budget figures mentioned by the author seem reasonable?

A researcher's sense that an event or situation described in a historical source is improbable might not be a sufficient basis for discounting the source. Most people can recall highly improbable events that actually have occurred during their lifetime.

Internal criticism requires researchers to judge both the reasonableness of the statements in a historical source and the trustworthiness of the person who made the statements. Criteria used to judge the trustworthiness of a source's author include (1) the author's presence or absence during the events being described, (2) whether her role was that of participant or observer, (3) her qualifications to describe such events accurately, (4) her level of emotional involvement in the situation, and (5) whether she might have a vested interest in the outcomes of the event.

Even competent and truthful witnesses often give different versions of events. When researchers discover widely differing accounts of an event, they need not conclude that all are equally true or false. As Edward Carr (1967) notes, "It does not follow that, because a mountain appears to take on different shapes from different angles of vision, it has objectively either no shape at all or an infinity of shapes" (pp. 30–31). Carr argues that the historian's task is to combine one or more witnesses' accounts, admittedly subjective, and interpret them (also a subjective process) in an attempt to discover what actually happened.

Historical accounts need to be checked carefully for **bias**, a set way to perceive events such that certain types of facts are habitually overlooked, distorted, or falsified. Individuals with strong motives for wanting a particular version of a described event to be regarded as "the truth" are likely to produce biased information. Historians try to appraise the likelihood of bias by examining such factors as the author's ethnic background, political party, religious affiliation, and social status. They also examine use of emotionally charged or intemperate language, which can reflect commitment to a particular position on an issue.

If researchers discover a difference between someone's public and private statements, the discrepancy does not necessarily mean that the public statements have no value as historical evidence. Rather, the discrepancy itself is evidence about the person making the statement and about the social environment in which the person functioned.

INTERPRETING HISTORICAL DATA

In explaining internal criticism, we noted that witnesses to an event report different impressions based on their competence, personal position, and relationship to the event. Historical researchers are in a similar position. Historians will write different histories about the past depending on the evidence they have chosen to collect and how they have interpreted it.

Because history inevitably involves interpretation, historical researchers continually reconstruct the past as their interests and questions change. For example, revisionist historians have become prominent voices in education in recent decades. As we explained earlier in the chapter, these researchers take a different view of educational history than the conventional or popular view.

Historical researchers need to be especially careful to avoid **presentism**, a bias in which the interpretation of past events is based on concepts and perspectives from more recent times. To avoid this bias, they need to discover how various concepts were used in the time period and setting that they are investigating, rather than attach present meanings to them. For example, the concept of *school principal* has changed over time, as you will find in the journal article reprinted at the end of this chapter.

Causal Inference in Historical Research

An essential task of historical research consists of investigating the causes of past events, as in the following examples of causal questions. What events gave rise to the intelligence testing movement? Why did U.S. educators so readily adopt the British open-classroom approach several decades ago? How did the role of school principals originate in this country? When did the concept of the "achievement gap" arise, and what forces led it to become a major focus of educational reform?

Causal inference in historical research is an interpretive process that results in a conclusion that one set of events brought about, directly or indirectly, a subsequent set of events. Historians cannot demonstrate through direct observation that one past event caused another, but they can make explicit the assumptions that underlie their causal inferences.

Some historians make the assumption that humans act similarly across cultures and time. Thus, they might use a currently accepted causal pattern to explain an apparently similar pattern in the past. For example, a researcher might find an instance in 19th-century U.S. education when students at a particular college stopped attending classes and began making public protests against college administrators. Suppose that the researcher also discovered that this event was preceded by administrative rulings at the college that diminished students' rights and privileges. He might infer that these rulings led to the student revolt, using as his rationale that a similar chain of events precipitated student protests in many U.S. colleges during the 1960s. Other historians believe, however, that historical events are unique, and therefore history does not repeat itself. In this view, occurrences at one point in time can illuminate, but not explain, occurrences at another point in time.

Historians invoke various types of causes in their attempts to explain past events. They might attribute past educational occurrences to the actions of certain key persons, to the operation of powerful ideologies, to advances in science and technology, or to economic, geographical, sociological, or psychological factors.

Some historians take an eclectic view and explain past events in terms of a combination of factors. For example, David Tyack (1976) studied the rise of compulsory education in the United States. He explained that until about 1890, Americans built a broad base of elementary schooling that attracted ever-growing numbers of children. During that period, most states passed compulsory attendance laws but did little to enforce them. Tyack calls this phase the *symbolic* stage of compulsory schooling.

Tyack concluded that a second stage, which he calls the *bureaucratic* stage, began in the United States shortly before the turn of the 20th century. He notes that during this era,

> school systems grew in size and complexity, new techniques of bureaucratic control emerged, ideological conflict over compulsion diminished, strong laws were passed, and school officials developed sophisticated techniques to bring truants into schools. By the 1920s and 1930s increasing numbers of states were requiring youth to attend high school, and by the 1950s secondary school attendance had become so customary that school-leavers were routinely seen as dropouts. (1976, p. 60)

The question arises—why did schooling in the United States gradually become compulsory under force of law? Tyack examined five causal interpretations to see how well each answered this question. For example, the ethnocultural interpretation argues that compulsory education came about because of the belief that it would inculcate a single "correct" standard of behavior. This interpretation is based in part on a recognition of efforts then being made to address challenges to the U.S. economy and culture resulting from the influx of immigrants from southern and eastern Europe. This influx provoked considerable concern among some of the religious and ethnic groups already established in the United States.

Another interpretation, drawn from the economic theory of human capital, states that compulsory schooling grew out of a belief that education would improve the productivity and manageability of the workforce.

Each of Tyack's interpretations of the main reason for the growing strength of compulsory schooling in the United States explains some historical evidence, leaves other evidence unexplained, and suggests new lines of research. Tyack notes that such alternative interpretations help historians "gain a more complex and accurate perception of the past and a greater awareness of the ambiguous relationship between outcome and intent—both of the actors in history and of the historians who attempt to recreate their lives" (1976, p. 89).

The more historians learn about the antecedents of a historical event, the more likely they are to discover possible alternative causes of the event.

Therefore, it probably is more defensible to identify an earlier event as *a* cause rather than *the* cause of a later event. Moreover, by their choice of language in the research report, historians can convey their interpretation of the strength of the causal link (e.g., "It was a major influence . . ." or "It was one of many events that influenced . . .") and of its certainty (e.g., "It is highly likely that . . ." or "It is possible that . . .").

Generalizing from Historical Evidence

Like other qualitative researchers, historical researchers do not seek to study all of the individuals, settings, events, or objects that interest them. Instead, they usually study only one case or several cases. The case that is chosen is determined partly by the availability of sources. For example, suppose that a historian wished to examine the diaries, correspondence, and other written records of elementary school teachers in the 1800s in order to understand teaching conditions during that time. The study necessarily would be limited to teachers whose writings had been preserved and to which the researcher could gain access.

Before generalizing the study's findings to other teachers of the period, the researcher should consider whether other teachers would have provided similar data. One way to determine this would be to examine how teachers in different circumstances viewed their teaching experience. For example, the researcher might ask whether teachers who wrote about their work for publication described similar conditions as did teachers who wrote about their work in private diaries and correspondence.

Another problem in historical interpretation involves the generalizability of historical data for one person. For example, a historian might discover a primary source in which an educator stated an opinion about a particular educational issue. The statement does not prove that this educator held the same opinion at a later or earlier time. The researcher must look for more data that will help establish whether the expressed opinion was characteristic of this educator.

Using Quantitative Materials in Historical Research

One reason for the growing use of quantitative materials in historical research is that conclusions based on large amounts of carefully selected quantitative data probably are more generalizable than conclusions based on case studies. Another benefit of quantitative materials is that they allow researchers to characterize the historical views and experiences of many people, which sometimes is referred to as the "common-man approach" to historical research. In contrast, older historical studies tend to focus on a few prominent individuals.

H. Warren Button (1979) referred to the common-man approach as "history from the bottom up—grassroots history" (p. 4). Because historical records typically give minimal attention to grassroots perspectives, Button argues that historians must mine every source to reflect those perspectives:

> For instance, for a quantitative study of Buxton, a black antebellum haven in Ontario, it is necessary to assemble data from perhaps fifteen thousand entries in the census manuscripts of 1861, 1871, and 1881; from town auditors' accounts, and church records. . . . The research necessity for compilation and statistical treatment, by unfortunate paradox, produces history almost without personalities, even without names. Still, this new history has and will produce new understandings and will counterweight our long-standing concern for "the better sort." (p. 4)

A study of this type is called a **quantitative history**, because researchers make use of a database, typically electronic, containing numerical data that are typically analyzed using a computer and statistical techniques.

FEATURES OF A HISTORICAL RESEARCH REPORT

Reports of historical research differ from other research reports. One of the main differences is that many of them are published as books rather than as journal articles. The reason for book publication is that historians often tell stories that have a broad sweep. For example, biographies of educators might encompass their entire lives. Certain phases of an educator's life, especially during their professional career, might require separate chapters. In describing critical life phases, the historian needs to make sense of the educator's actions and contributions by setting them in relevant contexts—political, economic, and cultural, among others—both at the local and broader levels.

Historical research studies that are published in journals do not follow the same format as quantitative studies and most qualitative studies. Instead, most of the article is a story: a chronology of events, the characters involved in them, the settings, and the larger forces in society that influenced the actions and thoughts of the characters. The researcher's interpretations are interwoven throughout the story.

The reprinted article at the end of this chapter, which concerns the history of the school principalship in the United States, illustrates this form of reporting. In the following sections, we will analyze another historical account. Our purpose is to note certain features that you are likely to find in educational histories.

Statement of Purpose

Tracy Steffes (2008) conducted a historical study of rural schools that were in operation from 1900 to 1933. Although more than a century has passed since the start of that period, her study of rural schools' problems and attempted solutions is relevant to current educational problems. The main problem of rural schools then was that they had vastly fewer resources compared to urban schools, an inequality still experienced in today's poor rural school districts.

As in some other historical reports, Steffes stated her purpose as a thesis, that is, as a proposition that she set forth and supported through evidence and argument:

> The Rural School Problem, this article argues, helped to stimulate and legitimate significant new interventions into local schools and define the forms of state aid, regulation, and bureaucracy in a formative period of state development. (p. 181)

In other words, Steffes proposed to demonstrate that a particular problem of practice led to the development of state departments of education and their particular ways of relating to local school systems. Most of the article provides historical evidence and interpretations to support this thesis.

Historical Chronology

Many reports of historical studies are organized chronologically, as in the rural school study. Steffes organized her report into four chronological sections, each having its own thematic label. The labels are shown in the following list, together with a summary of the significant events that each label encompasses:

- *Definition of the Rural School Problem.* A rural school system at the turn of the 20th century usually consisted of a single one-room school. Various groups gradually realized that these schools were lagging behind the sophisticated urban schools that were expanding as a result of industrialization. Educators and public leaders perceived that the gap between rural and urban schools might threaten the nation's economy and social fabric.

- *The Failure of Local School Reform to Solve the Rural School Problem.* Local reform efforts to improve rural schools met with limited success. These efforts, occurring in the 1910s and 1920s, included raising local taxes for schools and consolidating schools by closing down several small ones and building a larger, modern facility. Another effort involved replacing local school district control with county-level governance, which included a county board of education, a county superintendent and staff, and county taxation to fund schools. County governance worked to an extent, but the rural populace wanted to retain as much local control as possible.

- *Equalizing Opportunity in the Countryside: State Aid and Standards.* World War I revealed that draftees had high rates of illiteracy and physical unfitness. Public concern about this problem put pressure on states to take action. They needed to find a way to ensure that all schools, including rural schools, provided sound education. One of the main solutions was for states to provide financial aid to local school systems to support reforms such as the consolidation of schools. In the 1910s and 1920s, states increasingly tied financial aid to schools' adherence to state-defined standards. This solution had the effect of leaving behind low-performing school districts that could not raise matching funds for state aid or that made the investment to receive state aid but only met minimal state standards in return.

- *Leadership and Supervision: State Departments of Education.* As state governments took increasing responsibility for helping rural and other schools needing resources beyond local governments' ability to provide, many states began developing state departments of education. The average number of persons working in such departments grew from less than 3 in 1890 to almost 54 in 1930. These state departments increasingly took on the role of supervising local school districts. Supervisory personnel could not coerce conformity to state standards, but they found various ways to encourage and persuade local schools to meet state standards and implement "best practices."

This thematic chronology helps us see an evolving pattern in events involving local school districts, county districts, and state departments of education. The desire for local control meant that school communities were more likely to commit financial and emotional support to their schools, but it also resulted in some communities having low-performing schools. State departments of education faced the difficult task of helping these low-performing schools improve without resorting to coercive measures that would be seen as a violation of the near-sacred principle of local control.

Lessons to Be Learned from a Historical Study

Some historians interpret their findings but leave it to readers to draw their own implications for problems of practice. Others suggest lessons that can be learned from the findings, as does Tracy Steffes in her study of rural schools. She offers several lessons—but with the qualification that "the lessons to be learned from the relationship between local control and growing state centralization are neither simple nor straightforward" (2008, p. 219).

She observes that current interrelationships of local, state, and federal control over education are problematic. For example, researchers have found that educators are resistant to the requirements of the federal No Child Left Behind (NCLB) Act and state-mandated testing of students. Educators do not want federal and state governments overriding the local decision making of those closest to the students, namely, their parents and educators.

One of the main lessons that Steffes learned from her historical study is that local control of schools, with the support of county and state initiatives, can serve as a positive force for educational improvement but also as a negative force. Here is what she states about local control as a positive force:

> Local control harnessed local pride and boosterism in support of schooling which helped to encourage emulation of best practices as well as experimentation and innovation. . . . Perhaps most importantly, the close identification of a community with "its" local school helped to encourage higher levels of school spending and investment, even in the face of generalized anti-tax sentiment. (2008, p. 217)

She also writes about negative consequences:

> The system that emerged in this period did help to ease some rural and urban disparities and establish an absolute bottom limit, but it also accepted and further entrenched racial and economic inequality. Leaving enforcement to localities meant allowing them to ignore minority populations, and tying finance to local property tax in districts of unequal wealth meant that economic disparities would be a permanent and acceptable fixture of school governance. (2008, p. 218)

On the matter of minority populations, Steffes provides evidence that some rural school districts did not enforce school attendance for Mexican and African American students or provide them transportation to consolidated schools.

Steffes' history of rural schools from 1900 to 1933 does not tell us the best role for federal, state, and local governments in improving schools. What it does tell us is that some intergovernmental arrangements have had positive outcomes but also negative side effects. This knowledge can help us think more deeply about how to improve schools in the future. For example, we might conclude that no one level of control—local, state, or federal—is sufficient to improve education. Also, no one level of control can be dismissed as irrelevant. Educators and policy makers at all levels need to come together and figure out how to coordinate efforts to maximize positive outcomes and close loopholes that adversely affect some students or communities.

Historical Concepts

Earlier in the chapter, we noted that a historian might refer to concepts that were in use during the time period being studied. The researcher needs to avoid presentism by defining the concept as it was used in that time period, not today. For example, in describing the rise of state departments of education, Steffes claims that supervision was one of the "major projects of emerging state bureaucracies and they defined their roles in terms of it" (2008, p. 208).

The concept of supervision in education can have various meanings in today's world. Supervision might mean observing teachers or schools to assess whether they are meeting certain standards or, more simply, to check that they are not engaging in inappropriate actions. Supervision might also mean observing teachers or schools for the purpose of helping them to improve. To avoid the error of presentism, we need to check which of these meanings, or other meanings, were intended by use of the term in the past.

Because supervision was a central concept in the study, Steffes took care to explain its meaning in historical context:

> "Supervision" entailed both inspection and guidance and was designed to bring professional leadership to local school workers. Supervision required sending state officers into the field to observe teachers and local administrators at work, offer suggestions for improvement, diffuse new practices and ideas, and coordinate local efforts. . . . While couched as a program of improvement, supervision also carried a significant quest for greater uniformity of "best practices" as defined by the profession. (2008, p. 208)

This nuanced description of supervision as practiced in the early 1900s helps us understand it not from the perspective of our own experience but rather from the perspective of that particular time period.

EVALUATING HISTORICAL RESEARCH

Historical research studies in education tend to be more difficult to evaluate than other kinds of research. The reason is that reports of historical research generally do not include a discussion of the methodology used to collect evidence and interpret it. Nonetheless, it is important to read the reports with a critical perspective. The following questions can help you maintain this perspective as you read them.

- Does the report refer to primary sources?

    Interpretations of past events are likely to be more credible if they are based on the historian's examination of documents written by individuals who participated in or witnessed those events.

■ Does the report refer to the use of external criticism of primary sources?

It seems unlikely that documents of interest to educational historians are forgeries or of uncertain origin. However, if a document referring to a past event is essential to the study, it is worth asking whether there is any possibility that it is a forgery or written by someone other than the listed author.

■ Does the report refer to the use of internal criticism to check the accuracy of statements made in historical sources?

Earlier in the chapter, we stated five criteria for judging the trustworthiness of a source's author: (1) the author's presence or absence during the events being described; (2) whether she was a participant in or an observer of the events; (3) her qualifications to describe such events accurately; (4) her level of emotional involvement in the situation; and (5) whether she might have a vested interest in the outcomes of the event.

■ Do the historian's interpretations reflect bias?

Bias is certainly possible in historical research. Revisionist historians have identified evidence about past events that was overlooked or ignored by other historians. Check for indications, usually subtle, that the historian has a vested interest in portraying a particular view about an educational event.

■ Does the report include credible causal inferences?

Societal events and individual actions often are influenced by multiple factors. Check the historical report for interpretations that place undue weight on just one causal factor. Also, consider whether the causal inferences are supported by the evidence presented in the report.

■ Does the historian overgeneralize from the evidence presented in the report?

Historians generally focus on the study of particular individuals or events but use them to make generalizations about larger trends in education. Examine whether these generalizations are justified by the evidence presented in the report.

■ Does the historian use educational concepts in an appropriate manner?

Educational concepts in use today might have had a different meaning in the past. Therefore, determine whether the historian determined how these concepts were defined and used during the time encompassed by the study.

An example of
How Historical Research Can Help in Solving Problems of Practice

The Boston Globe, a newspaper in Boston, Massachusetts, reported on a new initiative to offer Spanish in elementary schools in the Massachusetts communities of Dover and Sherborn:

> Kindergartners in Dover and Sherborn will be learning Spanish in their classrooms next September if a plan first initiated by passionate parents four years ago is passed by the local school boards.
>
> The Elementary World Language Committee will take its proposal before the Dover and Sherborn school committees on Dec. 11. The plan calls for integrating Spanish into the kindergarten curriculum for 20 minutes four days a week during the next school year, and then expanding it over the following five years to include a half-hour of Spanish instruction in grades 1 through 5. . . .
>
> The committee considered adding French or Mandarin Chinese to the elementary curriculum but decided on Spanish because it is the second most-spoken language in the country, according to [school principal] Barbara Brown.
>
> Ishkanian, E. (2012, November 3). Dover, Sherborn adding Spanish at kindergarten level. Retrieved from http://www.boston.com/news/local/massachusetts/2012/11/04/dover-sherborn-study-adding-spanish-kindergarten-level/YBNRQnBbUjuFTVaeEFdkYJ/story.html

From a present-day perspective, we might ask what foreign language, or languages, are being taught in other school districts around the United States and in other countries. We might also ask what educators and the community see as the advantages and disadvantages of foreign-language instruction.

From a historical perspective, we can ask different yet equally interesting questions. Of particular interest might be the question of how different school districts chose particular foreign languages to include in the school curriculum and also the question of how and whether the choice of foreign languages changed over time. For example, a public high school on the Oregon coast includes Latin in its curriculum, but no other public high school in the region does so. How did this come to be? We do not know the answer, but the question is of great interest to us. Historical research on this and similar questions might help educators think more deeply about their foreign-language curriculum and whether and how it might be changed to better meet the needs and interests of their students.

A review of previous historical research should help to give us direction in deciding how to address the questions of how school districts chose to teach particular foreign languages and why these choices changed over time.

Suppose our literature review led us to decide to focus on the history of a school district that has a strong current commitment to foreign-language instruction at all grade levels, as appears to be the case in the school districts described above. After gaining the cooperation of local school officials, we could interview knowledgeable educators about their recollections of periods in the district's history when new foreign languages courses began being offered. We would ask them for the names of significant educators, committees, and community members and groups. We also would ask where significant documents were stored. These documents probably would include

curriculum guides, the minutes of school board meetings, and local newspapers. If the school district decided to offer a foreign language in response to outside forces, such as mandates from the state department of education or recommendations from national organizations for foreign language instruction, we would want to identify significant individuals and documents to include in our data-collection efforts.

As we collected data from these sources, we could start to construct a timeline for when particular foreign languages began to be taught, in which schools, and if and when they were terminated. We also would be identifying factors that influenced the selection of particular foreign languages to be taught. We would keep in mind that there might be several such factors, for example, an educator who made a strong case for teaching a particular foreign language, or a group of parents who wished to preserve their heritage by having a particular foreign language in the curriculum, or the community's response to current trends in world affairs, such as the ascendancy of a particular country or group of countries in the world's economy. In addition to being attentive to the voices of advocacy for particular foreign languages, we also want to search for dissenters and their rationales for not including a foreign language as part of the school curriculum.

The resulting history should provide a rich perspective on present and past forces that influenced the school district's foreign language curriculum over time. The findings might not be directly generalizable to other districts, but as is the case with other types of qualitative research, educators everywhere can read the history and form their own conclusions about how the study's findings can help them understand their own local situation. In particular, the study might help them think more deeply about their current foreign language curriculum and new directions it might take as new forces and needs come into play at local, national, and international levels.

SELF-CHECK TEST

1. All educational researchers can be regarded as historians, primarily because they
   a. review past research as a basis for designing their own research studies.
   b. study causal relationships among observed phenomena.
   c. interpret the practical significance of their research findings.
   d. suggest desirable directions for future research on the topics they have studied.

2. In historical research, the literature review typically
   a. is a relatively minor part of the research process.
   b. provides the research data.
   c. is conducted after the data have been analyzed.
   d. focuses on secondary sources.

3. In historical research, a private journal written by a 19th-century school principal most likely would be classified as a
   a. secondary source.
   b. document.
   c. relic.
   d. record.

4. In historical research, physical objects preserved from the period being studied are called
   a. records.
   b. secondary sources.
   c. repositories.
   d. relics.

5. The procedure for determining whether a source of historical data is authentic is called
   a. internal criticism.
   b. historiographical validation.
   c. external criticism.
   d. revisionism.

6. Internal criticism of documents is used to determine
   a. whether a document is a forgery.
   b. whether the author of a document has a consistent perspective on the events being described.

   c. the extent of a document's dissemination.
   d. the accuracy of the information in the text of documents.

7. In historical research, presentism refers to the
   a. belief that the present is more important than the historical past.
   b. use of contemporary concepts to interpret past events.
   c. belief that the future cannot be predicted based on study of past events.
   d. set of assumptions underlying revisionist history.

8. Historical researchers generally consider quantitative materials superior to other types of primary sources for examining
   a. the unique aspects of a historical event.
   b. the history of nonliterate cultures.
   c. population characteristics and trends during a historical period.
   d. accounts of prominent individuals of past periods.

9. Causal inference in historical research is a process by which researchers
   a. use interpretation to ascribe causality to a sequence of historical events.
   b. narrow the cause of a historical phenomenon to one set of factors.
   c. explain past events in terms of contemporary concepts.
   d. take a critical view of past practices that previously were viewed positively.

10. Generalizing from the historical study of one individual to other individuals in the same time period
    a. is not considered possible by revisionist historians.
    b. involves a process of internal criticism.
    c. involves a process of external criticism.
    d. is facilitated if the historian has access to documents pertaining to other individuals in the same time period.

CHAPTER REFERENCES

Button, H. W. (1979). Creating more usable pasts: History in the study of education. *Educational Researcher, 8*(5), 3–9.

Carr, E. H. (1967). *What is history?* New York, NY: Random House.

Donato, R., & Lazerson, M. (2000). New directions in American educational history: Problems and prospects. *Educational Researcher, 29*(8), 4–15.

Gonzalez, G. (2013). *Chicano education in the era of segregation*. Denton, TX: University of North Texas Press.

Grosvenor, I., & Lawn, M. (2001). Ways of seeing in education and schooling: Emerging historiographies. *History of Education, 30*, 105–108.

Iggers, G. G. (2005). *Historiography in the twentieth century*. Middleton, CT: Wesleyan University Press.

Katz, M. B. (1968). *The irony of early school reform: Educational innovation in mid-nineteenth century Massachusetts*. Cambridge, MA: Harvard University Press.

Kelen, L. G., & Stone, E. H. (1996). *Missing stories*. Salt Lake City, UT: University of Utah Press.

Lincoln, Y. S., & Guba, E. G. (1985). *Naturalistic inquiry*. Beverly Hills, CA: Sage.

Lugg, C. A., & Shoho, A. R. (2006). Dare public school administrators build a new social order?: Social justice and the possibly perilous politics of educational leadership. *Journal of Educational Administration, 44*(3), 196–208.

Sheumaker, H., & Wajda, S. T. (Eds.). (2007). *Material culture in America*. Santa Barbara, CA: ABC-CLIO.

Steffes, T. L. (2008). Solving the "Rural School Problem": New state aid, standards, and supervision of local schools, 1900–1933. *History of Education Quarterly, 48*(2), 181–220.

Tyack, D. B. (1976). Ways of seeing: An essay on the history of compulsory schooling. *Harvard Educational Review, 46*, 55–89.

RESOURCES FOR FURTHER STUDY

Barzun, J., & Graff, H. F. (2004). *The modern researcher* (6th ed.). Belmont, CA: Wadsworth.

> This is one of the classic books about historical research methodology. The authors provide a comprehensive description of historical researchers' work, including strategies for fact finding, criticism, interpretation, and reporting.

Henry, A. (2006). Historical studies: Groups/institutions. In J. L. Green, G. Camilli, & P. B. Elmore (Eds.), *Handbook of complementary methods in education research* (pp. 333–355). Mahwah, NJ: Lawrence Erlbaum.

> The author describes a revisionist approach to conducting historical research. She advocates for historians who are "on the margins" and marginalized groups who have been underrepresented or misrepresented in mainstream historical research.

Iggers, G. G. (2005). *Historiography in the Twentieth Century*. Middleton, CT: Wesleyan University Press.

> Historical research itself has a history. The author describes how the questions posed by historical researchers, their methods of inquiry, and their assumptions about society, culture, and the individual have changed in the past 200 years.

Janesick, V. J. (2010). *Oral history for the qualitative researcher*. New York, NY: Guilford.

> The author describes various purposes for doing oral historical research and methods for collecting, analyzing, and reporting oral history data.

Ramsey, P. J. (2007). Histories taking root: The contexts and patterns of educational historiography during the twentieth century. *American Educational History Journal, 34*(2), 347–363.

> The author identifies various cultural, social, and intellectual movements that have shaped the problems of education that historians have chosen to study and their interpretation of historical data. These movements include progressivism, psychoanalytic theory, and revisionism.

Rury, J. L. (2006). Historical research in education. In J. L. Green, G. Camilli, & P. B. Elmore (Eds.), *Handbook of complementary methods in education research* (pp. 323–332). Mahwah, NJ: Lawrence Erlbaum.

> The author provides an overview of current approaches to historical research and a good reference list for further study of particular topics.

Yow, V. R. (2005). *Recording oral history: A guide for the humanities and social sciences* (2nd ed.). Walnut Creek, CA: AltaMira.

> The author explains interviewing strategies and the ethical issues involved in oral history. The book includes an in-depth description of three types of oral history projects: community studies, biographies, and family histories.

Go to the Principal's Office: Toward a Social History of the School Principal in North America

Rousmaniere, K. (2007). Go to the principal's office: Toward a social history of the school principal in North America. *History of Education Quarterly, 47*(1), 1–22.

What *is* the role of the school principal? What *should* the role of the school principal be? Educators and others have struggled with these questions for decades.

The following article does not answer these questions directly but does put them into historical perspective.

As we see how the role of the school principal has evolved, we develop an understanding of the complex, conflicting demands that are placed on today's principals. With this understanding, we perhaps are in a better position to define the role so that principals can be more effective.

The article is reprinted in its entirety, just as it appeared when originally published.

Go to the Principal's Office: Toward a Social History of the School Principal in North America

KATE ROUSMANIERE

From Rousmaniere, K. (2007) Go to the principal's office: Toward a social history of the school principal in North America. *History of Education Quarterly, 47*(1), 1–22.

Of the many organizational changes that took place in public education in North America at the turn of the last century, few had greater impact on the school than the development of the principal. The creation of the principal's office revolutionized the internal organization of the school from a group of students supervised by one teacher to a collection of teachers managed by one administrator. In its very conception, the appointment of a school-based administrator who was authorized to supervise other teachers significantly restructured power relations in schools, realigning the source of authority from the classroom to the principal's office. Just as significant was the role that the principal played as a school based representative of the central educational office. Created as a conduit between the district and the classroom, the principal became an educational middle manager in an increasingly complex school bureaucracy.

The introduction of the principal's office radically changed the overall machinery of how public education was delivered from central authorities to the classroom. Located as the connecting hinge between the school and the district, the principal was critical to the success of newly designed school systems in the early twentieth century, in much the same way that the middle manager in business reinforced the development of corporate enterprise. Business historian Alfred Chandler describes how the creation of middle managerial structures helped to consolidate the control of independent businesses under a corporate umbrella. Modern administrative practices, including scientific management, greased the wheels of this development, providing managerial techniques, a hierarchical decision-making structure, and an occupational culture of rationality. Middle managers were the engine behind bureaucracy, providing the smooth transition of responsibilities—what Chandler described as "vertical integration"—from the central office to the shop floor.[1]

Like the foreman in the factory and the mid-level executive in the office building, the school principal was an administrator who was responsible for day-to-day building operations rather than strategic policy decisions. Standing between the district and the classroom, principals were, as C. Wright Mills described such white-collar positions, "the assistants of authority" whose power was derived from others, and who were responsible for implementing managerial decisions but had limited opportunities for influencing those decisions.[2] Like other middle managers, the principal had a "dual personality," standing "on the middle ground between management and employee," as both a loyal sergeant to a distant

---

[1] Alfred Chandler, *The Visible Hand: The Managerial Revolution in American Business* (Cambridge, MA: Belknap Press, 1977).
[2] C. Wright Mills, *White Collar: The American Middle Classes* (New York: Oxford University Press, 1951), 74.

supervisor and a local administrator who had to negotiate with workers in order to get the job done properly.[3] Larry Cuban aptly describes principals' historic and contemporary role as "positioned between their superiors who want orders followed and the teachers who do the actual work in the classrooms, . . . [principals'] loyalties are dual: to their school, and to headquarters."[4]

In this essay, I offer a framework for understanding the overall development of the principal's office in the United States and Canada from the late nineteenth century to the present. I argue that the school principal replaced the nineteenth century head teacher, exchanging an informal position of a teacher who took on administrative tasks with an administrator who supervised teachers. This is what I refer to as the development of the "principal's office:" the creation of both the administrative position of the principal *and* the physical office in the school building.

The essay is organized in the following way. First, I comment briefly on the historiography of the principal. Next, I introduce the nineteenth century predecessor to the principal—the head teacher, or principal teacher. I then describe how certain professionalization strategies led to the identification of the principal as the iconographic white man in the principal's office. I argue that the creation of the principal's office as the figurehead of North American schools involved the cementing of institutional and personal definitions of gender and race in school leadership. But ultimately, the middle manager location of the principal undermined its professional status. For all the efforts to lift the principal above the classroom teacher, the principal's office remained stubbornly embedded *in* the school, a middle manager position wedged between the classroom and the district.

Where Is the Principal's Office?

Given the significance of the principal's office in the development of modern schooling, it is surprising how little we know about it. There are no articles on the history of the public school principal in the *History of Education Quarterly*, the leading American journal in the field for the past forty-five years. In the *Historical Studies in Education* bibliography of over 850 references on the history of Canadian education published since 1980, there are only two essays specifically on the principal. A May 2006

survey of a leading history of education bibliographic listserve found no references to the principal out of 1,400 scholarly articles published since 1997.[5]

Whole volumes on the history of education refer to the historical development of school finance, curriculum, district policies, architecture, and student life; analyze the impact of desegregation, feminization, consolidation, and centralization; and describe the roles of teachers, superintendents, parent and community leaders, and government officials, with virtually no mention of the school building principal. The principal is missing from both the political history of school administration and the social history of schools. It's as if the principal did not exist at all, except to appear occasionally, without elaboration or explanation, as a spontaneous actor in the experience of a teacher or the development of a school.

The sole exception to this historiographical pattern is a pocket of studies on African American principals. Through the late twentieth century, black principals were completely excluded from predominantly white public schools in both the legally segregated southern United States and in the north where virtually no African American held a principalship in any school with even a minority white population until the 1960s. In their racially segregated school systems, black principals played a critical role, serving as important role models and respected servant leaders in their communities. Historians have examined black school leaders in racially segregated

---

[3]Nelson Lichtenstein, "'The Man in the Middle': A Social History of Automobile Industry Foreman," in *On the Line: Essays in the History of Auto Work,* ed. Nelson Lichtenstein and Stephen Meyer (Urbana: University of Illinois Press, 1989), 161–62; Geoff Mason, "Production Supervisors in Britain, Germany, and the United States: Back from the Dead Again?" *Work, Employment, and Society* 14, (2000): 626–27.

[4]Larry Cuban, *The Managerial Imperative and the Practice of Leadership in Schools* (Albany: SUNY Press, 1988), 61.

[5]h-education@h-net.msu.edu. This is not to say that the topic has been completely ignored. Recent scholarship on the history of the principalship in North America includes in addition to Larry Cuban's volume, Kathleen Brown, "Pivotal Points: History, Development, and Promise of the Principalship," in *Sage Handbook of Educational Leadership*, ed. Fenwick W. English (University of North Carolina: Sage Publications 2005), 109–141; Rebecca H. Goodwin, Michael L. Cunningham and Teresa Eager, "The Changes Role of the Secondary Principal in the United States: An Historical Perspective," *Journal of Administration and History* 37, (April 2005): 1–17; Thomas Fleming, "British Columbia Principals: Scholar-Teachers and Administrative Amateurs in Victorian and Edwardian Eras, 1872–1918," in *School Leadership: Essays on the British Columbia Experience, 1872–1995*, ed. Thomas Fleming (Bendall Books, 2001), 249–85; Thomas Fleming, "Our Boys in the Field: School Inspectors, Superintendents, and the Changing Character of School Leadership in British Columbia," in *Schools in the West: Essays in Canadian Educational History,* ed. Nancy M. Sheehan, J. Donald Wilson, and David C. James (Calgary: Detselig Enterprises, 1986), 285–303. Oral histories and biographical studies comprise a bulk of new scholarship on the history of the principal: Cecelia Reynolds, "Changing Gender Scripts and Moral Dilemmas for Women and Men in Education, 1940–1970," in *Women and School Leadership: International Perspectives,* ed. Cecilia Reynolds (Albany: SUNY, 2002), 29–48; James M. Wallace, *The Promise of Progressivism: Angelo Patri and Urban Education* (New York: Peter Lang, 2006).

schools with significantly more interest than any historians have expressed about white majority principals, and this research provides a unique model of scholarship on the historical significance of school leaders.[6]

Why has it been so easy for historians to side step the school principal? I suggest three reasons.

The first reason is that histories of educational administration are written primarily by scholars with limited historical training in order to frame prescriptive guidance for contemporary school leaders. The focus has been on categorizing occupational themes for contemporary reflection rather than the analysis and interpretation of historical evidence.[7] A second reason that the principal has been bypassed is that historians of education have tended to encapsulate the entire field of school administration in the popular historical trope of the "administrative progressive." This is the familiar argument that educational reformers in the late nineteenth century divided into two groups: pedagogical progressives who promoted a child centered, humanistic approach to education, and administrative progressives who advocated for the development of school systems driven by values of fiscal economy and organizational accountability. This division of educational history into administrative and pedagogical progressive camps was proposed by David Tyack over thirty years ago and has never been seriously revisited. We universally characterize the entirety of school leadership history by single phrases or metaphors such as "the cult of efficiency," "scientific management," and Tyack's own term "administrative progressives."[8]

Two points about the administrative progressive model are worth expanding here. First, in these histories, the occupational roles of principal and superintendent are often lumped uncritically together and seen as a one-dimensional cabal of administrative power.[9] Largely ignored are distinctions between building, local and central administrators. There are few fine-grained analyses of how administrative roles emerged and developed at all levels of the educational structure.[10] Secondly, these studies tend to focus on policy development and the institutionalization of bureaucratic authority through scientific management. The collapsing of all administrators into a pot of scientific management has colored our understanding of school organization so that we see the work of teachers and administrators as separate and antagonistic, driven by different values, ideologies, and purposes. In these studies of "system builders," we forget that local school administrators often had tenuous connections to central office power.

A final, impressionistic observation about why historians of education have ignored principals is simply a personal predilection against them. In our own life history, many of us remember an inspiring teacher, but we may remember the principal only for an unfortunate, and assuredly unfair, disciplinary encounter. For women and people of color the principal was often a position not of us, and not attainable.[11] Personal experience is reinforced by a long cultural history of alienation between school administration and classroom teaching: teachers who become administrators are often seen as crossing a boundary much like the River Styx—a one-way passage to a place not all that pleasant. The principal's office holds an unsavory tinge, and the people who sit in that office are viewed with some misgivings. Memory and methodology reinforce each other: when historians write about the introduction of scientific management and the consolidation

[6]Carol F. Karpinski, "Bearing the Burden of Desegregation: Black Principals and *Brown*," *Urban Education* 41, (May 2006): 237–276; Linda C. Tillman, "African American Principals and the Legacy of *Brown*," *Review of Research in Education*, (2005): 101–146; Adah Ward Randolph, "The Memories of an All-Black Northern Urban School: Good Memories of Leadership, Teachers, and the Curriculum," *Urban Education* 39, (November, 2004): 596–620 and "Resisting Oppression through Education: Ethel Thompson Overby, 1912–1958," *Journal of Black Studies* (forthcoming); Vanessa Siddle Walker, "Organized Resistance and Black Educators' Quest for School Equality," *Teachers College Record* 107, (March 2005): 355–a.

[7]H. Warren Button, "Doctrines of Administration: A Brief History," *Educational Administration Quarterly* 2, (Autumn 1966): 216–224; Phillip Hallinger, "The Evolving Role of American Principals: From Managerial to Instructional to Transformational Leaders," *Journal of Educational Administration* 30, (1992): 35–48; Lynn G. Beck and Joseph Murphy, *Understanding the Principalship: Metaphorical Themes, 1920s–1990s* (New York: Teachers College Press, 1993); Thomas E. Glass, et al., *The History of Educational Administration Viewed Through its Textbooks*, (Lanham, MD: Scarecrow, 2004).

[8]Ira E. Bogotch, "A History of Public School Leadership: The First Century, 1537–1942," in *Sage Handbook of Educational Leadership* ed. Fenwick W. English (Chapel Hill: University of North Carolina, Sage Publications), 7–33.

[9]The bulk of historical studies of educational administration are on district leadership: David Tyack and Elisabeth Hansot, *Managers of Virtue: Public School Leadership in America, 1820–1980,* (Boston: Basic Books 1982); Jackie Blount, *Destined to Rule the Schools: Women and the Superintendency, 1873–1995* (Albany: SUNY Press, 1998); Bruce Curtis, *True Government by Choice Men? Inspection, Education, and State Formation in Canada West* (Toronto: University of Toronto Press, 1992); Raymond E. Callahan, *Education and the Cult of Efficiency* (Chicago: University of Chicago Press, 1962).

[10]Kathleen Murphey's fine study of the late nineteenth century institutional development of Fort Wayne Indiana's school system is one of the few exceptions. Kathleen A. Murphey, "Common School or 'Our Best System'? Tracking School Reform in Fort Wayne, Indiana, 1853–75," *Historical Studies in Education* 11, (Fall 1999): 188–211. See also Michael F. Murphy, "Unmaking and Remaking the 'One Best System': London, Ontario, 1852–1860," *History of Education Quarterly* 37, (Fall 1997): 291–310.

[11]Blount, *Destined to Rule the Schools*, 153–56.

of authority in early twentieth century schools, the principal becomes folded into a battalion of upper level administrators who inflicted orders from distant offices.

Historians have largely side stepped the school principal as a central figure in the history of school life, as well as the history of school system development. A cursory overview of that history suggests that we cannot understand the development of early schools and early school systems without understanding the changing role of the principal.

The Making of the Principal Teacher

Before there was a principal's office, the school was essentially the teacher, and that teacher worked as instructor and building manager. The administrative structure of the school was simple: in the United States, a superintendent, and in Canada, an inspector, oversaw district operations from afar; local school boards exerted more immediate authority from the community. The teacher managed the school and taught students in a building consisting solely of classroom space. For the most part, the teacher worked alone, under broad administrative directives.

The first principals' positions were created in mid-nineteenth century urban districts to address the organizational demands of the new graded school where students were classified by age and achievement and placed in separate classrooms under a single teacher. With teachers and students divided into different graded compartments, a head teacher, or teaching principal, was assigned to act as an overarching authority to the whole, organizing the separate courses of study, administering discipline, and supervising the operation of all the classes in order to, as the American school reformer Henry Barnard wrote, "secure the harmonious action and progress of each department."[12] By the late nineteenth century in both America and Canada, most urban school systems had graded elementary and secondary schools with some form of a building administrator who reported to a district officer.[13]

The work of nineteenth century principals was based mostly on expediency, and not on the improvement of either learning or school operations. The principal's job was little more than a routine administrator: according to one historian, merely "a mechanic who was serving an unsophisticated machine."[14] Distinguishing leadership opportunities were few and far between. For example, in 1841, school trustees in Cincinnati, Ohio (one of the first cities that authorized the position) gave the principal the responsibility of monitoring examinations and seeing that the bell was rung for each class to come in; in 1847 the duty of ringing the bell for recess was added; the following year the principal was authorized to suspend pupils for profane language and to prevent pupils from leaving school without permission.[15]

There was no systematic process to the authorization of these first school principals. In his history of school administration in British Columbia, Thomas Fleming describes the "organizational incrementalism" whereby "one-room elementary schools grew room-by-room until they became institutions large enough to require supervision by a head teacher or principal." The process occurred over a century in North America "without any preconceived design for the shape of the institutions to come, without any overarching view of the structures required to manage such schools, and without much thought about who should manage them." Growing schools might be governed by the longest serving teacher, or the teacher most liked by the school board, or by the only teacher willing to do the work. Experience as a teacher was the sole prerequisite for the position. Fleming observes that "circumstance, rather than ambition, preparation, or talent" led to the identification of head teachers so that "supervisory and organizational chores were undertaken for decades by untrained individuals on a piecemeal basis, as something to be done before or after instruction."[16]

These early administrators worked in a world almost entirely free of job descriptions, legal guidelines, or professional support, and their relationship with both their superiors and their staff were unregulated, often leading to conflict. As the administrative framework of school districts developed, principals and district officers jostled for authority over their different pieces of the emerging educational enterprise. Local and district administrators argued over which office had the right to promote, assign, and examine pupils, hire and fire teachers, purchase books, and control

---

[12]"Henry Barnard on the significance of school grading," in *Education in the United States: A Documentary History*, Vol. 3, ed. Sol Cohen (New York: Random House, 1974), 1322; Frederick Dean McCluskey, "Introduction of Grading into the Public Schools of New England," *The Elementary School Journal* 21 (October 1920).

[13]David Tyack and Elisabeth Hansot, *Learning Together: A History of Coeducation in American Schools* (New Haven: Yale University Press, 1990), 82–83; Alison Prentice, *The School Promoters: Education and Social Class in Mid-Nineteenth Century Upper Canada,* (Toronto: McClelland and Stewart), 17; Charles E. Phillips, *The Development of Education in Canada* (Toronto: W. J. Gage and Co., 1957), 8.

[14]Rafael Alexander Lewy, "The Secondary School Principal in Theory: An Examination of Major Theoretical Trends of the Principalship in the United States Between 1917 and the Early Thirties," (Ph.D. diss., University of Illinois, 1965), 18.

[15]Paul Revere Pierce, *The Origin and Development of the Public School Principalship*, (Chicago: University of Chicago, 1935), 11–12, 26–27.

[16]Fleming, "British Columbia Principals," 251–52.

building maintenance.[17] School board minutes reveal squabbles at the most intricate levels of the work day. Ontario principals in 1909, for example, collectively objected to the Ministry of Education for requiring a specific method of examination of teachers' notebooks. Such "matters of detail," the principals argued, were local "questions of judgment."[18]

While battling intrusions from above, principals also defended their authority from those below. Relieved from the head teachers' menial duties of building maintenance, the principal now had to direct others to do that work, a managerial task that often caused discord within the building. Ontario principals in the 1890s believed that although some of their authority had increased, in other areas, including the heating and ventilation of the classroom, they were "powerless" and as a result, the occupants of schools were "being slowly poisoned" by negligent caretakers.[19] In some cities, regulations outlined the responsibilities of principal and engineer, such as in Chicago in 1905 where the Board wrote in excruciating detail about whose responsibility it was to open the school, keep the keys, sweep the halls, and monitor the furnace.[20] In relations with the local community, too, the principal's authority was not absolute: parents and teachers could, and did, appeal to district officials for review of a principal's decision on discipline or managerial practice.[21]

By the end of the nineteenth century, then, the principal teacher or head teacher, was a shadowy figure on the educational landscape. In one and two room schools in rural communities across North America, the principal simply did not exist, since staffing in local schools depended upon the fiscal resources and generosity of local school boards.[22] But urban schools were only marginally more systemic in their appointment of school leaders. In his 1892 expose of American urban schools, Joseph Rice described a variety of different responsibilities for principals, from Philadelphia where they were "lords and masters of their own schools" to Indianapolis where each school had a principal, but their duties barely extended beyond teaching and general supervision over the building. In some cities, one principal was in charge of a number of schools; in others, the principal was little more than a clerk whose main job was to keep attendance.[23]

The Making of the Principal's Office

Pivotal to the reshaping of the irregular head teacher into a professional office in the early twentieth century was the realignment of the principal's affinity away from the classroom teacher and towards the district officer. In 1923, Ellwood P. Cubberley described the significance of the principal's relationship with the district office as

> analogous in the business world to that of the manager of a town branch of a public utility to the general superintendent of the business; to that of the manager of a single department to the general manager of a department store; to that of the superintendent of a division of a railroad to the president of the company; or that of the colonel of a regiment to the commanding general of an army.[24]

The first step toward professionalizing the principal was to distinguish between mundane administrative tasks and supervisory responsibilities. The first, observed one reformer, "is mere shop keeping; the second is educational statesmanship."[25] Supervision enhanced [the] principal's cultural authority over the school: as Charles H. Judd saw it, only the principal's "true scientific supervision" would "convert the school into a laboratory of human engineering."[26] As Seattle's superintendent promised in 1933, all education would be improved by the principal's "well lubricated, frictionless operation of the machinery."[27] Supervision also increased [the] principal's actual authority to hire and fire, assign extra duties, and recommend teachers and staff for promotion. Later in the century, Willard Elsbree and Edmund Reutter specifically referred to these attributes when they described the principal as "a kind of foreman

[17]Pierce, *Origin and Development of the Public School Principalship*, 40–46, 50–51, 89–99; Lewy, "The Secondary School Principal," 23.

[18]Edwin C. Guillet, *In the Cause of Education: Centennial History of the Ontario Educational Association, 1861–1960* (Toronto: University of Toronto Press, 1960), 237.

[19]Guillet, *In the Cause of Education*, 135.

[20]Pierce, *Origin and Development of the Public School Principalship*, 52–53.

[21]See for example, "The Brantford 'School Difficulty'" and "An Inspector Investigates a Local Conflict," in Alison L. Prentice and Susan E. Houston, *Community School and Society in Nineteenth Century Canada*, 107–115, 122–27 (Toronto: Oxford University Press, 1975).

[22]D. A. Lawr and R. D. Gidney, "Who Ran the Schools? Local Influence on Education Policy in Nineteenth Century Ontario," *Ontario History* 72, (September 1980): 131–143.

[23]Joseph Mayer Rice, *The Public-School System of the United States* (New York: Arno Press, 1969), 113, 149.

[24]Ellwood P. Cubberley, "The Principal and the Principalship," *The Elementary School Journal* 23, (January, 1923): 342.

[25]Quoted in Leonard V. Koos, James M. Hughes, and Percival W. Huston, *Administering the Secondary School* (New York: American Book Company, 1940), 455.

[26]Quoted in Edward A. Krug, *The Shaping of the American High School, 1920–1941* (Madison: University of Wisconsin Press, 1972), 160.

[27]Worth McClure, "The Organizing Administrative Work of the School Principal," in *Modern School Administration: Problems and Progress*, ed. John C. Almack (Boston: Houghton Mifflin, 1933), 119.

who through close supervision helped to compensate for ignorance and lack of skill of his subordinates."[28]

And principals had an increasing number of subordinates in the expanding bureaucratic system. In their famous community study of Middletown, Robert and Helen Lynd pointed out that in 1890, the superintendent was the only person in the school system who did not teach; but by the 1920s there was "a whole galaxy of principals, assistant principals, supervisors of special subjects, directors of vocational education and home economics, deans, attendance officers, and clerks who do no teaching but are concerned in one way or another with keeping the system going."[29] The growing demands on principals to manage this staff led to their removal from the classroom: teaching principals remained prominent in smaller and rural schools, but by the mid-1930s, 70% of American urban principals in elementary schools had no teaching responsibilities.[30] Recognition of the new authority of the principal led to the construction of a separate principal's office that often included special accommodations for a secretary, filing clerks, and a waiting room.[31] By the 1920s, public address systems linked the principal's office with classrooms, emphasizing how the principal was both apart from, and constantly overseeing, teachers.[32]

The second step in the professionalization of the principal was the tightening of academic qualifications for the position, and specifically increasing the distinctions between administrator and teacher preparation. In 1906, Ellwood P. Cubberely, a newly minted graduate from one of the first doctoral programs in educational administration, proposed that each state offer an administrative certificate for educators seeking appointment to leadership positions, arguing that specified coursework in administration was an avenue toward "professionalizing educational leadership."[33] Between 1923 and 1934,

the number of American states that distinguished teacher from administrator certificates more than tripled from 7 to 27. By the 1950s one-third of all states and half of all Canadian provinces stipulated specific academic requirements for the principalship.[34] In the years after the Second World War, the new academic field of educational administration developed a knowledge base that increasingly distinguished administrative and pedagogical areas of research and that fragmented educational administrators into specialty groups—principals separated from superintendents and assistant superintendents, and from the panoply of other administrative experts in school finance, law, building management, and curriculum.[35] Such specialization solidified the identity of school administrators as uniquely prepared professionals with distinct skills. In 1962, an educator at the University of Calgary could conclude that "No longer is the administrator simply a teacher with intuitive understanding of some problems of school-community relationships."[36]

But these efforts to distinguish the principal from the teacher were compromised by the unavoidable fact that the principal remained in the school with teachers. Educational administrators struggled with this tension, constructing tortured arguments about how the principal both was and was not a teacher. For example, in 1910 Frank McMurry described principals as "professional leaders" whose primary affinity still should be to teachers, while at the same time they should also be "teachers of teachers."[37] The tangled irony of the principal's role was often symbolized by their physical office. Having left the classroom to address new administrative responsibilities, principals were then criticized for not paying enough attention to classroom matters. Such comments often referred specifically to the principal's office which, now that it was created to house the new building authority, was seen as the last place that the truly inspired principal should be. In 1924, Chicago's superintendent urged principals to get "out of the office chairs and into the work area."[38] Cubberley applauded the work of an elementary principal in Salt Lake City who was always

[28]Willard S. Elsbree and E. Edmund Reutter, Jr., *Principles of Staff Personnel Administration in Public Schools* (New York: Teachers College, 1954), 231.

[29]Quoted in David Tyack, *The One Best System: A History of American Urban Education* (Cambridge: Harvard University Press, 1974), 185.

[30]Bess Goodykoontz and Jessie A. Lane, *The Elementary School Principalship* (U.S. Department of the Interior Bulletin, 1938, no. 8), 9.

[31]Pierce, *Origin and Development of the Public School Principalship*, 47–48. See also Antonio Vinao, "The School Head's Office as Territory and Place: Location and Physical Layout in the First Spanish Graded School," in *Materialities of Schooling: Design, Technology, Objects, Routines*, ed. Martin Lawn and Ian Grosvenor (Oxford: Symposium Books, 2005), 56.

[32]Krug, *The Shaping of the American High School*, 162.

[33]As cited in Roal F. Campbell, Thomas Fleming, L. Jackson Newell, and John W. Bennion, *A History of Thought and Practice in Educational Administration* (New York: Teachers College Press, 1987), 75.

[34]Glass, *The History of Educational Administration Viewed through its Textbooks*, 62; W. N. Toombs, "Administrative Requirements of Principals and Superintendents," *Canadian Education and Research Digest, 2* (March 1962): 64.

[35]Keith Goldhammer, "Evolution in the Profession," *Educational Administration Quarterly* 19, (Summer 1983): 249–272; Frank W. Hart, "Special Certification as a Means of Professionalizing Educational Leadership," *Teachers' College Research* 27, (1925): 121; B. H. Peterson, "Certification of School Administrators in the United States," *School and Society* 45, (1937): 784–86.

[36]Toombs, "Administrative Requirements of Principals and Superintendents," 64.

[37]As quoted in Cuban, *The Managerial Imperative*, 6.

[38]As quoted in Pierce, *Origin and Development of the Public School Principalship*, 82.

"somewhere in the rooms busy with his work, instead, of sitting on his chair in his office."[39] Administrative reformers who assigned principals mountains of paper work now criticized principals for being a "Director of Routine" rather than leading "educational engineering and generalship."[40] Yet routine efficiency was also valued by district officials who were more likely to assess a principal on specific clerical matters than on instructional supervision or leadership style.[41]

Teachers' attitudes about the newly empowered school head also reflected the ambiguity of the principal's office. The increasing prestige of the principal concerned many teachers who reported abuses by their local administrator, what one teachers' council in Chicago in 1921 called the assumption on the part of some principals that their office carried with it "the right to be an autocrat, a boss, or a czar, instead of a leader in educational ideals."[42] When teachers began to form protective organizations in the early twentieth century, some excluded principals, seeing them as part of an encroaching administrative force that restricted the independence of the classroom teacher.

But teachers' antipathy to building principals was not universal. Teachers often expressed loyalty to their school head, appreciating the discipline and order provided by a principal who might act, as one Toronto teacher approvingly described it, as a "benevolent dictator."[43] Rural teachers in newly consolidated schools balanced their loss of autonomy in the one-room school with the relief from administrative and disciplinary responsibilities that their new principal assumed.[44] As Richard Quantz argued, some women teachers held complex attitudes about working relationships in their school house, leading many to accept their principal's authority.[45] Furthermore, the demands of teachers' organizations were primarily directed not at building principals but at district policies over salaries, pensions, tenure, and working conditions, and principals were largely powerless in determining these matters. Some teachers' associations did allow principals into their ranks, electing them as leaders in the organization, and filing grievances on their behalf.[46]

Nor were principals themselves easily seduced into the administrative hemisphere. Principals shared with teachers a common boss who was not always attuned to local contexts. Failure on the part of a principal to abide by a district officer's expectations might end a career: As one British Columbia principal was warned by a district official, "There are a lot of Siberia's out there" where a disobedient principal could be exiled.[47] Some principals shared teachers' concerns over district intrusions and were themselves committed activists for improving school funding, class size, and local autonomy, working with teachers to undermine the impact of district regulations.

The process of professionally distinguishing between principals and teachers was also complicated by the fact that principals were always required to have experience as teachers. Teachers' continued loyalty to principals was often rooted on their common experience in the classroom. In 1895, women teachers in a primary school in New York City objected to the appointment as principal of their school of a male grammar school teacher who had less experience than their own head teacher. The teachers argued that because their own Miss Eghert had been in their school for many years, she was "imbued with the atmosphere of the school," and best knew its needs and interests.[48] This experience qualified her for the position more than any outsider. Margaret Haley made a similar argument thirty years later in Chicago, when she criticized principals whose "sole claim to fitness for the position is that of having written an examination on academic subjects with particular emphasis on theory and method of teaching."[49]

Leading figures in new educational administration graduate programs disagreed, arguing that school administrators' work required "the endorsement of educational experts."[50] But even as academic qualifications for the principalship increased, experience in the classroom remained a requirement. For example, in the checklist of qualifications for the principalship that was devised by the Chicago Board of Examiners in 1930, an applicant's experience as a teacher was weighed as twice as important as a bachelors and masters degree.[51] Even as aspiring principals were

[39]As quoted in Cuban, *The Managerial Imperative*, 58–59.
[40]As quoted in Krug, *Shaping of the American High School*, 33.
[41]Cuban, *The Managerial Imperative*, 56.
[42]Group Council 29, Bryn Mawr School, Chicago, October 21, 1921, Box 48, Folder August–October 1921, Chicago Teachers' Federation General Files, Chicago Historical Society.
[43]Kristin R. Llewellyn, "Gendered Democracy Women Teachers in Post-War Toronto," *Historical Studies in Education* 18, (Spring 2006): 21.
[44]Margaret K. Nelson, "From the One-Room School House to the Graded School: Teaching in Vermont, 1910–1950," *Frontiers: A Journal of Women's Studies* 7, (1983): 14–20.
[45]Richard Quantz, "The Complex Visions of Female Teachers and the Failure of Unionization in the 1930s: an Oral History," *History of Education Quarterly* 25, (Winter, 1985): 439–458.

[46]John E. Lyons, "Ten Forgotten Years: The Saskatchewan Teachers' Federation and the Legacy of the Depression" in *Schools in the West*, ed. Sheehan et al., 113–129.
[47]Fleming, "Our Boys in the Field," 290.
[48]Wayne Urban, *Why Teachers Organized* (Detroit: Wayne University Press, 1982), 30.
[49]Margaret Haley's Bulletin, 31 January 1928, 107.
[50]As quoted in Callahan, *Education and the Cult of Efficiency*, 250–51.
[51]Pierce, *Origin and Development of the Public Principalship*, 175–76.

increasingly required to take written tests and submit academic credentials, their experience as teachers remained the prominent qualification.

By the mid twentieth century, the principal's office existed, but its professional status was uncertain. It was not always clear if the principal was a teacher or an administrator, or where the loyalties and professional attributes of the principalship lay. Standing on the middle ground between the district and the classroom, the principal was both and neither administrator and teacher.

The Making of the Man in the Principal's Office

Reformers' ambivalence about the professional status of the principal's office was accompanied by concerns about who sat in that office. The elementary principalship presented a special professional problem because, well into the twentieth century, it retained many of the characteristics of the old head teacher with its expansive job description, teaching responsibilities, and low status.[52] Most troubling was that the bulk of elementary principals were women. The elementary school had long been considered both the domain of women and an institution that resisted formal bureaucratic order. Compared with the secondary school with its subject areas, curriculum aligned toward vocational or collegiate preparation, and college educated teachers, the elementary school was a disordered mass of small children, integrated curriculum, and women teachers with insignificant certificates and Normal School degrees. As Marta Danylewycz and Alison Prentice argued in their study of women teachers in nineteenth century schools in Montreal and Toronto, bureaucratizing school systems institutionalized gender inequality, offering "radically different opportunities to the men and women who staffed the schools."[53] Because elementary schools were bureaucratized later than secondary schools, particularly in rural areas, women remained in those leadership positions for significantly longer. The result, as David Tyack and Elisabeth Hansot note, was that through much of the twentieth century, the elementary principalship offered women perhaps "the greatest opportunity for autonomy and educational leadership."[54]

In the United States between 1900 and the 1950s, over two-thirds of American elementary schools had women principals. Most of these positions were in rural schools, but women were also prominent in city schools, holding over three-fourths of elementary principalships in cities under 30,000, and well over half in many of the largest American cities.[55] In Canada, women elementary principals were particularly prominent in the west. Through the First World War, at least one half of all elementary principals in the city of Victoria were women, and through the 1940s almost 80% of elementary principals in Winnipeg were women.[56] In comparison, women were virtually excluded from the more prestigious and higher paying secondary school principal's office. In both Canadian and American cities, women secondary school principals could be counted on one hand, and were usually employed in all-girls' schools, small schools or vocational schools.[57]

Gendered differences in elementary and secondary school principalships were embedded in the structure of the two positions. High school principals were more likely than their peers in the elementary schools to have clerical help, separate conference rooms, and assistant principals; one 1929 study reported the suggestive finding that high school principals were three times more likely to dictate letters than were elementary principals, indicating that secondary principals were three times more likely to have a secretary to whom to dictate.[58] Even the earliest secondary schools required their principals hold an advanced degree, thereby excluding women who had limited access to universities, while elementary principals required only minimal qualifications through much of the twentieth century.[59] Elementary principals were more likely than secondary principals to teach

---

[52]Goodykoontz and Lane, *The Elementary School Principalship* 4, 7; James F. Hosic, "College Course for Elementary School Principals," *Teachers College Record* 27, (1926): 792.

[53]Marta Danylewycz and Alison Prentice, "Teachers, Gender, and Bureaucratizing School Systems in Nineteenth Century Montreal and Toronto," *History of Education Researcher* 24, (Spring 1984): 75–100.

[54]As quoted in Kathleen Weiler, *Country Schoolwomen: Teaching in Rural California, 1850–1950* (Stanford: Stanford University Press, 1998), 21.

[55]Tyack and Hansot, *Managers of Virtue*, 183; Goodykoontz and Lane, *The Elementary School Principalship*, 12; Pierce, *Origin and Development of the Public School Principalship*, 172.

[56]Fleming, "British Columbia Principals," 258–59; Mary Kinnear, "'Mostly for the Male Members': Teaching in Winnipeg 1933–1966," *Historical Studies in Education* 6, (Spring 1994): 5, 13.

[57]Kinnear, "Mostly for the Male Members," 5; Susan Gelman, "Women Secondary School Teachers: Ontario, 1871–1930," (Ph.D. diss., University of Toronto 1994), 88–91; Dan Harrison Eikenberry, "Status of the High School Principal" (Department of the Interior, Bureau of Education. Bulletin 1925, no. 24), 43; Frank Kale Foster, "Status of the Junior High School Principal," (Department of the Interior, Bureau of Education. Bulletin 1930, no. 18), 15, 46; Andrew Fishel and Janice Pottker, "Women in Educational Governance: A Statistical Portrait," *Educational Researcher* 3, (July–August 1974): 4–7; Cecelia Reynolds, "Naming the Experience: Women, Men and Their Changing Work Lives as Teachers and Principals," (Ph.D. diss., University of Toronto, 1987), 98–99.

[58]Goodykoontz and Lane, *The Momentary School Principalship*, 12; Fred C. Ayer, "The Duties of the Public School Administrator, III," *American School Board Journal* 78, (April 1929): 40.

[59]Peterson, "Certification of School Administrators," 785; Ontario Department of Education, A *History of Professional Certificates* (Ontario Department of Education Toronto, 1935), 68.

classes, be involved in direct interaction with children on the playground and lunch room, and in community and welfare organizations.[60] Early twentieth century architectural plans represented the occupational difference in material terms: the high school principal's office was positioned on the first floor, at the entrance to the school building to symbolize the principal as the public face of the school. In the elementary school, the principal's office was often on the second floor, embedded in the core of the school. Differential salaries reflected differential status: across Canada and the United States, elementary principals earned between two-thirds and three-fourths of secondary principals.[61] For those educators seeking promotion, experience as an elementary principal was considered less valuable than experience as a secondary principal. In turn of the century New York City, elementary principals were denied the opportunity even to apply for secondary principalship positions because, according to the school superintendent, the experience of managing an elementary school was simply not enough of a qualification for leading "a great city high school."[62]

To early twentieth century school reformers, the low status, expansive job description and continued feminization of the elementary principalship gave the position a decidedly unprofessional character. According to one observer in 1926, the elementary principalship, was not a professional position but merely "a function" that varied "with varying situations."[63] Reformers initiated a variety of strategies to redesign the elementary principalship, clarifying its job description, qualifications and credentialing processes, and replacing women principals with men.

In the 1920s, university programs in educational administration began to shape and categorize the work of the elementary school principal by offering specific courses on child study and elementary level administration.[64] Access to these programs was explicitly limited to men through recruitment practices and gender quotas in graduate programs. In both Canada and the United States, male veterans returning from the First and Second World Wars received tuition waivers for graduate courses.[65] Married men were

particularly targeted to resolve a perceived masculinity crisis caused by too many women in elementary schools. The athletic, married male principal offered school districts a vision of stability, heteronormativity, and professionalism.[66] Further excluding women from administration was that, although teaching experience remained a requirement for the principalship, experience in the elementary school was considered less favorably than in secondary schools, as seen in the New York City case noted earlier. And in the Chicago certification checklist of 1930 cited above, elementary teachers required two years more of teaching experience than secondary teachers to qualify for the principalship.[67] The work of elementary teaching, done primarily by women, was flatly counted as less significant for school leadership than similar work in the secondary school.[68]

Another strategy that effectively re-organized women out of the elementary principalship was school amalgamation and consolidation that systematically dismantled small elementary schools where women had been principals, and replaced them with large schools that were, in the words of one school reformer "large enough to be of interest to a man."[69] Kathleen Weiler describes how school consolidation excluded women principals in two rural counties in California between 1930 and 1950, when the number of women principals declined from almost twice the number of men principals, to one quarter.[70] A similar pattern occurred in Ontario where province-wide school consolidation in 1967 decreased the number of one-room schools from 1,400 to 500 in a two-year period.[71] Before the consolidation law was enacted, women held 26% of all principalships; three years later, they had dropped to 8%.[72]

[60]Ayer, "The Duties of the Public School Administrator," 40.

[61]Pierce, *Origin and Development of the Public School Principalship*, 188; salary estimates from the annual "Blue Books:" *Schools and Teachers of the Province of Ontario* (Toronto: Legislative Assembly of Ontario).

[62]Pierce, *Origin and Development of the Public School Principalship*, 163.

[63]Hosic, "College Courses for the Elementary Principal," 792; Goodykoontz and Lane, *The Elementary School Principalship*, 6.

[64]Hart, "Special Certification as a Means of Professionalizing Educational Leadership," 121; Goodykoontz and Lane, *The Elementary School Principalship*, 17–30.

[65]Ontario Department of Education, *History of Professional Certificates*, 50; Blount, "Manliness and the Gendered Construction of School Administration," 64.

[66]Jackie M. Blount, *Fit to Teach: Same-Sex Desire, Gender, and School Work in the Twentieth Century* (Albany: SUNY, 2005), 84. See also Catherine A. Lugg, "Sissies, Faggots, Lezzies, and Dykes: Gender, Sexual Orientation, and the New Politics of Education?" *Educational Administration Quarterly* 39, (February 2003): 95–134.

[67]Pierce, *Origin and Development of the Public School Principalship*, 175–76. There was also an "age penalty" that subtracted points for any principal applicant over the age of 54, thereby flatly denying experienced teachers credit for their years of work.

[68]For one unique exception to the exclusion of women through certification, see Anne Drummond, "Gender, Profession, and Principals: The Teachers of Quebec Protestant Academies, 1875–1900," *Historical Studies in Education* 2, (Spring 1990): 59–71.

[69]Cited in Blount, *Destined to Rule the Schools*, 123.

[70]Weiler, *Country Schoolwomen*, 240.

[71]Robert M. Stamp, *The Schools of Ontario 1876–1976* (Toronto: University of Toronto Press, 1982), 208.

[72]Shirley Stokes, "The Career Patterns of Women Elementary School Principals in Ontario," (master's thesis, University of Toronto, 1974), 1.

In cities, the amalgamation of schools led to similar results. In 1917 the Hamilton, Ontario school district had 20 elementary schools, four of which had women principals. Eleven years later, the total number of schools in the city had increased to 26, in spite of the fact that four schools had closed, and those were the very schools that had women principals in 1917. Of the original women principals, only one retained an administrative position at another, smaller school. (Notably, in 1965, Hamilton still had only four women principals, even though there were now 75 schools.[73])

By the 1960s, the principalship in both Canada and the United States had been culturally reconstructed to align with gendered norms. Institutional and personal definitions of manhood and womanhood played out in school staffs with the woman in the classroom and the man in the principal's office.[74] The impact of these processes on women principals was devastating. Across the United States, the number of women school principals plummeted from well over a half before World War II to less than a quarter in the 1970s. The percentage of women principals in Winnipeg declined between 1943 and 1956 from 46% to 33%. In 1967, in the urban area of Lower Mainland of British Columbia, 5 out of 250 principals were women; although 99 women continued to lead small rural schools in the region.[75] A 1968 survey of the elementary principalship in the United States reflected the legacy of this gendered professionalization process. Compared to their male peers in the principal's office, women principals had more experience as elementary teachers and longer tenure in the school system. But women principals were less likely to hold the formal professional credentials for the position, including a masters degree, a professional license, and membership in a professional association.[76]

The Making of the White Man in the Principal's Office

Until the late 1950s, American educational administrators worried less about black principals than they did about women because black principals were essentially invisible to the public school system. Employed only in racially segregated schools, black educators worked in almost complete isolation from whites, whether in legally segregated schools in the South, or in de facto segregated schools in the North. A number of scholars have argued that black schools in the South before the school desegregation mandates of the 1950s were fiscally impoverished but rich in community support. The unintended consequences of white neglect, argues Vanessa Siddle Walker and others, was that black schools built their own communities of academic excellence, commitment to students, and neighborhood support that were a beacon of achievement for African Americans.[77] Chief among the assets of the black school was the principal.

From the mid-nineteenth through the mid-twentieth century, black principals in racially segregated schools of the South were important role models and respected leaders in their communities, often comprising the bulk of the black middle class, and serving as central liaisons between the school and the family. The black principal was regarded as a professional, responsible for upholding the black school as the cultural symbol of the community's aspirations for its youth.[78] Ironically, black principals often had more authority than many of their white counterparts, due to the neglect of white school boards and superintendents. Ignored by district [offices], black principals could hire and fire teachers, design programs and command respect from parents, students, and staff.[79]

Black principals held local authority, but they had no independent financial power or access to resources outside the black community beyond what they could negotiate out of white administrators.[80] Furthermore, unlike many white principals, black principals at all levels were more likely to teach and be engaged in a wide variety of activities from teaching to community work to political advocacy. In this way, all black principals shared the same broad and diverse occupational responsibilities as white women elementary school principals. Similar too,

---

[73]*Schools and Teachers of the Province of Ontario.*

[74]Rosabeth Moss Kanter, *Men and Women of the Corporation* (New York: Basic Books, 1977); Angel Kwolek-Folland, *Engendering Business: Men and Women in the Corporate Office, 1870–1930* (Baltimore: Johns Hopkins University Press, 1994).

[75]Charol Shakeshaft, *Women in Educational Administration* (Newbury Park, CA: Sage, 1989), 20; Karin L. Porat, "The Woman in the Principal's Chair in Canada," *Phi Delta Kappan* 67, (December 1985): 297–98; Bernice McDonough, "Women Haven't a Chance in Our School System," *The B.C. Teacher 46*, (May-June 1967): 354–56; Kinnear, "Mostly for the Male Members," 3–5.

[76]Department of Elementary School Principals, National Education Association, *The Elementary School Principalship in 1968* (Washington, DC: Department of Elementary School Principals, 1968).

[77]Vanessa Siddle Walker, *Their Highest Potential: An African American School Community in the Segregated South* (Chapel Hill: University of North Carolina Press, 1996); Frederick A. Rodgers, *The Black High School and its Community*, (Lexington, MA: Lexington Books, 1975); Vivian Gunn Morris, *The Price They Paid: Desegregation in an African American Community* (New York Teachers College Press, 2002).

[78]Tillman, "African American Principals and the Legacy of *Brown*," 102; Jacqueline Jordan Irvine, "An Analysis of the Problem of Disappearing Black Educators," *The Elementary School Journal* 88, (May 1988): 509.

[79]Tillman, "African American Principals," 109.

[80]J. Irving and E. Scott, "The Professional Functions of Negro Principals in the Public Schools of Florida in Relation to Status," *The Journal of Negro Education* 13, (Spring 1944): 171, 73.

was that black principals received only a fraction of the salary of any white male principal.[81]

The maintenance of a segregated system of schooling ensured black principals a culturally significant role, and the dismantling of this system destroyed that. When Southern school districts were forced to desegregate after the Supreme Court's 1954 *Brown v. Board of Education* decision, white leaders complied by closing segregated black schools. The result all across the South was the destruction of thousands of community based black schools and staff. While black teachers became scarce under this process, black principals faced literal extinction. In the decade after *Brown,* the number of black principals in the South was reduced by 90%.[82] In the late 1960s, when the enforcement of desegregation was at its peak in the American South, black principals were eliminated with what one investigating body called "avalanche-like force and tempo."[83] Numbers show the stark reality that faced black principals: Between 1964 and 1971 in Alabama, the number of black secondary school principals fell from 134 to 14; in Virginia, from 107 to 16; in each Texas and North Carolina, 600 black principals lost their jobs. In Maryland, the number of black principals decreased by 27%, while the number of white principals increased 167%. Most of these former principals were reassigned to minor administrative jobs working under white principals, or returned to the classroom, or left education altogether.[84]

The ejection of the black principal from schools left the black community without one of its most professional icons. It interrupted the recruitment and promotion paths for young black teachers and excluded a voice advocating for black children at the administrative level. It meant not only the loss of one of the few professional positions reserved for highly educated African Americans, but also "a loss of tradition of excellence, a loss of black leadership as a cultural symbol in the black community, and a loss of expertise of educators who were committed to the education of black children."[85] The loss continues: in 2002, less than 10% of all American principals were African American, and only 4% were Hispanic,

at a time when students of color constitute a majority of enrollment in urban public school systems.[86] Even in urban schools with predominantly minority student populations, only one-third of all principals are African American.[87]

Conclusion: Go to the Principal's Office

The loss of the black principal mirrors the story of the removal of white women principals from elementary schools, and both cases speak to the impact of organizational change on school culture. The occupation of the principal in elementary schools and in black schools continued the tradition of the head teacher: the *educator* who took on administrative tasks, versus the *administrator* who supervised teachers. As the principalship became a more formalized position, it was designed to be more closely aligned to and responsive to district offices than to teachers' classrooms. The new configuration of the principal's office conformed with traditional social expectations for men, and its recruitment and hiring practices explicitly excluded women and people of color. But ironically, even as the principals' office marginalized others, the principal remained in a subsidiary position: marginalized in the middle of a vast bureaucracy.

As educational historians have long argued, the development of a bureaucratic school system in the late 19th and early 20th centuries created a seismic shift in the organizational character of North American schools. In this essay, I have traced the role of the principal in those massive organizational changes. I suggest that the peculiar position of the principal as a middle manager with a "dual personality," standing between the classroom and the district, provides a fresh insight into how school systems slowly lumbered into their contemporary model. The school principal continues to represents the on-going tension between central and local management, between policy development and policy implementation, and between the formal bureaucratic aspects of school administrative work and the informal, relational and immediate demands of daily school life. However much effort has been made to separate the principal from the teacher and to design it as an authoritative and professional profession, the principalship has remained tethered to the classroom and the teacher. That legacy continues in the workload of contemporary principals who juggle a diverse array of responsibilities from supervision of staff to instructional design to disciplining of students to community relations to crisis management. Not surprisingly, there is a shortage of school principals, and, also not

---

[81]Ibid.

[82]Johnny S. Butler, "Black Educators in Louisiana: A Question of Survival," *The Journal Negro Education* 43, (Winter 1974): 22.

[83]Cited in *Tillman,* "African American Principals," 112.

[84]Karpinksi, "Bearing the Burden of Desegregation," 251; Robert Hooker, "Displacement of Black Teachers in the Eleven Southern States," *Afro-American Studies* 2, (December 1971): 165–180; Simon O. Johnson, "A Study of the Perceptions of Black Administrators Concerning the Roles of the Black Principal in Florida During the Period 1973–78," *The Journal of Negro Education* 46, (Winter 1997): 53; Everett E. Abney, "The Status of Florida's Black School Principals," *The Journal of Negro Education* 43, (Winter 1974): 3–8.

[85]Tillman, "African American Principals," 112–13.

[86]Education Writers Association, "Searching for a Superhero: Can Principals Do it All?" Washington, DC: Educational Writers Association, 2002.

[87]Tillman, "African American Principals," 112–13.

surprisingly, a shortage of women and people of color expressing interest in the principalship. More historical studies of the school principal may provide further insight into the curious combination of marginality and centrality of the principal in school organization and culture.

ABOUT THE AUTHOR

Kate Rousmaniere is Professor of Educational Leadership at Miami University, Ohio. This essay was the History of Education Society Presidential Address delivered at the joint annual meeting of the History of Education Society and the Canadian History of Education Association, Ottawa, October 2006.

The author thanks the following for their help with the essay's conception and construction: Catherine Lugg, Jim Burchyett, Bob Hampel, Wayne Urban, Richard Quantz, Harry Smaller, Kim Underwood, Kathleen Knight Abowitz, Adah Ward Randolph, and Cecelia Reynolds.

CHAPTER SEVENTEEN

Mixed-Methods Research

PROBLEMS OF PRACTICE *in this chapter*

- What can be done to lessen the need for remedial courses in college?
- What is the best way for students to take notes while studying web-based material?
- How can curriculum content be framed so that it appeals to the way that students see the world?
- How can administrators make instruction in instrumental music more rewarding and effective for students and their teachers?
- How should a teacher respond to students when they make an error during classroom instruction in mathematics?
- How can educators reduce the stress experienced by high school students who have too many demands on their time?
- If a school is evaluated as being low-performing, what can be done to improve it?

IMPORTANT *Ideas*

1. Researchers need multiple research methods, because a method that is well suited for one purpose, such as the study of individuals' overt behavior, might be poorly suited for another purpose, such as the study of individuals' inner lives.
2. Mixed-methods researchers use both quantitative and qualitative techniques—either concurrently or sequentially—to address the same or related research questions.
3. Mixed-methods research designs differ from each other in (1) whether the quantitative and qualitative methods are used concurrently or sequentially and, if sequentially, which method is used first, (2) whether more emphasis is placed on qualitative methods or quantitative methods, and (3) whether an explicit theoretical perspective is used to guide the entire study.
4. Mixed-methods research designs vary depending on whether their purpose is (1) to use qualitative methods to explain quantitative findings, (2) to use a theoretical perspective to guide the design of the study and interpretation of its findings, or (3) to use qualitative and quantitative methods to triangulate findings.

5. The introductory section of a mixed-methods research report should explain the importance of the study, state the research questions or hypotheses that guided the study, and present a review of relevant literature.

6. In a mixed-methods study, the sampling procedures for the quantitative and qualitative components will vary; however, it is generally desirable to select a sample that represents a defined population.

7. Mixed-methods research imposes no restrictions on the types of measures that can be used.

8. Mixed-methods research reports include both quantitative results (typically based on statistical analyses) and qualitative results (typically based on the search for themes in observational or verbal data).

9. The discussion section of a mixed-methods research report should include a summary of the findings, reflections on the implications of the findings for research and practice, and a consideration of the study's limitations.

KEY TERMS

concurrent-triangulation research design

mixed-methods research

sequential-explanatory research design

sequential-transformative research design

THE NEED FOR MULTIPLE RESEARCH METHODS

No single research methodology, even experiments, is sufficient for examining all facets of education from all perspectives. For this reason, different communities of researchers have formed over time in order to study particular educational problems using their own special methods. We have described the primary research methods in Parts Three and Four of this book.

In the past 30 years or so, individual research methods have typically been grouped into two categories: quantitative and qualitative. Research methodologists have debated about how these two types of research differ and whether one is superior to the other. To a certain extent, qualitative research expanded in the 1970s and 1980s as a reaction to perceived inadequacies of quantitative research methods (Teddlie & Tashakkori, 2003).

Research in education and the social sciences has now reached the point where quantitative and qualitative research methodologies coexist in a state of mutual respect. Indeed, there is increasing awareness that both methodologies can be used in a single study to address the same research question. This type of inquiry typically is called mixed-methods research.

We define **mixed-methods research** as a type of study that uses both quantitative and qualitative techniques for data collection and analysis, either concurrently or sequentially, to address the same or related research questions. Given this definition, it is easy to see that you will need expertise in both quantitative and qualitative research methodology in order to design a mixed-methods study or to read a report of one. In fact, reports of mixed-methods studies appear increasingly in the research literature. Here are some examples:

Hong, J. S., & Espelage, D. L. (2012). A review of mixed methods research on bullying and peer victimization in school. *Journal of School Violence, 11*(1), 38–55.

Kington, A., Sammons, P., Day, C., & Regan, E. (2011). Stories and statistics: Describing a mixed methods study of effective classroom practice. *Journal of Mixed Methods Research, 5*(2), 103–125.

Meade, B. (2012). A mixed-methods analysis of achievement disparities in Guatemalan primary schools. *International Journal of Educational Development, 32*(4), 575–589.

Teague, G. M., Anfara, V. A., Jr., Wilson, N. L., Gaines, C. B., & Beavers, J. L. (2012). Instructional practices in the middle grades: A mixed-methods study. *NASSP Bulletin, 96*(3), 203–227.

Yeager, D. S., Bundick, M. J., & Johnson, R. (2012). The role of future work goal motives in adolescent identity development: A longitudinal mixed-methods investigation. *Contemporary Educational Psychology, 37*(3), 206–217.

As a starting point for explaining mixed-methods research, we will describe a problem of educational practice and show how it can be illuminated by using quantitative or qualitative methods, or both. To help us, we repeat here a table that first appeared in Chapter 1, here labeled Table 17.1, listing the key differences between quantitative and qualitative research methods. It lists key features of each approach and sets them in contrast to each other.

Our problem of educational practice comes from a newspaper article in *The Huffington Post* that reported research conducted by Complete College America, a national nonprofit organization whose goal is to increase the number of college graduates in the United States. The article reports that:

Each year, an estimated 1.7 million U.S. college students are steered to remedial classes to catch them up and prepare them for regular coursework. But a growing body of research shows the courses are eating up time and money, often leading not to degrees but student loan hangovers.

The expense of remedial courses, which typically cost students the same as regular classes but don't fulfill degree requirements, run about $3 billion annually. . . .

[Complete College America's] research shows just 1 in 10 remedial students graduate from community colleges within three years and a little more than a third complete bachelor's degrees in six years. (Hollingsworth, 2012)

TABLE 17.1 • Differences between Quantitative and Qualitative Research

Quantitative Researchers	Qualitative Researchers
Assume an objective social reality.	Assume that social reality is constructed by the participants in it.
Assume that social reality is relatively consistent across time and settings.	Assume that social reality is continuously constructed in local situations.
View causal relationships among social phenomena from a mechanistic perspective.	Assign human intentions a major role in explaining causal relationships among social phenomena.
Take an objective, detached stance toward research participants and their setting.	Become personally involved with research participants, to the point of sharing perspectives and assuming a caring attitude.
Study populations or samples that represent populations.	Study cases.
Study behavior and other observable phenomena.	Study the meanings that individuals create and other internal phenomena.
Study human behavior in natural or contrived settings.	Study human actions in natural settings.
Analyze social reality into variables.	Make holistic observations of the total context within which social action occurs.
Use preconceived concepts and theories to determine what data will be collected.	Discover concepts and theories after data have been collected.
Generate numerical data to represent the social environment.	Generate verbal and pictorial data to represent the social environment.
Use statistical methods to analyze data.	Use analytic induction to analyze data.
Use statistical inference procedures to generalize findings from a sample to a defined population.	Generalize case findings by determining their applicability to other situations.
Prepare impersonal, objective reports of research findings.	Prepare interpretive reports that reflect researchers' constructions of the data and an awareness that readers will form their own constructions from what is reported.

Source: Gall, M. D., Gall, J. P., & Borg, W. R. (2007). *Educational research: An introduction* (8th ed.). Boston, MA: Pearson. Reprinted by permission of the publisher.

The report documents what we consider to be a serious problem of practice. In the next sections, we explain how this problem can be addressed by posing different research questions, each requiring a different methodology—quantitative, qualitative, and mixed methods.

A Research Question That Requires a Quantitative Research Method

One question raised by Complete College America's research is whether the percentage of college students who need remedial instruction varies by the high school they attended. We raise this question because we wonder whether some high schools do a better job of preparing their students for college than others.

Answering this question clearly requires a quantitative study using descriptive research methodology (see Chapter 9). We might form a random sample of high schools from the population of all U.S. high schools, identify the students who graduated from each of the sampled high schools in a given year and completed at least one year of college, and then determine the percentage of students from each high school who required remedial instruction at their college.

A Research Question That Requires a Qualitative Research Method

The newspaper article that we mentioned includes a brief vignette about a particular student, Brandon True, and one of his instructors, Beth Gulley:

> Beth Gulley, an associate English professor who teaches remedial writing at the 22,000-student Johnson County Community College in northeast Kansas, acknowledges the remediation statistics are "pretty dismal." But she noted it sometimes takes students longer to graduate than the span of time the statistics track.
>
> "I think there is lots of hope," she said.
>
> Take her assistant Brandon True, who dropped a remedial math class twice before completing it and College Algebra. Now 23, he is taking a calculus-heavy class for aspiring video game designers and preparing to transfer to a four-year institution.
>
> "I was terrified," he recalled of his earlier math struggles. Because of those initial struggles, he feels like he truly understands the remedial writing students he helps. "I think they choke. It's scary."

These comments raise several research questions for us. We would like to know how Beth Gulley approaches her work as a teacher of remedial writing. What instructional methods does she use and why? What are her perceptions of students who need remediation? Why does she feel there is hope for these students?

We also would like to interview Brandon True to learn why mathematics terrified him. And we would want to learn what it means to "choke" or feel terror about mathematics or other academic subjects. We would want to interview other students in remedial classes to learn their perceptions about being labeled as remedial students, their views about what they need to succeed in college, and whether their high school met those needs. We wonder whether they feel in control of their education or victimized by an unfair system of schooling.

Answering these questions clearly calls for a qualitative research study using case study methodology. We are interested in particular individuals and their perceived reality. Moreover, our perspective is not neutral, because we are wondering about the fairness of the power relationships involved in high school and college instruction. Do students have any power to control the academic demands of their curriculum, and were they given information (e.g., the intellectual demands of college and careers) that would have helped them make informed decisions about which courses to take in high school and college? These questions suggest that we should approach our study from a critical theory perspective (see Chapter 14).

A Research Question Answerable by Either Quantitative or Qualitative Research Methods

Now we will consider a different question raised by the Complete College America research. Why do some high school graduates need to take remedial courses in college? It is not immediately clear whether this research question requires the use of a quantitative or qualitative research method. In fact, both types of methodologies can be used to address the question. Using Table 17.1, we outline two studies—one quantitative and the other qualitative—that could shed light on why some high school graduates need to take remedial courses in college.

Study of Cases versus Study of Populations or Samples

Our qualitative study will rely on the study of a single case. We will identify a high school that has an above-average percentage of graduates who require remedial instruction when they reach college. By intensive study of this school, we hope to discover factors that account for their graduates' need for remedial instruction.

Our quantitative study will rely on the study of two samples of college students. One sample will be college freshmen who do not need remedial instruction, and the other sample will be college freshmen who are enrolled in remedial courses. Both samples will be drawn from the same university. By studying these samples, we hope to identify factors that are associated with the need for remedial instruction.

Causality as Intentional versus Mechanistic

Qualitative researchers generally assume that people can form intentions to achieve certain goals. In other words, they can shape their own cause-and-effect relationships. In our qualitative study, then, we will interview selected high school students to determine what they are doing to prepare themselves for college. We also will interview some of their teachers about what they are doing to prepare students for college. We will synthesize what we learn from these interviews and then interview several college professors to determine their views of students' and teachers' preparation efforts.

Our quantitative study will involve a nonexperimental group comparison design (see Chapter 10), which makes no assumption about intentionality. We will compare our samples of remedial and nonremedial college freshmen on quantitative measures of personality characteristics, academic achievement, and study skills. Variables on which these two groups differ will be considered as possible causes of students' placement into remedial courses. In this research design, the factors are viewed as characteristics of students rather than as dynamic intentions that students continually form as active agents controlling their own destiny.

Discovery of Concepts or Theories versus Use of Known Concepts or Theories

In our qualitative study, we will make audio recordings of our student and teacher interviews. We might conduct additional interviews with school administrators and counselors, parents, classmates, and others, depending on what we learn from the initial interviews. Using the procedures of grounded theory (see Chapter 13), we will analyze the interview data by coding segments into categories and grouping them to identify constructs, themes, and patterns that should help reveal which factors possibly predispose students to need remedial instruction in college.

In our quantitative study, we will start by reviewing the research literature to determine what is already known about the factors causing students to need remedial college instruction. We also will learn how these factors have been measured quantitatively. In addition, we might identify other factors by examining relevant existing theories (e.g., theories of student motivation and self-concept). We will compare the two groups (remedial and nonremedial college freshmen) on the most promising factors. Factors on which the two groups differ will be viewed as possible causes of students' remediation status when they enter college.

In the qualitative study, then, the purpose is to discover concepts and theories. In the quantitative study, the purpose is to use known concepts and theories to create new research knowledge.

Analysis of the Illustrative Quantitative and Qualitative Studies

The preceding sections demonstrate how a quantitative study and a qualitative study might have contrasting features, yet address the same research question. We could elaborate on this analysis by using other features listed in Table 17.1, but hopefully they are sufficiently clear to enable you to do this analysis on your own.

Note that our analysis does not privilege either the quantitative or the qualitative research approach. Both of the outlined research studies have value and can contribute important knowledge that addresses our overriding research question: Why do some high school graduates need to take remedial courses in college? In particular, the use of qualitative data-collection techniques, such as interviews and observation, and quantitative data-collection techniques, such as tests and personality scales, provide a richer base of information than does either one on its own for shedding light on a particular research problem.

Note, too, that we have described each study as separate from the other. In fact, we could have designed this investigation as a single study, not two. It would simply be a larger study, requiring a "mix" of two methodologies—one quantitative and the other qualitative. Each methodology would complement the other in that each might identify different factors that result in college-level remedial instruction.

In the next sections, we analyze in more detail how quantitative and qualitative methods can be "mixed" in a single study so that they complement each other rather than constituting stand-alone studies.

TYPES OF MIXED-METHODS RESEARCH

As the mixed-methods approach to research has evolved in recent decades, researchers have created design variations that suit their particular purposes. Some researchers have developed typologies to classify these design variations and help other researchers realize their options when designing a mixed-methods study.

No single one of these typologies has become the accepted standard for mixed-methods researchers. However, there is one point of consensus: The term *mixed methods* applies only to studies that employ both quantitative and qualitative methods. Thus, a study that employed two quantitative research methods (e.g., descriptive research and an experiment) or two qualitative research methods (e.g., narrative study and critical ethnography) would not constitute a mixed-methods study. To be classified as mixed-methods research, the study must have design elements that genuinely reflect some or all of the features of both qualitative and quantitative research, as listed in Table 17.1.

Typologies of mixed-methods research designs have separate classifications for designs in which quantitative and qualitative methods are used concurrently and those in which they are used sequentially. Some typologies also distinguish between a sequential design in which quantitative

methods are used first and a sequential design in which qualitative methods are used first. Several of the typologies differentiate between mixed-methods studies by considering whether quantitative methods or qualitative methods were given more emphasis. Finally, a typology might discriminate between mixed-methods studies that are guided by a theoretical perspective and mixed-methods studies that are not.

In the following sections, we present several types of mixed-methods designs that appear to be particularly useful for developing knowledge to help educators solve problems of practice. We classify each example using typologies developed by John Creswell, Vicki Plano Clark, Michelle Gutmann, and William Hanson (2003). The examples illustrate three of the major mixed-method designs that they present.

Using Qualitative Methods to Explain Quantitative Findings

Researchers can design a quantitative research study in two phases. The first phase is a standard quantitative study using one of the designs described in Part Three of this book. The second phase is a qualitative study to help them understand the research findings of the first phase. The inclusion of this second phase can help the researchers understand their quantitative findings, especially if they are exploring educational phenomena about which little is known. Because this type of study includes both quantitative and qualitative methods, it qualifies as a mixed-methods design.

L. Brent Igo, Kenneth Kiewra, and Roger Bruning (2008) used this type of mixed-methods design in a study of students' note-taking behavior. The first phase of the study was an experiment involving students' note-taking behavior while studying text-based sources on the Internet. Previous research had found that the majority of students prefer to copy and paste selected sections of the text into a computer file (perhaps using software such as Microsoft Word) rather than typing their own notes.

However, at least one previous study cited by Igo and his colleagues found that most high school students in advanced placement courses preferred typing their own notes. Another study found that limiting the amount of web-based text that students could copy and paste was beneficial to learning.

Students were required to paste their notes into an electronic chart that allowed only seven words per cell. An explanation for the positive effect of this restriction is that limiting the amount of text that can be pasted requires students to engage in deep processing of the text in order to decide which words to copy and paste.

Igo and his colleagues designed an experiment in which college students were randomly assigned to four different treatment conditions. In each condition, students studied a 1,796-word web document about three learning theories. They copied and pasted their notes into an electronic chart containing 3 columns (one for each learning theory) and 11 rows (each row involving a different topic, such as definition, assumptions, and impact on instruction). Depending on the experimental condition to which they had been assigned, students could copy and paste (1) 7 words, (2) 14 words, (3) 21 words, or (4) an unlimited number of words into each cell.

After studying the text and copying and pasting (7, 14, 21, or an unlimited number of words) on day 1, students took three tests assessing recall of facts, concept recognition, and relational inferences on day 2. The researchers' hypothesis predicted that

> students assigned to the 7-word, 14-word, and 21-word copy-and-paste conditions will perform

better on tests assessing (a) cued recall of facts, (b) recognition of concepts, and (c) inferences regarding relationships among text ideas than students in the unrestricted copy-and-paste condition. (Igo et al., 2008, p. 153)

Their rationale for the hypothesis was that restrictions on note-taking compel students to engage in deeper cognitive processing of the text.

The test results are shown in Table 17.2. To the researchers' surprise, their hypothesis was not supported by the empirical results. Students in the unrestricted copy-and-paste condition demonstrated superior learning to students in two of the restricted conditions (14 words and 21 words), and they learned as well as students in the 7-word condition.

This unexpected finding led the researchers to pose the question, "Why did students in the unrestricted pasting group perform as well as those in the 7-word restricted pasting group?" (Igo et al., 2008, p. 157). They answered this question by using qualitative methods in the second phase of their study. They analyzed the students' note-taking charts and also interviewed 12 of the research participants—several from each of the four experimental conditions.

The researchers learned from their analysis of students' note-taking charts that students in the unrestricted condition copied and pasted many fewer

TABLE 17.2 • Means and Standard Deviations for Experimental Groups				
	Unrestricted	21-Word Restricted	14-Word Restricted	7-Word Restricted
Fact test				
M	4.77	2.63	2.00	4.87
SD	3.79	2.44	1.84	3.84
Relational test				
M	2.73	1.00	0.54	2.39
SD	2.41	1.45	0.88	2.21
Concepts test				
M	8.05	6.96	6.67	7.87
SD	2.88	2.42	2.44	2.32

Source: Igo, L. B., Kiewra, K. A., & Bruning, R. (2008). Individual differences and intervention flaws: A sequential explanatory study of college students' copy-and-paste note taking. *Journal of Mixed Methods Research, 2*(2), 149–168. Reprinted by permission of Sage Publications.

words per cell ($M = 24$) than was found in a previous research study ($M = 42$). Also, in the previous study, students who pasted the most words performed poorer on the posttests than students who posted the fewest words.

Thus, it appears that students in the unrestricted group in the present study were relatively selective in what they copied and pasted, even though they were free to paste as many notes as they wished. Their self-imposed selectivity means that they probably engaged in more cognitive processing of the text than the researchers expected.

Igo and his colleagues also interviewed students about their cognitive processes while copying and pasting and about whether they modified their notes after copying them into the chart cells and, if so, why. The researchers made verbatim transcripts of the interviews and then analyzed them.

The analysis revealed that three different processes can occur in the copy-and-paste method when studying web-based text. The student can read the text and copy a section (7, 14, 21, or unlimited words) into the chart cell; they can completely replace what they copied by copying another section of the text; or they can modify the copied section.

The researchers identified five themes in the transcripts, which, in brief, revealed that students in the unrestricted group focused almost entirely on the text, whereas students in the other three groups found themselves focusing both on the text and on the copy-and-paste restrictions, which sometimes proved to be distracting. For example, here is what one student in the unrestricted group stated: "I just put in the [sentence] that I thought fit the category best. . . . I didn't want to change what I had. . . . I just went with my instinct about it" (Igo et al., 2008, p. 161). In contrast, a student in the 21-word group stated: "In some cells, I had things that didn't need to be there. . . . I took them out," and "I usually took a couple of sentences that sounded good and then put them in [the cell] and trimmed them down to 14 words" (Igo et al., 2008, pp. 163–164).

The 7-word group expressed fewer copy-and-paste distractions than the 14-word and 21-word groups. This qualitative finding led the researchers to conclude that the lower frequency of distractions caused them to perform more like the unrestricted group. It also led them to conclude that the greater frequency of distractions encountered by the 14-word and 21-word groups caused them to have

the lowest learning levels of the four experimental groups.

Igo and his colleagues used their findings to make several practical recommendations to teachers whose students use the copy-and-paste method while reading web-based text. Primarily, they recommend that teachers prompt the students to be selective in how much of the text they copy and paste. They suggest that teachers might encourage students just to copy and paste key sentences or the main idea stated in a paragraph. The goal, in other words, is not note-taking for its own sake, but rather note-taking that facilitates deep processing of the information contained in the text.

According to the mixed-methods typology of Creswell and his colleagues (2003), the design of this study is sequential explanatory. According to them, a **sequential-explanatory research design** involves the collection and analysis of quantitative data followed by the collection and analysis of qualitative data, which are then used to explain the quantitative findings.

Using a Theoretical Perspective to Guide a Mixed-Methods Study

John Parmelee, Stephynie Perkins, and Judith Sayre (2007) conducted a mixed-methods study to explore how political ads affect college students. They used framing theory to guide their research design and interpretations. According to this theory, mass media and other social entities focus individuals' attention on certain events and not on others in order to shape their perceptions of social reality.

Robert Entman (1993) explained the framing process in these terms: "To frame is to select some aspects of a perceived reality and make them more salient in a communicating text, in such a way as to promote a particular problem definition, causal interpretation, moral evaluation, and/or treatment recommendation for the item described" (p. 52).

Parmelee and his colleagues drew on framing theory to help them understand why young people generally have a relatively low voter turnout in elections. The specific election of interest was the 2004 presidential election in which George W. Bush and John Kerry were the Republican and Democratic candidates, respectively.

Qualitative data collection and analysis constituted the first phase of the mixed-methods study. The researchers selected a sample of 32 college students, ages 18 to 28, which included registered Democrats, Republicans, and independents as well as nonregistered voters. The students were organized into four focus groups and shown eight political ads sponsored by Kerry's and Bush's campaigns. Each focus group was asked to discuss three main topics:

- In what ways have political ads successfully or unsuccessfully spoken to you in the past?
- How did the ads shown in the study speak to you?
- What would you do to make political ads better engage college students? (Parmelee et al., 2007, p. 188)

The researchers made an audiotape recording of each focus group discussion, created a verbatim transcript of each recording, and then analyzed the transcripts for themes using the method of constant comparison (see Chapter 13). The themes resulting from this qualitative analysis are shown in Figure 17.1.

Parmelee and his colleagues interpreted the themes to mean that the ads created frames of little relevance to college students. Also, negative ads confirmed their preexisting cynicism toward adult authority figures.

The quantitative phase of the study involved a content analysis of the eight Bush and Kerry television ads for issues that they mentioned. The content analysis revealed 13 issues: abortion, education, environment, health care, jobs, Medicare/Social Security, outsourcing, prescription drugs, stem cells, taxes, tuition assistance, terrorism, and the war in Iraq. The researchers also coded whether the ads were framed visually by showing 18- to 24-year-olds or by including statements that mentioned young adults.

The content analysis revealed that only one of the eight ads was framed to address college students. Furthermore, this ad covered only one of the 13 issues mentioned above. The researchers quoted one of the research participants, a 22-year-old college student, to convey the impact of this framing of the presidential television campaign:

> I just feel like all these ads are addressing the same thing, and they're kind of disregarding our age group. And it's kind of like a put-down, like we're not going to vote, you know? So maybe if they'd address it more towards our age group, we'd be more involved. (Parmelee et al., 2007, p. 191)

Parmelee and his colleagues explained these findings in terms of framing theory. They concluded that the framing of the political issues in the television ads had the effect of limiting their

FIGURE 17.1 • Emergent Focus Group Themes

1. Political advertising fails to engage participants because their issues are not addressed or are not addressed from their perspective:
   a. health insurance (they cannot afford health plans or had other concerns)
   b. educational issues (ads fail to include discussion of issues important to higher education, such as tuition assistance)
   c. the war in Iraq
   d. the war on terror
   e. jobs
   f. taxes
2. Ads ignore college student demographic in visual inclusion of actors from this demographic
3. Students cynical about negative nature of many ads
4. Students attracted to humor in some ads
5. Participants prefer to use Internet sites or other sources for political information
6. Suggested that political ads would be more relevant for this demographic if they discussed issues important to age group
7. Ads would gain legitimacy if they emphasized the importance of voting in general

Source: Parmelee, J. H., Perkins, S. C., & Sayre, J. J. (2007). "What about people our age?" Appling qualitative and quantitative methods to uncover how political ads alienate college students. *Journal of Mixed Methods Research, 1*(2), 183–199. Reprinted by permission of Sage Publications.

meaning and importance to college students, characterizing this effect as "the frame of omission" (2007, p. 192). The researchers mention several recommendations for changing this frame, such as having ads mention the relevance of the issues to young people and drawing on students' sensibilities and mannerisms.

Educators might draw other lessons from the study's findings for improving schooling. For example, they might review the social studies curriculum to determine whether issues of historical importance are framed in a manner that includes individuals of the same age group as the students and that motivates students by making reference to their particular way of seeing the world.

The researchers stated that their mixed-methods study was based on a sequential-transformative research design. According to Creswell and his colleagues (2003), a **sequential-transformative research design** involves the use of a theoretical perspective to guide both the qualitative and quantitative phases of data collection, analysis, and interpretation; either the qualitative or the quantitative phase can occur first. In the case of this study, framing theory was the theoretical perspective that guided the study's methodology and interpretation of the findings.

Using Qualitative and Quantitative Methods to Triangulate Findings

Kate Fitzpatrick (2011) conducted a mixed-methods study to learn how music teachers in urban schools go about their work. Her four research questions focused on (1) what music teachers in an urban setting know about the communities in which they teach; (2) the specialized skills such teachers need to be successful; (3) their attitudes and beliefs about teaching instrumental music in urban schools, and (4) the challenges and rewards they experience in their work.

Fitzpatrick collected data for her study in three phases. In the first phase, she conducted a focus-group interview, which is a qualitative research technique, with seven music teachers in the Chicago public schools. (Focus groups are discussed in Chapter 13.) She analyzed the interview data to derive themes relating to the four research questions.

In the second phase, Fitzpatrick used these themes to develop a survey questionnaire. All 153 music teachers in the Chicago public school system were surveyed, and 59 percent of the teachers completed them. Analysis of the responding teachers' characteristics revealed that they were sufficiently representative of the total population of 153 teachers. The majority of the questionnaire items involved a 5-point scale, where 5 represents the most positive or strongest belief. Administration of this type of questionnaire is a technique commonly used in quantitative research.

In the third phase of data collection, Fitzpatrick collected qualitative data from four teachers. This group included at least one teacher who was inexperienced (five years of teaching experience or less) and one who was experienced. It also included at least one teacher who worked in a struggling music program and one who worked in a thriving music program. The researcher interviewed each teacher for one hour, then observed each one for an entire school day, and finally conducted another interview to develop a better understanding of what she had observed. The usual methods of qualitative case-study research were used to derive themes from the resulting data that would shed light on the four research questions.

Fitzpatrick analyzed her quantitative and qualitative findings to determine points of agreement or contradiction relating to her four research questions. For example, with respect to the research question about the challenges and rewards of teaching instrumental music in urban schools, she found that the main challenges were a lack of freshman students (because they needed to focus on developing their math and reading skills); inadequate funding in some schools; problems in keeping music instruments in working order; and problems in recruiting students into the music program. For the most part, the qualitative data supported and amplified the quantitative findings.

The greatest rewards for the teachers, as indicated by the survey, were all student-centered: students' musical improvement, students' personal improvement, and general student success. Fitzpatrick comments that, "These student-focused rewards are confirmed by qualitative data" (p. 249). She illustrates this convergence of survey and interview findings with the example of comments by one of the teachers who were interviewed:

> But when you have the rewards, when you have those kids that can leave here and come back and still come back, and still come back and say,

"I remember when you showed me . . . ," or "If it wasn't for you telling me this or showing me that . . . ," those are your rewards, that's where your rewards are, that they actually got something out of it." (p. 250)

Fitzpatrick also found one major point of divergence between the quantitative and qualitative results. The quantitative survey data indicated that teachers' job satisfaction was moderately positive, but the qualitative data revealed that their daily work was a mix of challenges, frustrations, and rewards.

In the typology of Creswell and his colleagues (2003), Fitzpatrick's mixed-methods study followed a concurrent-triangulation design. A **concurrent-triangulation research design** involves collecting qualitative and quantitative data at approximately the same time and then determining whether the findings generated by analysis of each type of data corroborate the other.

Note that in this definition, we use the term *corroborate* to indicate that two sets of data analyses yield similar results. Researchers also use other terms that have the same meaning. Creswell and his colleagues (2003) use the terms *confirm*, *cross-validate*, and *corroborate* (p. 229) interchangeably to refer to the interpretation of quantitative and qualitative findings as similar or different. They use still another term, *triangulation*, in their label for this research design. We present all of these terms here because you might come across any or all of them in reading reports of mixed-methods research.

READING A MIXED-METHODS RESEARCH REPORT

Reports of mixed-methods studies vary in how they are organized. Quantitative and qualitative methods and results can be presented in various sequences, depending on the study's purpose. Nonetheless, there are commonalities across reports of mixed-methods research. To illustrate these commonalities, we use as our example a mixed-methods study by Meg Schleppenbach, Lucia Flevares, Linda Sims, and Michelle Perry (2007). The study examined a common problem of practice in mathematics instruction, namely, how teachers should respond to student errors during mathematics instruction.

Introduction

In the introductory section of a mixed-methods research report, the researchers should explain the importance of the study and the research questions to be answered or the hypotheses to be tested. They should provide a justification for the use of mixed methods to study these questions or hypotheses. They also should provide a review of relevant literature.

In the introduction to their research report, Meg Schleppenbach and her colleagues noted that the report, *Professional Standards for Teaching Mathematics*, published by the National Council of Teachers of Mathematics (1991), emphasizes the importance of student discourse in promoting students' learning of mathematics. Discourse does not primarily help students get more "right" answers but rather helps students think about and understand mathematics.

The researchers' primary purpose in conducting the study was to explore how students' errors in mathematics and teachers' responses to them can promote mathematical discourse and understanding. They focused on students' errors because their review of the literature suggested that this classroom phenomenon might have particular value for promoting these goals. For example, they cited an experiment (Borasi, 1994) that found students' errors, if used properly by teachers, could be "springboards for inquiry" into mathematical concepts and reasoning.

The researchers chose to examine students' errors from multiple perspectives. This goal was accomplished by observing how teachers in two different cultures, Chinese and American, respond to student errors. To keep the study focused, Schleppenbach and her colleagues framed three questions:

Do the instructional practices of Chinese teachers look different from those of U.S. teachers in terms of responses to errors? If so, how are they different? And finally, what can we learn from these differences? (2007, p. 134)

The researchers expanded on the third question by saying that they particularly wanted to learn whether some teacher practices are more effective than others in encouraging mathematical discourse, inquiry, and understanding. This statement demonstrates the researchers' interest in applying their research findings to educational practice.

Research Design

Schleppenbach and her colleagues did not explicitly label their research as a mixed-methods design. However, it is clear that the design involved the use of both quantitative and qualitative research methodology. They used quantitative research methods to collect observational data about teacher and student behavior in actual classroom settings. They also interviewed the teachers about the observed lesson and their philosophy of teaching and used qualitative methods to analyze interview responses.

Most important, the researchers integrated the two data sources to pursue a larger goal: "These [interview] statements and [classroom] practices were integrated into a presentation of four themes regarding beliefs and practices surrounding errors, with the goal being to examine how teachers' beliefs about the use of errors translated into inquiry-based practice regarding errors" (2007, p. 137). This statement indicates that the researchers did not subordinate quantitative data to qualitative data, or the reverse. Instead, they respected both types of data as sources for speculating about what teachers can do to promote student inquiry, discourse, and understanding during mathematics instruction.

Sampling Procedure

Mixed-methods research can accommodate various sampling procedures. The researchers' selection among these procedures will depend on the quantitative and qualitative methodologies they plan to use to address their research questions or hypotheses.

Whatever the sampling procedures, it is desirable to select a sample, at least for the quantitative phase of the study, that is representative of a defined population. By doing so, readers of the research report will be able to determine whether the findings are likely to generalize to the population of interest to them. Purposeful sampling strategies (see Chapter 13) generally are used for the qualitative phase of the study.

Schleppenbach and her colleagues selected their sample to represent various populations: 10 first-grade teachers and 14 fifth-grade teachers from China and 5 first-grade teachers and 12 fourth- and fifth-grade teachers from the United States. This sampling procedure enabled them to study student errors during instruction on two mathematical topics: place value in first grade and manipulation of fractions at the fourth- and fifth-grade level. Manipulation of fractions is taught at the fifth grade in China and at either the fourth or fifth grade in the United States.

The researchers acknowledged that the participating teachers constituted a convenience sample (see Chapter 5) rather than a randomly drawn sample from a defined population. For this reason, they state, "Because we did not randomly select the teachers, we naturally exercise caution in drawing inferences" (2007, p. 135).

The schools in which the teachers in the two countries worked were not matched. Therefore, we cannot be certain whether variations in student and teacher behavior reflect cultural or other factors. However, the researchers note that cross-cultural comparisons were not the key interest of their study. Rather, their interest was in observing a wide range of teacher behavior and beliefs in order to generate good ideas about how teachers might use student errors to promote mathematical inquiry, discourse, and understanding.

Measures

Mixed-methods research imposes no restrictions on the types of measures that are permissible. Any of the measures described in Chapter 5 or the chapters in Part Four can be used to collect data.

Schleppenbach and her colleagues used videotape to record 46 mathematics lessons taught by their sample of 24 Chinese teachers and 17 U.S. teachers. They analyzed only the parts of each lesson that involved whole-class instruction. Their twofold rationale for this decision was based on the difficulty of hearing verbal interaction during small-group work and seatwork and their belief that norms for discourse and inquiry are established most strongly for students during whole-class instruction.

The researchers' report does not include the questions they asked in the teacher interviews. Also, they do not indicate whether all teachers were asked the same questions and whether follow-up questions were asked following particular teacher statements. The researchers do state that the interview was designed to elicit teacher comments about how they prepared the lesson that was videotaped, the major points of the lesson, incidents during the lesson that surprised them, their methods for addressing student differences in mathematical ability, and their philosophy of mathematics instruction.

Results

Descriptive and inferential statistics generally are used to analyze the quantitative data in a mixed-methods study. Analytic techniques used in case study research (see Chapter 13) generally are applied to the qualitative data. The quantitative and qualitative analyses are often presented separately and then integrated in a subsequent section. This was the case in the study of mathematics instruction that we are using as an example.

Quantitative Results

Schleppenbach and her colleagues counted the number of student errors that occurred during whole-class instruction in each videotaped lesson. They also computed the amount of time that whole-class instruction occurred during the lesson. Dividing error frequency by the time measure yielded the variable, number of errors per minute.

The researchers found that the mean number of errors per minute varied little across lesson types (place value and fractions) and the teachers' country (China and the United States). The lowest mean number of errors per minute was 0.40 for U.S. place-value lessons (compared to 0.50 for the Chinese lessons), and the highest mean number of errors per minute was 0.55 for U.S. fraction lessons (compared to 0.44 for the Chinese lessons). We find, then, that students make errors while learning mathematics fairly frequently—approximately one every two minutes of whole-class instruction.

The researchers developed a coding scheme to categorize the types of responses that teachers made in response to student errors. Some of the response types are teacher statements, and others are teacher questions. These two categories and the subcategories under each of them are listed in the first column of Table 17.3. The statistics shown in this table are student errors in lessons about place value. Results for the lessons about fractions were similar.

TABLE 17.3 • Mean Proportion of Each Type of Teacher Response to Student Errors in Chinese and U.S. Lessons about Place Value

Type of Teacher Response	Mean Proportion for Chinese Teachers	Mean Proportion for U.S. Teachers	t value
Teacher Statement	.16	.34	2.65*
Tells the student the answer is wrong	.03	.10	0.92
Gives the correct answer	.08	.05	0.89
Ignores the error	.02	.05	0.77
Provides explanation or direction	.04	.14	2.32*
Students spontaneously correct themselves	.003	0.0 0	0.69
Teacher Question	.84	.66	2.65*
Re-asks the question	.28	.15	1.76
Clarifies the question	.11	.03	2.76*
Asks for an addition to the answer	.09	0.0 0	5.57**
Asks for certainty about the answer or agreement with it	.11	.25	3.33*
Redirects the question	.22	.24	0.28
Asks for student explanation of the answer	.03	0.0 0	1.61

*p < .05
**p < .001
Source: Based on Schleppenbach, M., Flevares, L. M., Sims, L. M., & Perry, M. (2007). Teachers' responses to student mistakes in Chinese and U.S. mathematics classrooms. *Elementary School Journal, 108*(2), 131–147. Reprinted by permission of the University of Chicago Press.

Schleppenbach and her colleagues found that teachers in both countries were more likely to respond to a student error with a question than a statement. Most commonly, they asked the same question of the same student who made the error or redirected the same question to another student.

The primary cultural difference revealed by the statistics in Table 17.3 is the relative emphasis on statements and questions after a student made a mathematical error. Although both Chinese and American teachers were more likely to respond to a student error with a question than a statement, Chinese teachers did so more often.

These quantitative results tell us something about the prevalence of student errors during mathematics instruction and how teachers respond to them. They provide a window into teachers' classrooms, but they do not tell us why teachers respond the way they do to student errors and whether one type of response is better than another. For answers, we need to look at the results of the researchers' qualitative analyses.

Qualitative Results

The researchers derived four themes from the interview data and from an analysis of the videotaped lessons.

1. *Creating a classroom environment that supports errors.* The teachers expressed the belief that student errors are a good way to help them discover the students' learning needs. Therefore, they try to convey to students that they should feel free to make errors. For example, one Chinese teacher stated:

> I won't discourage [the children who make mistakes] and will let them speak out their ideas confidently. It doesn't matter if you say it wrong. If only you dare say it, you're so great. In this way all the students can fully express themselves, and their problems can be exposed and resolved in a timely manner. (Schleppenbach et al., 2007, p. 140)

This belief in the value of student errors is supported by the researchers' quantitative finding that errors are, in fact, prevalent—approximately one every two minutes.

2. *Creating "good mistakes."* Some teachers in the sample deliberately asked questions that some students would answer incorrectly. For example, in a fractions lesson, a teacher asked students

how they would write "one whole." Evidently, students had just been taught that a fraction with the same numerator and same denominator equals 1. Therefore, some students stated that sixteen-sixteenths is "one whole." The teacher used this error as an opportunity to note that sixteen-sixteenths has 16 parts, and therefore is not a single whole thing.

The researchers commented that the elicitation of "good mistakes" might be a productive way for teachers to encourage mathematical inquiry and discourse among students.

3. *Review, review, and review again.* Some of the teachers commented that review is a powerful technique for helping students learn from their errors. For example, they refer to Chinese teachers' practice of having a student remain standing after they made an error. The teachers asked other students to provide the correct answer. Then the teachers asked the student who made the error to repeat the correct answer aloud.

This is a form of review in that the student who made the error had the opportunity to review it and replace it with the correct answer. Another type of review used by Chinese teachers is a remedial class where students who make repeated errors can receive instruction that addresses the learning problems that result in these errors.

4. *Students working through errors.* The researchers found in their quantitative results that Chinese teachers more often asked questions after a student error than did American teachers. They analyzed their qualitative data in search of an explanation for this cultural difference.

Their analysis led the researchers to this explanation:

> "We concluded that the emphasis on questions by the Chinese teachers was a matter of encouraging students to work through their errors rather than correcting their errors immediately" (Schleppenbach et al., 2007, p. 143).

The Chinese and American teachers who engaged in this practice did so in various ways, such as having students work on more problems to see if they could discover the errors in their thinking or by asking other students to help them.

Discussion

As is typical in reports of other kinds of research, reports of mixed-methods research often include a summary of their findings and extend them by exploring their implications for practice and further research. For example, Schleppenbach and her colleagues repeat their finding that errors in mathematics instruction are common and then speculate that "students' self-esteem does not suffer and they are better able to correct mistakes and learn more mathematics than when errors are discouraged" (2007, p. 145).

This speculation, which derives from the researchers' analysis of teacher interviews and videotaped lessons, can be tested by further research. Researchers can use qualitative or quantitative methods, or a combination of both, to determine whether student outcomes (self-esteem and mathematics learning) in classrooms where errors are encouraged and respected are different from student outcomes in classrooms where they are not.

The researchers also reflect on their findings about how teachers correct students' errors—whether to correct the error immediately or to ask questions that encourage students to work their way through the error to a correct answer. They state, "Obviously there is a fine line between giving students time to correct their errors and letting the discussion about an error go on too long" (Schleppenbach et al., 2007, p. 145). Researchers can speculate about what this "fine line" is and design a study to explore—quantitatively, qualitatively, or both—decision rules about when and for how long it is best to let students discover for themselves the source of their mathematical errors.

Educators, too, can reflect on the researchers' findings and consider experimenting with the way they handle students' errors in mathematics and other curriculum subjects. They can do this informally and collegially or more formally through action research (see Chapter 18).

Limitations of the research study are also considered in the discussion section of a report of a mixed-methods study. For example, Schleppenbach and her colleagues obtained richer quantitative and qualitative data by studying both Chinese and U.S. classrooms. However, their sampling approach still leaves room for further exploration using other cultures.

The researchers commented that "we did not see such high-level discourse practices surrounding errors as students debating each other about the plausibility of an error" (2007, p. 146). They noted that this type of practice is recommended by the National Council of Teachers of Mathematics and by experts on mathematics instruction. This limitation can be addressed by additional studies in which researchers identify classrooms where this practice occurs and study its possible strengths and weaknesses.

EVALUATING REPORTS OF MIXED-METHODS STUDIES

The most essential feature of mixed-methods research studies is that they employ both quantitative and qualitative methodologies. Therefore, in evaluating them, you can employ both Appendix 3 on evaluating a quantitative research report and Appendix 4 on evaluating a qualitative research report. In addition, you can pose the following questions specific to evaluating reports of mixed-methods studies.

- Did the researchers use both quantitative and qualitative methods in their study?

  If the answer to this question is no, it is not a mixed-methods study. Rather, it should be analyzed to identify which of the other research designs covered in this book was actually used.

- Did the researchers combine quantitative and qualitative methods so that they shed more light on the research problem than either method would have alone?

  In this chapter, we described three productive uses of a mixed-methods design: (1) using qualitative methods to explain quantitative findings; (2) testing the validity and utility of a theory to explain both quantitative and qualitative data; and (3) using qualitative and quantitative methods to triangulate research findings.

An example of

How Mixed-Methods Research Can Help in Solving Problems of Practice

Many adults complain about the fast pace of life today. There are so many demands on our time. Teenagers might be facing the same situation, as suggested by the following newspaper article:

HELP FOR OVERSCHEDULED TEENS?

Between school, sports and part-time jobs, many of today's teenagers have schedules that leave little breathing room. Some schools are trying to ease the pressure without sacrificing students' competitive edge.

After just six hours of restless sleep, 17-year-old Cassidy Brewin gets up. She grabs a smoothie, coffee, a handful of dry cereal. With a quick kiss from her mom, she rushes off to class. Between a schedule loaded with advanced-placement (AP) classes, soccer practice, a part-time job and homework that often keeps her up late, the Chanhassen High School senior knows the consequences of taking on too much.

"I've had a few mental breakdowns where I just sat and cried because I didn't know what to do first," she said. "I'm sick from the beginning of the year until spring. I've had pneumonia twice, whooping cough and bronchitis. I know it's because I get so stressed out."

The overscheduling of teenagers like Brewin has led some Twin Cities schools to intervene by imposing homework-free days, making relaxation techniques part of P.E. class or encouraging families to schedule a "night off" to spend more time together. At Brewin's school, the entire 1,500-member student body is required to take a 20-minute mental health break twice a week during the school day.

"High school has become college for a lot of students," said Chanhassen Principal Tim Dorway, who wears a bracelet with the message: "Balance. Perspective. Growth." "With their busy schedules, when are kids sleeping? They're sacrificing their bodies to get it all done. We see a lot of coffee and Rockstar energy drinks in our building."

The changes in the school came on the heels of an uptick in the number of students hospitalized for anxiety, depression and problems related to insomnia. Last year alone, three Chanhassen students fell asleep while driving, one while on the way to school in the morning.

"A lot of our kids are hurting," Dorway said. "What's the cost of trying to do everything all at once?"

Time for a break

When the bell rings at 9:36 a.m., the hallways and commons area of Chanhassen High fill with a crush of students ready to recharge. Students are encouraged to use the 20-minute break however they choose.

A group of boys play a game of hacky sack. Four girls grab coffees and giant pretzels from the snack cart. Some play "Guitar Hero" and "Angry Birds" in the media center. One student leans against a wall, eyes closed, ear buds in, listening to music.

Similar programs are being implemented throughout the metro area.

At Shakopee High School, students have a 20-minute flexible period each day when they can meet with teachers, read a book or just get their thoughts together.

"Our compulsion about scheduling every second of kids' time increases every decade," said Principal Kim Swift. "The pressures to achieve and do more are real and pervasive."

In Hopkins, a wellness committee helps students develop skills to cope with stress in healthy ways.

"High school has become kind of a pressure cooker," said Jane Kleinman, a health science teacher and curriculum coordinator for the Hopkins school district. "The stress on our kids has increased dramatically and the school environment is much more intense—it's like it's on steroids now."

Too late to turn back?

As author of the journal "The Case of Overscheduled Children," Bill Doherty has become something of an expert on the problem. The professor of family social science at the University of Minnesota praised the Chanhassen, Shakopee and Hopkins schools for trying to ease the pressure on students.

Doherty said that some schools, mainly in New York, also are eliminating AP classes to allow students to focus on learning rather than just cramming for exams. But he acknowledges the concern that letting up could cause students to be left behind in a competitive world.

"Both sides have legitimate worries," Doherty said. "We can't turn back the clock to a more innocent era, but we can try to offset it."

Nancy Krocak, mother to a college freshman and two juniors at Chanhassen High, straddles the deepening divide.

Like many other parents, she decries the speed of life for students. "It's just the insane schedules of these kids, which of course has been insane for the parents, too," she said.

To Chanhassen's attempts to relieve the stress on students, she says: "Amen. Particularly the no-homework nights, which gives us an opportunity to spend time as a family in the same house."

Still, she knows that doing well in school, taking part in extracurricular activities and volunteering are important for kids who want to get into the best colleges. So instead of cutting back on expectations, she's tried to make sleep a priority for her daughter. And she's taken both of her high school juniors to a massage therapist.

"As parents, we're conflicted. Of course we want our kids to be successful, but at what cost?" she asked. "We've gotten onto this path and I don't know if we can get off now."

Blanchette, A. (2012, November 28). Help for overscheduled teens? Retrieved from http://www.startribune.com/lifestyle/181240841.html

We might wonder whether Cassidy is one of a small number of students who are overscheduled and stressed, or whether the majority of high school students face the same situation. We might also wonder whether the techniques used in the Twin City schools (i.e., schools in Minneapolis and St. Paul, Minnesota) are effective in helping high school students lower their stress level. Mixed-methods research can provide answers to these questions, as we demonstrate below.

If we wish to determine the prevalence and nature of high school students' stress, we can start by selecting a representative sample of these students and administer one or more measures of stress to them. Various measures can be found in the research literature, for example, the Perceived Stress Reactivity Scale (Schlotz, Yim, Zoccola, Jansen, & Schulz, 2011). We would examine the data to determine the average level of stress in the sample, compare the average level (i.e., the mean score) with other populations for which statistics are available, and do an item analysis to determine whether the sample has unusually high scores on certain items. This phase of the study constitutes quantitative research.

We then might select a small number of students for case studies. For example, we might select a few high-achieving students with unusually high or low stress scores and do the same type of selection for average-achieving and low-achieving students. We would interview all students extensively about their home situation, life in and out of school, plans for life after high school, and unusual challenges that confront them. We would analyze each case separately and together, looking for thematic commonalities and differences across cases. This phase of the study constitutes qualitative research.

Finally, we would compare our quantitative and qualitative research results. In particular, we would focus attention on whether the case study results revealed types of stress experienced by students that were not assessed by the quantitative measure of stress. This comparison is characteristic of a concurrent-triangulation research design.

Another mixed-methods study suggested by the newspaper article would be an experiment testing the effectiveness of the interventions being tried out at Cassidy's high school—homework-free days, relaxation techniques, family "night offs," and mental health breaks in school. The experimental group would participate in the interventions, while students in the control group would follow their usual routines. Stress levels would be assessed by a quantitative measure before and after the experimental intervention. In the qualitative phase of the study, selected students in the experimental group would be interviewed to understand how they were reacting to the interventions. We would want to know whether particular stress-reduction techniques were beneficial and why, and also whether the students felt that they would integrate the techniques into their lifestyle after the experiment concluded.

This use of an experiment followed by a case study is characteristic of a sequential-explanatory research design.

The results of either of these two studies might be helpful to high school educators who are concerned about their students' stress levels and the potentially harmful effects. They might develop their own interventions or adopt those used in the schools described in the newspaper article.

SELF-CHECK TEST

1. At the present time, educational researchers generally believe that
   a. qualitative research belongs more to the humanities than to the sciences.
   b. quantitative research is more powerful than qualitative research in shedding light on problems of practice.
   c. quantitative and qualitative research can coexist in a state of mutual respect.
   d. the primary purpose of qualitative research is to act as a validity check on quantitative research findings.

2. Well-designed experiments that yield statistically significant findings about a problem of practice
   a. are sufficiently conclusive that mixed-methods research is not necessary.
   b. still leave important unanswered questions that can be addressed by multiple-methods research.
   c. can best be replicated through qualitative research studies.
   d. constitute a type of mixed-methods research if observational data are collected and quantified.

3. One advantage of mixed-methods research is that
   a. qualitative and quantitative measures typically provide a richer base of information than either one alone.
   b. some readers of a research report will find more meaning in statistical results, and other readers will find more meaning in case stories and themes.

   c. the value of qualitative research is heavily disputed, and therefore a qualitative study gains in legitimacy if supplemented by a quantitative component.
   d. research participants are more likely to take tests if they know they will also be interviewed.

4. Which one of the following studies is most legitimately an example of mixed-methods research?
   a. a correlational study followed by a pretest-posttest control-group experiment with randomization.
   b. a causal-comparison study followed by a correlational study.
   c. an ethnography followed by a narrative research study.
   d. a correlational study followed by case studies.

5. A mixed-methods study in which qualitative methods are used to explain previous quantitative findings can be classified as a
   a. sequential-explanatory design.
   b. sequential-exploratory design.
   c. sequential-transformative design.
   d. sequential-triangulation design.

6. A mixed-methods study that is guided by an explicit theoretical perspective can be classified as a
   a. sequential-explanatory design.
   b. sequential-exploratory design.
   c. sequential-transformative design.
   d. sequential-triangulation design.

7. The purpose of triangulation in a mixed-methods study is to determine whether
   a. the researchers have coded verbal transcripts similarly.
   b. the quantitative and qualitative findings support previous research on the same topic.
   c. there are points of convergence between the quantitative and qualitative results.
   d. the research participants agree with the researchers' depiction of themes in the qualitative data.

8. In a mixed-methods study,
   a. the same sampling procedure must be used to select a sample for both the quantitative and qualitative phases.
   b. it is inappropriate to use random sampling procedures.
   c. the cases to be studied in the qualitative phase should determine the sample that is selected for the quantitative phase.
   d. it is desirable to select a sample for the quantitative phase that is representative of a defined population.

9. In a mixed-methods study involving a sequential-transformative research design, a theoretical perspective is developed
   a. after data collection and is used to interpret the quantitative and qualitative results.
   b. before data collection and is used to guide the qualitative phase of the study.
   c. before data collection and is used to guide both the quantitative and qualitative phases of the study.
   d. by the researcher in collaboration with the research participants.

10. In mixed methods research studies,
   a. quantitative and qualitative data collection must occur concurrently.
   b. there are no requirements for sequencing quantitative and qualitative data collection in a particular order.
   c. quantitative data collection must precede qualitative data collection.
   d. the theoretical perspective is the primary factor in deciding how to sequence quantitative and qualitative data collection.

CHAPTER REFERENCES

Borasi, R. (1994). Capitalizing on errors as "springboards for inquiry": A teaching experiment. *Journal for Research in Mathematics Education, 25,* 166–208.

Creswell, J. W., Plano Clark, V. L., Gutmann, M. L., & Hanson, W. E. (2003). Advanced mixed methods research designs. In A. Tashakkori & C. Teddlie (Eds.), *Handbook of mixed methods in social and behavioral research* (pp. 209–240). Thousand Oaks, CA: Sage.

Entman, R. M. (1993). Framing: Toward clarification of a fractured paradigm. *Journal of Communication, 43,* 51–58.

Fitzpatrick K. R. (2011). A mixed methods portrait of urban instrumental music teaching. *Journal of Research in Music Education, 59*(3), 229–256.

Hollingsworth, H. (2012, May 28). Remedial college classes need fixing, say experts. *The Huffington Post.* Retrieved from http://www.huffingtonpost.com/2012/05/29/remedial-college-classes-_n_1552313.html

Igo, L. B., Kiewra, K. A., & Bruning, R. (2008). Individual differences and intervention flaws: A sequential explanatory study of college students' copy-and-paste note taking. *Journal of Mixed Methods Research, 2*(2), 149–168.

National Council of Teachers of Mathematics. (1991). *Professional standards for teaching mathematics.* Reston, VA: Author.

Parmelee, J. H., Perkins, S. C., & Sayre, J. J. (2007). "What about people our age?" Applying qualitative and quantitative methods to uncover how political ads alienate college students. *Journal of Mixed Methods Research, 1*(2), 183–199.

Schleppenbach, M., Flevares, L. M., Sims, L. M., & Perry, M. (2007). Teachers' responses to student mistakes in Chinese and U.S. mathematics classrooms. *The Elementary School Journal, 108*(2), 131–147.

Schlotz, W., Yim, I. S., Zoccola, P. M., Jansen, L., & Schulz, P. (2011). The Perceived Stress Reactivity Scale: Measurement invariance, stability, and validity in three countries. *Psychological Assessment, 23*(1), 80–94.

Teddlie, C., & Tashakkori, A. (2003). Major issues and controversies in the use of mixed methods in the social and behavioral sciences. In A. Tashakkori & C. Teddlie (Eds.), *Handbook of mixed methods in social and behavioral research* (pp. 3–50). Thousand Oaks, CA: Sage.

RESOURCES FOR FURTHER STUDY

Creswell, J. W., & Clark, V. L. P. (2011). *Designing and conducting mixed methods research* (2nd ed.). Thousand Oaks, CA: Sage.

   The authors have separate chapters for each major phase of a mixed-methods study: choosing a particular mixed-methods design, collecting data, analyzing and interpreting data, and writing a research report.

Hesse-Biber, S. (2010). *Mixed methods research: Merging theory with practice.* New York, NY: Guilford.

   This book is distinctive in that it emphasizes the qualitative side of the quantitative-qualitative nature of mixed-methods research. The author has separate chapters on interpretive, feminist, and postmodern approaches to designing and conducting a mixed-methods study. The author also includes a discussion of ethical considerations in doing mixed-methods research.

Tashakkori, A., & Teddlie, C. (Eds.). (2010). *Sage handbook of mixed methods in social and behavioral research* (2nd ed.). Thousand Oaks, CA: Sage.

   This book contains 31 chapters written by experts in mixed-methods research. If you are planning a mixed-methods study, the chapters on research designs, sampling strategies, data-collection strategies, methods of data analysis, and integrating mixed-methods results will be particularly useful.

A Portrait of Administrator, Teacher, and Parent Perceptions of Title I School Improvement Plans

Isernhagen, J. C. (2012). A portrait of administrator, teacher, and parent perceptions of Title I school improvement plans. *The Journal of At-Risk Issues, 17*(1), 1–7.

There continues to be an urgent need to help low-performing schools, particularly those with many students living in poverty, improve. Federal funds in the form of Title I grants are available to these schools. How are these funds being used by schools that receive them? What improvements are they able to make? What obstacles to improvement stand in their way? Do school administrators, teachers, and parents see the improvement process the same way? These are among the questions addressed by the study reported in the following journal article.

The researcher used a mixed-methods design for this study. Similar questions were addressed to the sample in both a questionnaire format (a quantitative research technique) and an interview format (a qualitative research format) at approximately the same time period. These features of the study would lead us to classify it specifically as a concurrent-triangulation mixed-methods design.

The article is reprinted in its entirety, just as it appeared when originally published.

A Portrait of Administrator, Teacher, and Parent Perceptions of Title I School Improvement Plans

JODY C. ISERNHAGEN

ABSTRACT As a nation we need to identify a set of practical tools to help schools meet the needs of diverse learners. Schools must improve learning for all students, including children living in poverty, students learning English for the first time, students with special needs, students that are mobile, and students with diverse backgrounds. It is critical to their success that decision making be based on real-time accurate data and include classroom interventions based on research. An increase in staff knowledge is required to promote a unified focus on strategies, targets, and data monitoring that is tied directly to the school mission, beliefs, and objectives for improvement.

Introduction

A Schoolwide Title I designation allows schools to utilize funds from Title I, Part A, and other federal education resources to upgrade the school's entire educational program and enhance academic achievement (Elementary and Secondary Education Act [ESEA], 1965). To qualify as a Schoolwide Title I school, at least 40 % of the student population must live in poverty. Title I concentrates on a results-based accountability approach. This allowed

> flexible use of Title I funds as opposed to targeting only qualifying students for academic assistance, reduced the fragmentation of programs and allowed schools to integrate services based on both the needs of the Title I students and other students within the building. (Stavem, 2008, p. 4–5)

Schoolwide Title I schools are required to develop a comprehensive plan within one year of obtaining Schoolwide Title I status (ESEA, 1965). The plans "must address the needs of all children in the school, but particularly the needs of children who are members of the target population of any federal education program whose funds are included in the Schoolwide program" (Stavem, 2008, p. 2).

This mixed methods research study examined the way Schoolwide Title I schools in Nebraska are implementing their Title I School Improvement Plans in order to identify needs, challenges, and successes within the Title I program. This research provides educators across the nation with information about the effectiveness of Title I School Improvement Plans, and could be used to offer improved assistance to Schoolwide Title I schools and their students. As a quarter of low-performing schools are rural schools (Manwaring, 2011, p. 18), these findings on school improvement have relevance beyond the state of Nebraska.

Purpose of Study

The purpose of the study was to examine administrative, teacher, and parent perceptions about their schools' Title I School Improvement Plans.

Literature Review

There is no doubt that improving schools in order to improve student achievement is extremely difficult work. It requires "strong leadership, a good plan and lots of communication with relevant stakeholders, including teachers and staff, families and community members" (Manwaring, 2011, p. 16). Robinson and Buntrock (2011) argue that schools that successfully improve have "high-impact leaders and the district capacity to initiate, support and enhance transformational change" (p. 22). Marzano's research supports this belief: "Leadership could be considered the single most important aspect of effective school reform" (2003, p. 172). Leadership influences practically every aspect of the school's organization: the teachers, students, parents, community, administration, and the overall school environment. Strong leaders not only encourage a change in school culture and the development of a clear focus, but are "key to the recruitment, retention, and development of effective teachers" (p. 26). It is important, therefore, that school leaders be given the flexibility to make personnel, schedule, and resource allocation changes (Duke & Jacobson, 2011; Robinson & Buntrock, 2011).

Inevitably, leaders seeking to turn around low-performing schools will face resistance in the form of deeply-entrenched behavior patterns of teachers, students, and parents (Heath & Heath, 2011). Overcoming these patterns means redefining how "administrators, staff and faculty think about and relate to work" (Ulrich & Woodson, 2011, p. 33). Robinson and Buntrock (2011) argue that stakeholders must "view turnaround status as a positive opportunity to transform their schools rather than a public rebuke for poor performance," and accordingly, turnaround schools must be "desirable places to work" (p. 26). Ulrich and Woodson (2011) discuss the need to forge an identity, purpose, personal relationships, and a positive work environment when trying to improve a school. They suggest that to transform schools in a meaningful way, school leaders must "recognize the interests and unique skills of those they lead and then encourage people to draw on their strengths to strengthen others" (p. 34). Duke and Jacobson (2011) describe successful leaders as having "boundless energy, infectious optimism, sincere regard for students, and an instinctive sense of where to focus resources and energy" (p. 38).

The consistent use of data derived from formative assessments is also necessary for low-achieving schools seeking to be successful (Robinson & Buntrock, 2011, p. 27). Without a good data collection and monitoring system, schools lose track of students' academic improvement and progress in meeting the standards; they can also fail to develop a focus for their school that is based on needs (Duke & Jacobson, 2011). While new teacher evaluation systems incorporating student achievement were "perhaps the most hotly debated education policy issue of the last year" (Manwaring, 2011, p. 18), it is also important that data is a part of teacher evaluation.

Heath and Heath (2011) describe a successful change pattern originally postulated for hospital administrators called the Rider-Elephant-Path game plan, wherein the rational "Riders" of a school are given a path to focus on, while the emotional "Elephants" are given a "jolt of energy and hope" to shake them out of a "culture of failure" (p. 32). According to DuFour (2007):

> When principals focus on creating an environment in which people are working toward a shared vision and honoring collective commitments, an environment in which the structures and supports foster collaborative efforts and continuous professional growth, an environment in which each teacher has someone to turn to and to talk to when confronted with challenges, they address one of the deepest yearnings in the hearts of most teachers: To make a positive difference in the lives of their students. (p. 46)

Methodology

This mixed-methods research study utilized both quantitative survey data and qualitative interview data collected in the winter and spring of 2010. Both the surveys and interview protocols explored seven themes: (a) Title I School Improvement Plans, (b) Clear Focus, (c) Classroom Interventions, (d) Professional Development, (e) Data/Monitoring, (f) Community Involvement, and (g) Overall Improvement.

Nebraska public school districts were divided into two categories, nonrural and rural, using Locale Codes defined by the Common Core of Data (National Center for Educational Statistics, 2010). Nonrural districts were defined as districts in cities, suburbs, and towns less than or equal to 35 miles from an urbanized area. Rural districts were defined as districts in rural areas as defined by the U.S. Census Bureau. Towns more than 35 miles from an urbanized area were also defined as rural for the purposes of this study. Of the 14 districts participating in surveys, one (7.1%) was classified as nonrural and 13 (92.9%) were classified as rural. Of the seven districts participating in interviews, one (14.3%) was classified as nonrural, and six (85.7%) were classified as rural.

Twenty schools in 14 districts that were currently in "Needs Improvement" status and four schools in four districts that had recently been in the category were invited to participate in surveys. Seventeen schools in "Needs Improvement" status and all four schools that had recently been in the category agreed to participate. Administrators and teachers from these 21 schools were surveyed using an online instrument regarding their perceptions of the Title I School Improvement Process. Administrators responded to a 51-item survey and teachers responded to a 53-item survey in the winter of 2010. Administrative and teacher survey responses ranged from 1 to 5 on the five-point Likert scale with "5" representing *strongly agree*. Of the 14 districts participating, eight (57.1%) returned surveys. Of the administrator surveys returned, 68.4% were from nonrural districts and 31.6% were from rural districts. Of the teacher surveys returned, 60.2% were from nonrural districts and 39.8% were from rural districts.

In addition, open-ended interviews were conducted with administrators, teachers, and parents in seven school districts. Detailed perceptions were collected using an interview protocol. Table 1 depicts the number of responses from both administrators and teachers in each identified theme. These sample districts were selected based on years in Title I (three schools were in their first year in the category, two schools had been in the category for two or more years, and two schools were no longer in "Needs Improvement"), geographic area, Free and Reduced Lunch (FRL) rate, and ethnicity. Forty-eight (48) individual interviews were conducted statewide during the spring of 2010. Interviews were conducted with administrators, teachers, and parents in both elementary and secondary settings. Up to five interviews were conducted within each school district.

Results

Administrators rated the category Title I School Improvement Plans 4.46, while teachers rated it 3.86. The Clear Focus category was rated 4.57 by administrators and 4.19 by teachers, the highest of any category. Administrators rated the Classroom Interventions category 4.53, while teachers rated it 4.11. Administrators rated the Professional Development category 4.39, while teachers rated it lower at 3.86. The Data/Monitoring category was rated 4.48 by administrators and 4.06 by teachers. The Community Involvement category was rated 3.69 by administrators and 3.31 by teachers, the lowest of any category. Administrators rated the Overall Improvement category 4.26, while teachers rated it lower at 3.84. Figure 1 shows administrators' and teachers' average ratings of the seven categories overall.

Title I School Improvement Plan

The average administrator response in this category was 4.46, higher than the 3.86 average teacher response in this category. However, administrators and teachers rated the same items as "strongly agree" and "strongly disagree." The item rated strongest by both teachers (4.41) and administrators (4.89) within this category was, "The planning process in my school is focused on improving student achievement." A male, nonrural secondary teacher explained, "Through our PLCs (Professional Learning Communities), through staff meetings, we discuss student achievement all the time. I might say, 'what are you doing to make that student achieve higher in your classroom than in mine, and vice versa?'" On the subject of administrator participation and leadership in the Title I process, administrators both rated themselves highly and received high ratings from teachers.

However, responses indicated that teacher involvement in the Title I process might be lacking. The item rated lowest by both teachers (3.18) and administrators

Table 1

Interview Themes and Total Coded Responses (2009–2010)

	Number of Coded Responses
Interview Question Themes	
Title I School Improvement Plans	160
Clear Focus	220
Classroom Interventions	349
Professional Development	152
Data/Monitoring	235
Community Involvement	214
Overall Improvement	124
Emerging Themes	
Collaborative Culture	161
Resources	290
Leadership	66
Challenges	64

Note. Demographic data on each of the quotes is included in the article under each theme.

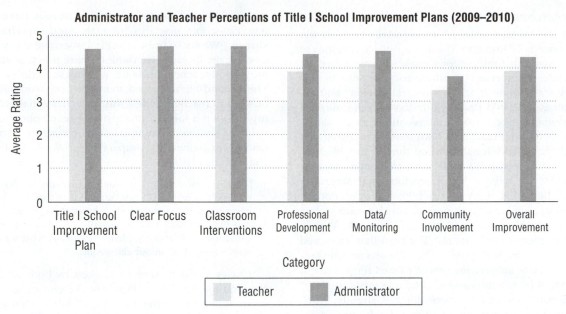

Administrator and Teacher Perceptions of Title I School Improvement Plans (2009–2010)

Figure 1 Survey of administrator and teacher perceptions of Title I School Improvement Plans (2009–2010).

(3.74) was "All teachers in my school were involved in the disaggregation of student data to identify Title I Goals." Teachers also gave their second-lowest rating (3.26) to the item "Teachers were involved in the identification of the Title I Goals." A nonrural female elementary teacher shared that at her school, "too few people [were] involved in school-wide goals." Although administrators more strongly agreed with this item (4.51), the second-lowest rating in the category given by administrators was for the item "Teachers in my school understand the Title I Goals and how to achieve these goals" (4.21). Teachers rated this item between "undecided" and "agree" at 3.81, their third-lowest rating.

Accordingly, there were mixed opinions about whether educators had clear understanding of their schools' Title I Plan and goals. For example, a female rural elementary teacher shared one goal that she was aware of, "I know that we needed improvement in reading." However, when asked "Do you know why you are in Title I?" she responded, "No, I don't think so."

Clear Focus

Educators acknowledged the importance of developing a clear focus on the areas they had identified as in need of improvement. The average administrator response (4.57) and average teacher response (4.19) in the Clear Focus category were the highest average responses given in any category. Administrators rated every item in this category between "agree" and "strongly agree," giving ratings that ranged between 4.47 and 4.74. Teachers rated most of the

items close to "agree," giving ratings that ranged between 3.89 and 4.49. This indicates that schools have strongly emphasized the concept of focus on standards and areas of need when developing curriculum and instruction. A female rural secondary Title I coordinator explained, "I think [teachers] are looking at the standards more closely and saying, 'By the time you leave this grade, you need to not just have been introduced to this standard, but have mastered it.' So I do think their teaching has become more standards-based."

Administrators gave the highest rating to the item "The curriculum in my school is aligned with state standards" (4.74). A male rural elementary principal explained.

> We set up time for staff to get together and review the curriculum and tie them to the state standards. Then we looked at our current curriculum and correlated it to the standards, and if we've got any gaps or overlaps, we look at how we can make adjustments.

Teachers gave this item the second-lowest rating in this category, but still agreed with the statement (4.09).

Teachers gave the highest rating to the item "Teachers in my school engage students in order to improve individual and group academic performance" (4.49). A female rural elementary reading coordinator stated.

> I feel like teachers have been a lot more engaged in the students' learning. They pay a lot more attention to what kids are doing on a daily basis and their test scores. Usually within two weeks, a teacher can say, "this kid's failing, what intervention can you help me put in place?"

Administrators rated this item similarly (4.47).

Classroom Interventions

Schools used a vast array of interventions to meet the learning needs of students. The average teacher response in the Classroom Interventions category was "agree" at 4.11, while the average administrator response in this category was higher at 4.53. In general teachers and administrators indicated that they understood the purpose and importance of classroom interventions. Both administrators (4.68) and teachers (4.30) most strongly agreed with the item "Additional learning time is provided for students who need it." A male rural elementary teacher explained, "We have a lot of teachers that stay after school to help kids, from 3:30 to 4:00 as needed. For 5th grade on up, we have tenth period, which means if they don't have work done, they stay and do work. There's an aide in there to help them." The item that was rated second highest by both groups was "Classroom interventions are used to achieve my school's Title I Improvement Goals" (4.19 by teachers and 4.63 by administrators).

Administrators and teachers differed slightly, however, on their assessment of their schools' use of resources and research-based interventions. The item rated lowest by teachers was "Both external and internal resources are used to develop research-based interventions" (3.98), while administrators gave it the third-highest rating of the category at 4.47. A female rural secondary teacher explained,

> Last year, I didn't even turn in the budget, because we had no money. This year I understand we've been cut $250,000 more. After a while you just go, 'happens every year.' What we're trying to do this year is just the bare minimum. The only thing I'm buying is a consumable vocabulary. The rest I will buy out of my own money.

The item producing the largest discrepancy between teacher and administrator means in this category was "Research-based interventions are implemented based on the data analyzed for my school's Title I Improvement Plan." Teachers were more likely to rate this item "agree" at 4.02, whereas administrators were in more enthusiastic agreement at 4.53. A male rural elementary principal stated, "We were using Response to Intervention (RTI) strategies and we charted all our growth. When we didn't see growth, we'd change the strategy, do something different in hopes of seeing gains."

Professional Development

Both teachers and administrators indicated that professional development at their schools needed to be improved. The average administrator response in the Professional Development category was 4.39, ranging from 4.26 to 4.53. The average teacher response was lower at 3.86.

Educators agreed that what professional development was available was helpful. Both administrators (4.53) and teachers (4.05) gave their strongest rating to "Professional development experiences have led to new classroom practices." A male rural superintendent shared, "We try to train in [APL Associates] every two or three years, because we think it's real, practical stuff that most good teachers probably use, but sometimes forget." The second-highest-rated item for both administrators (4.47) and teachers (4.03) was "Teacher collaboration in my school is a form of professional development used to enhance student learning." A female nonrural secondary teacher explained the impact of professional learning communities (PLCs):

> [The] PLC movement was huge for us. Before that, we were on our own. PLCs just brought it all together. That's when we really started to see a lot of changes: when we had that common time to actually sit, plan, talk about curriculum, talk about students, talk about what was and wasn't going well in our classrooms.

However, the item rated weakest by both administrators and teachers was "Teachers are encouraged to observe each other in the classroom." Administrators rated this 4.26, while teachers rated this item between "undecided" and "agree" (3.67). Although educators stated in interviews that such observations were important for teacher self-improvement, a nonrural male teacher indicated, "It is hard to arrange for the opportunities to make observing in fellow teacher's classrooms happen." The item rated second-lowest by both teachers (3.73) and administrators (4.32) was "Professional development needs at my school were based on analysis of data." Making sure that professional development decisions are based on data may be another area schools need to improve on.

Data/Monitoring

The use of data and the extent to which schools monitor student progress and plan curriculum and instruction varied; teachers and administrators gave a wide range of responses to this category. Administrator responses ranged from 4.16 to 4.89, with an average of 4.48. Teacher responses ranged from 3.72 to 4.38, with an average of 4.06. Educators (4.89 by administrators, 4.38 by teachers) agreed on the item rated strongest: "Data are essential to our school improvement process," showing that educators understand the importance of data to school improvement. A male rural principal explained, "We looked at different types of data sets. It all showed that our reading comprehension was going down as opposed to even staying level or going up. . . . It wasn't hard to say we had to make a change."

However, survey and interview results indicated that the actual use of data was not strong in all schools. The item rated weakest by administrators was "Teachers in my school adjust their instruction in order to attain our Title I Goals" (4.16), which teachers rated similarly (4.10). A male rural elementary principal stated,

Sometimes I question how much data-gathering you do. Sometimes I think it's too much. My core beliefs are that really good, effective teachers are going to be more effective than keeping score on kids all the time. I think we do too much assessment.

The items rated weakest by teachers were "Every classroom is implementing our Title I Goals" and "Administrators in my school monitor additional learning time for students to ensure success," both receiving a rating of 3.72. It should be noted that administrators either rated these items "agree" or "strongly agree," giving them both ratings of 4.47. This indicates that teachers and administrators are not in agreement as to the frequency and consistency of monitoring that is taking place in schools, with teachers feeling that less monitoring occurs than do administrators.

Community Involvement

The challenge posed by community involvement was made evident by the average administrator (3.69) and teacher (3.31) responses, which were the lowest of any category. Parent involvement was often low in Title I schools. Schools hoped to increase it by using diverse communication methods and expanding after-school programs. Administrators most strongly agreed with the item "The Title I Improvement Plan was communicated to all stakeholders" (4.47), also rated second highest by teachers (3.61). Schools—especially administrators—made a point of notifying parents and the community of the school's Title I status, as is required by the grant. A female rural elementary teacher stated, "I know our superintendent has put [information about Title I] in newsletters and in the paper. If parents have questions or want to observe a classroom, they're more than welcome to. We've had a few [come in], not very many at all."

The item rated strongest by teachers was "Community members have high expectations for student achievement" (3.65), which was not asked on the Administrator Survey. A male nonrural secondary teacher shared, "When schools and parents come together, there's always a benefit, because the student sees that it's not just the school trying to get you to learn this." A male rural elementary principal discussed parents' awareness of their children's achievement: "There's no reason our parents should not be fully aware of what their child's capabilities are."

However, parent and community engagement in the Title I process received low marks. The item rated lowest by both administrators and teachers was "Community members are engaged in decision making based on data that was analyzed." Administrators (3.16) and teachers (3.06) both rated this item mostly "undecided." The similar item "Community members were involved in identification of the Title I Goals" garnered similarly low ratings from administrators (3.37) and teachers (3.12). A nonrural female elementary principal stated, "Our community group is informed of the goals but did not take part in the decisions. We have parent and community groups but they don't actively work on the improvement plans."

Overall Improvement

The average administrator response in this category was 4.26, while the average teacher response was 3.84. Importantly, the item "Data shows that progress is being made in meeting our Title I Goals" received the strongest level of agreement within the category from both administrators (4.42) and teachers (4.04). A female nonrural secondary teacher provided the example using state writing scores:

Four years ago, 69% of our students were proficient in writing. Three years ago, after we started PLC work, we started this common planning, common assessment, big kick on writing in the classroom. That first year we went from a 69 % to a 95% proficient.

A female nonrural secondary Title I coordinator stated,

The 6th grade team set Smart Goals and the students were not making them. They were working so hard, they were doing everything correctly. The counselor and I were like, 'but look at that evidence of growth!' So they started charting both. They showed that maybe we didn't [meet the Smart Goals], but from where we were [at] pre-assessment and where we are [now], let's not forget that.

Administrators also rated "The use of our research-based interventions is leading to the attainment of our Title I Goals" the highest rating of 4.42. When a female rural elementary Title I coordinator was asked what she was seeing with the new reading program, she responded, "Huge improvements. The data I look at on a weekly basis, you can see their scores rising."

However, both administrators and teachers rated the item "Community members recognize improvement as a result of our Title I Improvement Plan" the lowest in this category. Teachers rated it between "undecided" and "agree" at 3.46, while administrators rated it "agree" at 4.05. The second-lowest rating was given to "During teacher evaluations, administrators in my school discuss with teachers about the way they are helping students in order to meet our Title I Goals," which administrators rated 4.16 and teachers rated 3.84.

Additional Themes

In addition to these seven themes, four additional themes emerged from the interviews: Collaborative Culture, Resources, Leadership, and Challenges.

Collaborative Culture

Educators emphasized the importance of a collaborative culture to the Title I School Improvement Process, as it allowed teachers to share resources, cooperate on a more cohesive curriculum, and support each other emotionally. A female rural elementary teacher explained, "With us being a small school, we are like a little family. Everybody here is on board. It's easy to ask if you have questions, easy to notice if somebody's confused. We all work really well at reaching that same goal. It's nice." She elaborated, "There's always a teacher that we can go to. It's mentoring, helping one another." A female rural secondary principal implied that steps taken during the Title I School Improvement Process might in and of themselves encourage collaboration: "There's a lot more collaboration between the disciplines and between the levels of the discipline than we've ever had before."

Collaboration took place across grade-levels, disciplines, and school buildings, but could be difficult to coordinate consistently. A male rural superintendent stated, "We had good conversations between our upper elementary and middle school people. We've not done as well with that recently." Teachers and administrators collaborated through formal, regularly scheduled meetings as well as informal conversations throughout the day. A male rural elementary principal explained, "Given the [small] size of our school, teachers go across the hallway and have grade interventions and intermingling. Even though we don't have official meetings, we simply stop and talk about how things are going in the classroom."

Resources

Through federal funding, the Title I School Improvement Process allows schools to use extra resources to support the implementation of their school improvement plans. Educators considered this a major benefit of participating in the Title I program. A female rural elementary teacher stated, "It's been a good thing for us to be in school improvement, because we get the opportunity to get more professional development and individual textbooks, which we need." Schools used these resources to attain new technology (e.g., interactive whiteboards, laptops, projectors, distance learning technology, reading and grading software): extra teachers (e.g., reading and math coaches, home-school coordinators, part-time teachers, and paraprofessionals); professional development opportunities; and new programs and interventions. Educational Service Units (ESUs), the Nebraska Department of Education (NDE), and consultants were also listed as helpful resources.

A female rural elementary Title I coordinator explained,

> When we were able to take advantage of this opportunity to develop a plan and have some funding to help us with research-based materials and strategies, and extra manpower to help deliver those services, then [it] became, as our principal referred to it, our reward for having [Title I status].

It is vital that schools learn how to manage these resources well. Educators stressed that this involves prioritization and accountability. A female rural elementary principal explained, "Don't go in and ask for something unless you can justify it. You know how you want to spend this money and what you expect to receive from it. That's the way it should be: accountability."

Leadership

Many educators pointed out the positive difference a good leader could make for a school in Title I "Needs Improvement" status. A female rural secondary principal explained, "It's trickle-down. It's important to [our superintendent] so it's important to me, and then it's important to the teachers, and then it's important to the kids."

Although administrators displayed a wide variety of leadership styles, teachers praised similar attributes: having an open door policy, being present in classrooms and hallways, being involved in the Title I process, and earning the respect of teachers and parents. A female rural secondary teacher explained that her principal was "really good about 'let's get together and talk about it.' . . . If you do a good job, you hear 'good job.' That makes a big difference." A female nonrural secondary teacher stated that communication with administrators at her school was "constant," and "They've made it a point to understand where we are in the curriculum. They know where we are in terms of pacing for every curricular area. Very, very involved."

High levels of administrative turnover can negatively impact the school improvement process. In these cases, teachers reported a decrease in staff collaboration and administrative involvement. A nonrural male elementary teacher shared, "Communication is a HUGE problem in my school. [Our] principal does not give information to teachers until the last minute, if even then." It is also inevitable that administrators will make mistakes. A female rural elementary principal explained, "Sometimes you do it and afterwards you think, 'I should have involved this person or that person,' or 'maybe that wasn't my job to do.' But that's part of being an administrator, you do some things right and you do some things not so right."

Challenges

Children from demographic subgroups have specific needs that must be taken into account. A female rural elementary principal explained that her students

> do not bond well with adults because they have basically raised themselves. They are, in their mind, adults already. If you are your own primary caregiver, it's difficult to go to school and look at someone else as a person who is going to inform you or change your life.

A male rural elementary principal stated: "Our kids don't understand what it takes to get to the next level, because they've never witnessed it at home."

For meeting these challenges, effective teachers are just as important as effective administrators. A female rural elementary teacher suggested, "Because some kids don't even have a kitchen table to do their homework, they need to stay here for half an hour and work with us." Still, educators expressed frustration that they could not eliminate these challenges. Regarding student mobility, a female rural elementary teacher shared:

> I wish there was a formula [for] what to do with children that move. It is hard to work so hard on a child, get them rolling, and they're gone. I don't care if they go to the best school in the state, they still miss out, they still have to adjust.

A male nonrural assistant secondary principal noted,

> [Our school] isn't like most schools in Nebraska. It's much more intense; you have to have a passion for it. The teachers said when I arrived, "it takes a special person to work at [our school]." It really doesn't take a special person to work here. To make an impact here, it takes a special person. To be a difference maker, it does take something special.

Conclusion

As illustrated by the survey findings and interview responses, Nebraska Title I "Needs Improvement" schools are focused on improving student learning. These results were categorized according to the themes of Title I School Improvement Plans, Clear Focus, Classroom Interventions, Professional Development, Data/Monitoring, Community Involvement, and Overall Improvement. Additionally, four themes emerged during interviews that were not examined by the survey: Collaborative Culture, Resources, Leadership, and Challenges.

The items "The planning process in my school is focused on improving student achievement" and "Professional development experiences have led to new classroom practices" were the highest-rated items by teachers and administrators in their respective categories. Given the focus on improving student achievement and providing new opportunities for teachers to implement interventions, it is worth noting that both teachers and administrators gave the highest rating in the Overall Improvement category to the item "Data shows that progress is being made in meeting our Title I Goals."

Teacher observation should be pursued as an opportunity for growth in schools, since both teachers and administrators gave "Teachers are encouraged to observe each other in the classroom" the lowest rating in the Professional Development category.

A major factor in the success of a Title I Plan is the involvement of parents and community. Both rural and nonrural educators indicated that engaging parents is difficult due to the many demands placed upon families with children in Title I programs. Teachers and administrators gave the item "Community members are engaged in decision making based on data that was analyzed" the lowest rating in the Community Involvement category. Engaging community members in the Title I School Improvement Process was even more difficult. This is evidenced by the finding that the item "Community members recognize improvement as a result of our Title I Improvement Plan" was the lowest-rated item in the Overall Improvement category by both teachers and administrators. One successful method of engaging parents was after-school programming. A female rural elementary parent who was also on the school staff explained, "A lot of parents call and say, '[my child] needs to go to the after-school program to complete their homework.' Some parents are really consistent and make sure their kid is here."

Administrators and teachers discussed the importance of focus in planning and implementing school improvement goals. A male rural elementary principal explained, "The more you can focus different aspects of different programs on the same thing is huge. I can really concentrate our efforts and improve one area at a time. Once you do that, you make a lot more progress." The area of greatest focus for the schools in this study was the use of interventions to positively impact learning. However, it is unclear how schools are using data to guide decisions about individual student needs.

It became evident in interviews that many challenges impact Title I students' learning. Many of their teachers indicated the need to depend on each other when trying to improve student performance, thus building a culture that encouraged collaboration. This culture allowed leaders to actively engage with staff and utilize new Title I resources and materials for professional development and student engagement.

REFERENCES

Duke, D. L., & Jacobson, M. (2011, February). Tackling the toughest turnaround—Low-performing high schools. *Phi Delta Kappan*, 92(5), 34–38.

DuFour, R. (2007). Collaboration is the key to unlocking potential. In V. von Frank (Ed.), *Creating a culture of professional learning* (pp. 44–46). Oxford, OH: National Staff Development Council.

Elementary and Secondary Education Act, as amended Title I, Part A; 20 U.S.C. 6301–6339, 6571–6578. (1965). Retrieved from U.S. Department of Education database from http://www2.ed.gov/policy/elsec/leg/esea02/pg2.html#sec1114.

Heath, C., & Heath, D. (2011, March). Overcoming resistance to change. *The School Administrator*, 3(68). 28–32.

Manwaring, R. (2011, March). School transformation: Can it work? *The School Administrator*, 3(68), 13–18.

Marzano, R. (2003). *What works in schools: Translating research into action*. Alexandria, VA: Association for Supervision and Curriculum Development.

National Center for Educational Statistics. (2010). *Common core of data (CCD): Identification of rural locales*. Washington, DC: U.S. Department of Education, Office of Educational Research and Improvement. Retrieved from http://nces.ed.gov/ccd/rural_locales.asp

Robinson, W. S., & Buntrock, L. M. (2011, March). Turnaround necessities. *The School Administrator*, 3(68), 22–27.

Stavem, J. (2008). *Revolving doors of Nebraska schools: A mixed methods study of Schoolwide Title I schools and systematic practices implemented to address the needs of highly mobile students* (Doctoral dissertation). University of Nebraska, Lincoln, NE.

Ulrich, D., & Woodson, B. A. (2011. March). Connecting hearts in the workplace. *The School Administrator*. 3(68), 33–37.

AUTHOR NOTE

Jody Isernhagen, Ed.D., is an Associate Research Professor at the University of Nebraska-Lincoln. Dr. Isernhagen has over 25 years experience as a teacher and administrator in public schools. She has written three books and numerous articles for educational journals. Her teaching and research interests focus primarily on school improvement and leadership.

CHAPTER EIGHTEEN

Action Research

PROBLEMS OF PRACTICE *in this chapter*

- What interventions can teachers use to reduce the incidence of bullying among their students?
- How can action research help urban school districts provide more rigorous academic preparation for all high school students, whether or not they plan to attend college?
- What is the benefit of reciprocal teaching over conventional instruction to social studies students?
- How can teachers improve middle school students' learning and motivation in performance-based courses like industrial arts?
- How can action science help university academic librarians address discrepancies between their espoused theories and their theories-in-use about promoting the information literacy of library patrons?
- How can action research help insiders and outsiders work together most effectively to improve educational practice?
- Should teachers assign homework to be done over holiday breaks from school?
- Is it effective for teachers to use close-reading strategies, which involve generating internal dialogue with the authors of assigned readings?

IMPORTANT *Ideas*

1. Action research is more closely tied to educators' practice than are other types of research, giving it the unique potential to solve problems of practice.
2. Educators can carry out action research projects for various purposes, including personal, professional, and political purposes.
3. After carrying out an action research project, educators can report their findings to colleagues in some form and decide on a new course of action for both improving practice and continuing their research.
4. Systematic data collection, analysis, and reflection distinguish action research from educators' other approaches to problem solving.

5. A well-done action research project gives educators both an increased understanding of new practices and empirical data about the effects of those practices on teaching and learning in a real-life setting.
6. Action research benefits educators by improving their theories of educational practice, their work with students, and their interactions with colleagues and educational stakeholders.
7. By following the principles of action science, educators can identify and address discrepancies between their espoused beliefs about educational practice and their actual behavior in practice.
8. Action research is carried out primarily by educators with an insider perspective on a problem of practice, but outsiders can help in designing the study, addressing insiders' feelings about the research problem, and contributing support for personal and social change.
9. Action researchers can use a number of validity criteria to help them design research to achieve maximum credibility and trustworthiness.

KEY TERMS

action research
action science
catalytic validity
collaborative action research
democratic validity
dialogic validity
espoused theory

insider
insider research
intentionality
outcome validity
outsider
participatory action research
practitioner research

process validity
reflection
self-study research
systematic practitioner
  research
teacher research
theory-in-action

THE HISTORY OF ACTION RESEARCH

Action research is a form of research carried out by educators in their everyday work settings for the primary purpose of improving their professional practice. This form of research corresponds to what some researchers call **practitioner research** or **self-study research** (Zeichner & Noffke, 2001), **teacher research** (Cochran-Smith & Lytle, 1999), and **insider research** (Kemmis & McTaggart, 2000). When researchers and participants collaborate in solving a problem of practice, it is sometimes called **participatory action research** (Reason & Bradbury, 2001).

Social psychologist Kurt Lewin (1946) helped popularize action research during World War II. He observed that much research resulted in scholarly publications that had little effect on professionals' work or on the broader society. Lewin developed action research as a form of investigation that community members and working professionals could do together to promote positive social change.

In one study, Lewin assembled small groups of housewives to consider the use of organ meats in family meals. At the time, the U.S. government was seeking to promote these cheaper cuts of meat because of a wartime shortage of meat supplies. Lewin's action research project showed the value of group discussion in changing housewives' attitudes and behaviors about this type of food.

Action research was popular in the social sciences during the 1940s and 1950s. Its use declined subsequently in the United States because most academic researchers, and the public as well, came to consider *research* as meaning primarily experiments carried out in laboratory settings. Australian and British educators brought action research back to the forefront in the 1960s, and they continue to use this approach extensively. Action research has once again become popular in the United States, especially among teachers who carry out studies as part of their teacher education preparation programs.

USING ACTION RESEARCH TO ADDRESS PROBLEMS OF PRACTICE

Table 18.1 summarizes the characteristics of action research compared to those of formal research. The comparisons highlight the relevance of action research as a tool for educators seeking to improve some aspect of their practice. The comparisons also show that action research has a different orientation and is simpler to carry out than formal research in every respect. In research design, action research remains close to teacher's everyday practice and helps them address the problems that concern them in that practice. In terms of researcher characteristics, it matches the skill sets of teachers very well.

Finally, the research characteristics are fairly easy for teachers to build into their daily practice, either on their own or with a colleague.

In general, teachers do not address their problems of practice through action research. Some teachers consider research, even action research, too difficult. However, based on our work with schools, we view action research as a much stronger foundation for addressing problems of practice than the other methods teachers typically use. It does take effort to collect and report research data, but, for two reasons, those data are well worth the effort. First, they allow teachers to see if they are really carrying out their practice in the ways they want to (see the section on Action Science, "Applying Action Science to Action Research," later in

TABLE 18.1 • Characteristics of Action Research Compared to Formal Research

	Action Research	Formal Research
Research Design		
Purpose	Solve a local problem of practice	Produce generalizable knowledge
Focus of study	A problem or goal related to one's own practice	A problem or question of general concern to educational researchers
Topic selection	Limited review of research literature, emphasizing secondary sources	Extensive review of research literature, emphasizing primary sources
Researcher Characteristics		
Researcher affiliation	One or more school-based educators, perhaps in collaboration with university faculty	Researchers in a university or research institute setting
Researcher qualifications	Practical experience with the problem; basic knowledge/experience in research	Substantial knowledge of the research literature and training in research methods
Research Characteristics		
Sample selection	Convenience sample of one's own clients/students	Random or representative sample from a defined population
Research method	Easily implemented procedures, emergent design, short time frame	Rigorous research design and controls, long time frame
Measures	Simple or available measures	Selection of measures based on evidence of validity and reliability
Data collection and analysis	Emphasis on descriptive statistics and practical significance of the results	Emphasis on in-depth qualitative coding and interpretation or on tests of statistical significance
Research report	Informal sharing with colleagues or publication through an online network	Published report or formal presentation at a conference
Application of results	Make changes to one's practice if the findings justify them	Add to the formal knowledge base of education

this chapter). Second, they are powerful tools for enabling teachers to improve the teaching-learning process.

EXAMPLES OF ACTION RESEARCH STUDIES

Action research studies are done by practitioners in various professional disciplines, including education. Educators might conduct studies for personal reasons or to fulfill their degree or licensure requirements. They might test a theory of their own or draw on other theoretical perspectives. Critical research, which advocates democratic changes in education (see Chapter 14), is one such theoretical perspective (Carr & Kemmis, 1988). The following sections present several examples of action research studies done by teachers.

Bullying in Middle School

Drosopoulos, J. D., Heald, A. Z., & McCue, M. J. (2008). *Minimizing bullying behavior of middle school students through behavioral intervention and instruction.* Chicago, IL: St. Xavier University. Retrieved from ERIC database. (ED500895), http://files.eric.ed.gov/fulltext/ED500895.pdf

Three teachers conducted this study as a master's degree requirement. They initiated the study by administering questionnaires to students and parents about the incidence of bullying in their experience. Among other findings, they learned that half of the students reported having been bullied at least once.

The teachers experimented with various interventions to reduce the incidence of bullying, including some that directly involved students as research participants. For example, the students created and posted anti-bullying posters in bullying "hot spots" in school, and they wrote and performed an anti-bullying rap song in class.

The teachers observed students at various locations in the school to determine the incidence of bullying before and after these interventions. They found that various types of bullying decreased overall by 31 percent, and name-calling decreased the most.

Teachers presented their own perceptions of the change. For example, one teacher stated:

> Once they were taught the definition of bullying, the many different kinds of bullying, and how it

can cause life long mental scars, most [students] were ashamed of the actions they had taken against other people at some point in the past. . . . [N]ow that I know the impact this intervention program has had on students, I will implement it every semester for the rest of my teaching career. (Drosopoulos et al., 2008, p. 70)

The teacher researchers submitted their paper to the Educational Resources Information Center (ERIC), and the full text is available on its website at files.eric.ed.gov/.

Developing Gateways for All High School Students to Excel

Murray, L. (2012). Gateways, not gatekeepers. *Educational Leadership, 69*(7), 60–64.

Linda Murray, a former superintendent of schools for a large urban school district, worked with the Education Trust-West to carry out an educational opportunity audit in nine California districts. The audit sought to uncover barriers to college readiness and develop a blueprint for action. Students, teachers, and parents participated in focus groups to clarify disconnects between students' aspirations for higher education and the courses they took in high school.

The blueprint for action included providing greater assistance to the many students who failed Algebra I and, even after repeated classes, never took further math classes. Districts created double blocks for students who needed more time to master the content and developed support classes that students could enter and then exit as soon as they mastered content standards. Sign language was added to meet the second-year world-language requirement. More time in school was provided through a seventh period, weekend classes, and tutorials built into a more academically oriented summer school.

In some districts, the number of units needed for graduation was raised, and all seniors needed to take capstone math and career and technical classes leading to a certificate. As a result of this action research project, in 1998, only 30 percent of seniors in Murray's district's high schools graduated with coursework and grades that qualified them for college; however, by 2008, that number had risen to 50 percent, with graduation rates among the highest in the United States for urban schools. The gap between the academic performance index for white and Latino students closed by 30 percent and by 41 percent for elementary students. Thus, the school audit and blueprint for action helped these districts raise their expectations for all seniors. Murray notes: "the reality is that whether students go to a four-year college or to other postsecondary training, they do, indeed, need the same rigorous academic preparation in high school" (p. 64).

The Effectiveness of Reciprocal Teaching

Holt, C. (2008). *Does reciprocal teaching increase student achievement in 5th grade social studies?* Action Research Network. Retrieved from http://actionresearch.altec.org

Crystal Holt, a teacher-researcher, conducted an action research study in her classroom of students who were struggling with social studies because of poor reading skills. She decided to try a teaching technique called *reciprocal teaching*, which had been found to be effective in formal research studies. With this technique, the teacher and students take turns in leading conversations about the meaning of text passages. The leader makes efforts to summarize the text, ask questions about it, clarify its statements, and predict what will come next.

Holt conducted an experiment with her 22 students in which half the students read textbook material, listened to the teacher talk about it, and took whole-group notes. The other half read the same textbook material but engaged in reciprocal teaching. She consulted with three other teachers in designing the reciprocal teaching intervention.

Holt found that the reciprocal teaching group made much greater gains from a pretest to a post-test on social studies than did the conventional instruction group. Moreover, she achieved an insight into her professional practice:

> Before doing this research, I had a lot of problems with students talking out and making inappropriate comments during instructional time. Now that I have implemented the reciprocal teaching technique into my daily routine I have noticed that the inappropriate talking has ceased while higher-order thinking and comments are coming more and more into play. I truly believe that the students behave better when given an outlet to talk.

These comments illustrate an important feature of action research. Although one can read about the benefits of a technique like reciprocal teaching in professional publications, action research makes these benefits tangible by enabling researchers to see changes occurring in their own workplace.

DESIGN FEATURES OF ACTION RESEARCH

Our explanation of how to design an action research project draws on the six-step model of action research developed by Jeffrey Glanz (1998). To his steps, we added a final step, namely, reporting the findings of action research. Action researchers do not always perform the steps in the order presented here. For example, some action researchers begin by taking a new action before collecting any data (Schmuck, 2006). Similarly, while reflection follows action taking in Glanz's model, reflection is appropriate at various points throughout a project.

Some models of action research describe a definite beginning and end. This description is generally accurate when action research is carried out as part of a degree or course requirement. However, when educators incorporate action research into their everyday work, it is more likely to become an ongoing cycle of activity.

We describe the typical steps in an action research project by referring to a study conducted by Wallace Shilkus (2001). This research addresses industrial arts education, an aspect of school curriculum that has become increasingly rare. However, in our view, this research study has continuing relevance because it demonstrates inventive actions and research strategies that teachers can use in any performance-based discipline, such as music, art, sports, robotics, and computer programming.

Step One: Selection of a Focus for the Study

Wallace Shilkus, an industrial arts middle school teacher, had recently returned as a student to graduate education after 17 years of teaching. Shilkus was "curious about the ways in which the industrial arts were relevant to middle school students" (2001, p. 143). He had several goals for his action research project, which he undertook as part of his coursework toward a master's degree. Specifically, he wanted to explore teaching methods to activate students' multiple intelligences and explore different ways to reach all students, including those who are hard to motivate.

Undertaking his research at a time when industrial arts was being cut from many schools' curriculum offerings, Shilkus also wanted to demonstrate the contribution of industrial arts to students' intellectual development, especially in middle school. He wanted to help others become aware of the importance of the "endangered subject" (p. 144) of industrial arts.

In his action research study, Shilkus used both what he called cross-tutoring and peer-tutoring to guide students' design and construction of CO_2-powered race cars. He arranged to have his seventh- and eighth-grade industrial arts "veteran" students first tutor fourth-grade "rookies" at his school and then tutor the adults in his own graduate education class.

Step Two: Data Collection

Shilkus's middle school students, their fourth-grade "rookie" partners, and his graduate school classmates all engaged in providing data for the action research project and sharing their discoveries to learn and help others learn.

He had observed in his transportation technology classes that a wide range of student abilities was needed to produce a successful CO_2-powered race car. He found Howard Gardner's theory of multiple intelligences (Gardner, 1983) helpful in defining the skills that students would need to learn to succeed in this class. Shilkus reports: "Student journal keeping assisted me . . . in identifying students' strengths and weaknesses" (2001, p. 145). This process was important because he wished to ensure pairings of students who would be compatible with each other. Also, Shilkus continually observed activities in his classroom and administered pre- and postsurveys to all three groups of research participants.

After analyzing each set of data, Shilkus added other data-collection strategies. He asked his adult classmates to make journal entries describing the classroom atmosphere. Also, he made a videotape of a two-hour lab in which the middle school students tutored the adults in the design and construction of their race cars, as well as a subsequent videotape of an elimination car race for all participants.

Step Three: Analysis and Interpretation of the Data

Shilkus wrote descriptions of students' design, construction, and tutoring activities in class, with specific examples:

> In many cases, I saw a marked improvement in class participation and behavior. Students were forming a tutoring system in the classroom too, not just with their tutees. I observed many students who asked for additional work; they wanted and enjoyed helping someone else. I was witnessing a form of community being born. (2001, p. 146)

At the elimination car race, "some members of my middle school class commented that the fourth-grade sketches were better than the adult sketches" (p. 148). A post-activity questionnaire revealed that participants liked making the cars more than designing them.

Adults reported insights that they gained from being in the role of student in an unfamiliar context. For example, the comment of a home economics teacher in Shilkus's graduate education class confirmed for him the importance of teachers being able to put themselves in their students' shoes when they design instruction: "I know now some of the frustrations my kids must feel in my sewing class. . . . As much as I like to think I can see things through a student's eyes, it's refreshing to be proved wrong on this point!" (2001, pp. 148–149). This teacher's comment illustrates how action research can clarify the discrepancy that often exists between a teacher's espoused theory, or beliefs, and theory-in-action, or what the teacher actually does in practice, which we discuss below in relation to action science.

Shilkus concluded from his research project that basing his teaching activities on the multiple intelligences framework helped him reach more of the hard-to-motivate students, promoted students' socialization skills, and appealed to their varied learning styles.

Step Four: Taking Action

Action research typically involves making changes in one's behavior and observing the consequences. As described, Wallace Shilkus engaged in a variety of actions: using both cross-tutoring and peer-tutoring, having veteran students tutor a fourth-grade class of "rookies," and having the veterans tutor the adults in his own graduate education class. Shilkus coached his veteran students in their role as tutors and helped the "rookies" and the adults take the role of industrial arts students, a role with which most of them were unfamiliar.

Step Five: Reflection

Reflection is a process by which educators step back from the fast-paced and problem-filled world of practice in order to ponder and possibly share with others ideas about the meaning, value, and impact of their practice. This type of reflection can lead educators to make new commitments, discover new topics to explore through action research, and achieve new insights into the strengths and weaknesses of their current practice. As an aspect of action science (described below), reflection also will help the action researcher discover possible discrepancies between what they believe they are doing in practice (their espoused theory) and what they are actually doing (their theory-in-action).

Shilkus does not specifically mention his use of reflection in his report, but he gives many examples of how his thought processes changed during and after the action research project. For example:

> I've noticed changes in myself and my students as a result of this project. Presenting information in different manners has made it possible to reach more students, not just the students who excel in traditional classes. . . . I can only hope my students learn as much as I did during this project. (2001, p. 149)

David Hobson (2001) views journaling as a critical tool for generating a "written record of practice" (p. 19). Figure 18.1 provides our summary of his suggestions for keeping an action research journal as a basis for reflection. In our view, if an action researcher thoroughly generates the information resulting from this form of journaling, the journal will approach a form of narrative research (see Chapter 15).

FIGURE 18.1 • Suggestions for Keeping an Action Research Journal

1. Use 8½" × 11" pages and put them in a three-ring binder so that pages can be removed, added, or rearranged. For ease of carrying, you might prefer a 6" × 9" binder, blank lesson plan book, Post-It note pad, or spiral-bound notebook.

2. Date and time each entry to facilitate viewing developmental processes over time. Start each entry on a new page so that the pages can be grouped to reflect recurring patterns or reconstruct sequences.

3. Make time for journaling by picking a regular time, free of interruption or by writing during class while your students are engaged in individual activity.

4. Use descriptive writing to record directly observed or experienced details for later review.

5. Use reflective writing to comment, associate, and make meaning.

6. Use double-entry journal writing with a description or activities in one column and reflection in the other column.

7. Keep a daily log to help reveal priorities and to note what absorbs your attention and what continuing issues predominate.

8. Name each important teacher you have known and describe each one. Look for commonalities; describe the stepping-stones in your experience of teaching and reflect on your development over time.

9. Examine the materials you have been reading that are related to your research, and bring the results of your investigations into your journal.

10. Develop a "journal of the journals," going back through your entire journal to seek themes and highlight passages, and have a friend read aloud to you the lines you have highlighted.

11. Ask your students to turn in "exit slips" at the end of each class reflecting on their learning, questions, and expectations.

Source: Based on Hobson, D. (2001). Action and reflection: Narrative and journaling in teacher research. In G. Burnaford, J. Fischer, & D. Hobson (Eds.), *Teachers doing research: The power of action through inquiry* (2nd ed., pp. 7–27). Mahwah, NJ: Lawrence Erlbaum.

Step Six: Continuation or Modification of Practices

The results of Shilkus's post-activity survey showed that his research participants preferred making the race car to designing it. Therefore, he decided that he needed to make the designing of the race car "even more interesting for my students" (2001, p. 148). His observations of the quality of his students' suggestions for the race car design and competition led him to add a critique unit to all of his car-racing classes. From the students' critiques, he learned that they appreciated seeing a finished product before they began their own car design and construction. Therefore, he changed his teaching unit to allow students to examine the cars being designed by others as they progress. This activity provides feedback and motivation to all of the students, both those designing the cars and those observing the design process.

Step Seven: Preparing a Report of the Findings

Wallace Shilkus's action research report is one of a number of detailed examples in *Teachers Doing Research* (Burnaford, Fischer, & Hobson, 2001). It is thus a polished, published example of action research, and it illustrates the value of being an action researcher while engaged in a professional development program. Through his program, Shilkus was able to interact with, learn from, and include as research participants his graduate student colleagues. He also received guidance from the course instructors who edited the book in which Shilkus's research report is published.

Reports of action research projects can be read, reported, or disseminated in other forms besides standard research reports in journals and books. Marilyn Cochran-Smith and Kelly Donnell (2006) observe that action research has led to "new ways to store, retrieve, code, and disseminate practitioners' inquiries in the form of CD-ROMs, Web sites, and other electronic innovations as well as new modes of public presentation and publication, such as multi-voiced conversations, readers theater, poetry, and so on" (p. 512). Free online education journals focusing on school-based action research include *Networks*, an online journal for teacher research.

Overall, we have found that many reports of action research are more like case stories (see

Chapter 13) than true action research reports, because the researcher makes only global statements about the results of new actions on students (e.g., "the students did much better when I used inquiry teaching than when I lectured"). They would make a far better case for evaluating the quality of their research by providing detailed descriptions of their changed actions, sample responses from student interviews or surveys, or numerical data useful for comparing student outcomes before and after the action research.

HOW ACTION RESEARCH DIFFERS FROM EDUCATORS' OTHER APPROACHES TO PROBLEM SOLVING

Table 18.1 describes how action research differs from formal research. Here, we consider briefly how action research differs from educators' typical approaches to solving problems of practice. Typically, teachers talk to colleagues, attend workshops, pick up ideas from professional magazines, or rely on their own hunches as a guide to trying something new in their practice.

The question must be asked: Do the ideas derived from these approaches actually affect student learning? Mixed evidence from the National Assessment of Educational Progress and the No Child Left Behind Act as to the overall quality of student learning in the United States suggests that such approaches, despite their popularity, are not highly effective. Action research possesses two important features beyond those of most other approaches to solving problems of practice—systematicity and intentionality.

Marilyn Cochran-Smith and Kelly Donnell (2006) used the concepts of systematicity and intentionality to clarify the unique characteristics of practitioner research, which is a form of action research. They describe systematicity, or **systematic practitioner research**, as "ordered ways of gathering and recording information, documenting experiences inside and outside of the contexts of practice, and making some kind of written record . . . [and] ordered ways of recollecting, rethinking, and analyzing events for which there are only partially written records" (p. 510).

Intentionality, in turn, "refers to the planned and deliberate rather than spontaneous nature of practitioner inquiry" (Cochran-Smith & Donnell, 2006, p. 510). Many teachers frequently examine assignments, test results, and other forms of student data routinely generated in schools. Action research encourages teachers to generate additional data to look at what specific new actions they take and what results they observe in students from those new actions. They thus can gather new data to highlight the specific relationships between their teaching choices and student learning.

In some reports of action research, the authors limit their description of findings to vague positive statements such as "students responded positively" or "did better" after a new action was undertaken. To have a stronger impact on their own and others' practice, authors of action research should explain specifically the actions they took, their research findings, and the procedures of data collection, analysis, and interpretation upon which they based these findings.

PURPOSES AND BENEFITS OF ACTION RESEARCH

Action research is sometimes regarded as having three main purposes—personal, professional, and political. As actual research studies cited in this chapter show, most educators carry out action research for reasons that blend these purposes. Below, we briefly summarize some of the benefits of action research, referring back to Wallace Shilkus's study (2001) to illustrate each one.

1. *Contributing to the theory and knowledge base that educators need to enhance their practice.* Educators who carry out action research learn to reconstruct educational theory and findings in terms that are understandable to them. Based on this understanding, they can develop more effective practices in their work settings. Shilkus's use of cross-tutoring and peer-tutoring illustrates his application of concepts from the theory of multiple intelligences to his teaching repertoire.

Educators who have the opportunity to try out new teaching strategies can in turn contribute to the teaching profession and to the educational research literature. For example, Madeline Hunter (1994) was the director of the laboratory school at the University of California at Los Angeles

when she began informally experimenting with ways to improve teachers' classroom instruction. Her individual creativity resulted in the development of a method of instruction called ITIP (Instructional Theory into Practice), which has had a major impact on teaching practice and has stimulated many formal research studies of its effectiveness compared to traditional teaching practice.

2. *Supporting the professional development of educators.* Shilkus's report shows how his action research increased his competence in applying research findings, carrying out research himself, guiding others in doing research, and reporting the results. Thus, he not only developed needed skills in doing research, but he also improved his ability to read, interpret, and apply the research of others. Furthermore, the education course that he completed while doing his research contributed to his completion of a master's degree.

3. *Building a collegial networking system.* **Collaborative action research** is carried out by two or more educators who are either involved in the same type of practice (e.g., elementary school teaching) or represent more than one type of practice (e.g., K–12 teachers and university teacher educators). The collaboration might also include participation of the clients whom the research activities are intended to impact in the conduct of the research itself.

For example, Wallace Shilkus's research collaborators included his own middle school students, the fourth-grade student "rookies" and their teacher, and his graduate education classmates. They were involved not only as research participants but also in the design and conduct of the research itself. Shilkus thus built a rich communication network, reducing the isolation often experienced by individual teachers and providing opportunities for future collaborative work.

4. *Helping identify problems and seek solutions in a systematic fashion.* Shilkus's action research required that he and his students and teaching colleagues define problems of practice clearly, identify and try out possible solutions systematically, and reflect on and share the results of their efforts. Thus, systematic action research enables educators to break out of the rut of institutionalized, taken-for-granted routines. It generates hope and motivation to solve seemingly intractable problems in the workplace.

5. *Having potential benefit for all levels and all areas of education practice.* Shilkus's study not only cut across two levels of schooling (fourth-graders and his middle school students), but it also included both his middle school and the university where he and his classmates were studying. Action research can be carried out in specific classrooms or departments, throughout an educational institution, or at the regional, national, or international level.

APPLYING ACTION SCIENCE TO ACTION RESEARCH

Action science, based on a theory developed by Chris Argyris and Donald Schön (1974), can help action researchers design their action research to produce effective change in their practice. **Action science** is an approach for helping educators discover and reconcile differences between their **espoused theory**, that is, their *beliefs* about how they deal with specific problems of practice, and their **theory-in-action**, that is, their actual *behavior* as they engage in their work.

For example, suppose that Sophie, a ninth-grade history teacher, believes that she fosters higher-order thinking when questioning her students. If, in fact, she actually asks mostly knowledge and comprehension questions, she is not addressing the higher cognitive levels that are specified in various models of thinking (e.g., Bloom, 1956; Wiggins & McTighe, 1998).

Action research can demonstrate this discrepancy and the problems it causes. Suppose that Sophie undertook action research to improve her questioning strategies. She would collect data on both her specific actions and students' responses to them. For example, she could videotape herself as she carries out a lesson for subsequent self-analysis—a method known as *microteaching* that was once widely used in teacher education (MacLeod, 1995). She could fill out an observation scale to assess the extent to which she carried out the actions that she intended to carry out. She also could ask colleagues or teacher educators from a university to observe and give her feedback.

Sophie could look specifically for instances that reveal differences between her espoused theory and her theory-in-action. Then she could take new actions to bring her behavior closer to her beliefs about what she wants to accomplish.

An example of research based on action science is the doctoral dissertation study of Paulette Kerr (2010). She investigated understandings and beliefs about information literacy and learning in 11 academic libraries and their parent universities. These libraries were recognized by the academic library community for exemplary instruction resources. Kerr identified the libraries' espoused theories by examining the libraries' policy documents. She identified theories-in-use by analyzing information literacy practices in the libraries' online tutorials and by interviewing information literacy educators at the libraries.

Kerr's analysis revealed several discrepancies in the libraries' espoused theories and theories-in-action. In particular, she found that the goals for information literacy were seldom realized in the actual information literacy practices of the libraries. The findings of this action science study can greatly benefit academic librarians by identifying problems of practice that can be addressed by follow-up action research studies.

THE INSIDER/OUTSIDER PERSPECTIVE IN COLLABORATIVE ACTION RESEARCH

Whether the promise of action research is realized depends to a great extent on the participants in action research projects. Some educators who engage in action research (typically, K–12 teachers) view themselves as **insiders**, that is, individuals with an internal perspective on the problems of practice being studied. Such individuals might view as **outsiders** individuals who are university professors or researchers from a research organization who have an external perspective on K–12 teachers' problems of practice. Stephen Kemmis and Robin McTaggart (2000) argue that reliance on the interpretations of outsiders might disempower teachers and might imply that "outsider" research is more valid than "insider" teacher research.

In a subsequent publication, Robin McTaggart (2002) addressed the insider/outsider issue from a different perspective. He argued that scholars such as university professors can add value to K–12 educators' practice through participatory action research endeavors. McTaggart argued that educational practice includes not only K–12 teaching but also all of the major functions of various educational systems or institutions, including curriculum development, administration, teacher education, and the conduct and publication of educational research. Because all educators engage in some aspect of practice, they can more successfully impact other aspects of practice through collaborative efforts. In other words, McTaggart argued that the new practices undertaken through action research must affect all levels of education—from the classroom to the university and beyond.

McTaggart identified three ways in which scholars like university professors, who are considered outsiders in relation to K–12 teaching, can contribute through action research to solving K–12 teachers' problems of practice. First, outsiders can help ensure that insiders adequately test the credibility of evidence in support of particular action research findings and interpretations, through engaging in "an ongoing sociopolitical process . . . in situ with participants" (2002, p. 9) that involves systematic data collection and analysis. Second, outsiders can support insiders and research participants in expressing feelings that might help or hinder their subsequent actions and determine how to take such feelings into account in the interests of social change. Third, outsiders can support the development of personal political agency among research participants and help build critical mass for a commitment to change.

McTaggart notes that outsiders' typical privileged institutional settings might deskill them for such collaborative roles with insiders. However, he asserts that outsiders, if they can "insinuate themselves into political life" (p. 14), will be able to become equal players with insiders in a truly participatory action research process.

EVALUATING THE CREDIBILITY AND TRUSTWORTHINESS OF ACTION RESEARCH PROJECTS

Action researchers need to consider ways to design and carry out their research so that the resulting actions and the reports about them are credible and trustworthy, both to the researchers and to others. Some action research projects rely primarily on quantitative research designs. You can evaluate these projects using the criteria shown in Appendix 3 and the design-specific criteria for descriptive research (Chapter 9), group comparison research (Chapter 10), correlational research (Chapter 11), and experimental research (Chapter 12).

Other action research projects rely primarily on qualitative research designs. You can evaluate these projects using the criteria shown in Appendix 4. The suggested strategies for evaluating case studies (Chapter 13) are also relevant. In addition, you can apply five validity criteria developed by Gary Anderson and Kathryn Herr (1999) for evaluating action research studies: (1) outcome, (2) process, (3) democratic, (4) catalytic, and (5) dialogic validity. We describe each of these validity criteria below, citing research studies and referring to specific strategies used in those studies to increase the various types of validity.

As you read about these criteria, keep in mind that you may learn of action research projects that are not presented in a complete, formal report. In such cases, you might interview the action researcher—and perhaps his colleagues and clients, too—in order to learn more about the project. That process should give you the necessary information to evaluate it.

Outcome Validity

Outcome validity concerns the extent to which actions occur that lead to a resolution of the problem that prompted the action research study. Rigorous action research, of course, seeks not only to solve a specific problem. It also aims to help researchers reframe the problem in a more complex way, which often leads to a new set of questions or problems to be addressed. Thus, this criterion also stresses the importance of reflection and the continuing introduction of new actions to address ongoing or emerging problems.

Lila Kossyvaki, Glenys Jones, and Karen Goldberg (2012) studied the effects of the interactive style used by staff members on young autistic children's spontaneous communication at school. In collaboration with the researchers, the staff developed an Adult Interactive Style Intervention (AISI) intended to promote the children's spontaneous communication. Two months later, each child was recorded for two hours across the same activities with staff using the AISI. All six children showed a statistically significant increase in their total initiations of communication with adult staff members. This increase is evidence of outcome validity for the intervention that the staff developed.

Process Validity

Process validity concerns the adequacy of the processes used in different phases of an action research project. Framing and solving problems in a way that promotes the researchers' ongoing learning is one aspect of process validity. Triangulation (the inclusion of multiple perspectives or data sources) also contributes to process validity. If the action research project is reported through narratives such as poems, folktales, or anecdotes, readers need to know whether these narratives depict accurately what occurred, instead of being purely subjective accounts or interesting exaggerations.

Martha Stevens (2001) carried out action research while teaching mainstreamed sixth-graders with learning disabilities. She used a continual process of exploration of students' learning, and corresponding change of her actions, to improve the learning environment. For example, she modified the curriculum to encourage greater self-management by students. Based on her review of research on teaching reading to students with learning disabilities, she also scaffolded information in the regular education texts for her students by recording it on audiotape and rewriting the assignments at a simpler reading level.

The fact that Stevens' explorations were ongoing and involved a literature review is evidence of a good process for developing interventions. Thus, we can conclude that this action research project had good process validity. It also had good outcome validity, as evidenced by six years of data reflecting good student progress in both reading and writing skills, including improvements in test scores and grades both in her classes and in mainstreamed settings.

Democratic Validity

Democratic validity refers to the extent to which an action research project is done in collaboration with all the parties who have a stake in the problem being investigated. It also involves determination of whether the multiple perspectives and material interests of all stakeholder groups have been taken into account. Multiple perspectives in this context are considered not as a basis for triangulation of data sources, but as an issue of ethics and social justice.

Wallace Shilkus's (2001) action research, described earlier, is an example of including multiple perspectives in the process of making industrial arts instruction an active learning endeavor for all participants. He included as data sources, and actually as co-researchers, not just his middle school students, but also fourth-grade "rookie" students and his graduate education classmates.

Catalytic Validity

Catalytic validity involves the extent to which an action research project reorients, focuses, and energizes participants so that they become open to a transformed view of reality in relation to their practice. Action researchers can strengthen this aspect of validity by keeping a research journal to record their reflections and changing perceptions.

This criterion also addresses the extent to which action research realizes an emancipatory potential. In other words, catalytic validity addresses an action research project's success in fostering the widespread engagement of educators and education stakeholders in an active quest for ending oppression and promoting social justice. (See Chapter 14 for a discussion of critical research, which typically has those objectives.)

For example, Eimear Enright and Mary O'Sullivan (2012) generated a participatory action research project with 41 female co-researchers and activists whose ages ranged from 15 to 19, within and beyond the walls of a secondary school. Their intentions were to engage with students to challenge the typical curriculum boundaries of physical education and also to connect with students' natural physical culture. They also examined the benefits and challenges of engaging in this sort of practical activism.

Enright and O'Sullivan found that their boundary-crossing approach to physical education helped students to find their own meanings in physical education and physical activity instead of viewing it primarily as a school requirement. Their report acknowledges that this type of boundary-crossing practice involves "a time- and thought-intensive pedagogical design, which will be challenging for many physical education teachers" (p. 255).

Dialogic Validity

Dialogic validity refers to the use of extensive dialogue with peers in the formation and review of the action researcher's findings and interpretations. It can be met by doing action research collaboratively. It also is enhanced by the researcher engaging in critical and reflective dialogue with other researchers or with a "critical friend" who serves as a sort of devil's advocate for alternative explanations of research data. Efforts to ensure the "goodness-of-fit" of the action research problem and findings with the intuitions of the practitioner community also improve dialogic validity.

Stevens' (2001) action research project, described above under process validity, involved an impressive amount of dialogue between her and her mainstreamed sixth-grade students, their parents, and other teachers. The other teachers' positive responses to her program outcomes and materials also reflect "goodness-of-fit" with the teaching community in her middle school.

An example of
How Action Research Can Help in Solving Problems of Practice

Students and others often question the value of homework, as illustrated in these excerpts from this newspaper article:

> For years, students, parents, teachers and Ph.D.s have debated the value of homework in general, yielding mixed but impassioned opinions. When it comes to giving homework over Thanksgiving and other school breaks, opinions are equally mixed—and passionate.
>
> Some teachers, such as English teacher [BN], don't give anything beyond extra credit or makeup work.
>
> Others, such as [SC], a second-grade teacher . . ., say they assign homework over breaks for students' own good.
>
> Schencker, L. (2008, November 26). School's out, but homework's not. *The Salt Lake Tribune.* Retrieved from http://www.sltrib.com/education/ci_11082337

The article also mentions parents, students, and professors who are either for or against assigning homework to be completed during holiday breaks from school. They express a surprising range of opinions about this issue. This controversy can stimulate an action research project, as we illustrate.

Suppose you are a teacher with the choice to assign or not assign homework over a holiday break. You know that students are expected to be prepared for school tests and for state competency examinations. On the pro side, you believe that homework helps them review and extend their learning beyond what you cover in class. On the con side, you feel that you and your students need a true break during holiday periods.

To help you decide on a strategy, you could first review some research on homework as to the pros and cons of assigning homework at all, and specifically assigning homework during school breaks. You also could talk to other teachers in your school and get their opinions. In the process, suppose that you discover another teacher at your grade level (Joan) who also wonders about the value of homework. You could do collaborative action research with Joan in one of her classes and one of your classes. Your goal would be to determine whether assigning homework over school breaks is a good idea and, if so, what type of homework is most appropriate.

You and Joan could design a questionnaire asking students to rate their attitudes about homework in general and homework over holiday breaks. It could also ask students to rate different types of homework as to how positively or negatively they would feel about having each type during a holiday break.

To help you find out more about individual students' attitudes, you could also include space for student comments on the questionnaire. If you ask students to sign their questionnaires, you could look for differences between the responses of higher-achieving and lower-achieving students.

When the next holiday break comes, you could give no homework while Joan tries out an approach to homework that students rated favorably. You could then have students in your class rate how positively they felt about getting no homework while the other class rates the approach Joan used. You also could give an examination on the curriculum material covered before the holiday break and compare the performance of the students who got homework during the break with the performance of students who were not assigned homework.

The findings from this action research project might help you and Joan develop a homework policy that fosters student learning. You and Joan could share the results with other teachers and with your students, which might reduce their resistance to homework that you assign in the future.

SELF-CHECK TEST

1. Action research has all the following purposes except
   a. supporting the professional development of education professionals.
   b. building theory and generalizable knowledge.
   c. building a collegial networking system among educators.
   d. helping practitioners identify problems and seek solutions systematically.

2. The quality of an action research project is *least* dependent on its
   a. use of well-designed methods of data collection and analysis.
   b. promotion of collaboration between the researcher and his or her colleagues.
   c. contribution to the knowledge base for education.
   d. impact on the researcher's practice.

3. Reflection by action researchers
   a. is particularly important at the start of an action research project.
   b. occurs primarily during data analysis and interpretation.
   c. involves pondering the meaning, value, and impact of one's actions.
   d. requires dialogue with the research participants.

4. The problem to be addressed by an action research project typically is identified by
   a. educators' consideration of issues limiting their achievement of work goals.
   b. reviews of the education literature.
   c. a systematic needs assessment.
   d. consultation with outsiders.

5. Action researchers who publish their studies in the research literature are primarily motivated by the desire to
   a. present generalizable findings to the widest possible audience.
   b. encourage other educators to undertake action research on problems of practice.
   c. demonstrate the rigor that action research can involve.
   d. enhance their status in their local educational context.

6. For an action research project to be considered a success, it is important that the researchers
   a. receive extensive preparation to develop their research knowledge and skills.
   b. thoroughly review the education literature before designing the action to be taken.
   c. discuss the theoretical implications of their results.
   d. apply the findings to their own practice.

7. According to Robin McTaggart, scholars can best contribute to collaborative action research with K–12 educators by
   a. promoting adherence to positivist principles of objectivity.
   b. providing structure for the research design.
   c. contributing to a critical mass for a commitment to change.
   d. all of the above.

8. Considering the multiple perspectives and interests of all stakeholders in an action research project is a strategy that directly increases its _____ validity.
   a. democratic
   b. catalytic

c. dialogic
d. process

9. Involving all stakeholders in the interpretation of the findings of an action research project is a strategy that directly increases its _____ validity.
    a. democratic
    b. catalytic
    c. dialogic
    d. process

10. Action science can best inform action research by
    a. identifying and resolving discrepancies between participants' espoused theories and theories-in-action.
    b. determining the appropriate participants for collaborative action research.
    c. enabling insiders to free themselves from disempowerment due to working with outsiders.
    d. increasing the political impact of research findings.

CHAPTER REFERENCES

Anderson, G. L., & Herr, K. (1999). The new paradigm wars: Is there room for rigorous practitioner knowledge in schools and universities? *Educational Researcher, 28*(5), 12–21, 40.

Argyris, C., & Schön, D. A. (1974). *Theory in practice: Increasing professional effectiveness.* San Francisco, CA: Jossey-Bass.

Bloom, B. S. (Ed.). (1956). *Taxonomy of educational objectives: Classification of educational goals. Handbook 1: Cognitive domain.* New York, NY: Longman.

Burnaford, G., Fischer, J., & Hobson, D. (Eds.) (2001). *Teachers doing research: The power of action through inquiry* (2nd ed.). Mahwah, NJ: Lawrence Erlbaum.

Carr, W., & Kemmis, S. (1988). *Becoming critical: Educational knowledge and action research.* London, UK: Falmer.

Cochran-Smith, M., & Donnell, K. (2006). Practitioner inquiry: Blurring the boundaries of research and practice. In J. L. Green, G. Camilli, & P. B. Elmore (Eds.), *Handbook of complementary methods in education research* (pp. 503–518). Washington, DC: American Educational Research Association.

Cochran-Smith, M., & Lytle, S. L. (1999). The teacher research movement: A decade later. *Educational Researcher, 28*(7), 15–25.

Enright, E., & O'Sullivan, M. (2012). Physical education "in all sorts of corners": Student activists transgressing formal physical education curricular boundaries. *Research Quarterly for Exercise and Sport, 83*(2), 255–267.

Gardner, H. (1983). *Frames of mind: The theory of multiple intelligences.* New York, NY: Basic Books.

Glanz, J. (1998). *Action research: An educational leader's guide to school improvement.* Norwood, MA: Christopher-Gordon.

Hobson, D. (2001). Action and reflection: Narrative and journaling in teacher research. In G. Burnaford, J. Fischer, & D. Hobson (Eds.), *Teachers doing research* (2nd ed., pp. 7–27). Mahwah, NJ: Lawrence Erlbaum.

Holt, C. (2008). *Does reciprocal teaching increase student achievement in 5th grade social studies?* Action Research Network. Retrieved from http://actionresearch.altec.org

Hunter, M. (1994). *Enhancing teaching.* New York, NY: Macmillan.

Kemmis, S., & McTaggart, R. (2000). Participatory action research. In N. K. Denzin & Y. S. Lincoln (Eds.), *Handbook of qualitative research* (2nd ed., pp. 567–605). Thousand Oaks, CA: Sage.

Kerr, P. (2010). *Conceptions and practice of information literacy in academic libraries: Espoused theories and theories in use* (Doctoral dissertation). Retrieved from ProQuest. (3418770)

Kossyvaki, L., Jones, G., & Guldberg, K. (2012). The effect of adult interactive style on the spontaneous communication of young children with autism at school. *British Journal of Special Education, 39*(4), 173–184.

Lewin, K. (1946). Action research and minority problems. *Journal of Social Issues, 2*(4), 34–46.

MacLeod, G. (1995). Microteaching in teacher education. In L. W. Anderson (Ed.), *International encyclopedia of teaching and teacher education* (2nd ed., pp. 573–577). Tarrytown, NY: Elsevier Science.

McTaggart, R. (2002). Action research scholar: The role of the scholar in action research. In M. P. Wolfe & C. R. Pryor (Eds.), *The mission of the scholar: Research and practice* (pp. 1–16). New York, NY: Peter Lang.

Reason, P., & Bradbury, H. (Eds.). (2001). *Handbook of action research: Participative inquiry and practice.* Thousand Oaks, CA: Sage.

Schmuck, R. A. (2006). *Practical action research for change* (2nd ed.). Thousand Oaks, CA: Corwin.

Shilkus, W. (2001). Racing to research: Inquiry in middle school industrial arts. In G. Burnaford, J. Fischer, & D. Hobson (Eds.), *Teachers doing research* (2nd ed., pp. 143–149). Mahwah, NJ: Lawrence Erlbaum.

Stevens, M. C. (2001). Laptops: Language arts for students with learning disabilities: An action research curriculum development project. In G. Burnaford, J. Fischer,

& D. Hobson (Eds.), *Teachers doing research* (2nd ed., pp. 157–170). Mahwah, NJ: Lawrence Erlbaum.

Wiggins, G., & McTighe, J. (1998). *Understanding by design*. Alexandria, VA: Association for Supervision and Curriculum Development.

Zeichner, K. M., & Noffke, S. E. (2001). Practitioner research. In V. Richardson (Ed.), *Handbook of research on teaching* (4th ed., pp. 298–330). Washington, DC: American Educational Research Association.

RESOURCES FOR FURTHER STUDY

Alber, S. M. (2011). *A toolkit for action research*. Lanham, MD: Rowman & Littlefield.

This book is about the collection and analysis of action research data. The author provides numerous fill-in-the-blank frames, forms, templates, and graphic organizers to guide action researchers in defining problems of practice and developing researchable questions.

Durrant, J., & Holden, G. (2006). *Teachers leading change: Doing research for school improvement*. Thousand Oaks, CA: Paul Chapman.

The authors provide practical guidance for integrating inquiry with practice, showing how to encourage collaboration and critical dialogue within and between schools. They describe how to do research focused on student, teacher, and organizational learning.

Herr, K. G., & Anderson, G. L. (2005). The action research dissertation: A guide for students and faculty. Thousand Oaks, CA: Sage.

The author provides an accessible roadmap that honors the complexity of action research and helps make action research by doctoral students a rewarding experience for both the researcher and the participants. The book addresses unique dilemmas faced by action researchers, including validity, positionality, design, write-up, ethics, and defense of the dissertation.

Klein, S. R. (Ed.). (2012). *Action research methods: Plain and simple*. New York, NY: Palgrave Macmillan.

The contributors to this book summarize methods to help readers understand and interpret action research data. They provide a balanced overview of quantitative and qualitative methodologies and methods for conducting action research within a variety of educational environments and community-based settings.

Stringer, E. T., Christensen, L. M., & Baldwin, S. C. (2010). *Integrating teaching, learning, and action research: Enhancing instruction in the K–12 classroom*. Thousand Oaks, CA: Sage.

The authors show how teachers can use action research as a natural part of the teaching-learning process. They focus on incorporating action research projects into classroom lessons in order to create a dynamic learning community.

Recognizing a "Different Drum" Through Close-Reading Strategies

Lassonde, C. A. (2009). Recognizing a "different drum" through close-reading strategies. *Networks: An On-line Journal for Teacher Research, 11*(1). Retrieved from http://journals.library.wisc.edu/index.php/networks/article/view/188

The following journal article reports a qualitative action research study that was published online. The author is a professor of education who collaborated with an eleventh-grade English teacher to improve his students' reading comprehension. They experimented with close-reading strategies, which involve generating internal dialogue with the authors of assigned readings. Students' drawings of their visualization of the theme of hearing a different drummer, based on a piece by Henry David Thoreau, show their expanding capacity to comprehend and personalize literature based on their own life experiences.

Recognizing a "Different Drum" Through Close-Reading Strategies

CYNTHIA A. LASSONDE
SUNY College at Oneonta

Every day 7,000 high-school students drop out of school (Alliance for Excellent Education, 2005). Students reading at basic levels are more prone to drop out than those reading at higher levels. According to the latest results on the National Assessment of Educational Progress 2005 Mathematics and Reading Trial Urban District Assessment, commonly called the "Nation's Report Card," the percentage of students reading below the basic level is high. Bob Wise, President of the Alliance for Excellent Education, has stated that

> For the most part, we stop teaching our children how to read when they leave third grade, and expect that they'll continue to expand vocabulary and comprehension skills on their own. While this may work for some students, others, especially those from low-income families, never make the necessary transition from *learning to read* to *reading to learn*. (Alliance for Excellent Education, 2005, p. 3, italics in original)

This statement indicates students are unable to comprehend the vocabulary or content of the material in their textbooks enough to succeed with academic tasks. To increase graduation rates, we must focus on ways to improve the reading skills that students need to deal with increasingly complex high school courses. In light of this, increasing students' reading comprehension should be one of the nation's primary education priorities.

Based on my concern over this critical issue of students' reading comprehension abilities, I decided to explore the development of comprehension skills through close-reading strategies by spending time in a high-school classroom in a small, rural school district in upstate New York. As a college professor from a nearby teacher-education institution, I contacted and worked with an eleventh-grade English teacher to develop a unit on individualism with the goal of fostering the growth and development of the students' abilities to generate a meaningful and insightful dialogue with the writer through close-reading strategies. More specifically, from September through November, I collaborated with a teacher who we will call Dan to take an up-close look at how a group of 17 students enrolled in a heterogeneously grouped section of English 11 developed critical thinking and reading comprehension skills across multiple genres within the context of a unit on individualism. The focus question was:

> How do students use close-reading strategies to develop comprehension and critical thinking around texts?

Defining Terms and Looking at Related Research

Key concepts to unpack in this study are *critical thinking* and *close reading*. Spears (2003) writes that critical thinking requires the reader to keep an open mind and suspend judgment until alternative points of view are considered. It involves developing a healthy skepticism about texts. Critical thinking has been referred to as the "new basics" in that it encourages readers to apply readings to the real world (Morrow, 2003). In this study, close reading is viewed as a group of strategies readers use to foster critical thinking as a response to texts. Close reading refers to the reader's use of various strategies to interpret text meaning. As one of the students succinctly described it in an exit survey, close reading involves delving "further than the words into a particular piece . . . to study the meaning and the message of the work."

Close-reading strategies were modeled and taught in this English 11 classroom. Such reading places emphasis on not only understanding vocabulary but on becoming sensitive to the nuances and connotations of particular passages, language use, syntax, and the unfolding of meaning in a text. Close readers pay attention to features such as the way sentences are constructed, the imagery that is used, semantics, cultural implications, structural importance, any emerging themes, and the view of the world the author offers. They consider small linguistic items such as figures of speech as well as larger issues of literary understanding such as tone and style. Following are two helpful websites that explain close reading and specific strategies further:

- **http://mason.gmu.edu/~rmatz/close_reading. htm** This website from George Mason University offers tips for close reading. It includes prompts and strategies such as paraphrasing and considering puns, metaphors, and puns.
- **http://uwp.duke.edu/wstudio/resources/genres/ close_reading.pdf** This Duke University site describes four steps for close reading: prereading/previewing/ mark-up, interpreting, critical reading/viewing, and writing.

Current research indicates the key features of effective middle- and high-school literacy instruction include that teachers consciously weave connections to students' lives as they teach strategies for how to make meaning of texts (Langer, 2000). Alvermann (2001) supports Langer's work by adding that effective instruction at this level develops readers' ability to talk and write about their comprehension of multiple genres. It encourages them to study and discuss the strategies they will use to respond to texts every day as life-long readers and writers. Students who are guided to practice and reflect upon the necessary skills needed to be close readers learn to apply these skills across texts and genres not only to perform well on high-stakes achievement tests but also to develop their literate lives.

Close readers interact with text as they participate in a silent dialogue with the writer to analyze, interpret, question, and perhaps challenge the writer's words. Based on transactional reader response theory (Rosenblatt, 1978), the reader's role is to draw upon past experiences and present understandings to organize personal responses to text. Following this theory, readers "evoke poems" as they develop a relationship with the text rather than accept the teacher's predetermined connections with the text. Reading instruction should go beyond the study of discrete skills and strategies. It should provide opportunities for readers to understand how skills and strategies

are integrated with life experiences (Langer, 2002). It is beneficial for adolescents' academic literacy to address issues of engagement.

Also relevant to this study is that one of the teacher's responsibilities and priorities was to prepare these students for the New York State English Regent's Examination. Integrating instruction, as the teacher has done through the unit on individualism that is the underlying thread of this study, allows teachers to shift the focus of test preparation from practice on the surface features of the test to meta-analysis of the knowledge and use of the strategies needed for students to be successful readers and writers of all texts (Langer, 2002). Integration provides opportunities for students to respond to texts in authentic, meaningful, and personal ways.

This research is a result of teacher research, described by Lassonde, Ritchie, and Fox (2008) as a method by which researchers "hold themselves accountable for their practices and students' learning as they take a close look at themselves as well as their philosophies and beliefs related to education" (p. 4). In this study, Cynthia and Dan asked intentional questions about teaching and learning, organized and collected information, focused on a specific inquiry, and engaged in reflection and discussion around their reflections, with the common goal of facilitating teaching and learning and maximizing student potential. It is appropriate that teacher research provided the frame through which this study was conducted. By providing this insider or "emic" perspective, the researchers were able to mix theory and practice (praxis). Teaching and researching within the classroom context allowed the researchers to examine the synthesis of the multiple layers of the processes of teaching and learning that resulted within this context. This examination provided opportunities to view and analyze the rich contextual factors that were relevant to this study, so the researchers could make active and informed decisions about their work.

The Unit on Individualism

To encourage students to use close-reading strategies to respond to texts, the classroom teacher and I developed a unit on individualism to use with eleventh-graders. The unit focuses on six different literary works representing a variety of genres, authors, and degrees of difficulty and complexity. The works also develop a common theme of the individual and individualism, a premise that is relevant to the adolescent who is struggling with self-identity and realization. Literary pieces were chosen to help students focus on how authors and their characters have dealt with this notion of individuality and what it means to be you. A list of the six pieces follows:

"Life," a poem by Nan Terrell Reed
"Initiation," a short story by Sylvia Plath
"The Sculptor's Funeral," prose from *The Troll Garden* (1905) by Willa Cather

Herman Melville's "Bartleby," a radio dramatization by Erik Bauersfeld

"anyone lived in a pretty how town," a poem by e.e. cummings

"Self-Reliance," an essay by Ralph Waldo Emerson

The pieces used in this unit were selected and sequenced to scaffold this group of eleventh-grade readers through the process of learning to read critically using close-reading strategies. Taken into consideration were the vocabulary and language used; diction; the complexity of the plot or theme; the use of metaphors and other literary devices (i.e., imagery, symbolism, and repetition); the organization; the relevancy to students' lives and experiences, and interests; and the structure and length of the pieces. The selections were intentionally chosen to connect with issues we perceived as relevant to this age group, population, and geographic region based on our combined extended personal and professional experiences. We felt students would be able, with assistance at first, to make connections that would lead them to insightful analysis and comprehension of several identity-related complex issues they were facing as male and female adolescents. We hoped the selections and ensuing discussions would help them clarify and develop informed positions and values. We sought to encourage them to develop an internal dialogue with texts and to feel confident and competent to voice this dialogue with peers.

Close-Reading Strategies that Were Taught and Modeled

Next, the strategies taught to the students to help them read these pieces more closely and critically were selected and sequenced so they could build upon each other to scaffold students' ability. With "Life," the students were guided to re-read for multiple purposes: first for enjoyment; second, for meaning and to predict the theme; third, to analyze the language, literary elements, diction, and content; fourth, for mood and tone; and finally, again, for enjoyment that comes from a better understanding than was possible with the first read. This process of re-reading was stressed and practiced with each succeeding piece. However, as the texts got more difficult, students were guided to "chunk" and re-read sections rather than rereading the whole piece with each step. For example, in "Bartleby," students re-read each act of the dramatization to monitor comprehension before moving on to the next act. With "Self-Reliance," they were instructed to chunk and reread based on their judgment and their self-monitoring of their comprehension.

Another strategy that was taught and scaffolded through students' application of the strategy to progressively more difficult texts as they were provided less guidance and were expected to work towards independent close reading was relating what they read to

personal and prior life and text experiences. Initially, they were encouraged to talk about connections they made to the content, particular phrases or passages, vocabulary, and so forth in a very broad aspect. These first small-group discussions paralleled brain-storming sessions in that all possibilities were considered and accepted. However, as they worked their way through the texts, they were taught to continually question whether the connections they were making were leading them toward logical and reasonable meanings. In other words, was it all making sense or had they somehow made an illogical connection that was leading them astray?

An additional strategy highlighted in this unit on individualism was honing students' written reflection and expression of their under-standing of each literary work. Writing was taught as a close-reading tool to support critical thinking. While reading "Life," the teacher modeled writing responses (i.e., interpretations, reactions, feelings, insights, constructed meanings, questions, observations, and reflections) to the poem in the margin while reading. Beginning with "Initiation," students were expected to respond through the use of a double-entry journal. The left side of the journal page noted concrete "happenings" from the text, while the right column of the page recorded the readers' responses. This strategy was modeled with the whole class the first day, and then its use was supported through "The Sculptor's Funeral." An additional strategy taught to the students was how to use a character web. With this, students analyzed a particular character by noting a) what the character said and did, b) what others said or felt about the character, c) how the character looks and feels, and d) how the reader feels about the character. These varied uses of writing as a tool to clarify understanding led to the expectation that students would combine their interpretations from the right side of the journal and from their character webs into a formal essay reflecting their interpretation and close reading of the text. Each of the strategies was first modeled, then guided, and finally students applied the strategies independently.

Other strategies students were taught to add to their toolbox of close-reading skills were using highlighters to note phrases or passages students felt were meaningful to them and would help them make personal and comprehensive meanings, using context clues to decipher meanings of vocabulary and passages they did not understand, and pulling out and examining the meanings and purposes behind particular literary devices (i.e., tone, theme).

Connections to the Standards and State Tests

This unit was designed to meet the principles of the *New York State English Language Arts Learning Standards* (available at the New York State Education Department's website at http://www.nysed.gov), which identify literary response and expression and critical analysis and evaluation as two of the four primary strands for reading, writing, listening, and speaking. These are skills that are also evaluated on the Comprehensive Examination in English in the literature-based tasks during the second session (Day 2) of the examination. In the first of the two tasks, students are provided with two literary passages that they are to read, respond to reading comprehension questions, and then write an essay developing a theme common to both selections. For the second task, students are to interpret a critical lens and apply that lens, that interpretation, to two works of literature from their own reading. These are complex tasks demanding students engage in not only literary response and expression but also critical responses and evaluation.

Methodology

The Participants

This qualitative study took place in a small, rural school district in upstate New York. The school's campus houses students in grades kindergarten through twelfth grade with approximately 100 students per grade level. Dan, a pseudonym used here for the teacher, has taught at the high school level in this district for over twenty years. He is the chairperson of the district's English Department and has taught introductory English at the local community college as an adjunct faculty member. Dan is a reflective practitioner who routinely examines his own practice by talking with colleagues and students. As the department chair, he is a teacher leader who values open communication among teachers and learners. Although he stated that he knows it is valuable to keep a teaching journal, he admits that he does not do so regularly. Because of limited time, Dan did not regularly keep a running journal account of his reflections on his teaching practices outside of this study. Dan was eager for this opportunity to participate in this collaboration. He saw our work as a way to examine and potentially improve his practice and, as a result, students' learning. Students' needs shape his pedagogy. He wants his students to develop as life-long readers and learners. He also feels responsible for helping his students with their success on the New York State Regent's Examination without reducing literacy instruction to the teaching of test-taking strategies.

My background is in literacy. I have taught at the college level for six years. My research interests include teacher research and self-study, and methods for working with striving readers and writers. I hold permanent certification to teach special education and reading in grades kindergarten through 12 and to teach as a classroom teacher from preschool through grade 6. Before teaching at the college level, I was an elementary teacher for over twenty years. Twelve of those years I taught Language Arts at the elementary level in the same school district as Dan. My relationship with Dan prior to this

collaborative effort was congenial. We had developed a mutual respect for each other's professional work and had opportunities to come together and share our ideas at various English Department meetings.

I approached Dan with interest in observing in his classroom based on his reputation in the district as a talented, knowledgeable, and well-respected teacher. For 10 weeks, from September through November, I visited Dan's classroom, sometimes as a detached observer and other times as a participant or facilitator of small-group discussions. We also regularly met outside of the classroom to reflect upon and discuss the curriculum and student responses. While we viewed our work together as collaboration, Dan stated he did not have the time to contribute to documenting the results of our work together. Therefore, while this paper represents our collaboration in the planning of the unit and during the data collection stage of the research process, Dan was not available to participate in the final data analysis, interpretation, and efforts at disseminating these findings. His availability, voice, and contributions were critical to this study.

The students in this grade 11 English class were varied in their physical appearance, preferences and interests, connections to each other and others, motivation to participate and succeed, dispositions and temperament, modes of thinking and learning, and literacy skills. Students also reported a wide range of variability in their personal uses of literacy. While several self-reported they were avid readers outside of the classroom, others stated they rarely picked up a book or other type of reading material outside of the classroom unless it was required reading. All stated that they had access to computers at home or school outside of class time and emailed or surfed the web at least two times per week for personal enjoyment. These variables influenced how and why students chose to adopt particular stances towards reading and the learning and practice of using close reading strategies, as well as how they progressed over time. While they were all of junior standing, several were supported by an in-class special education consultant teacher while others were enrolled in honors or Regent's sections in other content courses.

Data Collection and Analysis

Data sources consisted of classroom observations, teacher and researcher journal entries, videotaped visits to the classroom, informal interviews with several students and the push-in consultant special education teacher, collaboration between the teacher and the researcher, students' written assignments and journal entries, and pre- and post-survey responses. Dan shared regular journal reflections with me over the period. These reflections included self-study of his practices, of students' responses, and of our work together. Data was analyzed and discussed weekly and more fully at the end of the study.

Students were informed of the study and were given opportunities to ask questions. Signed consent forms were obtained from students and their families. Students were asked to complete a survey at the beginning of the study to determine their self-perceptions as readers. Also, they completed an exit questionnaire related to close-reading strategies. During the weeks of the study, several students were informally interviewed to clarify statements they had made during class and their developing understandings of critical thinking and the close-reading strategies they were practicing. The classroom consultant special education teacher also provided her insight as she responded to the researcher's questions during and after the observations.

Students' writing assignments were photocopied, analyzed, and coded for themes using Miles and Huberman's (1994) qualitative method of pattern coding and developing reflective remarks. Also, four readings were done using Gilligan's (1982) method of multiple readings. This method allowed the teacher and researcher to listen for variant voices, complex perspectives, and subtle meanings in the data. Following are the questions asked during each reading:

Reading #1 What strategies are the students using? How are they being used? What is the tone of the students' participation? (strategies and metacognition)

Reading #2 How are the students connecting to the unit's theme? (critical thinking and connection to their identities and lives)

Reading #3 What are the prominent recurring phrases, patterns, and themes?

Reading #4 What inquiries are emerging from the re-readings? What feelings and insights are the teacher and researcher developing as the data is read?

Results

Students used close-reading strategies to develop comprehension and critical thinking around texts in various ways, to different degrees, and for dual purposes (academic and personal). The title of this paper refers to recognizing a "different drummer." Representing diverse reading abilities, levels of interest, and degrees of motivation, as most classes do, these students collectively began to voice new identities for themselves as students and adolescents. This new self each unfolded is what I have come to call the different drummer within each student. In the process of learning and practicing specific strategies, the students began to think critically about the theme of individualization as they pulled ideas from the literature that paralleled their personal lives. Some did this more easily and more willingly than others, however.

How did this happen? Two dominant factors were noted in the multiple readings of the data. First, entwined with their perspectives of what it meant to be a reader and a "knower" capable of not just understanding but interpreting text had a great deal to do with their willingness to take on the role of questioning the author. Their confidence in their ability and being given "permission" to question the author seemed to influence their willingness to use the strategies, to connect to the text, and to take a critical look at their interpretations of the author's writing. Secondly, students' ability to comprehend the vocabulary used by the author as it led them to create a visual image of the piece as a whole affected their ability to engage in the author's work to the degree that they could effectively take a critical look. So what does this mean? The following section looks at each of these factors and how they were represented in the data and are supported by research.

To Be or Not To Be Skeptical: Permission to Question

As previously stated, to take a critical stance the reader must reserve judgment and carry a healthy skepticism that questions the text and the authority of the writer (Spears, 2003). During weeks one and two, there appeared a prevailing atmosphere of skepticism in the class, all right. But the skepticism that existed wasn't that to which Spears referred; it was students' doubt that they could transactionalize personal meanings from the text rather than find the "right" answer. Even though Dan and I explicitly encouraged them to make personal connections, they stubbornly continued to search for "the" meaning as if a text only had one meaning: that which the author (or perhaps their teacher) intended. By comparing survey data with students' writing from weeks 1 through 10, I noted those who made more progress in questioning the author were those who identified themselves as readers and said they read for pleasure outside of school. Further study would be needed to determine why that connection seemed to exist. Perhaps students who read for pleasure outside of school have a more personal connection to what it means to read and to be a reader. Data indicates these self-proclaimed readers did tend to take more risks in interpreting passages in class and in their written assignments for the readings. For example, following is an excerpt from an extensive and detailed analysis of "Life" that a self-proclaimed reader wrote:

> It started out optimistic, but ended on a longing note. The destruction of the dress metaphor into a rag is tied into the journal entry. There's a light tone. Vague but clear. Artsy, but poems are inherently artsy. Vocabulary is subtle until the end where she is absolute. She gets stronger as she goes on. You get a sense she's bitter. Flowing and beautiful turns into hardness. It deteriorates until she's bitter. Overall, I thought it was a beautiful study of life from a different aspect of

viewing it. It has to make you wonder what happened in this author's life to make her write this poem.

This student not only questioned the author's purpose for writing the poem but also the tone and vocabulary usage.

In contrast, students who identified themselves as nonreaders wrote more literal entries. Rather than sharing their overall impressions, many listed what individual lines or phrases meant. The meanings they shared were ones that were discussed previously in class. Little, if any, of their own voices were inserted into their journal and written assignments; and there was no evidence of questioning the author. For instance, one student wrote:

> The poem starts off with "They told me," giving an insight that other people's views were looked upon in this poem. "Somebody tangled the thread" shows people toil with your life and it can sometimes become hard. . . .

The entry continues on like this, listing phrases and interpreting them with comments heard from class discussions: a very this-is-what-the-poem-said, this-is-what-it-means approach. However, another self-proclaimed nonreader stated about "Life":

> Why didn't she just say that? Why do they have to make it so hard for you to figure out what they're saying? I don't get it!!!!!!!!

For this student, the craft of writing was a mystery. He expresses his frustration in his writing. He could not fathom why writing wasn't didactic and clear. He saw no purpose in spending time deciphering underlying meanings in texts or in writing in ways that would confuse people. To him, reading and writing, and perhaps being literate, meant conveying a message in ways others could clearly comprehend. While this student was questioning the author, his questions take the form of negating the author's craft rather than her message. He refers to "they," which implies his frustration with authors of all texts he struggles comprehending.

Over time, some students did make progress with risk taking and questioning the authors. We attribute that to our persistent encouragement during class discussions, Dan's feedback and acceptance of students' perceptions of text meaning in written assignments (see example below in Dan's feedback to KM), and the modeling of several self-proclaimed readers in the class who took the lead in questioning the text and negotiating personal interpretations of passages and texts during class discussions. Also, insightful journal entries were shared with the whole class as models of the possibilities for interpreting the texts. We did see less listing of ideas and repetition of plot summary in their writing through weeks 3 through 10. Students began to take more risks

in expressing overall themes, tone, and connections to their lives and their identities. Following is a student's response to "Initiation" along with Dan's feedback. Note how Dan's feedback encourages the student to think more critically about her connections to the poem.

KM: Popularity to me is a "social status" that friends and peers "rate" you upon. What makes you "popular" is a large amount of "popular" or well known friends, the latest material objects, also considered in popularity is physical appearance. The better you look, the more of a chance you have at being popular. . . . So I say get to know people before you judge them.

Dan's feedback: Can someone be popular AND be a good, decent person? Is it necessarily a bad thing to be popular? Were the people in "Initiation" bad people?

KM: Well, they weren't murderers but like my mother says they were good people doing bad things. I don't think popularity is always a bad thing. I think everyone has the potential to be a good, decent person. I just think popularity in high school is considered to be like power and that can either be used for good or abused and used as an excuse to ridicule "lesser" people and have it be ok.

Dan's feedback: If "popular" people ridicule or look down on others, I can't imagine why they'd be considered popular. (KM did not respond to this but went on to the next assignment.)

Furthermore, in our analysis of the pre- and post-surveys, students expressed an increase in their confidence in themselves as readers who could interpret difficult texts. They wrote these comments:

> We learned a lot of different ways to use to figure out what the author is trying to say. . . .I liked using the markers the best to highlight things I thought were important. I learned that you don't just highlight everything but you have to pick out really important things.
>
> When there are a lot of hard words, don't give up. You can do things like re-read and ask yourself what's going on.
>
> It used to be hard to understand some of the things we had to read in this class. Now I kind of get it.
>
> I already used a lot of the "tricks" we learned but I didn't really know what I was doing. Now when I don't understand something, like in the science book, I can say hey, I'll just reread it or use some kind of web or chart to help me visualize it.

A second dominant factor emerged from the evidence. That is, students' ability to comprehend the vocabulary used by the author as it led them to create a visual image of the piece as a whole affected their ability to engage in the author's work to the degree that they could effectively take a critical look. I refer to this as the vocabulary factor.

What's a "Scrivener" Anyway?: The Vocabulary Factor

Note that many of the texts chosen were written decades prior to the birth of these eleventh-graders. For example, written in 1905, "The Sculptor's Funeral" takes the reader to a time when train travel was common and characters "reckoned" and "conjectured." Vocabulary and dialect were challenging for most of the students. During a conversation with one student, she told me she relied heavily on using context clues to help her figure out what was going on. In her words, she

> could figure out what was going on even without knowing what every single word means. You kinda get an idea by what's happening in the story and what the characters are saying. . . . It helps a lot when people are talking cause they use words you can understand.

She didn't take the time to look up unfamiliar words because there were "just too many of them." While she thought using a dictionary probably would help her understand things better, she stated that she understood "enough." She thought she understood the piece enough to feel she had the gist of the story and could complete the assignment satisfactorily.

Interestingly the use of context clues wasn't always reliable. I believe because the contexts were related to situations that were antiquated, such as the job of a scrivener (one who copied manuscripts or public records), students struggled with making connections to contexts and texts with which they were familiar and could readily relate to. One student told me while reading "Bartleby" he had a picture in his head of a "scrivener as an office worker standing over a Xerox machine copying page after page." This visualization of the definition provided by the teacher lead to an interpretation of Bartleby as working in a much more modern, fast-paced type of business as might be found on Wall Street today. For him, he had no patience for the novella because he said no employer would stand for a worker preferring not to work. For him, the story lost all credibility; therefore, he wasn't interested in figuring out what meaning it carried. He was not engaged nor interested in developing any dialogue with the author.

On the other hand, Dan kept emphasizing to the students that the rich descriptions of these selected texts could be used to help them visualize the context and the characters. He proposed that visualization was a comprehension strategy that would allow them to pause, reflect, and respond in meaningful ways. When I asked a student what she thought her teacher meant by this, she said, "You can't make a picture or movie in your head if you don't understand what's going on. . . . It means, ya get the picture?"

In mid-October, Dan was thinking out loud about students and visualization as we prepared for class one morning. He said

> Students complain about too much description, but it's that description that allows them to see. They want immediate gratification like TV and computers. Technology that's image laden. Texts offer opportunities to make their own images, but they cannot make visions themselves. Will any of them be a Bill Gates when they can't visualize a story?

I thought, in particular, that his last question was insightful. I began to think of visualization was more than a method for improving comprehension; it represented the psychological ability to imagine and perceive an experience.

Evidence indicates that when students were able to negotiate the vocabulary within a text and use their prior knowledge in ways that did not interfere with close reading, they began to visualize the overall meaning of the text. However, the consultant special education teacher stated that sometimes she noted that students in the class were misinterpreting texts as a result of misapplying their prior knowledge. In particular, when students drew literal meanings from texts, the meaning they took from the text hindered their ability to negotiate metaphors and plots. For example, she remembered a student interpreting the phrase "he's as full as a tick" quite literally. Because he created the image of a blood-filled tick in his mind, he was seemingly unable to go beyond that vision to imagine other possibilities. Yet, this literal meaning did not make sense in the text. Therefore, we must teach students to self-monitor their connections to their prior knowledge about a word or context.

The Different Drummer

In the beginning of this article, I describe how students unfolded new selves as a result of this unit on individualism. To wrap up the unit, students read Henry David Thoreau. They were asked to draw their image of what it meant to them to hear a different drummer. Some of the images are provided here. It was clear in the ensuing class sharing of their images and discussion of the unit that students were able to peer into their lives and who they were as adolescents and readers as a result of their connections to the readings in this unit. Some comments made as students shared their drawings follow.

CB: If I choose not to drink beer with my friends, I'm making a choice. . . . I'm saying I don't have to follow everything you're doing. When you choose not to do something, like Bartleby, you're really making a choice anyway. (CB's drawing was Figure 1.)

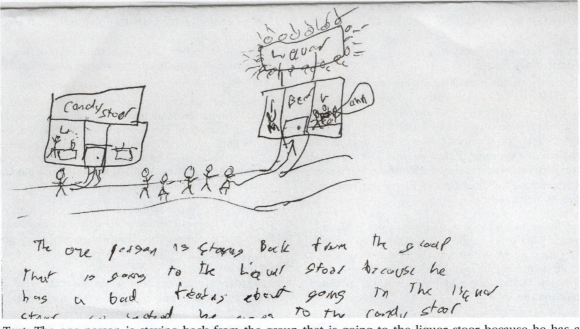

Text: The one person is staying back from the group that is going to the liquor stoor because he has a bad feeling about going in the liquor stoor so instead he goes to the candy stoor.

Figure 1 CB's Drawing

LG: Everybody's so worried all the time about what they look like and what they wear. I think like people who are Hip Hop or Goth and dress all the same as each other and stuff are trying to be different but end up just part of a group anyway . . . and, like they're not being different or themselves anyway. . . . but when people are totally far out there . . . ya know . . . totally different . . . it's like nobody will talk to them . . . they're like weird . . . thought of as weird . . . so people shut them out. . . . yeah, that's like the poem we read about the small town. (LG's drawing was Figure 2.)

Figure 2 LG's Drawing

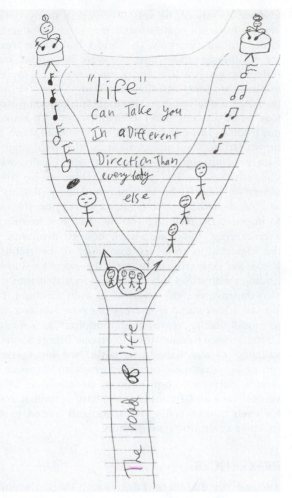

Figure 3 TB's Drawing

TB: You shouldn't be worried about following other people 'cause your life might take you down a different path. And that's all right. The Y in the picture kinda asks why you're taking the left or the right in the path. You can still go with your friends, but you have to ask why am I following them. See, I got that underlying message in my picture like the people who wrote this stuff. Ya get it? (TB's drawing was Figure 3.)

Conclusions

The students in this English 11 class were beginning to feel comfortable and competent in creating a dialogue around complex texts with the author, the teacher, and their peers. They voiced personal connections to texts by applying their interpretation of what those texts meant to situations they have or might find themselves in. LG applies the different drum metaphor to peers in the school

who dress Hip Hop or Goth. CB relates it to the peer pressure he might feel if asked to go into a liquor store. These drawings and comments are evidence the students were beginning to transactualize personal meanings from text through visualization and discussion. They were developing a healthy skepticism and means to look closely at author intent, context, and their role in deciphering text meaning.

Requiring students to draw their visualization of this reading was an afterthought in our development of the unit. Initially, the unit did not include this piece. After reflecting on students' responses and discourse about previous readings during our data collection, however, Dan and I decided to add this assignment to gain insight into the students' thinking processes. We wondered what would happen if we asked them to illustrate the internal dialogue they were having and then share that dialogue with their peers. We agreed that this component helped us gain insight into their internal dialogue. We think this might be an important next question upon which to focus a study as more data than what we have would be necessary to form solid conclusions about visualization strategies.

Implications for Education and Research

High-stakes testing has the potential to narrow literacy curriculum (NCTE, 2004). Instruction that focuses on preparing students to take required examinations tends to reflect a one-right-answer or main idea model of reading that contradicts current findings in research that substantiate more engaging approaches to literacy instruction. Dan avoided this test model of teaching reading even though he describes one of his priorities for this course is to prepare students to do well on the New York State English Regents examination. It seems, however, that students highly anticipated that the right answer was what Dan was expecting. It took a great deal of encouragement and practice to get them to feel comfortable in taking risks in making their own meanings and trusting their own interpretations through close readings. By week 10 of this study, students were finding out they did have something to offer. The meanings they were taking from texts were supported by the texts and by their prior knowledge, and they were meaningful to them. We saw students' faces spark and light up when their insights were shared, discussed, and affirmed by their peers and teachers. High-stakes tests must include opportunities for students' to practice and demonstrate their abilities to read critically with margin to transactualize meanings.

Furthermore, it is important as teachers to introduce students to new contexts and ideas. Part of our job is to expand their world. However, we have to keep in mind that to fully understand new ideas, students must be able to connect them to something they have in their prior knowledge, or, as Dan tells his students, to "hang our hats on something." We must encourage students to discuss and retrieve what they already know about the topic or something they can connect to the topic. Then, we must teach them to self-monitor whether their prior understanding is relevant in the particular text they are reading, being careful not to let a misapplication of prior knowledge hinder their negotiation of the text. For students to be able to transactualize text and create the "poem" that Rosenblatt (1978) talks about, text has to have personal meaning to them. As teachers, then, it is up to us to explicitly teach them strategies, such as those described in this article, to encourage them to make those connections and read closely.

Finally, this study adds to our understanding of collaboration and co-research. University-school partnerships commonly bring together college and K-12 faculty to ponder their teaching and students' resultant learning. This particular collaboration between Dan and I had its successes and its challenges. We did gain insight into the effectiveness of the unit. The evidence led to rich results that Dan has stated he will incorporate into the unit in future semesters and will shape his overall pedagogy. Dan also highly valued the time we spent just talking about the objectives and design of the curriculum. He stated that it helped him to clarify why he taught the way he did and how his teaching philosophy influenced his views on teaching strategies that would not only help students be successful on the State Regent's Examination but also apply to authentic life and workplace literacy demands. I was able to apply the results to my college classroom as well. I now look for the ways students seek meaning in course readings. I listen to their past experiences more intently than previously so I can better understand how they are interpreting text and classroom discourse. I no longer assume they are coming to the same understanding of text that I intend them to or assume they will based on the course and on my objectives. The professional development that occurred through this partnership mutually supported Dan and I to investigate our common questions and improve our teaching as it redefined what we understood about students' needs.

Time and personal objectives for the research became challenges to our collaborative efforts. They became barriers that limited our work together. I was able to donate time each week to meet with Dan and to be part of his class. As a professor at a university that values scholarship through research, my schedule allowed me the time to commit to this project. However, understandably, Dan's schedule as a high-school teacher required he teach the majority of the day. His "free" periods were dedicated to planning, assessing student work, and collaborating with colleagues.

Outside of school, he was involved in many personal and professional commitments that he, understandably, ranked as his priorities. Dan and I had similar reasons for wanting to collaborate. We were both interested in reflecting on practice and connecting it to theory to improve student learning; however, I had the added purpose of analyzing our findings for general purposes that could benefit other educators and disseminating our findings through publication. I attribute Dan's withdrawal from the collaboration in the final stages of data analysis and dissemination, specifically writing this article, to the fact that he had achieved his primary objective. That is, he had informed his pedagogy and as a result had concrete evidence to support the means to improve his teaching and his students' learning. As a researcher and tenure-track college professor with the expectation from my university to be published, I was the one who prioritized the need to share our findings with other educators in hopes that they could also improve the effectiveness of their teaching. I also saw an added value to sharing our research as a means to model teacher research methodology as a means of giving a voice to educators. Everyone brings something valuable to a collaborative table. We must learn to recognize what each member brings and respect each other's purposes, contributions, priorities, goals, and values. Dan and I continue to share a mutual respect for each other's goals and work and intend to work together again in the near future.

REFERENCES

Alliance for Excellent Education. (2005, December). Straight A's: Public education policy and progress, (5)23. Washington, DC.

Alvermann, D. E. (2001). Effective literacy instruction for adolescents. Executive Summary and Paper Commissioned by the National Reading Conference. Chicago, IL: National Reading Conference.

Gilligan, C. (1982). In a different voice: Psychological theory and women's development. Cambridge, MA: Harvard University Press.

Langer, J. (2002). Effective literacy instruction: Building successful reading and writing programs. Urbana, Illinois: National Council of Teachers of English.

Langer, J., Close, E., Angelis, J., & Preller, P. (2000). Guidelines for teaching middle and high school students to read and write well: Six features of effective instruction. Albany, NY: National Research Center on English Learning and Achievement.

Lassonde, C. A., Ritchie, G. V., & Fox, R. K. (2008). How teacher research can become your way of being. In C. A. Lassonde & S. E. Israel. (Eds.). Teachers Taking Action: A Comprehensive Guide to Teacher Research. Newark: DE: International Reading Association.

Miles, M. B., & Huberman, A. M. (1994). Qualitative data analysis: An expanded sourcebook. 2nd ed. Thousand Oaks, CA: Sage Publications.

Morrow, L. M., Gambrell, L. B., & Pressley, M. (Eds.). (2003). Best practices in literacy instruction, 2nd ed. New York: The Guilford Press.

NCTE's Commission on Reading. (2004, May). A call to action: What we know about adolescent literacy and ways to support teachers in meeting students' needs. Available online: http://www.ncte.org/about/over/positions/category/literacy/118622.htm

Rosenblatt, L. M. (1978). The reader, the text, the poem: The transactional theory of the literary work. Carbondale, IL: Southern Illinois University Press.

Spears, D. (2003). Developing critical reading skills, 6th ed. Boston, MA: McGraw Hill.

CHAPTER NINETEEN

Evaluation Research

PROBLEMS OF PRACTICE *in this chapter*

- Why have decades of program initiatives in STEM (science, technology, engineering, mathematics) produced little evidence that these programs are effective?
- What are the unmet needs of parents of children with an autism spectrum disorder?
- Should evaluation research be used to influence the direction of school reform initiatives?
- Should the evaluation of schools and teachers be focused primarily on how well students perform on achievement tests?
- Is the CIPP (Context-Input-Process-Product) model of evaluation worth the time and cost that it requires?
- What stakeholders need to be consulted when designing and adopting a new educational initiative?
- Should the R & D model be followed when developing any new educational programs or products?
- What can be done to overcome the negative reactions of teachers and administrators to state-led interventions for underperforming schools?
- Should schools buy tablet computers for all of their students and use electronic textbooks for all subjects?
- Is value-added teacher evaluation a sound method for determining whether a teacher is effective in the classroom?

IMPORTANT *Ideas*

1. Program evaluation is difficult because programs seldom are uniformly effective, and different stakeholders define effectiveness differently.
2. Programs typically include curriculum materials, instructional methods, assessment procedures, and a professional development component. In addition, each program functions within a distinct culture.
3. Evaluation research is value-laden and political at every stage of the process.

4. The identification of a program's stakeholders and their concerns is important in most evaluation studies.

5. The model of objectives-based evaluation focuses on how well a program helps students achieve specified learning objectives.

6. The model of needs assessment identifies discrepancies between an existing condition and a desired condition so that educators can decide whether to improve a current program or develop a new one.

7. The CIPP model of program evaluation encompasses the assessment of stakeholders' needs and problems, competing alternatives, work plans and budgets, program activities, and program effectiveness.

8. The model of responsive evaluation involves the use of qualitative methods to identify the issues and concerns of a program's stakeholders. Open, safe dialogue among stakeholders is critical to this evaluation model.

9. Research and development (R & D) is a systematic model for developing programs and products that are evidence-based. Formative and summative evaluation are integral components of this model.

10. Reports of evaluation studies generally follow the format of quantitative research reports, qualitative research reports, or mixed-methods reports.

11. The Joint Committee on Standards for Educational Evaluation, which includes representatives from 12 major educational organizations, has created a set of criteria for judging the quality of educational programs and products.

KEY TERMS

CIPP model
context evaluation
effectiveness evaluation
emergent design
evaluation research
formative evaluation
impact evaluation
input evaluation
Joint Committee on Standards for
    Educational Evaluation

meta-evaluation
National Assessment of
    Educational Progress
needs assessment
objectives-based evaluation
performance objective
process evaluation
product evaluation
program
program culture

program evaluation
research and development
    (R & D)
responsive evaluation
stakeholder
summative evaluation
sustainability evaluation
transportability evaluation
value-added teacher
    evaluation

THE USE OF EVALUATION RESEARCH IN EDUCATIONAL DECISION MAKING

In education, **evaluation research** (also called *program evaluation* or *program evaluation research*) is the process of using quantitative or qualitative methods or both to make judgments about the effectiveness of particular aspects of education. The process of arriving at these judgments is complicated because "effectiveness" is a multifaceted concept, meaning different things to different stakeholders. Also, educational programs and processes seldom are uniformly effective. Typically, they are found

to have benefits and drawbacks, and they might be effective only under certain conditions.

Despite its complexity, evaluation research has become increasingly important in education. Public schooling is essential in a democratic society, but it is also expensive. For this reason, the general public and policy makers want to know whether their money is well spent. In practice, this means that they want to focus funding on programs that work and eliminate those that do not.

The prominence of evaluation's role in governmental funding and decision making is illustrated by an evaluation review conducted by the Academic Competitiveness Council, an organization commissioned by the U.S. Congress. The following is an excerpt from the ERIC abstract of the Council's findings (Academic Competitiveness Council, 2007):

> The Academic Competitiveness Council (ACC) is responsible for reviewing the effectiveness of existing federally funded Science, Technology, Engineering, and Math (STEM) programs, and for improving the state of STEM education in the United States. To this end, it has conducted a review of program evaluations submitted by 115 STEM programs. The ACC's review revealed that, despite decades of significant federal investment in science and math education, there is a general dearth of evidence of effective practices and activities in STEM education, and there is evidence of ineffective duplication of efforts.

If educators take no action in response to this kind of evaluation, there is a risk that funding for science education and other educational programs will gradually diminish. This scenario could unfold if policy makers and other groups came to believe that educational programs in general, not just the ones evaluated by the Academic Competitiveness Council, are ineffective and not capable of improvement by education professionals.

Our illustration involves evaluation at a macro level. Closer to home, consider how evaluation research might affect you as an educator. During your career, you might be asked to learn about a new program and teach in it or administer it. For example, suppose you are teaching in a regular school and are asked to teach in a new charter school instead. Undoubtedly, you will be interested in what is known about the effectiveness of this new school. Who is it intended for? Is there evidence that it achieves the outcomes that are associated with its mission? Is there evidence that it produces better outcomes than traditional schools? What are the risks and drawbacks of this type of school? Would you be comfortable teaching in it?

A review of evaluation studies of this program might help you answer these important questions. If none are available, you and your colleagues will need to learn about the program as you implement it. Perhaps you will conduct action research (see Chapter 18) along the way. If the program is effective, all is well. If not, you might find yourself asking why the program was not researched beforehand to discover its pitfalls.

The purpose of this chapter is to help you learn about the effectiveness of programs not only from your personal experience with them but also from the findings of evaluation research.

EXAMPLES OF EVALUATION RESEARCH

Researchers do evaluation studies on many aspects of the education enterprise. The titles of the following journal articles suggest how wide the range is.

Bethea, S. L. (2012). The impact of Oakland Freedom School's summer youth program on the psychosocial development of African American youth. *Journal of Black Psychology, 38*(4), 442–454.

Leijten, P., Overbeek, G., & Janssens, J. M. A. M. (2012). Effectiveness of a parent training program in (pre)adolescence: Evidence from a randomized controlled trial. *Journal of Adolescence, 35*(4), 833–842.

Niehaus, K., Rudasill, K. M., & Adelson, J. L. (2012). Self-efficacy, intrinsic motivation, and academic outcomes among Latino middle school students participating in an after-school program. *Hispanic Journal of Behavioral Sciences, 34*(1), 118–136.

Stanat, P., Becker, M., Baumert, J., Ludtke, O., & Eckhardt, A. G. (2012). Improving second language skills of immigrant students: A field trial study evaluating the effects of a summer learning program. *Learning and Instruction, 22*(3), 159–170.

Wayman, J. C., Cho, V., Jimerson, J. B., & Spikes, D. D. (2012). District-wide effects on data use in the classroom. *Education Policy Analysis Archives, 20*(25). Retrieved from http://epaa.asu.edu/ojs/article/view/979

Williford, A., Boulton, A., Noland, B., Little, T. D., Karna, A., & Salmivalli, C. (2012). Effects of the KiVa anti-bullying program on adolescents' depression, anxiety, and perception of peers. *Journal of Abnormal Child Psychology, 40*(2), 289–300.

You can find many more examples of evaluation research at the website, What Works Clearinghouse (http://ies.ed.gov/ncee/wwc), described in Chapter 4. The U.S. Department of Education sponsors and funds this agency, reflecting its increasing emphasis on evaluation research to guide policy making and influence the direction of school reform initiatives.

Many evaluation studies, including those cited above, make use of the experimental method. This is because one of the primary questions that guides evaluation research is, "Does this program work?" Experimental research is well-suited for answering this question. However, some evaluation questions call for the use of other research methods. For example, the question, "Is this program needed?," might be best answered by a needs assessment, which is a type of evaluation research method described in this chapter.

PROGRAMS AS A FOCUS OF EVALUATION RESEARCH

A moment's reflection will help you realize that evaluation permeates the entire education enterprise. Teachers evaluate students' academic achievement and behavior. Administrators evaluate teachers. School boards evaluate school districts. School districts evaluate individual schools. Textbook adoption committees evaluate new textbooks.

Our focus in this chapter, however, is on methods for evaluating programs. We define a **program** as a systematic sequence of materials and activities designed to achieve explicitly stated goals and to be used in many different settings. In education, a program typically includes curriculum expressed in text materials and other media, instructional methods, assessment procedures, and perhaps a staff development component to help educators implement it properly. All of these components are packaged so that they can be implemented in many different school sites. For example, elementary textbook series in reading produced by major publishers qualify as programs under this definition, and so do systematic approaches to teacher evaluation.

Saville Kushner and Clem Adelman (2006) claim that programs include more than these components:

> [P]rograms typically exhibit a "program culture." This is to say that they have rules, rituals, roles, a tension between the individual and the collective, a recognizable texture to their social processes, and a broadly agreed boundary that demarcates thoughts and actions that are or are not of this program. . . . People fit into programs, but programs also fit into people's lives. (p. 712)

Based on this statement, we define **program culture** as the rules, rituals, and roles that accompany the technical specifications of a program and also the tensions that come into play when the needs and desires of individuals in the program conflict with these specifications.

Program culture becomes an important consideration when educators are asked to adopt a new program that will replace the one they are already using. These educators are likely to wonder how much work the adoption of the new program will add to their already-busy schedules. They might wonder, too, about the motivations of those promoting the new program, especially if they like the existing program. These concerns can be mitigated to an extent if evaluation evidence attesting to the program's effectiveness is available.

EVALUATION RESEARCH AS A POLITICAL ACTIVITY

All research involves values. For example, the fact that a researcher chooses to study one educational problem rather than another reflects a value judgment that one problem is more important, worthwhile, or interesting, or that it is more likely to attract funding and advance the researcher's careers.

Evaluation research is even more value-laden because researchers' explicit goal is to make value judgments about a program based on their empirical findings. Furthermore, individuals who are affected by the program will make value judgments about whether the evaluation was fair and relevant.

If everyone affected by a program shares the same values, an evaluation study is likely to proceed smoothly. However, this is seldom the case when educational programs are involved. An educational program has many features, and some might appeal to certain individuals and repel others. Therefore, individuals and groups are likely to compete with each other for power to make decisions about the program, such as whether to adopt or reject it, how to evaluate it to highlight its strengths, or, perhaps, how to evaluate it in order to minimize or conceal its weaknesses.

This competition, especially when the stakes are high, makes evaluation research an inherently political activity. The intensity of the politics can increase if the program has prominent cultural features—for example, a program for ethnic-minority groups designed and evaluated by ethnic-majority educators and researchers.

Because program evaluation is inherently political, researchers have found it helpful to identify all relevant stakeholders at the outset of an evaluation study. A **stakeholder** is an individual who is involved in the phenomenon that is being evaluated or who may be affected by the findings of an evaluation. Identifying all of the stakeholders affected by an educational program is not always easy. However, it is essential to be as inclusive as possible. Otherwise, some stakeholders' voices might be left unheard, thereby compromising the integrity of the evaluation study.

MODELS OF EVALUATION RESEARCH

In the course of doing evaluation studies over a period of decades, researchers have reflected on their work and created formal models of how evaluations should be done. Daniel Stufflebeam and Anthony Shinkfield (2007) identified and compared 26 of these evaluation models.

In the following sections, we describe five of these models, because they have achieved prominence in the literature and because they illustrate the range of variation among models. The variations are primarily in whether they focus on stakeholder perspectives and program culture or on the program's effectiveness in achieving measurable objectives.

If you plan to do a program evaluation, knowing about these models can help you decide which one best suits your purpose. If you are a stakeholder in an evaluation study, knowing about these models will give you a better sense of the study's goals and procedures.

Objectives-Based Evaluation

An **objectives-based evaluation** focuses on the extent to which an educational program helps students achieve the intended learning objectives associated with it. The **National Assessment of Educational Progress** (NAEP), described in Chapter 9, is an example of this evaluation model. NAEP is a federally funded project that annually determines how well students are performing on measures of learning objectives in reading, mathematics, science, writing, history, geography, and other school subjects.

NAEP is based on the model of curriculum, instruction, and evaluation developed by Ralph Tyler (1949), who claimed that school instruction should be organized around specific curriculum objectives and that the success of such instruction should be judged based on how well students achieve those objectives.

The U.S. school system largely follows the principles of Tyler's model to this day. Classroom, district, state, and federal assessments are, for the most part, evaluations of how well students perform on measures of curriculum objectives. Programs designed to tie teachers' incentive pay to student learning outcomes and programs to identify and remediate "failing" schools also exemplify the Tyler model.

Experiments can be considered to be a type of objectives-based evaluation if they compare the learning gains of students in an innovative program with those of students receiving a traditional program or no program. Some of these experiments are reviewed by the What Works Clearinghouse, which we described above, in an effort to provide educators with evaluation evidence about particular educational programs.

Needs Assessment

Needs assessment is a set of procedures for identifying and prioritizing needs related to societal, organizational, and human performance (McKillip, 1987). A *need* usually is defined as a discrepancy between a desired and an existing state or condition.

For example, Hilary Brown and colleagues (2012) conducted a needs assessment of 101 Canadian families who have a school-aged child with autism spectrum disorder. They wanted to identify needs that are not currently being met by the existing social service system. Several major unmet needs were identified. Seventy-eight percent of the families reported insufficient social activities for their child; 77 percent reported that they had insufficient information about available services; and 74 percent reported a lack of continuous service provision. These research results can help policy makers, educators, and others to target their resources so they can better serve the needs of families who are trying to provide the best possible environment for their children with autism spectrum disorder.

Needs assessment can be thought of as the first stage in program development. By evaluating existing conditions, researchers can determine whether they are satisfactory or in need of improvement. The availability of research data to establish a need should make it easier to argue for resources to improve existing programs or develop new ones.

The Context-Input-Process-Product (CIPP) Model

Stufflebeam (2003) developed the **CIPP model** to help educators evaluate programs, although the model also can be used to evaluate projects, personnel, institutions, and other entities. The acronym *CIPP* refers to four types of evaluation (context, input, process, product) that should be performed if one wishes to conduct a truly comprehensive assessment of a program as it unfolds over time.

- **Context evaluation** assesses needs, assets, and problems of the stakeholders, staff, and beneficiaries of a program.
- **Input evaluation** assesses competing alternatives, work plans, and budgets for the program under consideration.
- **Process evaluation** documents and assesses program activities.
- **Product evaluation** assesses whether the program succeeded.

Product evaluation has four subparts:

- **Impact evaluation** assesses whether the program reached the right target audience.
- **Effectiveness evaluation** assesses the quality and significance of the program's outcomes.
- **Sustainability evaluation** assesses whether the program is institutionalized successfully in the short term and long term.
- **Transportability evaluation** assesses whether the program can be adapted and institutionalized in other settings.

Stufflebeam (2007) developed sets of checklist items to guide evaluators and stakeholders through each of these types of evaluation as well as other aspects of evaluation, such as making contractual agreements for the evaluation and for writing a final report.

Guili Zhang and colleagues (2011) reviewed reports of previous uses of the CIPP model to evaluate programs and described their own use of the model to evaluate a service-learning program at a public university in the southeastern United States that integrates community service into the academic curriculum. The specific project that they evaluated within this program involved 26 preservice teachers who tutored kindergarten children with reading problems as part of a course on diagnostic/prescriptive reading instruction.

The specific evaluation methods they used within each component of the CIPP model are listed in Table 19.1. Although this approach to evaluation is complex and time-consuming, it yields rich data for designing a program that is likely to be effective, determining whether the program is effective, and identifying factors that led it to be effective or ineffective. Furthermore, the CIPP model is a helpful tool for program management, as Zhang and colleagues discovered.

> University-based service-learning projects involve multiple stakeholders and aim to meet the needs of service providers and community partners. Their complex and dynamic nature calls for an evaluation model [CIPP] that can *operationalize* the process and provide step-by-step systematic guidance. (p. 78).

Many program developers and administrators probably do not have the resources to perform a program evaluation that encompasses the entire CIPP model, as was done in the service-learning study. However, developers can review all of the elements within each of the four components (context, input, process, and product) and select those that are most important and feasible for their particular situation.

Responsive Evaluation

Stake (2004, 2011) developed one of the first qualitative approaches to evaluation. **Responsive evaluation** focuses on identifying and describing stakeholders' issues (i.e., points of contention among different stakeholders) and concerns (i.e., matters about which stakeholders feel threatened or want to substantiate). Concerns and issues tend to provide a wider and different focus for an evaluation study than the program objectives that are central to objectives-based evaluation.

The four phases of responsive evaluation are (1) initiating and organizing the evaluation, (2) identifying key issues and concerns, (3) gathering useful information, and (4) reporting results and making recommendations. During the first phase, stakeholders are identified; also, the evaluator and client negotiate a contract to specify such matters as the phenomena to be evaluated, the purpose of the evaluation, rights of access to records, and guarantees of confidentiality and anonymity.

In the second phase, key issues and concerns are identified through direct involvement with a

TABLE 19.1 • Using the CIPP Model to Guide a Service-Learning Tutoring Project

Standards for Quality Practice	Context, Input, Process, and Product Framework
Service-learning actively engages participants in meaningful and personally relevant service activites.	Context evaluation: Identify participants' needs. Input evaluation: Design project that is engaging and targets participants' needs.
Service-learning is intentionally used as an instructional strategy to meet learning goals and/or content standards.	Context evaluation: Identify learning goals. Input evaluation: Design project as an effective instructional strategy to meet learning goals.
Service-learning incorporates multiple challenging reflection activities that are ongoing and that prompt deep thinking and analysis about oneself and one's relationship to society.	Input evaluation: Design project that includes multiple challenging reflection activities. Process evaluation: Assess reflection activities through reflective journals, focus group interviews, and surveys on self-perceptions.
Service-learning promotes understanding of diversity and mutual respect among all participants.	Input evaluation: Design project that will promote understanding of diversity and mutual respect among all participants. Process evaluation: Formatively and summatively assess whether the project promoted understanding of diversity and mutual respect among all participants.
Service-learning provides youth with a strong voice in planning, implementing, and evaluating service-learning experiences with guidance from adults.	Context, input, process, and product evaluation: Involve participants in planning, implementing, and evaluating service-learning project.
Service-learning partnerships are collaborative, mutually beneficial, and address community needs.	Context evaluation: Identify participants' and community needs. Input evaluation: Design project that is mutually beneficial and allows participants to work collaboratively to address community needs.
Service-learning engages participants in an ongoing process to assess the quality of implementation and progress toward meeting specified goals, and uses results for improvement and sustainability.	Process and product evaluation: Engage participants in an ongoing process to assess the quality of implementation and progress toward meeting specified goals, and use results for improvement and sustainability.
Service-learning has sufficient duration and intensity to address community needs and meet specified outcomes.	Context evaluation: Identify community needs, and specify intended outcomes. Input evaluation: Design project with sufficient duration and intensity. Process and product evaluation: Assess whether community needs and specified outcomes are met.

Source: Zhang, G., Zeller, N., Griffith, R., Metcalf, D., Williams, J., Shea, C., & Misulis, K. (2011). Using the context, input, process, and product evaluation model (CIPP) as a comprehensive framework to guide the planning, implementation, and assessment of service-learning programs. *Journal of Higher Education Outreach and Engagement, 15*(4), 57–84. Reprinted by permission of the Journal of Higher Education Outreach and Engagement, https://jheoe.uga.edu.

variety of stakeholders. The evaluators seek to clarify the different stakeholders' values that underlie the issues and concerns expressed. For example, in examining a particular school system's governance structure, the evaluators might discover that some stakeholders value a high-quality curriculum and accountability, whereas others place greater value on equality of representation in decision making and a rational decision-making process.

In the third phase of the evaluation, the evaluators collect more information about the concerns, issues, and values identified by the stakeholders, descriptive information about the phenomena being evaluated, and standards to be used in making judgments about the stakeholders' concerns, issues, and values.

The final phase of a responsive evaluation involves preparing reports of results and recommendations. Frequently, features of a case study report (see Chapter 13) are used to describe the concerns and issues identified by stakeholders. The evaluators, in negotiation with stakeholders, then make judgments and recommendations based on the information that has been collected.

In doing a responsive evaluation, evaluators do not specify a research design at the outset of their work. Instead, they use an **emergent design**, meaning that the design of the evaluation changes as evaluators gain insights into stakeholders' primary issues and concerns. Consistent with the analytic methods associated with grounded theory (see Chapter 13), responsive evaluators continue obtaining information from stakeholders until the information they are receiving becomes redundant.

Dialogue among stakeholders is central to responsive evaluation. However, dialogue might or might not resolve issues and concerns about the program being evaluated. Tineke Abma (2006) claims that the goal of dialogue is not necessarily agreement. "Dialogue may lead to consensus, but it is also considered successful if personal and mutual understanding has increased or if the understanding of differences is enhanced" (p. 31). Abma's eight guidelines for responsive evaluators to follow in order to facilitate open dialogue among diverse stakeholders are listed in Figure 19.1.

All types of research methodology require researchers to be sensitive to the needs of their participants. The participants in program evaluation are stakeholders who are embedded in a political process, and, therefore, evaluators need to use guidelines, such as those presented in Figure 19.1, to ensure that the stakeholders feel safe in providing evaluative data. Participants are more likely to feel safe if they see that the evaluator respects them and if they know that there will be no political reprisals for anything they say.

Responsive evaluation is grounded in qualitative methodology, but it is not alone in this respect. Stufflebeam and Shinkfield (2007) describe other evaluation models that use qualitative methodology.

FIGURE 19.1 • Eight Guidelines for Creating Effective Dialogues among Stakeholders in a Responsive Evaluation Study

1. *Identify and include everyone who is a stakeholder in the program being evaluated.* Treat stakeholders as partners and collaborators in the evaluation. Pay particular attention to individuals who might feel silenced by other stakeholders.

2. *Show respect to all stakeholders.* Show respect to stakeholders, especially those who feel silenced or without power, by conducting in-depth, informal interviews with them on a one-to-one basis.

3. *Build trust.* Build trust by interviewing stakeholders and by participating, as equals, with them in activities on the stakeholders' own "turf."

4. *Examine the stakeholders' environment to determine their need for privacy.* Find out whether stakeholders have concerns that their comments about the program might put them in jeopardy. Respect their rights to privacy and anonymity.

5. *Form homogeneous discussion groups.* If certain stakeholders feel vulnerable, put them in their own discussion group. Seeing others who are like themselves might help stakeholders feel comfortable about expressing their concerns about the program.

6. *Use stories to create an open dialogue.* Ask stakeholders to share stories about experiences that convey their concerns about the program. Individuals often become more comfortable in a group if they share stories with each other.

7. *Avoid subtle mechanisms of exclusion.* Look for signs that certain stakeholders, especially those who have a lower status, are being excluded from participating in a group dialogue. Some members of a group might try to silence other members by nonverbal expressions or critical remarks; be sure to foster expression by everyone.

8. *Interact with all stakeholder groups.* If stakeholders form groups that have different status with respect to the program (e.g., administrators, staff, clients, community members), be impartial. A responsive evaluator should be a spokesperson for all of the groups and convey each group's distinctive perspective to the other groups.

Source: Based on Abma, T. A. (2006). The practice and politics of responsive evaluation. *American Journal of Evaluation, 27*(1) 31–43.

EDUCATIONAL RESEARCH AND DEVELOPMENT

Evaluation plays a key role in educational **research and development (R & D)**. Educational R & D is a systematic process for developing, improving, and assessing educational programs and materials (referred to hereafter as *products* or *product*). A term sometimes used to describe R & D, *research-based product development* conveys the fact that (1) the goal is to develop a product based as much as possible on research findings and (2) the development process itself will be research-based. The R & D process is widely used in medicine, engineering, and other fields where the product or process to be developed has life-and-death consequences or where product effectiveness is of paramount importance.

Dick, Carey, and Carey (2012) advocate the systems approach model of educational R & D. The 10 steps of this model are shown in Figure 19.2. Step 1 involves needs assessment, which we described in a previous section. In this context, a needs assessment is carried out in order to identify the goals of the product to be developed.

Step 2, instructional analysis, involves identification of the specific skills, procedures, and learning tasks that are seen as necessary to reach the instructional goals.

Step 3 is designed to identify the level of entry behaviors (sometimes called enabling objectives) that learners need to bring to the learning task. It also involves identification of other characteristics of the learners that might affect learning (e.g., specific personality traits such as test anxiety) and the settings in which the instruction will occur and in which the learned skills will ultimately be used.

During Step 4, the developers write **performance objectives**, which are descriptions of the behaviors that the learners will be able to demonstrate after instruction. Then assessment instruments to test achievement of the objectives are developed (Step 5); the appropriate instructional strategy is formulated (Step 6); and instructional materials are developed or possibly selected from available materials (Step 7).

Steps 8, 9, and 10 of the R & D systems model involve the distinction between formative and summative evaluation, which was formulated by Michael Scriven (1967). He found that, in practice,

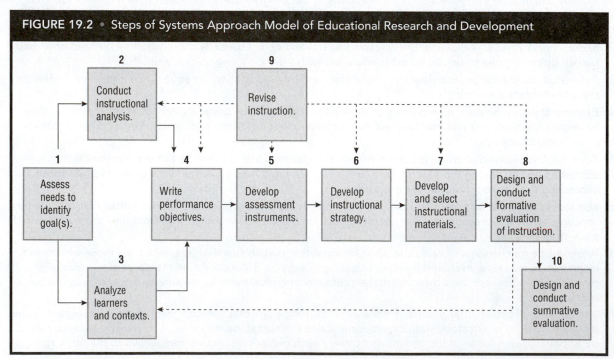

FIGURE 19.2 • Steps of Systems Approach Model of Educational Research and Development

Source: Based on Dick, W., Carey, L., & Carey, J. O. (2012). *The systematic design of instruction* (7th ed.). Boston, MA: Pearson. Adapted with permission from the publisher.

evaluation serves two different functions, which he called *formative evaluation* and *summative evaluation*.

Step 8, **formative evaluation**, involves collecting data about an educational product while it is under development. This is done to help the developers and evaluators decide whether the product needs revision before release and, if so, what revisions are necessary. Formative evaluation is also used to determine whether the prospects for an eventually effective product are low and, if so, to reach a decision about whether further product development should be terminated.

As shown in Figure 19.2, formative evaluation can occur at all of the earlier stages of the development process. For example, the developers might carry out a formative evaluation of the product's objectives during Step 4, examining such issues as the clarity and comprehensiveness of the objectives. Based on the results, they might eliminate some objectives, rewrite others, or add new objectives. Once they have developed instructional materials (Step 7), developers might do more formative evaluation and further revise the performance objectives, perhaps so that the wording of the objectives better matches the content of the instructional materials.

A more thorough formative evaluation is conducted when a prototype of the product (that is, a relatively complete but not polished set of the necessary elements) is available. This formative evaluation involves a field test of the product. Compared to implementation of the completed product, a field test is a trial of the product (1) with a smaller number of research participants, (2) more hands-on involvement of the developers, and (3) a more controlled environment than the real-life conditions in which the final product is meant to be used.

At some point in your career, you might find yourself involved in a formative evaluation of a program or product. Your knowledge about evaluation research will help you to be a good participant in the formative evaluation process. Your expert feedback can serve as one basis for improving the program or product so that it is effective for many other educators later on.

Step 10, summative evaluation, is conducted once the development process (i.e., Steps 1 through 9) has been completed. The purpose of **summative evaluation** is to determine whether the completed product achieves its objectives under real-life conditions. Summative evaluation also might involve comparing the effectiveness of the completed product with that of competing products.

Summative evaluation is usually carried out by someone other than the developers, but it also can be done by members of the development team if appropriate controls are used to minimize researcher bias. If a summative evaluation demonstrates that the product is effective, we can characterize it as being evidence-based. In Chapter 1, we explained that evidence-based practice is becoming increasingly important in education and other professional fields.

Most evaluation studies of programs that appear in the education literature are summative evaluations. As an educator examining the evaluation research literature, you probably will be most interested in summative evaluations of instructional programs, methods, and materials that have been tested under conditions similar to your work environment. These evaluations will help you determine whether these products will be effective under conditions similar to your own situation.

The authors of this book worked together at a federally funded laboratory many years ago to do research and development to create programs to improve various aspects of education (Hemphill & Rosenau, 1972). Expensive, multiyear efforts were required to complete all steps of an R & D cycle. If you want to develop your own product (e.g., software or a set of curriculum guides), you might be able to accomplish this goal as a thesis or dissertation by developing only part of the product and completing only some of the steps of the R & D cycle. One of our doctoral students conducted this type of study to develop a textbook on the history of Guam for use there. He developed and evaluated one part of the textbook to determine which of several approaches was most effective for students (Cunningham & Gall, 1990).

HOW TO READ AN EVALUATION RESEARCH REPORT

Many evaluation studies are done under contract for a school system, governmental agency, or other organization. These reports serve local purposes and might contain sensitive information. Therefore, they are rarely available in the published literature.

Some of the intended readers of these reports might have little knowledge of research methods and terms. Therefore, the evaluation reports are likely to be nontechnical. The emphasis is on the implications of the findings rather than on the methods used to generate them.

Other evaluation studies are conducted to assess programs that are widely used or that show promise of solving an important problem of practice. These studies generally are conducted with the intent that they eventually will be reported in wide-circulation educational journals. These are the kinds of reports that we consider here.

We start by noting that most evaluation studies use quantitative, qualitative, or mixed methods. If an evaluation study uses quantitative methods, the report will be organized like the reports of quantitative methods described in Part Three of this book. Many of these reports are experiments that are designed to test the effectiveness of a program.

If a program evaluation uses qualitative methods, on the other hand, it most likely will be a case study. Therefore, the report probably will be organized like the reports described in Chapter 13. An example is an evaluation study by Patrick McQuillan and Yves Salomon-Fernandez (2008). Their purpose was to determine how the staff of underperforming schools responded to state-led interventions to improve the students' academic achievement. The schools were underperforming as defined by the No Child Left Behind Act, which mandates that schools make adequate yearly progress toward proficiency for all students in English/language arts and mathematics by 2014. (This mandate is currently being contested by some states.)

The researchers collected qualitative data from staff at two underperforming middle schools and one underperforming high school. They interviewed 16 teachers and administrators at these schools, made observations at each school on two occasions, and analyzed various documents. The teachers and administrators constituted the stakeholders for this study

McQuillan and Salomon-Fernandez used the method of constant comparison based on grounded theory (see Chapter 13) to identify themes and patterns in the data. Their report lists 11 themes, each of which reflects the stakeholders' perspective on state-level interventions. Each theme is illustrated by interview comments made by the teachers and administrators. Figure 19.3 presents two of the

themes—one positive and one negative—to illustrate the results of this evaluation study.

These findings can help other stakeholders (e.g., federal officials and leaders of teacher organizations) understand the impact of external mandates on those who must implement them. Better solutions to problems of educational practice are more likely if all stakeholders can have their concerns and aspirations heard and respected.

EVALUATING EVALUATION RESEARCH AND USES OF EVALUATION IN EDUCATIONAL PRACTICE

You can judge the quality of most evaluation research reports by answering the questions listed in Appendix 3 (for a quantitative study), Appendix 4 (for a qualitative study), and Appendix 5 (for specific research designs).

In addition, you can refer to the authoritative standards for program evaluation developed by the **Joint Committee on Standards for Educational Evaluation** (Yarbrough, Shulha, Hopson, & Caruthers, 2010). The committee consisted of representatives from 17 major educational organizations, including the American Association of School Administrators, the American Educational Research Association, and the Canadian Evaluation Society.

The Joint Committee excluded the evaluation of educators from their consideration of program evaluation because they developed a separate set of personnel evaluation standards (Joint Committee, 2008). They also developed a separate set of standards for assessing evaluation practices in elementary and secondary classrooms (Joint Committee, 2002).

The evaluation of teachers has become an increasing matter of concern to policy makers and the community in recent years. In part, this concern arises from the persistent achievement gap between white and ethnic-minority students and the perceived need to hold teachers accountable for their students' performance in the classroom. **Value-added teacher evaluation** addresses these concerns by focusing on how much gain a teacher's students make on a standardized achievement test administered before and after they have received

---

FIGURE 19.3 • Themes and Quotes from a Report of a Qualitative Evaluation of a State-Level Intervention on Underperforming Schools

Theme 1: Benefits of State Intervention

Administrator Statement

"I can't tell you how much support, cooperation I've gotten from teachers. . . . Most people here spend a great deal of time after school, they go the extra mile. . . . This has forced [teachers] to examine what they do. . . . I thank [Massachusetts Comprehensive System] for bringing my staff together and making them even more unified. . . . This has been my most rewarding experience in education." (p. 17)

Teacher Statement

"It has had a positive impact in terms of the lower end of the teaching staff who didn't necessarily give a lot of thought and consideration to what they were doing. They've had to raise the bar. [In fact,] we've all stepped up to the [challenge]. . . . [W]e've been forced to look at ourselves and reflect more. And that's been the positive part." (p. 18)

Theme 2: Negative Impacts of Interventions on Schools

Teacher Statement

"We have not been able to operate as a real school because all our attention has been focused on doing what the DOE [Department of Education] wants. . . . It's not like we're doing things because it's best for our kids. . . . [I]t's always around the parameters set by the DOE. You do something and you have to think, 'Is this going to fit within the guidelines of DOE? Will it meet DOE expectations?'" (pp. 20–21)

Administrator Statement

"I'm constantly preparing information for the state and . . . it really takes me away from instruction and working in classrooms. . . . It takes a lot of energy. . . . It's a good thing to have oversight, but there are limits. . . . It's the most frustrating part of my job." (p. 21)

Source: McQuillan, P. J., & Salomon-Fernandez, Y. (2008). The impact of state intervention on "underperforming" schools in Massachusetts: Implications for policy and practice. *Education Policy Analysis Archives, 16*(18), 1–40.

---

instruction from the teacher. The amount of gain might be simply the difference between a student's pre-instruction and post-instruction score, followed by the computation of a mean gain of all the students who were in the teacher's class. This average gain is the "value" that the teacher adds to students' learning.

Various statistical adjustments to this simple model for calculating a teacher's value have been developed (Braun, 2005). These statistical adjustments and other aspects of the process of value-added teacher evaluation have proved to be controversial, especially when used as a basis for job dismissal (Amrien-Beardsley & Collins, 2012). Teachers are particularly important stakeholders in the process because they are the specific focus of the evaluation. Their concerns are the subject of the research article that is reprinted at the end of this chapter.

The study reported in the article involves an analysis of teacher concerns about values-added teacher evaluation. In effect, it is an evaluation of an evaluation. This type of evaluation is called a **meta-evaluation**, which we define as a research study that evaluates the quality and effectiveness of an evaluation program or evaluation study. Of course, the individuals responsible for an evaluation program or evaluation study can make their own judgments about the quality and effectiveness of their efforts. However, these judgments, which are a form of meta-evaluation, are subject to bias because in effect, the evaluators are evaluating their own work. Ideally, a meta-evaluation of an evaluation program or study should be conducted by an independent evaluator. Daniel Stufflebeam (2011) has developed a systematic process for conducting a systematic meta-evaluation.

An example of
How Program Evaluations Can Help in Solving Problems of Practice

Tablet computers (generally called tablets), together with electronic textbooks, are finding their way increasingly into schools. Reports of their purchase and use can be found on websites and in newspapers in the United States and other countries. For example:

- The Los Angeles Unified School District has approved a $30 million contract to purchase 30,000 iPad tablets for its students, provide teacher training and school support, and hire 15 technology experts. District officials hope that the tablets will improve students' success in university work and the job market. De Vore, A. (2013, June 21). LAUSD approves $30 mil for 30,000 iPads. Retrieved from http://www.nationalteachersalliance.org/dialogue/article/lausd-approves-30-mil-for-30000-ipads

- Litchfield High School in Litchfield, Connecticut, is giving Dell tablets to all enrolled students. In addition to a tablet, students are given a protective cover, a stylus, a detachable keyboard, and a power adaptor. Students will be offered presentations during flex periods so that can learn about the use of this equipment. Flynn, R. (2014, January 22). Parents learn about tablet computer that Litchfield High School students will receive. *The Register Citizen*. Retrieved from http://www.registercitizen.com/social-affairs/20140122/parents-learn-about-tablet-computers-that-litchfield-high-school-students-will-receive

- The country of Jamaica has a Tablet in Schools Pilot Project under which 30,000 tablets will be given to students across all grade levels in schools that are underperforming academically. The tablets will be Internet enabled, and project managers are working with publishers to convert their hard-copy textbooks into electronic books. Jamaica Observer

(2014, January 21). 37 schools to get tablet computers by May/June, state minister says. *Jamaica Observer*. Retrieved from http://www.jamaicaobserver.com/news/37-schools-to-get-tablet-computers-by-May-June–state-minister-says

- The Charlottesville, Virginia, school system has an initiative called BLAST (Blended Learning to Advance Student Thinking), which purchased 392 Fujitsu tablets and leased another 2,082 tablets for use by middle school and high school students. Teachers are using them to post notes, quizzes, discussion forums, and other class materials. They also are employing them for flipped instruction, which means that students study curriculum content on their tablet as homework and then use class time to work on problem sets and other learning activities that previously had been assigned as homework. Davis, M. E. (2013, January 23). Tablets in Charlottesville school prove successful. *The Daily Progress*. Retrieved from http://www.dailyprogress.com/news/tablets-in-charlottesville-schools-prove-successful/article_0509d7aa-8d58-5280-8d39-9627167f6f11.html

Educators, legislators, and the community might wonder, after reading these articles, whether the potential benefits of tablets are worth the cost. Are they a fad that will pass, or are they indeed the wave of the future? And will they improve student learning? Evaluation research can provide evidence to answer these questions, as we explain below.

Evaluators might start their research by using the methods of responsive evaluation to identify the stakeholders' issues and concerns. Their concerns likely will involve the costs and benefits of providing tablets to all students in a school. Do stakeholders perceive a real need for students to have tablets? Is ongoing funding available to provide tablets if they become lost, stolen, or broken? Who will be in charge of the inventory for these devices and of repairing them when they are broken? Can electronic textbooks replace all of the textbooks currently being used? Are electronic textbooks in line with state and national curriculum standards? Will students learn as much from their tablets as they learn from conventional textbook-based instruction? What can be done to address parents' concerns that students might develop an addiction to using their tablets to play video games or use them to access adult websites that parents find objectionable?

If the stakeholders want all of these questions answered, the CIPP model of program evaluation might be a good option. The stakeholders can go to the CIPP website described in this chapter and review the checklist items listed there. They can choose those parts of the model (impact, effectiveness, sustainability, transportability) that are most appropriate to their concerns. The evidence provided by CIPP-based evaluation can give stakeholders a fuller understanding of the use of tablet computers in schools. With this understanding, they can weigh the benefits of these devices against their costs and risks and develop an action plan that is defensible.

SELF-CHECK TEST

1. Program culture refers to the
   a. explicit and tacit views of those involved in a program evaluation study.
   b. the roles and relations between program developers and educators.
   c. the rituals, rules, and roles that come into play as individuals become involved with a program.
   d. the way a program is designed to accommodate the ethnic identities of the individuals who are the target audience for the program.
2. A stakeholder is
   a. the individual who initiates the request for an evaluation.
   b. anyone who will be affected by the evaluation findings.
   c. an evaluator who assesses a program by analyzing costs relative to benefits.
   d. an evaluator who uses personal interpretation to evaluate a phenomenon.
3. The work of the National Assessment of Educational Progress and the What Works Clearinghouse is based primarily on
   a. needs assessment.
   b. the CIPP model.
   c. objectives-based evaluation.
   d. all of the above.
4. Needs assessment typically involves
   a. measurement of the discrepancy between an existing condition and a desired condition.

   b. interviews of stakeholders to identify what they require for a program to function efficiently.
   c. estimation of the costs and benefits of a proposed intervention.
   d. the determination of which program, in a set of possible programs, should have priority for funding.
5. The CIPP model of evaluation focuses on
   a. stakeholder needs and problems.
   b. a program's work plans and budgets.
   c. a program's impact and transportability.
   d. all of the above.
6. A central feature of responsive evaluation is its
   a. focus on identifying the issues and concerns of stakeholders.
   b. specification of the evaluation design prior to data collection.
   c. concern with the goals and objectives of the program being evaluated.
   d. specification of procedures for reconciling the different perspectives of various stakeholders.
7. The primary purpose of formative evaluation in educational R & D is to
   a. demonstrate the effectiveness of a program under operational conditions.
   b. evaluate the program once the development process has been completed.
   c. obtain information to guide revision and further development of the program.

    d. satisfy the oversight mandates of the agency funding the program's development.

8. Unlike formative evaluation, summative evaluation of a program generally

    a. occurs throughout the R & D process.

    b. is conducted to determine whether development of the product should be discontinued.

    c. is conducted to determine why stakeholder groups have different views of the program's effectiveness.

    d. is conducted to determine the effectiveness of the completed program.

9. Reports of program evaluation studies

    a. are rarely published because the evaluation process reveals sensitive political matters that stakeholders wish to keep private.

    b. are published in professional journals only if the study involves the objectives-based model of evaluation.

    c. generally are organized more like reports of historical studies than like reports of case studies.

    d. generally are organized like reports of quantitative research studies and case studies.

10. The program evaluation standards of the Joint Committee on Standards for Educational Evaluation

    a. are suitable for the evaluation of teachers and school administrators.

    b. are suitable for use by teachers in constructing their own tests.

    c. were developed by a committee representing major educational organizations in the United States.

    d. does not specify ethical standards for conducting program evaluation because standards of this type differ greatly across school districts and other agencies.

CHAPTER REFERENCES

Abma, T. (2006). The practice and politics of responsive evaluation. *American Journal of Evaluation, 27*(1), 31–43.

Academic Competitiveness Council. (2007). *Report of the Academic Competitiveness Council.* Washington, DC: U.S. Department of Education. Retrieved from ERIC database. (ED496649)

Braun, H. I. (2005). *Using student progress to evaluate teachers: A primer on value-added models. Policy information perspective.* Princeton, NJ: Educational Testing Service. Retrieved from http://childparenting.about.com/gi/o.htm?zi=1/XJ&zTi=1&sdn=childparenting&cdn=parenting&tm=153f=00&su=p284.13.342.ip_&tt=2&bt=0&bts=0&zu=http%3A//www.ets.org/Media/Research/pdf/PICVAM.pdf

Brown, H. K., Quellette-Kuntz, H., Hunter, D., Kelley, E., & Cobigo, V. (2012). Unmet needs of families of school-aged children with an autism spectrum disorder. *Journal of Applied Research in Intellectual Disabilities, 25*(6), 497–508.

Cunningham, L. J., & Gall, M. D. (1990). The effects of expository and narrative prose on student achievement and attitudes toward textbooks. *Journal of Experimental Education, 58*(3), 165–175.

Dick, W., Carey, L., & Carey, J. O. (2012). *The systematic design of instruction* (7th ed.). Boston, MA: Pearson.

Hemphill, J., & Rosenau, F. S. (Eds.). (1972). *Educational development.* Eugene, OR: Center for Advanced Study in Educational Administration.

Joint Committee on Standards for Educational Evaluation. (2002). *The student evaluation standards: How to improve evaluations of students.* Thousand Oaks, CA: Corwin.

Joint Committee on Standards for Educational Evaluation. (2008). *The personnel evaluation standards: How to assess systems for evaluating educators.* Thousand Oaks, CA: Corwin.

Kushner, S., & Adelman, C. (2006). Program evaluation: A democratic process. In J. L. Green, G. Camilli, & P. B. Elmore (Eds.), *Handbook of complementary methods in education research* (pp. 711–726). Mahwah, NJ: Lawrence Erlbaum.

McKillip, J. (1987). *Need analysis: Tools for the human services and education.* Thousand Oaks, CA: Sage.

McQuillan, P. J., & Salomon-Fernandez, Y. (2008). The impact of state intervention on "underperforming" schools in Massachusetts: Implications for policy and practice. *Education Policy Analysis Archives, 16*(18), 1–40.

Scriven, M. (1967). The methodology of evaluation. In R. E. Stake (Ed.), *Curriculum evaluation: American Educational Research Association Series on Evaluation, No. 1* (pp. 39–83). Chicago, IL: Rand McNally.

Stake, R. E. (2004). *Standards-based and responsive evaluation.* Thousand Oaks, CA: Sage.

Stake, R. E. (2011). Program evaluation particularly responsive evaluation. *Journal of MultiDisciplinary Evaluation, 7*(15), 180–201.

Stufflebeam, D. L. (2003). *The CIPP model for evaluation.* In T. Kellaghan & D. L. Stufflebeam (Eds.), *The international handbook of educational evaluation* (Chapter 3). Boston, MA: Kluwer Academic Publishers.

Stufflebeam, D. L. (2007). *CIPP evaluation model checklist* (2nd ed.). Retrieved from http://www.wmich.edu/evalctr/archive_checklists/cippchecklist_mar07.pdf

Stufflebeam, D. L. (2011). Meta-evaluation. *Journal of MultiDisciplinary Evaluation, 7*(15), 99–158.

Stufflebeam, D. L., & Shinkfield, A. J. (2007). *Evaluation theory, models, and applications.* San Francisco, CA: Jossey-Bass.

Tyler, R. W. (1949). *Basic principles of curriculum and instruction: Syllabus for Education 360.* Chicago, IL: University of Chicago Press.

Yarbrough, D. B., Shulha, L. M., Hopson, R. K., & Caruthers, F. A. (2010). *The program evaluation standards: A guide for evaluators and evaluation users* (3rd ed.). Thousand Oaks, CA: Sage.

Zhang, G., Zeller, N., Griffith, R., Metcalf, D., Williams, J., Shea, C., & Misulis, K. (2011). Using the context, input, process, and product evaluation model (CIPP) as a comprehensive framework to guide the planning, implementation, and assessment of service-learning programs. *Journal of Higher Education Outreach and Engagement, 15*(4), 57–84.

RESOURCES FOR FURTHER STUDY

Altschuld, J. W., & Kumar, D. D. (2010). *Needs assessment: An overview.* Thousand Oaks, CA: Sage.

> The authors explain how to conduct a needs assessment and use the results to create an action plan for organizational change.

Evaluation Center at Western Michigan University. (n.d.). Evaluation checklists. Retrieved from www.wmich.edu/evalctr/checklists

> This website provides checklists that evaluators can use to design and conduct evaluation projects of various sorts. Each checklist is accompanied by a rationale grounded in the evaluation literature and lessons learned from practice.

Fitzpatrick, J. L., Sanders, J. R., & Worthen, B. R. (2010). *Program evaluation: Alternative approaches and practical guidelines* (4th ed.). New York, NY: Pearson.

> The authors explain the purposes of program evaluation and provide a detailed treatment of contemporary approaches to program evaluation. The book gives practical guidelines for planning, conducting, and using evaluations.

Patton, M. Q. (2002). *Qualitative research and evaluation methods* (3rd ed.). Thousand Oaks, CA: Sage.

> The author explains how to conduct an evaluation study using qualitative research methods. Among the topics covered are ethical issues in evaluation, focus groups, computer-assisted analysis of data, and criteria for judging the quality of qualitative evaluation studies. Another resource is his book about a specific type of evaluation: Patton, M. Q. (2012). *Essentials of utilization-focused evaluation.* Thousand Oaks, CA: Sage.

Sanders, J. R., & Sullins, C. D. (2006). *Evaluating school programs: An educator's guide* (3rd ed.). Thousand Oaks, CA: Corwin.

> This book is for educators who need to conduct mandated evaluations of school programs. The authors present a five-step model for evaluation that is efficient, responsive to No Child Left Behind guidelines, and oriented to school improvement.

What Did the Teachers Think? Teachers' Responses to the Use of Value-Added Modeling as a Tool for Evaluating Teacher Effectiveness

Lee, L. (2011). What did the teachers think? Teachers' responses to the use of value-added modeling as a tool for evaluating teacher effectiveness. *Journal of Urban Learning, Teaching, and Research, 7,* 97–103.

The following article reports a study that evaluates a type of teacher evaluation that is being used increasingly to evaluate teachers' performance in the classroom. It is called value-added teacher evaluation or, as it is called in the article below, value-added modeling. As we explain in this chapter, this type of teacher evaluation measures the amount of gain that students make in their scores on a standardized test that is administered before students are taught by a particular teacher and again after they have completed instruction from the teacher, which is typically the end of the school year. The greater the student gain, the more positive is the teacher's evaluation.

The researcher used a mixed-methods design, involving both quantitative and qualitative methods, to determine how well a particular value-added system of teacher evaluation was working in one school district. The study can be considered a meta-evaluation because it involved an evaluation of the use of a particular type of evaluation. It also can be considered a form of responsive evaluation because the researcher focused on the concerns of one group of stakeholders, namely, teachers, who were affected by the evaluation system.

What Did the Teachers Think? Teachers' Responses to the Use of Value-Added Modeling as a Tool for Evaluating Teacher Effectiveness

LINDA LEE
California State University, Los Angeles

ABSTRACT   The policy discourse on improving student achievement has shifted from student outcomes to focusing on evaluating teacher effectiveness using standardized test scores. A major urban newspaper released a public database that ranked teachers' effectiveness using Value-Added Modeling. Teachers, whom are generally marginalized, were given the opportunity to respond to their rankings. This research examines a subset of those teachers' perceptions about the use of standardized test scores in determining teacher effectiveness. It is important for policy makers to hear from those whom are the implementation level of such major policy shifts in education reform.

Keywords: Teacher Effectiveness; Teacher Attitudes; Teacher Response; Teacher Evaluation; Evaluation Methods; Value-Added Models; Accountability; Educational Policy; Elementary Education

Introduction

In August 2010, a major urban newspaper, the Los Angeles Times (*L.A. Times*), published a study on teacher effectiveness using a statistical method, Value-Added Modeling (Buddin, 2010). The results of the study were published in an online database, which showed individual rankings of teacher effectiveness, based on the teacher's students' progress on standardized test scores in English and math. The "value" a teacher adds or subtracts is based on the difference between a student's expected growth and actual performance on the tests. The database included about 6000 Los Angeles Unified School District teachers that taught at least 60 students in the third, fourth and fifth grades, during the 2003 to 2009 school years. The newspaper's statement on the purpose of publishing the information was ". . . it bears on the performance of public employees who provide an important service, and in the belief that parents and the public have a right to judge it for themselves" (Felch, et al., 2010).

The public release caused a stir, because, for the first time, the public was able to see quantifiable differences

Linda Lee is a doctoral candidate in the EdD Program in Educational Leadership at California State University, Los Angeles and an administrator at an urban elementary charter school. Ms. Lee can be reached at CSU Los Angeles, Division of Applied and Advanced Studies in Education, 5151 State University Drive, Los Angeles, CA 90032. E-mail: llee18@calstatela.edu.

amongst teachers. In tandem with the release of rankings, the newspaper gave teachers the opportunity to respond to the rankings and use of test scores in evaluating teacher effectiveness. In doing so, the L.A. Times provided the public with a rare opportunity to hear from the teachers, whom often when decisions on educational policy are made, are left out of the conversation. This is powerful in the sense that by "searching the margins… one finds the great potential of people expressing counter narratives and alternative proposals for policy" (Marshall & Gerstl-Pepin, p. 152). In the responses posted, teacher gave opinions, arguments, and suggestions about the use of Value-added Modeling. The purpose of this study is to analyze these responses, so that we can better understand some of the challenges and nuances of trying to measure a process as dynamic as teaching and learning. Understanding the teachers, who are the negotiators of the transactions between teaching and learning, is essential to illustrate some of the challenges the nation faces as it moves to evaluating and rewarding effective teachers, and, ultimately, the implications for producing educated citizens.

Unfortunately, effective evaluation of teachers has been an elusive task, where we have lacked the ability to discern effective and ineffective teachers. Weisberg, Sexton, Mulhern, & Keeling's (2009) study of twelve districts in four states showed that, in districts with binary evaluation ratings (satisfactory/unsatisfactory), more than 99 percent of teachers received a satisfactory rating. In districts with a broader range of ratings, 94 percent of teachers received one of the top two ratings and less than one percent received an unsatisfactory rating. A study on statewide policies on teacher evaluation in the mid-west region (Brandt, Thomas, & Burke, 2008) found that most states provided guidance to districts on evaluating their teachers, which included criteria ranging from who is responsible, to frequency of evaluation. However, the criteria were general to the status of the teacher, rather than teaching and learning. Similarly, the No Child Left Behind Act provided the requirement of having Highly Qualified teachers, but the qualification only went so far as tracking credential status. Meeting the definition of Highly Qualified neither predicted nor ensured that a teacher would be successful at increasing student learning.

In addition to having ineffective evaluation tools, efforts to increase student learning have been challenging. According to the National Center for Educational Statistics (Rooney et al., 2006), since the early 1990s, the achievement gaps between White and Black, and White and Hispanic, have shown little measurable change. The inability to close these gaps has resulted in looking beyond student achievement on standardized tests and is now sharply focused on teachers. The basic framework of logic, which is driving much of the nation's current efforts in closing the achievement gap,

is the notion that if you have good teachers, you will have good student achievement. Or, one can inversely infer: bad teachers are preventing our students from achieving. This notion of having teachers with different levels of effectiveness has become a major focal point in federal government's plan to "fix" the problem of low student achievement. The Blueprint for Reform (US Department of Education, 2010) ties teacher effectiveness with student test scores:

"We will elevate the teaching profession to focus on recognizing, encouraging, and rewarding excellence. We are calling on states and districts to develop and implement systems of teacher and principal evaluation and support, and to identify effective and highly effective teachers and principals on the basis of student growth and other factors." (p. 4). This has led to a drive to find a way to measure teacher effectiveness using standardized test scores as the tool.

Value-Added Modeling

One statistical method that policymakers see as a tool for teacher evaluations is Value-added Modeling (McCaffrey, Lockwood, Koretz, & Hamilton, 2003), a statistical method that calculates individual student growth by comparing his/her previous year's test score to his/her current year's score, and comparing that growth in relation to other students in that grade level. Policymakers around the nation are embracing the idea of using a value-added measurement tool because it seems to provide an objective measure in evaluating teacher effectiveness. However, researchers have cautioned the use of Value-Added Models (VAM) due to limitations and unsolved problems. For instance, Schochet & Chiang (2010) found that more than 90 percent of the variation in student gain scores is due to the variation in *student-level* factors, and strongly suggests that policymakers carefully consider system error rates in designing and implementing teacher performance measurement systems that are based on value-added models. Another factor, is the issue of missing data (van de Grift, 2009), where the results are only valid for the detection of schools with the highest raw scores and the highest learning gains. In addition, Papay (2011) found that the different tests did not rank individual teachers consistently. Because of these and other limitations, Baker et. al. (2010) argue that VAM should only be one component, and a comprehensive evaluation should be standards-based and include evaluation by supervisors and peers. Thus far, the discourse on determining teacher effectiveness with the use of VAM has mainly been at the policy and research levels. We need to solicit teacher perspectives to understand the subtleties involved with evaluating teaching and student learning. However, there are few conduits of influence where teachers can have their opinions heard. Often times, their viewpoints are mediated through others (e.g.

unions, administrators, associations) or not surfaced at all for the knowledge of the general public. Including teachers in the discourse is essential, as it can provide valuable information from those that are directly charged with increasing student achievement, information that would normally be missed when making policy decisions. Hence, this study will analyze the teachers' responses to the use of VAM in determining teacher effectiveness.

Research Question

What are the perceptions of teachers who are working in a large urban school district concerning the use of VAM in evaluating their effectiveness?

Sub questions: Do teachers differ in their opinions based upon their individual rankings? Is there a relationship between Overall Ranking and Years of Teaching Included?

Methodology

This is a mixed methods study that utilizes non-participant observation strategies through an unobtrusive research design due to the fact that the data set is publicly posted on the Internet. As of December 2010, 293 teachers posted responses. Only teachers who were part of the released rankings were allowed to post a response. Information collected from the database included: the submitting teacher's name, the time and date of the submission, teacher's VAM Overall Ranking, VAM ranking in English, VAM ranking in Math, number of years included in the ranking, the school they were employed at during the most recent standardized test administration, the schools where they were previously employed, and the teacher's response.

Each response was analyzed to determine whether the teacher was generally positive/agreed with the use of VAM, negative/disagreed, or neutral/mixed. For quantitative analysis, a frequency count determined the number of respondents at each of the five levels of rankings, ranging from least effective to most effective. Cross-tabulation was used to categorize the type of comment (Positive/Agree, Negative/Disagree, Neutral/Mixed) within each level of ranking. In addition, a correlation analysis examined teacher rankings in relation to the number of years teaching included in the study. Qualitatively, conventional content analysis (Hsieh & Shannon, 2005) was used to allow for categories to emerge from the data. As the responses were being read through, open coding was used to select content by marking key words, phrases, sentences and paraphrases of the responses. Units of code, ranging from single words to sentences, were gathered and then sorted into related categories. Several common categories were determined from the patterns of the units (e.g. arguments, opinions, outcomes, alternatives, etc.). These were then grouped into three main categories to determine common elements in the responses: knowledge, attitudes, and beliefs.

Findings

Quantitatively, frequency counts of each type of respondent (i.e. least effective, less, average, more, most effective) demonstrated a range of 17.4%–22.8%, which is approximate to the quintile breakdown used in VAM. Hence, there was a fair balance of responses from teachers at each of the five ranking levels. Upon analyzing the nature of the responses, it was found that the majority of the responses (221 of 293) were categorized as Negative/Disagree (see Table 1). The level that had the most categorized as Positive/Agree was the "Most Effective" level, where many responses indicated that the teachers were appreciative of having recognition of their efforts. Notably, although this level had the most positive/agree responses, the majority of the responses were negative/disagree towards the use of VAM.

An evaluation was made of the relationship between Overall Rank and years of teaching within the 6-year window using Pearson's correlation. The analysis showed that the results were not statistically significant, $r = .100$, $p > .05$. Therefore, no relationship between the ranking of the teacher and the years of teaching that were included could be determined (see Table 2).

In using conventional content analysis, initially, over 850 codes emerged through open coding. From the codes,

Table 1

Cross-tabulation of Overall Rank and Type of Comment

| | | Type of Comment | | | |
		Negative/Disagree	Neutral/Mixed	Positive/Agree	Total
Overall Rank	Least	45	2	3	51
	Less	50	4	7	61
	Average	48	9	8	65
	More	42	6	4	52
	Most	35	4	25	64
	Total	221	25	47	29

Table 2

Correlation Analysis of Overall Rank and Years Included

		Overall Rank	Years Included
Overall Rank	Pearson Correlation	1	.100
	Sig. (2-tailed)		.088
	N	293	293
Years Included	Pearson Correlation	.100	1
	Sig. (2-tailed)	.088	
	N	293	293

more than 300 patterns of text were identified. These patterns were then categorized into themes. Major themes were then classified into three categories: the knowledge, attitudes, and beliefs teachers had regarding the use of VAM for evaluation of effectiveness (see Figure 1).

Overwhelmingly, teacher attitudes towards the use of VAM was negative due to what they perceived as a disconnect in defining the education of the whole child with a test score in English and math. In particular, strong affective terminology was most used with regard to the public release of teacher names and rankings (e.g. demoralizing, resentment, public stoning, offensive, irreversible.) criticizing how the information was disseminated, and the lack of privacy for teachers. Many teachers were angered and felt that the newspaper was premature, irresponsible, and unfair. The responses also demonstrated that teachers had knowledge that validated many of the issues that already exist in the literature, such as the impact of student-level factors (e.g. special education

students, students with little room to improve, English Language Learners), parent-level factors (e.g. education level, support at home), teacher-level factors (e.g. team teaching, previous teacher effects, being on leave for part of the year, teaching to the test), and institution-level factors (e.g. type of curriculum, leadership, lack of random assignment of students). Implications that were raised included: increased competition amongst teachers; under-performing children being "unwanted"; "branding" teachers; narrowing of the curriculum; cheating as a means to "game" the system; and parental competition for those labeled as most effective teachers. Concepts introduced by teachers included: lack of recognition of their dedication and efforts; lack of resources to properly teach; influences of school culture; influence of teacher seniority on selection of classes; influence of school initiatives and programs; interference of district and union policies; year-round vs. traditional calendars; importance of administrator competence;

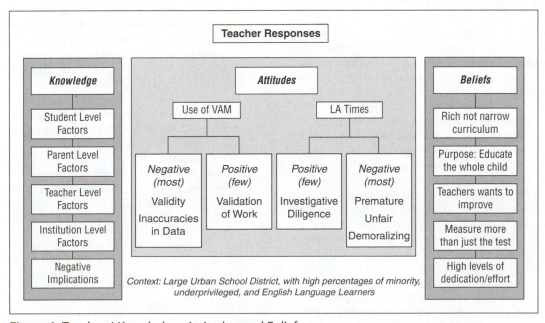

Figure 1 Teachers' Knowledge, Attitudes, and Beliefs

degradation of the level of collaboration found in professional learning communities; restrictive curriculum; and influence of lack of student motivation for doing well on the test. Teachers' beliefs surfaced issues about necessity of having a rich curriculum to develop a whole child, the purpose of education being the educating of an individual not a test score, the turning of education into a business model, and that teachers want to improve in their practice. Responses indicated that teachers welcomed a process for evaluation to improve practice, but it should be done privately, and that VAM should not be the sole tool for evaluation. They suggested including other measures such as classroom observations, parent feedback, student feedback, and portfolios.

Further investigation is warranted to understand what metrics teachers would apply to the things they deem important in the education of a child. Also, some teachers indicated the need to remove ineffective teachers, but what was lacking in the responses was how to identify ineffective teachers. Further study is needed in order to understand what criteria teachers would use to determine ineffectiveness, and whether those criteria would be similar to ones used to identify effectiveness. In addition, there is little reference in the literature to the issue of the social learning environment. The process of learning is not isolated to the relationship between the teacher and an individual student. Rather, learning is also constructed upon interaction with peers, and is a dynamic process that is also dependent upon interrelationships and interactions within and outside the classroom. Because these teachers work in an urban district that serves high percentages of minority, underprivileged, and English Language Learners, further exploration is needed how effectiveness can be measured when the challenges are compounded.

In conclusion, this study found that teachers identified many factors (e.g. institutional, teacher, parent and student level), which are outside of a teacher's control, that influence who and how they teach. Hence, the use of standardized test scores is not a valid measurement of teacher effectiveness. Most significantly, they argue for an evaluation that addresses the development of the whole child by fostering critical thinking, love of learning, and respectful citizenship, through a rich and diverse curriculum. An implicit assumption that can be made from their responses is that what VAM measures is not aligned to what teachers see as the purpose of education. This misalignment stems reform efforts in which there has been a substantial change in our purpose of education, where we have moved from the development of the individual as a basis for a democratic society, to the development of individuals as a currency for economic competitiveness. This misalignment is noteworthy for all of us, because society's definition of the purpose of education ultimately affects the type of educated citizen that is produced, and how that education is measured.

REFERENCES

Baker, E. L., Barton, P. E., Darling-Hammond, L., Haertel, E., Ladd, H. F., Linn, R. L., Ravitch, D., Rothstein, R., Shavelson, R. J., & Shepard, L. A. (2010). *Problems with the use of student test scores to evaluate teachers*. (EPI Briefing Paper #278). Washington, DC: Economic Policy Institute. Retrieved from http://www.epi.org/publications/entry/bp278

Brandt, C., Thomas, J., & Burke, M. (2008). *State Policies on Teacher Evaluation Practices in the Midwest Region. REL Technical Brief. REL 2008-No. 004:* Washington, DC: Institute for Educational Sciences.

Buddin, R. (2010). *How Effective Are Los Angeles Elementary Teachers and Schools?* Retrieved from http://documents.latimes.com/buddin-white-paper-20100908/

Felch, J., Ferrell, S., Garvey, M., Lauder, T. S., Lauter, D., Marquis, J., Pesce, A., Poindexter, S., Schwencke, K., Shuster, B., Song, J., & Smith, D. (2010). Los Angeles Teacher Ratings. *Los Angeles Times*. Available online from http://projects.latimes.com/value-added/

Hsieh, H. F. & Shannon, S. E. (2005). Three approaches to qualitative content analysis. *Qualitative Health Research* 15(9), 1277–1288

Marshall, C. & Gerstl-Pepin C. (2005). *Re-Framing Educational Politics for Social Justice*. New York: Pearson Education, Inc.

McCaffrey, D. F., Lockwood, J. R., Koretz, D. M., Hamilton, L. S. (2003). *Evaluating Value-Added Models for Teacher Accountability*. Santa Monica, CA: Rand.

Papay, J. P. (2010). Different test, different answers. The stability of teacher value-added estimates across outcome measures. *American Educational Research Journal, 48*(1), 163–193.

Rooney, P., Hussar, W., Planty, M., Choy, S., Hampden-Thompson, G., & Provasnik, S. (2006). *The Condition of Education*, 2006. NCES 2006-071. Washington, DC: National Center for Education Statistics.

Schochet, P. Z. & Chiang, H. S., National Center for Education, E., & Regional, A. (2010). *Error Rates in Measuring Teacher and School Performance Based on Student Test Score Gains. NCEE 2010-4004*. Washington, DC: National Center for Education Evaluation and Regional Assistance.

US Department of Education. (2010). *A Blueprint for Reform: The Reauthorization of the Elementary and Secondary Education Act*. Washington, DC: Author.

van de Grift, W. (2009). Reliability and validity in measuring the value added of schools. *School Effectiveness and School Improvement, 20*(2), 269–285.

Weisberg, D., Sexton, S., Mulhern, J., & Keeling, D. (2009). *The Widget Effect: Our National Failure to Acknowledge and Act on Differences in Teacher Effectiveness*. Brooklyn, NY: The New Teacher Project. Retrieved from http://widgeteffect.org

Self-Check Test Answers

Chapter 1: Using Research Evidence to Improve Educational Practice

1. b   2. d   3. a   4. d   5. c
6. b   7. b   8. a   9. d   10. c

Chapter 2: Doing Your Own Research: From Proposal to Final Report

1. b   2. d   3. a   4. c   5. a
6. b   7. d   8. c   9. a   10. d

Chapter 3: Conducting and Writing Your Own Literature Review

1. c   2. a   3. c   4. b   5. a
6. a   7. c   8. c   9. b   10. d

Chapter 4: Using Search Engines and Available Literature Reviews

1. b   2. b   3. a   4. d   5. c
6. a   7. d   8. b   9. b   10. a

Chapter 5: Analyzing and Evaluating Reports of Quantitative Research Studies

1. b   2. c   3. c   4. a   5. d
6. b   7. b   8. a   9. a   10. c

Chapter 6: Using Descriptive Statistics to Study Problems of Practice

1. b   2. d   3. b   4. c   5. a
6. b   7. d   8. a   9. c   10. d

Chapter 7: Tests of Statistical Significance

1. c   2. b   3. c   4. a   5. a
6. d   7. a   8. c   9. b   10. d

Chapter 8: The Practical Significance of Statistical Results

1. c   2. d   3. a   4. a   5. b
6. c   7. b   8. d   9. d   10. b

Chapter 9: Descriptive Research

1. c   2. c   3. a   4. c   5. b
6. b   7. c   8. c   9. d   10. a

Chapter 10: Group Comparison Research

1. b   2. d   3. d   4. c   5. b
6. d   7. a   8. c   9. a   10. c

Chapter 11: Correlational Research

1. a   2. b   3. d   4. b   5. d
6. b   7. c   8. b   9. a   10. b

Chapter 12: Experimental Research

1. c   2. c   3. c   4. d   5. a
6. b   7. d   8. c   9. a   10. b

Chapter 13: Case Studies in Qualitative Research

1. c   2. b   3. d   4. c   5. a
6. c   7. d   8. a   9. a   10. c

Chapter 14: Ethnography and Critical Research

1. a   2. d   3. a   4. b   5. a
6. d   7. d   8. c   9. b   10. b

Chapter 15: Narrative Research

1. c   2. a   3. d   4. d   5. c
6. d   7. b   8. a   9. d   10. a

Chapter 16: Historical Research

1. a   2. b   3. b   4. d   5. c
6. d   7. b   8. c   9. a   10. d

Chapter 17: Mixed-Methods Research

1. c   2. b   3. a   4. d   5. a
6. c   7. c   8. d   9. c   10. b

Chapter 18: Action Research

1. b   2. c   3. c   4. a   5. a
6. d   7. c   8. a   9. c   10. a

Chapter 19: Evaluation Research

1. c   2. b   3. c   4. a   5. d
6. a   7. c   8. d   9. d   10. c

APPENDIX 1

Guide for Outlining a Quantitative or Qualitative Research Proposal

This appendix consists of a list of items in the form of questions and directions. By completing each item, you can create an outline of a research proposal. The outline can then be elaborated into a formal research proposal.

1. Purpose of Study

A. The purpose of this study is to . . . (State the purpose succinctly in one or two sentences)

B. What previous research is your study most directly based on? (Select three to five publications that are absolutely central)

C. How does your study build on previous research?

D. How will your study contribute to educational research and practice?

2. Research Questions, Hypotheses, Variables, and Case Delineation

A. List your research questions or hypotheses.

B. If you propose to test hypotheses, describe briefly the theory from which the hypotheses were derived.

C. If your study is quantitative in nature, list the variables that you will study. For each variable, indicate whether it is an independent variable, a dependent variable, or neither.

D. If the study is qualitative in nature, describe the case features on which data collection and analysis will focus.

3. Literature Search

A. List the search engines and indexes that you will use to identify relevant publications.

B. List the keywords and descriptors that will guide your use of search engines and indexes.

C. Identify published literature reviews (if available) relating to your study.

4. Research Design

A. Describe the research design that you selected for your study: descriptive, group comparison, correlational, experimental, qualitative (case study or specific qualitative research tradition), evaluative, mixed-method, or action research.

B. If your study is quantitative in nature, what are the threats to the internal validity of your research design? (Internal validity means the extent to which extraneous variables are controlled so that observed effects can be attributed solely to the independent variable.) What will you do to minimize or avoid these threats?

C. If your study is quantitative in nature, what are the limitations to the generalizability (i.e., external validity) of the findings that will result from your research design? What will you do to maximize the generalizability of your findings?

552

D. If your study is qualitative in nature, what criteria do you consider to be relevant to judging the credibility and trustworthiness of the results that will be yielded by your research design?

5. Sampling

A. If your study is quantitative in nature, describe the characteristics of the population that you will study.

B. If your study is qualitative in nature, describe the phenomenon you wish to study and the cases that comprise instances of the phenomenon.

C. Identify your sampling procedure and sampling unit.

D. Indicate the size of your sample, and explain why that sample size is sufficient.

E. Indicate whether the sample will be formed into subgroups, and, if so, describe the characteristics of the subgroups.

F. If your study will involve the use of volunteers, explain whether their characteristics will affect the generalizability of the research findings.

6. Methods of Data Collection

A. For each of the variables that you plan to study (see 2.C), indicate whether you will measure it by a test, questionnaire, interview, observational procedure, or content analysis. Indicate whether the measure is already available or whether you will need to develop it.

B. For each measure stated above, indicate which types of validity and reliability are relevant and how you will check them.

C. If your study is qualitative in nature, indicate whether your data collection will focus on etic or emic perspectives, or both; state how you will collect data on each case feature that you have chosen for study (see 2.D); and explain the nature of your involvement in the data-collection process.

7. Data-Analysis Procedures

A. What descriptive statistics and inferential statistics, if any, will you use to analyze the data for each of your research questions or hypotheses?

B. If your study is qualitative in nature, indicate whether you will use an interpretational, structural, or reflective method of analysis.

8. Ethics and Human Relations

A. What risks, if any, does your study pose for research participants? What steps will you take to minimize these threats?

B. Will the study need to be approved by an institutional review board? If yes, describe the approval process.

C. How will you gain entry into your proposed research setting, and how will you get the cooperation of your research participants?

9. Time Line

A. Create a time line listing, in chronological order, all of the major steps of your study. Also indicate the approximate amount of time each step will take.

A P P E N D I X 2

Search Options in the ERIC Search Engine

We wrote this appendix to help you take full advantage of ERIC, the search engine most widely used by educators. Some of its capabilities are featured in other search engines, so once you know how to use them in ERIC, you will be able to take advantage of them in other search engines.

Since we updated this appendix in mid-2013, a federal shutdown of many agencies, including ERIC and its search engine, occurred in October 2013. As of January 2014, a simplified version of the search engine has reappeared, but its database does not include documents that have been published since mid-2013. Therefore, some features of ERIC described in this appendix are not currently available on ERIC's website. However, these features are available in other search engines for the ERIC database, notably, EBSCO and First Search. Therefore, in reading this appendix, keep in mind that you might not find some features at the present time, but they might become available later. Also, many of the features are available for other search engines for the education literature not associated with ERIC.

As you read the next sections, we recommend that you go to ERIC's website (eric.ed.gov) so that you can see the current search options on an actual computer screen as we describe them here.

Figure 1 shows a section of the first screen you see when you access the ERIC website. This screen, which is ERIC's home page, includes two windows, *Search Term(s):* and *Search In:*, which you can use to do what is called a *basic search* of the ERIC database of publications.

If you click on the "Advanced Search" link, you will see a new screen, part of which is shown in Figure 2. We will use the screen shown in Figure 2 to explain search options for ERIC. Once you understand these options, you will find it easier to do a basic or advanced search, whichever best serves your purpose.

To explain the search options, we show in Figure 3 an example of the bibliographic citation that ERIC provides about each publication in its database. The bibliographic citation constitutes what ERIC refers to as a *record*. We obtained this record by using the keyword phrase "questioning techniques" in an advanced search.

Drop-Down Menu for Keywords

If you look at Figure 2, you will see the phrase "Search for: Keywords (all fields)." Immediately to the right of this phrase are two tiny arrows, one pointing up and the other pointing down. These arrows indicate a drop-down menu, which you will see if you click on the phrase. The choices in the drop-down menu are Keywords (all fields), Title, Author, Descriptors (from Thesaurus), ERIC #, Source, Identifiers, ISBN, ISSN, Institution, Sponsoring Agency, and Publisher. As indicated by the following description of the drop-down choices, each one enables you to focus your search for relevant publications in a different way.

Keywords

A keyword is any word or phrase that you want ERIC to look for in its database. You can enter any keyword or key phrase in the window to the right

FIGURE 1 • ERIC Home Page

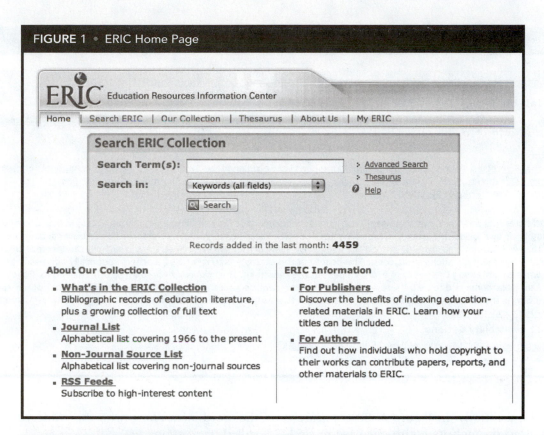

FIGURE 2 • ERIC Advanced Search Screen

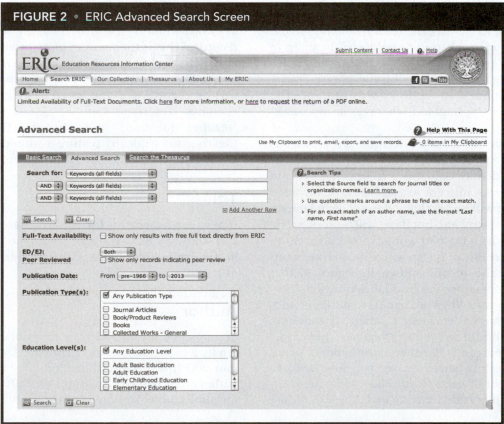

FIGURE 3 • An ERIC Bibliographic Citation

9. Asking the Right Questions: Teachers' Questions Can Build Students' English Language Skills (EJ782243)   🗑 Add

Author(s):	Hill, Jane D.; Flynn, Kathleen	**Pub Date:**	2008-00-00
Source:	Journal of Staff Development, v29 n1 p46-52 Win 2008	**Pub Type(s):**	Journal Articles; Reports - Descriptive
		Peer-Reviewed:	Yes

Descriptors:
Educational Strategies; Action Research; Second Language Learning; Language Skills; English (Second Language); English Instruction; Questioning Techniques; Limited English Speaking; Mainstreaming; Classroom Environment; Faculty Development; Teacher Role; Teaching Methods

Abstract:
This article presents an instructional strategy that helps teachers engage English language learners (ELLs) in learning, thus increasing their own belief that they can effectively teach English language learners, and proposes a professional development activity that will cement this strategy in teachers' minds. By using an action research strategy, teachers can increase their skills in targeting classroom questions to students. The beauty of this strategy is that it helps teachers specifically address the needs of ELLs while also meeting the needs of every student in the classroom. It allows teachers to integrate learning for ELLs in mainstream classrooms and to help these students achieve academic success at the same levels as their native English-speaking peers. Finally, it shows teachers one direction for creating a supportive environment for English language learners. (Contains 1 table.) ▲ Hide Full Abstract

Full-Text Availability Options:
Not available from ERIC | Find in a Library | Publisher's Web Site

of this item, as shown in Figure 2. ERIC's search engine will go through its entire database to find any record that contains this word or phrase in the text of any of its fields. (The term *field* refers to the information adjacent to each boldfaced heading in the record.) For example, we retrieved the record shown in Figure 3 by entering the phrase "questioning techniques" in the Keywords window. The phrase will be highlighted wherever it appears in the record.

If you put quotation marks around a phrase, as we did for "questioning techniques," the search engine will identify only those records that contain those two terms adjacent to each other. Each word in the phrase will be highlighted in yellow wherever it appears in the record, but there will be at least one instance in which the two words appear adjacent to each other in the order specified in the keyword window. In the record shown in Figure 3, that instance occurs under the field labeled Descriptors.

Suppose your keyword can have different endings. For example, consider teachers' questioning practices. Should we enter "teacher question," "teacher questions," "teacher questioning," or all three phrases? In such a case, we only need to enter the stem of each word followed by an asterisk (*), which is called a *wildcard*. The use of just

the word stem along with the wildcard sign (*) is called *truncation*.

When we entered "teacher questions" in the keyword window, the search engine retrieved 173 records. (This is the number of records for a search conducted in August 2013; ERIC content keeps increasing, so you are likely to obtain a larger number of records for the same search and other searches described below.) When we entered "teacher question*" it retrieved 1,108 records. Clearly, the wildcard feature resulted in a more comprehensive set of potentially useful records.

Title

If you are searching for a particular publication and know its title, you can select the Title option in the drop-down menu. You can enter all or part of the title.

Author

Perhaps you wish to identify all publications written by a particular author. Using the Author option, you will find these publications if you enter the author's last name (e.g., Brophy). ERIC will search for publications written by anyone whose last name is Brophy. If you wish to search for publications by a particular Brophy, for example, Jere Brophy, you can enter "Brophy, Jere" and select the Author option.

ERIC

This is a unique number that the ERIC staff assigns to the record for each publication in the database. The prefix for each ERIC # is either EJ, which indicates that the publication is a journal article (ERIC Journal), or ED (ERIC Document), which indicates that it is some other kind of publication.

Other Options in the Keyword Drop-Down Menu

You can click on the "Learn more" link in the "Search Tips" box of the Advanced Search screen to learn the meaning of the other search options of the keyword drop-down menu: Source, Identifiers, ISBN, ISSN, Institution, Sponsoring Agency, and Publisher.

Drop-Down Menu for Connectors

Look at Figure 2, and you will see three keyword drop-down menus. Next to two of them are two other drop-down menus labeled *AND*. The AND drop-down menu is an important aid for focusing your research. It includes three options: AND, OR, and NOT (OR and NOT are not shown in Figure 4.2.) These options sometimes are called *connectors* or *Boolean operators*, because they derive from a branch of mathematics known as Boolean logic. In the case of ERIC, a connector examines the relationship between two or more sets of publication records in the database.

To illustrate, we will continue to use the example of teachers' questioning practices. We retrieved 1,108 records when we entered *"teacher question**"* in the window for the first keyword drop-down menu. Suppose we wish to focus only on publications relating to teachers' questioning practices in mathematics education. Now, if we enter *"teacher question**"* as a keyword in the first window and *"mathematics instruction"* as a keyword in the second window, using AND as the connector, we retrieve 60 records. An AND connector identifies all publications in a database that have both keywords or both descriptors.

Suppose we are interested in publications about either teachers' questioning practices or discussion groups. We can search for these publications by using the OR connector. We enter the keyword "questioning techniques" in the first window and the keyword "discussion group" in the second window, selecting OR as the connector. The search retrieves 1,624 records. Use of the OR connector almost invariably will retrieve more records than an AND connector, because an AND connector requires that a publication record include both keywords. However, an OR connector requires only that a publication include one of the two keywords in the publication record.

The **NOT connector** in the pull-down menu is used when you wish to exclude a set of published records having a characteristic that is not relevant to your literature review. For example, suppose we are interested in teachers' questioning techniques during classroom instruction. Our search of the ERIC database using the keyword *"questioning techniques"* yields 5,345 records. As we examine the records, we find that some of them are about questions on tests, not questions asked during classroom interaction between teacher and students.

To exclude the records involving test questions, we redo the search by entering the keyword *"questioning techniques"* in one window, entering *test*** as a keyword in another window, and selecting NOT as the connector to the left of the second window. This search yields 4,381 results that are more relevant to our interests.

If you examine Figure 2, you will see a label "Add Another Row." By clicking on this label, you can add other keywords (or another option in the drop-down menu) and other connectors.

OTHER ADVANCED SEARCH OPTIONS IN ERIC

In the preceding section, we described some of the most important ways in which the advanced search option in ERIC allows you to define and focus your literature search. If you examine Figure 2, you will see additional search options, such as Publication Type(s) and Education Level(s). These options generally will not help you define the range of topics (as expressed by keywords) that your literature review will encompass, but they can help you limit your search to a manageable, but relevant, set of publication records.

Full-Text Availability

ERIC makes available at no cost the full text of some of the publications that are stored in its database. Full-text availability is shown on a line near the middle of Figure 2. If the full text is available, you can view it as a pdf document on your computer and save it as a pdf, a "portable document file" that can be opened by free software called Adobe Acrobat, in case you wish to view it again later or print a copy.

Publication Date

The vast majority of the documents in the ERIC database were published between 1966 and the present. You might find a small number published prior to 1966, depending on your topic. If you want to search for older literature, we advise you to go to the website, "Education Index Retrospective: 1929–1983." If your research problem has a psychological aspect, you can try using the search function at "PsycInfo," a website maintained by the American Psychological Association that includes publications dating back to the 1800s in its database.

In general, we recommend that you start your literature search in ERIC by going back two years at a time for ten years, and then perhaps five years at a time for older publications. By starting with the two most recent years, you can usually get a manageable number of records to review. Reading the abstracts for these records (a sample abstract is shown in Figure 3) will give you a sense of recent knowledge and practice on your topic of interest. Then you can select a few of the most relevant records and read the complete journal article or other type of publication. These publications are likely to include a review of the literature, which will give you a sense of the knowledge that has accumulated over time and its significance from the perspective of the author.

You can continue repeating this process two years at a time, using the Publication Date field (see Figure 2). By the time you have gone back 10 years, you should have a good sense of the way that knowledge about your topic of interest has developed and what the current state of knowledge is. You will also have a sense of who the leading

experts are based on the number and quality of their own publications and other publications in which they've been cited.

Publication Types and Education Levels

Figure 2 demonstrates that you can limit your ERIC search to certain types of publications and education levels. The default option, as you can see, is *Any Publication Type(s)* and *Any Education Level(s)*. These options are appropriate if you wish to do a comprehensive literature review. However, if you have a limited focus, you can use other options to exclude nonrelevant records and thereby save time.

Figure 2 shows only a limited number of options in the drop-down menus for *Publication Type(s)* and *Education Level(s)*. You will see that there are many other options in the drop-down menus by exploring ERIC's website.

Citation Pearl Growing

Suppose that the journal article cited in Figure 3 is directly relevant to your literature review. In this case, you would likely want to find other publications similar to it. A process to help you do this, called "citation pearl growing," uses a relevant article (the "pearl") to search for other relevant publications. One way to "grow" the pearl would be to examine the reference list for the article cited in Figure 3. At least some of these articles should be relevant to your topic.

Another way to "grow" the pearl is to examine the bibliographic citation for the article. The ERIC citation shown in Figure 3 includes 13 descriptors. A descriptor is a particular type of keyword tied to the ERIC thesaurus, which, at the time of this writing, is not available. However, you can use descriptors as keywords when searching for publications. You can select the most relevant descriptors and then conduct ERIC searches using each of these descriptors as the "Search for:" term in the advanced search window (see Figure 2). Because your "pearl" article (the article cited in Figure 3) was classified by the descriptor selected, it might well be that other relevant articles in the ERIC database were classified by the same descriptor.

Still another way to "grow" the pearl is to use the search function found on the website, "Web of Science," described in Chapter 4. It will look for other publications that have included the article cited in Figure 3 in their reference list. If another publication cited our "pearl" article in its reference list, the authors of that publication considered the article to be relevant to their research problem or problem of practice. Thus, the publication is likely to be relevant to our interest in questioning techniques.

Part of the rationale for citation pearl growing is that researchers and educators who are strongly interested in a particular problem of practice are likely to begin communicating with each other and reading each other's publications. Consequently, they will start citing each other's publications in their own writings. If you can find one relevant publication within this emerging community, you can use pearl growing as a strategy to find other relevant publications within the community.

KEEPING TRACK OF YOUR SEARCH

In reality, the search for relevant publications for a literature review is a trial-and-error process. In performing a search on ERIC, you might try different keywords, thesaurus descriptors, if available, connectors, and publication-year intervals until you find the ones that retrieve relevant publications. Also, you might end up using several different search engines, each in a different way.

The number of searches can increase rapidly, and it will be difficult to remember all of them. Consequently, you might repeat searches needlessly, wasting valuable time. Therefore, we recommend that you keep a log of your searches, noting such details as (1) the date you conducted the search; (2) the name of the search engine; (3) keywords,

descriptors, and connectors that defined the search; (4) additional limits on the search, such as publication type, education level, and publication-year interval; and (5) the number of publication records yielded by the search. It takes just a few minutes to enter this information for each search, but doing so can save hours later.

A good report of a literature review will include information about the search procedure so that readers can evaluate its soundness. If you have kept a detailed log of your searches, it will be easy to report this information.

FINDING THE FULL TEXT FOR A CITATION

You will note at the bottom of Figure 3 that an ERIC record helps you locate the publication (also called "full text") that it cites. The three aids are:

1. *Help Finding Full Text.* Some of the publications referenced in the ERIC database are available directly from ERIC. If that is the case, the first clickable button will state, "ERIC Full Text." Clicking that typically will show the complete publication as a pdf file.

2. *Find in a Library.* Clicking on this button will take you to screens with a list of libraries and online sources that have the publication.

3. *Publisher's Website.* This will take you to the website, if there is one, of the publisher of the document cited in the ERIC record. The website might give you additional information about the publication, including information about how to secure a copy of it.

APPENDIX 3

Questions to Ask Yourself When Evaluating a Report of a Quantitative Study

---

The following questions can help you evaluate each section of a quantitative research report. For each question, we indicate the type of information that you will need to identify in your report to answer the question, and we provide a sample answer. The examples are drawn from our experience in evaluating quantitative research studies.

Quantitative studies encompass various research designs. For design-specific questions to use in evaluating quantitative studies, see Appendix 5.

INTRODUCTORY SECTION

1. Are the research problems, methods, and findings appropriate given the researchers' institutional affiliations, beliefs, values, or theoretical orientation?

   Information needed. The researchers' institutional affiliation often is given beneath the title of a published research report, or it might appear at the end of the report or at the end of the journal in which the report appears. Also look for any information in the report that indicates the researchers' beliefs, values, or theoretical orientation with respect to education and how that affected their research.

   Example. Most of the researchers' prior work has focused on cognitive models

of learning. Therefore, they designed their research to show the advantages of cognitively oriented teaching methods compared to behaviorally oriented teaching methods.

2. Do the researchers demonstrate any favorable or unfavorable bias in describing the subject of the study (e.g., the instructional method, program, curriculum, etc. that was investigated)?

   Information needed. Identify any adjectives or other words that describe an instructional method, program, curriculum, and so forth in clearly positive or negative terms.

   Example. The researchers described the group of children who served as research participants as difficult to handle, unmotivated, and disorganized. No evidence was presented to support this characterization. In the absence of evidence, this description might indicate a negative attitude toward the children who were studied.

3. Is the literature review section of the report sufficiently comprehensive, and does it include studies that you know to be relevant to the problem?

   Information needed. Examine the studies mentioned in the report. Note particularly if a recent review of the literature relevant to the research problem was cited or if the researchers mentioned an effort to make their own review comprehensive.

Example. The researchers stated the main conclusions of a previously published comprehensive literature review on the instructional program that they intended to study. They demonstrated clearly how their study built on the findings and recommendations of this review.

4. Is each variable in the study clearly defined?

Information needed. Identify all of the variables (also called *constructs*) that were studied. For each variable, determine if and how it is defined in the report.

Example. One of the variables studied is intrinsic motivation, which is defined in the report as the desire to learn because it increases self-esteem. This definition is not consistent with other definitions in the research literature, which state that intrinsic motivation is the desire to learn because of the satisfaction that comes from the act of learning and from the content being learned.

5. Is the measure of each variable consistent with how the variable was defined?

Information needed. Identify how each variable in the study was measured.

Example. The researchers studied self-esteem but did not define it. Therefore, it was not possible to determine whether their measure of self-esteem was consistent with their definition.

6. Are the research hypotheses, questions, or objectives explicitly stated, and, if so, are they clear?

Information needed. Examine each research hypothesis, question, or objective stated in the report.

Example. The researcher stated one general objective for the study. It was clearly stated, but it did not provide sufficient information concerning the specific variables that were to be studied.

7. Do the researchers make a convincing case that a research hypothesis, question, or objective was important to study?

Information needed. Examine the researchers' rationale for each hypothesis, question, or objective.

Example. The researchers showed how the hypothesis to be tested was derived from a specific theory. They also showed that if the hypothesis was confirmed by the study, it would add support to the validity of the theory, which currently is being used to guide the design of new reading curricula.

METHOD SECTION

8. Did the sampling procedures produce a sample that is representative of an identifiable population or that is generalizable to your local population?

Information needed. Identify the procedures the researchers used to select their sample.

Example. The researchers selected several classes (not randomly) from one school. The only information given about the students was their average ability and gender distribution. We cannot tell from this description whether the sample is similar to students in our schools.

9. Did the researchers form subgroups to increase understanding of the phenomena being studied?

Information needed. Determine whether the sample was divided into subgroups and, if so, why.

Example. The researchers showed the effects of the instructional program for both boys and girls; this information was helpful. However, they did not show the effects for different ethnic subgroups. This is an oversight, because the program might have a cultural bias that could have an adverse effect on some ethnic subgroups.

10. Is each measure appropriate for the sample?

Information needed. Determine whether the researchers reported the population for whom the measure was developed.

Example. The ABC Reading Test was developed 20 years ago for primary grade students. The current study also involves primary grade students, but the test may no longer be valid because students and the reading curriculum have changed considerably over the past 20 years.

11. Is each measure in the study sufficiently valid for its intended purpose?

    Information needed. Examine any evidence that the researchers presented to demonstrate the validity of each measure in the study.

    Example. The XYZ Test was used because it purportedly predicts success in vocational education programs. However, the researchers presented evidence from only one study to support this claim, and it involved a vocational education program that was quite different from the one they investigated.

12. Is each measure in the study sufficiently reliable for its intended purpose?

    Information needed. Examine any evidence that the researchers presented to demonstrate the reliability of each measure in the study.

    Example. The researchers had observers rate each student's on-task behavior during Spanish instruction in a sample of 30 classrooms. Inter-rater reliability was checked by having pairs of observers use the rating system in the same five classrooms. The pairs typically agreed on 90 percent of their ratings, which indicates good reliability.

13. If any qualitative data were collected, were they analyzed in a manner that contributed to the soundness of the overall research design?

    Information needed. Determine whether the researchers reported qualitative information about the research participants, procedures, or findings.

    Example. In seeking to explain the absence of differences between the experimental and control groups' classroom behavior, the researchers mentioned information shared by the students' teacher that students in the control group classroom had reacted positively to the observer's presence.

14. Were the research procedures appropriate and clearly stated so that others could replicate them if they wished to do so?

    Information needed. Identify the various research procedures that were used in the study and the order in which they occurred.

    Example. The researchers administered three types of pretests during one class period the day before the experimental curriculum was introduced. The pretests, though brief, might have overwhelmed the students so that they could not do their best work. Also, some aspects of the experimental curriculum (e.g., the types of seatwork activities) were not clearly described in the research report, and the researchers did not indicate how soon the posttests were administered after the curriculum was completed.

RESULTS SECTION

15. Were appropriate statistical techniques used, and were they used correctly?

    Information needed. Identify the statistical techniques described in the report.

    Example. The researchers calculated the mean score for students' performance on the five tests that were administered. However, they did not give the range of scores (i.e., lowest score and highest score). This would be helpful information, because they studied a highly heterogeneous group of students. Also, the researchers did not compute a confidence interval for each mean.

16. Was the practical significance of statistical results considered?

    Information needed. Look for the presence of effect-size statistics or interpretation of descriptive statistics in terms of normative standards.

    Example. The researchers found a difference between the mean scores of the experimental and control groups on a measure of science achievement. They computed an effect-size statistic to determine the percentile of the average student in the experimental group relative to the score distribution of students in the control group.

DISCUSSION SECTION

17. Do the results of the data analyses support what the researchers conclude are the findings of the study?

    Information needed. Identify what the researchers considered to be the major findings of the study.

    Example. The researchers concluded that the experimental treatment led to superior learning compared to the control treatment, but this claim was true for only two of the four criterion measures used to measure the effects of the treatments.

18. Did the researchers provide reasonable explanations of the findings?

    Information needed. Identify how the researchers explained the findings of the study and whether alternative explanations were considered.

    Example. The researchers concluded that the narrative version of the textbook was less effective than the traditional expository version. Their explanation was that the story in the narrative version motivated students to keep reading, but that it also distracted them from focusing on the factual information that was included in the test. They presented no evidence to support this explanation, although it seems plausible.

19. Did the researchers relate the findings to a particular theory or body of related research?

    Information needed. Identify any theory or body of related research to which the researchers refer in discussing their findings.

    Example. The researchers discussed the conceptual implications of their findings in relation to theories about the effect of reinforcement on learning and task performance.

20. Did the researchers identify sound implications for practice from their findings?

    Information needed. Identify any implications for practice that the researchers identified from their findings.

    Example. The researchers claimed that teachers' morale would be higher if administrators would provide more self-directed staff development. However, this recommendation is based only on their questionnaire finding that teachers expressed a desire for more self-directed staff development. The researchers are not justified in using just this bit of data to claim that teachers' morale will improve if they get the kind of staff development they prefer. This type of claim requires evidence from experiments.

21. Did the researchers suggest further research to build on their results or to answer questions that were raised by their findings?

    Information needed. Identify any suggestions the researchers make for further study of the topic and the questions that such study might answer.

    Example. The researchers noted that students showed greater levels of problem behavior during the reversal phase of the single-case experiment than during the baseline phase. They recommended further research to explore the conditions under which such "post-reversal intensification" tends to occur.

APPENDIX 4

Questions to Ask Yourself When Evaluating a Report of a Qualitative Study

The following questions can help you evaluate each section of a qualitative research report. For each question, we indicate the type of information that you will need to identify in the report to answer the question, and we provide a sample answer. The examples are drawn from our experience in evaluating qualitative research studies.

Qualitative studies encompass various research designs. For design-specific questions to use in evaluating qualitative studies, see Appendix 4.

INTRODUCTORY SECTION

1. Are the research problems and methods appropriate given the researchers' institutional affiliations, beliefs, values, or theoretical orientation?

   Information needed. The researchers' institutional affiliation is often given beneath the title of a published research report, or it might be at the end of the report or at the end of the journal in which the report appears. Also, look for any information in the report that indicates the researchers' beliefs, values, or theoretical orientation with respect to education and how that affected their research.

   Example. The researchers taught in inner-city schools for many years before doing this

study. This experience would give them knowledge of the issues facing inner-city students and teachers.

2. Do the researchers demonstrate any favorable or unfavorable bias in describing the subject of the study (e.g., the instructional method, program, curriculum, etc. that was investigated)?

   Information needed. Identify any adjectives or other words that describe an instructional method, program, curriculum, and so forth in clearly positive or negative terms.

   Example. The researchers used a qualitative research method known as *educational connoisseurship and criticism* to study a high school football team. This method is inherently evaluative, so it is no surprise that the researchers made many judgments—both positive and negative—about the impact of the team on individual players.

3. Is the literature review section of the report sufficiently comprehensive? Does it include studies that you know to be relevant to the problem?

   Information needed. Examine the studies mentioned in the report. Note particularly if a recent review of the literature relevant to the research problem was cited or if the researchers described their efforts to make their own review comprehensive.

Example. The researchers completed their literature search prior to beginning data collection. This procedure is not desirable in qualitative research because questions and hypotheses are bound to arise as the data are collected. They should have done an ongoing literature search to discover what other researchers have found concerning the emerging questions and hypotheses.

RESEARCH PROCEDURES

4. Did the sampling procedure result in a case or cases that were particularly interesting and from which much could be learned about the phenomena of interest?

   Information needed. Identify the type of purposeful sampling the researchers used to select their sample.

   Example. The researchers used intensity sampling to select a high school principal who had received several awards and widespread recognition for "turning her school around." She was a good case to study given the researchers' interest in administrators' instructional leadership.

5. Were the data-collection methods used in the research appropriate for the phenomena that the researchers wanted to explore?

   Information needed. Examine any evidence that the researchers presented to demonstrate the soundness of their data-collection methods.

   Example. The researchers' primary data-collection method was participant observation. Several quotations suggest that they were accepted as honorary members of the groups they observed. Thus, it appears that they had good access to the kinds of events and behavior about which they wanted to collect data.

6. Was there sufficient intensity of data collection?

   Information needed. Identify the time period over which an individual, setting, or event was observed and whether the observation was continuous or fragmented. If documents were analyzed, identify how extensive the search for documents was and how closely

the documents were analyzed. If interviews were conducted, did the researchers build sufficient rapport with field participants before asking in-depth questions, and did they continue exploring sensitive topics in subsequent interviews in order to check their data?

Example. The researchers' goal was to learn how elementary school teachers established classroom routines and discipline procedures at the beginning of the school year. They observed each teacher every day for the first three weeks. This is a good procedure. They assumed, however, that routines and discipline procedures would be explained at the start of the school day, and so they observed only the first hour of class time. The validity of this assumption is questionable.

7. Were the data collected in such a way as to ensure a reflection of the field participants' emic perspective?

   Information needed. Examine any information that the researchers presented to demonstrate that they sought to reflect the emic perspective of field participants.

   Example. The researchers wished to learn about children's views of preschool but noted that children in the culture they studied often become uncomfortable when adults asked them questions in a formal setting. The researchers made the children more comfortable by setting up a playlike environment and asking questions unobtrusively as the interviewer and children played.

8. Did the researchers triangulate their data sources and data-collection methods to test the soundness of the findings?

   Information needed. Examine such information as whether the data obtained from two or more data-collection methods were compared for evidence of confirmation or of meaningful discrepancies.

   Example. The researcher obtained both observational data on students' self-references when they were with their peers and interview data about students' self-perceptions from one-on-one conversations with the researcher.

9. Were the research procedures appropriate and clearly stated so that others could replicate them if they wanted to?

   Information needed. Identify the various research procedures that were used in the study and the order in which they occurred.

   Example. The researchers' main data-collection procedure was to ask students questions as they attempted to solve mathematics problems. The problems and questions are available upon request, so it seems that the study could be replicated.

RESEARCH FINDINGS

10. Did the report include a thick description that gives a thorough sense of how various individuals responded to the interview questions and how they behaved?

    Information needed. Identify the amount of vivid detail that is included about what the individuals being studied actually did or said.

    Example. The researchers identified 10 issues that mentor-teachers faced in working with beginning teachers. Unfortunately, the issues were described in rather meager detail, with no examples of what they looked like in practice.

11. Was the research report written in a style that brings to life the phenomenon being studied?

    Information needed. Identify any use of visual or literary structures (e.g., drawings, use of similes or metaphors) or unusual genres (e.g., poetry, songs, storytelling) that are meant to convey the unique perspective of individuals in the field.

    Example. The historical research report included photographs to convey what one-room schools and their teacher and students looked like at the turn of the century. A typical school song of the period was included, as well as a harrowing newspaper account of a boy who became lost in the woods while on his way to school during the winter.

12. In summarizing the findings, did the report present any specific questions or hypotheses that emerged from the data that were collected?

    Information needed. Identify each research hypothesis or question that is stated in the report and how they are based on the study data.

    Example. The researchers focused almost entirely on writing a narrative account of the events leading up to the teachers' strike. There was no attempt to develop hypotheses about why these events happened, which could be tested in subsequent research.

13. If any quantitative data were collected, were they described and analyzed appropriately?

    Information needed. Identify any quantitative data in the report.

    Example. The researchers studied three teachers' aides and made such comments as "They spent most of their time helping individual children and passing out or collecting papers." Time is easily quantified, so the researchers could have collected some time data and reported means and standard deviations.

14. Did the researchers establish a strong chain of evidence?

    Information needed. Identify information in the report that explains the researchers' reasoning with respect to their decisions from the beginning to the end of the study.

    Example. The researchers wanted to study how recent immigrants adapted to the manner in which students interact with each other in inner-city high schools. They trained high school students from each immigrant culture to collect observational and interview data. They explained that they chose this method of data collection because they assumed the students would be able to obtain more valid data than adult researchers could obtain. This explanation seems reasonable, and therefore it contributes to the chain of evidence supporting the soundness of the study's findings.

15. Did the researchers use member checking to ensure that the information they presented about field participants was accurate and reflected the field participants' perceptions?

    Information needed. Identify information indicating that the researchers asked individuals to review statements in drafts of the researchers' report for accuracy and completeness.

Example. The researchers asked several members of each of the groups they studied—students, teachers, and parents—to review drafts of the report. An individual who spent considerable time on that task and provided helpful feedback was listed as one of the report authors.

DISCUSSION

16. Did the researchers reflect on their own values and perspectives and how these might have influenced the study outcomes and describe steps that were taken to minimize their effect?

    Information needed. Look for information in which the researchers describe their own thoughts or feelings about the phenomenon being investigated and how they took their personal reactions into account in collecting and analyzing the data.

    Example. The report referred to a discussion among the researchers about their personal disappointment at the ways some students treated other students during the research observations. It noted the researchers' agreement to behave in a respectful and friendly manner toward every individual in the field and then to journal about their personal feelings after each field session.

17. Were multiple sources of evidence used to support the researchers' conclusions?

    Information needed. Identify the researchers' conclusions and how each of them was supported by the data analyses.

    Example. The researchers concluded that textbook adoption committees were frustrated by the paucity of written information provided by publishers and their inability to question the publishers' representatives in person. This frustration was documented by analysis of interviews with selected members of the textbook adoption committees, field notes made by the researchers during committee meetings, and letters written by the chair of the committee to the director of textbook adoption in the state department of education.

18. Did the researchers provide reasonable explanations of the findings?

    Information needed. Identify how the researchers explained the findings of the study and whether alternative explanations were considered.

    Example. The researchers found that peer coaching did not work at the school they studied, and they attributed its failure to the lack of a supportive context, especially the lack of a history of collegiality among the teaching staff. Another plausible explanation, which they did not consider, is that the teachers received inadequate preparation in peer coaching.

19. Was the generalizability of the findings appropriately qualified?

    Information needed. Identify whether the researchers made any statements about the generalizability of their findings. If claims of generalizability were made, were they appropriate?

    Example. The researchers made no claims that the results of their case study could be generalized to anyone other than the teacher who was studied. It is unfortunate that they did not discuss generalizability, because the findings have significant implications for practice, if in fact they apply to other teachers. There are not enough data about the teacher's professional education for readers to generalize on their own.

20. Did the researchers identify reasonable implications for practice from their findings?

    Information needed. Identify any implications for practice that the researchers drew from their findings.

    Example. The researchers found that students who volunteer for community service derive many benefits from the experience. Therefore, they encourage educators to support community service programs for their students. This recommendation seems well grounded in their findings about the benefits of community service that students in their study received.

APPENDIX 5

Design-Specific Questions to Ask Yourself When Evaluating a Research Report

---

Appendix 3 lists questions that will help you evaluate any report of a quantitative study. Appendix 4 is similar, except that it applies to reports of qualitative studies. In this appendix, we list additional questions that apply to evaluating the specific research design used in a study. Most of the questions are drawn from the chapters in which each research design is discussed.

Descriptive Research Studies (Chapter 9)

- If the researchers generalize their findings from a sample to a population, have they taken steps to ensure that these generalizations are justified?
- If the sample was randomly drawn from a population, did the researchers present a measure of sampling error for their statistical results?
- Did the researchers develop their questionnaire, interview, or observation schedule by doing a pilot study?
- Did the researchers include relevant, clearly stated items in their measures?

Group Comparison Research (Chapter 10)

- Did the researchers specify a cause-and-effect model that links their variables?
- Are the comparison groups similar in all respects except for the variable on which they were selected to differ?

- Did the researchers draw tentative, rather than definitive, conclusions about whether observed relationships between independent and dependent variables are causal in nature?

Correlational Research (Chapter 11)

- Did the researchers specify a cause-and-effect model that links their variables?
- Were the researchers' conclusions about possible causal relationships expressed in tentative, exploratory language rather than as definite claims?

Group Experiments (Chapter 12)

- Did the researchers randomly assign the sample to the experimental and control conditions?
- Did the researchers check for attrition of research participants over the course of the experiment?
- Did the researchers check for threats to the internal and external validity of the experiment?
- Did the research participants follow the researchers' specifications for the experimental intervention or control conditions?
- Was the intervention sufficiently strong?

Single-Case Experiments (Chapter 12)

- Did the experiment contain sufficient data points?
- Did the experiment include a control condition?

Case Studies (Chapter 13)

- Is the study useful in the sense of being relevant to problems of practice?
- Is the emic perspective of the research participants represented in the report?
- Are quantitative data used, when relevant, to support qualitative observations?
- Did the researchers observe the case over a sufficiently long period of time?
- If data were coded, did the researchers check the reliability of the coding?
- Did the research participants check the report for accuracy and completeness?
- Did the researchers check whether the findings were supported by different data-collection methods, data sources, analysts, and theories?
- Did the researcher provide an in-depth description of the history, setting, participants, and culture within which the case was situated?
- Are the research questions, data, data analyses, and findings clearly and meaningfully related to each other?
- Do the researchers state personal assumptions, values, theoretical orientations, and biases that influenced their approach to the case study?

Ethnography and Critical Research (Chapter 14)

- Does the report include an emic perspective?
- Does the report include an etic perspective?

Narrative Research (Chapter 15)

- Did the researcher elicit sufficient detail about the participants' stories?
- Does the researcher provide a credible interpretation of the story?

Historical Research (Chapter 16)

- Does the report refer to primary sources?
- Does the report refer to the use of external criticism of primary sources?

- Does the report refer to the use of internal criticism to check the accuracy of statements made in historical sources?
- Do the historian's interpretations reflect bias?
- Does the report include credible causal inferences?
- Does the historian overgeneralize from the evidence presented in the report?
- Does the historian use educational concepts in an appropriate manner?

Mixed-Methods Research (Chapter 17)

- Did the researchers use both quantitative and qualitative methods in their study?
- Did the researchers combine quantitative and qualitative methods so that they shed more light on the research problem than either method would have alone?

Action Research (Chapter 18)

- Do the researchers state actions that occurred to solve the problem that prompted the study?
- Do the researchers validate their findings by triangulating them using multiple perspectives or data sources?
- Do the researchers explain how the study contributed to their professional development?
- Did the researchers collaborate with all of the individuals who have a stake in the problem being investigated?
- Do the researchers state how the project energized the participants so that they became open to new viewpoints about their work?
- Did the researchers engage in a dialogue with their peers in framing their findings and interpretations?

Evaluation Research (Chapter 19)

- Was the study informative, timely, and useful for the stakeholders?
- Was the evaluation design appropriate to the setting in which the study was conducted?
- Was the evaluation design cost-effective?
- Was the evaluation study conducted legally and ethically?
- Did the evaluation study produce valid, reliable, and comprehensive information for making judgments about the evaluated program's worth?

Glossary

A-B-A-B research design a single-case experiment in which researchers institute a baseline condition (*A*), administer the treatment (condition *B*), reinstate the baseline condition (the second *A*), and readminister the treatment (the second *B*), while measuring the target behavior repeatedly during all conditions.

A-B-A research design a single-case experiment in which researchers institute a baseline condition (*A*), administer the treatment (condition *B*), and reinstate the baseline condition (the second *A*), while measuring the target behavior repeatedly during all conditions.

abstract a brief summary of the information contained in a publication, usually written either by the author or an indexer for a search engine.

accessible population a population from which it is feasible to draw a sample.

action research (also called *insider research*, *participatory action research*, *practitioner research*, *self-study research*, *teacher research*) research that is carried out by practitioners, usually in their own workplace, to improve their professional practice.

action science in action research, the use of the theory of action to help professionals discover and address discrepancies between their espoused theories about how they work and their theories-in-action, which are the theories underlying their actual work behavior.

Adequate Yearly Progress (AYP) in the No Child Left Behind Act, a measure of whether schools are making sufficient gains each year toward the end goal of having all students in a school achieve proficiency on standardized tests of mathematics and reading.

age equivalent a score that represents a given raw score on a measure as the average age of the individuals in a norming group who earned that score.

agency in qualitative research, individuals' assumed ability to shape the conditions of their lives.

analysis of covariance a statistical procedure for determining whether the difference between the mean scores of two or more groups on a measure is statistically significant, after adjusting for initial differences between the groups on one or more pretests.

analysis of variance a statistical procedure for determining whether the difference between the mean scores of two or more groups on a measure is statistically significant.

AND connector a search engine feature that enables the user to identify only those bibliographic citations in a database that include both of two keywords.

anti-oppressive education an approach to educational inquiry and practice that involves questioning traditional educational practices in order to expose and correct underlying forms of cultural oppression maintained by such practices.

APA Presidential Task Force on Evidence-Based Practice a commission established by the American Psychological Association to determine research-based and expertise-based standards for psychologists to use in their professional practice.

applicability in case study research, an individual's judgment that a study's findings can be used to inform a problem of practice in other settings or to test a theory.

applied research research that is designed to yield findings that can be used directly to improve practice.

archive (also called *repository*) a facility for storing documents to preserve them in good condition and control access to them.

artifact see *relic*.

artificial dichotomy a variable that has only two values, both of them created by researchers or others.

attrition (also called *experimental mortality*) in experiments, the loss of research participants over the course of the experimental treatment.

audit trail a detailed record of a researcher's procedures so that other researchers can check the soundness of the study's methodology or use it to replicate the study.

bar graph a graphical display that shows the variability in a sample's scores on a variable through the use of a set of rectangles, with one side of each rectangle representing a particular score for the variable and the other side representing the number of cases in the sample that have this score.

baseline condition (also called the *A condition*) in single-case experiments, a period of time during which the individual's behavior is observed under natural conditions.

basic research research that is designed to understand processes and structures that underlie observed behavior.

behavior analysis in single-case experiments, a procedure for careful observation of an individual in a setting, typically for the purpose of determining dysfunctional behaviors and specifying desired behaviors.

behavior modification in single-case experiments, the use of techniques such as reinforcement, modeling, and discrimination training to increase or decrease the frequency of specified behaviors.

bell-shaped curve   see *normal probability distribution*.

bias   a mental set to perceive events in such a way that certain types of facts are habitually overlooked, distorted, or falsified.

bibliographic citation   a brief description of a publication that typically states its author, title, publisher, publication date, page numbers if an article or book chapter, and a brief abstract.

bibliographic index   a hard-copy guide to the literature at a specific location, such as a library or archive

bivariate correlational statistic   a statistic that describes the magnitude of the relationship between a sample's scores on two measures.

border pedagogy   in critical theory, an approach to educational practice that conceives the differences between individuals and ethnic groups as permeable and changing, as opposed to the more rigid, either/or nature of conventional social categories.

canonical correlation   a type of multiple regression analysis that uses a sample's scores on two or more measures to predict a composite of their scores on two or more criterion measures.

case   in qualitative research, a particular instance of a phenomenon, bounded in time and place, that is selected for study.

case focus   those aspects of the phenomenon on which data collection and analysis will concentrate.

case story   a description of a series of events that is meant to be informative and entertaining, but without evidence for its validity or applicability to other settings.

case study   a type of qualitative investigation that typically involves an in-depth study of instances of a phenomenon in its natural context, both from the participants' and researchers' perspective, and with concern for the validity and applicability of the findings.

catalytic validity   in action research, a judgment about the extent to which an action research project reorients, focuses, and energizes participants so that they become open to a transformed view of reality in relation to their practice.

categorical scale   (also called *nominal scale*) a measure whose values are categories that have the properties of being mutually exclusive and not orderable.

causal-comparative research   see *group comparison research*.

causal pattern   in case-study research, a systematic relationship that is observed between particular phenomena within a case or across cases and that is presumed to be causal.

causal relationship   (also called *cause-and-effect relationship*) in quantitative research, a hypothesis or empirical demonstration that one variable, which is the assumed cause and is measured at a certain point in

time, has an influence on another variable, which is the assumed effect and is measured at a later point in time.

ceiling effect   a situation in which a research participant earns the maximum score on a test or a score close to it because his achievement level exceeds the highest achievement level measured by the test.

central tendency   a point in a distribution of scores, such as the mean or median, that is representative of the scores in the distribution.

chain of evidence   a judgment of the soundness of a study's findings based on clear, meaningful links among the study's research questions, the raw data, the data-analysis procedures, and the findings.

chart essay   a visual presentation that focuses the audience's attention on particular findings from a research study or research review.

chi-square (χ^2) test   a nonparametric test of statistical significance that is used to accept or reject the null hypothesis when the data are frequency counts on two or more categorical scales.

CIPP model   see *Context-Input-Process-Product (CIPP) model*.

citation   see *bibliographic citation*.

citation manager   software that enables the user to store bibliographic citations and retrieve them easily.

citation pearl growing   the use of a relevant publication (the "pearl") to search for other relevant publications.

clinical expertise   the ability to make informed, ethical judgments about whether a particular professional practice is both evidence-based and appropriate for the needs of an individual student or other client.

closed-ended item   in an attitude scale or other measure, an item that requires an individual to make a forced choice between the options that it lists.

cluster sampling   the selection of naturally occurring groups, rather than individuals, to form a sample for a research study.

Cochrane Collaboration   an organization that synthesizes research findings on medical interventions in order to promote the practice of evidence-based medicine.

coding check   the determination of the reliability of data by calculating the level of agreement between different researchers who coded it into categories.

coding frame   in narrative research, an analytic framework for capturing the overall meaning of stories and the issues they raise.

Cohen's *d*   a measure of effect size calculated by subtracting the mean score of Group 1 from the mean score of Group 2 and then dividing this difference by the standard deviation (SD) of the scores from both groups.

cohort study   research in which a group of individuals is surveyed at multiple data-collection points, with the provision that a different sample from the group is included at each of the data-collection points, for the purpose of learning how and why the group changes over time.

collaborative action research a type of investigation in which different professionals, sometimes from different organizations or disciplines, work together to collect data about a problem of practice, analyze the data, report the results to stakeholders, and implement a plan of action to solve the problem.

commitment script in narrative research, story elements that indicate an early decision to focus one's life in a particular direction that appears to offer a unique advantage for the individual, sufficiently so that the individual is willing to confront obstacles that might arise along the way.

comparison groups in group comparison research, two or more samples that are selected because they naturally possess different levels of a variable; in experiments, two or more samples that are formed in order to test different interventions or control conditions.

concept a construct that is used to group individuals, events, or objects that share one or more attributes.

concurrent evidence of test validity (also called *concurrent validity*) the extent to which individuals' scores on a new test correspond to their scores on a more established test of the same construct, which is administered shortly before or after the new test.

concurrent-triangulation research design in mixed-methods research, the collection of qualitative and quantitative data at approximately the same time, followed by analysis of findings from both types of data to determine whether they corroborate each other.

concurrent validity see *concurrent evidence of test validity*.

confidence interval a range of values of a statistic calculated for a sample that is likely to include the corresponding parameter for the population from which the sample was drawn.

confidence limit the upper or lower value of a confidence interval.

conscientization in critical theory, a process in which individuals come to find their voice and courage to question and change their role in maintaining cultural processes that are not consistent with their basic values.

consequential evidence of test validity the extent to which the values implicit in the constructs measured by a test and its intended uses are consistent with the values of test takers, those who will use the test results to make decisions, and other stakeholders.

constant a construct that, when measured, yields the same value for all participants in a research study.

constant comparison in qualitative research, the process of comparing instances of data that have been classified by a particular code in order to discover commonalities in these data that reflect the meaning of the code and that differentiate it from other codes.

construct a concept that is inferred from commonalities among observed phenomena.

content analysis the study of the information contained in a document or other communication by developing categories to code the information and analyzing the frequency of each category.

content-related evidence of test validity (also called *content validity*) the extent to which the items in a test represent the domain of content that the test is designed to measure.

content validity see *content-related evidence of test validity*.

context evaluation in the CIPP model, assessment of the needs, assets, and problems of the stakeholders, staff, and beneficiaries of a program.

Context-Input-Process-Product (CIPP) model a type of evaluation research that is used to assess various aspects of a program—needs, problems, budgets, competing alternatives, functions, effectiveness—as it unfolds over time.

continuous variable a variable whose measurement, typically by an interval or ratio scale, includes an indefinite number of points along its continuum.

control condition in an experiment, a situation in which a group of research participants receives no intervention or an alternative intervention against whose performance the experimental group's performance is compared.

convenience sample see *volunteer sample*.

convergent evidence of test validity the extent to which individuals' scores on a test correlate positively with their scores on other tests that are hypothesized to measure the same construct.

correlational research a type of quantitative investigation that seeks to discover the direction and degree of the relationship among variables, typically by the use of correlational statistics.

correlation coefficient a mathematical expression of the extent to which a sample's distribution of scores on two or more measures are related to each other.

correlation matrix an array of rows and columns displaying the correlation coefficients for all pairs of variables that were measured in a research study.

criterion sampling the selection of a research sample by choosing only those individuals within a preliminary sample or population who satisfy a certain criterion.

criterion variable in experimental research, a variable that is measured after the intervention and that the intervention is intended to affect; in correlational research, a variable for which there is a measure that is administered to a sample to determine whether their scores on it can be predicted by their scores on other measures.

critical ethnography a qualitative research tradition that combines critical theory and ethnographic methods to study power relationships and forms of oppression in a culture.

criticalists researchers or theorists who use their investigations as a form of social or cultural criticism.

critical pedagogy any applied system of teaching and learning that is based on the goals and values of critical theory.

critical theory (also called *critical research*) a qualitative research tradition that seeks to understand the power relationships and forms of oppression in a culture and to use that understanding to emancipate members of the culture who are oppressed.

Cronbach's alpha a reliability coefficient used to quantify the extent to which an individual's scores across different items on a test are consistent with each other.

cross-sectional study a type of research in which changes in a population over time are studied by collecting data at one point in time from samples that vary in age or developmental stage.

crystallization see *triangulation*.

cultural acquisition the process by which individuals learn the concepts, values, skills, and behaviors that are in their culture.

cultural studies a qualitative research tradition that investigates the economic, legal, political, and other underpinnings of cultural phenomena as expressed in literature, art, history, and other disciplines.

cultural transmission the process by which the larger social structure intentionally intervenes in individuals' lives in order to promote or discourage the learning of particular concepts, values, skills, or behaviors.

culture the pattern of traditions, symbols, rituals, and artifacts that characterize a particular group of individuals and that they transmit from one generation to the next or from current members to newly admitted members.

curvilinear correlation a relationship between two variables, such that low and high values of variable A are associated with low values of variable B, and medium values of variable A are associated with high values of variable B; or the converse, where low and high values of variable A are associated with high values of variable B, and medium values of variable A are associated with low values of variable B.

database in a search engine, the citations for all of the publications or other items that it indexes.

deconstruction the critical analysis of texts, based on the assumptions that a text has no definite meaning, that words can refer only to other words, and that "playing" with a text can yield multiple, often contradictory interpretations.

democratic validity a judgment about the credibility of an action research project based on the extent to which the perspectives and interests of all stakeholders were taken into account.

dependent variable a variable that researchers hypothesize occurs after, and as an effect of, another variable (called the *independent variable*) that occurs naturally or as the result of an intervention.

descriptive research a type of quantitative investigation that seeks to portray characteristics of a sample or population by measuring variables specified by the researcher.

descriptive statistics mathematical techniques for summarizing and displaying a set of numerical data.

descriptor in a literature search, a term an individual uses to locate publications that have been classified by it; in ERIC, one of a list of terms created by its administrators.

dialectic in narrative research, an oppositional relationship between an important value or perspective in an individual's life story and a countervailing, equally powerful value or perspective.

dialogical data generation a stage of a critical ethnography project in which researchers collect data by having the research participants explore issues with their own vocabulary, metaphors, and ideas.

dialogic validity a judgment about the credibility of an action research project based on the extent to which colleagues shared in the development of the practitioner/researcher's findings and interpretations.

dichotomous variable a variable that has only two values.

differential analysis a method for determining whether an observed relationship between two variables for the entire research sample is the same for subgroups formed by using a moderator variable.

differential-selection effect in quasi-experiments, selecting participants for the experimental and control groups by a procedure other than random selection, with the consequence that the groups have different initial characteristics that affect the outcome variables.

directional hypothesis a prediction that one group of research participants will have a higher average score on a measure than another group.

direct observation the collection of data while the research participants are engaged in an event or everyday behavior.

discrete variable in contrast to a continuous variable, a variable that has fixed values with no intervals between them.

discriminant analysis a type of multiple regression used to determine how well a sample's scores on measures of several independent variables collectively predict their scores on a measure of a dependent variable whose scores are in the form of categories.

disruption in narrative research, an unexpected, difficult, or disturbing occurrence in one's life that is given meaning by an interpretive process.

document in historical research, a type of text material that is prepared for personal use rather than for an official purpose.

DOI an acronym for *digital object identifier*, which is a permanent link to a publication's location on the Internet.

ecological validity in experiments, the extent to which the findings can be generalized to the naturally occurring conditions of a local setting.

educational research the systematic collection and analysis of empirical data in order to develop various kinds of valid, generalizable knowledge—descriptions of educational phenomena; predictions about future events or performance; evidence about the effects of experimental interventions; and explanations of observed phenomena in terms of basic processes that underlie them.

Educational Resources Information Center (ERIC) a federally funded agency that maintains a search engine and database of bibliographic citations for education-related documents.

effect size a statistic that represents the magnitude of the difference between the average scores of two groups on a measure or the magnitude of the relationship between a sample's distributions of scores on two measures.

effectiveness evaluation in the CIPP model, a process for assessing the quality and significance of a program's outcomes for its participants.

emancipation in critical theory, a process of generating action and consciousness-raising in and toward oppressed cultural groups in order to free them from their oppression.

emergent design a form of evaluation in which the focus of evaluation changes as evaluators gain insights into stakeholders' primary issues and concerns.

emic perspective in qualitative research, the research participants' perceptions and understanding of their social reality.

empirical data direct observation, testing, or other measurements of the phenomena being studied.

epistemology the branch of philosophy that studies the nature of knowledge and the process by which knowledge is acquired and validated.

ERIC see *Educational Resources Information Center (ERIC)*.

espoused theory in action science, professionals' beliefs about how they deal with problems of practice.

ethnography the firsthand, intensive study of the features of a specific culture.

ethnology the comparative study of a particular phenomenon as it manifests itself in different cultures.

ethnoscience the study of a culture's semantic systems for the purpose of revealing the cognitive structure of the culture.

etic perspective in qualitative research, the researchers' conceptual and theoretical understanding of the research participants' social reality.

evaluation research (also called *program evaluation*) a systematic process for making judgments about the merit, value, or worth of programs, organizations, and other phenomena.

evidence-based practice the art of solving problems of practice through the integration of the best available research findings combined with the practitioner's clinical expertise and values.

Excel a software program, available in Office for Windows or Mac, for computing statistics commonly used in educational research.

experiment a type of quantitative investigation that involves the manipulation of a treatment variable to determine its effect on one or more dependent variables.

experimental condition in an experiment, a situation in which one or more individuals take part in an intervention to determine its effect on the dependent variable.

experimental method the use of experiments to empirically determine the effects of a particular intervention in either a natural or laboratory setting.

experimental mortality see *attrition*.

external criticism in historical research, the process of determining the authenticity of a historical source, that is, whether the apparent or claimed origin of the source corresponds to its actual origin.

external validity in quantitative research, the extent to which the results of a study can be generalized to individuals and situations beyond those involved in the study.

extraneous variable in experiments, a factor other than the treatment variable that has a possible effect on the dependent variable.

face validity the extent to which an informal inspection of a test's items indicates that they cover the content the test is claimed to measure.

factor (also called *latent variable*) in factor analysis, a mathematical expression of a feature shared by a particular subset of quantitative variables that have been found to be intercorrelated; in experimental design, a term synonymous with *independent variable*.

factor analysis a correlational procedure for reducing a set of measured variables to a smaller number of variables called *factors*.

factorial experiment an experiment having more than one factor or, in other words, more than one independent variable.

feminisms (also called *feminist research*) various forms of study of females' lived experience and the manner in which that experience is shaped by cultural forces.

fidelity of implementation see *treatment fidelity*.

fieldwork   in qualitative research, a researcher's collection of data while interacting with research participants in their natural settings.

fixed variables   in a group comparison design, a characteristic of individuals or groups that cannot be manipulated.

focus group   a type of group interview in which individuals, led by a skilled interviewer, talk to each other, expressing feelings and opinions that might not emerge if they were interviewed individually.

forgery   in historical research, a document or relic that is claimed to be the work of a particular individual but that was actually fabricated by someone else.

formal literature review   in research, a synthesis of what is known about a particular topic or problem, based on a systematic search for relevant publications, using standard search procedures and criteria for judging the soundness of the research findings that these publications report.

formative evaluation   a type of evaluation that is carried out while a program or product is under development, in order to decide whether and how it should be improved or whether it should be abandoned.

fugitive literature   publications that are not widely disseminated or easy to obtain.

futurology   in historical research, a type of investigation that uses such methods as analysis of past events and simulations in order to predict possible futures.

***F* value**   a statistic that is computed in an analysis of variance or covariance and used to decide whether to accept or reject a null hypothesis.

gain score   an individual's score on a posttest minus that individual's score on a pretest.

Glass's delta   in experiments, a measure of effect size calculated by subtracting the mean score of the control group from the mean score of the experimental group, and then dividing this difference by the standard deviation of the control group.

grade equivalent   a derived score that represents a student's raw score on a test as the grade level of students in a norming group who, on average, earned that score.

grounded theory   in qualitative research, the principle that researchers should develop theory inductively by examining their data directly and without external influence, rather than by creating a theory in advance of what they are studying.

group comparison research   (also called *causal-comparative research*) a type of quantitative investigation in which groups that differ on the independent variable are compared to determine whether they also differ on the dependent variable or in which groups that differ on the dependent variable are compared to determine whether they also differ on the independent variable.

group experiment   in experimental research, a design in which each treatment and control condition includes a sample of research participants rather than a single participant or a group of participants considered individually.

growth model   an approach to the measurement and statistical analysis of students' learning over time in order to assess their learning gain.

Guttman scale   a type of attitude measurement in which the attitude is conceptualized to have one dimension, and a set of items is constructed and placed in a sequence such that an individual who agrees with a specific item in the sequence also will agree with all previous items in the sequence.

Hawthorne effect   an improvement in the experimental group's performance because of the special attention it received from the researchers.

hegemony   a privileged group's dominance over subordinate groups through the cultural agencies they control.

hermeneutics   the study of how people interpret texts and other forms of communication.

hermeneutic circle   the process of understanding texts and other forms of communication as a whole by interpreting their various parts.

hierarchical linear modeling (HLM)   a statistical technique for determining whether the correlation between two variables is affected by different levels of nesting.

high-inference variable   a variable that requires the researcher to make an inference from observed behavior to underlying factors, such as cognitive and emotional processes, that it expresses.

high-stakes tests   assessments that hold schools, teachers, or students to certain accountability standards and that, if not met, can have adverse consequences for them.

histogram   a graphical display that shows the variability in a sample's scores on a variable through the use of a set of rectangles, with one side of each rectangle representing a specified range of scores for the variable and the other side representing the number of cases in the sample that has these scores.

historical research   a type of investigation that involves a systematic search for data to answer questions about a past phenomenon in order to better understand the phenomenon and its likely causes and consequences.

history effect   in experiments, the effect on the dependent variable of events that occur while the experimental intervention is in progress, but that are not part of the intervention.

holistic ethnography   a qualitative research tradition that seeks to provide a comprehensive description and analysis of the entire culture of a group of people who live close together in a specified geographical region.

human subjects review committee   see *institutional review board*.

hypothesis a prediction, derived from a theory or speculation, about how two or more constructs will be related to each other.

impact evaluation in the CIPP model, an assessment of whether a program reached the appropriate target audience.

independent variable a variable that researchers hypothesize occurred prior to, and had an influence on, another variable (the *dependent variable*).

in-depth study in qualitative research, the collection of a large amount of data, using various methods and extending over a substantial time period, in order to develop a deep understanding of a case.

inferential statistics mathematical procedures that enable researchers to make inferences about a population's characteristics based on the descriptive statistics that are calculated from data for a sample that was selected to represent the population.

informal literature review a quick search of the literature to get an overview or specific information about a topic of interest.

informed consent a procedure whereby potential participants in a research study have been informed about all of the possible risks and costs involved in participation, and no coercion is used to obtain their consent, including threats of possible negative consequences if they decline to participate.

input evaluation in the CIPP model, the assessment of competing alternatives, work plans, and budgets for a particular program.

insider in action research and qualitative research, a practitioner or other individual in the setting being studied who is viewed as having direct knowledge of the problem that is being investigated.

insider research see *action research*.

Institute of Education Sciences an agency of the U.S. Department of Education that has the mission of supporting scientifically based research to improve student learning outcomes.

institutional review board (also called *human subjects review committee*) a committee within a recognized institution that follows a protocol to ensure that research participants are protected from risk of harm.

instrumental rationality a preoccupation with means over ends; in critical theory, a term used to characterize research and theory that emphasizes prediction, control, and the maximization of productivity rather than emphasizing deliberation about which ends have the most value.

instrumentation effect in experiments, a change from the pretest to the posttest that is due to the use of different pretest and posttest measures rather than to the experimental treatment.

intentionality in action research, practitioner inquiry that is planned and deliberate rather than spontaneous.

interaction effect in experiments, a situation in which an independent variable has an effect on the dependent variable, but only under certain of the conditions specified in the experimental design.

internal criticism in historical research, the process of determining the accuracy and worth of the information contained in a historical source.

internal narrative in narrative research, the ongoing stream of thought and self-talk that most individuals engage in during many of their waking moments, whether they are conscious of it or not.

internalized oppression in critical theory, the process by which individuals unwittingly maintain their own lack of privilege through thoughts and actions consistent with a lesser social status.

internal validity in experiments, the extent to which extraneous variables have been controlled by the researchers such that any observed effects can be attributed solely to the treatment.

interpretational analysis in qualitative research, the process of examining data to identify constructs, themes, and patterns that can be used to describe and explain the phenomenon being studied.

interpretivism an epistemological position that social reality has no existence apart from the meanings that individuals construct for them in a continuous process as they participate in social reality.

inter-rater reliability the extent to which the scores assigned by one rater agree with the scores assigned by other raters who have observed the same events or analyzed the same tests or other materials.

interval scale a measure that lacks a true zero point and for which the distance between any two adjacent points is the same.

interview the collection of data through direct structured, semi-structured, or unstructured communication between the researcher and the individuals being studied.

item consistency the extent to which all of the items on a test measure the same construct, as determined by one of several correlational methods.

item response theory a theory of psychological measurement that assumes that individuals with different amounts of an ability will perform differently on an item measuring that ability; also, an approach to test administration in which the difficulty level of the items presented to each individual are matched with his or her ability level as determined by performance on earlier test items.

Joint Committee on Standards for Educational Evaluation a committee with representatives from 12 major educational organizations whose mission it is to create standards for evaluating the quality of educational programs.

key informant in qualitative research, an individual with special knowledge or status whom a researcher recruits to obtain an emic perspective of the social reality being studied.

keyword a word or phrase that a search engine will use to identify all entries in its database, such as bibliographic citations and website addresses, containing that word or phrase.

Kruskal-Wallis test of statistical significance a nonparametric test of statistical significance used to determine whether the observed difference between the distribution of scores for more than two groups on a measured variable is statistically significant.

Kuder-Richardson Formula 20 a procedure used to obtain a reliability coefficient based on the internal consistency of a measure, all of whose items are dichotomous, as is the case with most achievement tests.

latent variable see *factor*.

latent variable causal modeling see *structural equation modeling*.

Likert item a type of attitude measurement that asks respondents to read a statement and then record the intensity of their feeling about the statement on a line that typically has 5 points, ranging from strongly disagree to strongly agree.

Likert scale a set of Likert items that measure the same attitude and that can be summed to yield a total score or averaged to yield a mean score.

linear correlation a statistical approach for analyzing the distribution of a sample's scores on two measures, based on the assumption that as scores in one distribution increase, scores in the other distribution will also increase or decrease throughout the range of the score distribution.

line of best fit in correlational research, the line on a scattergram that allows for the best prediction of an individual's score on the y axis from knowing the score on the x axis.

Listserv a software program for managing Internet bulletin boards and discussion forums so that their subscribers can interact with each other.

literature review see *formal literature review, informal literature review, professional literature review*.

log in interviews, a record of the topics covered in a specific interview, accompanied by notations of any interesting occurrences (especially disruptions) and how they were handled.

logistic regression analysis a type of multiple regression in which a sample's scores on two or more measures are used to predict their scores on a categorical measure.

longitudinal research in quantitative research, a study that involves describing changes in a sample's characteristics or behavior patterns over a period of time.

low-inference variable a variable that requires the observer to examine a behavior and then decide whether it is an instance of a particular behavioral construct.

Mann-Whitney *U* test of statistical significance a nonparametric test of statistical significance used to determine whether the observed difference between the distribution of scores for each of two groups on a measured variable is statistically significant.

margin of error a range of values derived from a statistic for a random sample that is likely to include the corresponding population parameter.

matching procedure in experimental or group comparison research, a technique used to equate groups on extraneous independent variables so that if group differences are observed on a dependent variable, this effect cannot be attributed to the extraneous variables, but instead to the independent variable of interest to the researchers.

maturation effect in experiments, a change in scores from the pretest to the posttest that is due to developmental changes in the research participants during the course of an experiment rather than to the intervention.

mean a measure of central tendency that is calculated by summing the individual scores of the sample and then dividing the total sum by the number of individuals in the sample.

mean absolute deviation in a score distribution, the mean of all of the amounts by which each score deviates from the actual mean of the scores, ignoring whether the deviation from the mean is positive or negative.

meaning fields in critical theory, the possible intended meanings of a participant's statements or nonverbal behavior that others in the setting themselves might infer.

measurement error the difference between the scores that individuals actually obtain on a test and their true scores if it were possible to obtain a perfect measure of their performance.

median a measure of central tendency corresponding to the middle point in a distribution of scores.

member checking a procedure used by qualitative researchers to check their reconstruction of the field participants' emic perspective by having them review statements in the research report for accuracy and completeness.

meta-analysis a method for combining the statistical results from different quantitative research studies on the same phenomenon into a single statistic, an effect size.

meta-ethnography a method for synthesizing case studies that involves searching for concepts and themes in a set of studies about a particular phenomenon and then interpreting them.

meta-evaluation a research study that evaluates the quality and effectiveness of an evaluation study or a program of evaluation, such as a school district's teacher evaluation system.

microethnography   the study of specific aspects of the culture or a specific subgroup of members of the culture, instead of making a comprehensive study of the culture as a whole.

mixed-methods research   a type of study that uses both quantitative and qualitative techniques for data collection and analysis, either concurrently or sequentially, to address the same or related research questions.

mode   a measure of central tendency that identifies the most frequently occurring score in a distribution of scores.

moderator variable   in correlational research, a variable, Z, that affects the extent to which variable X predicts variable Y, such that the correlation between X and Y for some values of Z is different from the correlation between X and Y for other values of Z.

monological data collection   in critical ethnography, a stage of a research project in which only the researchers "speak," compiling a thick description of field participants' activities that is written from the perspective of an uninvolved observer.

multiple-baseline research design   in single-case experiments, using situations other than the naturally occurring condition as a baseline control for determining the presence of intervention effects.

multiple regression   a statistical procedure for determining the magnitude of the relationship between a criterion variable and a combination of two or more predictor variables.

multivariate correlation   the statistical analysis of the magnitude of the relationship between three or more variables.

multivariate descriptive statistics   a type of statistic that is used to describe the relationship between the distributions of scores on two or more measures.

multivocality   a situation in which the participants in a culture or societal group do not speak with a unified voice but instead express diverse interests and viewpoints.

narrative   in narrative research, a story in which a precise time line, made up of points in time during which particular events occurred, is established.

narrative identity   a sense of self that is grounded in the stories that an individual constructs from his or her experiences.

narrative research   the systematic description and interpretation of stories about life experiences.

National Assessment of Educational Progress (NAEP)   a congressionally mandated, large-scale, continuing assessment of what a representative sample of students in the United States know and can do in various subject areas.

Nation's Report Card   a publication issued periodically by the National Center for Education Statistics that uses the findings of achievement tests administered by the National Assessment of Educational Progress to inform various constituencies about the academic achievement of American elementary and secondary students.

needs assessment   a set of procedures for identifying and prioritizing needs, which are defined as discrepancies between desired and existing conditions.

negative correlation   a correlation between two score distributions, X and Y, for a sample such that the higher the score for variable X, the lower the corresponding score for variable Y is likely to be.

nesting   a situation in which a variable exists at several levels of organizational structure, such as students being "nested" in a classroom, classrooms being "nested" in a school, and schools being "nested" within a school district.

No Child Left Behind Act   a set of regulations approved by the U.S. Congress that impose various educational requirements on all states, including the requirement to specify standards of achievement in basic skills that all students in certain grades are expected to meet.

nominal scale   see *categorical scale*.

nonlinear correlation   a relationship between two variables such that the values of one variable have a predictable association with values of another variable, but the association is not best described by a straight line.

nonparametric test of statistical significance   a type of test of statistical significance that does not depend on assumptions about the distribution or form of scores on the measured variables.

normal curve   see *normal probability distribution*.

normal curve area   the amount of area in the normal curve between any two scores on the x axis.

normal probability distribution   (also called *normal curve* and *bell-shaped curve*) a distribution of scores that has the characteristic of being clustered around each side of the mean in a symmetrical bell-shaped curve when plotted on a graph.

normative-evaluative truth claims   in critical ethnography, assumptions about the world as it is or should be that reflect existing social agreements on the rightness, goodness, and appropriateness of various types of activities.

norming group   a large sample that represents a defined population and whose scores on a test provide a set of standards to which the scores of individuals who subsequently take the test can be referenced.

norm-referenced test   a test that is intended for widespread use and that is accompanied by tables of norms so that local users can compare their students' scores with those of students in the general population who are at the same age or grade level.

norms   unstated background sets of rules and assumptions that influence individuals' social acts.

NOT connector   a search engine feature that enables the user to exclude bibliographic citations in a database that have a particular keyword.

null hypothesis   a prediction that the researcher typically hopes to reject by using a test of statistical significance.

objectives-based evaluation   the use of quantitative or qualitative methods to determine how well a program helps students achieve specified learning outcomes.

objective truth claims   in critical ethnography, assertions that are open to multiple access, meaning that they are accessible to examination and therefore can be directly validated by various observers.

observer bias   an observer's mental set to perceive an event in such a way that relevant aspects of the event are overlooked, distorted, or falsified.

one-group pretest-posttest study   an experiment in which the entire sample receives an intervention, a pretest, and a posttest; a separate control group is not formed.

one-shot case study   an experiment in which the entire sample receives an intervention and a posttest; there is no control group or pretest.

one-tailed test of statistical significance   a test that evaluates the null hypothesis in one direction, for example, a test that considers the possibility that the mean score for population *A* is higher than the mean score for population *B*, but does not consider the possibility that the mean score for population *A* is lower than the mean score for population *B*.

online journal   a periodic publication, typically issued monthly or quarterly, that is available via the Internet.

open-ended item   in an attitude scale or other measure, an item that allows any response an individual wishes to make.

oral history   a type of historical research in which individuals who witnessed or participated in past events are asked to recount their recollections of those events.

OR connector   a search engine feature that enables the user to identify bibliographic citations in a database that include one or the other, or both, of two keywords.

ordinal scale   a measure whose different values can be placed in order of magnitude, but the difference between any two sets of adjacent values might differ.

outcome validity   in action research, a judgment about the extent to which new actions lead to a resolution of the problem that prompted the action research project.

outlier   a case that differs greatly in some manner from other cases that are studied.

outsider   in action research, an individual who works outside the setting being studied and who is viewed as having an external perspective on the problem of practice being investigated.

p   see *probability (p) value*.

panel study   research in which the same sample is surveyed at more than one data-collection point in order to explore changes in specific individuals and possible reasons for those changes.

parameter   a statistic that applies to the entire population rather than just to a sample.

parametric test of statistical significance   a test of statistical significance that depends on certain assumptions about the distribution and form of scores on the measured variables.

participant observation   in qualitative research, researchers' assumption of a meaningful identity within the group being studied while maintaining their role as observers collecting research data.

participatory action research   see *action research*.

path analysis   a multivariate statistical method for testing the validity of a theory about causal links between three or more measured variables.

pattern   in case study research, a systematic relationship between two or more types of phenomena within a case.

pdf file   an electronic copy of a document created by the software program Adobe Acrobat.

pearl growing   see *citation pearl growing*.

Pearson product-moment correlation coefficient (also called *r*) a widely used statistic that indicates the direction and magnitude of the relationship between a sample's distribution of scores on two measures.

peer-reviewed journal   in research, a periodical in which the articles have been evaluated by authorities for the quality and significance of the research, theory, or opinions that they report.

percentile rank   a type of rank score that represents a given raw score on a measure as the percentage of individuals in the sample whose score falls at or below that score.

performance ethnography   staged reenactments of cultural phenomena that have been discovered by ethnographers.

performance measure   a test that evaluates individuals' skill by having them complete a complex task, sometimes involving a real-life situation.

performance objective   in research and development, a specific statement of what learners will be able to do after receiving instruction provided by a systematic program.

phenomenon   in qualitative research, any process, event, or characteristic that will be the subject of inquiry.

Phi Delta Kappa/Gallup Polls   an annual national poll, jointly sponsored by the Gallup organization and the educational organization Phi Delta Kappa, to determine the public's attitude about various aspects of U.S. schools.

pie chart   a graphical display, in the form of a circle, of the variability in a sample's scores on a variable, with each section of the circle representing the percentage of the sample having that score.

population   the complete set of individuals, groups, events, or other entity that is specified as the subject of inquiry and from which a sample typically is drawn for detailed study.

population validity   the degree to which the results of a research study can be generalized from the specific sample that was studied to the population from which the sample was drawn.

positive correlation   a correlation between two score distributions, X and Y, such that the higher the score for variable X, the higher the corresponding score for variable Y.

positivism   an epistemological position that asserts that there is a reality "out there" that is available for objective study through scientific means similar to those that have been developed in the physical sciences.

postmodernism   a broad social and philosophical movement that questions the rationality of human action, the use of positivist epistemology, and any human endeavor (e.g., science) that claims a privileged position with respect to the search for truth.

posttest   in experiments, a measure that is administered following the intervention in order to determine the effects of the treatment.

posttest-only control-group experiment with randomization   an investigation that includes an intervention, a posttest, a group that receives the intervention, and one or more groups that do not receive the intervention or that receive another intervention, with random assignment of the sample to these groups.

posttest-only control-group experiment without randomization   an investigation that includes an intervention, a pretest and posttest, a group that receives the intervention, and one or more groups that do not receive the intervention or that receive another intervention, but without random assignment of the sample to these groups.

practical significance   in statistics, a statistical result that has meaningful consequences for individuals to whom the result applies.

practitioner research   see *action research*.

praxis   in critical theory, the process of transforming theory into practice so as to do the right thing and do it well in interacting with one's fellow human beings.

prediction research   an investigation that involves the use of data collected at one point in time to predict future behavior or events.

predictive evidence of test validity   (also called *predictive validity*) the extent to which the scores of individuals on a measure administered at one point in time predict their scores on a measure administered at a subsequent point in time.

predictive validity   see *predictive evidence of test validity*.

predictor variable   a variable that researchers measure at one point in time and then correlate with a criterion variable that is measured at a later point in time.

presentism   a type of bias in historical research that involves interpreting past events by using concepts and perspectives that originated in more recent times.

pretest   in experiments, a measure that is administered prior to an intervention in order to provide a basis for comparison with the posttest.

pretest-posttest control-group experiment with randomization   an investigation that includes an intervention, a pretest and posttest, a group that receives the intervention, and one or more groups that do not receive the intervention or that receive another intervention, with random assignment of the sample to these groups.

pretest-posttest control-group experiment without randomization   an investigation that includes an intervention, a pretest and posttest, a group that receives the intervention, and one or more groups that do not receive the intervention or that receive another intervention, but without random assignment of the sample to these groups.

primary source   in general research, a publication written by the individuals who actually conducted the investigation presented in the publication; in historical research, any source of information from witnesses or participants that has been preserved from the past.

privilege   in critical theory research, the disproportionate power, resources, and life opportunities that are granted to members of culturally dominant groups in a society; also, to grant such power to a specific group or individual.

probability (*p*) value   a mathematical expression derived from a sample's data that is used to accept or reject a null hypothesis about the population from which the sample was drawn.

process evaluation   in the CIPP model, an assessment of program activities.

process validity   the adequacy of the processes used in different phases of an action research project.

product evaluation   in the CIPP model, an assessment about the success of a program.

product-moment correlation coefficient   see *Pearson product-moment correlation coefficient*.

professional literature review   a synthesis of research findings in the literature about a particular problem of practice, but without the technical details found in a formal literature review.

program   a systematic sequence of materials and activities, usable in many settings, that are designed to achieve explicitly stated goals.

program culture   the rules, rituals, and roles that are involved in implementing a program.

program evaluation   see *evaluation research*.

progressive discourse   in science, the view that anyone at any time can offer a criticism about a particular research study's findings or methodology and that if it proves to have merit, it will be listened to and accommodated.

progressive story structure   in narrative research, a story in which the events demonstrate progress toward a goal.

proportional random sampling   a variation of stratified random sampling that is designed to ensure that the proportion of individuals in each subgroup in the sample is the same as their proportion in the population.

Publication Manual of the American Psychological Association   a book containing style specifications that are widely used in preparing dissertations, journal articles, and other reports in education.

purposeful sampling   in qualitative research, the process of selecting cases that are likely to be information-rich with respect to the purposes of a particular study.

***p* value**   see *probability value.*

qualitative research   generally, a type of inquiry grounded in the assumption that individuals construct social reality in the form of meanings and interpretations and that these constructions are transitory and situational; the primary methodology is to discover these meanings and interpretations by studying cases intensively in natural settings.

qualitative research tradition   an approach to inquiry involving a group of qualitative researchers and scholars who hold a similar view of the nature of social reality, the research questions that are important to ask, and the techniques needed to answer them.

quantitative historical materials   materials containing numerical information that are preserved and used as a primary source in historical research.

quantitative history   an approach to historical research typically involving the use of an electronic database containing numerical data that can be analyzed by statistical techniques.

quantitative research   inquiry that is grounded in the assumption that features of the social environment constitute an objective reality that is relatively constant across time and settings; the primary methodology for inquiry involves collecting numerical data about samples and subjecting these data to statistical analysis.

quasi-experiment   an experimental study in which research participants for the experimental and control groups are selected by a procedure other than random selection.

questionnaire   a set of questions in paper-and-pencil or computer format that typically measure many variables.

r   see *Pearson product-moment correlation coefficient.*

R & D   see *research and development.*

random assignment   in experiments, the process of assigning individuals or groups to the experimental and control conditions such that each individual or group has an equal chance of being in either condition.

random sample   a group in which each member of the group was chosen entirely by chance from the population.

randomized trial   (also called *randomized control trial*) an experiment involving random assignment of the sample to experimental and control groups, and with the implication that the experimental intervention is large-scale, conducted in real-life settings, and addressing outcomes that have societal significance.

range   a statistic that measures the amount of dispersion in a score distribution; it is equal to the difference between the highest and the lowest score plus 1.

rank   (also called *ranking*) a number that expresses the position of an individual's score on a measure relative to the positions of other individuals' scores.

ratio scale   a type of measurement in which the values of the variable can be ordered, the interval between any two adjacent values is equal, and there is a true zero point.

raw score   the numerical value that the individual obtains on the scale that the measure employs, without any further statistical manipulation.

reconstructionist   (also called *revisionist historian*) a historian who conducts research on aspects of the past that were missed or distorted in previous historical accounts.

reconstructive analysis   the process that critical ethnographers use to analyze the data collected during monological data generation in order to describe interaction patterns among field participants and the apparent meaning of those patterns.

record   in historical research, a type of document that is prepared with an official purpose, as contrasted with material prepared for personal use only.

reflection   in action research, the process by which practitioners step back from the world of practice and ponder and share ideas about the meaning, value, and impact of their work.

reflective analysis   in qualitative research, a type of data analysis in which researchers rely on their own intuition and personal judgment to analyze the data that have been collected.

reflexivity   in qualitative research, the researchers' act of inquiring about themselves as constructors and interpreters of the social reality that they study.

refutation   the process of submitting the knowledge claims of science to empirical tests that allow them to be challenged and disproved.

regressive story structure   in narrative research, a story in which the events present either obstacles to achieving a goal or possibly a defeat leading to abandonment of the goal.

relational pattern   in case study research, a systematic relationship, not presumed to be causal, that is observed between particular phenomena within a case or across cases.

reliability   the extent to which a test or other measure is free of measurement error.

reliability coefficient   a type of correlation coefficient that quantifies the extent to which a test or other measure is free of measurement error.

relic   (also called *artifact*) in historical research, any object whose physical properties provide information about the past.

replication research   the process of repeating a research study with different research participants under similar conditions in order to increase confidence in, and possibly extend, the original study's findings.

repository   (also called *archive*) a facility for preserving documents and controlling access to them.

reproduction   in critical theory, the view that many of the learning problems experienced by members of low-income and ethnic-minority groups result from educational practices that maintain and reinforce the cultural oppression of such groups.

research and development   (also called *R & D*) a systematic process involving the development of educational programs and materials through formative and summative evaluation.

research narrative   in narrative research, an organized interpretation of events.

response-process evidence of test validity   the extent to which the processes used by an individual in taking a test are consistent with the particular constructs that the test presumably measures.

responsive evaluation   a type of evaluation research that focuses on stakeholders' issues and concerns.

restorying   a process used in narrative research to convert a story told by an individual, or group of individuals, into a research narrative.

reversal phase   in single-case experiments, the process of withdrawing the treatment (condition *B*) so as to reinstitute the baseline condition (*A*).

revisionist historian   see *reconstructionist*.

r value   see *product-moment correlation coefficient*.

sample   a group of participants or other entity that is selected by random or nonrandom methods for inclusion in a research study.

sampling error   the difference between a statistic for a sample and the same statistic for the population from which the sample was randomly drawn.

scale   a set of numbers that represent the range of values of a variable.

scattergram   (also called *scatter plot*) a graph depicting the correlation between two measured variables, with the scores on one measured variable plotted on the *x* axis and the scores on the other measured variable plotted on the *y* axis of the graph.

scatter plot   see *scattergram*.

Scheffé's test   a type of *t* test that is used to compare pairs of means for three or more groups.

search engine   computer software that helps users sort through a database to identify documents or other items that satisfy user-specified criteria.

secondary source   in literature reviews, a publication in which the author reviews the writings of individuals who have studied a particular problem or topic; in historical research, a document or other communication in which an author who was not a direct witness describes an event.

selection-maturation interaction effect   in experiments, a change from the pretest to the posttest that is due to developmental differences between the experimental and control groups rather than to the intervention.

self-study research   see *action research*.

sequential-explanatory research design   in multiple-methods research, the collection and analysis of quantitative data followed by the collection and analysis of qualitative data, which are then used to explain the quantitative findings.

sequential-transformative research design   in multiple-methods research, the use of a theoretical perspective to guide both the qualitative and quantitative phases of data collection, analysis, and interpretation; either the qualitative or the quantitative phase can occur first.

simple random sampling   a procedure in which all of the individuals in the defined population have an equal and independent chance of being selected as a member of the sample.

single-case experiment   a type of experiment in which one or a few individuals participate in an intervention in order to determine its effect on one or more dependent variables.

skewness   a nonsymmetrical distribution of scores in which the majority of scores are clustered on one side of the mean, and the other scores trail off on the other side of the mean.

snowball sampling   in qualitative research, a type of sampling in which information provided by one or more initially selected cases leads to the selection of other individuals who are likely to yield relevant, information-rich data.

Solomon four-group experiment   an experiment in which a sample is randomly assigned to four groups that vary in whether they take a pretest and participate in the research intervention for the purpose of determining the effects of the pretest on the posttest and on the experimental or control conditions.

stable story structure   in narrative research, a story in which the events lead to little or no change in the individual's circumstances.

stakeholder   an individual who is involved in a program or activity that is being evaluated or who may be affected by or interested in the findings of the evaluation.

standard deviation   a statistic that indicates how much a set of scores deviates from the mean score.

standard error of measurement   a statistic that is used to estimate the probable range within which an individual's true score on a test falls.

standard score   an expression of an individual's raw score on a test or other measure in another form, namely, a score based on the standard deviation of the score distribution.

Standards for Educational and Psychological Testing a definitive guide, sponsored by several professional organizations, for determining the quality of tests and other measures.

statistic any number that describes a characteristic of a sample's scores on a measure.

statistical power the probability that a particular test of statistical significance will lead to the rejection of a false null hypothesis.

statistical regression the tendency for individuals who score either very high or very low on a measure to score nearer to the mean when the measure is readministered.

statistical significance an inference, based on a statistical analysis, that the results obtained for a research sample are of a sufficient magnitude to reject the null hypothesis.

status model a method of evaluating schools' ability to promote students' academic achievement in which students at a particular grade level are tested each year, so that the achievement test scores of students at that grade level in year X can be compared with the scores of students at the same grade level in year Y.

story in narrative research, an individual's account of events that occurred at specific times in the past.

stratified random sampling a procedure involving the identification of subgroups with certain characteristics in the population and then drawing a random sample of individuals from each subgroup.

structural equation modeling (also called *latent variable causal modeling*) a statistical procedure for testing the validity of a theory about the causal links among variables, each of which has been measured by one or more different measures.

subjective truth claims in critical ethnography, assertions by field participants about their state of being to which there is privileged access, meaning that only the individual has access to the experience on which the claim is based.

sum of squares the total amount of variability in a set of scores, determined by computing the sum of all of the squared deviations (each raw score minus the mean) for the scores.

summative evaluation a type of evaluation that is conducted to determine the worth of a fully developed program in a natural field setting, especially in comparison with competing programs.

survey research a form of descriptive investigation that involves collecting information about research participants' beliefs, attitudes, interests, or behavior using standard questionnaires, interviews, or paper-and-pencil tests.

sustainability evaluation in the CIPP model, an assessment of whether a program is institutionalized successfully in a particular setting in the short term and long term.

systematic practitioner research a type of action research that emphasizes educators' systematic, intentional use of data collection and analysis to improve their professional practice.

table of norms a presentation of possible raw scores for a test or other measure and, for each score, its age equivalent, grade equivalent, or other numerical value based on a norming group.

tacit knowledge implicit meanings that the individuals being studied either cannot find words to express or that they take so much for granted that they do not refer to them.

target population the entire group of individuals or other entities that have the characteristics of interest to researchers and to which they wish to generalize the findings of their study.

teacher research see *action research*.

test a measure of an individual's knowledge, understanding, or skill within a curriculum domain, typically yielding a total score for the number of items answered correctly.

testing effect in experiments, the effect of repeated administrations of a test or other measure on the posttest.

test of statistical significance a mathematical procedure for determining whether the researchers' null hypothesis can be rejected at a given probability level.

test-retest reliability (also called *test stability*) the extent to which individuals' scores on one administration of a test are consistent with their scores on another administration of the test after a delay.

test stability see *test-retest reliability*.

test validity the degree to which the interpretation of the scores yielded by a test are supported by relevant research evidence and theory.

tetrachoric correlation coefficient a statistic used to describe the magnitude of the relationship between two variables, both of which yield scores that can be split into artificial dichotomies.

text in critical theory, any cultural discourse, object, or event that possesses communicative value, but particularly those communications that express and maintain differences in privilege among cultural groups in society.

theme in qualitative research, a salient, recurrent feature of the case being studied.

theoretical saturation the outcome of the process of comparing theoretical constructs and empirical indicators of their meaning until additional data collection and analysis no longer contribute anything new about the phenomenon under investigation.

theory an explanation of observed phenomena in terms of a set of underlying constructs and principles that relate the constructs to each other.

theory-in-action in the theory of action, the rationale that explains the actual behavior of professionals as they engage in their work.

thick description in qualitative research, a richly detailed report that re-creates a situation and as much of its context as possible, including the meanings and intentions inherent in the situation.

transportability evaluation In the CIPP model, an assessment of whether a program can be adapted and institutionalized in other settings.

treatment condition in experiments, the intervention that is administered to the experimental group to determine its effect on the dependent variable.

treatment fidelity the extent to which the experimental intervention is implemented according to the specifications of the researchers or program developers.

trend study a research study that describes change in a population over time by selecting a different sample at each data-collection point from the population, which does not necessarily remain constant.

triangulation (also called *crystallization*) in qualitative research, the use of multiple data-collection methods, data sources, analysts, or theories to increase the soundness of research findings.

troubling in anti-oppressive education, the process of questioning widely accepted but oppressive cultural practices.

true dichotomy a variable that has only two values in reality.

true score the score on a test or other measure that an individual would receive if it were possible to obtain a perfect measure of the individual's performance, attitude, or other construct.

truncation a procedure for searching an electronic database for any words that contain the same stem, such as the stem *sign* retrieving *signature*, *signing*, and *signs*.

***t* test** a test of statistical significance that is used to determine whether the null hypothesis can be rejected with some degree of certainty.

***t* test for correlation coefficients** a *t* test that is used to accept or reject the null hypothesis that a correlation coefficient for a sample is zero or the null hypothesis that two correlation coefficients for a sample are chance fluctuations.

***t* test for independent means** a *t* test in which it is assumed that the two populations from which the two samples were drawn are not related to each other.

***t* test for related means** a *t* test in which it is assumed that the two populations from which the two samples were drawn are related to each other.

Tukey's test a type of *t* test for comparing pairs of means for three or more groups.

two-tailed test of statistical significance a test that evaluates the null hypothesis in both directions, for example, a test that considers the possibility that the mean score for population *A* is higher than the mean score for population *B* and also the possibility that the mean score for population *A* is lower than the mean score for population *A*.

Type I error the rejection of the null hypothesis when it is actually true.

Type II error the acceptance of the null hypothesis when it is actually false.

validity in research generally, the soundness of research findings based on the satisfaction of specific criteria for the research design that generated the findings; in testing, the degree to which evidence and theory support the interpretation of test scores in the context that they will be used.

value a discernible point in a variable.

value-added teacher evaluation an approach to evaluation of teachers' performance that focuses on the amount of gain that a teacher's students make on a standardized achievement test administered before and after they have received instruction from the teacher.

variable a quantitative expression of a construct indicating the possible number of ways that individuals or other entities can vary with respect to the construct.

variance a statistical measure of the extent to which scores in a distribution deviate from the mean, computed for a sample by dividing the sum of squares by the sample size minus one ($n - 1$).

voice in critical theory, the extent to which individuals occupying particular social categories are privileged, silenced, or empowered through the operation of discourses that maintain or contest dominant and subordinate cultures in a society.

volunteer sample (also called *sample of convenience*) a sample based on individuals' expression of willingness to participate in a research study rather than on a systematic sampling strategy.

What Works Clearinghouse an agency within the U.S. Department of Education that creates databases and user-friendly reports about research evidence relating to interventions that claim to improve student learning and other outcomes.

Wilcoxon signed-rank test a nonparametric counterpart of the *t* test of statistical significance.

wildcard a part of the truncation feature of search engines that involves the use of a symbol, typically an asterisk (*), to find all words in an electronic database that have the same stem.

***x* variable** an independent variable that researchers assume has a causal influence on another variable, called the dependent variable or *y* variable.

***y* variable** a dependent variable that researchers assume was caused by another variable, called the independent variable or *x* variable.

***z*-score** an expression of a raw score, called a standard score, that indicates the raw score's distance from the score distribution's mean in standard deviation units.

Name Index

Subject Index